M000025484

GLENCOE

Writer's Choice

Grammar and Composition

Grade 10

Glencoe

New York, New York Columbus, Ohio Chicago, Illinois Peoria, Illinois Woodland Hills, California

ACKNOWLEDGMENTS

Grateful acknowledgment is given authors, publishers, photographers, museums, and agents for permission to reprint the following copyrighted material. Every effort has been made to determine copyright owners. In case of any omissions, the Publisher will be pleased to make suitable acknowledgments in future editions.

Acknowledgments continued on page 982.

The **Facing the Blank Page** feature in this book was prepared in collaboration with the writers and editors of *TIME*.

6+1 Trait® is a registered trademark of Northwest Regional Educational Laboratory, which does not endorse this product.

The McGraw·Hill Companies

Copyright © 2005 by The McGraw-Hill Companies, Inc. All rights reserved. Except as permitted under the United States Copyright Act of 1976, no part of this publication may be reproduced or distributed in any form or means, or stored in a database or retrieval system, without the prior written permission of the publisher.

PRINTED IN THE UNITED STATES OF AMERICA

Send all inquiries to:
GLENCOE/MCGRAW-HILL
8787 Orion Place
Columbus, OH 43240-4027

ISBN 0-07-829818-0
(Student Edition)
ISBN 0-07-829811-3
(Teacher Wraparound Edition)

5 6 7 8 9 10 027/055 09 08 07

PROGRAM CONSULTANTS

Mark Lester is Professor of English Emeritus at Eastern Washington University. He formerly served as Chair of the Department of English as a Second Language, University of Hawaii. He is the author of *Grammar and Usage in the Classroom* (Allyn & Bacon, 2000) and of numerous other professional books and articles.

Sharon O'Neal is Associate Professor at the College of Education, Texas State University–San Marcos, where she teaches courses in reading instruction. She formerly served as Director of Reading and Language Arts of the Texas Education Agency and has authored, and contributed to, numerous articles and books on reading instruction and teacher education.

Jacqueline Jones Royster is Professor of English and Associate Dean at the College of Humanities at Ohio State University. She is also on the faculty at the Bread Loaf School of English at Middlebury College in Middlebury, Vermont. In addition to the teaching of writing, Dr. Royster's professional interests include the rhetorical history of African American women and the social and cultural implications of literate practices.

William Strong is Professor of Secondary Education at Utah State University, Director of the Utah Writing Project, and a member of the National Writing Project Advisory Board. A nationally known authority on the teaching of composition, he is the author of many volumes, including *Coaching Writing: The Power of Guided Practice* (Heinemann, 2001) and *Writing Incisively: Do-It-Yourself Prose Surgery* (McGraw-Hill, 1991).

Jeffrey Wilhelm, a middle and high school English teacher for thirteen years, is currently Associate Professor of English Education at Boise State University, where he specializes in adolescent literacy, with research interests in struggling readers and writers. He has been a National Writing Project site director for the past eight years. He has written eleven books on literacy education and numerous articles and chapters. He has won the NCTE Promising Research Award for *You Gotta BE the Book* and the Russell Award for Distinguished Research for *Reading Don't Fix No Chevys.*

Denny Wolfe, a former high school English teacher and department chair, is Professor of English Education, Director of the Tidewater Virginia Writing Project, and Director of the Center for Urban Education at Old Dominion University in Norfolk, Virginia. Author of more than seventy-five articles and books on teaching English, Dr. Wolfe is a frequent consultant to schools and colleges on the teaching of English language arts.

Advisors

Michael Angelotti
Professor of Instructional Leadership and Academic Curriculum, English/Literacy Education
College of Education
University of Oklahoma

Larry Beason
Associate Professor of English and Director of Freshman Composition Program
University of South Alabama

Charles Duke
Dean of Reich College of Education
Appalachian State University

Carol Booth Olson
Director
University of California, Irvine, Writing Project

Willis L. Pitkin
Professor of English
Utah State University

Judith Summerfield
Professor of English and Director of Freshman Year Initiative
Queens College
City University of New York

Bonnie S. Sunstein
Associate Professor of English and Education
College of Education
University of Iowa

Educational Reviewers

Lenore Croudy
Flint Community School
Flint, Michigan

John A. Grant
St. Louis Public Schools
St. Louis, Missouri

Vicki Haker
Mead Junior High School
Mead, Washington

Frederick G. Johnson
Georgia Department of Education
Atlanta, Georgia

Sterling C. Jones Jr.
Detroit Public Schools
Detroit, Michigan

Barry Kincaid
Raytown School District
Kansas City, Missouri

Evelyn G. Lewis
Newark Public Schools
Newark, New Jersey

M. DeAnn Morris
Crescenta Valley High School
La Crescenta, California

Anita Moss
University of North Carolina
Charlotte, North Carolina

Ann S. O'Toole
Chesterfield County Schools
Richmond, Virginia

Suzanne Owens
Glendale High School
Glendale, California

Sally P. Pfeifer
Lewis and Clark High School
Spokane, Washington

Marie Rogers
Independence High School
Charlotte, North Carolina

Barbara Schubert
Santa Clara County Office of Education
San Jose, California

Ronnie Spilton
Chattahoochee High School
Alpharetta, Georgia

Robert Stolte
Huntington Beach High School
Huntington Beach, California

Student Advisory Board

The Student Advisory Board was formed in an effort to ensure student involvement in the development of *Writer's Choice.* The editors wish to thank members of the board for their enthusiasm and dedication to the project. The editors also wish to thank the many student writers whose models appear in this book.

BOOK OVERVIEW

Part 1 Composition

Part 2 Grammar, Usage, and Mechanics

Part 3 Resources and Skills

Reference Section

CONTENTS

Part 1 Composition

UNIT 6

Persuasive Writing

UNIT 9

Troubleshooter 386

Problems and Solutions

Business and Technical Writing 412

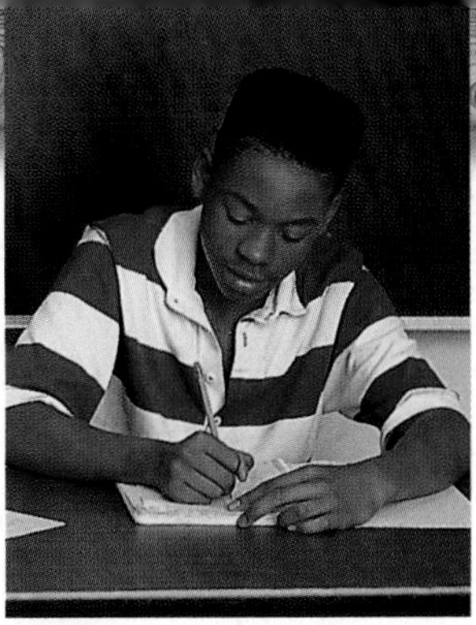

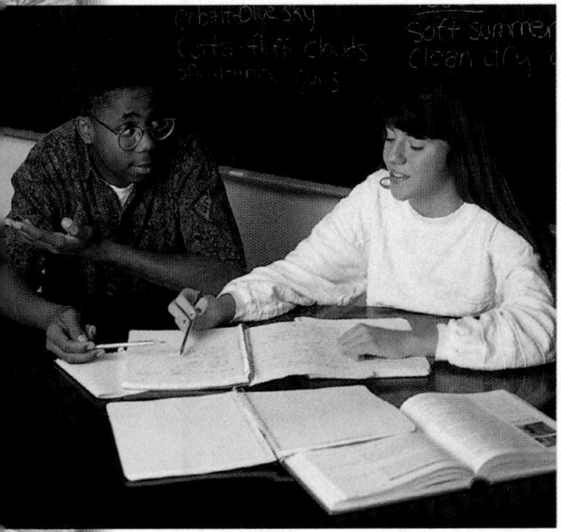

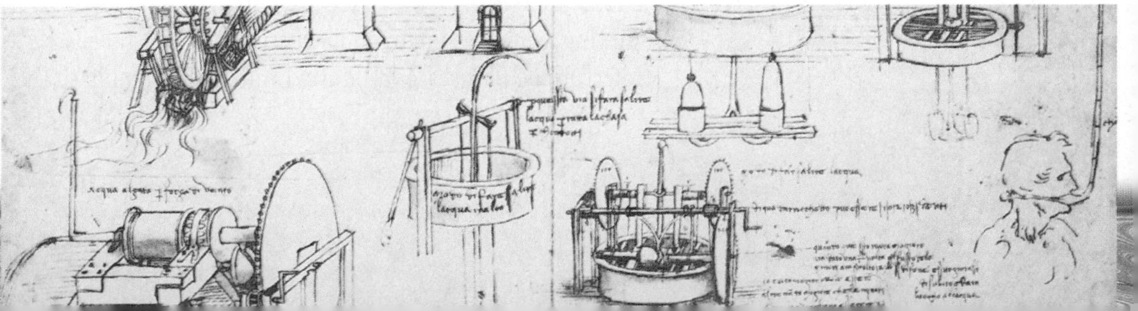

Part 2 Grammar, Usage, and Mechanics

UNIT 10 Parts of Speech

UNIT 13 Clauses and Sentence Structure 542

Instruction and Practice

UNIT 14 Diagraming Sentences 574

Instruction and Practice

UNIT 15 Verb Tenses and Voice 584

UNIT 16 Subject-Verb Agreement 612

UNIT 17 Using Pronouns Correctly 636

UNIT 21 Punctuation, Abbreviations, and Numbers....... 732

Part 3 Resources and Skills

COMPOSITION

UNIT 31

Electronic Resources 908

Instruction and Practice

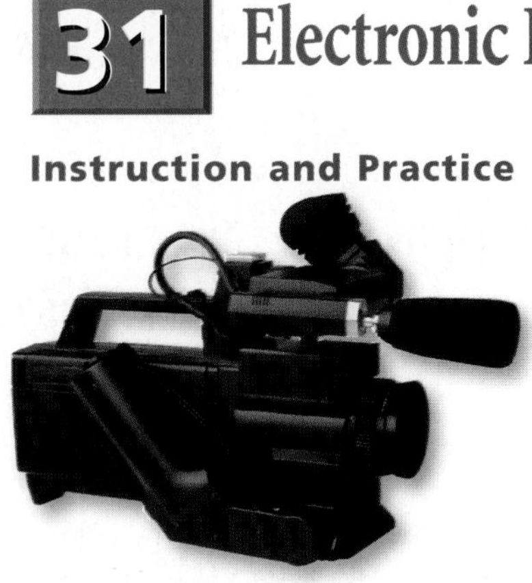

Quick Help

Reference Section *Fast answers to questions about writing, research, and language*

LITERATURE MODELS

Composition Models

Each literature selection is an extended example of the mode of writing taught in the unit.

Skill Models

Excerpts from outstanding works of fiction and nonfiction exemplify specific writing skills.

LITERATURE MODELS

Skill Models *continued*

Language Models

Each Grammar Review uses excerpts to link grammar, usage, or mechanics to literature.

FINE ART

Fine art—paintings, drawings, photos, and sculpture—is used to teach and stimulate ideas for writing.

GLENCOE

Writer's Choice

Grammar and Composition

Welcome to Writer's Choice!

Your writing and your choices are what this book is all about. Take a few minutes to get to know each of the book's four main parts: Composition; Grammar, Usage, and Mechanics; Resources and Skills; and the Writing and Research Handbook.

Part 1

Composition

How do you become a better writer? By writing! Four-page lessons give you the strategies you need to improve your writing skills. Each lesson focuses on a specific writing problem or task, offers clear instruction, shows models of effective writing, and—most importantly—provides a variety of writing activities for you to practice what you've learned.

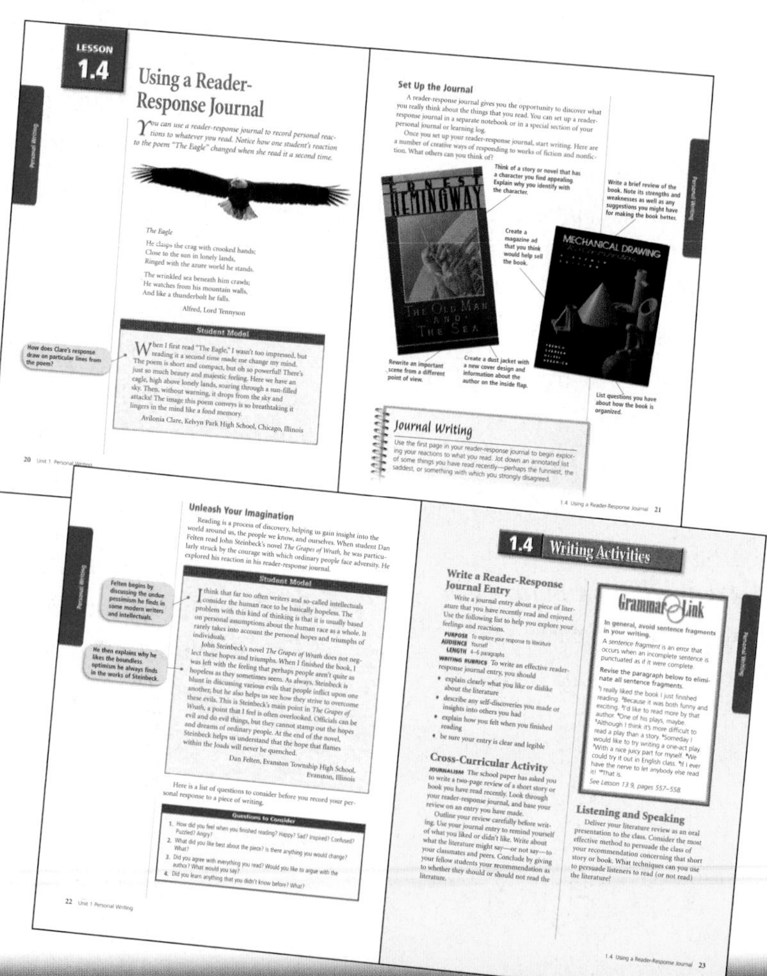

Part 2

Grammar, Usage, and Mechanics

Short focused lessons make learning grammar easy. Rules and definitions teach you the basics, while examples and literature models show you how the concepts are used in real-life writing.

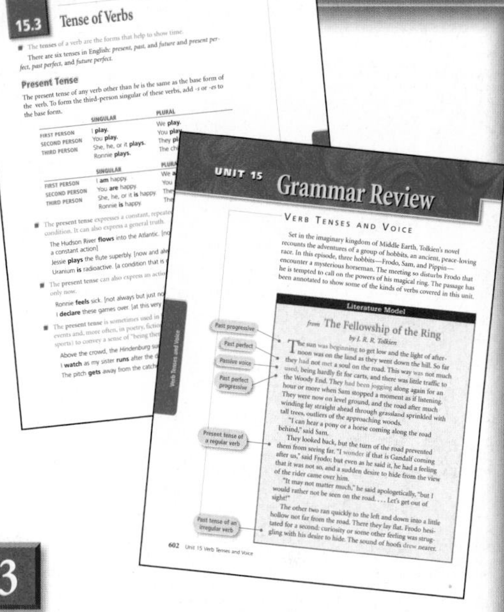
UNIT 15 **Grammar Review**

VERB TENSES AND VOICE

Set in the imaginary kingdom of Middle Earth, Tolkien's novel recounts the adventures of a group of hobbits, an ancient, peace-loving race. In this episode, three hobbits—Frodo, Sam, and Pippin—encounter a mysterious horseman. The meeting so disturbs Frodo that he is tempted to call on the powers of his magical ring. The passage has been annotated to show some of the kinds of verbs covered in this unit.

Literature Model

from The Fellowship of the Ring

by J. R. R. Tolkien

The sun was beginning to get low and the light of afternoon was on the land as they went down the hill. So far they had not met a soul on the road. This way was not much used, being hardly fit for carts, and there was little traffic to the Woody End. They had been jogging along again for an hour or more when Sam stopped a moment as if listening. They were now on level ground, and the road after much winding lay straight ahead through grassland sprinkled with tall trees, outliers of the approaching woods.

"I can hear a pony or a horse coming along the road behind," said Sam.

They looked back, but the turn of the road prevented them from seeing far. "I wonder if that is Gandalf coming after us," said Frodo; but even as he said it, he had a feeling that it was not so, and a sudden desire to hide from the view of the rider came over him.

"It may not matter much," he said apologetically, "but I would rather not be seen on the road. . . . Let's get out of sight!"

The other two ran quickly to the left and down into a little hollow not far from the road. There they lay flat. Frodo hesitated for a second: curiosity or some other feeling was struggling with his desire to hide. The sound of hoofs drew nearer.

602 Unit 15 Verb Tenses and Voice

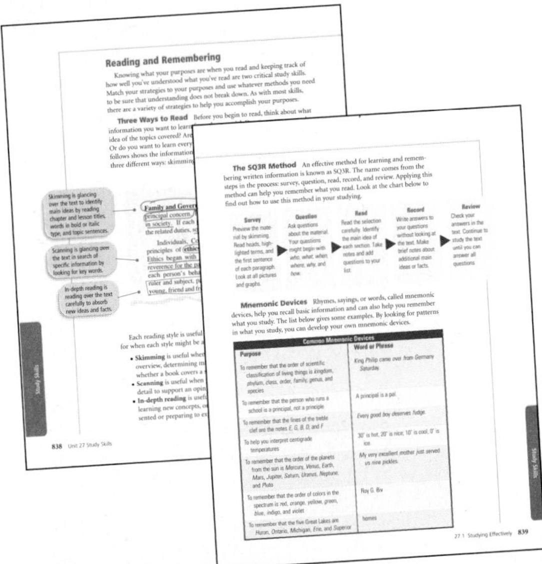
The SQ3R Method An effective method for learning and remembering written information is known as SQ3R. The name comes from the steps in the process: survey, question, read, record, and review. Applying this method can help you remember what you read. Look at the chart below to find out how to use this method in your studying.

Mnemonic Devices Rhymes, sayings, or words, called mnemonic devices, help you recall basic information and can also help you remember what you study. The list below gives some examples. By looking for patterns in what you study, you can develop your own mnemonic devices.

Common Mnemonic Devices	
Purpose	**Word or Phrase**
To remember that the order of scientific classification of living things is *kingdom, phylum, class, order, family, genus,* and *species*	*King Philip came over from Germany Saturday*
To remember that the person who runs a school is a principal, not a principle	A principal is a pal
To remember that the lines of the treble clef are the notes *E, G, B, D,* and *F*	*Every good boy deserves fudge*
To help you interpret centigrade temperatures	30° is hot, 20° is nice, 10° is cool, 0° is ice
To remember that the order of the planets from the sun is *Mercury, Venus, Earth, Mars, Jupiter, Saturn, Uranus, Neptune,* and *Pluto*	*My very excellent mother just served us nine pickles*
To remember that the order of colors in the spectrum is *red, orange, yellow, green, blue, indigo,* and *violet*	Roy G. Biv
To remember that the five Great Lakes are *Huron, Ontario, Michigan, Erie,* and *Superior*	homes

27.1 Studying Effectively 839

Part 3

Resources and Skills

Would you like to improve your study skills, learn how to give a speech, or get better at taking tests? The lessons in this part give you the skills you need to do all these things and more. Each lesson is complete, concise, and easy to use.

Writing and Research Handbook

This user-friendly handbook gives explanations, examples, and tips to help you write strong sentences, paragraphs, compositions, and research papers. Use it whenever you get stuck!

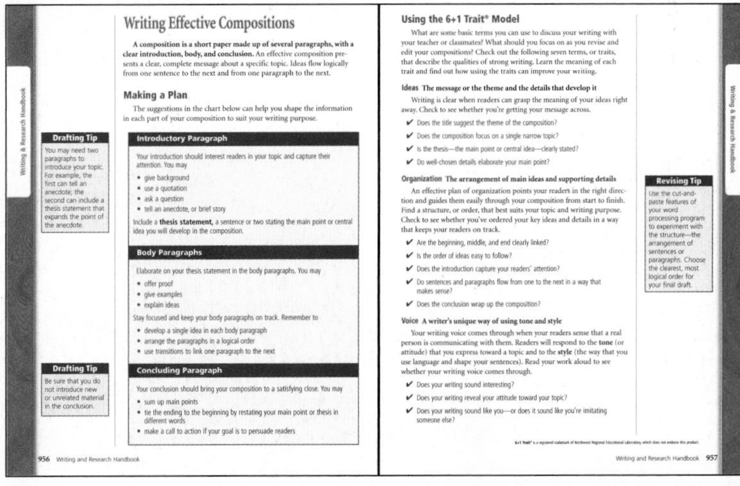
Writing Effective Compositions

A composition is a short paper made up of several paragraphs, with a clear introduction, body, and conclusion. An effective composition presents a clear, complete message about a specific topic. Ideas flow logically from one sentence to the next and from one paragraph to the next.

Making a Plan

The suggestions in the chart below can help you shape the information in each part of your composition to suit your writing purpose.

Introductory Paragraph

Your introduction should interest readers in your topic and capture their attention. You may
- give background
- use a quotation
- ask a question
- tell an anecdote, or brief story

Include a **thesis statement,** a sentence or two stating the main point or central idea you will develop in the composition.

Body Paragraphs

Elaborate on your thesis statement in the body paragraphs. You may
- offer proof
- give examples
- explain ideas

Stay focused and keep your body paragraphs on track. Remember to
- develop a single idea in each body paragraph
- arrange the paragraphs in a logical order
- use transitions to link one paragraph to the next

Concluding Paragraph

Your conclusion should bring your composition to a satisfying close. You may
- sum up main points
- tie the ending to the beginning by restating your main point or thesis in different words
- make a call to action if your goal is to persuade readers

Drafting Tip
You may need two paragraphs to introduce your topic. For example, the first can tell an anecdote; the second can include a thesis statement that expands the point of the anecdote.

Drafting Tip
Be sure that you do not introduce new or unrelated material in the conclusion.

956 Writing and Research Handbook

Using the 6+1 Trait® Model

What are some basic terms you can use to discuss your writing with your teacher or classmates? What should you focus on as you revise and edit your compositions? Check out the following seven terms, or traits, that describe the qualities of strong writing. Learn the meaning of each trait and find out how using the traits can improve your writing.

Ideas The message or the theme and the details that develop it

Writing is clear when readers can grasp the meaning of your ideas right away. Check to see whether you're getting your message across.
- ✔ Does the title suggest the theme of the composition?
- ✔ Does the composition focus on a single narrow topic?
- ✔ Is the thesis—the main point or central idea—clearly stated?
- ✔ Do well-chosen details elaborate your main point?

Organization The arrangement of main ideas and supporting details

An effective plan of organization points your readers in the right direction and guides them easily through your composition from start to finish. Find a structure, or order, that best suits your topic and writing purpose. Check to see whether you've ordered your key ideas and details in a way that keeps your readers on track.
- ✔ Are the beginning, middle, and end clearly linked?
- ✔ Is the order of ideas easy to follow?
- ✔ Does the introduction capture your readers' attention?
- ✔ Do sentences and paragraphs flow from one to the next in a way that makes sense?
- ✔ Does the conclusion wrap up the composition?

Voice A writer's unique way of using tone and style

Your writing voice comes through when your readers sense that a real person is communicating with them. Readers will respond to the **tone** (or attitude) that you express toward a topic and to the **style** (the way that you use language and shape your sentences). Read your work aloud to see whether your writing voice comes through.
- ✔ Does your writing sound interesting?
- ✔ Does your writing reveal your attitude toward your topic?
- ✔ Does your writing sound like you—or does it sound like you're imitating someone else?

Revising Tip
Use the cut-and-paste features of your word processing program to experiment with the structure—the arrangement of sentences or paragraphs. Choose the clearest, most logical order for your final draft.

Writing and Research Handbook 957

"The white mares of the moon rush along the sky
Beating their golden hoofs upon the glass heavens . . ."

—Amy Lowell

Albert Bierstadt, *Study for the Last of the Buffalo,* 1888

PART 1

Composition

"There, among the geraniums and pots of yerbubuena I would bring to them the news of the war."
—Mary Helen Ponce, "How I Changed the War and Won the Game"

UNIT 1

Personal Writing

Writing in the Real World

Journal writers, unlike other writers, usually compose just for themselves. Keeping a journal helps these writers to explore the world around them and to examine their own lives. It can also serve as a source of ideas for other types of writing. The following is a journal entry by Denise Chavez, an award-winning playwright, poet, and fiction writer.

The Personal Journals of Denise Chavez

By Denise Chavez

August 28
Beginning
9:00 a m Wednesday in my new notebook—the paper seems harsh, perhaps too crisp, but I am happy to be writing in this new Journal—it indicates to me a time of Beginning—it is the Birth of many new things in my life, although at the same time (ironically, comically.) it signifies perhaps too, the Death of many things . . . this time of year . . .

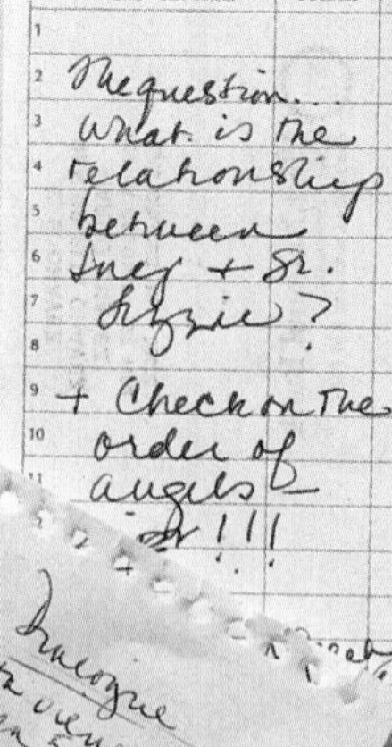

When Chavez forgets her journal and an idea hits her, she'll write on whatever is handy—whether a check stub or a restaurant napkin.

Author Denise Chavez

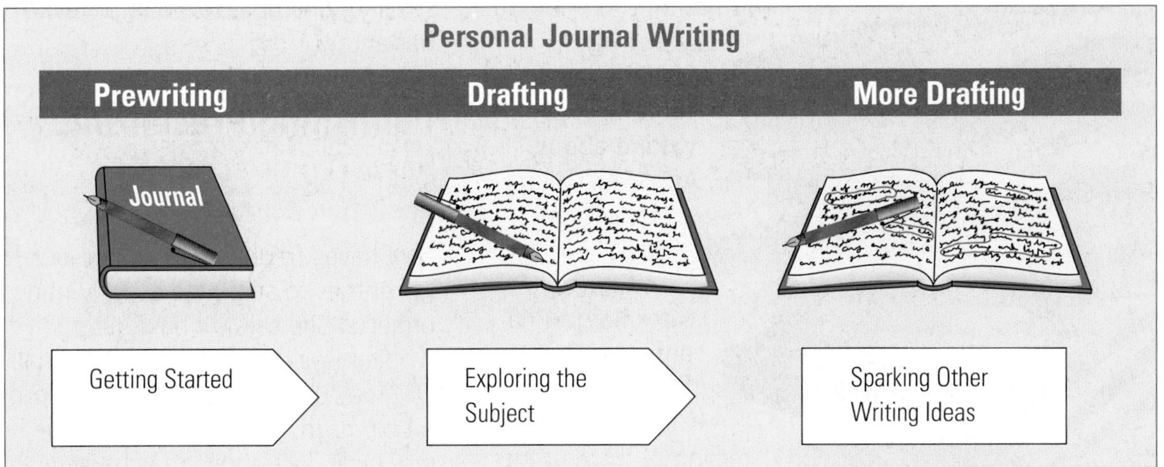

A Writer's Process

Prewriting:

Getting Started

Denise Chavez completes two or three personal journals each year, which she stores on a shelf in her back room. "I've kept a journal for almost as long as I can remember," she says; "I feel healthier and happier when I'm recording." Chavez's journals help her both to look within herself and to explore the world around her. "Writing a journal helps me keep abreast of what's going on in my life," explains Chavez. "Looking back over my journal, I can see patterns of my own behavior and personality. I've learned a lot by what I've loved and by what I've chosen. Keeping a journal is something I do for mental health."

Before beginning a new journal, Chavez gives it a title. She explains, "I may call it 'On the Road' or 'Becoming.' Each journal represents a chunk of time in which I'll be working on some personal goal, and the title gives me a point of focus. It's with great joy that I greet these new journals."

Drafting/Revising:

Exploring the Subject

Chavez usually writes in her journal just before going to bed, but she also carries her journal with her, in case she is inspired to jot something down. Chavez doesn't have to look far to find things to write about. She says, "I write more when I travel, but I don't have to go beyond my own house to find things to write about. We got a cat whom we named Pascualita.

A personal journal can be a record of your thoughts and memories. Whatever you choose to record, it's a place where you can try out your writing ideas in private.

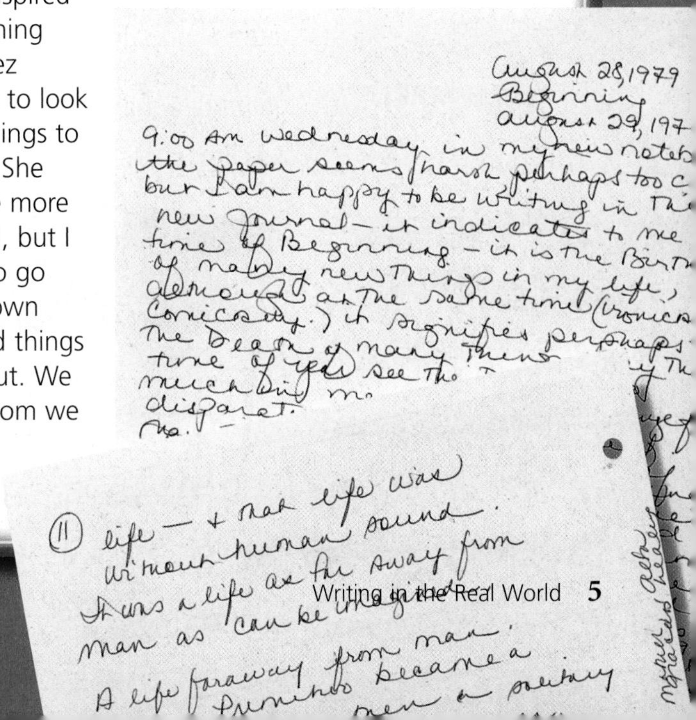

Writing in the Real World

This brought to mind an aunt of my mother's and I found myself writing about Aunt Pascualita for several days."

Chavez writes her journal entries in longhand. She says, "I like the physical feeling of moving the pen across the paper. I've always liked paper, the feel of it. I use artists' sketch pads, because I never write with lines. I think lines are very restrictive and don't allow for the organic, natural process. If I want to draw a picture or put in a newspaper clipping, I have room."

Years of journal keeping can result in a personal library of journals.

"Sometimes," she continues, "I write all the way around the page. That's when the writing is coming so fast, I can't stop. There's no time to flip the page. At other times, I may allow myself to put just one word on a page."

As she writes, Chavez pays little attention to grammar or spelling, since for her the ideas are more important than the syntax or spelling. She does not edit or revise her entries.

Publishing/Presenting:

Journal Writing Leads to Published Works

Chavez frequently uses her journal entries to stimulate other writing projects. She says, "I have seen whole plays come out of my journal. Or I may use the journal to work out problems in my plays, such as biographical data about the characters or the setting."

Chavez began working on her short story "Evening in Paris" in her journal. She says, "I had a deadline to get this story in to a magazine. I just started writing about Christmas and putting together some of the smells. I remembered that we always had a chicken for Christmas because we couldn't afford a turkey. I kept writing down things and I worked on it every day. Finally, I had pages of notes in my journal. When I began to write the story, I already had my guide, my road map, in the journal, so I was pretty sure of the road I'd be driving on as I wrote the story."

Chavez's journal writing exploration seems unlimited. She notes, "I never run out of things to write about. In fact, I'm booked for the rest of my life."

Denise Chavez's novel The Last of the Menu Girls *was also produced as a play.*

Examining Writing in the Real World

Analyzing the Media Connection

Discuss these questions about the journal entry on page 4.

1. How does Chavez begin her journal entry? Do you think this is a typical way for journal writers to begin? Why or why not?
2. Why do you think Chavez uses dashes in her entry instead of periods?
3. What subjects does Chavez explore in her entry?
4. How would you characterize the style of writing Chavez uses in her entry?
5. How might Chavez use this journal entry as a springboard for her professional writing?

Analyzing a Writer's Process

Discuss these questions about Denise Chavez's writing process.

1. What are some reasons that Chavez gives for keeping a journal?
2. When does Chavez write in her journal?
3. Describe Chavez's technique for drafting her journal entries.

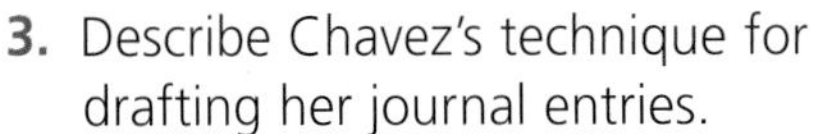

4. Where does Chavez get ideas for her journal writing?
5. What role do Chavez's journal entries play in her professional writing?

Use adjective clauses to create variety in sentence structure.

An *adjective clause* is a subordinate clause that modifies a noun or a pronoun. For example, Denise Chavez writes the following:

> *We got a cat* ***whom we named Pascualita.***

An adjective clause that is not needed to make the meaning of a sentence clear is set off by commas.

Add an adjective clause to each sentence below, using correct punctuation.

1. My brother James keeps a journal.
2. He writes a lot about sports and about our dog.
3. Sometimes he also writes for the school paper.
4. James wrote a great story about the basketball team.
5. The coach wants him to do a feature story about sports injuries.

See Lesson 13.5, pages 549–550.

LESSON 1.1

Writing to Discover Your World

Recording ideas and feelings in a personal journal is a risk-free way to learn about yourself and your world.

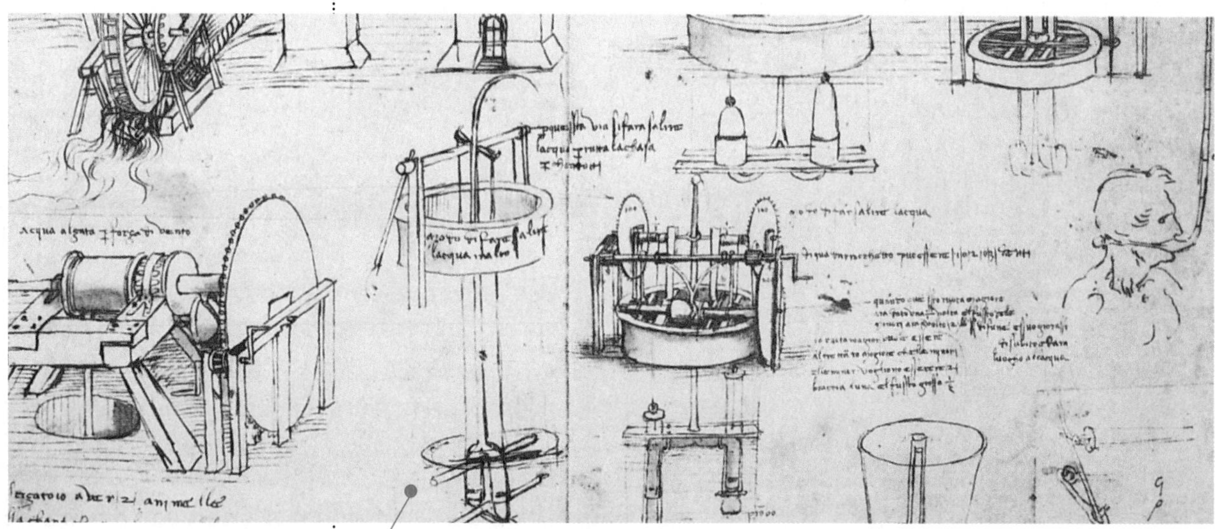

Da Vinci, Renaissance artist, filled his notebooks with detailed drawings and diagrams dealing with art, engineering, architecture, and other topics.

Plath, a modern American poet, wrote this entry when she was eighteen. What does this passage reveal about her reasons for keeping a journal?

Literature Model

Some things are hard to write about. After something happens to you, you go to write it down, and either you overdramatize it or underplay it, exaggerate the wrong parts or ignore the important ones. At any rate, you never write it quite the way you want to. I've just got to put down what happened to me this afternoon. I can't tell Mother; not yet, anyway. She was in my room when I came home, fussing with clothes, and she didn't even sense that something had happened. She just kept scolding and chattering on and on. So I couldn't stop and tell her. No matter how it comes out, I have to write it.

Sylvia Plath, *The Journals of Sylvia Plath*

Start Your Own Personal Journal

A personal journal is a place where you can try out your writing ideas without risk. You can follow your thoughts wherever they lead, explore new ideas, and sort out feelings. Here are some tips for getting started with your own personal journal.

Tips for Journal Writing

1. Write whatever comes to mind. Write about thoughts and memories that have special significance for you.
2. Write on a regular basis, either every day or every other day.
3. Date each journal entry for future reference.

Try Out New Writing Ideas

A journal is the ideal place for exploring personal thoughts and insights into situations. It is perfect for other kinds of writing, too. Some people experiment with poetry. Others try out ideas for stories and plays. You don't have to limit yourself to writing. You can include original cartoons, comic strips, even doodles. The following chart shows other kinds of items you can include in your journal.

Personal Journal Entries			
Unsent Letters	**Dear Gabby Letters**	**Tongue-in-Cheek Ads**	**Words and Music**
to parents or friends dealing with problems that you would like to discuss face to face—but can't	about problems that bug you (you might want to play Gabby and write the replies, too)	about diet and exercise, mixing sound advice about nutrition and health with good-natured humor	for original songs—pop, country, or rock-and-roll (the choice is up to you)

Journal Writing

People choose a variety of formats for their personal journals—spiral notebooks, loose-leaf notebooks, even computer disks. Decide which format will work best for you, and start your own personal journal. In your first entry, write what you hope journal writing will do for you.

Don't Be Afraid to Experiment

You will want to experiment with different ways of recording information in your journal. Da Vinci, for example, filled his notebooks with drawings and diagrams, and he wrote backward. The following examples demonstrate different ways of exploring the same early childhood experiences.

One way of exploring early childhood memories is to write freely about each experience as it comes to mind.

Another way is to create an experience map, with captions highlighting significant events.

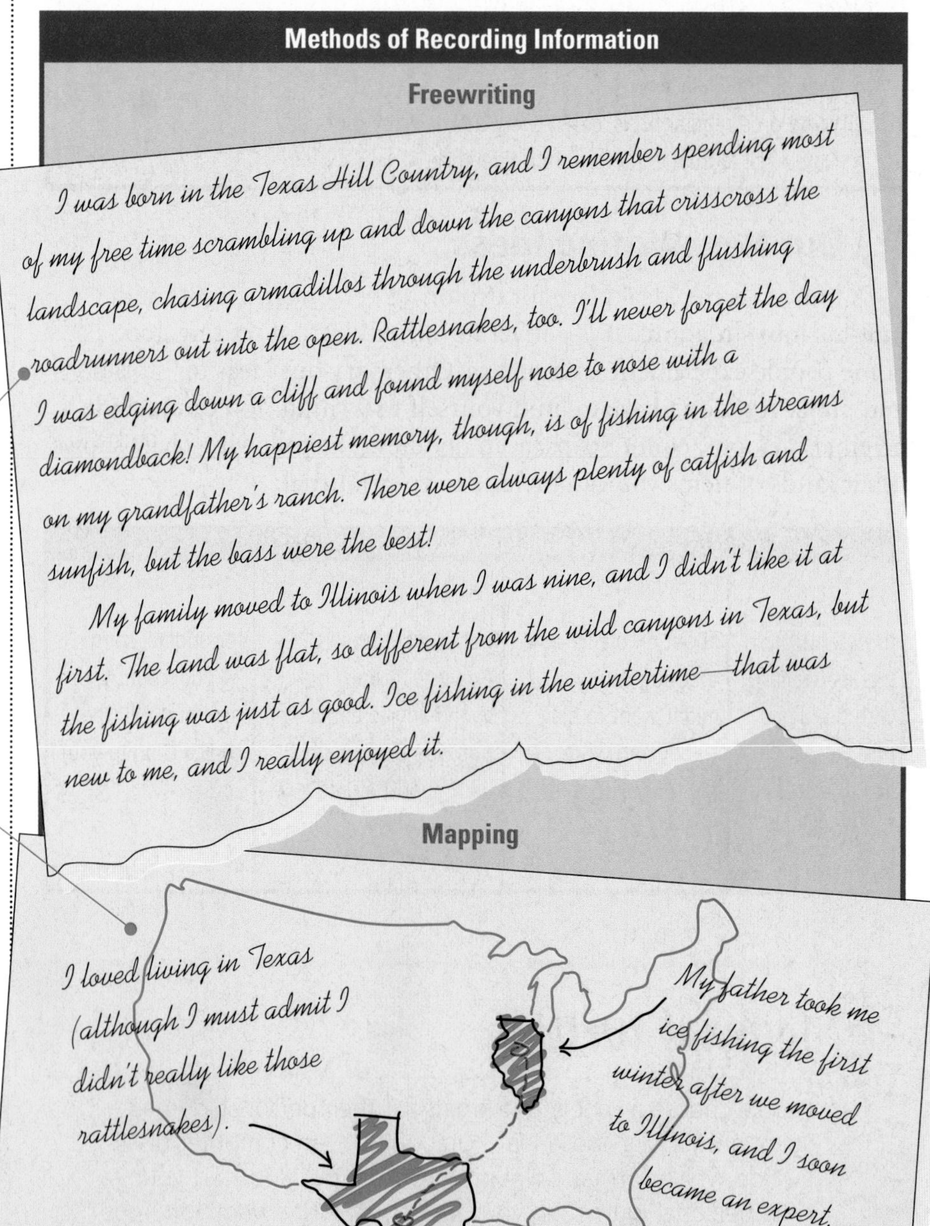

Methods of Recording Information
Freewriting
I was born in the Texas Hill Country, and I remember spending most of my free time scrambling up and down the canyons that crisscross the landscape, chasing armadillos through the underbrush and flushing roadrunners out into the open. Rattlesnakes, too. I'll never forget the day I was edging down a cliff and found myself nose to nose with a diamondback! My happiest memory, though, is of fishing in the streams on my grandfather's ranch. There were always plenty of catfish and sunfish, but the bass were the best!
My family moved to Illinois when I was nine, and I didn't like it at first. The land was flat, so different from the wild canyons in Texas, but the fishing was just as good. Ice fishing in the wintertime—that was new to me, and I really enjoyed it.
Mapping
I loved living in Texas (although I must admit I didn't really like those rattlesnakes).
My father took me ice fishing the first winter after we moved to Illinois, and I soon became an expert.

1.1 Writing Activities

Write a Journal Entry

The painting below shows an extended family at a birthday celebration. Examine the scene carefully. Then write your personal reactions in your journal.

PURPOSE Self-discovery
AUDIENCE Yourself
LENGTH 2–3 paragraphs

WRITING RUBRICS To write an effective journal entry, you should

- explore feelings and memories similar to those shown in the painting
- experiment with different ways of recording ideas
- be sure your writing is legible and that it is meaningful to you

Cooperative Learning

In a small group, assign each member a family role. Role-play for five minutes a family conversation—perhaps about an after-school activity.

Carmen Lomas Garza, *Cumpleaños de Lala y Tudi,* 1989

Avoid vague pronoun references.

Even your private writing should make sense when you reread it.

Revise each sentence below to make the pronoun reference clear.

1. Frank got maps for the Saturday hike to Nelson Park, which was a great idea.
2. That day they took along a picnic lunch, but it was cold.
3. Some folks climbed the firetower, which was a spectacular view.
4. The rangers had closed off one park trail, and that changes their plans.
5. The group wants to go on some longer hikes, and it will probably be during spring vacation.

See Lesson 17.6, pages 649–651.

Each group member should write a journal entry about the conversation from the point of view of the role he or she played. Share journal entries and compare reactions.

Listening and Speaking

Imagine you are one of the characters in the painting on this page. Write a journal entry for that character. What might the person be thinking or feeling at the celebration? Read your journal entry aloud to the class. Remember to speak clearly and to read at an appropriate speed.

LESSON 1.2

Using a Learning Log

A learning log is a special kind of journal that can help you clarify your ideas about concepts covered in various classes. The example below shows a page from a learning log for biology, written after a class discussion of nutrition.

The log entry begins with the date and a brief summary of the discussion in class.

The entry includes a notation. It could also have indicated a point for further exploration. What other kinds of notations might you make?

The entry ends with the class assignment.

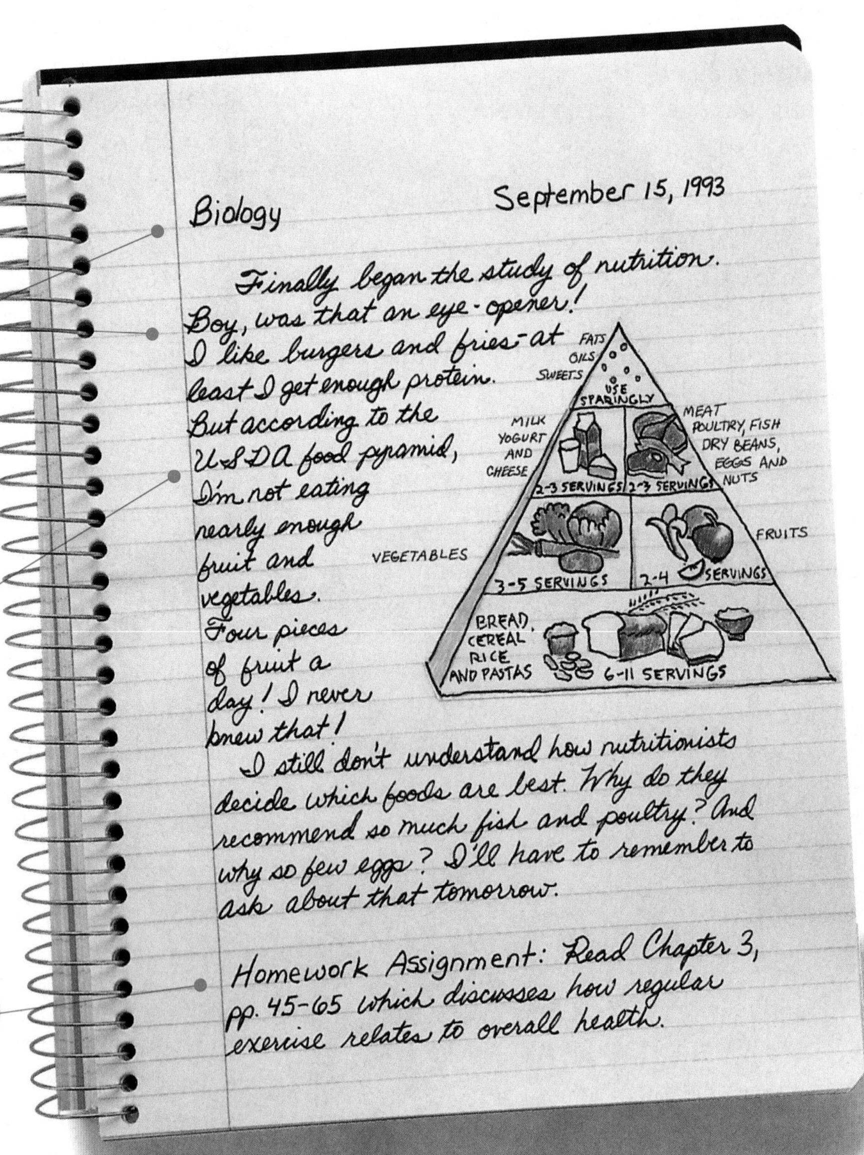

Biology
September 15, 1993
Finally began the study of nutrition. Boy, was that an eye-opener! I like burgers and fries—at least I get enough protein. But according to the USDA food pyramid, I'm not eating nearly enough fruit and vegetables. Four pieces of fruit a day! I never knew that!
I still don't understand how nutritionists decide which foods are best. Why do they recommend so much fish and poultry? And why so few eggs? I'll have to remember to ask about that tomorrow.
Homework Assignment: Read Chapter 3, pp. 45-65 which discusses how regular exercise relates to overall health.
FATS
OILS
SWEETS
USE SPARINGLY
MILK
YOGURT
AND
CHEESE
2-3 SERVINGS
MEAT
POULTRY, FISH
DRY BEANS,
EGGS AND
NUTS
2-3 SERVINGS
VEGETABLES
3-5 SERVINGS
FRUITS
2-4 SERVINGS
BREAD,
CEREAL
RICE
AND PASTAS
6-11 SERVINGS

Write on a Daily Basis

Learning logs work best when you use them on a day-to-day basis, with a separate section for each class. Here are a few tips for using a learning log to keep your studies on track.

Keeping a Learning Log			
Characterize	**Identify**	**Discuss**	**Evaluate**
the main ideas discussed in class. Did you learn anything new?	difficult concepts you want to examine further. Where can you go for help?	a controversial idea that came up in class. Where do you stand on this issue?	your progress on a weekly basis. How are you doing in this class?

Write to Learn

Writing can help you make sense out of new information in any subject area. You never fully know something until you can state it in your own words. The following chart shows some writing-to-learn techniques that you can use to clarify ideas and concepts. Remember that your goal is to make the information make sense to *you.*

A Variety of Writing Ideas	
Idea	**Example**
1. Try to summarize the significance of what you are studying in a single clear sentence.	1. "The study of nutrition teaches us how to select the best diet for better health and longer life."
2. Begin with a particular topic, start freewriting, and see where it leads.	2. "Diet and exercise, exercise and diet, that's all you hear about these days. . . . "
3. As you write, continue to ask why until you exhaust all questions.	3. "Why do we need so much fruit in our diet? For the vitamins, I know, but why are vitamins important?"
4. Set down your point of view, and then deliberately argue against it.	4. "I am dead set against junk food, but . . . "

Journal Writing

In your journal write at least two questions about today's class work in one of your school subjects. Note what you might do to answer your questions.

Personal Writing

Make a Learning Log Work for You

Jenny King found the following passage in her biology textbook difficult to understand, so she used her learning log to help clarify the ideas. She began by creating a diagram to show how ideas in the passage relate. Then she rewrote the passage in her own words.

Muscle strength does not depend on the number of fibers, but rather on their thickness and on how many of them contract at one time. Thicker fibers are stronger and contribute to muscle mass. Exercise stresses muscles slightly; as a result, the fibers increase in size.

Regular exercise can result in overall body fitness and endurance that can affect muscle strength. Body fitness is related to the condition of the heart and the number of capillaries in body tissue. One component of physical fitness is the efficiency of the heart in pumping blood to the tissues. Increased physical fitness results in a greater number of capillaries in the muscle tissue. Endurance is a measure of how long you can continue to exercise and depends on how much fuel your muscles can store. A muscle that is continually exercised is stronger and can store more fuel.

King made a diagram like this to show how the main ideas in the passage relate.

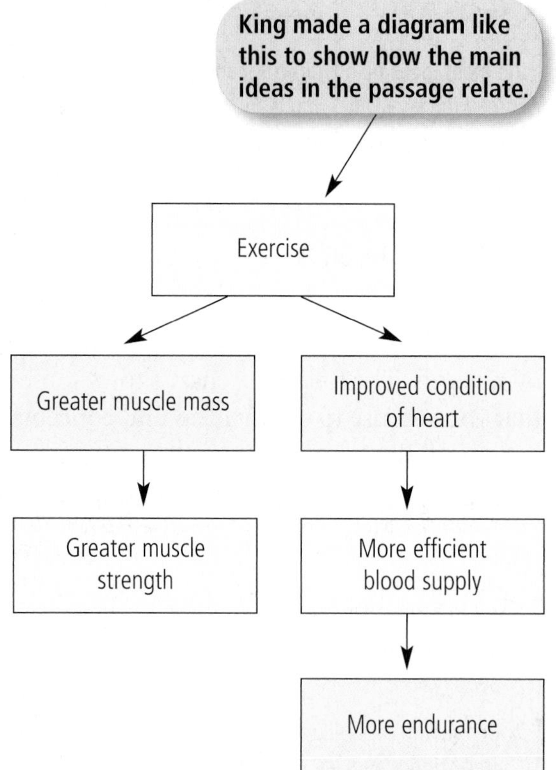

What evidence can you find that King used her diagram to rewrite the passage?

Student Model

Muscle strength depends on the thickness of muscle fibers, how many of the fibers contract at one time, and the amount of fuel stored within the muscle tissue. Exercise relates to all three categories. Exercising the muscles causes slight stress. This stress causes the muscle fibers to increase in thickness and controls the fiber contractions. Exercise also improves the condition of the heart and increases the number of capillaries in body tissue, including muscle tissue. These increased capillaries increase the amount of energy stored within the muscle; therefore, muscle endurance is increased.

Jenny King, Henry Clay High School, Lexington, Kentucky

1.2 Writing Activities

Write a Learning Log

Start using your learning log today in your English, history, or math class, and keep it going for a week. Then reread your log entries. Think about how they have helped you understand your class. Then write a log entry evaluating your experience.

PURPOSE To clarify concepts discussed in class
AUDIENCE Yourself
LENGTH 2–4 paragraphs

WRITING RUBRICS To write an effective learning log, you should

- write for at least three to five minutes for each class session
- begin each entry with a brief summary of the class discussion
- make notes for concepts you do not understand
- be sure your learning log is legible and that it is clear to you

Viewing and Representing

PEER REVIEW Share completed learning logs with your classmates. Discuss the various graphic organizers that you and others used. What makes these particular graphics effective? Discuss your responses in small groups.

Using Computers

If you have access to a personal computer, you may want to keep your learning log electronically. Set up separate files for different classes. As you experiment with writing-to-learn techniques, save and date entries.

Use commas to separate three or more words, phrases, or clauses in a series.

Muscle strength depends on the thickness of muscle fibers, how many of the fibers contract at one time, and the amount of fuel stored within the muscle tissue.

Add any needed comma or commas to each sentence below.

1. Our subway ride to the museum yesterday was long hot and crowded.
2. Over the weekend I had homework assignments for my science math history and English classes.
3. I can't decide whether to join the drama club the school debating team or a new after-school jazz club.
4. The jazz club will meet at our school at a neighboring school and at a professional jazz club downtown.
5. My music and German classes meet on Monday Wednesday and Friday.
6. We got to the museum at one stood in line for an hour and finally toured the exhibit with 35 fourth graders.
7. By Monday I have to memorize a poem finish a history paper plan my science project and make a poster.
8. I'm not sure whether the poem paper project or poster is the place to start.
9. My older brother says I am disorganized forgetful and hopeless.
10. Of course, he can't remember anyone's birthday our parents' anniversary or his own weekend plans.

See Lesson 21.6, page 743.

Personal Writing

LESSON

1.3

Keeping a Commonplace Book

A commonplace book is a collection of items that have some special significance for you personally and that may eventually become a source of writing ideas that you can use for other writing. The model shows entries from a commonplace book assembled by poet Sheila P. Donohue.

Personal Writing

August 18, '86

"I arrived at the end of the tulips, the beginning of the rose; I left as the gladiolas began."
Sharon, about Poland

Maybe the first sentence of a short story? – Idea of changes in the outside world representing emotional phases.

Late August

"Feed 'em, love 'em,
and leave 'em alone."
Dr. Spock on children

Hmm...

September 3, 1986

– Clam shells in piles decay,
the stench of still water
in their shiny throats.

– A quick eye for gulls
dive-bombing the shells and leaving
with a squawk and stiff
flick of wings

from a 9/12/85 draft –
the only interesting parts
Maybe use in a new poem

(Good place names ↑)

Donohue collected several quotations that help her clarify her view of the world.

What do Donohue's notes reveal about her reasons for keeping the quotations for future reference?

Start Your Own Commonplace Book

You can collect whatever you want in your commonplace book—quotations, song lyrics, jokes, menus—anything that you find interesting or thought-provoking. The following display shows other kinds of items you might keep in your book.

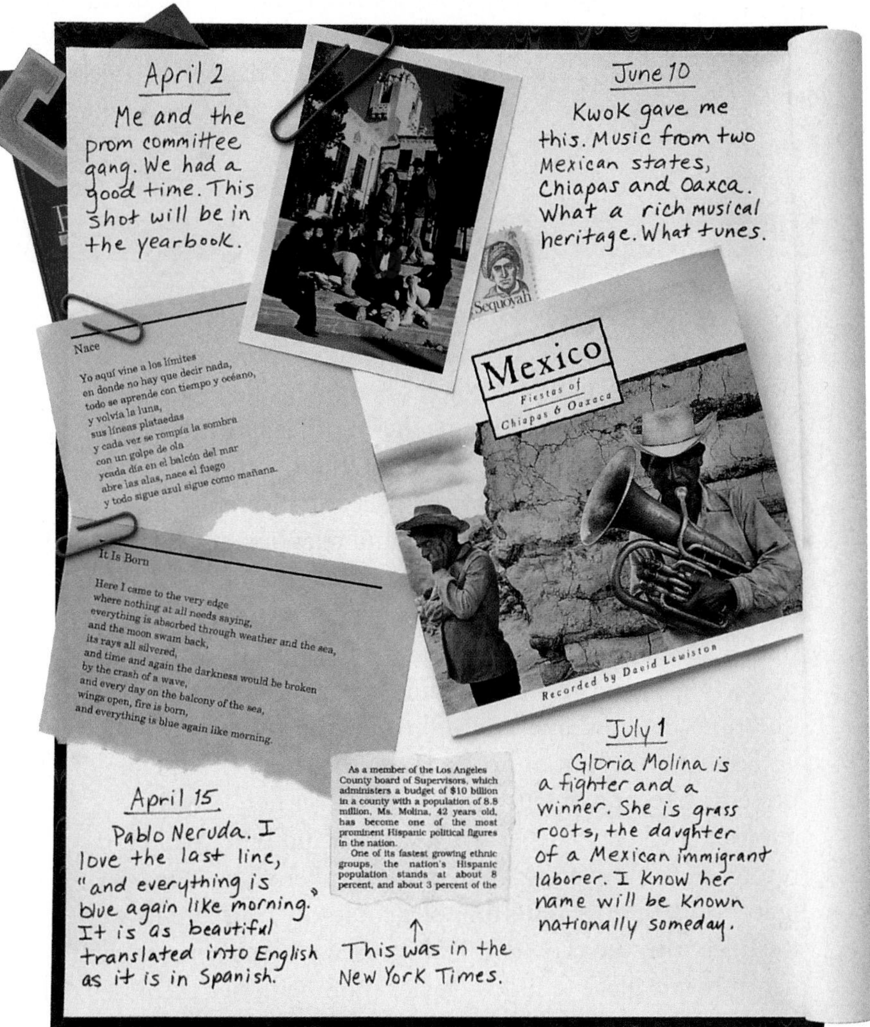

April 2
Me and the prom committee gang. We had a good time. This shot will be in the yearbook.
June 10
Kwok gave me this. Music from two Mexican states, Chiapas and Oaxca. What a rich musical heritage. What tunes.
Sequoyah
Mexico
Fiestas of Chiapas & Oaxaca
Recorded by David Lewiston
Nace
Yo aquí vine a los límites
en donde no hay que decir nada,
todo se aprende con tiempo y océano,
y volvía la luna,
sus líneas plataedas
y cada vez se rompía la sombra
con un golpe de ola
ycada día en el balcón del mar
abre las alas, nace el fuego
y todo sigue azul sigue como mañana.
It Is Born
Here I came to the very edge
where nothing at all needs saying,
everything is absorbed through weather and the sea,
and the moon swam back,
its rays all silvered,
and time and again the darkness would be broken
by the crash of a wave,
and every day on the balcony of the sea,
wings open, fire is born,
and everything is blue again like morning.
April 15
Pablo Neruda. I love the last line, "and everything is blue again like morning." It is as beautiful translated into English as it is in Spanish.
As a member of the Los Angeles County board of Supervisors, which administers a budget of $10 billion in a county with a population of 8.8 million, Ms. Molina, 42 years old, has become one of the most prominent Hispanic political figures in the nation.
One of its fastest growing ethnic groups, the nation's Hispanic population stands at about 8 percent, and about 3 percent of the
This was in the New York Times.
July 1
Gloria Molina is a fighter and a winner. She is grass roots, the daughter of a Mexican immigrant laborer. I know her name will be known nationally someday.

TIME

For more about the writing process, see **TIME Facing the Blank Page,** pp. 109–119.

Personal Writing

Journal Writing

Do some freewriting in your journal, assessing different kinds of items you might want to keep in your own commonplace book.

Explore Ideas for Writing

In her reading Nina Molumby ran across a quotation about responsibility. She wrote a note explaining why she thought the quotation worth saving, and she put the item in her commonplace book. Months later, Nina came across the item again, and it started her thinking. She decided to write a story about responsibility, but with a twist. She would show what could happen to a person who refused to take responsibility for her life.

Character—the willingness to accept responsibility for one's own life—is the source from which self-respect springs.

Joan Didion

Responsibility—that's a word you hear more and more these days:
"Take charge."
"Accept responsibility."
"Just say no."

Personal Writing

Student Model

Sophie sat at her desk in her room, thinking about her life. Last year her mother had left, leaving Sophie alone with her father. Their family problems had intensified over the years with her father's drinking, her mother's irrational behavior, and Sophie's poor performance in school. Eventually, Sophie stopped seeing her friends, replacing busy afternoons of swimming practice and telephone calls with solitude. The only thing that seemed to matter any more was her orchids. She poured into them all her love, since she was unable to share it with anyone else. They served as a barrier, protecting Sophie from her family problems, her teachers' questions, and her own fear of being vulnerable.

Sophie broke out of her daze and drifted back into the present. A feeling of frustration swept over her. Was she another crack-up like her parents? How did other people resolve their problems? All that her family had tried usually failed. Still, there was nothing she could do. Her parents were the ones with the problem. They caused all the agony, leaving her only one place to hide—in her room with her orchids. How could she accept responsibility for a life that was already ruined by others? As for self-respect, the only pride she had was in her plants.

Nina Molumby, Evanston Township High School,
Evanston, Illinois

Molumby's story revolves around a character named Sophie, whose life is on hold because of family troubles.

What echoes of Molumby's journal entry do you hear in these sentences?

As you look through your commonplace book for a writing idea, don't feel constrained by an annotation you wrote long before. It's just a starting point. Open your mind. Follow your ideas wherever they lead. If one leads nowhere, choose another.

1.3 Writing Activities

Write Commonplace Book Annotations

Set up your own commonplace book, and start collecting items that interest you. Look for things related to the themes of self-discovery and self-improvement. You can include such things as a cartoon, a photo, or lines from a song.

PURPOSE Self-discovery
AUDIENCE Yourself
LENGTH 4 or more annotations

WRITING RUBRICS To write an effective commonplace book, you should

- choose items that are important to you
- write a brief note explaining each item
- make notes for concepts you do not understand
- be sure your annotations are clear and legible

Spelling

LEARNING NEW WORDS As you gather information for your commonplace book, you will probably come across words that are new to you. When you first hear a new word, you can make a note of it, attempting to spell it correctly. Later, to be sure of the correct spelling, use a dictionary or spelling-checker software. Usually, you will be able to spell enough of a word to find it in a dictionary or with a spelling-checker. If you don't find the word at first, try other possible spellings. (Spelling-checker software will suggest possible spellings if you've spelled the word incorrectly.)

Grammar Link

A verb must agree with its subject, not with the predicate nominative that follows it.

In the student model, Nina Molumby correctly writes, *The only thing that seemed to matter . . . was her orchids.*

Complete each sentence to make the subject and verb agree.

1. In northern states, snowmobiles (is, are) a common form of winter transportation.
2. The puppies (is, are) an added expense for the family.
3. The first item on the agenda (was, were) the needs of the new tenants.
4. Baseball cards (is, are) his only topic of conversation.
5. The favorite dessert (was, were) strawberries with ice cream.

See Lesson 16.2, page 615.

Viewing and Representing

With a small group of classmates, create a "commonplace bulletin board" for the classroom. Choose a general theme for your collection. Have each group member contribute things he or she makes. Decide how to assemble the items for display.

LESSON 1.4

Using a Reader-Response Journal

Personal Writing

You can use a reader-response journal to record personal reactions to whatever you read. Notice how one student's reaction to the poem "The Eagle" changed when she read it a second time.

The Eagle

He clasps the crag with crooked hands;
Close to the sun in lonely lands,
Ringed with the azure world he stands.

The wrinkled sea beneath him crawls;
He watches from his mountain walls,
And like a thunderbolt he falls.

Alfred, Lord Tennyson

Student Model

When I first read "The Eagle," I wasn't too impressed, but reading it a second time made me change my mind. The poem is short and compact, but oh so powerful! There's just so much beauty and majestic feeling. Here we have an eagle, high above lonely lands, soaring through a sun-filled sky. Then, without warning, it drops from the sky and attacks! The image this poem conveys is so breathtaking it lingers in the mind like a fond memory.

Avilonia Clare, Kelvyn Park High School, Chicago, Illinois

How does Clare's response draw on particular lines from the poem?

Set Up the Journal

A reader-response journal gives you the opportunity to discover what you really think about the things that you read. You can set up a reader-response journal in a separate notebook or in a special section of your personal journal or learning log.

Once you set up your reader-response journal, start writing. Here are a number of creative ways of responding to works of fiction and nonfiction. What others can you think of?

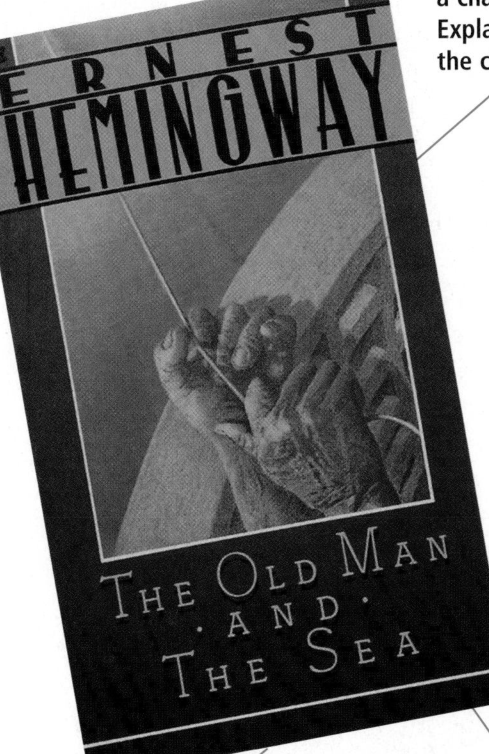

Think of a story or novel that has a character you find appealing. Explain why you identify with the character.

Create a magazine ad that you think would help sell the book.

Rewrite an important scene from a different point of view.

Create a dust jacket with a new cover design and information about the author on the inside flap.

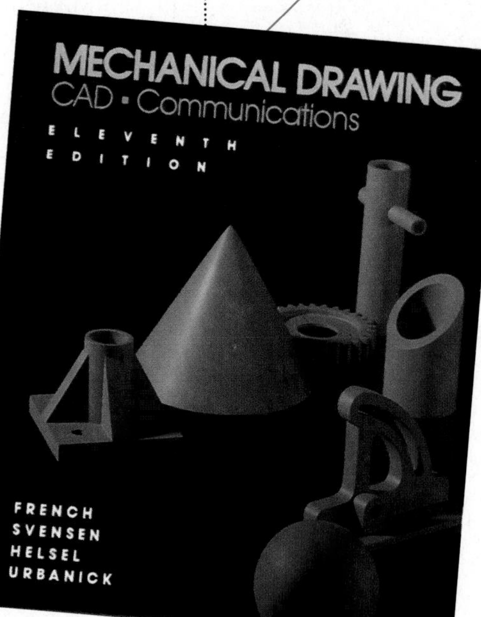

Write a brief review of the book. Note its strengths and weaknesses as well as any suggestions you might have for making the book better.

List questions you have about how the book is organized.

Journal Writing

Use the first page in your reader-response journal to begin exploring your reactions to what you read. Jot down an annotated list of some things you have read recently—perhaps the funniest, the saddest, or something with which you strongly disagreed.

Personal Writing

Unleash Your Imagination

Reading is a process of discovery, helping us gain insight into the world around us, the people we know, and ourselves. When student Dan Felten read John Steinbeck's novel *The Grapes of Wrath,* he was particularly struck by the courage with which ordinary people face adversity. He explored his reaction in his reader-response journal.

Felten begins by discussing the undue pessimism he finds in some modern writers and intellectuals.

He then explains why he likes the boundless optimism he always finds in the works of Steinbeck.

Student Model

I think that far too often writers and so-called intellectuals consider the human race to be basically hopeless. The problem with this kind of thinking is that it is usually based on personal assumptions about the human race as a whole. It rarely takes into account the personal hopes and triumphs of individuals.

John Steinbeck's novel *The Grapes of Wrath* does not neglect these hopes and triumphs. When I finished the book, I was left with the feeling that perhaps people aren't quite as hopeless as they sometimes seem. As always, Steinbeck is blunt in discussing various evils that people inflict upon one another, but he also helps us see how they strive to overcome these evils. This is Steinbeck's main point in *The Grapes of Wrath,* a point that I feel is often overlooked. Officials can be evil and do evil things, but they cannot stamp out the hopes and dreams of ordinary people. At the end of the novel, Steinbeck helps us understand that the hope that flames within the Joads will never be quenched.

Dan Felten, Evanston Township High School,
Evanston, Illinois

Here is a list of questions to consider before you record your personal response to a piece of writing.

Questions to Consider

1. How did you feel when you finished reading? Happy? Sad? Inspired? Confused? Puzzled? Angry?
2. What did you like best about the piece? Is there anything you would change? What?
3. Did you agree with everything you read? Would you like to argue with the author? What would you say?
4. Did you learn anything that you didn't know before? What?

1.4 Writing Activities

Write a Reader-Response Journal Entry

Write a journal entry about a piece of literature that you have recently read and enjoyed. Use the following list to help you explore your feelings and reactions.

PURPOSE To explore your response to literature
AUDIENCE Yourself
LENGTH 4–6 paragraphs

WRITING RUBRICS To write an effective reader-response journal entry, you should

- explain clearly what you like or dislike about the literature
- describe any self-discoveries you made or insights into others you had
- explain how you felt when you finished reading
- be sure your entry is clear and legible

In general, avoid sentence fragments in your writing.

A *sentence fragment* is an error that occurs when an incomplete sentence is punctuated as if it were complete.

Revise the paragraph below to eliminate all sentence fragments.

[1]I really liked the book I just finished reading. [2]Because it was both funny and exciting. [3]I'd like to read more by that author. [4]One of his plays, maybe. [5]Although I think it's more difficult to read a play than a story. [6]Someday I would like to try writing a one-act play. [7]With a nice juicy part for myself. [8]We could try it out in English class. [9]If I ever have the nerve to let anybody else read it! [10]That is.

See Lesson 13.9, pages 557–558.

Cross-Curricular Activity

JOURNALISM The school paper has asked you to write a two-page review of a short story or book you have read recently. Look through your reader-response journal, and base your review on an entry you have made.

Outline your review carefully before writing. Use your journal entry to remind yourself of what you liked or didn't like. Write about what the literature might say—or not say—to your classmates and peers. Conclude by giving your fellow students your recommendation as to whether they should or should not read the literature.

Listening and Speaking

Deliver your literature review as an oral presentation to the class. Consider the most effective method to persuade the class of your recommendation concerning that short story or book. What techniques can you use to persuade listeners to read (or not read) the literature?

LESSON
1.5

WRITING ABOUT LITERATURE

Responding to a Short Story

Novelist John Updike as a young man

Responding to a story in your reader-response journal can teach you something about yourself. Plot, theme, setting, and characters may evoke interesting opinions and connections. Notice how novelist John Updike responded to J. D. Salinger's stories.

Literature Models

It's in Salinger that I first heard, as a college student in the early Fifties, the tone that spoke to my condition. I had a writing teacher . . . who read aloud to us some of Salinger's stories as they appeared in *The New Yorker.* They seemed to me to say something about the energies of people and the ways they encounter each other that I did not find in the short stories of Hemingway or John O'Hara or Dorothy Parker or any of that "wised-up" style of short-story writing. Salinger's stories were not wised up. They were very open to tender invasions.

John Updike, *Picked-Up Pieces*

How does Updike signal in the first sentence the effect that J. D. Salinger's stories had on him?

Updike found Salinger's stories especially meaningful because they contain characters with whom he could identify.

"I looked down at Charles, who was now resting the side of his face on his chair seat. When he saw that I was looking at him, he closed his eyes, sleepily, angelically, then stuck out his tongue—an appendage of startling length—and gave out what in *my* country would have been a glorious tribute to a myopic baseball umpire."

J. D. Salinger, "For Esmé—with Love and Squalor"

Get into the Spirit

The best way to find out how you really feel about a piece of literature is to write a personal response in your reader-response journal. As you explore your feelings about and reactions to a piece, you may even discover that you have an opinion different from the one you originally had. The following graphic lists a variety of ways you can respond to a short story.

Ways of Responding to a Short Story	
Characters The individuals in a story	• Pick one character you like and write a dialogue between the two of you. • Write a letter to a character in the story, making connections with your life.
Setting The time and place of the action	• Tell why the setting of the story has a special appeal for you. • Create a drawing or painting depicting the setting of a major event.
Plot The sequence of events	• Tell what you like or don't like about the ending of the story. • Get a new perspective on the story by writing a different ending.
Theme The underlying meaning	• Compare the story with another story that has the same general theme. • Write about an experience of your own that had a similar meaning for you.

Journal Writing

What is the last story you read? Did you like it? Why or why not? Which story element influenced your reaction the most? What were the significant ideas expressed in the story? Spend a few minutes freewriting about your reaction in your reader-response journal.

Personal Writing

Respond in Your Own Way

Most people like stories that have a character with whom they can identify, so they usually begin their personal response there. Don't overlook other elements of a short story. Speculating about setting, plot, and theme can be just as fruitful in discovering why a story has special appeal for you.

The following model shows how student Robin Borland responded to the short story "A Sunrise on the Veld" by Doris Lessing. The story tells how a fifteen-year-old boy in southern Africa, rejoicing in his own good health, suddenly comes face to face with the unpredicability of death. This theme touched Borland deeply because it reminded her of a time when she herself had come face to face with mortality.

Student Model

Borland begins by providing a brief summary of the story theme.

To feel helpless is just about the worst emotion a person can experience, especially to feel helpless for the first time. At the beginning of "A Sunrise on the Veld," the boy is brimming with enthusiasm for life. He is completely unprepared for the reality of death—in himself or in any other living creature. Then he stumbles upon a buck covered with ants, and he watches, powerless, as the shadows of death swarm over the dying animal. Had he not been there, the same thing would have happened, yet now he is left scarred with an image of mortality—an image he had no inkling of up until this time.

She then connects the story theme with something that happened in her own life.

I came face to face with this reality when a close friend of mine passed away this year. He was seventeen and had been fighting kidney disease for over three years. I continued to visit him during that time, holding fast to an inner belief that everything would be fine. I believed that life is great, that everything is eternal, that nothing goes wrong in this great place. There was no way that my friend was going to die. But then he died.

Notice how she uses her own experience to gain a deeper understanding of the story. Borland expresses her voice by responding in a personal way to this story.

I know now that there was nothing I could have done. My visits weren't enough; the doctors weren't enough. I know how the boy in "Sunrise on the Veld" felt as he watched the ants swarm over the prey. The ants took away the boy's innocence. Death is unpredictable and unmerciful; it is not something that you can prepare for. It is the ultimate shock of feeling completely helpless.

Robin Borland, Evanston Township High School,
Evanston, Illinois

1.5 Writing Activities

Write a Reader-Response Journal Entry

Reread a favorite short story. Then write a creative response in your journal.

PURPOSE To respond creatively to a short story
AUDIENCE Yourself
LENGTH 4–6 paragraphs

WRITING RUBRICS To write an effective reader-response journal entry, you should

- respond specifically to the characters and the setting of the story
- consider the story's plot, theme, and significant ideas in your entry
- explain how you felt when you finished reading
- be sure your entry is clear and legible

Viewing and Representing

In your journal, write your response to the painting below. Is the scene realistic? What do you imagine is happening, and what might happen next? Respond in prose or poetry.

Using Computers

Work with a partner to research various readers' responses on the Internet. Choose a novel that you and your partner have read. Find out what other readers have to say about that novel on the Internet. You might start your search by visiting online bookstore sites. Are readers' reviews based on careful analysis of characters, setting, plot, and theme? Are the reviews based on subjective feelings? Do you agree with other readers' responses?

Avoid double negatives in writing.

Notice that Robin Borland uses only one negative word in a sentence.

There was no way that my friend was going to die.

Revise the sentences below to eliminate double negatives.

1. When the fire began, the Robinson family didn't notice no smoke.
2. When they saw the flames, they did not have no time to save their belongings.
3. There wasn't no room for the fire trucks to get through the street.
4. The Robinsons didn't have nowhere to sleep that night.
5. The place was a mess, but they felt lucky because they hadn't lost nothing that was really important to them.

See Lesson 18.6, page 673.

Henri Rousseau, *The Sleeping Gypsy*, 1897

UNIT 1

Writing Process in Action

Personal Writing

Personal Writing

Visit the Writer's Choice Web site at writerschoice.glencoe.com for additional writing prompts.

In preceding lessons you've learned about—and had the chance to practice—using personal writing to keep journals, learning logs, commonplace books, and reader-response journals. Now it's time to put together what you've learned. In this lesson you're invited to write a personal narrative about how you were changed as a result of something that happened to you—a turning point in your life.

Assignment

Context

Your new class journal, *Start Me Up,* is to serve as a source of models and inspiration for student writing. The class has chosen the issue of change and growth as the first topic for writing. Submission of articles for publication will be voluntary.

Purpose

To write a brief account of an incident or experience that caused you to change.

Audience

Yourself and maybe some of your peers

Length

1–2 pages

The following pages can help you plan and write your narrative. Read through them, and then refer to them when necessary, but don't feel limited by them. You are in charge of your own writing process.

Prewriting

First you need to select the right incident to write about—one that is clearly an experience that caused a change in you. If one does not immediately pop into your mind, you might get an idea by looking through your journal or commonplace book. Still stuck?

- Write the heads "People" and "Places," and list memories that come to mind in each category.
- Think back to earlier school years.
- Look at old photographs, or reminisce with your family or a close friend.

When you have selected one incident for your narrative, try to recall what happened as fully as possible. Make a list of specific details about the incident. The questions to the right may help you.

Prewriting Questions

- Who was involved in this incident?
- What happened, and where?
- How did I feel while it was going on?
- What did I learn from this experience?
- What might others learn from my telling about it?

Drafting

To begin drafting your narrative, simply tell what happened, step by step. Don't worry about how it sounds or the flow of the writing. Your goal in drafting is to set down your ideas without worrying about polishing them. A straight chronological retelling—writing in the order events took place—is often best, but you may want to experiment with other arrangements. You may want to take a humorous approach or use dialogue to make your narrative lively. Remember to tell why the event was important to you.

Since this is a personal narrative, it should include details that give readers a sense of who you are. Your narrative should sound like you, even if you are writing about something that happened to you a long time ago. You will also want to give the details that bring this particular incident to life. In the passage on the next page, notice how William Least Heat-Moon provides specific information and sensory details that tell how he is feeling and allow the reader to picture the scene clearly.

Drafting Tip

For more information about starting to get your ideas down on paper, see Lesson 1.1, page 8.

Literature Model

I turned up the heater to blast level, went to the back, and wrapped a blanket around the sleeping bag. I undressed fast and got into a sweatsuit, two pairs of socks, my old Navy-issue watch cap, a pair of gloves. When I cut the engine, snow already had covered the windshield. Only a quarter tank of gas. While the warmth lasted, I hurried into the bag and pulled back the curtain to watch the fulminous [related to thunder and lightning] clouds blast the mountain. That sky was bent on having a storm, and I was in for a drubbing.

William Least Heat-Moon, *Blue Highways*

Revising

To begin revising, read over your draft to make sure that what you've written fits your purpose and audience. Then have a **writing conference.** Read your draft to a partner or small group. Use your audience's reactions and the Revising Checklist below to help you evaluate your work.

Revising Tip

To give your peer reviewers some ideas about questions they might consider when responding to your personal narrative, see Lesson 1.4, page 22.

Revising Checklist

- Does my personal narrative tell my story clearly?
- Does it deal with my personal change or growth?
- Does it show why the incident was important to me?
- Does a sense of "me" come through?

Editing/Proofreading

Once you are satisfied with the content and style of your narrative, **proofread** it carefully for errors in grammar, usage, mechanics, and spelling. Use the questions at the right as a guide.

In addition to proofreading, use the self-evaluation list below to make sure your narrative does all the things you want it to do. When you're satisfied, make a clean copy of your narrative and proofread it once more.

Editing/Proofreading Checklist

- Have I avoided sentence fragments?
- Have I used commas correctly in a series?
- Have I avoided double negatives?
- Are my pronoun references clear?
- Have I checked spellings of any words I'm unsure of?

Self-Evaluation

Make sure your personal narrative—

- ✔ focuses on a situation that caused you to change
- ✔ orients readers with a clear narration of what happened
- ✔ uses personal frames of reference to personalize the incident
- ✔ explains why the experience was important to you
- ✔ follows standard grammar, usage, mechanics, and spelling

Publishing/Presenting

You may wish to offer your narrative for inclusion in the class journal along with those of your classmates. If you feel your sketch is too personal to share with such a wide audience, keep it with your personal journal.

Proofreading

For proofreading symbols, see page 84.

Journal Writing

Reflect on your writing process experience. Answer these questions in your journal: What do you like best about your personal narrative? What was the hardest part of writing it? What did you learn in your writing conference? What new things have you learned as a writer?

UNIT 1

Literature Model

FROM

Blue Highways
A Journey into America

by William Least Heat-Moon

William Least Heat-Moon is the pen name of writer William Trogdon, a Native American of Sioux ancestry. In 1978 Trogdon packed his small truck and began a journey across rural America—to discover both his country and himself. As you read this excerpt from his book Blue Highways: A Journey into America, *note what you think the author discovered about himself during his travels. Then complete the activities in Linking Writing and Literature on page 38.*

Somewhere out there was the Colorado River perfectly hidden in the openness. The river wasn't more than a mile away, but I couldn't make out the slightest indication of it in the desert stretching level and unbroken for twenty or thirty miles west, although I was only fifty miles above where it enters Grand Canyon. This side of the Colorado gorge[1] was once an important

1 **gorge** a steep narrow pass between great heights

Maynard Dixon, *Earth Knower,* C. 1932

Hopi[2] trail south, and, some say, the route Hopi guides took when they first led white men to the canyon. While the arid[3] path followed the river cleft,[4] water was an inaccessible four hundred feet down. Typically, the flexible Hopi solved the desert: women buried gourds of water at strategic points on the outward journey for use on the return.

The highway made an unexpected jog toward Navajo Bridge, a melding of silvery girders and rock cliffs. Suddenly, there it was, far below in the deep and scary canyon of sides so sheer they might have been cut with a stone saw, the naturally silted[5] water turned an unnatural green (*colorado* means "reddish") by the big settling basin a few miles upriver called Glen Canyon Dam. Navajo Bridge, built in 1929 when paved roads began opening the area, is the only crossing over the Colorado between Glen Canyon and Hoover Dam several hundred river miles downstream.

---

2 **Hopi** (hō′pē) a Native American group from northeastern Arizona
3 **arid** (ar′ id) dry and barren
4 **cleft** an opening or crevice
5 **silted** filled or clogged with fine-grained sediment

Literature Model

West of the gorge lay verdant[6] rangeland, much of it given to a buffalo herd maintained by the Arizona Game Commission; the great beasts lifted their heads to watch me pass, their dark, wet eyes catching the late sun. To the north rose the thousand-foot butt end of the Vermillion Cliffs; the cliffs weren't truly vermillion,[7] but contrasting with the green valley in the orange afternoon light, they seemed so.

In 1776, a few months after white-stockinged men in Philadelphia had declared independence, a Spanish expedition led by missionaries Francisco Silvestre Velez de Escalante and Francisco Atanasio Dominguez, returning from an unsuccessful search for a good northern route to the California missions, wandered dispiritedly along the Vermillion Cliffs as they tried to find in the maze of the Colorado a point to cross the river chasm.[8] They looked for ten days and were forced to eat boiled cactus and two of their horses before finding a place to ford; even then, they had to chop out steps to get down and back up the four-hundred-foot perpendicular walls. My crossing, accomplished sitting down, took twenty seconds. What I saw as a remarkable sight, the Spaniards saw as a terror that nearly did them in.

Escalante's struggles gave perspective to the easy passage I'd enjoyed across six thousand miles of America. Other than weather, some bad road, and a few zealous police, my difficulties had been only those of mind. In light of what was about to happen, my guilt over easy transit proved ironic.

I went up an enormous geologic upheaval called the Kaibab Plateau; with startling swiftness, the small desert bushes changed to immense conifers as the Kaibab forest deepened: ponderosa, fir, spruce. At six thousand feet, the temperature was sixty: a drop of thirty degrees in ten miles. On the north edge of the forest, the highway made a long gliding descent off the plateau into Utah. Here lay Kane and Garfield counties, a place of multicolored rock and baroque[9] stone columns and, under it all, the largest unexploited coalfield in the country. A land certain one day to be fought over.

At dusk I considered going into the Coral Sand Dunes for the night, but I'd had enough warmth and desert for a while, so I pushed north toward Cedar Breaks in the severe and beautiful Markagunt Plateau. The cool would refresh me. Sporadic splats of rain, not enough to pay attention to, hit the windshield. I turned onto Utah 14, the cross-mountain road to Cedar City. In the dim light of a mountainous sky, I could just make out a large sign:

ELEVATION 10,000 FEET
ROAD MAY BE IMPASSIBLE
DURING WINTER MONTHS.

So? It was nearly May. The rain popped, then stopped, popped and stopped. The incline became steeper and light rain fell steadily, rolling red desert dust off the roof; I hadn't hit showers since east Texas. It was good. The pleasant cool turned to cold, and I switched on the heater. The

---

6 **verdant** (verd′ ənt) green
7 **vermillion** (vər mil′ yən) a bright red or scarlet
8 **chasm** (kaz′ m) a deep crack in the earth's surface
9 **baroque** (bə rōk′) irregular in shape

Jaune Quick-To-See Smith, *Osage Orange,* 1985

headlights glared off snowbanks edging closer to the highway as it climbed, and the rain became sleet. That's when I began thinking I might have made a little miscalculation. I looked for a place to turn around, but there was only narrow, twisted road. The sleet got heavier, and the headlights were cutting only thirty feet into it. Maybe I could drive above and out of the storm. At eight thousand feet, the wind came up—a rough, nasty wind that bullied me about the slick road. Lear,[10] daring the storm to "strike flat the thick rotundity[11] of the world," cries, "Blow, winds, and crack your cheeks! Rage! Blow!" And that's just what they did.

A loud, sulphurous blast of thunder rattled the little truck, then another, and one more. Never had I seen lightning or heard thunder in a snowstorm. Although there were no signs, the map showed a campground near the summit. It would be suicide to stop, and maybe the same to go on. The wind pushed on Ghost Dancing[12] so, I was afraid of getting blown over the

---

10 **Lear** a legendary British king and the central character of a tragedy by William Shakespeare
11 **rotundity** (rō tun′ də tē) roundness or fullness
12 **Ghost Dancing** the name that the author uses for his 1975 Econoline van

invisible edge. Had not the falling snow taken away my vision, I might have needed a blindfold like the ones medieval travelers wore to blunt their terror of crossing the Alps. A rule of the blue road: Be careful going in search of adventure—it's ridiculously easy to find.

Then I was on the top, ten thousand feet up. UP. The wind was horrendous. Utah 14 now cut through snowbanks higher than the truck. At the junction with route 143, a sign pointed north toward Cedar Breaks campground. I relaxed. I was going to live. I puffed up at having beaten the mountain.

Two hundred yards up 143, I couldn't believe what I saw. I got out and walked to it as the raving wind whipped my pantlegs and pulled my hair on end. I couldn't believe it. There it was, the striped centerline, glowing through the sleet, disappearing under a seven-foot snowbank. Blocked.

Back to the truck. My heart dropped like a stone through new snow. There had to be a mistake. I mean, this wasn't 1776. The days of Escalante were gone. But the only mistake was my judgment. I was stopped on state 143, and 143 lay under winter ice.

I turned up the heater to blast level, went to the back, and wrapped a blanket around the sleeping bag. I undressed fast and got into a sweatsuit, two pairs of socks, my old Navy-issue watch cap, a pair of gloves. When I cut the engine, snow already had covered the windshield. Only a quarter tank of gas. While the warmth lasted, I hurried into the bag and pulled back the curtain to watch the fulminous[13] clouds blast the mountain. That sky was bent on having a storm, and I was in for a drubbing.

At any particular moment in a man's life, he can say that everything he has done and not done, that has been done and not been done to him, has brought him to that moment. If he's being installed as Chieftain or receiving a Nobel Prize, that's a fulfilling notion. But if he's in a sleeping bag at ten thousand feet in a snowstorm, parked in the middle of a highway and waiting to freeze to death, the idea can make him feel calamitously stupid.

A loud racketing of hail fell on the steel box, and the wind seemed to have hands, it shook the Ghost so relentlessly. Lightning tried to outdo thunder in scaring me. So did those things scare me? No. Not *those* things. It was something else. I was certain of a bear attack. That's what scared me.

Lightning strikes the earth about eight million times each day and kills a hundred and fifty Americans every year. I don't know how many die from exposure[14] and hypothermia,[15] but it must be at least a comparable number. As for bears eating people who sleep inside steel trucks, I haven't been able to find that figure. It made no sense to fear a bear coming out of hibernation in such weather to attack a truck. Yet I lay a long time, waiting for the beast, shaggy and immense, to claw through the metal, its hot breath on my head, to devour me like a gumdrop and roll the van over the edge.

---

13 **fulminous** (fool′ mə nəs) of or related to thunder and lightning
14 **exposure** (iks pō′ zhər) being overly exposed to extreme weather conditions
15 **hypothermia** (hī′ pə ther′ mēə) an extremely low body temperature

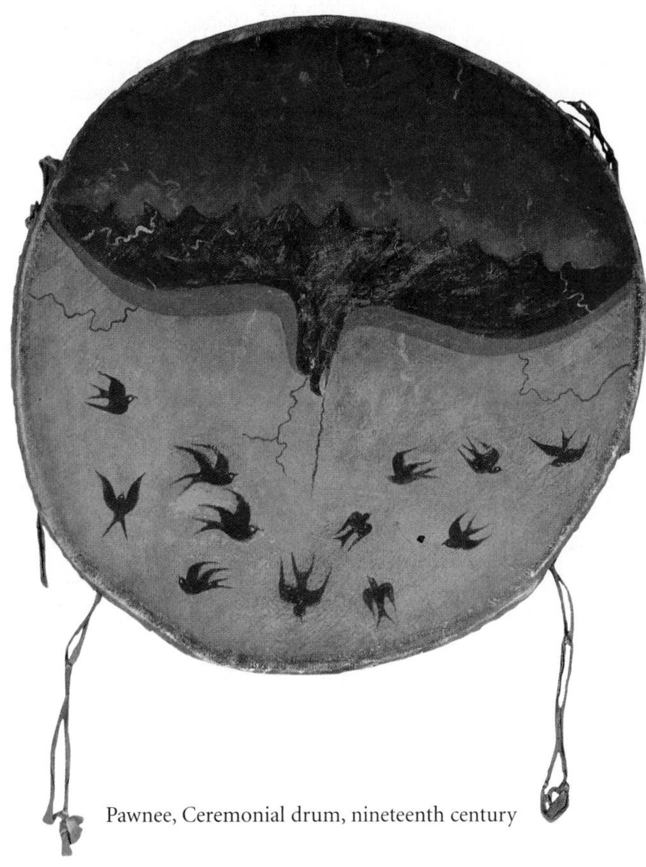

Pawnee, Ceremonial drum, nineteenth century

Perhaps fatigue or strain prevented me from worrying about the real fear; perhaps some mechanism of mind hid the true and inescapable threat. Whatever it was, it finally came to me that I was crazy. Maybe I was already freezing to death. Maybe this was the way it happened. Black Elk prays for the Grandfather Spirit to help him face the winds and walk the good road to the day of quiet. Whitman too:

O to be self-balanced for contingencies,
To confront night, storms, hunger, ridicule,
accidents, rebuffs, as the trees and animals do.

I wondered how long I might have to stay in the Breaks before I could drive down. The cold didn't worry me much: I had insulated the rig myself and slept in it once when the windchill was thirty-six below. I figured to survive if I didn't have to stay on top too long. Why hadn't I listened to friends who advised carrying a CB?[16] The headline showed darkly: FROZEN MAN FOUND IN AVALANCHE. The whole night I slept and woke, slept and woke, while the hail fell like iron shot, and thunder slammed around, and lightning seared the ice.

---

16 CB a citizens' band radio, sometimes used for communication among cars and trucks on highways

Linking Writing and Literature

Collect Your Thoughts

Think about what happens to Heat-Moon during the part of his journey he tells about in this selection. Then create two web diagrams. In the center of one diagram, write *his outer journey.* In the center of the other diagram, write *his inner journey.* Fill in the diagrams with details and ideas about each type of journey.

Talk About Reading

Talk with other students about the excerpt from *Blue Highways: A Journey into America.* Assign a group leader to keep everyone focused and a group secretary to take notes. Use the questions below to guide your discussion.

1. **Connect to Your Life** How does Heat-Moon's description of the experiences he has while traveling connect to your own life? Consider both the mental journey Heat-Moon makes and the challenges he faces as well as the physical landscape he travels through.
2. **Critical Thinking: Infer** What do you think Heat-Moon learns from this part of his journey? Back up your ideas with information from the text and with your own knowledge or experience.
3. **6+1 Trait®: Voice** Where in the selection do you think Heat-Moon's voice comes through most strongly? Read specific examples aloud. Does Heat-Moon's voice appeal to you? Why or why not?
4. **Connect to Your Writing** What makes a travel story engaging? Make a list of criteria to evaluate a piece of travel writing.

Write About Reading

Travel Journal Write one to three entries in a travel journal to describe a travel experience of your own. You may recount an actual journey that you've taken to a distant place or within your own city or neighborhood; or you might describe a journey you'd like to take. Tell about both your physical journey and your personal journey.

Focus on Voice As you describe your journey, let your own voice come through. Do you want to use irony? Capture your sense of humor on the page? Decide what tone or feeling you want to express that will make the writing unmistakably yours. Then experiment with word choice, anecdotes, and references to other writings to help make your voice come alive.

For more information on voice and the 6+1 Trait® model, see **Writing and Research Handbook,** pages 957–959.

6+1 Trait® is a registered trademark of Northwest Regional Educational Laboratory, which does not endorse this product.

UNIT 1 Review

Reflecting on the Unit

Summarize what you learned in this unit by answering the following questions.

1. What are the important functions of a personal journal in your development as an individual and as a writer?
2. How can a learning log help you become actively involved in your school work?
3. What is a commonplace book and what uses does it serve?
4. How can a reader-response journal help in both your reading and your writing?

Adding to Your Portfolio

CHOOSE A SELECTION FOR YOUR PORTFOLIO Look over the personal writing you have done in this unit. Select a completed piece of writing to put into your portfolio. The piece you choose should show one or both of the following:

- reactions to something you have seen, experienced, read, or studied
- your own personal thoughts and feelings

REFLECTING ON YOUR CHOICE Attach a note to the piece you chose, explaining briefly why you chose it and what you learned from writing it.

SET GOALS FOR YOUR WRITING How can you improve your writing? What skill will you focus on the next time you write?

Writing Across the Curriculum

MAKE A SCIENCE CONNECTION Choose a science concept that interests you, and write a learning log entry about it. Summarize what you already know about the subject. Identify aspects of the concept that you want to examine further. Discuss any controversial ideas that relate to the concept. Make a list of questions you have that relate to the concept. Use pictures, charts, or diagrams as part of your entry.

"He was sitting behind a brown table upon which stood piles of dust and cobweb-covered books and papers."

—**Mark Mathabane,** *Kaffir Boy*

UNIT 2

The Writing Process

Writing in the Real World

Skilled investigative reporters, like detectives, spend countless hours searching for the truth behind a story. Then they must be sure to use fair and accurate writing to present their findings. The following is an excerpt from an investigative newspaper story reporter Mark Trahant wrote for the *Arizona Republic.*

Trahant Investigates Nuclear Transport

by Mark Trahant

Investigative Reporter Mark Trahant

It's about an hour shy of dusk as the white 18-wheeler races toward the setting sun at speeds occasionally topping 70 mph.

The truck and its trailer are inconspicuous. There are no markings of any kind. But you can see its U.S. government license plates, an odd crop of antennas fenced in on the truck's roof and an escort of four sinister-appearing Chevy Suburbans that lead and follow the rig.

This is no ordinary truck. It's a "safe secure trailer" [SST] from the U.S. Department of Energy and probably is carrying a cargo of missile components, weapons-grade plutonium or hydrogen bombs. Behind the dark windows of the escort Suburbans are enough guns to launch a small war—including turret-mounted machine guns in some vehicles.

It's life in the nuclear lane on Interstate 40.

Tractor-trailers ferrying nuclear materials travel most of America's interstates as well as many main highways. The rig in the next lane could be carrying plutonium, uranium or a host of other products of fission.

The potential for accidents grows with each additional truck on the road. On . . . Interstate 85 in China Grove, N.C., a car crashed head-on into a tractor-trailer carrying low-level radioactive material.

One person was killed and more than 225 were evacuated for about five hours while officials surveyed the area for radioactive leaks. . . .

Federal investigators have found that many trucks on the highways—including those that carry nuclear freight—have serious mechanical problems. At the same time, the Department of Energy is considering a number of plans that would increase the amount of nuclear freight on public highways, especially in the Southwest, in the next two decades. . . .

A Writer's Process

Prewriting:

Investigating the Transports

Mark Trahant's interest in the transport of radioactive materials evolved from research he did on a New Mexico nuclear waste project—a plan to bury millions of cubic feet of plutonium waste in the desert near Carlsbad. While researching this topic, he met townspeople who said they saw nuclear transport trucks all the time. Soon after, he discovered that almost 3 million loads of nuclear freight crisscross U.S. highways each year.

Once his editor gave him the go-ahead for a story, Trahant dug up every bit of information he could on these nuclear transport trucks. "Successful investigative reporters are, above all, very good reporters," Trahant said. "They are curious. They want to see how a story affects people—the population of a city or county, as well as one person." They also have to doggedly seek out every side of the story. "Investigative reporters can't be seen as advocates of any side," Trahant stressed.

For four weeks, ten to eighteen hours a day, Trahant traveled, talked, listened, and read. He scoured four years' worth of transportation records and safety complaints in Denver, El Paso, and Phoenix federal courts. He conducted more than fifty interviews with people on all sides of the issue—the Department of Energy, experts on nuclear transport safety, scientists, peace activists, terrorism experts, and people who live on the main routes. He even tried, unsuccessfully, to talk to people in Texas at a major weapons manufacturing plant.

After a month of research, Trahant had four notebooks full of

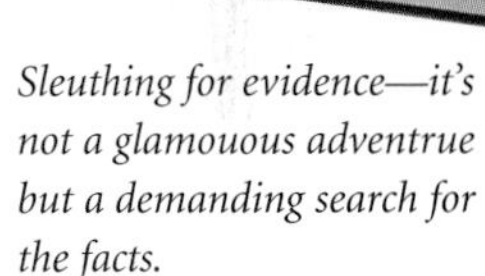

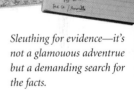

Sleuthing for evidence—it's not a glamouous adventrue but a demanding search for the facts.

notes and several file drawers of photocopied documents. At that point, he met with his editor, explained where the story was going, and asked for a full page in the newspaper.

Drafting/Revising:

Recording and Supporting Key Ideas

Trahant approached the job of drafting the story with a reporter's strategy—write it fast the first time; then rewrite. "Journalism is literature in a hurry," he said.

To open the piece, Trahant described the truck he clocked at 72 miles an hour, an anecdote he had marked "lead" in his notebook. Then he drafted the body of the story, keeping in mind three or four key ideas that presented all sides of the story and the need to interest readers. "Good writing is surprising [to the reader]," Trahant said. "It tells the reader something unusual, not expected. It's also concrete. It puts the reader there with examples of color, how something looked or sounded."

Reporter Mark Trahant defines journalism as "literature in a hurry."

Trahant closed with an attention-grabbing quotation, despite knowing that editors often cut stories from the end. "Most editors realize that a good story has a beginning, a middle, and an end," he said. After finishing a draft, Trahant went back and inserted supporting details and quotations. Then he read the story aloud, checking to be sure the language flowed smoothly.

Revising/Editing:

Making Necessary Changes

Three editors reviewed Trahant's article to ensure complete and fair coverage and to check for correct style and grammar. Then Trahant made his final revisions. Most newspapers ask an attorney to review very touchy stories before publication to be sure the paper won't be sued, but Trahant's piece went to press without legal review. "There was no real bad guy in this story," explained Trahant. His research pointed out two areas of public concern: the large percentage (20 percent) of all SSTs in poor mechanical condition and the growing potential for accidents as the number of trucks on the roads increases.

Publishing/Presenting:

Getting the Story Out

What did Trahant hope to accomplish by publishing this article? "I always hope my work will result in improvements, but I know one story won't change much," he said. "My job is to dig up the information and present it in an interesting way. I leave change to the public."

By the time a story reaches the morning breakfast table, an investigative reporter is following fresh leads for the next story and beginning the writing process again.

Examining Writing in the Real World

Analyzing the Media Connection

Discuss these questions about the article on page 42.

1. In your opinion, does the lead, or opening, of Trahant's article capture the reader's interest? Why or why not?
2. What details create a sense of drama and urgency in the story?
3. What tragedy does Trahant mention? For what reasons does he mention this tragedy?
4. In your opinion, does Trahant do a good job of persuading the reader that change is necessary? Why or why not?
5. Describe the style of writing Trahant uses in his article. How is it similar to or different from your own style of writing?

Analyzing a Writer's Process

Discuss these questions about Mark Trahant's writing process.

1. What prompted Mark Trahant to write an article about the transport of nuclear materials?
2. How did Trahant research his topic? What kinds of evidence did he gather?
3. What basic strategy did Trahant use in drafting his story?
4. Describe the steps Trahant followed in drafting his story? Why do you think he followed that order?
5. What did Trahant's editors look for in his story? How did Trahant view the outcome of his work?

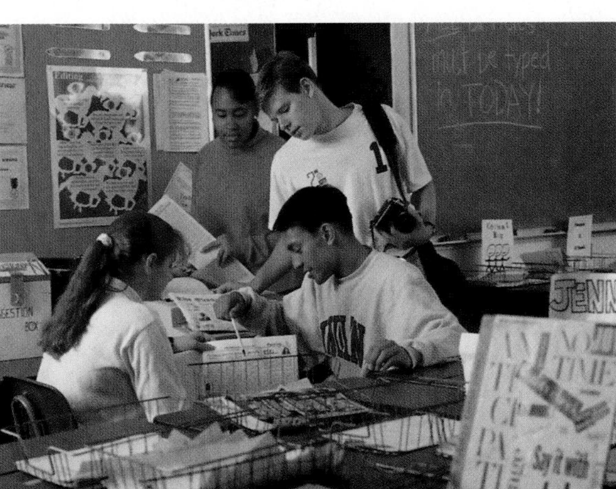

Make verbs agree with nouns of amount.

The verb that follows a noun of amount is plural if the noun refers to individual units: *Almost 3 million* ***loads*** *of nuclear freight* ***crisscross*** *U.S. highways.* The verb is singular if the noun refers to a single unit: *Three million* ***loads is*** *a lot.*

Complete each sentence with the correct form of the verb in parentheses.

1. Three-fourths of Trahant's article (focuses, focus) on nuclear transports.
2. One-and-a-half file drawers (was, were) full of photocopied documents.
3. Four weeks (is, are) a long time to spend gathering evidence.
4. The 100 inches of copy space (was, were) more than most articles get.
5. Twenty percent of all SSTs (was, were) in poor mechanical condition.

See Lesson 16.4, pages 618–619.

The Writing Process

LESSON 2.1

Stages of the Writing Process

The five stages of the writing process allow you to explore, investigate, and write about any topic. In the following pages you will follow the investigation and writing process of a high school student, Shella Calamba.

The Five Writing Process Stages

Writing is a process with different stages. Professional and student writers all follow processes made up of combinations of the stages shown below.

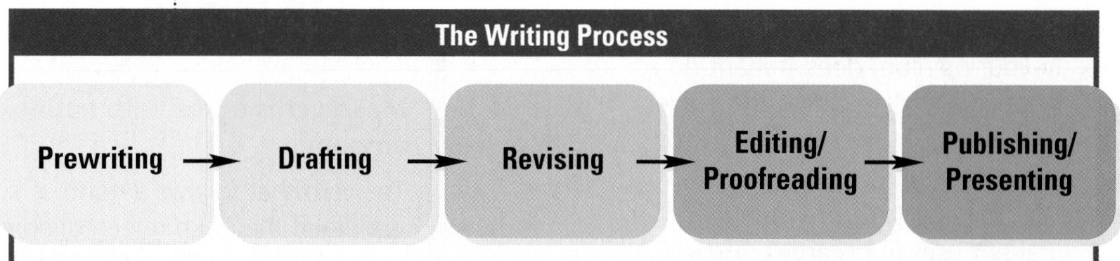

PREWRITING The first stage, called prewriting, is the idea stage. By probing your thoughts, you can discover a topic and a purpose for writing about it. This is the stage in which information or details are gathered and the paper is planned. Shella Calamba began investigating her family's history by using a prewriting technique called freewriting.

Exploring my family's history. Chinese and Spanish ancestors. Great-grandparents half Chinese. Great-grandfather Filipino. Great-grandmother very religious according to my mother. My mother was named after my great-grandmother, Josefa Parcarey. My great-grandfather was the mayor of the town. Both my grandparents were farmers. I could write about my mother's genealogy.

During the freewriting stage, Calamba's ideas are random and free flowing, but they lead to a writing topic.

DRAFTING Drafting is writing your ideas down in related sentences and paragraphs. The goal during drafting is to let your writing flow without worrying about grammar or mechanics. Notice how Calamba has combined related ideas in a paragraph.

> It is far from a coincidence that my mother was named after my great-grandmother, Josefa. My mother spent her early childhood years under my great-grandmother's watchful, firm eye. Later, she spent her teenage years in Manila, where she studied in high school and college.

How does Calamba give structure to her ideas in the drafting stage?

REVISING Revising means reading your draft closely, reminding yourself of your purpose, and reworking and clarifying your ideas, as Calamba did here.

> My great-grandfather was the mayor of a Philippine province. My great-grandmother, Josefa, a religious woman, taught my mother Latin prayers. They ~~would~~ *used to* pray together *every afternoon at precisely five*.
>
> My grandparents raised eight children. Two aunts ~~were~~ *became* teachers, and one ~~has~~ *owns* a store. My mother is a pharmacist in Chicago. One uncle is ~~in business~~ *a restaurant owner*, and one is a nurse in Australia.

In revising this passage, what details has Calamba added? What effect do they have? What other changes did Calamba make?

The Writing Process

Journal Writing

In your journal analyze your own writing process. Which of these first three stages do you find easy? What are your stumbling blocks? Do you always move straight forward, or do you sometimes return to a previous stage?

LESSON 2.2

Prewriting: Finding a Writing Topic

Writers may use various techniques to zero in on a topic. When asked to write a feature story on Native Americans in southern California, journalist Wayne Swanson began by jotting down some ideas. Compare his freewriting with the first part of his article to see how he used his notes.

Through his freewriting, Swanson focused on a topic—glimpses of a lost Native American heritage.

Sad truth, little left of Native American culture—time, conquest, conversion, development have buried. But long history, and if know where to look, possible to catch a glimpse of world before white people came.

So. I could focus on glimpses of their lost heritage, baskets and cemetery plots at missions, but also evidence of power that eradicated most of their history. Perhaps draw a picture of life along San Luis Rey valley. Where were their settlements? What did they do?

How did the comments in the prewriting notes about drawing a picture lead to this introduction?

Literature Model

Imagine a time when the San Luis Rey River ran freely, even in dry years. Imagine irrigated fields of corn and grain thriving in its valleys. Imagine small, self-sufficient villages up along the valley slopes, scattered all the way from the ocean to Mt. Palomar and beyond.

In other words, imagine San Diego County before European adventurers claimed it for their own. As development moves relentlessly up the valley, the evidence of this earlier era becomes ever harder to find. Nevertheless, glimpses remain. They remain in the landscape and in the efforts of Native Americans and others to hold on to what is left.

Wayne Swanson, "Exploring Proud Past of Indians"
Los Angeles Times

Discover Ideas

Like Wayne Swanson, you have countless ideas hidden in your mind, waiting to be uncovered. How can you get at them? There are several techniques you can use.

FREEWRITING Freewriting consists of writing nonstop for a set time, usually only five or ten minutes. The idea is to keep pace with your thoughts, getting them on paper before they vanish. Freewriting can start anywhere and go anywhere. Sometimes it begins with an assignment. Sometimes it grows out of a class discussion—for example, a biology class discussion on using animals in medical research. Read Shella Calamba's freewriting to see what ideas she uncovered as she thought about this topic.

Student Model

The role of animals in medical research is an interesting topic. But what aspect? Which animals are used and why? Maybe pick one species and describe an experiment done on it. I can include safety precautions involved in using animals. I could write about rights and laws that protect animals. Controversy surrounding animals and research. I could investigate this. I could give my own opinions on the vital role of animals in research.

Shella Calamba, Lincoln Park High School, Chicago, Illinois

Freewriting Tips

1. Let your thoughts flow—ideas, memories, anything that comes to mind.
2. Don't edit or judge your thoughts; just write them down. You can evaluate them later.
3. Don't worry about spelling, punctuation, grammar, or even sense; just keep writing.
4. If you stop, rewrite your last sentence, or write "I'm stuck" until a new idea pops up.

TIME

For more about the writing process, see TIME Facing the Blank Page, pp. 109–119.

Journal Writing

In your journal, spend five minutes freewriting about whatever comes to mind. Then make a list of the different ideas you came up with.

BRAINSTORMING You freewrite on your own, but like the students shown below, you can brainstorm ideas with others. The student at the right is tossing out a question, and the others will answer it. These ideas will lead to new ideas as each student's comment starts the others thinking. The result of this interplay of ideas is a list like the one below. You should allow a set amount of time, ten to fifteen minutes, for each brainstorming session.

Brainstorming Tips
1. Choose someone to list ideas as they are called out.
2. Start with a topic (such as inventions) or a question.
3. Encourage everyone to join in freely.
4. Accept all ideas; do not evaluate them now.
5. Follow each idea as far as it goes.

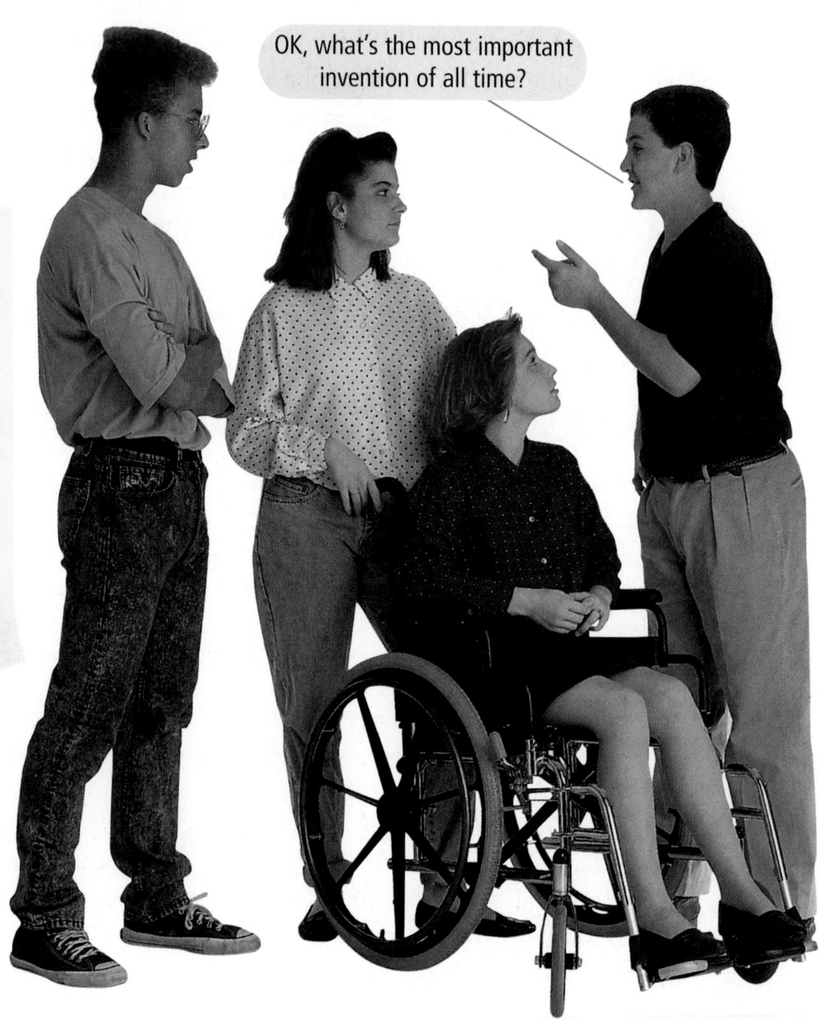

Inventions

- Most important inventions: wheel, internal-combustion engine, movable type, electricity, penicillin, telephone
- Unsuccessful inventions
- How inventions happen
- Inventions still needed

CLUSTERING Brainstorming is often a group activity, but you can also brainstorm by yourself. One way to focus your brainstorming is by clustering. Start by circling a word or phrase. Surround it with related ideas, and connect each of those ideas with others, creating groups, or clusters, of ideas. The following cluster started with one word, *inventions.*

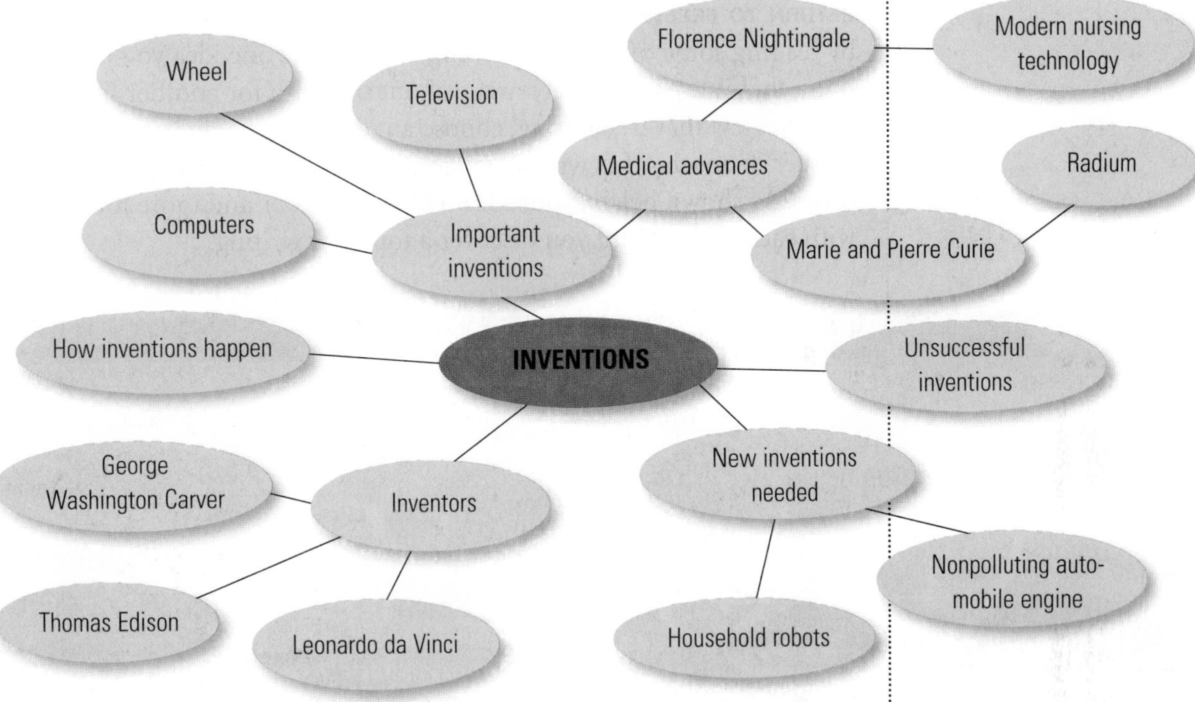

Clustering Tips

1. Start with a key word or phrase circled in the center of your paper.
2. Brainstorm to discover related ideas; circle each one, and connect it to the central idea.
3. Branch out with new ideas that refine existing ideas by adding details.
4. Review your chart, looking for ideas or clusters of ideas that interest you.

Journal Writing

Some writers prefer to work alone, while others like working in groups. Write in your journal about the pros and cons of group activities like brainstorming and individual efforts like freewriting and clustering. Which approach do you think works better for you? Why?

Narrow Your Focus

Prewriting techniques—freewriting, brainstorming, clustering—help you discover your thoughts and ideas, but they have another value, too. They can help you narrow a topic so that you can use it for a short piece of writing, even a single paragraph.

RETURN TO FREEWRITING Looping is one way to narrow your topic. Start by reading some of your freewriting, and choose one idea you touched upon that interests you. Freewrite about that idea for another five minutes. Review that freewriting, choose an idea from it, and try to focus it further in another freewriting session. Repeat the process two or three times. As shown below, your idea will be narrower and more focused with each "loop" until you discover a topic for writing.

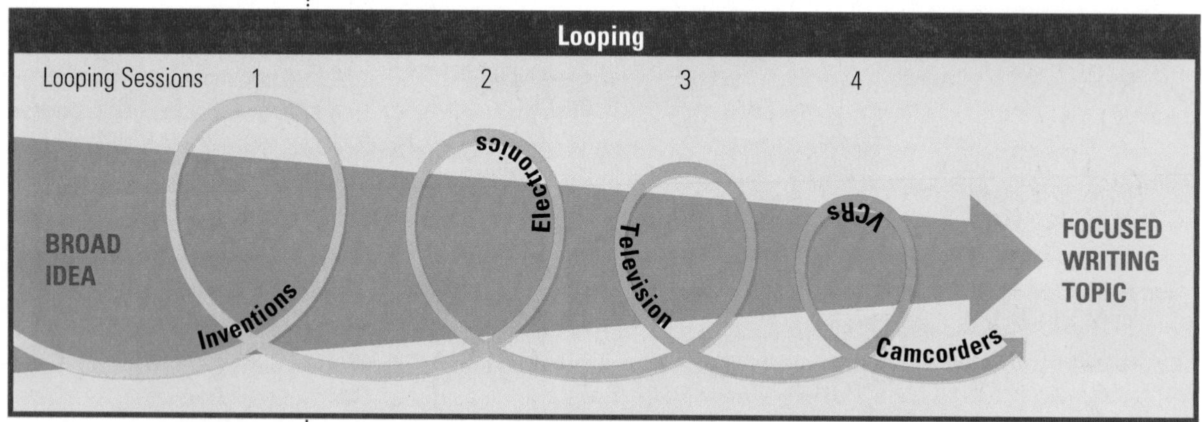

RETURN TO CLUSTERING Writing additional clusters is another way to narrow your topic. Look at the clustering you did to search for ideas, and choose an idea that seems promising—for example, "How inventions happen" from the cluster on page 53. Write it at the center of a new page, and start clustering again.

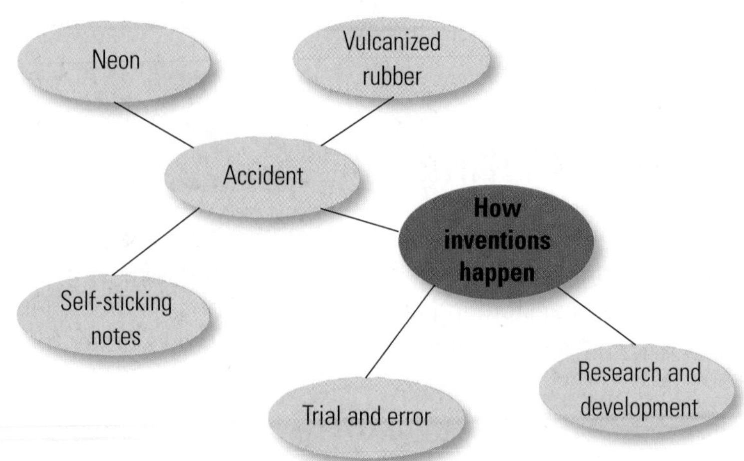

2.2 Writing Activities

Write to Find a Topic

As you study this unit, you will be writing an investigative report. Use the prewriting methods discussed in this lesson to choose two or three possible topics for your report.

PURPOSE To select writing topics
AUDIENCE Yourself
LENGTH 1-2 pages

WRITING RUBRICS To find a topic, you should

- freewrite and use different sources to collect ideas
- brainstorm to generate related ideas
- use looping and clustering to narrow your focus

Edna Jackson, *Kaaswoot*, 1983

Viewing and Representing

COOPERATIVE LEARNING In a small group, study the self-portrait on this page. The artist is of Native American and European descent. How does the portrait reflect the artist's dual heritage? Use your group's ideas to write a paragraph each about the painting.

Capitalize proper nouns.

Rewrite the following sentences, adding or dropping capital letters as necessary.

1. The aztec built majestic Temples and Palaces in Central Mexico.
2. They built the City of Tenochtitlán on a swampy Island in lake Texcoco.
3. By the Fifteenth Century, this city was one of the largest in the World.

See Lesson 20.2, pages 715–721.

Cross-Curricular Activity

ART Visit the Web site for the National Portrait Gallery. Write a paragraph comparing and contrasting two portraits. How is each figure shown (standing, seated, a head-and-shoulders view)? Does the figure hold anything? What do you learn about the subject by looking at the portrait?

LESSON 2.3

Prewriting: Identifying Purpose and Audience

Knowing your purpose and audience will help determine your main idea, or what you want a piece of writing to say. Mike had different purposes and audiences in mind as he wrote the postcards below.

Decide on Your Purpose

Deciding on a purpose will help you determine what to include in your writing. To clarify your purpose, answer these questions:

1. Why do I want to write about this topic?
2. Is my purpose to describe? Inform? Narrate? Amuse? Persuade?
3. Will I have more than one purpose in this piece of writing?

Purpose: to persuade
What is Mike's purpose in writing to his parents? How do his details reflect his purpose and audience?

Purpose: to inform

Purpose: to describe
How does Mike select details that relate to his friend's experience as he describes the Hall of Fame?

Identify Your Reader

Your audience is anyone who will be reading your writing. Sometimes you write just for yourself. More often, however, you write to share information with others. The audience may include a few friends or family members, your classmates, or the population at large.

The writers of both excerpts below wrote with a similar purpose, to inform. Note that each had a different audience in mind.

Literature Model

[The sports hero] exhibits that complete skill to which the amateur vainly aspires. Instead of being looked upon as a servile and ignoble being, because of the very perfection of his physical efforts, as the Athenians in Socrates' time looked upon the professional athletes and dancers, this new hero represents the summit of the amateur's effort.

Lewis Mumford, *Technics and Civilization*

What words and details does Mumford use to appeal to his scholarly, academic audience?

Literature Model

Pro football players are adults who fly through the air in plastic hats and smash each other for a living. I now know a bunch of them, and I think they are good folks.

Roy Blount Jr., *About Three Bricks Shy of a Load*

The writer's informal tone and choice of details appeal to a general-interest audience.

As you write, consider these questions about your audience:

1. Who will my audience be: What do I want to say to them?
2. What do my readers already know about my topic?
3. What types of information will interest my audience?

Journal Writing

Reread one sample of your recent writing and jot down your thoughts about these questions: How could I use the same ideas to write for a different purpose? How could I make this appeal to a different audience?

Write Your Main Idea Statement

With a topic, a purpose, and an audience in mind, you're almost ready to write. In the next step ask yourself, What's the most important idea? Answer the question in one sentence. That sentence will be your main idea statement.

No matter how big or small your writing project is—a single paragraph or a twenty-page research paper—you should write a main idea statement. It will tell what you want your entire piece to say and will help you choose appropriate details for your topic. Later, as you draft your piece, it will keep your writing on track. As the chart below indicates, the main idea statement is central to any writing; all other ideas depend on it.

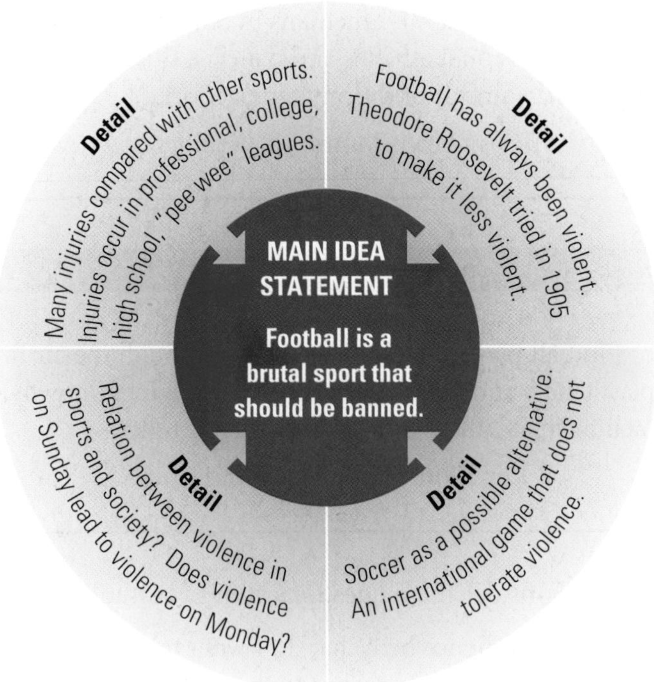

MAIN IDEA STATEMENT
Football is a brutal sport that should be banned.
Detail
Many injuries compared with other sports. Injuries occur in professional, college, high school, "pee wee" leagues.
Detail
Football has always been violent. Theodore Roosevelt tried in 1905 to make it less violent.
Detail
Relation between violence in sports and society? Does violence on Sunday lead to violence on Monday?
Detail
Soccer as a possible alternative. An international game that does not tolerate violence.

Now consider a different main idea statement about football: *Football is a game built on teamwork, discipline, and strategy.* To what audience might this topic appeal? What kinds of details could you use to develop the main idea?

Ask yourself the following questions as you develop your main idea statement for any piece of writing:

1. What point do I want to make?
2. Will my audience be interested in the idea?
3. Do I need to narrow my topic further?

2.3 Writing Activities

Identify Purpose and Audience

Before you make the final choice of topic for your investigative report, decide on your audience and your purpose.

PURPOSE To identify audience and purpose; to select a topic
AUDIENCE Yourself
LENGTH 1-2 pages

WRITING RUBRICS To focus your topic ideas, you should

- identify your purpose. Is it to point out a problem? encourage people to take some action? provide background information?
- identify your audience. Is it your classmates? your family? a club? readers of the school newspaper?

Listening and Speaking

COOPERATIVE LEARNING In a small group, brainstorm ideas for changes or improvements in your community. Then choose one idea about which you could write. Discuss how your writing might vary for different audiences. For example, how would you approach a good friend versus the CEO of a major corporation? Possible audiences to consider in your discussion include the following: the principal, your parents, the mayor, a restaurant owner, a friend, or the president of the United States. As a group, prepare a few samples that show how your writing would vary depending on the audience. Present the samples to the class.

Grammar Link

Tailor your writing style to your audience.

When you write for a young audience, try using simple sentences and easy-to-understand vocabulary.

Rewrite the following sentences into simple sentences. Change wording as necessary.

1. Despite the fact that writing can be complex and time-consuming, it is frequently quite enjoyable.
2. Acquaintances who no longer live in the area savor receiving letters from me.
3. Now and again I take advantage of e-mail, which is extraordinarily fast, to communicate with my friends.
4. My older sibling has created a screenplay that is being filmed in San Antonio, Texas.

See Lesson 13.3, pages 545–546.

Using Computers

On the Internet locate a speech by a past leader, such as Franklin D. Roosevelt or Martin Luther King Jr. Determine the intended audience and the purpose of the speech. With a partner, discuss how the speaker used language to reach the intended audience and what features of the speech make it memorable.

LESSON

2.4

Prewriting: Exploring a Topic

After you've identified a writing topic, explore it further by listing and organizing details, asking questions, and doing research.

Observe Closely

One good starting point for exploring a topic is simply to observe closely and list the details you see. What do you observe in this photo of 1960s students that reflects the social unrest of the time? List the details that you observe.

The next step is to arrange the items on your list into categories. For example, the details you listed about the photograph might fit into broad categories such as clothes, hairstyles, body language, and attitudes. The categories you choose depend on the details you observe and your writing goal. If you were going to describe a place—say, the campus where these students attended school—you might arrange your details according to the five senses, what you smell, hear, see, taste, and touch.

Ask Questions

Asking questions is another way of exploring a topic and is central to any investigation. Questions help you get at the facts of the matter. They also help you see your topic in new ways and probe its meaning. Jot down questions about your topic in a notebook or journal. Notice the three kinds of questions listed below.

Questions for Exploring a Topic

Factual	Creative	Personal
1. What did 1960s young people wear? Did they all dress alike? 2. What music did they listen to? What books and magazines did they read? 3. What events and causes were important to them, and why? 4. How are they similar to kids today? How are they different?	1. How do today's styles in clothing and music reflect the 1960s? 2. Would I feel at home in the 1960s? Why or why not? 3. What if one of the kids in the photo were my parent? 4. What kind of conversation might I have with a student from the 1960s? What would we ask each other?	1. Why do I want to know about 1960s students? 2. What can I learn from them? What could they learn from me? 3. What causes did 1960s kids support? Were their causes similar to mine? 4. What about their dreams?

Journal Writing

Observe something in the room around you and record details about it. Use one or more of the techniques explained in this lesson to find out as much as possible about the essential qualities of your subject.

Search Out Information

Outside sources of reliable information are important when you explore a topic. These sources include encyclopedias, books, articles, and a wide range of formal and informal sources. Are there Web sites, photographs, filmstrips, records, videos, TV programs, interviews, field trips, or other resources that would give you information about your topic? The more creative you are in searching out information, the more likely you are to find full and satisfactory answers to the questions about your topic.

Create an Idea Tree

As you gather your information, you may begin to wonder how it all fits together. Creating an idea tree can help you analyze your topic. An idea tree like the one below can often make the relationships among the parts of your topic stand out and may even show you a plan for organizing your writing.

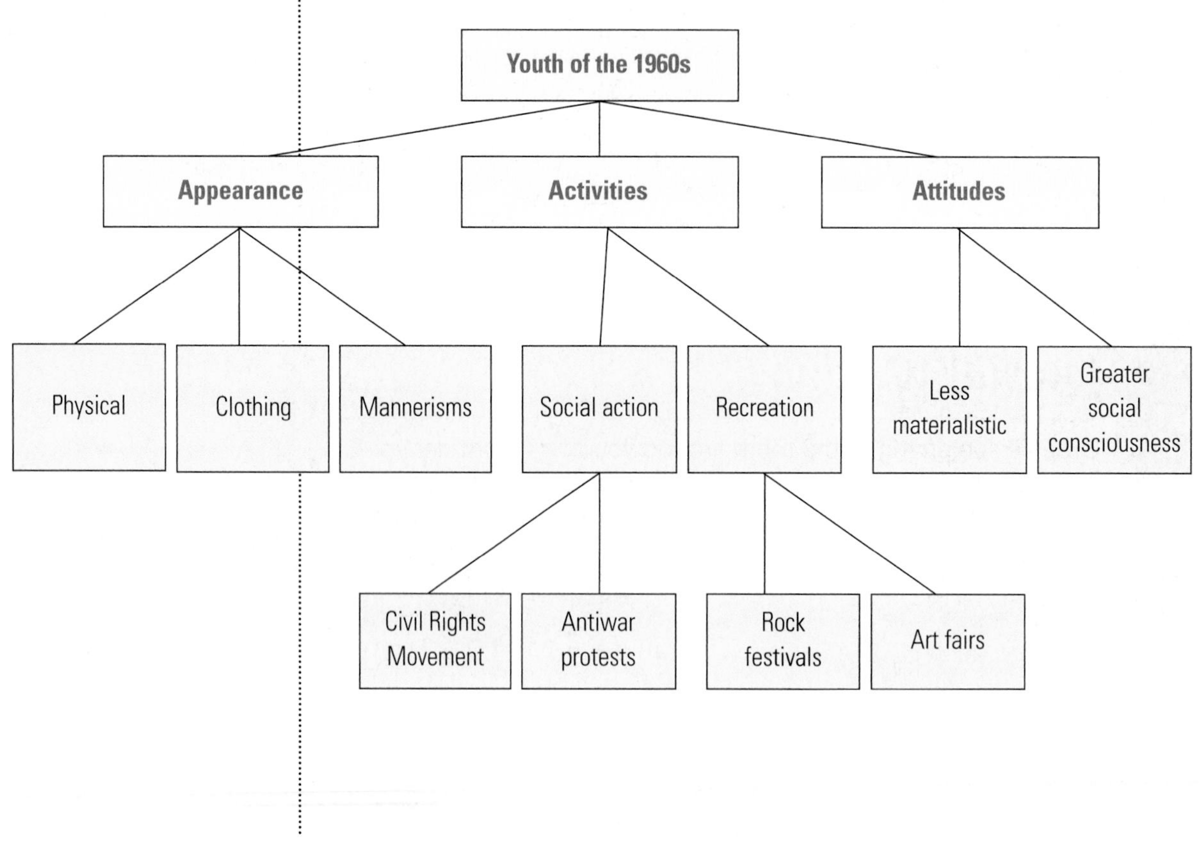

2.4 Writing Activities

Make a Plan for Writing

Look at the topic you chose for your investigative report, and begin to plan your writing. For help with planning your writing, see **Writing and Research Handbook,** page 956.

PURPOSE To plan your writing
AUDIENCE Yourself
LENGTH 1-2 pages

WRITING RUBRICS To develop an effective writing plan, you should

- identify your main idea
- list your main points, questions, details, or incidents
- arrange your ideas logically and in an order to suit your purpose

Cross-Curricular Activity

ART Study the painting on this page. What can you tell about the people pictured? How do you think the artist felt about these people? Write a list of questions you would like to answer by consulting an outside source for information about the artist, the place in which he lived, or the time period of the painting.

Vincent van Gogh, *The Potato Eaters,* 1885

Make verbs agree with compound subjects.

A compound subject that is joined by *and* is plural unless its parts are thought of as one unit, such as "ham and eggs."

Complete each sentence below by choosing the correct verb.

1. How (does, do) today's music and movies reflect the culture of the twenty-first century?
2. Both Tom Hanks and Brad Pitt (is, are) actors who are popular with teenagers.
3. Salsa and chips (is, are) a favorite snack.
4. The balanced budget amendment and health care reform (is, are) controversial issues.
5. By the mid-1990s, the House of Representatives and the Senate (was, were) controlled by the Republicans.

See Lesson 16.5, page 620.

Viewing and Representing

ELEMENTS OF DESIGN Find out more about van Gogh's paintings, including *The Potato Eaters.* How does he use light, color, and texture, and how does this change in his later work? View his works. Research his techniques and the topics he chose. Record notes and write a research summary.

LESSON 2.5

Prewriting: Interviewing

Interviewing someone is often the best way to get information on a topic. Successful interviews begin with carefully thought-out and organized questions.

ARE THERE ANY BIG DRAWBACKS IN BEING A ROCK STAR?
HUH?
I SAID, ANY DRAWBACKS?!
OH, YEAH... THERE'S SOME HEARING LOSS, BUT THAT'S NOT A PROBLEM.
MOST OF OUR FANS ARE HALF-DEAF NOW TOO...
©Jefferson Communications, Inc. 1986
Distributed by Tribune Media Services, Inc.
MACNELLY

Go Straight to the Source

An interview is a focused, structured encounter for which the interviewer has a topic and purpose firmly in mind. Interviewing is a vital part of prewriting for many writing projects, and the firsthand information you collect will add liveliness to your writing.

Journalist Wayne Swanson researched the Native American heritage of southern California for a newspaper feature story. His investigation took him to an archaeologist who is an expert on the subject. Here are some of the questions Swanson asked, along with their answers.

Q. How did you get involved in studying the Native Americans of southern California?

A. When I was in college, I went on an archaeological dig outside San Diego. When we discovered some artifacts, I felt an immediate link with the people. I wanted to learn more about them.

This question shows that Swanson has already done some research on his topic. But he wants to know more.

Q. Why has so little been written about them?

A. They did not fit the popular image of warriors on horseback. They had few confrontations with white people. Instead, they had a stable, self-sufficient culture.

Q. What is notable about these early Native Americans?

A. They are renowned for basketry and pottery making. They also had a remarkable knowledge of plants and pharmacology.

Ask Questions and Take Notes

As Swanson's interview shows, the success of an interview depends on asking good questions. Keep these points in mind when you prepare your interview questions:

1. Ask questions that require more than *yes* or *no* answers.
2. Ask questions that are clearly worded and easily understood.
3. Ask questions that relate directly to your topic and purpose.

DO BACKGROUND RESEARCH Before an interview you should do preliminary research about the person and the topic. Informed questions will get you informative answers. What do the questions below tell you about the interviewer's preparation?

Q: Why do we have so little evidence today of early Native American settlements?
A: They built few permanent structures and had few material possessions. In this warm climate they had no need for elaborate housing or warm clothing.

Q: How did the arrival of the Spanish affect the Native American people?
A: The Spanish impact was devastating. It drastically reduced the population. The Native Americans lacked immunity to common European diseases, and many died of smallpox, measles, and influenza.

Notes

Warm climate
didn't need sturdy
houses, warm clothes

"The Spanish impact
was devastating."
Many died of European
diseases.

DON'T WRITE EVERY WORD You want to capture your subject's ideas, but you don't have to become a human tape recorder. Listen carefully, and write down words and phrases that summarize the ideas. When the person makes a point in a way that stands out, write the exact words and enclose them in quotation marks. Even if you use a tape recorder, note taking can help you organize and summarize the information.

Journal Writing

Think about an interview you've read in a newspaper or magazine or watched on television. What questions helped to make the interview effective? List them.

ASK ON-THE-SPOT QUESTIONS Some of the best questions can't be planned in advance. Listen closely to the subject's answers and be aware of opportunities to ask follow-up questions. Notice in the graphic below the insight that is lost when the interviewer plows ahead with a prepared question instead of considering a follow-up question.

Prepared question: What is the state of the Native American heritage today?

A. Some aspects of Native American language and customs are lost with each generation. But the culture is resilient.

Next prepared question: How many Native Americans live in southern California

A. Many. About ten thousand in San Diego County alone.

Follow-up question: What do you mean by "resilient"?

A. The Native American culture never dies. It just reinvents itself.

Another follow-up question

FOLLOW THESE STEPS The following chart can help you plan and carry out an effective interview.

Set It Up
- Request an interview, explain your purpose, and make an appointment.
- Do background research about the person and the topic.
- Write a list of focused questions.
- Ask permission to tape the interview.

Listen More, Say Less
- Be polite, friendly, and businesslike.
- Listen well, and try not to interrupt. Let the person explain fully.
- Ask appropriate follow-up questions.
- In taking notes, summarize the main ideas, and quote well-stated remarks.

Get It All Down
- Listen to your tape. Review your notes. Then freewrite about your topic.
- If some information is unclear, check back with the person for clarification.
- Send the person a copy of your finished writing.

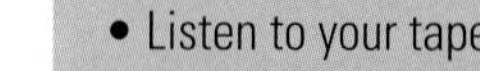

2.5 Writing Activities

Interview to Gather Information

Plan and conduct an interview to gather information about the topic of your investigative report. After the interview, summarize your findings.

PURPOSE To plan and carry out an interview
AUDIENCE Yourself
LENGTH 1-2 pages

WRITING RUBRICS To conduct an interview, you should

- set up the interview and explain your purpose to the person you will interview (your subject)
- research to learn about the subject and the topic
- accurately record main points and quotations during the interview

Using Computers

You might want to write up your interview as a script. You could also prepare a dialogue for a mock interview to perform in front of the class. Use a word processing program to put your questions and answers in a script format—indent the text after the name of the person speaking. Make one person's dialogue italic, and the other's bold. Such visual distinctions make it easier to keep your place on the page.

Enclose direct quotations in quotation marks.

When you take notes during an interview, enclose the subject's own exact words in quotation marks.

Rewrite any incorrect sentences below, adding quotation marks when they are needed.

1. In a recent interview, a telecommunications executive made this statement: The bottom line is that the information superhighway is changing the way we live.
2. She added that the information superhighway will dramatically affect the way we work and play.
3. The executive then went on to enumerate how the superhighway would transform the workplace.
4. What do you think will be the most significant change in the next five years? asked the interviewer.

See Lesson 21.9, pages 755–757.

Listening and Speaking

COOPERATIVE LEARNING Before conducting an interview for your investigative report, conduct a practice interview with a partner. Critique each other's questions and techniques to sharpen your performances.

LESSON 2.6

Drafting: Writing a Paragraph

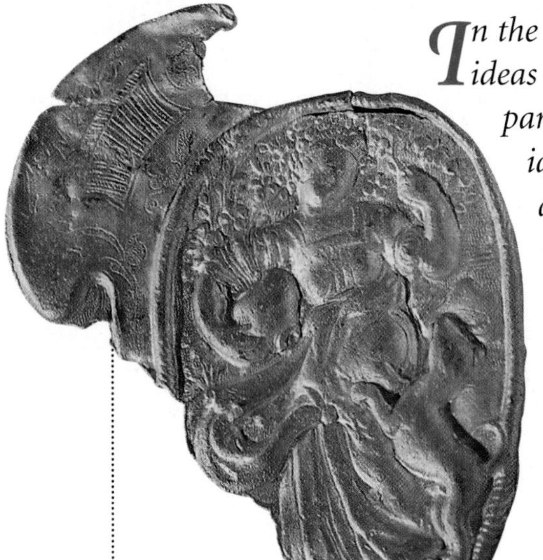

In the drafting stage, you write down your ideas in sentences and paragraphs. Each paragraph should have a topic or main idea sentence that is supported by details.

A paragraph is a group of related sentences that work together to develop one main idea. Notice how William Mathers states the main idea in each paragraph in the model below.

The first sentence introduces the main idea: the author finds a small metal object. The supporting sentences describe the object in detail.

The first sentence makes an observation about the nature of some items that were found. How do the following sentences support the first?

Literature Model

And then I catch a glimpse of metal—a small, luminous object poking from the sand. Probing carefully, I uncover a three-inch-wide fragment of hand-tooled gold plate. I am captivated by the image on the fragment: A woman in a swirling gown cradles a vase of flowers. Her left hand holds a cluster of roses. A small dog springs up at her feet. Floral designs embellish the fragment's border. . . .

Some items were touchingly personal. Along the edges of a small gold comb I made out "AÑOS 1618" inscribed in appliquéd gold dots. An abbreviated name, "DOÑA CATAL D GUSMA" (short for Doña Catalina de Guzmán) was also visible. Later research revealed that she was a widow residing in Manila in 1634. Had she been aboard the stricken vessel? What was her ultimate fate? No one knows.

William M. Mathers, *"Nuestra Señora de la Concepción"*

The Topic Sentence

In many paragraphs the main idea is stated in a topic sentence, and then all the details in the paragraph develop that idea. The wheel illustrates the vital role of a topic sentence in controlling the paragraph. All the details must not only be on the same topic, but must also help support the idea in the topic sentence.

In the literature model on the opposite page, the topic sentence comes at the beginning of each paragraph. Sometimes, though, the topic sentence comes at the end or in the middle. Wherever it is, it should tell two things: what your topic is and what your paragraph will say about it. Notice how Shella Calamba used a topic sentence to keep this paragraph on track.

Student Model

In investigating my mother's family history, I think I've discovered the origin of many of my own traits. My grandfather, who enjoyed listening to music as loud as any teenager today, willed me his love of music. My grandmother taught me to be responsible and open-minded. Because two of my aunts were teachers, I learned to value education. I inherited my dark, sarcastic sense of humor from one of my uncles. He would play bizarre practical jokes, and of many I was the victim. My interest in history and politics came from my great-grandfather, once the mayor of a small Philippine province. Finally, I credit my mother with teaching me to be independent, strong-minded, and determined in going after whatever goals I set.

Shella Calamba, Lincoln Park High School, Chicago, Illinois

The topic sentence states the main idea, which Calamba has supported with details—in this case, specific examples.

Journal Writing

Examine some of your topic sentences in a piece of your recent writing. Experiment with ways you could make your topic sentences better.

Elaborate with Supporting Details

The details you include in your supporting sentences should prove, clarify, or elaborate on your main idea. The types of details that you decide to use will vary, but they will generally fall into the categories shown in the following chart.

Kinds of Supporting Details	
Concrete details	The *Mayflower's* sails rustled, and the masts creaked in the breeze.
Examples	The heavy storm caused one more unhappy delay in the *Mayflower's* departure.
Incidents	Five months after the Pilgrims landed, the *Mayflower* sailed for home.
Facts or statistics	A Common House served as a townhouse, an arsenal, and a meetinghouse.
Reasons	The Pilgrims looked for a land where they could live and worship freely.

In some paragraphs all the supporting details are the same type, as in the student model on page 69. More frequently, a paragraph will contain two or more types of details, all working to support the main idea. In a family memoir, Bette Bao Lord used concrete details and reasons to develop a paragraph about her grandfather's grave site in China. How do the two kinds of details work together to create a sense of the present and the forever, rather than a sense of the past and time?

Concrete details describe the grave site.

What kinds of details explain why the grave site is important to the family?

Literature Model

Grandfather sleeps in the earth near Suzhou. He has mountains to shelter him from the wind, green farm lands to gaze upon, the shade of a bamboo grove, the vast tranquillity of Tai Hu Lake, and the singing mists just over the horizon. And he has a name. It is carved in stone. This man was born and lived and died. The stone will not be plowed under or smashed or abandoned or carted away. It will stand. It will endure. For my grandfather. For us. For my Chinese roots. So when one day the children of my children and their children, who won't speak Chinese, look Chinese or know China, visit this lone ancestor they will feel Chinese, as I did that afternoon at his grave.

Bette Bao Lord, *Legacies: A Chinese Mosaic*

2.6 Writing Activities

Write a Draft

You have planned for your investigative report. Now it is time to begin your draft. Just begin writing. Skip every other line to leave room for changes. Don't worry about correctness. At this stage, you are still exploring what you want to say.

PURPOSE To create a draft
AUDIENCE Yourself
LENGTH 1-2 pages

WRITING RUBRICS To write an effective draft, you should

- use your prewriting notes for ideas
- get your ideas down on paper
- add ideas that support or relate to your topic sentences

Cross-Curricular Activity

SOCIAL STUDIES Locate a photograph of a person in the newspaper. Read the accompanying article about why the person is pictured. Imagine that you are going to interview the subject as part of an investigative report. What would you ask, and how would you use the information? Then make a list of questions for the interview.

Viewing and Representing

COOPERATIVE LEARNING With a partner, select a painting from this book. Where are the figures placed, and how are they presented? Notice the title. What main idea does the painting express? Take notes on your reactions to the painting. Together, compose a topic sentence based on your responses and write a paragraph using the details you discussed.

Use commas after introductory phrases and clauses.

Shella Calamba said: *Because two of my aunts were teachers, I learned to value education.*

Rewrite the sentences below, adding commas where they are needed.

1. Working with the latest underwater equipment the salvage team explored the ocean bottom.
2. Because they were seeking whatever remained of the Spanish ship's cargo they spent over two years in the islands.
3. During the long search for the treasure many of the divers almost gave up hope.
4. By the time the project was completed the team had recovered almost 2,000 pieces of treasure.
5. Of the many items found a gold comb appliquéd with gold dots was the most interesting.

See Lesson 21.6, pages 743–751.

LESSON 2.7

Drafting: Organizing a Paragraph

Writers, like artists, put together pieces to create meaning. Just as the artist connected pieces of small snapshots to give his collage a meaning, a writer arranges and links details to express a main idea.

David Hockney, *Paul Explaining Pictures to Mie Kakigahara,* 1983

Order the Details

As you prepare to write, you accumulate many unconnected ideas and pieces of information. Before you begin to write, your task is to sort out and organize your main ideas and the details that support them.

When you arrange details to express a main idea in writing, you can use one of several kinds of order.

SPATIAL ORDER One student, Mark Center, explored a department store on a busy day. Later, he described the store in spatial order, arranging the details according to their closeness to each other.

Student Model

In the store's display window, two mannequins pose stiffly, showing off the season's newest styles. Inside, next to the window, an extravagant tropical tree reaches to the ceiling, its limbs spreading over racks of pastel plaid shorts and matching shirts. Behind the service counter, a salesman rings up a purchase for a distressed mother looking around for her child. The little girl is peering into a glass case filled with glittering jewelry. A few steps beyond, a thin, glamorous model tries to shower passing customers with perfume. A frantic father drags his two small boys onto an escalator, while they fuss and cry. The store's rear entrance is jammed with exhausted shoppers leaving and enthusiastic shoppers entering.

Mark Center, Jefferson Davis High School,
Montgomery, Alabama

Center begins with the display window in the front of the store and ends with the rear entrance.

What words does Center use to help his readers locate objects in this scene?

The Writing Process

OTHER KINDS OF ORDER Spatial order works well for descriptive writing, but when your primary purpose is to narrate, you will usually choose chronological order. Be aware of other types of order as well.

Four Kinds of Order

Chronological	Importance	Cause and Effect	Compare and Contrast

To explain how a medical researcher went about her work, arrange the steps in time order.	To persuade people to donate money for cancer research, end with your strongest argument.	To convince someone that a certain drug is harmful, explain what happened to some of its users.	To explain a new and unfamiliar medical procedure, compare it with a familiar one.

Journal Writing

List possible topics that would be best described by each of the five kinds of order presented in this lesson.

The Writing Process

Link the Details

Mark Center arranged his details about the department store in a logical order, but he also connected his ideas smoothly to each other and to the main idea. Mark used transition words and phrases as signposts to point his reader in the right direction. Notice how transitions help you follow the ideas in the paragraph below. It describes the discovery of a German battleship, the *Bismarck,* that sank in the North Atlantic in 1941.

Transition words and phrases—"soon," "then," "at last"—clarify the order of the events and add coherence. The words "this" and "these" add coherence by referring to something mentioned earlier.

Literature Model

We had been fooled by the debris from the clipper ship, but this time it would prove to be *Bismarck.* Following the trail northwestward, we soon encountered one of the battleship's four massive gun turrets. These had been held in place by the force of gravity, and they had fallen free when *Bismarck* capsized on her way to the bottom. Then at last on June 8 [1988] we came upon *Bismarck* herself, a great phantom shape resting in her grave three miles beneath the surface.

Robert D. Ballard, "The *Bismarck* Found"

The transition words and phrases you choose will depend on your topic and purpose. The chart below shows some transitions you can use to connect ideas that are related in different ways. Not every sentence, however, needs a transition word or phrase. Too many transitions will make your writing sound awkward and artificial.

Transition Words and Phrases

Time	first, when, until, next, before, later, finally, afterward, that night, meanwhile, then
Location	above, below, here, underneath, inside, next to, around the corner, in the distance
Importance	first, mainly, primarily, last, most important, secondly, next
Cause and Effect	as a result, because, consequently, for that reason, therefore, then
Compare	similarly, like, just as, also, in the same way
Contrast	but, even so, however, in contrast, on the other hand, unlike, on the contrary

2.7 Writing Activities

Plan Ordered Paragraphs

Review the draft of your investigative report. Pick out two of the main ideas and plan an ordered paragraph for each. For help with organizing paragraphs, see **Writing and Research Handbook,** pages 953–955.

PURPOSE To plan the structure of paragraphs
AUDIENCE Yourself
LENGTH 2 paragraphs

WRITING RUBRICS To develop an effective plan for your paragraphs, you should

- consider the order that best suits the content and purpose of the paragraphs
- arrange the supporting details in a suitable order
- use transitions to link details

Cross-Curricular Activity

HISTORY Look through the table of contents and the historical atlas of your U.S. history textbook. Locate information and maps showing the territorial growth of the country. Use the information and maps to write a report describing the expansion of the United States from 1783 to 1853. You can tell about the events in chronological order; in spatial order, tracing expansion from east to west or north to south; or in order of importance.

Viewing and Representing

VISUALS Present to the class the main points of your report from the Cross-Curricular Activity, along with a visual in the form of a map, a chart, or a time line. Make sure that your visual is clear and legible and that it clarifies information in your report.

Use a semicolon to separate main clauses joined by a conjunctive adverb (such as *however, therefore*) or by an expression (such as *for example* or *in fact*).

In such sentences the expression or adverb is also set off by a comma:

Divers finally located the sunken ship; however, it took more than 40 years.

This type of sentence structure is often useful when you write using transitions.

Rewrite the following sentences, using correct punctuation.

1. Each supporting detail in a paragraph is like a piece of a jigsaw puzzle in fact it may have little meaning by itself.
2. Spatial order works well for descriptive writing however it seldom works for narrative writing.
3. The relationship between sentences needs to be made clear for that reason transition words are often used to tie ideas together.
4. Transition words clarify the order of supporting details therefore they add coherence to your writing.
5. Not every sentence needs a transition furthermore too many transitions may make your writing awkward.

See Lesson 21.5, page 740, and Lesson 21.6, pages 746–748.

The Writing Process

Revising: Checking Unity and Coherence

When you revise your writing, work with a peer reviewer. Check unity; all sentences and details should help support the main idea. Also check for coherence, adding transitions to connect ideas.

All writers, even famous ones, keep trying to improve their writing. Here's how author E. B. White revised the conclusion of an essay about the day American astronauts first set foot on the moon.

still holds the key to madness

kiss in every land

The moon stil belongs to lovers, and lovers are everywhere--not
just in America. What a pity we couldn't have planted some
precisely this unique, this incredible
emblem that ~~exactly~~ expressed the occasion, even if it were
nothing more than a white banner, with the legend: ~~"Hello, everybody"~~-y."
that simply said
"At last!"

handkerchief, symbol of the common cold, which, like the moon, belongs to all mankind

This humorous ending adds unity by supporting the idea that the moon belongs to everyone, not just Americans.

Evaluate Your First Draft

Writers need to evaluate their first drafts objectively, at times ruthlessly. Often it helps to put your draft aside, returning to it a few days later. Then you can look at it objectively, asking yourself questions like the ones in the chart.

Questions to Consider
1. Is my writing interesting?
2. Is it easy to follow?
3. What do I like best about it?
4. How can I make it better?

Your fellow writers are facing the same challenges, and you can help one another. A classmate can serve as a peer reviewer, who points out what works well in your draft and what does not. Here are three ways to work with a peer reviewer.

Working with a Peer Reviewer

1. Read your first draft aloud; then discuss it with a peer reviewer.	2. Let your peer reviewer read your first draft silently, making comments right on the page.	3. Give your peer reviewer an evaluation form to fill out.

Journal Writing

How successful are you at evaluating your own work? List ways in which a peer reviewer can help you. What other strategies might help you revise more successfully?

Use a Peer Reviewer's Comments

A peer reviewer can spot problems you may not be able to see. Notice how a peer reviewer's comments, shown in the margin, helped one writer.

I'd like to know when Bly was born.

I really like your introduction, but this detail about the name of the town doesn't seem to belong here.

How did the editor come up with that name?

Nellie Bly, who was born ^in 1867^ in Cochran Mills, Pennsylvania, became the first celebrated woman investigative reporter in the United States. "Nellie Bly" was actually just her pen name. Her real name was Elizabeth Cochran. ~~I guess her family must have owned the town they lived in, because it had the same name.~~ Her pen name was suggested by the managing editor at The Pittsburgh Dispatch, where she was a reporter. ^He took the name from a song by Stephen Foster.^

The paragraph below needed more extensive changes. Again, read the peer reviewer's suggestions in the margin. Which change corrected a problem in unity?

I don't think this sentence belongs here.

Shouldn't this sentence come after the first one?

What were the conditions like?

In 1887, Nellie had joined the New York World. ~~At the Dispatch, she had written about slum life and divorce.~~ ~~She~~ ^Nellie^ pretended to be insane so that she could be admitted to Blackwell's Island, an insane asylum near New York. The World specialized in "muckraking," journalism that exposed corruption and scandal. She saw ~~the conditions~~ ^the horrifying and inhumane treatment of the helpless inmates^ firsthand. Her story brought about reforms at Blackwell's Island.

Revise for Unity

In a unified paragraph, all sentences work together to support the main idea. When you revise, look at each paragraph to see whether every sentence relates to your main idea. Any sentences that introduce irrelevant ideas should be eliminated. The questions below will help you revise your paragraphs for unity.

Checking for Unity

1. Does my topic sentence accurately state what I want to say about my topic? Can it be more tightly focused?
2. Have I fully supported my topic sentence? Do I need to add details?
3. Do all supporting statements relate to the topic sentence? Should any be eliminated?

Examine the changes this writer made in response to her peer reviewer's comments. Which changes add unity to her writing? Which changes add detail to support her topic sentence?

Bly's ~~biggest~~ *greatest* triumph was her attempt to beat the record for traveling around the world set by Phileas Fogg in Jules Verne's novel Around the World in Eighty Days. ~~This popular book was made into an equally popular movie.~~ Bly sailed *from New York* on November 14, 1889. She rode ~~on many forms of transportation~~ *ships, trains, sampans, horses, and burros* as she circled the globe. She returned to New York 72 days, 6 hours, 11 minutes, and 14 seconds later. *She had beaten the record and given her readers a thrilling adventure to share.*

This is an interesting fact, but I don't think it relates to your topic sentence.

I think your readers would like to know what kinds of transportation.

Journal Writing

Look at a recent piece of writing and examine it for unity. In your journal experiment with ways you can change specific paragraphs to add unity to your writing.

Revise for Coherence

In a coherent paragraph, sentences are clearly and logically connected to each other. Look over your writing to see whether your paragraphs flow smoothly from one idea to the next. These questions can help you revise your paragraphs for coherence.

Checking for Coherence
1. Does each sentence follow in a logical order?
2. Would another means of organizing my ideas work better?
3. Do transition words and phrases clarify the relationships between ideas?

Notice how changes in the following paragraph reflect the peer reviewer's comments shown in the margin. How do the changes add coherence to the writing?

I think you're getting the story out of sequence here.

This belongs near the sentence where you mention the contest.

While Bly circled the globe, the editors at the World made her journey a national story. ~~In fact,~~ when she returned to San Francisco, a special train waited to carry her to New York. In addition to daily stories about Bly's exploits, the World, aiming to increase its circulation, held a contest. Whoever came closest to guessing the time of her journey would win a ~~prize~~. The contest worked. The World received almost one million contest entries from readers who were following Bly's race around the world. Steaming across the country, the train was met at every stop by large crowds, brass bands, and fireworks. ~~What's more, the contest winner would get a~~ trip to Europe. Bly's triumph sparked the nation's imagination.

2.8 Writing Activities

Revise for Effective Paragraphs

Take another look at the draft of your investigative report. Work with a peer reviewer. Then revise your paragraphs, incorporating useful peer reviewer suggestions. For help with writing unified paragraphs, see **Writing and Research Handbook,** pp. 953–955.

PURPOSE To revise for paragraph unity
AUDIENCE Yourself
LENGTH Changes on the draft

WRITING RUBRICS To revise for unity in each paragraph, you should

- make sure that all the sentences are about one main idea
- check to see whether the paragraph needs a topic sentence
- see whether transition words are needed

Using Computers

To check your use of transitions, convert all your transition words and phrases into boldface type. Check for awkward transitions, and see where transitions may be needed. When you have finished revising, convert the entire file back to regular text.

When revising for clarity, look for misplaced or dangling modifiers.

In your sentences, place modifiers as close as possible to the words they modify so that your meaning is clear. For example, in the model on page 80 the writer states:

> *Steaming across the country, the train was met at every stop by large crowds, brass bands, and fireworks.*

The reader understands that the modifier describes the train.

Rewrite the sentences below, correcting the misplaced or dangling modifier in each.

1. The main character in Jules Verne's novel *Around the World in Eighty Days*, reporter Nellie Bly wanted to break the travel record of Phileas Fogg.
2. She rode on horses and camels traveling around the world.
3. Beating Fogg's record, newspaper readers shared Bly's thrilling experience.
4. While circling the globe, the editors at the *World* made Bly's journey a front-page story.

See Lesson 18.7, pages 674–679.

Listening and Speaking

COOPERATIVE LEARNING To review paragraphs with a partner, try reading aloud first to evaluate content. After arranging your paragraphs as they will appear in the finished product, read the paragraphs aloud again and check for unity and coherence.

LESSON

2.9

Editing/Proofreading: Toward a Final Version

The fourth stage in the writing process is editing/proofreading. Like the framers of the United States Constitution, shown below, you correct your errors so that they do not distract the reader from your ideas.

"So, then . . . Would that be 'us the people' or 'we the people'?"

Edit to Correct Sentence Errors

Begin the editing stage by taking a careful look at your sentences. Make sure that each sentence expresses a complete thought in a way that is grammatically correct. Compare the edited draft below with the checklist. Which sentence-editing guidelines did the writer apply?

Sentence-Editing Checklist

1. Have I avoided sentence fragments?
2. Have I avoided run-on sentences?
3. Are all pronouns used correctly?
4. Are all verbs used correctly?
5. Have I avoided double negatives?
6. Have I avoided wordiness?

Scientists ~~who are~~ searching for clues about what ~~it was that~~ caused the extinction of the dinosaurs ~~has~~ *have* debated various theories. One theory suggests that dinosaurs became extinct suddenly, after a gigantic comet or meteor collided with the earth. The impact spewed debris into the atmosphere. The sunlight was blocked for months. Temperatures dropped, *and* many species of plants and animals

Journal Writing

Perhaps you have found yourself in this situation: a teacher likes the content of your paper but has given you a lower mark because of errors. "But you know what I meant," you complain. "Why does it matter how I said it?" Write a response from your teacher's point of view.

The Writing Process

Proofread for Spelling and Mechanics

Proofreading is the part of editing that focuses on spelling and on mechanics—capital letters and punctuation marks. Use the checklist below to identify errors. Use the proofreading symbols as a kind of shorthand to mark needed changes.

Proofreading

Checklist

1. Does each sentence have the right end punctuation?
2. Are commas and semicolons used as needed?
3. Are other punctuation marks used as needed?
4. Are all words spelled correctly?
5. Are possessives and contractions written correctly?
6. Are capital letters used as needed?

Symbols

Symbol	Meaning
∧	Insert
ℓ	Remove
⌒‿	Exchange
¶	New paragraph
⊙	Add period
∧ with comma	Add comma
≡	Uppercase
/	Lowercase
⌒ ‿	Close space

What change does each proofreading symbol indicate?

¶ Until recently, many scientists theorized that the extinction of the dinosaur was a gradual process. One theory held that poisons slowly built up in earth's vegetation over the years, ~~slowly~~ killing the dinosaurs. Another theory was that mamals ate the dinosaur eggs still another theory was that dinosaurs could not adapt to gradual changes in earth's climate and plant life. Today, however most scientists think that a sudden and catastrophic event--perhaps caused by a crashing Meteor or colliding planet--caused the extinction of dinosaurs.

Proofreading is the last part of the editing process. Your investigation of your subject, which may have started with just a glimpse of an idea, has resulted in a fully developed piece of writing. Now is the time to prepare your final version and present your writing to its audience.

2.9 Writing Activities

Edit Your Draft

When you are satisfied that your investigative report says what you want it to say, it is time to edit your writing.

PURPOSE To edit and proofread
AUDIENCE Yourself
LENGTH Changes on the draft

WRITING RUBRICS To edit and proofread your draft, you should

- use the editing and proofreading checklists from this lesson
- proofread for one kind of error at a time
- use proofreading symbols

Using Computers

Sharpen your keyboard skills as well as your proofreading skills by having a paragraph from this textbook read aloud to you while you sit at your computer. As you listen to the passage, type it as a document in your word processing program. Later check for typographical errors you may have made, as well as errors in punctuation, spelling, and capitalization.

Listening and Speaking

COOPERATIVE LEARNING Work with a partner to read aloud various stages of your edited investigative reports. Listening to a report can help make grammatical errors and errors in usage more obvious because oral expression is influenced by such conventions of English.

Make sure subjects and verbs agree in person and number.

Check subject-verb agreement as you edit your work. Be especially careful with sentences in which phrases intervene between the subject and the verb. For example, look at the first sentence of the model on page 83. The subject, *scientists,* is plural. The writer changed the verb to its plural form to agree with the subject.

Rewrite the sentences below to make subjects and verbs agree.

1. Scientists from all over the world is studying the effects of climate changes.
2. This scientist, in addition to many of his colleagues, believe that severe climate changes caused the extinction of dinosaurs.
3. An ice age thousands of years ago probably were responsible for migrations of early people.
4. Perhaps the poisons slowly building up in the earth's vegetation was the cause of dinosaurs disappearing.
5. A definitive answer to this question, as well to the reason for migrations, continue to elude scientists.

See Lessons 16.1, page 614; and Lesson 16.6, pages 621–622.

LESSON 2.10

Publishing/Presenting: Sharing Your Writing

Presenting your work—sharing it with others—is the final stage in the writing process. You may think your job is done when you hand your work in to your teacher; but other avenues are available to help you get the word out.

Shown below are just a few possible places where you could present your work. When you've spent the time and effort to put your thoughts on paper, you owe it to yourself—and your potential readers—to share your ideas.

Prewriting: "None of my friends are cooks. How can I interest them in salsa recipes?"

Drafting: "A description of a rock concert will grab my readers' attention."

Revising: "My cousin doesn't use a computer. I'd better explain how to use a mouse."

Editing/Proofreading: "Is it *o-s-m-o-s-e-s?* Mr. Dorn teaches science, so I'd better spell it right."

Publishing/ Presenting: "Hey, I think I've got it now. Got a minute to listen to this?"

Reach Your Audience

Whenever you write, you're writing for an audience. As the photos suggest, your audience should affect every stage of your writing process. Your audience can be yourself when you write in your journal or a friend when you scribble a note. It can be the large and far-flung audience you reach by publishing your work. Who might learn from your writing, be entertained or persuaded by it, or be interested in some other way by your work? Here are some ways to present what you write.

Places to Publish

Publication	Audience
School publications: literary magazine, newspaper, yearbook	Your fellow students
General-interest newspapers and magazines	The general student and adult population
Special interest newsletters and magazines	People interested in a particular subject: hobby, sport, cause, career
Computer networks: on-line bulletin boards, special-interest networks	Computer users linked by common interests

Journal Writing

Choose a piece of writing from your journal. Write about the audience you'd like to present it to and how you'd prepare it.

The Writing Process

Publish Together

Today it's easier than ever for writers to see their work in print. Desktop publishing allows anyone with access to a computer and a printer to produce high-quality graphic art and professional-looking layouts. Even without a computer, you can create interesting and effective publications—with just a typewriter and a copy machine.

What type of publication could your class produce? Would you like to produce a literary magazine that will be a forum for stories, poetry, and reviews? Or a general magazine covering topics of interest to your class? Or perhaps a series of special reports, each covering one topic or issue in depth? Look at the examples below for ideas your class might use to create its own publication.

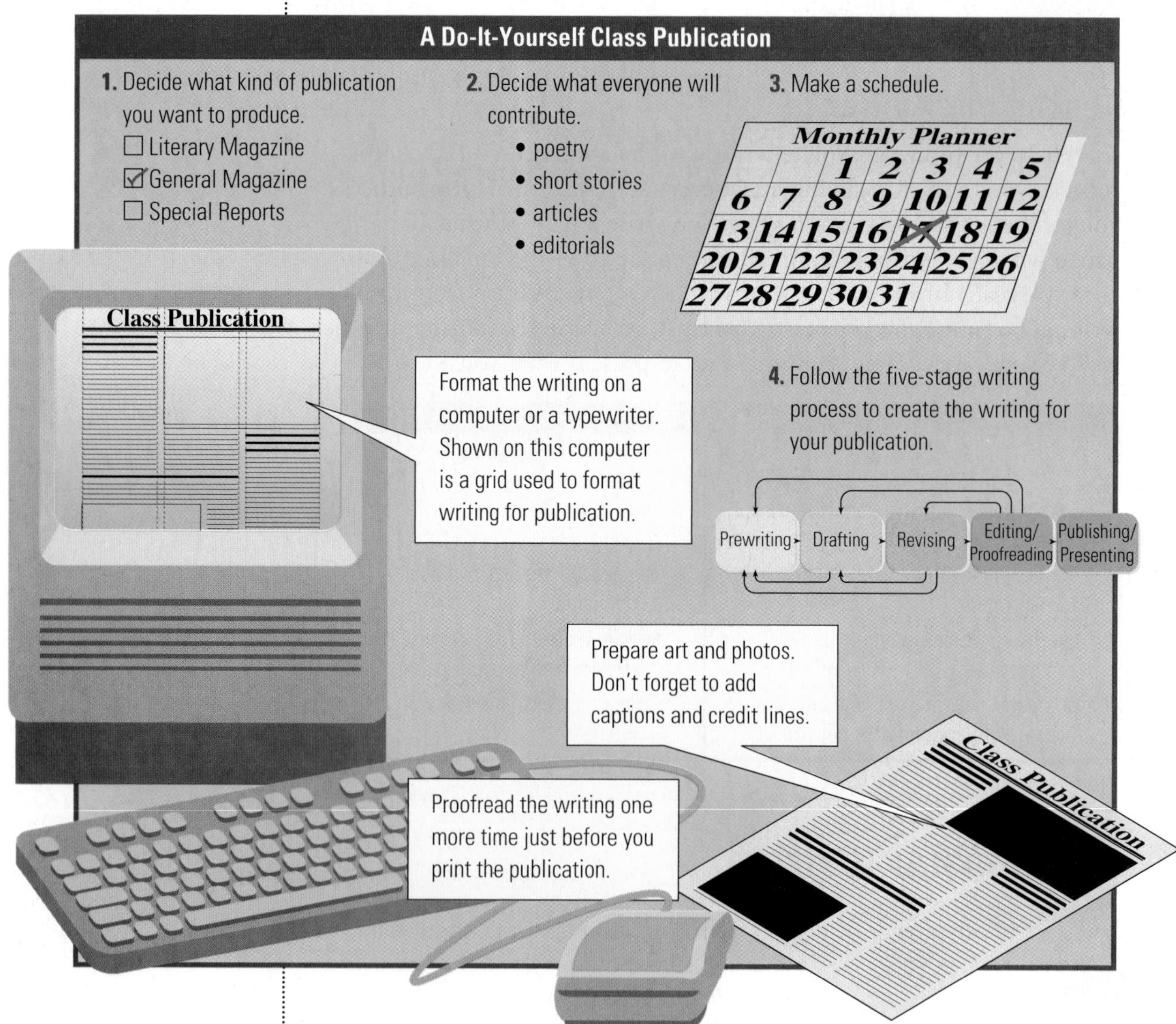

A Do-It-Yourself Class Publication
1. Decide what kind of publication you want to produce.
☐ Literary Magazine
☑ General Magazine
☐ Special Reports
2. Decide what everyone will contribute.
• poetry
• short stories
• articles
• editorials
3. Make a schedule.
Monthly Planner
1 2 3 4 5
6 7 8 9 10 11 12
13 14 15 16 17 18 19
20 21 22 23 24 25 26
27 28 29 30 31
Class Publication
Format the writing on a computer or a typewriter. Shown on this computer is a grid used to format writing for publication.
4. Follow the five-stage writing process to create the writing for your publication.
Prewriting
Drafting
Revising
Editing/ Proofreading
Publishing/ Presenting
Prepare art and photos. Don't forget to add captions and credit lines.
Class Publication
Proofread the writing one more time just before you print the publication.

2.10 Writing Activities

Present Your Writing

You have taken your report through prewriting, drafting, revising, and editing/proofreading. Now it's time for sharing your writing!

PURPOSE To present your finished work
AUDIENCE The audience you chose when you began to write
LENGTH Whatever is appropriate for your purpose

WRITING RUBRICS To prepare your writing for final presentation, you should

- use a format that is appropriate for your audience and purpose
- include illustrations or other images if desired
- make your paper neat and legible

Using Computers

You might present your final investigative report in the form of a Web page on the Internet. (First check your school's policy.) Investigate Web page–building software, and choose the one most appropriate for your purpose and audience. Before publishing, check your report once more for accuracy in content, spelling, and grammar.

Grammar Link

Use correct punctuation for each part of a business letter.

When you submit a piece of your writing to the editor of a publication, you should write a cover letter to go with it. Be sure to use the correct form and punctuation for your letter.

Use commas to separate city from state, day from year, the addressee's name from his or her title, and after the closing. Use a colon after the greeting. Use correct punctuation with abbreviations.

Write the parts of the business letter below using correct punctuation.

1. 120 N Merrill Street
   Park Ridge IL 60068
   March 6 1997
2. Mr. Paul Oscar Feature Editor
   The Shore Weekly
   1 Sunrise Lane
3. Westport CT 06880
4. Dear Mr. Oscar
5. Sincerely yours

See Lesson 21.4, page 739; Lesson 21.6, pages 749–750; and Lesson 21.13, pages 766–768.

Viewing and Representing

COOPERATIVE LEARNING In a small group, brainstorm to create a list of magazines and other publishing vehicles, including electronic ones, in which you and your classmates might publish your writings. Begin by considering the audiences that might be interested in individual and class writing samples. Present your list to the class. Visit your library and check out publications that feature student writing to display in the classroom.

LESSON 2.11

WRITING ABOUT LITERATURE

Analyzing Point of View

Point of view is the angle from which you see people, objects, or events. In the cartoon you see what is outside the window from the point of view of Gladys Murphy. In other words, you see only what she sees. In a short story or novel, point of view controls what the reader knows.

"Hello, Emily. This is Gladys Murphy up the street. Fine, thanks . . . Say, could you go to your window and describe what's in my front yard?"

Identify Point of View

The paragraphs that follow tell the same story from different points of view. Read them to discover the three main points of view that story writers use: first-person, third-person limited, and third-person omniscient (all-knowing). The paragraph is part of a mystery story involving a police investigation. The characters are the detective, Sergeant Rivera, and the suspect, Carson. For each version ask these questions: Who is the narrator, or the teller of the story? How much is known to the narrator, and therefore to the reader?

First Person

We walked to the swimming pool. I leaned against the diving board, wondering if now were the moment to spring my trap, to ask Carson just how his emerald stickpin had wound up on the floor of Jasmine Tsing's abandoned car. Carson sank into the *chaise longue,* clearly puzzled by my silence. I knew he thought he'd left no clues, no evidence along that secluded stretch of Evergreen Road. Time and time again, he told me that he'd never even met Jasmine Tsing. Carson had no idea that a small chunk of fiery green crystal was about to call him a liar.

The writer has Rivera tell the story from his own point of view, using the first-person pronouns *I* and *me.* This point of view allows readers to know the character better and gives a "you-are-there" feeling.

Third-Person Limited

They walked to the swimming pool. As Rivera leaned against the diving board, Carson sank into the *chaise longue.* Why, he wondered, was Rivera so silent? Carson was certain he had left no clues, no evidence along that solitary stretch of Evergreen Road where Jasmine Tsing's abandoned car had been discovered. No, he told himself, Rivera couldn't possibly suspect him. Hadn't he told the police more than once that he'd never met Jasmine Tsing?

A third-person limited narrator tells the story from one character's point of view—in this case, Carson's. What does the reader learn about other characters' thoughts and feelings? What clues are given?

Third-Person Omniscient

They walked to the swimming pool. Rivera leaned against the diving board, wondering if now were the moment to spring the trap, to ask how Carson's emerald stickpin had wound up on the floor of Jasmine Tsing's abandoned car. Carson sank into the *chaise longue.* He was puzzled by Rivera's silence but certain he'd left no clues, no evidence along that secluded stretch of Evergreen Road. Hadn't he told the police more than once that he'd never even met Jasmine Tsing?

A third-person omniscient narrator knows everything about the characters. How does this affect the way the reader views the characters?

When you are planning an analysis of point of view in a story, your prewriting begins with reading the work closely. Then you are ready to use the following questionnaire.

Questionnaire on Point of View

1. What point of view is used—first-person, third-person limited, or third-person omniscient?
2. How does the point of view affect your attitude toward the characters and the events?
3. How does the point of view affect your overall understanding of the story?
4. How would the story be different if the author had told it from another point of view?
5. What point of view would you use if you were writing this story? Why?

Journal Writing

Use the questionnaire to analyze point of view in a favorite short story. Do you view the story differently now? Explain your answer.

Draft Your Analysis

Once you've completed the questionnaire, you are ready to draft your analysis of the point of view in a story or novel. You've seen that first-person point of view uses the pronoun *I.* Third-person point of view, limited or omniscient, uses *he, she,* and *it.* But as you will see in Katherine Wise's analysis of Willa Cather's *My Ántonia,* point of view goes far beyond grammar: it is an essential part of the author's style.

Student Model

Willa Cather and Jim Burden were crossing Iowa on the same train. They began talking about the small Nebraska town where they had grown up together. In her introduction to the novel *My Ántonia,* Cather says that the conversation kept centering around a Bohemian girl who, better than anyone else, seemed to epitomize their prairie childhood. Over the years Burden had written down the things he remembered about her, and he showed his manuscript to Cather. He had entitled it *Ántonia* but after a little thought changed it to *My Ántonia.* From there came what is considered Willa Cather's greatest work.

Wise provides background by referring to Cather's introduction.

Cather tells the story through Jim Burden's eyes. But they become her eyes, too. The book is so real that you keep flipping back to the introduction to see that yes, this was written by Cather, and that no, this is not a biography—it is a novel.

According to Wise, the story is told through whose eyes? What effect does this create?

Cather is able to maintain this feeling of reality because as the narrator she remains completely objective. She describes everything through Jim's eyes, but she never states what his feelings or emotions are. This seems strange at times, but it would not have been as sincere if Cather had tried to apply her own feelings to Jim, or if she had tried to imagine what his feelings might be. Instead her objectivity emphasizes the fact that the book is not about Jim, but about Ántonia.

Burden and Cather had "agreed that no one who had not grown up in a little prairie town could know anything about it." But they proved themselves wrong. Cather took me there—to Black Hawk, Nebraska—swept away on the prairie winds of her words. Her writing is as plain, simple, and harsh as the land it is about, and just as beautiful.

This paragraph describes the student's strong personal response to a powerful story.

Katherine Jane Wise, Perrysburg High School,
Perrysburg, Ohio

2.11 Writing Activities

Write from a Particular Point of View

Look at the painting and its title below. Write a short description of what might be happening in the scene from one of these points of view: the first-person point of view of one of the people pictured, third-person limited, or third-person omniscient.

PURPOSE To explore point of view
AUDIENCE Your classmates
LENGTH 2 paragraphs

WRITING RUBRICS To present point of view correctly, you should

- make the point of view clear
- keep the point of view consistent
- use pronouns correctly

Cross-Curricular Activity

MUSIC In a small group, listen to the lyrics of a ballad. Discuss the point of view used in the song and why that point of view may have been chosen by the lyricist.

Sofonisba Anguissola,
Three of the Artist's Sisters Playing Chess, 1555

Listening and Speaking

NARRATIVE Consider the viewpoint of different characters in a story. Discuss which viewpoints offer the most interesting perspectives on story events. Then take turns telling parts of the story as first-person narration by different characters.

Grammar Link

Be consistent in presenting point of view when writing.

When you write in the first person, use the pronouns *I* and *we.* In the third person, refer to characters as *he, she, one,* and *they.* In the second person, use *you.* The writer of the first-person narration in the model on page 90 used pronouns consistently:

I leaned against the diving board, wondering if now was the moment to spring ***my*** *trap. . . .*

Revise each sentence below to eliminate the incorrect shifts in pronouns.

1. When you analyze first-person point of view, we decide how much we can learn from the first-person narrator.
2. If they are writing from a third-person point of view, you can narrate the actions and words of all the characters.
3. If a story captures one's curiosity, your interest usually follows.
4. When one is interested in a story, I keep on reading.
5. She and I like reading the same kinds of books in their spare time.

See Lesson 17.5, page 644.

UNIT 2

Writing Process in Action

The Writing Process

The Writing Process

WRITING Online

Visit the Writer's Choice Web site at writerschoice.glencoe.com for additional writing prompts.

In preceding lessons you learned about the five stages of the writing process—prewriting, drafting, revising, editing/proofreading, and publishing/presenting. You also had an opportunity to practice each of these stages. Now you will use the writing process to put together a piece of writing about your personal history or heritage.

Assignment

Context

As part of a world history assignment, class members have been asked to write about some aspect of their personal history or heritage. Suggested topics include family histories, descriptions of family or relatives, and autobiographical accounts. The goal of the assignment is to show how you are part of history and of the history-making process.

Purpose

To briefly describe a particular aspect of your personal history or heritage

Audience

Your teacher and peers, and perhaps your family members

Length

1-2 pages

For advice on how to approach this assignment, you will find the next few pages helpful. You can come back to these pages as you write, getting help where and when you need it. Don't feel limited by the suggestions here. You're in charge of your own writing process.

Prewriting

Do you remember listening spellbound to a tale about your past or your family's past? Maybe you have your own stories—memories that hold their shape and color despite the passage of time. Search your memory for a story you'd like to explore. If you're looking for an idea, try the prewriting suggestions.

Next, review the assignment. Your main purpose is to inform your readers about an aspect of your personal history or heritage. Is there anything else you want to accomplish? For example, do you want to persuade your readers to be proud of their own roots? Also keep in mind the needs of your audience. Be sure to provide enough background information so that family relationships and other details that you take for granted will make sense to your teacher and classmates.

Then, work on a main idea statement to help you choose details and keep your writing on track. To find details, start with family photo albums or videos. Interview family members and family friends to get firsthand information. Make notes on what you learn to help you as you draft.

Prewriting Options

- Read your journal. Look for autobiographical entries.
- Prewrite about yourself. Try to answer the question, Who am I?
- Brainstorm with family members.
- Create an idea tree. Start by circling the word family.

Prewriting Tip

For tips on interviewing, see Lesson 2.5, pages 64–67.

Drafting

Now it's time to start getting your story down on paper. Review your prewriting notes and main idea statement. Then find a place to jump in—either at the beginning, or at the part that is clearest in your mind, even if that's somewhere in the middle. The goal of drafting is to get your ideas down, even if they're not exactly in the right order or in a polished form.

How will you organize your draft? If you're telling a story about your past, chronological order may be your best choice. If you are describing a special place, you may want to use spatial order.

As you write, look for ways you can use details to intrigue your readers. In his autobiography, Alex Haley, the author of *Roots,* introduces his readers to the strange sounding words that were clues to his African heritage. Read the following passage and notice Haley's effective use of details.

Drafting Tip

For examples of different types of supporting details, see Lesson 2.6, page 70.

Literature Model

Anyway, all of this is how I was growing up in Henning at Grandma's, listening from behind her rocking chair as she and the other visiting old women talked of that African . . . who said his name was "*Kintay,*" and said "*ko*" for banjo, "*Kamby Bolong*" for river, and a jumble of other "*k*"-beginning sounds that Grandma privately muttered. . . .

Alex Haley, "My Furthest-Back Person—The African"

Once you've got everything down, take a break from your writing, even if you're not particularly satisfied with your draft. You'll be able to evaluate your draft more objectively after a few hours or a day away from it.

Revising

To begin revising, read over your draft to make sure that what you've written fits your purpose and audience. Then have a **writing conference.** Read your draft to a partner or small group. Use your audience's reactions and the Revising Checklist below to help you evaluate your work.

Revising Tip

For advice on how to work with a peer reviewer, see Lesson 2.8, page 77.

Revising Checklist

- Does my writing reveal something interesting about my personal history?
- Have I narrowed my topic to get a tight focus?
- Is each paragraph coherent and unified?
- Will my writing appeal to my audience—my teacher and peers?

Editing/Proofreading

When you have revised your writing for basic content and organization, **proofread** it carefully for grammar, usage, and mechanics errors that can distract readers. Use the questions at the right as a guide.

Now use the Self-Evaluation list below to judge your overall work. When you're satisfied with your personal history, make a clean copy of it and proofread one more time.

Editing/Proofreading Checklist

- Have I capitalized proper nouns, especially names of places and people?
- Have I made sure that all pronouns are correct?
- Have I added commas and semicolons where they are needed?
- Have I set off direct quotes with quotation marks?
- Have I checked carefully for possible misspellings?

Self-Evaluation

Make sure that your personal history —

- ✔ describes an aspect of your life or heritage
- ✔ uses an appropriate method of organization
- ✔ includes supporting details, humor, or suspense to maintain audience interest
- ✔ reveals something interesting about your background
- ✔ follows correct grammar, usage, mechanics, and spelling

Publishing/Presenting

If you choose to do so, share your writing with the class. You also may want to publish your writing in a local history journal or in a magazine that publishes students' writing.

Proofreading

For proofreading symbols, see page 84.

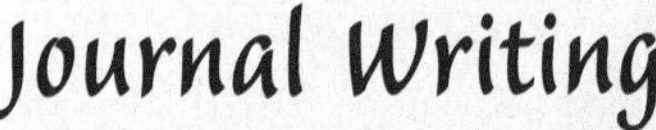

Reflect on your writing process experience. Answer these questions in your journal: What do you like best about your personal history? What was the hardest part of writing it? What did you learn in your writing conference? What new things have you learned as a writer?

UNIT 2

Literature Model

The Writing Process

FROM

My Furthest-Back Person

Alex Haley wrote the tremendously popular Roots, *an account of seven generations of his own African American family. In the following autobiographical selection, Haley provides a glimpse of his own writing process as he shows how he got the original idea for* Roots. *As you read, note how he began researching the full story. Then try the activities in Linking Writing and Literature on page 107.*

My Grandma Cynthia Murray Palmer lived in Henning, Tenn. (pop. 500), about 50 miles north of Memphis. Each summer as I grew up there, we would be visited by several women relatives who were mostly around Grandma's age, such as my Great Aunt Liz Murray who taught in Oklahoma, and Great Aunt Till Merriwether from Jackson, Tenn., or their considerably younger niece, Cousin Georgia Anderson from Kansas City, Kan., and some others. Always after the supper dishes had been washed, they would go out to take seats and talk in the rocking chairs on the front porch, and I would scrunch down, listening, behind Grandma's squeaky chair, with the dusk deepening into night and the lightning bugs flicking on and off above the now shadowy honeysuckles. Most often they talked about our family—the story had been passed down for generations—until the whistling blur of lights of the southbound Panama Limited train whooshing through Henning at 9:05 p.m. signaled our bedtime.

So much of their talking of people, places and events I didn't understand: For instance, what was an "Ol' Massa," an "Ol' Missus" or a "plantation"? But early I gathered that white folks had done lots of bad things to our folks, though I couldn't figure out why. I guessed that all that they talked about had happened a long time ago, as now or then Grandma or another, speaking of someone in the past, would excitedly thrust a finger toward me, exclaiming, "Wasn't big as *this* young 'un!" And it would astound me that anyone as old and grey-haired as they could relate to my age. But in time my head began both a recording and picturing of the more graphic scenes they would describe, just as I also visualized David killing Goliath with his slingshot, Old Pharaoh's army drowning, Noah and his ark, Jesus feeding that big multitude with nothing but five loaves and two fishes, and other wonders that I heard in my Sunday school lessons at our New Hope Methodist Church.

The furthest-back person Grandma and the others talked of—always in tones of awe, I noticed—they would call "The African." They said that some ship brought him to a place that they pronounced "'Naplis." They said that then some "Mas' John Waller" bought him for his plantation in "Spotsylvania County, Va." This African kept on escaping, the fourth time trying to kill the "hateful po' cracker" slave-catcher, who gave him the punishment choice of castration or of losing one foot. This African took a foot being chopped off with an ax against a tree stump, they said, and he was about to die. But his life was saved by "mas' John's" brother—"Mas' William Waller," a doctor, who was so furious about what had happened that he bought the African for himself and gave him the name "Toby."

Crippling about, working in "Mas' William's" house and yard, the African in time met and mated with "the big house cook named Bell," and there was born a girl named Kizzy. As she grew up her African daddy often showed her different kinds of things, telling her what they were in his native tongue. Pointing at a banjo, for example, the African uttered, "*ko*"; or pointing at a river near the plantation, he would say, "*Kamby Bolong.*" Many of his strange words started with a "k" sound, and the little, growing Kizzy learned gradually that they identified different things.

When addressed by other slaves as "Toby," the master's name for him, the African said angrily that his name was "*Kintay.*" And as he gradually learned English, he told young Kizzy some things about himself—for instance, that he was not far from his village, chopping wood to make himself a drum, when four men had surprised, overwhelmed, and kidnaped him.

So Kizzy's head held much about her African daddy when at age 16 she was sold away onto a much smaller plantation in North Carolina. Her new "Mas' Tom Lea" fathered her first child, a boy she named George. And Kizzy told her boy all about his African grandfather. George grew up to be such a gamecock[1] fighter that he was called "Chicken George," and people would come from all over and "bet big money" on his cockfights. He mated with Matilda, another of Lea's slaves; they had seven children, and he told them the stories and strange sounds of their African great-grandfather. And one of those children,

---

1 **gamecock** (gām′ käk′) a rooster bred and trained to fight other roosters in events called cockfights

Tom, became a blacksmith who was bought away by a "Mas' Murray" for his tobacco plantation in Alamance County, N.C.

Tom mated there with Irene, a weaver on the plantation. She also bore seven children, and Tom now told them all about their African great-great-grandfather, the faithfully passed-down knowledge of his sounds and stories having become by now the family's prideful treasure.

The youngest of that second set of seven children was a girl, Cynthia, who became my maternal Grandma (which today I can only see as fated). Anyway, all of this is how I was growing up in Henning at Grandma's, listening from behind her rocking chair as she and the other visiting old women talked of that African (never then comprehended as *my* great-great-great-great-grandfather) who said his name was "*Kin-tay,*"and said "*ko*" for banjo, "*Kamby Bolong*" for river, and a jumble of other "k"-beginning sounds that Grandma privately muttered, most often while making beds or cooking, and who also said that near his village he was kidnaped while chopping wood to make himself a drum.

The story had become nearly as fixed in my head as in Grandma's by the time Dad and Mama moved me and my two younger brothers, George and Julius, away from Henning to be with them at the small black agricultural and mechanical college in Normal, Ala., where Dad taught.

To compress my next 25 years: When I was 17 Dad let me enlist as a mess boy in the U.S. Coast Guard. I became a ship's cook out in the South Pacific during World War II, and at night down by my bunk I began trying to write sea adventure stories, mailing them off to magazines and collecting rejection slips for eight years before some editors began purchasing and publishing occasional stories. By 1949 the Coast Guard had made me its first "journalist"; finally with 20 years' service, I retired at the age of 37, determined to make a full time career of writing. I wrote mostly magazine articles; my first book was "The Autobiography of Malcom X."

Then one Saturday in 1965 I happened to be walking past the National Archives building in Washington. Across the interim years I had thought of Grandma's old stories—otherwise I can't think what diverted me up the Archives' steps. And when a main reading room desk attendant asked if he could help me, I wouldn't have dreamed of admitting to him some curiosity hanging on from boyhood about my slave forebears. I kind of bumbled that I was interested in census records of Alamance County, North Carolina, just after the Civil War.

The microfilm rolls were delivered, and I turned them through the machine with a building sense of intrigue, viewing in different census takers' penmanship an endless parade of names. After about a dozen microfilmed rolls, I was beginning to tire, when in utter astonishment I looked upon the names of Grandma's parents: Tom Murray, Irene Murray . . . older sisters of Grandma's as well—every one of them a name that I'd heard countless times on her front porch.

It wasn't that I hadn't believed Grandma. You just *didn't* not believe my Grandma. It was simply so uncanny actually seeing those names in print and in official U.S. Government records.

Howardena Pindell, *Autobiography: Water/Ancestors, Middle Passage/Family Ghosts,* 1988.

Library. (Whenever black attendants understood the idea of my search, documents I requested reached me with miraculous speed.) In one source or another during 1966 I was able to document at least the highlights of the cherished family story. I would have given anything to have told Grandma, but sadly, in 1949 she had gone. So I went and told the only survivor of those Henning front-porch storytellers: Cousin Georgia Anderson now in her 80's in Kansas City, Kan. Wrinkled, bent, not well herself, she was so overjoyed, repeating to me the old stories and sounds; they were like Henning echoes: "Yeah, boy, that African say his name was '*Kin-tay*'; he say the banjo was 'ko,' an' the river 'Kamby-Bolong,' an' he was off choppin' some wood to make his drum when they grabbed 'im!" Cousin Georgia grew so excited we had to stop her, calm her down, "You go' head, boy! Your grandma an' all of 'em—they up there watching what you do!"

That week I flew to London on a magazine assignment. Since by now I was steeped in the old, in the past, scarcely a tour guide missed me—I was awed at so many historical places and treasures I'd heard of and

During the next several months I was back in Washington whenever possible, in the Archives, the Library of Congress, the Daughters of the American Revolution read of. I came upon the Rosetta stone[2] in the British Museum, marveling anew at how Jean Champollion, the French archaeologist, had miraculously deciphered its ancient demotic and hieroglyphic[3] texts. . . .

The thrill of that just kept hanging around in my head. I was on a jet returning to New York when a thought hit me. Those strange, unknown-tongue sounds, always part of our family's old story . . . they were obviously bits of our original African "Kin-tay's" native tongue. What specific tongue? Could I somehow find out?

Back in New York, I began making visits to the United Nations Headquarters lobby; it wasn't hard to spot Africans. I'd stop any I could, asking if my bits of phonetic sounds held any meaning for them. A couple of dozen Africans quickly looked at me, listened, and took off—understandably dubious about some Tennessean's accent alleging "African" sounds.

My research assistant, George Sims (we grew up together in Henning), brought me some names of ranking scholars of African linguistics. One was particularly intriguing: a Belgian- and English-educated Dr. Jan Vansina; he had spent his early career living in West African villages, studying and tape-recording countless oral histories that were narrated by certain very old African men; he had written a standard textbook, "The Oral Tradition."

So I flew to the University of Wisconsin to see Dr. Vansina. In his living room I told him every bit of the family story in the fullest detail that I could remember it. Then, intensely, he queried me about the story's relay across the generations, about the gibberish of "k" sounds Grandma had fiercely muttered to herself while doing her housework, with my brothers and me giggling beyond her hearing at what we had dubbed "Grandma's noises."

Dr. Vansina, his manner very serious, finally said, "These sounds your family has kept sound very probably of the tongue called 'Mandinka.'"

I'd never heard of any "Mandinka." Grandma just told of the African saying "*ko*" for banjo, or "*Kamby Bolong*" for a Virginia river.

I was awed at so many historical places and treasures I'd heard of and read of.

Among Mandinka stringed instruments, Dr. Vansina said, one of the oldest was the "*kora.*"

"*Bolong,*" he said, was clearly Mandinka for "river." Preceded by "Kamby," it very likely meant "Gambia River."

Dr. Vasina telephoned an eminent Africanist colleague, Dr. Philip Curtin. He said that the phonetic "*Kin-tay*" was correctly spelled "Kinte," a very old clan that had originated in Old Mali. The Kinte men traditionally were blacksmiths, and the women were potters and weavers.

---

2 **Rosetta** (rō zet′ ə) **stone** an ancient tablet found in Egypt with inscriptions in both Greek and Egyptian, thus giving researchers a key to understanding ancient Egyptian writings

3 **demotic** (di mot′ik), **hieroglyphic** (hī′ ər ə glif′ik) two ancient Egyptian systems of writing

Literature Model

I knew I must get to the Gambia River.

The first native Gambian I could locate in the U.S. was named Ebou Manga, then a junior attending Hamilton College in upstate Clinton, N.Y. He and I flew to Dakar, Senegal, then took a smaller plane to Yundum Airport, and rode in a van to Gambia's capital, Bathurst. Ebou and his father assembled eight Gambia government officials. I told them Grandma's stories, every detail I could remember, as they listened intently, then reacted. "'*Kamby Bolong*' of course is Gambia River!" I heard. "But more clue is your forefather's saying his name was '*Kinte*.'" Then they told me something I would never even have fantasized—that in places in the back country lived very old men, commonly called *griots,* who could tell centuries of the histories of certain very old family clans. As for *Kintes,* they pointed out to me on a map some family villages, Kinte-Kundah, and Kinte-Kundah Janneh-Ya, for instance.

The Gambian officials said they would try to help me. I returned to New York dazed. It is embarrassing to me now, but despite Grandma's stories, I'd never been concerned much with Africa, and I had the routine images of African people living mostly in exotic jungles. But a compulsion[4] now laid hold of me to learn all I could, and I began devouring books about Africa, especially about the slave trade. Then one Thursday's mail contained a letter from one of the Gambian officials, inviting me to return there.

Monday I was back in Bathurst. It galvanized[5] me when the officials said that a griot had been located who told the *Kinte* clan history—his name was Kebba Kanga Fofana. To reach him, I discovered, required a modified safari: renting a launch to get upriver, two land vehicles to carry supplies by a roundabout land route, and employing finally 14 people, including three interpreters and four musicians, since a *griot* would not speak the reversed clan histories without background music.

The boat Baddibu vibrated upriver, with me acutely tense: Were these Africans maybe viewing me as but another of the pith-helmets?[6] After about two hours, we put in at James Island, for me to see the ruins of the once British-operated James Fort. Here two centuries of slave ships had loaded thousands of cargoes of Gambian tribespeople. The crumbling stones, the deeply oxidized[7] swivel cannon, even some remnant links of chain seemed all but impossible to believe. Then we continued upriver to the left-bank village of Albreda, and there put ashore to continue on foot to Juffure, village of the *griot.* Once more we stopped, for me to see *toubob kolong,* "the white man's well," now almost filled in, in a swampy area with abundant, tall, saw-toothed grass. It was dug two centuries ago to "17 men's height deep" to insure survival drinking water for long-driven, famishing coffles[8] of slaves.

---

4 **compulsion** (kəm pul′ shən) a driving force
5 **galvanized** (gal′ və nīzd′) excited, as if by an electric shock
6 **pith-helmets** (pith′ hel′ mət) a reference to earlier European explorers of Africa, who wore such helmets
7 **oxidized** (ok′sə dīzd′) rusted
8 **coffles** (kô′ fəlz) groups of slaves fastened or driven together

Walking on, I kept wishing that Grandma could hear how her stories had led me to the "*Kamby Bolong.*" (Our surviving storyteller Cousin Georgia died in a Kansas City hospital during this same morning, I would learn later.) Finally, Juffure village's playing children, sighting us, flashed an alert. The 70-odd people came rushing from their circular, thatch-roofed, mud-walled huts, with goats bounding up and about, and parrots squawking from up in the palms. I sensed him in advance somehow, the small man amid them, wearing a pillbox cap and an off-white robe—the *griot.* Then the interpreters went to him, as the villagers thronged around me.

And it hit me like a gale wind: every one of them, the whole crowd, was *jet black.* An enormous sense of guilt swept me—a sense of being some kind of hybrid[9] . . . a sense of being impure among the pure. It was an awful sensation.

It was as if some ancient scroll were printed indelibly within the griot's *brain.*

The old *griot* stepped away from my interpreters and the crowd quickly swarmed around him—all of them buzzing. An interpreter named A. B. C. Salla came to me; he whispered: "Why they stare at you so, they have never seen here a black American." And that hit me: I was symbolizing for them twenty-five millions of us they had never seen. What did they think of me—of us?

Then abruptly the old *griot* was briskly walking toward me. His eyes boring into mine, he spoke in Mandinka, as if instinctively I should understand—and A. B. C. Salla translated:

"Yes . . . we have been told by the forefathers . . . that many of us from this place are in exile . . . in that place called America . . . and in other places."

I suppose I physically wavered, and they thought it was the heat; rustling whispers went through the crowd, and a man brought me a low stool. Now the whispering hushed—the musicians had softly begun playing *kora* and *balafon,* and a canvas sling lawn seat was taken by the *griot,* Kebba Kanga Fofana, aged 73 "rains" (one rainy season each year). He seemed to gather himself into a physical rigidity, and he begin speaking the *Kinte* clan's ancestral oral history; it came rolling from his mouth across the next hours . . . 17th- and 18th-century *Kinte* lineage details, predominantly what men took wives; the children they "begot," in the order of their births; those children's mates and children.

Events frequently were dated by some proximate singular physical occurrence. It was as if some ancient scroll were printed indelibly within the *griot's* brain. Each few sentences or so, he would pause for an interpreter's translation to me. I distill here the essence:

The *Kinte* clan began in Old Mali, the men generally blacksmiths ". . . who conquered fire," and the women potters and weavers. One large branch of the clan

---

9 **hybrid** (hī′ brid) the offspring of individuals of unlike genetic background, such as of people of different races

moved to Mauretania from where one son of the clan, Kairaba Kunta Kinte, a Moslem Marabout holy man, entered Gambia. He lived first in the village of Pakali N'Ding; he moved next to Jiffarong village; ". . . and then he came here, into our own village of Juffure."

In Juffure, Kairaba Kunta Kinte took his first wife, ". . . a Mandinka maiden, whose name was Sireng. By her, he begot two sons, whose names were Janneh and Saloum. Then he got a second wife, Yaisa. By her, he begot a son, Omoro."

The three sons became men in Juffure. Janneh and Saloum went off and found a new village, Kinte-Kundah Janneh-Ya. "And then Omoro, the youngest son, when he had 30 rains, took as a wife a maiden, Binta Kebba.

"And by her, he begot four sons—Kunta, Lamin, Suwadu, and Madi . . ."

Sometimes, a "begotten," after his naming, would be accompanied by some later occurring detail, perhaps as ". . . in time of big water (flood), he slew a water buffalo." Having named those four sons, now the *griot* stated such a detail.

"About the time the king's soldiers came, the eldest of these four sons, Kunta, when he had about 16 rains, went away from this village, to chop wood to make a drum . . . and he was never seen again . . ."

Goose-pimples the size of lemons seemed to pop all over me. In my knapsack were my cumulative notebooks, the first of them including how in my boyhood, my Grandma, Cousin Georgia and the others told of the African "*Kin-tay*" who always said he was kidnaped near his village—while chopping wood to make a drum . . .

I showed the interpreter, he showed and told the *griot,* who excitedly told the people; they grew very agitated. Abruptly then they formed a human ring, encircling me, dancing and chanting. Perhaps a dozen of the women carrying their infant babies rushed in toward me, thrusting the infants into my arms—conveying, I would later learn, "the laying on of hands . . . through this flesh which is us, we are you, and you are us." The men hurried me into their mosque[10], their Arabic praying later being translated outside: "Thanks be to Allah for returning the long lost from among us." Direct descendants of Kunta Kinte's blood brothers were hastened, some of them from nearby villages, for a family portrait to be taken with me, surrounded by actual ancestral sixth cousins. More symbolic acts filled the remaining day.

When they would let me leave, for some reason I wanted to go away over the African land. Dazed, silent in the bumping Land Rover, I heard the cutting staccato[11] of talking drums. Then when we sighted the next village, its people came thronging to meet us. They were all—little naked ones to wizened[12] elders—waving, beaming, amid a cacophony[13] of crying out; and then my ears identified their words: "*Meester Kinte! Meester Kinte!*"

Let me tell you something: I am a man. But I remember the sob surging up from

---

10 **mosque** (mäsk) a Muslim place of worship
11 **staccato** (stə kä′ tō) a pattern of rapid, abrupt sounds with quick, distinct breaks
12 **wizened** (wiz′ ənd) withered, wrinkled
13 **cacophony** (kə kof′ ə nē) jarring, dissonant sounds

my feet, flinging up my hands before my face and bawling as I had not done since I was a baby . . . the jet-black Africans were jostling, staring . . . I didn't care, with the feelings surging. If you really knew the odyssey of us millions of black Americans, if you really knew how we came in the seeds of our forefathers, captured, driven, beaten, inspected, bought, branded, chained in foul ships, if you really knew, you needed weeping . . .

Linking Writing and Literature

Collect Your Thoughts

Think about the kind of person Kunta Kinte, Haley's "furthest-back person," was. Jot down a description of him, including as many details as you can. Then write an explanation of how Kunta Kinte was able to influence his family for many, many generations.

Talk About Reading

Talk with a group of classmates about the excerpt from "My Furthest-Back Person—The African." Assign a group leader to maintain the group's focus and a secretary to take notes. Use the questions below to guide your discussion.

1. **Connect to Your Life** To which parts of this essay did you connect most strongly? Why? Which parts of the essay helped you learn something new?
2. **Critical Thinking: Interpret** Why do you think Haley felt it was so important to find both written and oral evidence of his family's history and then to record that history in his book *Roots?*
3. **6+1 Trait®: Sentence Fluency** Do Haley's sentences flow smoothly from one to another? Use examples from the selection to support your answer.
4. **Connect to Writing** Do you find Haley's biographical account interesting? Does it capture your attention? Explain. Then make a list of criteria to help evaluate a biographical account.

Write About Reading

Biographical Essay Write a four- to eight-paragraph essay about a person who had a strong influence on your life or on the life of someone in your family. If that person lived before you were born, include information on how you learned about that person.

Focus on Sentence Fluency Your biographical essay will be more engaging if you make your sentences flow smoothly. As you write, model your essay on the parts of Haley's essay that you thought have the most fluid sentences. As you revise, look for ways to make the sentences flow even more smoothly. You might vary the beginnings of your sentences and the length of your sentences and make clearer transitions between sentences.

For more information on sentence fluency and the 6+1 Trait® model, see **Writing and Research Handbook,** pages 957–959.

6+1 Trait® is a registered trademark of Northwest Regional Educational Laboratory, which does not endorse this product.

UNIT 2 Review

Reflecting on the Unit

Summarize what you learned in this unit by answering the following questions.

1. What are the five stages of the writing process?
2. What are the important elements of each stage?
3. What techniques, tools, or procedures can help you successfully complete each stage of the process?
4. What are some of the main things to consider when you analyze point of view in literature?

Adding to Your Portfolio

CHOOSE A SELECTION FOR YOUR PORTFOLIO Look over the writing you have done during this unit. Select a completed piece of writing to put in your portfolio. The piece you choose should show some or all of the following:

- a specific audience and writing purpose
- a clear topic sentence or sentences supported by appropriate details
- a logical ordering of ideas
- unity and coherence
- careful editing and proofreading

Reflecting on Your Choice

Attach a note to the piece you chose, explaining briefly why you chose it and what you learned from writing it.

SET GOALS How can you improve your writing? What skill will you focus on the next time you write?

Writing Across the Curriculum

MAKE A SOCIAL STUDIES CONNECTION Scan your government textbook or a magazine or newspaper for topics relating to local, state, or national politics. Choose a subject that interests you. Write two related topic sentences and list details that will help support each. Try to include each type of supporting detail: a concrete detail, an example, a fact or statistic, and a reason. Then follow the other stages of the writing process. Use your topic sentences and supporting details to draft, revise, and edit two unified paragraphs that describe a political issue. Write legibly and be sure to check for errors in spelling and grammar. You may wish to present your finished writing to an audience of other students.

TIME

Facing the Blank Page

Inside the writing process with TIME writers and editors

Writing for TIME

The stories published each week in TIME are the work of experienced professionals. The writing is strong; the facts are accurate; the grammar, spelling, and punctuation are error-free (or close!). Behind the scenes, however, there is another story to be told. As these pages reveal, TIME staffers struggle with many of the same challenges that students face in the messy, trial-and-error process that is writing: selecting among topics; finding information; getting organized; starting to draft; and then revising, revising, and revising some more.

Is there a secret to the quality of writing in TIME? Beyond experience and hard work, the key lies in collaboration. As the chart on these pages illustrates, writers are assisted at each stage of the process by other members of the staff in a kind of "group journalism" that has become the magazine's hallmark. The writers and editors teach and learn from one another every week; student writers can do the same. Try out and adapt the writing and collaboration strategies presented in "Facing the Blank Page" to discover what works for you.

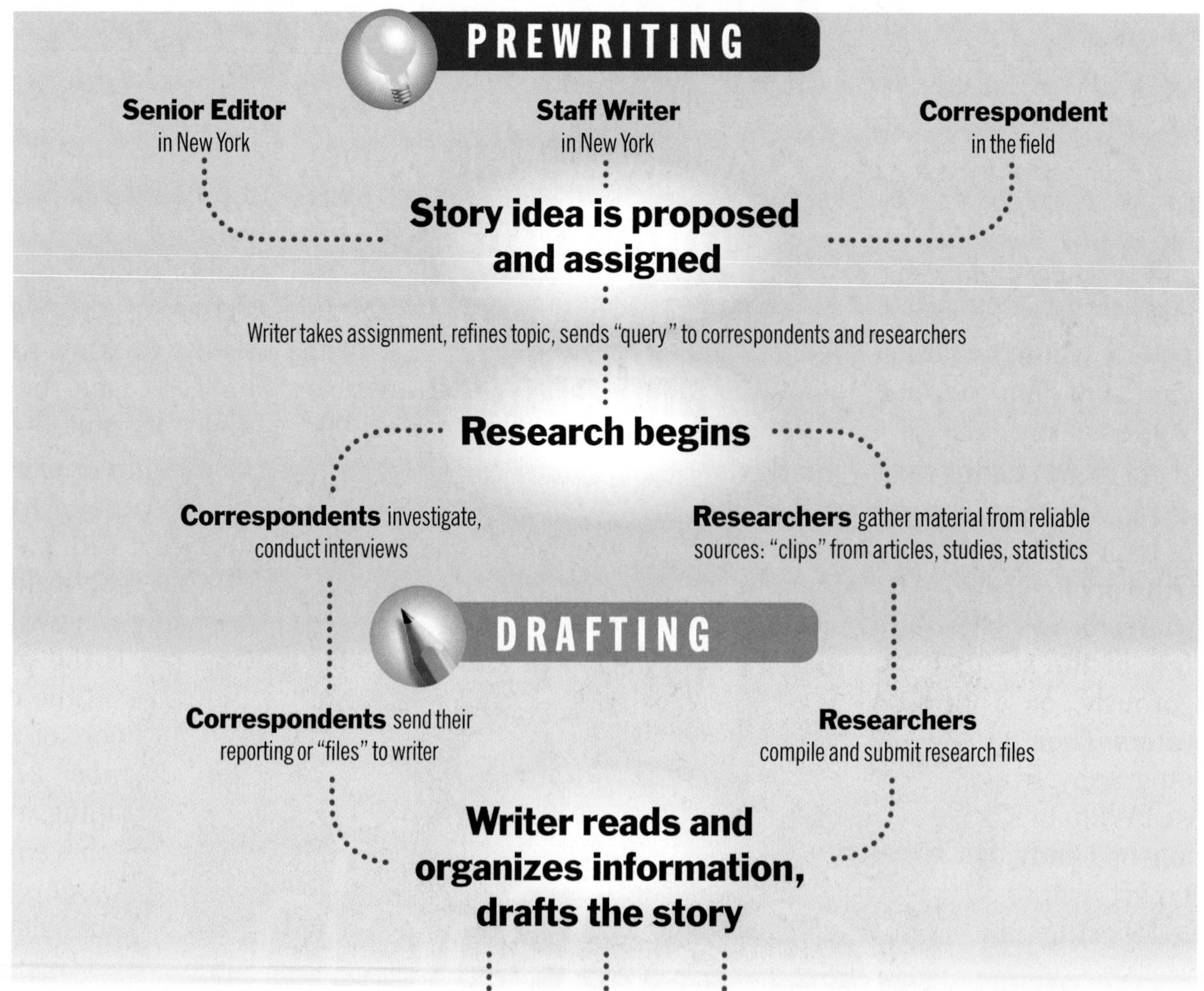
PREWRITING
Senior Editor in New York
Staff Writer in New York
Correspondent in the field
Story idea is proposed and assigned
Writer takes assignment, refines topic, sends "query" to correspondents and researchers
Research begins
Correspondents investigate, conduct interviews
Researchers gather material from reliable sources: "clips" from articles, studies, statistics
DRAFTING
Correspondents send their reporting or "files" to writer
Researchers compile and submit research files
Writer reads and organizes information, drafts the story

REVISING

Editor reads draft, asks for revisions

Correspondents check interpretation, make suggestions ⟷ **Writer revises, resubmits for comments** ⟷ **Researchers** check accuracy, details

Writer and editor revise again, "green" (edit for length)

EDITING AND PROOFREADING

Checks for conformity to TIME style and conventions ⟷ **Copy Desk** ⟷ Checks and corrects grammar, mechanics, spelling

PUBLISHING AND PRESENTING

Managing Editor chooses to print, hold, or "kill" (omit) story

Circulation of TIME rises or falls ⟷ **Readers respond to published story** ⟷ E-mail and letters to the editor

Prewriting

Getting Started: Freewriting

In the early stages of writing an essay or article for TIME, contributor Lance Morrow uses freewriting to help him discover what the focus of his piece should be.

Lance Morrow:

"A great help to me in writing is making notes. I record information or snippets of quotations from books or sources and then I think, 'Hey, what about that? Well, that's interesting, but where does it lead?' I follow that road, and then that idea leads down another road. So I go down the next road a bit. And then I put it all into notes. By writing, you are forming your own thinking. You are assembling the materials, but you are also defining the questions that you want to address. What's important here? What is the essence?

What you want to do is honestly accompany the idea. Don't pre-cook the ideas in a piece of writing—test yourself. Test your assumptions. Don't think that you've got it when you start out on the journey, because, to me, the whole point is that you learn in the process of writing."

KEITH BEDFORD

Lance Morrow: Test your assumptions.

WRITING TIP

Facing the Essay

"There is a feeling that the essay is an imposing form. Don't be intimidated by it. An essay is simply a somewhat organized exercise in discussing, having a conversation about a particular subject. Approach the essay the way you would approach discussing this subject with an intelligent, reasonably well-informed friend."

—Lance Morrow

LEARNING FROM THE WRITER

TRY IT OUT

Try Morrow's freewriting technique. At the top of a blank piece of paper, name an issue in school, local or national news, or an important topic you have discussed in any one of your classes. On the next line, write a statement or a question about this topic. Then continue to write freely, allowing one idea or argument to lead to another. Write without stopping for 15 minutes. Now stop, reread your writing, and circle the word, phrase or sentence that answers Morrow's question: What's important here? What is the essence?

HOW I WRITE

1. Is freewriting a technique that works for you? Have you ever tried it before? What other strategies have you used to find the focus for a piece of writing?

2. Review the work in your writing folder and journal. Identify a piece of writing in which you tested yourself and challenged your assumptions. Specifically, what did you learn in the process of writing?

Thinking and writing freely can also help you organize ideas before drafting. Here is a technique that works for television critic James Poniewozik.

JAY COLTON FOR TIME

James Poniewozik: Writing freely to find a structure.

James Poniewozik:

“I don’t use outlines, but what I often do is just free-associate on a page. I will freely write down the dozen topics or points that should be mentioned at some point in the piece, and then maybe I’ll write numbers by them—either to show their relative importance or to put them in what seems to make for a smooth flow of the article.

And an order emerges: I say, ‘I should start with this, and then I’ll jump to this, and this segues to this,’ and so on. Then I can start to write.”

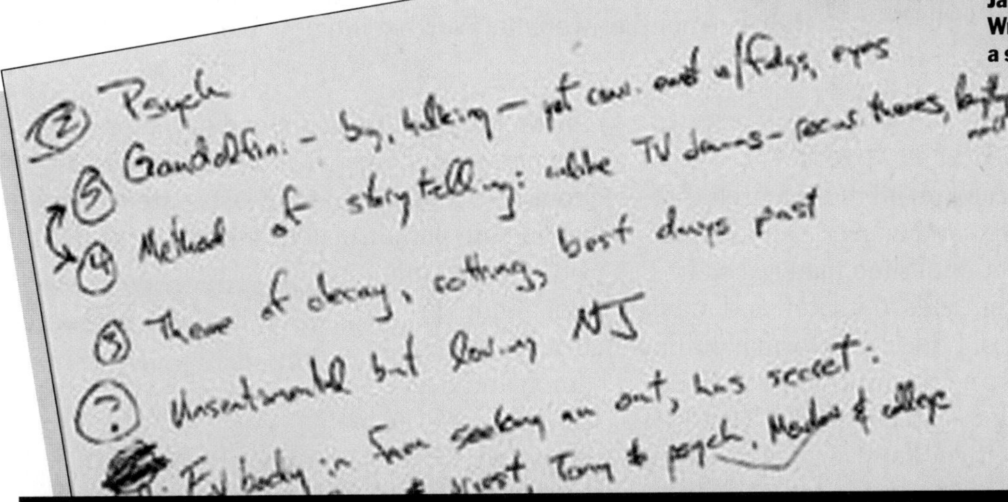

LEARNING FROM THE WRITER

TRY IT OUT

1. Review by the numbers. Poniewozik’s reviews of television shows appear frequently in TIME. The notes above are for a piece he wrote naming *The Sopranos* the best television program of 1999. Use his writing strategy to prepare your own review. Think of a program you have seen recently. Now “free-associate” on a sheet of paper: describe characters and plot, offer analysis and comparisons, tell about your personal response to the show. Get down on paper every point you might wish to make about this program. Then look back over your writing and number items as Poniewozik did. Does an order for a review emerge? Write the review!

2. Compare Poniewozik’s technique to the suggestions for finding and focusing a topic presented in Lesson 2.2. Which strategy works best for you?

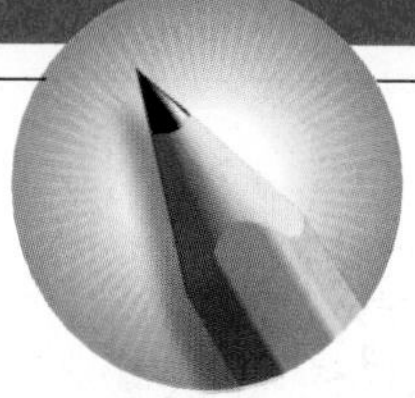

Drafting

The Flow of Ideas: Leads and Transitions

Jesse Birnbaum: Each sentence calls forth the next.

MARIANNE BARCELLONA

When a TIME staff writer is ready to begin drafting, he or she faces a desk piled high with material supplied by the research department, along with "files" or reports written by TIME correspondents around the country and around the world. From here, no two writers proceed in exactly the same way.

Recalls writer Jesse Birnbaum, "The late Paul O'Neill, a famous writer at TIME, would take all the folders on his desk, read them twice, and then put them all away. He would sit down and write the cover story without ever once looking back at the material. His idea was that the things you remembered were the things that were worth saying, and that the details you didn't remember were not worth telling the reader about."

Birnbaum's own method is different, and easier to test as a model:

"I will try to absorb all the research that has been gathered and arrive at an idea for the story. I might underline material as I read, so that I can refer to it later, and maybe make some notes. I don't do a formal outline. For me, there is an organization I can find without working too mechanically. That is: get your lead written, know what you want to say, and let every sentence call forth the next idea."

When each sentence and paragraph leads to the next, the result is a coherent, organized draft. A story or review by Jesse Birnbaum is held together by logical and elegant transitions between paragraphs and ideas.

Birnbaum on transitions:

"Transitions move the reader on to another subject from the end of the preceding paragraph. One way to find good transitions is to look back at the last sentence, or maybe the penultimate sentence of the previous paragraph. Get a thought from that paragraph and evoke the idea, or even a key word, from what came before. Pause and look back to help you find a transition into your next subject, the next scene.

Finally, as you go toward the end, it helps organize a story to evoke (in your last paragraph or last sentence) a thought that was made in your lead."

TIME LEXICON

Lead: The opening paragraph or paragraphs of a piece, designed to draw in the reader and show the reader what the story will be about. "The lead," says Birnbaum, "is a road map for the rest of the story."

LEARNING FROM THE WRITER

Read this excerpt from one of Jesse Birnbaum's book reviews in TIME:

Roads Not Taken: What If Some of Our History Had Happened a Little Differently?

Military history is a gallimaufry of choices and chance, of opportunities taken, of roads forsaken.

It is this truism that drives *What If?*, a collection of essays by 34 military historians, journalists and novelists, all indulging in "counterfactual" conjecture.

In 334 B.C., for example, the 22-year-old Macedonian King Alexander charged with his cavalry into the ranks of Persian forces at the Granicus River in what is now Turkey. A Persian soldier clubbed Alexander with an ax, but before he could deal a second and fatal blow, the King's bodyguard killed him.

What if Alexander had died at Granicus? Goodbye to all the conquests of Alexander the Great, says Princeton historian Josiah Ober. The Persian Empire would have overtaken the known world. The great promise of Hellenism would have lost its way; the growing Roman Empire would have atrophied; Judea would have remained a backwater, Jesus merely "a local religious figure," and Christianity and Judaism insignificant provincial oddities. There would have been no need for a Martin Luther, no Reformation, no Renaissance, no Enlightenment, no Western culture.

In 1944 General Dwight Eisenhower was prepared to invade Normandy on June 5, but when his weather officer predicted storms over the English Channel, Ike postponed D-day for 24 hours. What if the Channel weather had not abated on June 6? World War II chronicler Stephen Ambrose argues that without air cover and paratrooper support, the first waves of Allied troops would have been incapable of fighting. Hitler could have held his positions, and Operation Overlord, the master plan for reconquering Europe, would have disintegrated.

—Jesse Birnbaum

DISCUSSION

1. How does Birnbaum's lead work as a "road map" for the reader and the writer?

2. Study his transitions. How does the first sentence of each paragraph harken back to a word or an idea in the preceding paragraph?

3. Look at one paragraph closely and evaluate Birnbaum's writing. Does each sentence "call forth the next idea"? Cite an example or counter-example.

TRY IT OUT

1. Select a piece of writing from your portfolio and evaluate it as you did Jesse Birnbaum's writing. Do the paragraphs follow a logical organization? Are there transitions to lead the reader smoothly from one paragraph to the next? Identify one paragraph that would benefit from a clearer transition and revise it.

2. Recall and describe how you organized the writing of this piece. How does your writing strategy compare to Jesse Birnbaum's? Could his approach work for you? Why or why not?

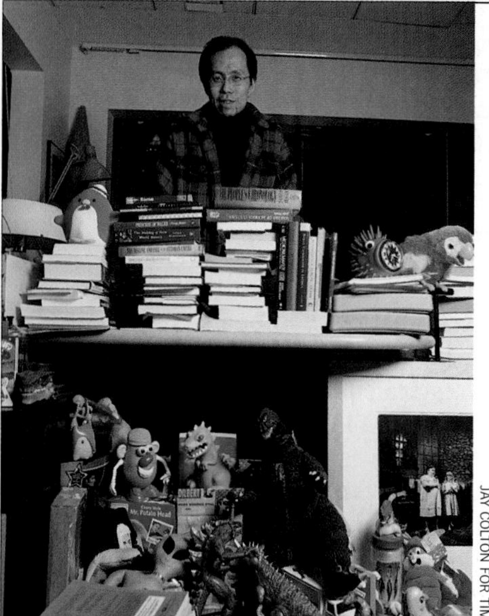

JAY COLTON FOR TIME

Howard Chua-Eoan: Even the best writers need an editor.

Revising

The Editor's Role

TIME magazine works in much the same way that many writing classes do: through collaboration, conferences, and peer review. TIME's writers revise with the help of their editors and fellow writers.

Senior Editor Howard Chua-Eoan:

"Someone has to read your copy to make sure the point you're trying to get across gets put across. You might think you've made your point clearly, but then when someone else reads it—which is always the test—and it's not clear, then you've got to go back and do it over again—all of it, or perhaps just a sentence or two.

Even the best writers need an editor, because sometimes you think you've figured everything out, but you've slid over an essential step in reasoning a story. An editor can say, 'I know what you're trying to do, and I agree with it, but you're missing how you get from this point to that point.'

Students should focus on whether or not the message gets across. Next, see if the message is delivered coherently. Then ask: Is there a structure embedded in the story that holds it together? The structure is very important; how you begin the story, the paragraph where you say what the story is all about, what it means. Details, quotes, style should be left to the writer's discretion."

WRITING TIP

"When you write, it's important to have structural elements firmly in place, but then you should experiment. If you can just do a story, you're not special. But if you can do special things within the existing structure—that's what's great."

—Howard Chua-Eoan

LEARNING FROM THE EDITOR

DISCUSSION

1. What is the role of an editor at TIME? Have you ever had a good editor?

2. How is a classroom writing conference similar to or different from the writer/editor relationship at TIME?

TRY IT OUT

1. Questions for revision. Based on Howard Chua-Eoan's advice, make a list of questions to help you and your listeners in a writing conference. Use them to help revise a piece of writing in progress.

2. Recall a time when you freely experimented with your writing. What did you try to do? Was it successful? How can you, your teacher, and your classmates encourage each other to experiment with your writing this year?

Sentence Variety: Making It Move

Time Correspondent James Willwerth was asked to give one essential tip for writers. Jim grabbed a marker and explained:

"This is my advice. Here is 'straight-line writing': 'Bill went to the store to get some bread.' That's a fine, declarative sentence. But in the next sentence, instead of using another straight declarative, vary it and write: 'Because he had to get some bread, Bill went to the store.' That variety is the wavy line. If you front-load some sentences with clauses, back-load others, and use the straight declarative, too, then your narrative moves. Your narrative has some rhythm to it."

LEARNING FROM THE WRITER

Side by Side in Santa Paula: One School's Success

Math teacher Zbigniew Zielina was puzzled by the silence. It was early in the school year, he was about to begin his algebra class, and the Santa Paula High School instructor detected none of the loud talk and scraping chairs that usually marked his students' entrance. He turned to investigate. "I see 30 kids quietly copying the questions," he recalls. "They were ready to work. In all my years, I have never seen this."

Until last September, no one in Santa Paula, Calif., had. That's when the tiny (population: 27,000) farm community, about 65 miles northwest of Los Angeles, decided to integrate its college-prep and "general" education students so that slow, average and accelerated learners would sit side by side. It is a bold experiment. Segregating students by ability—a vintage classroom organizational tool known as "tracking" or "ability grouping"—is practiced in at least 80% of U.S. high schools, according to the National Center for Education Statistics. But in Santa Paula, anger at the grouping system had smoldered for decades. "This is a small town that's been run the same way forever," says special-programs teacher Lisa Salas. **—James Willwerth**

TRY IT OUT

1. Does Jim Willwerth follow his own advice? Look closely at the lead paragraphs from Willwerth's story, "Side by Side," above. Does Willwerth vary the length and structure of his sentences? Find an example. Identify the longest and shortest sentences in the paragraph. Transform the longest into two or three short, declarative sentences. Combine his shortest with the sentence that comes before or after it. Read the sets of sentences together. Why do you think Willwerth made the choices he did?

2. Analyze a sample of your writing. Take a paragraph you have written, from either a work-in-progress or a completed piece in your portfolio. Would James Willwerth call your paragraph "straight-line writing" or "wavy-line writing"? Why?

Now rewrite the paragraph by adding more variety to the length and structure of the sentences. Your goal is to find the right balance for your own writing. Read the paragraphs aloud to a partner, but don't specify which is the original. Which version does your partner feel has more movement and rhythm?

Editing and Proofreading

Following the Rules—and Breaking Them!

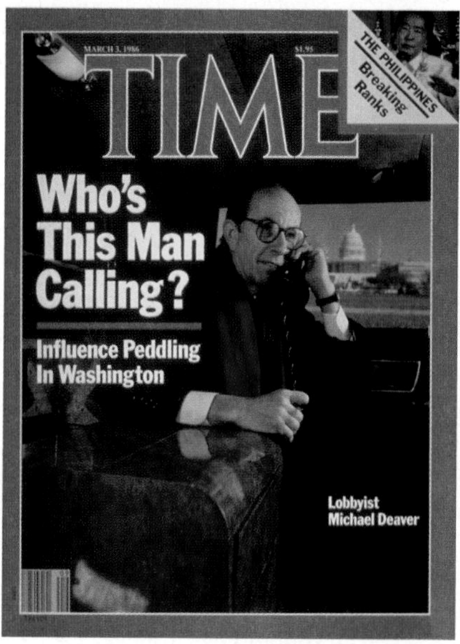

It is the job of TIME's copy editors to ensure that every article, caption, and headline appearing in the magazine is correct. The Copy Desk catches and changes misspellings and errors in grammar and usage.

Imagine that you are a copy editor at TIME. On Saturday, the cover of Monday morning's magazine lands on your desk. The cover text—"Who's This Man Calling?"—contains an error. Can you find it?

Deputy Copy Chief Judy Paul spotted it right away:

"We told the editors that the first word should be *whom*. But changing it to *whom* made the line awkward. We suggested to the editors that they rewrite the cover line to work around the problem, but they said, 'No. We're going to go with it.' A Managing Editor always gets what he wants, so we left it alone. We received a slew of letters on that one. *Who's This Man Calling?* was technically incorrect. We were incorrect on the cover! But that was a conscious decision, not a mistake.

At TIME, if there is a good reason for breaking a usage rule, we will sometimes go ahead and break the rules. But if you just do it because you like it, that's a problem."

LEARNING FROM THE EDITOR

DISCUSSION

1. Explain why the cover line was incorrect. For help, refer to Lesson 17.4.

2. Look closely at the cover photo, title, and subtitle. Write an alternative that works around the *who/whom* usage problem.

3. In your daily speech, do you use *who* and *whom* correctly? Give an example of a common misuse of *who* or *whom* in spoken English.

4. On paper, do you use the two pronouns correctly? Why is there more emphasis on correct usage of pronouns in written English than in spoken English?

5. Why do you think TIME's editors chose to run this cover as originally written? Would you have made the same choice? Do magazines and newspapers have a special responsibility to follow standard usage rules at all times?

TRY IT OUT

Hunt for usage errors. Go on a search for usage errors in print. Begin at a newspaper and magazine rack, scanning cover titles and subtitles, headlines, and advertising copy. Pay attention to signage in stores and on the street. For every error you identify, write a corrected version. Which errors do you think are the result of a conscious decision to break standard usage rules?

Publishing and Presenting

Rewards and Challenges

"Writing," admits Senior Editor Janice Simpson, "is very, very hard work." Does getting published make it all worthwhile?

JAY COLTON FOR TIME

Janice Simpson: Going into other people's worlds.

Janice Simpson reflects:

"It isn't necessarily being published that I find rewarding. What drew me to journalism was the fact that I'd actually get paid to be a dilettante! I like going into other people's worlds. I like finding out about those worlds. Then I tell other people about them. Journalism still excites me because it allows me to do that.

Yes, writing is hard work, but there's also an element of fun about what we do, and the best writing reflects that joy. That joy is transmitted in writing, in finding the right word. I think we've all had the experience of reading something and thinking, 'Aha! Let me write that down. That's just the way I feel about it.' When that happens, the writer has transmitted some of the joy he or she is feeling, some of the emotion, to you, the reader. And that's very much what writing and storytelling and journalism are about."

Janice Simpson's first "official" published piece of writing appeared when she was 15. Simpson was the *Portland Press-Herald* correspondent for her high school in Portland, Maine.

TEEN-AGE

. . . Express'd

Waynflete-Hyde Seminar Explores Christianity

By JANICE SIMPSON

Who was Jesus? Master, teacher, heretic, son of man, or forerunner of the Hippie movement? All of these titles, except the last, have been attributed to Jesus in the Gospels. But

ally accepted. One does, however, need to begin somewhere; Dean Brown suggests that it be with the search for the historical Jesus.

Everyone has his own concept of Jesus. Dean Brown likens this to the test in which a person looks at an ink blot and

what we want Him to be. It is, Dean Brown noted, easier to create one's own version of something than to look for the correct one.

Dean Brown conceded that the search wouldn't be an easy one, for the Gospels, our earliest record of Jesus, never come out and tell us who He was. And

JOURNAL WRITING

REFLECT ON WRITING AND READING

1. Describe a time you found satisfaction in learning about other people's worlds as either a writer or a reader.

2. Recall a time when you had an "Aha!" experience as a reader. What was the genre: comic strip, novel, article? Write about your response.

3. Do you agree that writing is "very, very hard work"? When has hard work paid off for you as a writer? Are some forms of writing easier than others? Why?

"The jungle was wide and full of twitterings, rustlings, murmurs, and sighs. Suddenly it all ceased, as if someone had shut a door."

—Ray Bradbury, "A Sound of Thunder"

UNIT 3

Descriptive Writing

Writing in the Real World

To create a vivid picture of a place, travel writers use descriptive writing. Good descriptive writing includes details that appeal to one or more of the senses. The following is an excerpt from a travel book about countries located near the equator. It was written by Thurston Clarke.

from *Equator*

by Thurston Clarke

Travel Writer Thurston Clarke

MY CLOTHES ARE EXHAUSTED, thin as silk from being slapped on rocks and scorched by irons heated over charcoal. I slip them on and smell, I think, the equator: sweat, charcoal, and low tide.

Souvenirs litter my rooms. There is a paper clip from Albert Schweitzer's desk, a box with a pop-out snake, and a chunk of propeller from a plane crashed on a Pacific atoll by Amelia Earhart, or so I was told. I have a T-shirt saying Happy Trails, in Indonesian. I won it racing Baptist missionaries up a Borneo hill. I keep pencils in a soapstone box from Somalia, as white and square as the houses of Muqdisho. I weight papers with a gold-flecked rock from a Sumatran mine. My wife says it is fool's gold.

I have become a connoisseur of heat. There is the heat that reflects off coral and scorches and softens the face like a tomato held over a fire. There is the greasy heat of a tropical city, a milky heat that steams a jungle river like a pan of nearly boiled water, a blinding heat that explodes off tin roofs like *paparazzi's* flashbulbs, . . .

. . . Before a journey a map is an impersonal menu; afterwards, it is intimate as a diary. Before, I had stared at my maps and wondered if there was still a Jardin Botanique in the middle of Zaïre. Did passenger ships sail between Sumatra and Borneo? . . . And what should I make of the black dots signaling a "difficult or dangerous" road? Now I know, and these maps have become as comfortable as my canvas boots. I enjoy touching them, imagining I can feel, as if printed in Braille, the mountains, rivers, roads, and railways, all the familiar contours of the longest circular route on earth.

Why do maps attract the finger? . . . What child has not traveled by spinning a globe? I owned an illuminated one. I switched it on and darkened the room and it became the glowing, revolving planet that introduced travelogues and newsreels. Then I closed my eyes, stabbed at it with a finger, and imagined going wherever I landed.

My journey began this way on a snowy February evening in New York when I grabbed a globe off a friend's bookshelf and spun it into a whirling bouquet of continents and oceans.

A Writer's Process

Prewriting:
Researching and Traveling

Clarke spent several months organizing his expedition to South American, African, and Asian countries located on the equator. Research took up a major portion of his time. "I spent two or three months in libraries, reading about each country, especially newspaper articles," he said.

As he read the articles, Clarke jotted down the names of missionaries, politicians, Peace Corps workers, and other individuals. "It's important to have a couple of people to call who live in a place," he said. "They can give you a briefing about the country, tell you where to go, and what to avoid, describe the political situation, and introduce you to other people." Clarke's research also helped him develop a loose itinerary for a series of trips that lasted about eight months.

Clarke decided to travel west to east beginning in the small city of Macapá, Brazil. In Macapá, he found the Park of the Equator—a place with a long wall faced in blue tiles and a garden. Clarke would return to this park two years later "to complete the circle."

Wherever he went, Clarke jotted down his first impressions. "First impressions are very important for any writer," he said. "I schedule nothing the first day. I take long walks and notice everything new, scary, wonderful. I jot down a few words about something that strikes me. If I hear a conversation I want, I write a summary. In the evening I expand my notes into a paragraph or two about what impressed me."

Drafting/Revising:
Putting the Trip into Words

When Clarke revisited Macapá, the Park of the Equator had been replaced by an "eight-story concrete slab." Clarke decided the time had come for him to return home and start writing.

By the time Clarke sat down to write, much of the book had already taken shape in his mind. "The trip itself defines the book, so as I experienced and did things they determined the book," he reflected. Still, Clarke had to choose material from a dozen notebooks and the newspaper clips he collected along the way. "Travel books depend on variety," he said. "So I used my best, most interesting stuff." With this rule in mind, Clarke began to write. "I always write a first draft fast, just to get something down. Often the sentences run on, there's a lot of repetition, and the transitions aren't very good. I just keep moving to get a first draft," he said.

Revising/Editing:
Adding the Finishing Touches

Once he finished a draft, Clarke started revising. "I really think of writing as editing," Clarke explained. "I edit so many times that the writing happens for me when I edit. That's when I put in the transitions and play with the copy. I enjoy editing a lot."

During this phase, Clarke took care to create powerful descriptions, using active verbs—not adjectives. "If you're describing a landscape or a city, there are always things going on; there's always motions and movement," he said. For example, Clarke wrote: "My first sunset . . . was a classic equatorial one, with the sun hesitating an instant as if taking a deep breath, before jumping into the sea. The wind dropped, clouds froze, and the sails of a native canoe sagged. The sun fell and the lagoon turned silver."

Clarke revised manuscript six or seven times, a process that took almost a year. The manuscript Clarke sent to the publisher was about 650 well-crafted pages. "I never submit a book until it's absolutely ready." said Clarke. Clarke's editor asked him to make no major changes to his manuscript —except to cut it down. With his editor's help, Clarke trimmed 20,000 words from *Equator.*

The task of writing does not end with a polished manuscript. Often substantial changes are required before a book can be published.

Examining Writing in the Real World

Analyzing the Media Connection

Discuss these questions about the book excerpt on page 122.

1. What sensory details does Clarke use in the opening paragraph? To what senses do they appeal?
2. What purpose does the list of souvenirs serve?
3. What figure of speech does Clarke use in describing heat? How does its use add to the description?
4. List some active verbs that enrich Clarke's writing. How do they contribute to the overall effect of the piece?
5. Clarke describes a spinning globe as "a whirling bouquet of continents and oceans." What does this description suggest about his feelings about globes?

Analyzing a Writer's Process

Discuss these questions about Thurston Clarke's writing process.

1. How did Clarke prepare for his trip?
2. Why was it important for Clarke to jot down his first impressions?
3. What approach did Clarke take in writing a first draft?
4. How does Clarke define writing? Do you agree with his definition? Why or why not?
5. Why does Clarke consider active verbs important in travel writing?

Use strong verbs.

Strong verbs, not adjectives, create powerful descriptions such as this one:

> *The wind* ***dropped,*** *clouds* ***froze,*** *and the sails of a native canoe* ***sagged.***

Rewrite these sentences, replacing weak verbs with stronger ones to paint a vivid picture, making other changes too.

1. As the wind blew, the trees moved.
2. A convertible that looked as if it were held together with bandages and tape came in our direction.
3. Its driver had on an orange jumpsuit and matching cap that caught the eye of everyone on the street.
4. When the car got closer to us, the driver motioned.
5. We couldn't hear what he said over the racket his car was making.

See Lesson 10.3, page 453.

A river meanders through the grasslands around Kampala, Uganda.

Descriptive Writing

LESSON

3.1 Writing to Describe

Good descriptive writing depends on the creation of vivid word pictures and the organization of those pictures into an effective pattern. Note how Stephen King organizes details in the following passage to let the reader "see" the scene.

King helps bring the scene to life with vivid images like "lightning flared in a blue sheet" and "thunder exploded a bare moment later."

Is "hearing the tendons in her neck creak like dirty doorhinges" an effective image? Why?

Literature Model

Lightning flared in a blue sheet, giving Anderson a shutter-click of what she had come to think of—as her neighbors did—as her dooryard. She saw the truck, with the first drops of rain on its windshield; the short dirt driveway; the mailbox with its flag down and tucked securely against its aluminum side; the writhing trees. Thunder exploded a bare moment later, and Peter jumped against her, whining. The lights went out. They didn't bother dimming or flickering or messing around; they went out all at once, completely. They went out with *authority.*

Anderson reached for the lantern—and then her hand stopped.

There was a green spot on the far wall, just to the right of Uncle Frank's Welsh dresser. It bobbed up two inches, moved left, then right. It disappeared for a moment and then came back. . . .

She turned toward Peter, hearing the tendons in her neck creak like dirty doorhinges, knowing what she was going to see. The light was coming from Peter's eye. His left eye. It glared with the witchy green light of St. Elmo's fire drifting over a swamp after a still, muggy day.

Stephen King, *The Tommyknockers*

Organize Details in Spatial Order

Good descriptive writing depends on the effective use of details for elaboration and the organization of those details into meaningful patterns. One natural way of organizing descriptive writing is to arrange details in spatial order—that is, left to right, front to back, near to far, clockwise, or counterclockwise. How did Iowa writer Sharon Oard Warner organize the details of her description?

Grammar Tip

When you write descriptions, you can use prepositional phrases, as Warner does, to establish spatial relationships between objects. For more information about prepositional phrases, see Lesson 12.1, page 523.

Literature Model

The pediatric waiting room is divided into two unequal sections by a length of Plexiglas that juts out into the middle of the room. A table at one end keeps people from walking into the flat edge. Orange and brown upholstered chairs line both sides of this transparent wall, back to back, as though some enormous game of musical chairs is about to begin. The smaller section of the room is reserved for well patients, and a prominent sign directs the rest of us to the other side.

When I carried Jancey in this morning, I stopped in the entrance, momentarily confused. Some redecorating had gone on since our last visit. A large oval braided rug covered an expanse of institutional carpet in the unwell section, and a baby not much older than Jancey was seated in the middle of it. While I watched, he crawled to the edge and then back again, as though the rug were an island and he was marooned.

Sharon Oard Warner, "A Simple Matter of Hunger"

"Island" and "marooned" reinforce the sense of rigidly divided space.

Journal Writing

Experiment with spatial organization of details by writing a brief description of a special place or secret hideaway where you go to get away from it all.

Descriptive Writing

Organize Details According to Importance

Writers sometimes arrange details in order of importance, from the least important detail to the most important. This lets the description build to a climax, leaving the strongest image for the end. In the passage below, African American writer Eugenia Collier recalls several details about childhood summers that made a lasting impression on her.

Beverly Buchanan, *Barnesville,* 1989

In this case, order of importance means moving from the general and pervasive—"dust"—to the specific and sharply focused—"a brilliant splash of sunny yellow."

Literature Model

When I think of the home town of my youth, all that I seem to remember is dust—the brown, crumbly dust of late summer—arid, sterile dust that gets into the eyes and makes them water, gets into the throat and between the toes of bare brown feet. I don't know why I should remember only the dust. Surely there must have been lush green lawns and paved streets under leafy shade trees somewhere in town; but memory is an abstract painting—it does not present things as they are, but rather as they *feel.* And so, when I think of that time and that place, I remember only the dry September of the dirt roads and grassless yards of the shanty-town where I lived. And one other thing I remember, another incongruency of memory—a brilliant splash of sunny yellow against the dust—Miss Lottie's marigolds.

Eugenia Collier, "Marigolds"

Focus on the Topic Sentence

Topic sentences are as important in writing descriptions as in any other form of writing. Where you place your topic sentence—at the beginning of the paragraph or at the end—depends upon the effect you want to achieve. The model below begins with a topic sentence, setting the stage for a scary night for two children.

Literature Model

We were afraid at night in the winter. . . . The upstairs of our house was not finished. A brick chimney went up one wall. In the middle of the floor was a square hole, with a wooden railing around it; that was where the stairs came up. On the other side of the stairwell were the things that nobody had any use for anymore. . . . I had told Laird, as soon as he was old enough to understand such things, that bats and skeletons lived over there; whenever a man escaped from the county jail, twenty miles away, I imagined that he had somehow let himself in the window and was hiding behind the linoleum.

Alice Munro, "Boys and Girls"

The topic sentence states the main idea—the children were afraid at night—and the rest of the paragraph describes why they were afraid.

The next paragraph takes a different approach, beginning leisurely and developing a vivid picture one detail at a time. Everything builds toward the topic sentence at the end.

Model

Tall bookshelves stood at attention along the right wall; the books toed a straight line. Two uncomfortable chairs were deployed strategically across the room. Matching brass trays holding paper clips and pens were set up across the front of the desk. Rosa's office clearly revealed her personality.

What can you infer from the description about Rosa's personality?

Journal Writing

Find a paragraph that begins with a topic sentence. Rewrite the paragraph with the topic sentence at the end. Compare the two versions. Explain which you like better.

Put It All Together

After you've created your images and organized them around a topic sentence, you should have an effective description. Notice how student Lonn Rider used specific and vivid details to create a clear image of a favorite place.

The topic sentence states the main idea: to describe Picture Canyon and explain why it has a special effect on people.

In what order does Rider arrange his details in describing Picture Canyon? What details does he use?

Transition words such as "overhead," "on either side," and "looking ahead" help the reader follow the organization.

Student Model

Picture Canyon, though not the most beautiful of places, has a special, enigmatic effect on people. As you enter the canyon, the soft golden sandstone walls begin to build and loom overhead until they meet the electric-blue skyline. Native American drawings etched inside the canyon cover sheer cliff walls on either side, illustrating a past long since forgotten. The rugged floor of the canyon is scattered with multitudes of small, algae-covered ponds with a few weather-beaten, sandstone roadways. Looking ahead, there are small, wind-twisted pine trees with a multitude of squirrels feeding on the pea-sized piñon nuts. Each playfully eats his fill and stores the excess in bulging cheeks. As the sun sets over the horizon, the jagged, golden rock formations on the skyline seem to radiate an eerie, golden energy known only to a few infrequent visitors and to the Native Americans who lived in the canyon centuries ago.

Lonn Rider, Centennial High School, Pueblo, Colorado

Like Rider, you can enhance your descriptions by carefully organizing your ideas and supporting details. Follow these guidelines when you write your own descriptive paragraphs.

Revising Tip

When you revise your writing, add transition words to help the reader follow the organization of your descriptive details. For help refer to Lesson 2.7, page 72.

Guidelines for Descriptive Writing

1. Gather vivid details that will help you re-create a scene or an experience for your readers.
2. Decide which kind of organization will be more appropriate for your subject—spatial order or order of importance.
3. Write a topic sentence, and decide whether it will be more effective positioned at the beginning or the end of the paragraph.
4. Use appropriate transitions to make the organization and relationships among ideas clear.

3.1 Writing Activities

Write a Descriptive Paragraph

Write a description of the painting below that is so specific that someone who has never seen it would immediately recognize it. Use the guidelines on page 130 to help you.

PURPOSE To describe a painting
AUDIENCE Someone who has never seen it
LENGTH 1 paragraph

WRITING RUBRICS To write an effective descriptive paragraph, you should

- use specific details
- order details spatially or by order of importance
- write a clear topic sentence

Listening and Speaking

COOPERATIVE LEARNING Write a paragraph about a possession you had in your early childhood. Describe the object's most unusual features, without naming the object. Read your paragraph aloud with those of a group, identify the objects, and discuss which specific details helped identify the objects.

Blackbear Bosin, *Prairie Fire, 1953*

Grammar Link

Use prepositional phrases to show spatial relationships.

The literature models in this lesson used prepositional phrases, such as "in the middle of the floor," to establish spatial relationships.

Clarify position or location by adding at least one prepositional phrase to each sentence below.

1. A bookcase stood.
2. An overstuffed blue chair squatted.
3. A patchwork quilt of primary colors covered the bed.
4. Clothes were strewn in heaps.
5. A matching chair and desk of oak faced the window.

See Lesson 12.1, pages 523–524.

Cross-Curricular Activity

SCIENCE Work with a partner to research information about the role of fire in maintaining the prairie environment. Write a few paragraphs and present your facts to the class.

LESSON 3.2

Observing and Taking Notes

Striking, image-creating details bring a place to life. The most effective way to "capture" such details is through direct observation and note taking. What direct observations were used to enliven this description of an Indian restaurant in Queens, New York?

Specific visual images like "red plastic tables," "yellow turmeric stains," and "styrofoam bowls" evoke a strong sense of place.

What do words like "wheaty," "bitter," and "sting" add to the description of the scene:

Literature Model

Adam is in an Indian restaurant in Queens, little red plastic tables with yellow turmeric[1] stains on them, styrofoam bowls of dal[2] and chicken curry, slippery with orange oil.

Adam's fingers tear a chapati[3] and dip it into the dal. He gulps it down, the smoothness of the dal mixing with the wheaty taste of the chapati. He eats some chicken, carefully licking all the masala[4] from his fingers, almost tasting each spice alone, the sweet cinnamon and cardamom, the bitter cumin and coriander, the sting of the chilies. The smell makes him so homesick his eyes start watering. He thinks of his grandmother's chicken curry.

"Food all right, sir? Not too spicy?"

Adam swallows. The chicken is so sweet. He looks up at the waiter. "It's perfect," he says.

The waiter looks worried. "You want some yogurt, sir? To make it less spicy. Some raita. That is yogurt with cucumber in it. You know, cucumber."

"No, thank you," says Adam, smiling. "I know what raita is."

"Oh yes, a lot of Europeans eat Indian food now. It's very popular in England as well. Yes, I can see you know how to eat like an Indian," leaning on the table now, he hangs the wet cloth over the back of the chair. "Me, I like American food. I never eat here. I eat at McDonald's or Kentucky Chicken. It's so funny, isn't it? Indians like American food and Americans like Indian food."

Ameena Meer, "The Only Living Boy in New York."

1 **turmeric** (tur′mer ik) an orange-colored spice
2 **dal** (däl) lentil sauce
3 **chapati** (chə pät′ē) bread
4 **masala** (mə säl′a) spice mixture

Use Direct Observation

Revisiting a scene through memory is one kind of observation, but you can get a better sense of a place if you revisit the location in person. In both cases you will want to consider the same questions as you think about re-creating the scene in words: What is the most striking thing about the scene? What colors do you see? What sounds do you hear? What scents do you smell? What will you have to include in the description so that your readers will see what you saw, feel as you felt?

Take Notes

If you don't have a photographic memory, draw a sketch, make a video, or take notes in your personal journal. Do whatever you think will help you re-create the scene later when you sit down to write. Here is a set of notes that student Michelle Kalski took in preparation for writing a description of her favorite getaway spot.

Prewriting Tip

You may want to record your observations in a notebook. Keep a list there of your first impressions.

Sight

green grass, sunlight and shadows, sun-kissed water, rippling waves, white sails, cobalt-blue sky, cotton-fluffy clouds, snow-white gulls

Sound	*Smell*	*Touch*
chirping birds,	*fresh greenery,*	*soft summer breeze,*
whispering trees	*fragrant pines*	*clean dry grass*

Journal Writing

Look carefully around you right now. Think about the questions above under "Use Direct Observation." Make notes answering these questions.

Write from Notes

The student model below shows how Kalski used her notes to write a descriptive paragraph. She began with a topic sentence stating the main idea. She then organized the supporting details in order of importance, saving strong, mood-capturing details for the end.

Publishing Tip

You might want to get together with others to create a poster display of your descriptive writing.

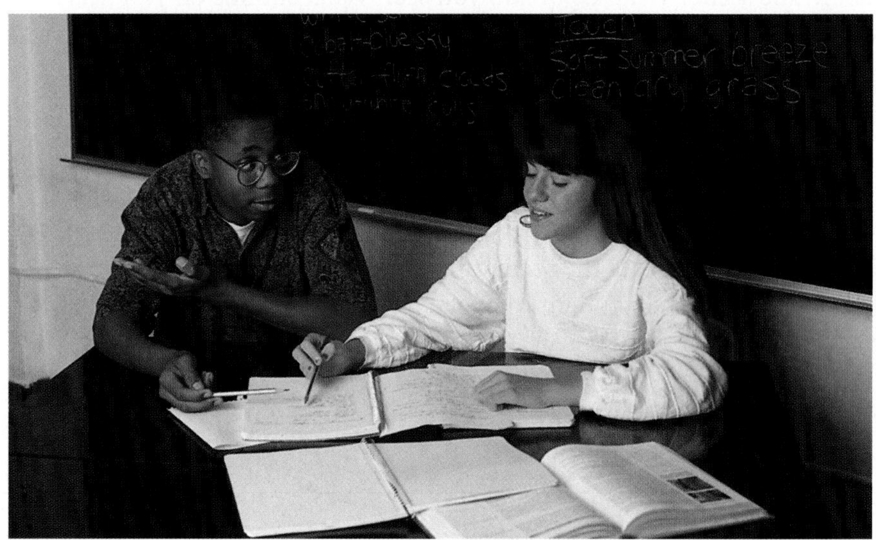

Student Model

School is out in gorgeous weather, and there isn't much to worry about except sleeping too late into the afternoon. I head out to my favorite spot, a small patch of space to separate me from the busy lives of all the bustling people. As I lie there, the green dry grass plays hide and seek with my fingers and toes. Sun and shade spot me like tie-dye configurations, while a warm breeze keeps me company. The trees overhead say "Hello," as if they were old friends; they shade and protect me just in case the sky might fall. I feel a warm sun penetrating through the trees, making conversation with the breeze as if they'd known each other for a thousand years. I'm surrounded and encompassed by nature. I look over the glistening lake and see ripples kissing the water's surface. Scattered cotton clouds on blue wait to absorb everything around in just one season. The only things heard are birds chirping and the breeze and trees discussing old times. Peace is all around until sunset and later on.

Michelle Kalski, Evanston Township High School, Evanston, Illinois

Kalski relied on her notes for specific sensory details like "green dry grass," "warm breeze," and "glistening lake."

How do original and unusual details make this passage more effective?

3.2 Writing Activities

Write About a Painting

The painting on this page portrays an interesting impression of Fifth Avenue in New York. Take notes on the style, colors used, and effect of the painting. Then write a descriptive paragraph about the painting.

PURPOSE To observe and describe a painting
AUDIENCE Your teacher
LENGTH 1 paragraph

WRITING RUBRICS To write an effective descriptive paragraph, you should

- compose a topic sentence for your paragraph
- use observation and list details
- include details that appeal to different senses

Listening and Speaking

COOPERATIVE LEARNING In a small group, explore an outdoor location. Ask each group member to take detailed notes about the plant and animal life in one section. Write the combined notes into a group description.

Using Computers

SPELLING To refine your spelling skills, work with a partner to check each other's spelling on printouts of your paragraphs. Then verify any suggested spelling corrections using the spell-check feature on the computer.

Form possessive pronouns correctly.

Possessive pronouns do not use apostrophes. Do not confuse the possessive pronoun *its* with the contraction *it's* (it is):

"It's perfect," he [Adam] says.

Choose the right words to complete each sentence below.

1. (Her's, Hers) is the backpack that's bigger than (your's, yours).
2. This canvas backpack is (he's, his).
3. The backpacks left on the bus must be (their's, theirs).
4. (Our's, Ours) were not on the bus.
5. Ted's backpack is torn; (it's, its) time for him to find (it's, its) replacement.

See Lesson 17.1, pages 637–638.

Childe Hassam, *Fifth Avenue*, 1919

LESSON 3.3

Using Energetic Verbs

Cartoonists highlight words like BAM, POW, and BWHOOOOOSH. You can bring the same kind of energy to your own writing by using specific, action-packed words.

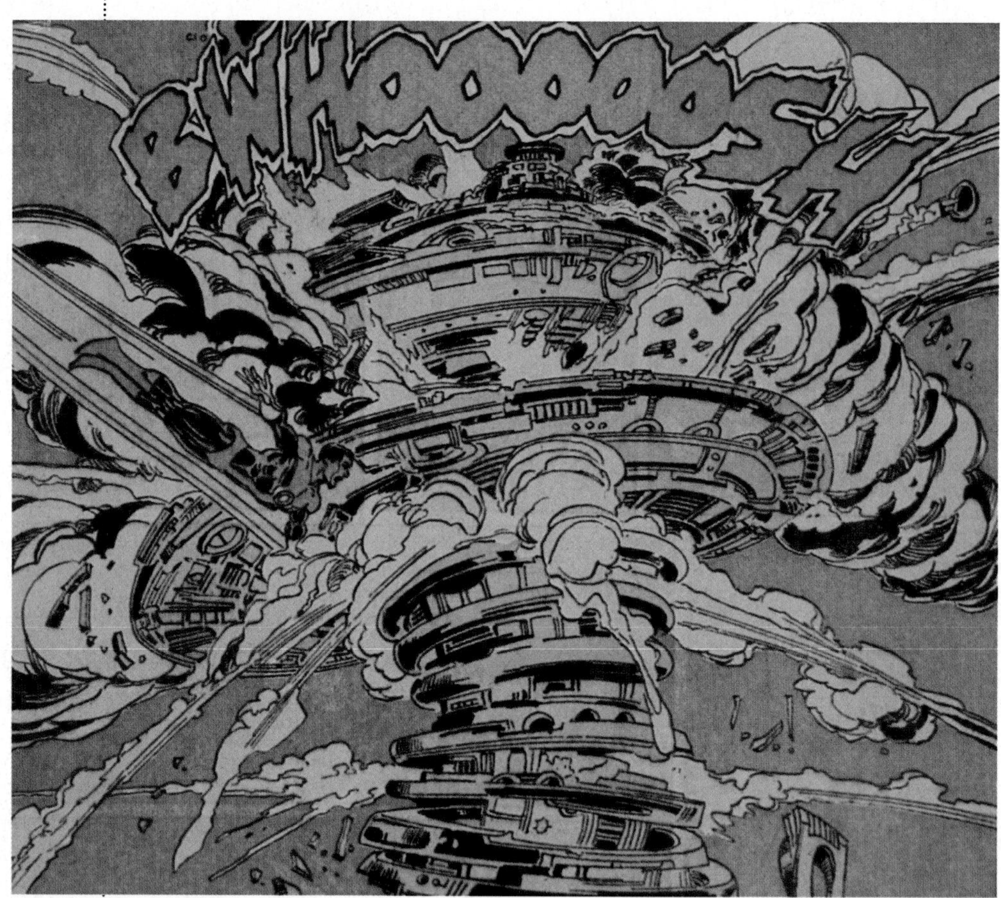

Choose Exact Verbs

Exact verbs create mood and strong mental images in descriptive writing. Notice how the writers of the following models have used energetic verbs.

Literature Model

The nights now are full of wind and destruction; the trees plunge and bend and their leaves fly helter skelter until the lawn is plastered with them and they lie packed in gutters and choke rain pipes and scatter damp paths.

Virginia Woolf, *To the Lighthouse*

Literature Model

The crowds are thick on the sidewalks and street vendors work on nearly every block. The litter baskets—they look like volcanoes of trash that have just erupted—are overloaded from a Sunday's use. Debris is strewn over the pavement and in the gutters. A wind stirs up scraps and creates a funnel of newspaper that swirls up in a mad ballet.

McCandlish Phillips, *City Notebook*

What verbs in these passages create strong mental pictures? What pictures do they create?

To choose just the right verb to use in a particular situation, do what many professional writers do—use a thesaurus, which is a collection of synonyms. Just keep in mind that synonyms are not necessarily interchangeable. For example, you wouldn't write "The horse *jogs*" when you mean "The horse *gallops,*" even though *jog* and *gallop* are both synonyms for *run.*

Sometimes you may not be certain of the precise meanings of synonyms. See the thesaurus entry at the right, for example. You might have to consult a dictionary to find the exact meanings of *aggrandize* and *augment.*

INCREASE—V.

Increase, enhance, aggrandize, augment; intensify, step up, raise, boost.

grow, surge, swell, fill out, inflate; skyrocket; overgrow, spread.

Vocabulary Tip

During the revising stage, replace verb-adverb pairs with a single verb. For instance, change "Pablo smiled happily" to "Pablo beamed."

Journal Writing

Choose a recent entry in your journal. Underline all the verbs. Replace them with more vivid ones. How does this change your entry?

Revise with Exact Verbs

The best time to check the effectiveness of your verbs is in the revising stage, after you've gotten all your ideas down. Notice how much the replacement verbs in the following model strengthen the images the writer is trying to create. The guidelines below the model provide a plan for systematically checking and improving verbs.

Model

It stopped raining at noon, but clouds continued to ~~flow~~ *sweep* down the craggy mountain into the valley below. Despite the weather, we were determined to hike up at least one mountain in Switzerland. We ~~climbed~~ *trudged* up the steep slope behind the Klausen Pass Hotel, picking our way through fields of sharp rock and over spongelike clumps of wet lichen. After an hour of heavy climbing, we ~~sat~~ *plopped* down on a chilly slab to revive ourselves with water and chocolate. Suddenly, the clouds that had been moving down the mountain spread over our slope, enveloping us in mist. Like it or not, we knew we had to turn back. Disappointed, we ~~walked~~ *stumbled* blindly downward until we came to the road to our hotel.

"Sweep" gives a better feeling of relentless motion than "flow."

How is "trudged" better than "climbed"?

What does "plopped" tell you?

"Stumbled" calls up a more vivid mental image than "walked." How does "stumbled" build on the impression created by "plopped" and "trudged"?

Guidelines for Revision

1. Read your first draft carefully, highlighting each verb with a yellow marker.
2. Scrutinize each verb. Does it call up a vivid mental picture? If not, try to substitute one that does.
3. Consult a thesaurus for help in finding specific, interesting verbs.

Grammar Tip

When you get to the editing stage, pay particular attention to consistency of tenses. See Lessons 15.3–15.6, pages 589–599.

3.3 Writing Activities

Write with Energetic Verbs

Use one of the following verbs to help you visualize an activity in a location with which you are familiar: *slide, kick, skip, lunge, swoop, shriek, whirl, toss.*

Picture both the location and the action. Write a description of what you visualized. First, make a list of striking details you want to include in the description. Then, write a first draft, using your details to create a vivid word picture. Revise your paragraph, replacing simple verbs with action-packed verbs where appropriate. Consult a thesaurus if you need help finding synonyms. For help with word choice, see **Writing and Research Handbook,** page 958.

PURPOSE To use action verbs to describe
AUDIENCE Yourself and your teacher
LENGTH 1 paragraph

WRITING RUBRICS To use action verbs to describe, you should

- choose exact verbs
- use verbs that are descriptive and energetic
- replace overused, uninteresting verbs

Using Computers

If your computer has an electronic thesaurus, use it to help you choose energetic verbs. The electronic thesaurus will quickly give you options for synonyms of verbs, or any other words, that you highlight. The thesaurus may even replace the original word automatically with the new word you have chosen.

Use verbs correctly.

Even vivid verbs will not be effective if you do not use them correctly. Remember to use the past form without a helping verb (I *went*) and the past participle form with a helping verb (I *have gone*). Remember also to use the correct verb in confusing pairs such as *lie* and *lay.*

Rewrite each sentence below, inserting the correct form of the verb in parentheses.

1. I have (grew, grown) up reading English writer Virginia Woolf.
2. She (wrote, written) several excellent novels, including *To the Lighthouse.*
3. I have (read, readed) most of Virginia Woolf's books.
4. I have sometimes (thunk, thought) that they are among my favorites.
5. Occasionally, Woolf's characters have (drove, driven) me crazy.

See Lessons 15.1 and 15.2, pages 585–588.

Listening and Speaking

COOPERATIVE LEARNING Working in a small group, take turns reading your descriptive paragraphs aloud without identifying the place in your description. Have your listeners guess the place or type of place you have written about.

LESSON

3.4

Describing from Vantage Points

The term vantage point *refers to the location from which a writer observes a scene. A writer can describe a scene from a stationary vantage point or, if the scene continually changes, from a moving vantage point. Which vantage point would be used to describe the cockpit below? the scene outside it?*

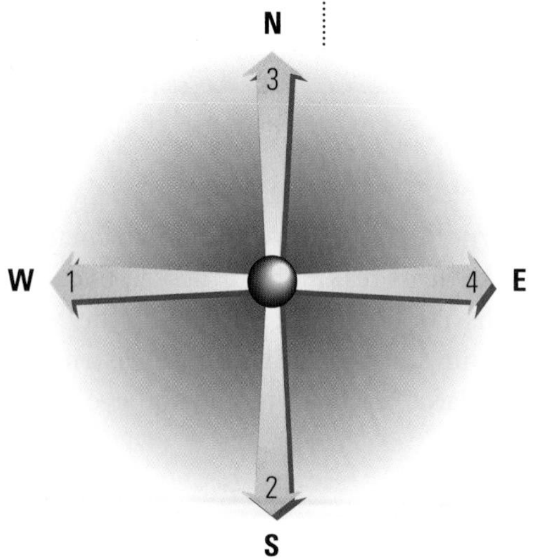

Stationary Vantage Points

A stationary vantage point is a fixed position from which to view a scene. In the following model, American writer Edward Abbey describes a scene from such a vantage point. He views a mountain landscape from a central focus, describing the view to each compass point in turn, first west, then south and north, and finally east. The graphic at the left diagrams this spatial organization.

Literature Model

The view is open and perfect in all directions except to the west where the ground rises and the skyline is only a few hundred yards away. Looking toward the mountains I can see the dark gorge of the Colorado River five or six miles away, carved through the sandstone mesa, though nothing of the river itself down inside the gorge. Southward, on the far side of the river, lies the Moab valley between thousand-foot walls of rock, with the town of Moab somewhere on the valley floor, too small to be seen from here. Beyond the Moab valley is more canyon and tableland stretching away to the Blue Mountains fifty miles south. On the north and northwest I see the Roan Cliffs and the Book Cliffs, the two-level face of the Uinta Plateau. . . . To the east, under the spreading sunrise, are more mesas, more canyons, league on league of red cliff and arid tablelands, extending through purple haze over the bulging curve of the planet to the ranges of Colorado—a sea of desert.

Edward Abbey, "The Most Beautiful Place on Earth"

What words give you a sense of direction in this passage?

Prewriting Tip

Creating a diagram before you begin drafting a description can help you focus your writing. Use arrows and numbers to show the ordering of specific details.

Journal Writing

Think about your daily trip to school. List details you would use to describe that trip. In your journal write a few sentences about your trip. Experiment with creating a graphic for organizing a description of your trip from a stationary vantage point.

Moving the Vantage Points

A moving vantage point occurs when the position of the viewer continually changes. Usually a writer switches to chronological, or time, order when describing a scene from a moving vantage point. The diagram graphically shows the model's chronological organization.

Moving along points on a path, you describe each scene as you come upon it.

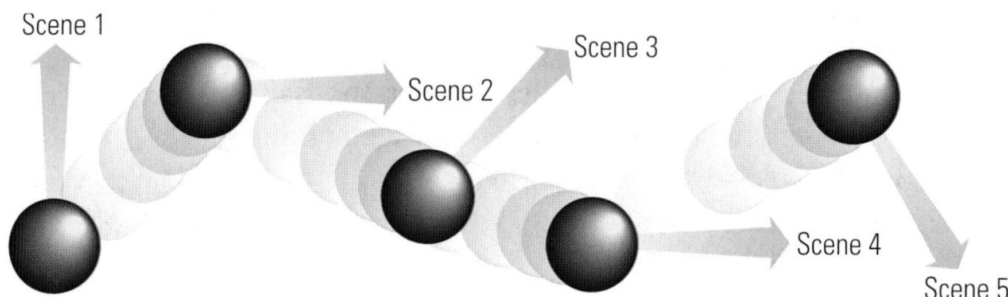

You can get a better feel for the chronological nature of Abbey's organization by comparing the description with the diagram.

Literature Model

I drove twelve miles farther north on the highway until I came to a dirt road on the right, where a small wooden sign pointed the way: ARCHES NATIONAL MONUMENT EIGHT MILES. I left the pavement, turned east into the howling wilderness. Wind roaring out of the northwest, black clouds across the stars—all I could see were clumps of brush and scattered junipers along the roadside. Then another modest signboard:

WARNING: QUICKSAND
DO NOT CROSS WASH WHEN WATER IS RUNNING

The wash looked perfectly dry in my headlights. I drove down, across, up the other side and on into the night. Glimpses of weird humps of pale rock on either side, like petrified elephants, dinosaurs, stone-age hobgoblins. Now and then something alive scurried across the road: kangaroo mice, a jackrabbit, an animal that looked like a cross between a raccoon and a squirrel—the ringtail cat. Farther on a pair of mule deer started from the brush and bounded obliquely through the beams of my lights, raising puffs of dust which the wind, moving faster than my pickup truck, caught and carried ahead of me out of sight into the dark. The road, narrow and rocky, twisted sharply left and right, dipped in and out of tight ravines, climbing by degrees toward a summit which I would see only in the light of the coming day.

Edward Abbey, "The Most Beautiful Place on Earth"

Vocabulary Tip

When you revise descriptions written from a moving vantage point, you can make chronological order clearer by using transitions that suggest the passage of time: *until, later, then, after.*

3.4 Writing Activities

Write from a Moving Vantage Point

Write a description of a place from a moving vantage point, such as a landscape viewed from a train window or a canyon as you climb down into it.

PURPOSE To describe a scene from a moving vantage point
AUDIENCE Your classmates
LENGTH 2–3 paragraphs

WRITING RUBRICS To describe a scene from a moving vantage point, you should

- select an interesting scene to describe
- use chronological order to describe the moving scene
- use transitions when your vantage point changes

Cross-Curricular Activity

GEOGRAPHY Think of a city that you have studied recently or one with which you are familiar. Choose one stationary vantage point from which to describe a view of the city. Write a paragraph telling what you see from that vantage point. Then select an area of the city that you might like to walk through, and write a paragraph describing sites from that moving vantage point. Decide which description communicates a better sense of the city.

Grammar Link

Make subjects agree with verbs in inverted sentences.

A subject must agree with a verb even when it follows that verb.

To the east, under the spreading sunrise, ***are*** *more* ***mesas****. . . .*

Rewrite any faulty sentence below so that the verb agrees with the subject. Do not confuse subjects with objects of prepositions that precede the verb.

1. Behind the emerald hills, in the distance, loom the hazy shapes of a snow-capped mountain range.
2. There is adventures to be found in those mountains.
3. Here comes two backpackers.
4. There go another two backpackers in the distance.
5. On the mountain lives deer and bears.
6. Near my house is two national parks.

See Lesson 16.3, pages 616–617.

Listening and Speaking

SPELLING Work with a partner and use a dictionary or the spell-checking feature on your computer to make sure that your descriptions are spelled correctly. Correct your misspellings and discuss what your most common spelling errors have in common. How might you avoid these errors in your future writing?

LESSON 3.5

Descriptive Writing

WRITING ABOUT LITERATURE

Responding to Imagery in Poetry

The images a poet uses enable readers to share the poet's unique experience of the world. How would you respond to the images in the following poem? By writing your own poem? By painting a picture such as the one on page 145?

TIME

For more about the writing process, see **TIME Facing the Blank Page,** pp. 109–119.

Literature Model

Corsons Inlet

I went for a walk over the dunes again this morning
to the sea,
then turned right along
  the surf
        rounded a naked headland
        and returned

  along the inlet shore:

it was muggy sunny, the wind from the sea steady and high,
crisp in the running sand,
  some breakthroughs of sun
 but after a bit

continuous overcast:

the walk liberating, I was released from forms,
from the perpendiculars,
      straight lines, blocks, boxes, binds
of thought
into the hues, shadings, rises, flowing bends and blends
        of sight . . .

A. R. Ammons

Respond Creatively

Sometimes people are so affected by a poem that they feel a need to respond in a creative way. For example, some people turn poetic images into pictures—pencil sketches, watercolors, even quilts. Others pick an image and respond by choreographing a dance. The following chart shows four other creative ways of responding to imagery in a poem.

Creative Responses to Poetic Images

1. Create a collage that expresses the image's meaning to you.
2. Use your journal to explore the feelings the image arouses in you.
3. Write a poem based on an image that inspires you.
4. Read the poem aloud for a friend or group of classmates.

Arthur Dove, *Sunrise*, 1924

Prewriting Tip

You may want to discuss your idea for responding to a poem with a classmate before working it out on your own. Such interaction will help you clarify and focus your own ideas.

Grammar Tip

When you revise poems you have written as responses, add vivid adjectives to bring images to life. For more information about adjectives, see Lesson 10.4, pages 460–465.

Journal Writing

Think about different ways of responding to a favorite poem. In your journal, discuss which of the responses listed above would work best for you.

Descriptive Writing

Respond to Poetry

Sometimes it isn't easy to respond to a poem. New York poet Kenneth Koch found a way to help his students—children as young as 8 and adults as old as 98. Koch taught reading poetry and writing poetry as one subject. The two were brought together by "poetry ideas," suggestions for writing that echo the theme of a poem being studied.

Sonia Terk Delaunay, *Electric Prisms,* 1914

To see how to apply Koch's idea, look back at the selection "Corsons Inlet" on page 144. Notice how Ammons contrasts the changing shapes and movement of nature—the dunes, the sea, the wind, and the sun—with the rigid perpendiculars, straight lines, and binds of his own thinking. One writer took that as his "poetry idea": how thinking often gets in the way of really seeing.

The writer uses Ammons's images of nature as a springboard for the new poem.

Why does the poet suddenly include the image of a diner counter? What does it point to?

In the second stanza the writer details how thinking gets in the way of seeing.

Model

I wish the hard part
would be forms. Catching the trees right,
getting the sea to cooperate
Or the sun, coaxing the sun out
when everything is right
and you want it shining.
But all this is easy, soothing, and natural.
As bright and spotless as a diner counter.

The real difficulty is eyeing the flat,
plain, and level. Scaffolding,
the high wires, the firefighter's ladders,
disarrange the subject. Then
an ocean has thoughts; the wind
calls collect, a whispering relative. Your signature
is on everything
saying names and hiding shapes.

3.5 Writing Activities

Write a Response Poem

Write a poem in response to one of the images in the poem at the beginning of this lesson or to an image in another poem of your own choosing. First, find a "poetry idea" in the original poem. Then, freewrite to build on this idea.

PURPOSE To respond to a poetic image
AUDIENCE Yourself and your teacher
LENGTH 1 page

WRITING RUBRICS To write an effective poem, you should

- choose a subject that lends itself to descriptive words and images
- list impressions as you visualize your subject
- use your list of impressions to help you write
- use vivid adjectives to create your images

Using Computers

As you are writing your poem, you might experiment with how the words look on the page. Try breaking your lines at different places. Try a different typeface or size. The shape and size of the letters can affect the "feel" of your poem. Print out different versions of your poem and compare them. If you want to achieve a special effect, change the typeface of only one line or word. Use tabs or alignment commands to scatter your text across the page. See which changes bring the most meaning to your poem.

Use clear, precise adjectives to improve your descriptions.

Adjectives such as *muggy, flowing,* and *soothing* from the models in this lesson help create precise word pictures. Look at this example by A. R. Ammons:

> *it was* ***muggy sunny****, the wind from*
> *the sea* ***steady*** *and* ***high,***
> ***crisp*** *in the* ***running*** *sand . . .*

Revise the following sentences by adding at least one vivid adjective to each.

1. I walked over the dunes.
2. The sea grass grew.
3. The sea beckoned me.
4. The waves lapped the shore.
5. A boat bobbed, straining at its anchor.
6. The sun barely penetrated the mist.
7. The air tickled my nose.
8. I laughed.

See Lesson 10.4, pages 460–465.

Listening and Speaking

COOPERATIVE LEARNING After drafting your poem, work with a partner to review each other's work. Read each other's poems and make suggestions for improvement. How might you make images more "real"? What other words might you use to make a description more vivid? Incorporate some of your partner's suggestions into your final draft. Then read your completed poems aloud.

Descriptive Writing

LESSON 3.6

WRITING ABOUT LITERATURE

Analyzing Setting in a Short Story

Setting is the environment—the time and place—in which the action of a story takes place. When you analyze setting, you describe the setting and then look at how it relates to other important elements of the story.

The graphic below illustrates some important uses of setting. Consider these uses when you analyze the setting of any story.

Uses of Setting

Use	Example	Explanation
To create mood	*During the whole of a dull, dark, and soundless day in the autumn of the year, when the clouds hung oppressively low in the heavens, I had been passing alone, on horseback, through a singularly dreary tract of country, and at length found myself, as the shades of evening drew on, within view of the melancholy House of Usher.* Edgar Allan Poe, "The Fall of the House of Usher"	The setting creates a mood of depression and impending doom.
To affect action	*The house was very still about me and yet alive, as if it breathed softly. . . . I shivered and crept to the wide-open window. The faint dawn light, scarcely less than darkness, showed only the silhouette of the birch trees. The moon was down. The garden was totally indistinct.* Iris Murdoch, "The Italian Girl"	The setting is crucial as a backdrop for the action.
To develop character	*"It's pretty over there," she said. . . . "I go there all the time. Ride over. Especially the graveyard. Down where Spring Creek runs into the Clear Fork. Daddy says it's dangerous because of the copperheads but I go there anyway."* A. C. Greene, "The Girl at Cabe Ranch"	The setting conveys information about the main character.

Look for Connections

Relating the setting of a story to other elements such as mood, plot, and character, you may find that the setting tells about the other elements. For example, setting may foreshadow disaster or create an atmosphere of terror. The contrast between two settings in a story—a farmhouse and a city apartment, for instance—may reveal a character's feelings. The details of setting—color of walls, neatness of a desk, contents of a drawer—may provide important information about a character.

Setting may also be used as an active participant in a story—for example, a mountain that must be scaled. In this case the setting is something that a character must struggle against. Below is a questionnaire that you can use to help you analyze a story setting.

Grammar Tip

As you analyze story setting, notice the author's use of adverbs to present a more vivid picture of place. For more information about adverbs, see Lesson 10.5, pages 466–472.

Descriptive Writing

Analyzing a Story Setting

General	1. What is the name of the story? 2. Where does most of the story action take place? When does it take place? Is there historical significance to the setting?
Setting and Mood	3. What is the general mood of the story? Cheerful or gloomy? Comforting or threatening? Hopeful or despairing? 4. How does the story setting contribute to the mood?
Setting and Plot	5. What is the plot in the story? 6. Is the setting crucial to the plot? Would it matter much if the story had a different setting? Does the description of the setting change as the story progresses?
Setting and Character	7. Who is the main character in the story? What is this person like? 8. How do we learn about the main character? Does the author convey any important information about the main character through setting?

Journal Writing

Use the questionnaire to begin analyzing setting in a favorite short story. Answer the questions as thoroughly as possible.

Create Your Analysis

After you identify the connections between setting and the other story elements, plan an effective analysis. Use the questionnaire on page 149 as a guide while developing your main points and the support for your arguments. Notice how the questionnaire relates to the following model. Below the model is a set of guidelines you can use to write your own essay about setting in a short story.

Descriptive Writing

The introductory paragraph points out that setting plays a major role in the story.

How does the writer use direct quotations from the story?

How does the writer use evidence from the story to support and elaborate on the arguments of the analysis?

Model

In some stories setting isn't very important. It's only background to the main action. In other stories, however, setting plays a major role, creating a unifying thread that touches everyone and everything. Such is the case with the setting in "Chee's Daughter."

Chee is a Navajo who always tries to live in harmony with nature. He has a "feeling of wholeness and of oneness with the sun and earth and growing things." As the story begins, we learn that Chee's wife has died, leaving a three-year-old daughter who, according to Navajo custom, now lives with the mother's relatives.

The story revolves around Chee's efforts to get his daughter back, and the plot and the setting are intertwined every step of the way. For example, the story begins in the cold of winter, so when Chee first asks the grandparents if the daughter can stay with him, we know what the answer will be: a frigid no. We soon learn, however, that "spring-time transformed the mesas," and we realize immediately that it will transform Chee, too. He has a new plan—to place his trust in the land, grow a bountiful harvest, and exchange the food for the child. In the end, Chee's faith is vindicated, and he gets his daughter back.

Guidelines for Writing About Setting

1. Read the story carefully, completing the questionnaire as you go.
2. Write an introductory paragraph that states the main idea of your essay.
3. Use information from the questionnaire in developing your major points.
4. Cite specific evidence from the story to support and elaborate on your argument.
5. End with a brief paragraph summarizing your conclusions.

3.6 Writing Activities

Write a Setting Analysis

Select a painting from this book. Think of a general plot for a story that could accompany the painting. Then write an explanation of how the painting's setting affects the story.

PURPOSE To analyze setting
AUDIENCE Your teacher
LENGTH 2-3 paragraphs

WRITING RUBRICS To write an effective analysis of setting, you should

- describe the mood created by the setting
- explain how the setting might affect the actions or feelings of the characters
- cite details from the artwork to support and elaborate on your views

Cross-Curricular Activity

HISTORY Read a short story that takes place in a specific historical period. Write an analysis of how the story's setting, including the historical context, affects the story's mood, action, and character development. Elaborate on your analysis with detailed references to the text.

Grammar Link

Use strong adverbs to make descriptions more precise.

Notice how Edgar Allan Poe uses the adverbs *oppressively, alone,* and *singularly* in the model on page 148.

Revise the following sentences by adding at least one vivid adverb to each. (You may make other changes, too, if you wish.)

1. The thunder faded into the distance.
2. Gray clouds raced overhead.
3. The countryside lay sodden and silent.
4. The weary plop of a horse's hooves reached my ears.
5. A solitary rider approached.

See Lesson 10.5, page 466.

Listening and Speaking

ILLUSTRATING Imagine moving the figures from the painting you used for your setting analysis to a different setting. It might be the beach or an amusement park. Orally describe the scene you imagine. Be sure to provide vivid details. What mood describes your setting? How does the setting affect the characters?

UNIT 3

Writing Process in Action

Descriptive Writing

Descriptive Writing

WRITING Online

Visit the Writer's Choice Web site at **writerschoice.glencoe.com** for additional writing prompts.

In preceding lessons, you've learned how to describe a place by choosing a vantage point, observing and organizing details carefully, and using energetic verbs. You've also had a chance to write a poem and an essay about story setting. In this lesson you'll put together what you've learned by describing a place that you know well.

Assignment

Context

A student from another state is moving to your school. Your principal has sent the student a variety of orientation materials—class schedules, copies of the school newspaper, last year's yearbook. The student writes back, politely explaining that what she or he really wants is a description of the new school that will allow her or him to "see" the place and the people in it. You've been asked to respond to this request.

Purpose

To write a description of your school that will convey what it's like from a student's point of view

Audience

A student moving to your school from another state

Length

1 to 2 pages

You will find the next few pages helpful as you plan and write your description. Read through the pages, and refer to them as you need to, but remember that they are only guidelines. After all, you're in charge of your own writing process.

Prewriting

How will you describe your school? What details will you use to present a picture of the building? What details will bring the people in the school to life for your future schoolmate? The questions on the right may help you choose details and a method of organizing the details that will help you write a vivid description.

Jot down notes of details as they occur to you. If you decide to describe the school from a moving vantage point, walk through the building, noting any striking images to include in your description. If necessary, research facts by checking with the school administration.

Once you've collected your details, decide which ones you want to use, and organize your notes. Does a fact or an image stand out? If so, use that for your lead—the first sentence or two that will grab your reader's attention. Look at the lead that Gretel Ehrlich uses in this description of her subject, Wyoming. Note how this passage presents a general picture of Wyoming and uses a quotation to sharpen the picture.

Prewriting Questions

- What images—verbal snapshots—will allow my reader to see the school as I see it?
- What personal anecdotes or quotations can I include?
- What facts and statistics will provide useful information?
- What vantage point would give life to my description?

Literature Model

To live and work in this kind of open country, with its hundred-mile views, is to lose the distinction between background and foreground. When I asked an older ranch hand to describe Wyoming's openness, he said, "It's all a bunch of nothing—wind and rattlesnakes—and so much of it you can't tell where you're going or where you've been and it don't make much difference."

Gretel Ehrlich, *The Solace of Open Spaces*

Drafting Tip

To review how to organize details, see Lesson 2.7, pages 72–75, and Lesson 3.1, pages 126–131.

Drafting

To begin drafting, imagine where you are—the place you'll begin your tour or where you will stand to describe all that you see around you—or look at your lead. Then just start writing.

As you write, be aware of details unique to your school that might need special explanation. Try to look at your school with a "fresh" eye so you can make the description clear for the new student.

Visualize what you are describing. Use your notes to help you remember details, but don't stop writing at this stage to find the perfect verb or image. If you get stuck, take a break, talk about your description with a friend, or start over.

Revising Tip

If you are having trouble with word choice, consult the Guidelines for Revision chart, Lesson 3.3, page 138.

Revising

To begin revising, read over your draft to make sure that what you've written fits your purpose and audience. Then have a **writing conference.** Read your draft to a partner or small group. Use your audience's reactions and the Revising Checklist below to help you evaluate your work.

Revising Checklist

- Did I use a lead that grabbed the reader?
- Did I select good details and organize them logically around topic sentences?
- Were the images I used clear and striking?
- Did I use exact, energetic verbs to enliven my description?
- Did I write from a vantage point that made sense?

Editing/Proofreading

When you are satisfied with your description, **proofread** it carefully for errors in grammar, usage, mechanics, and spelling. Use the quotations at the right as a guide.

In addition to proofreading, use the Self-Evaluation guidelines to make sure your writing describes the school well. When you feel that it does, make a clean copy of your description and proofread it one more time.

Editing/Proofreading Checklist

- Have I used verbs correctly?
- Have I formed possessive pronouns correctly?
- Do my subjects and verbs agree?
- Have I used precise, vivid word choices?
- Have I checked spellings of any words of which I'm unsure?

Self-Evaluation

Make sure your description—

- ✔ uses a strong lead
- ✔ uses different kinds of vivid supporting details
- ✔ uses strong verbs and good transitions
- ✔ follows correct grammar, usage, mechanics, and spelling

Editing, like revising, is best accomplished in a series of passes through your work. It's easier to watch for one type of error than to be on the lookout for ten kinds. The guidelines for editing presented in Lesson 2.9, pages 82–85 can also help. Don't let the fact that you know your work lull you into missing obvious errors.

Proofreading

For proofreading symbols, see page 84. Use the spell-check and grammar-check features on the computer to examine your work.

Publishing/Presenting

You might want to have someone from another state read your description. Your reader might be a friend who has moved away, a relative, or a pen pal. Feedback from such a reading would tell you how well your description works.

Journal Writing

Reflect on your writing-process experience. Answer these questions in your journal: What do you like best about your description? What was the hardest part of writing it? What did you learn in your writing conference? What new things have you learned as a writer?

Literature Model

FROM

The Solace of Open Spaces

by Gretel Ehrlich

In this excerpt from her book The Solace of Open Spaces, *Gretel Ehrlich, who lives on a ranch in Wyoming, uses descriptive writing to portray her adopted home state, its land, and its people. Pay particular attention to the images, the facts, and the anecdotes Ehrlich uses to engage the reader in her description. Then try the activities in Linking Writing and Literature on page 162.*

To live and work in this kind of open country, with its hundred-mile views, is to lose the distinction between background and foreground. When I asked an older ranch hand to describe Wyoming's openness, he said, "It's all a bunch of nothing—wind and rattlesnakes—and so much of it you can't tell where you're going or where you've been and it don't make much difference." John, a sheepman I know, is tall and handsome and has an explosive temperament. He has a perfect intuition about people and sheep. They call him "Highpockets," because he's so long-legged; his graceful stride matches the distances he has to cover. He says, "Open space hasn't affected me at all. It's all the people moving in on

Frederic Remington, *The Fall of the Cowboy,* 1895

it." The huge ranch he was born on takes up much of one county and spreads into another state; to put 100,000 miles on his pickup in three years and never leave home is not unusual. A friend of mine has an aunt who ranched on Powder River and didn't go off her place for eleven years. When her husband died, she quickly moved to town, bought a car, and drove around the States to see what she'd been missing.

Most people tell me they've simply driven through Wyoming, as if there were nothing to stop for. Or else they've skied in Jackson Hole, a place Wyomingites acknowledge uncomfortably because its green beauty and chic affluence[1] are mismatched with the rest of the state. Most of Wyoming has a "lean-to" look. Instead of big, roomy barns and Victorian houses, there are dugouts, low sheds, log cabins, sheep camps, and fence lines that look like driftwood blown haphazardly into place. People here still feel pride because they live in such a harsh place, part of the glamorous cowboy past, and they are determined not to be the victims of a mining-dominated future.

1 **chic affluence** (shēk′ af′ lo͞o əns) stylish wealth

Most characteristic of the state's landscape is what a developer euphemistically[2] describes as "indigenous growth right up to your front door"—a reference to waterless stands of salt sage, snakes, jack rabbits, deerflies, red dust, a brief respite of wildflowers, dry washes, and no trees. In the Great Plains the vistas look like music, like Kyries[3] of grass, but Wyoming seems to be the doing of a mad architect—tumbled and twisted, ribboned with faded, deathbed colors, thrust up and pulled down as if the place had been startled out of a deep sleep and thrown into a pure light.

I came here four years ago. I had not planned to stay, but I couldn't make myself leave. John, the sheepman, put me to work immediately. It was spring, and shearing time. For fourteen days of fourteen hours each, we moved thousands of sheep through sorting corrals to be sheared, branded, and deloused.[4] I suspect that my original motive for coming here was to "lose myself" in new and unpopulated territory. Instead of producing the numbness I thought I wanted, life on the sheep ranch woke me up. The vitality of the people I was working with flushed out what had become a hallucinatory[5] rawness inside me. I threw away my clothes and bought new ones; I cut my hair. The arid country was a clean slate. Its absolute indifference steadied me.

Sagebrush covers 58,000 square miles of Wyoming. The biggest city has a population of fifty thousand, and there are only five settlements that could be called cities in the whole state. The rest are towns, scattered across the expanse with as much as sixty miles between them, their populations two thousand, fifty, or ten. They are fugitive-looking, perched on a barren, windblown bench, or tagged onto a river or a railroad, or laid out straight in a farming valley with implement stores and a block-long Mormon church. In the eastern part of the state, which slides down into the Great Plains, the new mining settlements are boomtowns, trailer cities, metal knots on flat land.

Despite the desolate look, there's a coziness to living in this state. There are so few people (only 470,000) that ranchers who buy and sell cattle know one another statewide; the kids who choose to go to college usually go to the state's one university, in Laramie; hired hands work their way around Wyoming in a lifetime of hirings and firings. And despite the physical separation, people stay in touch, often driving two or three hours to another ranch for dinner.

Seventy-five years ago, when travel was by buckboard or horseback, cowboys who were temporarily out of work rode the grub line—drifting from ranch to ranch, mending fences or milking cows, and receiving in exchange a bed and meals. Gossip and messages traveled this slow

---

2 **euphemistically** (yo͞o fə mis′ tik lē) using a word or phrase in place of another that is distasteful or offensive

3 **Kyries** (kēr′ ē āz) parts of Church liturgy, often set to music

4 **deloused** (dē lousd′) rid of lice

5 **hallucinatory** (hə lo͞o′ sə nə tor′ ē) characterized by, or producing, sights or sounds that are not really present

Ann Taylor, *Red Riding,* 1982

circuit with them, creating an intimacy between ranchers who were three and four weeks' ride apart. One old-time couple I know, whose turn-of-the-century homestead was used by an outlaw gang as a relay station for stolen horses, recalls that if you were traveling, desperado or not, any lighted ranch house was a welcome sign. Even now, for someone who lives in a remote spot, arriving at a ranch or coming to town for supplies is cause for celebration. To emerge from isolation can be disorienting.[6] Everything looks bright, new, vivid. After I had been herding sheep for only three days, the sound of the camp tender's pickup flustered me. Longing for human company, I felt a foolish grin take over my face; yet I had to resist an urgent temptation to run and hide.

Things happen suddenly in Wyoming, the change of seasons and weather; for people, the violent swings in and out of isolation. But good-naturedness is

6 **disorienting** (dis ôr′ i ent′ ing) causing one to lose one's bearings

concomitant with severity.[7] Friendliness is a tradition. Strangers passing on the road wave hello. A common sight is two pickups stopped side by side far out on a range, on a dirt track winding through the sage. The drivers will share a cigarette, uncap their thermos bottles, and pass a battered cup, steaming with coffee, between windows. These meetings summon up the details of several generations, because, in Wyoming, private histories are largely public knowledge.

Because ranch work is a physical and, these days, economic strain, being "at home on the range" is a matter of vigor, self-reliance, and common sense. A person's life is not a series of dramatic events for which he or she is applauded or exiled but a slow accumulation of days, seasons, years, fleshed out by the generational weight of one's family and anchored by a land-bound sense of place.

In most parts of Wyoming, the human population is visibly outnumbered by the animal. Not far from my town of fifty, I rode into a narrow valley and startled a herd of two hundred elk. Eagles look like small people as they eat car-killed deer by the road. Antelope, moving in small, graceful bands, travel at sixty miles an hour, their mouths open as if drinking in the space.

The solitude in which westerners live makes them quiet. They telegraph thoughts and feelings by the way they tilt their heads and listen; pulling their Stetsons into a steep dive over their eyes, or pigeon-toeing one boot over the other, they lean against a fence with a fat wedge of Copenhagen beneath their lower lips and take in the whole scene. These detached looks of quiet amusement are sometimes cynical, but they can also come from a dry-eyed humility as lucid as the air is clear.

Conversation goes on in what sounds like a private code; a few phrases imply a complex of meanings. Asking directions, you get a curious list of details. While trailing sheep I was told to "ride up to that kinda upturned rock, follow the pink wash, turn left at the dump, and then you'll see the water hole." One friend told his wife on roundup to "turn at the salt lick and the dead cow," which turned out to be a scattering of bones and no salt lick at all.

Sentence structure is shortened to the skin and bones of a thought. Descriptive words are dropped, even verbs; a cowboy looking over a corral full of horses will say to a wrangler, "Which one needs rode?" People hold back their thoughts in what seems to be a dumbfounded silence, then erupt with an excoriating[8] perceptive remark. Language, so compressed, becomes metaphorical. A rancher ended a relationship with one remark: "You're a bad check," meaning bouncing in and out was intolerable, and even coming back would be no good.

What's behind this laconic[9] style is shyness. There is no vocabulary for the subject of feelings. It's not a hangdog[10] shyness, or anything coy—always there's a robust spirit in evidence behind the

---

7 **is concomitant with severity** (kon kom′ ə tənt) (sə ver′ ə tē) is related to harshness
8 **excoriating** (eks kôr′ ē āt′ ing) harsh; abrasive
9 **laconic** (lə kon′ ik) brief or succinct in speech
10 **hangdog** ashamed; cringing

restraint, as if the earth-dredging wind that pulls across Wyoming had carried its people's voices away but everything else in them had shouldered confidently into the breeze.

I've spent hours riding to sheep camp at dawn in a pickup when nothing was said; eaten meals in the cookhouse when the only words spoken were a mumbled "Thank you, ma'am" at the end of dinner. The silence is profound. Instead of talking, we seem to share one eye. Keenly observed, the world is transformed. The landscape is engorged with detail, every movement on it chillingly sharp. The air between people is charged. Days unfold, bathed in their own music. Nights become hallucinatory; dreams, prescient.[11]

---

11 **prescient** (prē′ shē ənt) able to know of things before they occur

Linking Writing and Literature

Collect Your Thoughts

Draw a Venn diagram, labeling one circle *Wyoming* and the other circle with the name of the town where you live. Jot down notes about Gretel Ehrlich's Wyoming and your town: their similarities and differences. Think about how the place where you live is similar to and different from the Wyoming that Ehrlich describes. How do you think those similarities and differences affect the way you responded to this excerpt?

Talk About Reading

Talk with other students about the excerpt from *The Solace of Open Spaces.* Assign a group leader to maintain the group's focus and a secretary to take notes. Use the questions below to guide your discussion.

1. **Connect to Your Life** What did you learn about Wyoming from reading this selection? Now reflect on important places in your life. How are your feelings about each of these places similar to or different from Ehrlich's feelings about Wyoming?
2. **Critical Thinking: Analyze** Reread the title of the book from which this selection comes. Do you think the title fits the selection? Why or why not?
3. **6+1 Trait®: Word Choice** How does Gretel Ehrlich use words to paint pictures of Wyoming? List some specific images that you found memorable.
4. **Connect to Writing** What makes a descriptive essay effective? Make a list of criteria for evaluating descriptive essays.

Write About Reading

Description of a Place Write a five- to eight-paragraph descriptive essay about a place that has had a strong impact on your life. The place may have had a positive effect, as Wyoming had on Gretel Ehrlich, or it may have had a negative effect, such as a place of tragedy or a place that evokes fear.

Focus on Word Choice Make your essay highly evocative of the place you are describing through careful choice of facts, quotes, anecdotes, and descriptive details. Use precise verbs and specific, colorful adjectives that give readers a true sense of the place.

For more information about word choice and the 6+1 Trait® model, see **Writing and Research Handbook,** pages 957–959.

6+1 Trait® is a registered trademark of Northwest Regional Educational Laboratory, which does not endorse this product.

UNIT 3 Review

Reflecting on the Unit

Summarize what you learned in this unit by answering the following questions.

1. How can you gather details for descriptive writing?
2. What are some effective ways to organize descriptive details to create effective images?
3. How can choice of verbs affect the vitality of your writing?
4. How does vantage point relate to description of a place?
5. What are some important elements in analyzing the setting of a story?

Adding to Your Portfolio

CHOOSE A SELECTION FOR YOUR PORTFOLIO Look over the descriptive writing you have done during this unit. Select a completed piece of writing to put into your portfolio. The piece you choose should show some or all of the following:

- descriptive details arranged in an effective order
- a basis in observation and note taking
- precise, vivid verbs
- the use of a clear vantage point

REFLECT ON YOUR CHOICE Attach a note to the piece you chose, explaining briefly why you chose it and what you learned from writing it.

SET GOALS How can you improve your writing? What skill will you focus on the next time you write?

Writing Across the Curriculum

MAKE A GEOGRAPHY CONNECTION Think about the description of your school that you wrote and about Gretel Ehrlich's description of Wyoming. What images spring to mind when you think about your town or county? Take notes and organize your descriptive details. Create a lead using colorful images, quotations, anecdotes, or background facts. Then write a two- or three-paragraph description of your town or county. Use topic sentences to focus the details in your paragraphs and action-packed verbs to make your vision come to life for the reader. Write legibly and check spelling for your final copy.

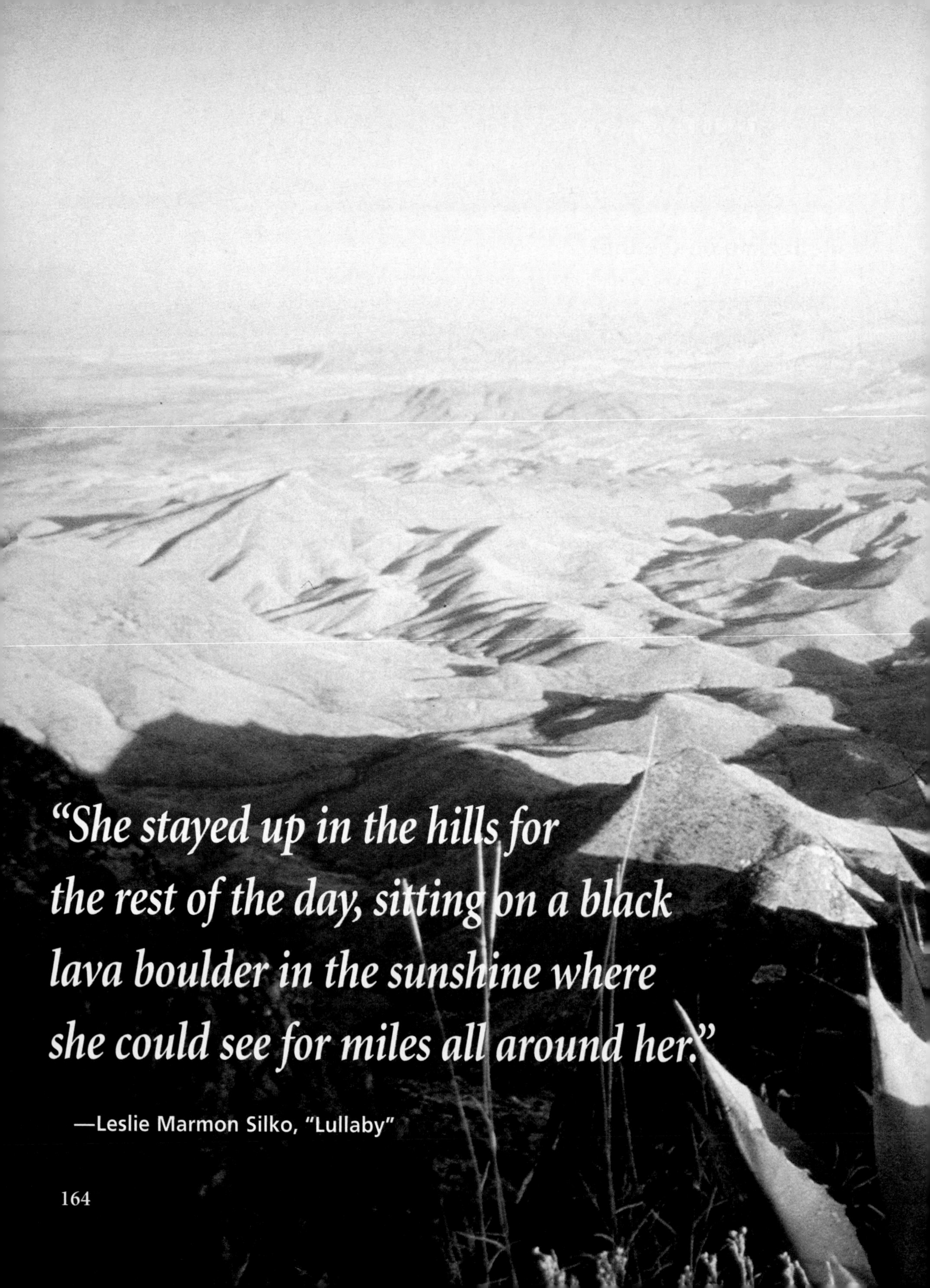

"She stayed up in the hills for the rest of the day, sitting on a black lava boulder in the sunshine where she could see for miles all around her."

—Leslie Marmon Silko, "Lullaby"

UNIT 4

Narrative Writing

Writing in the Real World

Like a story written for a book, a story created for the stage has characters, a plot, and a setting. In the case of a told story, however, character and plot are usually emphasized more than setting is. The following excerpt is from a work written for the stage by storyteller Bobby Norfolk. It is based on classical scholar Edith Hamilton's written version of the myth of Perseus.

From "Perseus and the Gorgon"

by Bobby Norfolk

Perseus stood up in the king's court and shouted: "I will go off and bring back the head of Medusa!" Everyone gasped. "The boy must be mad!" someone said. No man in his right mind would try to kill Medusa. Medusa was one of the Gorgons. She stood about eight feet tall and had scales of green hue. Her fingernails were long and sharp, and she had canine teeth that hung from her mouth—used for tearing flesh from bone. Her hair was a mass of living snakes, hissing and twirling about constantly. Medusa had a long serpentlike tail that [dragged] behind her for six feet. That was not the most hideous thing about Medusa however. She had blood-red eyes that lit up when any person looked upon her. That person would immediately turn into stone. . . .

. . . Perseus was guided by Hermes, over ocean and sea to the Terrible Sisters' Island. As fate would have it, the Terrible Sisters were all asleep when Perseus found them. In the mirror, he could see them clearly, hideous creatures with scales, and hair, a mass of twisting snakes. Perseus hovered low enough to be within striking distance of Medusa. The two messengers were with him, and gave Perseus explicit instructions on which monster was Medusa. Two of the Gorgons were immortal, [hence] only Medusa could be killed. Perseus carefully aimed his sword by way of the mirror at the Gorgon's neck, and hovering above the trio, [launched] his surprise attack.

With one fell swoop, . . . Perseus cut the head of Medusa off and it landed on the floor of the cave. He then flew down low enough to grab the head up and place it in [his] pouch. The other Gorgons were enraged upon finding their sister slain and tried to pursue the attacker, but using his cloak of invisibility, Perseus was able to avoid the Gorgons.

A Writer's Process

Prewriting

Finding the Story

Some storytellers write their own stories. Others retell narratives that they have heard or read. Storyteller Bobby Norfolk, for example, finds most of his stories in books. "I live in libraries and bookstores," he says.

After rereading Edith Hamilton's *Mythology,* Norfolk chose to retell the tale of Perseus, one of the heroes of Greek mythology, "because it was the most visual of all the myths. This one gets as close as you can to classic horror," he explains, "so I knew kids would relish it."

As told by Edith Hamilton, the story of Perseus unfolds like a fairy tale. Perseus's extraordinary adventures begin with his boast that he will slay Medusa, a monster with "snaky hair," who turns people who look at her into stone. Naturally, Perseus needs help to accomplish this task, which comes from three witches and several Greek gods. Norfolk says, "As I read the story, I visualized the three witches who had to share one eye, and Perseus's meeting with the Greek gods. I knew I could convey these vivid images to my listeners."

Drafting/Revising

Adapting the Story

To adapt Hamilton's tale for the stage, Norfolk expanded the dialogue. He also supplied details to emphasize the scene that he considered the climax of the story—when the king and his court are turned into stone all at once. In Norfolk's adaptation, a series of pantomimes shows five or six courtiers becoming petrified in turn. This technique extends the action and underlines the climactic moment.

In addition to adding dialogue and highlighting plot elements, Norfolk also enlarged upon the descriptions of several characters. Hamilton describes Medusa's locks as "snaky hair, most horrible to mortals." Norfolk's version supplies many other vivid details his listeners can visualize as he speaks.

The foundation of world literature lies in the stories of ancient mythology.

Edith Hamilton's book Mythology *inspired Norfolk to create his version of the Perseus tale.*

Revising/Editing

Fine-Tuning the Story

No matter how often storytellers practice and revise a story, storytelling is an improvisational art. As they perform, storytellers make many

Portraying various moods and gestures, Norfolk performs the tale of Perseus.

adjustments. "As I tell my story," notes Norfolk, "I look around the audience and gauge their response. Sometimes I insert a modern reference, as in describing Perseus. I say he's built like Hulk Hogan, and then I growl and flex my muscles. The first time I told this story, I made clicking noises as the three witches in turn plucked the eye out of their forehead. The kids all said 'oooh,' so I knew that part had to stay. They also loved the part where I act out Medusa. I made my ten fingers the snakes wriggling on my head. I hissed like a snake, and then I did hand movements like silhouettes on the wall, rising through the air."

Storytellers, like other kinds of writers, revise their stories numerous times. In their case, however, the audience serves as editor. "If I don't get a satisfactory reaction," states Norfolk, "I know I have to rework my story. I usually get an audience's rapt attention. If people are glancing off, I know they have mentally strayed. But if the story is hot, if the audience is very upbeat, then I know I've done the right thing. That's how I critique myself."

Publishing/Presenting

Performing the Story

The style a storyteller uses to perform a story is comparable to the style an author uses to write. Some authors write using spare prose, just as some storytellers tell their tales with little fanfare. Not Bobby Norfolk. Norfolk's dramatic storytelling style incorporates his skills in acrobatics and sound effects so that his audience can "see, hear, taste, touch, and smell the story."

Norfolk pantomimes Medusa's snaky hair.

While many storytellers publish or produce tapes of their stories, they may still continue to change them with each telling. Norfolk has written down his version of "Perseus and the Gorgon," but the storyteller says, "I've revised the story since I originally performed it. If you saw it, you would probably notice some parts that are different from my written version."

Norfolk performs at Miller Plaza in Chattanooga to celebrate the county library's summer reading program.

Examining Writing in the Real World

Analyzing the Media Connection

Discuss these questions about the excerpt on pages 166–167.

1. How does Norfolk use concrete details to create terrifying images of Medusa's fingernails and teeth?
2. What verbs does Norfolk use to describe the movements of Medusa's hair? Why might he have chosen these particular verbs?
3. What, according to Norfolk, was most hideous about Medusa?
4. What does this excerpt reveal about Perseus as a character?
5. Norfolk calls the Perseus myth "the most visual of all the [Greek] myths." Why?

Analyzing a Writer's Process

Discuss these questions about Bobby Norfolk's writing process.

1. Where does Bobby Norfolk find most of his stories?
2. What changes did Norfolk make to Hamilton's version of the myth in adapting it for storytelling?
3. Why did Norfolk make changes to Hamilton's version?
4. For what reasons does Norfolk revise his story as he tells it?
5. Describe Norfolk's style of storytelling. Why might his approach to storytelling engage an audience?

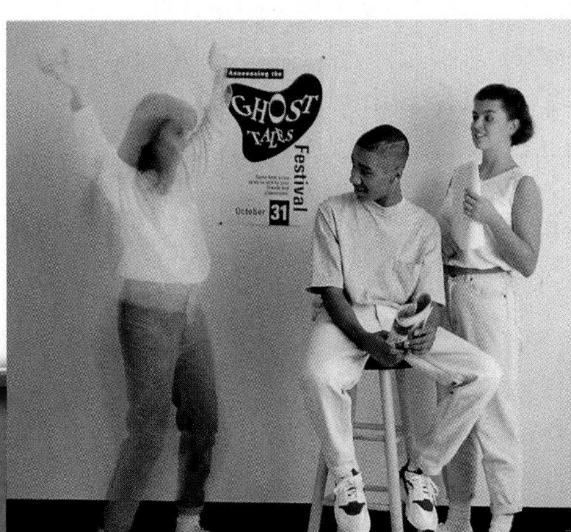

Use participles, correctly punctuated, to add lively details to a story.

A *participle* is a verb form used as an adjective. Introductory participles and participial phrases and those that are not essential to the meaning of a sentence are set off by commas.

> *Her hair was a mass of* ***living*** *snakes,* ***hissing*** *and* ***twirling*** *about constantly.*

Use each present participle below in a sentence. Insert commas where necessary.

1. screeching
2. whining
3. snaking
4. clutching
5. hammering
6. honking
7. snarling
8. glistening
9. sprinting
10. rumbling

See Lesson 12.3, pages 527–531, and Lesson 21.6, pages 743–751.

LESSON

4.1

Narrating a Personal Experience

Narrative Writing

A personal narrative allows you to focus on important events of your life and their significance. Notice how Amber Sumrall uses first person and chronological order in relating an event from early childhood.

Literature Model

When I was five we went to Yosemite for our first vacation. As my mother and father sat outside our cabin in Tuolomne Meadows reading the newspaper I played near the river with Bear, dipping his furry feet into the icy water. He was my best friend; I took him everywhere, could not fall asleep at night without him. Suddenly the current swept him out of my hands. I ran screaming and crying to my father, "Daddy, hurry, Bear's gone down the river." In a matter of seconds he'd tossed his newspaper aside and followed me to the place where I last saw Bear. Leaping from boulder to boulder he seemed to be flying down the creek, his red flannel shirt billowing like a flag, finally disappearing from view. When he returned an hour later, drenched and disheveled, he had Bear in his hands. Until that moment I had never been conscious of loving my father. I wonder if he realized then just how thoroughly Bear had taken his place. And if he knew what a disaster it would be for both of us if he'd returned empty-handed.

Amber Coverdale Sumrall, "Home Stretch"

After setting the scene, Sumrall narrates the event vividly and dramatically.

What meaning did the event have for the writer? Why does she remember it so vividly? Explain in your own words.

Find Ideas for Your Personal Narrative

A personal narrative, such as the one you just read, comes directly from the writer's experience; it tells a real-life story. It also takes readers beyond the events to the meaning of those events. Two strategies—charting and mapping—can help you find ideas for personal narratives.

Charting involves making a chart of events grouped in categories. It includes such categories as important firsts, like the first day of school or a first date; turning points, like moving or joining a team; worst times, such as a disastrous summer job or an unfriendly sleepover.

Mapping involves making a map of your life. Draw a winding path showing high and low points, turning points, roads not taken. How would your personal map compare with the one below?

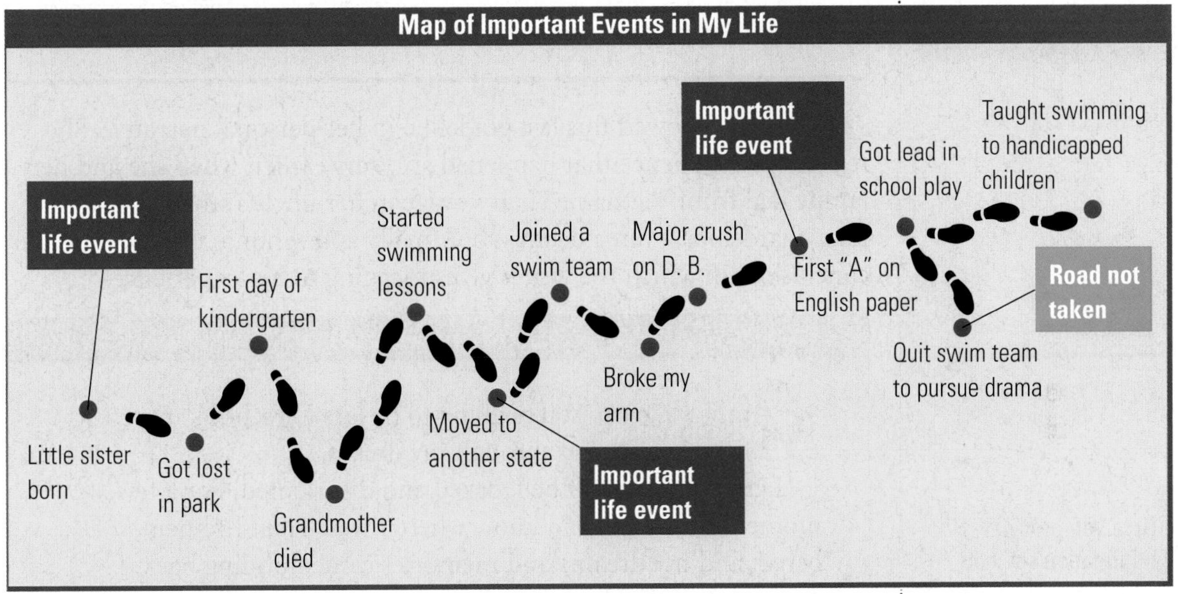

Journal Writing

Explore ideas for a personal narrative by charting and mapping. In your journal try out each strategy for about ten minutes. Compare the results. Write a few sentences about which strategy uncovered more of your memories and why.

Narrative Writing

Write Your Personal Narrative

After you find a personal experience to write about, use a prewriting strategy such as brainstorming to recall as many details as possible. Complete your prewriting by deciding what meaning your experience had for you. Then follow these guidelines to write your narrative.

Grammar Tip

When you revise your personal narrative, check for correct use of first-person pronouns. For help, see Lesson 17.1, pages 637–638.

Guidelines for Writing a Personal Narrative

1. In prewriting, list the events chronologically—the order in which they happened.
2. Maintain a first-person point of view, using the pronoun *I*.
3. Enliven your narrative with specific facts and details.
4. Use language—concrete nouns, vivid verbs, precise adjectives—to help readers share your excitement, sorrow, or anger.
5. Build a conclusion that expresses your thoughts and feelings about your experience and tell what it means to you.

Van Ngo followed this last guideline in her personal narrative. She related an experience that happened six years earlier, when she and her family fled from Vietnam. Their voyage in her uncle's small boat meant many hardships, even a death—but finally a new home. Following is her conclusion, in which the writer gives meaning to her experience.

Student Model

Mimi, wake up. You're going to be late for school," my mom's voice cut through my dream.

I got slowly out of bed, dazed and disoriented. For a few moments, I didn't even know where I was. Then I remembered, and my dreams and memories came flooding back. I remembered that long journey and the day after my cousin's death when we finally found land. We'd landed on a Malaysian island and stayed for sixteen months before being sponsored by St. Mary's Church in Ohio. The Lord had answered all our prayers!

Here Van provides information she had intentionally omitted earlier in order to focus on the sea voyage.

Six years have passed, but I still occasionally have dreams about my long journey to America. I feel so lucky and grateful that we found land and a new life in America. I learned that life should be appreciated and loved. Above all, I learned never to give up hope.

The experience has more than one meaning for Van. What does she say is the most important lesson she learned?

Van Ngo, Thomas Jefferson High School, Alexandria, Virginia

First appeared in *Merlyn's Pen: The National Magazine of Student Writing*

4.1 Writing Activities

Write a Personal Narrative

Charles Dickens began his famous novel *A Tale of Two Cities* with these words: "It was the best of times, it was the worst of times." Write a narrative about your own personal best time or worst time. Use mapping or charting to choose an event.

PURPOSE To write a personal narrative
AUDIENCE English class
LENGTH 3–4 paragraphs

WRITING RUBRICS To write an effective personal narrative, you should

- present events chronologically
- maintain a first-person point of view
- build to a conclusion that explains what the experience meant to you
- use *I* and *me* correctly

Cross-Curricular Activity

SCIENCE Read James Thurber's account of his continuing failure in biology class. Then write a short narrative about an experience you've had in a science class. Read your narrative aloud to a small group.

> I never once saw a cell through a microscope. This used to enrage my instructor. He would wander around the laboratory pleased with the progress all the students were making in drawing the involved and, so I am told, interesting structure of flower cells, until he came to me. I would just be standing there. "I can't see anything," I would say. He would begin patiently enough, explaining how anybody can see through a microscope, but he would always end up in a fury, claiming that I could too see through a microscope but just pretended that I couldn't.
>
> James Thurber, *My Life and Hard Times*

Use *I* and *me* correctly.

Personal writing involves much use of first-person pronouns. In compound constructions be particularly careful to use *I* for subjects and *me* for objects.

> *. . . followed* ***me*** *to the place where* ***I*** *last saw Bear.*

Complete each sentence below by adding *I* or *me*.

1. Chin and ____ have bicycled together before.
2. Yet this was a major trip for both him and ____.
3. Vanessa's description of a family bike trip had so impressed Chin and ____ that we decided to follow the same route.
4. My parents made my friend and ____ sandwiches for two days' lunches.
5. Since we had arranged to stay with Chin's uncle overnight, Chin and ____ planned to eat dinner and the next day's breakfast with his uncle's family.

See Lesson 17.1, pages 637–638.

Viewing and Representing

COOPERATIVE LEARNING After everyone has read an account of a humorous experience in science class, work together to create a graph or chart that shows the types of humorous events that have taken place in science classes.

LESSON

4.2

Developing a Fictional Narrative

Like any other narrative, a fictional narrative tells a story. A short story is a tightly constructed narrative built around a complication. Note the characters, the setting, the events that form the plot, and the point of view from which the story below is told.

Literature Model

They went out from the house. The sun turned the sweat of Durante to hot water and then dried his skin so that his clothes felt transparent. "Tony, I gotta be mean," said Durante. "Stand right there where I can see you. Don't try to get close. Now listen. The sheriff's gunna be along this trail sometime today, looking for me. He'll load up himself and all his gang with water out of your tanks. Then he'll follow my sign across the desert. Get me? He'll follow if he finds water on the place. But he's not gunna find water."

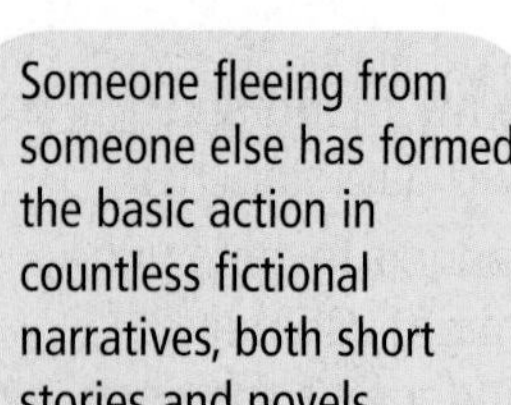

Someone fleeing from someone else has formed the basic action in countless fictional narratives, both short stories and novels.

"What you done, poor Dick?" said Tony. "Now look, I could hide you in the old wine cellar where nobody—"

"The sheriff's not gunna find water," said Durante. "It's gunna be like this."

He put the rifle to his shoulder, aimed, fired. The shot struck the base of the nearest tank, ranging down through the bottom. A semicircle of darkness began to stain the soil near the edge of the iron wall.

Tony fell on his knees. "No, no, Dick! Good Dick!" he said. "Look! All the vineyard. It will die. It will turn into old, dead wood, Dick. . . ."

Durante, ruthless and single-minded, confronts kind, trusting Tony. Through the ages, writers have told stories about the struggle between good and evil.

"Shut your face," said Durante. "Now I've started, I kinda like the job."

Max Brand, "Wine on the Desert"

The Elements of a Short Story

This lesson will focus on the short story, one kind of fictional narrative. It is created in the writer's imagination and tells about some made-up event or occurrence. In a short story, an event or series of events forms the **plot.** The events happen to **characters,** usually people. They happen in a time and place—**the setting**—and are told from a certain angle, or **point of view.** In the chart below, examine the elements that make up the short story "Wine on the Desert."

Elements of a Narrative

Element	Explanation	Example
Plot	The plot is the story's action and events. Most plots focus on a problem faced by the main character.	Durante is being pursued by the sheriff. He destroys Tony's water tanks to solve this problem.
Character	The characters of a story are the people or animals involved in the plot.	Tony and Durante are the characters. The sheriff is pursuing Durante, but doesn't appear in the story.
Setting	The setting is the time and place in which the events of a story happen. Setting can create mood or atmosphere.	The desert setting of "Wine on the Desert" creates an atmosphere of starkness and danger.
Point of View	Point of view is the particular vantage point from which the story is told.	"Wine on the Desert" is told from Durante's point of view.

Prewriting Tip

A story's point of view is usually chosen during prewriting. For more about point of view, see Lesson 2.11, on pages 90–93.

Journal Writing

Think of a short story you've read recently. In your journal summarize the plot, characters, setting, and point of view. Explain how any one of these elements contributes to the short story.

Narrative Writing

Add Other Story Elements

Plot, character, setting, and point of view provide the basic language for talking about a story. But there are other, equally important, story elements. Jon Franklin, Pulitzer-Prize-winning feature story writer, says that a story "consists of a sequence of actions that occur when a sympathetic character encounters a complicating situation that he [or she] confronts and solves." In other words, a story centers around a problem, or **complication,** and its solution, or **resolution.**

THE COMPLICATION The most attention-grabbing element of a story is the complication. The complication may be external: Leo struggles to keep his boat afloat in a storm. Or it may be internal: Lisa is torn between loyalty and honesty when her friend shoplifts. Above all, the problem must be basic to human experience, and the central character must care deeply about it.

THE RESOLUTION A story's plot moves forward in a series of actions resulting from the complication and moving toward the resolution, which is the solution to the character's problem. The resolution must grow out of the story; a character's problem can't be solved by having the roof cave in on the villain. Often, the resolution teaches the character—and the reader—a lesson about coping with the world.

News photos that present actual events can spark ideas for fictional narratives. A photo of a farm blighted by drought illustrates a problem. A photo of a daring rescue from a burning building illustrates both a problem and a solution. To a writer, the photo of a skating competition on this page could suggest a story complication; the photo of the winner could suggest a resolution.

Kristi Yamaguchi

Find a Story Idea

For many short-story writers, thinking of a good idea is the hardest part about writing. However, good ideas are everywhere, in other people's lives and in your own life. Behind almost every action in real life lies an attempt to solve a problem or conflict. The chart below shows some strategies for using real-life problems and solutions to find and evaluate story ideas.

Using Complications To . . .	
Find Story Ideas	**Evaluate Story Ideas**
• Look for external problems: Kelly's father was ill. • Look for internal problems: Ana had to make a moral decision. • Look for action: What action did Otis take to solve a problem? • Look for motivations: Why did Anita quit her job?	• Does the complication concern basic human experiences such as love, hate, loyalty, faith, sorrow, pain, survival, death? • Does the complication matter deeply to the character? • Does the complication create an opportunity for the character to learn something?

Using Resolutions To . . .	
Find Story Ideas	**Evaluate Story Ideas**
• Look for newspaper stories about achievement. • Look for changes in a person, condition, or situation. • Work backward from a resolution to a complication—if someone received an award, ask how.	• Does the resolution grow directly out of the complication? • Is the resolution the result of a character's own efforts? • Does the resolution teach readers a lesson about how to deal with life? • Does the character change or grow by resolving the complication?

Journal Writing

List four or five problems that would make interesting stories. Then list possible solutions for each problem. Ideas might come from your own experience, from photos, or from other sources.

TIME

For more about the writing process, see **TIME Facing the Blank Page,** pp. 109–119.

Narrative Writing

Develop Your Story

A short story can start with a problem or solution. You decide who the characters are, what problems they confront, how they solve them, and what they learn. Refer to the chart and the excerpt from Jeanine Skendzel's "Summer's End" for development ideas.

Drafting Tip

In drafting your story, you usually relate the events in chronological order—but not always. "Summer's End," for example, tells the central event through a flashback that "looks back" at an earlier event.

How to Write a Story	
• Create a character. • Confront the character with a problem.	• Show the character reacting to the situation. • Allow the character to resolve the problem.

Student Model

We're heading to our cottage on Scenic Lake. A dull ache pounds in my head, and my stomach churns in rhythm with the motor. I stretch out comfortably halfway across the seat until I accidentally hit my sleeping sister, Tracy. Just a few months ago we could hardly fit in this back seat: that's when my brother, Drew, was here. He would take up half the seat alone. The pain stabs me and the memories quickly flood back.

How does Skendzel prepare you in this paragraph for the problem that is the basis of her story's plot?

We're diving for Drew's waterproof wristwatch as we do every year. Drew or I throw the watch as far as possible and the other person dives to find it. Since Drew is seventeen and I'm only fourteen, he holds an unfair advantage, but I never complain. This time it's my turn to throw it. He has already beaten me three times today by thirty seconds each, so this particular time I secretly throw the watch behind me. Drew bobs up and down the dock, searching for a glint of silver in the hot summer sun.

What details demonstrate that Skendzel is interested not only in the actions and events but also in how actions and events affect her characters?

"Come on, Ben! What'd ya do with it?" he frustratedly whines. I foolishly grin back, pleased that I have finally outwitted him at something. Grabbing my arm, he strongly twists it into a horrible snake bite.

"Tell me, Ben, or you know what's coming," he whispers, checking for our parents. We glare at each other, flashing our ugliest poses. Finally, we break down laughing and I point happily toward the watch.

"You little . . . " is all I hear before he sprints off the dock and pulls into a flawless dive.

Jeanine Skendzel, Traverse City Senior High School, Traverse City, Michigan. First appeared in *Merlyn's Pen: The National Magazine of Student Writing*

4.2 Writing Activities

Write the Solution for a Story Problem

In his short story "The Lady, or the Tiger?" Frank Stockton presents the following unresolved complication:

A young man dared to love a princess. He was brought to an arena, where he must open one of two identical doors. Behind one, a fierce, hungry tiger was waiting; behind the other, a beautiful lady—not the princess—was waiting to marry him.

Write an ending to the story.

PURPOSE To create a story resolution
AUDIENCE Your English class
LENGTH 1 paragraph

WRITING RUBRICS To write a dramatic solution for a story problem, you should

- clearly identify and describe the characters and their actions
- resolve the conflict
- use correct spelling and grammar

José Gamarra, *Five Centuries Later,* 1986

Cross-Curricular Activity

FINE ART Freewrite about the scene in the painting. Consider the plants, people, water, and lighting. Jot down story ideas that the painting suggests. Choose one idea, and plan a short story about it.

Listening and Speaking

COOPERATIVE LEARNING Work together with a partner to create a dramatic telling of the story you invented about the painting. Make sure that your story contains a problem and a possible solution that would be appropriate for your audience.

Grammar Link

Make verbs agree with compound subjects.

When you have a compound subject joined by *or* or *nor* or *either . . . or* or *neither . . . nor,* the verb always agrees with the subject nearer the verb.

Drew or I ***throw*** *the watch . . . .*

Choose the correct form of the verb for each sentence below.

1. Fur or feathers (covers/cover) many living creatures.
2. Neither people nor a bird (is/are) cold-blooded.
3. Either feathers or hair (keeps/keep) the body warm.
4. However, neither a fur coat nor feathers nor warm blood alone (identifies/identify) a mammal.

See Lesson 16.5, page 620.

LESSON 4.3

Organizing a Fictional Narrative

After you've identified your story idea, a main character, and a problem, you're ready to plan your story. Creating a story outline or diagram can help you organize the events for your plot.

Plan Your Story

Look at the outline for a story called "Same Difference," written by student Yannie ten Broeke. Note how it orders the events of the plot.

Outline for a Story	
1. Introduce a main character.	Mrs. Kreager, a poor, elderly woman
2. Introduce a problem (complication, conflict).	Mrs. Kreager, who lives alone in a city apartment, walks to the park on her birthday to feed the pigeons.
3. List the actions and events (in chronological order, the order in which they happen).	1. Mrs. Kreager gathers bread crumbs in a small bag. 2. She goes to the park to feed the pigeons. 3. She tries to feed Henry, her pet pigeon.
4. Tell the climax (the point of highest tension in the story).	When Sam, a younger pigeon, keeps Henry from eating, Mrs. Kreager accidentally hits Henry. Henry will never recover.
5. Suggest the resolution (how the problem is solved or not solved).	Mrs. Kreager leaves the park, never to return.

With the elements shown in the outline, Yannie ten Broeke has forged a moving story that focuses on cheerful, plucky Mrs. Kreager, whose one pleasure is feeding pigeons in the park. Read from her story's ending.

Student Model

Henry fell over on his side, stunned, and made no attempt to get to his feet. Mrs. Kreager's eyes opened wide with horror, and her hands covered her mouth. She lurched with such quickness that all the pigeons scattered, leaving an immobile Henry. She put him in her hands, and although he was not dead, it seemed he had given up life. . . .

She stood up, still clutching the warm little body, and began to walk home, leaving the bag on the bench to be thrown away by the Park Service and the stick to be found by some child in search of an imaginary Excalibur. She knew she would not be back.

Yannie ten Broeke, Rutgers Preparatory School, Somerset, New Jersey. First appeared in *Merlyn's Pen: The National Magazine of Student Writing*

Do you think the resolution solves the problem? Why or why not?

Narrative Writing

A plot diagram like the one below can be a handy tool to help you visualize the structure of the story you will write. Notice how the diagram reflects the basic structure of a story.

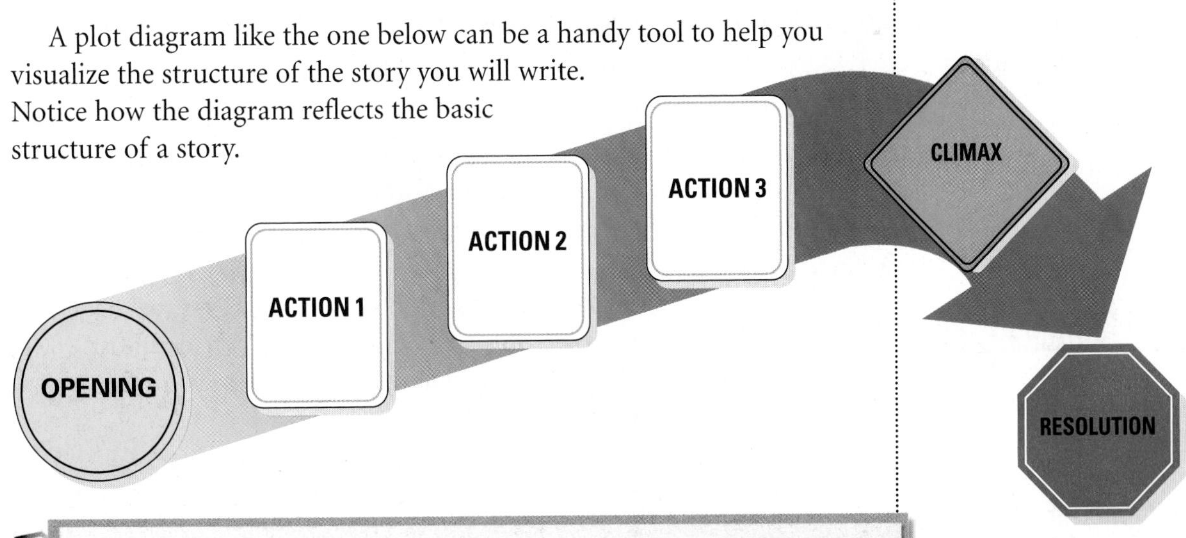

Journal Writing

Use the diagram above to examine a short story you've read. List the main character, the complication, the main events, the climax, and the resolution.

Draft Your Opening

Once you have a story outline, your next step is to draft your opening. Does the story opening below snag your interest? If so, how?

What main character does the writer introduce in his opening?

Notice how the opening also establishes a setting—both time and place. What details show that the day begins as an average one for Kevin?

What problem or complication does the writer introduce?

Literature Model

I reached over and shut off the insistent buzzing of my bedside alarm clock. I sat up, swung my feet over the edge of the bed, and felt for my slippers on the floor. Yawning, I walked toward the bathroom. As I walked by the corner of my room, where my computer table was set up, I pressed the on button, slid a diskette into the floppy drive, then went to brush my teeth. By the time I got back, the computer's screen was glowing greenly, displaying the message: *Good Morning, Kevin.*

I sat down before the computer table, addressed the keyboard and typed: *Good Morning, Louis.* The computer immediately began to whirr and promptly displayed a list of items on its green screen.

Today is Monday, April 22, the 113th day of the year. There are 254 days remaining. Your 14th birthday is five days from this date.

Math test today, 4th Period.

Your history project is due today. Do you wish print-out: Y/N?

I punched the letter *Y* on the keyboard and flipped on the switch to the computer's printer. At once the printer sprang to life and began *eeek*ing out page one. I went downstairs to breakfast. . . .

When I returned to my room to shower and dress for the day, my history project was already printed out. I had almost walked by Louis, when I noticed there was a message on the screen. It wasn't the usual:

Printout completed. Do you wish to continue: Y/N?

Underneath the printout question were two lines:

When are you going to get me my voice module, Kevin?

I blinked. It couldn't be. There was nothing in Louis's basic programming that would allow for a question like this.

T. Ernesto Bethancourt, "User Friendly"

Grammar Tip

"User Friendly" is told from a first-person point of view, with Kevin the *I* of the story. When drafting, be careful to maintain your point of view and not to shift pronouns. See Lesson 17.5, pages 644–648.

4.3 Writing Activities

Write a Story Opening

Plan an original short story for your school's literary magazine based on the painting shown here. Write a plot diagram and the opening for the story you will submit.

Richard Bosman, *Flight*, 1981–82

PURPOSE To write a story opening that introduces character, setting, and complication

AUDIENCE Readers of the school literary magazine

LENGTH 3–4 paragraphs

WRITING RUBRICS To write an effective plot diagram and story opening, you should

- chart the conflict, action, climax, and resolution of the plot
- draft your opening, making sure to establish character, setting, point of view, and conflict
- use correct spelling and grammar

Using Computers

Use your computer's drawing software to create the plot diagram for your story. Make sure to include the conflict, action, climax, and resolution.

Listening and Speaking

COOPERATIVE LEARNING In a small group, find a short story in your literature book or another source. After reading the story, discuss the resolution and possible alternative resolutions. Which resolution seems most satisfying? Why?

Grammar Link

Use commas to separate three or more items in a series.

Note how Bethancourt uses commas to separate parts of a series in this sentence from "User Friendly."

> *I sat up, swung my feet over the edge of the bed, and felt for my slippers on the floor.*

Rewrite the following sentences, inserting commas as necessary.

1. My little brother scowled stamped his right foot stuck out his lower lip and announced that he was mad.
2. His face was pale wrinkled and angry.
3. He cast furious glances at me at our mother and toward the cat.
4. I bristled my mother looked puzzled and the cat stalked away.
5. "I want milk bread jelly and peanut butter right now," announced the little tyrant.

See Lesson 21.6, pages 743–751.

LESSON

4.4 Writing Dialogue

It's about time they let us speak for ourselves! If I hear myself described one more time as a puffed-up, blustering fool, I'll . . .

At least they gave you a personality. I'm portrayed so vaguely that if I ever get to open my mouth, I won't know what to say, much less how to say it.

A dialogue is a conversation between two or more persons. Note how Mary Lavin uses dialogue in the model below to bring characters and events to life.

Literature Model

A neighbor passed.

"Waiting for Packy?" said the neighbor, pleasantly, and he stood for a minute to take off his hat and wipe the sweat of the day from his face. He was an old man.

"It's a hot day!" he said. "It will be a hard push for Packy on that battered old bike of his. I wouldn't like to have to face into four miles on a day like this!"

"Packy would travel three times that distance if there was a book at the other end of the road!" said the widow, with the pride of those who cannot read more than a line or two without wearying.

The minutes went by slowly. The widow kept looking up at the sun.

"I suppose the heat is better than the rain!" she said, at last. "The heat can do a lot of harm too, though," said the neighbor, absent-mindedly, as he pulled a long blade of grass from between the stones of the wall and began to chew the end of it. "You could get sunstroke on a day like this!" He looked up at the sun. "The sun is a terror," he said. "It could cause you to drop down dead like a stone!"

The widow strained out further over the gate. She looked up the hill in the direction of the town.

How does the dialogue create a vivid sense of time and place?

The dialogue shows the widow's deep pride in Packy.

The dialogue contains a subtle foreshadowing, or hint of possible trouble to come. What is it?

Where does the dialogue contain another hint of possible danger?

"He will have a good cool breeze on his face coming down the hill, at any rate," she said.

The man looked up the hill. "That's true. On the hottest day of the year you would get a cool breeze coming down that hill on a bicycle. You would feel the air streaming past your cheeks like silk. And in the winter it's like two knives flashing to either side of you, and peeling off your skin like you'd peel the bark off a sally-rod [willow twig]." He chewed the grass meditatively. "That must be one of the steepest hills in Ireland," he said. "That hill is a hill worthy of the name of a hill." He took the grass out of his mouth. "It's my belief," he said, earnestly looking at the widow—"it's my belief that that hill is to be found marked with a name in the Ordnance Survey map!"

"If that's the case," said the widow, "Packy will be able to tell you all about it. When it isn't a book he has in his hand it's a map."

"Is that so?" said the man. "That's interesting. A map is a great thing. A map is not an ordinary thing. It isn't everyone can make out a map."

The widow wasn't listening.

"I think I see Packy!" she said, and she opened the gate and stepped out into the roadway.

Mary Lavin, "The Story of the Widow's Son"

The dialogue adds liveliness and realism. Even this unnamed old man has a personality—warm, friendly, interested in people and places.

How does this part of the dialogue advance the plot?

Narrative Writing

Use Dialogue to Advance Your Story

Good dialogue can serve many purposes in a narrative. Mary Lavin uses it to create a sense of time and place, tell about character, foreshadow possible trouble, and move the plot along. When you write a story, you can use dialogue for all these purposes—and more.

Revising Tip

In revising, read your dialogue aloud to test whether it sounds like real conversation. Keep revising and rereading until your characters' words sound right.

Journal Writing

Find and examine some dialogue in a novel or short story. Explore the purposes of the dialogue by writing what it reveals about the setting, the characters, or the plot.

Write Dialogue

Essentially, a dialogue is a series of direct quotations. A direct quotation is a character's own words enclosed in quotation marks. An indirect quotation is a report of what someone said. Compare the following quotations.

Direct quotation: "I think I see Packy!" she said.
Indirect quotation: The widow said that she thought she saw Packy.

In a dialogue, the words that identify the speaker, such as "said the widow," are called tag lines. Without tag lines, readers might have trouble figuring out who is saying what. Too few tag lines can make a dialogue confusing; too many tag lines can make it choppy.

Mary Lavin uses the verb *said* eleven times in the passage you read. You might think that the story would be more interesting if she had substituted synonyms such as *replied* and *remarked.* However, Lavin chose her verbs carefully. Later, to emphasize the difference in the widow's tone of voice, she used vivid verbs in her tag lines:

> "He's only in a weakness!" *screamed* the widow. . . . "Get a doctor!" she *cried.*

Grammar Tip

If you need to review the mechanics of writing dialogue, see Lesson 21.9, pages 755–757.

In addition to tag lines, your dialogue can include descriptions of characters' facial expressions, tone of voice, gestures, and mannerisms. Here is an example:

> "The heat can do a lot of harm too, though," said the neighbor, absent-mindedly, as he pulled a long blade of grass from between the stones of the wall and began to chew the end of it.

The following guidelines will help you write effective dialogue in your fictional narratives.

Guidelines for Writing Dialogue

1. Make sure your dialogue has a purpose: to reveal character, to highlight the relationships between characters, to intensify the action, to add suspense, or a combination.
2. Write dialogue in words and phrases appropriate to each character. Consider the character's age, personality, and educational background. Consider the character's emotional state.
3. Use dialogue to reveal character and personality. What are this character's beliefs? Desires? Fears? Is the character shy? Honest? Nervous? Ignorant? Boastful?
4. Make your dialogue sound like real conversation by using interruptions and pauses.
5. Make your dialogue easy to follow by using clear tag lines and correct paragraphing and punctuation.

4.4 Writing Activities

Write a Dialogue

Recall an interesting conversation you heard or took part in. Then write a fictional dialogue based on what you remember.

PURPOSE To create a dialogue
AUDIENCE Your teacher and classmates
LENGTH 1-2 pages

WRITING RUBRICS To write realistic dialogue, you should

- reveal something about your speakers
- use appropriate words and phrases for each speaker
- use clear tag lines and correct paragraphing, punctuation, and capitalization

Listening and Speaking

With a partner, write a short dramatic scene based on this painting. Rehearse your dialogue and then present it to your class.

Gilberto Ruiz, *The Good News Call,* 1986

Viewing and Representing

COOPERATIVE LEARNING In a group of four, make a video of one of the dialogues you wrote for the activities on this page. One person should direct the production, one person should operate the camera, and the other two should act out the dialogue. Share your completed video with the class.

Grammar Link

Capitalize and punctuate direct and indirect quotations correctly.

Reread Mary Lavin's dialogue and page 186. Then rewrite the following sentences correctly. Write *correct* for any sentence that needs no changes.

1. Abraham Lincoln gave a speech in which he said the ballot is stronger than the bullet.
2. In a later speech, Lincoln said that nobody had ever expected him to be President.
3. I feel somewhat like the boy in Kentucky who stubbed his toe while running to see his sweetheart Lincoln replied in answer to a question in 1862. The boy said he was too big to cry, and far too badly hurt to laugh.
4. These words of Lincoln are in John Bartlett's *Familiar Quotations* my teacher said. do you know what that book is?
5. I've heard of it I admitted but I don't know whether I've ever seen it.

See Lesson 20.1, pages 713–714 and 21.9, pages 755–757.

LESSON

4.5

Theme and Anecdote

An anecdote is a brief story that makes a point. The theme of a work is its main idea or underlying message. Look for the point that Will Steger makes with this anecdote.

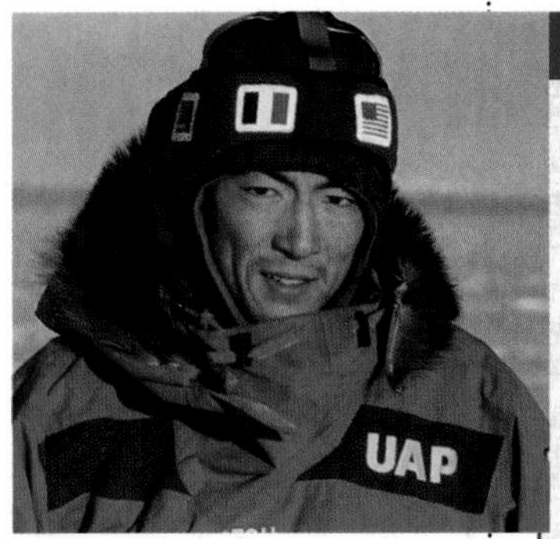

How is this anecdote a story within a story? Why do you think Steger decided to use it as his introduction?

Why does Steger use a direct quotation in his anecdote? Why not just say "I called Keizo by name"?

Literature Model

Tears of frustration and despair blinded me more than the stinging wind or snow. For 24 hours a storm had pinned us in our camp only 16 miles from our goal—the far edge of Antarctica. We had come too far, endured too much suffering, to lose a man now, I thought bitterly. We had to find him.

We clung to a long rope as we searched; the end was tied to a sled to keep us from straying, as he had, into the raging whiteout. "Keizo!" I yelled into the blizzard. "Keizo! . . . Keizo!"

Faintly I heard the others shouting his name as they too groped in a tethered arc around the tents and sleds. Our Japanese teammate, Keizo Funatsu—gentle, compassionate Keizo—had crawled out of his tent at 4:30 the afternoon before to check on his dogs. By six we knew he was lost. We searched into the night, calling and listening, flashlight beams futile against the swirling snow.

Now in the first faint wash of daylight we were searching again.

It was unthinkable that one of us could be gone after what we had come through together for nearly seven months: Trudging, antlike, across 3,700 miles of brutal terrain, from sea level to lonely elevations above 11,000 feet . . . battered for weeks by continuous storms . . . winds that howled at 90 miles an hour.

We had challenged a foreign place, a place not meant for warm-blooded animals. Antarctica's terrible interior tries to turn men into its own image—frozen. Yet this endurance test had forged a deep and permanent bond among us: six dissimilar men from six nations, attempting to complete the first crossing of the continent by dogsled.

I envisioned the worst—carrying Keizo these last few miles wrapped in the flag of his homeland—and my stomach knotted in anguish. "Keizo!" I bellowed, over and over again.

I couldn't believe it when I glimpsed him—a wraith emerging from the driving curtain of snow. "I am alive," he said. In seconds we were clutching each other. Both of us were crying.

Keizo is a skilled survivor. Once lost, he scraped a shallow trench with pliers, the only tool he had, and curled up in it like a sled dog, allowing the blizzard to bury him. And there, with Zen-like calm, he waited for 13 hours, until he heard our calls.

It was then—but only then—that I was certain our expedition was a success.

Will Steger, "Six Across Antarctica," *National Geographic*

How does this last sentence suggest the point of the anecdote?

Narrative Writing

Understand the Theme

Steger's anecdote forcefully introduces his article. It also illustrates his theme, or main idea: Six men from dissimilar cultural backgrounds could work together under some of the cruelest conditions on the planet.

The chart below explains some of the characteristics of a theme. Notice that it discusses themes in fiction as well as nonfiction.

The Characteristics of a Theme

A theme is . . .	A theme is not . . .
• A theme is a general insight about life or human nature. • In nonfiction, a theme is often stated, as in Steger's article. • In fiction, a theme is usually implied, as in a story in which the events show how love overcomes prejudice.	• A theme is not the topic or subject of the work. • A theme is not a summary of a plot or story line. • A theme is not a moral or lesson about life, though it may suggest one.

Journal Writing

Find a theme in something you have written. In your journal express the theme as a general statement about life or human nature.

Use Anecdotes to Support the Theme

An anecdote in fiction is a story within a story. Claire Edwards has included the following anecdote in "Kay," a fictional story about the death of the narrator's best friend, an event that happened when both girls were teenagers. Underlying Edwards's story is a theme about a strong friendship that the narrator believes will endure forever. Notice how this anecdote supports the theme.

This anecdote has all the elements of any narrative. Can you identify the characters, the setting, the complication, and the resolution?

This last sentence expresses the point of the anecdote. How does the anecdote support the theme of the whole story?

Student Model

Kay and I met on the first day of third grade. Fate brought us together—literally! We collided on the front steps of our school building, and I ended up dropping all my new books. A freckled face peered into mine and gasped, "Oh, I'm sorry! Would you believe this is the second time today I've bumped into someone? I'm not always this clumsy, but I woke up late, and my mom made me eat all my breakfast, bite by bite. It took such a long time, and I don't think I'm quite fully awake yet. By the way, my name's Katherine Montgomery, but all my friends call me Kay." It was only a matter of weeks before Kay and I were inseparable.

Claire Edwards, New Trier East Township High School, Winnetka, Illinois. First appeared in *Merlyn's Pen: The National Magazine of Student Writing*

Revising Tip

In revising, make your anecdote short and lively. Cut out unnecessary details, but keep those that make your writing interesting. A peer reviewer can help you make cuts.

When writing either nonfiction or fiction, think of anecdotes you might use to support your theme. For example, a nonfiction article about the importance of animals to children could include an anecdote about the writer's own pet. A fiction story about a teenager who works in a restaurant could include a humorous anecdote showing how his job teaches him valuable lessons about people. Once you have an idea for an anecdote, answer the following questions to plan it.

Prewriting Your Anecdote

- What is the setting?
- Who are the characters?
- What problem, challenge, or conflict do they face?
- How is the problem solved?
- What's the point?

4.5 Writing Activities

Write an Anecdote

Adults often tell young children stories about lessons learned through experience. These stories are anecdotes. Write an anecdote for young children based on your own experience.

PURPOSE To write an anecdote
AUDIENCE Young children
LENGTH 4-6 paragraphs

WRITING RUBRICS To write a meaningful anecdote, you should

- illustrate a theme or lesson
- reveal the setting, characters, conflict, and resolution
- make the point of your anecdote clear
- ensure that your word choice is appropriate for a young audience

Using Computers

Anecdotes, like jokes, benefit in special ways from revision, since they succeed best when they are brief and lively, saying much in little space. Use the copy feature of your word-processing program to help you revise your anecdotes. Make several copies of the original, and revise each one, creating different versions. Compare them, and select the best version. If you're unsure which is really your best, print out two you like, and ask a peer reviewer to read and respond to them.

Listening and Speaking

After you have written your anecdote, practice reading it aloud before presenting it to the class. Decide how you will tell the story. Use storytelling techniques to make your anecdote more interesting. After all the presentations, the class should create a questionnaire to elicit students' views on the characteristics of successful presentations.

Use and punctuate appositives and appositive phrases correctly.

An *appositive* is a noun or pronoun placed next to another noun or pronoun to provide additional information. An *appositive phrase* is an appositive plus any words that modify it.

Add at least one appositive or appositive phrase to each sentence below. Use commas as needed.

1. In 1832, Charles Darwin sailed from England on the HMS *Beagle.*
2. Darwin collected 68 different species of small beetles in a forest outside Rio de Janeiro.
3. During the next three years, the *Beagle* sailed south to round Cape Horn and north again up the coast of Chile.
4. The expedition eventually came to the Galápagos Islands where Darwin made more studies of wildlife.
5. There Darwin found cormorants, iguanas, and tortoises that were very different from those on the mainland.

See Lesson 12.2, pages 525–526.

Narrative Writing

LESSON 4.6

WRITING ABOUT LITERATURE

The Plot Summary

Narrative Writing

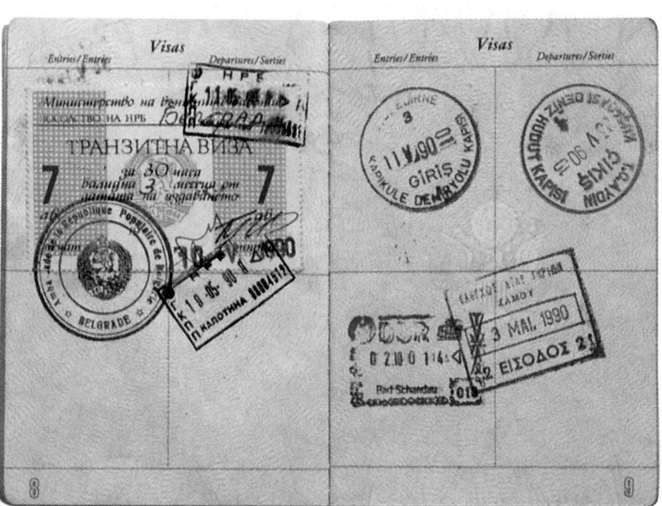

A plot summary is a shortened version of a story built around the main character's problem. Like a traveler's passport, it shows important stopping points but does not tell whether the trip was enjoyable. As you read the plot summary of "The Most Dangerous Game," note how it summarizes the narrative elements of the story.

Literature Model

The short story "The Most Dangerous Game," by Richard Connell, pits two great hunters against each other. Rainsford, the main character, falls from a yacht and swims to an island owned by General Zaroff. We as readers see the events through Rainsford's eyes. Zaroff, bored with hunting animals, hunts men instead. Rainsford's horror grows as he finds himself the unwilling quarry in Zaroff's deadly game.

According to the rules of that game, Rainsford must elude his foe for three days or be killed. He begins his flight in panic, then gathers his wits and draws on his vast knowledge of hunting. Rainsford knows terror when Zaroff tracks his intricate trail but deliberately saves him for another day's sport. The next day, Rainsford escapes death and wins his

What elements of the plot does the summary introduce in the first paragraph?

foe's respect by building ingenious traps that wound Zaroff and kill one of his dogs. The third day, Zaroff pursues him with a pack of ferocious dogs led by his savage servant, Ivan. Rainsford's last trap misses its intended victim but kills the servant. Finally, knowing he cannot outrun the dogs, Rainsford leaps into the sea.

The climax comes later that night. Retiring to his bedroom, Zaroff finds himself face to face with Rainsford, who swam across the cove to the chateau. Surprised, the general congratulates Rainsford for winning the game. Rainsford lets his enemy know the game isn't over, and both men realize that the loser will be fed to the dogs. We know who that is in the last sentence, when Rainsford decides that he "never slept in a better bed."

Notice that the second paragraph sums up the main events that build suspense.

What is the writer's purpose in this third paragraph?

Narrative Writing

Why Write a Plot Summary?

A plot summary is intended to sum up the main events in a story—specifically, the main character's problem and how it is resolved. It does not include personal opinion or evaluation.

Plot summaries can be valuable in a number of ways. Read the chart for ideas of how to use summaries.

Uses of a Plot Summary
• Preparing a plot summary will help you recognize the story line and other narrative elements.
• Writing the summary will help you clarify your understanding of action, complication, resolution, and theme.
• Reading the plot summary later will help you review for a test.

Journal Writing

Think of a movie or TV program you saw recently. How would you summarize it in two or three sentences for a friend? Write your summary in your journal.

Write a Plot Summary

As with most writing you do, prewriting is crucial to preparing a plot summary. The first step is to read the work carefully. As you read, take notes regarding the elements listed in the chart below. Most plot summaries, including both of the models in this lesson, are organized as shown. Notice the focus on the main character's problem.

Paragraph 1
List the title, author, main character(s), setting, and point of view. Then describe the main character's problem.

→

Paragraph 2
Explain the main events in chronological order (the order in which they happen).

→

Paragraph 3
Describe the climax or turning point, when readers know how the problem will be solved and how the story ends.

Literary terms, such as *complication* and *climax,* can help you summarize the story line, but their use isn't necessary. In her plot summary below, Laurie Valle used very literary terms.

Revising Tip

In revising your plot summary, be sure to verify your facts and organization against the original work.

Student Model

The Story of an Hour" by Kate Chopin begins with a delicate situation. Louise Mallard, who has a serious heart condition, must be told that her husband is dead. Her sister Josephine and her husband's friend Richards have come to her home, where they gently break the news of the tragic railroad accident.

Louise retires to her bedroom, overcome with weeping. Alone, she thinks about the accident and the effect it will have on her life. The reader learns that she did not love her husband. She feels no grief at his death but rather, exultation. Now she is free, able to run her own life.

Then Brently Mallard walks through the door unscathed. He was not on the train at all and was, in fact, very far from the accident. The irony of the situation is in the way Louise Mallard dies. The doctor says her sudden death is from "heart disease—joy that kills." But the reader knows it isn't joy that kills Louise Mallard. Instead, seeing her husband alive has destroyed her new sense of freedom, killing her joy and causing her death.

Laurie Valle, Edison High School, Edison, New Jersey

Although the plot summary is written in Valle's own words, it includes this brief quotation. Why did Valle choose to use these words from the story?

How does Mrs. Mallard's story illustrate irony, a contrast between what appears to be true and what really is true?

4.6 Writing Activities

Write a Plot Summary

Summarize the plot of a short story you read or a movie you saw recently.

PURPOSE To summarize a short story or movie
AUDIENCE Your classmates
LENGTH 3 paragraphs

WRITING RUBRICS To write an effective plot summary, you should

- describe setting, point of view, and the main character's conflict
- explain the important events up through the climax and resolution
- exclude personal opinions
- use verbs in the present tense

Cross-Curricular Activity

WORLD HISTORY History is usually told as a narrative, with the events related in chronological order. Summarizing requires careful reading, so a useful technique for studying history is to summarize the story line of a chapter or unit in your history text. Try it. Write a one- to two-page summary of the material that will be covered on your next history test.

Viewing and Representing

CREATING AN AD Use one of the plot summaries you wrote to create a print ad for the work. Make sure that your ad is visually appealing. Illustrate your print ad and display it in the classroom.

Avoid unnecessary shifts in verb tenses.

When summarizing or analyzing literature, use verbs in the present tense. Note how Laurie Valle uses the present tense when speaking of Louise Mallard.

Louise Mallard . . . ***has*** *a serious heart condition.*

Then note the verbs in the rest of Valle's plot summary.

Revise the plot summary below, correcting shifts from the present tense.

1. In "The Most Dangerous Game," General Zaroff played a deadly game in which he hunts people, not animals.
2. Rainsford, the main character, tried to escape from Zaroff, who hunted him.
3. Although Zaroff finds Rainsford on the first day, Rainsford is not killed because Zaroff wanted to track him for one more day.
4. On the second day Rainsford fought back and made a clever trap, which kills one of Zaroff's tracking dogs.
5. On the final day of the hunt, Rainsford escaped from the dogs and jumps into the sea.
6. He will be the victor, though, because he will become the hunter and confront Zaroff when he least expected it.

See Lesson 15.6, pages 598–599.

LESSON 4.7

WRITING ABOUT LITERATURE

Analyzing Conflict

One way to understand a story is to examine its conflict, or the struggle between opposing forces. Read the analysis below of W.W. Jacobs's "The Monkey's Paw." Who or what are the opposing forces in the conflict?

Edvard Munch, The Scream, 1893

The analysis begins with this thesis sentence, which is a statement about the nature of the conflict.

Literature Model

In the short story "The Monkey's Paw," members of an ordinary family come into conflict with fate. The family suffers because they try to change their lives by using the magic in the monkey's paw.

Mr. White is intrigued with magic and the unknown, so he rescues the paw when his guest, Morris, throws it into the fire. Later, Mr. White's first wish is granted. When the Whites hear of their son's death, they realize the awful truth of the fakir's[1] words: "that fate ruled people's lives, and that those who interfered with it did so to their sorrow."

As readers, we know that the monkey's paw always brings tragedy. Before the action of the story, the paw had caused one death and left Morris with terrible memories. Still, much of our interest in this story is created by its suspense. We don't know what the tragedy will be, or how it will happen, and we care about this family. We identify with Mrs. White in her desire to get her son back, but we know the monkey's paw can bring nothing good, even if he returns. In the end, the Whites have learned a great deal about fate, but with their knowledge has come the sorrow that the fakir had promised.

1 fakir: (fə kir′) a Hindu or Muslim holy man

According to the analysis, readers can predict which side of this conflict will win. What causes the suspense that makes readers want to read on?

Recognize Conflict

Most stories focus on a complication, a problem in the main characters' lives. Usually, the complication is a conflict, a struggle between opposing forces. The conflict can be important (two soldiers fight to the death) or petty (a sister and brother argue over their inheritance). The conflict can be external (a family fight to save their house from a flood) or internal (a girl is torn between love for her mother and desire for independence). Conflict engages readers by creating suspense, a desire to find out what happens. The suspense ends when the conflict is resolved and readers know which opposing force will prevail.

Near the story's beginning, the conflict motivates the characters, leading them to act. By the story's end, the characters have usually learned something significant. The chart below gives examples of conflicts found in fiction.

Revising Tip

In prewriting a conflict analysis, you may find it helpful to discuss the story with another person who has read it.

Conflicts in Fiction

Kind	Example	Plot
Person vs. Person	"The Most Dangerous Game" by Richard Connell	Rainsford, who has become General Zaroff's unwilling prey, must elude his hunter for three days or be killed.
Person vs. Nature	"To Build a Fire" by Jack London	A man struggles to keep from freezing to death in the extreme cold of winter in the Klondike region of western Canada.
Person vs. Society	"The Lottery" by Shirley Jackson	A woman is selected by lot for death by stoning in a ritual mandated and carried out by the community.
Person vs. Self	"Through the Tunnel" by Doris Lessing	A boy struggles to overcome his fear of drowning in order to satisfy his desire to swim through an underwater tunnel.
Person vs. Machine	"Trucks" by Stephen King	People who are being held hostage by trucks must decide whether to meet the trucks' demands.
Person vs. the Supernatural	*The Odyssey* by Homer	Odysseus is delayed in his return to Ithaca by various characters, including the sea god Poseidon.

Journal Writing

Why do you think conflict is an element of most good fiction? Is it because readers can identify with conflicts they have experienced? Is it because the resolution of conflict gives meaning to events? Explore these questions in your journal.

Narrative Writing

Grammar Tip

When you revise your analysis, you might discover places to use direct quotations to support your ideas. For information about punctuating direct quotations, see Lesson 21.9, pages 755–757.

Write About Conflict

As you prepare to write a conflict analysis, first pinpoint the conflict. Use the questions in the chart below to help you plan your analysis.

Questions About Conflict

1. What are the opposing forces in the conflict?
2. Is the conflict external, internal, or both?
3. How does the writer create and maintain interest in the conflict?
4. How is the conflict resolved?
5. What new understanding do the characters reach as a result of the conflict and its resolution? What new understanding do readers discover?
6. How does the conflict help the author develop the story's theme?

A conflict analysis is not a plot summary. Refer to the plot only as it relates to the conflict, as Cary Chaffee does in the analysis below.

What is the thesis statement in Chaffee's analysis, and what is its purpose?

Why do you think the writer chose to quote from the story? What do the direct quotations add to her analysis?

Student Model

In the short story "Eveline," from James Joyce's *Dubliners,* the conflict is internal; it is Eveline versus herself. Eveline's dilemma—whether to stay in an unhappy home or seize an opportunity to escape to another place and a better life—is with herself alone. It is a conflict that many readers will recognize. Like many people, Eveline must choose between security and happiness.

Eveline lives a terrible life. On her job she is unappreciated, and in her home she is little more than a household drudge. Her father, a drunkard, has recently begun to threaten her with the same kind of violence he once used on her brothers. Now she has a chance to escape. "Why should she be unhappy? She had a right to happiness."

Eveline realizes, though, that no matter how bad things are, she is secure at home with her father. "It was hard work—a hard life—but now that she was about to leave it she did not find it a wholly undesirable life." Eveline's inner struggle makes readers want to urge her to marry her lover and be happy. Her uncertainty creates suspense. In her decision to stay, readers can discover a theme: you can become happy only by taking risks.

Cary Chaffee, Quartz Hill High School, Quartz Hill, California

4.7 Writing Activities

Write a Conflict Analysis

Write an analysis of the conflict in one of the following short stories: "The Use of Force" by William Carlos Williams; "Barn Burning" by William Faulkner; or "Through the Tunnel" by Doris Lessing.

PURPOSE To analyze conflict in a short story
AUDIENCE Your teacher and classmates
LENGTH 3-4 paragraphs

WRITING RUBRICS To write an effective analysis, you should

- identify the conflict and the forces involved in it
- explain the development of the conflict and its resolution
- tell what new understandings the characters and the reader reach

Listening and Speaking

COOPERATIVE LEARNING In a small group discuss the elements of conflict in the painting *Salmon Run.* Brainstorm to list examples of conflict in nature: animal vs. environment; one animal species vs. another; conflict among animals of the same species. What resolutions are possible in these conflicts?

Using Computers

Conduct research on the Internet or various newsmagazines to find out more about a conflict between two groups over an environmental issue. Create a poster presentation, using printouts from your research, additional photographs, and text that shows how this conflict might be resolved.

Form possessive nouns correctly.

The writer of the conflict analysis of "The Monkey's Paw" used a number of singular possessive nouns. To refer to the paws of more than one monkey, you would write "*monkeys'* paws."

Complete each sentence below with the correct possessive form.

1. The teacher collected one (class's, classes') papers.
2. She announced that all (student's, students') writing had improved.
3. Each (paper's, papers') subject was conflict.
4. Many (paper's, papers') thesis statements related to the nature of the conflict analyzed.
5. Mrs. (Harris's, Harris') comments were generally favorable.

See Lesson 21.11, pages 760–762.

Melissa Miller, *Salmon Run,* 1984

Narrative Writing

Writing Process in Action

WRITING Online

Visit the Writer's Choice Web site at writerschoice.glencoe.com for additional writing prompts.

Narrative Writing

In preceding lessons you've learned about the basics of narrative writing—character, setting, plot, point of view, conflict, and resolution. You've also had a chance to practice writing parts of narratives, as well as plot summaries and conflict analyses. Now it's time to put together everything you've learned. In this lesson, you're invited to plan a short story of your own and to write the beginning of it.

Assignment

Content

You are a faithful reader of *To Be Continued . . .*, a magazine that publishes serialized student fiction in short monthly installments. You plan to submit a story to the magazine. In the first installment of your story, you will introduce the characters, setting, plot, and the complication you plan to develop in the succeeding installments.

Purpose

To write a narrative that could serve as an introduction to a longer work of fiction

Audience

Editors and teenage readers of *To Be Continued . . .*

Length

1-2 pages

You will find the next few pages helpful for planning your story and writing its first installment. Begin by reading through the pages, but don't feel you have to remember everything on them. You can refer back to the pages as you need to. After all, you're in charge of your own writing process.

Writing Process in Action

Prewriting

If you have trouble coming up with an idea, the prewriting options shown here may help.

After choosing your idea, do the following:

- Make notes to identify characters, setting, point of view, and the basic events of your plot.
- Freewrite about your story's plot.
- Outline or diagram the basic events of your story.
- Decide whether you will use a first-person, third-person limited, or third-person omniscient narrator, and, if limited, from which character's point of view you will tell the story.

Prewriting Options

- Skim your journal for ideas.
- Brainstorm with family members or friends.
- Browse through newspapers and magazines to find references to interesting characters or real-life problems and solutions.
- Select a theme, conflict, or character type that interests you.

Drafting

Sometimes writers don't tell a story from its beginning. Look at what Rudolfo A. Anaya does in these opening paragraphs of his novel *Tortuga.*

Literature Model

I awoke from a restless sleep. For a moment I couldn't remember where I was, then I heard Filomón and Clepo talking up front and I felt the wind sway the old ambulance. I tried to turn my body, but it was impossible. Upon waking it was always the same; I tried to move but the paralysis held me firmly in its grip.

I could turn my head and look out the small window. The cold winter rain was still falling. It had been only a gray drizzle when we left the hospital, but the farther south we went into the desert the sheets of icy rain became more intense. For a great part of the trip we had been surrounded by darkness. Only the flashes of lightning which tore through the sky illuminated the desolate landscape.

Rudolfo A. Anaya, *Tortuga*

Prewriting Tip

If you want to review creating a story outline or plot diagram, see Lesson 4.3, pages 180–183.

Drafting Tip

For help in structuring your introduction as an anecdote, see Lesson 4.5, pages 188–191.

Anaya introduces the main elements of his narrative—the character and complication—in the first paragraphs of his book. Later he will have to go back in time to explain the origin of the complication—how the boy came to be paralyzed—and move forward in time to resolve the complication.

However you start your story, you need to construct a beginning that grabs your reader, moves the story along, lets readers get to know your characters, and gives them some idea of what lies ahead. Since you are writing the first installment of a continuing narrative, you can't really wrap up your story at the end. You can and should, however, leave your readers eager to find out more. Think about raising a compelling question, introducing a mysterious character, or even creating a suspenseful cliff-hanger.

Revising

Revising Tip

If your peer reviewers suggest that more or better dialogue would improve your story introduction, see Lesson 4.4, pages 184–187.

To begin revising, read over your draft to make sure that what you've written fits your purpose and audience. Then have a **writing conference.** Read your draft to a partner or small group. Use your audience's reactions and the Revising Checklist below to help you evaluate your work.

Revising Checklist

- Did I introduce characters, setting, plot, and complication?
- Was the complication or conflict introduced potentially interesting to my audience?
- Did I end in a way that made my audience want to continue reading?
- Did I present a clear and consistent point of view?

Editing/Proofreading

When you are satisfied with your story introduction, proofread it carefully for errors in grammar, usage, mechanics, and spelling. Use the questions at the right as a guide.

In addition to proofreading, use the self-evaluation list below to make sure your story introduction does all the things you want it to do. When you feel that it does, make a clean copy of your story and proofread it one more time.

Editing/Proofreading Checklist

- Have I punctuated appositives, participles, and their phrases correctly?
- Have I punctuated direct quotations correctly?
- Have I formed possessive nouns correctly?
- Have I used commas to separate items in a series?
- Have I checked spellings of any words of which I'm unsure?

Self-Evaluation

Make sure your narrative introduction—

- ✔ focuses on an interesting complication
- ✔ establishes setting, characters, and conflict
- ✔ has a compelling beginning and ending
- ✔ ends in a way that keeps the reader guessing
- ✔ uses dialogue and/or anecdotes effectively
- ✔ is written from a consistent point of view
- ✔ follows correct grammar, usage, mechanics, and spelling

Publishing/Presenting

Many magazines publish student writing. Check such references as *Writer's Market* to identify publications and determine their policy for submissions. If you decide to send your chapter to a real magazine, attach a brief letter informing the editors that you are submitting your story for publication. Be sure to include your address and phone number so that they can respond to your work.

Proofreading

For proofreading symbols, see page 84.

Journal Writing

Reflect on your writing process experience. Answer these questions in your journal: What do you like best about your narrative introduction? What was the hardest part of writing it? What did you learn in your writing conference? What new things have you learned as a writer?

Literature Model

FROM

Tortuga

by Rudolfo A. Anaya

Mexican American writer Rudolfo A. Anaya, who was born in New Mexico, says he learned "from the old storytellers" in his native state "how to re-create the narrative and pass it on." In this beginning to the third novel of his trilogy about growing up a Mexican American in the Southwest, notice how the author creates mood while introducing characters and plot. Then complete the activities in Linking Writing and Literature on page 212.

Literature Model

I awoke from a restless sleep. For a moment I couldn't remember where I was, then I heard Filomón and Clepo talking up front and I felt the wind sway the old ambulance. I tried to turn my body, but it was impossible. Upon waking it was always the same; I tried to move but the paralysis held me firmly in its grip.

I could turn my head and look out the small window. The cold winter rain was still falling. It had been only a gray drizzle when we left the hospital, but the farther south we went into the desert the sheets of icy rain became more intense. For a great part of the trip we had been surrounded by darkness. Only the flashes of lightning which tore through the sky illuminated the desolate landscape.

For a great part of the trip we had been surrounded by darkness. Only the flashes of lightning which tore through the sky illuminated the desolate landscape.

I had slept most of the way; the rain drumming against the ambulance and the rumble of the distant thunder lulled me to sleep. Now I blinked my eyes and remembered that we had left at daybreak, and Filomón had said that it would be mid-afternoon before we arrived at the new hospital.

Your new home, he had said.

Home. Up north, at home, it would be snowing, but here it was only the dark, dismal rain which swept across the wide desert and covered us with its darkness. I tried to turn again, but the paralysis compounded by the bone-chilling cold held me. I cursed silently.

"It's never been this dark before," I heard Clepo whisper.

"Don't worry," Filomón answered, "it'll get better before it gets worse. You have to know the desert to know rain don't last. It can be raining one minute and blowing dust devils[1] the next. But the clouds are beginning to break, see, to the west."

I turned my head and looked out the window. In the distance I could see the bare outline of a mountain range. Around us the desert was alkaline[2] and white. Only the most tenacious shrubs and brittle grasses seemed to grow, clinging to the harsh land like tufts of mouldy hair. Overhead, the sun struggled to break through the clouds. To the east, a diffused, distorted rainbow stretched across the vast, gray sky.

I remembered the rainbows of my childhood, beautifully sculptured arches reaching from north to south, shafts of light so pure their harmony seemed to wed the sky and earth. My mother had taught me to look at rainbows, the mantle[3] of the Blessed Virgin Mary she called them. When a summer thunderstorm passed she would take me out and we would stand in the thin drops which followed the storm. We would turn our faces up to the sky, and the large, glistening drops of rain would pelt our faces. She would open her mouth and hold out her tongue to receive the large, golden drops. She would stir the muddy ponds and pick up the little

---

1 **dust devils** small whirlwinds of dust
2 **alkaline** (al′ kə līn) containing mineral salts
3 **mantle** a cloak or cape

frogs which came with the rain. "They are like you," she told me, "blessed by the rain, children of the water." When I was hurt she would take me in her arms and sing . . . .

Sana, sana
colita de rana
Si no sanas hoy
sanarás mañana . . . [4]

And her touch could drive away the worst of pains. But then the paralysis had come, and suddenly her prayers and her touch were not enough. Her face grew pale and thin, her eyes grew dark. "It is God's will," she had said.

"It's clearing now," Filomón said, "see, the sun is beginning to break through!"

"Yes, the sun!" Clepo shouted. He was Filomón's assistant, a small impish man with hunched shoulders. I noticed he limped when they loaded me on the ambulance.

"I think I see the top of the mountain!" Filomón cried cheerfully.

I was fully awake. The last images of the dreams faded as the darkness of the rain moved over us and eastward. Only occasional peals of thunder rumbled across the sky. Beneath us the ambulance rocked like a ship. Memories of my life moved in and out of my troubled consciousness. My mother's face appeared again and again. She had cried when they loaded me on the ambulance, but she knew it was necessary. The doctors there had helped as much as they could. Now, they insisted, they had to move me to this new hospital in the south where they specialized in taking care of crippled children. If there was any hope of regaining the use of my stiff limbs, it was there. So early in the morning they wheeled me on a gurney[5] to the outpatient area, loaded me onto Filomón's ambulance and the journey began.

My mother's face appeared again and again. She had cried when they loaded me on the ambulance. . . .

"There!" Filomón shouted again, "There's the mountain!"

I tried to turn my head to see, but I couldn't. "What mountain?" I asked.

"Tortuga Mountain," he said and looked back, "it's right by the hospital. Don't worry, I'll stop so you can see it." He sounded happy, revived, after the long, monotonous drive across the desert. I felt a sense of urgency as he pulled the ambulance onto the shoulder of the road. We bounced along until he found the right spot, then he stopped the ambulance and turned off the motor. He climbed over the seat to where I lay strapped on the small cot.

---

4 **Sana, sana / colita de rana / Si no sanas hoy / sanarás mañana . . .** Spanish for "Get well, get well / little frogtail / If you don't get well today / you will tomorrow . . . ."

5 **gurney** (gur′nē) a wheeled stretcher or cot used to move hospital patients

"Ah, Filo," Clepo grumbled, "you've stopped here every time we bring a new kid. Don't you ever get tired of showing them that . . . mountain?"

"It's always a new kid," Filomón smiled as he loosened the straps that held me, "and each kid deserves to see the mountain from here. I want the boy to see it."

Filomón was an old man with a deep wrinkled face and rough, calloused hands, but he moved like a younger man as he lifted me tenderly so I could look out the window and see the mountain.

"There it is," he nodded, "that's Tortuga." His eyes sparkled as he looked at the volcanic mountain that loomed over the otherwise empty desert. It rose so magically into the gray sky that it seemed to hold the heavens and the earth together. It lay just east of the river valley, and the afternoon sun shining on it after the rain covered it with a sheen of silver.

His eyes sparkled as he looked at the volcanic mountain that loomed over the otherwise empty desert.

"It's a magic mountain," Filomón whispered, and I felt his heart beating against me as he held me. "See!" he whispered, "See!" I tried to see beyond the volcanic slabs and granite boulders which formed the outline of a turtle, I tried to sense the steady rhythm of his pulse which seemed to be draining into the giant mountain, but I couldn't. I was too tired, and my faith in magic had drained out the night the paralysis came and in the ensuing nights and days which I spent without movement on the hospital bed.

I shook my head.

"That's okay," he smiled, "it comes slowly sometimes. But now at least you know it's there—" He seemed very tired. It had been a long trip for him too. He had had to keep the ambulance on course through one of the worst storms I could remember. But now we were almost there.

"Where's the hospital?" I asked.

"It's on this side of the river, you can't see it from here. See the smoke rising in the valley? That's Agua Bendita.[6] It's a small town, but people come from all over to bathe in the mineral waters from the springs which drain from the mountain—"

"It's a town full of old arthritics," Clepo giggled, "old people who think they can escape the pains of old age by dipping themselves in the mountain's water, but they can't run fast enough from death!" He slapped his thigh and laughed.

Filomón didn't answer. He sat beside the cot and looked out the window into the desert. "Even as terrible as the storm was for us, it will be good for the plants in the spring. After a good, wet winter the desert blooms like a garden," he nodded and rolled a cigarette. There was something about the

---

6 **Agua Bendita** (ä′ gwä ben dē′ tä) Spanish for "holy water"

way he spoke, the strength of his face, that reminded me of someone I had known—my grandfather perhaps, but I hadn't thought of him in years.

"These old villages cling to the river like the beads of a rosary,"[7] he continued, thinking aloud.

"Whoever crosses this desert has a lot of praying to do," Clepo agreed, "it's a journey of death."

"No, a journey of life. Our forefathers have wandered up and down this river valley for a long, long time. First the Indians roamed up and down this river, then others came, but they all stopped here at this same place: the springs of Tortuga, the place of the healing water—"

"Whoever crosses this desert has a lot of praying to do," Clepo agreed, "it's a journey of death."

He talked and smoked. The dull sun shone through the window and played on the swirling smoke. I was fully awake now, but I felt feverish, and I couldn't help wondering what a strange day it had been to ride all this way with the old man and his assistant. I shivered, but not from the cold. The inside of the ambulance was now stifling. It glowed with white smoke and golden light which poured through the window. Filomón's eyes shone.

"How long have you been bringing kids to the hospital?" I asked.

"As long as I can remember," Filomón answered. "I bought this old hearse[8] in a junk yard and I fixed it up like an ambulance. I've been transporting kids ever since."

"We get thirty dollars a kid, dead or alive," Clepo laughed. "And we get to hear a lot of interesting stories. We've taken every kind of diseased body there is to the hospital. Why, Filo and I could become doctors if we wanted to, couldn't we Filo? But we don't know anything about you. You slept most of the way." He leaned over the seat and peered at me.

"He's tired," Filomón said.

"Yeah, but he's awake now," Clepo grinned. "So how did he get crippled? I know it ain't polio, I know polio. And how come his left hand is bandaged, huh? There's quite a story there, but he hasn't said a word!"

He seemed put out that I had slept most of the way and had not told the story of my past. But since the paralysis the past didn't matter. It was as if everything had died, except the dreams and the memories which kept haunting me. And even those were useless against the terrible weight which had fallen over me and which I cursed until I could curse no more.

---

7 **rosary** (rō′ zər ē) a string of beads used in prayer to keep count
8 **hearse** an automobile used to carry the corpse during a funeral

Literature Model

Rufino Tamayo, *Interior with Alarm Clock*, 1928

"Do you take the kids back?" I asked.

"No, we don't!" Clepo said, "That's against the rules!"

"I picked you up," Filomón reminded him.

"I was hitch-hiking," Clepo said smartly, "somebody would have picked me up."

"You were lost. I found you in the middle of a sandstorm, crying. Lucky for you I came along."

"I wasn't crying, I had sand in my eyes," Clepo insisted.

Filomón smiled. "It doesn't matter, you've been a good assistant." That seemed to satisfy Clepo, he grunted and sat back down. Filomón drew close and looked at me. "We can't take anybody back, that's not our job. But when you get better you can make the trip back home by yourself. Just wait till spring, and you'll be better. I know it looks bad now, but in the spring the river comes alive and the desert dresses like a young bride. The lizards come out to play in the warm sun, and even the mountain moves—" He touched my forehead with his fingers, then he leaned close to me and I felt his forehead touch mine, perhaps he was just leaning to retrieve one of the straps to tie me up again, but I felt his forehead brush mine, and I felt a relief from the paralysis which I hadn't felt since it came. Then he tied the strap and climbed back into the driver's seat.

. . . I couldn't move. I could only turn my head and watch the mountain across the valley.

"Filomón says you gotta keep your eyes on the mountain," Clepo said to fill in the silence.

"Well, it's helped us," Filomón answered, "it's been our faith in this wasteland . . . and it's helped a lot of kids. There's a strong power there."

He started the ambulance and let it coast down the long slope of the hill into the valley. I knew he was still looking at the mountain, still feeling the strange power that resided there for him.

"The water from the mountain springs is holy," he mused aloud, "long ago the place was used as a winter ceremonial ground by the Indians. They came to purify themselves by bathing in the warm waters . . . the water of the turtle . . . Later, when the Spaniards came, they called the springs Los Ojos de la Tortuga,[9] and when they discovered the waters could cure many illnesses they called the village Agua Bendita . . ."

"Who lives here?" I asked. We had entered the edge of the small town. Through the window I could see the tops of rundown gas stations, motels and cafes. There was a dilapidated movie house, a brownstone hotel, and many signs which

---

9 **Los Ojos de la Tortuga** (lōs ō′ hōs dā lä tôr to͞o′ gä) Spanish for "the eyes of the turtle"

creaked in the wind as they advertised the hot mineral baths.

"Mostly old people who come for the baths, people who work at the hospital, and a few of the old people who try to make a living from the small farms along the river—"

Filomón turned the ambulance and I caught a glimpse of a weathered sign that read *Crippled Children and Orphans Hospital.* The arrow pointed up the hill, so from the highway which ran through the small town we had to turn up the hill again towards the washed-out buildings which huddled together at the top. I struggled to turn to see more, instinctively, as I had so many times before, but it was useless, I couldn't move. I could only turn my head and watch the mountain across the valley. An air of hopelessness brooded over the dull mountain as the remaining winter clouds huddled at its peak. It seemed lost and out of place in the immense desert which surrounded it, and I wondered what secret rested in its core. Whatever it was, it was something that made Filomón's voice ring with hope and made his eyes sparkle even after the fatigue of the long journey.

Literature Model

Linking Writing and Literature

Collect Your Thoughts

Now that you've finished reading this excerpt from *Tortuga,* think about how the narrator might have felt as he drove to the hospital. Jot down some of the hopes and fears he might have had.

Talk About Reading

Talk with other students about this excerpt from *Tortuga.* Assign a group leader to maintain the group's focus and a secretary to take notes. Use the questions below to guide your discussion.

1. **Connect to Your Life** What experience from your own life can help you relate to the narrator? Your experience might be a time away from home, a challenge that you faced, or an illness. How was your experience similar to that of the narrator? How was it different?
2. **Critical Thinking: Evaluate** Which of the three characters in this excerpt from *Tortuga* did you like best? Why? Explain how the author's description of this character contributes to the narrative.
3. **6+1 Trait®: Conventions** Look for sentences on pages 208–211 containing conjunctions that either join the clauses of a compound sentence or begin a sentence. For each sentence you identify, evaluate why the author wrote the sentence the way he did.
4. **Connect to Writing** After reading this selection, what qualities do you think a narrative that describes a personal experience should have? Make a list of criteria for a good personal narrative. Save the list and refer to it next time you write a personal narrative.

Write About Reading

Narrative Writing What do you think happens to the narrator after he enters the hospital? What happens next to Filomón and Clepo? Write a narrative that continues the story of one or more of these characters.

Focus on Conventions As you write, be conscious of your use of conventions. For example, decide what ideas you want to emphasize by using conjunctions either to join sentences or to begin sentences. Make your writing strong and correct by checking for any errors in spelling, grammar, and punctuation.

For more information on conventions and the 6+1 Trait® model, see **Writing and Research Handbook,** pages 957–959.

6+1 Trait® is a registered trademark of Northwest Regional Educational Laboratory, which does not endorse this product.

UNIT 4 Review

Reflecting on the Unit

Summarize what you learned in this unit by answering the following questions.

1. What are the characteristics of personal narrative writing, and what strategies can help you find ideas for your personal narratives?
2. What are the basic elements of a work of fiction, and what characterizes plot?
3. How does dialogue serve narrative writing?
4. What is an anecdote? How can anecdotes serve theme in fiction and nonfiction?
5. What are the important aspects of plot summary and conflict analysis and the uses of each?

Adding to Your Portfolio

CHOOSE A SELECTION FOR YOUR PORTFOLIO Look over the narrative writing you have done during this unit. Select a completed piece of writing to put into your portfolio. The piece you choose should show some or all of the following:

- the basic narrative elements—characters, setting, plot, and point of view
- a character in a conflict or complication that leads to a climax and a resolution
- dialogue that advances plot or reveals character
- an anecdote that reinforces the theme of the story

Reflecting on Your Choice

Attach a note to the piece you chose, explaining briefly why you chose it and what you learned from writing it.

SET GOALS How can you improve your writing? What skill will you focus on the next time you write?

Writing Across the Curriculum

MAKE A LITERATURE CONNECTION Select a work of literature you read in class this year—a story, novel, or personal narrative. Then write a one- or two-page story introduction that would get someone interested in reading the story. Include setting, characters, complication, and resolution.

"What disruptions would occur if a warming or cooling trend were to shrink or expand the winter sea ice? Presumably ocean currents would shift, perhaps causing drastic shifts in climate."

—Jane Ellen Stevens, "Exploring Antarctic Ice"

UNIT 5

Expository Writing

Writing in the Real World

Expository Writing

MEDIA Connection

Magazine Article

Like other kinds of exposition written for a general audience, science writing uses plain talk and concrete examples to bring a subject to life. The following is an expository article by Anastasia Toufexis, health and behavior editor at *Time* magazine.

from "Drowsy America"

by Anastasia Toufexis

At 7 A.M. or 6 or maybe even 5, the blare of the alarm breaks the night, and another workday dawns. As an arm gropes to stop the noise and the whole body rebels against the harsh call of morning, the thought is almost always the same: *I have to get more sleep.* That night, after 17 or 18 hours of fighting traffic, facing deadlines and racing the clock, the weary soul collapses into bed once again for an all-too-brief respite. And just before the slide into slumber, the nagging thought returns: *I have to get more sleep.*

Millions of Americans make this complaint, but how many do anything about it? Sleep is a biological imperative, but do people consider it as vital as food or drink? Not in today's rock-around-the-clock world. Not in a society in which mothers work, stores don't close, assembly lines never stop. . . .

To some night owls, the very idea of spending more than 20 years of one's life in idle snoozing is appalling. Listen to Harvey Bass. Between a job as a computer-systems manager in New York City and free-lance consulting, he gets no more than five hours of sleep a night and sometimes only two. He admits that the schedule occasionally leaves him with a "tingling around my head." Even so, he says, "if I live a normal life span, I will have lived 20% more than the average person because I'm awake."

That may sound like an attractive exchange, but scientists are increasingly making the case that forgoing rest is a foolish and often perilous bargain. In fact, evidence is mounting that sleep deprivation has become one of the most pervasive health problems facing the U.S. . . . [S]tudies show that mental alertness and performance can suffer badly. "Sleepiness is one of the least recognized sources of disability in our society," declares Dr. Charles Pollak, head of the sleep-disorder center at Cornell University's New York Hospital. . . . "[P]eople who don't get enough sleep can't think, they can't make appropriate judgments, they can't maintain long attention spans."

Such mental fatigue can be as threatening as a heart attack. Recent evidence indicates that drowsiness is a leading cause of traffic fatalities and industrial mishaps.

A Writer's Process

Prewriting

Getting the Facts

In preparing her story on sleep, Toufexis enlisted the help of correspondents in six *Time* bureaus around the country. She sent each one a query explaining the gist of the story, a list of questions to research, and the names of a few information sources.

Toufexis worked with a team in order to gather information from all around the country. "There would be no way to get national coverage unless we had an enormous amount of time [for me to] travel around the country, stopping in each and every place to get experts' views and analyses of their research plus finding people locally," she explained.

Local people—pilots, students, stockbrokers, truck drivers, working moms—were critical to the story. "We didn't want a dry academic treatise on the lack of sleep," Toufexis said. "We wanted to humanize the problem, make it alive."

Toufexis did considerable reading herself, in books, in *Time*'s clip folder of articles on sleep, in professional journals, and in her bulging file of reports on sleep research. She also interviewed several experts in the field.

After a month of detective work, Toufexis and her team had a stack of research material standing a foot and a half high that revealed a national health problem. The problem ranged from scary tales of sleepy airplane pilots to statistics showing that up to 200,000 truck accidents a year may be related to fatigue.

Press conferences, such as the one on "America's Sleep Debt," sometimes offer a forum for individuals to present their research on a topic.

Drafting/Revising

Selecting and Condensing Facts

Before trying to turn the mountain of data into a lively article, Toufexis laid some important groundwork. She organized her notes into topics. Then she typed the most important facts, studies, and quotes into her computer. The result: three or four pages of information for each topic. Next, Toufexis noted the length her story should be—4,000 to 5,000 words.

Toufexis's first challenge was to write a gripping lead. "Within the first two or three paragraphs, I have to be clear about why I'm doing the story so I can get people interested," she said. "Then I try to hit them with the billboard: Why is this important? How does it affect you?" For this article, Toufexis chose to begin with the common experience of struggling awake to an alarm clock.

With her lead resolved, Toufexis began writing. She presented her main idea and selected key research to support it. She explained the research clearly and then illustrated it with examples from her interviews. For instance, she cited one study that found that adolescents need at least nine and a half hours of sleep a night. Do they get it? Toufexis answered this question with two examples. One example came from a fifteen-year-old from California who was horrified at the notion of sleeping nearly ten hours a night. The second example came from teachers who were interviewed and described "sleepy youngsters arriving late to class. . . . "

After selecting and condensing material, Toufexis had a complete draft. It was still "way too long, portions were unbalanced, but the draft was finished," Toufexis said. She let the draft sit for a couple of days before starting to revise.

All over the country, the correspondents found that school, part-time work, and social demands keep teens from getting necessary sleep.

Revising/Editing

Checking Accuracy and Sense

After a week of revising her story, Toufexis released it to the senior editor, who edited it for interest and sense. The magazine's managing editor and other high-level editors also reviewed the story, as did the correspondents, who were asked to respond to a list of fact-checking questions.

The week before Toufexis's story ran, she and a researcher worked long hours improving the story by responding to questions of grammar, punctuation, sense, and style raised by *Time*'s copyeditors. As the deadline neared, Toufexis and her researcher fit the story to the layout, wrote captions, and held a final review with the science editor. Finally, "Drowsy America" was ready for publication.

Publishing/Presenting

Making People Aware

Was all the effort worth it? "I hope my work has an impact," Toufexis said, "but for the most part, I work to get a piece of information across. If I make people aware that a subject is something they should think of, I've done my job."

Through collaborative effort, a large group of people made this cover story possible.

Examining Writing in the Real World

Analyzing the Media Connection

Discuss these questions about the article on page 216.

1. How does Toufexis capture the reader's interest with her opening paragraph?
2. What example of parallelism does Toufexis use in the second paragraph? How does it contribute to the impact of the article?
3. Why do you think Toufexis includes the anecdote about Harvey Bass?
4. How do the quotations from a sleep-disorder expert advance the story?
5. Why do you think Toufexis choose the title "Drowsy America" for her article? How appropriate is this title?

Analyzing a Writer's Process

Discuss these questions about Anastasia Toufexis's writing process.

1. For what reason did Toufexis enlist the help of other *Time* correspondents?
2. How did Toufexis and her team gather information on sleep deprivation?
3. How did Toufexis organize the data she and her team collected?
4. Describe Toufexis's writing process. Do you think it is effective? Why or why not?
5. What was the role of each editor who reviewed Toufexis's article?

Expository Writing

Vary sentence structure to create interest.

Reread the media connection. Note how the sentences vary in structure and in length. In addition to simple sentences, there are compound sentences: *It was "way too long, portions were unbalanced, but it was finished,"* . . . There are also complex sentences: *As the deadline neared, Toufexis and her researcher fit the story to the layout. . . .*

Follow these directions to create different types of sentences.

1. Write a simple sentence or choose one in the media connection.
2. Rework it, making it a compound sentence.
3. Rework the simple sentence again to make it part of a complex sentence.
4. Rework your compound sentence into a compound-complex sentence.
5. Write a fifth related sentence, and tell what type of sentence it is.

See Lesson 13.3, pages 545–546; and Lesson 13.4, pages 547–548.

LESSON

5.1 Writing to Inform and Explain

Expository writing is what you use to give directions, explain a new term or idea, compare one thing to another, or explain how to do something. In the model below, Mary Crow Dog and Richard Erdoes explain the importance of the tiyospaye[1] *in Lakota Sioux society.*

Literature Model

The topic sentence defines "tiyospaye."

Supporting sentences use comparison and several examples to explain the specific qualities of a tiyospaye.

At the center of the old Sioux society was the *tiyospaye,* the extended family group, the basic hunting band, which included grandparents, uncles, aunts, in-laws, and cousins. The tiyospaye was like a warm womb cradling all within it. Kids were never alone, always fussed over by not one but several mothers, watched and taught by several fathers. The real father, as a matter of fact, selected a second father, some well-thought-of-relative with special skills such as a hunter or medicine man, to help him bring up a boy, and such a person was called "Father" too. And the same was true for the girls. Grandparents in our tribe always held a special place in caring for the little ones, because they had more time to devote to them, when the father was out hunting, taking the mother with him to help with the skinning and butchering.

Mary Crow Dog and Richard Erdoes, *Lakota Woman*

1 tiyospaye tē′ yō shpä′ yā

Choose a Kind of Expository Writing

An essay is the most general form of expository writing. The introduction of an essay includes a thesis statement, a one-sentence summary of purpose. The body is made up of one or more paragraphs of details that support the thesis. The conclusion states the implications of the thesis. Within the general essay format, the specific kind of exposition you write depends on your goal, as the chart shows.

Six Kinds of Expository Writing

Kind	Attribute	Examples
Process Explanation	Uses step-by-step organization to explain how something happens, works, or is done	How do you run a computer program? How are homes built? How does the human body process food?
Cause and Effect	Identifies the causes and/or effects of something and examines the relationship between causes and effects	What causes freckles? What causes sunspots? What are the effects of poverty on children?
Comparison and Contrast	Examines similarities and differences to find relationships and draw conclusions	Compare jazz and rap, or blues and country music. Compare and contrast basketball and ballet.
Definition	Explains a term or concept by listing and examining its qualities or characteristics	What is hypothermia? What is "grandstanding"? What was the Harlem Renaissance?
Classification	Organizes subjects into categories and examines qualities or characteristics of those categories	What organisms are considered fungi? How would you characterize the writing of Stephen King?
Problem and Solution	Examines aspects of a complex problem and explores or proposes possible solutions	How can your community increase literacy? What can be done to protect wilderness areas?

Journal Writing

If you were asked to write about any aspect of school life for your school's newspaper, what would you write about? Choose a topic and tell which kind of expository writing would help you meet your goal.

Grammar Tip

In the editing stage, check that words used to represent themselves have been italicized or underlined. For more information about italics, see Lesson 21.10, pages 758–759.

Expository Writing

Revising Tip

Whenever you revise expository writing, ask yourself whether using a different kind of exposition would help you develop your topic more clearly or completely.

Combine Various Kinds of Exposition

To fully explore the qualities and characteristics of a topic, you will most often need to use a combination of expository types. In the following passage, authors Betsy Armstrong and Knox Williams write about an avalanche-prone area in Switzerland. The authors begin by explaining how forests tend to inhibit avalanches. Then they discuss what happens when areas are deforested for building or heating purposes. Finally, the authors describe how reforestation can prevent avalanches. As you read, try to pick out the specific kinds of expository writing the authors use.

Literature Model

What is the cause-and-effect relationship between human settlement and an increase in avalanches?

In many cases, the villagers made the avalanche problem worse. Before settlement, dense forests covered many of the steep slopes above the valleys. The forests inhibited large avalanches, since catastrophic avalanches do not originate in a heavy forest, and avalanches traveling into such a forest will often slow as the snow encounters the trees. [A forest] tends to diminish the speed of the snow and break up the avalanche. However, villagers often cut down the forests for building and heating purposes. In many areas the trees never grew back, leaving the slopes bare and smooth—a perfect track for the run of a snow avalanche. A prime example of deforestation is in the valley of Ursental in central Switzerland. Above the town of Andermatt, there remains just a wedge of trees, while the remainder of the steep slope is bare. Up valley, near the Furka Pass, is the town of Hospental, which also maintains its own protective wedge of trees. As the story is told, the inhabitants of the valley systematically cut down the forests that covered the steep slopes on both sides. Almost too late they realized their mistake: they saw that on the bare, treeless slopes, huge avalanches began descending to the valley floor, making travel between towns extremely dangerous. All tree-cutting stopped and the wedges of trees above the towns were preserved. Reforestation, the systematic planting of trees, continues today in the Ursental, to thicken the wedges that are periodically thinned by avalanches.

How do the writers explain reforestation in Ursental, Switzerland, as the solution to a problem?

Betsy Armstrong and Knox Williams, *The Avalanche Book*

5.1 Writing Activities

Write an Explanation of an Event

Examine the painting *Castle of Cards.* Who do you think the four people are, and how might they be related? What's going on? Write an essay explaining the event you see in the painting.

PURPOSE To explain an event portrayed in a piece of art
AUDIENCE Your teacher and classmates
LENGTH 2–3 paragraphs

WRITING RUBRICS To write an effective explanation of an event, you should

- combine the kinds of exposition you use
- include an introduction, a body, and a conclusion

Using Computers

SPELLING Check your explanation for correct spelling. List any consistent spelling errors you make and store them in the spell-check section labeled "Options" on your computer so that these words will be automatically checked and corrected in the future.

Zinaida Serebriakova, *Castle of Cards,* 1918

Grammar Link

Make subjects and verbs agree in inverted sentences.

Subjects and verbs must agree in inverted sentences—sentences in which the subject follows the verb. The selection from *Lakota Woman* begins with this inverted sentence:

At the center of the old Sioux society was the tiyospaye. . . .

Rewrite each sentence below, adding the verb that agrees with the subject.

1. There (is, are) usually many people in an extended family group.
2. Included in the extended family (is, are) in-laws and grandparents.
3. Hovering behind the children in that photograph (stands, stand) several mothers.
4. Under the huge tree (sits, sit) that young boy's second "father."
5. Here (comes, come) the cousins now.

See Lesson 16.3, pages 616–617.

Cross-Curricular Activity

SCIENCE In a small group, select a natural phenomenon: hurricane, earthquake, glacier, iceberg, sunspots, or any other you'd like to explore. Work together to compile a list of questions based on the six kinds of exposition. Divide the questions among group members. Do some basic research using your science textbook, and write a paragraph answering your question. Then combine the paragraphs into a fact sheet on your subject to share with the class.

Expository Writing

LESSON 5.2 Knowing Your Audience

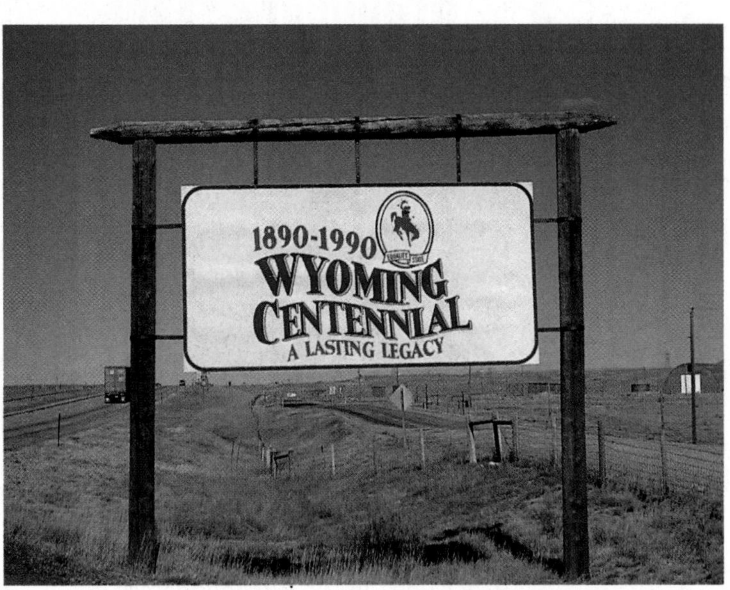

Identifying your audience will help you focus your writing and choose details. In the model below, one-time California film-maker Gretel Ehrlich explains her attraction to a place that her audience, most of them city dwellers, regard as isolated and desolate.

Ehrlich provides two examples to show what she means when she says the people are "tenderhearted about quirky behavior."

This quotation brings a sense of immediacy to the writing. How might Cliff's comment help Ehrlich's readers to understand her words "strong on scruples"?

Literature Model

In all this open space, values crystallize quickly. People are strong on scruples but tenderhearted about quirky behavior. . . . A friend, Cliff, who runs a trapline in the winter, cut off half his foot while chopping a hole in the ice. Alone, he dragged himself to his pickup and headed for town, stopping to open the ranch gate as he left, and getting out to close it again, thus losing, in his observance of rules, precious time and blood. Later, he commented, "How would it look, them having to come to the hospital to tell me their cows had gotten out?"

Accustomed to emergencies, my friends doctor each other from the vet's bag with relish. When one old-timer suffered a heart attack in hunting camp, his partner quickly stirred up a brew of red horse liniment and hot water and made the half-conscious victim drink it, then tied him onto a horse and led him twenty miles to town. He regained consciousness and lived.

Gretel Ehrlich, *The Solace of Open Spaces*

Write to Someone

Thinking about your particular audience for each piece of expository writing will help you zero in on what your readers need to know. Even if your main readers are your teachers, you should remember every teacher is different. Think about what each teacher is looking for as you complete your assignments.

Besides teachers, classmates and other peers will often read and critique your writing. In addition, when you write personal notes, letters to friends, job or college applications, or news stories for the school paper, you must consider various readers. The following questions can help you develop a feel for your audience.

Revising Tip

A peer editor can give you valuable feedback on how well you have responded to the needs of your audience.

Understanding Your Audience	
Interest	• Does this audience care about my topic already, or must I convince them of its importance? • Will I need to find ways to overcome apathy or dislike of my topic? • If this audience has a strong interest in my topic, how can I move forward swiftly to maintain their interest?
Background	• How much does this audience already know about my topic? • Do I need to define basic terms and concepts? • Do I need to probe deeply for new insights in order to tell this audience something it doesn't already know, or should I concentrate on clarifying the main points?
Vocabulary	• Should I use formal or informal language to reach this audience? • Should I present my points in nontechnical language? • Will my audience be able to follow complex explanations, or should I keep sentences short and simple?

Journal Writing

Using the chart above, analyze a piece of writing you have already completed. Would you change anything now? Record your reactions in your journal.

Expository Writing

Use Details to Appeal to Your Audience

Identifying your audience is just the first step. Here are some strategies you can use to support your main ideas and make connections clear to your audience.

Grammar Tip

When editing expository writing, check that all proper nouns and proper adjectives are capitalized, as in the literature model. To review capitalization rules, see Lessons 20.2 and 20.3, pages 715 and 722.

Supporting Details and Good Connections	
Examples	Support main ideas with vivid, interesting examples to help readers grasp unfamiliar information or relate information to their own experiences.
Facts and Statistics	Use facts and statistics to help readers understand the magnitude of an issue, set the time frame, provide historical background, or support technical points.
Comparisons	Use analogies, metaphors, similes, and other forms of comparison to help readers understand unfamiliar concepts by relating them to something readers *do* understand.
Quotations	Use engaging quotations from experts on your topic to clarify meanings or lend authority to your writing. Or use a relevant quotation at the beginning of your writing to set the tone.

Literature Model

Statistics help give readers a sense of the vastness of the continent.

Africa occupies 20 percent of the earth's land surface, or 11.7 million square miles. Only Asia is larger. Africa is 5,000 miles long, reaching from the God-forsaken deserts of the north to the lush wine country in the south, and 4,600 miles wide. Its coastline measures 18,950 miles—shorter than Europe's because of the absence of inlets and bays—and the equator cuts Africa just about in half. Africa's climate varies wildly, from temperate in the high plateaus, to tropical along the coastal plains to just plain intolerable in the sizzling deserts.

Lamb compares the size of the Sahara and the United States. What does this comparison tell you that statistics alone cannot?

The coastal strip around Africa is narrow, and the interior plateaus are characterized by wide belts of tropical rain forest, wooded savanna and grassland plains. In the far north is the Sahara, the world's largest desert. It covers one quarter of the continent, an area as large as the United States mainland. In the far south is the Kalahari Desert, the world's seventh largest. The highest point in Africa is Mount Kilimanjaro in Tanzania, 19,340 feet tall and snow-capped the year round. . . .

David Lamb, *The Africans*

5.2 Writing Activities

Write an Explanation of a Painting

Look carefully at the painting on this page and read the title. Write a short explanation of what is happening in the picture. Your audience is a foreign exchange student unfamiliar with the game of baseball. Think about what your audience needs to know.

PURPOSE To explain baseball to someone unfamiliar with the game
AUDIENCE A foreign exchange student
LENGTH 2–3 paragraphs

WRITING RUBRICS To write an effective explanation of a painting, you should

- use language that your audience will understand
- use details to support your main idea
- make good, clear connections

Cross-Curricular Activity

SCIENCE In a small group, choose a complex biological term, such as *ecosystem, biodiversity,* or *molecular.* Each of you should choose a different audience—for example, a younger child, a parent, or a biology teacher—and write a paragraph defining the term. Compare definitions to identify techniques each writer used to reach a particular audience.

Viewing and Representing

COOPERATIVE LEARNING After you have defined your term, work as a group to illustrate your term for your audience. Use appropriate materials to represent your expository paragraphs visually.

Avoid sentence fragments.

A *sentence fragment* is an incomplete sentence punctuated as if it were a complete sentence.

Rewrite the following items, correcting all sentence fragments.

1. Expository writing can be dry and boring. Often lacks feeling.
2. Your readers have different levels of knowledge. And varying degrees of interest in your topic.
3. What kind of language should you use to reach a younger audience? Probably informal.
4. Regardless of their background. Make sure that your audience understands technical terms you introduce.
5. Support your main ideas with comparisons. For example, analogies, metaphors, and similes.

See Lesson 13.9, pages 557–558.

Jacob Lawrence, *Strike,* 1949

LESSON

5.3

Writing About a Process

Expository Writing

When you explain a process, you describe the steps involved in completing it. Notice the details James Wagenvoord uses in his explanation.

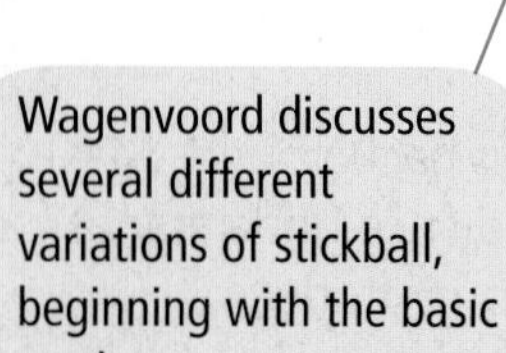

Wagenvoord discusses several different variations of stickball, beginning with the basic version.

What kinds of details does Wagenvoord use to characterize stickball?

Literature Model

Stickball's a little closer to the big game than stoopball. Instead of playing the width of a street, it stretches down the block as far as a hollow Spaldeen can be powered with a cut-off broom handle. It's often an impressive distance. There are neighborhood variations upon variations. If there's a basic version it's the street game—the hitter flipping the ball into the air, fixedly eyeing its bounce in front of him, and then, as it rises to its apex, stepping into the ball to slash at it with the bat. When the ball is smashed into the playing area, the standard baseball rules take over—again with variations. A ball landing and staying on the rooftop—fair or foul—is an automatic out. But a fair ball skimming off fire escapes, window frames, and dribbling down building faces is in play. There's a version of the game called slow pitch which, with a pitcher, becomes baseball except for the size of the ball and the narrow bat. And there's "off the wall," a tailoring of the classic to interior courtyards, a reversed mirror-image form. The pitcher stands behind the batter, outfielders ranging behind them and all facing the same wall, as the batter waits for his crack until a pitch has been flung at the wall and rebounds to him. His hit is in play the moment that, on the fly, it again strikes the wall. Then stoopball bounce rules take over. One bounce before being caught is a single, and a home run is four bounces or a smash hopelessly beyond reach of the defenders.

James Wagenvoord, *Hangin' Out: City Kids, City Games*

Explain One Step at a Time

When you write about a process, you must take care to remember all the little details. Unless you can describe the process completely and accurately, your readers will be left in the dark. You must also take into consideration the level of knowledge of your readers. If they know little about the process, you may need to define basic terms and concepts. If your readers are familiar with the process, you don't want to bore them with general information they already know. The following steps can help you write about a process.

Explaining a Process	
1. Investigate	Watch someone perform the process, do it yourself, ask questions about it, or read about it. Take notes as you go.
2. Observe	Identify the main parts of the process and the specific steps needed to carry it out.
3. Arrange	Put the steps in chronological order. You may wish to "walk through" the process mentally to make sure nothing is missing.
4. Elaborate	Decide what background information and examples you need to include so that your audience will understand your explanation. Be sure to define any unfamiliar terms.
5. Polish	Use transitions such as *first, next, meanwhile, then, finally,* and *last* to point the way as you write.
6. Review	Check to make sure your explanation is complete, clear, and accurate.

Journal Writing

What steps do you take to get ready for a party or a school dance? Try listing the steps in your journal. Be careful not to leave anything out or take anything for granted. You may be surprised at how complex such a routine process turns out to be.

Expository Writing

Revise Your Explanation

When you revise an explanation, your main goals are clarity, completeness, and accuracy. Make sure that the information you present and the way you present it are appropriate for your audience.

The first draft below is taken from an essay that explains the stages of building a house. It is intended for a general audience with no specific background in home building. What changes would you make in order to improve the passage's clarity and appropriateness for that audience?

Prewriting Tip

Explaining a process to a peer editor before writing can help you identify steps or essential background information you may have overlooked.

Model

Next, workers bolt wooden sills to the top of the foundation. Floor joists are placed across the foundation on the sills, and the floorboards are nailed to the top of the joists, forming the bottom layer of the floor. Each wall frame is lifted into place along the sill and braced temporarily. When all the outside walls have been set in place, they are nailed together and braced permanently.

Grammar Tip

When describing a process, be sure to use the same verb tense throughout the explanation. For help, see Lesson 15.6, pages 598–599.

When the writer reviewed the draft, she made some vocabulary changes. She realized her readers might not know some basic terms, such as *sills* and *joists.* Also, they might understand the process more easily if she drew attention to the distinct stages of the process. Notice the changes she made.

Model

The next step is to build the frame. Workers start by bolting wooden sills, called base plates, to the top of the foundation. These sills support the outside walls. Next, floor joists, or support beams, are placed across the foundation on the sills, and the floor boards are nailed to the top of the joists, forming the bottom layer of the floor.

At this point the structure is solid enough to hold the wall frames. Carpenters assemble each wall frame separately. Then each one is lifted into place along the sill and braced temporarily. When all the outside walls have been set in place, they are nailed together and braced permanently.

How does the topic sentence in each paragraph make the steps of the process clearer?

The writer also defines terms that she knows might be unfamiliar.

5.3 Writing Activities

Write a "How-to" Article

Write a 2- to 3-paragraph explanation of a process you are very familiar with, such as how to care for tropical fish or how to train for a 10K race. Assume that your audience is fellow students who are unfamiliar with the process.

PURPOSE To explain a familiar process to somebody unfamiliar with it
AUDIENCE Other students
LENGTH 2–3 paragraphs

WRITING RUBRICS To write an effective "how-to" article, you should

- arrange the steps in chronological order
- explain one step at a time
- tailor your explanation to your audience
- proofread your article

Viewing and Representing

COOPERATIVE LEARNING In a small group, discuss processes in M. C. Escher's *Day and Night* shown on this page. Refer to a process that is portrayed in the picture, a process used by the artist to achieve his effects, or both. Then each member should write a paragraph about the picture. Share and compare responses.

Using Computers

With a partner, search the Internet for other works by M. C. Escher and critical responses to his art. In three or four paragraphs, summarize how you found the information and what you learned about Escher's art and reputation. Share your findings and processes with the class.

Grammar Link

Use exact action verbs.

James Wagenvoord uses forms of strong, exact action verbs—*powered, flipping, eyeing, slash, smashed, flung.*

Rewrite the explanation below, using exact verbs. (You may make other changes, too.)

1. In football, two teams try to get possession of the ball and move it across their opponent's goal line for a touchdown.
2. The offensive team, led by a quarterback, must go ten yards in four downs to keep the ball.
3. The defending team runs after the ball carrier to keep him from advancing.
4. When a player gets a touchdown, his team has six points.
5. The team gets another point if its kicker sends the ball over the goal posts.

See Lesson 3.3, pages 136–139, and Lesson 10.3, pages 453–459.

M. C. Escher, *Day and Night,* 1938

Expository Writing

LESSON 5.4

Writing About Cause and Effect

Cause-and-effect writing explains relationships between events or facts—specifically, that one event or fact caused another. In the model below, reporter Frank Trippett describes several revolutionary effects of air conditioning.

Expository Writing

Trippett begins by identifying the cause and then explains the effects.

Trippett gives details about a series of effects of air conditioning.

Literature Model

In fact, air conditioning has substantially altered the country's character and folkways. . . . Many of its byproducts are so conspicuous that they are scarcely noticed. To begin with, air conditioning transformed the face of urban America by making possible those glassy, boxy, sealed-in skyscrapers on which the once humane geometries of places like San Francisco, Boston and Manhattan have been impaled. It has been indispensable, no less, to the functioning of sensitive advanced computers, whose high operating temperatures require that they be constantly cooled. Thus, in a very real way, air conditioning has made possible the ascendancy of computerized civilization. . . . It has also reshaped the national economy and redistributed political power simply by encouraging the burgeoning of the sultry southerly swatch of the country, profoundly influencing major migration trends of people and industry. Sunbelt cities like Phoenix, Atlanta, Dallas and Houston (where shivering indoor frigidity became a mark of status) could never have mushroomed so prosperously without air conditioning; some communities—Las Vegas in the Nevada desert and Lake Havasu City on the Arizona-California border—would shrivel and die overnight if it were turned off.

Frank Trippett, "The Great American Cooling Machine"

Identify the Relationship

In a simple chronological relationship, one event simply follows another in time. In a cause-and-effect relationship, however, one event *causes* another—for example, according to Frank Trippett, the birth of skyscrapers occurred because of air conditioning. You can test for a cause-and-effect relationship by asking the following: If the "cause" hadn't happened, would the "effect" have happened?

Cause-and-effect relationships are not always simple and straightforward. One cause can have several effects; one effect can result from several causes. Individual causes and effects can also form a chain of events, each one leading to the next. The graphic below will help you to visualize these relationships.

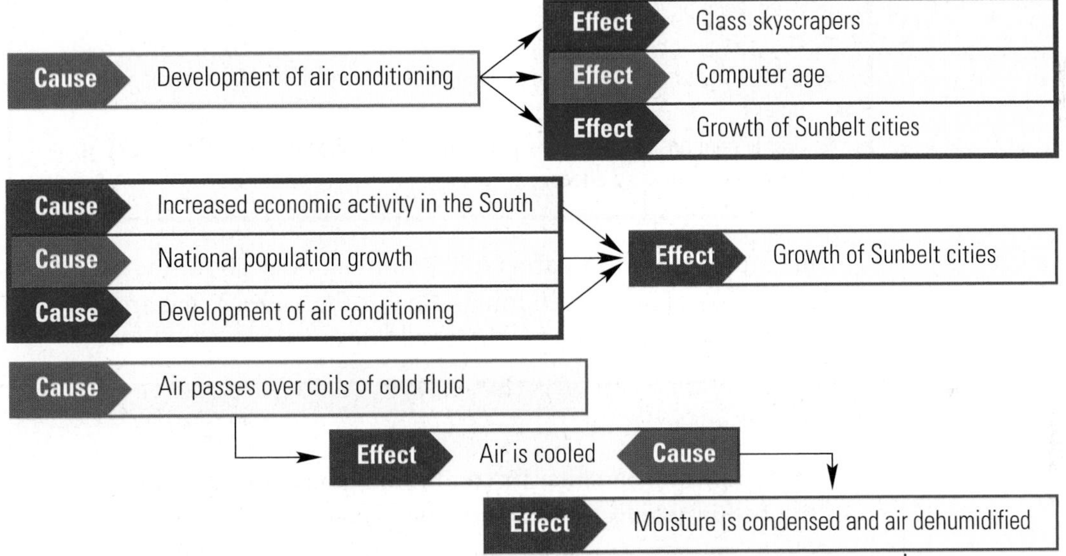

When you write about cause-and-effect relationships, you generally use one of two patterns of organization. With the cause-and-effect pattern, you start by explaining the cause (or causes) and then proceed to the effects. In the effect-to-cause pattern, you examine the effect (or effects) first and then explain what caused them.

Journal Writing

In your journal brainstorm a list of positive and negative effects of the computer. Then write a short paragraph exploring this question. On the whole, have the effects of the computer on modern society been beneficial or harmful?

Vocabulary Tip

Transitions such as *accordingly, as a result, consequently, therefore,* and *thus* can help you show connections between causes and effects.

Explore Relationships

Examining causes and effects is a skill frequently used in the natural and social sciences and in journalistic writing. The following guidelines can help you explore cause-and-effect relationships.

Guidelines for Writing a Cause-and-Effect Essay

1. Test the cause-and-effect relationship. Does one action actually *cause* another to happen, or does one merely follow the other?
2. Explore the cause-and-effect relationship. How are causes and effects related? What are the most significant aspects of the relationship?
3. Choose a focus. Do you want to emphasize causes, effects, or both?
4. Gather details. Find examples, facts and statistics, and other details to explain the cause-and-effect relationship. Keep in mind the interest level and prior knowledge of your audience.
5. Organize your writing. Should you use cause-to-effect order or effect-to-cause order? Or should you explain a chain of causes and effects in chronological order?
6. Clarify relationships. Use paragraphing and transitions to draw distinctions between causes and effects.

This cause-and-effect paragraph is from an essay about the benefits and drawbacks of air conditioning. What is the cause? What are the effects? What transitions show these relationships?

Model

Despite its benefits, air conditioning has caused its share of problems as well. Air conditioners require tremendous amounts of power. Consequently, as more homes and businesses installed air conditioning, power utilities were forced to increase their capacities. Some coal-burning utilities began burning far more fuel to meet the demand. As a result, pollution increased. Other utilities began ambitious nuclear power projects. Some citizens, concerned about the safety of nuclear power, protested. As a result, many of these projects were halted or forced to exceed their budgets to meet new safety requirements. In many large cities, even increased utility capacity could not keep up with the demand. Summer became a time of frequent "brownouts," when certain parts of a city would experience brief periods of reduced power. In some cases, power would be lost completely.

Which phrases help to show the relationship between causes and effects?

This specific example elaborates on one effect.

5.4 Writing Activities

Write a Cause-and-Effect Paragraph

The following poems, both by Robert Frost, contain causes and effects. Choose one of the poems and write a paragraph explaining its meaning in terms of cause and effect.

PURPOSE To explain a cause-and-effect relationship in poetry
AUDIENCE Your English teacher
LENGTH 1 paragraph

WRITING RUBRICS To write an effective cause-and-effect paragraph, you should

- identify the cause-and-effect relationship
- use a pattern of organization from the chart on page 233
- clarify relationships with clear transitions

Fire and Ice
Some say the world will end in fire,
Some say in ice.
From what I've tasted of desire
I hold with those who favor fire.
But if it had to perish twice,
I think I know enough of hate
To say that for destruction ice
Is also great
And would suffice.

Dust of Snow
The way a crow
Shook down on me
The dust of snow
From a hemlock tree

Has given my heart
A change of mood
And saved some part
Of a day I'd rued.

Viewing and Representing

COOPERATIVE LEARNING With a small group, create visuals of the poems, depicting important causes and effects. Share your work.

Make verbs agree with indefinite pronoun subjects.

Some indefinite pronouns are singular and require singular verbs; others are plural and take plural verbs. Note how the indefinite pronoun subject *many* is used in this sentence from the model on page 232. "*Many* of its byproducts *are* . . . scarcely noticed." There are also indefinite pronouns whose number depends on the nouns to which they refer.

Write sentences using each of the ten indefinite pronouns below as the subject. Make each subject agree with a present-tense verb.

1. nothing	**2.** some
3. several	**4.** one
5. each	**6.** few
7. both	**8.** everyone
9. most	**10.** either

See Lesson 16.7, pages 623–625.

Using Computers

Many word-processing programs include an outlining feature that enables you to create an outline and a skeleton "draft" at the same time.

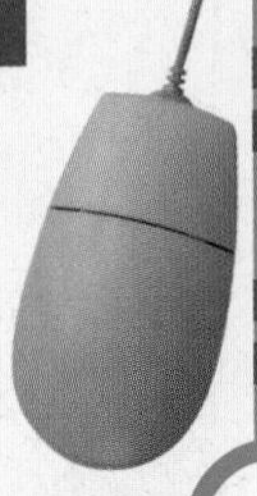

Expository Writing

LESSON

5.5

Comparing and Contrasting

When you compare two or more subjects, you explain how they are similar. When you contrast them, you explain how they are different. Note how writer Phil Sudo uses comparison and contrast to discuss the likes and dislikes of a Japanese exchange student studying in the United States.

Expository Writing

高等学校

The first sentence introduces the main ideas—"the radical differences" between Japanese and U.S. schools.

Sudo compares features of Japanese and U.S. schools: study habits, teacher-student relationships, social life.

Student Model

Life in America has exposed Naohiko to the radical differences between Japanese and U.S. schools. [In the United States] students rarely study more than two hours a night. In part, that's because so many have part-time jobs. "In my high school in Japan, they said we couldn't get jobs. 'If you get a job, you can't study,' they said." But also, he says, some students [in the United States] take advantage of the free environment. "I don't understand why it's so easy to skip class," says Naohiko. . . .

On the positive side, . . . is the open curriculum. "Here we can choose our classes and choose our teachers. In Japan, I didn't like teachers and they didn't like students. In America, a teacher is like a friend."

He also likes the social aspects of school. He has an American girlfriend, and goes to school dances. "In Japan, school is for studying. There's not many good experiences. In America, we get a lot of good experiences. It makes a lot of nice memories."

Phil Sudo, *Scholastic Update*

When comparing and contrasting, you do more than list similarities and differences. You investigate relationships and draw conclusions.

Create Graphic Organizers

In preparing to write a comparison-contrast essay, you may find two kinds of graphic organizers particularly useful.

VENN DIAGRAMS A Venn diagram can help you explore similarities and differences in your subjects. Here's how to create a Venn diagram:

1. Draw two intersecting circles. 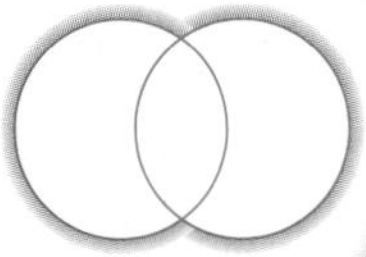
2. In the left-hand circle, list features unique to Subject A. In the right-hand circle, list features unique to Subject B.
3. Where the circles overlap, list the important features that both subjects share.

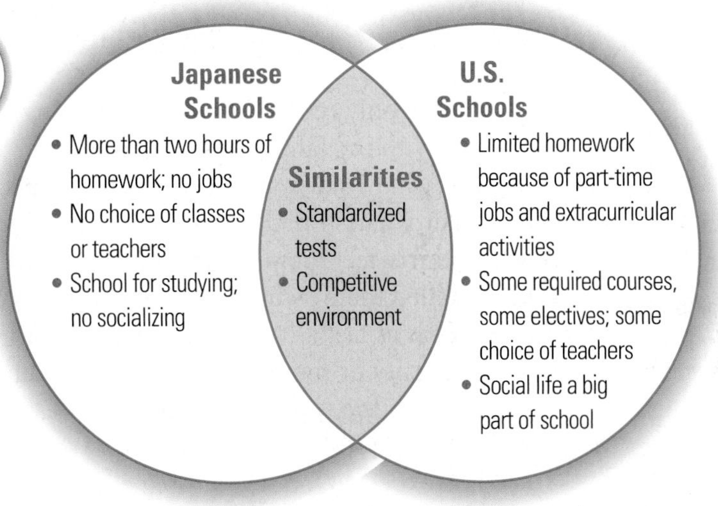

Japanese Schools
- More than two hours of homework; no jobs
- No choice of classes or teachers
- School for studying; no socializing

Similarities
- Standardized tests
- Competitive environment

U.S. Schools
- Limited homework because of part-time jobs and extracurricular activities
- Some required courses, some electives; some choice of teachers
- Social life a big part of school

COMPARISON FRAMES If you know the categories you want to compare and contrast, use a comparison frame. Follow these steps:

. Write the two subjects being compared as headings.

. List the categories you will compare and contrast.

. Fill in the boxes.

	Subjects	
Categories	**U.S. Schools**	**Japanese Schools**
Study Habits	Limited homework because of activities and jobs	Often more than two hours of homework; no jobs
Student Choice	Some required courses and some electives	Courses prescribed by government
Social Life	Social life an important aspect of school	School for studying, not socializing

Grammar Tip

When comparing two items, use the comparative form of a modifier. For help, see Lesson 18.1, pages 663–665.

Journal Writing

How would you compare and contrast two things, such as rugby and football, or two movies? In your journal, create a Venn diagram or comparison frame.

Expository Writing

Organize Your Comparison

Sudo's essay comparing Japanese and U.S. high schools uses the feature-by-feature method of organization. Another method, shown in this model, discusses all aspects first of one subject and then of the other. The chart below clarifies each method.

How do the first two sentences set the stage for a contrast?

The writer compares by presenting subjects separately. The first subject is her expectations. The second subject is her actual observations.

What is the purpose of the last sentence?

Model

The only reason I cared about going to Florida on vacation with my family was to see the killer whales at Sea World. But what I saw was not what I had expected. I pictured the killer whales I had seen on television: huge creatures—twenty to thirty feet long—with shiny backs and white bellies. I recalled them swimming freely through ocean waters at speeds as fast as twenty-five miles an hour in groups as large as twenty or more, stopping occasionally for a joyful roll through the water or a leap above the surface.

The killer whales I saw at Sea World certainly looked as I had expected, but everything else about them surprised and disappointed me. They lived in tanks—gigantic to you and me, but puny compared to the vast ocean. They traveled at rates that never even approached their top ocean speeds and were alone or in pairs rather than in large groups. Their flips and leaps were commanded by the trainer and didn't seem quite so joyful and free. After a short time, all I felt was sadness for these captives of an environment not their own.

Grammar Tip

Eliminate any double comparisons—that is, comparisons that add both the ending *-er* or *-est* and the word *more* or *most* to the modifier. See Lesson 18.3, pages 668–669.

How to Organize a Comparison-Contrast Essay

Feature by Feature	Subject by Subject
1. Study Habits A. Japan B. United States **2.** Student Choice A. Japan B. United States **3.** Social Life A. Japan B. United States	**1.** What I expected A. Swimming in ocean B. Groups of twenty or more C. Free, joyful actions **2.** What I observed A. Confined to tanks B. Alone or in pairs C. Actions on command

5.5 Writing Activities

Write a Comparison-Contrast Article

Write an article comparing and contrasting the abstract painting below with the realistic floral painting on page 243 in regard to color, composition, and total effect on the viewer. First, explore similarities and differences in a Venn diagram. Then, list your categories and information in a comparison frame.

PURPOSE To compare and contrast two paintings
AUDIENCE Your classmates and teacher
LENGTH 2–3 paragraphs

WRITING RUBRICS To write an effective comparison-contrast article, you should

- use an appropriate method of organization
- draw clear conclusions
- check your spelling and sentence structure

Avoid double comparisons.

The comparative form of an adjective or adverb is formed with *-er* or *more/less.* Using both together creates an incorrect double comparison.

Rewrite each sentence below to eliminate the double comparison.

1. U.S. schools are more easier than Russian schools.
2. Russian students have homework more frequenter than American students.
3. Russian teachers are less friendlier than American teachers.
4. Russian schools offer more fewer electives than U.S. schools.
5. American students attend social events more oftener than do Russian students.

See Lesson 18.3, pages 668–669.

Cross-Curricular Activity

SCIENCE Write an article comparing and contrasting the optimist's view of the future of the planet with that of the pessimist. The optimist thinks that the environment will be saved by people who are committed to recycling and ending pollution. The pessimist thinks that the environment is in decline and that people have neither the capacity nor the commitment to adequately care for the planet.

Alma Thomas, *Iris, Tulips, Jonquils and Crocuses,* 1969

Listening and Speaking

MAKING A SPEECH Deliver your article on the future of the environment as a speech to a specific audience of people unfamiliar to you, such as retired NASA scientists, a group of kindergartners, or a U.S. Senate committee. Ask your classmates if they can identify the audience you are aiming at and how effectively you adapted your article to this audience.

LESSON

5.6 Writing Effective Definitions

Basic definitions of words can be found in dictionaries. To present more elaborate concepts of words, however, lengthier writing is often needed. Notice how Wendell Berry gives both a formal and a personal definition of "family farm" in this excerpt from an essay.

What is Berry's definition of a family farm?

What two types of farm does Berry exclude from his definition?

Literature Model

What I shall mean by the term "family farm" is a farm small enough to be farmed by a family and one that *is* farmed by a family, perhaps with a small amount of hired help. I shall *not* mean a farm that is owned by a family and worked by other people. The family farm is both the home and the workplace of the family that owns it. . . .

Furthermore, the term "family farm" implies longevity in the connection between family and farm. A family farm is not a farm that a family has bought on speculation and is only occupying and using until it can be profitably sold.

Wendell Berry, "A Defense of the Family Farm"

Write a Formal Definition

A formal definition places a word or subject in a general category and examines how it differs from other words in its category. One way to get started in writing a formal definition is to create a word map.

Word Map

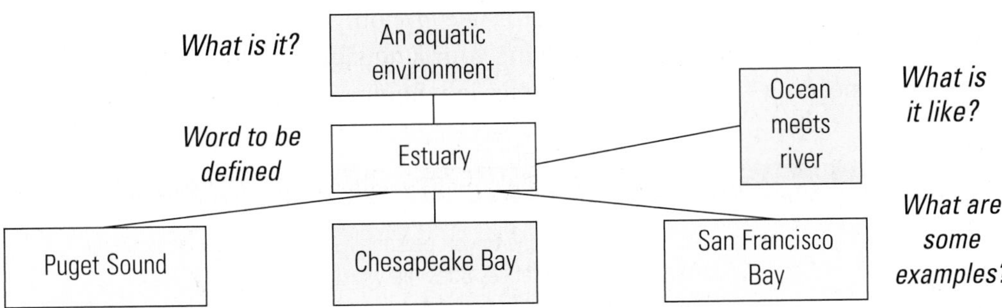

Naming your word's general category (What is it?) helps identify its broadest, most basic meaning. Naming other words in the same category (What is it like?) helps pinpoint the meanings that are unique to your word. Citing examples helps clarify the specific qualities included in the meaning of your word.

The word map above was helpful in writing this definition of *estuary*. As you read the definition, refer to the word map.

Model

Puget Sound, San Francisco Bay, and Chesapeake Bay may seem to be just busy waterways in the middle of large urban areas; but they have something else in common as well. They are all estuaries, aquatic environments with unique combinations of physical surroundings and life forms.

Estuaries are located where rivers and oceans meet, and the mixing of salt water from the ocean and fresh water from the river produces a unique environment. In addition, the action of ocean tides creates currents that deposit sediments and organic debris, making estuaries rich in minerals and nutrients. These conditions also make estuaries productive breeding grounds for shellfish.

Familiar examples help readers picture the meaning of the term being defined.

The explanation about oceans and rivers shows how estuaries are related to these other aquatic environments.

Journal Writing

Experiment with writing formal definitions. Create a word map for one or more of the following words: *horror movie, personal computer, frog, medicine.*

Expository Writing

Vocabulary Tip

You may find that you need to combine the techniques of writing formal and personal definitions to fully explore the meaning of some words.

Write a Personal Definition

Formal definitions of words like *love* only scratch the surface. An informal definition—involving your language, your style, your meaning—can often do a better job. Look at the guidelines below.

Guidelines for Writing Personal Definitions

1. Examine what the word means to you personally. How does the word affect you? What feelings or experiences does the word bring to mind?
2. Examine other viewpoints. What is the dictionary definition? What other personal definitions can you find? How is your definition different from others?
3. Find details to support your definition.

Notice the techniques this writer used to develop a personal definition of the term *environmentalist.*

Model

A dictionary definition "anchors" the personal definition and provides a basis for comparison.

I consider myself an environmentalist. According to the dictionary, an *environmentalist* is interested in preserving and improving the environment, and I certainly fit that description. To me, however, being an environmentalist requires a greater commitment than just being "interested."

Examples elaborate on the personal definition.

For me, every day is Earth Day. I try to buy only those products that are packaged in biodegradable materials. I recycle paper, aluminum, and plastics. I persuaded my brother and sister-in-law to stop buying disposable diapers for my nephew Mark. My biggest accomplishment, however, was getting my parents to stop using weed killers on our lawn. No more pesticides for us. If we see a few weeds, that's OK. We can live with weeds.

Some environmental activists are more extreme. They chain themselves to trees in the forest to keep them from being cut down. They lie down in front of bulldozers. They ride out in boats to interfere with commercial fishing and nuclear testing. I support their goals, but not their tactics. I believe we've done enough violence to the environment without doing more harm to one another. I just want future generations to live in a world that is a little cleaner and a little less threatening than the one I am growing up in.

5.6 Writing Activities

Write a Definition

The style of the painting shown on this page is sometimes called *photorealism.* Look at the painting closely, and use it to write your own definition of photorealism. Before you write your definition, prepare a word map.

PURPOSE To define *photorealism,* using a painting as an example
AUDIENCE Your teacher and classmates
LENGTH 1–2 paragraphs

WRITING RUBRICS To write an effective definition, you should

- identify feelings and experiences the word or painting brings to mind
- use details to support your definition
- make sure your writing is legible and clear

Listening and Speaking

COOPERATIVE LEARNING In a small group, prepare a presentation on current slang. Brainstorm to generate a list of terms, starting with words for *good* and *bad.* Assign each student to compose several creative definitions and examples. Share your definitions within the group. Then present them as an oral reading to the class.

Ben Schonzeit, *Parrot Tulip,* 1976

Grammar Link

Use precise nouns to clarify meaning.

When you write definitions, use specific nouns to make clear what you mean. Note how precise nouns are used as supporting details in the model definitions.

Rewrite the definitions for the italicized words below, replacing the general nouns with nouns that are more exact.

1. A *community* is a collection of things.
2. A *habitat* is a place where things live and grow.
3. *Ecologists* are people who study science.
4. *Air* is the item all things breathe.
5. *Water* is another thing all things need to live.

See Lesson 10.1, pages 439–444.

Using Computers

Investigate similarities and differences in definitions among various Internet sites and software such as Encyclopaedia Britannica, Encarta, and Webster's Dictionary. Choose six words to look up using each research tool and note the respellings, origins, and definitions provided for each word. Write a summary of your findings.

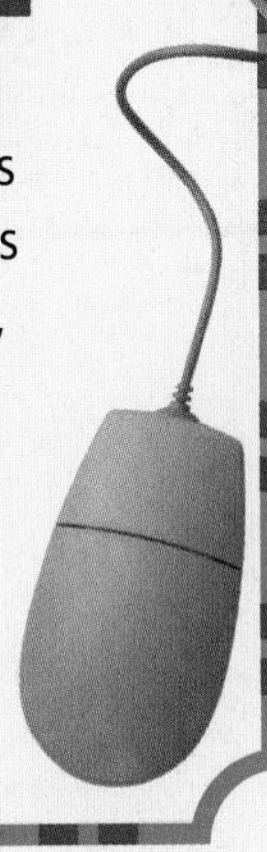

LESSON
5.7

Using Graphs in Exposition

Expository writers often use graphs to present information that may be too difficult or boring to present in words. Notice how the graph below shows that the population of Phoenix more than doubled from 1960 to 1990.

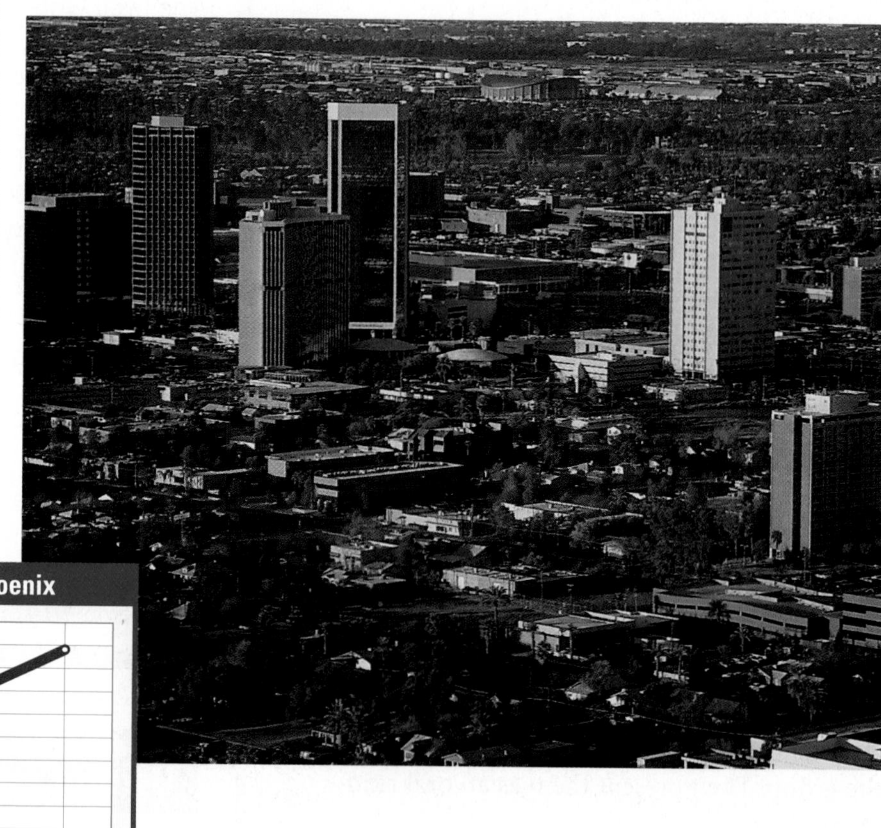

Population Growth in Phoenix

Population (in thousands)

1000
500
0

1960 1970 1980 1990

Use Graphs for Clarification

Writing filled with statistics can be deadly, with numbers cluttering up the sentences, making them hard to read and understand. Study the two examples on the next page carefully. Which model does a better job of presenting the information about the 10 largest cities in the United States—the one with the graph or the one without?

Model: Text Only

The census figures show that New York is still the nation's largest city, with 7.3 million people, even though the city's population shrank by almost a half million between 1960 and 1990. Los Angeles became the second largest city, growing by one million people to 3.5 million, and Chicago dropped to third. Houston edged past Philadelphia—now in the fifth position—to become the fourth largest city, and San Diego jumped to sixth place, ahead of Detroit, Dallas, Phoenix, and San Antonio. Phoenix, number 29 on the list in 1960, rose to ninth.

Burying statistics in a paragraph makes the data hard to find and hard to follow.

Model: Text and Graph

The latest census figures reveal a reshuffling of the order of the nation's largest cities. As the graph below shows, New York remains by far the nation's most populous city, and Los Angeles has moved past Chicago into second place. Other cities to make the top ten were Houston, Phoenix, and San Diego. Baltimore, which was sixth in 1960, failed to make the top ten this time around.

Presenting the statistics in a graph enables the reader to take in the information at a glance.

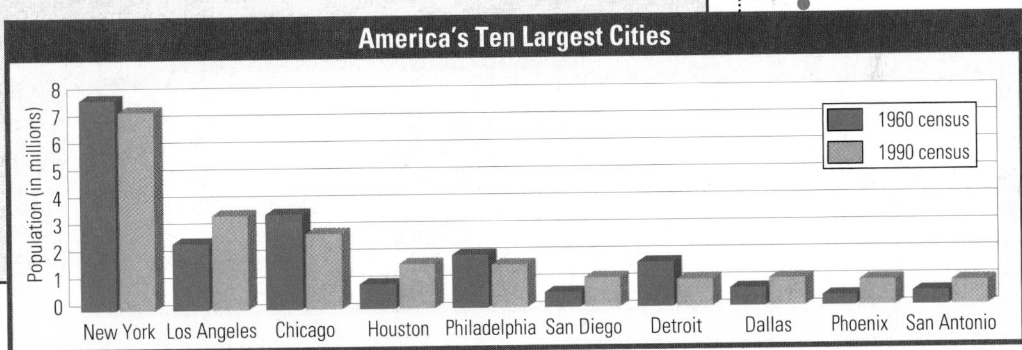

The bar graph helps readers visualize the information. It allows readers to see which cities are larger and also how much larger.

Journal Writing

List some kinds of data that can be graphed, such as height, weight, test scores, and so on. What is the advantage to presenting this kind of information in a graph?

Presenting Tip

Include a graph, diagram, map, or other graphic with your final draft to enhance a reader's understanding of your exposition.

Choose the Right Graph

You can choose specific types of graphs to clarify different relationships among statistics. Examine the models below. Then use the guidelines below the models to determine when and how to include graphs in your expository writing.

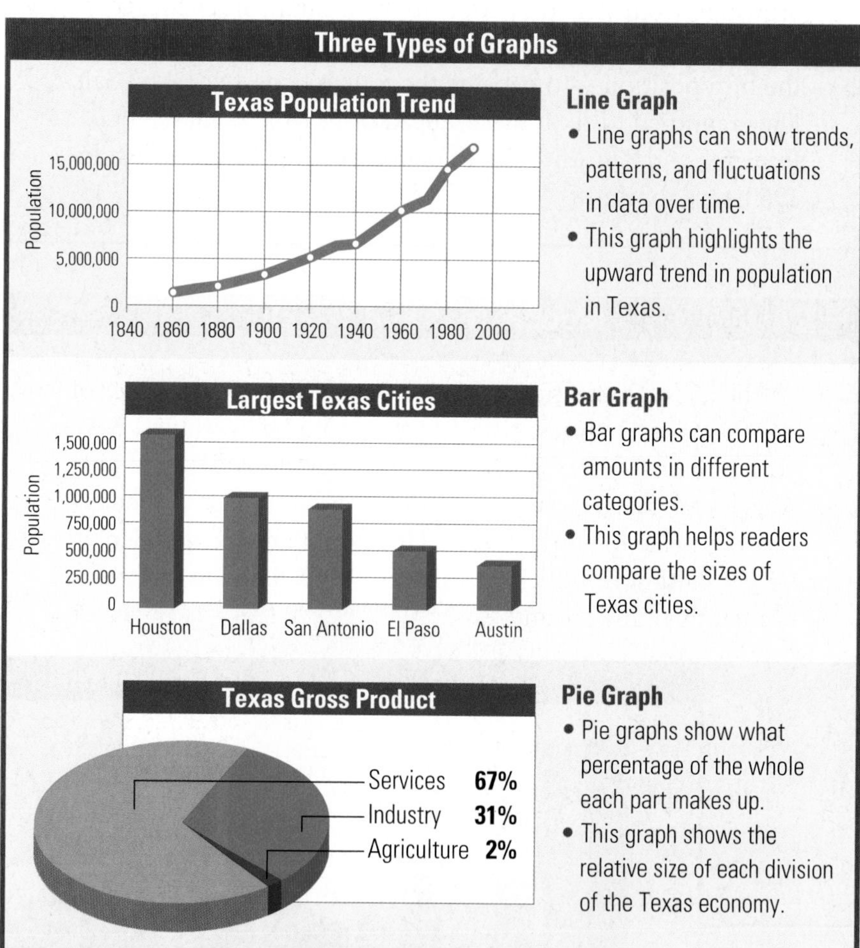

Three Types of Graphs
Texas Population Trend
Population
15,000,000
10,000,000
5,000,000
0
1840 1860 1880 1900 1920 1940 1960 1980 2000
Line Graph
• Line graphs can show trends, patterns, and fluctuations in data over time.
• This graph highlights the upward trend in population in Texas.
Largest Texas Cities
Population
1,500,000
1,250,000
1,000,000
750,000
500,000
250,000
0
Houston Dallas San Antonio El Paso Austin
Bar Graph
• Bar graphs can compare amounts in different categories.
• This graph helps readers compare the sizes of Texas cities.
Texas Gross Product
Services 67%
Industry 31%
Agriculture 2%
Pie Graph
• Pie graphs show what percentage of the whole each part makes up.
• This graph shows the relative size of each division of the Texas economy.

Revising Tip

Make sure that readers recognize how the graph relates to the text. If necessary, add a specific reference or caption to make the connection clear.

Guidelines for Making Graphs

1. Examine your data to determine whether or not a graph will help. Can you present the data more clearly in a graph than in sentences alone?
2. Decide whether you want to emphasize trends, comparisons, or parts of a whole. Choose the type of graph that meets your needs.
3. Add titles and labels that explain the information you are presenting.

5.7 Writing Activities

Write to Compare Information

Write a paragraph in which you compare and contrast the average high and low temperatures in Flagstaff and Phoenix and their implications for travelers. Use the graph for information. For help with organizing, see **Writing and Research Handbook,** page 954.

PURPOSE To compare and contrast high and low temperatures using a graph to present information

AUDIENCE Travelers

LENGTH 1 paragraph

WRITING RUBRICS To write an effective comparison, you should

- include facts from the graph
- organize your information in a coherent manner

Viewing and Representing

COOPERATIVE LEARNING Work together with a partner to construct one of the graphs discussed in this lesson: line graph, bar graph, or pie graph. Choose a meaningful subject and decide which graph would be most appropriate. Make your graph clear and legible.

Using Computers

Your electronic spell-checker can help you proofread, but you have to be careful. For example, if you've used the wrong homonym, such as *here* when you meant *hear,* your spell-checker will not catch the error. Be sure to check manually the proper nouns not in the spell-checker.

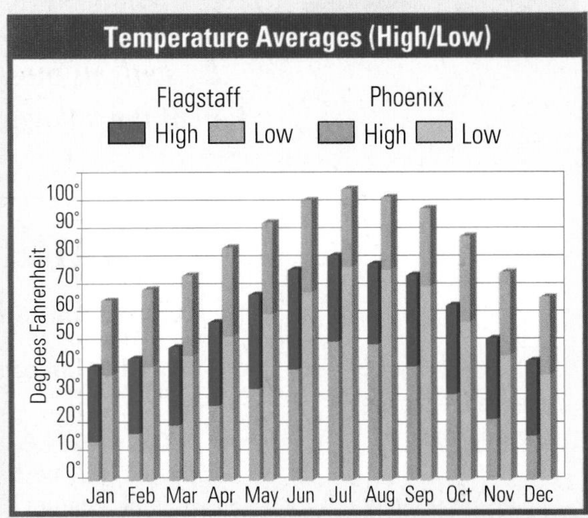

Capitalize names and titles in a graphic correctly.

Capitalize all proper nouns in a graphic, including the beginning and key words in its title.

Rewrite the following sentences, adding capital letters as necessary.

1. The time line shows the establishment of the massachusetts bay colony, virginia, maryland, and other english colonies.
2. The title of the diagram is how a bill becomes a law.
3. The map shows bull run, gettysburg, vicksburg, and other battle sites of the civil war.
4. The line graph compares the population growth rate of hispanics, african americans, asians, and other ethnic groups.

See Lesson 20.2, pages 715–721, and Lesson 20.3, pages 722–725.

Expository Writing

Expository Writing

LESSON 5.8

Writing a News Article

The primary purpose of a news story is to inform; thus, it presents its most important information first. Note the organization of the following article.

The first paragraph—the lead—captures attention and summarizes the main points of the story.

In what order are paragraphs arranged in this article?

2 Condors to Fly Free Late in '91

Release plans follow unexpected success of captive breeding

By Gina Lubrano
Staff Writer

LOS ANGELES — Two California condors will be reintroduced into the wilds of Ventura County late this year in a gamble that the once nearly extinct birds can live free, officials said yesterday.

"The time is now for the condors' return," said Marvin Plenert, Pacific regional director of the U.S. Fish and Wildlife Service.

"We have the birds. We have the site. We have the expertise, and we have the dedication."

Chocuyens, hatched at the San Diego Wild Animal Park on May 29, and Hoi-Ne-Wut, hatched at the Los Angeles Zoo three weeks earlier, are the million-dollar babies selected for release.

"Frankly, we will be taking a gamble," Plenert said. "The chance of losing a young condor faced with the uncertainties of life in the wild is extremely high."

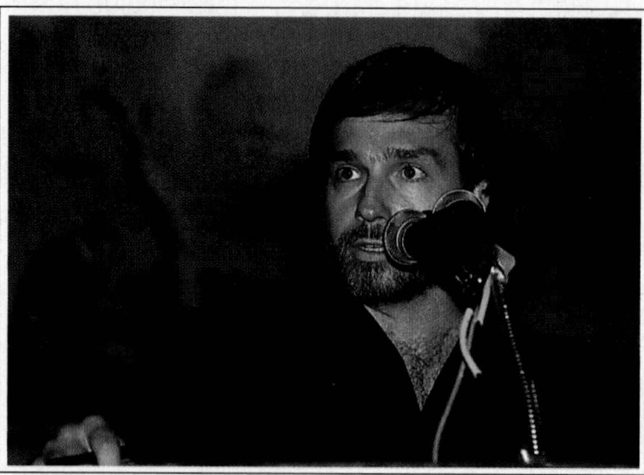

Marc Weitzel, manager of the Hopper Mountain National Wildlife Refuge in Ventura County, tells where two endangered California condors will be released into the wild.

TIME

For more about the writing process, see TIME Facing the Blank Page, pp. 109–119

Get the Facts

Most of the details in a news story are facts—statements, events, and observations that can be proved or disproved. The readers of news articles—a broad, general-interest audience—want to know what happened, not what the writer's opinions are. The goal of a news article is to answer six basic questions, the five *W*s and an *H*.

5 *W*s and *H*	
Who?	Who did it? Who caused the action? Who else is affected?
What?	What happened? What was the action? What were the reactions?
When?	When did it take place? When will related actions occur?
Where?	Where did it happen? What was the scene like?
Why?	Why did it happen? Why is it significant?
How?	How did it happen? How does it work? How will it affect people?

Start with a Lead

An effective lead, or opening paragraph, attracts attention and provides a capsule summary of the article—all in the space of a sentence or two. The lead presents the essential facts, answering some or all of the six basic questions. Notice which questions are answered in this lead.

Two California condors will be reintroduced into the wilds of Ventura County late this year in a gamble that the once nearly extinct birds can live free, officials said yesterday.

WHO?
WHAT?
WHERE?
WHEN?
WHY?

Journal Writing

As you go about your daily activities, try to see things through the eyes of a reporter. What news do you see in your classes, in the cafeteria, and on your way to and from school? In your journal practice writing leads about two or more scenes, trying to answer as many of the six basic questions as possible.

Present the Details

The events in a fictional story usually build up to a climax or turning point, often the most important event in the story. Reporters turn this pattern upside down. They start with a lead that sums up the most important event and relate other events in decreasing order of importance. This organization makes it easier for editors to make last-minute cuts in the story. Read Michael Han's story to see how it follows this pattern. Then review guidelines for writing a news article.

How does Michael's lead draw readers into the story? Which of the five *W*s does he answer in the lead?

After presenting the most important part of the story at the beginning, Michael adds less important material.

Student Model

The Cookeville Cavaliers head into their game at Warren County tonight with a new football coach and a new enthusiasm.

"I'm looking forward to the season," said senior Jerald Bryant. "I think it's going to be a great one."

Jake Libbey begins his second stint as the head football coach of the Cavaliers with what could best be described as a "rebuilding" year. The team has only 32 players, 17 of them seniors.

The season began last Friday here in Cookeville with a win against Hillsboro. The Cavaliers are staring at a demanding schedule with five away games, including Oakland and McGavock. The Homecoming game will be against Riverdale on October 5.

"We are just going to have to take this schedule one game at a time," said Coach Libbey. "We can't look before us or behind us. We're really going to have to rise to the occasion with courage and desire."

Michael Han, Cookeville High School, Cookeville, Tennessee

Grammar Tip

As you gather information for a news article, listen for direct quotations, which will add authority and interest to your writing. Set off direct quotes with quotation marks. For information on using quotation marks, see Lesson 21.9, pages 755–757.

Guidelines for Writing a News Article

1. Gather information that will add authority and interest to your writing.
2. Write a strong lead. Grab the reader's attention and summarize your main points.
3. Present information in order of importance. Start with the most important points.
4. Be fair. Cover all sides of the story, and keep your own opinions out of your article.
5. Make sure your facts are accurate and that proper names are spelled correctly.

5.8 Writing Activities

Write a News Article

Imagine that you were a reporter who was present on the historic day when the Berlin Wall was opened. Write a news article using these facts:

- Wall is opened November 9, 1989.
- At an all-night celebration, people dance on the wall itself.
- People travel freely between East and West Berlin for the first time since 1961.
- At exactly midnight, people begin crossing.
- The wall is twenty-six miles long.
- Tens of thousands of East and West Berliners swarm across the wall.
- Some chisel off pieces for souvenirs.
- One elderly East Berliner who crosses over the wall is overheard saying, "I can't believe I'm here. We have dreamed of this."

PURPOSE To write a news story about a major historical event
AUDIENCE Readers of your local newspaper, all ages
LENGTH 2–3 paragraphs

WRITING RUBRICS To write an effective news article, you should

- write a strong lead
- present details in decreasing order of importance
- avoid personal opinions

Using Computers

In revising, if you discover a misspelled word that you use again and again, save time by using the Search and Replace feature of your word-processing program.

Grammar Link

Punctuate direct quotations correctly.

Note how the writer punctuated this direct quote in her news article about condors:

"Frankly, we will be taking a gamble," Plenert said. "The chance of losing a young condor . . . is extremely high."

Rewrite the following sentences, adding or correcting punctuation as necessary.

1. For years, the Japanese assumed that their cities were earthquake resistant, a news reporter commented.
2. "Twenty seconds of terror shattered that belief" said one reporter, "when a 7.2 earthquake hit Kobe, Japan, in 1995"
3. A government official admitted, I never felt so powerless in my life.
4. A second official confessed, "The government's initial response was pure panic and confusion."
5. "Revamping disaster-relief plans and revising building codes are the only way to avoid future disasters" seismologists warn.

See Lesson 21.9, pages 755–757.

Listening and Speaking

BROADCAST NEWS Rewrite your news article or a news article on another event as a TV report for the nightly news. Deliver your report in the style of a network news anchor. Discuss with the class the major difference between a written news article and a TV news report.

LESSON

5.9

Taking an Essay Test

Do you react like the character in the cartoon when you have to take an essay test? In this lesson you will learn some ways to examine test questions and compose illuminating answers.

Expository Writing

© 1986 Tribune Media Services, Inc. All Rights Reserved

Look at the sample test below. How would you go about answering the following questions?

Answer all the questions below. You will have one hour to complete this test.

1. Define the term biome. (20 points)
2. Discuss the characteristics of desert biomes. (20 points)
3. Compare the qualities of tropical savannas to those of temperate grasslands. (20 points)
4. Analyze the factors that affect the distribution of biomes. (40 points)
5. Describe the vegetation found in the tropical rain forest.
6. Summarize the problems facing tropical rain forests today.

Develop a Plan of Attack

When you sit down to take a test like the one on the previous page, don't jump right in and start writing answers. Instead, take a moment to look over the individual questions and the test as a whole. That way you can make plans that will help you answer all the questions in the time available. Keep the following steps in mind.

Read the directions. Are you expected to answer *all* the questions, or do you have a choice? How much time do you have to complete the test?

Read each question. Which ones will be easier or will take less time to answer? Are you unprepared to answer any of the questions?

Note the point value for each question. Are some questions worth more than others? Does the test include any extra credit questions?

To avoid the problem of time being up while you are still writing answers, estimate how much time you will need for each question. Consider both how much you know about the subject and how many points the question is worth. The greater the point value, the more time you should plan to devote to the question, especially if it's one about which you know a great deal. The graphic below shows one way to divide your time among four unequally weighted questions. How might your time allotment vary if you knew little about question 2?

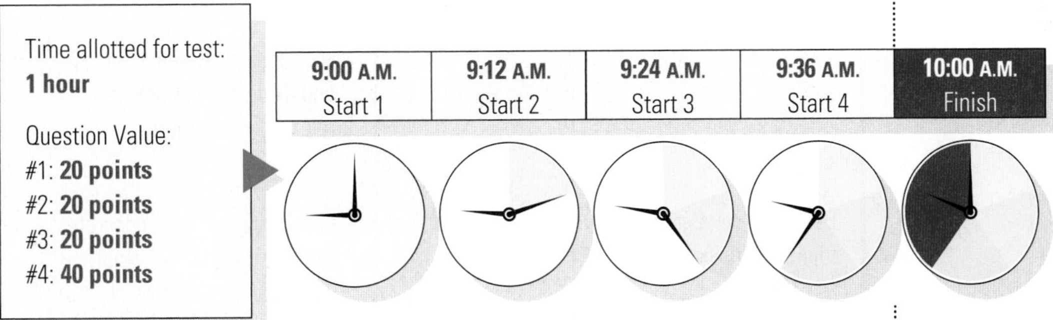

Journal Writing

In your journal, reflect on your test-taking experiences. Write about some ways that previewing tests and budgeting your time could help you improve your performance.

Expository Writing

Understand the Questions

Make sure you understand each question before you start to respond. Focus on key words that tell exactly what you have to do. Below are some questions that include common key words and some strategies for answering the questions.

Key Words in Essay Questions

Question	Key Word	Strategy for Answering
Define the term *biome.*	**Define**	Tell what the term means, and explain what distinguishes it from other similar terms.
Discuss the characteristics of desert biomes.	**Discuss**	Look at your subject from several viewpoints, and provide facts and other details to explain its characteristics or qualities.
Compare the qualities of tropical savannas with those of temperate grasslands.	**Compare**	Tell how two or more subjects are alike and how they are different. Support your ideas with details and examples.
Analyze the factors that affect the distribution of biomes.	**Analyze**	Identify the important parts of your subject, examine each part, and explain how each part relates to the others.
Describe the vegetation found in tropical rain forests.	**Describe**	Create and organize concrete sensory images that vividly illustrate the qualities of your subject.
Summarize the problems facing tropical rain forests today.	**Summarize**	Present the main points or concepts of your subject, and give a brief explanation for each.

Write a Thesis Statement

An effective thesis statement, a sentence that communicates the main idea you intend to develop in an answer, can point you in the right direction as you begin writing. Such a statement also tells the reader how you will respond to the key word in the question and helps you determine what types of details you must include to develop your essay. Often you can rephrase the question as a statement and indicate how you will respond to it, as in the example below.

2. Discuss the characteristics of desert biomes. (20 points)

Desert biomes are characterized by a variety of harsh conditions, chief of which is a lack of water.

Create a Plan

Since you probably will not have much time to revise your answer, it pays to plan what you intend to say before you start writing. Your plan should be simple, logically organized, and easy to follow. Create an outline, a cluster diagram, or a comparison-contrast chart to identify and organize your main points. Notice how brief your organizing plan can be.

2. Discuss the characteristics of desert biomes. (20 points)

A. Amount of precipitation
B. Range of temperatures
C. Types of plants
D. Types of animals

Journal Writing

Look at the questions in the chart on the previous page. In your journal, write thesis statements for several by rewording the questions and anticipating how you might respond to them.

Drafting Tip

As you write, keep looking back at your thesis statement to remind yourself of your focus.

Expository Writing

Draft Your Answer

Because your time is limited, you need to use a simple, straightforward format for writing your answer. Your thesis statement, which introduces your main idea, can serve as your first sentence. Then you can let your outline or graphic aid guide you as you compose your answer, adding solid facts and other supporting details that elaborate on your thesis. Remember to use appropriate transition words and phrases to connect ideas. Finally, end your answer with a brief conclusion that restates your main ideas.

The answer begins with the thesis statement. Each paragraph addresses a topic that supports the thesis. The conclusion restates the main point.

What specific details are used to support generalizations?

2. Discuss the characteristics of desert biomes. (20 points)

Desert biomes are characterized by harsh conditions, including a lack of water. Deserts get little rain, so plants are few and widely scattered. The soil is often mainly sand. The lack of ground cover affects temperatures. The land heats up rapidly during the day and cools off rapidly at night, so temperature ranges are extreme.

Plants and animals have adapted to the desert in various ways. Some plants, such as the saguaro cactus, store water in their tissues during rains and use it later in dry periods. Others, such as the desert dandelion, grow only when there is enough moisture. Many desert animals are nocturnal, sleeping in the shade during the day.

In the harsh conditions of desert biomes, only hardy plants and animals survive.

Editing Tip

Even though time is limited, be sure to proofread your work. Pay special attention to the spelling and usage of those key terms and concepts on which you are being tested.

There's no getting away from essay tests; you will face them throughout your school years. By following the steps summarized below, you can probably improve your performance.

Guidelines for Taking an Essay Test

1. Preview the test by reading all directions and questions.
2. Budget your time, using the point value of each question as a guide.
3. Prepare a thesis statement and brief outline or graphic aid before you begin drafting your essay.
4. Start your essay with your thesis statement, follow your outline, and support each point with specific facts and details. Conclude by restating your thesis.

5.9 Writing Activities

Write an Essay Answer

Read the following excerpt from *Sand County Almanac,* and take the essay test that follows it. Allow yourself thirty minutes. Read the whole test before you begin.

PURPOSE To take an essay test on literature
AUDIENCE Your English teacher
LENGTH 3–6 paragraphs

When I was a boy, there was an old German merchant who lived in a little cottage in our town. On Sundays he used to go out and knock chips off the limestone ledges along the Mississippi, and he had a great tonnage of these chips, all labeled and catalogued. The chips contained little fossil stems of some defunct water creatures called crinoids. The townspeople regarded this gentle old fellow as just a little bit abnormal, but harmless. One day the newspaper reported the arrival of certain titled strangers. It was whispered that these visitors were great scientists. Some of them were from foreign lands, and some among the world's leading paleontologists. They came to visit the harmless old man and to hear his pronouncements on crinoids, and they accepted these pronouncements as law. When the old German died, the town awoke to the fact that he was a world authority on his subject, a creator of knowledge, a maker of scientific history. He was a great man — a man beside whom the local captains of industry were mere bushwhackers. His collection went to a national museum, and his name is known in all the nations of the earth.

Aldo Leopold, *Sand County Almanac*

Essay Test

- Compare and contrast what the German merchant was like with what people in the town thought he was like. (60 points)
- Summarize Leopold's main point in telling this story. (40 points)

WRITING RUBRICS To write an effective answer to an essay question, you should

- budget your time and plan your answers
- study the key words in each question
- write a clear thesis statement

Use commas in compound sentences to avoid run-ons.

Commas and coordinating conjunctions are needed between the clauses in a compound sentence.

Rewrite the following compound sentences, adding commas as necessary.

1. Energy cannot be created or destroyed yet it can change form.
2. Energy is needed to maintain all aspects of life for you use it even when you sleep.
3. All living things get their energy from the sun but plants get it directly.
4. Energy conversions always involve a loss nor is any conversion 100-percent efficient.

See Lesson 21.6, pages 743–751.

Cross-Curricular Activity

PROOFREADING In a small group, exchange essay answers and check for misspelled words and illegible writing. Discuss common strengths and weaknesses.

Listening and Speaking

COOPERATIVE LEARNING In a small group, brainstorm for essay questions on a science topic you are studying. Discuss various ways of responding to the questions.

LESSON 5.10

WRITING ABOUT LITERATURE

Comparing and Contrasting Literature

There are many approaches you can take in comparing and contrasting works of literature. For example, you might compare this modern fable with a traditional fable.

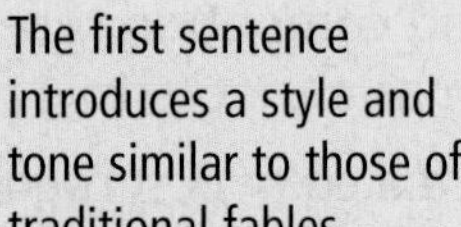

The first sentence introduces a style and tone similar to those of traditional fables.

Literature Model

There was once a town in the heart of America where all life seemed to live in harmony with its surroundings. The town lay in the midst of a checkerboard of prosperous farms, with fields of grain and hillsides of orchards where, in spring, white clouds of bloom drifted above the green fields. In autumn, oak and maple and birch set up a blaze of color that flamed and flickered across a backdrop of pines. Then foxes barked in the hills and deer silently crossed the fields, half hidden in the mists of the fall mornings.

Along the roads, laurel, viburnum and alder, great ferns and wildflowers delighted the traveler's eye through much of the year. Even in winter the roadsides were places of beauty, where countless birds came to feed on the berries and on the seed heads of the dried weeds rising above the snow. The countryside was, in fact, famous for the abundance and variety of its bird life, and when the flood of migrants was pouring through in spring and fall, people traveled from great distances to observe them. Others came to fish the streams, which flowed clear and cold out of the hills and contained shady pools where trout lay. So it had been from the days many years ago when the first settlers raised their houses, sank their wells, and built their barns.

Then a strange blight crept over the area and everything began to change. Some evil spell had settled on the community: mysterious maladies swept the flocks of chickens; the cattle and sheep sickened and died. Everywhere was a shadow of death. The farmers spoke of much illness among their families. In the town the doctors had become more and more puzzled by new kinds of sickness appearing among their patients. There had been several sudden and unexplained deaths, not only among adults but even among children, who would be stricken suddenly while at play and die within a few hours.

There was a strange stillness. The birds, for example—where had they gone? Many people spoke of them, puzzled and disturbed. The feeding stations in the back yards were deserted. The few birds seen anywhere were moribund; they trembled violently and could not fly. It was a spring without voices. On the mornings that had once throbbed with the dawn chorus of robins, catbirds, doves, jays, wrens, and scores of other bird voices there was now no sound; only silence lay over the fields and woods and marsh. . . .

No witchcraft, no enemy action had silenced the rebirth of new life in this stricken world. The people had done it themselves.

Rachel Carson, *Silent Spring*

Most traditional fables end with a moral. Carson's fable ends with an accusation. How does her accusation serve as a kind of moral?

Expository Writing

Evaluate Literary Elements

Depending on what your precise topic is, your literary analysis will examine some or all of the elements listed below.

Analyzing Basic Elements of Literature

Element	Question to Ask
Theme, or central focus	Does the work address a universal problem or teach a moral?
Style	Is the language formal or informal, figurative or objective?
Tone	Is it serious? Sad? Humorous?
Setting	What is the role of time and place?
Plot	What is the main conflict?
Characters	How do we know what the characters are like?

Prewriting Tip

It is often helpful to write down your initial impressions about a piece of literature as you read.

Journal Writing

Reread a short literary piece you've read recently. In your journal, note what you see now that you hadn't seen before.

Grammar Tip

When comparing literary pieces, use quotation marks to set off the titles of short works, such as short stories and poems. Italicize, or underline, the titles of longer works, such as novels. See Lesson 21.9, page 755, and 21.10, page 758.

Make Your Point

After you've identified the elements on which you will focus, examine similarities and differences about each element. Look also for direct quotations you can use to help you make your points and elaborate on them. Use these guidelines to help you.

Guidelines for Writing a Literary Comparison and Contrast

1. Write an introductory paragraph stating your main idea.
2. Use information from your reading to shape your writing.
3. Include quotations, when appropriate, to support and elaborate on your points.
4. Write an effective conclusion, summing up your main idea in a sentence or two.

The following model compares and contrasts Rachel Carson's fable with the traditional form of the fable. Note how it uses the guidelines.

Model

For thousands of years, people have told fables to teach a lesson or to pass on wisdom. Fables were part of the oral tradition of many early cultures, and the well-known Aesop's fables date to the sixth century B.C. Yet, the form of the fable still has value today, as Rachel Carson demonstrates in "A Fable for Tomorrow."

Carson uses a simple, direct style common to fables. In fact, her style and tone are seemingly directed at children. "There was once a town in the heart of America where all life seemed to live in harmony with its surroundings," her fable begins, borrowing some familiar words from many age-old fables. Behind the simple style, however, is a serious message intended for everyone.

In contrast to traditional fables, Carson's story ends with an accusation instead of a moral. She warns of the environmental dangers facing society, and she teaches that people must take responsibility for saving their environment.

The themes of traditional fables often deal with simple truths about everyday life. In contrast, Carson's theme is a more weighty warning about environmental destruction. Nevertheless, Carson proves that a simple literary form that has been passed down through the ages can still be used today to draw attention to important truths.

The form of Carson's fable is compared to that of traditional fables.

How does this quotation contribute to the overall passage?

What does the writer contrast at the end? How does the writer achieve this effect?

5.10 Writing Activities

Write a Comparison-Contrast Essay

The two poems on this page were both written by William Carlos Williams. Write a comparison-contrast essay about the two poems.

PURPOSE To compare and contrast works of a poet
AUDIENCE Your English teacher and classmates
LENGTH 2 paragraphs

WRITING RUBRICS To write an effective comparison-contrast essay, you should

- identify key elements in each poem
- explore similarities and differences for each element
- identify quotations to support your points
- check your spelling

This Is Just to Say
I have eaten
the plums
that were in
the icebox

and which
you were probably
saving for breakfast

Forgive me
they were delicious
so sweet
and so cold

The Red Wheelbarrow
so much depends
upon

a red wheel
barrow

glazed with rain
water

beside the white
chickens

Using Computers

To write effective literary criticism, you must find the right words to express your meaning. If your word-processing program has an electronic thesaurus, be sure to use it, especially in revising.

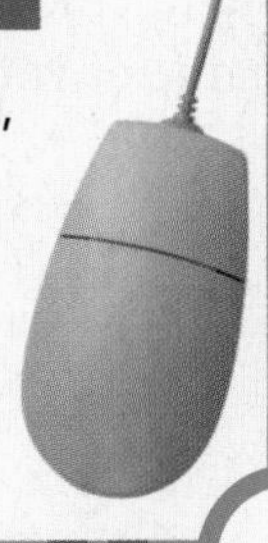

Grammar Link

Make clear and complete comparisons.

In the model, note how the student clearly states one difference between Rachel Carson's fable and more traditional fables:

In contrast to traditional fables, Carson's story ends with an accusation instead of a moral.

Rewrite each sentence below to correct the unclear comparison.

1. Rachel Carson, a marine biologist, wrote more books on the environment than any scientist.
2. She has had more influence on environmental beliefs than anyone.
3. Carson portrayed people's role in silencing the rebirth of new life as greater than witchcraft or enemy action.
4. Traditional fables deal with simpler truths than Carson.
5. Still, in their own way yesterday's fables are as valuable as today.

See Lesson 18.4, page 670.

Viewing and Representing

COOPERATIVE LEARNING Work with a partner to create a visual image to represent the poems. Discuss the following questions with your partner before you start. How will you depict the ideas in each poem? What materials will you use to create your images? Display your work along with the text of each poem.

UNIT 5

Writing Process in Action

WRITING Online

Visit the Writer's Choice Web site at writerschoice.glencoe.com for additional writing prompts.

Expository Writing

In preceding lessons you learned about the different kinds of expository writing, the purpose of each, and ways to make exposition informative and engaging. You've had a chance to write comparison-contrasts, definitions, and news articles. Now you are invited to write a practical or whimsical explanation of a process that is familiar and enjoyable for you.

Assignment

Context

You are a member of a team of writers selected to write a book entitled *How to Do Just About Anything.* You have been asked to write an entry explaining a process with which you are familiar and that you enjoy. The subject you select can be practical or whimsical, and your writing style should be light and engaging.

Purpose

To write a practical or whimsical explanation of a familiar process

Audience

Teenagers and adults who read general-interest books

Length

1–2 pages

The guidelines on the following pages can help you plan and write your book entry. Read through the guidelines, and then refer back to them as you complete this assignment. However, don't feel tied down by them. Remember, you're in charge of your own writing process.

Prewriting

A good way to find a topic is to think about your talents and your interests. Let your mind wander for a few minutes. Additional ways to probe your thoughts are listed to the right.

Once you've found a topic, think about what you want to accomplish with this piece. You might want to clear up misconceptions about something, persuade readers to look at your process in a new light, or just entertain your readers. Try freewriting to explore how you really feel about your topic; develop a main idea statement.

Next, think about your audience. The fact that you will be writing for a general readership means you can't assume readers will have any prior knowledge of your process. It also means they probably won't have enough interest to wade through piles of dry facts.

Prewriting Options

- Freewrite about your areas of expertise. Explore jobs, hobbies, sports, and school subjects.
- List "how to" topics.
- Hold a brainstorming session with your classmates.

Drafting

The challenge in explaining a process is to make your writing more than just a monotonous list of steps. The key is finding a way to make your writing flow. Start by figuring out how to break down your subject. What are the major terms and concepts you need to explain? What are the processes related to these concepts?

Next, think about how you can weave the concepts and processes into an engaging expository essay. Don't let yourself get bogged down in technicalities. Keep your audience in mind, and consider what details will grab their attention and maintain their interest. Note how naturalist writer Sue Hubbell mixes factual data with first-person observations in the model that follows.

Prewriting Tip

To gain better understanding of your audience, ask yourself the questions listed in Lesson 5.2, page 224.

Drafting Tip

For tips on writing about a process, see Lesson 5.3, pages 228–231.

Literature Model

In early springtime, the bees' need for pollen may be greater than what is available, and then they will compulsively gather up almost any fine granular material—sawdust, bits of plastic packing materials, ashes—whether it is useful to them or not. I often see them at the bird feeder, picking through the wild bird feed. At that time of year, I often get a telephone call from a dairy farmer who lives near one of my beeyards.

"Hey, Sue," he says. "How about coming over and feeding your bees? They're in the calf feed again."

Sue Hubbell, *A Book of Bees . . . and How to Keep Them*

Revising Tip

For additional tips on revising expository writing, see Lesson 5.3, page 230.

Revising

To begin revising, read over your draft to make sure that what you have written fits your purpose and your audience. Then have a **writing conference.** Read your draft to a partner or small group. Use your audience's reactions to help you evaluate your work so far. The questions in the Revising Checklist can help you and your listeners.

An easy way to check your explanation for completeness is to visualize yourself actually doing the process. Walk through each step of the process mentally, checking your work as you go. Sharing your draft with a peer reader is another way to identify holes in your explanation. Ask for feedback about steps that are unclear, terms that are unfamiliar, background information that would be helpful.

Next, look closely at how your explanation flows. Make sure you use strong topic sentences to tell readers where you are headed with each paragraph. Within paragraphs, use transitions to move readers along the steps of the process.

Revising Checklist

- Is my explanation complete, clear, and accurate?
- Are the steps of the process easy to follow?
- Have I used a writing style that a general audience will enjoy?
- Have I defined any unfamiliar terms and concepts?

Editing/Proofreading

Once you have revised your article for basic content and organization, **proofread** it carefully for errors in grammar, usage, mechanics, and spelling. Use the questions at the right as a guide.

In addition to proofreading, use the list below to make sure your explanation does all the things you want it to do. When you're satisfied, make a clean copy of your explanation and proofread it one more time.

Editing/Proofreading Checklist

- *Have I avoided sentence fragments and run-on sentences?*
- *Do my subjects and verbs agree?*
- *Have I used correct capitalization?*
- *Have I made any comparisons clear and logical?*
- *Have I checked carefully for possible misspellings?*

Self-Evaluation

Make sure your exposition—

- ✔ focuses on explaining a process
- ✔ presents steps in a clear, easy-to-follow order
- ✔ uses terms and concepts related to the process in an appropriate way
- ✔ uses a light, engaging style of writing
- ✔ follows correct grammar, usage, mechanics, and spelling

Proofreading

For proofreading symbols, see page 84.

Publishing/Presenting

With your classmates, compile a class "how to" book. Create a cover, table of contents, and an introduction for the volume. Have interested classmates either draw or find illustrations to include in the book.

Journal Writing

Reflect on your writing process experience. Answer these questions in your journal: What do you like best about your process explanation? What was the hardest part of writing it? What did you learn in your writing conference? What new things have you learned as a writer?

Literature Model

FROM

A Book of Bees . . . and How to Keep Them

by Sue Hubbell

Sue Hubbell, a self-taught naturalist, spends much of the year on her Missouri farm, taking care of her 300 beehives and approximately 12 million bees. As you read the selection below from A Book of Bees . . . and How to Keep Them, *note how Hubbell reaches out to her readers as she guides them through the beekeeper's year. Then try the activities in Linking Writing and Literature on page 274.*

Literature Model

Spring for bees, and so for beekeepers as well, has nothing to do with the calendar. In protected hollows even in the Missouri winter, bees can find a bit of springtime in flowers with enough pollen to feed the first young bees growing from the eggs the queen has begun to lay.

Various species of maples, all members of the genus *Acer,* with their delicate blossoms ranging from yellow-green to red, are one of the earliest to bloom. Maples are tall trees, and their blossoms are borne high in the crowns, where they often are not seen by humans. The bees, of course, have no trouble in finding them. The American hazel, *Corylus americana,* is a smaller tree—hardly more than a shrub—that is another early source of pollen, and easier for us to see. It grows wild throughout most of temperate North America and produces the nuts we call filberts. In late winter and early spring when most other plants are at rest, hazel generously produces pollen on long, dangling catkins.[1] In the winter, I like to stop on my walk down to the mailbox and draw one of the yellowish brown catkins between my thumb and forefinger and watch the powdery golden pollen collect in my palm. On days warm enough, bees, having declared it springtime, will be on the catkins collecting pollen.

Skunk cabbage, *Symplocarpus foetidus,* with its coarsely sheathed flower and supposedly vile odor, makes spring for bees in February in northern parts of the country. If a walker in the wet woods or swamps takes the time to look inside the skunk-cabbage spathe[2] on a mild day, he will usually find a honeybee there, packing pollen into the carrying baskets on her back legs.

Mature adult bees are carbohydrate feeders. They live on nectar and honey, which are almost exclusively carbohydrate in composition except for a few traces of minerals, vitamins and other materials. But young and developing bees need protein to grow muscles, glands and other tissues, and it is pollen—variously rich in protein, depending on its source—that provides it.

It takes about three weeks for a bee to grow from egg to adult. Three days after the queen bee has laid an egg, it hatches out into a nearly white larva that, throughout its instars, or developmental stages, has a ferocious need for food high in protein. Bee larvae don't move around looking for food as some insects do in their early stages; they are not wriggly caterpillars as are those of moths or butterflies. They merely lie passively in their cells, growing, changing. They are small animals, with disproportionately large stomachs waiting to be filled by nurse bees—young adults just emerged from pupation.[3] These nurse bees feed on the gathered pollen and produce secretions from their hypopharyngeal[4] glands (glands under the pharynx), which they will use as food for the developing larvae.

---

1 **catkins** (kat′ kinz) drooping, scaly spikes that hang down from trees such as poplars and birches
2 **spathe** (spāth) a leaflike part of a plant that encloses a fleshy spike or tiny flower
3 **pupation** (pyoo pā′ shən) the developmental stage between larva and adult insect
4 **hypopharyngeal** (hī′ pō fə rin′ jē əl) [for pronunciation only; see above for definition]

Vincent van Gogh, *View of Arles,*

In recent years, vendors of nostrums[5] to the health-food industry have been delighted by Ronald Reagan's public consumption of pollen, and pollen has become a hot item in health-food stores. Claims are made that humans who eat pollen are stronger, sexier, livelier and more cheerful, but there is no good medical evidence to back up these claims so far. And as a matter of fact, some people have experienced severe allergic reactions after eating it.

---

5 **nostrums** (näs′ trəmz) medicines, sometimes sold with exaggerated claims of what they can do

Pollen from a hay-fever sufferer's local area is also said to cure him of his allergy. I have an open mind. I am an empiricist.[6] I have hay fever. And, after all, bee venom[7] does help my arthritis. So one summer, when my eyes were running and I was sneezing exquisitely from ragweed, I gathered and ate pollen from my bees. Pollen has a bitter taste. It is no fun to eat, but in the interests of testing the efficacy[8] of the stuff I dutifully continued to eat it—and to sneeze. It is possible pollen may cure someone else's hay fever, but it doesn't cure mine.

I am always eager to start working with the bees in the spring. I miss them in the winter and want to be back with them again. But I sternly remind myself I can do more harm than good if I open their hives before the daffodils bloom, so when the crocuses flower around my cabin I have to content myself with crouching down beside those purple, white and yellow blossoms to watch the field bees gathering pollen.

Each worker bee is covered with stiff hairs. These catch the granules when the bee brushes against the flower's pollen-bearing anthers.[9] She is soon covered and stops to use her two front pairs of legs to comb the sticky pollen from her body and pack it into the baskets on her rear pair of legs. When her legs are heavy with their wads of pollen she returns to her hive to unload. House bees arrange the pollen granules in the honeycomb cells around the developing bee larvae, where it is conveniently available to the nurse bees.

In the springtime, a typical frame of brood—as beekeepers call developing bees—contains a large central semicircle of cells containing eggs and larvae in various stages. The eggs and larvae are there to see, but the oldest brood, stomachs full, have spun themselves cocoons in which to pupate, and are hidden from human eyes, sealed in their cells by a tough, velvety brown covering, from beneath which they will emerge as adults. The entire semicircle of brood is bordered by a ring of pollen-filled cells, which in turn is surrounded by honey, or, as the season progresses, nectar.

In this part of the country most of the early pollen collected is yellow and makes a bright ring around the fuzzy brown sealed brood area. But as the season advances and the days lengthen, more pollen sources are available. Serviceberry, *Amelanchier arborea,* frosts the slopes of the hills near the rivers with white blossoms. Redbud, *Cercis canadensis,* flourishes in the wood's understory, with dramatic purplish red clusters of blossom. Henbit, *Lamium amplexicaule,* which everyone except beekeepers think of as an unwelcome weed, covers the ground with a low-growing thatch of purple-blue flowers. The wild fruit trees—plum, cherry and peach—bloom extravagantly. These flowers all have different-colored pollens, and the pollen cells ringing the bees' brood are as various: scarlet, pale green, yellow, and orange—as beautiful as a stained-glass window.

---

6 **empiricist** (em pir′ ə sist) one willing to learn through experiment and observation
7 **venom** (ven′ əm) a secreted poison
8 **efficacy** (ef′ i kə sē) effectiveness
9 **anthers** (an′ thərz) pollen sacs

In early springtime, the bees' need for pollen may be greater than what is available, and then they will compulsively gather up almost any fine granular material—sawdust, bits of plastic packing material, ashes—whether it is useful to them or not. I often see them at the bird feeder, picking through the wild bird feed. At that time of year, I often get a telephone call from a dairy farmer who lives near one of my beeyards.

"Hey, Sue," he says. "How about coming over and feeding your bees? They're in the calf feed again."

He's always a little embarrassed. The first time he called me, years ago, was on a day in autumn. There were, he insisted, bees flying all around the inside of his milking shed. He didn't want to spray them with insecticide, but he was going to have to do that unless I could lure them out.

It sounded like an odd way for bees to behave, but I drove over to his place. There they were, golden-striped fuzzy insects flying around inside his barn, darting here and there. They looked like bees, but they didn't act like bees, so I captured one in my hand. The creature did not sting me as a honeybee would have done and on close scrutiny its beelike appearance disappeared. Moreover, the insect had only a single pair of wings, not two sets, as a bee has. The two wings, a single pair, puts any insect into the zoological order Diptera (which means two-winged), the order of flies. Honeybees belong to the order Hymenoptera (or membrane-winged), which includes not only all the bees but also wasps, ants and other similar insects.

I wasn't sure which flies these were in the milk barn, because I don't know much about Diptera, but I know that there were a number of fly species that mimic bees in appearance. I showed the farmer the single pair of wings and told him that this and the others in the air were flies, not bees. He was interested, and asked more questions than I could answer. When I got home, I photocopied as much information about bee-mimicking flies as I could find on my bookshelves and sent it to him. Now when he calls he always makes sure that the insect about which he is lodging a complaint is indeed a honeybee.

The first time he found bees in his calf feed he was worried that they were after the calves, and might sting and frighten them. I assured him that the bees were not the least concerned with the calves but were looking for the pollen they needed as food in the springtime. As soon as some pollen-bearing flower bloomed, I told him, the bees would disappear from the calf feed, but in the meantime I'd try giving them a pollen substitute that might satisfy them.

Beekeeping-supply companies sell a commercial pollen substitute made of a combination of protein-rich materials such as soy flour and brewers' yeast. This powder can be mixed with honey to make into patties, which can be squished down between the top bars on the frames of the upper hive bodies. Many beekeepers recommend the feeding of pollen substitute as a regular routine, and for a number of years I made up patties and fed them to all my hives. In some parts of the country where there is not a dependable source of pollen this may

Vincent van Gogh, *View of Arles with Irises*, 1888

Ernest Lawson, *Garden Landscape,* ca. 1895

be a good practice, but I have concluded that it is not worth the expense or time here in the Ozarks. Bees prefer the real thing—fresh pollen—and although a day or two in these hills may pass when they can't find any, something usually bursts into bloom and they scorn the substitute, leaving it to molder inside the hives. So I stopped feeding pollen substitute, and find that productivity of my hives is no poorer for doing so. Indeed, the per-hive yield of honey from my bees has grown greater in what appears to be a direct relationship to the decrease in the number of times I open the hives. The less I disrupt and fiddle with the bees, the more they can concentrate on making honey.

Now when the dairy farmer calls, more as a public-relations gesture then anything else, I go to the health-food store and buy fifty-nine cents' worth of soy flour, take it over to the hives near his place, lift off the outer cover of each hive and sprinkle some of it on the inner cover. I did that a few days ago, and today I stopped by his place to give him a jar of honey as a recompense[10] for the nuisance my bees had caused him.

I asked if the bees had stopped coming to the calf feed.

"Yep. They've left. Thank you kindly for feeding them."

"No trouble. Thank you for calling me and letting me know. I don't like the bees to be a bother to you."

Then I drove over to the hives and lifted up the telescoping covers. The soy flour stood unused on the inner covers, and I shook it off on the grass. The bees had not wanted it. Flowers have begun to bloom somewhere, and the bees, their rear legs wadded with golden pollen, are flying into the hives so heavily loaded they find it hard to stay airborne.

The farmer is happy. The calves are happy. The bees are happy.

I sit down beside the end hive and watch the bees flying in with their loads of pollen, which will assure the development of the thousands of young bees needed to gather nectar and make honey in the months to come.

The sun is shining on my back as I watch, and I can feel its warmth. The air is fragrant. There are flowers in bloom everywhere today.

And I am happy.

---

10 **recompense** (rek′ əm pens′) something given to make up for an inconvenience

Literature Model

Linking Writing and Literature

 Collect Your Thoughts

What type of person do you think Sue Hubbell is? From reading this essay, what do you think are some of her values? How are they similar to and different from your values? Write a few sentences about this in your reading journal.

 Talk About Reading

Talk with other students about this excerpt from *A Book of Bees . . . and How to Keep Them.* Assign a group leader to maintain the group's focus and a secretary to take notes. Use the questions below to guide your discussion.

1. **Connect to Your Life** What did you learn about the life of a beekeeper from reading this essay? How can you use one or two of the things that you learned from this essay in your own life?
2. **Critical Thinking: Analyze** How would you describe the mood of this selection? What specific words and images help create this mood?
3. **6+1 Trait®: Organization** In which section of this selection do you think Hubbell's organization is the strongest? What specific aspects of the writing make the organization in this section so strong?
4. **Connect to Writing** The next time you want to explain something in writing, which—if any—of Hubbell's techniques might help you make your explanation interesting and clear?

 Write About Reading

Expository Writing Write a one- to three-page explanation of how to care for a pet, a plant, or a prized possession. As you write your essay, create a clear mood, as Hubbell did, and bring out a specific theme.

Focus on Organization Review the different types of organizational structures and decide which structure best fits with the topic, mood, and theme of your exposition. Then order your ideas according to the organizational structure you choose. Be sure to use signal words, clear language, and paragraph breaks to present information logically. You want your essay to inform your readers but be interesting and meaningful as well, so include relevant examples, anecdotes, and descriptions in your writing.

For more information on organization and the 6+1 Trait® model, see **Writing and Research Handbook,** pages 957–959.

6+1 Trait® is a registered trademark of Northwest Regional Educational Laboratory, which does not endorse this product.

UNIT 5 Review

Reflecting on the Unit

Summarize what you have learned in this unit by answering the following questions.

1. What are six kinds of expository writing, and what is the basic purpose of each?
2. What are some of the ways cause-and-effect writing can be organized?
3. What types of graphic organizers can help you organize information for a compare-contrast essay?
4. How do graphs and charts clarify explanations?
5. How can you use the words in essay questions to plan your answer?
6. What steps can you take to improve your performance on essay tests?

Adding to Your Portfolio

CHOOSE A SELECTION FOR YOUR PORTFOLIO Look over the expository writing you have done during this unit. Select a completed piece of writing to put in your portfolio. The piece you choose should show some or all of the following:

- a specific audience and writing purpose
- a well-expressed thesis statement
- supporting details that appeal to readers' level of knowledge and interest
- logical organization and clear connections
- a combination of expository types

REFLECT ON YOUR CHOICE Attach a note to the piece you chose, explaining briefly why you chose it and what you learned from writing it.

SET GOALS How can you improve your writing? What skill will you focus on the next time you write?

Writing Across the Curriculum

MAKE A HISTORY CONNECTION Scan your history textbook for a historical event or occurrence that can be described as a process, such as the building of a stockade or the election of a president. Write a brief essay explaining the process. Be sure to explain any unfamiliar terms.

"Let us rise up tonight with greater readiness. Let us stand with a greater determination. And let us move on in these powerful days, these days of challenge to make America what it ought to be."

—Martin Luther King, Jr.,
"I've Seen the Promised Land"

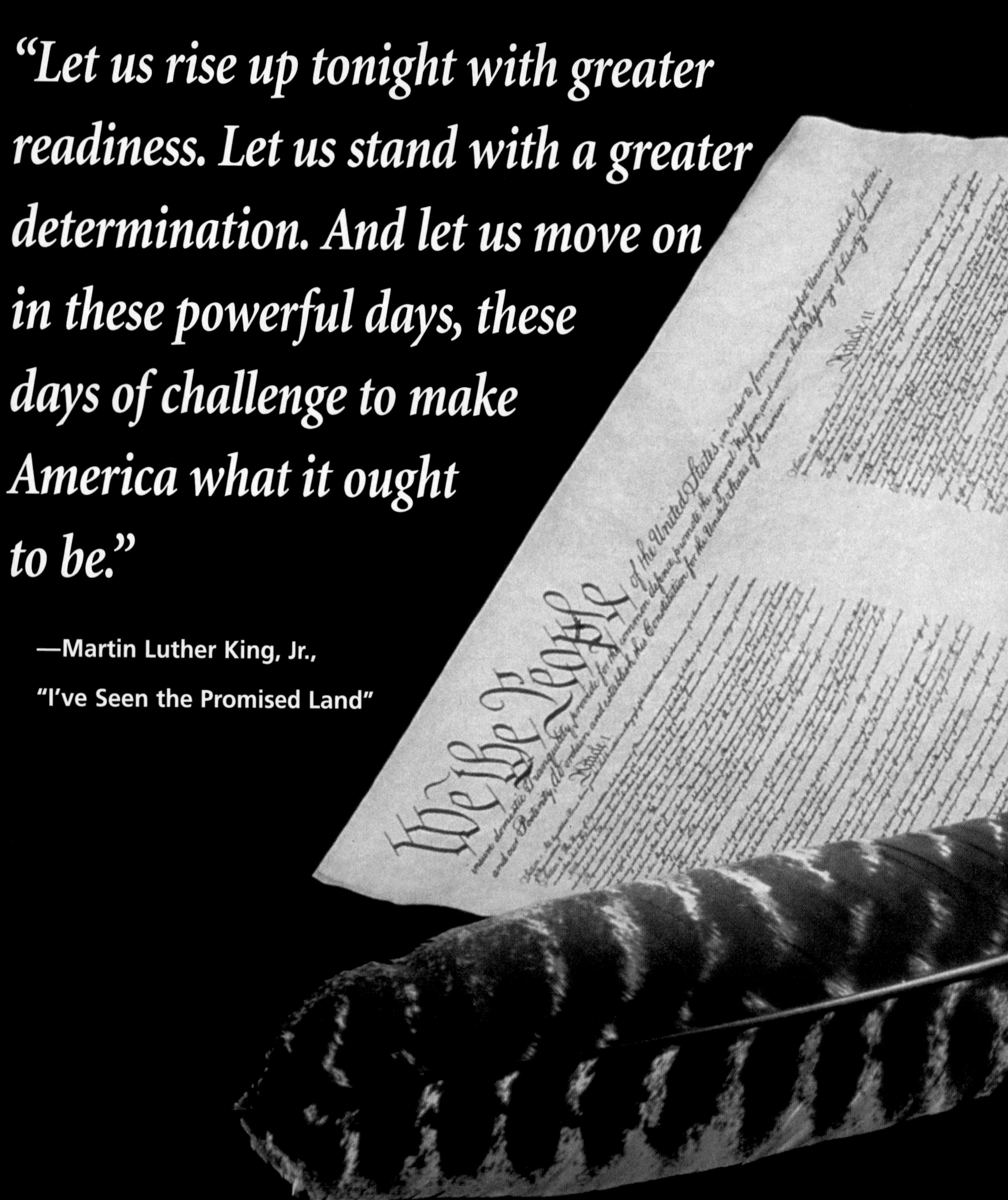

UNIT 6

Persuasive Writing

Writing in the Real World

In persuasive writing, the writer tries to influence the reader to accept an idea, adopt a point of view, or perform an action. Effective persuasive writing is unified by one central idea. Advertisements are great examples of persuasive writing. The ads on this page are part of a campaign for Chicago's Museum of Contemporary Art (MCA). The ads were created by Mitchiner, Ross and Kahn, a Chicago advertising agency.

Membership at the MCA: What Will It Do To You?

by the advertising agency of Mitchiner, Ross and Kahn

A Writer's Process

Prewriting

Finding the Main Idea

Before developing the MCA ad campaign, the Mitchiner, Ross and Kahn team did some basic homework. They studied campaigns for other art museums and looked at figures showing who visits the MCA. They also went to the museum themselves to see, according to senior art director Steven Wohlwender, "how to get your average Joe to come look at contemporary art."

The main theme for the MCA campaign began with a drawing. "I'd drawn this goofy little face with a strange reaction on it," explains Wohlwender, "based on the people I'd seen at the museum. And Marshall Ross, our creative director, simply said, `What will it do to you?'"

"That question started out being a headline for just one ad, but then Ross said, `This should be the main theme because it works for everything.' And the rest of us saw the light."

Assistant creative director Amy Krouse Rosenthal calls "What will it do to you?" an idea with "legs." That expression means the idea can "walk into" a wide range of media, including brochures, banners, bus posters, and newspaper ads. She adds, "We want the people who see these ads to get off their bottoms, go to the museum, and get zapped in the brain."

The idea generated in Wohlwender's sketch of a goofy face was carried through several design stages and ultimately appeared in a variety of formats, from T-shirts to café table tents.

Drafting

Seeing the Picture

The members of the advertising team decided to use photographs of real faces instead of sketches because they believed photos would be more persuasive than drawings. As Wohlwender puts it, "Photography is real. These people look real. The photographer even picked people off the street and told them to give a reaction as if they were looking at art."

"We wanted to make the ads appeal to as broad a group as possible," said Wohlender. "The museum told us what kind of people they wanted shown in terms of ages and ethnic groups they were targeting. The photographer went out and got ten people in each category. You don't want people who look like models, of course. These people look real. We wanted people looking at any one of these ads to be able to say, 'This museum is for me.'"

Revising/Editing

Choosing the Right Words

Every word used in an ad must contribute to persuading the audience. For example, Krouse Rosenthal says the word *you* was crucial to this campaign because "it makes you think about yourself." In selecting words for the campaign, the ad team made a conscious decision to keep the language informal.

For the MCA ad campaign, it was crucial to use humor and informal language.

Krouse Rosenthal explains that if the ads had used lofty language, some readers might have felt excluded from the museum experience.

Publishing/Presenting

Getting the Message Out

As part of the campaign, the MCA sent out a booklet to prospective members filled with funny, irreverent questions relating to the main idea, "What will it do to you?" Wohlwender says, "Usually people will read just one line and throw away a piece of junk mail. We tried to write [the booklet] so people would keep turning the pages."

The ads created for the Museum of Contemporary Art were supposed to run for only a year. Within eight months, however, museum attendance had skyrocketed by 42 percent and membership by 16 percent—rises that represented the biggest leaps in the museum's history. As a result, the ads were slated to run indefinitely.

Examining Writing in the Real World

Analyzing the Media Connection

Deconstruct, or analyze, the ads on pages 278–280 by discussing the following questions.

1. What question do the ads ask? How does each ad answer that question?
2. What is the effect of the word *you* in the ads? Would the word *us* or *them* have the same effect? Why or why not?
3. What is the central idea developed in the ads?
4. In your opinion, what immediate effects do the photographs have? Why?
5. For what reasons do you think these ads were so successful?

Analyzing a Writer's Process

Discuss these questions about the advertising team's writing process.

1. What is the purpose of the MCA ad campaign?
2. How did the advertising team come up with an idea for the campaign?
3. Why did the team decide to use photographs in the ads?
4. What kind of language did the team incorporate in the ads? Why?
5. How did the ad campaign affect attendance and membership?

Make pronouns agree with antecedents.

A pronoun must agree with its antecedent in gender, number, and person.

> *The advertising* ***team***
> *decided to use photographs . . .*
> *because* ***they*** *believed . . .*

Rewrite each sentence to correct the pronoun use.

1. Our class wants to go to the Museum of Contemporary Art, where you can see an exhibit of Georgia O'Keeffe's paintings.
2. I always rent an audiotape so that you know what to look for when you study a painting.
3. My friend and I plan to visit the museum gift shop, where you can buy prints of your favorite paintings.
4. Many students recognize that you can do firsthand research for a report in a museum.
5. Do you think that someday you'll visit the museum?

See Lesson 17.5, pages 644–648.

Persuasive Writing

Persuasive Writing

LESSON 6.1

Understanding Persuasive Writing

In persuasive writing, you try to convince readers to agree with your opinion and possibly to take action. In the following excerpt, a former Federal Communications Commission chairman appeals to both reason and emotion to persuade broadcasters that television is a "vast wasteland."

Literature Model

When television is bad, nothing is worse. I invite you to sit down in front of your television set when your station goes on the air and stay there without a book, magazine, newspaper, profit-and-loss sheet, or rating book[1] to distract you—and keep your eyes glued to that set until the station signs off. I can assure you that you will observe a vast wasteland.

You will see a procession of game shows, violence, audience participation shows, formula comedies about totally unbelievable families, blood and thunder, mayhem, violence, sadism, murder, Western badmen, Western good men, private eyes, gangsters, more violence and cartoons. And, endlessly, commercials—many screaming, cajoling, and offending. And, most of all, boredom. True, you will see a few things you will enjoy. But they will be very, very few. And if you think I exaggerate, try it.

Is there one person in this room who claims that broadcasting can't do better?

Newton Minow, Address to the Broadcasting Industry

How would you summarize Minow's opinion in your own words?

What specific examples does Minow use to support his opinion?

In what way does this final question challenge the particular audience to whom Minow spoke?

1 rating book: a book that rates TV programs by the number of households viewing them

Recognize Persuasive Writing

When you write persuasively, you express an opinion and try to convince your readers to agree with you. Sometimes you'll want your readers to take action. In persuasive writing, audience is all-important, as the speech about television illustrates. Newton Minow aimed his message at broadcast executives, the very people responsible for television programming.

Every day you see and hear countless persuasive messages: a billboard ad for a popular brand of jeans, a radio spot for a movie the critics are raving about, bumper stickers calling attention to a cause or a candidate. Below are some of the places where you encounter persuasive messages. Can you think of others?

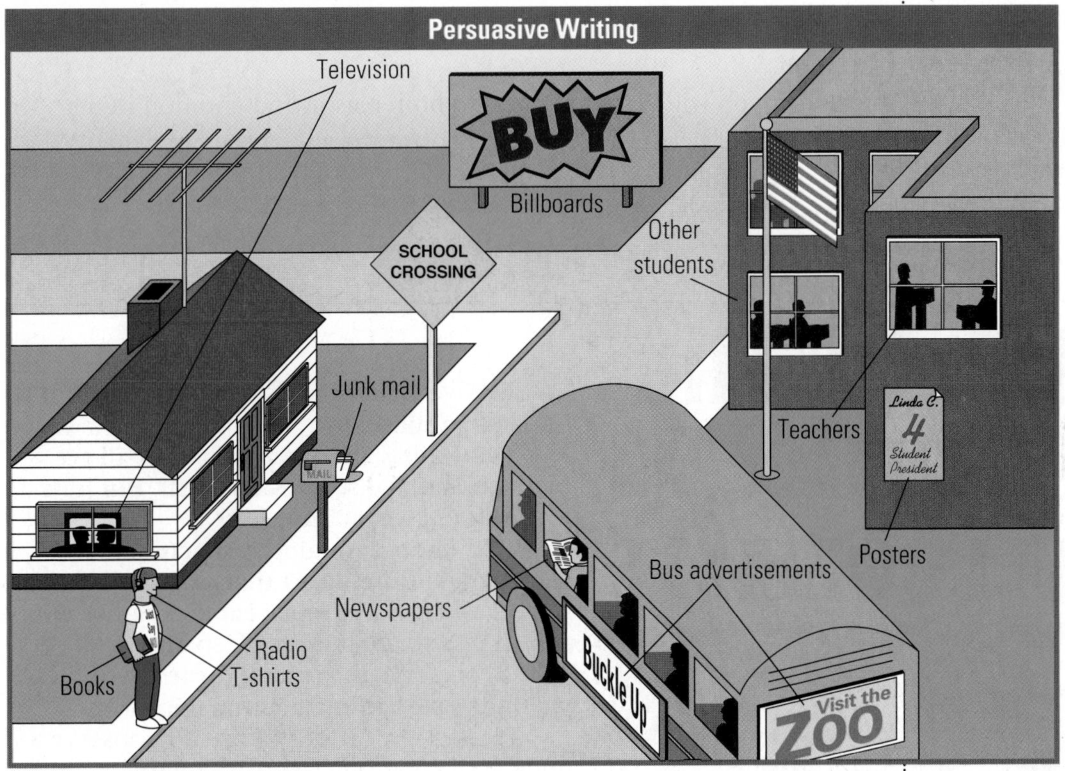

Journal Writing

Persuasive appeals are so widespread that you probably tune many of them out as you go about your business. Think back over the past day, and try to remember all the persuasive appeals you heard or saw. List them in your journal.

Give Your Persuasive Writing an Edge

> **Grammar Tip**
>
> When revising a piece of persuasive writing, determine whether the modifiers you have used are vivid and strong enough to support your opinion. For basic information on modifiers, see Lessons 10.4 and 10.5, pages 460–472.

Like other types of writing, persuasive writing consists of a topic, a main idea about the topic, and supporting details. However, your main idea in persuasive writing has an edge to it. It's an opinion that you want others to adopt. Therefore, you need to pay special attention to your audience, presenting your supporting ideas in a way that will persuade your audience to accept your opinion.

You can support your opinion with two main kinds of details: appeals to reason and appeals to emotion. To appeal to reason, use facts, statistics, expert opinions, and examples that validate your position. To appeal to emotion, use words that generate strong positive or negative responses. For example, if you want to persuade readers to favor a candidate, you might applaud his "courageous" stand on the issues; if you want to discredit that same candidate, you might attack his "foolhardy" position.

Often you will want to appeal to both reason and emotion in the same piece of persuasive writing. Look at the advertisement below. What kind of appeal does the headline make? What part of the ad appeals to reason? To emotion?

AND ON THE EIGHTH DAY, WE BULLDOZED IT.

Elusive jaguars, rarest orchids, colorful birds-of-paradise.

Rainforests are haven to half of all the plant and animal species on earth. But how much time do they have left?

Fifty thousand rainforest acres are lost each day worldwide. At that rate, the last traces of original, irreplaceable paradise will vanish in a single human lifespan.

To preserve the splendid variety of life we must save the endangered rainforests.

Please support our efforts to conserve a miracle of creation. Tomorrow won't wait.

Save the rainforests and safeguard the survival of half of the species on earth, including our own. Here's my donation of ☐ $25 ☐ $50 ☐ $75 ☐ $100 ☐ ________

NAME ________

ADDRESS ________

CITY ________ STATE ____ ZIP ____

RAINFOREST ACTION NETWORK

300 BROADWAY, SAN FRANCISCO, CA 94133

Public Media Center

6.1 Writing Activities

Write an Opinion

Express your opinion of the painting below in a brief essay that could be published in an art gallery brochure. Use the details in the painting to support your opinion.

PURPOSE To express and support an opinion
AUDIENCE Visitors to an art gallery
LENGTH 2–3 paragraphs

WRITING RUBRICS To express a convincing opinion in writing, you should

- present your opinion in a main idea statement
- use supporting ideas that appeal to both reason and emotion
- pitch your argument to a particular audience

Viewing and Representing

DECONSTRUCTING MEDIA In a small group, analyze the quality of commercial TV programming. Assign each member to either read a recent article on current TV programming or view different channels for a few hours. Meet to discuss your findings and collaborate on a one-page response to Newton Minow's statements on page 282.

Jonathan Franklin, *Mad Hatters,* 1990

Avoid sentence fragments in your writing.

A *sentence fragment* is an incomplete sentence punctuated as if it were a complete sentence:

Elusive jaguars, rarest orchids, colorful birds-of-paradise.

Though sentence fragments may be effective in advertising, do not use them in formal writing.

Rewrite to correct the fragments.

1. Television, labeled a "vast wasteland" by Newton Minow.
2. Insulting comedies, violent detective shows, irrelevant talk shows, and endless commercials. The list goes on.
3. There are a few shows that entertain and inform. Such as *Sixty Minutes.*
4. Cable television, supposedly an improvement over network programs.

See Lesson 13.9, pages 557–558.

Listening and Speaking

Present your findings from the Viewing and Representing activity as a persuasive speech. Aim your speech at a particular audience of people you do not know, such as the parents of young children, teachers at another school, or workers in the television industry. Present your completed speech to the class and ask them to identify your intended audience.

LESSON

6.2

Evidence in Persuasive Writing

In persuasive writing you need to support your viewpoint with facts and relevant opinions. As you read these two contrasting views of MTV, look for supporting evidence.

Literature Model

MTV is primarily a triumph of marketing. Who would have thought, say, eleven years ago, that TV audiences would sit still for a channel showing nothing but commercials separated by commercials? Those music videos are essentially ads designed to sell records. In between them, MTV places real commercials to sell seven thousand different kinds of jeans and hair glop.

Not for nothing has MTV earned the nickname "Empty-V." Instead of denying that emptiness, however, MTV celebrates it. Members of the viewing audience are frequently assured that they are not to be bothered with matters of consequence. "MTV News," which is shown frequently each day, is "news" about rock stars, pop stars and silly celebrities—puff and fluff spun in the hype mills of Hollywood.

Tom Shales, "MTV Has Shallow Look of Success"

Which of Shales's word choices helps to reinforce his negative opinion of MTV?

Literature Model

Almost since its inception, MTV has been rightly applauded by a grateful record industry for revitalizing pop music, boosting album sales and creating a thriving new market for home music videos. (MTV helped boost sales of music videos to a record $172.3 million last year, up $55 million from 1989. . . .)

MTV has also been hailed for revolutionizing TV (it is largely credited with inspiring the tone of the "Miami Vice" series), and for making its 1981 slogan "You'll never look at music the same way again," a reality. . . .

Eager to counter the many charges of vacuousness and puffery that have plagued it, MTV has also aired public service programs about political, social and environmental issues, even winning a prestigious Peabody Award for its two-hour retrospective on the '80s, "Decade."

George Varga, "Is It MTV, or Is It 'Empty-V'?"

What facts does Varga use to portray MTV in a more positive light?

Use Facts and Opinions

Persuasive writing is more than just a statement of your opinion. You need to back up your opinion with evidence—facts and opinions that support your viewpoint. Facts are statements, statistics, observations, and examples that can be verified, or proved. Evaluate a fact by answering these questions: Is it accurate? Is it up to date? Is it relevant?

Opinions are personal judgments. They may be supported by facts, or they may be simply personal preferences. Their value depends upon the qualifications of the person stating them. Evaluate an opinion by answering these questions: Is the opinion-giver qualified, with specific knowledge of the subject? Is the opinion-giver biased, with something to gain from supporting a certain viewpoint?

Both facts and opinions can be open to interpretation. Different people draw different conclusions from the same evidence. The key is to decide how valid the evidence is.

Prewriting Tip

Both clustering and brainstorming can help you generate facts and opinions for persuasive writing, but you need to evaluate the evidence you generate.

Journal Writing

What's your opinion on MTV? In your journal, list several facts and opinions that you could use to support your view.

Prepare Arguments

In persuasive writing, an argument is the position you take on an issue, along with the evidence you use to support your position. Often your evidence will include a mix of facts, statistics, expert opinions, and personal opinions that anticipate opposing viewpoints.

The excerpt below is from an ad by the makers of jewel boxes, the plastic packages in which compact discs are sold. The ad writer seeks to convince record companies that jewel boxes are the best packaging for CDs. What evidence supports the position? Is it convincing?

Grammar Tip

When editing, check that verbs and indefinite pronouns, such as *one* and *some,* agree in number. For more information about indefinite pronouns as subjects, see Lesson 16.7, pages 623–625.

Literature Model

The People's Choice

As the makers and advocates of the jewel box, we believe the best alternative to the longbox already exists. One that's proven internationally—sell CDs in the jewel box, alone.

We're not the only ones who believe this. Peter Gabriel and Raffi are just two of the artists who agree. And with successful "jewel box-only" releases, they've proved the viability of that option.

But most important is the opinion of CD buyers like you—the people who should have the final say in any CD packaging decision. In a recent survey by *CD Review* magazine, they found that 84% of CD buyers preferred the sturdy, plastic jewel box to an alternative, paperboard package. . . .

Environmental Protection

Of course, some argue that an alternative package will be better for the environment. But the facts don't support their position.

Consider that last year alone at least 50 million unsold CDs were returned by retailers. Not a problem with the jewel box—the discs, artwork and booklets can be removed, and the jewel boxes could be re-used or recycled.

But proposed alternative CD packages can't be re-used or recycled, because they're made of paperboard and plastic glued together and pre-printed for just one release. If those 50 million returns were in an alternative package, the packages would have only one place to go—into the garbage.

JAM (Jewelbox Advocates and Manufacturers)

6.2 Writing Activities

Write an Editorial

Write an editorial for your school newspaper on security measures, testing student athletes for drug use, or some other controversial school issue of your choice.

PURPOSE To express and support an opinion on a school issue
AUDIENCE Readers of the school newspaper
LENGTH 3–4 paragraphs

WRITING RUBRICS To write an effective editorial, you should

- state your position on the issue
- support your position with facts and valid opinions
- anticipate and respond to possible opposing viewpoints

Cross-Curricular Activity

ART The painting on this page is by Mandy Martin, an Australian known for expressing her views on environmental issues through her art. In this painting, she tries to show the negative effect of the mining industry on the environment. Does she succeed? Use observations about the painting along with your personal judgment to write an evaluation of how well the painting fulfills its purpose.

Listening and Speaking

Review copies of your local newspaper and choose an issue of importance to people in your community. Through careful research, develop your own opinion about the topic and prepare a two-minute persuasive speech. Be sure to build a sound argument based on fact and expert opinion. You might want to include quotations from appropriate sources. Present your speech to the class and ask them to evaluate your argument.

Make collective noun subjects and verbs agree.

A collective noun can be singular or plural. When writing about MTV's *audience,* for example, you would use a singular verb to refer to a group as a whole but a plural verb to refer to group members acting as audiences.

Write the correct form of the verb in parentheses.

1. The crowd (roar, roars) its approval.
2. The crowd (have, has) to pass through the gate, one at a time.
3. The band (is, are) warming up.
4. The band (take, takes) their places on stage.
5. Our whole group (is, are) shocked by the news about the lead singer.

See Lesson 16.4, pages 618–619.

Mandy Martin, *Powerhouse,* 1988

Persuasive Writing

LESSON 6.3

Presenting an Opinion

The models below present opposing viewpoints on the issue of high school classes watching commercial television programs. Try to identify the position each writer takes and the audience to which each argument is targeted.

Summarize Berry's opinion in one sentence.

Literature Model

I have no objection to television commercials being shown to a "captive" audience of students in school, especially when the commercials are tastefully done. . . .

The furor over Channel One advertising baffles me. Ads are everywhere in our building and have been for years. The clocks, the No. 2 pencils, the computers, even the footballs have company logos. . . .

The things we use have to be paid for by somebody. Many school systems like mine would never have this kind of equipment except through a program like this.

Betty Berry, *NEA Today*

Summarize March's opinion in one sentence.

Literature Model

Schools are marketplaces for ideas, not commercial turf. The opposite concept—that schools should provide a captive audience for commercials "endorsed" by educators—is repulsive. *Educators present all sides of an issue—we don't "sell" one point of view. . . .*

The *Wall Street Journal* reports that American teenagers spent $55 billion in 1988. Harnessing that purchasing power can give an advertiser a big advantage in the marketplace.

Jennifer March, *NEA Today*

Take a Meaningful Stand

To write persuasively, you must take a stand on a topic you have some knowledge of and then support your position with relevant evidence. For instance, both Berry and March drew on their many years of teaching experience to present specific arguments for and against commercials in classroom programs.

In addition to knowing your subject, you need to make sure that a genuine difference of opinion exists between you and your audience. Taking a stand against pollution would probably not be worth your time, since few people would disagree. Taking a stand in favor of a specific antipollution measure, such as mandatory carpooling, is more controversial since some people may oppose your position. Once you have an arguable topic, express your opinion in a clear thesis statement such as this: Mandatory carpooling regulations should be adopted to ease air pollution.

Prewriting Tip

Discuss your opinion and your audience with a peer. Ask for ideas about how to get through to the audience you have in mind.

Persuasive Writing

Examine Your Audience

Knowing your audience is the essence of persuasive writing. After all, you're trying to influence their opinions and sometimes even change their actions. The questions in the chart may help you decide what you need to know about your audience.

Drafting Tip

For examples of the kinds of details to use to support a position, see Lesson 5.2, pages 224–227.

Evaluating Your Audience

- What is the current attitude of my audience? Are they likely to agree or disagree? Do they care about the issue, or will I have to overcome their apathy?
- What do they already know about the issue? Do I need to provide background or clear up misconceptions?
- What types of evidence will have the strongest impact on my audience? Will facts and statistics do the job? Should I include informed opinions?
- What do I want my audience to do: change their thinking, take action, or simply recognize the validity of my viewpoint?

Journal Writing

Make notes in your journal about some audiences you could write for, including how your choice of an audience affects your argument. If you presented your opinion about watching commercials in school, what information would appeal to your classmates, your teachers, your parents, and the members of your school board?

State Your Case

Your success in persuasive writing will depend on stating your case well, and that means organization. Persuasive writing often follows the four-step plan below.

Drafting Tip

As you draft persuasive writing, think about the order of your arguments. You can leave your readers with a stronger impression if you save your best argument for last.

Guidelines for Persuasive Writing			
Introduce the issue	**State your opinion**	**Support your position**	**Draw your conclusion**
Describe the issue, and supply any background needed to help readers understand it.	Take your stand in a clear, direct thesis statement	Present your evidence—facts, opinions, or both—and respond in opposing viewpoints.	End by summarizing your ideas and, if appropriate, giving a clear call to action.

Public-service advertisements often use the approach suggested above to draw attention to a cause or to seek financial support. In your opinion, how well does the following ad make its case?

How effective is this headline and why?

What facts does this ad include, and how do they provide strong support for the ad's purpose?

What specific action does this ad call for in its conclusion?

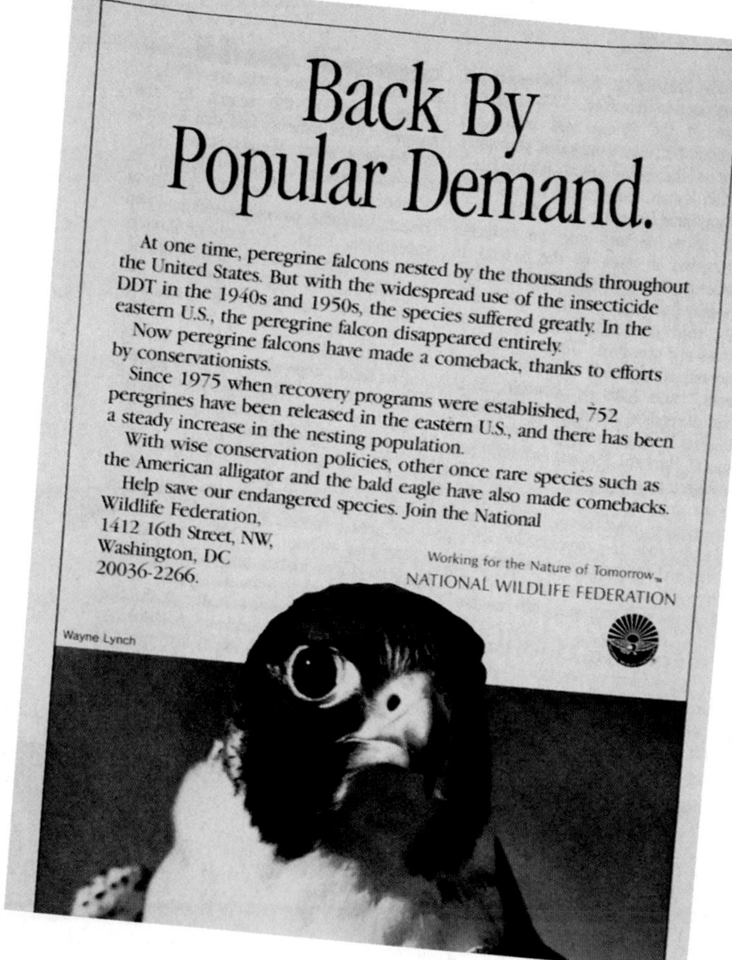

Back By Popular Demand.
At one time, peregrine falcons nested by the thousands throughout the United States. But with the widespread use of the insecticide DDT in the 1940s and 1950s, the species suffered greatly. In the eastern U.S., the peregrine falcon disappeared entirely.
Now peregrine falcons have made a comeback, thanks to efforts by conservationists.
Since 1975 when recovery programs were established, 752 peregrines have been released in the eastern U.S., and there has been a steady increase in the nesting population.
With wise conservation policies, other once rare species such as the American alligator and the bald eagle have also made comebacks.
Help save our endangered species. Join the National Wildlife Federation,
1412 16th Street, NW,
Washington, DC
20036-2266.
Working for the Nature of Tomorrow.
NATIONAL WILDLIFE FEDERATION
Wayne Lynch

6.3 Writing Activities

Write a Letter

Write a letter to your school principal stating your position on this topic: Your school should (should not) receive or continue to receive daily television news broadcasts. As your evidence, use the information below, the information on page 290, and your own ideas.

PURPOSE To write a letter supporting or opposing TV news in the classroom
AUDIENCE Your school principal
LENGTH 2–3 paragraphs

WRITING RUBRICS To write an effective persuasive letter, you should

- explain the issue
- state your position in a thesis statement
- support your position
- draw your own conclusion
- gear your argument to your audience

Pro

__ In exchange for requiring students to watch the television news, with commercials, schools are lent TV equipment.

__ Many high school students lack knowledge of current events.

__ A study by the producer of the news program found that students who had watched it had a "significantly better" knowledge of world and national events than did other students.

Con

__ The contract requires students to watch the news program every day.

__ When the contract expires, the television equipment must be returned.

__ Schools have no control over what kinds of information and commercials are presented during the broadcasts.

Use specific nouns and strong modifiers.

Schools are marketplaces for ideas, not commercial turf.

Revise the sentences below, using specific nouns and strong modifiers.

1. Some schools have a lot of things and some don't.
2. School funds should come from many sources.
3. Taxes on many items could be raised.
4. Certain people think that a new tax plan will result in better schools.

See Lesson 10.1, pages 439–444; Lesson 10.4, pages 460–465; and Lesson 10.5, pages 466–472.

Using Computers

Store your facts and opinions in your word-processing program. Enter the information, give it a heading, and box it so that it looks like a note card. Then, organize your notes grouping them under ideas or headings.

Cross-Curricular Activity

EARTH SCIENCE With a partner, draft a letter to the publisher of an environmental newsletter or magazine, presenting a well-supported argument about a current environmental issue. Revise and edit the letter carefully.

LESSON 6.4

Writing a Product Evaluation

Using persuasive techniques, writers prepare evaluations of a broad range of products and services. Reading a product evaluation such as this one could help you find the right in-line skates.

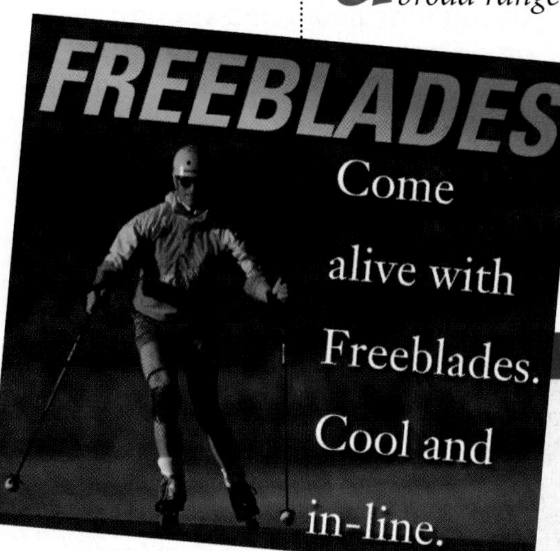

FREEBLADES
Come alive with Freeblades. Cool and in-line.

Literature Model

The hottest roller skates around don't look much like the skates most grownups remember from their childhood. The hardware most resembles flashy ski boots with a line of plastic wheels down the center of the sole. They're known formally as in-line skates. . . .

We tested nine skates in time trials around a paved running track, in our parking lot, and along some country roads. We also rolled on an exercise treadmill and measured the amount of force needed to keep rolling along. . . .

The hard, molded-plastic boots provide good ankle support—provided you can pull the laces tight enough. That wasn't always easy to do, we found. . . .

Beginners might well look low in the Ratings [of specific models], to skates at less than $100. (Just make sure the boots feel comfortable to you.)

Those skates may not roll quite as easily or rapidly as higher-priced models. But then, you may not want a lot of speed as a beginner. Once the original wheels and bearings wear out, you can swap them for a good set for about $100. Changing wheels is fairly easy.

"In-Line Skates: They Aren't Just for Kids," *Consumer Reports*

The article begins by explaining what the product is.

What kind of testing did the evaluators do?

What are the report's recommendations? How might they help a consumer?

Set a Goal

Product evaluations that you write can serve various purposes. You can judge the quality of a particular brand or service; you can compare several brands or services for the purpose of rating them; or you can evaluate the usefulness of a product itself, making a judgment about whether it's worth purchasing *any* brand. Setting a goal at the outset will help you determine what types of evidence you need to gather.

Develop Standards for Evaluation

A product evaluation must be backed up with evidence. You need to develop standards you can use to evaluate the product and then determine how well the product measures up to your standards. *Consumer Reports* evaluates products by running them through a series of tests. You yourself can't conduct that type of evaluation, but you *can* go to product users for evidence. Conduct an informal survey, asking your friends, neighbors, and family to answer questions about the product you plan to evaluate. You can adapt the chart below to fit your product.

Standards for Evaluating Products

Price	Is the price reasonable? How does it compare with those of similar products?
Features	What are its most important features? Are any desirable features missing? Are any of its features unnecessary?
Workmanship	Is the product well made? Is anything easily broken?
Design	Is it good-looking? Is it easy to use?

Based on the information from your survey, you can make informed judgments about the product. You can then prepare a written report to help other consumers make the right choices.

Prewriting Tip

A comparison frame can help you organize your evidence for a product evaluation. See Lesson 5.5 on pages 236–239.

TIME

For more about the writing process, see **TIME Facing the Blank Page,** pp. 109–119.

Journal Writing

Think of a product you bought recently, and evaluate it according to the standards in the chart above for price, features, quality, and design. Would you have purchased the product if you first had evaluated it according to these standards? Write your answer in your journal.

Use Visual Evidence

Photos and other illustrations can add vital information about a product. For example, the *Consumer Reports* evaluation of film-processing services noted that photographers sometimes blame themselves for what are actually problems in processing. To illustrate processing problems, *Consumer Reports* used the following photos as visual evidence.

The film was underexposed in printing, so the print has low contrast and washed-out colors.

Here the film was processed correctly, so the print has sharp edges and bright colors.

Once you've completed your investigation, you'll need to present your findings. Here are some guidelines you can follow to make your evaluation helpful to your readers.

Writing a Product Evaluation	
Introduce it	What product or service are you evaluating?
State your main idea	Are you judging one product or service? Are you comparing two or more?
Explain your methods	Did you examine the product or service? Did you survey its users?
State your findings	What are your standards? How well did the product or service measure up?
Make a recommendation	Should people buy the product or use the service?

Grammar Tip

When editing a product evaluation, check that antecedents of pronouns, such as *this, that, which,* and *it* are clearly stated. For more information about pronoun references, see Lesson 17.6, pages 649–651.

6.4 Writing Activities

Write an Evaluation of a Place

Write an article for a travel magazine. Evaluate a place you have visited, such as an amusement park, a museum, or a zoo.

PURPOSE To write an evaluation of a travel destination
AUDIENCE Readers of a travel magazine
LENGTH 3–4 paragraphs

WRITING RUBRICS To write an effective evaluation of a place, you should

- state your main ideas
- identify your standards for evaluating the place
- explain how you gathered your data
- state your findings and make a recommendation
- provide visual evidence if possible

Cross-Curricular Activity

COOPERATIVE LEARNING Work in a small group to evaluate a product or service popular among teenagers—for example, jeans, CD players, or fast-food restaurants. Draw up a list of standards for evaluating your product or service. Then have each member use the standards to conduct an informal survey of friends and classmates. Record individual findings and pool the results of the surveys. Then prepare a product evaluation, having each member write one part of the report.

Grammar Link

Use *good/well* and *bad/badly* correctly.

Good and *bad* are adjectives. They precede nouns and follow linking verbs. Use *well* as an adjective to mean "in good health." Otherwise *well* and *badly* are adverbs and modify action verbs.

Beginners might well look . . . in the ratings . . . swap them for a good set. . . .

Complete each sentence below by adding *good, well, bad,* or *badly.*

1. We have recently been told that butter may be ____ for us.
2. Eating a bucket of unbuttered popcorn is not ____ for you either.
3. Foods saturated with fat or brimming with salt can make you feel ____.
4. Experts debate whether people need vitamins to eat ____.
5. Federal standards for nutrition supplements are enforced ____.

See Lesson 18.5, pages 671–672.

Viewing and Representing

CREATE A BROCHURE Develop a travel brochure using photographs or drawings of a particular place. Consider what visuals would most likely convince others to visit. Label the images with persuasive captions and display your brochure for teachers and classmates to view and evaluate.

LESSON 6.5

Creating an Ad

A strong ad is carefully worded to grab the attention of its intended audience. At what audience is the ad below aimed? Do you think it successfully "sells" advertising?

Persuasive Writing

How does the headline grab your attention?

The ad appeals to reason and emotion as it answers common arguments against advertising.

Does the ad present its strongest argument at the end? Support your opinion.

THIS AD IS FULL OF LIES.

LIE #1: ADVERTISING MAKES YOU BUY THINGS YOU DON'T WANT. Advertising is often accused of inducing people to buy things against their will.

But when was the last time you returned home from the local shopping mall with a bag full of things you had absolutely no use for? The truth is, nothing short of a pointed gun can get *anybody* to spend money on something he or she doesn't want.

No matter how effective an ad is, you and millions of other American consumers make your own decisions. If you don't believe it, ask someone who knows firsthand about the limits of advertising. Like your local Edsel dealer.

LIE #2: ADVERTISING MAKES THINGS COST MORE. Since advertising costs money, it's natural to assume it costs *you* money. But the truth is that advertising often brings prices down.

Consider the electronic calculator, for example. In the late 1960s, advertising created a mass market for calculators. That meant more of them needed to be produced, which brought the price of producing each calculator down. Competition spurred by advertising brought the price down still further.

As a result, the same product that used to cost hundreds of dollars now costs as little as five dollars.

LIE #3: ADVERTISING HELPS BAD PRODUCTS SELL. Some people worry that good advertising sometimes covers up for bad products.

But nothing can make you like a bad product. So, while advertising can help convince you to try something once, it can't make you buy it twice. If you don't like what you've bought, you won't buy it again. And if enough people feel the same way, the product dies on the shelf.

In other words, the only thing advertising can do for a bad product is help you find out it's a bad product. And you take it from there.

LIE #4: ADVERTISING IS A WASTE OF MONEY. Some people wonder why we don't just put all the money spent on advertising directly into our national economy.

The answer is, we already do.

Advertising helps products sell, which holds down prices, which helps sales even more. It creates jobs. It informs you about all the products available and helps you compare them. And it stimulates the competition that produces new and better products at reasonable prices.

If all that doesn't convince you that advertising is important to our economy, you might as well stop reading.

Because on top of everything else, advertising has paid for a large part of the magazine you're now holding.

And that's the truth.

ADVERTISING.
ANOTHER WORD FOR FREEDOM OF CHOICE.
American Association of Advertising Agencies

Get Your Audience's Attention

Advertisements have a clear purpose—to persuade people to buy a product or service or to support a point of view, idea, or candidate. The goals of advertising can be summed up in the acronym AIDA: a good ad must attract *A*ttention, arouse *I*nterest, create *D*esire, and get *A*ction. Study this chart to see how AIDA works.

AIDA	
Attention	Use an attention-getting headline or striking design to draw readers in.
Interest	Present evidence to show why readers should be interested. Use facts and opinions to explain the product's features and show how it's different from the competition—and better.
Desire	Appeal to your readers' reason and emotions to make them want your product.
Action	End with a clear call to action—buy the product, give money to the cause, vote for the candidate.

Revising Tip

In advertising, a few words go a long way. Keep your message short and to the point.

Create an Audience Profile

You want your ad to succeed, and that means reaching the right audience: those who are likely to use your product, service, or idea. An audience profile gives you the information you need to tailor your ad to the desired audience. All it takes is asking a few simple questions.

Audience Profile	
Age group	How old are the people who might use your product or service?
Education level	Does your product or service appeal to people with a certain level of education?
Buying power	Does your product or service appeal to people with a certain level of income?
Attitudes	What opinions and interests characterize your audience?
Life style	What entertainment characterizes your audience?
Needs	What are the needs of your audience?

Journal Writing

Find a magazine or newspaper ad that you think is effective, and paste it in your journal. Prepare an audience profile for the ad, answering as many questions as you can from the chart above.

Persuasive Writing

Choose the Right Words

Vocabulary Tip

When looking for the right word, you may want to use a thesaurus. For information about how to use this reference, see Lesson 24.2, pages 816–817.

Grammar Tip

When editing copy for an ad, make sure that a noun of amount, such as *hundreds,* agrees in number with its verb. For more information about verb agreement with special subjects, see Lesson 16.4, pages 618–619.

To arouse your audience's interest and create desire for the product, you need to use the right words. Mark Twain once said, "The difference between the right word and the nearly right word is the same as that between lightning and the lightning bug."

Use Precise Words Ad writers choose words carefully. Wear Champions running shoes, and you won't just run fast; you'll "glide effortlessly." Devine Cookies aren't simply delicious; they're "honey-sweet and taste-tempting." The Rapmaster isn't just a new radio; it's "a state-of-the-art sound system." Concrete nouns, strong action verbs, and colorful adjectives and adverbs help to create a desire for your product, service, or idea.

Recognize Connotations You're writing an ad for the Fataway exerciser. Do you promise customers a "scrawny body" or a "lean body"? *Scrawny* and *lean* have similar meanings; both are synonyms of *thin.* But the connotations of the words—their positive or negative associations—are strikingly different. Since persuasive writing appeals to emotion as well as to reason, you can enhance your message by keeping connotations in mind. What word choices help to make the following ad effective?

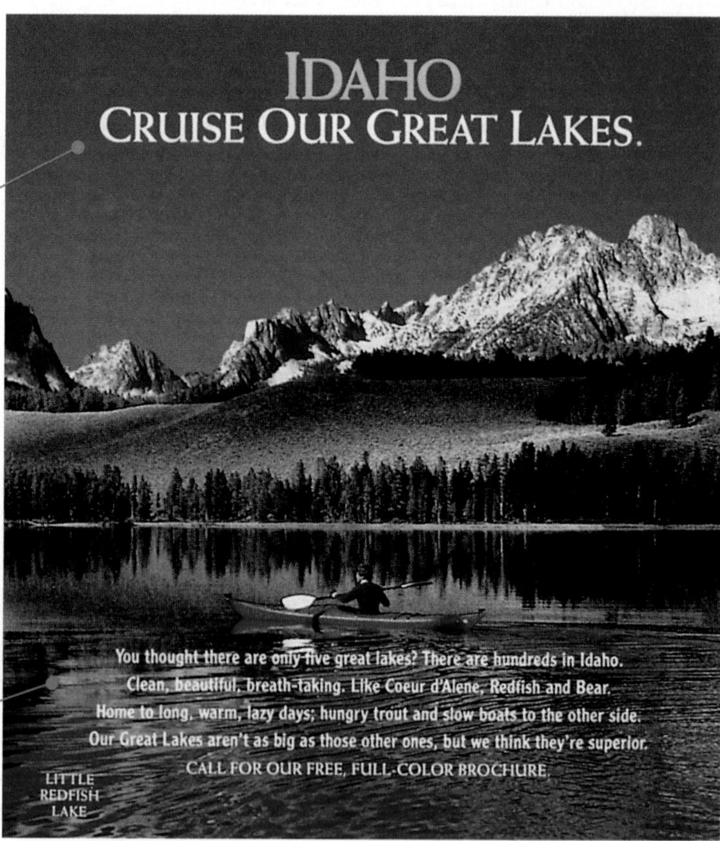

IDAHO
CRUISE OUR GREAT LAKES.
You thought there are only five great lakes? There are hundreds in Idaho.
Clean, beautiful, breath-taking. Like Coeur d'Alene, Redfish and Bear.
Home to long, warm, lazy days; hungry trout and slow boats to the other side.
Our Great Lakes aren't as big as those other ones, but we think they're superior.
CALL FOR OUR FREE, FULL-COLOR BROCHURE.
LITTLE REDFISH LAKE

Words paint an attractive picture of Idaho's lakes and suggest a relaxing travel destination.

Ad writers capitalize on double meanings. How does this ad play on two meanings of "great lakes"?

6.5 Writing Activities

Write an Ad

Write a one-page ad for your local newspaper. You can create an ad for an exhibit of paintings, for a travel agency, a soap, a perfume, a cleaning service, or for a product, service, or idea of your choice.

PURPOSE To create an advertisement
AUDIENCE Readers of the local newspaper
LENGTH 1 page

WRITING RUBRICS To write an effective ad, you should

- appeal to your desired audience
- write an attention-getting headline
- present evidence
- appeal to readers' reason and emotion
- end with a clear call to action
- use precise words with appropriate connotations

Using Computers

Use computer software to create text and visuals for your ad. Present your completed voting ad to the class. Discuss with classmates the persuasive elements in each ad. Which design elements seem to be more persuasive? Explain.

Claude Monet, *Les Coquelicots (Wild Poppies)*, 1873

Cross-Curricular Activity

GOVERNMENT You are working on an advertising campaign urging citizens to register to vote in the upcoming election. Your task is to create an advertisement targeted specifically to people who have just turned eighteen and are eligible to vote for the first time. Write the ad copy and design a full-page ad. Include an appropriate graphic.

Make indefinite pronouns and the personal pronouns referring to them agree in number and person.

Pronouns referring to indefinite pronouns should be singular if the indefinite pronoun is singular and plural if it is plural. If the gender of a singular indefinite pronoun is unknown, you may wish to rephrase to avoid "he or she."

Rewrite the sentences to make the personal and indefinite pronouns agree.

1. Most of the consumers assume that you cannot be swayed by advertising.
2. Few of the men think that he has been forced to buy products or services against their will.
3. Others of them have purchased an item because he or she was influenced by an ad.
4. Neither of the girls bought this item because they believed the ad.
5. None of us should blame the advertiser, however, if they buy a shoddy product twice.

See Lesson 17.5, pages 644–648.

Persuasive Writing

LESSON

6.6 Writing a Letter of Complaint

Persuasive Writing

"Try to imagine how much I care!"

When you write a letter of complaint, you usually want to persuade someone to solve a problem. In the letter below, notice how the writer calmly identifies the problem, offers evidence, and proposes a reasonable solution.

Student Model

Summarize Reis's complaint in a sentence.

I purchased an automatic dishwasher, model 98765, from B & A Appliance Service Center on April 18. On May 2 the washer began leaking water from the bottom.

What evidence does Reis present to justify her complaint?

Right away, I called B & A and explained the problem. I also explained my warranty, which entitles me to parts and labor for a full year from the purchase date. The next day B & A sent two repairmen, but they were unsuccessful, and the washer still leaked. I called again, and on May 6 the same men came back but still could not fix the washer. On May 8, I received a bill for $59.03 from B & A for parts and labor. I now have called and visited your store on several occasions. Mr. Black, the department manager, insists that I am responsible for paying the bill.

What solution does Reis suggest? Is her suggestion reasonable?

I am enclosing a copy of my original receipt, my warranty, and the repair bill. I believe I am not responsible for these charges. My washer still leaks, so I request that B & A live up to the terms of the warranty and fix it. If it cannot be fixed, please replace it with another washer of the same make and model. I hope we can come to an agreement on this matter.

Teresa Reis, Quartz Hill High School, Quartz Hill, California

Identify the Problem and a Solution

When you write a letter of complaint, you are trying to solve a problem. Your goals are to explain your problem, convince your reader that you have a valid complaint, and propose a reasonable solution. Your letter can follow this simple pattern.

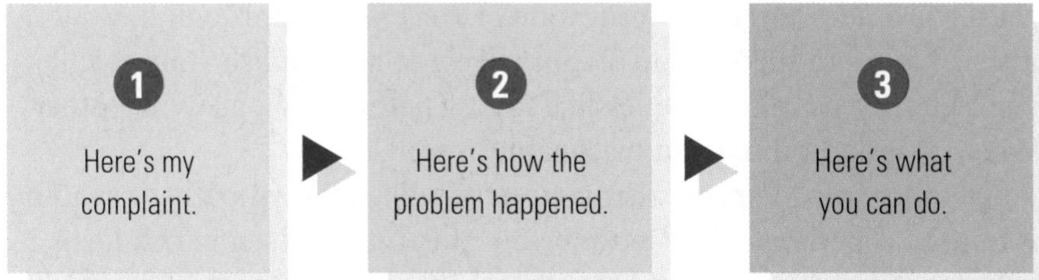

1
Here's my complaint.
2
Here's how the problem happened.
3
Here's what you can do.

Persuasive Writing

In the model letter on the opposite page, Teresa Reis has presented these three ideas in three paragraphs. Some complaints have a long history, and, therefore, the letter must be longer. Other complaints can be explained in one paragraph. Whatever its length, your letter should have the same three parts.

First open with a clear statement of the problem, usually in a sentence or two. Make it brief but complete. No one can help you without understanding what your problem is.

Next tell your story. In a paragraph or two, explain what happened, describing any previous attempts to correct the problem. This middle section is usually a narrative, so arrange the details in chronological order, the order in which they happened. Include dates and names, but avoid unnecessary details. Enclose any relevant evidence, such as a photocopy of the manufacturer's warranty.

In your final paragraph, explain specifically what you want done. If the solution you propose is a reasonable one, you are likely to get the results you want. The key word here is *reasonable.* A reasonable solution is one that the person or company can agree to without going to an excessive amount of trouble or expense.

Revising Tip

Ask a peer reviewer whether your letter offers adequate evidence and whether your proposed solution is reasonable.

Journal Writing

Set aside a page in your journal. Label the page "Complaints," and keep a running list of ideas for complaint letters. Over a period of time, you may find that the same complaint appears again and again. When that happens, it may be time to compose and mail that letter of complaint.

Persuasive Writing

Use a Businesslike Tone and Form

When you are writing a letter of complaint, chances are you're angry. Your first impulse may be to strike back with sarcasm, insults, even threats. ("I'll never shop in your stupid store again, and I'll tell all my friends to stay away, too.") To write an effective letter of complaint, you need to keep your emotions under control. Remember, your goal is to get the problem corrected. Your tone of voice comes through in writing just as it does in speech. You're more likely to accomplish your goal if your letter has a calm, businesslike tone. That way, you allow the other side to respond calmly and reasonably as well.

Another way to ensure that your letter will get a sympathetic reading is to use proper form. The letter below illustrates the semiblock form, a popular style for a business letter that will help you get results.

Presenting Tip

Some complaints fail because they are not directed to the right person. If possible, find out who has the authority to solve your problem, and address your letter to that person.

123 Washington Way
Irving, NY 12034
July 27, 1992

Sales Manager
Bemus Music Store
1 Trailblazer Way
Portland, OR 97202

Dear Sir or Madam:

On July 15, I ordered the tape Ice Rink, by Carrie Carey. Today it came, but it broke the first time I played it.

When I inserted the tape and pushed the play button on my tape player, I heard the beginning of the first number, but no more. When I removed the tape, I could see that it was broken. I played some other tapes to make sure my player had not caused the problem, but it worked perfectly.

I am enclosing a copy of the receipt, and I am returning the defective tape in a separate package. Please send me another copy.

Yours truly,

Peter Bianco

Peter Bianco

Grammar Tip

When editing a letter, check that you have used commas correctly. For information about commas in letter writing, see Lesson 21.6, pages 743–751.

6.6 Writing Activities

Write a Complaint Letter

Think about problems with products and services you or members of your family have had. Write a letter of complaint about a problem of your choice or about one listed below. Follow correct business-letter format.

(1) You paid $299 for a new camera. The next week the manufacturer announced that it was discontinuing the model and replacing it with a more advanced one at an introductory price of $250.

(2) You washed a new sweater as directed on the label, but the sweater shrank two sizes.

(3) You and some friends waited to be served in a restaurant for almost an hour. When the food came, it was cold.

PURPOSE To write a letter of complaint
AUDIENCE Person or company
LENGTH 3 paragraphs

WRITING RUBRICS To write an effective letter of complaint, you should

- state the complaint clearly and briefly
- explain what happened
- propose a reasonable solution
- use a businesslike tone
- use correct business-letter form

Listening and Speaking

COOPERATIVE LEARNING In small groups, read aloud your letters of complaint. Discuss and evaluate them for effective argument, clear and concise language, and business-like tone.

Use the past and past perfect tenses correctly.

Use the past tense to describe an action that was started and completed in the past. Use the past perfect tense to show that a past action began and ended before another past action began.

Write the correct form of each verb in parentheses.

1. By the time I (go) shopping for a cordless phone, I (research) the product in several consumer magazines.
2. However, the sales clerk (convince) me to buy a different model than the one that I (choose).
3. When I (arrive) home, I knew that I (make) a terrible mistake.
4. I (want) these special features long before they (become) popular.

See Lesson 15.3, pages 589–592, and Lesson 15.4, pages 593–595.

Using Computers

The electronic spelling checker in your word processing program can be a great help in proofreading. Be especially careful, though, since your spelling checker won't help you if you've misspelled a proper noun, such as the name of the company, or if you've used the wrong homonym, such as *you're* instead of *your.*

LESSON 6.7

WRITING ABOUT LITERATURE

Reviewing a Nonfiction Book

Book reviews are a type of product evaluation. The reviewer gives an opinion, supported with evidence, about whether a book is worth a reader's time and money.

Answer Questions in a Review

Readers ask two basic questions about any nonfiction book: What's it about? and Is it any good? As a reviewer, your job is to answer those questions. Begin by assuming that your readers are unfamiliar with the book. Summarize the book's contents—its subject and the author's purpose in writing. You may also need to provide background information about the author and subject, though such information isn't always necessary. Reviewers who write for *Rolling Stone*, for example, can assume that their readers have a basic knowledge of rock-and-roll, so they spend less time on background than they would for the general public.

Prepare by Taking Notes

A good nonfiction review says more than whether the reviewer liked the book; it explains why, presenting specific reasons to support its position. The best way to write such a review is to respond to the book as you are reading it. Take notes—in your reader-response journal if you have one—about ideas and opinions. Quote whole sentences that are striking. Also take notes on your own responses: Do you agree or disagree with the author? Are you surprised, angered, encouraged, or discouraged by the book's message? You may wish to reread the book, or key parts of it, to grasp the author's meaning fully. The questions below can help you reflect on your reading.

Grammar Tip

When quoting whole sentences from a book, use quotation marks to set off direct quotes. When summarizing statements in your own words, you do not need quotation marks. For information on how to use punctuation with quotations, see Lesson 21.9, pages 755–757.

Questions for Book Reviewers

1. Why do I think the author wrote this book and what did I learn from it?
2. What would I like to know more about? Less about?
3. What was memorable about the book?
4. Did I find the book factual? Believable?
5. Was I persuaded to agree with the author?
6. How has the book affected my attitude on the topic?
7. How did the author's style affect the book's message?
8. Who would benefit most from reading this book?
9. Would I choose to read other books by this author?

Journal Writing

You and your friends probably give each other mini-reviews of books, movies, and music. Think about discussions you've had. In your journal explain what information helps you the most in choosing books, movies, and music for yourself.

Find a Focus

Once you've finished reading, use your notes to help you write a statement of opinion—a thesis statement—to focus your book review. For a nonfiction book, your statement of opinion will sum up the author's purpose and state whether you recommend the book. Then in the body of the review consider these points: Was the purpose a worthy one? How well did the author achieve it? Should others read the book? In the review below, notice how David Fricke's enthusiasm comes through.

Grammar Tip

When you use the book's title in your review, remember to underscore it to indicate italics. For more about writing titles, see Lesson 21.10 on pages 758–759.

Persuasive Writing

Literature Model

Sam Phillips did not set out to make rock & roll history when he founded Sun Records in 1952. History came to him, walking through the doors of his converted storefront studio, the Memphis Recording Service, in the form of Elvis Presley, Jerry Lee Lewis, Roy Orbison, Johnny Cash and Carl Perkins, among others. But as Colin Escott and Martin Hawkins explain in *Good Rockin' Tonight,* Phillips presided over the birth of rock & roll because he had the instinctive wisdom to recognize the wealth of talent at his doorstep, the indefatigable energy to record as much of it as possible and the discriminating genius to select the pick of the litter to bear Sun's immortal yellow rooster-at-dawn logo. . . .

The first paragraph provides important historical background and an overview of the book's content.

But the most impressive thing about *Good Rockin' Tonight* is that its narrative drive is every bit as contagious as the music it celebrates. "Long on feel and short on contrivance" is how Escott, in his preface, describes the explosive hybrid of blues, country, gospel and rockabilly that came to be known as the Sun Sound. It is an apt description of the book as well. *Good Rockin' Tonight* reads like a day at Phillips's office, with its breathless parade of frantic farm-boy rockers, blustery blues singers and hillbilly crooners passing daily in front of the Sun microphones. . . .

What details in the review give readers a feel for the liveliness of the author's style?

Phillips . . . wasn't a great businessman; his biggest stars had all left the label by 1963. But the breadth of his vision and the depth of his faith in the music he recorded and released is eloquently documented here. From Sun-rise to Sun-set, *Good Rockin' Tonight* is the last word on the first great rock & roll record label.

Explain the purpose of the last sentence, referring to both its content and its style.

David Fricke, "Sam Phillips and the Birth of Rock & Roll,"
Rolling Stone

6.7 Writing Activities

Write a Book Review

Select a nonfiction book you have read, and write a review of it for your school newspaper. First, consider your audience's knowledge and interest level. Then, make notes about the author's opinions, ideas, and style and about your responses.

PURPOSE To write a book review
AUDIENCE High school students and teachers
LENGTH 1–2 paragraphs

WRITING RUBRICS To write an effective book review, you should

- write a thesis statement summarizing the author's purpose and your opinion of the book
- include your own response to the book
- include supporting details and references to the text

Cross-Curricular Activity

MUSIC Find a review of any nonfiction book about music or musicians. Read the review carefully. Then use the information in the review to write 100–200 words of text for the jacket of the book. If necessary, provide background information about the author and the subject and quote striking sentences from the review.

Viewing and Representing

Look at a number of book jackets in your school library or local bookstore, carefully reading the pertinent text information inside the jackets. Choose a book jacket whose design you do not find appealing and redesign it. Present your book jacket to the class, explaining the reasons for your new design.

Punctuate and capitalize titles correctly.

BOOK TITLE: *Good Rockin' Tonight*

BOOK REVIEW: "Sam Phillips and the Birth of Rock & Roll"

Write the titles below correctly. Underline the titles that should be italicized.

1. one writer's beginnings [book]
2. an electronic job hunt [magazine article]
3. U.S. news & world report [magazine]
4. the charge of the light brigade [short poem]
5. great lady on a white horse [short story]
6. playing through [magazine article]
7. new forces of nationalism [chapter in a book]
8. the world almanac and book of facts [book]
9. the new york times [newspaper]
10. long day's journey into night [play]
11. the new york public library desk reference [book]
12. the rime of the ancient mariner [long poem]
13. a midsummer night's dream [play]
14. a perfect day for bananafish [short story]
15. the waves [book]

See Lesson 20.2, pages 715–721; Lesson 21.9, pages 755–757; and Lesson 21.10, pages 758–759.

Persuasive Writing

Writing Process in Action

Visit the Writer's Choice Web site at writerschoice.glencoe.com for additional writing prompts.

Persuasive Writing

In preceding lessons, you have learned the techniques of persuasive writing. You have learned about how to present and support an opinion, create an ad, and write a product evaluation and a complaint letter. Now it's time to apply what you've learned. In this lesson you're invited to write a letter persuading someone in authority to change a rule in a game or sport that you enjoy playing or watching.

Assignment

Context

Years of playing or watching have convinced you that a rule change would enhance a certain sport or game. You have decided to write a letter to the people who have the power to change the rules. You want to persuade them to adopt the rule change you propose.

Purpose

To write a brief persuasive essay on a rule change you propose for a sport or game you play or enjoy watching

Audience

The rules committee, governing body, or manufacturer of the sport or game you want to change

Length

1 to 2 pages

The following pages can help you plan and write your letter. Read through them and then refer back to them as you write. However, do not feel tied down by these guidelines. Remember you're in charge of your own writing process.

Prewriting

Should professional football make greater use of instant replays? Should Pin the Tail on the Donkey be changed to Tape the Tail on the Donkey to avoid cruelty to animals? Maybe an idea for a rule change came to mind the minute you read this assignment. If not, the suggestions on the right may help you.

When you have identified a rule change to propose in your letter, spend some time exploring the change to see if it is a reasonable one. Consider potential short- and long-term consequences and the effect of the change on players and spectators.

Once you have chosen your topic, express your position clearly and directly in a thesis statement. Then think about how to approach your audience. You will be writing to the people responsible for the rules of the game, so you know that you won't need to provide background information and clarify terms. You will, however, need to present compelling and convincing evidence to support your position.

When gathering evidence, look for facts and valid opinions. Although facts are generally the stronger kind of evidence, it might be difficult to find hard facts to support your position. Therefore, you may have to cite the opinions of experts who have specific knowledge of your sport or game.

Prewriting Options

- Freewrite about sports and games you know well.
- Ask "What If" questions: What if soccer players could use their hands?
- Brainstorm with classmates.

Prewriting Tip

To gain a better understanding of your audience, use the questions in Lesson 6.3, page 291.

Drafting

In persuasive writing more than in other kinds of writing, your effectiveness depends upon both what you say and how you say it. Choose a tone that is appropriate for the point you want to make. Then, as you write, choose specific words with strong positive or negative connotations to bolster your argument.

Now you are ready to state your case. Begin with an introduction that will create interest in your topic and motivate your audience to read on. Then state your position clearly and precisely. In the model on the next page, note how Mark Mathabane introduces his position on the emergence of power rackets on the professional tennis circuit.

Drafting Tip

For suggestions about using precise words and words with strong connotations, see Lesson 6.5, page 300.

Literature Model

The U.S. Open, America's premier tennis event, is under way and at the end of its two hectic weeks of fierce competition, new champions will be crowned in the men's and women's fields. But one of the hottest controversies on the professional tennis circuit will remain unresolved: the threat to the integrity of the game proposed by the new breed of power rackets. . . . Over the past three or four years, these rackets have transformed the sport of tennis from one of skill and finesse to one of sheer power.

Mark Mathabane, "A Plague on Tennis"

As you provide evidence in support of your position, be sure to respond to opposing viewpoints. Ignoring arguments against your viewpoint makes your case weaker.

Once you have presented your evidence, write a conclusion that puts an exclamation point on your argument. You want your readers to act on your proposal, so you need to leave them with a convincing call to action.

Revising

To begin revising, read over your draft to make sure that what you've written fits your purpose and audience. Then have a **writing conference.** Read your draft to a partner or small group. Use your audience's reactions to help you evaluate your work so far. The Revising Checklist can help you and your listeners.

Revising Checklist

- Is my position stated in a clear thesis statement?
- Is the supporting evidence convincing? Have I addressed opposing viewpoints?
- Are the facts and opinions relevant and credible?
- Does the conclusion relate to the evidence?
- Is the tone appropriate?

Revising Tip

When revising your letter, you may need to qualify or limit your arguments to avoid generalizations. For example, state that "*Some* experts believe . . . ," not "*Everyone* believes . . ."

Editing/Proofreading

Once you are happy with the content of your letter, **proofread** it carefully for errors in grammar, usage, mechanics, and spelling. Use the questions at the right as a guide.

In addition to proofreading, use the list below to assess your letter. When you're satisfied, make a clean copy and proofread it one more time.

Editing/Proofreading Checklist

- Have I avoided sentence fragments?
- Do pronouns and antecedents agree?
- Are *good/well* and *bad/badly* used correctly?
- Are the tenses and numbers of my verbs correct?
- Have I checked carefully for possible misspellings?

Self-Evaluation

Make sure your persuasive letter —

- ✔ focuses on a rule change in a sport or game you know well
- ✔ addresses potential problems and consequences of the rule change
- ✔ follows a plan that includes a strong thesis statement and a clear call for action
- ✔ uses valid evidence and logical reasoning
- ✔ follows correct grammar, usage, mechanics, and spelling

Proofreading

For proofreading symbols, see page 84. The electronic spelling and grammar checkers in your word processing program can help you edit and proofread your letter.

Publishing/Presenting

You're almost ready to send your letter off to the powers that be. But what if your proposal is rejected? That doesn't have to be the end. How about submitting a letter to the editor of a newspaper or a magazine that is read by fans of the sport or game of your choice?

Journal Writing

Reflect on your writing process experience. Answer these questions in your journal: What do you like best about your persuasive letter? What was the hardest part of writing it? What did you learn in your writing conference? What new things have you learned as a writer?

UNIT 6

Literature Model

A Plague on Tennis

by Mark Mathabane

Mark Mathabane, a black South African, escaped his country's oppressive apartheid system on a tennis scholarship that sent him to the United States. As you read the excerpt below, look for evidence Mathabane uses to support his views on the emergence of power rackets in professional tennis. Then try the activities in Linking Writing and Literature on page 318.

Literature Model

The U.S. Open, America's premier tennis event, is under way and at the end of its two hectic weeks of fierce competition, new champions will be crowned in the men's and women's fields. But one of the hottest controversies on the professional tennis circuit will remain unresolved: the threat to the integrity of the game posed by the new breed of power rackets.

A power racket is much bigger than a traditional racket. It's almost two rackets welded together. Its "sweet spot"—the best place for the ball to be struck, in the center of the racket head—is abnormally large.

Over the past three or four years, these rackets have transformed the sport of tennis from one of skill and finesse to one of sheer power. They have removed a compelling reason for players to develop all-round games, as did champions of the past.

The nature of tennis today is, in a word, power.

"Power-hitters" like Andre Agassi, Ivan Lendl, Jennifer Capriati and Monica Seles typify this change. Some tennis experts, among them the commentator Bud Collins and the champion Jimmy Connors, have gone so far as to call for a ban on power rackets at high levels of competition.

When I took up tennis in the early 1970's the sport was synonymous with wooden rackets. The players I idolized, enjoyed watching, and sought to emulate—Arthur Ashe, Stan Smith and Rod Laver—all relied on wooden rackets to carve out illustrious

Charles March Gere, *The Tennis Party,* 1900

careers and win major championships, including Wimbledon and the U.S. Open.

Their talent and finesse on the court were unmistakable. They served, volleyed and hit ground-strokes flat, sliced or with topspin, and whenever the occasion demanded, they played delicate touch strokes, such as angled drop shots. In sum, they possessed all-round games. They were the closest thing to the "complete player" and a delight for spectators to watch.

The demise of wooden rackets changed all that. The nature of tennis today is, in a word, power. The new rackets can generate so much power in the hands of just about anyone that players of modest abilities are transformed into giant-killers on the court, capable on any given day, usually in the early rounds, of defeating the game's finest.

Are power rackets good for tennis? The weekend player has certainly benefited from them. Their large "sweet spot" can compensate for poor vision, awkward footwork and lapses in concentration. But at the professional level these rackets have had a ruinous effect. After all, the true test of a champion is not whether he or she can hit the ball at 100 miles an hour. Racket control, variety of strokes, footwork, concentration, conditioning and above all, the ability to out-think one's opponent, are the marks of great champions.

One need only recall the impeccable styles and court acumen[1] of players like Althea Gibson, Don Budge, Margaret Court, Yvonne Goolagong and Billie Jean King to get the point.

Most tennis fans I know would rather watch the symphonic[2] play that was characteristic of these players than the "boom-boom" tennis matches of their modern replacements. With a few notable exceptions such as John McEnroe, Martina Navratilova, Boris Becker and Zina Garrison, most tennis professionals today play predictable, insipid[3] and monotonous tennis.

. . . most tennis professionals today play predictable, insipid and monotonous tennis.

Their robotic games are hopelessly lacking in variety. Armed with rackets that behave like cannons on the court, all these players are content to do, all day if need be, is keep firing the same "boom-boom" missiles until their opponents drop dead.

Some people have argued that power rackets are a great equalizer and enable small players like Michael Chang to compete with big, tall players like Boris Becker. I disagree. I believe that a player of Michael Chang's talents can compete with the best using any racket.

I know it's unrealistic to expect a return to wooden rackets. For players and racket manufacturers, there's simply too much money in the new rackets. But one would hope that for the sake of the lovely sport of tennis, already tarnished by commercialism and unsportsmanlike behavior, professional tennis players and racket makers would curb the mania[4] for more powerful rackets.

I know it's unrealistic to expect a return to wooden rackets.

Something can be learned from major league baseball's insistence on wooden bats. The rule recognizes that it should be the batter's ability, not the bat, which drives that pitch out of the ball park. The same should apply to tennis. Fans at the U.S. Open and other major tournaments around the world deserve to watch tennis at its best. And the best tennis remains that provided by players with complete games.

---

1 **acumen** (əkyoo′ mən) shrewdness
2 **symphonic** (sim fän′ ik) harmonious; having all parts combined in a pleasing arrangement
3 **insipid** (in sip′ id) dull and lifeless
4 **mania** (mā′ nē ə) a persistent enthusiasm; a craze

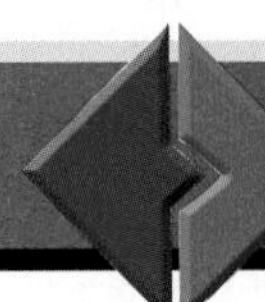

Linking Writing and Literature

Collect Your Thoughts

Whom do you think Mark Mathabane is trying to persuade in this essay? What is he trying to persuade them to do? Do you think he will be successful? Jot down your prediction in your notebook.

Talk About Reading

Talk with other students about "A Plague on Tennis." Assign a group leader to maintain the group's focus and a secretary to take notes. Use the questions below to guide your discussion.

1. **Connect to Your Life** What did you learn from this essay about the sport of tennis and its evolution? What controversies surround other sports that you are familiar with? In each case, what do you think would be the best action to resolve the controversy?
2. **Critical Thinking: Evaluate** Do you think Mathabane crafted a good title for this essay? Explain.
3. **6+1 Trait®: Ideas** Which of the ideas, arguments, or evidence that Mathabane presented did you find most interesting? Why did this capture your interest?
4. **Connect to Writing** After reading this selection, what qualities do you think good persuasive writing should have? Make a list of criteria for evaluating persuasive essays.

Write About Reading

Persuasive Writing Write a one- to three-page persuasive essay on a sports controversy of interest to you. Or, as an alternative, you could write about a political controversy of local, regional, or national significance. Before you begin writing, identify a controversy and your opinion of it. In a prewriting chart, list a few reasons for your opinion. Then note examples that support each reason.

Focus on Ideas Remember that you want to present your opinion clearly in the introduction of your essay. Make sure your ideas are strong and support your position. Use interesting and informative supporting details to elaborate on your main ideas, and be sure to end your essay with a strong conclusion.

For more information about ideas and the 6+1 Trait® model, see **Writing and Research Handbook,** pages 957–959.

6+1 Trait® is a registered trademark of Northwest Regional Educational Laboratory, which does not endorse this product.

UNIT 6 Review

Reflecting on the Unit

Summarize what you have learned in this unit by answering the following questions.

1. What are some characteristics of good persuasive writing?
2. Why is knowing your audience so important in this type of writing?
3. When creating an ad, what four goals should you keep in mind?
4. What is an effective three-step plan to follow when writing a letter of complaint?
5. How is a book review like a product evaluation?

Adding to Your Portfolio

CHOOSE A SELECTION FOR YOUR PORTFOLIO Look over the persuasive writing you have done during this unit. Select a completed piece of writing to put in your portfolio. The piece you choose should show some or all of the following:

- a position supported with facts and opinions that have been evaluated
- evidence that appeals to both reason and emotion
- an awareness of the audience to whom the writing is targeted
- a clear thesis statement, supporting details, and a conclusion calling for action
- precisely chosen words with appropriate connotations

REFLECT ON YOUR CHOICE Attach a note to the piece you chose, explaining briefly why you chose it and what you learned from writing it.

SET GOALS How can you improve your writing? What skill will you focus on the next time you write?

Writing Across the Curriculum

MAKE A HISTORY CONNECTION Scan the opinion page in your local and national newspapers. Find an editorial or a letter to the editor on a historical or political topic of interest to you. Read the editorial carefully and then draft a letter composed of two or three paragraphs to the editor of the paper, supporting or opposing the writer's position.

"Then came a shower of ash. . . ."

—George Russell, "Colombia's Mortal Agony"

UNIT 7

Research Paper Writing

Research Paper Writing

LESSON 7.1

Prewriting: Planning and Researching

Like a detective, the writer of a research paper must search for the facts. You need to gather data and let the evidence lead you to a conclusion.

Evaluation Rubric

By the time you complete Lesson 7.1, you will have

- selected a research paper topic that is neither too broad nor too narrow
- identified a central idea for your paper
- identified appropriate authoritative sources of information
- created complete, accurate source cards
- taken notes from your sources in order to avoid plagiarism

Types of Research Papers

Research papers come in many forms. The following chart lists the most common forms.

Types of Research Papers	
Summary	The writer explores a topic by summing up the opinions of other writers but does not express an opinion about it.
Evaluative	The writer states an opinion and backs it up with evidence found in primary and secondary sources.
Original	The writer does original research on a topic and reports on his or her findings.
Combination	The writer combines approaches, such as evaluating the research of others and then conducting original research.

Draw Up a Schedule

Set a schedule for yourself. A good research paper can't be written in a weekend. The schedule below shows how you might divide your time among the stages of the writing process.

Two Weeks	Two Weeks	One Week	One Week
Planning, researching, and outlining March 28	Drafting April 10	Revising April 24	Editing and presenting May 1

May 8 paper due!

Select a Topic

After making a schedule, select a topic. Spend some time in the library skimming books and encyclopedia articles. Researching and writing will be easier if you are curious about the topic you choose and if you find an approximate focus for your paper.

Amy Colleen Bryan, a student at Lexington High School in Lexington, Virginia, was interested in the sinking of the *Titanic* in 1912. Throughout this unit, you will see examples of notes, outlines, and drafts, and Amy's final paper in Lesson 7.6.

Besides your interests, consider what resources are available. If you have only one source on a topic, you will have only one viewpoint. On the other hand, selecting, condensing, and interpreting a mountain of information about a broad topic is difficult. This diagram shows how to identify an appropriate research paper topic.

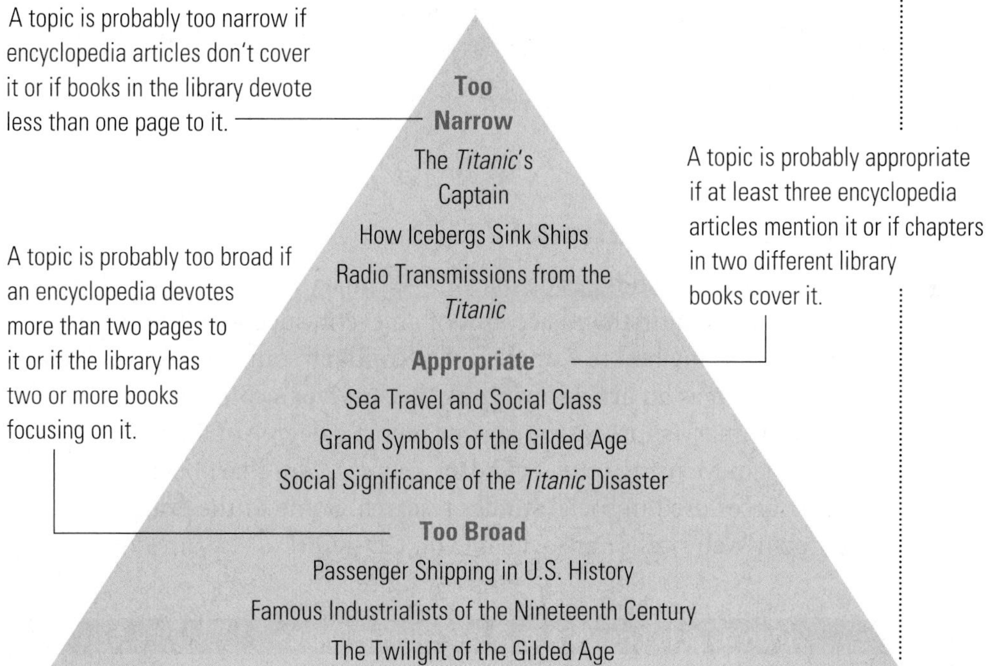

A topic is probably too narrow if encyclopedia articles don't cover it or if books in the library devote less than one page to it.
Too Narrow
The Titanic's Captain
How Icebergs Sink Ships
Radio Transmissions from the Titanic
A topic is probably appropriate if at least three encyclopedia articles mention it or if chapters in two different library books cover it.
Appropriate
Sea Travel and Social Class
Grand Symbols of the Gilded Age
Social Significance of the Titanic Disaster
A topic is probably too broad if an encyclopedia devotes more than two pages to it or if the library has two or more books focusing on it.
Too Broad
Passenger Shipping in U.S. History
Famous Industrialists of the Nineteenth Century
The Twilight of the Gilded Age

Examine the Topic

As you continue to read about your topic, you will begin to determine your central idea. Examine your topic from various points of view. Amy might have considered the following perspectives: How did the owners of the *Titanic* respond to the disaster? What did survivors recall about the sinking? Whom did investigators blame for the tragedy? Don't worry if some angles lead to dead ends. For now just try to think critically about the topic from several perspectives.

Drafting Tip

As you define special terms in your paper, you may want to review the characteristics of a good definition. See Lesson 5.6, pages 240–243.

To set a path for research, identify three to seven questions to answer first. As you answer these questions, you will discover others, as the diagram below shows. Let your central idea guide you in selecting questions.

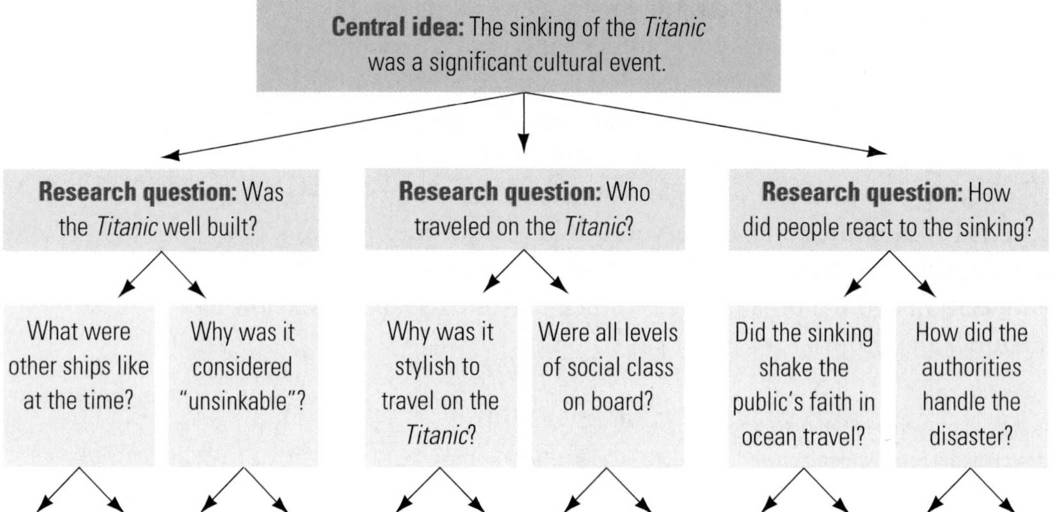

Locate Information

You may use two types of sources—primary and secondary. A **primary** source is a firsthand account of an event, such as a *Titanic* survivor's testimony before Congress. A **secondary** source is a secondhand account, such as an article analyzing the survivor's comments. If possible, use primary sources to give your report a degree of authority that's hard to achieve using only secondary sources. The chart below lists some basic sources used in social studies research. Some of the examples have their own Web sites or are available on CD-ROM.

Sources of Information on Social Studies Topics

Type	Definition	Examples
Periodicals	Magazines and journals devoted to history and written for nonscholarly audiences	*American Heritage* focuses on topics in United States history. *Zillions* covers consumer and economic issues of interest to many students.
Reference Books	Specialized works that provide excellent background information on social studies topics	*Encyclopedia of American History* lists and describes events in U.S. history. *Encyclopedia of World History* lists significant world events in chronological order.
News Updates	Publications that provide information on current events and people	*Facts on File* is an up-to-date review of current events. *Current Biography* provides detailed biographies of important people in the news.

Develop a Working Bibliography

As you begin your research, you will need to develop a working bibliography, a record of the books, articles, and other sources you will consult for your paper. Record the publication data for each appropriate source—including the publishing company, city, and date of publication—in a computer file or on a three-by-five-inch index card, as shown below. Number each source file or card in the upper right corner so that when you take notes, you can jot down the number of the source in which you find information. Preparing complete source files or cards now will help you compile your works-cited list at the end of your paper. Write notes to yourself as well, as shown on the magazine source card below.

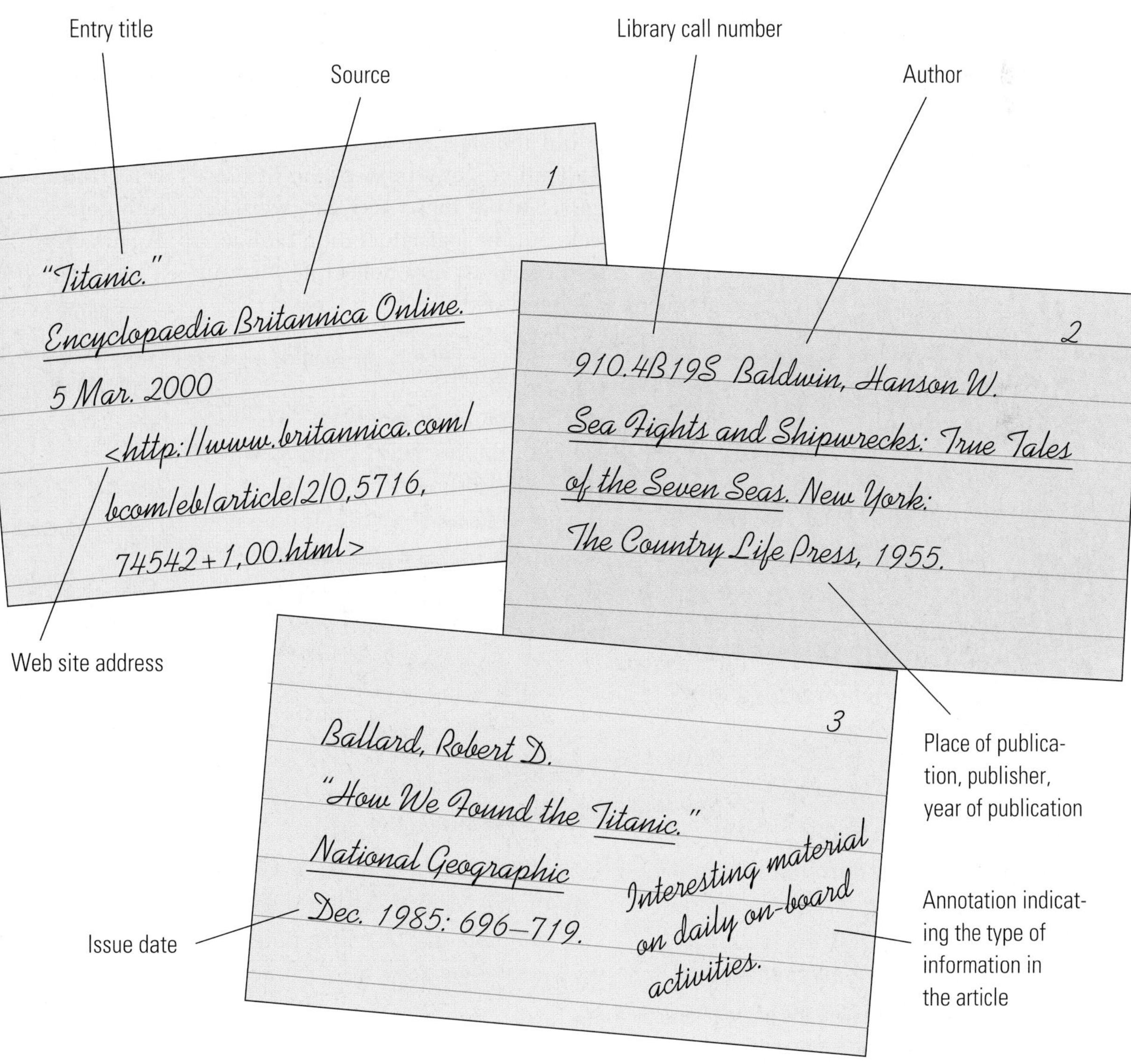

Entry title
Source
Library call number
Author
1
"Titanic."
Encyclopaedia Britannica Online.
5 Mar. 2000
<http://www.britannica.com/bcom/eb/article/2/0,5716,74542+1,00.html>
2
910.4B19S Baldwin, Hanson W.
Sea Fights and Shipwrecks: True Tales of the Seven Seas. New York:
The Country Life Press, 1955.
Web site address
3
Ballard, Robert D.
"How We Found the Titanic."
National Geographic
Dec. 1985: 696–719.
Interesting material on daily on-board activities.
Place of publication, publisher, year of publication
Issue date
Annotation indicating the type of information in the article

Research Paper Writing

Take Notes

Grammar Tip

When taking notes, remember to use quotation marks to enclose direct quotes. For more information about quotation marks, see Lesson 21.9, pages 755–757.

Just as you use cards when developing your working bibliography, you can use cards when taking notes. As you find a piece of information that answers one of your research questions, write it on a four-by-six-inch note card. In the upper right-hand corner of the note card, write the number of the source from the working bibliography.

You might want to put your initials by any of your own thoughts that you jot down on note cards. By initialing your own comments, you will be able to keep straight which information comes from other sources and which comes from your own interpretation.

Three ways of taking notes—paraphrasing, summarizing, and writing direct quotations—are shown below.

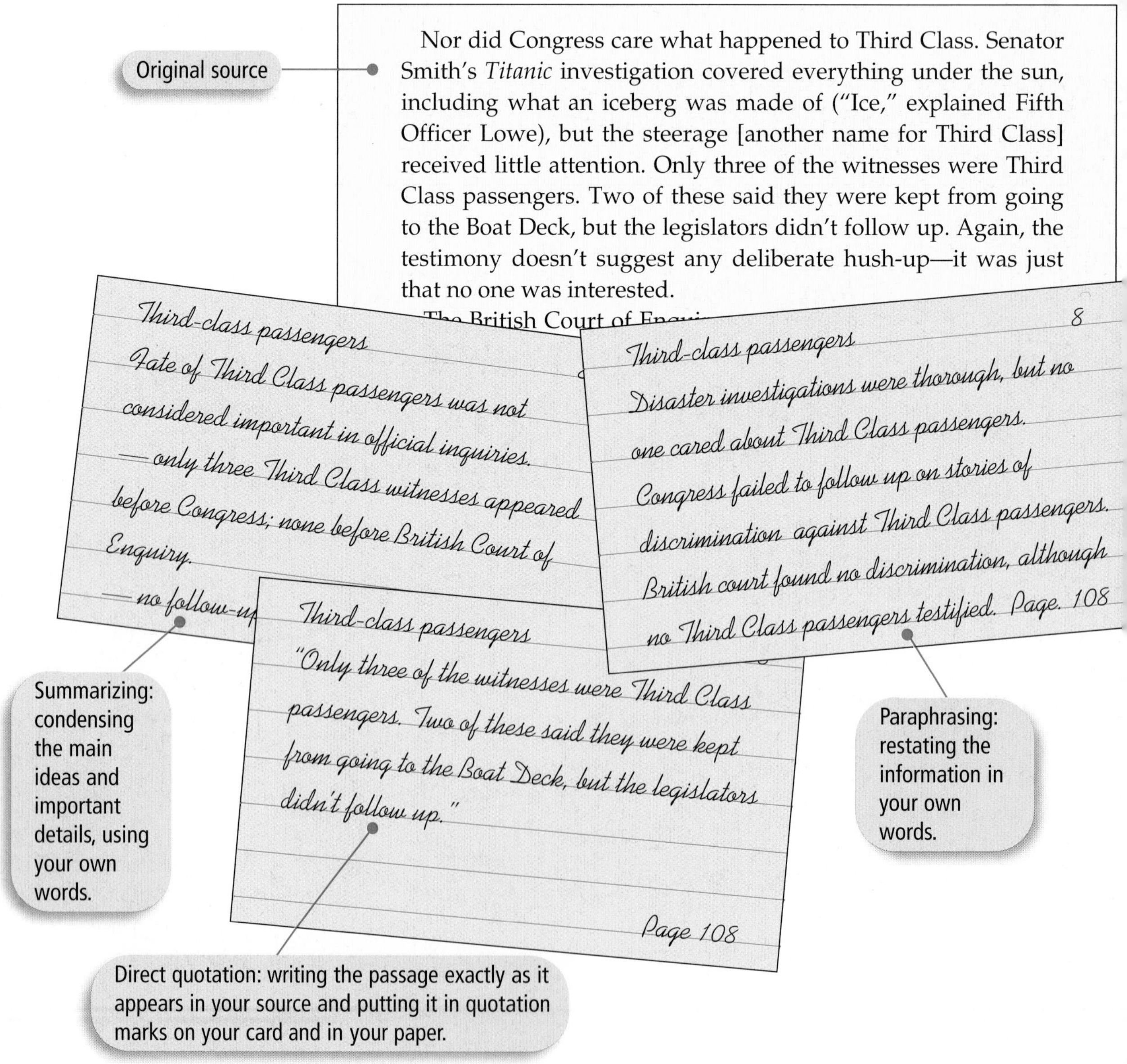

Original source

Nor did Congress care what happened to Third Class. Senator Smith's *Titanic* investigation covered everything under the sun, including what an iceberg was made of ("Ice," explained Fifth Officer Lowe), but the steerage [another name for Third Class] received little attention. Only three of the witnesses were Third Class passengers. Two of these said they were kept from going to the Boat Deck, but the legislators didn't follow up. Again, the testimony doesn't suggest any deliberate hush-up—it was just that no one was interested.

The British Court of Enqu...

Third-class passengers

Fate of Third Class passengers was not considered important in official inquiries.

—only three Third Class witnesses appeared before Congress; none before British Court of Enquiry.

—no follow-u...

Summarizing: condensing the main ideas and important details, using your own words.

Third-class passengers 8

Disaster investigations were thorough, but no one cared about Third Class passengers. Congress failed to follow up on stories of discrimination against Third Class passengers. British court found no discrimination, although no Third Class passengers testified. Page. 108

Paraphrasing: restating the information in your own words.

Third-class passengers

"Only three of the witnesses were Third Class passengers. Two of these said they were kept from going to the Boat Deck, but the legislators didn't follow up."

Page 108

Direct quotation: writing the passage exactly as it appears in your source and putting it in quotation marks on your card and in your paper.

Examine Sources Critically

Because each source you use is written by a person with particular interests, knowledge, and values, be alert to each author's bias. Find sources that approach your topic from different angles. Asking the following questions will help you critically evaluate your sources.

Questions About Sources

1. What is the author's purpose in writing the book or article?
2. Has new information been discovered since the source was written?
3. Are the views of the author often disputed by others knowledgeable on the topic?
4. Would someone from another culture, religious group, economic class, or time period view the events differently?

Grammar Tip

When editing and proofreading, you will be correcting capitalization and punctuation. To make this task easier, be sure to use correct capitalization and punctuation in your notes.

Avoid Plagiarism

Presenting someone else's ideas or expressions as your own is plagiarism, a form of cheating. Even when unintentional, plagiarism is a serious offense. You must give credit to the sources of information you use in your paper. To avoid plagiarism, keep clearly documented notes so you know where you found each piece of information. Lesson 7.4 will teach you how to credit your sources accurately.

7.1 Writing Activities

Skills Practice

1. Write a brief explanation of why each topic below is too broad, too narrow, or about right for a seven-page research paper.

- the Mongol Empire under Genghis Khan
- the controversy over the death penalty
- the childhood of Indira Gandhi
- African independence movements since 1945

2. For each general area, suggest two topics appropriate for a seven-page research paper:

- great leaders in African history
- relations between China and Japan
- cultural diversity in South America
- railroads in United States history

Your Research Paper

Begin the process of writing a research paper, following the directions below.

- Select a research paper topic that interests you and do some preliminary reading to help you narrow the topic appropriately.
- Write at least five research questions.
- Conduct library research and prepare source cards, using the *MLA Handbook for Writers of Research Papers* and the examples on pages 325 and 340 as guides to recording publication information accurately.
- Take legible notes from the sources you've gathered and make sure to properly cite the source of each idea.

LESSON 7.2

Prewriting: Outlining

Evaluation Rubric

By the time you complete Lesson 7.2, you will have

- made a formal outline or graphic organizer that indicates an appropriate method of organization for your paper
- drafted and revised a thesis statement that provides a clear focus for your writing

Your rapidly growing pile of note cards is threatening to bury you. What do you do? It's simple. You learn the lesson that military generals throughout history have learned. If you break up your opposition into smaller units, you can quickly take control of the situation.

Develop an Outline

An outline is a summary of the main points and the ideas that support them. Soon after you have begun your research—before your pile of note cards is too big—you can start to outline your paper. Outlining will help you organize your information and further focus your research efforts.

A Working Outline As you take notes, look for ways to classify the facts and ideas you find. For example, look for similar features, such as two facts about the role of an individual in a historical event. Begin to group the note cards as you classify them.

As you make decisions on how to organize your cards, you are developing the information you need to write a working outline. The reasons you use to categorize your cards will become the headings on your working outline. If some cards do not fit under the headings, set them aside. Later you can decide whether to keep or discard them.

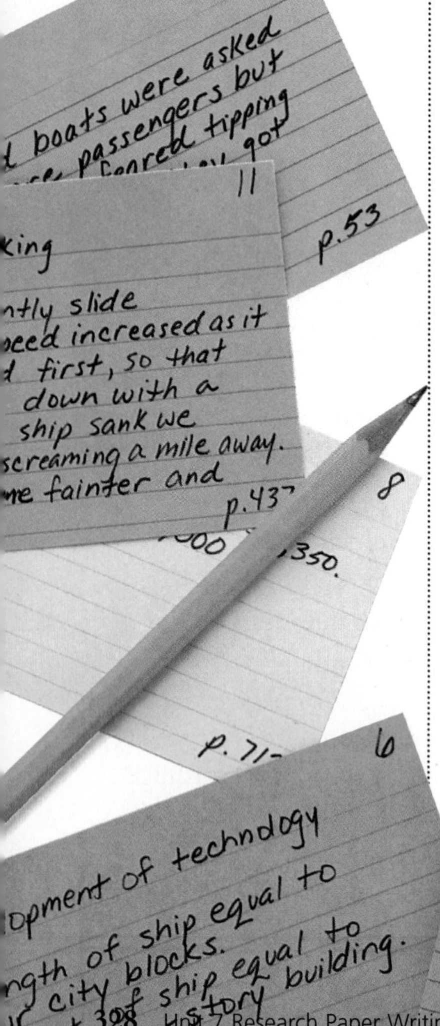

Think of this first outline as a preliminary sketch. As you continue your research, revise your working outline and your central idea to reflect new information. If a heading seems to be less important than it did earlier, make it a subheading or discard it altogether. Try creating your outline on a computer so you can easily make changes as you continue researching. The annotations on the example show how to organize headings and information.

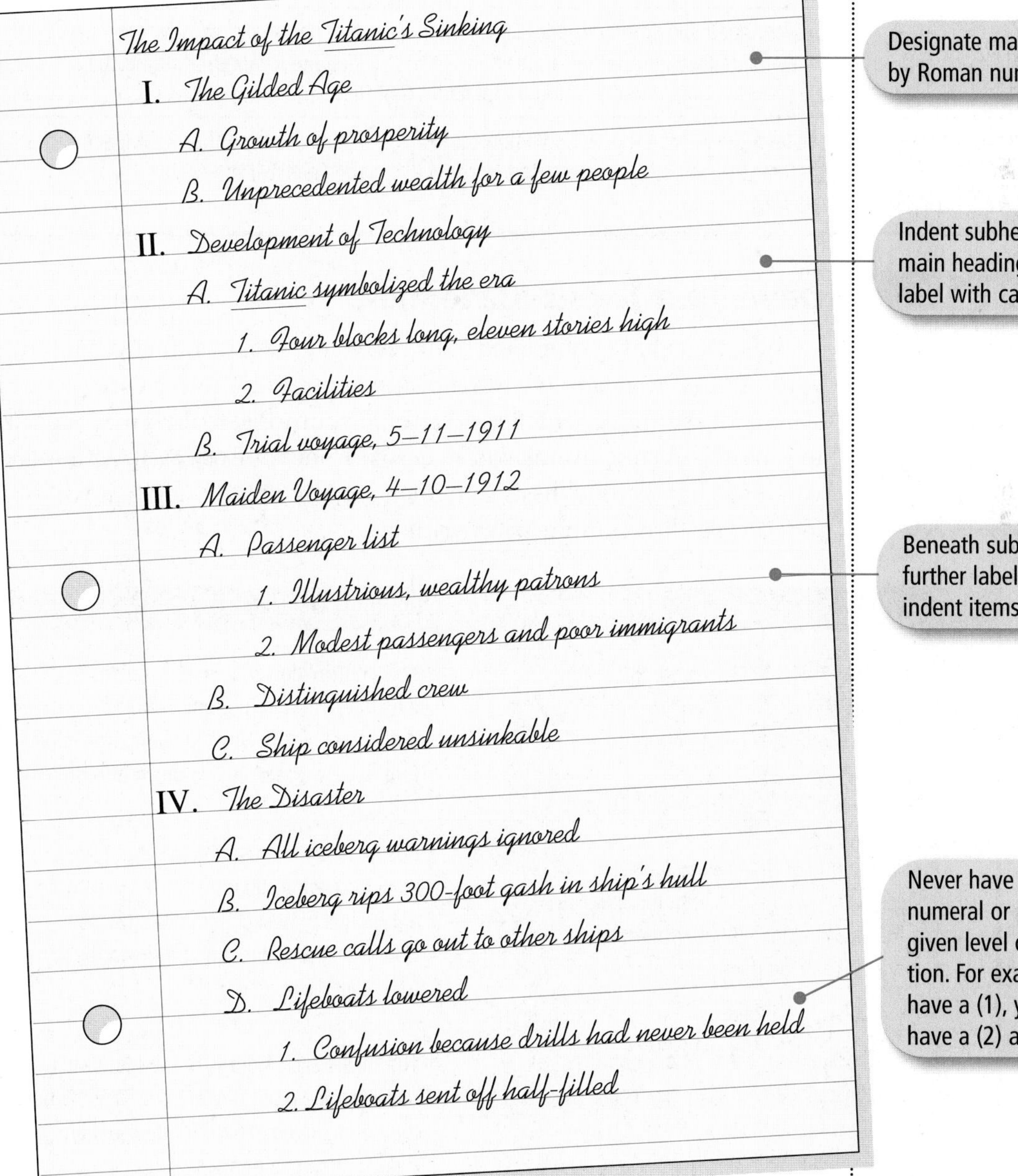

The Impact of the Titanic's Sinking
I. The Gilded Age
A. Growth of prosperity
B. Unprecedented wealth for a few people
II. Development of Technology
A. Titanic symbolized the era
1. Four blocks long, eleven stories high
2. Facilities
B. Trial voyage, 5–11–1911
III. Maiden Voyage, 4–10–1912
A. Passenger list
1. Illustrious, wealthy patrons
2. Modest passengers and poor immigrants
B. Distinguished crew
C. Ship considered unsinkable
IV. The Disaster
A. All iceberg warnings ignored
B. Iceberg rips 300-foot gash in ship's hull
C. Rescue calls go out to other ships
D. Lifeboats lowered
1. Confusion because drills had never been held
2. Lifeboats sent off half-filled

Designate main headings by Roman numerals.

Indent subheads under main headings and label with capital letters.

Beneath subheads, further label and indent items.

Never have just one numeral or letter at a given level of organization. For example, if you have a (1), you must have a (2) as well.

Three Methods of Organization As you categorize your note cards, begin to consider ways to organize the information within each category. Three of the most common methods of organization are described below. Note that Amy Bryan uses the chronological method in her outline.

Methods of Organization		
Method	**Description**	**Example**
Chronological	Information arranged according to when it happened; often used in papers describing historical changes	A paper surveying China's changing policies under Mao Zedong toward the former Soviet Union
Cause and Effect	Items arranged showing how one development directly influenced another; often used in papers explaining why something happened	A paper analyzing how each new idea led to another during the Industrial Revolution
Cumulative	Items arranged according to how important or how familiar each one is; often used in papers evaluating results	A paper evaluating the impact of the Gulf War of 1991

Prewriting Tip

For further help in developing a thesis statement, you may wish to review Lesson 2.3, pages 56–59.

Develop a Thesis Statement

When you have completed your research, prepare a final version of your outline. You can now rewrite your central idea into a concise thesis statement—a single sentence describing your topic and your approach to it based on conclusions you've drawn from your research. Although you may change your thesis statement slightly in later stages, it will provide a clear direction for your writing.

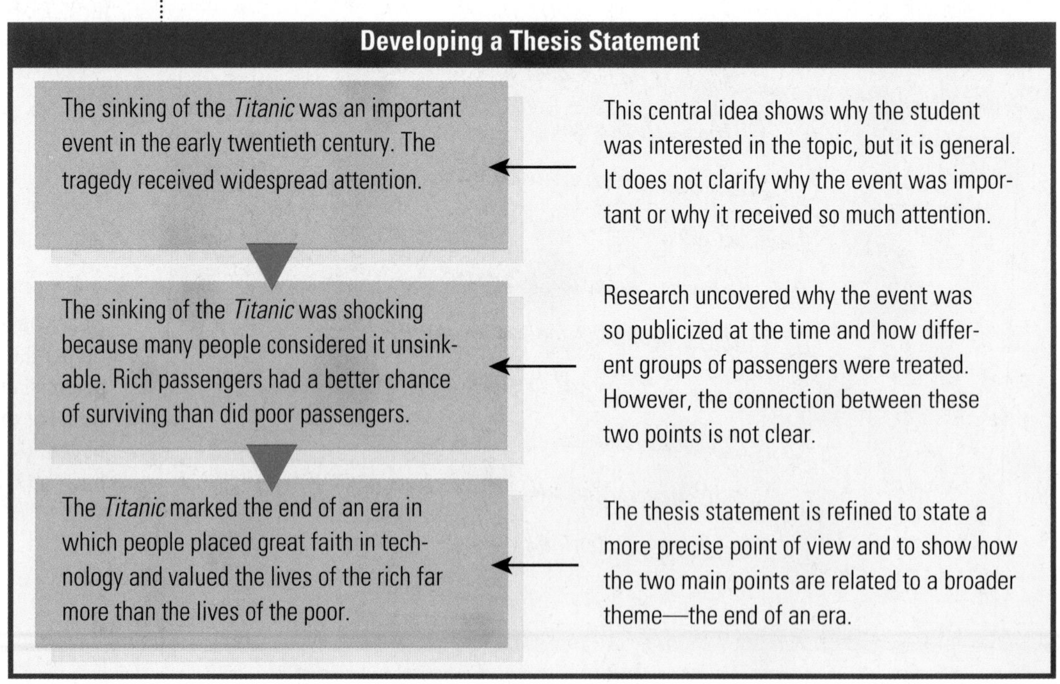

Developing a Thesis Statement
The sinking of the *Titanic* was an important event in the early twentieth century. The tragedy received widespread attention.
This central idea shows why the student was interested in the topic, but it is general. It does not clarify why the event was important or why it received so much attention.
The sinking of the *Titanic* was shocking because many people considered it unsinkable. Rich passengers had a better chance of surviving than did poor passengers.
Research uncovered why the event was so publicized at the time and how different groups of passengers were treated. However, the connection between these two points is not clear.
The *Titanic* marked the end of an era in which people placed great faith in technology and valued the lives of the rich far more than the lives of the poor.
The thesis statement is refined to state a more precise point of view and to show how the two main points are related to a broader theme—the end of an era.

The type of thesis statement you use will depend upon the type of paper you write. The chart below lists some types of thesis statements.

Four Types of Thesis Statements	
Original	Used to demonstrate new information that you have developed
Evaluative	Used when stating your opinion on a topic
Summary	Used when your paper primarily reports the ideas of others
Combination	Utilizes two of the three other categories listed in this chart

7.2 Writing Activities

Skills Practice

1. Create a chronological outline by organizing the statements below under the given headings.

Headings

I. Pre-Berlin Wall Political Divisions

II. The Wall as a Physical Barrier

III. Beginnings of Reunification

Statements

- The Berlin Wall was erected in 1961.
- After World War II ended in 1945, Berlin was divided and occupied by the four major Allied powers.
- Many people defected from East Germany by escaping to West Berlin in the 1950s.
- The Berlin Wall prevented free movement between East Germany and West Berlin until 1989.
- The Berlin Wall was dismantled in December 1989.
- East Germany was created in 1949.
- In the 1980s, the Soviet Union reduced its influence over East Germany.

2. Organize the following notes into cause-and-effect order.

- Because of trade, Mali prospered.
- Because of scholars, Mali became an intellectual center.
- In the 1300s, the West African kingdom of Mali controlled trade across the Sahara.
- Because of its prosperity, Mali was able to recruit scholars to live there.

3. Write a thesis statement for the outline you developed in 2 above.

Your Research Paper

Continue working on your research paper. Complete the following steps.

- Arrange your note cards in groups according to subject.
- Identify main ideas and use them as the main headings in a formal outline or graphic organizer.
- Complete your outline or graphic organizer, adding subheadings and details.
- Write a thesis statement that states the main idea you will develop in your paper.

Research Paper Writing

LESSON 7.3

Drafting

Evaluation Rubric

By the time you complete Lesson 7.3, you will have

- drafted your research paper, making sure that your ideas logically progress from one idea to the next
- written an interesting introduction that includes your thesis statement
- created a conclusion that integrates your ideas and brings your paper to a close

According to legend, a mid-nineteenth-century historian who lived in London would not begin writing until he had read every book available on the topic he was researching. Today that task would be nearly impossible. So many books—not to mention journals, magazines, newspapers, and Web sites—exist that it would be ambitious to read everything written about even a narrow topic. At some point, like every researcher, you must begin to write.

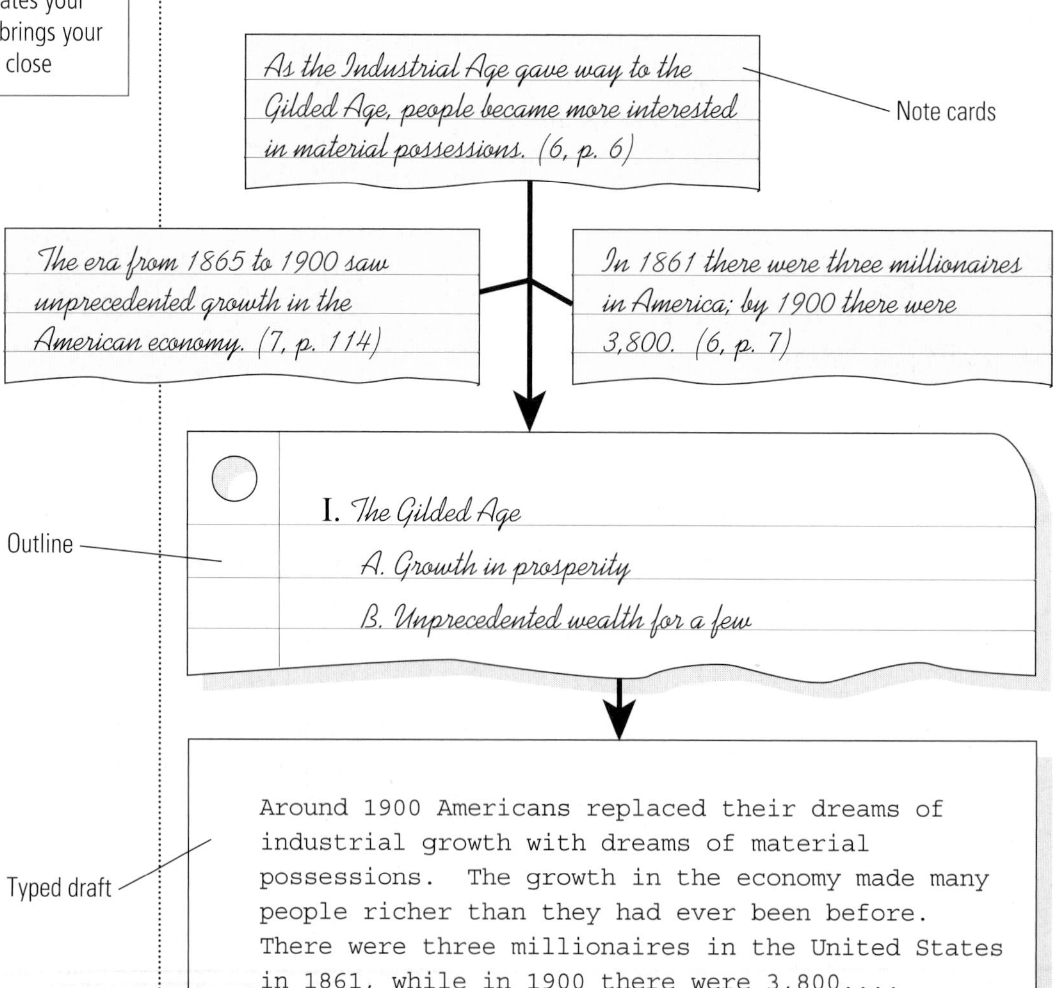

As the Industrial Age gave way to the Gilded Age, people became more interested in material possessions. (6, p. 6)
Note cards
The era from 1865 to 1900 saw unprecedented growth in the American economy. (7, p. 114)
In 1861 there were three millionaires in America; by 1900 there were 3,800. (6, p. 7)
Outline
I. The Gilded Age
A. Growth in prosperity
B. Unprecedented wealth for a few
Typed draft
Around 1900 Americans replaced their dreams of industrial growth with dreams of material possessions. The growth in the economy made many people richer than they had ever been before. There were three millionaires in the United States in 1861, while in 1900 there were 3,800....

Use Your Outline and Notes

In writing your first draft, use your outline as a map to guide the direction of your writing. Write at least one paragraph for each main heading in your outline. As shown on the preceding page, you can combine information from several cards to help you state one idea. Keep your ideas flowing logically from one to the next but don't get bogged down by details or by trying to find the perfect words to express your ideas. This is only your first draft—you will revise it later.

As you take information from note cards and insert it into your draft, also insert the number of the note card next to the information. You will then have a clear and accurate record of your sources to use in the final version of your paper.

As you write, you may run into some difficulty in handling a large quantity of information. The chart below gives advice for overcoming some problems that commonly occur in the early stages of drafting.

Grammar Tip

Your paper will be more interesting to read if you vary your sentences. Before you revise your first draft, look at examples of sentence structures you might use. See Lessons 13.3 and 13.4, pages 545–548.

Drafting: Problems and Solutions

Problem		Solution
I have a large stack of note cards. How do I handle so many notes?	▶	Read through them and remove anything that duplicates another note or that contains only irrelevant material. Set them aside for possible use later.
I have many notes on some aspects of my topic but very few on others. What should I do?	▶	Conduct more research, or look again at your outline to see if you can write a good paper with the notes you now have. If so, revise your outline.
Do I have to write the first part of the paper first, the second part second, and so on?	▶	Write in whatever way is easiest for you. If you write sections out of sequence, pay close attention when you revise to the transitions between sections and to how forcefully you are building your argument.
How can I overcome writer's block when I sit down to write my first draft?	▶	Don't worry about finding the perfect words. Just get the ideas down. You can always improve your writing in your next revision.
I seem to run out of time before I get very far into my writing. How should I plan my time?	▶	Set aside at least three hours for nothing but writing your paper. Eliminate distractions by going to the library or asking your family not to disturb you.

Write an Introduction and a Conclusion

A good paper has an identifiable introduction and conclusion. An effective introduction attracts and holds the reader's attention; it should also contain your thesis statement, which clearly describes the topic or central idea of the paper. A few suggestions for how to start your introduction are shown below. Each describes a way to capture the attention of your readers.

Tips for Writing Introductions	
Summarize	Providing an overview of the main headings in your outline will make your reader comfortable with the topic.
Describe	Include an unusual fact or amusing anecdote about your topic. This will entertain your reader and show your topic from a new perspective.
Pose a Question	If you are writing about the Civil War, for example, ask your reader to imagine what the United States would be like today if the South had won.
Use a Quotation	An eyewitness opinion often is more emotional and gripping than comments by later analysts.
Describe a Scene	In the model paper for this lesson, the writer describes the eerie underwater wreckage of the *Titanic,* transporting the reader to the decks of the once elegant ship.

Your conclusion should pull the paper together and alert the reader that you are finishing your argument. As with the introduction, a conclusion can be written in many different ways. Since it is the last part of your paper, use the conclusion to summarize your main point for your reader. Amy Bryan concludes her paper with a quotation that addresses the question asked in her thesis statement.

Tips for Writing Conclusions

1. Summarize your main points to refresh the reader's memory of your arguments.
2. Reexamine the topic and its effects. Did your opinion on the topic change as you researched it? Did any part of your research surprise you?
3. Consider the future. How does your research put your topic in a new light? What questions for further research can you think of?

7.3 Writing Activities

Skills Practice

Use the following outline entries and note cards to write a cohesive paragraph about the early life of former South African president Nelson Mandela. Your audience is a group of seventh-grade students. Use only the entries and note cards that you need to write one good paragraph.

Outline Entries

I. Early years marked Mandela as a leader and a lover of democracy
   A. Adopted by the chief of the Thembu
      1. Listened to many legal cases
      2. Went to school to study law
   B. Suspended from school for leading a student strike
   C. Urged by adoptive father to stop the strike
      1. Father wanted him to become chief of the Thembu
      2. Father had arranged a marriage for him

Note Cards

Mandela's father was the second-most-important leader of the Thembu. On his deathbed, his father asked Chief David Dalindyebo to take Mandela into his care.

The Thembu, though governed by a chief, had a long heritage of democracy. Mandela heard these stories at tribal meetings with his father.

Despite the South African government's attempts to diminish the authority of the tribal leaders, Dalinyebo still heard and decided on many legal issues. Mandela often sat in on the court deliberations.

Chief Dalindyebo was grooming Mandela to become chief of the Thembu.

Mandela went to Fort Hare College in 1938 to get a bachelor of arts degree, the first step toward getting a law degree.

In 1940 the authorities at Fort Hare College decided to lessen the responsibilities of the student council.

- Mandela was a member of the council.
- He led a student strike in protest and was suspended.

Chief Dalindyebo urged him to stop the strike and return to class. The chief also had chosen a wife for Mandela.

Your Research Paper

Draft your research paper, completing the following steps. For additional help with writing effective research papers, see **Writing Research Handbook,** pages 960–962.

- Begin by writing the section about which you feel most confident.
- Using the main and subordinate headings in your outline as a guide, pull information from your note cards. Provide clear transitions from one idea to the next.
- Write an introduction that captures your reader's attention and includes a thesis statement that states the direction your paper will take.
- Write a conclusion that reinforces your thesis and the main points of your paper.

LESSON 7.4

Citing Sources

When did Christopher Columbus first sail to the Americas? The answer is common knowledge: 1492. When did the industrial revolution begin? Not everyone's answer would be precisely the same. When you write a research paper to answer such a question, you must know when to tell your readers where you got your information and when you can assume they know and accept your information.

Evaluation Rubric

By the time you complete Lesson 7.4, you will have

- learned what information in your paper does and does not need to be documented
- chosen an appropriate method for citing your sources
- correctly cited your sources in the body of your paper

Document Appropriately

The information you include in your research paper must be properly documented. In other words, you need to identify where you found the information. By citing the sources of all ideas, statements, and quotations that you have used, you allow your reader to judge the validity of the information. For example, information quoted from a respected historical journal will carry more weight than a statement quoted from a television dramatization.

Why Document By citing your sources properly, you acknowledge those people whose ideas you are using. Since they developed the facts, opinions, and analyses that you have borrowed, they deserve a mention in your work.

In addition, by citing your sources properly, you avoid plagiarism—the presentation of someone else's ideas or statements as your own. You should cite your source whether you use the information word for word or you paraphrase it.

What Not to Document While you want to credit others for their work, you don't have to cite the source of common knowledge. Examples of common knowledge include widely accepted facts, such as that the Andes are in South America or that the Magna Carta was signed in 1215. Widely known proverbs, famous quotations, and simple definitions are also common knowledge. The following chart gives examples of statements and whether or not they need documentation.

Documenting Your Information		
Type of Information	**Citation?**	**Explanation**
Direct quotation: The sinking of the *Titanic* "signaled the end of the Edwardian era in all its cocky opulence."	Yes	The source of each direct quotation should be given because the words are clearly borrowed from someone else.
Opinion: Americans equated size with security and excess with success.	Yes	This is a paraphrase of another author's conclusions. Sources of conclusions and other opinions should be cited.
Opinion: Completed in 1912, the *Titanic* was considered the most luxurious ship of its day.	No	The luxuriousness of the ship is an opinion widely enough accepted that is common knowledge.
Statistics: The *Titanic* was four city blocks long and eleven stories high.	Yes	Phrasing the measurements in terms familiar to general readers was the work of another writer, so the source should be cited.
Data: The ship sailed out of London and was to reach New York one week later.	No	General information about the trip could be found in several reference Works. None of this information comes from one particular work.

Revising Tip

As you revise your paper and move information from one part of the paper to another, be careful to move the documentation with the information. For more help with citing sources within your paper, see **Writing and Research Handbook,** page 962.

Format Citations Properly

Documenting your sources will be easy if you have accurately completed and numbered your source cards and note cards during the prewriting stage. All the information you need should be right at your fingertips. (If you've missed something, return to the library to find your sources again.)

You can cite your sources in one of three ways: footnotes, endnotes, or parenthetical documentation, which is recommended by the Modern Language Association of America (or MLA). Parenthetical documentation is generally preferred because the reader does not have to search for the citation. The instruction and models in this unit conform to the MLA guidelines; however, check with your teacher and use the method that he or she prefers.

Parenthetical Documentation with a Works-Cited List

A works-cited list is an alphabetized list of the sources that you have used in writing your research paper. In your paper, after each quotation, summary, or paraphrase of information from a source, you must include within parentheses a reference to a source and, when appropriate, a page reference. This citation points readers to the corresponding entry in your works-cited list.

Research Paper Writing

Drafting Tip

For more information about italicizing (underlining) titles or using quotation marks, see Lessons 21.9 and 21.10, pages 755–759.

When you drafted your paper, taking information from your note cards, you jotted down the corresponding number of the source from which you took the information. Now you can replace those numbers with proper parenthetical documentation. Place the citation as close as possible to the borrowed information. The parenthetical reference usually should be positioned where a pause would naturally occur, such as just before a comma or at the end of a sentence (but before the final period), as shown in this example:

In 1861 there were three millionaires in the United States; in 1900 there were 3,800 (Wade 7).

The examples that follow and Amy Bryan's final draft of her research paper on pages 349–356 provide guidance and models for using parenthetical documentation to cite sources in text.

PARENTHETICAL DOCUMENTATION GUIDELINES

1. (Lord 108)

Put the author's last name and the page reference in parentheses. If you're using two or more works by different authors with the same last name, include the author's first name or initial.

2. (Kingston and Lambert 145)

For a work by two or three authors, put the authors' last names and the page reference in parentheses. If a work has more than three authors, use the last name of the first author, followed by *et al.*, and the page reference: (Kingston et al. 145).

3. (*White Star 110*)

If a source does not have an author, use a shortened form of the title in parentheses. Provide a page reference if possible.

4. (Angier, "Haunting Images" 58)

If you use more than one source by the same author, include the author's last name followed by a comma, the source title or a shortened form of it, and a page reference.

5. (Lord 171–172; *Secrets*)

If you use a piece of information that you found in more than one source, cite each work as you normally would, inserting a semicolon between the entries.

6. (109)

When you use the author's name in the sentence that includes the information you need to document, provide only a page reference in parentheses, as shown in this example: As Walter Lord noted, "The *Titanic* was the last stand of wealth and society in the center of public affection" (109).

7. ("Titanic")

If you use a nonprint source, such as a videocassette, a film, or an article published online (the example above is for an article published by *Encyclopaedia Britannica Online*), name the work in running text or, in parentheses, give readers the information they need to find the complete citation in the works-cited list.

Vocabulary Tip

When you edit your paper, check the spelling of the names of authors you cite against your list of works cited for possible misspellings.

Research Paper Writing

Format Your List of Works Cited

Whichever form of citation you use, at the end of the paper you should include a list of works cited. Unlike your working bibliography, the works-cited list includes only those sources that you use in your final paper. Although you may have consulted many additional sources for background and other general information, these sources should not be included on this final list.

Record the publication information from your source cards, following the formats shown on the next page and in Amy Bryan's works-cited list on pages 355–356. If you use a source that is not modeled in this unit, consult your teacher or the *MLA Handbook for Writers of Research Papers.*

The following are some general tips for formatting works-cited lists.

Formats for Works-Cited Entries

1. Arrange entries in alphabetical order according to the author's or editor's last name. Write the name in reverse order—last name first. For works with two or more authors, reverse only the first author's name.
2. If no author or editor is given, alphabetize the entry by the title, disregarding the word *a, an,* or *the* at the beginning of a title.
3. When more than one work by an author is listed, use three hyphens followed by a period rather than repeat the author's name.
4. Begin each entry at the left margin. If an entry runs more than one line, indent every line five spaces after the first.
5. Book and magazine titles should be in italics or else underlined.
6. Article titles should be enclosed in quotation marks.

Research Paper Writing

Use a shortened form of the publisher's name—for example, "Knopf" for "Alfred A. Knopf, Inc." Use the abbreviation "UP" for "University Press." (See the entry under "Bishop" in the chart.)

The chart below shows how to format different types of entries in a works-cited list. Some examples are from Amy Bryan's paper.

Works-Cited Entries	
Source	**Example of Entry**
Book with one author	Baldwin, Hanson W. *Sea Fights and Shipwrecks: True Tales of the Seven Seas.* New York: Country Life Press, 1955.
Book with two or three authors	Kingston, Jeremy, and David Lambert, *Catastrophe and Crisis.* New York: Facts on File, 1979.
Book with no author	*The White Star Triple Screw Atlantic Liners Olympic and Titanic.* New York: Arco, 1970.
Book with an editor but no single author	Kuntz, Tom, ed. *The Titanic Disaster Hearing: The Official Transcripts of the 1912 Senate Investigation.* New York: Pocket Books, 1998.
A selection in an anthology	Bishop, Mrs. H. D. "The *Titanic:* From a Lifeboat, 15 April 1912." *Eyewitness to History* Ed. John Carey. Cambridge: Harvard UP, 1987. 436–437.
Encyclopedia article	"Titanic." *Encyclopedia Americana.* 1998.
Magazine article	Ballard, Robert D. "How We Found the *Titanic.*" *National Geographic* Dec. 1985: 696–719.
Newspaper article	"New Liner *Titanic* Hits an Iceberg." *New York Times* 15 Apr. 1912: A1.
Personal interview	Watkins, Eliza. Personal interview. 30 October 1999.
Lecture, address, or sermon	Baker, A. B. Sermon. Trinity Church, Princeton. 21 Apr. 1912.
Radio broadcast	"*Titanic* Photo Book." Narr. Bob Edwards. *Morning Edition.* Natl. Public Radio. WBEZ, Chicago. 15 Apr. 1998.
Online resource	"Titanic." *Encyclopaedia Britannica Online.* 5 Mar. 2000 <http://www.britannica.com/bcom/eb/article/2/0,5716,74542+1,00.html>.
CD-ROM	Garzke, William H., Jr. "Titanic." *World Book Multimedia Encyclopedia.* CD-ROM. Chicago: World Book, 1999.
Web site	*The Virginia Newspaper Project Exhibit of the Titanic.* 11 Nov. 1999 <http://www.lva.lib.va.us/pubserv/vnp/titanic/titanic1.htm>.

7.4 Writing Activities

Skills Practice

1. For each piece of information below, tell whether you think source documentation is necessary. Explain the reasons for your answer.

- Kemal Ataturk ruled Turkey from 1923 to 1938.
- Ataturk declared, "Our thoughts and our mentality will become civilized from head to toe."
- According to one historian, Ataturk was more concerned with reforming his country than with increasing his power.
- The status of Turkish women was raised during Ataturk's rule.
- Radical changes instituted by Ataturk threatened to destroy traditional Turkish culture.

2. Each of the following entries from a list of works cited contains two mistakes in punctuation. Copy each entry, correcting the punctuation as you do so.

- Ghareeb, Edmund. *The Kurdish Question in Iraq.* Syracuse, Syracuse UP. 1981.
- "British Views of Disunion." *New York Times:* 8 Feb. 1861:8
- Koch, Adrienne and William Peden, eds. *The Life and Selected Writings of Thomas Jefferson.* New York: The Modern Library, 1944.
- Lih, Lars T. "Gorbachev and the Reform Movement." *Current History* October 1987: 310

3. Using parenthetical documentation, write the citation that would appear in the text for each of the following sources:

- a quotation from page 21 of *Abuse of Power* by Theodore Draper
- a quotation from page 17 of *England Under the Tudors* by G. R. Elton, one of three books by Elton used in the paper
- a quotation from page 100 of *The Mau Mau from Within,* by Donald J. Barnett and Karari Njama
- a quotation from page 19 of an article in *Time* magazine, "Six Minutes," with no author listed

Your Research Paper

Continue working on your research paper by completing the following steps.

- Insert proper documentation within the body of your paper. If you're using parenthetical documentation, replace the note card numbers that correspond to your source cards with a proper citation in parentheses.
- Create a draft of your works-cited list.
- Ensure the accuracy of your documentation and your works-cited list by following the formats outlined in this lesson and in the *MLA Handbook for Writers of Research Papers.*

LESSON

7.5

Revising

Even the Declaration of Independence, one of the most powerfully written documents in United States history, needed revision. Thomas Jefferson, the Declaration's author, knew what every good writer knows: almost anything you write can be improved through revision. Your first draft is an important beginning, but you should plan to make changes to it.

Evaluation Rubric

By the time you complete Lesson 7.5, you will have

- evaluated your research paper draft for both content and mechanics
- reviewed the paper's organization and reorganized the content to ensure coherence, logical progression, and support for ideas
- refined your writing style to suit the requirements of the research paper and to meet the needs of your audience

Improve Your Paper

When you revise your first draft, work on mechanics, word choice, transitions, and presentation of ideas. Remember that in a formal research paper, you should write in a voice and a style that are appropriate to your audience and purpose. The following chart describes problems you may face and offers possible solutions to them.

Revising: Questions and Answers

Questions		Identifying What Needs Revising
Have I given the first draft a clear focus?	▶	Review your thesis statement to be sure it is clearly stated.
Have I accomplished what I set out to do in this paper?	▶	Skim your paper, looking for and deleting irrelevant information. Add ideas that readers might need to follow your reasoning.
Do my paragraphs flow logically and smoothly?	▶	Read the last sentence of each paragraph and the first sentence of the following paragraph. If the flow of ideas is not smooth, add transitions.
Have I used someone else's ideas without credit?	▶	Scan your paper, reading each sentence that does not contain a citation. Add documentation if necessary.
Do my examples and supporting details help clarify my main point?	▶	Replace the questionable examples or details with direct and appropriate ones.
Have I used terms that are not familiar to the average reader?	▶	Scan your paper, picking out specialized terms or unusual words. Review your definitions or explanations of each of these terms or words.
Is my choice of words interesting and appropriate?	▶	Delete redundant words and phrases. If a word is repeated often, find synonyms for it. Replace vague terms with more precise ones.
Are my introduction and conclusion effective?	▶	Read your first and last paragraphs. Each should highlight the main point of the paper.

Using proofreading marks like the ones modeled on the next page saves time during revision and makes your copy easier to read. To review proofreading symbols, see page 411.

Drafting Tip

As you revise your paper, try to keep a mental note of the types of changes you make most often. This can help you when you begin drafting another paper.

Revising Tip

For examples of different kinds of supporting details you can use when revising your first draft, see Lesson 2.6, pages 68–71.

Using synonyms avoids repetition of word "Titanic."

Combine sentences to avoid repetition and present related information together.

"Reportedly" is more concise than "it was reported."

Revise to improve the flow of the sentence.

Using pronouns avoids repetition.

Add a phrase to create or improve the transition between paragraphs.

Change verb so the number agrees with the subject.

The ~~Titanic~~ ship also ~~had~~ carried a ~~good~~ distinguished crew. The captain of the Titanic was Edward Smith, and ~~He~~ was a favorite among high-society Americans, ~~He also~~ who had been captain of the Olympic, the Titanic's sister ship. Upon sailing, ~~it was reported that~~ Second Officer C. H. Lightoller reportedly said, "It was clear to everyone on board that we had a ship that was going to create the greatest stir British shipping circles had ever known" (218). When a woman asked a deckhand ~~was~~ if the Titanic was really "unsinkable," ~~the deckhand~~ he replied, "God himself could not sink this ship" (Friedrich 70).

~~They had~~ This overconfident attitude was matched by perfect weather for the first four days of sailing. Then at 9:00 A.M. ~~in the morning~~ on April 14, the Titanic received iceberg warnings from ~~another ship,~~ the Coronia. Two more warnings ~~was~~ were received that afternoon, yet Captain Smith dismissed all three, ~~He~~ never decreasing the ship's speed of 22 knots or changing its course. At 7:30 P.M. ~~another ship,~~ the Californian, warned the Titanic of ice.

Revise Your Paper

Certain writing problems are common in research papers. Try exchanging papers with a partner to get another perspective on your work and to provide your partner with feedback. Review the points in the following checklist as you revise your paper.

Checklist for Revising a Research Paper

1. How can you strengthen your thesis statement so that it provides a clear focus for the paper?
2. How can your main ideas be better organized to ensure coherence and logical progression? What irrelevant or repetitious ideas can you delete?
3. Which ideas could be better supported with information from sources?
4. How can you strengthen the transitions between ideas and paragraphs?
5. Have you written in a voice and style that is consistent throughout—and is appropriate, given your audience and purpose?
6. Have you varied your sentence structures and used lively verbs so that your paper isn't boring?
7. What technical terms still need to be defined?
8. Which frequently used words can be replaced with appropriate synonyms?
9. Have you cited your sources correctly in the body of your paper?
10. Is your works-cited list accurate, complete, and properly formatted?

7.5 Writing Activities

Skills Practice

Each of the following pairs of statements includes an excerpt from a first draft of a social studies paper and a new bit of information that the writer found after completing the first draft. Use the new information to help you revise the italicized information in each first-draft excerpt.

- **First draft:** In 1960 forty-three-year-old John Kennedy became president of the United States. *As the youngest person ever to serve* as president, he brought great energy to government.

  New information: Theodore Roosevelt was only forty-two years old when, following the assassination of President McKinley, he became president in 1901.
- **First draft:** Jimmy Carter defeated Gerald Ford in the 1976 presidential election. Carter served as president *until 1980.*

  New information: Carter served only one term as president, from 1977 to 1981.

Your Research Paper

Revise your research paper. Complete these steps and use the Checklist for Revising a Research Paper to guide you.

- Clarify your thesis statement if necessary, making sure that it adequately sets a purpose and direction for the paper.
- Evaluate the organization of your draft and decide how you can improve the flow of ideas.
- Conduct additional research if necessary to support your data.
- Strengthen your transitions to ensure that your paper is coherent.

LESSON 7.6

Editing and Presenting: A Model Paper

Research Paper Writing

After Thomas Jefferson revised the Declaration of Independence, he commissioned a final version in elegant, flowing handwriting. Although the ideas in the Declaration were powerful, Jefferson still took time to prepare a perfect document that would help him win support for his ideas. To win the most support for your research paper, you should follow Jefferson's example.

Prepare the Final Copy

After you have made your paper as clear, logical, and coherent as you can, focus your attention on editing. Proofread your paper, watching for mistakes in citations, grammar, spelling, punctuation, and word usage. Read your paper aloud to catch mistakes that you might miss by reading silently. Once your research paper is free of errors, you can type or print your final copy. The checklist below can help you remember to examine all the important aspects of your final version.

Evaluation Rubric

By the time you complete Lesson 7.6, you will have

- proofread your paper, identifying and correcting errors in grammar, punctuation, and spelling
- confirmed that every summary, paraphrase, and quotation is properly credited to a source and checked that every source you used is listed in a properly formatted works-cited list
- created a clean final copy that is free of errors and ready to present to your audience

Editing and Presenting Checklist

1. Have I organized my ideas clearly?
2. Have I explained or defined any words that may be unfamiliar to the reader?
3. Have I discussed my topic completely and fairly?
4. Have I checked the paper for missing words or letters?
5. Have I considered the proper meaning of the words I've used?
6. Have I corrected all grammar and punctuation mistakes?
7. Is each word spelled and capitalized correctly?
8. Is the paper neat and easy to read?

Present Your Paper

Bryan 1

Amy Colleen Bryan
Ms. Meryl Wilk
English Composition
26 April 2000

The *Titanic:*
Was It the End of an Era?

Writer's last name and the page number should appear on each page, one-half inch from the top and one inch from the right edge of the paper.

Writer's name, teacher's name, course name, and date should appear on the first page, one inch from the top of the page and one inch from the left edge of the paper.

The title should be centered on the page.

You may want to create a cover for your paper or enclose it in a special folder. A separate title page should include the title of your paper, your name, your teacher's name, the course name, and the date on which you submit the paper. If you don't have a separate title page, put this information on the first page of your paper, as shown here. The last page of your paper is always the list of works cited.

Give some thought to whether your paper would be enhanced by the use of any visuals, such as copies of photographs or works of art, diagrams, time lines, or charts. These materials may be attached to the end of your paper, before the works-cited list.

Your teacher may ask you to submit a variety of materials along with your final paper. You may be asked to submit your note cards, your final outline (which should not include your introduction and conclusion), or a summary statement. Make sure that you know what's expected of you well in advance of the final due date. You don't want any last-minute surprises!

7.6 Writing Activities

Skills Practice

1. On a separate paper, rewrite the following sentences to make them clearer.

- Each of the United States is represented by two people in the Senate.
- The first Europeans to explore the Great Lakes were missionaries and fur-trapping operations.

2. Copy the following sentences, and correct the problems of word usage and writing style.

- The Great Depression through millions of people out of work.
- Andrew Jackson was tough, shrewd, and had experience as a soldier.

3. Read these sentences and identify misleading comments or poorly constructed thoughts.

- Because his plantation relied on the efforts of enslaved persons, Thomas Jefferson probably would have sided with the Confederates in the American Civil War.
- Gandhi was beloved by the Indian people because of his nonviolent principles, and he had admirers around the world as well.
- The purchase of Alaska increased the mineral wealth of the United States, and gold was soon discovered in the Canadian Yukon.

Your Research Paper

As you prepare the final version of your research paper, use the student model on the following pages as a guide. Read the call-out notes in the side column and use the student model to help you understand each note and to answer any questions you find there. Pay special attention to the following strategies:

- Presenting Tip
- Grammar Tip
- Editing Tip

Also, note how the Works-Cited list is presented. As you create your own list, refer back to the Formats for Works-Cited Entries on page 339 and the examples in the Works-Cited Entries chart on page 340.

Prepare the final version of your research paper, and hand it in to your teacher. Be sure to include any additional materials that your teacher requires.

Student Model

The *Titanic:* Was It the End of an Era?

Amy Colleen Bryan

"All around us there was this twisted mass of wreckage and tons of coal spread around. And then there was this lady's shoe. It was incredible, just haunting" (Lemonick 70). On September 1, 1985, marine geologist Dr. Robert Ballard, with the help of U.S. and French researchers, found the *Titanic* 13,000 feet below the surface of the Atlantic Ocean. Using sonar and a robot submarine, Dr. Ballard located the ship about 500 miles south of Newfoundland, where it had sunk seventy-three years before. Thirteen thousand feet below the surface the water is totally black with no marine life and a temperature of 39° F, yet the *Titanic* had been well preserved. It was sitting upright covered with silt, and although it split in half during the sinking, the grand staircase, railings and wooden deck were still intact, the planks still visible. On closer investigation, Ballard's crew found five cases of wine with the corks still in them, china plates, wash basins, chamber pots, and luggage.

Completed in 1912, the *Titanic* was considered the most luxurious ship of its day. The *Titanic* has been called a "monument to the Gilded Age" (Marbach 46) and its sinking "signaled the end of the Edwardian era in all its cocky opulence" (Angier, "*Titanic* Find" 68). Was the sinking of the *Titanic* really the end of an era?

The two decades before World War I have been labeled the Gilded Age for a number of reasons. After the American Civil War, as westward expansion resumed, industry expanded and many Americans discovered wealth for the first time. Around 1900 the optimistic "dream" for industrial growth turned into an optimistic dream for material possessions (Wade 6). Many people were richer than ever before. In 1861 there were three millionaires in the United States; in 1900 there were 3,800 (Wade 7). Americans equated size with security and excess with success (Wade 29). They wanted to expand technologically and materially. They prized business success and placed faith in extravagance.

(continued)

Remember to underline titles when appropriate in your text and works-cited list; or use italics if you're using a word processing program. (See Lesson 21.10 on pages 758–759 for reminders about appropriate punctuation of titles.)

Bryan grabs her reader's attention by describing vivid scenes of the wreck.

How does this background information help the reader?

Bryan states her thesis as a question she is trying to answer in her paper.

Research Paper Writing

Transitions help the reader follow the course of events.

Why, do you think, did Bryan put the dimensions of the *Titanic* in these terms?

Presenting Tip

Including a diagram or a photograph of the *Titanic* in the final draft would enhance a reader's understanding of the dimensions of the ship.

In the beginning of the 1900s there were no movie, radio, or television stars to idolize, so "the public depended on the socially prominent people for all the vicarious glamour that enriches drab lives" (Lord 109–110). In fact the rich lifestyle of the Gilded Age existed for very few. Those who did fit the description held a wealth almost beyond comprehension, a wealth that has never quite been repeated. The life and fate of the rich and famous received the most attention. John Jacob Astor IV, the richest man in America, possessed thirty million dollars (an amount almost equivalent to $350,000,000 in today's money). Benjamin Guggenheim followed with twenty million and Isidor Straus and George Widener each had ten million (Davie 45).

Besides material growth, the time around 1900 was full of invention and technology, from automobiles to rubberbands (*Secrets*), and it seemed like the *Titanic* was the epitome of this era, symbolizing all that this time had to offer.

Work began on the *Titanic* in 1909 at Harland & Wolff's shipping yards in Belfast, Ireland. It took three thousand men two years to build. When completed, the ship was made of 46,000 tons of steel and measured 882.5 feet long and 105.7 feet high. Comparatively speaking, the *Titanic* was four city blocks long and eleven stories high (Lord 170). The inside of the ship contained facilities ranging from Turkish baths and tennis courts to sun parlors, a theater, and a miniature golf course.

As news of the extravagant technological wonder spread throughout the world, it soon became known as the "unsinkable" *Titanic.* Experts considered the ship "unsinkable" because of its vast size and the strength and stiffness of the floor; the keel, longitudinals, and inner and outer bottoms were greater in size, weight, and thickness than in any other ship; the floor extended up the sides of the ship so as to "frame" it; the whole length of the hull was stiffened by deep web frame girders; the hull was divided into sixteen watertight compartments, four of which could be flooded and the ship would still float; the deck beams were ten inches thick and held to the sides with steel; and the elaborate pipe systems could delay the rise of water ("Experts" 981). The structural stability of the ship, unparalleled for its time, was ready to be tested in open waters.

The *Titanic* set sail from Belfast Harbor on May 11, 1911. Her trial voyage lasted eight hours, and upon her return, her builders were confident that she was indeed "unsinkable." She left Southampton at twelve noon on April 10, 1912, on her maiden voyage. She was to reach New York City one week later.

There were approximately 2,207 passengers on board when the *Titanic* left the harbor (Friedrich 70), 706 of whom were immigrants traveling to the United States for the first time (Baldwin 47). About 350 of the biggest names in American and British society were on the first-class list ("*Titanic* in Peril"). These people paid $4,350 for their seven-day trip, an amount almost equivalent to $50,000 in today's money (Ballard 712). The passenger list included General John Jacob Astor IV and his wife; Major Archibald Butt, military aide to President William Howard Taft; John B. Thayer, Vice-President of the Pennsylvania Railroad; Charles M. Hays, President of Grand Trunk Railways in Canada; Mr. And Mrs. Isidor Straus, owners of Macy's Department Store; and J. Bruce Ismay, chairman and managing director of the White Star Line.

The ship also carried a distinguished crew. The captain of the *Titanic* was Edward Smith, who had been a captain of the *Olympic,* the *Titanic's* sister ship, and was a favorite among high-society Americans. Upon sailing, Second Officer C. H. Lightoller reportedly said, "It was clear to everyone on board that we had a ship that was going to create the greatest stir British shipping circles had ever known" (218). When a woman asked a deckhand if the *Titanic* was really "unsinkable," he replied, "God Himself could not sink this ship" (Friedrich 70).

This over-confident attitude was matched by perfect weather for the first four days of sailing. Then at 9:00 A.M. on April 14, the *Titanic* received iceberg warnings from the *Coronia.* Two more warnings were received that afternoon, yet Captain Smith dismissed all three, never decreasing the ship's speed of 22 knots or changing its course. At 7:30 P.M. the *Californian* warned the *Titanic* of ice. Second Operator Harold Bride ignored these signals because he was figuring accounts. Around 9:30 P.M. Commander Lightoller ordered Frederick Fleet to get up in the crow's nest to watch for icebergs. At 11:00 P.M. the *Californian* again warned the *Titanic*

(*continued*)

Bryan converts amounts of money to modern equivalences so the reader can understand their significance.

Grammar Tip

When editing your paper, check that you have used commas correctly. For information about comma usage, see Lesson 21.6, pages 743–751.

What form of organization does Bryan use in describing the voyage?

Research Paper Writing

about ice. First Operator Phillips, who relieved Bride, told the *Californian* operator to shut up and leave him alone because he was busy (Baldwin 49). The *Titanic* still steamed full speed ahead at 22 knots.

Up in the crow's nest, at 11:40 P.M., 1300 miles from New York City, Fleet saw an iceberg looming in the distance. The officer on the bridge gave the order to turn the ship hard to starboard. The orders were too late. There was a faint jarring that lasted for ten seconds. The result was a 300-foot gash along the starboard side of the hull. Five water-tight compartments had been flooded, enough to sink the ship. The first wireless call for help went out at 12:15 A.M. The *Virginian,* the *Carpathia,* and the *Baltic* received the call and started for the ship. Evans, the wireless operator for the *Californian,* had turned off his signals and retired to bed fifteen minutes before. Ironically, the *Californian* was less than ten miles from the *Titanic* (Angier, "Haunting" 58).

At 12:45 A.M. the first distress rocket was fired, and the first lifeboat was lowered. Launching arrangements were confused; because no lifeboat drills had been held beforehand, loading was random. Women and children were given first priority along with the first-class passengers in general (Kingston and Lambert 145). Half-filled boats were asked to take more passengers but did not; they feared tipping and sinking once they got into the water (Baldwin 53). Lifeboat 6 had a capacity of sixty-five passengers but left with only twenty-eight (Baldwin 53). Lifeboat 1 had a capacity of forty people but left with only twelve ("*Titanic* Diary"). Two of these passengers were women, the rest men—among them were three millionaires and J. Bruce Ismay.

At 1:40 A.M. the crew fired the last rocket into the air and at 2:05 A.M. lowered the last lifeboat, "collapsible D," into the water. Benjamin Guggenheim and his valet came on deck in full evening dress, saying "We've dressed in our best and are prepared to go down like gentlemen" (Friedrich 70). When Astor tried to board a lifeboat with his wife, he was refused; he told her he would meet her later.

Around 2:10 A.M. the wireless operator sent the last call for help. As the ship sank at 2:20 A.M., Mrs. H. D. Bishop observed from a lifeboat, "It began to slide gently downwards. Its speed increased as it went down head first, so that the stern shot down with a rush. . . . As the ship sank we could

Eyewitness descriptions carry more power than an analysis from a secondary source.

Use ellipses to indicate that material has been omitted from quotations.

hear the screaming a mile away. Gradually it became fainter and died away" (437).

Many lifeboats made little attempt to help other survivors in the water. Fireman Harry Senior was swept off the ship as it went down. Later he explained, "I tried to get aboard a boat, but some chap hit me over the head with an oar. There were too many people in her" (435).

The *Carpathia* arrived at dawn to pick up survivors. By 8:50 A.M. the *Carpathia* was headed for New York City with 705 *Titanic* passengers (Lord 171–172; *Secrets*). The total death count was 1,502.

When the news reached American newspapers, the *New York Times* was so confident that the *Titanic* was unsinkable that it carried only a small front page story about the accident ("New Liner"). However, on April 16 when the news was confirmed, the stories filled up the entire front section of the *New York Times* for five consecutive days. New York City swarmed with people trying to find out who had survived. The *New York Times* ran front page stories on the rich and famous who were on board, with an entire article devoted to John Jacob Astor alone; almost as an afterthought the 1,800 others who might have died were listed (Lord 110).

The shock of this calamity raised many questions. Almost immediately after the disaster, both the United States and Great Britain set up investigations. Through these investigations, the injustices that occurred on the *Titanic* that night were made public. These were conditions that would "never get by the social consciousness (or news sense) of today's press" (Lord 108). There were lifeboats for only half the passengers on board, and of the 1,500 people in the water, only 13 were picked up by lifeboats (Kingston and Lambert 145). Greatly debated was the treatment of the second-class, third-class, and steerage passengers. Of the women in first-class, only 4 of 143 drowned (3 by choice); 15 of 93 women in second-class drowned; and 81 of 179 women in third-class drowned. All except 1 of 30 children in first- and second-class survived, but only 23 of the 76 children in steerage survived (Lord 107).

For the most part the third-class passengers had to fend for themselves. Some in third-class thought that access to the lifeboats was a privilege of the first- and second-classes (Lord 108–109). Unbelievably, there was a higher loss of third-class

(*continued*)

Editing Tip

It is common practice to not italicize the article preceding the title of a magazine or newspaper.

How does this sentence help the reader?

Why is this sentence a helpful lead-in to the paragraph?

Research Paper Writing

children than first-class men (Lord 108). A steward stationed on the third-class deck testified that some men were kept locked below deck until almost 1:15 A.M. Thirty-four percent of the first-class men were saved, while only eight percent of the second-class and twelve percent of the third-class survived (Davie 45). When lawyers investigated the situation, however, White Star Line was indifferent, as were the press and even Congress. The British enquiry said it found no discrimination (Lord 108).

The investigation procedures for each country were very different but ultimately resulted in the same conclusions. Some recommendations that resulted from the investigations were: life preservers and regulation lifeboats for all passengers on board, lifeboat drills, a wireless operator on duty at all times, and a double-skin for the hull, longitudinal bulkheads, and water-tight decks. The United States and British governments set up the International Ice Patrol and the first International Convention for the Safety of Life at Sea was begun in London in 1913 ("Titanic").

Laws at sea changed, but also Americans realized that in their haste to progress, they had sacrificed safety; in their quest for material possessions, they had forgotten the spiritual. In a sermon given at Princeton University the Sunday after the *Titanic* disaster, Reverend A. B. Baker said:

Set off any quotations longer than three lines by indenting the entire passage.

> Was there not something of self-confidence and self-sufficiency in the contention that it was perfectly safe, that it could outride any ocean storm and come unharmed through any danger to which it might be exposed? . . . It will not do to put our confidence in ships nor in anything that represents the boastful progress of the age.

In this disaster the world had lost a number of the noted wealthy. As a result many Americans changed their view of wealth and success. The *Titanic* was the "last time the special position of First Class was accepted without question" (Lord 109). Many Americans quickly realized that prominent people under stress could be selfish and conceited (Lord 109). As Walter Lord noted, "The *Titanic* was the last stand of wealth and society in the center of public affection" (109). The First World War and later the Depression made sure of that. After the *Titanic* disaster it was more difficult for Americans to be as confident of technology and progress. The *Titanic* "mirrored" the Gilded Age. It had seemed to be the peak of all

Since the author's name is given in the text, only the page number is needed in the citation.

technology, wealth, and luxury. Life after its sinking was never the same.

Many people have tried to pinpoint reasons for the *Titanic* disaster. The chance is one in a million that a ship will hit an iceberg and sink to the ocean floor (Beasley 174). Was this disaster destined by fate? Had people become so sure of themselves that Divine Intervention was needed to put them back in their place?

The Gilded Age was a period of extremes—growing wealth and growing technology. The sinking of the *Titanic* shocked Americans back to reality. It made them retrace their steps and look at the world in a different light, a world where it was harder to be so confident and sure of oneself. Dr. Charles H. Parkhurst tried to explain the reason for this tragedy by saying:

> The two sore spots which really run into one another and which constitute the disease that is gnawing into our civilizations are the love of money and the passion for luxury. These two combined are what sunk the *Titanic* and sent 1500 souls prematurely to their final account ("Religious Views" 939).

Bryan ends her paper with a strong quotation.

Works Cited

Angier, Natalie. "After 73 Years, a *Titanic* Find." *Time* 16 Sep. 1985: 68.

—. "Haunting Images of Disaster." *Time* 23 Sep. 1985: 58.

Baker, A. B. Sermon. Trinity Church, Princeton. 21 Apr. 1912.

Baldwin, Hanson W. *Sea Fights and Shipwrecks: True Tales of the Seven Seas.* New York: Country Life Press, 1955.

Ballard, Robert D. "How We Found the *Titanic.*" *National Geographic* Dec. 1985: 696–719.

Beasley, Lawrence. *The Loss of the* Titanic. London: Philip Allan, 1929.

Bishop, Mrs. H. D. "The *Titanic:* From a Lifeboat, 15 April 1912." *Eyewitness to History.* Ed. John Carey. Cambridge: Harvard, 1987. 436–437.

Presenting Tip

In your final works-cited list, cite only those sources from which you actually used information in your research paper. Your teacher may ask you to include a brief annotation for each work cited in which you explain the source's content and usefulness.

Davie, Michael. Titanic: *The Death and Life of a Legend.* New York: Knopf, 1986.

"Experts on the *Titanic* Wreck." *Literary Digest* 11 May 1912: 981.

Friedrich, Otto. "When the Great Ship Went Down." *Time* 16 Sep. 1985: 70.

Kingston, Jeremy, and David Lambert. *Catastrophe and Crisis.* New York: Facts on File, 1979.

Lemonick, Michael D. "Treasures Reclaimed from the Deep." *Time* 2 Nov. 1987: 70.

Lightoller, Commander. Titanic *and Other Ships.* London: Ivor Nicholson and Watson, 1935.

Lord, Walter. *A Night to Remember.* New York: Holt, 1955.

Marbach, William D. "The Sea Gives Up a Secret." *Newsweek* 16 Sep. 1985: 46.

"New Liner *Titanic* Hits an Iceberg." *New York Times* 15 Apr. 1912: A1.

"Religious Views of the *Titanic.*" *Literary Digest* 4 May 1912.

Secrets of the Titanic. Dir. Nicholas Nixon. With Martin Sheen. Videocassette. National Geographic Society Video, 1986.

Senior, Harry. "The *Titanic:* A Fireman's Story, 15 April 1912." *Eyewitness to History.* Ed. John Carey. Cambridge: Harvard, 1987. 434–435.

"Titanic." *Encyclopaedia Britannica Online.* 5 Mar. 2000 <http://www.britannica.com/bcom/eb/article/2/0,5716,74542+1,00.html>.

"Titanic Diary." *Encyclopedia Titanica.* Sept. 1996. 4 Mar. 2000 <http://atschool.eduweb.co.uk/phind/lifeboats/boat_01.html>.

"*Titanic* in Peril on Leaving Port." *New York Times* 11 Apr. 1912: A1.

Wade, Wyn Craig. *The* Titanic—*End of a Dream.* New York: Rawson, Wade, 1979.

TIME

For more about the writing process, see **TIME Facing the Blank Page,** pp. 109–119.

UNIT 7 Review

Reflecting on the Unit

Summarize what you learned in this unit by answering the following questions.

1. What are the important elements of planning and researching a paper?
2. How and why do you outline the information gathered during your research?
3. What is the purpose of a thesis statement?
4. What are the important steps to follow when you draft a research paper?
5. How and why should you document information you use in your paper?
6. What techniques can help you revise and present your paper effectively?

Adding to Your Portfolio

Look over the research paper you prepared during this unit and add it to your portfolio. The final draft of your paper should show some or all of the following:

- an appropriate research topic and a useful working bibliography
- a clear thesis statement supported with adequate details
- an effective introduction and a strong conclusion
- clarity, logic, and coherence
- proper documentation of sources

REFLECT ON YOUR CHOICE Write a brief note to explain what you learned from writing your research paper. Attach the note to your paper.

SET GOALS How can you improve your writing? What skill will you focus on the next time you write?

Writing Across the Curriculum

MAKE A SCIENCE CONNECTION One type of research paper is an evaluative paper. In such a paper, the writer states an opinion and backs it up with evidence found in primary and secondary sources. Scan the newspaper, a weekly newsmagazine, or a science journal, and choose an issue or topic that interests you. Draft a central idea statement presenting your opinion on the topic. Locate supporting evidence—facts and educated opinions—in primary and secondary sources. Then outline the contents of the paper and write a thesis statement and opening paragraph for it.

"About three minutes after Ms. Bear walked into the cannery, twenty of the twenty-four workers were climbing out . . ."
—Robert H. Abel, "Appetizer"

UNIT 8

Sentence Combining

Style Through Sentence Combining

What do you have in common with writers such as James Baldwin, Annie Dillard, James Thurber, Amy Tan, and Rudolfo Anaya? Like them, you have a distinctive writing style, a way of communicating your personality. Developing a clear, expressive writing style requires practice, of course. By writing regularly in your journal and trying out different types of writing—poems, essays, stories, letters to the editor—you develop a range of skills. Another excellent approach for developing style is sentence combining.

Unlock Your Style

Sentence combining is a research-tested writing strategy that enables you to explore options, make choices, and develop style. This process of combining short sentences into more complex ones is the focus of this unit. Your goal, however, is not to make long sentences, but to make good ones. Sometimes you will find that longer, more complex sentences enable you to express your ideas with precision and clarity. At other times, shorter is better.

The point is that sentence combining helps you understand your stylistic options. Instead of being locked into one type of sentence and "playing it safe" with a short, choppy style that reads like a first-grade reader, you can make choices as a writer. Practice in combining unlocks your style by making you aware of writing choices.

Learn the Drill

In sentence combining, you express the same information in different ways by using four combining strategies: (1) deleting repeated words; (2) using connecting words; (3) rearranging words; and (4) changing the form of words. Consider this cluster of short, basic sentences to see how they might be combined differently.

Sentence combining is a writing strategy.
The strategy has been tested by research.
It enables students to explore options.
It enables students to make choices.
It enables students to develop style.

As you scan these sentences, your brain goes to work, drawing upon your knowledge of language. You can use the four combining strategies to express these ideas in fewer words. Look at the example below.

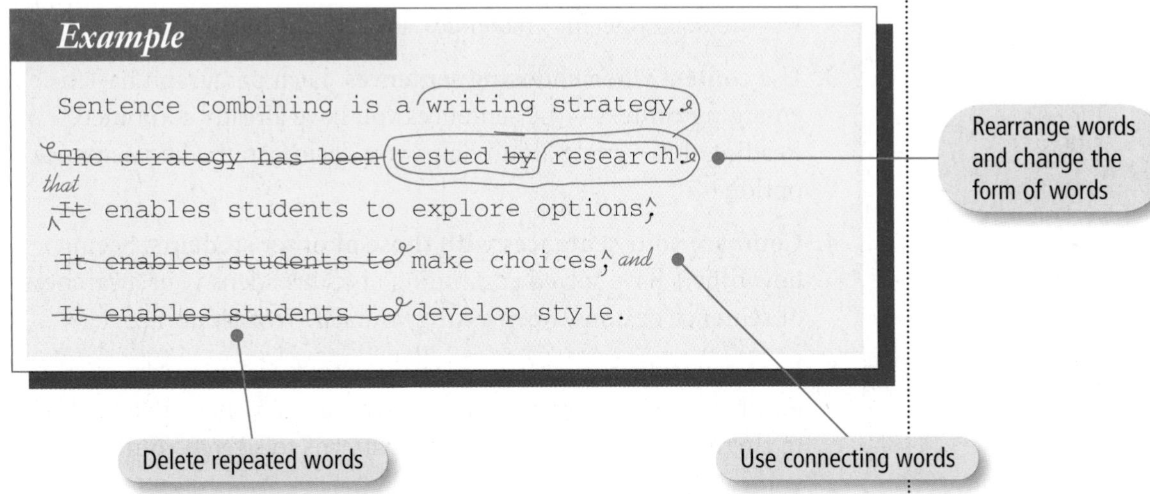
Example
Sentence combining is a writing strategy
The strategy has been tested by research.
that
It enables students to explore options;
It enables students to make choices; and
It enables students to develop style.
Rearrange words and change the form of words
Delete repeated words
Use connecting words

Notice how editing produces the sentence that starts the section headed "Unlock Your Style" on page 360. Note the parallel structure of the three verbs—explore, make, and develop—that makes the sentence effective. But there are many other ways to combine these sentences. Read the ones below aloud, listening to differences in style:

1. Sentence combining is a writing strategy that has been tested by research; as options are explored and choices are made, students develop style.
2. Sentence combining, a writing strategy that has been tested by research, enables students to develop style by exploring options and making choices.
3. Enabling students to explore options, make choices, and develop style, sentence combining is a strategy for writing that has been tested by research.

All of these sentences communicate basically the same message, but each one has a different emphasis. Which is "best"? The answer to that question depends on the *context,* your *purposes* as a writer, and your sense of *audience.* Put simply, your choice of the "best" sentence depends on what sounds right to you.

Follow the Hints

Sentence combining is easy and fun. On the next page are some basic suggestions that you might try as you explore style.

1. **Whisper sentences to yourself.** As you work with clusters of sentences, try saying them aloud. This process is faster than writing, and it helps you decide on a "best sentence" to write down.
2. **Work with a partner.** By trying out sentences on a partner—and hearing your partner's ideas—you often discover new, interesting ways to solve specific challenges. Feel free to borrow ideas.
3. **Use context when choosing sentences.** Each paragraph has an emerging context—the sentences you have already combined. Reading this context aloud helps you decide on the best sentence option.
4. **Compare your sentences with those of other students.** Seeing how others have solved combining tasks broadens your awareness of sentence options. Keep asking yourself, "Which do I prefer?"
5. **Look for stylistic patterns in your writing.** Calculate the average number of words per sentence; study your sentence openers; listen to rhythms in your style. Try new patterns to stretch yourself.
6. **Take risks.** Learning to make clear, effective sentences also means taking risks and making mistakes. It actually makes *sense* to accept mistakes—even *welcome* them—as you combine sentences. After all, mistakes provide feedback for your language learning. As you learn from them, you develop an expressive style, a voice of personal authority. You come to know yourself as a writer.

As you can see, sentence combining involves the skills of talking to yourself, making judgments, and holding what you say in your short-term memory so that you can transcribe it. These are oral skills as much as they are writing skills. Good writers trust their "inner voices."

Style and Focus Workshop

Looking ahead in this unit, you will find two kinds of sentence combining. The exercises in sections 8.1 through 8.4 present clusters of short sentences, with spaces between the clusters. The exercises in section 8.5, drawn from literature selections in this book, are set up in an unclustered format.

Sections 8.1 to 8.4 give you practice in making descriptive, narrative, expository, and persuasive paragraphs. You can combine each cluster into a single sentence, but you can also leave a cluster partially combined—or combine clusters with others. The idea, always, is to take risks and create the best sentences you can. The exercises on facing pages deal with the same topic or situation. Think of these exercises as "bookends" for the writing you will do. After you have combined sentences, your task is to connect the paragraphs into a longer essay or story. Doing so will help you transfer sentence-combining skills to your own writing.

Section 8.5 invites you to test your skills against those of professional writers. As you do these unclustered exercises, you will need to figure out which ideas logically belong together. After you have done the sentence combining, you can check your version against the author's original. By studying the similarities and differences between the two passages, you will learn a great deal about your own style. Sometimes you will prefer the professional writer's sentences. Why, specifically, are they "better" than yours? However, you will sometimes prefer your own style. Can you build on this writing skill, trying it out in your own stories and essays? Either way, you will learn to write better.

Explore Your Own Style

The whole point of sentence combining practice is to improve your revising and editing skills. Practice in sentence combining helps you see that sentences are flexible tools for thought, not rigid structures cast in concrete. The simple fact that you feel confident in moving sentence parts around increases your control of revising and editing. To acquire this sense of self-confidence—one based on your real competence in combining and revising sentences—you can try strategies like those shown below.

1. **Vary the length of your sentences.** Work for a rhythmic, interesting balance of long and short sentences, remembering that short sentences can be dramatic.
2. **Vary the structure of your sentences.** By using introductory clauses on occasion—and by sometimes tucking information in the middle of a sentence—you can create stylistic variety.

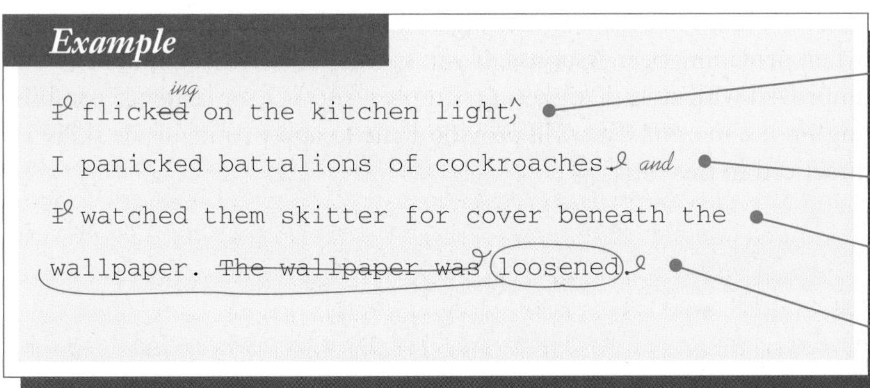

Example
I flicked on the kitchen light;
I panicked battalions of cockroaches. and
I watched them skitter for cover beneath the
wallpaper. The wallpaper was loosened.
ing
Open with an introductory participial phrase by deleting the subject and changing *flicked* to *flicking*.
Use a connecting word.
Create a main clause with a compound predicate.
Delete and rearrange words.

Author's Original Version Flicking on the kitchen light, I panicked battalions of cockroaches and watched them skitter for cover beneath the loosened wallpaper.

from *Growing Up* by Russell Baker

Use **parallelism,** or similar grammatical structure, in the remaining sentence parts. Note how the repeated participial phrases create a consistent, distinctive rhythm. For more on parallelism, see **Writing and Research Handbook,** pages 951–952.

Use commas to separate phrases in a series.

Delete repeated words.

3. **Use parallelism for emphasis.** Experiment with repeated items in a series—words, phrases, and clauses—to understand how structural patterns work and how you can use them to advantage.

Example

Writers did not have to trudge through town.
~~They were not~~ peddling from canvas bags,
~~They were not~~ defending themselves against angry
dogs, ~~They were not~~ being rejected by surly
strangers.

Author's Original Version Writers did not have to trudge through town peddling from canvas bags, defending themselves against angry dogs, being rejected by surly strangers.

from *Growing Up* by Russell Baker

4. **Use interruption for emphasis.** Colons, semicolons, dashes, commas, parentheses—all of these are useful tools in your stylistic toolkit. Knowing how to use them well will help you.

5. **Use unusual patterns for emphasis.** That you might sometimes reverse normal sentence patterns may never have occurred to you, but using such a strategy can work—if you know how to do it right.

When it comes time to rework a draft, it's important to apply what you have learned about combining and revising. The same holds true when providing peer response. If you spot a passage that could be improved with stylistic tinkering, simply write *SC* (for sentence combining) in the margin. This will provide a cue to apply some of the skills practiced in this unit.

LESSON 8.1 Description

Exercise A: Playoff Game

Directions Combine each cluster of numbered items into one or more sentences. Combine clusters if you wish.

1.1 The gym was jammed with students.
1.2 The gym was jammed with townspeople.
1.3 The gym was jammed with TV equipment.
1.4 The gym was sweltering.

2.1 Signs festooned the walls.
2.2 The signs were made of butcher paper.
2.3 The signs were huge.
2.4 The walls were cinderblock.

3.1 A hometown band erupted into sound.
3.2 The sound was brassy.
3.3 The sound was discordant.
3.4 Cheerleaders bounded into action.
3.5 They were like marionettes.
3.6 The marionettes were perky.

4.1 They danced in syncopation.
4.2 Their syncopation was well rehearsed.
4.3 They danced from left to right.
4.4 They brought the crowd to its feet.

5.1 Voices chanted in unison.
5.2 The voices were hoarse.
5.3 The voices were excited.
5.4 Voices finally became a chorus.
5.5 The chorus was screaming.
5.6 The chorus had one mind.

6.1 The score was tied.
6.2 It was the fourth quarter.
6.3 There were only minutes left to play.

7.1 Noise rose in crescendo.
7.2 The crescendo was thundering.
7.3 It was like a tidal wave of sound.

Extension What else do you picture happening in this scene? Use your description to link "Playoff Game" to "Final Seconds."

Grammar Tip

Try opening either cluster 4 or 5 with a participial phrase. For more on participial phrases, see page 527.

Exercise B: Final Seconds

Directions Combine each cluster of numbered items into one or more sentences. Combine clusters if you wish.

1.1 A referee's whistle made a shriek.
1.2 The shriek was high-pitched.
1.3 It pierced the jeers.
1.4 It pierced the groans.
1.5 The groans came from local fans.

2.1 Police braced themselves.
2.2 Security guards braced themselves.
2.3 They were braced for any move.
2.4 The move might signal trouble.

3.1 The hometown coach paced restlessly.
3.2 He chewed a thumbnail.
3.3 He was on the sidelines.
3.4 Both teams took positions down court.
3.5 They were awaiting a foul shot.
3.6 It could decide the conference title.

4.1 The opposing star was cocky.
4.2 The opposing star was grinning.
4.3 The opposing star toed the foul line.
4.4 He bounced the ball twice.
4.5 He spun it through his fingertips.

5.1 He shrugged off the catcalls.
5.2 He barely eyed the basket.

6.1 The shot lofted up in an arc.
6.2 The arc was soft.
6.3 The arc was high.
6.4 It dragged the crowd to its feet.

7.1 It hit the back of the rim.
7.2 It bounced against the backboard.
7.3 The backboard was glass.
7.4 The backboard was like a rising moon.

Extension Describe what you see happening after this scene. Share your text with a writing partner.

Exercise C: Canyon Trail

Directions Combine each cluster of numbered items into one or more sentences. Combine clusters if you wish.

1.1 The canyon trail crossed logs.
1.2 The trail was shadowy.
1.3 The logs were moss covered.
1.4 It passed through thickets of ferns.

2.1 Wildflowers grew in clumps of yellow.
2.2 Wildflowers grew in clumps of purple.
2.3 The clumps were cheerful.
2.4 The clumps were bright.
2.5 The clumps were along the river's edge.

3.1 Huge boulders lay in the white water.
3.2 The water was rushing.
3.3 They were like hippos.
3.4 The hippos were sleeping.

4.1 The trail finally became a clearing.
4.2 The clearing was grassy.
4.3. It was filled with sunlight.
4.4 It was filled with insects.
4.5 The insects hummed.

5.1 Maple trees swelled with life.
5.2 Aspen tees swelled with life.
5.3 Leaves uncurled from buds.
5.4 The leaves were golden.
5.5 The buds were tiny.

6.1 The sky above was like a hole.
6.2 The sky was cobalt-blue.
6.3 The hole was deep.
6.4 It was rimmed by treetops.

7.1 The air smelled sweet.
7.2 The air smelled fiercely green.
7.3 It was a first taste of spring.

Extension Move farther into the clearing, describing what you see and sense around you. Link your description to "Throwaway."

Vocabulary Tip

In cluster 7, try *a first taste of spring* at the beginning, in the middle, and at the end of the sentence. Which position do you think works best?

Exercise D: Throwaway

Directions Combine each cluster of numbered items into one or more sentences. Combine clusters if you wish.

1.1 The car lay rusting.
1.2 The car lay abandoned.
1.3 It was at the bottom of a ravine.
1.4 It was near the stream's edge.

2.1 Scabs of paint had lifted off.
2.2 The scabs were black.
2.3 The paint was oxidized.
2.4 This revealed blotches of primer.
2.5 The primer was gray.

3.1 The driver's door hung open.
3.2 It was permanently ajar.
3.3 Bullet holes ventilated the windows.

4.1 Inside was a single shoe.
4.2 It was under the dashboard.
4.3 Its leather was cracked.
4.4 Its leather was twisted.
4.5 Inside was a *Life* magazine.
4.6 It was from 1948.

5.1 Springs pushed through seats.
5.2 The springs were coiled.
5.3 The seatcovers were worn.
5.4 The seatcovers were fabric.

6.1 The car smelled dead.
6.2 It was now home to mice.
6.3 It was now home to birds.
6.4 It was now home to seasons.
6.5 The seasons changed.

7.1 Once its fenders had been stroked.
7.2 Once its interior had been caressed.
7.3 That day was long gone.

Vocabulary Tip

As you begin to combine sentences in each cluster, reread your sentence from the cluster before. How does the language in that sentence relate to the new cluster?

Extension What thoughts does the old car prompt about forgotten lives—or about recycling? Share the text you create with a writing partner.

LESSON 8.2

Narration

Exercise A: Solo

Directions Combine each cluster of numbered items into one or more sentences. Combine clusters if you wish.

1.1 The mood was festive.
1.2 The mood was energetic.
1.3 The mood was focused on homecoming weekend.
1.4 This was felt especially on the dance floor.

2.1 A jazz band had played for two hours.
2.2 The playing was inspired.
2.3 The audience was chanting for more.
2.4 The audience was appreciative.

3.1 The soloist stepped into the lights.
3.2 He mouthed his thanks to the audience.
3.3 He laced his fingers around his trumpet.
3.4 His fingers were long.
3.5 The trumpet was gleaming.

4.1 The applause grew louder.
4.2 The applause grew more enthusiastic.
4.3 He raised the trumpet.
4.4 He grinned at the flashbulbs.
4.5 The flashbulbs were exploding.

5.1 Faces below him shone expectantly.
5.2 The faces were radiant.
5.3 He nodded a cue to the drummer.
5.4 The cue was decisive.
5.5 The drummer was nearby.

6.1 Sound swirled through the room.
6.2 The notes of the solo were crisp and clear.
6.3 The solo was intricate.
6.4 The drum and bass provided a beat.
6.5 The beat was steady and insistent.

7.1 Each player in turn picked up the tune.
7.2 The players were talented.

Extension Narrate what happens next in the "Solo" scenario. Link this narrative to the accompanying "Good Vibrations" exercise.

Grammar Tip

In cluster 3, try using one or two participial phrases (beginning with *stepping, mouthing,* or *lacing*) as modifiers for the base sentence. For more on participial phrases, see page 527.

Sentence Combining

Exercise B: Good Vibrations

Directions Combine each cluster of numbered items into one or more sentences. Combine clusters if you wish.

1.1 Music surged through the room.
1.2 Music vibrated through the room.
1.3 It drew in the listeners.

2.1 Students moved their feet in patterns.
2.2 The patterns were rhythmic.
2.3 Students shuffled on the wax.
2.4 The wax was dusty.

3.1 Students tapped to the sound.
3.2 Students swayed with the sound.
3.3 Their bodies made shadows on the walls.
3.4 The shadows were moving.

4.1 The boys betrayed concentration.
4.2 Their faces were tight-lipped.
4.3 Their heads bobbed.
4.4 Their heads dipped.
4.5 Their arms hung loose.

5.1 The girls danced with ease.
5.2 Their ease was practiced.
5.3 They whirled with the music.
5.4 They turned with the music.
5.5 The music was irresistible.

Grammar Tip

In cluster 6 try an appositive—a phrase that describes the song's windup. For more on appositives, see page 525.

6.1 On stage the trumpeter closed his eyes.
6.2 He threw himself into the song's windup.
6.3 The windup was a final chorus.
6.4 The chorus was triumphant.

7.1 The musicians took their bows.
7.2 The musicians were exultant.
7.3 The musicians beamed at the dancers.
7.4 The dancers cheered in unison.
7.5 The dancers clapped in unison.

Extension What next? Narrate effective endings for "Solo" and "Good Vibrations." Share your text with a writing partner.

Exercise C: The Crow

Directions Combine each cluster of numbered items into one or more sentences. Combine clusters if you wish.

1.1 Mona reached for the travel alarm clock.
1.2 The travel alarm was palm-sized.
1.3 It was beside her bed.
1.4 She squinted at the numbers.

2.1 A crow screamed on the window sill.
2.2 Its screaming was brazen.
2.3 It welcomed the day's first light.
2.4 The light was a thin skin of gray.
2.5 The skin was on the landscape.

3.1 Each morning the crow did not stay long.
3.2 It stayed only for a few moments.
3.3 The moments were raucous.

4.1 It delivered its message.
4.2 It began a fixed routine.
4.3 It first bounced between the pines.
4.4 It floated to the lawn.
4.5 The lawn was dewy.
4.6 It then fussed over the dumpster.
4.7 The dumpster was next door.

5.1 Its work was finished.
5.2 The crow always spread its feathers.
5.3 The feathers were glossy.
5.4 The feathers were black.
5.5 It always headed east.

6.1 She watched its ritual once again.
6.2 She knew it was time for her work.
6.3 Her work was a run toward town.
6.4 The run was through quiet streets.

7.1 Mona had heard the crow call her name.
7.2 She now needed to get started.

Extension Narrate Mona's getting out of bed in clear, precise detail. Use your narration to link "The Crow" to "Training Run."

Vocabulary Tip

Notice the strong, specific nouns, verbs, and adjectives in each cluster. Do your combined sentences make good use of these words? For more information on strong nouns, verbs, and adjectives, see pages 439, 453, and 460.

Sentence Combining

Exercise D: Training Run

Directions Combine each cluster of numbered items into one or more sentences. Combine clusters if you wish.

1.1 Outside the air was cool.
1.2 It was still.
1.3 There was no hint of breeze.

2.1 Mona bent down.
2.2 She tightened her shoelaces.
2.3 She began her leg stretches.
2.4 She took time to loosen her calves.
2.5 She took time to loosen her thighs.
2.6 She took time to work out all the kinks.

3.1 Then she set off on her usual course.
3.2 She jogged easily at first.
3.3 She jogged through the damp grass.
3.4 She let her body set its own pace.

4.1 Patches of light filled the sky.
4.2 The light was creamy.
4.3 She picked up the pace.
4.4 She settled into a rhythm.
4.5 The rhythm was loping.

5.1 Sweat blossomed on her forehead.
5.2 Sweat blossomed on her arms.
5.3 Her lungs gulped for oxygen.

6.1 She turned off her usual course.
6.2 She cut through the town cemetery.
6.3 She bounded down a gravel path.
6.4 The gravel was crunchy.
6.5 She bounded past stone markers.
6.6 The markers were faceless.

7.1 Finally Mona slowed to a walk.
7.2 She listened to inner whispers
7.3 She felt herself being drawn east.

Extension To complete the story, narrate what happens next. Share your text—"The Crow" plus "Training Run"—with a writing partner.

Grammar Tip

To open cluster 6 with participial phrases, use *turning* and *cutting* as key words. For more on participial phrases, see page 527.

LESSON 8.3

Exposition

Exercise A: Car Culture

Directions Combine each cluster of numbered items into one or more sentences. Combine clusters if you wish.

1.1 Cars serve practical ends.
1.2 They get us from place to place.
1.3 They also serve as objects of ornament.
1.4 They are much like clothing.

2.1 Cars make statements.
2.2 The statements are about who we are.
2.3 The statements are about what we value.
2.4 They create a "public identity."

3.1 A sports car projects a lifestyle.
3.2 The lifestyle is carefree.
3.3 The lifestyle is romantic.
3.4 A station wagon projects an image.
3.5 The image is family-oriented.

4.1 An economy runabout suggests thrift.
4.2 An economy runabout suggests efficiency.
4.3 It zips nervously through traffic.
4.4 A luxury sedan makes a different statement.
4.5 It guzzles gas.
4.6 It wallows toward its destination.

5.1 Such images shape our thinking.
5.2 They are reinforced by advertising.
5.3 The advertising is relentless.
5.4 They influence how we see others.
5.5 They influence how we see ourselves.

6.1 We may make snap judgments about people.
6.2 The judgments are based on their automobiles.
6.3 We may choose a car to satisfy our fantasies.
6.4 We may choose a car to impress others.

7.1 Judging books by their covers is dangerous.
7.2 So is judging drivers by their cars.

Extension Write about a personality that *differs* from his or her car (see cluster 7). Relate your text to "Car Culture."

Grammar Tip

In clusters 1, 3, and 4, try several connectors—*but, yet, however, while, although*—before settling on one. For information on the correct punctuation, see pages 740 and 743–747.

Sentence Combining

Exercise B: Car Colors

Directions Combine each cluster of numbered items into one or more sentences. Combine clusters if you wish.

1.1 Early car buyers had one choice of color.
1.2 The color was "basic black."
1.3 Today's consumer has many color options.

2.1 Psychologists contend something.
2.2 Car colors can reveal personality traits.
2.3 These traits are basic.
2.4 Car colors can express "hidden selves."

3.1 Red appeals to attention seekers.
3.2 Red is a fiery color.
3.3 They may be impulsive.
3.4 They may be aggressive.

4.1 Cautious people often choose brown.
4.2 The people are analytical.
4.3 Active types often like yellow.
4.4 These types may have an artistic bent.

5.1 Blue is associated with steadiness.
5.2 Blue is associated with consistency.
5.3 It appeals to many introverts.
5.4 It appeals to some extroverts.

6.1 Drivers often choose white.
6.2 The drivers may be critical.
6.3 The drivers may be compulsively neat.
6.4 The drivers may be safety conscious.

7.1 Green typically appeals to romantics.
7.2 Green typically appeals to intellectuals.

8.1 And black is a "power color."
8.2 It appeals to sophisticates.
8.3 The sophisticates are self-confident.
8.4 They wish to be taken seriously.

Extension Based on what you know about cars and colors, write about the kind of car—and color—that you might choose for yourself. Relate what you write to "Car Colors."

Exercise C: Cholesterol Facts

Directions Combine each cluster of numbered items into one or more sentences. Combine clusters if you wish.

1.1 Many of us have heard of cholesterol.
1.2 Its dangers have been widely publicized.
1.3 Few of us know much about it.

2.1 Cholesterol is found in the bloodstream.
2.2 Cholesterol is found in all body tissues.
2.3 It is a fatlike substance.
2.4 It is white and waxy.

3.1 It is used in the outer membrane of cells.
3.2 It is used as a sheath around nerve fibers.
3.3 It is used as a building block for hormones.
3.4 It is clearly essential to life.

4.1 Our bodies convert fats into cholesterol.
4.2 Our bodies convert proteins into cholesterol.
4.3 Our bodies convert carbohydrates into cholesterol.
4.4 Our bodies also ingest it directly from various foods.

5.1 The body manufactures its own cholesterol.
5.2 We don't have to consume it to stay healthy.

6.1 Confusion surrounds cholesterol.
6.2 There are two types of the substance.
6.3 One type is called HDL.
6.4 The other type is called LDL.

7.1 HDL is "helpful" cholesterol.
7.2 LDL is "harmful" cholesterol.

8.1 HDL takes cholesterol back to the liver.
8.2 The cholesterol is in the bloodstream.
8.3 The liver reprocesses or excretes the substance.

9.1 But LDL circulates cholesterol through the body.
9.2 It accumulates on arterial walls.

Extension Develop a character sketch or dramatic incident to introduce "Cholesterol Facts" and "More Cholesterol Facts."

Sentence Combining

Exercise D: More Cholesterol Facts

Directions Combine each cluster of numbered items into one or more sentences. Combine clusters if you wish.

1.1 Cholesterol is found primarily in meat.
1.2 Cholesterol is found primarily in dairy products.
1.3 Many Americans know this fact.

2.1 Plant foods contain no harmful cholesterol.
2.2 These foods include vegetables.
2.3 These foods include fruits.
2.4 These foods include grains.
2.5 These foods include nuts.

3.1 One can decrease cholesterol intake.
3.2 This is done by eating more plant foods.
3.3 This is done by cutting back on animal products.
3.4 Animal products include meats and poultry.
3.5 Animal products include dairy goods.
3.6 Animal products include eggs.

4.1 But one must also eat less saturated fat.
4.2 Fat is found in both plant and animal foods.
4.3 Fat stimulates one's cholesterol production.

5.1 Beef is high in saturated fat.
5.2 Some pork is high in saturated fat.
5.3 Poultry skin is high in saturated fat.
5.4 Whole milk is high in saturated fat.
5.5 So is coconut oil.
5.6 So is palm oil.

6.1 Finns and Americans have diets.
6.2 The diets are rich in saturated fat.
6.3 Both groups have very high cholesterol levels.
6.4 This makes them world leaders in heart disease.

7.1 The Japanese have the world's lowest level of cholesterol.
7.2 The Japanese have the world's lowest level of heart disease.
7.3 Their diets are extremely low in saturated fat.

Extension Write a concluding paragraph for "Cholesterol Facts" and "More Cholesterol Facts." Then share your text with a writing partner.

Vocabulary Tip

In clusters 4, 5, and 6, try causal connectors such as *because, since, therefore, consequently,* and *so.* For more information on punctuation with causal connectors, see pages 746 and 748.

LESSON

8.4 Persuasion

Exercise A: Success Story

Directions Combine each cluster of numbered items into one or more sentences. Combine clusters if you wish.

1.1 A bald eagle spreads its wings.
1.2 The eagle is white maned.
1.3 Its wings are enormous.
1.4 It soars on the morning wind.

2.1 This predator faced extinction in 1963.
2.2 This predator is magnificent.
2.3 It is America's national bird.
2.4 Only four hundred pairs of eagles remained in 1963.
2.5 The eagles were in the lower forty-eight states.

3.1 America had been home to thousands of bald eagles.
3.2 They were decimated by loss of habitat.
3.3 They were decimated by illegal hunting.
3.4 They were decimated by the use of DDT.

4.1 Eagles were at the top of the food chain.
4.2 They were especially vulnerable to DDT.
4.3 DDT affected their ability to reproduce.

5.1 The ban on DDT gave eagles a chance.
5.2 Breeding programs gave eagles a chance.
5.3 Strict law enforcement gave eagles a chance.
5.4 Their numbers slowly began to build.

6.1 By the mid 1990s, the number of nesting pairs had increased.
6.2 There were about 4,500 in the lower forty-eight states.
6.3 The bald eagle's status was upgraded to threatened.
6.4 It was hoped that by 2000 the bald eagle could be removed from the threatened list.

7.1 Some people feared that removing the bird from the list would expose it to new harms.
7.2 Government acts continue to protect the species.
7.3 The Migratory Bird Treaty Act is one such act.
7.4 The Bald and Golden Eagle Protection Act is another.

Extension What does the eagle's success story suggest about the spirit of the country it symbolizes? Develop a follow-up paragraph.

Grammar Tip

To experiment with subordinate clauses, try using *because* as a connector in cluster 4 and *although* as a connector in cluster 6. For more on subordinate clauses, see page 544.

Exercise B: Continuing Threat

Directions Combine each cluster of numbered items into one or more sentences. Combine clusters if you wish.

1.1 Predators are part of the ecosystem.
1.2 The ecosystem is on public rangelands.
1.3 Western ranchers graze their sheep there.

2.1 Ranchers lose about 500,000 sheep annually.
2.2 This is about 5 percent of their flocks.
2.3 The loss is to coyotes.
2.4 The loss is to wild dogs.
2.5 The loss is to other predators.

3.1 These predators include eagles.
3.2 The eagles feed mainly on fish.
3.3 The eagles feed mainly on small game.
3.4 The eagles also dine on spring lamb.

4.1 Some ranchers have fought back.
4.2 They are frustrated by predator attacks.
4.3 They are angered by economic losses.
4.4 They have injected carcasses with poisons.
4.5 The poisons are illegal.

5.1 Their targets have mainly been coyotes.
5.2 Their targets have mainly been dog packs.
5.3 They have also killed hundreds of eagles.
5.4 The eagles have eaten the meat.
5.5 The meat is toxic.

6.1 At issue are questions of land use.
6.2 At issue are questions of public policy.
6.3 Ranchers pay fees for grazing rights.
6.4 Ranchers contribute much to local economies.

7.1 A final point must be underscored.
7.2 Bald eagles are protected by law.
7.3 There are threats to their safety.
7.4 The threats are serious.

Extension Should taxpayers support the losses of ranchers to keep them from resorting to extreme measures? Develop a follow-up paragraph that presents your point of view.

Exercise C: Ozone Problem

Directions Combine each cluster of numbered items into one or more sentences. Combine clusters if you wish.

1.1 We have too much ozone at ground level.
1.2 We have too little ozone in the stratosphere.
1.3 The stratosphere is ten to twenty-five miles above us.

2.1 Both types of ozone are chemically alike.
2.2 One is a dangerous component of smog.
2.3 Smog results from burning fossil fuels.
2.4 The other serves as a natural screen.
2.5 It protects us from the sun's radiation.

3.1 Something is unfortunate.
3.2 The ozone in smog cannot reach the stratosphere.
3.3 It might do some good there.
3.4 It might reduce the greenhouse effect.

4.1 The ozone screen is destroyed by compounds.
4.2 The ozone screen is in the upper atomosphere.
4.3 The compounds are synthetic.
4.4 The compounds are called chlorofluorocarbons (CFCs).

5.1 CFCs have a wide range of industrial uses.
5.2 They serve as coolants for refrigerators.
5.3 They serve as coolants for air conditioners.
5.4 They serve as foaming agents for food packages.
5.5 They serve as foaming agents for mattresses.
5.6 They serve as solvents in microchip production.

6.1 CFCs are released during product use.
6.2 CFCs eventually rise into the stratosphere.
6.3 Radiation breaks them down, releasing chlorine.
6.4 Chlorine has an effect on ozone.
6.5 The effect is devastating.

7.1 CFCs take decades to reach the stratosphere.
7.2 We do not know the full extent of their damage.
7.3 The damage is continuous.

Extension Write a paragraph that introduces "Ozone Problem" by focusing on the problem in an everyday situation.

Vocabulary Tip

To create an adverb in cluster 3, add *-ly* to *unfortunate.* For sentence variety, try opening cluster 6 with *released.*

Exercise D: Ozone Solutions

Directions Combine each cluster of numbered items into one or more sentences. Combine clusters if you wish.

1.1 NASA has found holes in the ozone layer.
1.2 The holes are ominously vast.
1.3 The holes are over Antarctica and the Arctic.

2.1 Scientists have predicted something.
2.2 Increased radiation will lead to more melanoma.
2.3 Melanoma is an especially deadly skin cancer.
2.4 The radiation may also damage crops on earth.
2.5 This damage includes plankton in the oceans.

3.1 Ozone depletion is a worldwide problem.
3.2 Its solution depends on cooperation.
3.3 The cooperation must be international.
3.4 Its solution depends on consumer awareness.

4.1 Governments must agree to timetables.
4.2 The timetables phase out CFC production.
4.3 American consumers must curtail CFC use.

5.1 Air conditioners cause most of our CFC emissions.
5.2 The air conditioners are in automobiles.
5.3 One should go to service stations.
5.4 The stations are equipped to recycle CFCs.

6.1 One should avoid food-packaging products.
6.2 The products are made from plastic foam.
6.3 They are often found in fast-food restaurants.

7.1 One should check labels on aerosol cans.
7.2 This is to ensure that the cans are environmentally safe.

8.1 One should also choose a refrigerator.
8.2 The refrigerator should be energy efficient.
8.3 It will release fewer CFCs into the atmosphere.
8.4 It eventually wears out and is discarded.

Extension Link "Ozone Problem" and "Ozone Solutions" and write a conclusion. Then share your text with a writing partner.

LESSON **8.5**

Literature Exercises

Exercise A

Directions Scan the sentences below, which are adapted from *Blue Highways* by William Least Heat-Moon. Decide which of the numbered sentences belong together, and combine them in your own way. Then compare your sentences with the originals on pages 34–35.

1. It was nearly May.
2. The rain popped.
3. It then stopped.
4. It popped.
5. It stopped.
6. The incline became steeper.
7. Light rain fell steadily.
8. It rolled red dust off the roof.
9. The dust was from the desert.
10. I hadn't hit showers since east Texas.
11. It was good.
12. The pleasant cool turned to cold.
13. I switched on the heater.
14. The headlights glared off the snowbanks.
15. The snowbanks were edging closer to the highway.
16. The highway climbed.
17. The rain became sleet.
18. That's when I began thinking something.
19. I might have made a little miscalculation.
20. I looked for a place to turn around.
21. There was only narrow road.
22. The road was twisted.
23. The sleet got heavier.
24. The headlights were cutting only thirty feet into it.
25. Maybe I could drive above and out of the storm.
26. The wind came up at eight thousand feet.
27. It was rough.
28. It was nasty.
29. It bullied me about the road.

Grammar Tip

Read quickly through all sentences to get a sense of the entire piece before you begin combining.

Exercise B

Directions Scan the sentences below. Some are from *My Furthest-Back Person: The African,* by Alex Haley. The numbered sentences are adapted from Haley's original. Decide which of the numbered sentences belong together, and combine them in your own way. Then compare your sentences with the originals on page 105.

> About the time the king's soldiers came, the eldest of these four sons, Kunta, when he had about 16 rains, went away from this village to chop wood to make a drum . . . and he was never seen again . . .

1. Goose-pimples seemed to pop all over me.
2. They were the size of lemons.
3. My cumulative notebooks were in my knapsack.
4. The first of them included something.
5. In my boyhood my Grandma told of the African "*Kin-tay.*"
6. In my boyhood Cousin Georgia told of the African "*Kin-tay.*"
7. In my boyhood others told of the African "*Kin-tay.*"
8. Kin-tay always said he was kidnapped near his village.
9. He was chopping wood to make a drum.
10. I showed the interpreter.
11. He showed and told the *griot.*
12. The *griot* excitedly told the people.
13. They grew very agitated.
14. They then formed a human ring.
15. This happened abruptly.
16. They were encircling me.
17. They were dancing.
18. They were chanting.
19. Perhaps a dozen of the women rushed in toward me.
20. They were carrying their infant babies.
21. They thrust the infants into my arms.
22. I later learned something.
23. This conveyed "the laying on of hands."
24. "This flesh is part of us."
25. "We are you."
26. "You are us."

> The men hurried me into their mosque, their Arabic praying later being translated outside: "Thanks be to Allah for returning the long lost from among us."

Exercise C

Directions Scan the sentences below. One comes directly from *The Solace of Open Spaces,* by Gretel Ehrlich. The numbered sentences are adapted from Ehrlich's originals. Decide which numbered sentences belong together, and combine them in your own way. Then compare your sentences with the originals on page 160.

1. Conversation goes on.
2. It sounds like a code.
3. The code is private.
4. A few phrases imply a complex of meanings.
5. You ask directions.
6. You get a list of details.
7. The list is curious.
8. I was trailing sheep.
9. I was told something.
10. "Ride up to that kinda upturned rock."
11. "Follow the pink wash."
12. "Turn left at the dump."
13. "Then you'll see the water hole."

> One friend told his wife on roundup to "turn at the salt lick and the dead cow," which turned out to be a scattering of bones and no salt lick at all.

14. Sentence structure is shortened.
15. It expresses the skin and bones of a thought.
16. Descriptive words are dropped.
17. Even verbs are dropped.
18. A cowboy will say something to a wrangler.
19. The cowboy is looking over a corral.
20. The corral is full of horses.
21. "Which one needs rode?"
22. People hold back their thoughts.
23. It seems to be a dumbfounded silence.
24. Then they erupt with a remark.
25. The remark is perceptive.
26. The remark is excoriating.
27. Language is compressed.
28. It becomes metaphorical.
29. A rancher ended a relationship with one remark.
30. "You're a bad check."
31. This meant that bouncing in and out was intolerable.
32. This meant that even coming back would be no good.

Exercise D

Directions Scan the sentences below. One comes directly from *A Book of Bees . . . And How to Keep Them,* by Sue Hubbell. The numbered sentences are adapted from Hubbell's original. Decide which numbered sentences belong together, and combine them in your own way. Then compare your sentences with the originals on page 269.

1. Each worker bee is covered with hairs.
2. The hairs are stiff.
3. These hairs catch the granules.
4. The bee brushes against the flower's anthers.
5. The anthers bear pollen.
6. She is soon covered with pollen.
7. She stops to use her two front pairs of legs.
8. She combs the pollen from her body.
9. The pollen is sticky.
10. She packs it into the baskets.
11. The baskets are on her rear pair of legs.
12. Her legs become heavy.
13. The heaviness is wads of pollen.
14. She returns to her hive to unload.
15. House bees arrange the pollen granules.
16. The arrangement is in the honeycomb cells.
17. The cells are around the bee larvae.
18. The larvae are developing.
19. The pollen is available to the nurse bees.
20. The availability is convenient.

> In the springtime, a typical frame of brood—as beekeepers call developing bees—contains a large central semicircle of cells containing eggs and larvae in various stages.

21. The eggs and larvae are there to see.
22. The oldest brood have spun themselves cocoons.
23. Their stomachs are full.
24. They pupate [develop] within the cocoons.
25. They are hidden from human eyes.
26. They are sealed in their cells by a covering.
27. The covering is tough and velvety brown.
28. They will emerge as adults from beneath it.
29. The entire semicircle of brood is bordered by a ring.
30. The ring is of cells filled with pollen.
31. The ring in turn is surrounded by honey.
32. It is surrounded by nectar as the season progresses.

Exercise E

Directions Scan the sentences below. One comes directly from "A Plague on Tennis," by Mark Mathabane. The numbered sentences are adapted from Mathabane's original. Decide which numbered sentences belong together, and combine them in your own way. Then compare your sentences with the originals by Mathabane on page 361.

1. I took up tennis in the early 1970s.
2. The sport was synonymous with wooden rackets.
3. The players all relied on wooden rackets.
4. I idolized the players.
5. I enjoyed watching them.
6. I sought to emulate them.
7. They included Arthur Ashe.
8. They included Stan Smith.
9. They included Rod Laver.
10. The rackets enabled them to carve out illustrious careers.
11. The rackets enabled them to win major championships.
12. The championships included Wimbledon.
13. The championships included the U.S. Open.
14. Their talent on the court was unmistakable.
15. Their finesse on the court was unmistakable.
16. They served and volleyed.
17. They hit ground strokes flat.
18. They hit ground strokes sliced.
19. They hit ground strokes with topspin.
20. The occasion made its demands.
21. They played delicate touch strokes.
22. These included angled drop shots.
23. In sum, they possessed all-around games.
24. They were the closest thing to the "complete player."
25. They were a delight for spectators to watch.
26. The demise of wooden rackets changed all that.
27. The nature of tennis today is expressed in a single word.
28. The word is "power."

The new rackets can generate so much power in the hands of just about anyone that players of modest abilities are transformed into giant-killers on the court, capable on any given day, usually in the early rounds, of defeating the game's finest.

Sentence Combining

UNIT 9

Troubleshooter

Use Troubleshooter to help you correct common errors in your writing.

Troubleshooter

9.1 Sentence Fragment

Problem 1

Fragment that lacks a subject

frag *Jamal is very athletic. Plays a great game of tennis.*

SOLUTION Add a subject to the fragment to make it a complete sentence.

Jamal is very athletic. He plays a great game of tennis.

Problem 2

Fragment that lacks a complete verb

frag *Sabra saw a bright light in the sky. A meteor with brilliant colors.*

frag *We can hardly hear ourselves think. Ruth trying out her new set of drums.*

SOLUTION A Add a complete verb or a helping verb to make the sentence complete.

Sabra saw a bright light in the sky. A meteor with brilliant colors was flashing by.

We can hardly hear ourselves think. Ruth is trying out her new set of drums.

SOLUTION B Combine the fragment with another sentence.

Sabra saw a bright light in the sky—a meteor with brilliant colors.

With Ruth trying out her new set of drums, we can hardly hear ourselves think.

Troubleshooter

Problem 3

Fragment that is a subordinate clause

frag *José often succeeds. Because he is persistent.*

frag *I am reading a book by Alice Walker. Who is one of my favorite writers.*

SOLUTION A Combine the fragment with another sentence.

José often succeeds because he is persistent.

I am reading a book by Alice Walker, who is one of my favorite writers.

SOLUTION B Rewrite the fragment as a complete sentence, eliminating the subordinating conjunction or the relative pronoun and adding a subject or other words necessary to make a complete thought.

José often succeeds. He is persistent.

I am reading a book by Alice Walker. She is one of my favorite writers.

Problem 4

Fragment that lacks both a subject and a verb

frag *Kate felt ill and left the theater. Before the end of the movie.*

SOLUTION Combine the fragment with another sentence.

Kate felt ill and left the theater before the end of the movie.

If you need more help in avoiding sentence fragments, turn to Lesson 13.9, pages 557 – 558.

Troubleshooter

9.2 Run-on Sentence

Problem 1

Comma splice—two main clauses separated only by a comma

run-on *Paula told me the answer to the riddle, I have forgotten what she said.*

SOLUTION A Replace the comma with an end mark of punctuation, such as a period or question mark, and begin the new sentence with a capital letter.

Paula told me the answer to the riddle. I have forgotten what she said.

SOLUTION B Place a semicolon between the two main clauses.

Paula told me the answer to the riddle; I have forgotten what she said.

SOLUTION C Insert a coordinating conjunction after the comma.

Paula told me the answer to the riddle, but I have forgotten what she said.

Problem 2

Two main clauses with no punctuation between them

run-on *The lights flickered a few times then they went out.*

SOLUTION A Separate the main clauses with an end mark of punctuation, such as a period or a question mark, and begin the second sentence with a capital letter.

The lights flickered a few times. Then they went out.

SOLUTION B Separate the main clauses with a semicolon.

The lights flickered a few times; then they went out.

SOLUTION C Insert a comma and a coordinating conjunction between the main clauses.

The lights flickered a few times, and then they went out.

Troubleshooter

Problem 3

Two main clauses with no comma before the coordinating conjunction

run-on *Ilona would like to own a pet but she is allergic to most animals.*

run-on *My brother just started playing soccer and he wants me to play as well.*

SOLUTION Insert a comma before the coordinating conjunction to separate the two main clauses.

Ilona would like to own a pet, but she is allergic to most animals.

My brother just started playing soccer, and he wants me to play as well.

If you need more help in avoiding run-on sentences, turn to Lesson 13.10, pages 559–561.

Troubleshooter

9.3 Lack of Subject-Verb Agreement

Problem 1

A subject that is separated from the verb by an intervening prepositional phrase

agr *A complex system of roads link the two cities.*

agr *The sounds of the traffic keeps her awake.*

Do not mistake the object of a preposition for the subject of a sentence.

SOLUTION Make the verb agree with the subject, which is never the object of the preposition.

A complex system of roads links the two cities.

The sounds of the traffic keep her awake.

Problem 2

A predicate nominative that differs in number from the subject

agr *Grapes is his favorite snack.*

SOLUTION Ignore the predicate nominative, and make the verb agree with the subject of the sentence.

Grapes are his favorite snack.

Problem 3

A subject that follows the verb

agr *On the wall hangs two handsome watercolors.*

agr *There goes the last two bicyclists.*

SOLUTION In an inverted sentence look for the subject *after* the verb. Then make sure the verb agrees with the subject.

On the wall hang two handsome watercolors.

There go the last two bicyclists.

Troubleshooter

Problem 4

A collective noun as the subject

agr *The soccer team have won consistently.*

agr *The group has different views on the issue.*

SOLUTION A If the collective noun refers to a group as a whole, use a singular verb.

The soccer team has won consistently.

SOLUTION B If the collective noun refers to each member of a group individually, use a plural verb.

The group have different views on the issue.

Problem 5

A noun of amount as the subject

agr *Five dollars are too much for that item.*

agr *Five pennies makes a nickel.*

SOLUTION Determine whether the noun of amount refers to one unit and is therefore singular or whether it refers to a number of individual units and is therefore plural.

Five dollars is too much for that item.

Five pennies make a nickel.

Problem 6

A compound subject that is joined by *and*

agr *Copper and zinc makes brass.*

agr *Rice and beans are a healthful main dish.*

SOLUTION A If the parts of the compound subject do not belong to one unit or they refer to different people or things, use a plural verb.

Copper and zinc make brass.

SOLUTION B If the parts of the compound subject belong to one unit or if both parts refer to the same person or thing, use a singular verb.

Rice and beans is a healthful main dish.

Problem 7

A compound subject that is joined by *or* or *nor*

agr *Neither my cousins nor my aunt resemble her.*

SOLUTION Make the verb agree with the subject that is closer to it.

Neither my cousins nor my aunt resembles her.

Problem 8

A compound subject that is preceded by *many a, every,* or *each*

agr *Many a bluejay and robin have visited that feeder today.*

When *many a, every,* or *each* precedes a compound subject, the subject is considered singular.

SOLUTION Use a singular verb when *many a, each,* or *every* precedes a compound subject.

Many a bluejay and robin has visited that feeder today.

Problem 9

A subject that is separated from the verb by an intervening expression

agr *My karate class, as well as Kazuo's swimming class, take place on Saturday.*

Certain expressions, such as *as well as, in addition to,* and *together with,* do not change the number of the subject.

SOLUTION Ignore an intervening expression between a subject and its verb. Make the verb agree with the subject.

My karate class, as well as Kazuo's swimming class, takes place on Saturday.

Problem 10

An indefinite pronoun as the subject

agr *Each of the contestants receive a gift.*

Some indefinite pronouns are singular, some are plural, and some can be either singular or plural, depending upon the noun they refer to. (See page 647 for a list of indefinite pronouns.)

SOLUTION Determine whether the indefinite pronoun is singular or plural and make the verb agree.

Each of the contestants receives a gift.

If you need more help with subject-verb agreement, turn to Lessons 16.1 through 16.7, pages 613–625.

Troubleshooter

Troubleshooter

9.4 Lack of Pronoun-Antecedent Agreement

Problem 1

A singular antecedent that can be either male or female

ant *An attorney must protect his clients' interests.*

Traditionally a masculine pronoun was used to refer to an antecedent that might be either male or female. This usage ignores or excludes females.

SOLUTION A Reword the sentence to use *he or she, him or her,* and so on.

An attorney must protect his or her clients' interests.

SOLUTION B Reword the sentence so that both the antecedent and the pronoun are plural.

Attorneys must protect their clients' interests.

SOLUTION C Reword the sentence to eliminate the pronoun.

An attorney must protect every client's interests.

Problem 2

A second-person pronoun that refers to a third-person antecedent

ant *Isaiah drinks milk because it supplies you with calcium and protein.*

Be sure not to refer to an antecedent in the third person using the second-person pronoun *you.*

SOLUTION A Use the appropriate third-person pronoun.

Isaiah drinks milk because it supplies him with calcium and protein.

SOLUTION B Use an appropriate noun instead of a pronoun.

Isaiah drinks milk because it supplies people with calcium and protein.

Troubleshooter

Problem 3

A singular indefinite pronoun as an antecedent

ant *Each of the mothers brought (their) own child to the zoo.*

ant *Neither of the boys at the table finished (their) dinner.*

Each, everyone, either, neither, and *one* are singular and therefore require singular personal pronouns.

SOLUTION Don't be fooled by a prepositional phrase that contains a plural noun. Determine whether the indefinite pronoun antecedent is singular or plural, and make the noun agree.

Each of the mothers brought her own child to the zoo.

Neither of the boys at the table finished his dinner.

If you need more help with pronoun-antecedent agreement, turn to Lesson 17.5, pages 644–648.

Troubleshooter

9.5 Lack of Clear Pronoun Reference

Problem 1

A pronoun reference that is weak or vague

ref *The musicians played, which we enjoyed.*

ref *Economists differ about how to improve the economy, and that has led to inconsistent economic policies.*

ref *The author argues at length that there is life on other planets, but it is not convincing.*

Be sure that *this, that, which,* and *it* have clear antecedents.

SOLUTION A Rewrite the sentence, adding a clear antecedent for the pronoun.

The musicians played several old songs, which we enjoyed.

SOLUTION B Rewrite the sentence, substituting a noun for the pronoun.

Economists differ about how to improve the economy, and their disagreement has led to inconsistent economic policies.

The author argues at length that there is life on other planets, but his theory is not very convincing.

Problem 2

A pronoun that could refer to more than one antecedent

ref *When Nelson gave his father the book, he beamed with pleasure.*

ref *The parents met with the teachers, and they asked whether the principal could be present.*

SOLUTION A Rewrite the sentence, substituting a noun for the pronoun.

When Nelson gave his father the book, the boy beamed with pleasure.

SOLUTION B Rewrite the sentence, making the antecedent of the pronoun clear.

The teachers asked whether the principal could be present at their meeting with the parents.

Troubleshooter

Problem 3

The indefinite use of *you* or *they*

ref *In court you are innocent until proved guilty.*

ref *In that store they have some excellent bargains.*

SOLUTION A Rewrite the sentence, substituting a noun for the pronoun.

In court defendants are innocent until proved guilty.

SOLUTION B Rewrite the sentence, eliminating the pronoun entirely.

That store has some excellent bargains.

If you need more help in making clear pronoun references, turn to Lesson 17.6, pages 649–651.

9.6 Shift in Pronoun

Problem

An incorrect shift in person between two pronouns

pro *Kenji and Jeanne are going on a trip to the mountains, where you can hike and breathe fresh air.*

pro *I like movies that keep you guessing.*

pro *When one examines the card catalog, you find a wealth of information.*

Incorrect pronoun shifts occur when a writer or speaker uses a pronoun in one person and then illogically shifts to a pronoun in another person.

SOLUTION A Replace the incorrect pronoun with a pronoun that agrees with its antecedent.

Kenji and Jeanne are going on a trip to the mountains, where they can hike and breathe fresh air.

I like movies that keep me guessing.

When one examines the card catalog, one finds a wealth of information.

SOLUTION B Replace the incorrect pronoun with an appropriate noun.

Kenji and Jeanne are going on a trip to the mountains, where vacationers can hike and breathe fresh air.

I like movies that keep the audience guessing.

If you need more help in eliminating incorrect pronoun shifts, turn to Lesson 17.5, page 646.

Troubleshooter

9.7 Shift in Verb Tense

Problem 1

An unnecessary shift in tense

shift t *Jan opens the can and savored the aroma.*

shift t *Otis left the room just as we arrive.*

When two or more events occur at the same time, be sure to use the same verb tense to describe both or all events.

SOLUTION

Jan opens the can and savors the aroma.

Otis left the room just as we arrived.

Problem 2

A lack of correct shift in tenses to show that one event precedes or follows another

shift t *By the time the coach sent him in, Julius sat on the bench for an hour.*

When events being described have occurred at different times, shift tenses to show that one event precedes or follows another.

SOLUTION Shift from the past tense to the past perfect tense to indicate that one action began and ended before another past action began. Use the past perfect tense for the earlier of the two actions.

By the time the coach sent him in, Julius had sat on the bench for an hour.

If you need more help with shifts in verb tenses, turn to Lesson 15.4, pages 593–595, and Lesson 15.6, pages 598–599.

Troubleshooter

9.8 Incorrect Verb Tense or Form

Problem 1

An incorrect or missing verb ending

tense *Last Saturday night, I cook for the family.*

tense *Have you ever want to study modern dance?*

SOLUTION Add *-ed* to a regular verb to form the past tense and the past participle.

Last Saturday night, I cooked for the family.

Have you ever wanted to study modern dance?

Problem 2

An improperly formed irregular verb

tense *Emilio swinged the bat but missed the ball.*

tense *Mr. Caruso teached violin lessons.*

Irregular verbs form their past tense and past participle in some way other than by adding *-ed.* Memorize these forms, or look them up.

SOLUTION

Emilio swung the bat but missed the ball.

Mr. Caruso taught violin lessons.

Problem 3

Confusion between the past form and the past participle

tense *The committee has chose Juana as chairperson.*

tense *He has broke our school's high-jump record.*

SOLUTION Use the past participle form of an irregular verb, not the past form, when you use the auxiliary verb *have.*

The committee has chosen Juana as chairperson.

He has broken our school's high-jump record.

Problem 4

Improper use of the past participle

tense He (swum) across the lake.

tense The school choir (sung) beautifully at the class assembly.

tense The bell (rung.)

The past participle of an irregular verb cannot stand alone as a verb. It must be used with the auxiliary verb *have.*

SOLUTION A Add the auxiliary verb *have* to the past participle to form a complete verb.

He has swum across the lake.

The school choir has sung beautifully at the class assembly.

The bell has rung.

SOLUTION B Replace the past participle with the past form of the verb.

He swam across the lake.

The school choir sang beautifully at the class assembly.

The bell rang.

If you need more help with correct verb forms, turn to Lesson 15.1 and Lesson 15.2, pages 585–588.

Troubleshooter

Troubleshooter

9.9 Misplaced or Dangling Modifier

Problem 1

A misplaced modifier

mod *The insects fascinated the children with their long antennae.*

mod *Hanging on the wall, Tamiko saw her painting.*

mod *The cat hissed at the goldfish staring at the fishbowl.*

Modifiers that modify the wrong word or seem to modify more than one word in a sentence are called misplaced modifiers.

SOLUTION Move the misplaced phrase as close as possible to the word or words it modifies.

With their long antennae, the insects fascinated the children.
Tamiko saw her painting hanging on the wall.
Staring at the fishbowl, the cat hissed at the goldfish.

Problem 2

The adverb *only* misplaced

mod *Sylvia only orders soup as an appetizer.*

The meaning of your sentence may be unclear if *only* is misplaced.

SOLUTION Place the adverb *only* immediately before the word or group of words it modifies. Note that each time *only* is moved in the sentence, the meaning of the sentence changes.

Only Sylvia orders soup as an appetizer.
Sylvia orders only soup as an appetizer.
Sylvia orders soup only as an appetizer.

Problem 3

A dangling modifier

mod *(By paying attention to the instructions,) the bookcase was assembled easily.*

mod *(Concerned about making mistakes,) the driving lesson went surprisingly well.*

mod *(Standing on the mountaintop,) the view was breathtaking.*

Dangling modifiers do not logically seem to modify any word in the sentence.

SOLUTION Rewrite the sentence, adding a noun to which the dangling phrase clearly refers. Often you will have to add other words to make the meaning of the sentence clear.

By paying attention to the instructions, Rachel easily assembled the bookcase.

Concerned about making mistakes, Duane felt that his driving lesson went surprisingly well.

Standing on the mountaintop, Ted found the view breathtaking.

If you need more help with misplaced or dangling modifiers, turn to Lesson 18.7, pages 674–679.

Troubleshooter

9.10 Missing or Misplaced Possessive Apostrophe

Problem 1

Singular nouns

poss *That artists painting is James favorite.*

SOLUTION Use an apostrophe and an *-s* to form the possessive of a singular noun, even one that ends in *-s*.

That artist's painting is James's favorite.

Problem 2

Plural nouns ending in *-s*

poss *The officers quarters are in that building.*

SOLUTION Use an apostrophe alone to form the possessive of a plural noun that ends in *-s*.

The officers' quarters are in that building.

Problem 3

Plural nouns not ending in *-s*

poss *Womens shoes are sold on the third floor.*

SOLUTION Use an apostrophe and an *-s* to form the possessive of a plural noun that does not end in *-s*.

Women's shoes are sold on the third floor.

Problem 4

Pronouns

poss Anyones guess is as good as mine.

poss I see every painting but your's.

SOLUTION A Use an apostrophe and an *-s* to form the possessive of a singular indefinite pronoun.

Anyone's guess is as good as mine.

SOLUTION B Do not use an apostrophe with any of the possessive personal pronouns.

I see every painting but yours.

Problem 5

Confusion between *its* and *it's*

poss That car has lost it's front bumper.

poss Its always good to try new things.

The possessive of *it* is *its. It's* is the contraction of *it is.*

SOLUTION Do not use an apostrophe to form the possessive of *it.* Use an apostrophe to form the contraction of *it is.*

That car has lost its front bumper.

It's always good to try new things.

If you need more help with apostrophes and possessives, turn to Lesson 17.1, page 638, and Lesson 21.11, pages 760–762.

Troubleshooter

Troubleshooter

9.11 Missing Commas with Nonessential Element

Problem 1

Missing commas with nonessential participles, infinitives, and their phrases

com *The team defeated trudged wearily to the bus.*

com *The waves gleaming in the sunlight pounded the beach.*

com *To be sure I have no experience with this kind of problem.*

SOLUTION Determine whether the participle, infinitive, or phrase is truly not essential to the meaning of the sentence. If it is not essential, set off the phrases with commas.

The team, defeated, trudged wearily to the bus.

The waves, gleaming in the sunlight, pounded the beach.

To be sure, I have no experience with this kind of problem.

Problem 2

Missing commas with nonessential adjective clauses

com *Kai-chi who comes from Shanghai is studying piano.*

SOLUTION Determine whether the clause is truly not essential to the meaning of the sentence. If it is not essential, set off the clause with commas.

Kai-chi, who comes from Shanghai, is studying piano.

Problem 3

Missing commas with nonessential appositives

com *Mr. Lomawaima our anthropology professor will speak on Hopi customs.*

SOLUTION Determine whether the appositive is truly not essential to the meaning of the sentence. If so, set off the appositive with commas.

Mr. Lomawaima, our anthropology professor, will speak on Hopi customs.

Problem 4

Missing commas with interjections and parenthetical expressions

com *Oh I know what you mean.*

com *Derrick I believe offered to help with the scenery for the play.*

SOLUTION Set off the interjection or parenthetical expression with commas.

Oh, I know what you mean.

Derrick, I believe, offered to help with the scenery for the play.

If you need more help with commas and nonessential elements, turn to Lesson 21.6, pages 743–751.

Troubleshooter

9.12 Missing Comma in a Series

Problem

Missing commas in a series of words, phrases, or clauses

s com *Birches maples and hemlocks covered the sides of the mountain.*

s com *The motor sputtered coughed whined and finally died.*

s com *The ivy crept up the wall around the drainpipe and over the roof.*

s com *Lila sat nervously, biting her lip frowning and drumming her fingers on the table.*

s com *The rain stopped the clouds rolled away and the sun came out.*

SOLUTION When there are three or more elements in a series, use a comma after each element, including the element that precedes a conjunction.

Birches, maples, and hemlocks covered the sides of the mountain.

The motor sputtered, coughed, whined, and finally died.

The ivy crept up the wall, around the drainpipe, and over the roof.

Lila sat nervously, biting her lip, frowning, and drumming her fingers on the table.

The rain stopped, the clouds rolled away, and the sun came out.

If you need more help with commas in a series, turn to Lesson 21.6, page 743.

Proofreading Symbols		
⊙	Lieut Brown	Insert a period.
∧	No one came the party.	Insert a letter or a word.
∧ ;	The bell rang the students left for home.	Insert a semicolon.
≡	I enjoyed paris.	Capitalize a letter.
/	The Class ran a bake sale.	Make a capital letter lowercase.
⁀ ‿	The campers are home sick.	Close up a space.
(sp)	They visited N.Y. (sp)	Spell out.
∧ ,	Sue please help.	Insert a comma.
∾	He enjoyed feild day.	Transpose the position of letters or words.
#	alltogether	Insert a space.
℘	We went to to Boston.	Delete letters or words.
∨ ∨	She asked, Who's coming?	Insert quotation marks.
/=/	mid January	Insert a hyphen.
¶	"Where?" asked Karl. "Over there," said Ray.	Begin a new paragraph.
∨	She liked Sarahs glasses.	Insert an apostrophe.

Troubleshooter

Business and Technical Writing

Contents

Business Letters

People write business letters to apply for jobs, complain about poor service, order products, say thanks, request help or information, and express opinions. Knowing how to write an effective business letter is a valuable skill—one that you will use your whole life.

Why Write Business Letters?

You will probably write a number of business letters while you are still in high school, perhaps to apply for a job, to request information from businesses or government agencies, or to express your opinions on subjects of interest to you.

Business writing is a special form of expository writing. The most important thing to know about business writing is that it needs to be *efficient.* The reader should be able to grasp the meaning of a business letter quickly and with a minimum of effort. A letter that is long and complicated simply will not be read. You are much more likely to get the results you want if your letter is brief and clearly written.

Business letters use relatively formal language. The style is conversational but polite. Keep in mind that the impression the letter makes on the reader will certainly affect how he or she responds. Correct grammar, spelling, and punctuation are musts.

Business letters are usually single spaced and written on one side of a page only. However, you may double space a very short business letter so that it fills up more of the page. If the letter goes to two pages, number pages after the first as follows, with the name of the recipient, the date, and the page number, all flush with the left margin and at the top of the page:

```
R. Mandel

10/23/01

Page 2
```

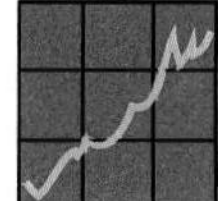

Activity

Bring an example of a business letter to class. In small groups, evaluate your letters. How effective are they? What do the letters have in common? Present the results of your discussion to the rest of the class by creating a set of criteria for an effective business letter.

Styles of Business Letters

Two basic styles are used for most business letters. These are the block style and the modified block style.

Block Style The use of conventional styles or formats in business writing lets readers know exactly what to expect and where to look for important information. The most commonly used style is block format. In this style, all parts of the letter are aligned at the left margin.

Notice that this letter is brief, clear, and carefully organized to meet the needs of the reader. The writer has asked for what she wants in the first paragraph and provided her reader with all the basic information needed to make a decision.

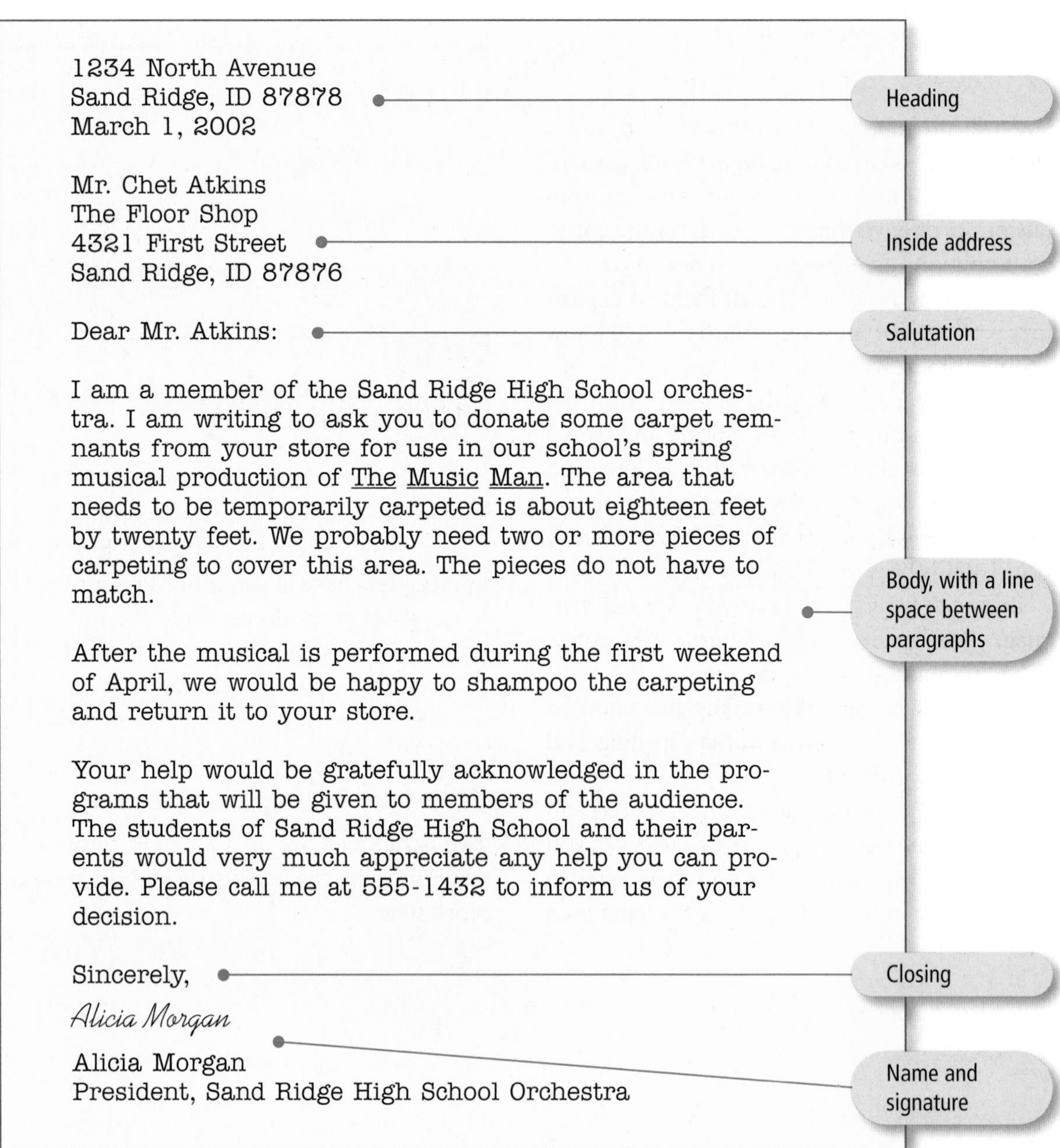

1234 North Avenue
Sand Ridge, ID 87878
March 1, 2002

Mr. Chet Atkins
The Floor Shop
4321 First Street
Sand Ridge, ID 87876

Dear Mr. Atkins:

I am a member of the Sand Ridge High School orchestra. I am writing to ask you to donate some carpet remnants from your store for use in our school's spring musical production of The Music Man. The area that needs to be temporarily carpeted is about eighteen feet by twenty feet. We probably need two or more pieces of carpeting to cover this area. The pieces do not have to match.

After the musical is performed during the first weekend of April, we would be happy to shampoo the carpeting and return it to your store.

Your help would be gratefully acknowledged in the programs that will be given to members of the audience. The students of Sand Ridge High School and their parents would very much appreciate any help you can provide. Please call me at 555-1432 to inform us of your decision.

Sincerely,

Alicia Morgan

Alicia Morgan
President, Sand Ridge High School Orchestra

Modified Block Format Some writers prefer modified block format. With this format, the date and closing are indented to the right. Paragraphs are indented and do not have a line space between them. Here is the same letter in the modified block format.

1234 North Avenue
Sand Ridge, ID 87878
March 1, 2002

The writer's address and the date are indented.

Mr. Chet Atkins
The Floor Shop
4321 First Street
Sand Ridge, ID 87876

Dear Mr. Atkins:

I am a member of the Sand Ridge High School orchestra. I am writing to ask you to donate some carpet remnants from your store for use in our school's spring musical production of The Music Man. The area that needs to be temporarily carpeted is about eighteen feet by twenty feet. We probably need two or more pieces of carpeting to cover this area. The pieces do not have to match.

After the musical is performed during the first weekend of April, we would be happy to shampoo the carpeting and return it to your store. Your help would be gratefully acknowledged in the programs that will be given to members of the audience.

Paragraphs are indented.

The students of Sand Ridge High School and their parents would very much appreciate any help you can provide. Please call me at 555-1432 to inform us of your decision.

Sincerely,

Alicia Morgan

Alicia Morgan,
President, Sand Ridge
High School Orchestra

The closing is indented and aligned with the return address.

Personal Letter Format Although most business letters are written to strangers, some are more personal. Personal letters are usually handwritten, not typed. They are less formal in format and tone.

1234 North Avenue
Sand Ridge, ID 87878
March 1, 2002

Dear Uncle Chet,

Do you remember that I play violin in the Sand Ridge High School Orchestra? Well, we have a problem, and we were hoping you could help by donating some carpet remnants from your store.

This spring the school is producing <u>The Music Man.</u> During practice we found out that it's sometimes hard to hear the singers because the orchestra is too loud. We have to find a way to deaden the music, and we thought putting carpeting on the floor under us might work.

Do you think you can find some old pieces of carpet that we could use? Everyone here would sure appreciate it. Please give me a call if you can help. We will be happy to shampoo the carpeting and return it to your store after the production is over, and we will acknowledge your help in the program given to members of the audience.

I look forward to seeing you and Aunt Teri at Mom and Dad's anniversary party.

Love,

Alicia

The salutation is informal and followed by a comma.

The tone of the body of the letter is informal.

The closing is personal.

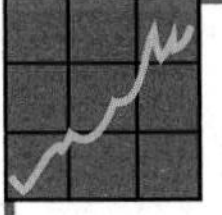

Activity

Imagine that you have completed a science project that you would like to enter in a science fair. Locate the name and address of the appropriate organization and write a business letter requesting specific information about procedures for entering, forms that need to be completed, dates and locations, and any other information needed to participate in the fair. Use either the block or modified block style.

PURPOSE To write a business letter requesting information
AUDIENCE Science fair officials
LENGTH 1 page

Writing Rubrics

In writing a letter requesting information, you should

- write clearly and to the point
- state your request in the first paragraph of the letter
- use polite but conversational language
- use correct business letter format
- check your letter for grammar, spelling, and mechanics

Types of Business Letters

People write business letters for many purposes. They may be requesting information or assistance, complaining, expressing an opinion about a product or service, apologizing, or applying for a job. The basic form of the letter remains unchanged regardless of the purpose, but each type of letter will be organized and structured somewhat differently. Your style may also change depending on your purpose.

Request The key to writing a letter requesting information or action is to ask for what you want in the first paragraph and to provide directions to the recipient as to how to respond in the paragraphs that follow. If you are requesting several items, it is helpful to indicate what you want in a bulleted list.

Please send the following items:
- two dozen test tubes
- four Bunsen burners
- one dozen small beakers
- six large beakers

Another kind of request, more difficult than placing an order or asking for information, is a personal request for assistance. To write this type of letter, you should:

- acquaint the reader with the basics of the situation
- provide details
- make it easy for the reader to do as you ask

> I am writing to ask if I may change the time of my driving lesson from 7:00 p.m. to 4:00 p.m. My father has been taking me to my lesson, but his work schedule has changed, making it difficult for me to make the 7:00 time. The 4:00 time would allow me to walk to my lesson after school. If you do not have an opening then, please let me know at what other times you have openings so that we can work out a mutually convenient time.

The tone of your letter should be respectful but not pleading or demanding.

Complaint If you are writing to complain about a product or service, first decide what you want the company to do about your complaint. Do you want an apology, a replacement, or a refund?

Explain the problem and ask for exactly what you want in the first paragraph. If your tone is polite, you are more likely to get a positive response. If your letter is formal, you convey to the reader that your complaint is to be taken seriously.

> I recently ordered the enclosed book from your online service. As you can see, the book is damaged. I would like you to send me a replacement as soon as possible.

Opinion When you state your opinion in a letter, your goal is to persuade the recipient to adopt your point of view. Begin by stating what you believe. If you are disagreeing with another point of view, state the opposing position as clearly and as accurately as possible. This strategy avoids giving the impression that you are attacking a point of view that you do not appreciate or understand.

Whenever you express your opinion, your credibility as a writer is especially important. Be sure your facts are correct and your writing is error free.

> I am opposed to the construction of a new strip mall on the north edge of town. I am aware that the town's population is growing and more places to shop are needed. However, there are many buildings in the downtown area that are currently empty. The town should make use of existing buildings rather than spoil the scenic open spaces north of town. Doing so will also help to bring life back to the downtown area and help keep it from becoming run down.

Note the effort the writer makes to show an understanding of the other point of view. Remember, the more controversial the issue, the more important it is that the tone of the letter be reasonable.

Apology To write an effective apology, never trivialize the concern of the person making the complaint or make excuses. Too often, people who write apologies say things like "I'm very sorry for any inconvenience you experienced," but to the person who bothered to complain, inconvenience is probably much too weak a word to describe the experience. The person complaining also doesn't want to hear about how "busy we were" or how "hard we try." Apologize, simply and directly.

> You are correct. We checked our files and you were scheduled for a haircut last Thursday. As our way of saying we are sorry, we will not charge you for your next haircut. We are very sorry for the trouble you experienced and are checking our procedures so that we do not make the same mistake again.

Notice that the writer takes the complaint seriously and doesn't offer excuses for the error.

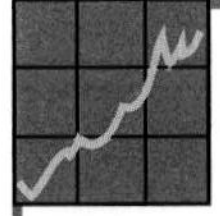

Activity

Write a letter to your school newspaper expressing your opinion about an issue that concerns you. You might write about a traffic problem, the need to clean up the halls, or how to make use of a vacant classroom. Before you write, take some time to investigate the issue and understand the opposing position or positions. Use either a block or a modified block format.

PURPOSE To write a letter expressing an opinion about an issue
AUDIENCE Readers of school newspaper
LENGTH 1 page

Writing Rubrics

To write an effective letter, you should

- state your opinion clearly in a reasonable tone
- provide evidence or reasons to support your opinion
- give a fair picture of the opposing points of view
- use correct business letter form
- check the letter for grammar, spelling, and mechanics

Memos, E-mail, and Applications

Written business communication can take forms other than formal letters.

Business Memos

People who work in a school, business, or other organization use memos to communicate with one another. Memos share many of the characteristics of the business letter but are usually less formal.

The memo format is designed to be as efficient as possible. The heading is double spaced and contains essential information for the reader, including who wrote the memo and what it is about. The rest of the document is single spaced with a line space between paragraphs. The content is direct and to the point. Typically, a memo is one page or less. It delivers its message immediately and directly.

One of the advantages of the memo format is that the recipient can write his or her response on the memo itself and return it. If you choose, you can end the memo with the word *Response:* or *Comment:* to make it clear that you expect only a quick, handwritten note in response.

To: Committee Chairpersons

From: Lisa Hopkins *LH*

Date: February 4, 2002

Re: Committee Chairpersons Meeting

We need to schedule the quarterly meeting for all of the school's committee chairpersons. Will Thursday afternoon at 3:00 P.M. in the library work for you? Please let me know as soon as possible.

It is important that you make every effort to attend the meeting, since we need to begin discussing plans for the class party. Thank you.

Instead of a signature at the end, the writer initials his or her name in the heading.

Re is an abbreviation for *regarding*. The subject of the memo goes here.

All text is flush left.

There is no closing, since the writer is identified in the heading.

E-mail

Of all the forms of business communication, e-mail is by far the most informal. E-mail often reads like a transcript of a conversation.

As e-mail becomes more and more common in business and elsewhere, writers need to analyze their audiences. The use of sentence fragments, colloquial language, and abbreviations may be fine for friends, but they are not appropriate for most business exchanges.

For anyone other than a close friend, an e-mail should be similar to a memo in format and style. The subject line, in fact, is even more important, since busy readers use the subject line to decide whether to open the message.

Clarity and directness are also important. Answering "I can come" to an e-mail may be more puzzling than helpful. If you are answering an e-mail, repeat enough of the original message to remind the recipient of the context, so he or she doesn't have to guess what you are writing about.

Remember that e-mail may not be private. Companies can access the e-mail of employees, and recipients of e-mail can easily forward what you have written. Before you know it, your "private" message may end up on a bulletin board that boasts 250 "hits" a day.

Because you cannot always format an e-mail as you can a letter (and because the format can sometimes be garbled in transmission of the e-mail), more formal communications should be done in a word processing program and e-mailed as an attachment. In most e-mail programs, sending an attachment requires simply that you click on a button marked *attachment*, insert the path and file name, and click OK.

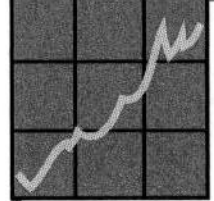

Activity

Pretend you are a member of a student committee that has been asked to make recommendations about the best place to hold a school-sponsored dance or concert. Write a memo to members of the committee asking that they poll classmates and gather their own ideas prior to the first meeting. Be sure to include the date and time of the meeting.

PURPOSE To write a memo
AUDIENCE Committee members
LENGTH 1 page or less

Writing Rubrics

To write an effective memo, you should

- convey your message clearly and concisely
- use the correct memo format
- include all necessary information
- proofread the memo

Applications

To apply for almost any job, secure a library card, get a driver's license, rent an apartment, open a bank account, or attend a college, you will need to fill out an application. The application conveys an impression of you as a person. Many applicants have been passed over because of typographical or spelling errors on a job application.

Volunteer Application Form

Thank you for considering volunteer work at the Lincoln Animal Shelter.

Name: ______________________ Date: ______________

Address: ____

City: ________________ State: _____ ZIP Code: _______

Phone: _________ Fax: __________ E-mail: ___________

DOB: ____________ SSN: _________________________

Best time to reach you: ____________________________

Education (circle highest level completed):
7 8 9 10 11 12

Is this experience for school credit? Yes No

School Name and address: __________________________

____

Why do you want to volunteer? _____________________

____

____

Describe previous volunteer experience.

____

____

Signature: ____

Be sure that the form is filled out neatly in black ink.

Abbreviations commonly used on applications include DOB (date of birth) and SSN or SS# (social security number).

Include hyphens in your social security number.

If the information asked for does not apply to you, write *n/a* in the blank.

In completing an application form, read through the entire document before writing anything. Follow instructions carefully.

Neatness counts. If possible, request more than one copy of the form so you can redo it if necessary.

Don't leave blank spaces. If something does not apply, write *n/a* (not applicable) in the space. Blank spaces suggest that you have something to hide or that you did not carefully read the form.

Complete the form in ink, preferably black ink.

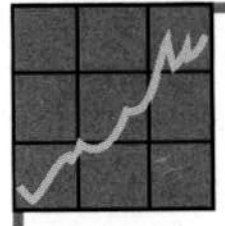

Activity

Fill out one or more practice applications. You can obtain blank forms from a local bank, the Registry of Motor Vehicles, the public library, potential employers, or parents. Work in a small group to evaluate and critique each other's work.

PURPOSE To complete at least one sample application
AUDIENCE Your classmates
LENGTH Length of the application(s)

Writing Rubrics

To effectively prepare an application form, you should

- answer each question
- correctly place information on the form
- write neatly and legibly
- check spelling and punctuation

Using the Computer as a Writing Tool

Computers can be used to research information, create and format documents, and present data graphically. The instructions given for these functions in this section are general; every software program performs some or all of these tasks a little differently. The easiest way to learn these functions is by reading the instruction manual or using the Help menu.

Making Tables and Graphs

Your word processing program can be used to display information and data in tables and graphs. In most cases, you can create either with a few keystrokes.

Tables Tables are used to present facts and figures in an easy-to-read format. Tables organize information into columns and rows. Columns are the vertical elements in a table and rows are the horizontal elements. Cells are the individual boxes that contain data.

To make a table in a word processing program, use the Help menu or the Tables pull-down menu. Then select the number of rows and columns you need. In most cases you will need one "extra" row to provide headings for each of the columns. If necessary, you can insert and delete rows and columns after you have created your table. You can also adjust the appearance of the table by adding borders and shading or color. Here is an example of a table.

Prefix	Meaning	Examples
re-	again	restate, restart
ante-	coming before	anteroom, antecedent
un-	not	unclean, undone
sub-	below	subcommittee, submarine

Graphs While a table can help readers quickly find and compare data, graphs highlight a comparison by showing it pictorially. You can use your word processing program to display information and data in tables or graphs. Keep in mind that in many software programs, graphs are referred to as charts. To learn to use the capabilities of your computer software, read the instruction manual that comes with your software or use the Help menu.

A **bar graph** shows data plotted along two axes. The vertical axis is the Y axis, and the horizontal is the X axis. Bar charts are used to showcase comparisons. The example bar graph shown here compares the number of students enrolled in various science classes. Notice how the size of the bars allow you to quickly rank the classes from smallest to largest enrollment.

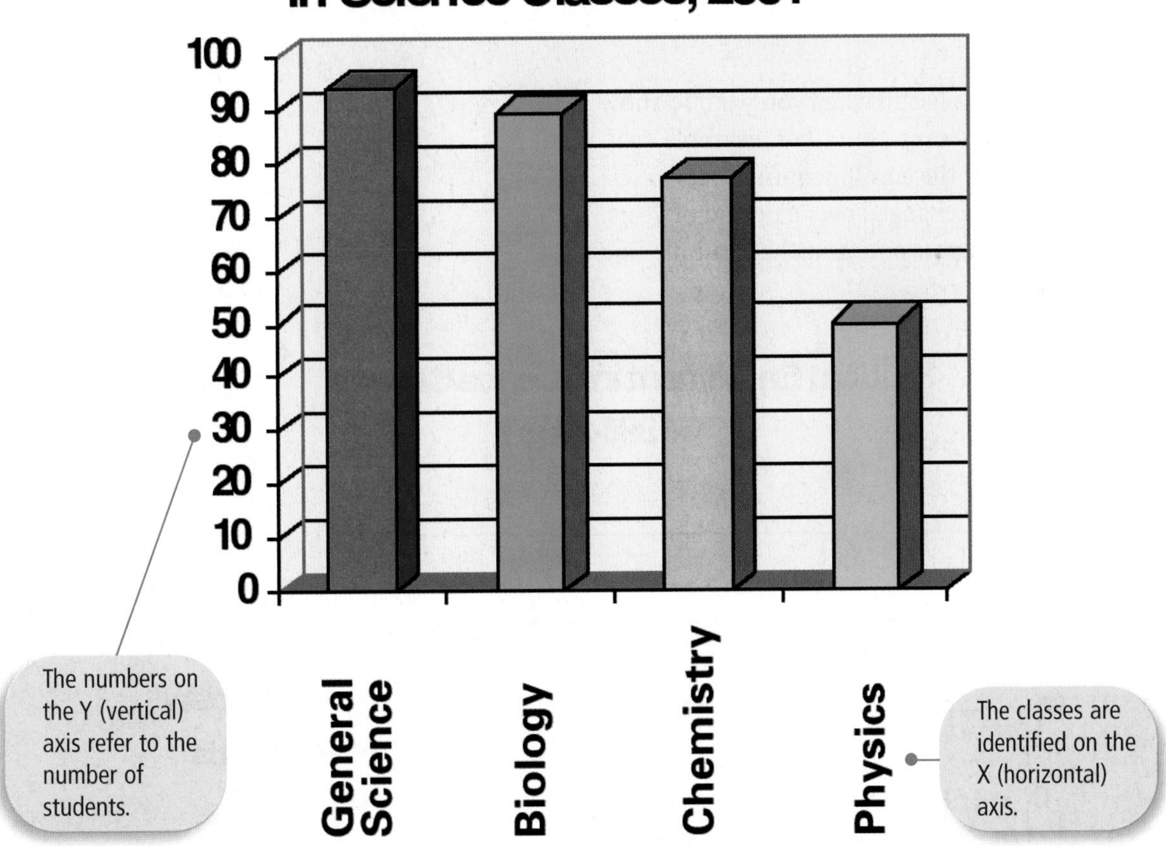

A **circle graph,** or pie chart, shows the relationship of parts to a whole. In the circle graph shown, for example, the complete circle stands for all the students enrolled in a science class. The segments represent the percentage of students in each type of science class.

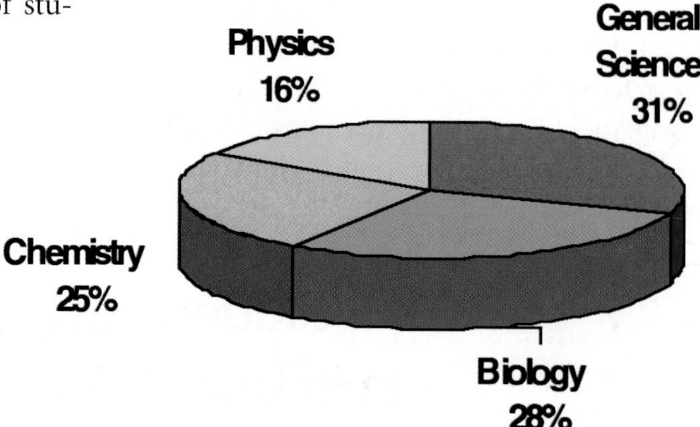

A **line graph** is useful when you want to show changes in data over time. For example, you might show how the enrollment numbers in science classes have changed over a period of years. What trends do you notice in the example line graph?

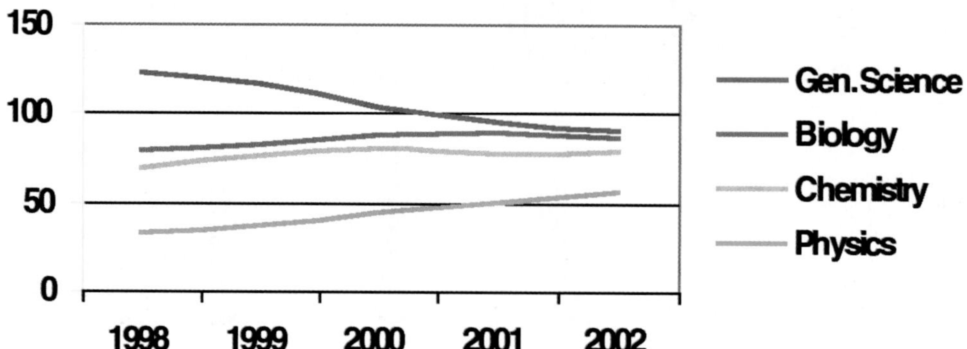

Creating graphs, or charts as they are called in word processing programs, is easy. You can enter data directly in a table designed to work with the charting function. When the data is entered, you choose the kind of chart you want, enter a title and—if needed—a legend, and click OK. The word processor creates the graph for you and inserts it into your document. If you discover a problem once your graph has been inserted into the document, simply double click on the graph to return to the editing function. Usually, you can switch between one type or style of graph and another once the data is entered to see which best conveys the point you are trying to make.

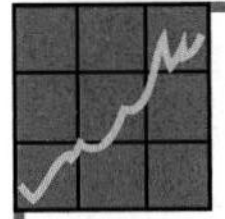

Activity

Gather statistical data for publication in a magazine. You may choose any topic that interests you. Examples of the kinds of things you might research include the most popular CDs or movies among young adults; the most popular sports among young adults in selected states; or driver's education policies at various high schools across the United States. The possible topics are countless.

Research your topic and write a report that presents the data not only in words but also in at least two different graphic formats: tables, charts, or graphs. Document your sources.

PURPOSE To gather, use, and present data in graphic form
AUDIENCE Readers of a student magazine
LENGTH 2–3 pages

Writing Rubrics

To prepare an effective table, chart, or graph, you should

- choose data that can be presented pictorially
- select a format appropriate for the audience
- present the data using the most effective graphic form
- include a descriptive title, labels, and/or legend
- proofread for accuracy

Creating Organization Charts and Flowcharts

Organization charts show how individuals, positions, or departments within an organization are related to one another. Check your Help menu to see if your program has a function or template to help you create organization charts. If your program does not allow you to create them automatically, you can use the drawing tools to make a chart. To make an organization chart, click on the appropriate icons to create boxes and lines similar to those shown in the example chart. You can choose either a vertical (portrait) or horizontal (landscape) orientation from Page Setup in the File menu. Once you have determined a structure, type in the names, titles, and other information you need. The example shows the basic organization of a student government.

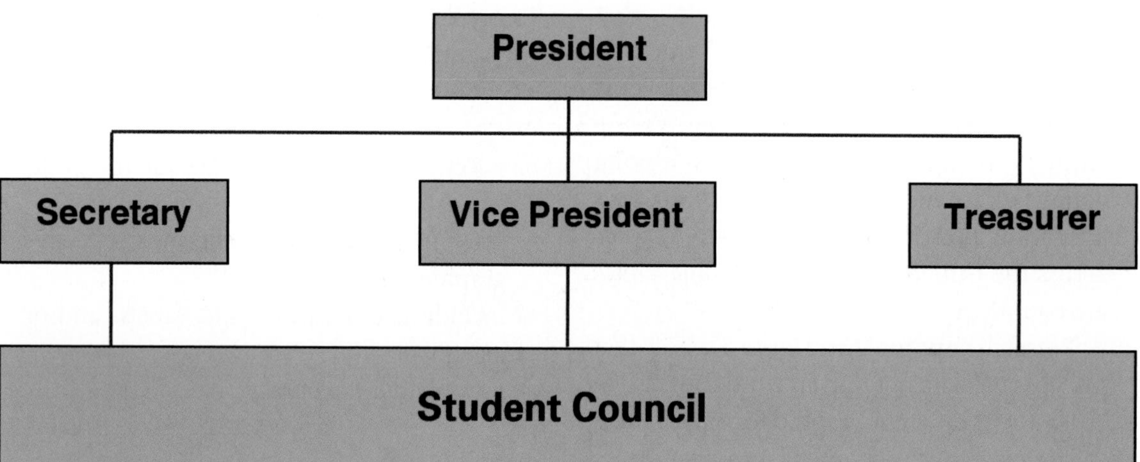

Be careful not to show too much information in one chart or one box; your information should be easy to see and understand. Start each box the same way. Be sure to include a title for your chart.

Flowcharts highlight a different kind of relationship; they show the stages in a process. They often use arrows to show progress from one step to the next. For flowcharts, be consistent in the kind of information you enter in each box. For example, each box might include a single step or a single action in a process. The example describes how you can use your word processing software to create a flowchart.

How to Create a Flowchart

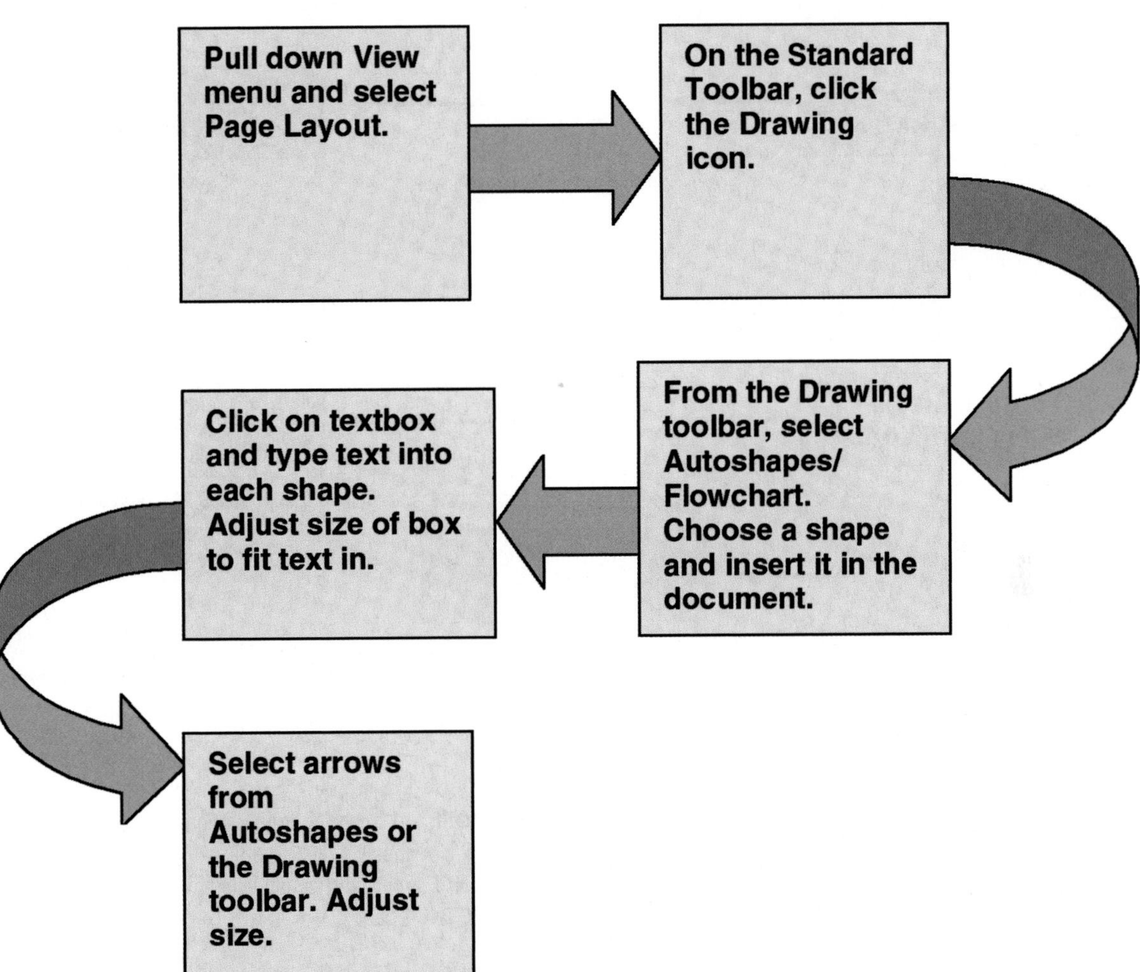

Pull down View menu and select Page Layout.
On the Standard Toolbar, click the Drawing icon.
From the Drawing toolbar, select Autoshapes/ Flowchart. Choose a shape and insert it in the document.
Click on textbox and type text into each shape. Adjust size of box to fit text in.
Select arrows from Autoshapes or the Drawing toolbar. Adjust size.

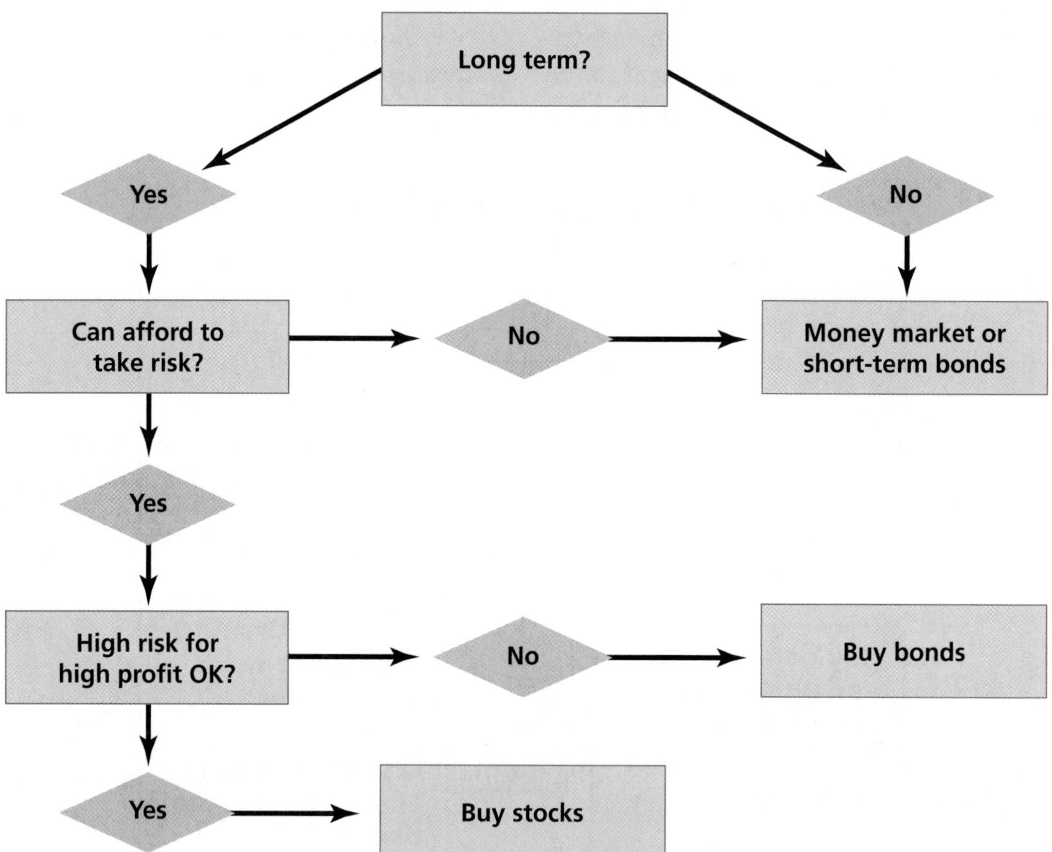

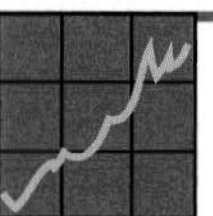

Activity

Choose one option:

- Use a computer to make an organization chart showing the structure of your student council or some other school group. Show each level of the organiztion.
- Use a computer to make a flowchart that explains a process with which you are familiar, such as how to do a science experiment, how to set up a VCR, or how to decorate a cake. Show all steps in the process.

PURPOSE To create an organization chart or a flowchart
AUDIENCE Your teachers and classmates
LENGTH 1 page

Writing Rubrics

To create an effective chart, you should

- identify each step and its place in the process
- write a title for the chart
- use the correct format
- label consistently
- check for accuracy

Technical Writing

Technical writing puts scientific or technical information into language that is easy to read and understand. Accuracy, consistency, clarity, and brevity are important characteristics of technical writing.

Elements of Technical Writing

Accuracy While errors in all kinds of writing are to be avoided, errors can be a calamity in technical writing. Putting a decimal point in the wrong place in a manual written for computer engineers can lead to millions of dollars worth of damage.

Consistency Technical writers and editors use a uniform style, so that words are consistently capitalized and units of measure are the same throughout the document. In some cases, inconsistencies may just be annoying, but in other cases they can spell disaster.

It is also important to be consistent in the names that you give to objects and processes. If your document tells the reader to "rotate" an object, then you should continue to use the word *rotate* rather than synonyms such as *spin, turn,* or *twist.* By doing so, you lessen the chance that your reader might become confused.

Most companies that issue technical documents and reports have a style manual to help writers maintain a consistent style. These manuals deal with such issues as capitalization, abbreviations, punctuation, and how to write numbers and equations.

Clarity Technical writers must be aware of their audience. Language appropriate for an audience of engineers may baffle nontechnical readers. On the other hand, if a document is intended for specialists, translating technical jargon into everyday language will unnecessarily complicate the writing.

Brevity Technical writers know that their readers want to gather relevant information as quickly as possible. Therefore, they often use short sentences, bulleted or numbered lists, and brief paragraphs to convey information. They also divide the text into multiple sections that make it easier to find specific information.

Many technical reports and papers begin with an abstract that summarizes the document in one tightly written paragraph. Many readers rely on abstracts not only to get the information they need but also to help them decide if the document is one they need to read in its entirety.

Technical writers are careful to organize reports so that readers can easily find the sections they need. Tables of contents guide the reader, and chapters are divided into clearly labeled sections. Abstracts provide a quick summary, and appendices include details too cumbersome to be included in the body of the report.

Technical writers also help their readers by presenting as much information as possible in charts, graphs, tables, or other graphic forms.

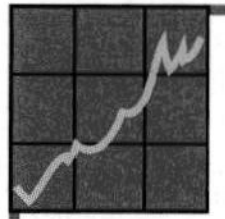

Activity

Suppose that your school newspaper is planning to include brief summaries of computer software reviews. Prepare a summary to submit to your school paper.

Read a review of a piece of new software on the Internet or in a computer magazine and write an abstract of no more than 250 words. The abstract should thoroughly summarize the review, reflecting its major points and conclusions. Be sure to write the abstract in your own words, although you can quote from the original as necessary.

PURPOSE To write an abstract of a software review
AUDIENCE Readers of your high school paper
LENGTH 250 words or less

Writing Rubrics

In writing an effective abstract, you should

- summarize the major points of the original review
- clearly state the conclusion
- write clearly, simply, and succinctly
- proofread your work carefully

Writing Instructions

Instructions are a form of technical writing. In order to give meaningful instructions, you have to understand the process you are describing thoroughly and completely. Then you must recall what it was like not to understand the process so you can explain it to others. In thinking about the process, divide it into clearly delineated steps. Then place those steps in an order that avoids repetition of steps or the need to backtrack. Below are some key recommendations from technical writers of how-to manuals.

Tips for Technical Writing

- Show or describe the finished product so the reader knows the goal.
- List all required parts and tools. You don't want to send the reader down to the basement in the middle of a project because you forgot to mention that your process requires a hot-glue gun or a stapler.
- Label each step clearly: (*Step One: Open the view menu.*)
- Write imperative sentences. (*Select page layout.*)
- Spell out even those steps that you think ought to be obvious. (*Turn on your computer.*)
- Check for errors or omissions by following your directions exactly as they are written.
- Have someone else follow the steps to help you identify instructions that may be confusing or difficult to understand.

We often write or follow instructions in science laboratory classes. The following box presents an example of instructions that were written for a biology mini-lab.

What happens to plant cells in a hypertonic solution?

Plant tissue is normally rigid or crisp because of the turgor presssure within the cells. When plant cells lose their turgor pressure, the plant wilts. What happens on the cellular level when a plant cell is exposed to hypertonic solution?

Procedure

1. Use forceps to take a leaf from the tip of an *Elodea* sprig, and place it on a slide with a drip of water. Apply a coverslip.
2. Use your microscope to observe it first with low power and then with high power. Draw a cell and its contents.
3. Place a drip of 3% salt solution on the slide near one side of the coverslip. Place a piece of paper towel on the opposite side of the coverslip to draw out the plain water and pull the salt water underneath the coverslip.
4. Observe the cell for a few minutes and then sketch it.

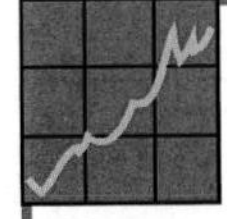

Activity

Write a brief "how-to" manual to teach your classmates to perform a step-by-step process. Select a process that you know well but which others may not know. Consider such processes as changing a set of spark plugs, adjusting the gears on a racing bike, firing a clay pot, or giving medication to an uncooperative cat or dog.

PURPOSE To write a "how-to" manual
AUDIENCE Your teacher and classmates
LENGTH 2–4 pages

Writing Rubrics

In writing effective instructions, you should

- list tools and equipment needed
- place steps in sequential order
- label each step
- use visuals effectively
- write clearly
- take into account the level of knowledge of the audience
- proofread for vague language and for errors in grammar, usage, and spelling
- test for omissions

— Collaborative Writing in the Business World —

Today, many organizations stress collaboration and teamwork, insisting that employees analyze and solve problems in groups, evaluate each other's performance, and report to management as one voice.

Businesses use teams because people in groups tend to generate more and better ideas than individuals. Creativity is enhanced when people share ideas in open discussion. There are few experiences more satisfying than a team experience in which everyone contributes to create a first-class product. Collaboration can be rewarding and enjoyable if group members work well together.

However, if the participants do not know how to work together effectively, collaborating on a project can be a frustrating and time-consuming process. Also, whenever people work together in groups, there is a risk that those who are more outgoing may silence those who are quiet but have much to contribute.

Active Listening

Working effectively in groups requires active listening. To listen actively:

- Make sure that everyone's point of view is not only heard but also understood.
- Don't interrupt, and try not to disagree until the other person has fully expressed his or her views.
- Ask open-ended questions and paraphrase the answers to be sure you have understood what the other person is saying.
- If necessary, ask follow-up questions to clarify the other person's ideas.

Once a group has been assigned a task, it should agree on the purpose and audience. Be as concrete and specific as possible: (For example, *The purpose of this report is to convince students of the dangers of smoking.*) Do not assume everyone understands the rules of group work. Discuss them thoroughly and record the statements the group has mutually agreed to.

Then list the tasks involved in completing the assignment. Discuss the strengths of group members, and assign various aspects of the project based on what each person does best. One person may be especially good at research on the Internet; another may be more knowledgeable about library reference sources; someone may know how to create professional-looking graphics.

Watch out for potential problems within the group. If someone is not pulling his or her weight or is refusing to participate, meet as a group to discuss the problem and find a solution.

Assign portions of the writing to individuals, or have each person draft the entire report and pull the best parts from each individual attempt. Then have the entire group suggest revisions and proofread the final project.

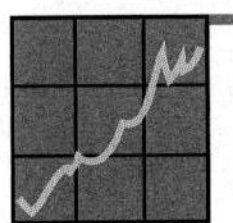

Activity

Working in small groups, create a history of your school, neighborhood, or community. It should show what the place was like in at least three different time periods.

The report may be presented in any manner you choose, but it must be a group project. Focus equally on visual images and words. You may tell the whole story of the place from its beginnings to today or highlight selected periods. Include visual aids to enhance your presentation.

PURPOSE To prepare an oral report about a particular place.
AUDIENCE Classmates
LENGTH 5–10 minutes

Writing Rubrics

To prepare an effective collaborative presentation, you should

- collect enough information to tell a coherent story
- present the information in both words and pictures so your audience can grasp key events easily
- assign tasks based on members' strengths

"I'm fishing this beautiful stream in Alaska, catching salmon, char and steelhead, when this bear lumbers out of the woods and down to the stream bank."

—Robert H. Abel

Jan Plaskosinski, *The Animal Kingdom*

PART 2

Grammar, Usage, and Mechanics

UNIT 10

Parts of Speech

10.1 Nouns

- A **noun** is a word that names a person, a place, a thing, or an idea.

PERSON	woman, man, Juanita Brown, great-grandfather
PLACE	planet, Texas, farm, high school
THING	dolphin, parrot, ivy, bookmark
IDEA	success, affection, freedom, courage

- A **concrete noun** names an object that occupies space or that can be recognized by any of the senses. Concrete nouns are things you can see, hear, taste, touch, smell, or feel.

thorn	stars	thunder	gas	milk
child	drum	velvet	headache	dove

- An **abstract noun** names an idea, a quality, or a characteristic.

excitement	honesty	innocence	happiness	harmony
truth	bravery	softness	fear	peace

Most nouns can take either a singular or a plural form, depending upon whether they name *one* person, place, thing, or idea or *more than one.*

SINGULAR	desk, bench, sky, wolf, man
PLURAL	desks, benches, skies, wolves, men

The possessive form of a noun can show possession, ownership, or the relationship between two nouns.

SINGULAR POSSESSIVE	PLURAL POSSESSIVE
the **girl's** coat	the **girls'** coats
a **business's** debts	those **businesses'** debts
a **prince's** crown	the **princes'** crowns
a **man's** voice	the **men's** voices

Exercise 1 Identifying Nouns

Find the twenty nouns that appear in the following paragraph, and write them on your paper.

Musical Flair

[1]When Seiji Ozawa, the colorful principal conductor of the orchestra, performs, the auditorium is usually overflowing. [2]He performs with a stylish blend of intelligence, fierce concentration, and theatricality. [3]As the famed director leads the orchestra through fast, loud, and dramatic passages, his baton flashes like a sword, and his thick mop of black hair bobs furiously up and down. [4]There are no sheets of music on the podium as he conducts because he routinely memorizes the entire score of each work.

Exercise 2 Supplying Abstract and Concrete Nouns

For each concrete noun in items 1–10, write an abstract noun that names an idea with which the concrete noun can be associated. For each abstract noun in items 11–20, write a concrete noun that has the quality of the abstract noun.

SAMPLE ANSWERS dancer—grace
redness—tomato

1. quarterback
2. scream
3. perfume
4. pepper
5. bruise
6. dog
7. binoculars
8. teeth
9. lamb
10. book
11. intelligence
12. friendliness
13. darkness
14. aroma
15. stupidity
16. anger
17. hospitality
18. noise
19. celebration
20. luck

Exercise 3 Writing Singular and Plural Nouns

On your paper, write the plural form of each singular noun below. If you need help, consult a dictionary.

1. lesson
2. cheese
3. tax
4. boy
5. radio
6. brush
7. half
8. country
9. aptitude
10. woman
11. church
12. concern
13. stereo
14. city
15. child
16. calf
17. business
18. moose
19. valley
20. envelope

Exercise 4 Writing Possessive Forms of Nouns

On your paper, write each of the following phrases, supplying the possessive form of the italicized noun.

1. my three *sisters* bedrooms
2. the *men* tailor
3. a *friend* misfortune
4. the *bus* fumes
5. several *galaxies* stars
6. the *mice* squeals
7. the *wives* trip
8. the *video* stars
9. the *boy* parents
10. the *children* behavior

Exercise 5 Adding Nouns to Categories

On your paper, add one more noun to each group of nouns listed below.

SAMPLE tulips, roses, carnations, ______
ANSWER tulips, roses, carnations, peonies

1. lion, gorilla, orangutan, ______
2. hatred, hostility, battle, ______
3. aunt, cousin, great-grandmother, ______
4. plateau, mountain, river, ______
5. neighbors, strangers, merchants, ______
6. justice, democracy, fairness, ______
7. library, theater, convention center, ______
8. Jenny's, Kim's, Mariana's, ______
9. potatoes, noodles, bread, ______
10. mathematics, sociology, anthropology, ______
11. sensitivity, kindness, concern, ______
12. Paris, Buenos Aires, Kuala Lumpur, ______
13. container, plate, dish, ______
14. teacher, doctor, private investigator, ______
15. courage, honor, decency, ______
16. planet, space, solar system, ______
17. insect, bird, reptile, ______
18. defendant, witness, prosecutor, ______
19. possibility, prospect, opportunity, ______
20. Thomas, Derek, Anthony, ______

Exercise 6 Completing Sentences with Nouns

On your paper, complete each sentence by filling in the blanks with nouns. Be sure that your completed sentences make sense.

1. The two ______ bought new ______.
2. The ______ coat was made of ______.
3. The ______ watched a(n) ______.
4. Her ______ seems to be her best ______.
5. Seven ______ sat on the ______.
6. My three ______ moved to a new ______.
7. The ______ shoes were covered with ______.
8. In ______ I enjoy the ______ and the ______.
9. One ______ stood alone on his ______.
10. ______ are at the ______.

Proper and Common Nouns

- A **proper noun** is the name of a particular person, place, thing, or idea.
- A **common noun** is the general—not the particular—name of a person, place, thing, or idea.

Proper nouns are capitalized, whereas common nouns are not usually capitalized.

TYPE OF NOUN	PROPER NOUNS	COMMON NOUNS
PERSON	Aunt Shirley, Uncle Arnold	relatives
	General Powell, General Lee	generals
PLACE	Atlantic Ocean, Pacific Ocean	oceans
	Mars, Venus, Jupiter	planets
THING	Labor Day, Fourth of July	holidays
	The Lion King, Aladdin	movies
IDEA	Buddhism, Judaism	religions
	Middle Ages, Great Depression	eras

Parts of Speech

Exercise 7 Matching Proper Nouns with Common Nouns

On your paper, match proper nouns 1–10 on the left with common nouns *a–j* on the right. Then match proper nouns 11–20 with common nouns *k–t.*

1. Santa Fe	**a.** actor
2. *National Geographic*	**b.** continent
3. Kleenex	**c.** gorge
4. Shakespeare	**d.** magazine
5. Denzel Washington	**e.** skyscraper
6. Florence Griffith-Joyner	**f.** author
7. Africa	**g.** athlete
8. the Grand Canyon	**h.** city
9. the Empire State Building	**i.** tissue
10. Linda Ronstadt	**j.** singer
11. Theodore Roosevelt	**k.** automobile
12. Islam	**l.** computer
13. Grammy	**m.** comedian
14. Canada	**n.** country
15. Chrysler	**o.** historical movement
16. Macintosh	**p.** play
17. Industrial Revolution	**q.** president
18. *Hamlet*	**r.** religion
19. David Letterman	**s.** state
20. Mississippi	**t.** award

Collective Nouns

■ A **collective noun** names a group.

army	committee	(the) public
team	choir	(a) pride (of lions)

You can consider collective nouns either singular or plural, depending upon the meaning you wish to convey. If a collective noun refers to a group as a whole, it is considered singular. If a collective noun refers to the individual members of a group, it is considered plural. Note the differences in the meaning in the following examples:

SINGULAR The **committee** wants our attention.
PLURAL The **committee** have gone their separate ways.
SINGULAR The **class** likes to read plays.
PLURAL The **class** take their seats.

Exercise 8 Identifying Collective Nouns

On your paper, list the five collective nouns in the following paragraph.

Observing the Wonders of Ocean Life

[1]After the crew of the merchant ship finish their chores, they love to watch the sea. [2]Occasionally at night a swarm of plankton makes the ocean glow softly. [3]A young sailor watches in amazement as a pod of feeding whales suddenly breaks the calm surface. [4]Only a few days earlier, along the coast of California, the sailors had spotted a herd of sea lions frolicking in the waves. [5]The varied population of the sea never ceases to delight the young sailor.

Exercise 9 Using Plural and Singular Collective Nouns

On your paper, complete the sentences in each pair by writing one of the collective nouns listed below. Indicate how the noun is used by writing *plural* or *singular.*

family jury audience club people infantry

1. a. The ______ struggle into their coats after the play.
b. The ______ applauds when the curtain falls.
2. a. The ______ meets every other Thursday.
b. The ______ vote for a chairperson and treasurer every two years.
3. a. The ______ plans a vacation.
b. The ______ each have different chores.
4. a. The ______ disagree on a verdict.
b. Has the ______ reached a decision?
5. a. ______ have different characteristics.
b. This ______ has created a great civilization.

Parts of Speech

Exercise 10 Classifying Common Nouns, Proper Nouns, and Collective Nouns

On your paper, classify each of the following nouns by writing *common, proper,* or *collective.* Some nouns belong in more than one category.

1. Uncle John
2. assembly
3. uncle
4. juror
5. Cape May
6. troop
7. major
8. crowd
9. flock
10. Niagara Falls
11. scout
12. Hilton Hotel
13. chorus
14. University of California
15. class
16. manager
17. Fifteenth Amendment
18. person
19. committee
20. Renaissance

Exercise 11 Completing Sentences with Different Kinds of Nouns

On your paper, complete each sentence by filling in the twenty-five blanks with the kinds of nouns specified in *italic* typeface. Be sure that your completed sentences make sense.

1. *Proper* left her *common* in the *concrete.*
2. The practice of *common* has become popular with the *common collective.*
3. The *common collective* proved its *abstract* at the *common.*
4. Near the *common* I saw three *common* run across the *concrete.*
5. *Proper* is a famous *common.*
6. Environmental *abstract* is a serious *abstract* for anyone who cares about humankind.
7. A *common collective* of zebras and a *common collective* of ostriches are only two of the spectacular sights on the plains of East *proper.*
8. I was thrilled to be able to watch *proper* practice *common* before the game.
9. The *common collective* voted for the *common.*
10. His *common* was born in *proper* on *proper* 4, 1932.

Exercise 12 Creating Sentences with Nouns

Write five sentences about one of your favorite places. Rely especially on concrete nouns to convey a vivid picture of the place.

10.2 Pronouns

■ A **pronoun** is a word that takes the place of a noun, a group of words acting as a noun, or another pronoun. The word or group of words that a pronoun refers to is called its **antecedent.** A pronoun must agree in number and gender with its antecedent.

When **she** was still a young girl, Sylvia Plath decided to become a writer. [The pronoun *she* replaces the noun *Sylvia Plath.*]

George Orwell wrote *Animal Farm* and *1984* in the 1940s. **Both** remain immensely popular today. [The pronoun *both* takes the place of the nouns *Animal Farm* and *1984.*]

Phillis Wheatley published **her** first poem at the age of sixteen and soon found **herself** a celebrity. [The pronouns *her* and *herself* take the place of the noun *Phillis Wheatley.*]

There are a limited number of pronouns, about seventy-five, in English. They fall into one or more of the following categories: personal and possessive pronouns, reflexive and intensive pronouns, demonstrative pronouns, interrogative pronouns, relative pronouns, and indefinite pronouns.

Exercise 13 Identifying Pronoun Antecedents

On your paper, write the antecedent of each italicized pronoun.

Emily Dickinson

1. In *her* poems, Emily Dickinson wrote about love, nature, and immortality.
2. "I never saw a Moor" and "The Sky is low—the Clouds are mean" are *both* about nature.
3. For many years, Emily's father did not support *her* interest in poetry.
4. Emily, her brother Austin, and her sister Vinnie grew up in Amherst, Massachusetts. *They* continued to live there as adults.
5. Emily seldom left Amherst. *She* spent many years as a recluse.
6. Some of Emily's acquaintances urged *their* friend to publish her poems.
7. Emily sent a few poems to a poetry critic at *The Atlantic Monthly* and asked for *his* opinion.
8. *They* corresponded until Emily's death in 1886.
9. Emily found beauty in nature and all *its* variations.
10. Emily once wrote of *herself:* "I am small, like the Wren."

Personal and Possessive Pronouns

■ A **personal pronoun** refers to a specific person or thing by indicating the person speaking (the first person), the person being spoken to (the second person), or any other person or thing being spoken about (the third person).

Personal pronouns, like nouns, are either singular or plural.

Personal Pronouns		
	Singular	**Plural**
FIRST PERSON	I, me	we, us
SECOND PERSON	you	you
THIRD PERSON	he, him she, her it	they, them

FIRST PERSON Thomas went with **me** to the game. [*Me* refers to the person speaking.]

SECOND PERSON Ask Gina to show **you** the article. [*You* refers to the person being addressed.]

THIRD PERSON **He** gave **them** a poor excuse. [*He* and *them* refer to the persons being discussed.]

Third-person singular pronouns express **genders.** *He* and *him* are masculine; *she* and *her* are feminine; *it* is neuter (neither masculine nor feminine).

The **possessive pronouns** in the following chart take the place of the possessive forms of nouns.

Possessive Pronouns		
	Singular	**Plural**
FIRST PERSON	my, mine	our, ours
SECOND PERSON	your, yours	your, yours
THIRD PERSON	his her, hers its	their, theirs

The first form of each pronoun in the preceding chart can be used before a noun. The second form is used alone, like a noun.

USED BEFORE A NOUN This is **her** radio.
Its battery is new.

USED ALONE This radio is **hers.**

Exercise 14 Identifying Personal and Possessive Pronouns

On your paper, list the personal or possessive pronoun in each of the following items. Then identify the pronoun as *personal* or *possessive.*

Ancient Rome

1. The Romans built a forum in the center of each city and used it for public activities.
2. Their houses had little furniture and usually only a single door as protection against thieves.
3. The father of a Roman family had total power over all members of his household.
4. Roman parents selected marriage partners for their children.
5. As a student in a school in ancient Rome, you would have used a wax tablet for writing.
6. Your day would have started before dawn.
7. For entertainment, citizens went to races and bet on a chariot and its driver.
8. Some entertainment was bloody. It involved gladiators fighting to the death.
9. Wealthy people had servants and often sent them to do the shopping.
10. Servants were often enemy soldiers captured in battle. They tended gardens, served meals, and taught the children.
11. Men and women wore a gown called a tunic. It hung to the knees or below.
12. Men dressed in white, but women dyed their clothing various colors.
13. Romans made few scientific discoveries, but they did collect scientific information.
14. Pliny the Elder assembled scientific knowledge of his day.
15. Most Romans lived by farming. They used crop rotation to enrich soil.
16. Romans invented concrete, which provided a strong building material for their structures.
17. Many roads crisscrossed the Roman Empire. They helped hold the empire together.
18. Augustus was the first emperor of Rome. He built an elaborate arch in the middle of town to celebrate a victory in battle.
19. His uncle was Julius Caesar.
20. A Roman woman of noble birth had an important role. She looked after the house and all the servants.

Exercise 15 Using Personal and Possessive Pronouns

Improve the following paragraph by replacing each underlined word or group of words with a personal or possessive pronoun. Write your answers on your paper.

Navajo Chants

[1]Two friends and <u>the writer of this article</u> attended a lecture on Native American history and culture. [2]<u>The writer's</u> two friends especially enjoyed the lecture, since <u>the lecture</u> was presented by <u>the two friends'</u> mother, who is an expert on the subject. [3]<u>The lecturer's</u>

Parts of Speech

comments about the importance of music in Navajo religious ceremonies interested the writer of this article. [4]Navajo religious ceremonies regularly feature a male singer, or medicine man, who is a highly respected member of the singer's community. [5]The music is designed to provide healing for tribe members. [6]The singer has a great responsibility, for the singer's chant (which may take several days to complete) must be performed perfectly. [7]Otherwise the chant will not carry its healing powers. [8]The reader of this passage would have loved to hear the demonstration of the Navajo mountain chant. [9]The demonstration was fascinating.

Reflexive and Intensive Pronouns

You form the reflexive and intensive pronouns by adding *-self* or *-selves* to certain personal and possessive pronouns.

Reflexive and Intensive Pronouns		
	Singular	**Plural**
FIRST PERSON	myself	ourselves
SECOND PERSON	yourself	yourselves
THIRD PERSON	himself, herself, itself	themselves

- A **reflexive pronoun** refers, or reflects back, to a noun or pronoun used earlier in the sentence. A reflexive pronoun always adds information.

  I almost exhausted **myself** working for her in the campaign.

  Today, for the first time in months, she is **herself.**

  As a team they have no faith in **themselves.**

- An **intensive pronoun** adds emphasis to another noun or pronoun.
- An **intensive pronoun** does not add information to the sentence. If it is omitted, the meaning of the sentence will still be the same.
- An **intensive pronoun** is often placed directly after its antecedent.

  You **yourself** told me to stop.

  Rita **herself** met us.

  However, an **intensive pronoun** may come anywhere in the sentence.

  I baked the bread **myself.**

  We will bake it **ourselves.**

Parts of Speech

Exercise 16 Identifying Antecedents of Reflexive and Intensive Pronouns

On your paper, write the antecedent of the italicized pronoun in each of the following sentences.

SAMPLE John Tyler and his wife, Julia, wrote a poem and set it to music *themselves.*

ANSWER John Tyler and his wife, Julia

Presidents and Their Families

1. During her college years, Pat Nixon supported *herself* as a bank teller and also worked as a movie extra.
2. Mamie Eisenhower and her friends often amused *themselves* by playing cards.
3. To entertain *himself* at his father's inauguration, Charles Taft read a book.
4. The White House *itself* was the focus of much of Jacqueline Kennedy's reading before she actually moved in.
5. Because Gerald Ford *himself* had laryngitis, he asked his wife to extend his congratulations to President-elect Jimmy Carter.

Exercise 17 Distinguishing Between Reflexive and Intensive Pronouns

On your paper, write the reflexive or intensive pronoun in each of the following sentences. Then identify each pronoun as *reflexive* or *intensive.*

Marie Curie

1. As a child, Marie threw herself into her studies.
2. Learning itself was her passion.
3. By the time she married Pierre Curie, he had already made himself a reputation as a well-known physicist.
4. When working with radioactive compounds, even Marie herself was surprised at how much radioactivity they gave.
5. Recognizing the significance of his wife's work, Pierre convinced himself to abandon his research and help Marie.
6. Marie often had to defend herself from attacks made against her because she was a woman scientist.
7. During World War I, Marie promoted the use of the X-ray machine for medical purposes. The doctors themselves were not immediately convinced of the machine's usefulness.
8. Marie's contribution to science was invaluable, but the work itself may have led to her untimely death.
9. Because so little was known about radioactivity, Marie did not realize that she needed to protect herself from polonium radiation.
10. Did Marie congratulate herself when she was appointed as a delegate to the League of Nations?

Demonstrative Pronouns

■ A **demonstrative pronoun** points out specific persons, places, things, or ideas.

Demonstrative Pronouns		
SINGULAR	this	that
PLURAL	these	those

■ A **demonstrative pronoun** can come before or after its antecedent. An antecedent may also be understood.

BEFORE ANTECEDENT	**This** is the hat I want.
	These are the potatoes left over from dinner.
AFTER ANTECEDENT	My old shoes are nicer than **those.**
UNDERSTOOD ANTECEDENT	Show me **that** [thing] again.

Exercise 18 Completing Sentences with Reflexive, Intensive, and Demonstrative Pronouns

Supply the appropriate reflexive, intensive, or demonstrative pronoun for each blank. On your paper write the pronoun and identify it as *reflexive, intensive,* or *demonstrative.*

Recollecting the Harlem Renaissance

1. Actually, I ______ suggested a field trip to New York City to learn more about Countee Cullen and the Harlem Renaissance.
2. Our class polled ______ to determine whether there was interest in the trip.
3. ______ was the most one-sided vote I had ever seen.
4. We surprised ______ by raising enough money to allow the entire class to spend one day and night in New York.
5. During the 1920s and 1930s, Countee Cullen, Langston Hughes, Zora Neale Hurston, W. E. B. Du Bois, and Jean Toomer all lived and supported ______ in Harlem.
6. ______ are only a few of the hundreds of writers, musicians, and artists who helped make Harlem vibrant.
7. The class set two specific goals: they were to find the site of the historic Cotton Club ______ and to locate the building where Countee Cullen grew up.
8. Our teacher reminded us that Cullen ______ had been a schoolteacher in New York's public schools.
9. After walking four miles, we treated ______ to a picnic in Riverside Park.
10. Back home again, we all said, "______ was a trip we shall never forget."

Parts of Speech

Interrogative and Relative Pronouns

- An **interrogative pronoun** is used to form questions.

who? whom? whose? what? which?

Who are those strangers?
Whom should I invite?
Whose did you borrow?
What did you say?
Which of these personal computers shall I buy?

The intensive forms of the interrogative pronouns are *whoever, whosoever, whomever, whichever,* and *whatever.*

Whoever told you that? **Whatever** did you say?

- A **relative pronoun** is used to begin a special subject-verb word group called a subordinate clause (see Unit 13).

who	whose	whomever	that	what
whom	whoever	which	whichever	whatever

The pilot **who** landed the plane is my cousin. [The relative pronoun *who* begins the subordinate clause *who landed the plane.*]

The plane, **which** landed late, carried our friends. [The relative pronoun *which* begins the subordinate clause *which landed late.*]

Exercise 19 Distinguishing Between Interrogative and Relative Pronouns

On your paper, list the interrogative and relative pronouns that appear in the following sentences, and label each pronoun as *interrogative* or *relative.* (Some sentences have more than one interrogative or relative pronoun.)

Frida Kahlo

1On a quiz show, I heard the question "Which of the modern Mexican artists had a museum named after her?" 2It was then that I first heard of Frida Kahlo, whose paintings include *The Broken Column.* 3Kahlo, who in her youth was in a highway accident that forced her to abandon her dream of becoming a doctor, became an artist instead. 4Whoever sees her work is enchanted by its bright colors and vibrant forms. 5It is clear, however, that Kahlo's paintings often contain images of figures in pain. 6One might ask, What was it that gave her the strength to continue painting after the accident had left her in constant pain? 7After her death in 1954, her husband, Diego Rivera, who was also a celebrated painter, gave Kahlo's home to the Mexican government for use as a museum.

8In recent years, much has been written about Frida Kahlo, whose art is now displayed in galleries worldwide. 9The book that tells the story of her life with Diego Rivera is especially fascinating. 10Whoever wrote it must have known both artists well.

Indefinite Pronouns

- An **indefinite pronoun** refers to persons, places, or things in a more general way than a noun does.

Jacob seems to know **everyone** at school. [The indefinite pronoun *everyone* refers to people in general.]

I'm going to bake **something** special. [The indefinite pronoun *something* does not indicate to what it specifically refers.]

We served the bread, not knowing **some** was stale. [The indefinite pronoun *some* has the specific antecedent *bread.*]

Some Indefinite Pronouns				
all	each	many	nothing	somebody
another	either	most	one	someone
any	enough	much	other	something
anybody	everybody	neither	others	
anyone	everyone	nobody	plenty	
anything	everything	none	several	
both	few	no one	some	

Exercise 20 Identifying Different Kinds of Pronouns

(a) On your paper, list in order the 25 pronouns that appear in the following paragraph.
(b) Identify each pronoun as *personal, possessive, reflexive, intensive, demonstrative, interrogative, relative,* or *indefinite.*

The Riddle of the Sphinx

[1]The Sphinx was a mythical monster that had the body of a lion and the head of a woman. [2]The people of Thebes were under her control, and anyone who met her had to answer a riddle correctly or die. [3]This was the riddle: what walks on four legs in the morning, on two legs at noon, and on three legs at night? [4]Many tried, but none could solve the riddle. [5]Then Oedipus, himself a Greek hero, confronted her. [6]When he correctly answered the riddle, the enraged Sphinx threw herself from a cliff. [7]The people of Thebes, whose deliverance Oedipus had won, were so grateful they made him king. [8]In our time everyone knows the answer to the riddle. [9]It is you and I and all of humankind. [10]We crawl on hands and knees as babies, travel on two legs in our youth, and use a cane to support ourselves in old age.

Exercise 21 Creating Sentences with Different Kinds of Pronouns

Write 10 sentences about a favorite meal that you shared with friends or members of your family. Try to use pronouns from all the categories you have studied in this lesson.

10.3 Verbs

■ A **verb** is a word that expresses action or a state of being and is necessary to make a statement.

Business people **work.**
The curtain **closed** too soon.
Artists **are** creative.

A verb has the ability to express time—present, past, and future—by means of *tense.*

PRESENT TENSE	We **hear** a car outside.
PAST TENSE	We **heard** a car outside.
FUTURE TENSE	We **will hear** a car outside.

Exercise 22 Completing Sentences with Verbs

On your paper, write twenty complete sentences by supplying a verb for each blank.

Hawks as Hunters

1. The solitary hawk ______ slowly, high above the green valley.
2. It ______ black against the blue sky.
3. Sensing the hawk's presence, the rodents ______ in the grass.
4. Riding rising air currents, the hawk barely ______ its wings.
5. Its flight ______ effortless.
6. With its piercing eyes, the hawk ______ the countryside in search of food.
7. A hawk ______ eight times more acutely than a human being.
8. Some hawks will even ______ at night, catching bats on the wing.
9. Hawks are territorial birds that ______ their nests from other hawks.
10. Most hawks ______ their nests high in trees.
11. Some hawks ______ by themselves or in small flocks.
12. Cooper's Hawks often ______ on telephone poles.
13. The osprey, a type of hawk, ______ fish almost exclusively.
14. Hawks ______ for the slightest movement in the grass below.
15. The red-tailed hawk ______ mainly on small rodents.
16. Many bird watchers ______ Hawk Mountain in Pennsylvania.
17. Experienced bird watchers ______ hawks flying in the distance.
18. Hawks ______ hooked bills and strong talons.
19. Bird watchers ______ different kinds of hawks by their coloring and silhouettes.
20. Hawks ______ larger than most other birds.

Action Verbs

- An **action verb** tells what someone or something does.

PHYSICAL ACTION	The huge lineman **leads** the charge through the defense.
MENTAL ACTION	The coaches **plan** the team's strategy before each game.

- A **transitive verb** is an action verb that is followed by a word or words that answer the question *what?* or *whom?*

Chipmunks **climb** small trees to get at berries and nuts. [The action verb *climb* is followed by the noun *trees,* which answers the question *climb what?*]

- An **intransitive verb** is an action verb that is *not* followed by a word that answers the question *what?* or *whom?*

Chipmunks also **climb** much of the time simply to escape from their enemies. [The action verb is followed by words that tell *when* and *why.*]

To decide whether a verb in a sentence is transitive or intransitive, ask *what?* or *whom?* after the verb. If the answer is given in the sentence, the verb is transitive. If the answer is not given in the sentence, the verb is intransitive.

Many action verbs can be either transitive or intransitive, depending on how they are used in a sentence.

TRANSITIVE	Jill usually **ate** her sandwich in the cafeteria. [*Sandwich* tells what Jill ate.]
INTRANSITIVE	Jill **ate** right before class today. [*Right before class today* tells when Jill ate.]

Some verbs have only transitive or intransitive uses. A dictionary will indicate how a verb may be used.

Exercise 23 Identifying Action Verbs

On your paper, write the action verb that appears in each of the following sentences. Indicate how the verb is used by writing *transitive* or *intransitive.*

Hints for Backpackers

1. Backpackers often carry contour maps on a hike.
2. Contour lines on a map identify the elevation of each spot.
3. Numerals on a contour line tell an area's distance above sea level.
4. On steep slopes, contour lines run close together.
5. Rivers, creeks, and rills always flow downward across the contour lines of a map.
6. Hills and valleys show vividly on a contour map.
7. The abbreviation *BM* (for *bench mark*) indicates the location of a tablet with the exact elevation of that spot.
8. Surveys by the United States Geological Survey place at least two bench mark tablets in each township.
9. Hikers use bench marks for reference.
10. With the help of a contour map, compass, and bench marks, backpackers find the right track.

Exercise 24 Identifying and Using Transitive and Intransitive Verbs

On your paper, write the verb that appears in each of the following sentences. Label each verb *transitive* or *intransitive,* depending on how it is used in the sentence. Then write five new sentences, using each transitive verb as an intransitive verb and each intransitive verb as a transitive verb.

SAMPLE I type my poetry assignments for English class.
ANSWER type, transitive
I type slowly but accurately.

The Challenge of Haiku

1. Most of my classmates wrote poems that rhyme.
2. Barbara and I, however, each composed a haiku—three lines, with seventeen syllables of unrhymed verse.
3. The great Japanese poet Bashō lived in the seventeenth century.
4. The simplicity of Bashō's verses awakened in many readers a love of all poetry, especially haiku.
5. What other poet thought as simply and clearly as Bashō?

Exercise 25 Creating Sentences with Action Verbs

Choose five of the action verbs that you identified in Exercise 23. For each verb write one sentence.

Linking Verbs

- A **linking verb** links, or joins, the subject of a sentence (often a noun or pronoun) with a word or expression that identifies or describes the subject. A linking verb does not show action.

The most commonly used linking verb is *be* in all its forms—*am, is, are, was, were, will be, has been, was being.*

I **am** a musician.
That singer **is** an artist.
The days **were** hot.
Those **are** mosquitoes.

Several verbs other than the forms of *be* can also act as linking verbs.

Other Linking Verbs			
appear	grow	seem	stay
become	look	sound	taste
feel	remain	smell	

The cake **tastes** good.
He **grew** taller over the summer.
She **felt** good about the election results.
He **seems** better today.

Parts of Speech

Exercise 26 Completing Sentences with Linking Verbs

On your paper, write a linking verb to complete each sentence below. Try to use as many different linking verbs as possible.

Weather in the Great Lakes

1. The weather around the Great Lakes ______ quite cold in the winter.
2. The summers, however, ______ either cool or very hot.
3. The weather ______ most pleasant in the fall.
4. The days ______ warm even though the nights ______ colder.
5. People ______ happiest about the weather when the sun shines.

Exercise 27 Identifying Linking Verbs

On your paper, write the linking verb that appears in each of the following sentences.

The United States Flag

1. After World War II, the flag of the United States became a familiar symbol around the world.
2. Before the American Revolution, most colonial flags looked similar to the British flag.

3. The traditional story about Betsy Ross's role in the creation of the first U.S. flag now appears unlikely.
4. Francis Hopkinson, a delegate to the Continental Congress, was probably the designer of the first American flag.
5. The stripes in the flag, an idea from a colonial patriot group's flag, are symbolic of the thirteen original colonies.
6. Though not official, a flag with thirteen stars in a circle is often representative of the nation's early years.
7. The colors red, white, and blue on the flag are traditional.
8. After years of confusion about where to place each new star, the positions of the flag's stars became official by presidential order in 1912.
9. By government regulation, an American flag is part of every public building and school.
10. The U.S. flag is always the flag on the right in a parade or display with other flags.
11. No other flags are more prominent than the U.S. flag.
12. The blue field of stars appears uppermost in any display.
13. Most of these regulations seem helpful for the preparation of official exhibits about the flag's history.
14. A flag with a rattlesnake on it was once a symbol of the American colonies.
15. Many of the state flags, like the U.S. flag, are red, white, and blue.

Exercise 28 Identifying Action and Linking Verbs

On your paper, list ten verbs that appear in the following paragraph. Identify each verb as either *action* or *linking.*

Jesse Owens, Gold Medalist

[1]Jesse Owens was one of the first superstars in track and field. [2]As a junior high school student in Cleveland, Ohio, in the 1920s, Owens sprinted 100 yards in 10 seconds. [3]A few years later, he captured the entire nation's attention with a 10.3-second 100-yard dash at East Technical High School. [4]His fame increased during his years as an athlete at Ohio State University. [5]Owens's performance in four events on May 25, 1935, seemed extraordinary. [6]At the age of 22, he shattered world records for the 220-yard dash, the 220-yard low hurdles, and the broad jump. [7]A new record in a fourth event, the 100-yard dash, was just out of his reach. [8]Jesse Owens's fame peaked the following year at the 1936 Olympics in Berlin, Germany. [9]In the presence of the Nazi dictator, Adolf Hitler, Owens won gold medals in four events. [10]Hitler's lack of acknowledgment of the achievements of this famous African American only heightened the world's appreciation of Owens's success.

Verb Phrases

The verb in a sentence may consist of more than one word. The words that accompany the main verb are called **auxiliary,** or helping, **verbs.**

■ A **verb phrase** consists of a main verb and all its auxiliary, or helping, verbs.

The forms of *be* and *have* are the most common auxiliary verbs. They help the main verb express the various tenses.

I am walking. **I have walked.** **I had been walking.**

Auxiliary Verbs			
FORMS OF *BE*	am, is, are, was, were, being, been		
FORMS OF *HAVE*	has, have, had, having		
OTHER AUXILIARIES	can, could	may, might	shall, should
	do, does, did	must	will, would

In addition to expressing time, the other auxiliary verbs are used to express different shades of meaning.

She **might wait.** We **would have played.**
He **could win.** I **must be going.**

Exercise 29 Identifying Verb Phrases

On your paper, write each verb phrase that appears in the following sentences. (Two of the sentences have more than one verb phrase.) Put parentheses around the auxiliary verbs in each phrase. (Words that interrupt a verb phrase are not considered part of the verb phrase.)

San Antonio's April Fiesta

1. For a long time now, the April fiesta has been the highlight of the year in San Antonio.
2. The fiesta may be the world's most enjoyable party, and it attracts visitors from all over.
3. People can enjoy excellent Spanish and Mexican meals while they are listening to delightful music.
4. They might hear country swing, country rock, or Dixieland.
5. The fiesta must begin in front of the Alamo on a Saturday.
6. It may last ten days.
7. Always the highlight, the Battle of Flowers Parade has attracted people since 1891.
8. During the fiesta all of San Antonio's diverse cultures can display themselves and have done so brilliantly over the years.
9. The pomp and lavishness of the fiesta could humble the royalty of Europe.
10. Tourists will long remember the lights, flowers, and music.

Exercise 30 Completing Sentences with Verb Phrases

On your paper, complete the following sentences by replacing each blank with a verb phrase. Be sure that your completed sentences make sense.

Florida

1. Florida ______ the "sunshine state."
2. Because of environmental problems, many native animals in Florida, such as the manatee and the Florida panther, ______ in number.
3. Tourists ______ to Florida by the warm climate, beautiful beaches, and many entertainment centers.
4. With the opening of Disney World, central Florida ______ from a quiet rural area to a world-renowned tourist destination.
5. The Apollo 11 moon rocket ______ from the Kennedy Space Center near Titusville.
6. Each night the beautiful sunset ______ by the many people congregated in Key West's Mallory Square.
7. St. Augustine, the oldest city in America, ______ in 1564.
8. Miami became an important city after railroads ______ to link it with cities farther north.
9. Many ships ______ at the port in Jacksonville.
10. High-technology and electronics industries ______ in the Melbourne–Palm Bay area.

Exercise 31 Completing Sentences with Different Kinds of Verbs

On your paper, complete each sentence in the following paragraph by supplying a verb. The kind of verb to use in each case is indicated in italics. Be sure that your completed sentences make sense.

Hobbies

Because people [1]*action verb* more leisure time than ever before, hobbies [2]*verb phrase* in popularity. Preferences for hobbies [3]*action verb* greatly from person to person. Whereas some people [4]*action verb* sculpture, others [5]*linking verb* most content when they [6]*verb phrase* an old car. Photography [7]*action verb* to many people, some of whom [8]*action verb* darkrooms, where they [9]*verb phrase* their own film. Hobby stores [10]*action verb* model planes that actually [11]*action verb* even though they [12]*verb phrase* very fragile. People who [13]*action verb* for a hobby [14]*linking verb* quite pleased when they [15]*verb phrase* their work at an art show. Anyone [16]*verb phrase* a philatelist, which [17]*linking verb* the term for a person who [18]*action verb* stamps. The more a philatelist's collection [19]*action verb*, the more valuable it [20]*linking verb*.

Exercise 32 Creating Sentences with Vivid Verbs

On your paper, write five sentences about one of your favorite outdoor activities. Choose very specific action verbs and verb phrases to convey vividly a sense of the activity.

10.4 Adjectives

HOW BEAUTIFUL THE TULIP IS!
THAT BEAUTIFUL TULIP WON FIRST PRIZE.
THE TULIP IS BEAUTIFUL.
THE FLORIST CONSIDERED IT BEAUTIFUL.
THE TULIPS, BEAUTIFUL IN THE SUNLIGHT, DANCED IN THE WIND.

■ An **adjective** is a word that modifies a noun or pronoun by limiting its meaning.

An adjective may describe a noun or pronoun by answering one of these questions: *What kind? Which one? How many? How much?*

QUESTION	ADJECTIVES	
What kind?	**green** sweater	**sunny** Greece
	tall woman	**pure** joy
Which one?	**this** book	**these** islands
	that child	**those** rules
How many?	**four** oceans	**few** farmers
	many rings	**both** principals
How much?	**more** money	**no** time
	enough salad	**little** patience

Adjectives appear in various positions in the sentence.

How **beautiful** the tulip is!
That **beautiful** tulip won first prize.
The tulip is **beautiful.**
The florist considered the tulip **beautiful.**
The tulips, **beautiful** in the sunlight, danced in the wind.

The words *a, an,* and *the* are special kinds of adjectives called **articles.** *A* and *an* are called **indefinite articles.** *The* is called the **definite article.**

INDEFINITE	We camped near **a** river.
	Kim ate **an** orange.
DEFINITE	We camped near **the** river.
	Kim ate **the** orange.

Forms of Adjectives

Many adjectives have different forms to indicate their degree of comparison. The **positive degree** is the simple form of the adjective. The **comparative degree** compares two persons, places, things, or ideas. The **superlative degree** compares more than two persons, places, things, or ideas.

POSITIVE	COMPARATIVE	SUPERLATIVE
slow	slower	slowest
healthy	healthier	healthiest
strenuous	more strenuous	most strenuous

Comparative adjectives of two or more syllables are usually formed by placing the words *more* or *most* before the positive form.

Exercise 33 Identifying Adjectives and the Nouns They Modify

In the following sentences, identify the adjectives and the nouns they modify. Do not include definite and indefinite articles. On your paper, list the words in two columns, one labeled *adjectives* and the other labeled *nouns they modify.*

SAMPLE Bells are musical instruments that originated in ancient China.

ANSWER	**ADJECTIVES**	**NOUNS THEY MODIFY**
	musical	instruments
	ancient	China

A Short History of Bells

1. Some of the earliest bells had rich ornamentation.
2. Such bells were used originally to provide an atmosphere of mystery to religious ceremonies.
3. It was once thought that ringing a bell would drive away deadly diseases.
4. The Chinese and Japanese decorated temples with bells that made a delicate sound in the slightest breeze.
5. The ancient Goths stirred reluctant soldiers to military order with the ringing of bells.
6. Women in Persia once wore little bells as jewelry.
7. Bells have also been used to warn off a nearby enemy or other danger.
8. The practical Greeks used bells to announce the arrival of fish fresh from the sea.
9. If we heard a bell in a busy supermarket today, we would consider the sound bizarre.
10. In Rome no bells advertised merchandise, but many bells tolled the news when an emperor died.
11. In ancient Greece and Rome, bells were hung on the tomb and funeral carriage of a king.
12. In Burma bells were hung in the pagodas to drive away evil spirits.
13. In Africa healers hung a bell over the doorway of the house of a sick person.
14. The Celts became more famous than the Romans for making melodic chimes.
15. Since the sixth century, Christians have had a great enthusiasm for bells.
16. Bells were once hung in some churches as a protection against violent storms.
17. In Italy special towers, or *campaniles,* were constructed for particularly immense bells.
18. In England a local officer rang a bell to announce a late curfew, a fire, a meeting, or even a certain deadline.
19. A crier in a town would ring a bell to attract a large crowd and then shout the latest news.
20. Today we hear fewer bells because most of them have been replaced by electronic methods of communication.

Proper Adjectives

■ A **proper adjective** is formed from a proper noun and begins with a capital letter.

Duke Ellington was an **African American** composer.
The term ***Victorian*** *era* refers to the years 1837 to 1901.

Proper adjectives are often created by adding the following suffixes: *-an*, *-ian*, *-n*, *-ese*, *-ish*, and *-ic*. In some cases, the noun and adjective forms are the same.

PROPER NOUNS	PROPER ADJECTIVES
Queen Elizabeth I	Elizabethan
Indonesia	Indonesian
Japan	Japanese
Spain	Spanish

Some words that began as proper adjectives have been used for so long that their origins have been forgotten or disregarded. Such words have become **common adjectives** that begin with lowercase letters.

PROPER NOUNS	COMMON ADJECTIVES
Italy	italic
Rome	romantic
Puritan	puritanical
Bohemia	bohemian

Exercise 34 Forming Proper Adjectives from Proper Nouns

Write a proper adjective for each proper noun below. Consult a dictionary if necessary.

1. Asia
2. Sigmund Freud
3. King George
4. Greece
5. Turkey
6. Mars
7. Java
8. Charles Dickens
9. Siberia
10. Brazil
11. China
12. Canada
13. William Shakespeare
14. Malta
15. Ireland
16. Iceland
17. Andrew Jackson
18. Hungary
19. King Edward
20. Europe
21. Britain
22. Boston
23. Nepal
24. Norway
25. Paris

Nouns Used as Adjectives

In some cases, nouns are used as adjectives. A noun used as an adjective answers one of these questions: *What kind? Which one?*

NOUNS	NOUNS AS ADJECTIVES
music	**music** critic (What kind of critic?)
city	**city** bus (What kind of bus?)
history	**history** lesson (Which lesson?)
United States	**United States** flag (Which flag?)

Sometimes possessive nouns are used as adjectives.

Kate's parrot the **river's** source the **story's** end **Don's** restaurant

Exercise 35 Identifying Adjectives and Nouns Used as Adjectives

On your paper, list the adjectives in the following sentences. Do not include definite and indefinite articles. If the adjective is also a noun, write *noun* in parentheses.

SAMPLE In the early 1900s, there were few laws against child labor.
ANSWER early, few, child (noun)

Chicago's "Newsies"

1. In the first part of this century, the newspaper business was thriving in Chicago.
2. The newspapers' success was due largely to a sensational style of journalism.
3. A small army of children sold these papers to commuters in the downtown section of the city.
4. These so-called newsies were not street urchins but ordinary kids who wanted to earn a little money after school.
5. They came from every ethnic group in the city.
6. Before the daily supply of papers arrived, the newsies would often play a baseball game.
7. As soon as rush hour began, they went to work.
8. Industrious little hustlers appeared where carefree children had stood.
9. The eager children stationed themselves along streets with the heaviest pedestrian traffic.
10. Some set up shop outside department stores and subway stations.
11. Those newsies who succeeded had a good business sense and an aggressive sales pitch.
12. On a slow day, some of the newsies made up false news headlines to attract customers.
13. The children lived for the great headlines, the large red type that sold editions.
14. The newsies had to anticipate probable sales before they purchased any newspapers.
15. However, they made more money by begging for tips from big spenders.
16. The excitement of street life provided a break from the stuffy classroom.

17. Social reformers feared that the children's lifestyle would lead them to serious crime later on.
18. Few boys, however, became real criminals in the adult world.
19. These industrious children raised themselves from poverty to prosperity.
20. Most of them ended up as successful business executives because of the work ethic they had developed on Chicago's streets.

Pronouns Used as Adjectives

Some pronouns can also be used as adjectives. **Possessive adjectives** are possessive pronouns that answer the question *which one?*

There are seven possessive pronouns that can also be used as adjectives: *my, your, her, his, its, our,* and *their.*

Woody wrecked **his** car in the crash.
Roller-blading is **our** idea of fun.
The Millers cultivated **their** garden.
Your photo turned out well.

Demonstrative adjectives are pronouns that answer the questions *which one? how many?* and *how much?*

She went to **that** concert. They took **those** classes.

Interrogative adjectives are pronouns that are used to ask questions.

Which concert did she hear?
What grade did he get?
Whose party was best?

Exercise 36 Identifying Adjectives and Pronouns Used as Adjectives

On your paper, list the twenty adjectives that appear in the following passage. Count possessive pronouns as well as regular adjectives in this exercise but do not count the words *a, an,* and *the.*

A Farmer and His Land

[1]There was a bright, full moon in the clear sky, and the sunset was still shining faintly in the west. [2]Dark woods stood all about the old . . . farmhouse, save down the hill, westward, where lay the shadowy fields which John Hilton, and his father before him, had cleared and tilled with much toil—the small fields to which they had given the industry and . . . affection of their honest lives. [3]John Hilton was sitting on the doorstep of his house. [4]As he moved his head in and out of the shadows, . . . one could see his good face, rough and somewhat unkempt, as if he were indeed a creature of the shady woods and brown earth, instead of the noisy town.

From "The Hiltons' Holiday" by Sarah Orne Jewett

Exercise 37 Identifying Different Kinds of Adjectives

On your paper, write the twenty-five adjectives, including articles, that appear in the following paragraph.

The Hawaiian Islands

[1]Hawaii is a chain of 132 islands. [2]These beautiful islands extend 1,523 miles. [3]Major islands include Maui, Oahu, and Hawaii, an island that is famous for active volcanoes. [4]Although there are a number of islands, Hawaiian people live only on major ones. [5]Kahoolawe has no inhabitants. [6]It is used only for naval purposes. [7]Minor islands, some only as big as great rocks, are too small and infertile to support human life. [8]Hawaii's population displays a mixture of origins. [9]Diversity is one of its sources of vitality. [10]Much of the population is of Asian descent.

Exercise 38 Expanding Sentences with Adjectives

Rewrite the following sentences, adding at least two appropriate adjectives to each one. In your fifteen sentences, include at least one comparative or superlative adjective, one noun used as an adjective, and one pronoun used as an adjective.

An Audio Demonstration

1. Music filled the showroom of the electronics store.
2. A salesman showed a speaker system to my two friends and me.
3. Though we liked the size and appearance of the speakers, we were obviously more interested in the sound.
4. The salesman played tapes to demonstrate the speakers' power, clarity, and versatility.
5. First, my friends and I listened to a song by Loretta Lynn.
6. Seconds later, we heard the notes of a Mozart piano concerto.
7. When the piano, bass, and drums of an Aretha Franklin song kicked in, we noticed a number of feet beginning to tap.
8. Before long, bodies began to sway, and customers started to mouth the words of the song.
9. I almost expected the singer to appear out of nowhere.
10. My friends and I are fans of soul music from the 1960s and 1970s—especially the music of Aretha Franklin.
11. She has a way of making music that touches the hearts and souls of all people.
12. As much as I loved the sound that came through those speakers, I knew that I would never own them, for their price was astronomical.
13. My speakers at home have problems that I guess I will have to endure a bit longer.
14. I wonder whether that store will ever have a sale on speakers.
15. I'll look for advertisements in the weeks ahead.

Exercise 39 Creating Sentences with Adjectives

Write five sentences about a favorite food. Use at least two descriptive adjectives in each sentence.

10.5 Adverbs

■ An **adverb** is a word that modifies a verb, an adjective, or another adverb by making its meaning more specific.

Adverbs that Modify Verbs

Adverbs add meaning to verbs and verb phrases by answering the questions *when? where? how?* and *to what degree?*

ADVERBS THAT MODIFY VERBS

QUESTION	VERB	ADVERB
When?	fly	fly **now**
	had arrived	had arrived **early**
Where?	jump	jump **aside**
	was charging	was charging **forward**
How?	argued	argued **effectively**
	will speak	will speak **clearly**
To what degree?	finish	finish **completely**
	would have known	**hardly** would have known

When modifying a verb, an adverb may appear in various positions in relation to the verb.

" Nothing can stop me now,"

Tom said tirelessly.

Eventually the train will arrive at the station.

The train will **eventually** arrive at the station.

The train will arrive at the station **eventually.**

Negative words also function as adverbs modifying verbs.

Adverbs include the word *not* and the contraction *-n't.* Other negative words can also function as adverbs of time, place, and degree.

The cow is **not** in the barn.
The cow is **nowhere** in sight.
I **never** saw a purple cow.
The cow **hardly** chews her cud.

Exercise 40 Identifying Different Kinds of Adverbs

On your paper, write each of the twenty adverbs in the paragraph below. Then write the verb that each adverb modifies.

SAMPLE Hercules performed difficult tasks easily because of his strength.
ANSWER easily—performed

The Labors of Hercules

[1]People usually equate the word *Hercules* with physical strength, and today I learned the Greek myth behind the name. [2]As a child, Hercules earnestly studied the sports of chariot racing, wrestling, and archery. [3]He grew steadily in physical strength but never improved his self-control. [4]Once he attacked his music teacher in a fit of rage; for this misdeed he was sent off to the countryside by the king of Thebes. [5]There he lived in the fresh air and increased his strength daily. [6]As an adult, he still possessed a hot temper and a violent streak. [7]Then the Greek gods sternly ordered him to perform twelve difficult tasks that had not been completed by anyone else. [8]He slew a savage lion and brought back its skin as his initial task. [9]Next he somehow found the land of the Amazons and took away the precious belt of Hippolyta, the queen of the Amazons. [10]Hercules finally tamed his unruly temper, and afterward he became the national hero of Greece. [11]We often refer to difficult tasks as "the labors of Hercules."

Exercise 41 Positioning Adverbs That Modify Verbs

Rewrite each of the following sentences, adding the verb-modifying adverb that appears in parentheses. Then write each sentence again, this time placing the same adverb in a different position.

SAMPLE At the end of the steep trail, we beheld the ruins of Machu Picchu. (finally)
ANSWER **a.** At the end of the steep trail, we finally beheld the ruins of Machu Picchu.
b. Finally, at the end of the steep trail, we beheld the ruins of Machu Picchu.

The Lost City of the Inca

1. The ancient Inca city of Machu Picchu was discovered by an American archeologist in 1911. (surprisingly)
2. Hiram Bingham had searched for the city before finding it. (tirelessly)
3. News of the fabulous discovery began to spread. (soon)
4. Archaeologists had found such a splendid site before. (seldom)
5. The Inca held on to Machu Picchu until the sixteenth century. (tenaciously)
6. The Spanish conquistador Francisco Pizarro conquered the Inca Empire in 1533. (ruthlessly)
7. The sacred city of Machu Picchu was abandoned. (then)
8. It has survived earthquakes and erosion. (fortunately)
9. The world has seen finer stonework than that of Machu Picchu. (never)

Adverbs That Modify Adjectives

Adverbs can give additional meaning to adjectives. An adverb that modifies an adjective answers the question *to what degree?*

QUESTION	ADJECTIVE	ADVERB
To what degree?	beautiful	**very** beautiful
	shy	**rather** shy
	optimistic	**unusually** optimistic
	clean	**thoroughly** clean

Adverbs that modify adjectives generally appear directly before the word they modify.

The train is **extremely** late.

June felt **rather** weak.

Will pitches **incredibly** fast.

My **very** best friend moved.

Exercise 42 Identifying Adverbs That Modify Adjectives

On your paper, list the adverb in each sentence that modifies an adjective. Then write the adjective the adverb modifies.

Hot-Air Ballooning

1. Hot-air ballooning is a somewhat recent sport craze in the United States.
2. The first flight in history was accomplished by the truly talented Montgolfier brothers at Annonay, France, in 1783.
3. It must have seemed a particularly risky undertaking because this was the first time people had defied gravity.
4. Within a few years, balloonists substituted hydrogen gas for hot air because hydrogen was greatly superior in buoyancy.
5. The world's first air force was an understandably small balloon corps established by the French in 1794.
6. In 1793 Jean Pierre Blanchard made the very first balloon flight in America.
7. As late as the 1930s, balloon flights and races were extremely popular events.
8. In the 1960s, ballooning enjoyed a quite amazing revival.
9. The new generation of enthusiasts returned to hot air because they determined that it was much safer than hydrogen.
10. To the spectator, balloons look simply spectacular as they float silently over a large city.

Adverbs That Modify Adverbs

Sometimes adverbs are used to give extra meaning to other adverbs. An adverb that modifies an adverb answers the question *to what degree?*

QUESTION	ADVERB	ADVERB
To what degree?	walked **slowly**	walked **quite** slowly
	always wins	**almost** always wins
	call **often**	call **too** often

An adverb that modifies another adverb appears directly before the modified word.

They were **only** partially convinced.
The play ended **somewhat** abruptly.
Please speak **more** slowly.
I know him **very** well.

Exercise 43 Identifying Adverbs That Modify Other Adverbs

On your paper, list the adverb in each sentence that modifies another adverb. Then write the adverb that is being modified.

The Bermuda Triangle

1. The tabloid press quite frequently writes about bizarre events in an area known as the Bermuda Triangle.
2. Their stories depict most vividly a long list of strange occurrences that presumably have taken place there.
3. Journalists ask their readers to imagine a line that runs somewhat approximately from Melbourne, Florida, to Bermuda, to Puerto Rico, and back to Florida.
4. They claim that within this triangle a large number of ships and airplanes have too often disappeared under mysterious circumstances.
5. It is known that storms move into this area very quickly.
6. Violent downward air currents occur there more frequently than in other places.
7. Scientists, however, are almost unanimously dubious about such tales.
8. They reiterate rather patiently that no such peculiarities exist.
9. They cannot understand why people nearly always accept hearsay over scientific evidence.
10. Nevertheless, readers of these tales remain convinced that we have just barely begun to understand the menace of the Bermuda Triangle.

Forms of Adverbs

Like adjectives, some adverbs have different forms to indicate degree of comparison. The comparative form of an adverb compares two actions. The superlative form of an adverb compares more than two actions.

For adverbs of only one syllable, add *-er* to make the comparative form and *-est* to make the superlative form.

POSITIVE	COMPARATIVE	SUPERLATIVE
plays **hard**	plays **harder**	plays **hardest**
climbed **high**	climbed **higher**	climbed **highest**

When an adverb ends in *-ly,* use the word *more* to form the comparative and *most* to form the superlative.

POSITIVE	COMPARATIVE	SUPERLATIVE
walks **slowly**	walks **more slowly**	walks **most slowly**
smiles **easily**	smiles **more easily**	smiles **most easily**

Some adverbs do not form the comparative and superlative in the regular manner.

POSITIVE	COMPARATIVE	SUPERLATIVE
skates **well**	skates **better**	skates **best**
dances **badly**	dances **worse**	dances **worst**
knows **little**	knows **less**	knows **least**
goes **far**	goes **farther**	goes **farthest**

Parts of Speech

Exercise 44 Using Comparative and Superlative Forms of Adverbs

On your paper, write the comparative and superlative form of each adverb below. Then write a sentence using each of those forms.

SAMPLE hard
ANSWER harder, hardest
He threw the ball harder than Peter, but I threw it hardest of all.

1. thoroughly
2. eagerly
3. low
4. well
5. near
6. badly
7. close
8. angrily
9. quickly
10. curiously

Distinguishing Between Adverbs and Adjectives

Some words can be either adverbs or adjectives, depending on how they are used in a sentence. To distinguish between these two parts of speech, remember that an adjective modifies a noun or pronoun, and an adverb modifies a verb, an adjective, or another adverb.

I arrived **late.** (adverb)
The bus was **late.** (adjective)

She ate **early.** (adverb)
She had an **early** date. (adjective)

You can sometimes distinguish an adverb from an adjective by remembering that many adverbs are formed by adding *-ly* to an adjective.

a **rare** book
ADJ. NOUN

a **great** treat
ADJ. NOUN

rarely find
ADV. VERB

greatly appreciate
ADV. VERB

Not all words that end in *-ly* are adverbs. Some are adjectives in their own right (*lonely, deadly*), and some are adjectives formed by adding *-ly* to the noun.

NOUN	ADJECTIVE ENDING IN *-LY*
brother	**brotherly** love
state	a **stately** home

Parts of Speech

Exercise 45 Distinguishing Between Adverbs and Adjectives

On your paper, identify each of the italicized words as an *adverb* or an *adjective.*

Nostalgia

1. My mother often speaks *nostalgically* about her childhood.
2. She and her two sisters enjoyed a *leisurely* existence in a small town.
3. Mother says her town was a *neighborly* place in which to live.
4. Most people she knew cared *little* for expensive cars and exotic vacations.
5. As she was the youngest, Mother was always getting *sisterly* advice from the other two.
6. They lived *close* to a park where the girls loved to skip rope and play jacks.
7. They felt *close* to each other because they got along so well.
8. Every night, the three young girls went to bed very *early.*
9. Their father told them, "The *early* bird catches the worm."
10. Now Mother's life is more *worldly,* but she misses those simpler times.

Exercise 46 Identifying Different Kinds of Adverbs

On your paper, write each of the twenty adverbs that appear in the following paragraph. Then write the word or words that each adverb modifies.

A Great African American Dancer

[1]While she was still a child, Pearl Primus came to the United States from Trinidad. [2]Later she attended college in New York and apparently planned to be a doctor. [3]She never expected to be a dancer. [4]Her obvious talent very quickly distinguished her. [5]Soon she won a scholarship and was studying dance exclusively. [6]Subsequently, she worked with Martha Graham, Doris Humphrey, and other masters of modern dance. [7]When she performed professionally, she received rave reviews everywhere for her beautiful dancing. [8]Critics justifiably called her the finest new dancer of 1943. [9]Primus was greatly interested in African dance and is widely credited with the introduction of African motifs into American dance. [10]Her quite frequent trips to the Caribbean and Africa helped her substantially, and she translated African dances meaningfully for all audiences. [11]At the age of 60 Primus had hardly slowed her pace. [12]She creatively developed programs for the handicapped and worked persistently on her doctoral degree. [13]In 1978 she finally received it.

Exercise 47 Completing Sentences with Adverbs

A Tom Swifty is a sentence in which an adverb comments in a humorous way on an action or object mentioned in a quotation. Note the relationship between each adverb and quotation in the following examples:

"I cleaned my room," Leroy said **tidily.**
"This picture has no color," complained Andrea **drably.**

Tom Swifties

Write the Tom Swifties in items 1–5 on your paper, completing each with an adverb that comments on the quotation. Then write five Tom Swifties of your own, using the adverbs provided in items 6–10. Consult a dictionary if necessary.

1. "Don't burn yourself!" Min warned ______.
2. "Nice job of sanding," said the carpenter ______.
3. "These flowers were just picked," the florist said ______.
4. "Is the pond frozen yet?" asked Luis ______.
5. "That lemon made my mouth pucker!" Robin exclaimed ______.
6. dully
7. crisply
8. softly
9. blandly
10. coolly

10.6 Prepositions

■ A **preposition** is a word that shows the relationship of a noun or pronoun to some other word in a sentence.

The garage is **behind** the house. [*Behind* shows the spatial relationship between the house and the garage.]

The engine purred **after** the adjustment. [*After* tells the time relationship between the purring and the adjustment.]

It started **with** ease. [*With* relates the verb *started* to the noun *ease.*]

Commonly Used Prepositions				
aboard	behind	except	opposite	under
about	below	excepting	out	underneath
above	beneath	for	outside	until
across	beside	from	over	unto
after	besides	in	past	up
against	between	inside	pending	upon
along	beyond	into	regarding	with
amid	but*	like	respecting	within
among	by	near	since	without
around	concerning	of	through	
as	despite	off	throughout	
at	down	on	to	
before	during	onto	toward	

*meaning "except"

■ A **compound preposition** is a preposition that is made up of more than one word.

Compound Prepositions		
according to	because of	next to
ahead of	by means of	on account of
along with	in addition to	on top of
apart from	in front of	out of
aside from	in spite of	owing to
as to	instead of	

Phrases that begin with a preposition usually end with a noun or pronoun, called the **object of the preposition.**

He gave me a book **of poetry.**
Mei Ying sat **next to me.**
I was talking **with Mei Ying.**

Exercise 48 Identifying Prepositions

On your paper, list the prepositions that appear in each of the following sentences. Remember that some prepositions are made up of more than one word. (The numeral in parentheses at the end of each item indicates the number of prepositions in that sentence.)

A Special-Effects Pioneer

1. Willis O'Brien, a creator of special effects for the early film industry, pioneered the use of rubber and clay models in movies. (4)
2. Shooting the film frame by frame and changing the position of the model slightly between shots, he created illusionary movement. (3)
3. By means of this method, O'Brien shot an experimental film with a clay dinosaur that "roamed" through a miniature set. (3)
4. Since the dinosaur's movements looked too choppy in this first attempt, O'Brien shot a second version, using dinosaurs made from rubber and metal instead of clay and wood. (3)
5. Six years after this film, which was distributed throughout the United States, O'Brien worked on a full-length movie concerning dinosaurs in a South American jungle. (5)
6. During one scene, a brontosaurus is brought across the ocean to London, where it escapes and runs around the city. (4)
7. In addition to his dinosaur models, O'Brien used scenery painted onto glass panes that he positioned in front of the action. (3)
8. Because of O'Brien's skill, models and sets were transformed into believable monsters and jungles on the movie screen. (3)
9. Years later, another movie showed a giant gorilla on top of the Empire State Building, high above the frightened crowds. (2)
10. This giant gorilla, which we now know as King Kong, was created by O'Brien. (2)

Exercise 49 Using Prepositional Phrases

Use each of the following prepositional phrases in an original sentence. Then combine your sentences into a coherent paragraph or two. You may combine your sentences in any order.

1. according to his directions
2. underneath the dining-room table
3. near the back door
4. on top of the map
5. outside the house
6. between you and me
7. beyond belief
8. throughout the evening
9. on the highway outside of town
10. against my better judgment

Some words may be used as either prepositions or adverbs. A word is used as a preposition if it has a noun or pronoun as its object. A word is used as an adverb if it does not have an object.

WORD USED AS PREPOSITION	WORD USED AS ADVERB
He left his friends **behind** the stadium.	He left his friends **behind.**
I finally took my boots **off** the step.	I finally took my boots **off.**
The bike is **outside** the garage.	The bike is **outside.**

Exercise 50 Completing Sentences with Prepositions and Adverbs

On your paper, complete each sentence by writing any preposition or adverb that makes sense. Then write whether you used the word as a *preposition* or an *adverb.* Use the charts on page 473 to help you choose appropriate words.

SAMPLE I lost my balance and fell _____.
ANSWER over—adverb

White-Water Rafting

1. Our first exposure to white-water rafting was ______ the Nantahala River.
2. The Nantahala is a swift-flowing river ______ Great Smoky Mountains National Park.
3. Friends had told us that nothing else compares to the thrill ______ white-water rafting.
4. Our guide warned us not to leave our life jackets ______.
5. Our equipment was a large rubber raft ______ six long oars.
6. We learned how to direct our raft to the right or left, and even how to turn it completely ______.
7. As we started, we felt very chilly ______ the bright sun.
8. At first we were nervous because we were afraid of tipping the raft ______.
9. Soon we relaxed and began to joke with the people in the raft ______ us.
10. ______ our successful experience this time, we plan to ride an even wilder river in the future.

Exercise 51 Creating Sentences with Prepositions

Choose five prepositions from the lists on page 473. Use each one in a sentence. Add adjectives and adverbs wherever necessary.

10.7 Conjunctions

■ A **conjunction** is a word that joins single words or groups of words.

Coordinating Conjunctions

■ A **coordinating conjunction** joins words or groups of words that have equal grammatical weight in a sentence.

Coordinating Conjunctions						
and	but	or	nor	for	yet	so

She designs **and** builds.
He writes in French **but** not in English.
Practice writing, **or** you will never improve.
She had no homework, **nor** did she have basketball practice.

Exercise 52 Identifying Coordinating Conjunctions

On your paper, write the coordinating conjunction(s) that appear in each of the following sentences.

Baseball, an Integrated Sport

[1]Many people know something about the history of baseball in our country, but the story of African Americans and baseball is often neglected. [2]The history of African Americans and baseball began sometime during the Civil War, for it was then that black soldiers learned to play the game. [3]In 1885 a group of waiters from the Argyle Hotel in Babylon, New York, met and organized a paid baseball team. [4]All of the team's players were African American, yet they called themselves the Cuban Giants. [5]Their choice, they thought, was to pretend that they were Hispanic or face discrimination. [6]By the turn of the century, African Americans were playing on several college teams in the northern and the western sections of the country. [7]The 1920s was an important era for minorities and baseball, for several African American teams were organized during that decade. [8]Among them were the Homestead Grays, the American Giants, the Kansas City Monarchs, and the St. Louis Stars. [9]The great Jackie Robinson could have chosen to play on an African American team, but in 1947 he joined the Brooklyn Dodgers, becoming the first African American to play in the major leagues in the twentieth century. [10]Prejudice didn't deter African American baseball heroes such as Jackie Robinson, nor were they discouraged by the low pay that they received during those early years.

Correlative Conjunctions

■ **Correlative conjunctions** work in pairs to join words and groups of words of equal weight in a sentence.

Correlative Conjunctions		
both . . . and	just as . . . so	not only . . . but (also)
either . . . or	neither . . . nor	whether . . . or

The relationship between words or groups of words is emphasized by using correlative conjunctions rather than coordinating conjunctions.

COORDINATING CONJUNCTIONS	CORRELATIVE CONJUNCTIONS
You **and** I must go.	**Both** you **and** I must go.
You **or** I must go.	**Either** you **or** I must go.
	Neither you **nor** I must go.
We saw Tokyo **and** Kyoto.	We saw **not only** Tokyo **but also** Kyoto.

Exercise 53 Identifying Correlative Conjunctions

On your paper, write both parts of the correlative conjunctions that appear in the following sentences.

Special-issue Stamps

[1]A great many countries issue special stamps either to honor a famous person or to commemorate an important event. [2]Some countries print specially priced stamps in order both to celebrate an event and to generate extra funds. [3]Either original art or reproductions of famous paintings may decorate the special stamps. [4]A special 1893 stamp was not only a tribute to the discovery of America but also the first commemorative stamp issued by the United States. [5]Other stamps have honored both famous leaders and important occasions. [6]Neither the Apollo space program nor the nation's bicentennial passed without a special stamp. [7]During the International Year of the Child, another significant event, children's art appeared on both postage stamps and holiday seals. [8]Neither the American Lung Association, which used children's art on its holiday seals, nor the design sponsors chose the themes for the seals. [9]Each school chosen to take part decided on its own whether to tell its students exactly what to draw or simply to suggest a holiday theme. [10]Just as these holiday seals celebrated children's art, so the postage stamps from many other countries continue to do so.

Subordinating Conjunctions

■ A **subordinating conjunction** joins two clauses, or ideas, in such a way as to make one grammatically dependent upon the other.

The idea, or clause, introduced by a subordinating conjunction is considered subordinate, or dependent, because it cannot stand alone as a complete sentence.

We cheered the tall ships **because** they were so glorious.
We cheered the tall ships **when** they arrived.
Whenever the ships sail again, we will want to see them.
We will want to see them **if** they sail again.

Common Subordinating Conjunctions			
after	as though	provided (that)	until
although	because	since	when
as	before	so long as	whenever
as far as	considering (that)	so that	where
as if	if	than	whereas
as long as	inasmuch as	though	wherever
as soon as	in order that	unless	while

Parts of Speech

Exercise 54 Identifying Subordinating Conjunctions

Write the subordinating conjunction that appears in each sentence below. Remember that some subordinating conjunctions are made up of more than one word.

Harold Krents, a Success Story

1. Considering that Harold Krents was totally blind by his eighth birthday, his achievements are extraordinary.
2. Life is not easy when one's vision is impaired.
3. When he was in high school, Krents's classmates elected him president of his school.
4. Because Krents was brilliant, he was accepted by Harvard.
5. Before he went to college, Krents spent the summer as an arts counselor at camp.
6. Whereas others had difficulty finding their way around the tents in the dark, Krents moved about easily and kept the campers quiet after taps.
7. As soon as he had graduated *cum laude* from Harvard University, Krents was accepted at Harvard Law School.
8. Krents met his future wife while she was reading for visually challenged law students.
9. Krents was very surprised when his draft board mistakenly classified him 1-A.
10. After he heard Krents's story, Leonard Gershe wrote the play *Butterflies Are Free.*

Conjunctive Adverbs

■ A **conjunctive adverb** is used to clarify the relationship between clauses of equal weight in a sentence.

Conjunctive adverbs tend to be stronger and more precise than coordinating conjunctions.

COORDINATING CONJUNCTION	The ships sailed away, **but** they left us with happy memories.
CONJUNCTIVE ADVERB	The ships sailed away; **nevertheless,** they left us with happy memories.

Conjunctive adverbs have several uses:

TO REPLACE *AND*	also, besides, furthermore, moreover
TO REPLACE *BUT*	however, nevertheless, still
TO STATE A RESULT	consequently, therefore, so, thus
TO STATE EQUALITY	equally, likewise, similarly

Exercise 55 Completing Sentences with Conjunctive Adverbs

On your paper, write each of the following sentences, replacing the blank with an appropriate conjunctive adverb that makes the sentence meaningful. In most cases, there is more than one correct answer.

The Early Inuit

1. Some people think that the Inuit are native to Alaska; ______, they actually came from Siberia about five thousand years ago.
2. Some people think the Inuit crossed from Siberia to Alaska by sea; ______, others say that they walked over a land bridge.
3. The early Inuit hunted caribou; ______, they moved often to follow the herds.
4. They lived in one of the coldest, darkest, and most desolate regions of the world; ______, their life was harsh.
5. The Inuit invented many words to describe minute changes in the weather; ______, they had a rich vocabulary of hunting terms.
6. Some Inuit carvings may have magical or religious associations; ______, archaeologists are not certain of this.
7. It is hard to imagine the Inuit without sled dogs; ______, the Inuit learned to train dogs only about nine hundred years ago.
8. The Inuit thought that nothing should be wasted; ______, they made dozens of useful objects from the animals they killed.
9. Traditional Inuit clothing, made from caribou hides and sealskins, is light and warm; ______, it is waterproof.
10. Many people refer to these people as *Eskimos;* ______, the group itself uses the term *Inuit.*

Exercise 56 Identifying Different Kinds of Conjunctions

On your paper, write the conjunction in each of the following sentences. Label each conjunction as *coordinating, correlative,* or *subordinating.* Some sentences contain more than one conjunction.

The Constellations

1. Because the earth revolves around the sun, different constellations can be seen at different times of the year.
2. While it can be very helpful in locating constellations, you must learn how to use a star map effectively.
3. Astronomers use both binoculars and telescopes to observe the stars.
4. When you look at a constellation, you may see a planet wandering through it.
5. Although there are eighty-eight constellations, only about two dozen constellations are visible at any time.
6. Since the earth revolves around the sun, some constellations can be seen only during certain seasons.
7. An observer at the North or South Pole can see only one hemisphere of stars.
8. Greeks and Romans named stars after animals and mythological characters.
9. Both Leo and Taurus are constellations named for animals.
10. Not only Orion but also Perseus is a constellation named for a Greek hero.
11. Many people think the Big Dipper is a constellation, but it is actually part of the large constellation called the Great Bear.
12. Although the Little Dipper is small, it contains the most important star in our skies, the North Star.
13. Just as you can use the Big Dipper to find the North Star, so you can use the Big Dipper to find Regulus, the brightest star in the constellation Leo.
14. As soon as you find the Great Square of Pegasus, find Andromeda and Cassiopeia.
15. You may be able to find the Andromeda Nebula, the most distant object visible to the unaided eye, if the night is clear.
16. The constellation Cassiopeia is thought to represent either the mythological queen Cassiopeia or her throne.
17. In the constellation Taurus the Bull, the Pleiades look like a tiny cloud, yet they are actually a group of stars.
18. After you find the Pleiades, look for the star Aldebaran in the bull's head.
19. Night and day are the same length when the sun reaches the bottom of the Pisces constellation.
20. This happens about March 21 and marks the beginning of spring.
21. If you find three bright stars in a straight line, you are looking at Orion.
22. After you spot the belt of three stars, look below it to find the Orion Nebula.
23. Orion has not only the reddish star Betelgeuse but also the bluish white star Rigel.
24. Castor and Pollux are stars in the constellation Gemini.
25. Because Gemini is part of the zodiac, planets wander into the constellation and often put on an impressive show.

Exercise 57 Completing Sentences with Different Kinds of Conjunctions

On your paper, replace each blank with the kind of conjunction stated in parentheses at the end of each sentence.

SAMPLE The country drained by the Flathead River is ______ a valuable ecological area ______ an important recreation area. (correlative conjunction)

ANSWER The country drained by the Flathead River is both a valuable ecological area and an important recreation area.

The Flathead River

1. The Flathead River lies mostly in the United States; ______, its headwaters are in Canada. (conjunctive adverb)
2. The lands drained by the Flathead River are forest, ______ they are populated by about two-thirds of the remaining grizzly bears. (coordinating conjunction)
3. ______ the threatened grizzly bear ______ the Rocky Mountain wolf inhabit the Flathead wilderness. (correlative conjunction)
4. The north fork of the Flathead River is eventually joined by ______ the middle fork ______ the south fork. (correlative conjunction)
5. ______ you visit the North Fork valley, you may meet Mary McFarland, a veterinarian. (subordinating conjunction)
6. From Mary McFarland's window, you can see mountains ______ you turn. (subordinating conjunction)
7. ______ a Dolly Varden trout ______ a rare cutthroat trout is a likely catch along the Flathead River. (correlative conjunction)
8. Otters play along the Flathead River, ______ bald eagles soar overhead. (subordinating conjunction)
9. ______ it leaves the wild country, the Flathead River meanders through rich farmlands into Flathead Lake, west of the Missouri. (subordinating conjunction)
10. ______ the Flathead emerges from the lake, it turns to join the Clark Fork River. (subordinating conjunction)

Exercise 58 Creating Sentences with Different Kinds of Conjunctions

Think of a favorite room that you have known or read about, in which there are many interesting articles and pieces of furniture. Write several sentences about that room, using as many conjunctions as possible.

10.8 Interjections

■ An **interjection** is a word or phrase that expresses emotion or exclamation.

An interjection has no grammatical connection to the other words in the sentence and is set off from the other words by an exclamation point, a question mark, or a comma.

Different emotions are expressed by different interjections.

surprise	**Oh,** didn't you know?
delight	**Ah,** your father knows the recipe.
confusion	**What?** I didn't know that.
pain	**Ouch!** That hurts.
joy	**Wow!** This is great.

Interjections are used mostly in speech. They should be used sparingly in writing.

Exercise 59 Using Interjections

On your paper, fill each blank in the following items with an appropriate interjection from the following list:

wow	hey	gee whiz	help	hi
oh my	golly	good luck	hush	whew

1. ______, the movie is about to begin.
2. ______! The sink is overflowing.
3. ______! We hope to see you at the finish line.
4. ______, we just moved into the house next door.
5. ______! How did you manage to catch that pass?
6. ______! I'm glad that test is over.
7. ______! What an incredible view there is from here!
8. ______, I wish you'd told me that sooner.
9. ______! Where do you think you're going with my bicycle?
10. ______, what a gorgeous picture that would make!

Exercise 60 Identifying Parts of Speech

On your paper, write the part of speech of the italicized word in each of the following sentences.

Seashells

1. Anyone out for a stroll on a beach may find *wonderful* shells.
2. For even better discoveries, *look* in tidal pools.
3. Seashells are often more *numerous* after a storm.
4. Some seashells are *collectors'* items.
5. Such items are *usually* large, beautiful, and not well known.
6. Seashells, unlike stamps and coins, rarely increase *in* value.
7. *These* are the leading families of collectibles: cones, cowries, volutes, murexes, slit shells, and scallops.
8. Prehistoric people *often* used large univalve shells as pots or ladles.
9. Conch shells were sounded like trumpets, *not only* to call buffalos or warriors *but also* to frighten evil spirits or to accompany a funeral.
10. *Which* Central American people "milked" a particular live seashell for its purple dye?
11. In many ancient cultures cowrie shells were used as money *because* of their small size, beautiful shape, and luster.
12. The Chinese used cowries as *their* money from about 2000 B.C. to 600 B.C.
13. *Ah,* how beautiful are some of the seashells depicted in art!
14. Native Americans made wampum belts from shells of the quahog clam, *and* they used the belts as money or to record important events.
15. Pen shells have a tuft of silky threads with which they anchor *themselves* to the bottom of the sea.
16. Some historians think that Jason's Golden Fleece was material woven from *the* pen shells' silky threads.
17. Shells, especially scallop shells, are often used in the decorative arts; *moreover,* the theme is repeated in architecture.
18. Painted during the *Renaissance,* one of Sandro Botticelli's greatest works depicts Venus being gently blown to shore on the lower half of a fluted shell.
19. *Anyone* can see this painting at the Uffizi Gallery in Florence, Italy.
20. Shells truly *are* one of nature's wonders.

Exercise 61 Using Parts of Speech

On your paper, write a paragraph about a collection or hobby of your choice. Describe the hobby, using at least one example of each of the eight parts of speech. Use as many types of the parts of speech as possible—for example, proper and abstract nouns, subordinating conjunctions, and conjunctive adverbs.

Grammar Review

Parts of Speech

The Sound of Waves, by the prolific Japanese writer Yukio Mishima, tells the story of the love between a young boy and girl who live in a fishing village in Japan. World War II has just ended, and the villagers are slowly rebuilding their lives. This scene describes how the women of the island dive for abalone. The passage has been annotated to show the parts of speech covered in this unit.

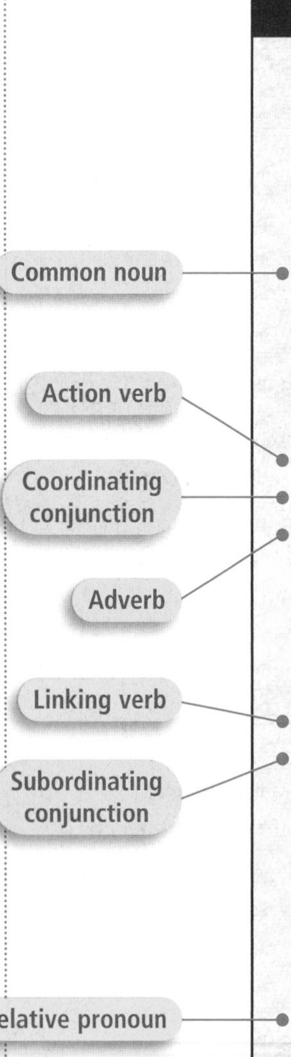

Literature Model

from The Sound of Waves

by Yukio Mishima

translated from the Japanese by Meredith Weatherby

The young girls of the island faced the arrival of the diving season with precisely the same heart-strangling feeling city youths have when confronted by a final school-term examinations. Their games of scrambling for pebbles on the bottom of the sea close to the beach, begun during the early years of grade school, first introduced them to the art of diving, and they naturally became more skillful as their spirit of rivalry increased. But when they finally began diving for a living and their carefree games turned into real work, without exception the young girls became frightened, and the arrival of spring meant only that the dreaded summer was approaching.

There was the cold, the strangling feeling of running out of breath, the inexpressible agony when water forced its way under the water-goggles, the panic and sudden fear of collapsing that invaded the entire body just when an abalone was almost at the fingertips. There were also all kinds of accidents; and the wounds inflicted on the tips of the toes when kicking off against the sea's bottom, with its carpet of sharp-edged shells, to rise to the surface; and the leaden languor that possessed the body after it had been forced to dive almost beyond endurance. . . . All these things had become sharper and sharper in the remembering; the terror had become all the more intense in the repeating. And often sudden nightmares would awaken the girls from sleep so deep as seemingly to leave no room for dreams to creep in. Then, in the dead of night, in the darkness surrounding their peaceful, dangerless beds, they would peer at the flood of sweat clenched within their fists.

It was different with the older divers, with those who had husbands. Coming out of the water from diving, they would sing and laugh and talk in loud voices. It seemed as though work and play had become united in a single whole for them. Watching them enviously, the young girls would tell themselves that they could never become like that, and yet as the years passed they would be surprised to discover that, without their quite realizing it, they themselves had reached the point where they too could be counted among those lighthearted, veteran divers.

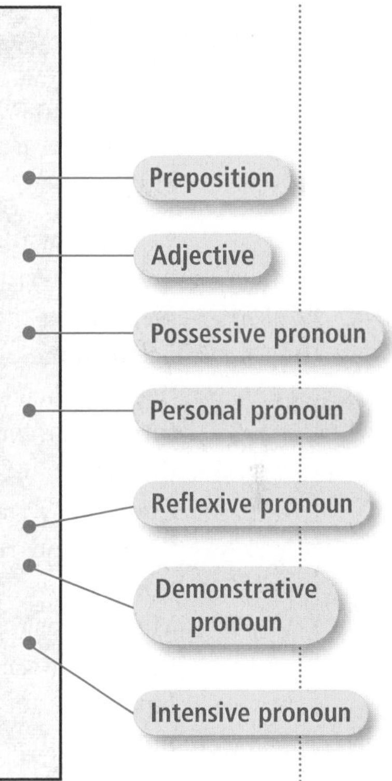

Review: Exercise 1 Identifying Nouns

The following sentences elaborate on ideas or images suggested by the passage from *The Sound of Waves.* On your paper, identify each noun and write in parentheses *common, proper,* or *collective,* depending upon how it is used in the sentence.

1. On one side of the country lies the Pacific Ocean.
2. On the other side is the Sea of Japan.
3. Many islanders depend upon the ocean for jobs.
4. On Song Island the women dive for abalone.
5. The young girls play games at the beach.
6. Crowds scramble for stones at the bottom of the ocean.
7. Sometimes teams compete for prizes.
8. The competition often improves the girls' diving skills.
9. Later the lighthearted contests become work.
10. Do the young women still enjoy their dives?
11. The search for a colony of abalone is no longer a game.
12. Suddenly the new crew of divers fears the cold waters of the Pacific Ocean.
13. Cuts from the sharp edges of the shells are very painful.
14. The young workers also fear the feeling of exhaustion after a dive.
15. In spring the girls dread the start of the new diving season.

Review: Exercise 2 **Identifying Pronouns**

The paragraph below describes the Japanese literary tradition from which Yukio Mishima emerged. On your paper, list the twenty-five pronouns used in the paragraph.

[1]The Japanese literary tradition out of which Mishima emerged is itself quite interesting. [2]It reflects many of the characteristics of the Japanese people, such as their love of tradition and sensitivity to nature. [3]These elements occur in the oldest existing manuscripts, which date to the eighth century. [4]During the Heian period (794–1185), most of the people who wrote literature were members of the nobility. [5]Of these, the greatest were women, and the greatest of all was Murasaki Shikibu. [6]In her masterpiece, *The Tale of Genji,* she writes about herself and the court life of which she was a part. [7]Drama and poetry have also played important roles in this literary tradition. [8]The verse form that is known as *haiku* was developed in the 1600s by Matsuo Bashō, who established its strict rules. [9]Whoever reads the best of these is entranced by their ability to stimulate the imagination. [10]In modern Japan, Mishima and others like him have blended their own literary tradition with that of Western culture.

Review: Exercise 3 **Using Pronouns Effectively**

The paragraph below is based on passages from *The Sound of Waves* that are not reprinted in this textbook. On your paper, rewrite each sentence in the paragraph, substituting pronouns for nouns when a pronoun would make good sense. Do not substitute a pronoun for a noun if the pronoun makes the sentence unclear.

[1]As the day drew to a close, the young women of Song Island gathered at the harbor, where the young women often helped the returning fishers. [2]The fishers had been out in the fishers' boats all day, hoping to fill the fishers' boats with a good catch. [3]The men still had to transfer the men's fish to the boat owned by the Fishers' Cooperative. [4]Then the men had to pull the men's heavy boats up onto the beach, where the boats were kept on wooden frames. [5]The frames were called abacuses because of the frames' shape. [6]The girls dragged the frames down to the shoreline, and the men slipped the frames under the backs of the men's boats. [7]When the boats were safe for the night, the men and women could go home for the men's and the women's evening meal. [8]Later the men would visit the public baths because the men did not have baths in the men's homes. [9]Once a week, the unmarried young men attended a meeting of the Young Men's Association. [10]There the young men argued politics and discussed various projects that the young men thought would be good for civic improvement.

Review: Exercise 4 Identifying Verbs and Verb Phrases

The following sentences are adapted from the literary passage. Write on your paper any simple verbs and any verb phrases that appear in the sentences, and label them accordingly.

SAMPLE By early morning, the women and girls had assembled on the beach.
ANSWER had assembled—verb phrase

1. The older women were laughing about the events of the previous evening.
2. The young girls wore more solemn expressions.
3. Some of them might have been remembering their nightmares.
4. Others were probably recalling the carefree dives of earlier years.
5. The women did not waste a moment.
6. They quickly scrambled onto the boats and sailed offshore.
7. Before long the splash of divers in the water could be heard.
8. Then each diver was alone with her thoughts.
9. At noon they would meet again on the beach and eat lunch.
10. After lunch they would return to their daily search for abalone.

Review: Exercise 5 Identifying Transitive and Intransitive Verbs

The following sentences contain verbs that appear in the passage from *The Sound of Waves.* For each item, write *transitive* or *intransitive* on your paper, depending upon the way the italicized verb is used in the sentence.

SAMPLE The divers *faced* a challenge of enormous proportions.
ANSWER transitive

1. They *confronted* the difficulty of diving in heavy seas.
2. More experienced divers *introduced* the younger ones to advanced safety precautions.
3. The younger women's excitement *increased* in anticipation of a bold adventure.
4. Each diver *approached* the event with extreme caution.
5. Fear *overwhelmed* some of the young women.
6. The older divers *possessed* experience and a healthy respect for nature.
7. Watching the older women *awakened* an unexpected strength in the younger divers.
8. They all *peered* into the dark water.
9. All of them *clenched* their teeth at the start of the dive.
10. After a strenuous but successful venture, the divers *sang* songs of the sea and laughed.

Review: Exercise 6 Identifying Adjectives

The following sentences are about abalone. On your paper, write the adjectives that appear in each sentence. Count pronouns and proper adjectives but do not count the words *a, an,* and *the.* After each adjective write a dash and the word that the adjective modifies.

SAMPLE Abalone is valuable for three reasons.
ANSWER valuable—abalone; three—reasons

1. The fleshy body, or foot, inside the shell makes a tasty meal.
2. The dishlike shell of the abalone is lined with gray mother-of-pearl.
3. From this lustrous substance fancy buttons are made.
4. Like oysters, abalone can also produce valuable pearls.
5. Handsome pearls develop when foreign objects accidentally lodge inside a shell.
6. The shellfish reacts by coating the object with several layers of mother-of-pearl.
7. The entire process may take three years.
8. Although most pearls are white, other colors are found.
9. Between 1893 and 1919, an artificial method of pearl production was developed by Japanese experimenters.
10. Pearls produced by this method must still grow inside shellfish, but the foreign object is inserted by human hands.

Review: Exercise 7 Expanding Sentences with Adjectives

The following sentences elaborate on ideas suggested by the passage from *The Sound of Waves.* On your paper, rewrite each sentence, adding adjectives in the places indicated by carets. Although there are no specific correct answers, you should base your choices on what you have learned from reading the passage.

SAMPLE In July the days were ∧ and ∧.
ANSWER In July the days were warm and sunny.

1. At Garden Beach, the ∧ divers prepared to enter the ∧ water.
2. ∧ rowboats took the ∧ women from the shore to ∧ water.
3. Away from the ∧ beach, the water was ∧.
4. A ∧ woman wearing a ∧ turban was the first to dive.
5. Taking a ∧ gulp of air, she plummeted into the ∧ ocean.
6. On the ocean floor, she felt ∧ and ∧.
7. Working quickly, the ∧ diver grabbed ∧ abalone.
8. A ∧ push carried her to the surface, where a basket bobbed on a ∧ rope tied to her waist.
9. A few ∧ strokes brought her to the basket, which was soon full of ∧ abalone.
10. In seconds the ∧ diver was ready for another ∧ descent to the bottom of the ocean.

Review: Exercise 8 Identifying Adverbs

The sentences below are about octopus fishing, another typical industry of the islands off the coast of Japan. On your paper, write each adverb that appears in these sentences. After each adverb, write a dash and the word that the adverb modifies.

SAMPLE The fishers headed sleepily toward their boat.
ANSWER sleepily—headed

1. The master of the boat was always cheerful.
2. Because of his good humor, his two assistants willingly worked for him.
3. Soon the three reached the village's fishing grounds.
4. There they found the other boats from the village.
5. A bitterly cold wind chilled the fishers as they worked.
6. Laboriously the boys pulled heavy traps from the ocean.
7. In twenty traps, they did not find a single octopus.
8. Eventually a full trap was collected.
9. The master and his assistants then grew optimistic.
10. By afternoon they were quite happy with the day's catch.

Review: Exercise 9 Using Adverbs

The following sentences are based on a passage from *The Sound of Waves* that is not reprinted in this textbook. On your paper, rewrite each sentence, substituting an appropriate adverb for the prepositional phrase in italics. The adverb should express the same idea as the prepositional phrase.

SAMPLE As the fishers left their boats, they laughed and sang *with boisterous energy.*
ANSWER As the fishers left their boats, they laughed and sang boisterously.

1. A young fisher strolled along the beach *in an unhurried manner.*
2. He was carrying a halibut, which he would *in a short time* deliver to the lighthouse keeper.
3. The boy noticed a girl leaning *in a calm way* against some boat frames.
4. Her manner of dress suggested that she had *at some recent time* been working.
5. The boy regarded her *with curiosity,* for he had never seen her before.
6. The girl stared at the sky *with an intent look.*
7. *In a purposeful way* the boy passed quite near the stranger.
8. He stood before her and stared at her *in a rude manner.*
9. *To a surprising degree* the mysterious young woman remained motionless.
10. Finally, the boy turned *in an abrupt manner* and moved on.

Grammar Review

Review: Exercise 10 **Identifying Prepositions**

The following sentences are based on passages from *The Sound of Waves* that are not reprinted in this textbook. On your paper, list the prepositions that appear in each sentence. Remember that some prepositions are made up of more than one word. (The numeral in parentheses at the end of each item indicates the number of prepositions the sentence contains.)

1. At home the young fisher thought about the girl on the beach. (3)
2. He had never seen her before that day. (1)
3. He was tormented by thoughts of her lovely face. (2)
4. One day, because of high winds, none of the fishing boats left the shore. (2)
5. In his free time, the young man was doing chores for his mother. (2)
6. A few days earlier, she had gathered firewood and left it inside a concrete tower on the mountain. (2)
7. Her son climbed to the tower and looked for the small bundle with his mother's name on it. (4)
8. After a few minutes in the tower, he heard a sound. (2)
9. He hurried up the stone steps and quickly arrived at the top of the tower. (3)
10. There, above the tower, was the girl. (1)

Review: Exercise 11 **Completing Sentences with Prepositions**

Each of the sentences below elaborates on the passage from *The Sound of Waves*. On your paper, rewrite each sentence, replacing the blank with a preposition that completes the word or phrase in italics and makes sense in the sentence. In some cases, there may be more than one preposition that makes sense.

SAMPLE The young girls thought fearfully ______ *the diving season.*
ANSWER The young girls thought fearfully about the diving season.

1. As children, they ran joyfully ______ *the rocky island coast.*
2. Grabbing pebbles ______ *the ocean floor* was a favorite pastime.
3. Gradually their childish games had become contests ______ *skill.*
4. When diving turned into their life's work, however, they became frightened ______ *it.*
5. ______ *a dive* they often felt that they were strangling.
6. Broken shells ______ *the ocean floor* rubbed their toes raw.
7. ______ *a dive* the girls were exhausted.
8. Did they tell their friends ______ *their nightmares?*
9. The older divers did their job ______ *such fears.*
10. They usually came up from a dive laughing and talking ______ *themselves.*

Parts of Speech

Review: Exercise 12 Completing Sentences with Conjunctions

The following sentences describe Japan, where *The Sound of Waves* is set. On your paper, replace each blank with an appropriate conjunction according to the directions in parentheses. Choose your conjunctions from the list that precedes the exercise. There are more conjunctions listed than you will need.

SAMPLE Japan's geography ______ history are closely intertwined.
(Add a coordinating conjunction.)

ANSWER Japan's geography and history are closely intertwined.

CONJUNCTIONS

and but or nor for
both . . . and neither . . . nor
although as long as as soon as because if so that until

1. Japan is a nation of islands ______ large ______ small.
(Add a correlative conjunction.)
2. There are four main islands ______ many hundreds of smaller ones.
(Add a coordinating conjunction.)
3. Japan's rugged mountains create a beautiful landscape ______ leave farmers little land for cultivation.
(Add a coordinating conjunction.)
4. Thus, ______ Japan's soil is fertile, only a small percentage of it is farmed.
(Add a subordinating conjunction.)
5. ______ the island nation has a long coastline, fishing has always been a popular occupation.
(Add a subordinating conjunction.)
6. In the seventeenth century, Japan almost completely closed its borders to foreigners ______ it could protect itself from outside influence.
(Add a subordinating conjunction.)
7. Japan's rulers were able to maintain a policy of isolation ______ Japanese ports stayed closed to foreign ships.
(Add a subordinating conjunction.)
8. ______ the United States sent Commodore Matthew Perry to open trade with Japan in 1853, Japan was secluded from the outside world for 250 years.
(Add a subordinating conjunction.)
9. The Japanese government had a choice: it could fight Perry's fleet ______ submit peacefully and open its ports.
(Add a coordinating conjunction.)
10. ______ the Meiji Constitution of 1889 modernized Japanese society, Japan became a major world power.
(Add a subordinating conjunction.)

Review: Exercise 13 **Rewriting Sentences with Conjunctive Adverbs**

The sentences below are about the land of Japan. On your paper, rewrite each sentence, using a conjunctive adverb. Choose your adverbs from the list on page 479.

1. Many people think Japan is one large island; it is actually hundreds of islands.
2. Much of Japan is steep, mountainous terrain; arable farmland is scarce.
3. Japan has a meager supply of minerals but is one of the world's richest nations.
4. Volcanic eruptions take place frequently; earthquakes are common occurrences.
5. Japanese trees are often cultivated as miniatures; gardens are often designed as smaller versions of the surrounding landscape.
6. The main island, Honshu, is less than two hundred miles wide at its greatest width; no part of Japan is more than one hundred miles from the sea.
7. Few inlets are found on the east coast north of Tokyo, but south of Tokyo are many of the best harbors.
8. Every valley in Japan has a stream; no long navigable rivers exist in Japan.
9. Some scenic Japanese lakes are located in river valleys; most of the lakes are mountain lakes.
10. In the Japanese mountains, there are about 200 volcanoes, and only about 50 are still active.

Review: Exercise 14

Proofreading

The following passage describes the artist Andō Hiroshige, whose work appears on the opposite page. Rewrite the passage, correcting the errors in spelling, capitalization, grammar, and usage. Add any missing punctuation. There are twenty-five errors.

Andō Hiroshige

[1]Andō (or Ichiyū-sai) Hiroshige (1797–1858) was the son of a fire-brigade cheif. [2]Shortly after the death of his mother—she died when her son was twelve—Hiroshige inherited his fathers post. [3]He eventually abandoned the position so that he could consentrate on painting, his real love.

[4]Unlike painter's in Europe and America, japanese artists explored a limited number of themes according to strict rules of representation. [5]Hiroshige experiment with a variety of pictorial themes, including portraits and historical scenes, before settling on Landscapes. [6]He focused on this subject throughout his' long and productive life.

[7]Hiroshige's landscapes are gentle lyrical, and subdued in tone. [8]In many of his prints, the stark beauty of the Japanese landscape are softened by a

human presence. [9]Peasants trudge home in great drifts of snow or villagers hurry, heads bowed, through a rainstorm. [10]Variations in weather and the Seasons is depicted with care and precision.

[11]When he was thirty-five, Hiroshige embarked on the more ambitious project of his career. [12]He begun a series of fifty-five woodblock prints illustrating scenes along the great highway that linked the city of kyoto to Edo (now known as Tokyo). [13]These prints established Hiroshige as one of the master's of his day. [14]His later pictures of birds and flowers seems tentative and sentimental by comparison.

[15]The woodblock prints for which Hiroshige is famous was a technical feat. [16]Each color is printed separately by rubbing paper against the woodblock or by running the block through a press. [17]The first prints, generally the clearest and most subtly colored, becomed the most valuable.

[18]*Imagiri Promontory from Maizaka* is typical of Hiroshiges mature style. [19]It's harmonious composition projects a mood of stillness and calm. [20]Hiroshige was particularly famous for his deep blues and reds which are subtle yet vivid. [21]One can imagine in such a scene the diver's described in *The Sound of Waves.*

Andō Hiroshige, *Imagiri Promontory from Maizaka,* 1833

Parts of Speech

Review: Exercise 15

Mixed Review

The biography of Yukio Mishima below is followed by twenty sentences. Rewrite each one, replacing the blank with an appropriate word. Use the directions in parentheses.

Yukio Mishima

Yukio Mishima is the pen name of Kimitake Hiraoka, one of the most famous writers of modern Japan. Born in 1925, Mishima was weak and sickly as a child. He was highly intelligent, however, and took an interest in literature early in life. His first work was published in 1941, when he was just 16. Because he was so young, he decided to take a pen name. *Confessions of a Mask,* published in 1949, established Mishima's reputation as an author. From that time on, he devoted himself to writing. *The Sound of Waves,* published in 1954, was inspired by a vacation in the Greek islands. This romantic story is the happiest of Mishima's forty novels. Mishima also wrote plays, essays, and short stories. He died in 1970.

1. The ______ writer Yukio Mishima was born in 1925. (Add a proper adjective.)
2. As a child, Mishima suffered from poor ______. (Add a common noun.)
3. At the same time, he was ______ successful in his schoolwork. (Add an adverb.)
4. At an early age, Mishima ______ interested in literature. (Add a linking verb.)
5. ______ he reached his eighteenth birthday, his writing had already been published in a magazine. (Add a subordinating conjunction.)
6. To conceal his youth, he ______ a pen name. (Add an action verb.)
7. ______ 1949 writing became a full-time career for Mishima. (Add a preposition.)
8. Mishima wrote *The Sound of Waves* after a trip to ______. (Add a proper noun.)
9. This happy ______ romantic novel was made into a movie. (Add a coordinating conjunction.)
10. Yukio Mishima wrote ______ kinds of works. (Add an adjective.)
11. ______ Yukio Mishima ______ Kimitake Hiraoka are names used by the same person. (Add a pair of correlative conjunctions.)
12. ______ his death, Mishima produced forty novels. (Add a preposition.)
13. He enjoyed the Greek islands; ______, the story they inspired was his happiest. (Add a conjunctive adverb.)
14. By the age of sixteen, Mishima ______ his first novel. (Add a verb phrase.)
15. A common theme ______ his novels is conflict. (Add a preposition.)
16. The novel ______ established Mishima as an author. (Add an intensive pronoun.)
17. Mishima is a famous writer in Japanese ______. (Add an abstract noun.)
18. We will ______ know what else he might have written. (Add a negative adverb.)
19. ______ work is admired by readers everywhere. (Add a possessive pronoun.)
20. ______ should read Mishima's books. (Add an indefinite pronoun.)

Writing Application

TIME

For more about the writing process, see **TIME Facing the Blank Page,** pp. 109–119.

Adverbs in Writing

In this passage from Ralph Ellison's short story "Flying Home," a farmer and his son have come across a pilot who has fallen from a small plane. Notice how Ellison uses adverbs to help convey the pilot's shock and confusion. Examine the passage, focusing especially on the italicized adverbs.

> Sounds come to him *dimly*. . . . He lay rigid, hearing their breathing and trying to weave a meaning between them and his being stretched *painfully* upon the ground. He watched them *warily*, his mind traveling *back* over a painful distance. Jagged scenes, *swiftly* unfolding as in a movie trailer [preview], reeled through his mind, and he saw himself piloting a tailspinning plane and landing and falling from the cockpit and trying to stand. *Then*, as in a great silence, he remembered the sound of crunching bone.

Techniques with Adverbs

Try to apply some of Ralph Ellison's writing techniques when you write and revise your own work.

❶ Use adverbs to clarify actions or behavior. In Ellison's passage, for example, the adverb *painfully* helps explain why the pilot is confused.

WITHOUT ADVERB . . . his being stretched upon the ground . . .

ELLISON'S VERSION . . . his being stretched *painfully* upon the ground . . .

❷ Use adverbs to emphasize a point. Compare the following descriptions of the pilot's memories.

WITHOUT ADVERB Jagged scenes, unfolding as in a movie trailer, reeled through his mind . . .

ELLISON'S VERSION Jagged scenes, *swiftly* unfolding as in a movie trailer, reeled through his mind . . .

❸ Try to choose adverbs that contribute to the mood, or atmosphere, that you are trying to convey.

WITHOUT ADVERBS He watched them, his mind traveling over a painful distance.

ELLISON'S VERSION He watched them *warily*, his mind traveling *back* over a painful distance.

Parts of Speech

Practice Practice these techniques by revising the following passage, using a separate sheet of paper. Add adverbs in the places indicated with carets (^).

Afternoon teas at Mrs. Chan's apartment are ^ to be missed. Mrs. Chan ^ brings out her finest china and ^ sets it on the kitchen table. Her best cloth napkins are ^ folded at each place. She ^ prepares delicate almond cakes and pork dumplings to serve to her guests. Each woman comes to the tea ^ dressed. The women chat ^, and newcomers are ^ welcome. When tea is over, the guests ^ leave. Everyone ^ agrees to come back next week.

UNIT 11

Parts of the Sentence

11.1 Simple Subjects and Simple Predicates

- A **sentence** is a group of words expressing a complete thought.

The two basic parts of every sentence are the *subject* and the *predicate.*

- The **subject** is the part of the sentence about which something is being said.
- The **predicate** is the part that says something about the subject.

Both the subject and the predicate may consist of more than one word.

- The **simple subject** is the key noun or pronoun (or group of words acting as a noun) that tells what a sentence is about.
- The **simple predicate** is the verb or verb phrase that tells something about the subject.

A simple predicate that is a verb phrase consists of the verb and any helping verbs.

SIMPLE SUBJECT	SIMPLE PREDICATE
Condors	soar.
Spring	will come.
Coretta Scott King	is speaking.
Nora	sang.
Breakfast	is served.

You find the simple subject by asking *who?* or *what?* about the verb. For example, in the first sentence above, the noun *condors* answers the question *what soar?* In the second sentence, *spring* answers the question *what will come?*

Exercise 1 Identifying Simple Subjects and Simple Predicates

On your paper, write the simple subject and simple predicate of each sentence. Underline the simple predicate.

1. American teenagers spent about $88 billion in 1993.
2. The amount increased to approximately $99 billion in 1994.
3. The cause for the increase was partly an increase in the number of teenagers in the United States.
4. Money came from parents, jobs, allowances, and gifts.
5. Many teens hold jobs after school, on weekends, and during school vacations.

Parts of the Sentence

11.2 Complete Subjects and Complete Predicates

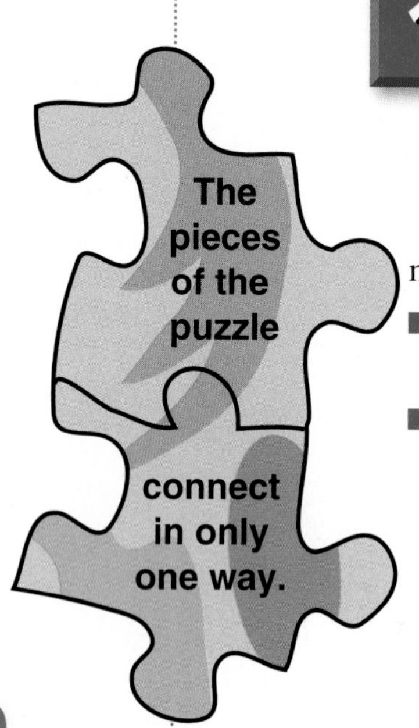

The
pieces
of the
puzzle
connect
in only
one way.

In most sentences, the addition of other words and phrases expands or modifies the meaning of the simple subject and the simple predicate.

- The **complete subject** consists of the simple subject and all the words that modify it.
- The **complete predicate** consists of the simple predicate and all the words that modify it or complete its meaning.

COMPLETE SUBJECT	COMPLETE PREDICATE
The condors of California	soar gracefully in the sky.
A welcome spring	will come after a cold winter.
Coretta Scott King	is speaking first.
My sister Nora	sang a lullaby.
A late breakfast	was served at the same time as lunch.

Exercise 2 **Identifying Complete Subjects and Complete Predicates**

Write the following sentences on your paper. Underline each complete subject once and each complete predicate twice.

Canobie Lake Park

1. Canobie Lake Park in the southeastern section of New Hampshire opened in 1902.
2. Many people consider Canobie Lake Park one of the most beautiful amusement parks in the United States.
3. The pleasant grounds feature tree-lined walkways, flower gardens, and a lake.
4. Guests to the park are especially amused by the 150-passenger paddle-wheel riverboat.
5. The eighty-acre park is regarded as one of the popular entertainment centers in New England.
6. The entire family will find something to enjoy there.
7. Visitors love the antique carousel with its beautiful hand-carved horses.
8. Young and not-so-young thrill seekers ride the park's four roller coasters again and again.
9. Small children squeal in delight at the costumed characters throughout the park.
10. The park presents high-tech fireworks and musical performances all summer long.

Exercise 3 Identifying Subjects and Predicates

On your paper, write each of the following sentences, and draw a vertical line between the complete subject and the complete predicate. Then underline the simple subject once and the simple predicate twice.

SAMPLE ANSWER One of the most important leaders of the abolitionist movement | was Frederick Douglass.

Frederick Douglass, Champion of Equality

1. Frederick Douglass dedicated his life to the fight for racial equality.
2. He was born enslaved in Tuckahoe, Maryland, around 1818.
3. Douglass escaped from slavery in 1838.
4. The brave young man spoke at an antislavery meeting in Massachusetts in 1841.
5. The enthusiastic reaction to his speech led to a series of lecture engagements.
6. Douglass worked for civil rights for African Americans.
7. His activities included the publication of an antislavery newspaper.
8. President Abraham Lincoln conferred with Douglass during the Civil War.
9. The proud African American served as United States minister to Haiti from 1889 to 1891.
10. The United States owes a great debt to Douglass and his tireless struggle for civil rights.

Exercise 4 Expanding Subjects and Predicates

Expand each of the following sentences by adding words and phrases to both the simple subject and the simple predicate. Write your sentence. Then underline the simple predicate in each sentence. (There are many ways to expand each sentence.)

SAMPLE Sky darkened.
ANSWER The previously clear sky darkened suddenly to a furious yellowish-gray.

1. Wind screeched.
2. Rain began.
3. Leaves flew.
4. Trees bent.
5. Windows rattled.
6. Water dripped.
7. Gutters overflowed.
8. Waves crashed.
9. Clouds raced.
10. Sky lightened.

11.3 Compound Subjects and Compound Predicates

A sentence may have more than one simple subject or simple predicate.

Compound Subjects

■ A **compound subject** is made up of two or more simple subjects that are joined by a conjunction and have the same verb.

The conjunctions most commonly used to join the subjects in a compound subject are *and* and *or.*

Shall **you** and **I** go to the nature preserve tomorrow?
Eagles and **owls** hunt for food.
A **cardinal** or a **robin** will be frightened by these hunters.

Correlative conjunctions may be used to join compound subjects.

Neither the two **eagles** nor the lone **owl** is hunting.
Both the **eagle** and the **owl** are strong fliers.

When more than two words are included in the compound subject, the conjunction is usually used only between the last two words, and the words are separated by commas.

Eagles, owls, and **vultures** are birds of prey.

Parts of the Sentence

Exercise 5 Identifying Compound Subjects

On your paper, write the compound subject in each sentence.

1. Two peach baskets and a gym set the stage for the world's first basketball game in 1891.
2. Two teams and an old soccer ball put the play into motion.
3. Nets and backboards were early additions to the game.
4. Men and women played basketball in the early years of its development.
5. Stanford and California met in 1896 for the first women's intercollegiate match.

Exercise 6 Expanding Subjects

(a) Write five sentences. In each one, use a simple subject and a simple predicate.
(b) Expand each sentence by making the subject compound.

SAMPLE ANSWER
a. Toni Morrison wrote several highly successful novels.
b. Toni Morrison and Alice Walker wrote several highly successful novels.

Compound Predicates

■ A **compound predicate** (or **compound verb**) is made up of two or more verbs or verb phrases that are joined by a conjunction and have the same subject.

Eagles **soar** and **plunge.**
Suki either **is** here already or **will be** here soon.

In compound verbs that contain verb phrases, the helping verb may not be repeated before the second verb.

We **have lost** or at least **misplaced** the map.
Tyrone **will buy** a stamp, **mail** the letter, and **hurry** home.

Some sentences have both a compound subject and a compound predicate.

S **S** **P** **P**
Eagles and **condors soar** and **plunge** in the sky.

S **S** **P** **P**
Either **you** or **I have lost** or **misplaced** the map.

Exercise 7 **Identifying Compound Predicates**

On your paper, write the compound predicate in each of the following sentences.

Cats

1. Many cats are faithful pets and make friendly companions.
2. Cats seem independent and sometimes resist training.
3. They generally are fed canned food but may prefer fish or meat.
4. Cats are good hunters and prey on small creatures.
5. Cats climb trees, run fast, and walk on narrow ledges.
6. Their pride, however, keeps them from foolish behavior and sometimes makes them stubborn.
7. An arched back with puffed-out fur is caused by fear or initiated by anger.
8. These physical changes make the cat's appearance larger, give the impression of ferocity, and intimidate enemies and prey.
9. Cats usually approach their prey very stealthily and then pounce.
10. The Birman is easygoing, does not stray far, and appears very affectionate and even-tempered.

Exercise 8 **Expanding Predicates**

(a) Write five sentences. In each one, use a simple subject and a simple predicate.
(b) Expand each sentence by making the predicate compound.

SAMPLE ANSWER **a.** The horse jumped the fence.
b. The horse jumped the fence and trotted away.

Exercise 9 Identifying Subjects and Predicates

On your paper, write the simple subject and the simple predicate from each sentence. Underline the simple predicates. Note that some subjects and predicates are compound.

The Mound Builders

1. Several North American cultures built large mounds of earth thousands of years ago and used them as burial places and foundations for buildings.
2. The Adena, the Hopewell, and the Mississippians were the three major groups of mound builders.
3. Much time and much effort were devoted to the construction of each mound.
4. Large quantities of dirt and stone were the primary construction materials of the mound builders.
5. Each mound builder carried loads of dirt on his back and transported them to the burial sites.
6. No horses, oxen, or carts assisted the workers in their difficult task.
7. Jewelry or pipes for the deceased were often buried in the mounds.
8. Many large mounds still stand in the midwestern United States and Canada.
9. The Giant Serpent Mound near Hillsboro, Ohio, resembles a huge, sinuous snake and is approximately a quarter of a mile long.
10. Monk's Mound near Cahokia in southern Illinois covers about sixteen acres and is about one hundred feet high.

Exercise 10 Writing Compound Subjects and Predicates

On your paper, expand each of the following sentences by making both the subject and the predicate compound. (You may need to make other changes, too.)

SAMPLE Worms crawl.
ANSWER Worms and insects crawl and hide.

Gardening

1. Carly fertilized the garden.
2. Mulch had covered the ground.
3. A garden rake can break up the soil.
4. Crocuses arrive in early spring.
5. Peonies come in many colors.
6. Lilacs flower in late spring.
7. Cottonwoods spread their seeds widely.
8. Some lilies bloom in late June.
9. Sunlight makes a good garden.
10. Carly starts her garden plans earlier each year.

11.4 Order of Subject and Predicate

The subject comes before the verb in most sentences in English. Some exceptions to this normal word order are discussed below.

Commands and Questions

The subject *you* is understood rather than expressed in the case of commands or requests.

[You] **Jump!** [You] **Tear** it down. [You] **Ask** her, please.

Questions frequently begin with a verb or helping verb.

Is he right? **Will** you **visit** your cousin?

Other questions often begin with the words *who, what, when, where, why,* or *how.*

What does she want? **Why** did he go to the gym?

Notice that the subject generally follows the verb or helping verb.

To find the subject of a question, rearrange words to form a statement.

SUBJECT	PREDICATE
He	is right.
You	will visit your cousin.
She	does want.
He	did go to the gym.

Exercise 11 Identifying Subjects and Predicates in Commands and Questions

On your paper, write the simple subject and the simple predicate of each of the following sentences. (Remember that the simple predicate may contain one or more helping verbs.) If the sentence is a command, write (*You*) as the subject.

1. Can anyone name three main types of musical instruments?
2. Notice the string instruments, wind instruments, and percussion instruments.
3. Give me an example of a string instrument.
4. What kind of sound does a woodwind make?
5. Beat a drum for a good idea of percussion sound.
6. In what ways are a drum and a xylophone similar?
7. Is a piano a string instrument or a percussion instrument?
8. Study these parts of a saxophone.
9. Do you see the reed in the mouthpiece slot?
10. Watch it carefully.

Inverted Order

A sentence written in **inverted order,** where the predicate comes before the subject, serves to add emphasis to the subject.

PREDICATE	SUBJECT
Over the mount **soared**	the two **eagles.**
Beyond the eagles **was**	a **condor.**

Remember that a word in a prepositional phrase can never be the subject.

When the word *there* or *here* begins a sentence and is followed by the verb *to be,* the subject generally comes after the predicate. (The sentence appears in inverted order.) Keep in mind that *there* and *here* are almost never the subject of a sentence.

PREDICATE	SUBJECT
There **are**	three **owls** in the nest.
Here **is**	my **sister.**

Parts of the Sentence

Exercise 12 Reordering Sentences

On your paper, rewrite each of the following sentences so that the complete subject comes before the predicate. Then underline the simple subject once and the simple predicate twice. (Remember that both subjects and predicates may be compound.)

The Invention of Motion Pictures

1. In the late 1800s began the development of motion pictures.
2. From George Eastman, the American inventor, came flexible celluloid film.
3. There were two machines invented by Thomas Edison for use with George Eastman's new film.
4. With Edison's kinetoscope came a brief success.
5. Through a peephole could be seen strips of "moving" pictures.
6. There were several short films made in Edison's studio.
7. In and out of the Kinetoscope Parlor in New York City streamed intrigued customers.
8. There was a new projection machine invented by Thomas Armat.
9. On Armat's projector were shown the earliest commercial motion pictures.
10. From these early efforts came a new and popular art form.

Exercise 13 Analyzing Subjects and Predicates

Copy each of the following sentences, draw a vertical line between the complete subject and the complete predicate, and label each. Then underline the simple subject once and the simple predicate twice. Write *(You)* for an understood subject. Finally, indicate with the letter *C* or *I* those sentences that are either a command *(C)* or written in inverted order *(I)*. (Not all sentences will be labeled *C* or *I*.)

SAMPLE ANSWER

S | P
(You) | Look at that clothing. **C**

P | S
On the hat rack is | a huge sombrero. **I**

P | S
There are | many beautiful Mexican costumes. **I**

Traditional Dress in Mexico

1. Some residents of Mexican villages still wear traditional types of clothing.
2. Many of these styles of clothing date back many centuries.
3. Look at the young boy in the cornfield.
4. On his head is a wide-brimmed straw hat, or sombrero.
5. The sombrero serves as excellent protection against the intense Mexican sun.
6. There are several other types of protective clothing for men and women.
7. A poncho, or blanket with a slit in the center for the head, is popular with men in cold or rainy weather.
8. Notice the rebozos, or fringed cotton shawls, covering the heads of those village women near the fountain in the plaza.
9. There are some special costumes for holidays and other occasions.
10. Look at the handsome suits worn by the cowboys, or *charros,* from Guadalajara.
11. Here is an example of a traditional Mexican outfit.
12. The material for the suit of a *charro* may be doeskin or velvet.
13. There are a short jacket, or bolero, and tight pants with gold buttons down the sides of the legs.
14. A shirt, boots with spurs, and a large sombrero complete the costume.
15. Among popular women's costumes is the beautiful *china poblana.*
16. It may have been named for a seventeenth-century Chinese princess.
17. The costume includes a full cotton skirt, a colorful blouse, and a wide sash.
18. There are many people in modern styles.
19. A common shoe is the *huarache.*
20. Many Mexican city dwellers no longer wear traditional clothing.

11.5 Complements

■ A **complement** is a word or group of words that completes the meaning of a verb.

The four kinds of complements are *direct objects, indirect objects, object complements,* and *subject complements.*

Direct Objects

■ A **direct object** answers the question *what?* or *whom?* after an action verb.

The verb in a sentence usually indicates the action being performed by the subject. That action may be received by or directed toward someone or something: the direct object. Direct objects are nouns, pronouns, or words acting as nouns; and they may be compound. Only transitive verbs have direct objects.

Roberto bought **tomatoes.** [Roberto bought *what?*]

Sandra likes **me** very much. [Sandra likes *whom?*]

Ralph reported his **discovery.** [Ralph reported *what?*]

Roberto bought plum **tomatoes** and red-leaf **lettuce.** [Roberto bought *what?*]

Exercise 14 Identifying Direct Objects

On your paper, write the action verb that appears in each of the following sentences. Then list any direct objects.

Francisco Pizarro, a Spanish Conqueror

1. Francisco Pizarro, a sixteenth-century Spanish explorer, won much fame and fortune for his country.
2. Around 1520 Pizarro heard rumors of a vast and rich empire in the central highlands of South America.
3. In 1524 Pizarro began an expedition to the west coast of South America.
4. Bad weather hindered him in his first visit to the region.
5. In 1528, however, Pizarro located the Inca and their extensive empire.
6. Signs of gold and other riches in the Inca capital of Cuzco pleased the explorer greatly.
7. In 1532 Pizarro captured Atahualpa, a great Inca ruler, in the town of Cajamarca.
8. The Incas gave a vast quantity of gold and silver objects to Pizarro in order to save Atahualpa.
9. In the end Pizarro heartlessly killed the Inca ruler.
10. After the death of Atahualpa, Pizarro conquered the Inca and their capital city.

Indirect Objects

- An **indirect object** answers the question *to whom? for whom? to what?* or *for what?* after an action verb.

In most cases, a sentence can have an indirect object only if it has a direct object as well. The indirect object always appears after the verb and before the direct object.

We gave **students** awards. [We gave awards *to whom?*]

Trisha gives **homework** her full attention. [Trisha gives her full attention *to what?*]

Angela bought **Soo** and **Gloria** lunch. [Angela bought lunch *for whom?*]

Exercise 15 Identifying Direct and Indirect Objects

On your paper, write the direct object in each of the following sentences. Then write and underline any indirect objects. (There may be more than one indirect object in a sentence, or there may be none at all.)

Kristi Yamaguchi, Olympic Champion

1. Kristi Yamaguchi, a fourth-generation Japanese American, showed many female athletes and Asian Americans the rewards of dedication.
2. At age four, Yamaguchi started ballet study and ice-skating lessons.
3. She entered her first ice-skating competition at age eight.
4. As a young skater, Yamaguchi won many titles and medals.
5. She gave the audience and judges the best free-skate performance of her career.
6. Yamaguchi completed six triple jumps in this program.
7. At the 1992 Winter Olympics, Yamaguchi brought the United States a gold medal in figure skating.
8. Having won her Olympic gold medal just a month earlier, Yamaguchi provided her hometown a thrill by winning a second consecutive world championship.
9. She joined a professional tour in 1993.
10. Yamaguchi's artistry and athleticism have given her family, her country, and many audiences great pride and much pleasure.

Exercise 16 Using Direct and Indirect Objects

On your paper, rewrite the following sentences so that each contains both a direct and an indirect object. Write a *D* above each direct object and an *I* above each indirect object.

1. Book groups offer meetings on a regular basis.
2. Members give information about a wide variety of books.
3. One by one, each member tells his or her impressions of the book.
4. Sometimes the members write about the book.
5. Book groups also offer the possibilities of new friendships.

Object Complements

- An **object complement** answers the question *what?* after a direct object. That is, it *completes* the meaning of the direct object by identifying or describing it.

You will find object complements only in sentences that contain a direct object *and* include one of the following action verbs or a similar verb that has the general meaning of "make" or "consider":

appoint	choose	elect	prove
call	consider	name	vote

An object complement follows a direct object and may be an adjective, a noun, or a pronoun.

Engineers find plans **essential.** [adjective]

Nations often make their bridges **symbols.** [noun]

The citizens call that privilege **theirs.** [pronoun]

Mozelle considers me a **close friend** and **helpful adviser.** [nouns with modifiers]

Exercise 17 Identifying Object Complements

On your paper, write the object complements that appear in the following sentences. (Two sentences have two object complements, and one sentence has none.)

Japanese Prints

1. Art historians and critics consider many Japanese prints masterpieces.
2. A museum curator calls seventeenth-century Japanese prints irreplaceable and priceless.
3. Some scholars think the early black-and-white prints particularly delicate and expressive.
4. Harunobu, a master of the print, found children a worthy subject.
5. Somehow he rendered the children interesting.
6. An eighteenth-century printmaker, Harunobu, made color prints popular.
7. Some collectors prefer Utamaro's color prints.
8. Many in the art world have named Utamaro a master.
9. Quite often Utamaro made women his subjects.
10. Some artists consider the art of printmaking fascinating.

Exercise 18 Using Object Complements

On your paper, complete the following sentences with object complements. Then write the letter *A, N,* or *P* to identify each object complement as an adjective, noun, or pronoun.

1. The selfish children considered all the toys ____.
2. Drivers found the traffic ____.
3. Sunshine made the meadow ____.
4. The highway patrol called the storm ____.
5. Pilots considered the weather ____.
6. Vacationers thought the fog ____.

Parts of the Sentence

Subject Complements

■ A **subject complement** follows a subject and a linking verb and identifies or describes the subject.

The two kinds of subject complements are *predicate nominatives* and *predicate adjectives.*

■ A **predicate nominative** is a noun or pronoun that follows a linking verb and points back to the subject to identify it further.

Engineers are **scientists.**

The engineer on this project is **she.**

Although predicate nominatives most often appear in sentences containing forms of the linking verb *be,* a few other linking verbs (for example, *become* and *remain*) can be followed by a predicate nominative.

San Francisco is a **city.**

Monday remains a **holiday** for us.

Tanya became a famous **singer** and **dancer.**

■ A **predicate adjective** follows a linking verb and points back to the subject and further describes it.

Engineers are **inventive.**

Engineers must be highly **responsible.**

Predicate adjectives may follow any linking verb.

The hikers had become very **weary.**

The team looks **ready** for the game.

Lena seems **eager** and **determined.**

I feel quite **chilly.**

Exercise 19 Identifying Predicate Nominatives

On your paper, write the predicate nominatives that appear in the following sentences. (If a sentence has no predicate nominative, write *none.*)

The trail looked suspicious!

George Mason

1. George Mason was a statesman during the Revolutionary War era.
2. Born in Virginia, Mason became a brilliant student of law.
3. Mason was not a supporter of slavery.
4. Public officials appreciated Mason's legal genius.
5. Mason's work became the basis for Thomas Jefferson's Bill of Rights.

Exercise 20 Identifying Predicate Adjectives

On your paper, write the simple subject and predicate adjective in each of the following sentences. If a sentence has no predicate adjective, write *none.*

Rabies

1. The behavior of an animal with rabies seems strange.
2. A rabid animal grows irritable.
3. It ventures fearlessly into contact with people.
4. The sick animal looks normal.
5. Its appearance often does not change.
6. The animal's strange actions, not its appearance, should be watched often.
7. Do not go near a strange-acting animal.
8. An animal with rabies feels unusually restless.
9. A normally friendly animal may become unfriendly.
10. Call an authority about a possibly rabid animal.

Exercise 21 Identifying Subject Complements

On your paper, write all the subject complements that appear in the following sentences. Identify each as a *predicate nominative* or a *predicate adjective.* (One sentence has more than one subject complement; other sentences have none.)

The Farmer's Market

1. A farmer's market is a place for the sale of the produce of local farmers.
2. In many communities, these markets have become quite popular.
3. With the eager crowds, colorful stands, and shouting vendors, a farmer's market seems festive.
4. Locally grown fruits and vegetables, arranged on open stands, look crisp and fresh.
5. Breads and rolls, often still warm from the oven, smell delicious.
6. The farmers must be early risers.
7. Many of them sell preserves or handicrafts as well as fruits and vegetables.
8. Their loud sales pitches always sound persuasive.
9. Spend a morning at a farmer's market.
10. Soon you will be a regular customer.

Exercise 22 Using Subject Complements

On your paper, complete each of the following sentences by adding a noun, a pronoun, or an adjective. (You may also add other words.) Write *PN* or *PA* to identify the complement as a predicate nominative or predicate adjective.

1. The most interesting type of character created by Hollywood is ____.
2. The lives of Hollywood-created characters seem ____.
3. In real life, however, most people remain ____.
4. Many of the situations of Hollywood characters appear ____.
5. Compared to these situations, ordinary people's lives look ____.

Exercise 23 Identifying Complements (Part 1)

On your paper, write the complements that appear in the following sentences. Next to each complement, write the kind of complement it is: *direct object, indirect object, object complement, predicate nominative,* or *predicate adjective.*

Batik and Tie-dyeing

1. Batik is a method of fabric decoration.
2. The batik artist applies wax to parts of the cloth.
3. The artist then gives the cloth a dye bath.
4. The bath dyes the unwaxed part a vivid color.
5. The part of the cloth with wax resists the dye.
6. This method gives the cloth intricate designs.
7. The colors of batik appear rich and often subtle.
8. The process of tie-dyeing is similar but easier.
9. Common to both of these crafts is the resist-dyeing technique.
10. The tie-dye artist ties string around the cloth in different places.
11. The artist then dyes the fabric a color.
12. The tied areas give the cloth its design.
13. This design often appears random.
14. Usually, the fabric does not resist the dye uniformly.
15. Uneven dyeing makes the final product quite beautiful.

Exercise 24 Identifying Complements (Part 2)

On your paper, write the complements that appear in the following paragraph. Next to each complement, write the kind of complement it is: *direct object, indirect object, object complement, predicate nominative,* or *predicate adjective.*

The Mystery of Lightning

[1]Lightning was mysterious to the ancient Greeks. [2]In fact, for them lightning was a weapon used by their chief god, Zeus. [3]According to mythology, the Greeks gave Zeus the thunderbolt. [4]Many persons today still consider lightning scary. [5]Of course, the reasons for this fear seem sound. [6]During a storm, lightning strikes the earth about one hundred times a second. [7]Sometimes lightning strikes the tallest tree in a field. [8]Lightning may cause fire. [9]In addition, in the United States alone, lightning kills approximately one hundred people every year. [10]Lightning can be both mysterious and dangerous.

Exercise 25 Writing Sentences with Complements

Write four sentences about an environmental concern, such as acid rain, air pollution, noise pollution, deforestation, or oil spills. In each sentence, use at least one of the four kinds of complements: *direct object, indirect object, object complement,* and *subject complement.* Label the complements.

UNIT 11 Grammar Review

PARTS OF THE SENTENCE

Cairo is the home of Naguib Mahfouz [nä gēb′ mä fooz′]. His novel *Palace Walk* traces the fortunes of a middle-class Cairo family in the years between the two world wars. In this scene, the youngest son of the family, Kamal, is on his way home from school. The passage has been annotated to show some of the parts of the sentence covered in this unit.

Literature Model

from Palace Walk

by Naguib Mahfouz

translated from the Arabic by William Maynard Hutchins and Olive E. Kenny

He reached the pastry shop and stretched out his hand with the small change he had hung on to since morning. He took a piece of pastry with the total delight he experienced only on such a sweet occasion. It made him frequently dream of owning a candy store one day, not to sell the candy but to eat it. He continued on his way down al-Husayn Street, munching on the pastry with pleasure. He hummed and forgot he had been a prisoner all day long, not allowed to move, not to mention play or have fun. . . .

On his way, he passed by the tobacco store of Matoussian. He stopped under its sign, as he did every day at this hour, and raised his small eyes to the colored poster of a woman reclining on a divan with a cigarette between her crimson lips, from which rose a curling plume of smoke. She was leaning her arm on the windowsill. The curtain was drawn back to reveal a scene combining a grove of date palms and a branch of the Nile. He privately called the woman Aisha after his sister, since they both had golden hair and blue eyes. Although he was just going on ten, his admiration for the mistress of the poster was limitless. How often he thought of her enjoying life in its most splendid manifestations. How

Direct object (piece)

Compound predicate (hummed, forgot)

Simple subject (curtain)

Object complement (Aisha)

Subject complement (predicate adjective) (limitless)

Parts of the Sentence

often he imagined himself sharing his carefree days in that luxurious room with its pristine view that offered her, in fact both of them, its earth, palms, water, and sky. He would swim in the green river valley or cross the water in the skiff that appeared ghostlike far off in the picture. He would shake the palm trees till the dates fell around him or sit near the beautiful woman with his eyes gazing at her dreamy ones.

He left the vaulted section of the alley for the other half. At the end he could see Palace Walk and the entrance of Hammam al-Sultan. Then his eyes fell on his home's dark green wooden grilles and the large door with its bronze knocker. His mouth opened in a happy smile at the wide variety of amusements this place harbored for him. Soon the boys from all the neighboring houses would run to join him in his wide courtyard, with its several chambers, surrounding the oven room. There would be fun and games and sweet potatoes.

At that moment he saw the Suarès omnibus slowly crossing the street heading for Palace Walk. His heart leaped. Pleasure at his own cleverness filled him. At once he tucked his book bag under his left arm and reached to catch it. He jumped on the back steps, but the conductor did not let him enjoy his pleasure for very long. He came and asked the boy for his fare, giving him a suspicious, challenging look. Kamal told him ingratiatingly that he would get off as soon as it stopped but could not while it was moving. The conductor turned from him and yelled to the driver to stop the vehicle. He was angrily scolding Kamal, but when he looked away the boy seized the opportunity to tread on the instep of his foot, take a swing at him, and hop to the ground. He shot off in flight.

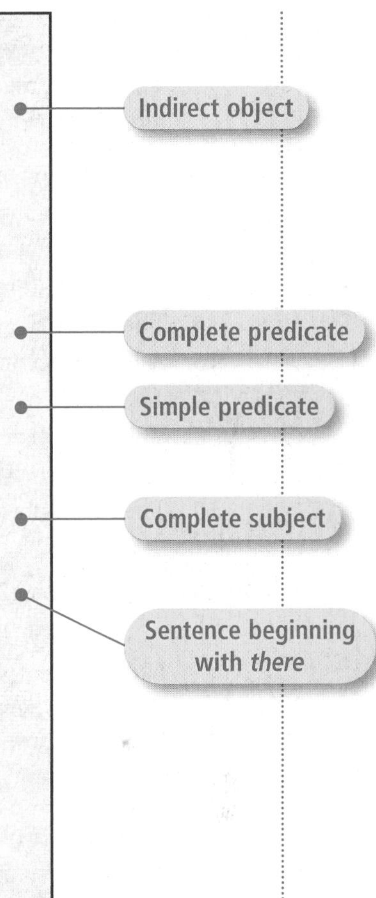

Review: Exercise 1 **Identifying Simple Subjects and Predicates**

For each of the following sentences, write the simple subject and simple predicate. Underline the simple predicate.

1. The young boy bought a pastry at a shop on his way home.
2. The tobacco store of Matoussian had a beautiful woman on its sign.
3. Kamal privately called the woman Aisha after his sister.
4. Dreams of a luxurious life filled his imagination.
5. The entrance to Hammam al-Sultan was nearby.

Review: Exercise 2 **Identifying Complete Subjects and Predicates**

The following sentences are based on the excerpt from *Palace Walk.* Copy each sentence and draw a line between the complete subject and complete predicate.

1. The woman on the poster seemed exotic to the small boy.
2. She was reclining on a divan and leaning her arm on a windowsill.
3. A scene with a grove of date palms and a view of the Nile could be seen behind her.
4. Kamal's sister had blond hair and blue eyes, just like the woman on the poster.
5. The boy privately called the woman Aisha.
6. A life of luxury similar to the view in the picture beckoned to Kamal.
7. The water of the Nile in the poster looked good for a swim or a sail in a skiff.
8. The dates from the palm trees might fall around him and the beautiful woman.
9. Thoughts of this wondrous life filled his mind for many minutes.
10. The young boy finally continued on his way home.

Review: Exercise 3 **Writing Sentences with Complete Subjects and Complete Predicates**

Each of the following partial sentences elaborates on an idea suggested by the passage from *Palace Walk.* Write either a complete subject or a complete predicate to complete each sentence. Do not repeat the exact wording from the novel. Your sentence should make sense within the context of the passage.

SAMPLE The young boy ______.
ANSWER was walking home from school.

1. The pastry shop ______.
2. ______ took the change from Kamal.
3. His precious purchase ______.
4. The happy young boy ______.
5. ______ was another favorite place.
6. ______ caught his eye.
7. The magnificent room in the poster ______.
8. ______ was located near Palace Walk.
9. ______ would soon be playing in the large courtyard.
10. The oven room ______.
11. The Suarès omnibus ______.
12. ______ filled with pleasure at his cleverness.
13. ______ jumped on the back of the bus.
14. The conductor ______.
15. ______ was the boy's response.

Review: Exercise 4 **Writing Sentences with Compound Subjects and Compound Predicates**

On your paper, write a complete sentence to answer each of the following questions. Begin your sentence with the subject and follow the instructions in parentheses. Underline and label the simple or compound subject and the simple or compound predicate. Draw a line separating the complete subject from the complete predicate.

SAMPLE What foods gave Kamal great pleasure? (Use a compound subject.)

ANSWER Pastry (COMPOUND SUBJECT) and other sweets | gave (SIMPLE PREDICATE) Kamal great pleasure.

1. Who lived in the city of Cairo? (Use a compound subject.)
2. What two shops were special to Kamal? (Use a compound subject.)
3. What did the young boy do after leaving the pastry shop? (Use a compound predicate.)
4. What two women had the same coloring? (Use a compound subject.)
5. What was the woman in the poster doing? (Use a compound predicate.)
6. What could be seen outside the woman's window? (Use a compound subject with three different nouns.)
7. What would Kamal and his friends do in Kamal's courtyard? (Use a compound predicate.)
8. What are three things Kamal did on his way home? (Use a compound predicate with three different verbs.)
9. Who had an unpleasant encounter on the back steps of the bus? (Use a compound subject.)
10. What gave Kamal particular pleasure on his walk? (Use a compound subject with three different nouns.)
11. What three features of Kamal's house promised amusement? (Use a compound subject with three different nouns.)
12. Who might have been riding on the bus with Kamal? (Use a compound subject with two different nouns.)
13. What did Kamal do to the conductor when the man turned his head? (Use a compound predicate with two different verbs.)
14. How might the passengers have reacted to Kamal's antics? (Use a compound predicate with two or three different verbs.)
15. Who would probably be having dinner at Kamal's house that night? (Use a compound subject with three different nouns.)

Review: Exercise 5 Writing Inverted Sentences

The sentences below are based on the excerpt from *Palace Walk.* On your paper, rewrite each sentence in inverted order, following the instructions in parentheses.

1. Kamal walked through the streets of Cairo. (Begin the sentence with *Through the streets of Cairo.*)
2. Fascinating sights, sounds, and smells were all around him. (Begin the sentence with *There were.*)
3. Nothing was more wonderful than the excitement and freedom of a stroll through the busy city. (Begin the sentence with *There was.*)
4. The luscious aroma of sweet cakes wafted out of one of the shops. (Begin the sentence with *Out of one of the shops.*)
5. The eager boy marched into the shop. (Begin the sentence with *Into the shop.*)
6. Kamal proceeded down the busy street. (Begin the sentence with *Down the busy street.*)
7. An enchanting poster was above the tobacco store. (Begin the sentence with *There was.*)
8. Thoughts of a luxurious life floated into Kamal's head. (Begin the sentence with *Into Kamal's head.*)
9. A bus, with its promise of new adventure, moved toward him. (Begin the sentence with *Toward him.*)
10. A suspicious conductor was on the bus. (Begin the sentence with *There was.*)
11. The angry conductor strode toward the boy. (Begin the sentence with *Toward the boy.*)
12. An unpleasant frown was on his face. (Begin the sentence with *There was.*)
13. A furious glitter was in his eyes. (Begin the sentence with *There was.*)
14. The mischievous young boy smiled into the angry face. (Begin the sentence with *Into the angry face.*)
15. Words that were lies fell from his mouth. (Begin the sentence with *From his mouth.*)
16. The wrathful conductor turned away from the boy. (Begin the sentence with *Away from the boy.*)
17. A curious quiet was throughout the bus. (Begin the sentence with *There was.*)
18. The angry man bellowed into the silence. (Begin the sentence with *Into the silence.*)

19. The laughing boy hopped from the bus.
(Begin the sentence with *From the bus.*)
20. A narrow alley, a place to escape, was nearby.
(Begin the sentence with *There was.*)

Review: Exercise 6 **Writing Sentences with Predicate Nominatives and Predicate Adjectives**

The pairs of words that follow are derived from the passage from *Palace Walk.* For each pair, write a sentence that uses the first word as the subject and the second word as a predicate adjective or a predicate nominative. Do not use the exact wording from the novel, and be sure to add more than just a verb to the pair of words.

SAMPLE city, home
ANSWER The city of Cairo was Kamal's home.

1. Kamal, hungry
2. pastry, delicious
3. boy, happy
4. stop, tobacco store
5. person, woman
6. admiration, endless
7. scene, attractive
8. home, place
9. bus, challenge
10. conductor, angry

Review: Exercise 7 **Writing Sentences with Direct and Indirect Objects**

Each of the following groups of words describes an incident related to the passage from *Palace Walk.* Each word is labeled *S* (for *subject*), *DO* (for *direct object*), or *IO* (for *indirect object*). On your paper, write a sentence using these words, but do not use the exact wording from the novel. Try to add modifiers or prepositional phrases to make your sentences more interesting.

SAMPLE boy (S), merchant (IO), money (DO)
ANSWER The young boy gave the merchant some money.

1. baker (S), schoolboy (IO), delicacy (DO)
2. sweets (S), Kamal (IO), pleasure (DO)
3. Kamal (S), candy store (DO)
4. poster (S), boy (IO), delight (DO)
5. Kamal (S), woman (IO), affection (DO)
6. Kamal (S), home (DO)
7. home (S), amusements (DO)
8. mother (S), his friends (IO), sweet potatoes (DO)
9. schoolboy (S), bus (DO)
10. conductor (S), Kamal (IO), question (DO)

Review: Exercise 8 **Writing Sentences with Direct Objects and Object Complements**

Each word in the following groups is labeled *S* (for *subject*), *DO* (for *direct object*), or *OC* (for *object complement*). On your paper, write a sentence using these words. Try to add modifiers such as prepositional phrases to make your sentences more interesting.

SAMPLE Kamal (S), walk (DO), fun (OC)
ANSWER Kamal found his walk home from school fun.

1. boy (S), sweets (DO), treat (OC)
2. proprietor (S), boy (DO), funny (OC)
3. Kamal (S), woman (DO), beautiful (OC)
4. passengers (S), Kamal (DO), rude (OC)
5. friend (S), story (DO), funny (OC)

Review: Exercise 9

Proofreading

The following passage describes the artist Henri Matisse, whose painting appears on the opposite page. Rewrite the passage, correcting any errors in spelling, grammar, and usage. Add any missing punctuation. There are twenty-five errors.

Henri Matisse

[1]Born in northern France, Henri Matisse (1869–1954), who intended to become an attorney studied law. [2]He was recovering from illness in 1890 and he decided to amuse himself by painting. [3]He immediatly took to painting. [4]Which became his lifelong passion.

[5]In Paris in 1905, he showed some of his' works to the public at a revolutionary exhibit. [6]Critics labeled Matisse and the other artists in the exhibit *fauves* a French word meaning "wild beasts." [7]The name sticked. [8]Became the movement's unofficial leader.

[9]Matisse worked for years to refine fauvist ideas and technics. [10]His pictures were simple, fluid and colorful. [11]For the fauves and their supporters, color and light was the keys to a painter's power. [12]Sometime during the year of 1908, Matisse says, "What I am after, above all, is expression." [13]As he entered his later years, he frequently abandoned the use of paint altogether and he chose instead to make collages in brilliant hues.

[14]Matisse tooked his first trip to Morocco in 1912. [15]He was inspired by Africas architecture ancient cultures, and landscape.

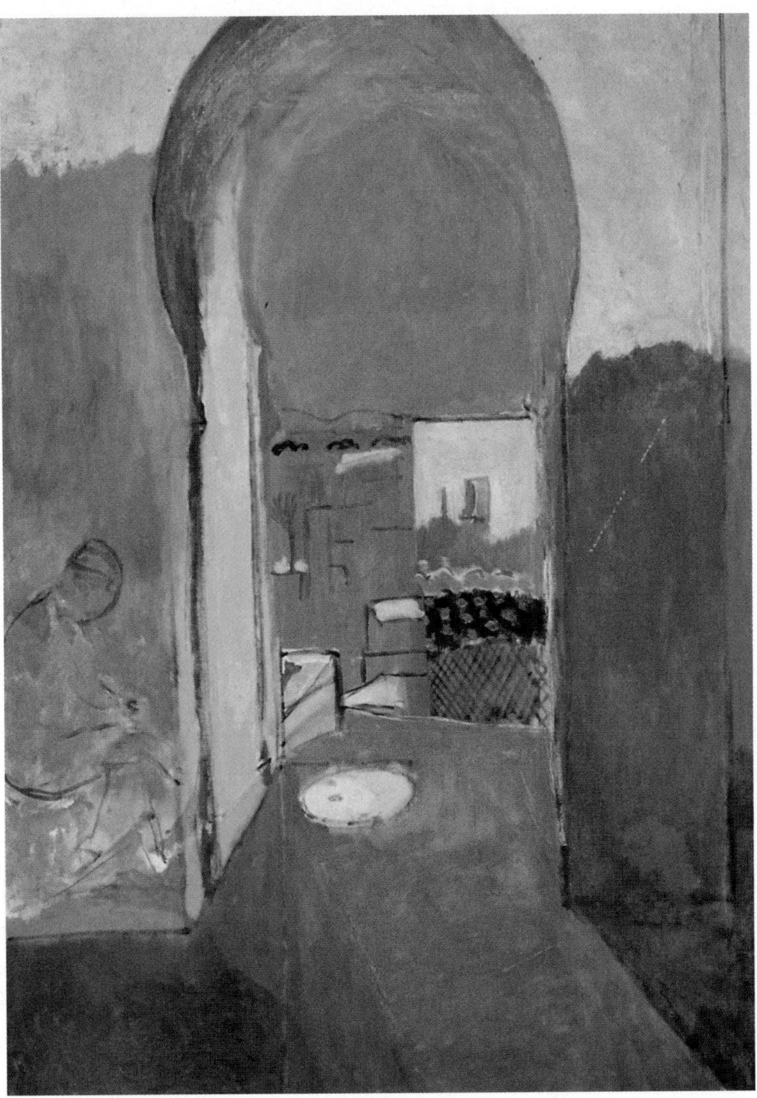

Henri Matisse, *The Casbah Gate,* 1912

[16]Matisse produces many powerful works in Morocco, including *The Casbah Gate.* [17]He painted the scene, useing brilliant colors. [18]He produced a mood based on color, light and form.

[19]Like the author of *Palace Walk,* Matisse using carefully chosen and rendered details, managed to convey a strong sense of place. [20]The shape of the archway in *The Casbah Gate* suggest the locale. [21]The pictures pale greens pinks, and roses reflects the pure light of the city. [22]Both the passage from *Palace Walk* and the scene in *The Casbah Gate* raises a sense of expectancy, almost as if the viewer were on the edge of a new and glorious adventure.

Review: Exercise 10

Mixed Review

The following sentences describe the life of Naguib Mahfouz. Rewrite each sentence on your paper according to the instructions that appear after each item. Make sure your answers are complete sentences.

Naguib Mahfouz

1. The Egyptian author Naguib Mahfouz was born *in 1911* in the city of Cairo. (Rewrite the sentence so that the phrase in italics, which is part of the complete predicate, appears in another position.)
2. Vivid sketches of Cairo are in his books. (Rewrite to begin with *There are.*)
3. In Mahfouz's books, the change in Cairo is depicted. (Add *and its people* to the complete subject.)
4. Mahfouz describes Egypt's political history. (Add *and depicts the desperate lives of the oppressed* to the complete predicate.)
5. This talented author has written numerous novels. (Add *and stories* to create a second direct object.)
6. Because of Mahfouz, the novel and short story have become modern genres in Arabic literature. (Add *popular* as a modifier of the subject complement.)
7. From his novels have come sixteen Egyptian movies. (Rewrite the sentence so that it begins with the complete subject.)
8. Winner of the Nobel Prize for Literature in 1988, Mahfouz gives a realistic view of urban Egyptian life. (Add *his readers* as an indirect object.)
9. With the translation of his books into English, Mahfouz has become increasingly popular in the United States. (Add *and respected* to create a second predicate adjective.)
10. Praised as Egypt's finest modern writer, Mahfouz has won honors. (Add *high* as a modifier of the direct object.)
11. Mahfouz offers detailed images of the luxury longed for by Cairo's impoverished population. (Add *his readers* to serve as an indirect object.)
12. These dreams contrast sharply with the reality of their lives. (Add another simple subject and a conjunction to form a compound subject.)
13. Mahfouz's words give an accurate picture of Cairo's architecture. (Add *the reader* to provide an indirect object.)
14. Readers from other cultures gain an understanding of twentieth-century Egyptian culture. (Add *excellent* to modify the direct object.)
15. Through reading Mahfouz's work, students of modern Egyptian culture can enhance their understanding of present-day Egyptian life. (Rewrite the sentence so that the complete subject comes before the complete predicate.)

Writing Application

Sentence Patterns in Writing

As you read the following passage from "Through the Tunnel" by Doris Lessing, notice how effectively the author varies the length of her sentences and their word order. Pay particular attention to the italicized sentences.

> *Jerry swam out to the big barrier rock, adjusted the goggles, and dived. . . .*
>
> *Under him, six or seven feet down, was a floor of perfectly clean, shining white sand, rippled firm and hard by the tides.* Two grayish shapes steered there, like long rounded pieces of wood or slate. *They were fish.* He saw them nose toward each other, poise motionless, make a dart forward, swerve off, and come around again. *It was like a water dance.* A few inches above them the water sparkled as if sequins were dropping through it.

Techniques with Sentence Patterns

Try to use Lessing's techniques when you write and revise your work.

1. Use compound subjects or predicates to tie ideas together.

CHOPPY SENTENCE Jerry swam out to the big barrier rock. He adjusted the goggles. He dived.

LESSING'S VERSION Jerry swam out to the big barrier rock, adjusted the goggles, and dived.

2. Achieve sentence variety by occasionally inverting word order.

GENERAL SENTENCE ORDER A floor of . . . white sand was under him, six or seven feet down.

LESSING'S VERSION Under him, six or seven feet down, was a floor of . . . white sand . . .

3. Vary the length of your sentences to maintain the reader's interest. Occasionally use a very short sentence to accent a point.

MONOTONOUS PATTERN Two grayish shapes steered there. They were like rounded pieces of wood or slate. The grayish shapes were fish.

LESSING'S VARIATION Two grayish shapes steered there, like long rounded pieces of wood or slate. They were fish.

TIME

For more about the writing process, see TIME Facing the Blank Page, pp. 109–119

Parts of the Sentence

Practice Practice these techniques by revising the following passage, adapted from "Through the Tunnel," combining ideas to create a pleasing variety of sentence lengths.

He put on his goggles. He fitted them tight. He tested the vacuum. His hands were shaking. Then he chose the biggest stone. He slipped over the edge of the rock. He looked up once at the empty sky. He filled his lungs once, twice. Then he sank fast to the bottom with the stone. He let it go. He began to count. No strain was on his lungs.

UNIT 12

Phrases

12.1 Prepositional Phrases

- A **phrase** is a group of words that acts in a sentence as a single part of speech.
- A **prepositional phrase** is a group of words that begins with a preposition and usually ends with a noun or pronoun, called the **object of the preposition.**

I voted **against the idea.** [*Idea* is the object of the preposition *against.*]

The elevator is necessary **for us.** [*Us* is the object of the preposition *for.*]

The poet Nikki Giovanni was born **in 1943.** [The date *1943* is the object of the preposition *in.*]

For lists of common prepositions, see page 473.

You may find adjectives and other modifiers appearing between the preposition and its object. Note also that a preposition may have more than one object.

The elevator goes **to the cool, dark basement.** [adjectives added]

The elevator goes **to the basement and the penthouse.** [two objects]

A prepositional phrase can act as an adjective or an adverb in a sentence. Used as an adjective, a prepositional phrase modifies a noun or a pronoun. Used as an adverb, it modifies a verb, an adjective, or an adverb.

Take the elevator **on the right.** [adjective phrase modifying the noun *elevator*]

Which **of these elevators** is working? [adjective phrase modifying the pronoun *which*]

After the meeting, you should take this elevator **to the lobby.** [adverb phrases modifying the verb phrase *should take*]

The elevator is helpful **to us.** [adverb phrase modifying the adjective *helpful*]

We sometimes work late **into the night.** [adverb phrase modifying the adverb *late*]

Exercise 1 Identifying Prepositional Phrases

On your paper, write each prepositional phrase that appears in the following sentences. (Some sentences have more than one prepositional phrase.)

Art in Nature

1. Great environmental art is alive on the Great Plains.
2. From an airplane, the vast cultivated fields resemble works of abstract art.
3. The varied designs are the result of modern farming methods.
4. The plowed fields are basically hilly and rectangular in shape.
5. Farmers plow along the natural contours of the land.
6. Red, brown, and black patterns with a variety of textures result from the plowing.
7. Irrigation equipment often pivots around a central water source.
8. This technique produces huge circular areas of bright green.
9. No one on the Great Plains has consciously planned these designs.
10. They are the bonus of the collaboration between the farmer and nature.

Exercise 2 Identifying Adjective and Adverb Phrases

On your paper, write the word or words each prepositional phrase in Exercise 1 modifies. Then write whether each phrase is acting as an *adjective* or an *adverb.*

Exercise 3 Expanding Sentences with Prepositional Phrases

On your paper, copy and expand the following sentences by adding at least one adjective phrase and one adverb phrase to each.

SAMPLE The loud music blared.
ANSWER The loud music on the car stereo blared through the open windows.

1. The deep blue lake glimmers.
2. No one told me.
3. The two wild horses galloped.
4. The workers piled up the bricks.
5. The dancers rehearsed tirelessly.
6. The engine stopped suddenly.
7. The Dalmatian and the boxer always run.
8. A strong wind is blowing the papers.
9. That old building collapsed.
10. The geese were flying south.

Exercise 4 Using Prepositional Phrases in Writing

On your paper, write five sentences that include prepositional phrases. Underline each prepositional phrase; label it as an *adjective* or an *adverb.*

SAMPLE The tennis club <u>at school</u> meets <u>on Thursday</u>.
ANSWER at school, adjective; on Thursday, adverb

Phrases

12.2 Appositives and Appositive Phrases

- An **appositive** is a noun or a pronoun that is placed next to another noun or pronoun to identify or give additional information about it.

  My friend **Myles** sent me a postcard from England. [The appositive *Myles* identifies the noun *friend.*]

- An **appositive phrase** is an appositive plus any words that modify the appositive.

  Joanne rode a hydrofoil across the English Channel, **the body of water between England and France.** [The appositive phrase, in bold type, identifies *English Channel.*]

Appositives or appositive phrases that are not essential to the meaning of a sentence should be set off by commas.

Myles's sister **Jean** lives there. [The appositive *Jean* is essential because Myles has more than one sister.]

Myles's only brother, **Timothy,** now lives in Ireland. [The appositive *Timothy* is not necessary to identify the brother.]

Usually an appositive or appositive phrase follows the noun or pronoun it identifies or explains. Occasionally an appositive phrase precedes the noun or pronoun.

A talented artist, Myles would like to become an illustrator of children's books.

Exercise 5 **Identifying Appositives and Appositive Phrases**

On your paper, write the appositives and appositive phrases in the following sentences.

1. My cousin Andrea broke her leg.
2. She was visited in the hospital by Dan and Rosalia, two friends from school.
3. During her hospital stay, my mother took Andrea a get-well gift, a very cute toy bear.
4. Andrea stayed in the hospital, Memorial Hospital Center, for two days.
5. On Andrea's cast, her sister Camille drew an appropriate cartoon, a rabbit on skis tumbling down a hill.

Phrases

Exercise 6 Identifying Appositives and Appositive Phrases

On your paper, write the appositive or appositive phrase that appears in each sentence. Then write the noun or pronoun that is identified or expanded by the appositive or appositive phrase. (Two sentences have more than one appositive or appositive phrase.)

Leaders in Their Fields

1. Sandra Day O'Connor, the first female justice on the United States Supreme Court, was appointed by President Reagan.
2. A familiar figure on the evening news was Connie Chung, a Chinese American.
3. The Native American Maria Tallchief became a highly accomplished ballerina.
4. Ntozake Shange, an African American author and university professor, wrote a wonderful novel, *Betsey Brown.*
5. The United States Representative to the United Nations from 1981 to 1985 was Jeane Kirkpatrick, a teacher and scholar.
6. The anthropologist Margaret Mead made her reputation by studying native peoples of the South Pacific.
7. Anna Mary Robertson Moses, a farm wife untrained in art, became the famous painter Grandma Moses.
8. The tennis player Althea Gibson was the first African American to win a national American tennis tournament.
9. Chita Rivera, an American actress, has starred in many movies and musicals.
10. Pearl Buck, who received the Nobel Prize for Literature in 1938, is known for *The Good Earth,* her novel about China.

Exercise 7 Expanding Sentences with Appositive Phrases

On your paper, expand the following sentences by adding an appositive or an appositive phrase to each one. Be sure to use commas where necessary.

SAMPLE Matthew Henson went on the first expedition to the North Pole.
ANSWER Matthew Henson, an African American explorer, went on the first expedition to the North Pole.

1. My sister's dog is a champion.
2. My grandfather is my idol.
3. For my birthday, my cousin gave me a compact disc.
4. Sasha's friends look almost like twins.
5. On Sundays, we always have the same dessert.
6. The film is my favorite.
7. My brother volunteered to read to Elizabeth.
8. Mary preferred to take the old road.
9. My favorite singer is going on tour this summer.
10. Mike will help Mrs. Scott shovel her sidewalk.

12.3 Verbals and Verbal Phrases

- A **verbal** is a verb form that functions in a sentence as a noun, an adjective, or an adverb.
- A **verbal phrase** is a verbal plus any complements and modifiers.

The three kinds of verbals are *participles, gerunds,* and *infinitives.* All of these types can be expanded into phrases.

Participles and Participial Phrases

- A **participle** is a verb form that can function as an adjective.

Present participles always end in *-ing.* Although *past participles* often end in *-ed,* they can take other forms as well. Many adjectives commonly used in sentences are actually participles.

The **freezing** rain slowly turned to hail.

The **heated** argument occurred among the **losing** players.

A participle can be used as an adjective or as part of a verb phrase.

PARTICIPLE AS ADJECTIVE	The **married** couple have jobs.
PARTICIPLE IN VERB PHRASE	The judge **has married** the couple.

- A **participial phrase** contains a participle plus any complements and modifiers.

Participial phrases can be used in various positions in a sentence. They always act as adjectives.

Pete Sampras **playing tennis** draws large crowds.

Sampras, **disappointed with his first serve,** vowed to improve his game.

Sitting quietly during one of Sampras's games, his fans watch him intently.

Graciously accepting a trophy from the sponsors, he smiled at the crowd.

In general, a participial phrase at the beginning of a sentence is followed by a comma.

Phrases

Exercise 8 Identifying Participles and Participial Phrases

On your paper, write the participle or the participial phrase that acts as an adjective in each sentence. Then identify the word or words each one modifies.

Fashions from Other Lands

1. Americans looking for more variety often adopt the fashions of other countries.
2. The demand for goods imported from other lands is often great.
3. Chinese textile mills export silk decorated by hand.
4. A wool scarf woven in Ecuador is warm and colorful.
5. Brides prize lace veils made by French nuns.
6. Fine cotton fabrics used for men's shirts come from Egypt.
7. Batik cloth made in Malaysia makes beautiful warm-weather dresses and shirts.
8. Freshwater pearls imported from Japan are used for necklaces and earrings.
9. Rings from gold mined in Australia are prized by American women and men.
10. India exports gold hoops for pierced ears.
11. Embroidered blouses from Mexico contain intricate floral designs.
12. Leather processed in Italy is used in elegant shoes and purses.
13. Aquamarines and topaz mined in Brazil make beautiful jewelry.
14. Sweaters crafted by Irish workers are heavy and durable.
15. Shoppers can find interesting fashions from just about anywhere in the world.

Exercise 9 Writing Sentences with Participial Phrases

Use each of the following phrases in a sentence. Use the phrase as a participle, not as part of a verb phrase. Place your participial phrase as close as possible to the noun or pronoun it modifies. Then underline that noun or pronoun.

SAMPLE limping down the empty road
ANSWER Limping down the empty road, the lost <u>dog</u> looked pathetic.

1. panting in the midday heat
2. whining and whimpering with pain
3. frozen in his tracks
4. broken in two places
5. carrying him home on my shoulders
6. reaching our front porch
7. yelling for someone's help
8. hearing my call
9. sprawled helplessly on the porch floor
10. gathering up the dog in her arms
11. grabbing two soft blankets
12. comforted by our tender care
13. arriving at the veterinarian's office
14. known for his skill with animals
15. wagging his tail with glee

Phrases

Gerunds and Gerund Phrases

- A **gerund** is a verb form that ends in ***-ing*** and is used in the same way a noun is used.

  Reading is my favorite pastime. [gerund as subject]

  Dana enjoys **running.** [gerund as direct object]

  Jin gives **studying** top priority. [gerund as indirect object]

  How much time do you devote to **exercising?** [gerund as object of a preposition]

  My preference is **dancing.** [gerund as predicate nominative]

  Her hobbies, **skiing** and **hiking,** are strenuous and healthful. [gerunds as appositives]

- A **gerund phrase** is a gerund plus any complements and modifiers.

  Students are responsible for **mastering their subjects.**

jumping!

Both a present participle and a gerund end in *-ing.* A present participle is used as an adjective, whereas a gerund is used as a noun.

Listening to the radio, Yusuf worked faster. [present participle]

Listening to the radio helps Yusuf work faster. [gerund]

Exercise 10 Identifying Gerunds and Gerund Phrases

On your paper, list the gerunds and gerund phrases that appear in the following sentences. (Some of the sentences have more than one gerund or gerund phrase.)

The Yanomamo

1. Surviving is a challenge for the Yanomamo, a people from the tropical forests of South America.
2. For centuries, the Yanomamo have lived by raising crops, gathering fruits and nuts, and hunting.
3. Living in remote jungle areas had prevented the Yanomamo from having contact with modern civilization.
4. The Yanomamo look for a way of protecting themselves from the greed of the outside world.
5. Mining and ranching have begun to intrude on the lands of the Yanomamo.
6. Contact with outsiders has endangered the Yanomamo by exposing them to diseases.
7. Contracting unfamiliar illnesses is becoming all too common among the Yanomamo.
8. Coping with an indifferent government is another challenge for them.
9. Fighting to save the environment is one Yanomamo project.
10. Saving their homeland is their goal.

Infinitives and Infinitive Phrases

- An **infinitive** is a verb form that is usually preceded by the word *to* and is used as a noun, an adjective, or an adverb.

When the word *to* appears before the base form of a verb, it is part of the infinitive form of the verb and not a preposition.

To sleep is relaxing. [infinitive as subject]

Every baby needs **to crawl.** [infinitive as direct object]

Her wish is **to succeed.** [infinitive as predicate nominative]

I had a tendency **to doze.** [infinitive as adjective]

He was eager **to rest.** [infinitive as adverb]

- An **infinitive phrase** contains an infinitive plus any complements and modifiers.

To hike the Appalachian Trail is my sister's dream.

We decided **to dress for the party.**

The committee voted **to appoint Jennifer president.**

Exercise 11 Identifying Infinitives and Infinitive Phrases

On your paper, write the infinitive or infinitive phrase that appears in each of the following sentences. (One sentence has two infinitive phrases.)

Mary Harris Jones, Labor Leader

1. One of the most remarkable figures to join the American labor movement was Mary Harris Jones.
2. In 1880, at the age of 50, Jones decided to change her life.
3. After abandoning her work as a teacher and dressmaker, she proceeded to become a union organizer.
4. Her custom was to travel from place to place in a black gown and bonnet.
5. She worked in the cotton mills of the South to gather evidence for her campaign against child labor.
6. In 1915 she went to New York City to help the garment and streetcar workers.
7. In a speech, she said, "I want you to pledge yourselves . . . to stand as one . . . "
8. She led young millworkers to Washington to plead for child labor laws.
9. Mary Jones helped to organize the 1919 steel strike.
10. Mother Jones, as she was sometimes called, was able to make a vigorous speech before a camera on her hundredth birthday.

Exercise 12 Using Infinitive Phrases

Jot down five action verbs. Then write each one in an infinitive phrase in an original sentence. Underline the infinitive phrases.

Exercise 13 Identifying Verbal Phrases

On your paper, write the verbal phrases that appear in the following sentences. Write whether each phrase is a *participial phrase,* a *gerund phrase,* or an *infinitive phrase.*

Kachina Dolls

1. The word *kachina* is used by the Pueblo peoples in the southwestern United States to name one of the spirit gods.
2. Carving and painting kachina dolls, artists reflect the doll's importance to the people.
3. Used in ceremonies, the dolls are part of the people's beliefs.
4. Raising and planting crops are the most common purposes for ceremonies featuring kachinas.
5. Asking for rain, the people use the dolls.
6. Often, men dressed as kachinas dance in ceremonies.
7. Children watching the dance are not supposed to recognize their fathers dressed as the spirit.
8. Another kachina, a singing kachina, appears on housetops to make announcements.
9. Healing kachinas may be part of ceremonies held for people who are ill.
10. Passing the dolls from one generation to the next, people strengthen the belief in the dolls' powers.
11. Children of the Southwestern pueblos know they are not to play with kachina dolls.
12. Some kachinas bring surprising and exciting gifts to the children, making them feel a part of the ceremonies.
13. The gifts may be fruits and sweets for them to enjoy or toys that remind them of hunting skills.
14. Incorporating their religious beliefs into everyday life is important for the people.
15. In more recent times, artists have begun making kachina dolls to sell to tourists.
16. Some feel that having a singing kachina or a deer kachina may help the buyer understand the purpose of the spirit dolls.
17. Becoming familiar with various spirits may enable a person to respect the beliefs of the native peoples.
18. Many places offering kachinas for sale are approved by the Pueblo peoples.
19. Raising money through sales is important to many communities.
20. However, there are some members of the Southwestern peoples who are reluctant to see their sacred objects sold as souvenirs.

Exercise 14 Using Verbal Phrases

On your paper, write the following verbal phrases in original sentences. Write whether each is used as a *participial phrase,* a *gerund phrase,* or an *infinitive phrase.*

1. collecting money for a canned food drive
2. to set up a contest between classes
3. asking the community
4. to provide a nutritious meal
5. satisfied with the effort

Phrases

UNIT 12

Grammar Review

PHRASES

The Stuff of Heroes is about a young boy named Gervasio, who learns about bravery firsthand during the Spanish Civil War. Gervasio's family is divided by the conflict, which began in 1936 and lasted for three bitter years. This excerpt from the novel contains a vivid description of two friends of Gervasio's from school. The excerpt, translated from the Spanish, has been annotated to show the kinds of phrases covered in this unit.

Literature Model

from The Stuff of Heroes

by Miguel Delibes

translated from the Spanish by Frances M. López-Morillas

In those days the gang gained two new members, also left-overs from the Jesuits' departure: Dámaso Valentín and Eduardo Custodio. Dámaso wore his hair in a brush cut; his thin, elastic lips and the open smiling expression of his light brown eyes brought an enormous joie de vivre to the group. The youngest of five brothers, all of whom had left home, he lived with his widowed mother and two old servants in the most aristocratic part of town. Perhaps because life was easy for him and his weekly allowance double that of his friends, Dámaso was always smiling, and when he did so he displayed a notched front tooth (souvenir of a childhood fall) which he daintily caressed with the tip of his active red tongue. An adaptable and generous boy, he accepted enthusiastically any plan suggested by his friends and his prosperity even allowed him to place his small personal properties at the group's disposal. This was the case of the hard rubber ball with which, shortly after they had met him, they began to play after school on the sidewalk that ran alongside the park, defying the zeal of the municipal guards.

Prepositional phrase (adjective phrase): of his light brown eyes

Prepositional phrase (adverb phrase): with his widowed mother and two old servants

Appositive phrase: An adaptable and generous boy

Participial phrase (past participle): suggested by his friends

Participial phrase (present participle): defying the zeal of the municipal guards

Phrases

Eduardo Custodio was the other; pale, slow, and roundabout in speech, with a touch of humor, he suffered from a premature aging that showed in his nearsightedness, his heavy eyelids, his limpness, and a certain stiffness of the legs for which he tried to compensate with tenacity and pride when he played soccer, his great passion. He did not use glasses, and usually combated his myopia by pulling at the outside corner of his eye to make images clearer, and when he went to the movies or some other kind of show he used opera glasses that had belonged to his great-grandmother.

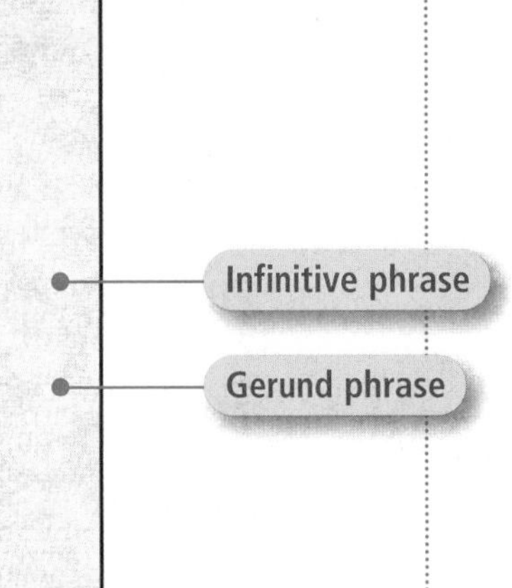

Review: Exercise 1 — Expanding Sentences with Prepositional Phrases

The following sentences describe an imaginary street scene. Read through the sentences quickly to get an idea of the scene, and then rewrite each sentence, adding at least one prepositional phrase, used as an adjective or an adverb, to each sentence.

SAMPLE Today was market day.
ANSWER Today was market day in the small Spanish town.

1. The town had a spacious plaza.
2. The fountain was a gathering place.
3. Farmers brought fresh potatoes and melons.
4. Farmhands arranged their produce.
5. Storekeepers exhibited their wares.
6. Some merchants displayed bundles.
7. Weary teams pulled heavy wagons.
8. Men carefully unloaded the wagons.
9. Fishmongers arranged their freshest fish.
10. The pearly scales gleamed.
11. Weavers exhibited woolen rugs.
12. Each rug had been carefully woven.
13. The leather merchant sold belts.
14. He also sold gloves.
15. A breeze cooled the air.
16. The hot sun cast shadows.
17. Baskets decorated the greengrocer's stall.
18. Wooden crates overflowed.
19. A noisy group assembled.
20. They splashed their hands and ran off.

Phrases

Review: Exercise 2

Expanding Sentences with Appositives and Appositive Phrases

The sentences below elaborate on ideas suggested by the passage from *The Stuff of Heroes.* Rewrite each sentence, incorporating the words in parentheses as an appositive or an appositive phrase. Use a comma or commas to set off the appositive or appositive phrase from the rest of the sentence.

SAMPLE Dámaso and Eduardo were the two new members of the gang. (leftovers from the Jesuits' departure)

ANSWER Dámaso and Eduardo, leftovers from the Jesuits' departure, were the two new members of the gang.

1. Dámaso Valentín brought to the group great verve, along with a taste of prosperity. (a high-spirited boy)
2. He lived with his mother. (a widow)
3. Dámaso's family lived in a house in the nicest part of town. (relatively affluent aristocrats)
4. Dámaso's constant smile revealed a notched front tooth. (the result of a fall)
5. The others in the group could usually count on Dámaso's generosity. (less affluent boys)
6. After school, the group would play on the sidewalk with a hard rubber ball. (a possession of Dámaso's)
7. Eduardo Custodio's nearsightedness and stiff legs made him seem old before his time. (middle-aged infirmities)
8. Eduardo played soccer with tenacity. (his great passion)
9. At the movies, he used opera glasses. (relics of his great-grandmother's day)
10. In many ways, Eduardo was the opposite of the lighthearted Dámaso. (a slow and cautious boy)
11. While Dámaso was quick, Eduardo was slow. (a deliberate and arthritic boy)
12. At soccer, Eduardo's self-discipline moved him beyond his limitations. (a game that punishes the slow)
13. He always played for a goal. (proof of his athletic skills)
14. The others admired Eduardo's persistence. (a quality that made him one of the best players)
15. Eduardo's dignity earned him respect. (a trait not often found in one his age)
16. Pride kept Eduardo from wearing glasses. (a symbol of weakness in his opinion)
17. In sharp contrast to Eduardo was Dámaso. (a vibrant and healthy boy)
18. Dámaso seemed to float through the ups and downs of daily life. (a very different sort of person)
19. His background gave him a favorable view of the world. (a life of comfort)
20. Dámaso was immensely likable. (an easy-going and kindly boy)

Review: Exercise 3 Expanding Sentences with Participial Phrases

The following sentences describe scenes in *The Stuff of Heroes.* Combine the sentences, changing the sentence in parentheses into a participial phrase. Be sure to place the participial phrase near the word that it modifies.

SAMPLE Dámaso and Eduardo found their school closed.
(They were beginning the new school year.)

ANSWER Beginning the new school year, Dámaso and Eduardo found their school closed.

1. The Jesuits shut their schools.
(The Jesuits were expelled from Spain by the government.)
2. Dámaso and Eduardo sought new friends.
(Dámaso and Eduardo were feeling self-conscious in their new school.)
3. Gervasio warmly greeted his two new classmates.
(Gervasio was seeing new faces.)
4. Gervasio's circle of friends gained two new members.
(The circle of friends was welcoming Dámaso and Eduardo.)
5. Dámaso quickly made friends with everyone.
(Dámaso was smiling his customary smile.)
6. Dámaso looked sleek and contemporary.
(Dámaso was wearing his hair in a brush cut.)
7. Dámaso's friends often visited his house.
(The house was located in an aristocratic part of town.)
8. Dámaso's mother was generous.
(She was giving him double the weekly allowance of his friends.)
9. The boy had an easy life. (He was experiencing little hardship.)
10. The municipal guards once caught Gervasio's gang.
(The boys were playing ball on the sidewalk alongside the park.)
11. One of Gervasio's relatives used his influence on the boy's behalf.
(The relative was conferring with a sergeant of the guards.)
12. The police freed the boys and returned their ball.
(The police were dropping the charges.)
13. Eduardo Custodio was pale and slow.
(He was suffering from premature aging.)
14. Eduardo never made excuses for himself.
(He was often vexed by the stiffness in his legs.)
15. He did not wear eyeglasses. (He was hiding his nearsightedness.)
16. The violence of civil war would soon interrupt the boy's sheltered lives.
(The violence was provoked by a miners' strike.)

Review: Exercise 4 **Writing Sentences with Gerund Phrases**

Each of the following items consists of a question followed by a phrase in parentheses that answers the question. For each item, write a sentence that answers the question, using the words in parentheses as a gerund phrase.

SAMPLE What helps explain Spain's role in Europe today? (understanding Spanish history)
ANSWER Understanding Spanish history helps explain Spain's role in Europe today.

1. What was Spain's goal at one time? (creating a vast colonial empire)
2. What set off Spain's decline? (losing its Latin American colonies)
3. What divided the country before World War II? (fighting a bloody civil war)
4. By what means did Franco unify Spain? (ruling the country as a dictator)
5. Many people opposed Franco for what action? (accepting military aid from Hitler)
6. What made Spain an outcast in postwar Europe? (being ruled by a fascist dictator)
7. Many Spaniards feared what turn of events? (returning to civil war)
8. What brought political reforms to Spain? (restoring the monarchy in 1975)
9. What did King Juan Carlos favor? (liberalizing Franco's harsh policies)
10. What finally made Spain a full participant in Western European society? (joining the European Economic Community in 1986)
11. What has begun to improve the standard of living in Spain? (participating in free trade with other countries)
12. What made Spain attractive to the United States during the cold war? (Franco's opposing the Soviet Union and communism)
13. How did the United States help Spain during the cold war? (loaning Franco's government millions of dollars)
14. What did Spain do to help the United States during the cold war? (allowing the United States to set up military bases in Spain)
15. What was the purpose of the American military bases in Spain? (defending Europe against possible Soviet attack)
16. What improved Spain's standing with other nations? (joining the United Nations in 1955)
17. How did the United States help Spain during its time of economic hardship? (donating millions of dollars in aid)
18. What helped pull Spain out of its economic difficulties in the early 1960s? (undertaking a financial reform program)
19. What was Spain's reward for undergoing financial reform? (receiving membership in the European Economic Community)
20. To what can the Spanish people now look forward? (becoming an even more prosperous and respected nation)

Review: Exercise 5 **Writing Sentences with Infinitive Phrases**

The following sentences are based on passages from *The Stuff of Heroes* that are not reprinted in this textbook. Each item consists of a question followed by a phrase in parentheses that answers the question. For each item, write on your paper a sentence that answers the question, using the words in parentheses as an infinitive phrase.

SAMPLE What was Gervasio's childhood dream? (to be a crusader)
ANSWER Gervasio's childhood dream was to be a crusader.

1. What was Gervasio's great desire? (to perform deeds of courage)
2. What did he hope to do? (to battle the enemy)
3. What did these ambitions only manage to do? (to give him goose flesh)
4. What did Gervasio's fervor make his classmates want to do? (to laugh at his zeal)
5. When rebels attacked, what was Gervasio's plan? (to shoot stones from his slingshot at the attackers)
6. What did Gervasio have to do to become a hero in his own eyes? (to participate fully in the battle)
7. What was Gervasio able to do because he began his career as a hero? (to feel triumphant)
8. Later, when the civil war broke out, what did Gervasio, Dámaso, and Eduardo volunteer to do? (to join Franco's navy)
9. According to Dámaso, what was the greatest honor? (to die for the cause)
10. What did a torpedo attack force Gervasio to do? (to confront paralyzing fear)
11. What would Gervasio be able to do if he performed courageous deeds? (to fulfill a personal goal)
12. What was Gervasio's personal goal? (to prove to himself that he was brave)
13. What did his thoughts of bravery continue to do? (to show him how frightened he really was)
14. What did Gervasio's classmates continue to do? (to ridicule his enthusiasm)
15. When he used his slingshot, what was Gervasio's hope? (to have accurate aim)
16. What did Gervasio have to do to gain self-respect? (to fight bravely)
17. As a hero, what would Gervasio have to do? (to take on more responsibility)
18. What did Gervasio, Dámaso, and Eduardo want to do during the civil war? (to become sailors)
19. What might be necessary when fighting for a cause? (to sacrifice oneself for one's beliefs)
20. What would Gervasio be able to do by engaging in armed conflict? (to meet his fear and work through it)

Review: Exercise 6 **Writing Sentences with Phrases**

On your paper, write sentences according to the directions that follow. Make your sentences relate to *The Stuff of Heroes,* but do not copy sentences from the passage.

SAMPLE Write a sentence that includes a prepositional phrase used as an adjective.
ANSWER The *Stuff of Heroes* is a book about a young boy named Gervasio.

1. Write a sentence using a prepositional phrase that is an adverb.
2. Write a sentence that begins with an appositive phrase.
3. Write a sentence in which a participial phrase modifies the direct object.
4. Make a gerund phrase the subject of a sentence.
5. Write a sentence using an infinitive phrase as a noun.

Review: Exercise 7

Proofreading

The following passage describes Henri Cartier-Bresson, the photographer whose work appears on the opposite page. Rewrite the passage, correcting the errors in spelling, grammar, and usage. Add any missing punctuation. There are twenty-five errors.

Henri Cartier-Bresson

[1]Born in Chanteloup, France, in 1908 the photographer Henri Cartier-Bresson ranks among the worlds great photojournalists. [2]The son of a wealthy thread manufacturer he began drawing and painting when he was very young. [3]Recuperating from an illness at the age of twenty-three he discovered photography.

[4]Cartier-Bresson beleived that a photographer should record life as it is, not as the photographer wants it to be. [5]Disliking the posed pictures common in studio photography he liked to capture the "decisive moment" of a situation the moment in which the essence of a scene is revealed. [6]During the year of 1933, he bought his first Leica camera a small instrument equipped with a quiet shutter. [7]This camera enabled you to take photographs quickly easily, and inconspicuously. [8]Indebted to the great films of the past Cartier-Bresson learned to choose expressive images for his photos. [9]Trained as a painter he always carried a sketch pad along with his camera.

[10]In the decade of the 1930s, Cartier-Bresson documented the lives of people in Mexico worked with the great French film director Jean Renoir, and made his own documentory about Spanish hospitals. [11]Captured by the Germans during World War II he escaped from prison on his third attempt. [12]Later, he helped establish Magnum a photo agency. ➡

Henri Cartier-Bresson, *Seville,* 1933

[13]*Seville* is typical of Cartier-Bressons documentary style. [14]Taken through a break in a wall the photograph shows a group of children playing in a poor neighborhood in Seville a city in Spain. [15]The composition is extrordinary and seemingly casual. [16]All the elements in the picture hangs in a delicate balance.

[17]Writing about the Spanish Civil War in *The Stuff of Heroes* Miguel Delibes describes children who are forced to endure hardships. [18]Each of the boys in Delibes's story manage to survive by creating their own imaginary world. [19]This world mirrors the real worlds conflict, yet it is also full of humor and joy.

Review: Exercise 8

Mixed Review

The biographical sketch of Miguel Delibes [mē gel′ dā lē′ bes] that appears here is followed by ten numbered sentences. Use the facts in the sketch to revise the ten items, following the guidelines that appear in parentheses at the end of each sentence. Be sure to place any phrase you add near the word it modifies.

Miguel Delibes

Miguel Delibes is one of Spain's most admired novelists. He was born in 1920 in Valladolid in the province of Castile, and most of his novels are set in that region. During Delibes's youth, Spain was torn by a civil war (1936–1939). General Francisco Franco's Nationalist forces, supported by Nazi Germany and Fascist Italy, battled the leftist Republican forces, which were aided by the Soviet Union. Franco emerged victorious, ruling Spain as a dictator until 1975. During the civil war, Delibes served as a volunteer in Franco's army.

After the war, Delibes earned degrees in law, business, and journalism. His first novel, *The Cypress Casts a Long Shadow,* won the Nadal Prize in 1947. This early success inspired Delibes to become a writer in addition to pursuing an academic career. Six of his many novels and works of nonfiction have been translated into English, including his most popular novel, *El Camino* (1950), published in English as *The Path.* Delibes's novel *The Stuff of Heroes* (1987) is a coming-of-age story based on his experiences as a school boy in Valladolid and as a volunteer in the civil war. Through Gervasio, its main character, the novel explores the meaning of heroism, bravery, and loyalty against the backdrop of divided allegiances within a family and a nation.

1. Miguel Delibes is a popular and admired novelist.
   (Add an adjective prepositional phrase.)
2. Delibes was born in the province of Castile. He sets most of his fiction in that region.
   (Combine the sentences by turning the first sentence into a participial phrase.)
3. The Spanish civil war began. (Add an adverb prepositional phrase.)
4. Spain was torn by something. It was fighting between fascists and socialists.
   (Combine the sentences by turning the second sentence into a gerund phrase.)
5. What did Delibes volunteer to do during the civil war?
   (Respond with a sentence that includes an infinitive phrase.)
6. After the war, Delibes devoted himself to something. He was studying law, business, and journalism.
   (Combine the sentences by turning the second sentence into a gerund phrase.)
7. *The Cypress Casts a Long Shadow* won the 1947 Nadal Prize.
   (Add an appositive phrase.)
8. Delibes was inspired by this prestigious award. Delibes decided to write more novels.
   (Combine the sentences by turning the first sentence into a participial phrase.)
9. Six of Delibes's works have been translated. (Add an adverb prepositional phrase.)
10. In *The Stuff of Heroes,* Gervasio is the name.
    (Add an adjective prepositional phrase.)

Writing Application

TIME

For more about the writing process, see TIME Facing the Blank Page, pp. 109–119

Phrases in Writing

William Least Heat-Moon uses many phrases in this passage from *Blue Highways: A Journey Into America*. Read the passage, focusing especially on the italicized phrases.

The highway made an unexpected jog toward Navajo Bridge, *a melding of silvery girders and rock cliffs.* Suddenly, there it was, far below *in the deep and scary canyon of sides so sheer* they might have been cut *with a stone saw,* the naturally silted water turned an unnatural green . . . *by the big settling basin a few miles upriver* called Glen Canyon Dam. Navajo Bridge, *built in 1929 when paved roads began opening the area,* is the only crossing *over the Colorado* between Glen Canyon and Hoover Dam several hundred miles downstream.

Techniques with Phrases

Try to apply some of William Least Heat-Moon's techniques in your own work.

1. Use prepositional phrases to explain location and to add precision.

GENERAL WORDS Suddenly, there it was, far below . . .

LEAST HEAT-MOON'S VERSION Suddenly, there it was, far below *in the deep and scary canyon* . . .

2. Consider whether appositive phrases can make your writing more vivid. For example, Least Heat-Moon uses an appositive phrase to help readers picture the Navajo Bridge.

GENERAL WORDS The highway made an unexpected jog toward Navajo Bridge. . . .

LEAST HEAT-MOON'S VERSION The highway made an unexpected jog toward Navajo Bridge, *a melding of silvery girders and rock cliffs.*

3. Use verbal phrases to improve the flow of your sentences and to show relationships between ideas.

REPETITIVE SENTENCES Navajo Bridge was built in 1929 when paved roads began opening the area. Navajo Bridge is the only crossing . . .

LEAST HEAT-MOON'S VERSION Navajo Bridge, *built in 1929 when paved roads began opening the area,* is the only crossing . . .

Practice Practice these techniques by expanding the following paragraph. Use prepositional phrases, appositive phrases, and verbal phrases to make ideas more precise and vivid.

My friends and I stood on the rim of the canyon. The sun was setting. The canyon walls reflected the soft rays. Different shades of red blended into each other. Long shadows crossed the ground. Long shadows hid some of the detail on the canyon's floor. In the distance we could see a small village. An old man rode his horse next to the river. A solitary woman tended a fire. Smoke from the fire rose. A lone eagle soared in and out of the gorge. The only noise I could hear was the slight breeze. It was rustling the leaves on the trees nearby.

UNIT 13

Clauses and Sentence Structure

13.1 Main Clauses

■ A **clause** is a group of words that has a subject and a predicate and that is used as a part of a sentence.

Clauses fall into two categories: *main clauses,* which are also called *independent clauses,* and *subordinate clauses,* which are also called *dependent clauses.*

■ A **main clause** has a subject and a predicate and can stand alone as a sentence.

There must be at least one main clause in every sentence. Both of the clauses in each of the following examples are main clauses because both can stand alone as sentences.

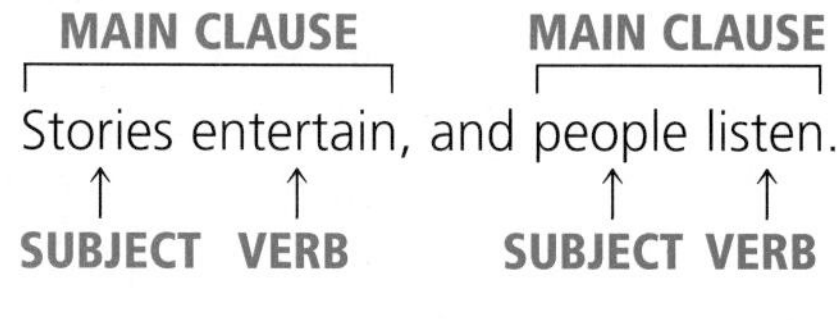

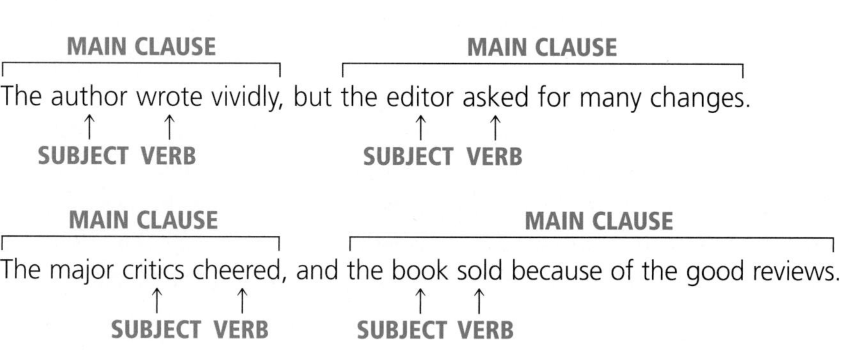

Exercise 1 Identifying Main Clauses

On your paper, copy the following sentences and mark each main clause. Then write *S* below each subject and *V* below each verb. Be sure that each clause you mark can stand alone as a sentence.

SAMPLE ANSWER

The book reached the bookstores, and the advertising campaign began.
S V S V

1. The publishers advertised, and the bookstore owners responded.
2. The book's cover was a striking design, and the author was pleased.
3. The author toured, and television hosts interviewed her.
4. Sometimes she gave readings, but few people attended.
5. Eventually sales increased, and the author celebrated.

13.2 Subordinate Clauses

■ A **subordinate clause** has a subject and a predicate but cannot stand alone as a sentence.

In order for a subordinate clause to make sense, it must be attached to a main clause. Many subordinate clauses begin with subordinating conjunctions or relative pronouns. (Subordinating conjunctions are listed on page 478, and relative pronouns are on page 451.)

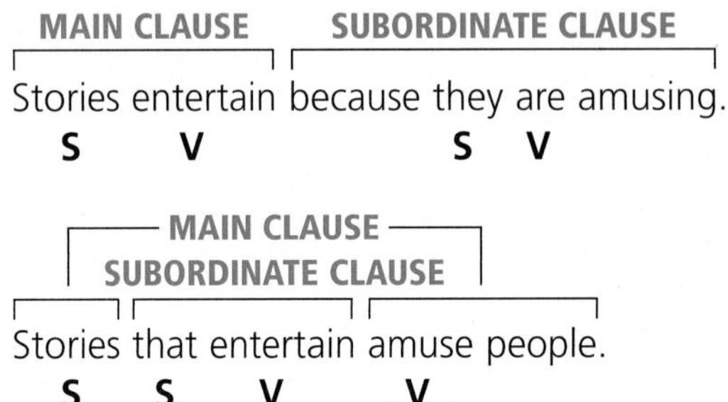

In the first example, the subordinate clause, *because they are amusing,* is attached to the main clause, *Stories entertain.* The subordinate clause is introduced by the subordinating conjunction *because,* which is placed before *they are amusing.* Note that the subordinate clause does not express a complete thought even though it has a subject and a predicate.

In the second example, the subordinate clause comes between the subject and the verb of the main clause. This subordinate clause begins with the relative pronoun *that,* which also serves as the subject of the clause.

Exercise 2 Identifying Clauses

Each of the following sentences has a clause that appears in italics. On your paper, indicate whether the clause is a *main clause* or a *subordinate clause.*

Mahalia Jackson, Gospel Singer

[1]Mahalia Jackson was an African American singer *who became popular worldwide as a performer of gospel music.* [2]*Although she was strongly associated with religious music,* her vocal style was influenced by blues. [3]*Jackson grew up in New Orleans,* where she sang in a church choir. [4]*When she was 16 years old,* Jackson moved to Chicago. [5]*She worked at odd jobs* during the first years that she lived in the city. [6]*Because she possessed a powerful, beautiful voice,* record companies soon offered her contracts. [7]In the 1950s, she gave a series of gospel concerts across the United States *that drew huge audiences.* [8]*Jackson performed internationally* after her United States tours proved so successful. [9]*Although she was a popular gospel star,* Jackson was also very much concerned with politics. [10]*Since she viewed song as an inspiration for peace,* she performed at many civil rights rallies and marches.

13.3 Simple and Compound Sentences

■ A **simple sentence** has only one main clause and no subordinate clauses.

A simple sentence may contain a compound subject or a compound predicate or both. The subject and the predicate can be expanded with adjectives, adverbs, prepositional phrases, appositives, and verbal phrases. As long as the sentence has only one main clause, however, it remains a simple sentence.

Stories entertain. [simple sentence]

Stories and riddles entertain. [simple sentence with compound subject]

Stories entertain and amuse. [simple sentence with compound predicate]

Stories and riddles amuse and entertain. [simple sentence with compound subject and compound predicate]

Stories about the Old West entertain adults and children alike. [simple sentence expanded]

■ A **compound sentence** has two or more main clauses.

Each main clause of a compound sentence has its own subject and predicate, and these main clauses are usually joined by a comma and a coordinating conjunction (such as *and, but, or, nor, yet,* or *for*).

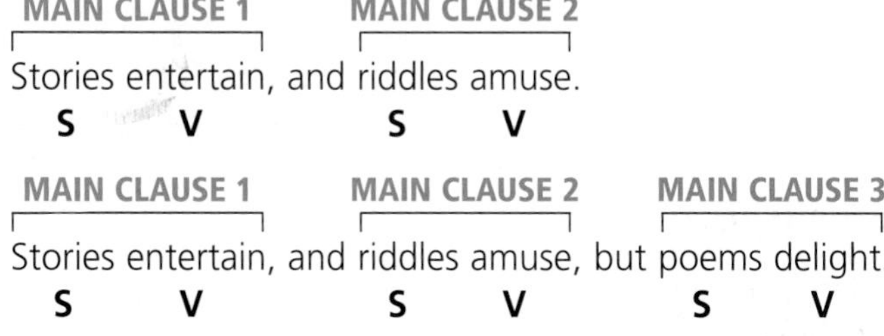

Semicolons may also be used to join the main clauses in a compound sentence.

MAIN CLAUSE 1

Few wild animals live in China's densely populated plains;

MAIN CLAUSE 2

in remoter areas, wildlife is abundant.

Bob shrieked, and Mary cried, but Dan laughed.

Compound Sentence

Exercise 3 Identifying Simple and Compound Sentences

On your paper, write *simple sentence* or *compound sentence* to identify each sentence. (Remember that a single main clause can have a compound subject and a compound predicate.)

Currier and Ives

1. Nineteenth-century American scenes and customs were recorded and preserved by the firm of Currier and Ives.
2. Nathaniel Currier was a printer, and James Ives was an executive.
3. The two men produced "cheap and popular pictures."
4. Currier favored current events; he produced prints of ships, battles, and news events.
5. Ives had broader interests and generally favored country scenes.
6. Together they published color lithographs depicting every facet of American life.
7. Currier and Ives produced thousands of lithographs, and each print was rich in color and detail.
8. Many prints showed city life, but others depicted life in the country.
9. In the last century, many Americans lived in the country, and many events took place outdoors.
10. Currier and Ives's prints show Americans at work and at play in the nineteenth century.

Exercise 4 Writing Simple Sentences

On your paper, combine each pair of ideas below into a simple sentence. Remember that each sentence must have only one main clause, although the sentence may have a compound subject or predicate.

Grandma Moses

1. Grandma Moses was born in 1860.
   She was an American painter.
2. She embroidered all her life.
   She didn't take up painting until the age of 78.
3. Moses had no formal art training.
   She possessed great natural talent.
4. Farm scenes and old-fashioned farm activities are her subjects.
   Her paintings are simple and colorful.
5. Moses' talent flourished.
   She died at the age of 101.

Exercise 5 Writing Compound Sentences

Use the information in each item from Exercise 4 to write a compound sentence. Remember that each sentence must have two or more main clauses. The clauses may be joined by a comma and a coordinating conjunction—or by a semicolon.

13.4 Complex and Compound-Complex Sentences

- A **complex sentence** has one main clause and one or more subordinate clauses.

MAIN CLAUSE

I like Toni Cade Bambara's stories

S V

SUBORDINATE CLAUSE

because they have real-life characters.

S V

SUBORDINATE CLAUSE MAIN CLAUSE SUBORDINATE CLAUSE

When I read her stories, I enjoy them because they are true to life.

S V S V S V

- A **compound-complex sentence** has two or more main clauses and at least one subordinate clause.

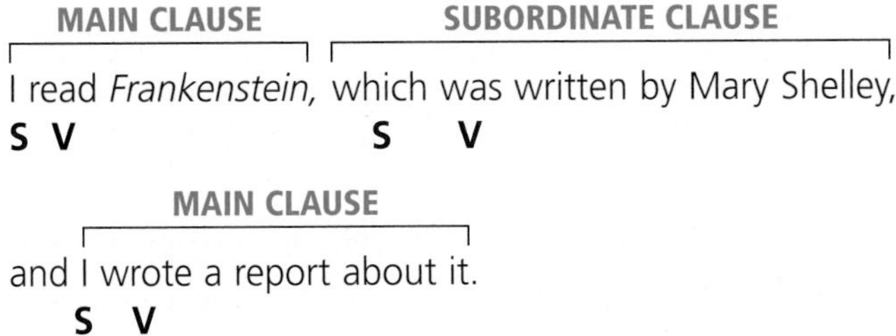

MAIN CLAUSE
SUBORDINATE CLAUSE
I read *Frankenstein,* which was written by Mary Shelley,
S V
S V
MAIN CLAUSE
and I wrote a report about it.
S V

Exercise 6 **Identifying Subordinate Clauses**

On your paper, write the subordinate clause from each of the following sentences. If a sentence has no subordinate clause, write *none.*

1. American pioneers built their houses out of the materials that were readily available.
2. Settlers in heavily forested regions erected log cabins, and newcomers on the treeless plains built sod houses.
3. When they journeyed across the continent, the pioneers lived in their covered wagons.
4. Native Americans of the woodlands built wooden houses, but Native Americans of the Great Plains preferred tepees because they were easy to move.
5. Today Americans who live in the Southwest often build their houses of adobe.

Exercise 7 Identifying Complex and Compound-Complex Sentences

On your paper, write the subordinate clause from each of the following sentences. Indicate whether each sentence is a *complex sentence* or a *compound-complex sentence.*

Adobe Homes

1. When people in New Mexico build their homes, they sometimes use adobe.
2. Adobe is the Spanish name for sun-dried bricks, which are made according to an ancient process.
3. Workers who manufacture adobe mix sandy clay with water and a small amount of straw.
4. After the clay, water, and straw are thoroughly mixed together, the adobe is shoveled into wooden forms and molded into rectangular bricks.
5. The blocks bake in the sun for about two weeks, and the result is strong adobe bricks that can be used for construction.
6. Once the bricks are dry, workers remove the forms.
7. Traditional adobe houses are covered with mud, but modern adobe homes are sometimes covered with a plasterlike material that is called stucco.
8. Many people prefer adobe houses, since they remain cool in hot weather.
9. Although adobe is a popular building material in the southwestern United States, it is not good for very damp or cold areas.
10. If adobe is exposed to frequent rains, the bricks will eventually crumble.

Exercise 8 Writing Simple, Compound, Complex, and Compound-Complex Sentences

Use your own knowledge and the information below to write four original sentences about mobile homes. Write *simple, complex, compound,* or *compound-complex* to identify each sentence you write. (You should write one sentence of each kind.)

Mobile homes are easily moved.
Some people travel in them.
Some people live in them.
They are pulled by cars or trucks.
They became popular during a wartime housing shortage.
They can be connected to utilities.
One quarter of all new single-family dwellings are mobile homes.
Their length varies from 12 to 30 feet.
Communities regulate their placement.
They were once called trailers or caravans.
Sites in mobile-home parks are usually rented.

Exercise 9 Creating Sentences with Various Structures

On your paper, write a simple sentence. Then rework it, making it a compound sentence. Rework the simple sentence again, making it part of a complex sentence. Finally, rework your compound sentence into a compound-complex sentence. Label your four sentences.

13.5 Adjective Clauses

■ An **adjective clause** is a subordinate clause that modifies a noun or a pronoun.

An adjective clause usually follows the word it modifies.

The horror story **that has always been my favorite** is "The Black Cat."

The writer **whom my sister likes best** is Yoshiko Uchida.

I like a writer **who surprises me.**

The detective
who works
under
cover
was unrecognizable.

Adjective clauses may be introduced by the relative pronouns (*who, whom, whose, that,* and *which*) and by the subordinating conjunctions *where* and *when.*

The Elizabethan Age spans the time **when Elizabeth I ruled.**

That is the house **where I was born.**

At times the relative pronoun is dropped at the beginning of an adjective clause.

This is a story **every science enthusiast should read.** [The relative pronoun *that* has been omitted.]

Some adjective clauses are called *essential clauses,* or *restrictive clauses.* Without them the meaning of the sentence would be unclear.

Edgar Allan Poe is the only American writer **who always fascinates me.** [essential clause]

"The Black Cat" is the story **that I like best.** [essential clause]

Some adjective clauses are *not* needed to make the meaning of the sentence clear. Such clauses are called *nonessential clauses,* or *nonrestrictive clauses.* A nonessential clause is always set off with commas.

Edgar Allan Poe, **who is my favorite author,** wrote "The Black Cat." [nonessential clause]

"The Black Cat," **which was written by Edgar Allan Poe,** is my favorite short story. [nonessential clause]

The word *that* usually introduces an essential clause; the word *which* usually introduces a nonessential clause.

"The Black Cat," **which I like best,** is thrilling. [nonessential clause]

I like a story **that thrills me.** [essential clause]

Exercise 10 Identifying Adjective Clauses and the Words They Modify

On your paper, write the adjective clause that appears in each of the following sentences. Then write the word that the clause modifies. (In one sentence, the relative pronoun has been dropped.)

The Story of O. Henry

1. William Sydney Porter wrote stories under a pseudonym, which is another word for a pen name.
2. Porter, who lived from 1862 to 1910, used the pseudonym O. Henry.
3. Porter contributed a number of articles to a humor magazine, which he had founded in Texas in 1894.
4. He wrote a daily column that was humorous and witty.
5. As O. Henry, Porter published many stories that were sympathetic and touching.
6. He created unusual plots that ended in surprising ways.
7. *The Four Million,* which is a collection of O. Henry's short stories, was published in the year 1906.
8. "The Gift of the Magi" is a story many people enjoy.
9. Another O. Henry work that is very popular is "The Third Ingredient."
10. Readers who enjoy poignant humor will delight in the short stories of O. Henry.

Exercise 11 Identifying Essential and Nonessential Clauses

For each sentence in the pairs below, write the adjective clause and then identify it as an *essential clause* or a *nonessential clause.*

Sally Ride: First U.S. Woman in Space

1. **a.** The 1983 U.S. space mission that received the most public attention was the six-day voyage in June of the *Challenger* space shuttle.
   b. The *Challenger* space shuttle, which went on a six-day mission in June 1983, received much public attention.
2. **a.** Sally Ride, who was flight engineer on the *Challenger,* became the first U.S. woman to enter outer space.
   b. The U.S. woman who first entered outer space was *Challenger* flight engineer Sally Ride.
3. **a.** The background that Ride had in astrophysics helped her qualify for NASA's space program.
   b. Ride's doctorate in astrophysics, which she earned from Stanford University, helped her qualify for NASA's space program.
4. **a.** Sally Ride used a remote-control mechanical arm, which she had helped design, to retrieve a satellite in space.
   b. To retrieve a satellite in space, Sally Ride used the remote-control mechanical arm that was 50 feet in length.
5. **a.** Today's astronauts are people who have training in specific fields.
   b. Today's space program is using mission specialists, who are astronauts with training in specific fields.

13.6 Adverb Clauses

■ An **adverb clause** is a subordinate clause that modifies a verb, an adjective, or an adverb. It tells *when, where, how, why, to what extent,* or *under what condition.*

I studied hard **before I took the test.** [The adverb clause modifies the verb *studied.* It tells *when.*]

I was happy **because I passed the test.** [The adverb clause modifies the adjective *happy.* It tells *why.*]

I can study better **if there is no noise.** [The adverb clause modifies the adverb *better.* It tells *under what conditions.*]

Adverb clauses are introduced by subordinating conjunctions, such as those listed on page 478. Remember that an adverb clause may either precede or follow the main clause. When the adverb clause comes first, separate it from the main clause with a comma. The first example above might have been written as follows:

Before I took the test, I studied hard.

At times words may be left out of an adverb clause. The omitted words, however, are understood, or implied. Adverb clauses from which words are omitted are called *elliptical adverb clauses.*

She can swim faster **than I [can swim].**
The news made José happier **than [it made] me [happy].**

Exercise 12 **Identifying Adverb Clauses**

On your paper, write the adverb clause that appears in each of the following sentences.

Squanto, Friend of the Pilgrims

1. Although he led a life of hardship, Squanto, a Pawtuxet from Massachusetts, accomplished a great deal.
2. After he was kidnapped by a group of English explorers in 1614, Squanto was taken to Spain.
3. He was taken to Spain so that he could be sold there as an enslaved person.
4. Once the opportunity arose, Squanto escaped to England.
5. As soon as it was safe, Squanto returned home to Massachusetts.
6. When Squanto met the Pilgrims at Plymouth in 1621, they were hungry and discouraged.
7. The Wampanoag were angry because the Pilgrims had taken their corn.
8. Since he spoke fluent English, Squanto became a peacemaker for the two groups.
9. As if that were not enough, Squanto also taught the Pilgrims about corn.
10. No one could have worked more tirelessly than he.

Exercise 13 Identifying Adverb Clauses

On your paper, write the adverb clause that appears in each sentence in the paragraph below. In one of the sentences, the adverb clause is elliptical.

King Philip's War

[1]Metacomet, better known as King Philip, felt threatened when the Puritan settlements began to spread. [2]Like Squanto, in earlier times he had aided the Pilgrims so that they could survive in a harsh new environment. [3]When tensions arose between the Native Americans and the colonists, the colonists forced Metacomet to swear fidelity to the colony. [4]After Metacomet allegedly caused the death of a suspected English spy, three of Metacomet's men were hanged in retaliation. [5]"King Philip's War," a series of battles, began as Metacomet's troops staged raids along the Massachusetts-Connecticut frontier. [6]Metacomet's soldiers were brave because, in their opinion, they were defending their homelands. [7]Metacomet might have been more successful if his fighting force had been larger. [8]The Native Americans fought as fiercely as the Puritans, but the Puritans were better armed and more numerous. [9]Before he was killed by one of his own men, Metacomet had destroyed several towns. [10]When the surviving Native Americans saw the futility of their efforts, they surrendered and the war ended.

Exercise 14 Adding Adverb Clauses to Sentences

On your paper, rewrite each of the following sentences, adding an adverb clause either before or after the main clause. Consult the list of subordinating conjunctions on page 478 for ideas.

SAMPLE I remember the story of one particular Native American.

ANSWER Whenever I think about colonial America, I remember the story of one particular Native American.

OR

I remember the story of one particular Native American whenever I think about colonial America.

1. The Pilgrims did not know how to survive in America.
2. Squanto was able to communicate with the Pilgrims.
3. Metacomet had been friendly with the Pilgrims.
4. Metacomet decided to wage war.
5. The Native American troops were discouraged.
6. Life was more secure for the Puritans.
7. New England's population grew steadily.
8. The New England colonists lived longer, healthier lives.
9. The Native American population decreased.
10. The Native Americans might still be the only Americans in New England.

13.7 Noun Clauses

■ A **noun clause** is a subordinate clause used as a noun.

Like a noun or a pronoun, a noun clause can have different functions in a sentence: it can act as a subject, a direct object, an indirect object, an object of a preposition, or a predicate nominative.

NOUN
Farmers often eat home-grown food.
S

NOUN CLAUSE
Whoever lives on a farm often eats home-grown food.
S

NOUN
A drought affects crops.
DO

NOUN CLAUSE
A drought affects whatever grows outdoors.
DO

In the preceding examples, each noun clause forms an inseparable part of the sentence's main clause (the entire sentence).

The following are some of the words that can be used to introduce noun clauses.

how	whatever	which	whoever
that	when	whichever	whose
what	where	who, whom	why

The following are additional examples of noun clauses.

Give **whoever comes to the door** a donation for Farmer's Aid. [indirect object]

This is **how most farmers plant their crops.** [predicate nominative]

Crops are fertilized with **whatever will make them grow fast and strong.** [object of a preposition]

The subordinating conjunction *that* is sometimes dropped at the beginning of a noun clause.

I believe [that] **nobody works harder than farmers.** [The subordinating conjunction *that* is omitted.]

Clauses and Sentence Structure

Exercise 15 Identifying Noun Clauses

On your paper, write the noun clauses that appear in each of the following sentences. (Some of the sentences have two noun clauses each.)

The History of Kites

1. Whoever has flown a kite knows that kite flying can be fun.
2. Few people realize that kites are not only for children.
3. What many may not know is that kites have existed for ages.
4. No one knows for sure where kites were invented, but they probably first appeared in China.
5. Folklorists tell us that the Chinese military of about two thousand years ago attached bamboo pipes to their kites.
6. The result was that the noise from the wind in the pipes panicked the enemy soldiers on the ground below.
7. In Hamamatsu, Japan, the three-day kite-flying festival in early May brings pleasure to whoever attends.
8. What attracts people to this festival is seeing so many brightly painted kites taller than themselves.
9. That the Hamamatsu festival is popular is proved by what is now a centuries-old tradition.
10. Do you agree that kite flying is an enjoyable activity?

Exercise 16 Writing Sentences with Noun Clauses

On your paper, complete the following sentences about baseball by replacing the blanks with noun clauses. Begin each noun clause with the word in parentheses.

SAMPLE Do you know (why) ________________?

ANSWER Do you know why baseball is America's favorite sport?

Baseball

1. Many people agree (that) ______________________.
2. (Whoever) ______________________ can go to first base.
3. (How) ______________________ is exciting to watch.
4. The umpire decides (who) ______________________.
5. A fast-paced game with lots of action is (what) ______________________.
6. Few fans understand (when) ______________________.
7. The catcher and the pitcher consult about (whose) ______________________.
8. The batter's biggest worry is (where) ______________________.
9. His excuse for striking out is (whatever) ______________________.
10. The coach has decided (which) ______________________.

Exercise 17 Identifying Subordinate Clauses

On your paper, write the subordinate clause in each sentence. Then write *adverb clause, adjective clause,* or *noun clause* to indicate the kind of clause it is.

A Historic Court Decision

[1]*Brown* v. *Board of Education of Topeka* was a legal case that changed the face of America's schools. [2]What began as a local matter in 1951 had gained national attention by 1954. [3]Because his daughter could not attend an all-white school, an African American parent sued the Topeka Board of Education. [4]Thurgood Marshall, who later became the first African American justice on the Supreme Court, represented the student's father, Oliver Brown. [5]Marshall was an attorney whom people respected. [6]In 1954 the Court ruled that segregated schools deprived minorities of an equal education. [7]Chief Justice Earl Warren declared that segregation violated a citizen's right to equal protection under the law. [8]After the decision was announced, schools across the country changed their policies. [9]Many schools adopted a policy of integration, which allowed children of different ethnic backgrounds to learn together. [10]Few Supreme Court cases have had a greater impact on American society than this one.

Exercise 18 Adding Adjective, Adverb, and Noun Clauses to Sentences

On your paper, combine the following pairs of sentences by turning one of them into a subordinate clause. Write the sentence. Then write *adjective clause, adverb clause,* or *noun clause* to identify the kind of clause you created.

SAMPLE (a) A boomerang is a throwing stick.
(b) A boomerang was used originally by Australian Aborigines.

ANSWER A boomerang is a throwing stick that was used originally by Australian Aborigines. (adjective clause)

Boomerangs

1. (a) A boomerang returns to the thrower.
   (b) It rotates horizontally in flight.
2. (a) Early European travelers wrote in their diaries.
   (b) The Aborigines used boomerangs to trap game.
3. (a) The use of boomerangs declined.
   (b) More sophisticated hunting weapons were introduced by the British.
4. (a) Every year the Smithsonian Institution stages a boomerang festival.
   (b) It takes place on the mall in Washington, D.C.
5. (a) The term *boomerang* is sometimes used as a verb.
   (b) It means "to result in harm to the user or doer."

Exercise 19 Writing Subordinate Clauses in Sentences

On your paper, write four original sentences. In the first one, use an adverb clause. In the second one, use an adjective clause. In the third one, use a noun clause as a subject. In the fourth one, use a noun clause as a direct object.

13.8 Four Kinds of Sentences

■ A **declarative sentence** makes a statement.

A lion is chasing the ostriches.

The huge birds run fast.

The declarative sentence is the most frequently used type of sentence. It normally ends with a period.

■ An **imperative sentence** gives a command or makes a request.

Look at the fleeing ostriches.

Please take pictures of them.

In an imperative sentence, the subject "you" is understood. An imperative sentence usually ends with a period, but it may end with an exclamation point if it expresses strong emotion.

■ An interrogative sentence asks a question.

What did the lion chase?

Is the lion chasing the ostriches?

An interrogative sentence ends with a question mark.

■ An **exclamatory sentence** expresses strong emotion.

What a good time we had!

How ferocious the lion looks!

An exclamatory sentence ends with an exclamation point.

Exercise 20 Identifying and Punctuating Four Kinds of Sentences

On your paper, write *declarative, imperative, interrogative,* or *exclamatory* to identify each sentence below. Then write the correct end mark of punctuation.

1. Have you ever been to an African game park
2. What a wonderful adventure it is
3. Kruger National Park is located in the northeastern part of South Africa, not far from the Limpopo River
4. If you go, you should plan to spend the night in one of the thatch-roofed huts
5. Don't ever get out of your car to take pictures of the elephants

Exercise 21 Creating Four Kinds of Sentences

On your paper, write four sentences about a recent news story. Use one declarative, one imperative, one interrogative, and one exclamatory sentence. Remember to punctuate each sentence correctly.

13.9 Sentence Fragments

- In general, avoid sentence fragments in your writing. A **sentence fragment** is an error that occurs when an incomplete sentence is punctuated as though it were a complete sentence.

There are three things you should look for when reviewing your work for sentence fragments. First, look for a group of words without a subject. Next, be alert for a group of words lacking a verb, especially a group that contains a verbal rather than a complete verb. Last, make sure that you have not mistaken a subordinate clause for a complete sentence.

You will often be able to correct a sentence fragment by joining it to a main clause that precedes or follows the fragment. At times you may have to add missing words to make a complete sentence.

FRAGMENT	Woodpeckers ate suet from my bird feeder last winter. **Seemed to be particularly fond of it.** [lacks subject]
COMPLETE SENTENCE	Woodpeckers ate suet from my bird feeder last winter, and they seemed to be particularly fond of it.
FRAGMENT	**A large bird with blue feathers eating from the feeder for weeks.** [lacks complete verb]
COMPLETE SENTENCE	A large bird with blue feathers has been eating from the feeder for weeks.
FRAGMENT	I filled the feeder with sunflower seeds. **Which both the jays and the cardinals seem to like.** [has subordinate clause only]
COMPLETE SENTENCE	I filled the feeder with sunflower seeds, which both the jays and the cardinals seem to like.

Professional writers sometimes use sentence fragments. They do so for special effect—to add emphasis or to convey realistic dialogue. They use sentence fragments *carefully* and *intentionally.* In most of the writing you do, however, including your writing for school, you should avoid sentence fragments.

Exercise 22 Identifying Sentence Fragments

On your paper, write whether each numbered item is a *complete sentence* or a *sentence fragment.*

Mexico City

[1]Can you guess which city is the largest in the world? [2]Mexico City, with more than 21 million inhabitants. [3]There are few cities with greater problems related to rapid growth. [4]Once the capital of the Aztec Empire, built on an island in the center of a lake. [5]Then the arrival of the Spanish, surprising the Aztecs. [6]The Spaniards conquered the city because of their superior weapons. [7]Also because of their alliances with traditional enemies of the Aztecs. [8]Many residents of modern Mexico City are descendants of the Aztecs and of other groups native to the area. [9]Or else of the Spaniards who came to Mexico in the sixteenth century and intermarried with the native population. [10]Modern Mexico City: a blend of Native American and Spanish, American and European, modern and traditional.

Exercise 23 Correcting Sentence Fragments

Revise the preceding paragraph by correcting each fragment. Wherever possible, combine the fragments with other sentences in the paragraph. You may need to change some words as well.

Exercise 24 Writing Sentences from Sentence Fragments

On your paper, rewrite each sentence fragment below to create a complete sentence. You may add or change words as needed. Make sure that your sentences make sense.

The Aztec

1. The Aztec, a native civilization that rose to a position of dominance.
2. A warlike group with an excellent military organization.
3. Settled on an island in Lake Texcoco.
4. In the thirteenth century in the valley of central Mexico.
5. When they established a tribute-collecting empire that included most of present-day Mexico and extended south to what is now Guatemala.
6. Which continued to the time of the Spanish conquest.
7. Montezuma I's attempts to find food for the growing population of Tenochtitlán.
8. Conquering war captives and acquiring luxury goods.
9. Before Hernán Cortés arrived in 1519.
10. A civilization that was flourishing.
11. Despite some discontent with autocratic policies, the many groups that made up the Aztec civilization.
12. As they grew in political status.
13. Communal land ownership with each farm supporting a few families.
14. Worked at irrigating, terracing, and fertilizing the land.
15. Helped by some native groups, Cortés, who defeated the Aztecs in 1521.

13.10 Run-on Sentences

■ Avoid run-on sentences in your writing. A **run-on sentence** is two or more complete sentences written as though they were one sentence.

There are three basic kinds of run-on sentences.

1. The most common type of run-on sentence is a **comma splice.** A comma splice occurs when two main clauses are separated by a comma instead of a period or a semicolon. You can correct a comma splice by replacing the comma with an end mark and starting the new sentence with a capital letter. You can also correct a comma splice by adding a coordinating conjunction.

   RUN-ON Tanya and Naoko are both going to work as camp counselors this summer, they are looking forward to the experience.

   CORRECT Tanya and Naoko are both going to work as camp counselors this summer**. T**hey are looking forward to the experience.

   CORRECT Tanya and Naoko are both going to work as camp counselors this summer**, and** they are looking forward to the experience.

2. A second type of run-on sentence occurs when two main clauses are written with *no* punctuation between them. To correct this kind of run-on, separate the main clauses with a mark of end punctuation or with a semicolon. Another way to correct the error is by adding a comma and a coordinating conjunction between the main clauses.

   RUN-ON Tanya and Naoko feel the job has many advantages working with children is one of them.

   CORRECT Tanya and Naoko feel the job has many advantages**. W**orking with children is one of them.

   CORRECT Tanya and Naoko feel the job has many advantages**;** working with children is one of them.

   CORRECT Tanya and Naoko feel the job has many advantages**, and** working with children is one of them.

3. A third type of run-on sentence occurs when the comma is left out before a coordinating conjunction that joins two main clauses. Correct this error by simply adding a comma before the coordinating conjunction.

   RUN-ON They will enjoy what they will be doing and they will be earning money too.

   CORRECT They will enjoy what they will be doing**,** and they will be earning money too.

Exercise 25 Distinguishing Between Run-ons and Correct Sentences

On your paper, write *run-on sentence* or *correct* to identify each of the following items.

Taos: An Artist Colony

1. Taos, a relatively small town in the north-central section of New Mexico, is one of the oldest settlements in the United States.
2. It was founded in 1615 and it became an important trading center on the Santa Fe Trail during the nineteenth century.
3. An ancient Pueblo village lies north of the town, a Spanish farming center, Ranchos de Taos, lies to the south.
4. Since the early 1900s, Taos has been a noted artist colony and has attracted many well-known artists, including Georgia O'Keeffe.
5. In 1949 O'Keeffe established her home in Taos, its atmosphere and its beautiful scenery inspired some of her finest work.

Exercise 26 Correcting Run-on Sentences

On your paper, write each of the following sentences, correcting the run-ons. Watch for the three types of run-on errors shown on page 559. You may choose from among the several ways of correcting run-ons that you have learned.

Georgia O'Keeffe: An American Artist

1. The American artist Georgia O'Keeffe became famous for her paintings of natural objects, her canvases are stunning.
2. The objects she painted appear huge and overwhelming her enlarged flowers and stones seem unique.
3. Her paintings are energetic, strong, and realistic nevertheless, most of them have an abstract quality.
4. O'Keeffe's colors are bold and startling, a patch of blue and green on a field of white looks stark and compelling.
5. Most of her paintings remain popular with art lovers, her work is intense, realistic and unique.
6. O'Keeffe was greatly influenced by the landscape of the American Southwest and there are many recognizable southwestern images in her paintings.
7. Many people think only of the Southwest when they think of Georgia O'Keeffe yet she also painted cityscapes.
8. O'Keeffe married the American photographer Alfred Stieglitz the wedding took place in 1924.
9. Stieglitz operated two art galleries in New York City and he often displayed his wife's work in them.
10. He also took many photographs of O'Keeffe, these are well-known today.

Exercise 27 Review: Correcting Sentence Fragments and Run-on Sentences

On your paper, write the following items, correcting all sentence fragments and run-on sentences. Write *correct* for any sentences that do not need revision.

Gemstones

1. Gemstones are minerals in crystal form, they occur naturally as chemical elements or compounds.
2. The value of a gem is based on certain properties beauty, durability, and rarity are three of these.
3. Diamonds being the hardest natural substance in the world. They cannot be scratched by any other substance.
4. Two gemstones come from corundum. Which is harder than any other substance except diamonds.
5. The red variety is called ruby and the blue variety is called sapphire.
6. One of the costliest gemstones of all is emerald, which is a kind of beryl.
7. A good emerald stone has a deep green color and is free of flaws. May cost several thousand dollars per carat.
8. The most common of all minerals is quartz. Which may crystallize into such gemstones as citrine, amethyst, tiger eye, and agate.
9. Some gemstones come from living things, among these are pearls, amber, and coral.
10. Gems have continued to fascinate people for ages. Their beauty and value make them among the most exciting and intriguing of objects.

Exercise 28 Review: Correcting Sentence Structure

On your paper, write the following paragraphs, correcting all sentence fragments and run-on sentences.

Lasers

[1]The word *laser* from the expression "light amplification by stimulated emission of radiation." [2]Both radio waves and light waves are forms of energy nevertheless, neither weak radio waves nor weak light waves harms us. [3]Producing and transmitting intense light being the basic purpose of a laser. [4]Either a rare metal or a rare gas used for the intensification of light waves. [5]Chromium and helium were used in early lasers, today various kinds of lamps produce the light that lasers intensify. [6]Electrons and light waves interacting to make the light extremely intense.

[7]Lasers have many practical applications, they are used in everything from surveying equipment to high-tech "smart" weapons. [8]Lasers by eye surgeons and cardiac specialists. [9]In photography, three-dimensional images called holographs produced with lasers. [10]We can thank lasers for the latest developments in the communications revolution, compact discs, videodiscs, and fiber-optic telephone cables are but three examples of laser technology at work.

Grammar Review

Clauses and Sentence Structure

Set in the mid-nineteenth century, Willa Cather's novel *Death Comes for the Archbishop* tells the story of Bishop Jean Latour, who has left his parish in France and returned to New Mexico, where he had served as a young man. In this scene, the bishop awakes in the same small room he had lived in years earlier, and he muses about the past. The passage has been annotated to show some of the clauses and sentence structures covered in this unit.

Literature Model

from Death Comes for the Archbishop

by Willa Cather

He felt a great content at being here, where he had come as a young man and where he had done his work. The room was little changed; the same rugs and skins on the earth floor, the same desk with his candlesticks, the same thick, wavy white walls that muted sound, that shut out the world and gave repose to the spirit.

Adverb clause

Compound sentence

Simple sentence

Noun clause

As the darkness faded into the gray of a winter morning, he listened for the church bells,—and for another sound, that always amused him here; the whistle of a locomotive. Yes, he had come with the buffalo, and he had lived to see railway trains running into Santa Fé. He had accomplished an historic period.

In New Mexico he always awoke a young man; not until he rose and began to shave did he realize that he was growing older. His first consciousness was a sense of the light dry wind blowing in through the windows, with the fragrance of hot sun and sage-brush and sweet clover; a wind that made one's body feel light and one's heart cry "To-day, to-day," like a child's.

Beautiful surroundings, the society of learned men, the charm of noble women, the graces of art, could not make up to him for the loss of those light-hearted mornings of the desert, for that wind that made one a boy again. He had noticed that this peculiar quality in the air of new countries vanished after they were tamed by man and made to bear harvests. Parts of Texas and Kansas that he had first known as open range had since been made into rich farming districts, and the air had quite lost that lightness, that dry aromatic odor. The moisture of plowed land, the heaviness of labor and growth and grain-bearing, utterly destroyed it; one could breathe that only on the bright edges of the world, on the great grass plains or the sage-brush desert.

That air would disappear from the whole earth in time, perhaps; but long after his day. He did not know just when it had become so necessary to him, but he had come back to die in exile for the sake of it. Something soft and wild and free, something that whispered to the ear on the pillow, lightened the heart, softly, softly picked the lock, slid the bolts, and released the prisoned spirit of man into the wind, into the blue and gold, into the morning, into the morning!

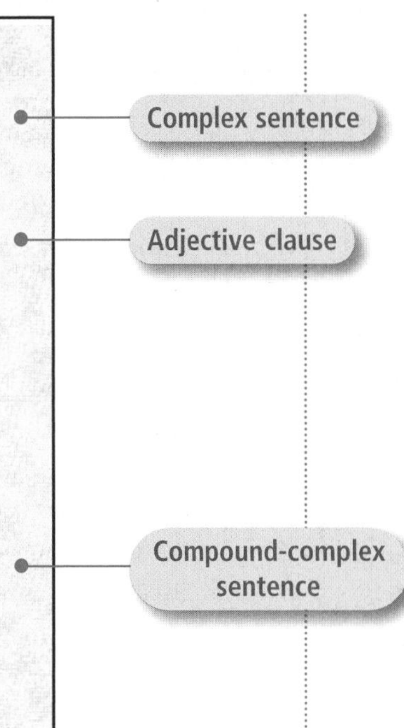

Review: Exercise 1 Identifying Main and Subordinate Clauses

The following sentences are based on the passage from *Death Comes for the Archbishop.* Each sentence contains a clause that appears in italics. On your paper indicate whether the italicized clause is a *main clause* or a *subordinate clause.*

1. *Because Bishop Jean Marie Latour had once lived in the room,* he felt at home there.
2. *The room had changed remarkably little,* even though many years had passed.
3. The furnishings *that he recalled so well* still stood in the room.
4. The bishop awoke, began to shave, and reflected about the land and *why he felt so content there.*
5. The bishop, *who was now an old man,* felt almost like a boy again in his former surroundings.
6. He experienced a feeling of newness and vigor *whenever he breathed the light, dry morning air of New Mexico.*
7. The source of the invigorating air was the country around him, *which was still untamed.*
8. Other places had once produced this remarkable effect, but *they no longer did.*
9. A sense of newness disappeared *after an area was developed.*
10. Although progress brought with it many civilized comforts and pleasures, *it also carried a high price.*

Review: Exercise 2 **Identifying Compound, Complex, and Compound-Complex Sentences**

The following sentences provide some background details from the novel *Death Comes for the Archbishop.* On your paper, write whether each sentence is *compound, complex, or compound-complex.*

1. In the late 1840s, after the Mexican War, the Catholic Church renewed its interest in New Mexico because the territory had just become part of the United States.
2. Missionaries had been working there since 1500, but control over Church activities was limited.
3. A new bishop could renew the Church there if the right man could be found.
4. A few years after the Mexican War, a young French priest who had just been elevated to the position of bishop was sent to Santa Fe, New Mexico.
5. Bishop Latour was exhausted when he finally arrived in New Mexico, for the trip had taken nearly a year.
6. There was a railroad out of New York, but it ended in Cincinnati, Ohio.
7. From Ohio, Bishop Latour had gone by boat to Galveston on the Texas coast, and then he had traveled across Texas.
8. He needed both strength and flexibility, or he would not succeed in his job.
9. After Bishop Latour had worked effectively in the area for many years, he retired.
10. Now he had come back to New Mexico, for he knew that he would soon die.
11. Willa Cather modeled Bishop Latour on two real priests who had lived in New Mexico during the nineteenth century.
12. John B. Lamy went to Santa Fe as bishop in 1846, and Joseph P. Machebeuf, who later became bishop of Colorado, accompanied Lamy as his able assistant.
13. Lamy instituted extensive reforms, and religious conditions in New Mexico improved greatly during his time there.
14. A few years after his arrival, Lamy built the Cathedral of Saint Francis of Assisi, which stands today in Santa Fe as an impressive landmark.
15. When Cather first visited New Mexico, she was impressed with the history of the Catholic Church in the region, but she didn't have enough facts to write about it.
16. She went back often, for the subject continued to fascinate her.
17. On one trip, she discovered a book about the life of Father Machebeuf; this book inspired her to write her own book.
18. The book also contained detailed information about Bishop Lamy because the two men were colleagues and friends.
19. Father Machebeuf's letters gave Cather a sense of the mood in which these two missionaries accepted the hardships of desert life.
20. She titled *Death Comes for the Archbishop,* the writing of which she called "a happy vacation from life," after a painting by Albrecht Dürer.

Review: Exercise 3 Writing Sentences with Adjective Clauses

The sentences that follow elaborate on ideas in the passage from *Death Comes for the Archbishop.* On your paper, rewrite each sentence, adding an adjective clause that answers the question in parentheses. Your clause must begin with a relative pronoun (see the list that follows), and it must contain a verb. Your sentence should make sense within the context of the passage but should not use Cather's exact words. There may be more than one answer.

RELATIVE PRONOUNS who whom whose which that

SAMPLE He was a bishop. (What had he done?)
ANSWER He was a bishop who had worked in New Mexico for many years.

1. Bishop Latour was back in New Mexico. (How did he feel about being there?)
2. The old rugs, desk, and candlesticks were still in the room. (From what time did the bishop remember these items?)
3. He took comfort from the solid white walls. (How did the walls make him feel?)
4. He was an aging man. (How did he feel when he came to New Mexico?)
5. The room was cooled by a gentle wind. (What did the wind bring in?)
6. Bishop Latour had almost forgotten his age. (How did his body feel that morning?)
7. He had abandoned many cultural advantages. (How did they compare with the benefits of the desert?)
8. To the bishop, the desert had a special wind. (What was special about the wind?)
9. The air in places like Texas and Kansas had lost its lightness. (What was happening to those places now?)
10. The bishop could find this special air only in open, undeveloped areas. (What could this air do for the bishop?)
11. When he looked around the room, he saw the rugs and skins on the floor. (How did the room look compared to before?)
12. The walls were painted white. (What did the walls do to sound?)
13. He listened to the whistle of the locomotive. (How did the sound of the whistle make him feel?)
14. The sun shone through the window. (How did the sun feel on his skin?)
15. Bishop Latour had once lived in other surroundings. (How did he remember them?)
16. He had enjoyed the society of men. (What sort of men were they?)
17. The special air of the desert floated in on the morning breeze. (What did the air smell of?)
18. The air whispered in his ear. (What qualities did the air have?)
19. His spirit was released. (How had his spirit felt before?)
20. His spirit was caught up in the morning. (What color was the morning?)

Review: Exercise 4 Writing Sentences with Adverb Clauses

The sentences that follow elaborate on ideas suggested by the passage from *Death Comes for the Archbishop.* On your paper, rewrite each sentence, adding an adverb clause that answers the question in parentheses. Your clause must begin with one of the subordinating conjunctions listed below, and it must contain a verb. The sentence should make sense within the context of the passage but should not use Cather's exact words. There may be more than one answer for each item.

SUBORDINATING CONJUNCTIONS

after	as if	in order to	though	whenever
although	because	since	until	where
as	before	than	when	wherever

SAMPLE The room was familiar to Latour. (Why?)
ANSWER The room was familiar to Latour because he had lived there before.

1. Bishop Latour felt quite happy. (Why?)
2. He listened for church bells. (When?)
3. He had first come to New Mexico during an earlier period in the territory's history. (When?)
4. Bishop Latour felt like a young man. (When?)
5. He realized that he was old. (When?)
6. That morning the aging bishop became aware of the fragrant wind from his window. (When?)
7. The light, dry wind made the bishop feel eager and full of life. (To what extent?)
8. The bracing mornings of the desert had been worth his sacrifice of the comforts of civilization. (Why?)
9. Unfortunately, the air in a new, untamed country lost its freshness and lightness. (When?)
10. For example, the dry, fragrant air had changed in parts of Texas and Kansas. (When?)
11. The bishop's room seemed little changed. (Why?)
12. The walls gave repose to the spirit. (How?)
13. He was amused. (Why?)
14. The air had lost that dry, fresh fragrance. (When?)
15. It was still quite possible, however, for one to breathe the fresh, sweet air. (Where?)
16. The special air would very likely disappear. (When?)
17. He had to come back to die in exile. (Why?)
18. His heart lightened. (Why?)
19. The air whispered in his ear. (When?)
20. His spirit was outdoors. (Where?)

Review: Exercise 5 Identifying Noun Clauses

The following sentences describe the history of New Mexico. On your paper, write the noun clauses that appear in the sentences. Two of the sentences have two noun clauses each.

1. Whoever is familiar with the Southwest recognizes that New Mexico's history makes it one of the most intriguing states in the country.
2. Does this reference book tell whether the earliest human settlements in New Mexico date from ten thousand years ago or twenty thousand years ago?
3. Pueblos and cliff dwellings were built by whoever originally inhabited the region.
4. How these structures were built can be determined by examining the remaining ruins.
5. What historians also know is that the Navajo and Apache later moved down to New Mexico from the north.
6. The sixteenth century was when the Spanish explorers and Catholic missionaries arrived.
7. The explorers believed that they would find huge amounts of gold in the Americas.
8. Have you read about how the Spaniards treated the Native Americans?
9. What had become part of Mexico's territory in 1821 was ceded to the United States in 1848, after the Mexican War.
10. This history of settlement and conquest tells us why three cultures come together in New Mexico today: Native American, Spanish, and Anglo-American.
11. The history of New Mexico in the nineteenth century is the story of how the area became a United States territory.
12. The opening of the Santa Fe Trail meant that more pioneers could travel to New Mexico.
13. The trading post at Santa Fe was an important stopover for whoever journeyed west along the trail.
14. A major turning point in the Civil War was when the Union troops defeated the Confederates at Glorieta Pass.
15. Why do historians think that the battle of Glorieta was important?
16. That the Union victory kept the Southwest from joining the Confederacy is of major significance.
17. The newly built railroads provided transportation to wherever New Mexicans wanted to go.
18. Why so many settlers poured into New Mexico in the 1890s is a question that has many answers.
19. The increase in population is why New Mexico was admitted to the Union as the forty-seventh state in 1912.
20. What attracts people to this state today is its climate, its scenery, and its rich mix of peoples and cultures.

Review: Exercise 6 Writing Four Kinds of Sentences

The following sentences develop an idea or image suggested by the passage from *Death Comes for the Archbishop.* On your paper, identify each of the following sentences as *declarative, imperative, interrogative,* or *exclamatory.* Then rewrite each sentence in the form noted in parentheses. There may be more than one answer.

SAMPLE He took the train from New York to Cincinnati.
(Rewrite in the imperative form.)

ANSWER declarative
Take the train from New York to Cincinnati.

1. How fascinating New Mexico's history is! (Rewrite as a declarative sentence.)
2. New Mexico was annexed to the United States in 1848. (Rewrite as an interrogative sentence.)
3. Did New Mexico formerly belong to Mexico? (Rewrite as a declarative sentence.)
4. Did you investigate the earliest human settlements in New Mexico? (Rewrite as an imperative sentence.)
5. Bishop Latour's first trip to New Mexico took much longer than such a journey would today. (Rewrite as an interrogative sentence.)
6. What a long and difficult journey it was! (Rewrite as a declarative sentence.)
7. Take a ship from New Orleans to Galveston. (Rewrite as a declarative sentence.)
8. How many hardships Latour endured on the way! (Rewrite as an interrogative sentence.)
9. Did Latour have to travel through the Rio Grande Valley? (Rewrite as a declarative sentence.)
10. Bishop Latour worked hard at his mission. (Rewrite as an imperative sentence.)
11. Was the landscape wild and beautiful? (Rewrite as an exclamatory sentence.)
12. Savor the air of this country while you still can. (Rewrite as a declarative sentence.)
13. The bishop loved the desert. (Rewrite as an exclamatory sentence.)
14. How familiar and comforting his old room seemed! (Rewrite as an interrogative sentence.)
15. Latour always felt the gentle wind in the morning. (Rewrite as an imperative sentence.)
16. Make your home in the desert, Bishop Latour. (Rewrite as an interrogative sentence.)
17. How light and fragrant the air was! (Rewrite as an interrogative sentence.)
18. The bishop knew that he had come to the desert to die. (Rewrite as an interrogative sentence.)
19. Did the air make the old man feel like a boy again? (Rewrite as an exclamatory sentence.)
20. He traded the comforts of civilization for something better—his freedom. (Rewrite as an imperative sentence.)

Review: Exercise 7 Correcting Sentence Fragments

The following paragraph describes a scene related to the passage from *Death Comes for the Archbishop.* On your paper, revise the paragraph, correcting sentence fragments by combining sentences, adding words (a subject or a verb), or changing a verb form.

SAMPLE The man who came to Santa Fe.
ANSWER The man who came to Santa Fe had lived there before.

[1]Waking in his old room, felt happy. [2]A white-walled room, filled with familiar furnishings, such as his old rugs, desk, and candlesticks. [3]Also familiar sounds floating in from the outside. [4]For example, the locomotive whistle that always amused him. [5]Most important of all, however, was the wondrous fresh wind from the desert. [6]Made him feel young and spirited like a boy. [7]Actually, an elderly man seeking the wild desert. [8]Because he could not do without its magic air. [9]Would that air last forever? [10]Not after the primitive area tamed.

Review: Exercise 8 Correcting Run-on Sentences

On your paper, revise the following sentences, correcting run-ons. Write *correct* if the sentence does not contain run-ons.

SAMPLE New Mexico's stunning landscapes attract tourists from all over the world its colorful history fascinates scholars from many fields.
ANSWER New Mexico's stunning landscapes attract tourists from all over the world. Its colorful history fascinates scholars from many fields.

1. New Mexico has been inhabited for at least 10,000 years early rock carvings can still be found near the Sandia Mountains and the present-day town of Folsom.
2. The landscape of New Mexico is varied and spectacular; it includes not only sandy deserts but also snowy mountains, forests, buttes, and mesas.
3. The population has exploded recently yet New Mexico remains one of the least populous states in the country.
4. More than 38 percent of New Mexico's population is of Spanish or Mexican origin, another 9 percent is made up of Navajo, Pueblo, and other Native American groups.
5. New Mexico includes vast open spaces, but nearly three quarters of the total population is concentrated in urban areas such as Albuquerque and Santa Fe.
6. The Spanish first came to New Mexico in search of gold however, missionary work became the main activity in the 1600s.
7. Navajos were treated harshly their relations with the Spanish were often hostile.
8. In 1848 New Mexico was made a U.S. territory, in 1912 it became a state.
9. The railroad reached New Mexico in 1878 and the population began to expand.
10. The architecture, art, and crafts of the area are exceptional, the arts of three cultures have flourished—and often blended—there.

Review: Exercise 9 **Correcting Sentence Structure**

The following paragraph describes places of interest in New Mexico. On your paper, revise the paragraph, correcting sentence fragments and run-on sentences. Some sentences are correct, but you may wish to combine them with other sentences. Try to vary your sentence structure and use correct punctuation.

[1]New Mexico has dozens of fascinating places to visit, they range from lush forests to steep ski slopes and include art museums and ancient communities. [2]In the southern part of the state, Carlsbad Caverns National Park, which contains the largest cavern yet discovered. [3]Also in the south is White Sands National Monument, it is a rare gypsum desert. [4]White sand into huge dunes. [5]The most spectacular sight in Albuquerque is the hot-air balloon fiesta. [6]Takes place in October. [7]North of Albuquerque is Santa Fe, its many shops, museums, beautiful old mission churches, and stunning opera house. [8]Nearby the ancient cliff dwellings of the Anasazi people, slightly higher up is the village of Los Alamos, where the first atomic bomb was developed. [9]Scattered through the state are pueblos, Native Americans have lived there for centuries. [10]The two most populous Native American groups in New Mexico are the Navajo and the Apache and many of them live on large reservations.

Review: Exercise 10

Proofreading

The following passage describes the artist Georgia O'Keeffe, whose painting appears on the opposite page. Rewrite the passage, correcting the errors in spelling, grammar, and usage. Add any missing punctuation. There are twenty-five errors.

Georgia O'Keeffe

[1]Georgia O'Keeffe (1887–1986) is born in Sun Prairie, Wisconsin. [2]When she was only seventeen, she begun her formal training at the Art Institute of Chicago. [3]Two years later, she went to New York City to continue her study of art and she remained in the city for several years. [4]During the winters from 1912 to 1918, she teached school in Texas. [5]Was drawn to its dramatic landscape and enormous skies.

[6]O'Keeffe lived in New York for a time and she made her first paintings of nature there. [7]These paintings were not realistic they were filled with flat patterns and bold colors. [8]O'Keeffe began spending your summers in New Mexico in 1929. [9]Moved there permanently in 1949. [10]She refined her lush, highly abstract style in New Mexico and it was there that she painted her most memorable works. [11]Her landscapes often present unusual perspectives which make the

viewer feel suspended in air. [12]Other paintings focus closely on a single image, such as a flower or the weather-beaten skul of an animal.

[13]Many critics in the art world considers O'Keeffe one of the forerunners of American abstract art. [14]She deliberately exagerated the shape, proportion, size, and color of the objects and scenes that she painted. [15]What huge flowers she painted [16]Her paintings, particularly those made in New Mexico have a spiritual quality.

[17]*Gate of Adobe Church* (1929) is typical of O'Keeffes abstract style. [18]She captures in this picture which has broad sweeps of color and a simple design, the mood and sense of a place. [19]She paints with uncluttered simplicity which evokes a quiet spirituality an energetic clarity, and a radiant warmth. [20]O'Keeffe's strong sense of place is strikingly similar to Willa Cathers. [21]Indeed, *Death Comes for the Archbishop* is filled with concrete, evocative images of the Southwest [22]Some of the most striking images is evoked by the main character of the novel a French bishop who has returned to New Mexico because he misses the dry, warm wind and the hot sun. [23]Can you feel the hot southwestern sun in this picture

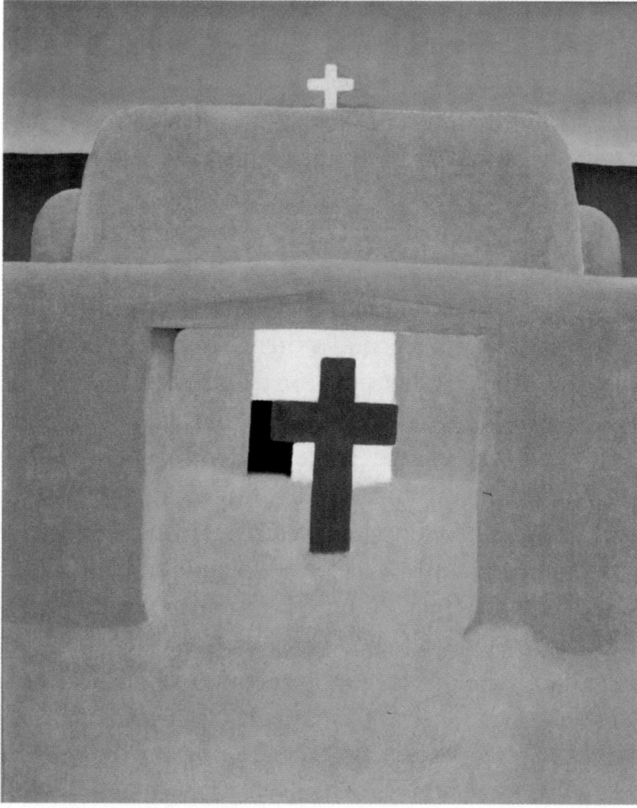

Georgia O'Keeffe, *Gate of Adobe Church,* 1929

Review: Exercise 11

Mixed Review

The items that follow describe the life of Willa Cather. On your paper, revise each item in the manner indicated in parentheses.

SAMPLE Willa Cather often wrote about pioneers. Cather grew up on the Nebraska frontier. (Combine the sentences by turning the second sentence into an adjective clause beginning with *who.*)

ANSWER Willa Cather, who grew up on the Nebraska frontier, often wrote about pioneers.

Willa Cather

1. Willa Cather was born in Virginia in 1873. Her family moved to Nebraska in 1882. (Rewrite as a compound sentence.)
2. In Red Cloud, Nebraska, she lived among European immigrants. They were beginning a new life. (Combine the sentences by turning the second sentence into an adjective clause beginning with *who.*)
3. Cather attended the University of Nebraska at Lincoln. She began to recognize her talent for writing. (Combine the sentences by turning the first sentence into an adverb clause beginning with *When.*)
4. She graduated from the university in 1895, and she moved across the continent to Pittsburgh. She began working on the staff of the *Pittsburgh Leader.* (Rewrite as a compound-complex sentence.)
5. Did Cather work next as principal of a Pittsburgh high school? (Rewrite as a declarative sentence.)
6. In 1912 Cather decided something. She would become a writer of novels. (Combine the sentences by turning the second sentence into a noun clause beginning with *that.*)
7. It was then that Cather left her position as managing editor of *McClure's,* the well-known magazine published in New York. (Rewrite as an interrogative sentence.)
8. Cather was awarded the Pulitzer Prize for her novel *One of Ours* (1922). Deals largely with World War I. (Eliminate the fragment by creating a complex sentence.)
9. Her early novels were based on her memories of pioneer life. Many of her later works focused on the anguish of creative people trapped in small-town life. (Combine the sentences by turning the first sentence into an adverb clause beginning with *Although.*)
10. From 1925 to 1931, she produced four great novels. These novels include *The Professor's House* (1925), *My Mortal Enemy* (1926), *Death Comes for the Archbishop* (1927), and *Shadows on the Rock* (1931). (Combine the sentences by turning the second sentence into an adjective clause beginning with *which.*)

Writing Application

Sentence Structure in Writing

In *Tortuga* Rudolfo A. Anaya uses a variety of sentence types not only to capture the reader's interest but also to develop a pleasing rhythm and an appropriate mood. In the following passage, notice the structure of Anaya's sentences and the kinds of clauses he uses.

> I remembered the rainbows of my childhood, beautifully sculptured arches reaching from north to south, shafts of light so pure their harmony seemed to wed the sky and earth. My mother had taught me to look at rainbows, the mantle of the Blessed Virgin Mary she called them. When a summer thunderstorm passed, she would take me out and we would stand in the thin drops which followed the storm. We would turn our faces up to the sky, and the large, glistening drops of rain would pelt our faces. She would open her mouth and hold out her tongue to receive the large, golden drops. She would stir the muddy ponds and pick up the little frogs which came with the rain.

Techniques with Sentence Structure

Try to apply some of Anaya's writing techniques when you write and revise.

❶ Avoid using the same sentence structure repeatedly.

SAME STRUCTURE A summer thunderstorm passed . . . She would take me out . . . We would stand . . .

ANAYA'S VERSION When a summer thunderstorm passed, she would take me out and we would stand . . .

❷ To emphasize some ideas and downplay others, put some ideas into subordinate clauses.

EQUAL ATTENTION We would stand in the thin drops [of rain]. The drops of rain followed the storm.

ANAYA'S VERSION . . . we would stand in the thin drops which followed the storm.

TIME

For more about the writing process, see TIME Facing the Blank Page, pp. 109–119

Clauses and Sentence Structure

Practice Practice these techniques by revising the following series of sentences and sentence fragments. Decide which ideas to stress and which to downplay. Use a variety of sentences.

I looked out the window of my car. I had stopped. By the side of the road. In the distance, a bare outline of mountain range. All around was the white, alkaline desert. Only the hardiest shrubs and grasses could grow on the desert. The cold winter rain continued. It had been only a drizzle. It had drizzled when I left home. Then the rain had turned icy. It had become more intense. Suddenly the rain stopped, the sun struggling to break through the clouds. The clouds were gray and heavy. Minutes passed. A glorious, glowing rainbow in the east. I sat entranced. The sight reminded me of other rainbows. I had enjoyed rainbows as a child.

UNIT 14

Diagraming Sentences

14.1 Diagraming Simple Sentences

■ **Diagraming** is a method of showing how the various words and parts of a sentence function and relate to the sentence as a whole.

You begin to diagram a sentence by finding the simple subject. After you have found the subject, find the action or linking verb that goes with it. Write the subject and the verb on a horizontal line, called a baseline. Separate the subject and the verb with a vertical line that bisects the baseline. This line indicates the division between the complete subject and the complete predicate.

Senators meet.

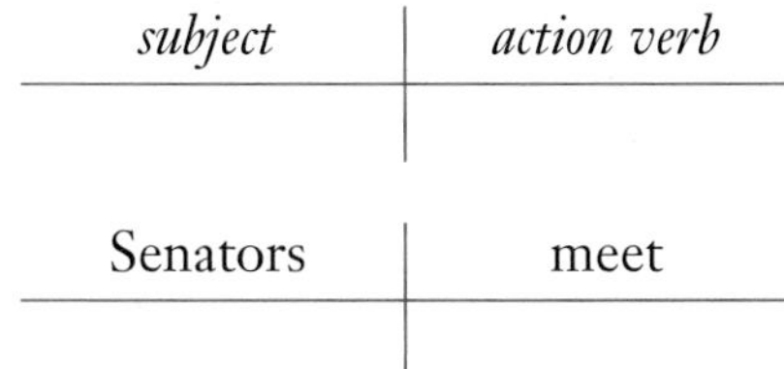

Compound Subjects and Verbs

A compound subject or verb is placed on two horizontal lines, with the conjunction on a dotted vertical line connecting the horizontal lines. To diagram a simple sentence with a compound subject and a compound verb, follow the model diagram below. Note how the compound elements extend from the baseline.

Staffers and senators will meet and decide.

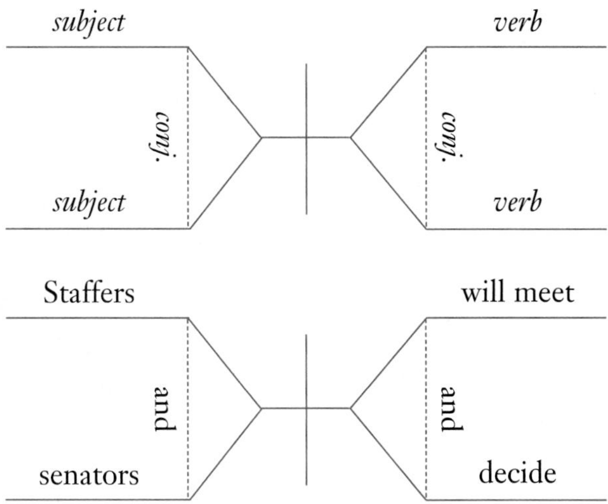

Diagraming Sentences

Direct Objects and Indirect Objects

To diagram a simple sentence with an indirect object and a direct object, follow the model diagram below.

Experts have given senators advice.

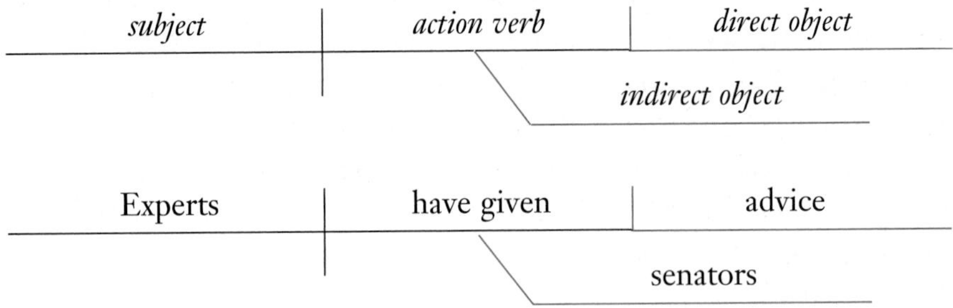

Object Complements

To diagram a simple sentence with an object complement, follow the model diagram below.

Everyone considered her important.

subject | action verb | direct object \ object complement

Everyone | considered | her \ important

Subject Complements

To diagram a simple sentence with a subject complement (a predicate nominative or a predicate adjective), follow the model diagram below.

Senators are legislators.

subject | linking verb \ subject complement

Senators | are \ legislators

Senators should be helpful.

Senators | should be \ helpful

Adjectives and Adverbs

To diagram a simple sentence with adjectives and adverbs, follow the model diagram below.

The more experienced senators meet regularly.

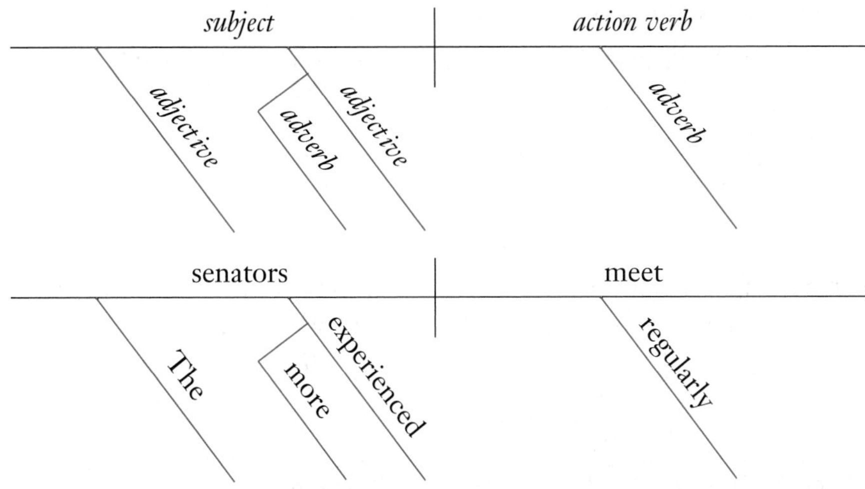

Exercise 1 **Diagraming Simple Sentences**

Using the preceding models as a guide, diagram the following sentences.

1. An informed citizen votes thoughtfully.
2. The voters gave the candidate a landslide.
3. Rich and poor elected him president.
4. A president is powerful but may seem hesitant.
5. Newspapers called the election an easy victory.
6. Friends and associates sent the winner their congratulations.
7. The elated president-elect spoke happily.
8. The country was now the primary concern.
9. She felt the responsibility keenly.
10. The future would not be easy.

14.2 Diagraming Simple Sentences with Phrases

Prepositional Phrases

Place the preposition on a diagonal line that descends from the word the prepositional phrase modifies. Place the object of the preposition on a horizontal line that joins the diagonal. The diagonal line on which the preposition is placed should extend somewhat beyond the horizontal on which the object of the preposition is placed, forming a "tail."

In their work, carpenters of today use tools with electric power.

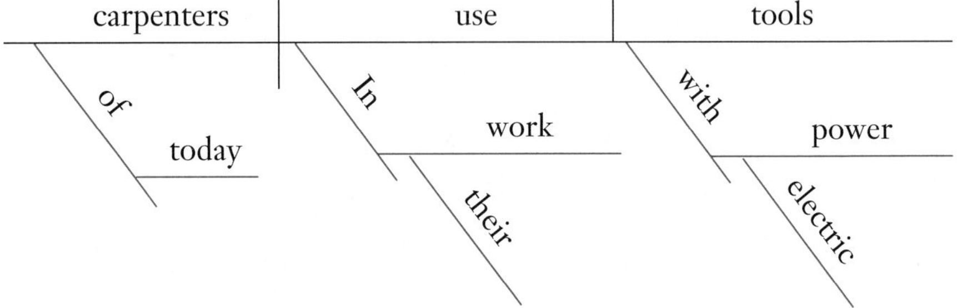

Appositives and Appositive Phrases

Place an appositive in parentheses after the noun or pronoun it identifies. Beneath it add any words that modify the appositive. Any words that modify the noun or pronoun itself, and not the appositive, should be placed directly beneath the noun or pronoun.

Argentina is proud of beautiful Buenos Aires, its cosmopolitan capital.

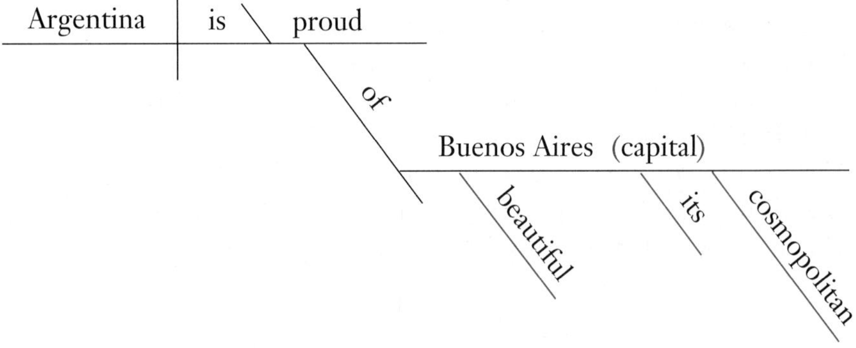

Diagraming Sentences

Participles and Participial Phrases

The line on which the participle is placed descends diagonally from the word the participle modifies and then extends to the right horizontally. The participle is written on the curve, as shown below. Add any modifiers, objects, and complements to the horizontal line in the same way that you would show the modifiers, objects, and complements of an action verb.

Whistling, the carpenter completed the work, happily driving the last two nails.

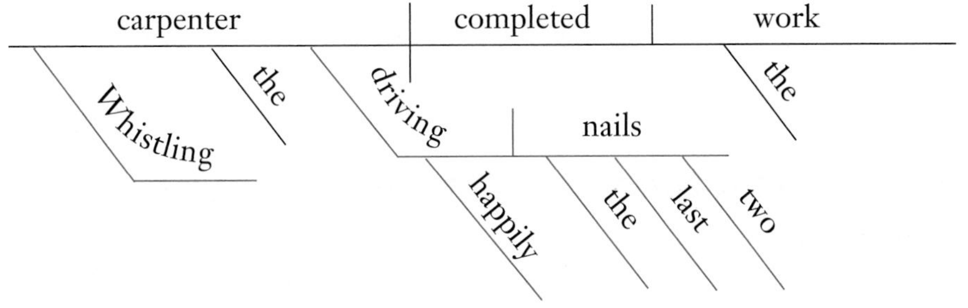

Gerunds and Gerund Phrases

Place a gerund on a "step," and add complements and modifiers in the usual way. Then set the gerund or the gerund phrase on a "stilt," and position the stilt in the diagram according to the role of the gerund in the sentence. (Remember that a gerund can be a subject, a direct object, an indirect object, a predicate nominative, an object of a preposition, or an appositive.)

Mitering is a common way of forming corner joints.

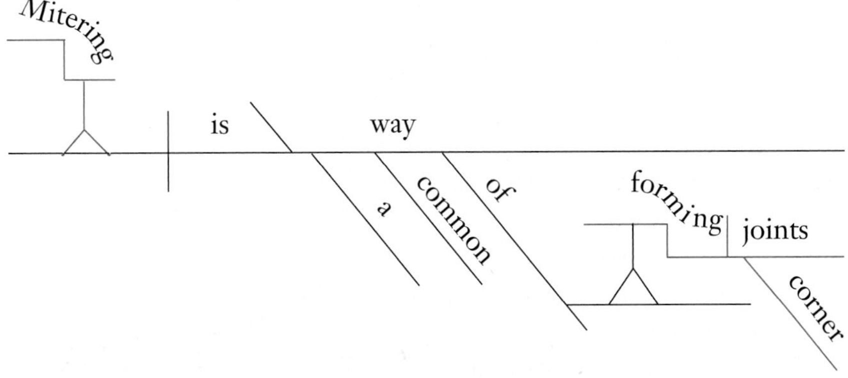

Diagraming Sentences

Infinitives and Infinitive Phrases as Adjectives or Adverbs

When an infinitive or an infinitive phrase is used as an adjective or an adverb, it is diagramed like a prepositional phrase.

Carpenters struggled to meet the deadline.

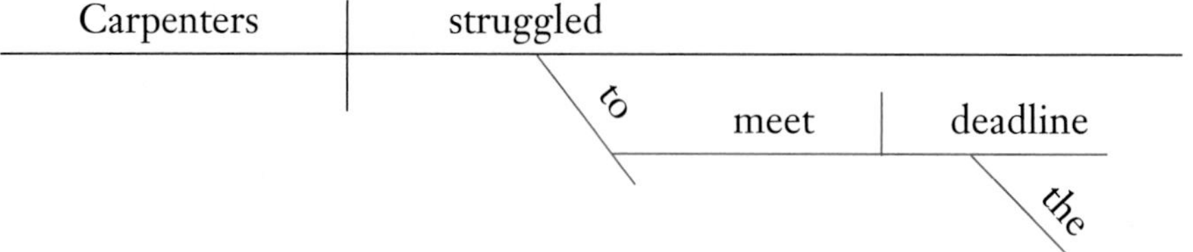

Infinitives and Infinitive Phrases as Nouns

When an infinitive or an infinitive phrase is used as a noun, it is diagramed like a prepositional phrase and then placed on a "stilt" in the subject, direct object, or predicate nominative position.

To work is to know satisfaction.

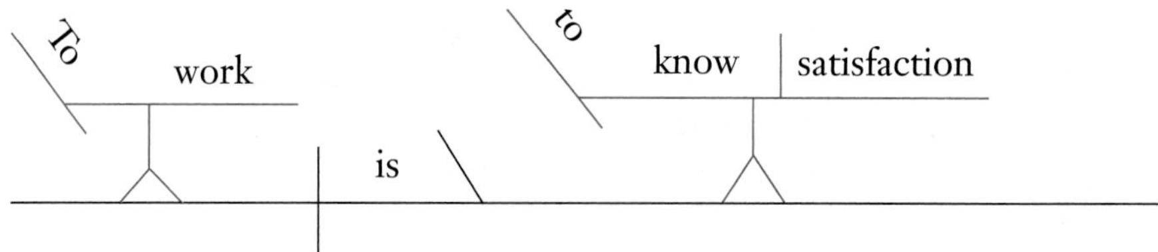

Diagraming Sentences

Exercise 2 **Diagraming Simple Sentences with Phrases**

Using the preceding models as a guide, diagram the following sentences.

1. A plumber from town installed pipes for water.
2. The pipes, copper tubing cylinders, arrived by heavy truck.
3. Several shingles, damaged by the wind, needed repairs.
4. Driving nails can be hard work.
5. To measure accurately is to save work.
6. The trade and craft of carpentry require working with lumber.
7. To build a house is to know joy.
8. Exhausted, the cabinetmaker finished by sanding carefully.
9. Crafting decorative woodwork requires a delicate touch.
10. Roofers, often unappreciated, work carefully to prevent costly leaks.

14.3 Diagraming Sentences with Clauses

Compound Sentences

Diagram each main clause separately. If the clauses are connected by a semicolon, use a vertical dotted line to connect the verbs of each main clause. If the main clauses are connected by a conjunction, place the conjunction on a solid horizontal line, and connect it to the verbs of each main clause by vertical dotted lines.

Mechanics like to fix objects, but carpenters must learn to build.

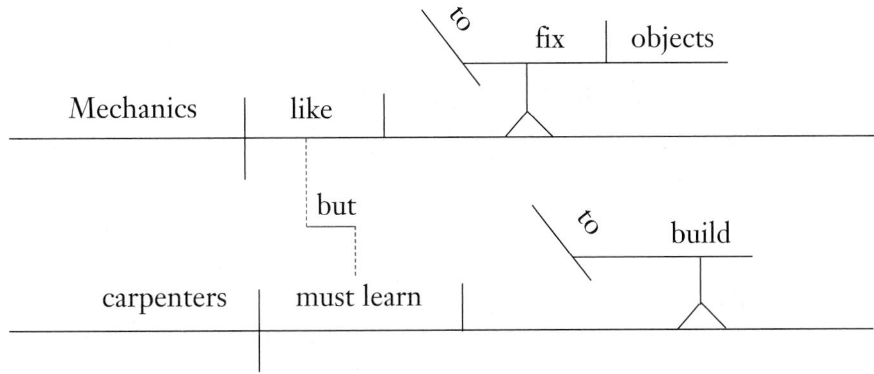

Complex Sentences with Adjective Clauses

Place the main clause in one diagram and the adjective clause beneath it in another diagram. Use a dotted line to connect the relative pronoun or other introductory word in the adjective clause to the modified noun or pronoun in the main clause.

The carpenter whom you hired fixed the shelves that were uneven.

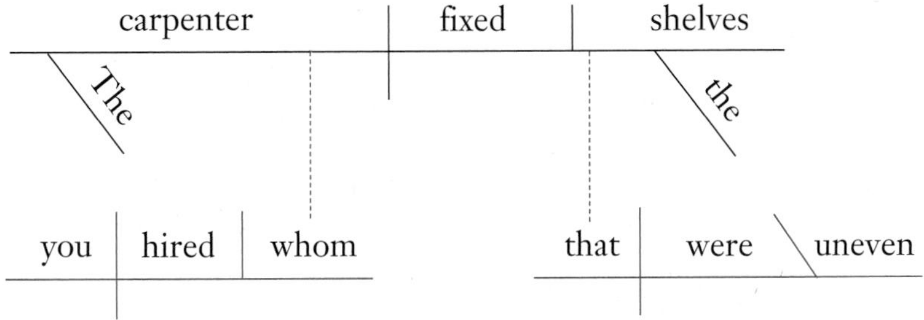

Diagraming Sentences

Complex Sentences with Adverb Clauses

Place the main clause in one diagram and the adverb clause beneath it in another diagram. Place the subordinating conjunction on a diagonal dotted line, connecting the verb in the adverb clause to the modified verb, adjective, or adverb in the main clause.

Before they cut the wood, carpenters make a design.

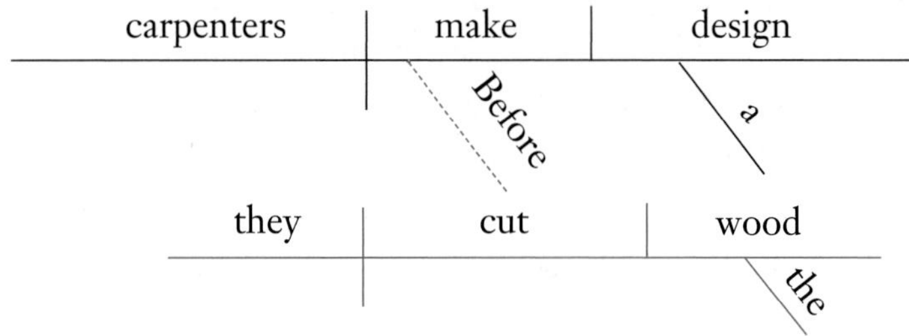

Complex Sentences with Noun Clauses

First decide what role the noun clause plays within the main clause. Is it the subject, direct object, predicate nominative, or object of a preposition? Then diagram the main clause, placing the noun clause on a "stilt" in the appropriate position. Place the introductory word of the clause in the position of the subject, object, or predicate nominative within the noun clause itself. If the introductory word merely begins the noun clause, place it on a line of its own above the verb in the noun clause, connecting it to the verb with a dotted vertical line.

NOUN CLAUSE AS SUBJECT

What that carpenter builds is especially sturdy.

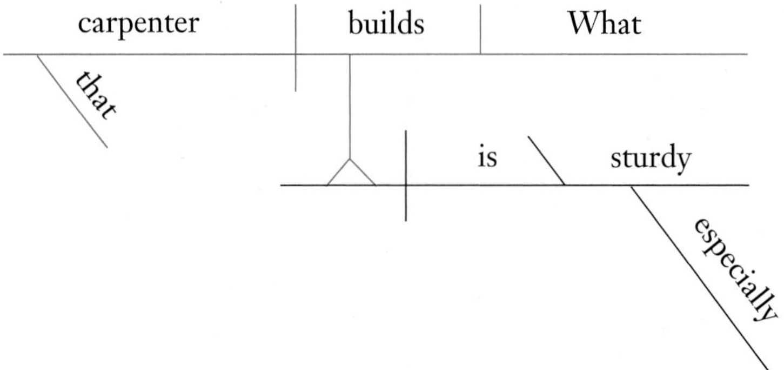

Diagraming Sentences

NOUN CLAUSE AS DIRECT OBJECT

We know that the mechanic fixes machines.

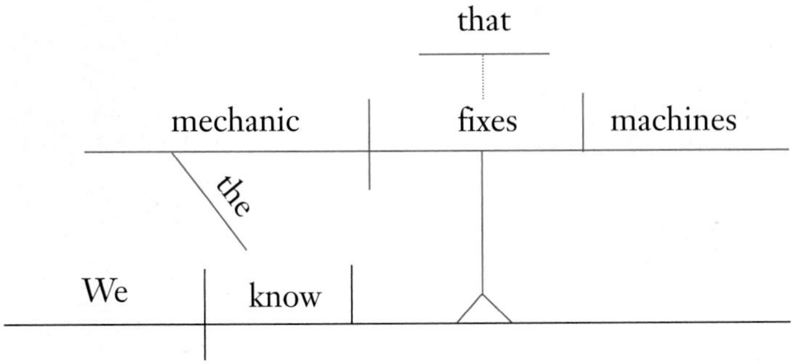

NOUN CLAUSE AS OBJECT OF A PREPOSITION

The carpenter builds cabinets for whoever wants them.

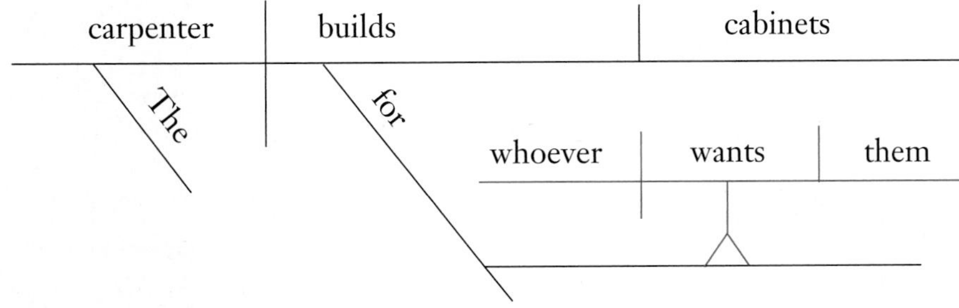

Exercise 3 Diagraming Sentences with Clauses

Using the preceding models as a guide, diagram the following sentences.

1. Carpenters work with wood, and masons work with stone.
2. The wood that we use is yellow pine.
3. When you design a house, you think about spaces.
4. An architectural style is what you must choose next.
5. That tastes in style vary is common knowledge.
6. The colonial style is popular with whoever values tradition.
7. Some people like whatever their neighbors like.
8. Before people move, they decide on a style.
9. When you travel in the West, you see more modern houses.
10. The style that I prefer is really a combination.

UNIT 15

Verb Tenses and Voice

15.1 Principal Parts of Verbs

■ All verbs have four **principal parts**—a *base form,* a *present participle,* a *simple past form,* and a *past participle.* All the verb tenses are formed from these principal parts.

Principal Parts of Verbs			
Base Form	**Present Participle**	**Past Form**	**Past Participle**
sail	sailing	sailed	sailed
soar	soaring	soared	soared
work	working	worked	worked
sing	singing	sang	sung
be	being	was, were	been
hit	hitting	hit	hit

You can use the base form (except the base form of *be*) and the past form alone as main verbs. The present participle and the past participle, however, must always be used with one or more auxiliary verbs to function as the simple predicate.

Carpenters **work.** [base or present form]

Carpenters **worked.** [past form]

Carpenters **are working.** [present participle with the auxiliary verb *are*]

Carpenters **have worked.** [past participle with the auxiliary verb *have*]

Exercise 1 **Using Principal Parts of Verbs**

Copy and complete each of the following sentences with the principal part of the verb that is indicated in parentheses.

1. Most plumbers ___ hot water heaters. (base form of *repair*)
2. Our plumber is ___ the kitchen sink. (present participle of *repair*)
3. Last month, he ___ the dishwasher. (past form of *repair*)
4. He has ___ many appliances in this house. (past participle of *repair*)
5. He is ___ his work. (present participle of *enjoy*)

15.2 Regular and Irregular Verbs

- A **regular verb** forms its past form and past participle by adding *-ed* to the base form.

Regular Verbs		
Base Form	**Past Form**	**Past Participle**
soar	soared	soared
climb	climbed	climbed
ski	skied	skied

When a suffix beginning with a vowel is added to the base form of some regular verbs, the verbs undergo spelling changes.

regulate + **-ed** = regulat**ed** try + **-ed** = tri**ed**

stop + **-ed** = stopp**ed** grin + **-ed** = grinn**ed**

- An **irregular verb** forms its past form and past participle in some way other than adding *-ed* to the base form.

Irregular Verbs		
Base Form	**Past Form**	**Past Participle**
be	was, were	been
beat	beat	beaten
become	became	become
begin	began	begun
bite	bit	bitten *or* bit
blow	blew	blown
break	broke	broken
bring	brought	brought
burst	burst	burst
buy	bought	bought
catch	caught	caught
choose	chose	chosen
come	came	come
do	did	done
draw	drew	drawn
drink	drank	drunk
drive	drove	driven
eat	ate	eaten
fall	fell	fallen
feel	felt	felt
find	found	found
fly	flew	flown

Irregular Verbs		
Base Form	**Past Form**	**Past Participle**
freeze	froze	frozen
get	got	got *or* gotten
give	gave	given
go	went	gone
grow	grew	grown
hang	hung *or* hanged	hung *or* hanged
have	had	had
hold	held	held
know	knew	known
lay*	laid	laid
lead	led	led
leave	left	left
lend	lent	lent
lie*	lay	lain
lose	lost	lost
put	put	put
ride	rode	ridden
ring	rang	rung
rise*	rose	risen
run	ran	run
say	said	said
see	saw	seen
set*	set	set
shake	shook	shaken
shrink	shrank *or* shrunk	shrunk *or* shrunken
sing	sang	sung
sink	sank *or* sunk	sunk
sit*	sat	sat
speak	spoke	spoken
spend	spent	spent
spring	sprang *or* sprung	sprung
steal	stole	stolen
swim	swam	swum
swing	swung	swung
take	took	taken
teach	taught	taught
tear	tore	torn
tell	told	told
think	thought	thought
throw	threw	thrown
wear	wore	worn
weave	wove	woven
win	won	won
write	wrote	written

*For more detailed instruction on *lay* versus *lie,* see Unit 19.

*For more detailed instruction on *raise* versus *rise* and *sit* versus *set,* see Unit 19.

Exercise 2 Using the Principal Parts of Verbs

On your paper, write the principal part of the verb that is indicated in parentheses.

The History of Words

1. The number of words in the English language has ____________ over the centuries. (past participle of *grow*)
2. Most words in our language have ____________ through changes in spelling or meaning. (past participle of *go*)
3. Etymologists, who study the history of words, have ____________ interesting clues to the present meanings of words. (part participle of *find*)
4. Two Latin words meaning "not speaking" ____________ the word *infant.* (past form of *become*)
5. An ancient word meaning "blood" has ____________ down to us as the word *red.* (past participle of *come*)
6. The word *ketchup* comes from the Malaysian name for a fish sauce that sailors ____________ to England in the seventeenth century. (past form of *bring*)
7. Long ago people sometimes ____________ their last name on the basis of their profession; it is easy to understand why the names Baker, Carpenter, Miller, Taylor, Wheelwright, and Smith were often selected. (past form of *choose*)
8. Celtic families often ____________ their last name with Mac or Fitz, meaning "son of." (past form of *begin*)
9. The name John has ____________ various forms in different languages around the world, including Jean, Giovanni, Juan, Hans, and Ivan. (past participle of *take*)
10. The Spanish have ____________ us such English words as *brocade, canyon, mosquito, plaza,* and *vanilla.* (past participle of *give*)
11. In the school library, I ____ a dictionary that dealt with the origin of words and phrases. (past form of *see*)
12. My English teacher ____ me his copy of this intriguing reference work. (past form of *lend*)
13. This dictionary ____ to rest many of my misconceptions about language and word usage. (past form of *lay*)
14. The authors of the dictionary have ____ many best-selling references, including the Berlitz language books. (past participle of *write*)
15. One of the authors ____ the advisory editor of a standard dictionary. (past form of *be*)
16. His syndicated newspaper column, "Words, Wit, and Wisdom," has ____ the interest of more than 12 million readers. (past participle of *catch*)
17. The dictionary has ____ my curiosity about the origins of many everyday words and expressions. (past participle of *satisfy*)
18. I never ____ that the abbreviation *COD* stands for "collect on delivery" in the United States and "cash on delivery" in Britain. (past form of *know*)
19. *Hamburger* ____ its name from the city of Hamburg, Germany, and was originally called "Hamburg steak." (past form of *take*)
20. The baseball term *duster* refers to a ball that a pitcher has ____ hard and close to the batter to make the batter step back from the plate. (past participle of *throw*)

15.3 Tense of Verbs

■ The **tenses** of a verb are the forms that help to show time.

There are six tenses in English: *present, past,* and *future* and *present perfect, past perfect,* and *future perfect.*

Present Tense

The present tense of any verb other than *be* is the same as the base form of the verb. To form the third-person singular of these verbs, add *-s* or *-es* to the base form.

	SINGULAR	PLURAL
FIRST PERSON	I **play.**	We **play.**
SECOND PERSON	You **play.**	You **play.**
THIRD PERSON	She, he, or it **plays.**	They **play.**
	Ronnie **plays.**	The children **play.**

	SINGULAR	PLURAL
FIRST PERSON	I **am** happy.	We **are** happy.
SECOND PERSON	You **are** happy.	You **are** happy.
THIRD PERSON	She, he, or it **is** happy.	They **are** happy.
	Ronnie **is** happy.	The children **are** happy.

■ The **present tense** expresses a constant, repeated, or habitual action or condition. It can also express a general truth.

The Hudson River **flows** into the Atlantic. [not just now but always: a constant action]

Jessie **plays** the flute superbly. [now and always: a habitual action]

Uranium **is** radioactive. [a condition that is generally true]

■ The **present tense** can also express an action or condition that exists only now.

Ronnie **feels** sick. [not always but just now]

I **declare** these games over. [at this very moment]

■ The **present tense** is sometimes used in historical writing to express past events and, more often, in poetry, fiction, and reporting (especially in sports) to convey a sense of "being there."

Above the crowd, the *Hindenburg* suddenly **bursts** into flame.

I **watch** as my sister **runs** after the ducks and **slips** in the mud.

The pitch **gets** away from the catcher and **bounces** into the fence.

Verb Tenses and Voice

Past Tense

■ Use the **past tense** to express an action or condition that was started and completed in the past.

The team **defeated** its opponent.

The rivalry **seemed** fierce.

Victory **tasted** sweet.

My friends and I **led** the cheers.

Except for *be,* nearly all verbs—regular and irregular—have just one past-tense form, such as *climbed* or *became.* When you use the past tense of *be,* however, you must choose between the forms *was* and *were.*

	SINGULAR	PLURAL
FIRST PERSON	I **was** happy.	We **were** happy.
SECOND PERSON	You **were** happy.	You **were** happy.
THIRD PERSON	He, she, or it **was** happy.	They **were** happy.

Exercise 3 Using the Present Tense in Sentences

On your paper, write a sentence using each of the following present tense verbs. The content of your sentence should express the kind of present time indicated in parentheses.

SAMPLE does (now and always)
ANSWER He does his laundry on Saturdays.

1. works (now and always)
2. sound (just now)
3. is (generally true)
4. says (at this moment)
5. sing (always)
6. finishes (a single sports event)
7. prefer (just now)
8. reads (now and always)
9. changes (generally true)
10. elect (historical present)

Exercise 4 Using the Past Tense in Sentences

On your paper, write two paragraphs. In the first, use the past tense of verbs 1–5; in the second, use the past tense of verbs 6–10. In your paragraphs, use the verbs in any order.

1. give
2. think
3. choose
4. take
5. know
6. beat
7. try
8. run
9. put
10. win

Future Tense

■ Use the **future tense** to express an action or condition that will occur in the future.

To form the future tense of any verb, use *shall* or *will* with the base form: *I shall talk; you will come.*

I **shall write** my essay tonight.

Angela **will mail** the application.

You **will see** me tomorrow.

There are other ways to express future time besides using *shall* or *will.*

1. Use *going to* with the present tense of *be* and the base form of a verb.

   Angela **is *going to* mail** the application.

   You **are *going to* see** me tomorrow.

2. Use *about to* with the present tense of *be* and the base form of the verb.

   I **am *about to* write** my essay.

   Angela **is *about to* mail** the application.

3. Use the present tense with an adverb or an adverb phrase that shows future time.

   Frank **sails *tomorrow.***

   Frank **sails *on the fifteenth of next month.***

Exercise 5 **Using Expressions of Future Time**

On your paper, write the verb in each sentence below in the future tense. Try to use at least two other ways of expressing future time besides adding *shall* or *will* to the base form of the verb.

India's Classical Dances

1. Two classmates and I presented a report about the classical dances of India.
2. First Chandra spoke about *Bharata natyam,* the sacred Hindu dance form.
3. She described its complex movements for the hands, arms, and torso.
4. Chandra demonstrated several of the hand and arm movements.
5. Then Lan described two other highly stylized Indian dance forms: *kathakali,* a dramatic style from southern India, and *kathak,* an ancient dance from northern India.
6. He told us about the *kathakali*'s link to early Hindu mythology.
7. He also presented a videotape of an authentic performance of *kathakali,* showing the dance's strong rhythms and rapid turns.
8. Then it was my turn to describe *manipuri,* a dignified dance from northeastern India.
9. I taught the students a few of the difficult movements typical of *manipuri* dancers.
10. Finally Chandra danced a pantomime from the *Bharata natyam* tradition.

Exercise 6 Expressing Future Time in Sentences

Write five statements or predictions about the future. Your sentences may be as realistic or as fantastical as you wish. Remember to vary the ways in which you express future time.

SAMPLE ANSWERS Film companies are going to produce all-day movies.
In-line skating is about to become the very next craze.
On Friday I fly to Puerto Rico.

Exercise 7 Changing Verb Tenses

Change the tense of the italicized verb in each sentence below, following the directions in parentheses. Write the correct tense on your paper.

1. The local minor league baseball team, the Panthers, *is* one of the least profitable teams in its league. (Change to the past tense.)
2. At that time, two major investors *take* over the ownership and management of the team. (Change to the past tense.)
3. Bill Smith, a former major leaguer, *left* his job as an insurance executive to take over the day-to-day operation of the team. (Change to the present tense.)
4. With a winning record and a whole series of giveaway programs, the Panthers' profits *soar.* (Change to the future tense.)
5. In 1997 the team *won* their first championship ever. (Change to the present tense.)
6. The Panthers eventually *become* the most consistent winner in their division. (Change to the past tense.)
7. Tom Flowers, the Panthers' former star pitcher, *beats* the World Series winners in his first major league game. (Change to the past tense.)
8. Baseball fans *find* it difficult to buy tickets for the Panthers' final play-off game. (Change to the past tense.)
9. Bill Smith says that the team *will release* their aging shortstop to make room for another player. (Change to another form showing future time.)
10. Early in the regular season, the team *falls* well behind their arch rivals, the Comets. (Change to the past tense.)
11. Real fans *knew* the team's misfortunes might last a bit longer. (Change to the present tense.)
12. They think that the departure of Tom Flowers *poses* a threat to the team's chances. (Change to the future tense.)
13. Every year, the team *lost* several players to the major leagues. (Change to the present tense.)
14. Attendance *dropped* at all the other ballparks in the league. (Change to the present tense.)
15. Even more success came to the management team that *oversees* the Panthers' business operations. (Change to the past tense.)

15.4 Perfect Tenses

Present Perfect Tense

■ Use the **present perfect tense** to express an action or condition that occurred at some *indefinite* time in the past.

To form the present perfect tense, use *has* or *have* with the past participle of a verb: *has studied, have chosen.**

*Do not be confused by the term *present perfect;* this tense expresses past time. Present refers to the tense of the auxiliary verb *has* or *have*.

She **has listened** to the recording.
They **have bought** a new home.

The present perfect tense can refer only to past time that is indefinite. You cannot add adverbs such as *yesterday* to make the time more specific.

He **has arrived** from Nebraska.

To refer to completed past time, you usually use the simple past tense.

He **arrived** from Nebraska yesterday.

You can also use the present perfect tense to show that an action or a condition *began* in the past and *continues* into the present. This use usually involves adverbs of time or adverb phrases.

He **has spoken daily** from his campaign headquarters.
Special guards **have remained** at the embassy **around the clock.**

Exercise 8 Using the Present Perfect Tense

(a) On your paper, rewrite each of the following sentences, changing the verb tense from past to present perfect. (b) Add adverbs or adverb phrases to each sentence to show that an action or condition began in the past and continues into the present.

SAMPLE We looked for a new car.
ANSWER **a.** We have looked for a new car.
b. We have looked for a new car for two weeks.

1. He taught swimming classes.
2. Movie critics praised the film.
3. The state highway was under repair.
4. Our art class studied portrait painting.
5. The towering waves cascaded over the craggy shore.
6. The student council met with the principal.
7. The senior class sponsored a schoolwide fundraising project.
8. Several students served meals at the shelter for the homeless.
9. The counselor drove them to their after-school jobs.
10. Many teachers worked on a special exhibit for the library.

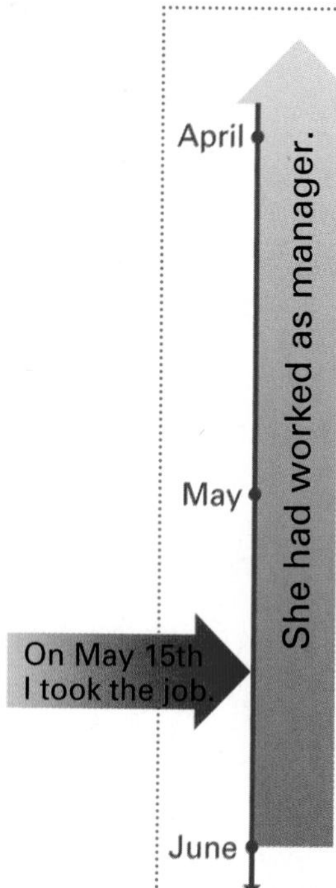

Past Perfect Tense

■ Use the **past perfect tense** to indicate that one past action or condition began *and* ended before another past action started.

To form the past perfect tense, use *had* with the past participle of a verb: *had guessed, had driven.*

PAST PERFECT / PAST

She **had worked** as manager before I **took** the job. [She worked; she stopped working; I worked.]

PAST / PAST PERFECT

By the time I **arrived,** several actors **had auditioned.** [They auditioned; they finished auditioning; I arrived.]

PAST / PAST PERFECT

Before I **fell,** I **had noticed** the sticky spots on that section of the floor. [I noticed; I stopped noticing; I fell.]

Exercise 9 Using the Past Perfect Tense

Decide which verb in each sentence should be in the past perfect tense. Write the past perfect form of that verb on your paper.

1. She served as mayor of our city for years when she decided to run for Congress.
2. Once she carefully analyzed the pros and cons of entering the race, she called a press conference to announce her decision.
3. Although still young for a politician, she wished she made the decision to enter politics earlier.
4. She told the press she already discussed the decision to run for office with her family.
5. By 6:00 P.M. on election day, she stopped in more than a hundred towns throughout her district.
6. By the week that the election was over, her campaign cost much more than she had calculated.
7. By the time she moved to Washington, D.C., she completed the selection of all members of her staff.
8. When she was sworn in, her chief of staff already accepted job applications from hundreds of job hunters.
9. When her old friends visited her in March, the first-year representative already drafted her first piece of legislation.
10. She organized her entire reelection campaign by the time August arrived.

Future Perfect Tense

- Use the **future perfect tense** to express one future action or condition that will begin *and* end before another future event starts. To form the future perfect tense, use *will have* or *shall have* with the past participle of a verb: *will have talked, shall have talked.*

By June I **will have worked** here two months. [Two months will be over before another future event, the coming of June, occurs.]

Exercise 10 Using the Future Perfect Tense

Use each phrase and verb below to write a sentence in the future perfect tense.

SAMPLE By early May—plant
ANSWER By early May, I will have planted 100 bulbs.

1. By next Sunday—give
2. Before the beginning of summer—buy
3. By the time I vote for the first time—watch
4. Before Susan's birthday—make
5. By New Year's Day—stop

Exercise 11 Writing the Perfect Tenses

On your paper, write the perfect-tense verb indicated in parentheses after each sentence.

African American Folktales

1. Folklorists _____ African American folktales for years. (present perfect of *collect*)
2. African Americans who _____ to this country as enslaved people later adapted West African folktales to suit the circumstances of their new culture. (past perfect of *come*)
3. The folktales about Brer Rabbit, for instance, grew out of trickster tales that African Americans _____ in their native West Africa. (past perfect of *learn*)
4. In the near future, some variations of West African folktales _____ in this country for more than 200 years. (future perfect of *survive*)
5. The African American inhabitants of the Georgia Sea Islands _____ variations of West African tales for many generations. (present perfect of *tell*)
6. Once African Americans _____ Western religions, they invented many preacher tales. (past perfect of *adopt*)
7. These religious tales _____ many African American ballads and spirituals. (present perfect of *influence*)
8. Writers such as Zora Neale Hurston found inspiration in folktales that _____ themselves into the fabric of African American culture. (past perfect of *weave*)
9. Many blues singers _____ from folktales themes that describe or allude to the hardships inherent in African American life. (present perfect of *take*)
10. It is likely that all American children _____ some African American folktales by the time they grow up. (future perfect of *hear*)

15.5 Progressive and Emphatic Forms

- Each of the six tenses has a **progressive** form that expresses a continuing action.

To make the progressive forms, use the appropriate tense of the verb *be* with the present participle of the main verb.

PRESENT PROGRESSIVE	They ***are*** **listening.**
PAST PROGRESSIVE	They ***were*** **listening.**
FUTURE PROGRESSIVE	They ***will be*** **listening.**
PRESENT PERFECT PROGRESSIVE	They ***have been*** **listening.**
PAST PERFECT PROGRESSIVE	They ***had been*** **listening.**
FUTURE PERFECT PROGRESSIVE	They ***will have been*** **listening.**

- The present and past tenses have additional forms, called **emphatic,** that add special force, or emphasis, to the verb.

To make the emphatic forms, use *do, does,* or *did* with the base form.

PRESENT EMPHATIC	I ***do*** **listen.**
PAST EMPHATIC	I ***did*** **listen.**

Exercise 12 Using the Progressive and Emphatic Forms

For each sentence, write the progressive or the emphatic form of the verb in parentheses. Choose the form that makes more sense in the sentence.

Miami's Cuban Community

1. For decades the city of Miami (attract) many visitors from the Caribbean.
2. Since the late nineteenth century, when Miami was first developed as a resort, wealthy Cubans, Venezuelans, and Colombians (come) to Miami on vacation.
3. Today many poor Nicaraguans and Mexicans (settle) in Miami, but the largest Spanish-speaking community in the city is Cuban.
4. Before 1959 few (anticipate) a large influx of Cubans fleeing Castro's new regime.
5. Nevertheless, it is clear now that the Cuban revolution of 1959 (have) a major impact on the population of Miami.
6. Today more than half a million people of Cuban descent (live) in Dade County, where Miami is located.
7. By the year 2000, almost as many people (speak) Spanish as English in Miami and the nearby communities.
8. Bilingualism (become) increasingly common among people who now work here.
9. Many Cubans who fled their homeland (hope) at first to return to their country.
10. Many Cuban Americans, however, (decide) that Miami is now their permanent home.

Exercise 13 Review: Using Verb Tenses and Forms

On your paper, complete each of the following sentences by writing the tense or form indicated in parentheses.

Kwanzaa

1. In 1966 Dr. Maulana Karenga ____ Kwanzaa as a way for African Americans to reflect on and celebrate their rich heritage. (past tense of *create*)
2. Since its inception this nonreligious and nonpolitical holiday ____ worldwide acceptance. (present perfect progressive form of *gain*)
3. Dr. Karenga ____ the annual celebration around African cultural and social experiences, particularly the traditional festival of first fruits. (past perfect tense of *develop*)
4. By the end of the weeklong celebration, African Americans ____ the Nguzo Saba, the Seven Principles of Kwanzaa. (future perfect tense of *observe*)
5. The Seven Principles ____ a set of values that emphasize accountability, reliability, and concern for one another. (present tense of *be*)
6. Prior to December 26, the first day of the celebration, millions of African Americans ____ weeks preparing the basic Kwanzaa symbols. (future progressive form of *spend*)
7. One is the Mkeka, or place mat, which ____ tradition. (present tense of *represent*)
8. Another symbol is Vibunzi, an ear of corn, which ____ to symbolize each child in the family. (present perfect tense of *come*)
9. Estimates indicate that 15 to 18 million people ____ this holiday in recent years. (past progressive form of *celebrate*)
10. Many students ____ to celebrate Kwanzaa along with their traditional religious holidays. (present perfect tense of *choose*)

Exercise 14 Review: Identifying Verb Tenses and Their Uses

On your paper, explain the difference in meaning between the sentences in each of the pairs below. Name the tense(s) used in each sentence.

SAMPLE **a.** Did she live in Washington long?
b. Has she lived in Washington long?

ANSWER In sentence *a* the action occurred in the past and has ended—past. In sentence *b* the action occurred in the past and is continuing—present perfect.

1. **a.** They went to Utah for vacation.
   b. They have gone to Utah for vacation.
2. **a.** We planned a trip to Virginia to visit friends.
   b. We were planning a trip to Virginia to visit friends.
3. **a.** Marisa did work in New Mexico.
   b. Marisa has worked in New Mexico.
4. **a.** She has been visiting them in Texas.
   b. She visited them in Texas.
5. **a.** Earl is traveling through Colorado.
   b. Earl has been traveling through Colorado.

15.6 Compatibility of Tenses

- Do not shift, or change, tenses when two or more events occur at the same time.

INCORRECT During the storm the dam **broke,** and the river **reaches** flood level. [The tense shifts from the past to the present.]

CORRECT During the storm the dam **broke,** and the river **reached** flood level. [Now it is clear that both events happened at nearly the same time in the past.]

- Shift tenses only to show that one event precedes or follows another.

INCORRECT By the time the game **ended,** she **bowled** six strikes. [The two past-tense verbs give the mistaken impression that both events—the ending of the game and the bowling of the strikes—happened at the same time.]

CORRECT By the time the game **ended,** she **had bowled** six strikes. [The shift from the past tense (*ended*) to the past perfect tense (*had bowled*) clearly indicates that the bowling of six strikes happened before the game ended.]

- Keep a statement about a general truth in the present tense even if other verbs are in the past tense.

CORRECT Then he **remembered** that Christmas **is** on December 25.

Verb Tenses and Voice

Exercise 15 Choosing Compatible Tenses

Find the first verb that appears in each sentence below. Then choose and write the correct tense of the second verb in parentheses.

SAMPLE Jaime had jogged daily after school, but he (has found, found) exercising in the evening difficult.

ANSWER found

1. Before Jaime began his morning workouts, he (felt, had felt) sluggish and lazy.
2. Then he remembered that exercise (gives, gave) a person more energy.
3. It has been almost a year since he (had bought, bought) a student membership in the gym.
4. If he has time this summer, he (plans, will have planned) to enroll in a diving class.
5. In the summer, he works at a hotel and also (teaches, will teach) tennis.

Exercise 16 Making Tenses Compatible

First find the two verbs that appear in each of the following sentences. Then rewrite each sentence, making the second verb compatible with the first verb.

Two Opera Stars

1. Victoria de los Angeles was born in Barcelona, Spain, in 1923, where she later had studied music at the Barcelona Conservatory.
2. After she had completed the six-year course at the conservatory in only three years, she makes her concert debut in 1944.
3. Although the public knows her by her stage name, her real name was Victoria Gómez Cima.
4. She took private voice lessons for five years and then wins first prize in an international singing contest in Switzerland.
5. De los Angeles soon discovered that she has offers for concert appearances from all over Europe and America.
6. By the time she made her debut in New York in the fall of 1950, the public already heard many favorable things about her.
7. She had recorded many of her most brilliant roles before she had left the stage in 1969.
8. After she retired from opera, de los Angeles had devoted herself to musical recitals.
9. She began her recitals with operatic arias and was ending them with Spanish flamenco songs.
10. De los Angeles mastered French, Italian, and German and was excelling in each language.
11. Julia Migenes is a popular soprano who gains fame for her memorable performance as Carmen in the film version of the opera.
12. Although she was not nominated for an Oscar, she receives a Grammy for her performance.
13. She appeared in the film with the tenor Placido Domingo, who is performing the role of Don José.
14. The *London Financial Times* called Migenes "mesmerizing" and describes her delivery as "straight and from the heart."
15. Migenes has played many leading roles; two of these will be Jenny in *The Fall of Mahagonny* and the title role in the opera *Lulu.*
16. When the Metropolitan Opera presented *Lulu,* PBS televises it.
17. Migenes will perform at the Kennedy Center where she sang excerpts from her most famous roles.
18. She introduced a program that features popular music, such as French *chansons* and the music of Brecht and Weill.
19. She enjoys performing the music of Leonard Bernstein, who had become one of her favorite composers.
20. Nowadays, Migenes often treats her audiences to several Gershwin songs that will be among her personal favorites.

15.7 Voice of Verbs

- An action verb is in the **active voice** when the subject of the sentence performs the action.

  The trainer **teased** the lion.

- An action verb is in the **passive voice** when its action is performed on the subject.

  The lion **was teased** by the trainer.

The active voice is generally stronger, but sometimes the passive voice is preferred or even necessary. Use the passive voice if you do not want to call attention to the performer, if you do not know who the performer is, or if the performer is unimportant.

The window **was broken.** [You may not want to identify the culprit.]

The roses **were sent.** [You do not know who the sender is.]

All the cards **were sold.** [It doesn't matter who sold them.]

To form the passive voice, use a form of the auxiliary verb *be* with the past participle of the verb. The tense of the auxiliary verb determines the tense of the passive verb.

The lion **is teased** by the trainer. [present tense, passive voice]

The lion **was being teased.** [past progressive tense, passive voice]

The lion **will have been teased** by the trainer. [future perfect tense, passive voice]

Exercise 17 Identifying Active and Passive Voice

For each sentence, write the verb and identify its voice as *passive* or *active.*

1. In 1977 Leslie Marmon Silko published *Ceremony,* a powerful novel.
2. In the book, the life of a Native American veteran of World War II is described.
3. Stories about her own Pueblo tribe are often related by Silko.
4. The young Silko was told many stories by her great-aunts and great-grandmother.
5. Silko's writing often depicts the differences between Native American and white cultures.
6. The Bureau of Indian Affairs ran Silko's school in Old Laguna, New Mexico.
7. This school was attended by many children from the nearby Pueblo reservation.
8. The University of New Mexico granted Silko a diploma in 1969.
9. The idea of a career in law initially tempted Silko.
10. Eventually, a career as a writer was chosen by her instead.

Exercise 18 Identifying and Writing Active and Passive Voice

On your paper, rewrite the sentences below, changing the active voice to the passive or the passive voice to the active. For some passive voice sentences, it may not be necessary to include the performer of the action.

SAMPLE Several popular folk songs were performed by the band.
ANSWER The band performed several popular folk songs.

Joan Baez, Folksinger

1. A musical career was launched by Joan Baez in 1960.
2. An entire generation was touched by her music and her message.
3. In the late 1950s, a teaching job was offered by the Massachusetts Institute of Technology to Joan's father, Dr. Alberto Vicio Baez.
4. One evening Joan was taken by her father to a coffeehouse in Cambridge's Harvard Square.
5. For the first time, the songs of some popular young folksingers were heard by Joan.
6. From then on, she focused her attention on the guitar and traditional folk ballads.
7. A music promoter saw her performance in a Cambridge coffeehouse.
8. Joan was booked by the promoter into the Gate of Horn, a club in Chicago.
9. There she was invited by singer Bob Gibson to a folk festival in Newport, Rhode Island.
10. As a result of her solo performance, record deals were offered to Joan by several recording companies.
11. A small recording company called Vanguard was chosen by Joan.
12. During the fall of 1960, several weeks were spent by Joan Baez in a recording studio in New York City.
13. Constant touring followed the success of her first album, a major hit nationwide.
14. The Democratic party asked Joan to a gala for President John F. Kennedy.
15. During the 1960s, their country's involvement in the Vietnam War was protested by many young Americans.
16. The anger and frustration of young Americans from all backgrounds was reflected in the music of Joan Baez.
17. Her singing revealed deep feelings about peace and war and injustice.
18. Her audiences were moved by such songs as "Blowin' in the Wind" and "We Shall Overcome."
19. In 1966 the Reverend Martin Luther King Jr. was joined by Joan Baez in escorting African American children to their newly integrated school.
20. Many young people joined activist and singer Baez in her efforts for political reform.
21. In 1974 an album of Spanish-language songs was released by Joan.
22. The album featured songs of love and death from Central and South America.
23. Joan dedicated the album to her father.
24. Throughout the years, albums of diverse musical styles, including country and western, have been recorded by Joan.
25. Audiences of all ages are still thrilled by her voice and her music.

UNIT 15 Grammar Review

Verb Tenses and Voice

Set in the imaginary kingdom of Middle Earth, Tolkien's novel recounts the adventures of a group of hobbits, an ancient, peace-loving race. In this episode, three hobbits—Frodo, Sam, and Pippin—encounter a mysterious horseman. The meeting so disturbs Frodo that he is tempted to call on the powers of his magical ring. The passage has been annotated to show some of the kinds of verbs covered in this unit.

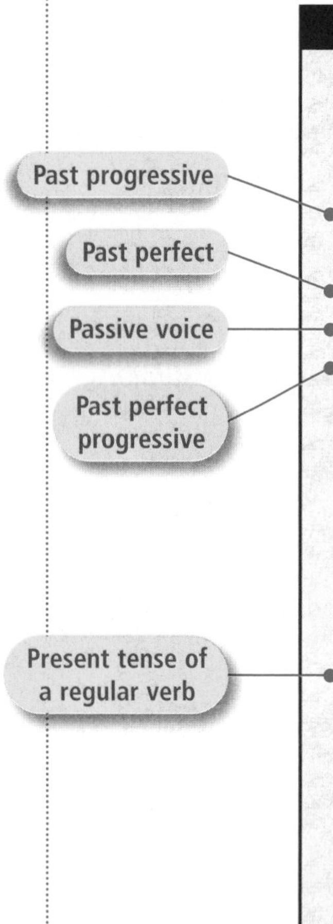

Literature Model

from The Fellowship of the Ring

by J. R. R. Tolkien

The sun was beginning to get low and the light of afternoon was on the land as they went down the hill. So far they had not met a soul on the road. This way was not much used, being hardly fit for carts, and there was little traffic to the Woody End. They had been jogging along again for an hour or more when Sam stopped a moment as if listening. They were now on level ground, and the road after much winding lay straight ahead through grassland sprinkled with tall trees, outliers of the approaching woods.

"I can hear a pony or a horse coming along the road behind," said Sam.

They looked back, but the turn of the road prevented them from seeing far. "I wonder if that is Gandalf coming after us," said Frodo; but even as he said it, he had a feeling that it was not so, and a sudden desire to hide from the view of the rider came over him.

"It may not matter much," he said apologetically, "but I would rather not be seen on the road. . . . Let's get out of sight!"

The other two ran quickly to the left and down into a little hollow not far from the road. There they lay flat. Frodo hesitated for a second: curiosity or some other feeling was struggling with his desire to hide. The sound of hoofs drew nearer.

Just in time he threw himself down in a patch of long grass behind a tree that overshadowed the road. Then he lifted his head and peered cautiously above one of the great roots.

Round the corner came a black horse, no hobbit-pony but a full-sized horse; and on it sat a large man, who seemed to crouch in the saddle, wrapped in a great black cloak and hood, so that only his boots in the high stirrups showed below; his face was shadowed and invisible.

When it reached the tree and was level with Frodo the horse stopped. The riding figure sat quite still with its head bowed, as if listening. From inside the hood came a noise as of someone sniffing to catch an elusive scent; the head turned from side to side of the road.

A sudden unreasoning fear of discovery laid hold of Frodo, and he thought of his Ring. He hardly dared to breathe, and yet the desire to get it out of his pocket became so strong that he began slowly to move his hand. . . . At that moment the rider sat up, and shook the reins. The horse stepped forward, walking slowly at first, and then breaking into a quick trot.

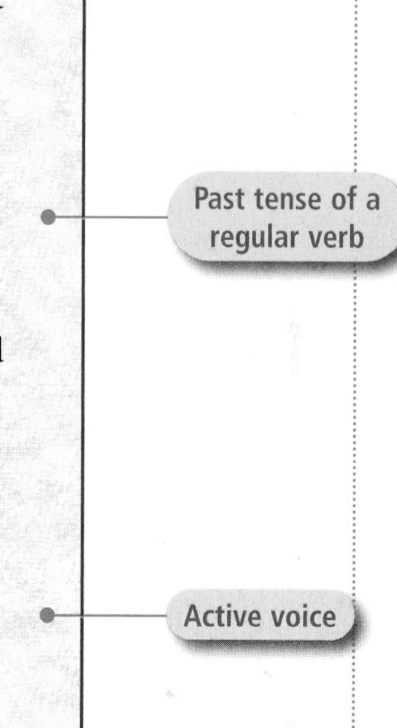

Review: Exercise 1 **Identifying Principal Parts**

The following sentences are based on *The Fellowship of the Ring.* Each sentence contains a verb in one of four forms: (a) the base form, (b) the past form, (c) the present participle, or (d) the past participle. At the end of the sentence is a second verb in parentheses. On your paper, write the form of the verb in italics. Then write the verb in parentheses in the same form as the original verb.

1. Their spirits *fall* at the approach of sunset. (sink)
2. The hobbits had *started* their journey too late in the day. (begin)
3. They *locate* a deserted road over the hill. (find)
4. The road *stretched* toward the dark woods ahead of the hobbits. (lead)
5. Few carts had *traveled* on the road in recent years because of its poor condition. (drive)
6. So far they had not *met* a soul along the road. (see)
7. In the fading light, Frodo and the other hobbits nervously *hurried* down the hill. (go)
8. Each hobbit had *carried* a few belongings from home in a pack on his back. (take)
9. Despite the rough road, they were *jogging* steadily toward the Woody End. (run)
10. Sam *heard* the sound of a horse's hoofs. (catch)

Review: Exercise 2 Using the Present, Past, and Future Tenses

Each of the following sentences elaborates on ideas suggested by the passage from *The Fellowship of the Ring.* On your paper, write each verb, changing the tense according to the instructions in parentheses. Use only the present, past, and future tenses; with the exception of *will* to express the future tense, do not use any helping verbs.

SAMPLE The hobbits *remain* in hiding.
(Change to the future tense.)

ANSWER will remain

1. Frodo *has* a Ring with magical powers. (Change to the past tense.)
2. Frodo *began* a dangerous journey through the imaginary kingdom of Middle Earth. (Change to the present tense.)
3. Frodo *thinks* admiringly of the powerful wizard Gandalf during his journey. (Change to the past tense.)
4. An unexpected noise *breaks* through the still air. (Change to the past tense.)
5. At the sound of the horseman, a sudden fear *will come* over Frodo. (Change to the past tense.)
6. After a slight hesitation, Frodo *told* the other hobbits of his nervousness. (Change to the present tense.)
7. The hobbits *fly* in different directions. (Change to the future tense.)
8. Frodo *sank* swiftly into a patch of tall grass. (Change to the present tense.)
9. His companions *went* to the left side of the road to find a place to hide. (Change to the present tense.)
10. Curiosity about the approaching horseman soon *will arise* in Frodo. (Change to the past tense.)
11. Before long Frodo *saw* a black horse—no mere hobbit-pony—and its rider. (Change to the future tense.)
12. The looming horseman *wore* a long black cloak and hood. (Change to the present tense.)
13. The horseman *speaks* to no one. (Change to the future tense.)
14. The rider's face *draws* back within the folds of his hood. (Change to the past tense.)
15. Frodo *remembers* the magic Ring in his pocket. (Change to the future tense.)
16. Frodo *will think* about the Ring in his pocket. (Change to the present tense.)
17. The horseman *will give* the horse's reins a shake. (Change to the past tense.)
18. The travelers *will take* greater precautions after this incident. (Change to the present tense.)
19. Perhaps Gandalf *comes* to their assistance. (Change to the future tense.)
20. The hobbits *will feel* nervous during the night. (Change to the present tense.)

Review: Exercise 3 Using the Perfect Tenses

Each of the following sentences is based on passages from *The Fellowship of the Ring* that are not reprinted in this textbook. On your paper, write the italicized verb in the tense indicated in parentheses, using the past participle of the main verb and the appropriate form of the helping verb *have.*

SAMPLE Before he started his journey, Frodo ∧ his house. (past perfect tense of *sell*)

ANSWER had sold

1. Frodo ∧ the magical Ring that is in his pocket from his uncle Bilbo. (present perfect tense of *inherit*)
2. Bilbo found the Ring in a cave, where Gollum, a wicked creature, ∧ it earlier. (past perfect tense of *lose*)
3. Before Gollum obtained the Ring, it ∧ to Sauron the Great, an evil power. (past perfect tense of *belong*)
4. A brave man named Isildur ∧ the Ring from Sauron's hand, but Isildur later lost the Ring in a river. (past perfect tense of *cut*)
5. Gollum murdered his friend Deagol, who ∧ the Ring from the river bottom. (past perfect tense of *got*)
6. Gandalf, a friendly wizard, ∧ Frodo of the Ring's unusual powers. (present perfect tense of *warn*)
7. Over the course of time, the Ring ∧ greed in each of its possessors. (present perfect tense of *foster*)
8. Gollum and Sauron's followers ∧ for the Ring for many years. (present perfect tense of *search*)
9. By the time the hobbits reach Mount Doom, perhaps some elves ∧ them. (future perfect tense of *help*)
10. Soon the Black Riders, Sauron's enthusiastic followers, ∧ Frodo. (future perfect tense of *attack*)

Review: Exercise 4 Using Verb Tenses in Writing

Choose a story that you have read recently or one that you have seen in the movies or on television. On your paper, write five sentences summarizing the story and describing the main characters. In each sentence, use at least two verbs that are compatible in tense. Write the verbs and label the tenses. Use all six verb tenses in your sentences.

SAMPLE ANSWER Last Saturday I saw a movie that I had heard about for weeks.
saw—past tense; had heard—past perfect tense

Review: Exercise 5 Using the Progressive and Emphatic Forms

On your paper, rewrite the following sentences, inserting the italicized verb in the form indicated in parentheses. Use the present participle of the main verb with the appropriate tense of the auxiliary verb *be,* or use the base form of the main verb with the appropriate form of *do.*

1. The sun has set in the distance, and twilight soon ∧ . (future progressive form of *come*)
2. An unfamiliar territory ∧ the group of adventurous hobbits. (present emphatic form of *surround*)
3. For many miles, the strange road ∧ down a steep hill. (past progressive form of *wind*)
4. Sam ∧ to the thunder of a horse's hoofs. (past progressive form of *listen*)
5. The horse ∧ briskly along the road just behind the travelers. (past progressive form of *gallop*)
6. Unfortunately, the bend in the road ∧ a view of any approaching rider. (present emphatic form of *obscure*)
7. The hobbits soon ∧ into hiding places near the edge of the road. (past progressive form of *dash*)
8. Frodo's heart ∧ fiercely against his chest. (past progressive form of *pound*)
9. Before long Frodo ∧ over the roots of a tree at the mysterious rider. (past progressive form of *peer*)
10. The horseman's dark and sinister appearance ∧ threatening. (past emphatic form of *seem*)
11. The rider ∧ his head. (present progressive form of *bow*)
12. The rider's hooded head ∧ from one side of the road to the other. (present progressive form of *turn*)
13. The rider ∧ the air for an elusive scent. (present progressive form of *sniff*)
14. After such a ride, dust ∧ to the horseman's cloak and saddle. (future progressive form of *cling*)
15. The horse ∧ heavily when it stops running. (future progressive form of *pant*)
16. In spite of his anxiety, Frodo ∧ about the identity of the mysterious rider. (present emphatic form of *wonder*)
17. Frodo ∧ his hand gradually toward the Ring in his pocket. (future progressive form of *move*)
18. Frodo truly ∧ against his uncontrollable desire for the Ring. (present emphatic form of *struggle*)
19. Frodo indeed ∧ the motives of the black-cloaked rider. (present emphatic form of *suspect*)
20. Evidently, the horseman ∧ the hobbits on their journey. (present progressive form of *follow*)

Review: Exercise 6 Making Tenses Compatible

The following sentences are based on the passage from *The Fellowship of the Ring* and other passages from the novel that are not reprinted in this textbook. On your paper, rewrite the sentence, changing the tense of the italicized verb to a form that makes the tenses of the verbs in the sentence compatible.

SAMPLE Before the horseman appeared, the hobbits *jumps* into hiding places.
ANSWER Before the horseman appeared, the hobbits had jumped into hiding places.

1. The mysterious figure sniffed the air as he *pauses* beside Frodo's concealed body.
2. As Frodo longingly *touches* his Ring, he remembered Gandalf's warning.
3. Before he disappeared, Gandalf *explains* the Ring's dangerous powers.
4. To the hobbits' relief, the horse broke into a trot while Frodo *watches.*
5. After the horseman rides away, Frodo *walked* toward his companions.
6. By the time Frodo reached his friends, they *stood* up.
7. The hobbits *discuss* the horseman who had frightened them.
8. Sam's father *saw* a stranger similar to the horseman before the hobbits left on their journey.
9. Frodo knew that the evil creature Gollum *left* his cave months ago in search of the Ring.
10. Frodo wondered whether Sauron *sends* the rider as a spy.

Review: Exercise 7 Changing the Voice of Verbs

The following sentences are based on *The Fellowship of the Ring.* First, identify each sentence as being in the *passive voice* or the *active voice.* Then rewrite each sentence, changing the active voice to the passive or the passive voice to the active.

SAMPLE The horseman's head was covered by a dark hood.
ANSWER passive voice; A dark hood covered the horseman's head.

1. The landscape of Middle Earth is described clearly by the novel's author, J. R. R. Tolkien.
2. A gray light bathed the lonely meadow.
3. The grassland around the bumpy road was sprinkled with tall trees.
4. The branches of a large tree overshadowed the road.
5. The curvy road was used by few people.
6. The rapid clatter of the horse's hooves alarmed Frodo and his friends.
7. Giant tree roots hid the small hobbits from view.
8. A great black cloak concealed most of the horseman's enormous body.
9. Suddenly Frodo was seized by a desire for his Ring.
10. The trembling hobbits were terrified by the horseman.

Review: Exercise 8 **Using Verb Tense, Form, and Voice**

Using details from the passage or your own ideas, write a sentence about each pair of nouns. Use the verb tense, form, or voice indicated in parentheses.

SAMPLE hobbits, road (past perfect progressive)
ANSWER The hobbits had been trudging along the road for an hour.

1. meadow, woods (present tense, passive voice)
2. sun, day (past progressive)
3. horse, rider (present perfect progressive)
4. sounds, fear (past emphatic)
5. hobbits, home (future progressive)

Review: Exercise 9

Proofreading

The following passage describes the artist Samuel Palmer, whose painting appears on the opposite page. Rewrite the passage, correcting the errors in spelling, usage, and grammar. Add any missing punctuation. There are twenty-five errors.

Samuel Palmer

[1]Samuel Palmer (1805–1881), the son of a bookseller who lived on the outskirts of London shown an early talent for painting. [2]By the time Palmer was fourteen, he has already had works accepted by the Royal Academy in London. [3]At the age of seventeen, he meets the artist John Linnell, who encourages him to study European art. [4]Linnell had a strong personal and professional influence on the young man and Palmer marries Linnell's daughter in 1837. [5]The relationship between the two men become difficult, however, because of Linnell's bossy and violent personality.

[6]Landscapes were Palmer's chief interest and he painted them with a keen eye. [7]He fills his notebooks with detailed drawings that expressed a deeply spiritual view of nature. [8]His view of life was strongly influenced by his friendship with William Blake the visionary English poet and painter. [9]Unfortunately, when Palmer died, many of his early sketches are destroyed by his son.

[10]*Early Morning* was finded among the few early sketches of Palmer's that had not been destroyed. [11]The gentle land scape depicted early in the morning. [12]Palmer has drawed each leaf, stone, and hillock with care and precision. [13]Rounded shapes predominate, some examples are the oak tree on the left, the cottage roof behind the wheat fields the sloping hills, and even Palmers signature

at the bottom of the canvas. [14]In a hollow below the tree sit a group of people. [15]Some critics beleive that the rabbit might symbolize the abundance of nature.

[16]Palmer often drawed his landscapes with a mythological quality, much like the settings in J. R. R. Tolkien's *The Fellowship of the Ring.* [17]He has wove elements of both realism and fantasy into the scene pictured in *Early Morning.* [18]Both Palmer and Tolkien was deeply spiritual men. [19]Both choosed to portray the sanctity of nature and the power of the human spirit.

Samuel Palmer, *Early Morning,* 1825

Review: Exercise 10

Mixed Review

The following sentences describe the life of the author J. R. R. Tolkien [täl′ kēn]. Rewrite each sentence, following the instructions in parentheses.

1. As a youth, J. R. R. Tolkien learns Greek and Latin and developed his own alphabet. (Change the first verb to make the tenses compatible.)

2. He also studies Finnish, and he invented the imaginary language of Quenya. (Correct the error caused by the use of the present tense.)
3. By the time Tolkien entered college, he already demonstrated an exceptional talent for languages. (Change the second verb to the past perfect.)
4. The gifted young student was awarded a scholarship by Oxford University. (Rewrite the sentence in the active voice.)
5. His studies of *Beowulf,* an early English epic, intensified his interest in Old English literature. (Rewrite the sentence in the passive voice.)
6. While Tolkien was still a student, he already gathered ideas for his future books about a mythological kingdom. (Change the second verb to the past progressive form.)
7. Elves, dwarfs, hobbits, and goblins truly inhabit this kingdom. (Change the verb to the present emphatic form.)
8. *The Hobbit,* the first book that Tolkien wrote about Middle Earth, appears in 1937. (Replace the inappropriate present tense.)
9. The idea of hobbits came to Tolkien as he graded exams at Oxford. (Change the second verb to the past progressive form.)
10. Some scholars think Tolkien's fantasies are reflecting the battle between good and evil in the real world. (Change the second verb from the present progressive to the present.)
11. A reviewer once observed that Tolkien will tap his readers' most common nightmares and fantasies. (Change the second verb to the present tense.)
12. Tolkien is called a "colonizer of dreams." (Change the verb to the active voice.)
13. He presents his readers with a viable alternative to the madness of the real world. (Change the verb to the present emphatic form.)
14. He introduced the word *hobbit,* which find its way into our everyday language. (Change the second verb to make the tenses compatible.)
15. In *The Hobbit,* Bilbo Baggins discovered, or perhaps steals, the One Ring of Power. (Change the second verb to make the tense compatible with that of the first.)
16. The last of the trilogy, which Tolkien names *The Return of the King,* was published in 1956. (Change the first verb to make the tenses compatible.)
17. Readers have been awaiting the publication of the final book for years. (Change the present perfect progressive to the past perfect progressive form.)
18. Critics believe that Tolkien's trilogy is one of the great literary achievements of our time. (Change the first verb to the present emphatic form.)
19. Sixty years later the story of the hobbits does remain profoundly relevant. (Change the verb form to the simple present tense.)
20. Tolkien's epic fantasy classic will delight readers for generations. (Change the verb to the future progressive form.)

Writing Application

TIME

For more about the writing process, see TIME Facing the Blank Page, pp. 109–119

Verbs in Writing

In this passage from *Roots: The Saga of an American Family,* Alex Haley explains how he began researching the story of his African American ancestors. As you read, note Haley's use of verbs.

The microfilm rolls *were delivered,* and I turned them through the machine with a building sense of intrigue, viewing in different census takers' penmanship an endless parade of names. After about a dozen microfilmed rolls, I *was beginning* to tire, when in utter astonishment I looked upon the names of Grandma's parents: Tom Murray, Irene Murray . . . older sisters of Grandma's as well—every one of them a name that I'd heard countless times on her front porch.

It *wasn't* that I *hadn't believed* Grandma. You just *didn't* not *believe* my Grandma. It was simply so uncanny actually seeing those names in print and in official U.S. Government records.

Techniques with Verbs

When you write and revise your own work, try to use verbs in some of the ways that Haley uses them.

1. Use the emphatic form for emphasis or to make a point. Notice how Haley uses the negative for additional emphasis.

UNEMPHATIC VERSION You just believed my Grandma.

HALEY'S VERSION You just *didn't* not *believe* my Grandma.

2. Use a verb form that correctly conveys your exact meaning. Compare the difference in meaning of these two sentences.

PAST TENSE VERSION After about a dozen microfilmed rolls, I *began* to tire.

HALEY'S VERSION After about a dozen microfilmed rolls, I *was beginning* to tire.

Verb Tenses and Voice

Practice Practice these techniques by revising the following passage on a separate sheet of paper. Choose an appropriate tense, form, and voice for each verb in parentheses. Make other changes to the passage that you think are needed.

When Alex Haley was seventeen, he enlisted in the U.S. Coast Guard with the permission of his father. During World War II, he (serve) on a warship. After he (write) adventure stories set on the high seas, he (submit) them to the editors of various magazines. For eight years, Haley (collect) rejection slips. Occasionally one of his stories (purchase) and (publish).

Haley retired from the Coast Guard after serving for twenty years, the last several years as a journalist. Now he (be) ready to begin a full-time career as a writer. He (begin) writing mostly magazine articles. In 1965 Haley (collaborate) on his first book, *The Autobiography of Malcolm X,* which was highly acclaimed. After twelve years of research and travel, Haley (produce) *Roots,* the winner of a special citation awarded by the Pulitzer Prize committee in 1977.

UNIT 16

Subject-Verb Agreement

16.1 Intervening Prepositional Phrases

■ A verb must agree with its subject in person and number.

Number can be singular or plural. Singular words indicate one and take a singular verb. Plural words indicate more than one and take a plural verb.

To show agreement, most verbs change form only in the present tense: when the subject is third-person singular, an *-s* (or *-es*) is added to the base verb.

SINGULAR	PLURAL
She **learns.**	They **learn.**
He **watches.**	They **watch.**

An exception is the linking verb *be,* which changes form in both the present tense and the past tense.

SINGULAR	PLURAL
The dog **is** happy.	The dogs **are** happy.
The apple **was** sour.	The apples **were** sour.

In order to show agreement with third-person subjects, the auxiliary verbs *be, have,* and *do* change form in verb phrases.

SINGULAR	PLURAL
She **is learning.**	They **are learning.**
She **has gone** home.	They **have gone** home.
Does he **live** in Virginia?	**Do** they **live** in Virginia?

Exercise 1 **Making Subjects and Verbs Agree**

On your paper, write the simple subject from each of the following sentences. Then write the verb form in parentheses that agrees with the subject.

The Class Party

1. Chandra, Bill, and Marco (is planning/are planning) the class party.
2. Carla (offers/offer) her house for the party.
3. The class representatives (votes/vote) to have the party on a Saturday.
4. Three students (visits/visit) the mall for ideas on decorating.
5. A teacher (volunteers/volunteer) to chaperone.
6. All class members (plans/plan) to attend the party.
7. They (knows/know) the food will be good.
8. It (is being/are being) made by student volunteers.
9. The volunteers (has been/have been) preparing sample dishes.
10. Everybody's favorite so far (was/were) the vegetarian deep-dish pizza.

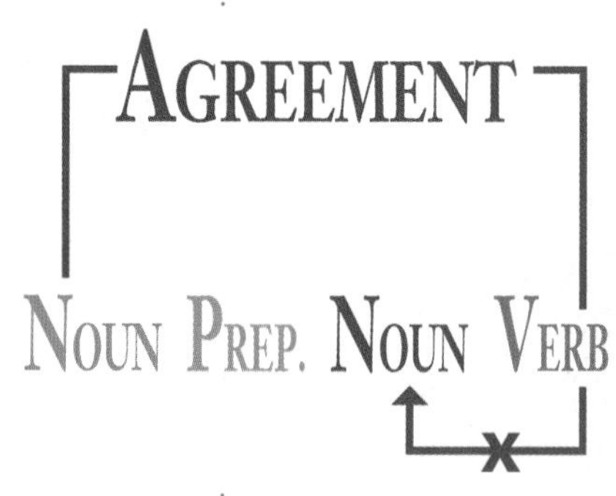

■ Do not mistake a word in a prepositional phrase for the subject of a sentence.

The subject of a sentence is never the object of a preposition. The verb must agree with the simple subject of the sentence, not with the object of a preposition.

The ***color*** of the roses **pleases** us. [The subject, *color,* is singular; *of the roses* is a prepositional phrase; the verb, *pleases,* is singular because it agrees with the singular subject.]

The ***flowers*** for the bouquet **are** pretty. [The subject, *flowers,* is plural; *for the bouquet* is a prepositional phrase; the verb, *are,* is plural because it agrees with the plural subject.]

Exercise 2 **Making Subjects and Verbs Agree When Prepositional Phrases Intervene**

On your paper, write the simple subject in each of the following sentences. Then write the verb form in parentheses that agrees with the subject.

Elizabeth Keckley

1. A report for one of my history classes (is/are) about Elizabeth Keckley, an African American who became the dressmaker for and confidante of First Lady Mary Todd Lincoln.
2. Keckley in her early years (was/were) enslaved in Virginia.
3. A daughter of the family (was/were) fond of Keckley and brought her to St. Louis to live.
4. Keckley's talents in the art of dressmaking (was/were) so considerable that she was able to help support the family.
5. In 1855 Keckley, with the help of loans from her customers, (was/were) able to purchase her freedom.
6. To me, Keckley's irrepressible longings for freedom and dignity (seems/seem) extraordinary.
7. Keckley's faith in herself and in her abilities (was/were) rewarded, for she moved to Washington, D.C., and became the dressmaker of President Lincoln's wife.
8. Keckley, as a personal friend of the Lincolns, (was/were) privy to many family matters at the White House.
9. Her opinions about the White House (was/were) published in 1868 in a book entitled *Behind the Scenes.*
10. The success of this determined woman (continues/continue) to inspire people today.

16.2 Agreement with Linking Verbs

- Do not be confused by a predicate nominative that is different in number from the subject. Only the subject affects the number of the linking verb.

The last ***course* was** strawberries with cream. [The singular verb, *was,* agrees with the singular subject, *course,* not with the predicate nominative, *strawberries.*]

The main ***courses*** for the dinner **were** a selection of fish dishes. [The plural verb, *were,* agrees with the plural subject, *courses,* not with the predicate nominative, *selection.*]

Baskets of flowers **were** the decoration at the banquet. [The plural verb, *were,* agrees with the plural subject, *baskets,* not with the predicate nominative, *decoration.*]

My favorite ***part*** of musicals **is** the duets. [The singular verb, *is,* agrees with the singular subject, *part,* not with the predicate nominative, *duets.*]

Exercise 3 Making Linking Verbs Agree with Their Subjects

On your paper, write the simple subject or subjects in each of the following sentences. Then write the form of the verb in parentheses that agrees with the subject.

Modern Circuses

1. For many people the joys of the circus (is/are) a pleasure that they never outgrow.
2. Circuses (remains/remain) a popular form of entertainment in many countries.
3. The circuses of ancient Rome (was/were) actually a group of chariot races performed in a ring.
4. Perhaps the first of the modern circuses (was/were) a one-ring show by Philip Astley, an eighteenth-century horse trainer.
5. In the eighteenth and nineteenth centuries, circus performers (was/were) the elite among popular entertainers.
6. The most exotic part of all circuses (is/are) the wild animals.
7. The feats of an acrobat or a trapeze artist (seems/seem) an impossibility to most of us.
8. A clown's acrobatic leaps (appears/appear) an easy trick, but in fact they are quite difficult to perform.
9. The strains of the calliope (is/are) a joyous sound, don't you think?
10. To me, an irresistible temptation (is/are) the aromas of popcorn and roasted peanuts.

16.3 Agreement in Inverted Sentences

■ In an **inverted sentence**—a sentence in which the subject follows the verb—take care in locating the simple subject and make sure that the verb agrees with the subject.

Because an inverted sentence often begins with a prepositional phrase, the object of the preposition may easily be mistaken for the subject. In an inverted sentence, however, the subject follows the verb.

V S
SINGULAR Near the trees **sleeps** the ***camper.***

V S
PLURAL Near the trees **sleep** the ***campers.***

Inverted sentences may also begin with the word *there* or *here. There* or *here* is almost never the subject of a sentence.

V S
SINGULAR There **is** a ***camper*** on the mountain.

V S
Here **comes** the last ***runner.***

V S
PLURAL There **are** ***campers*** on the mountain.

V S
Here **come** the last two ***runners.***

In interrogative sentences, the subject may come after an auxiliary verb. In this case, you will find the subject between the auxiliary verb and the main verb.

V S V
SINGULAR **Does** that ***eagle*** **live** in the mountains?

V S V
PLURAL **Do** those ***mountains*** **contain** eagles?

V S V
SINGULAR **Is** the ***tent*** **pitched** in the right place?

V S V
PLURAL **Are** the ***tents*** **pitched** in the right place?

Exercise 4 Making Subjects and Verbs Agree in Inverted Sentences

On your paper, write the simple subject in each of the following sentences. Then write the form of the verb in parentheses that agrees with the subject.

Blues from the Delta

1. In many a rock musician (beats/beat) the heart of a blues musician from the region of the United States known as the Mississippi Delta.
2. There (was/were) a dozen or more influential blues musicians born in the Mississippi Delta in the first two decades of this century.
3. In the group work songs of cotton-field workers (lies/lie) the roots of the Delta blues.
4. On the plantations of the Delta (was/were) heard the music of Robert Johnson, Muddy Waters, and John Lee Hooker, among others.
5. (Do/Does) these names seem familiar to you?
6. Unfortunately, there (is/are) few recordings of the very early musical pieces of some of these blues artists.
7. There (was/were) several musicians who carried the blues north, especially to Chicago, in the 1940s and 1950s.
8. (Was/Were) blues singers Howlin' Wolf and Muddy Waters performing in Chicago?
9. In the blues (lives/live) a sense of hope, strength, and survival.
10. In the debt of Delta blues musicians (is/are) artists as diverse as the Rolling Stones, Robert Cray, and Whitney Houston.

Exercise 5 Using Subject-Verb Agreement

On your paper, write the simple subject in each of the following sentences. Then write the form of the verb in parentheses that agrees with the subject.

SAMPLE There (is/are) much history to be found in Boston and its surroundings.
ANSWERS history is

Bunker Hill

1. One of many famous monuments (stands/stand) above Boston's waterfront.
2. Perhaps the most famous one of the Revolutionary War monuments (is/are) this one on Bunker Hill.
3. South of Bunker Hill and the monument (rises/rise) Breed's Hill.
4. Although the battle fought here was named for Bunker Hill, the true site of the first of many Revolutionary War conflicts (was/were) Breed's Hill.
5. Along the base of Breed's Hill (stretches/stretch) the old battle lines.
6. Among the American leaders in that conflict (was/were) Colonel William Prescott.
7. The hastily organized colonial militiamen (was/were) the "irregular" army that faced the better-organized British force.
8. One outcome of the Battle of Bunker Hill (was/were) the colonists' moral triumph.
9. Several patriotic songs and my favorite poem (is/are) based on the story of the Battle of Bunker Hill.
10. There (is/are) always many tourists at the historical site.

16.4 Agreement with Special Subjects

Collective Nouns

■ A **collective noun** names a group. Consider a collective noun singular when it refers to a group as a whole. Consider a collective noun plural when it refers to each member of a group individually.

SINGULAR The ***squadron*** of planes **soars.**
PLURAL The ***squadron*** **land** one at a time.

SINGULAR The ***crowd*** **cheers.**
PLURAL The ***crowd*** **rush** to find their seats.

Special Nouns

■ Certain nouns that end in *-s,* such as *mumps, measles,* and *mathematics,* take singular verbs.

SINGULAR ***Mathematics*** **interests** many people.

■ Certain other nouns that end in *-s,* such as *scissors, pants, binoculars,* and *eyeglasses,* take plural verbs.

PLURAL The ***scissors*** **were** defective.
Your ***pants*** **are** too short.

■ Many nouns that end in *-ics* may be singular or plural, depending upon their meaning.

SINGULAR ***Politics*** **is** often interesting. [one subject of interest]
PLURAL His ***politics*** **are** shameless. [more than one action of a political nature]

Exercise 6 **Making Verbs Agree with Special Subjects**

On your paper, write the simple subject of each sentence. Then write the form of the verb in parentheses that agrees with each subject.

1. The team (was/were) victorious in the state finals.
2. The audience (is/are) expressing their opinions about the play.
3. Diabetes (is/are) a disorder of the body's insulin production.
4. The headphones (is/are) on the table.
5. His ethics (was/were) questioned by the local newspaper.

Nouns of Amount

- When a noun of amount refers to a total that is considered as one unit, it is singular. When it refers to a number of individual units, it is plural.

SINGULAR Four ***dollars*** **is** a fair price. [one amount]
PLURAL Four ***dollars*** **lie** on the sidewalk. [four individual bills]

SINGULAR Two ***months*** **is** the waiting period. [one unit of time]
PLURAL Two ***months*** **have gone** by. [two individual time periods]

Titles

- A title is always singular, even if a noun within the title is plural.

SINGULAR ***Little Women*** **delights** readers of all ages.

SINGULAR ***Cakes and Bagels*** **is** my favorite bakery.

Exercise 7 Making Verbs Agree with Special Subjects

On your paper, write the simple subject in each sentence. Then write the form of the verb in parentheses that agrees with the subject.

Traditional Japanese Sports

1. After two hours, the audience at this demonstration of Japanese sports still (wears/wear) expressions of interest on their faces.
2. In traditional Japanese sports, each team (obeys/obey) strict rituals and rules.
3. More than 1,000 years (has/have) passed since Japanese men began to wrestle in the style known as sumo.
4. Statistics (confirms/confirm) that the average weight of a sumo wrestler is 300 pounds.
5. Fifteen feet (is/are) too far for the average person to throw or push a man weighing several hundred pounds, yet sumo wrestlers routinely perform this feat.
6. *Graceful Giants* (is/are) a good title for a sumo-wrestling film.
7. My binoculars (helps/help) me to appreciate the precise movements of the judo wrestlers.
8. While watching the sword game called *kendo,* a crowd of American spectators (is/are) apt to wonder at the significance of the stylized gestures.
9. Now a family of five (presents/present) individual demonstrations of *kyudo,* or Japanese archery.
10. The whole family (has/have) extraordinary poise and skill.

16.5 Agreement with Compound Subjects

Compound Subjects Joined by *And*

- A compound subject that is joined by *and* or *both . . . and* is plural unless its parts belong to one unit or they both refer to the same person or thing.

PLURAL The ***lawyer*** *and* the ***client*** **are** conversing.
Both the ***book*** and the ***movie*** **are** enjoyable.

SINGULAR ***Ham*** *and* ***eggs*** **costs** two dollars. [The compound subject is a single unit.]
Her ***husband*** *and* ***partner*** **consults** her. [One person is both husband and partner.]

Compound Subjects Joined by *Or* or *Nor*

- With compound subjects joined by *or* or *nor* (or by *either . . . or* or *neither . . . nor*), the verb always agrees with the nearer subject.

PLURAL *Neither* the ***lawyer*** *nor* the ***clients*** **are talking.**
Either the ***lawyer*** *or* the ***clients*** **are talking.**

SINGULAR *Either* the ***lawyer*** *or* the ***client*** **is talking.**
Neither the ***lawyers*** *nor* the ***client*** **is talking.**

Many a, Every, and *Each* with Compound Subjects

- When *many a, every,* or *each* precedes a compound subject, the subject is considered singular.

SINGULAR *Many a* ***man, woman,*** and ***child*** **knows** hunger.
Every ***eagle, owl,*** and ***parrot*** **fascinates** me.
Each ***eagle*** and ***owl*** **is soaring.**

Exercise 8 Making Verbs Agree with Compound Subjects

On your paper, write the correct form of each verb in parentheses.

1. The writer and his researcher (is/are) working together.
2. Neither the editor nor her assistants (has/have) read the manuscript.
3. Both the book and the article (explains/explain) an important historical event.
4. Every history book, article, and biography by that author (interests/interest) me.
5. Either the biographies or the history book (has/have) won a prize.

16.6 Intervening Expressions

Certain expressions, such as *accompanied by, as well as, in addition to, plus,* and *together with,* have a meaning that is similar to that of *and,* but they do not form a compound subject. These intervening expressions introduce phrases that modify the subject but do not change its number.

SINGULAR ***Snow,*** as well as sleet and ice, **makes** driving difficult.

PLURAL ***Sunshine and warm weather,*** in addition to a day off, **lift** the spirit.

The couple, along with a chaperone, is going to the prom.

- If a singular subject is linked to another noun by an intervening expression, such as *accompanied by,* the subject is still considered singular.

SINGULAR ***Water,*** in addition to food, **is** essential on a camping trip.
The ***father,*** as well as his daughter, **is arriving.**
Rain, accompanied by wind and thunder, **is** predicted for tomorrow.
Practice, plus talent, **makes** perfect.
The ***movie,*** together with the book, **tells** a compelling story.

Exercise 9 **Making Subjects and Verbs Agree When Expressions Intervene**

On your paper, write the simple subject of each sentence, as well as the form of the verb in parentheses that agrees with the subject.

The Cabots

1. John Cabot's life, as well as his voyages, (is/are) somewhat of a mystery to historians.
2. John Cabot, as well as his son Sebastian, (was/were) sent to explore the Americas.
3. Before Columbus's voyage, John Cabot, plus other navigators, (was/were) planning a westward voyage to Asia.
4. John, accompanied by 18 men, (was/were) scheduled to sail from England in 1497.
5. Five ships in the royal fleet, in addition to John's ship, (was/were) prepared to leave on a second voyage in 1498.
6. A crew mutiny, together with a lack of supplies, (appears/appear) to have doomed the voyage.
7. In 1525 Sebastian Cabot, accompanied by three Spanish vessels, (was/were) expected to develop trade with the Orient.
8. However, Cabot, as well as all his men, (was/were) diverted by news of great wealth in South America.
9. Unfortunately, three years, plus tremendous effort, (was/were) wasted, and Cabot was blamed for the failed expedition.
10. Sebastian Cabot, as well as his father, never (seems/seem) to have attained his exploration goals.

Exercise 10 Making Verbs Agree with Their Subjects

On your paper, write the correct form of each of the verbs in parentheses.

Struggle for Independence

1. Peru, in addition to other regions of South America, (was/were) ruled by Spain from the 1530s until early in the nineteenth century.
2. The famous Venezuelan Simón Bolívar, as well as the leaders José de San Martín and Antonio José de Sucre, (was/were) foremost in the fight for South American independence.
3. Bolívar's imagination and skills as a military tactician (remains/remain) highly regarded by historians today.
4. This statesman and soldier (was/were) also the author of two great political tracts, *El Manifesto de Cartagena (The Manifesto of Cartagena)* and *La Carta de Jamaica (The Letter from Jamaica).*
5. Napoleon Bonaparte's European victories over Spain, in addition to the unrest in South America, (was/were) crucial in weakening Spain's power around the globe.
6. Between 1808 and 1819, many a devastating battle and dizzying shift of power (was/were) witnessed on the continent of South America.
7. After neither the United States nor Great Britain (was/were) willing to provide military aid, Bolívar successfully appealed to Haiti in 1815 for money and weapons.
8. Neither flooded flatlands nor ice-covered mountains (was/were) able to stop Bolívar's army from ambushing and defeating the Spanish in New Granada in 1819.
9. In later years, Colombia and Peru (was/were) ruled by a dictatorship imposed by the Liberator, as Simón Bolívar became known.
10. Unfortunately, neither Bolívar's parents nor his wife (was/were) alive to witness his triumphs.

Exercise 11 Writing Sentences with Compound Subjects and Intervening Expressions

On your paper, write 10 sentences, using one of the following items as the subject of each sentence. Make each subject agree with a present-tense verb.

1. peanut butter and jelly
2. neither the plaintiff nor the defendants
3. both the *Times* and the *Chronicle*
4. Mother or her cousin
5. many a soldier and sailor
6. every boy and girl
7. each book and article
8. players as well as coaches
9. helmets, together with knee pads,
10. flowers, in addition to crepe paper,

16.7 Indefinite Pronouns as Subjects

■ A verb must agree in number with an indefinite pronoun subject.

Indefinite pronouns can be singular or plural, as indicated on the following chart.

Indefinite Pronouns			
Always Singular	each anything nothing everything one something	everyone either someone anyone no one	nobody everybody neither somebody anybody
Always Plural	several many	few	both
Singular or Plural	some most	all none	any

Singular indefinite pronouns take singular verbs. Plural indefinite pronouns take plural verbs.

SINGULAR When we checked, ***everything*** **was** as it should be.
Someone at the door **wants** to talk to you.

PLURAL ***Many*** in my class **are** good in Spanish.
Several of my friends **were** at the party.

As indicated on the chart, some indefinite pronouns can be singular or plural, depending upon the nouns to which they refer.

SINGULAR ***All*** of the money **is** gone. [*All* refers to *money,* a singular noun.]
Most of the cake **was** gone by noon. [*Most* refers to *cake,* a singular noun.]

PLURAL ***All*** of the children **want** dessert. [*All* refers to *children,* a plural noun.]
Most of the students **were** in favor of the field trip. [*Most* refers to *students,* a plural noun.]

Subject-Verb Agreement

Exercise 12 Making Verbs Agree with Indefinite Pronoun Subjects

On your paper, write the simple subject of each sentence and the form of the verb in parentheses that agrees with the subject.

Consumer Regulation

1. Most of us (is/are) consumers.
2. Someone (needs/need) to inform consumers about product safety and quality.
3. Everyone (wants/want) to save money.
4. Some of the people (says/say) we need better standards and more product regulation.
5. No one (expects/expect) poor quality products.
6. Both of these agencies (protects/protect) consumers.
7. Several of today's advertising claims (is/are) credible.
8. Despite all the new products manufactured each year, few (is/are) recalled.
9. Anyone with complaints (has/have) the opportunity to write or call the Better Business Bureau.
10. Not all of the consumers (considers/consider) Ralph Nader the symbol of consumer protection.

Exercise 13 Writing with Indefinite Pronoun Subjects

On your paper, write 10 sentences, using one of the following indefinite pronouns as the subject of each sentence. Make each subject agree with a present-tense verb.

SAMPLE each
ANSWER Each of the teachers has a master's degree.

1. everyone
2. several
3. few
4. nobody
5. one
6. many
7. anything
8. either
9. both
10. anybody

Exercise 14 Writing with Indefinite Pronoun Subjects

For each indefinite pronoun listed below, write two sentences, using the pronoun as the subject of both sentences. In the first sentence of each pair, use a singular present-tense verb. In the second sentence, use a plural present-tense verb.

SAMPLE none
ANSWER (a.) None of the pudding is for me.
(b.) None of the fans are happy with the call.

1. some
2. all
3. any
4. most
5. none

Exercise 15 Writing Sentences with Indefinite Pronoun Subjects

On your paper, write a paragraph about something funny or amusing that happened to you or someone else. Use at least five indefinite pronouns as subjects. Make each subject agree with a present-tense verb.

Exercise 16 Correcting Errors in Subject-Verb Agreement

The following sentences contain twenty errors in subject-verb agreement. Locate the sentences with errors and rewrite those sentences using the correct verb form. (Not every sentence has an error.)

The Circus

1. In the center of the field are a large circus tent, as well as cages of animals.
2. The crowd buy their tickets, and soon each of the animals are led from the cages.
3. One little boy, accompanied by his parents, stare in astonishment at a large bear.
4. On the grass is people eating picnic lunches.
5. There is dishes piled with chicken.
6. Bread and butter seems to be a part of everyone's meal.
7. In most cases, the dessert course of these lunches are made with fruit.
8. Suddenly someone shouts, "Here comes the performers!" and this nineteenth-century American circus begin.
9. The originator of modern circuses was the Englishman Philip Astley.
10. In eighteenth-century Europe, neither traveling troops of acrobats nor the traditional county fair were able to compete with Astley's circus.
11. The diversity of acts were amazing to the audience.
12. Gymnastics was one of Astley's most popular spectacles.
13. Many of Astley's circuses were established during his lifetime.
14. Although much has changed, circuses remain a major event in most towns today.
15. Many a young boy and girl have been delighted by the exotic animals and amazing performers of a circus.
16. All of the circuses today seems to travel from place to place.
17. Most still has animal acts, although some of them have eliminated these shows.
18. For me, animals, together with a good clown, is the heart of the circus.
19. Every trained elephant, dog, and large cat fascinate me.
20. Most of the people in the audience of a circus agree with me.
21. The audience usually cheer loudest for a good animal act.
22. The origin of circuses, according to my encyclopedia, were in ancient Rome.
23. There, a circus was a stadium; today, a circus are both a public entertainment and a circular arena.
24. In the United States, Phineas T. Barnum, one of the greatest promoters, were responsible for opening the first circus, the "Greatest Show on Earth."
25. The most famous circus of all such spectacles were probably the one Barnum formed when he merged with a rival and established Barnum and Bailey.

UNIT 16 Grammar Review

Subject-Verb Agreement

In his novel *Elsewhere, Perhaps,* the Israeli author Amos Oz captures the contradictions of contemporary life in his native country. Set on a kibbutz, or collective farm, near the Israeli frontier, the novel describes how a small, close-knit group copes with the threat of enemy fire and with the individuals' own conflicting dreams and desires. The passage, which has been translated from the Hebrew, has been annotated to show some examples of subject-verb agreement covered in this unit.

Literature Model

from Elsewhere, Perhaps

by Amos Oz

translated from the Hebrew by Nicholas de Lange

You see before you the kibbutz of Metsudat Ram: Its buildings are laid out in strict symmetry at one end of the green valley. The tangled foliage of the trees does not break up the settlement's severe lines, but merely softens them, and adds a dimension of weightiness.

Agreement between a singular noun subject and the singular verb ***does break*** with a plural object of a preposition intervening between subject and verb

The buildings are whitewashed, and most of them are topped with bright red roofs. This color scheme contrasts sharply with that of the mountain range, which completely blocks the view to the east, and at the foot of which the kibbutz lies spread. The mountains are bare and rocky, cut by zigzagging ravines. With the sun's progress their own shadows spill gradually down these folds, as if the mountains are trying to relieve their desolation with this melancholy shadow play.

Agreement between a plural indefinite pronoun subject and the plural form of ***be***

Along the lower terraces on the slope stretches the border between our land and that of her enemies.

An inverted sentence with agreement between a singular noun subject and the singular form of ***stretch***

This border, prominently marked on the maps with a thick green line, is not visible to the observer, since it does not correspond to the natural boundary between the lush green valley and the bleak, bare mountains. The soil of Israel overflows the limits of the valley and spreads up the lower slopes toward the barren heights. So the eye and the mind—or, more precisely, geology and politics—come to be at odds with one another. The kibbutz itself stands some two miles from the international frontier. We cannot define the distance more precisely without entering into the blood-stained controversy over the exact location of this line.

The landscape, then, is rich in contrasts, contrasts between appearances and reality and also inner contrasts within the appearances. These can be described only by the term "contradiction." There is a kind of enmity between the valley, with its neat, geometrical patchwork of fields and the savage bleakness of the mountains. Even the symmetrical architecture of Kibbutz Metsudat Ram is no more than a negation of the grim natural chaos that looks down on it from above.

Agreement between a compound noun subject and the plural form of *come*

An inverted sentence with agreement between a singular noun subject and the singular form of *be*

Review: Exercise 1 Making Subjects and Verbs Agree When Prepositional Phrases Intervene

Each of the following sentences elaborates on the passage from *Elsewhere, Perhaps.* Rewrite each sentence on your paper, following the directions in parentheses. In some cases, you will need to change the form of the verb to make the sentence correct; in other cases, the verb will remain the same.

SAMPLE The description of the scene offers many contrasts. (Change *description* to *descriptions.*)

ANSWER The descriptions of the scene offer many contrasts.

1. The fertile soil of the valley supports several kinds of trees. (Change *soil* to *soils.*)
2. The mountains near the building sites are quite barren. (Change *sites* to *site.*)
3. The ravine on the mountainside creates many shadows. (Change *ravine* to *ravines.*)
4. The red of the rooftop shines brightly. (Change *rooftop* to *rooftops.*)
5. The white walls of the structures glisten in the sun. (Change *structures* to *structure.*)
6. The scene to the east offers only mountains. (Change *scene* to *scenes.*)
7. The views in other directions include much farmland. (Change *views* to *view.*)
8. At Metsudat Ram, the people farm the land. (Move the prepositional phrase so that it comes directly after the subject.)
9. Fear of the enemy haunts the kibbutz dwellers. (Change *the enemy* to *enemies.*)
10. Near the mountains, the border separates the kibbutz from enemy lands. (Move the first prepositional phrase so that it comes directly after the subject.)

Review: Exercise 2 **Writing Sentences with Intervening Prepositional Phrases**

The following sentences describe a landscape similar to the one in the passage from *Elsewhere, Perhaps.* On your paper, rewrite each sentence, adding an appropriate prepositional phrase in the place indicated by the caret and choosing the correct form of the verb in parentheses.

1. A river ∧ (provides/provide) clear, pure water.
2. The foliage ∧ (makes/make) a beautiful sight.
3. Wildflowers ∧ (grows/grow) here and there.
4. People ∧ (farms/farm) the land.
5. The rich soil ∧ (produces/produce) abundant crops.
6. Cows ∧ (grazes/graze) in the valley.
7. The mountain ∧ (is/are) bare and rocky.
8. Ravines ∧ (makes/make) a zigzag design.
9. The colors ∧ (contrasts/contrast) with those of the valley.
10. The landscape ∧ (presents/present) many such contrasts.

Review: Exercise 3 **Making Linking Verbs Agree with Their Subjects**

Each of the following sentences describes *Elsewhere, Perhaps.* On your paper, rewrite each sentence, following the directions in parentheses. If necessary, change the number of the linking verb.

1. The subject of *Elsewhere, Perhaps* is Israeli kibbutz life. (Change *life* to *dwellers.*)
2. The kibbutz's inhabitants are fictional characters. (Change *fictional characters* to *a fictional creation.*)
3. The kibbutz's name is pure invention. (Change *kibbutz's name* to *characters' names.*)
4. The novel's setting is northern Israel. (Change *northern Israel* to *the northern farmlands.*)
5. The kibbutz remains a dangerous place to live. (Change *The kibbutz* to *These communities.*)
6. The kibbutz dwellers' neighbors are often enemies. (Change *enemies* to *the enemy.*)
7. This passage about Metsudat Ram is mostly description. (Change *This passage* to *These details.*)
8. The descriptions become a study in contrast. (Change *descriptions* to *description.*)
9. The contrasts are reflections of the novel's conflicts. (Change *reflections* to *a reflection.*)
10. The book's main conflicts are the private struggles of the characters. (Change *conflicts* to *focus.*)

Review: Exercise 4 Making Subjects and Verbs Agree in Inverted Sentences

Each of the following sentences describes the kibbutz of the passage from *Elsewhere, Perhaps.* First, write each sentence on your paper, choosing the correct form of the verb in parentheses. Then write each sentence in inverted order, making any necessary adjustments to the verb.

SAMPLE Metsudat Ram (is/are) near the Golan Heights.
ANSWER Metsudat Ram is near the Golan Heights.
Near the Golan Heights is Metsudat Ram.

1. The kibbutz (stands/stand) near the Syrian border.
2. The settlement (sprawls/sprawl) among the trees.
3. The buildings (lies/lie) in a symmetrical pattern.
4. The kibbutz (shines/shine) in white and red.
5. The mountains (is/are) near the kibbutz.
6. The people (lives/live) beside the mountain.
7. Several ravines (cuts/cut) across the mountain.
8. Rich soil (spreads/spread) up the lower slopes.
9. Dark and eerie shadows (looms/loom) on the mountainside.
10. The Syrian frontier (winds/wind) along the terraces.

Review: Exercise 5 Making Verbs Agree with Special Subjects

The following sentences are about a family touring Jerusalem, Israel. First, on your paper write the subject in each sentence and then the form of the verb in parentheses that agrees with that subject.

SAMPLE A family (is/are) on tour in Israel not by itself but with a group.
ANSWER family is

1. Three weeks (has/have) passed since the family arrived in Israel.
2. Measles (is/are) the reason the youngest child had to stay home.
3. The group (learns/learn) many facts about Jerusalem from the tour guide.
4. Forty-two square miles (is/are) the city's total area.
5. Statistics (shows/show) that the city has benefited from a multitude of pilgrims and tourists.
6. *Interesting Sights in Jerusalem* (is/are) the name of the book the guide recommends to the group.
7. The majority (wants/want) to see the Old City in East Jerusalem before viewing the more modern West Jerusalem.
8. The family (goes/go) off in opposite directions to see different parts of the city.
9. Binoculars (is/are) handy for surveying areas of the Old City.

10. Approximately 40 feet (is/are) the height of the stone walls surrounding the Old City.
11. One hundred sixty feet (is/are) the length of the Wailing Wall, the holiest Jewish shrine in Jerusalem.
12. A congregation of Christian pilgrims (gathers/gather) outside the Church of the Holy Sepulcher.
13. Two hours (flies/fly) by as they tour the Dome of the Rock, an ancient mosque.
14. The group (disagrees/disagree) over what to do the next day.
15. The crowd in the *souks,* or markets, (is/are) definitely another sight worth seeing in the Old City.
16. The throng in the narrow streets (buys/buy) souvenirs in the small, dark shops.
17. Seventeen thousand (is/are) the approximate number of students attending Hebrew University in Jerusalem.
18. Economics (is/are) one of the most important subjects taught there.
19. The tour group also (enjoys/enjoy) viewing the Knesset, the Israeli parliament.
20. "The People of Jerusalem" (is/are) a magazine article that describes the city's three populations—Jewish, Moslem, and Christian.

Review: Exercise 6 Making Verbs Agree with Compound Subjects

Each of the following sentences describes the nation of Israel. On your paper, rewrite each sentence, following the directions in parentheses. Make any necessary adjustments to the form of the verb and to any other words.

SAMPLE Haifa is among Israel's largest cities. (Add *and Tel Aviv* to the complete subject.)

ANSWER Haifa and Tel Aviv are among Israel's largest cities.

1. The Mediterranean Sea and the Dead Sea lie off Israel's borders. (Delete *and the Dead Sea* from the complete subject.)
2. Jordan and Syria border Israel. (Delete *and Syria* from the complete subject.)
3. Saudi Arabia is also among Israel's neighbors in the Middle East. (Add *and Egypt* to the complete subject.)
4. Tel Aviv is a multilingual city in Israel. (Add *and Jerusalem* to the complete subject.)
5. Many a tourist visits Israel each year. (Add *and historian* to the complete subject.)
6. Virtually every Israeli city has a rich history. (Add *and village* to the complete subject.)
7. The Dead Sea and the Rift Valley also attract many visitors. (Delete *and the Rift Valley* from the complete subject.)
8. Hot, dry summer weather and fairly mild winters help to create a pleasant climate. (Delete *and fairly mild winters* from the complete subject.)
9. Desert irrigation and swamp drainage have produced many farmlands. (Delete *and swamp drainage* from the complete subject.)
10. Tourism is vital to Israel's economy. (Add *and agriculture* to the complete subject.)

Review: Exercise 7 Making Subjects and Verbs Agree When Expressions Intervene

The following sentences are about Hebrew, the language in which Amos Oz writes. On your paper, rewrite each sentence, correcting any errors in subject-verb agreement. If the sentence contains no errors, write *correct.*

1. Hebrew, together with Arabic, are spoken in Israel.
2. Yiddish, in addition to Hebrew, are the language of some Israeli authors.
3. The German language, plus the Hebrew alphabet and some Slavic words, form the basis of Yiddish.
4. Jewish traditions from Eastern Europe, as well as the Jewish culture of the Mediterranean countries, have influenced the manner in which Hebrew is pronounced.
5. The chief difference between Eastern European and Mediterranean Hebrew, in addition to the sound of certain vowels, lie in the way some words are pronounced.
6. Hebrew, as well as Arabic, is a Semitic language.
7. This pair of languages, together with Aramaic, have common roots.
8. Ancient Egyptian, plus several modern Ethiopian tongues, is distantly related to the Semitic languages.
9. The Hebrew alphabet, unlike the English alphabet, includes only consonants.
10. The letters of the alphabet, together with symbols used to indicate the vowels, forms words that can be sounded out phonetically.

Review: Exercise 8 Making Verbs Agree with Indefinite Pronoun Subjects

The following sentences describe Israel's collective communities, or *kibbutzim* (the plural of *kibbutz*), as well as Israel's cooperative communities, or *moshavim* (the plural of *moshav*). On your paper, rewrite each sentence, replacing the indefinite pronoun in italics with the pronoun in parentheses. If necessary, change the number of the verb.

1. *Some* of the kibbutz members raise crops or livestock. (Several).
2. *Many* of the other members run small businesses for kibbutz residents. (Some)
3. *All* are welcome to join a kibbutz. (Anyone)
4. *Each* of the kibbutz residents shares in ownership of the collective's property. (All)
5. *Most* of Israel's farmers live in cooperative communities called moshavim. (Many)
6. In a moshav, *all* of the families own a separate plot of land. (each)
7. *Both* of these kinds of communities involve group effort. (Either)
8. *Many* in the group are ready and willing to contribute. (Everybody)
9. *None* are allowed to shirk responsibilities. (No one)
10. *Each* of these kinds of communities is important to the Israeli economy. (Both)

Review: Exercise 9 **Making Verbs Agree with Indefinite Pronoun Subjects**

The following sentences are about Israel's kibbutzim and moshavim. On your paper, write the subject and the correct form of the verb in parentheses for each sentence.

1. No one on the kibbutzim (work/works) for personal profit.
2. Everything on a kibbutz, except personal possessions, (is/are) collectively owned.
3. Each of the members (labors/labor) to capacity.
4. Everyone (receives/receive) according to need.
5. Most of the rooms in the kibbutz (is/are) communal.
6. Most of each community (is/are) cooperatively owned.
7. (Is/Are) all of the kibbutzim entirely agricultural?
8. (Has/Have) none established manufacturing industries?
9. (Does/Do) all of the children attend school?
10. (Does/Do) all of this moshav belong to its residents?

Review: Exercise 10

Proofreading

The following passage describes the artist Elias Newman, whose painting is reproduced on the opposite page. On your paper, rewrite the passage, correcting the errors in spelling, grammar, and usage. Add any missing punctuation. There are twenty errors.

Elias Newman

[1]Elias Newman was born in 1903 in the Russian-ruled city of Stashow located in Poland. [2]When he is ten, Newman and his family immigrated to the United States. [3]Growing up in New York City, he studyed at the National Academy of Design and the Educational Alliance Art School.

[4]Newman traveled too Europe and the Middle East in 1925. [5]He lived for four years in Palestine (now Israel) a country for which he felt a great kinship. [6]During Newman's stay there, Jerusalem and Tel Aviv was the sites of his solo exhibitions.

[7]Newman returned to New York but he also became involved in the art community of Rockport, Massachusetts, where he had a summer studio. [8]In addition, he begun working with the New York Artists' Equity Association, a leading organization of artists in America. [9]One of Newman's great contributions to the arts have been his work to raise funds for artists in financial need.

[10]Newman's other main endeavor, in addition to helping artists, have been his art. [11]His landscapes of Palestine is among his most famous works. [12]Using water-

Elias Newman, *Wadi Musserara,* 1926

colors and oil pigments, he create simple and forceful paintings. [13]One critic said of Newmans work, "It has an elusive richness and a depth that may well be part of Palestine's experience." [14]Newman's career have included more than a hundred one-person exhibitions, and he has received many awards.

[15]*Wadi Musserara* suggest the light and color of a rural landscape in the Middle East. [16]The elements of the landscape conveys movement and design. [17]The green field and plants in the foreground of this painting becomes a directional device to lead the viewer's eyes first to the meandering river and then into the arid hills far in the background.

[18]The pasage from Amos Oz's novel *Elsewhere, Perhaps* have as its setting an Israeli landscape very similar to the one depicted in Newman's painting. [19]Oz's description of the whitewashed buildings bare mountains, and "zigzagging ravines" could very well be a caption for Newman's work.

Review: Exercise 11

Mixed Review

The following sentences describe the life of Amos Oz. For each sentence, write on your paper the subject and the appropriate form of the verb in parentheses.

Amos Oz

1. Amos Oz, together with Nobel Prize winner Shmuel Yosef Agnon, (numbers/number) among Israel's best-known writers of fiction.
2. The author of *Elsewhere, Perhaps* (was/were) born in 1939 in Jerusalem.
3. Most of Oz's life since his teenage years (has/have) been lived in a kibbutz.
4. He and his wife and children (has/have) recently moved from northern Israel.
5. Their home (is/are) now in Israel's southern desert lands.
6. Amos Oz's last name, though not his birth name, (means/mean) "strength" in Hebrew.
7. Most of Oz's fiction (takes/take) place in modern Israel.
8. The relationship between Jews and Arabs (is/are) a dominant concern in Oz's work.
9. From his kibbutz experiences (comes/come) his clear understanding of human conflicts and emotions.
10. *Touch the Water,* as well as Oz's earlier novel *Elsewhere, Perhaps,* (depicts/depict) kibbutz life.
11. Each of these books (has/have) won praise from critics.
12. The most successful of Oz's novels (is/are) *My Michael,* which describes the psychological turmoil of an Israeli wife in a troubled marriage.
13. Oz's poetic novels (is/are) a reflection of the struggles of Israeli life.
14. Many of Oz's own experiences on a kibbutz (forms/form) the basis of his literary work.
15. A large part of Oz's literary earnings (has/have) been given to Kibbutz Hulda.
16. There (is/are) an element of religious poetry running through each of Oz's novels.
17. Oz's favorite writer of all American writers (is/are) Herman Melville.
18. The conflicts in Israel (is/are) the setting for many of Oz's stories.
19. The Jewish community (has/have) praised Oz's novels and short stories.
20. Oz, in addition to several other noted authors, (writes/write) all of his books in Hebrew.
21. Politics (has/have) played an important role in Oz's life.
22. Both Israelis and readers around the world (has/have) learned about life on a kibbutz.
23. Neither *My Michael* nor *Elsewhere, Perhaps* (has/have) been made into a motion picture.
24. Amos Oz, along with Isaac Bashevis Singer, (has/have) written stories about specifically Jewish topics.
25. The novels of Amos Oz (is/are) the topic for discussion in class today.

Writing Application

TIME

For more about the writing process, see TIME Facing the Blank Page, pp. 109–119

Subject-Verb Agreement in Writing

In this passage about the cable channel MTV, Tom Shales demonstrates correct subject-verb agreement. Examine the passage, focusing especially on the italicized subjects and verbs.

> Not for nothing *has MTV earned* the nickname "Empty-V." Instead of denying that emptiness, however, MTV celebrates it. *Members* of the viewing audience *are* frequently *assured* that they are not to be bothered with matters of consequence. *"MTV News,"* which is shown frequently every day, *is* "news" about rock stars, pop stars and silly celebrities—puff and fluff spun in the hype mills of Hollywood.

Techniques with Subject-Verb Agreement

Try to apply some of Tom Shales's writing techniques when you write and revise.

❶ In inverted sentences, remember that the subject follows the verb.

NON-INVERTED SENTENCE MTV has earned the nickname "Empty-V" not for nothing.

SHALES'S CORRECT USE Not for nothing has MTV earned the nickname "Empty-V."

❷ Be alert to prepositional phrases and other expressions that fall between a subject and its verb.

INCORRECT USE Members of the viewing audience is frequently assured. . . .

SHALES'S CORRECT USE Members of the viewing audience are frequently assured . . . .

❸ Remember that certain nouns that end in *-s* take singular verbs.

INCORRECT USE "MTV News," which is shown frequently each day, are "news" . . .

SHALES'S CORRECT USE "MTV News," which is shown frequently each day, is "news" . . .

Practice Apply these techniques and others you have learned in this unit by revising the following paragraph. On your paper, rewrite the paragraph, filling each blank with a verb in the present tense. Make other changes too. Write at least one sentence as an inverted sentence.

The islands known as the West Indies ______ in the Caribbean Sea. Trinidad and Tobago, the southernmost nation in the island chain, ______ the home of a type of music known as calypso. During the carnival held each February, many of the country's calypso singers ______ before a large crowd. Most of their music ______ improvised lyrics, and many of the lyrics ______ satirical. Each of the calypso singers ______ a distinct style, and all of them ______ how to please an audience. There ______ many recordings of calypso music. Both tourists and residents ______ recordings of the music to enjoy later. Nothing ______ more memorable about the island republic of Trinidad and Tobago than its calypso music.

Subject-Verb Agreement

UNIT 17

Using Pronouns Correctly

17.1 Case of Personal Pronouns

- Pronouns that are used to refer to persons or things are called **personal** pronouns.
- Personal pronouns have three **cases,** or forms, called **nominative, objective,** and **possessive.** The case of a personal pronoun depends upon the pronoun's function in a sentence (whether it is a subject, an object, a complement, or a replacement for a possessive noun).

Study the chart to recall the case forms of the different personal pronouns.

Personal Pronouns			
Case	**Singular Pronouns**	**Plural Pronouns**	**Function in Sentence**
NOMINATIVE	I, you, she, he, it	we, you, they	subject or predicate nominative
OBJECTIVE	me, you, her, him, it	us, you, them	direct object, indirect object, or object of preposition
POSSESSIVE	my, mine, your, yours, her, hers, his, its	our, ours, your, yours, their, theirs	replacement for possessive noun(s)

Exercise 1 Identifying Pronoun Case

On your paper, write each personal pronoun in the sentences below. Then tell what case each is, and how it functions in the sentence.

SAMPLE My father and I took him to a basketball game last Saturday afternoon.

ANSWER My—possessive, replacement for possessive noun; I—nominative, subject; him—objective, direct object.

1. We arrived early so that he could see the players shoot practice shots.
2. Our seats put Dad, him, and me near the half-court line.
3. One player smiled at us as she stopped to tie her shoes.
4. She knew that they would be playing their biggest game of the season that day.
5. He held up his pennant and waved it excitedly at her.

Use these rules to avoid errors with the case of personal pronouns.

1. Use the nominative case for a personal pronoun in a compound subject.

   Ann and **I** play tennis. **She** and **I** are equally matched.

2. Use the objective case for a personal pronoun in a compound object.

   Ann challenged Juan and **her.** She talked to Sue and **me.**

   Hint: When choosing the correct pronoun in a sentence with a compound subject or object, it is helpful to say the sentence to yourself without the conjunction and the other subject or object.

The ball bounced toward Ann and me.

3. After a form of the linking verb *be,* use the nominative case of a personal pronoun.

   The winner was **he.** Ann hoped that it would be **she.**

Today this rule is changing. In informal speech, people often use the objective case after a form of the linking verb *be;* they say *It's me* or *It was him.* Some authorities even advise using the objective case in informal writing to avoid appearing pretentious. In formal writing, however, always use the nominative case after a form of the verb *be.*

4. Do not spell possessive pronouns with apostrophes.

   This paddle is **yours.** The table is **ours.**

Remember that *it's* is a contraction for *it is.* You should not confuse *it's* with the possessive pronoun *its.*

It's my watch that is lying on the dresser.

Its band must be replaced.

5. Use possessive pronouns before gerunds (*-ing* verb forms used as nouns).

   Your singing relaxes the baby. He is amused by **my** talking.

Exercise 2 Choosing the Correct Case Form

For each sentence, write the correct personal pronoun from each pair in parentheses.

Satchel Paige, a Legendary Pitcher

1. When Marisa offered to help me with my report on a famous athlete, (she/her) and (I/me) chose Satchel Paige, one of the greatest baseball pitchers of all time.
2. It was (he/him) who became one of the first African Americans in the American League.
3. (He/Him) and Jackie Robinson were among the first African American athletes to play for major-league teams.
4. What impressed Marisa and (I/me) is that Paige never gave up.
5. To (she/her) and (I/me), Paige and his fellow African American players are true heroes.

17.2 Pronouns with and as Appositives

■ Use the nominative case for a pronoun that is in apposition to a subject or a predicate nominative.

The candidates, **she** and **Mr. Gomez,** will run for that office. [*Candidates* is the subject.]

The candidates are two people from our district, **Ms. Pierce** and **he.** [*People* is the predicate nominative.]

■ Use the objective case for a pronoun that is in apposition to a direct object, an indirect object, or an object of a preposition.

The crowd favored the local pair, **Hilda** and **her.** [*Pair* is the direct object.]

I gave my friends **Floyd** and **him** a ticket. [*Friends* is the indirect object.]

The officials talked to both groups of players, **them** and **us.** [*Groups* is the object of the preposition *to.*]

■ When a pronoun is followed by an appositive, choose the case of the pronoun that would be correct if the appositive were omitted.

We athletes want to win the cash prize. [*We* is the correct form because *we* is the subject of the sentence.]

It was **we athletes** who practiced for such long hours. [*We* is the correct form because *we* is the predicate nominative.]

The school awarded **us athletes** a handsome trophy. [*Us* is the correct form because *us* is the indirect object.]

The prize was divided evenly among **us athletes.** [*Us* is the correct form because *us* is the object of the preposition *among.*]

Hint: When you are confused about which pronoun to use, try saying the sentence aloud without the appositive.

Exercise 3 Using Pronouns with and as Appositives

For each sentence in the following paragraph, write the correct pronoun from the pair in parentheses.

An Artistic Triumph

[1]In 1959 two New York City theater critics, Brooks Atkinson and (he/him), praised *A Raisin in the Sun,* Lorraine Hansberry's play about the struggles of an African American family. [2]The acting by the stars, Sidney Poitier, Diana Sands, Ruby Dee, and (she/her), was widely applauded. [3]The play was also praised by two famous American playwrights, Tennessee Williams and (he/him). [4]Even today (we/us) young actors are very fortunate to be able to work with such a well-written script. [5]The character of Beneatha, a young girl searching for her identity, had a great impact on one young actor, (I/me).

Exercise 4 Using Pronouns Correctly with and as Appositives

For each of the following sentences, write the correct personal pronoun from each pair in parentheses.

The Game of Tennis

1. (We/Us) American tennis players claim that tennis was invented in the United States.
2. Jason and (she/her) told us that modern tennis was first played in Britain.
3. In preparing a report for our social studies class, the research team, Owen, Marjorie, and (I/me), discovered that the ancestor of tennis was a twelfth-century French handball game.
4. It was two student teachers, Ms. Liu and (she/her), who pointed us to the right sources.
5. It was a surprise to (we/us) hard-working researchers to learn that a version of the French game, called real tennis, is still played in Britain today.
6. Apparently Major Walter Clopton Wingfield, an English gentleman, introduced modern lawn tennis at a party on his estate in 1873—a fact that intrigued (we/us) investigators.
7. We learned from Claire and (he/him) that the game was brought to America in 1874 by Mary Ewing Outerbridge, who had learned to play during a visit to Bermuda.
8. An article found by two of our school librarians, Ms. Denver and (she/her), said that the tennis court was originally shaped like an hourglass.
9. The chief librarian, Mr. Wolfe, also gave (we/us) researchers several articles that made our report a resounding success.
10. (We/Us) proud students sent a copy of our report to our advisors Ms. Denver, Ms. Bueno, and (he/him).
11. The librarians and (we, us) students decided to submit the report to a student research contest.
12. Entry forms were filled out by Owen and (I, me) and co-signed by teachers Ms. Bueno and (he, him).
13. A letter came in about six weeks to (we, us) anxious researchers.
14. It was addressed to Mr. Wolfe and (she, her), as well as to (we, us).
15. (We, Us) three—Marjorie, Owen, and (I, me)—had won third prize.

17.3 Pronouns After *Than* and *As*

- In elliptical adverb clauses using *than* and *as,* choose the case of the pronoun that you would use if the missing words were fully expressed.

You finished the puzzle faster than **he.** [The nominative pronoun *he* is the subject of the complete adverb clause *than he finished the puzzle.*]

The movie frightened John as much as **them.** [The objective pronoun *them* is the direct object of the complete adverb clause *as much as it frightened them.*]

Some sentences can be completed with either a nominative or an objective pronoun, depending on the meaning intended.

Tony angered Dana more than I [angered her].

Tony angered Dana more than [he angered] me.

In informal speech, people often use the objective rather than the nominative form in sentences, such as *My sister is six years younger than me.* In your writing, however, you should be careful to use the correct case.

Exercise 5 Using the Correct Pronoun After *Than* and *As*

Each sentence contains an italicized word or group of words. Write on your paper the correct pronoun to substitute for the words in italics.

SAMPLE Polar bears are more maternal than *other animals.*
ANSWER they

The Good Mother

1. Mother polar bears seem to take parenting more seriously than *some other animals.*
2. Few animals provide as much parental care as *mother polar bears.*
3. Nothing is as important to polar bear cubs as *their mother.*
4. The mother polar bear needs to care for herself as well as *the cubs.*
5. After one-and-a-half years, the cubs will be as independent as *their mother.*
6. In the meantime, they are more dependent on their mother than *many animals.*
7. When the cubs are born, their eyes are not yet open, and the cubs are not as large as *one of their mother's paws.*
8. It will be years before the cubs are as large as *their mother.*
9. A fully grown polar bear may weigh well over nine hundred pounds—as much as *five large people.*
10. The adult polar bear hunts and eats fish as skillfully as *seals.*

Using Pronouns Correctly

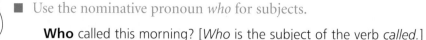

17.4 *Who* and *Whom* in Questions and Subordinate Clauses

Who will receive my letter?

■ Use the nominative pronoun *who* for subjects.

Who called this morning? [*Who* is the subject of the verb *called.*]

Tell us **who is in charge here.** [*Who* is the subject of the noun clause *who is in charge here.*]

To **whom** it may concern.

■ Use the objective pronoun *whom* for the direct or indirect object of a verb or verbal or for the object of a preposition.

Whom are you telling? [*Whom* is the direct object of the verb *are telling.*]

Whom did she want to tell? [*Whom* is the direct object of the verbal *to tell.*]

Whom did you give the report? [*Whom* is the indirect object of the verb *did give.*]

Jaime asked her **whom** she had seen at the party. [*Whom* is the direct object of the verb *had seen* in the noun clause *whom she had seen at the party.*]

Bette Bao Lord is a writer about **whom** I know very little. [*Whom* is the object of the preposition *about* in the adjective clause *about whom I know very little.*]

When a question contains an interrupting expression, such as *do you think,* it helps to omit the interrupting phrase to determine whether to use *who* or *whom.*

Who do you think gave the best oral report? [Think: *Who* gave the best oral report? *Who* is the subject of the verb *gave.*]

Whom do you think you are asking? [Think: *Whom* are you asking? *Whom* is the direct object of the verb *are asking.*]

When speaking informally, people often use *who* instead of *whom* in sentences like *Who are you calling?* In writing and in formal speech, you should distinguish between *who* and *whom.*

Exercise 6 Choosing *Who* or *Whom*

For each sentence in the following paragraphs, write on your paper the correct pronoun from the pair in parentheses.

Stories from Greek Mythology

a. [1](Who/Whom) do you think the Greeks honored as the goddess of agriculture? [2]Hades, (who/whom) ruled the underworld, admired Persephone, the daughter of Demeter, and he kidnapped her. [3]Persephone, (who/whom) Hades made queen of the underworld, could not escape. [4]Demeter, (who/whom) had grown angry at the loss of her daughter, refused to allow any crops to grow. [5]Hades was persuaded by Zeus, (who/whom) the gods must obey, to let Persephone return for part of each year so that the crops would grow.

b. [1](Who/Whom) did you say was the supreme architect and inventor of his time, according to Greek mythology? [2]King Minos of Crete kept a terrible monster called the Minotaur, for (who/whom) he commanded Daedalus, a skilled craftsman, to build a labyrinth where the monster could safely be kept. [3]King Minos was delighted with Daedalus, (who/whom) he would not allow to leave Crete lest Daedalus reveal the secret of the labyrinth he had designed. [4]Daedalus therefore used feathers and wax to build wings for himself and his son, Icarus, (who/whom) Daedalus warned not to fly too close to the sun. [5]Icarus, (who/whom) was a vain and foolish boy, ignored his father's warning and did fly too near the sun; consequently, the wax in the wings melted, causing him to fall to his death in the sea.

Exercise 7 Using *Who* or *Whom* in Sentences

On your paper, write the correct word *who* or *whom,* to complete each sentence.

The Pueblo, a Native American People

1. Reuben and his older sister, Lara, _______ is a college professor, visited several Pueblo villages in Arizona and New Mexico last summer.
2. Reuben, for _______ the trip was a dream fulfilled, had saved money to pay his way.
3. He had been interested in these Native Americans, _______ many others also admire, for a long time.
4. His sister, _______ he had begged to take him on this trip, studies Native Americans.
5. The Pueblo, _______ are an ancient people, actually consist of several different groups, each speaking a different language.
6. Besides the Hopi, Acoma, Laguna, Taos, and Tewa nations, there is the Zuñi group, for _______ one of the Pueblo languages is named.
7. According to Reuben's sister, _______ many Native Americans honor for her scholarly work, the Pueblo are best known for their large adobe dwellings.
8. Their conquerors, the Spanish, _______ the Pueblo grudgingly tolerated, named the people after their dwellings (*pueblo* is the Spanish word for "village").
9. _______ do you think is the Pueblo individual Reuben most admires?
10. He admires Popé, the leader _______ drove the Spanish off the Tewa lands in 1680.

17.5 Pronoun-Antecedent Agreement

■ An **antecedent** is the word or group of words to which a pronoun refers or that a pronoun replaces. All pronouns must agree with their antecedents in number, gender, and person.

Agreement in Number and Gender

■ A pronoun must agree with its antecedent in number (singular or plural) and gender (masculine, feminine, or neuter).

The antecedent of a pronoun may be a noun, another pronoun, or a phrase or clause acting as a noun. In the examples that follow, the pronouns appear in bold type and their antecedents appear in bold italic type:

Emily Brontë published **her** novel, *Wuthering Heights,* in 1847. [singular feminine pronoun]

Emily, Charlotte, and ***Anne Brontë*** published **their** collected poems in 1846. [plural pronoun]

Langston Hughes published **his** first volume of poetry, *The Weary Blues,* in 1926. [singular masculine pronoun]

Simon J. Ortiz and ***Diana Chang*** have also published poems that reflect **their** backgrounds. [plural pronoun]

The ***spruce,*** because of **its** soft wood, is used to make paper. [singular neuter pronoun]

Spruce and ***aspen*** are economical to raise because of **their** rapid growth. [plural pronoun]

When the gender of the antecedent is not known or when it may be either masculine or feminine, a masculine pronoun has traditionally been used.

A ***skier*** must keep **his** legs strong and limber.

This usage has changed, however, and many people now prefer to use gender-neutral wording. If you do not wish to use a masculine pronoun, you can frequently reword the sentence in one of three ways: (1) by using *he or she, his or her,* and so forth, (2) by using a plural pronoun, or (3) by eliminating the pronoun.

A ***performer*** must understand **his** role.

A ***performer*** must understand **his or her** role.

Performers must understand **their** roles.

A ***performer*** must understand a role. [no pronoun]

Agreement in Person

■ A pronoun must agree in person with its antecedent.

Do not use the second-person pronoun *you* to refer to an antecedent in the third person. Use either an appropriate third-person pronoun or a suitable noun.

POOR Richard and Clara are going to a store where you can buy brand-name clothing at reasonable prices.

BETTER Richard and Clara are going to a store where **they** can buy brand-name clothing at reasonable prices.

BETTER Richard and Clara are going to a store where **shoppers** can buy brand-name clothing at reasonable prices.

When the antecedent of a pronoun is another pronoun, the two pronouns should agree in person. Avoid shifting pronouns unnecessarily, as from *they* to *you*, *I* to *you*, or *one* to *you*.

POOR **They** spent several days in Rome, where ~~you~~ could sense history along every street.

BETTER **They** spent several days in Rome, where **they** could sense history along every street.

POOR **I** learned that ~~you~~ cannot see all of Rome in two days.

BETTER **I** learned that **I** cannot see all of Rome in two days.

POOR If **one** reads newpapers, ~~you~~ will understand current events.

BETTER If **one** reads newpapers, **one** will understand current events.

BETTER If **you** read newspapers, **you** will understand current events.

Exercise 8 Making Pronouns and Antecedents Agree

On your paper, complete the following sentences by replacing each blank with an appropriate possessive pronoun. Then write the antecedent of each pronoun that you supply.

Pablo Neruda, Chilean Poet

[1]Like any poet who understands _______ life and times, Pablo Neruda touched deep emotional chords. [2]At the age of twelve, he met Gabriela Mistral, a famous Chilean poet, who introduced him to some of _______ favorite authors. [3]Both Neruda and Mistral have been honored for _______ achievements; both poets won the Nobel Prize for Literature. [4]When I read Neruda's beautiful verses about the forests and glaciers of southern Chile, I renewed _______ vow to visit Chile someday. [5]My brother and I want to take a trip to Isla Negra; _______ intention is to visit the house in which Pablo Neruda lived for many years.

Exercise 9 Making Pronouns and Antecedents Agree

In each of the following sentences, find each personal pronoun and its antecedent. (Some sentences have more than one personal pronoun.) Then revise the sentence in one or more ways to correct the problem or problems in pronoun-antecedent agreement.

The Art of Raku

1. A person who is good at making pottery may like to test their skills by learning to make *raku,* a kind of Japanese earthenware.
2. For centuries a handful of Japanese *raku* artists have been perfecting his craft and passing it down from generation to generation.
3. Students who wish to learn to make *raku* will find that the art tests his patience, for the ceramics often break.
4. The potter throws their *raku* bowls, dries them and paints them with glaze, and then fires them one by one in a kiln until they are red-hot.
5. A *raku* expert may also take their glowing pots from the kiln and throw them into cold water to crack the glaze, but in the process their pots often shatter.

Exercise 10 Making Pronouns and Antecedents Agree in Person

On your paper, rewrite each of the following items, eliminating the inappropriate use of *you* by substituting a third-person pronoun or a suitable noun or nouns. You may also have to change other words.

Life in Ancient Greece

1. The ancient Greeks ate only two meals a day. You ate in midmorning and then again at sunset.
2. Men and women in ancient Greece wore tunics. They wore a brown one for work, but you wore a bleached one for special occasions.
3. There were three social classes in Athens, where you might be a citizen, an enslaved person, or a resident alien.
4. The women in ancient Greece led a more restricted life than the men did. You spent a great deal of your time in the home.
5. Children in the city of Athens attended school, where you learned to wrestle, handle weapons, sing, read, and write.
6. The ancient Greeks were the first to develop the idea of democracy, and they encouraged you to play an active role in government.
7. Only citizens could participate in government. The ancient Greeks usually denied you citizenship unless your father was a citizen.
8. A person could not own land in ancient Greece unless you were a citizen.
9. The people of ancient Greece valued learning. You could hear the world's finest orators, philosophers, and poets there.
10. The Greeks were dominant in the eastern Mediterranean for several centuries. You could hardly travel anywhere without seeing their influence.

Agreement with Indefinite Pronoun Antecedents

- In general, use a singular personal pronoun when the antecedent is a singular indefinite pronoun, and use a plural personal pronoun when the antecedent is a plural indefinite pronoun.

Indefinite Pronouns				
Always Singular	each either neither one	everyone everybody everything no one	nobody nothing anyone anybody	anything someone somebody something
Always Plural	several others	few	both	many
Singular or Plural	some none	all	any	most

Neither of the men wants to drive **his** car to work.

Each of the girls rides **her** bicycle to school.

Several of the neighbors make **their** commute by train.

Note that the number of the personal pronouns is not affected by the plural nouns in the prepositional phrases—*of the men, of the girls.* The personal pronouns *his* and *her* are singular because *neither* and *each,* their antecedents, are singular. When speaking, however, people often use the plural pronoun *their* in such sentences.

INFORMAL ***Neither*** of the men drove **their** cars to work.

Use gender-neutral wording when no gender is specified.

Everyone should ride **his or her** bicycle to school.

If you find the sentence above a bit awkward, the best solution may be to reword the sentence. You might replace the singular indefinite pronoun with a plural one or with an appropriate noun, or you might omit the personal pronoun altogether.

All should ride **their** bicycles to school.

All students should ride **their** bicycles to school.

Everyone should ride a bicycle to school. [no pronoun]

Exercise 11 Making Pronouns Agree with Indefinite Pronoun Antecedents

Write the singular or plural personal pronoun that correctly completes each sentence.

The Reign of Italian Opera

1. Nearly all of the audiences in eighteenth-century Europe selected opera as _______ first choice of contemporary music.
2. Most of the European composers in the 1700s used Italian librettos, or poetic text, in _______ music.
3. Each of the writers used language and melody to give _______ characters depth.
4. One of the male playwrights introduced comic situations in _______ operas.
5. Each of Goldoni's characters stated _______ point of view at the end of each comic act.
6. Few of the French intellectuals gave _______ approval to Italian opera until the comic opera *La serva padrona* was presented in Paris.
7. One of the French aristocrats wanted _______ government to censor the Italian operas.
8. Almost everyone wanted _______ city to build beautiful new opera theaters in the eighteenth century.
9. Several of the nobility held _______ private parties in the large halls of the Italian opera theaters.
10. In the nineteenth century, Guiseppe Verdi wrote _______ greatest masterpieces for Italian-style opera.

Exercise 12 Making Pronouns Agree with Indefinite Pronoun Antecedents

On your paper, write *correct* for each sentence that is correct. Then revise each incorrect sentence to make it correct. Most sentences can be revised in several ways.

African Sculpture

1. Many of the societies in Africa are known for the splendor of its sculptures.
2. Very few of the traditional African sculptors made their figures and masks from stone; most used wood, ivory, clay, and different metals.
3. Practically all of the sculptures in an African society played its own prominent role in the life of the people.
4. All the households of the Ijo people of Nigeria had a statue of their guardian spirit.
5. All of the children of the Teke people of the Congo River valley would be protected by his own spirit figure.
6. Some of the Yoruba people's ancient brass sculptures with its naturalistic representations of royal figures and their attendants fascinated archaeologists.
7. Almost all of the traditional societies in Africa created statues to honor their dead.
8. When portrayed in a statue, each of the kings of the Kuba tribe would sit stiffly with their legs crossed.
9. Many of the central African societies followed a tradition in which its women made pottery while its men created sculptures.
10. Anyone studying African sculpture can discover for themselves the majestic beauty that was part of the daily lives of African people.

17.6 Clear Pronoun Reference

■ Make sure that the antecedent of a pronoun is clearly stated and that a pronoun cannot possibly refer to more than one antecedent.

Luisa is a fine athlete, and ? was obvious from her gymnastic feats.

Vague and Ambiguous Pronoun Reference

Do not use the pronouns *this, that, which,* and *it* without a clearly stated antecedent.

VAGUE Luisa is a fine athlete, and **this** was obvious from her gymnastic feats. [What was obvious from her gymnastic feats? Her athletic ability was obvious, but the words *athletic ability* have not been specifically mentioned.]

CLEAR Luisa is a fine athlete, and **her athletic ability** was obvious from her gymnastic feats.

VAGUE Katrina and Yuki were arguing, **which** started from a misunderstanding. [What started from a misunderstanding? An argument started, but *argument* does not appear in the sentence.]

CLEAR Katrina and Yuki were having an argument, **which** started from a misunderstanding.

VAGUE Earl wants to be a doctor because **it** interests him. [What interests him? Medicine does, but *medicine* has not been specifically mentioned.]

CLEAR Earl wants to be a doctor because **medicine** interests him.

If a pronoun seems to refer to more than one antecedent, either reword the sentence to make the antecedent clear or eliminate the pronoun.

UNCLEAR ANTECEDENT When the apples fell among the leaves, **they** were hidden. [Which word is the antecedent of *they?* Were the apples or the leaves hidden?]

CLEAR ANTECEDENT The apples were hidden when **they** fell among the leaves.

NO PRONOUN When the apples fell among the leaves, **the apples** were hidden.

NO PRONOUN The fallen apples were hidden among the leaves.

Indefinite Use of Pronouns

- Avoid the indefinite use of the pronouns *you* and *they.*

INDEFINITE	In areas that get little rain, **you** must irrigate the crops.
CLEAR	In areas that get little rain, **farmers** must irrigate the crops.
INDEFINITE	In some companies, **they** do not work on Fridays during the summer months.
CLEAR	In some companies, **employees** do not work on Fridays during the summer months.

Exercise 13 Replacing Unclear Pronoun References

On your paper, rewrite each sentence to eliminate the use of the unclear pronoun reference. The pronoun you should replace is indicated in italics.

Gothic Art

1. *You* call medieval Italian art Gothic because the Goths invaded Italy during the Middle Ages.
2. Gothic cathedrals originally had simple lines, but *they* became increasingly ornate.
3. Gothic architects used stained-glass windows, and *they* told religious stories.
4. In Gothic cathedrals, *they* used flying buttresses, stone structures against the outside walls, to help support the vaulting.
5. When painters illustrated Gothic manuscripts, *they* sometimes depicted royal families.

Exercise 14 Making Pronoun References Clear

On your paper, rewrite the following sentences, making all pronoun references clear. In some cases, you may choose to eliminate the pronoun entirely.

Coping with Stress

1. In most industrial societies, they are affected by stress.
2. People can feel anxious about both joyful and sad events, and this affects their health.
3. The Alexanders went on vacation with the Harrises last summer, and they felt anxious about spending so much money.
4. When my brother Richard beat his best friend in a tennis tournament, he suffered a great deal of stress.
5. Richard's spectacular performance at the tournament made him feel guilty, and this surprised everyone.
6. When Mrs. Wong told Carrie that the company they worked for was closing, she became depressed.
7. When a family moves to a new city, it can cause anxiety.
8. In psychology books, they often discuss stress.
9. When doctors recommend that patients maintain a good diet and exercise to alleviate stress, they know it will help.
10. Scientists are evaluating the effects of stress on health, and it will have much impact on the medical profession.

Exercise 15 Review: Using Pronouns Correctly

On your paper, rewrite the following sentences, eliminating any mistakes in the use of pronouns. Each item has one error.

Special Effects

1. My brother Roy and me know much about special effects.
2. Each of us has their own special area of knowledge.
3. Desmond told me that they made the cyclone in *The Wizard of Oz* with a tube of fabric moved by a wind machine.
4. Whom did you say made the shark robots for *Jaws?*
5. One robot was used for side views of the shark, while another was used for the famous close-ups of it's jaws.
6. Actors depend upon special makeup to change their appearance, which most people take for granted.
7. In *Driving Miss Daisy,* the stars grow thirty years older; them aging so believably is partly due to great makeup.
8. No one was more surprised than me to discover that the very first movies had special effects.
9. *A Trip to the Moon* was made by the Lumière brothers; it was them who first used special effects to simulate space travel.
10. I guess my favorite special effect occurs during the moment in *Star Wars* when you see the spaceship reach the speed of light.
11. *Star Wars* was made by filmmaker George Lucas, who we all recognize as a trailblazer in the field of special effects.
12. What makes each of his films so remarkable is their use of computer animation.
13. The special-effects breakthroughs in *The Abyss* and *Terminator 2* seemed remarkable to we film buffs, Roy and me.
14. George Lucas is also one of the innovators whom is involved in making computer games of his films.
15. X-Wing is a space-combat simulator. The player pilots his or her Rebel Alliance craft against Darth Vader's Imperial Forces, which is a lot of fun.
16. The game is produced in 3-D, and their sound effects respond to the player who makes the choices.
17. Do you remember Princess Leia, who had a high-pitched voice? It is her whose whiny commands the game simulates.
18. I, who love computer games, am grateful to George Lucas for him creating this game.
19. Games of the future will let we players move more dramatically and control the actions of their characters more completely.
20. No one could be happier than I to hear that everyone will, in effect, be able to direct the outcome of their own game.

UNIT 17

Grammar Review

USING PRONOUNS CORRECTLY

Written by the West African writer and teacher William Conton, *The African* tells the story of a young man named Kisimi Kamara, who excels in his studies in West Africa and England and launches a successful political career. In this passage, which has been annotated to show some of the kinds of pronouns covered in this unit, Kisimi describes the village where he grew up.

Literature Model

from The African

by William Conton

My name is Kisimi Kamara.

Pronoun in the nominative case used as a subject

Pronoun in the possessive case

I was born at the height of a rainy season, in the village of Lokko in the British West African colony of Songhai. My father cultivated an acre of tired red soil round our hut and fished a near-by muddy stream, wringing from these unimpressive resources a livelihood which most of the other villagers regarded as enviable. I was the second son and the fifth child in a family of eleven, and my childhood was consequently quite unspoilt. . . .

The pronoun *us* is followed by the appositive *children.* As the object of a preposition, the pronoun appears in the objective case.

Pronoun *who* in the nominative case used as the subject of *looked*

We lived right on the main road; and, it being the first house you came across as you entered the village, now and then a car or lorry would draw up to obtain water for a hissing radiator or for parched throats, or to buy some of my mother's goods. That was always a tremendous event for us children. We grew to tell quite a long way ahead, from the note of the engine, whether or not the driver was looking for somewhere to stop; and we would race out to inspect with solemn awe the wheezing machines we believed to be possessed of some mighty spirit, the conjuring up of which had been done in a distant land called Britain. The supercilious drivers who looked so knowingly under bonnets and chassis during the halt we thought of as a type of high priest, ministering to this spirit; and we would hand them a leaking kerosene tin of muddy well-water with almost as much reverence as a server passing the bishop the holy water. The dust-covered passengers, however, we somehow despised rather than envied; for they seemed so helpless and unhappy, whether they were in the first-class compartment beside the driver, or in the second-class behind.

In fact not one of us would have allowed himself to be carried a yard away from home in any mechanical contraption of any kind. Our world was then a supremely secure one; and we felt instinctively that those flying lorries, with their cloaks of red dust billowing behind them, came from another world that was not nearly so secure or safe; that they were in some way harbingers of evil. . . .

The village we all loved so well consisted of perhaps twenty mud houses grouped in compounds on either side of the main road. Each compound contained four or five houses arranged in a hollow square. One of these compounds, the biggest by far, was the chief's. His was the only house with corrugated iron roofing. Not even his wives' houses in the same compound had this luxury.

The pronoun *they* in the nominative case is used as a subject. The pronoun agrees in number with its antecedent, *passengers.*

Pronoun in the objective case used as the object of a preposition

Agreement in number and gender between the possessive pronoun *his* and its antecedent, *chief's*

Review: Exercise 1 Choosing the Correct Pronoun Case

The following sentences elaborate on ideas suggested by the passage from *The African.* Write each sentence on your paper, replacing each italicized word or group of words with an appropriate pronoun. Note that the sentences are written, as the passage is, from Kisimi Kamara's first-person point of view.

1. Of the children in our household, the second-oldest son was *Kisimi.*
2. Despite our meager resources, many villagers envied *Kisimi* and my family.
3. The acre of land that surrounded the family hut was *my family's property.*
4. Similarly, the land around our neighbors' huts was *our neighbor's property.*
5. My father tried to make the soil productive, but *my father's* struggles had little effect.
6. Unfortunately, the tired red soil had lost much of *the soil's* fertility.
7. The best house in the village belonged to the chief, for it was *the chief* who wielded the greatest power.
8. Our neighbors and *my family* lived on the main road that led through the village.
9. Visitors to our village were rare, but it was not *the visitors* who fascinated us.
10. It was their vehicles that fascinated my brothers and *Kisimi.*

Review: Exercise 2 Using Pronouns Correctly with and as Appositives

The following sentences are based on passages from *The African* that are not reprinted in this textbook. For each sentence, determine whether the italicized pronoun appears in the proper form. If it does not, write the pronoun as it should appear. If it is used properly, write *correct.* Note again that the sentences are written from Kisimi Kamara's point of view.

SAMPLE The villagers, my parents and *them,* worked hard to feed their families.
ANSWER they

1. My mother devoted much attention to her children, my eight brothers and sisters and *I.*
2. Two members of the family, my elder brother and *her,* ran a small shop in the village.
3. All the men of the village, my father and *them,* fished and cultivated the land.
4. *Us* children were not all able to attend school, for some had to stay home and work.
5. The students, my friends and *me,* enjoyed special status.
6. An American missionary named Miss Schwartz taught the pupils, my friends and *I.*
7. Learning English was important to *us* students, for we knew that it would help us.
8. The two American missionaries, Miss Schwartz and *her,* lived in a bungalow.
9. A Scotsman named Jim Anderson often brought these Americans, Miss Schwartz and *she,* news from district headquarters.
10. I listened to the conversations of these English speakers, the two women and *he.*

Review: Exercise 3 Using Pronouns After *Than* and *As*

Rewrite each sentence below, substituting the correct pronoun for the words in italics. Note that the sentences are written from Kisimi Kamara's point of view.

SAMPLE The children who could not attend school were less fortunate than *Kisimi.*
ANSWER The children who could not attend school were less fortunate than I.

1. Because I was able to go to school, I was luckier than *most other village children.*
2. Since all the students were interested in new things, helping out in the teacher's home appealed to me as much as to *the other students.*
3. No volunteers were ever more eager than *the other students and Kisimi.*
4. No one, however, was more anxious to help out than *Kisimi.*
5. The sea of volunteers surprised no one more than *Miss Schwartz.*
6. When Miss Schwartz chose me, no one was happier than *Kisimi.*
7. Few students in the village school did as well as *Kisimi.*
8. The schools in the capital were much larger than *the small village schools.*
9. The prospect of attending secondary school in the capital pleased no one more than *Kisimi and the other students.*
10. When my father left with me for my new school in the capital, no one was more proud than *my father.*

Review: Exercise 4 Choosing *Who* or *Whom*

The following sentences are about Sierra Leone, the West African nation where William Conton has spent most of his life. For each sentence, write the correct pronoun from the pair in parentheses.

1. Sierra Leone was named by Pedro de Sintra, a Portuguese explorer (who/whom) we know lived in the fifteenth century.
2. De Sintra, (who/whom) every schoolchild in Sierra Leone studies, named the country Serra Lyoa, or Lion Mountains.
3. (Who/Whom) did you say are the modern inhabitants of Sierra Leone?
4. There are many people for (who/whom) Sierra Leone is home.
5. The Sierra Leone Creoles, (who/whom) many linguists have studied, are descendants of formerly enslaved people who returned to their native Africa.
6. The Creoles, (who/whom) make up about 2 percent of Sierra Leone's population, developed their own language, Krio.
7. Based on English, Krio also contains African words spoken by the many groups (who/whom) settled in Sierra Leone.
8. Natives of Sierra Leone, each of (who/whom) may speak a different language, often use Krio to communicate when they get together.
9. The many people in the country (who/whom) speak English, the official language of Sierra Leone, also communicate in English.
10. Do you know (who/whom) controlled Sierra Leone during the colonial period?
11. Sierra Leone's people, (who/whom) Britain ruled for more than a century, won their independence in 1961.
12. (Who/Whom) did you tell that the country is bordered on the west by the Atlantic Ocean?
13. I don't know (who/whom) knew that the highest mountain in Sierra Leone is 6,390 feet high.
14. Subsistence farmers (who/whom) produce maize and rice make up a substantial portion of the rural population.
15. Cocoa and coffee are agricultural exports that are profitable for those farmers (who/whom) have larger farms.
16. To (who/whom) do you think go the profits from the export of diamonds and iron?
17. Major population groups include the Mende, Temne, Limba, and Susu, all of (who/whom) are indigenous to the region.
18. Members of the house of representatives, (who/whom) are elected by the people, come from all groups in the country.
19. Did you tell me (who/whom) the first president of the country was?
20. Does anyone in this class know (who/whom) was the most recently elected president of Sierra Leone?

Review: Exercise 5 Making Pronouns and Antecedents Agree

Each sentence below contains an example of pronoun-antecedent agreement. On your paper, rewrite the sentences according to the directions given in parentheses, changing the pronouns if necessary. In some cases, you will also have to change the form of the verb or another word. Note that the sentences are written from Kisimi Kamara's point of view.

SAMPLE The village compounds have their huts arranged in a square. (Change *The village compounds* to *My family's compound.*)

ANSWER My family's compound has its huts arranged in a square.

1. I spent my youth in a small African village called Lokko in the British West African colony of Songhai. (Change *I* to *My brothers and I.*)
2. My father farmed his own land and reaped from it a meager harvest. (Change *My father* to *My father's friends.*)
3. My mother spent her days cooking, sweeping, washing, and caring for her children. (Change *My mother* to *The women in the village.*)
4. She and my sister also spent many of their waking hours pounding rice. (Change *She and my sister* to *She.*)
5. At the end of the day, my father slept in his hammock, which hung from the veranda roof. (Change *my father* to *my parents.*)
6. The babies of the village were carried on their mothers' backs. (Change *The babies of the village* to *The baby in our family.*)
7. Our mothers hoped that their children would receive a good education. (Change *Our mothers* to *My mother.*)
8. Our teachers, Miss Schwartz and Miss Costello, did their best to teach us English. (Change *Our teachers, Miss Schwartz and Miss Costello* to *My teacher, Miss Schwartz.*)
9. English was important to us because it gave us a chance for a better future. (Change *English* to *Our studies.*)
10. I wanted to go to the capital, where I could study in a big secondary school. (Change the first *I* to *The students.*)
11. A house in our village had its walls made of mud. (Change *A house* to *The houses.*)
12. Only the chief had his house covered with corrugated iron roofing. (Change *Only the chief had* to *Only chiefs could have.*)
13. Drivers along the road might pull their cars into the village for water. (Change *Drivers* to *An occasional driver.*)
14. A child who spotted a car or truck would quickly tell his or her friends. (Change *A child* to *Children.*)
15. We never wanted to put our bodies into those strange vehicles. (Change *we* to *I.*)

Review Exercise 6 Making Pronouns Agree with Indefinite Pronoun Antecedents

The following sentences are about the storytelling tradition of West Africa. Each sentence contains an example of pronoun-antecedent agreement. Rewrite the sentences according to the directions in parentheses, changing the pronouns if necessary. In some cases, you will also have to change the verb. (See page 647 for a list of singular and plural indefinite pronouns. Remember that some pronouns may be either singular or plural, depending upon the context.)

SAMPLE Each of the storytellers has his or her favorite stories. (Change *Each* to *All*.)
ANSWER All of the storytellers have their favorite stories.

1. Most of the folktales from West Africa have their roots in oral tradition. (Change *Most* to *Many.*)
2. All of these stories involve their characters in exciting events. (Change *All* to *Each.*)
3. In addition, each of the tales has its educational aspects. (Change *each* to *several.*)
4. Much of this body of traditional storytelling also has its historical significance. (Change *Much* to *Most.*)
5. Many of West Africa's people call their storytellers *griots.* (Change *Many* to *Some.*)
6. People in a rural village give their warmest welcome to a visiting storyteller. (Change *People* to *Everyone.*)
7. Most of the children are glad when a griot comes to entertain them. (Change *Most* to *Each.*)
8. No one in the village can deny a fascination with the griot's tales. (Change *No one* to *Few.*)
9. Each of the storytellers usually asks listeners to join in his or her performances. (Change *Each* to *All.*)
10. The listeners and the griot enjoy their roles a great deal. (Change *The listeners and the griot* to *Both.*)
11. Most of the griots travel from village to village telling their stories. (Change *Most* to *Each.*)
12. Some of the tales have their origin in stories told generations ago. (Change *Some of the tales* to *Either this tale or that.*)
13. Each one of the griots tells the stories in his or her own way. (Change *Each one* to *All*)
14. A good storyteller incorporates gestures into his or her storytelling. (Change *A good storyteller* to *Many storytellers.*)
15. Have most of this storyteller's tales found their way into print? (Change *tales* to *body of work.*)

Using Pronouns Correctly

Review: Exercise 7 **Correcting Vague or Ambiguous Pronoun References**

The following sentences are based on ideas in the passage from *The African.* Each sentence contains a vague or an ambiguous pronoun reference. On your paper, rewrite each sentence to eliminate the unclear pronoun reference. You may have to change only one or two words, or you may find it necessary to revise the entire sentence.

1. Kisimi Kamara was born into a large family in a small African village, which made him an unspoiled child.
2. They had poor land, but other families found the Kamaras' livelihood enviable.
3. Cars stirred up dust as they drove down the dry mud roads, and that must have surprised the children at first.
4. The children watched as the drivers examined their broken-down cars, and they were perplexed by the mechanisms under the hood.
5. Kisimi's father and the village chief both had mud houses, but his roof was made of corrugated iron.

Review: Exercise 8

Proofreading

The following passage describes the artist Clementine Hunter, whose work is reproduced on the opposite page. Rewrite the passage, correcting the errors in spelling, grammar, and usage. Add any missing punctuation. There are twenty-five errors.

Clementine Hunter

[1]The African American artist Clementine Hunter (1887–1988) was borned at the Hidden Hill Plantation near Cloutierville, Louisiana. [2]When she was fifteen, her and her parents moved to nearby Melrose Plantation. [3]She worked in the kitchen and her father and her worked in the cotton fields as well. [4]When Hunter and she family arrived in Melrose, the plantation was being restored.[5]It soon became a monument to a vanishing way of life, attracting writers artists, and tourists.

[6]Hunter made her first paintings on window shades, jars, gourds, skillets and other objects. [7]A French businesman named François Mignon, whom visited Melrose in 1938, grew interested in the place and eventually became the plantations' resident librarian. [8]Mignon noticed one of Hunter's paintings and was astonished at their simple power.

[9]Mignon became Hunters mentor and supporter. [10]Her continued to produce works documenting plantation life—it's harvests, holidays, baptisms and funer-

Clementine Hunter, patchwork quilt, 1938

als. [11]Her style was abstract and she cared little for proportion or perspective. [12]In the quilt pictured above, Hunter stitched together small swatches of fabrik to produce a lively scene of rural life.

[13]Clementine Hunter's skillful use of simple materials and uncluttered dezigns brought she great success. [14]Sold nearly all of her works. [15]Her was presented with an honorary doctorate of fine arts from Northwestern State University in Natchitoches, Louisiana, in 1986.

[16]Hunter grew up in poverty in a small, self-contained world and she recorded what she experienced in rich detail. [17]Kisimi Kamara, the narrator of William Conton's *The African* also spent his youth in a poor and confined world, yet he found great beauty in it. [18]Both Hunter and Kisimi Kamara, whom is much like Conton, were keen observers of the world around him.

Review: Exercise 9

Mixed Review

The following sentences describe aspects of William Conton's life and work. For each sentence, choose the proper pronoun from the pair in parentheses, and write it on your paper.

William Conton

1. William Conton, (who/whom) we know was born in the tiny West African nation of Gambia, has spent most of his life in Sierra Leone.
2. Readers enjoy Conton's fiction, from which (you/they) can learn a great deal about West African life.
3. Most of Conton's short fiction made (its/their) first appearance in West African journals.
4. Conton's novel *The African* describes the life of an ambitious young man named Kisimi Kamara, (who/whom) Conton resembles in many ways.
5. For example, both Conton and (he/him) went to college in England.
6. Both men, (he/him) and Conton, returned to West Africa in the 1950s, when many independence movements in Africa were growing.
7. Neither of the two West African men was unaffected by (his/their) experiences during those exciting years.
8. All of the people living at that time had (his/their) own vivid stories to tell.
9. Despite the similarities between the author and Kisimi, Conton had a more privileged upbringing than (he/him).
10. Conton was the son of an Anglican minister (who/whom) encouraged him to read at an early age.
11. (His/Him) having such a strong interest in writing no doubt stems from his early love of books.
12. As the child of a rural farm family, Conton's character Kisimi is far less sophisticated than (he/him).
13. Each of the men, Conton and the character Kisimi, nevertheless accomplished many of (his/their) ambitions.
14. Much of Conton's reputation is due to (his/him) holding high office in Sierra Leone.
15. (Who/Whom) do you think served as Sierra Leone's minister of education?
16. The minister of education was none other than (he/him), William Conton.
17. For that reason, Conton had little time to be a prolific author; nevertheless, in Sierra Leone few writers are as famous as (he/him).
18. In 1949 Conton married Bertha Thompson; (she/her) and Conton met when he was teaching in Freetown, the capital of Sierra Leone.
19. In fact, education was the chosen field of both Contons, William and (she/her).
20. The culture of West Africa owes some of (its/it's) richness to the vivid writings of William Conton.

Writing Application

TIME

For more about the writing process, see TIME Facing the Blank Page, pp. 109–119

Personal Pronouns in Writing

In the following excerpt from her novel *Song of Solomon,* author Toni Morrison tells about a landlord named Macon Dead and a man named Sonny. As you read, notice the many personal pronouns and focus especially on how the author avoids unclear pronoun references.

Macon Dead dug in *his* pocket for *his* keys, and curled *his* fingers around *them,* letting *their* bunchy solidity calm *him. They* were the keys to all the doors of *his* houses (only four true houses; the rest were really shacks), and *he* fondled *them* from time to time as *he* walked down Not Doctor Street to *his* office. At least *he* thought of it as *his* office, and even painted the word OFFICE on the door. But the plate-glass window contradicted *him.* In peeling gold letters arranged in a semicircle, *his* business establishment was declared to be Sonny's Shop. Scraping the previous owner's name off was hardly worth the trouble since *he* couldn't scrape *it* from anybody's mind.

Techniques with Personal Pronouns

Try to apply some of Toni Morrison's writing techniques when you write.

1. Use pronouns to avoid repetition of names and words.

REPEATED WORDS . . . dug in his pocket for his *keys,* and curled his fingers around the *keys,* letting the *keys'* bunchy solidity . . .

MORRISON'S VERSION . . . dug in his pocket for his *keys,* and curled his fingers around *them,* letting *their* bunchy solidity . . .

2. Make sure each pronoun you use has a clear antecedent.

UNCLEAR ANTECEDENT . . . *his* business establishment was declared to be Sonny's Shop. Scraping *his* name off was hardly worth the trouble . . .

MORRISON'S VERSION . . . *his* business establishment was declared to be Sonny's Shop. Scraping *the previous owner's* name off was hardly worth the trouble . . .

Practice Apply the techniques above by revising the following passage on a separate sheet of paper. The passage has been adapted from *Song of Solomon.* Eliminate awkward repetition by using personal pronouns, but also be certain that all your pronoun references are clear.

When Mrs. Bains closed the door, Macon Dead went back to the pages of Macon's accounts book, running Macon's fingertips over the figures and thinking with the unoccupied part of Macon's mind about the first time Macon had called on Ruth Foster's father. Macon had had only two keys in Macon's pocket then, and if Macon had let people like the woman who had just left have such people's way, Macon wouldn't have had any keys at all.

Using Pronouns Correctly

UNIT 18

Using Modifiers Correctly

18.1 The Three Degrees of Comparison

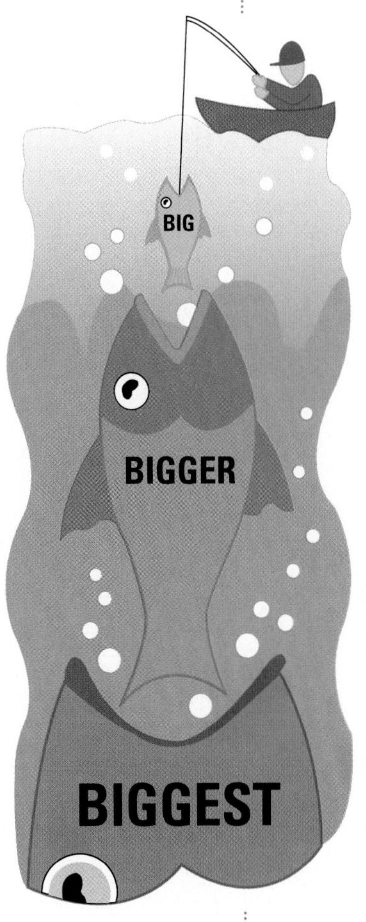

- Most adjectives and adverbs have three degrees of comparison: the positive, or base, form; the comparative form; and the superlative form.
- The **positive** form of a modifier cannot be used to make a comparison. (This form appears as the entry word in a dictionary.)
- The **comparative** form of a modifier shows two things being compared.
- The **superlative** form of a modifier shows three or more things being compared.

POSITIVE	The mechanic's hands are **rough.** The canary sang **happily.**
COMPARATIVE	The mechanic's hands are **rougher** than mine. My canary sang **more happily** than my neighbor's canary.
SUPERLATIVE	Of the three, his hands are **roughest.** The orange canary sang **most happily** of all.

Exercise 1 **Identifying Degrees of Comparison**

Write the comparative adjectives and adverbs in the following sentences on your paper. Then indicate the degree of comparison by writing *comparative* or *superlative* after each one.

Early Egyptian Rulers

1. The ancient Egyptians believed that their leaders would rule more wisely than other rulers.
2. One of the most capable rulers was Hatshepsut, the first woman leader in history and a strong leader.
3. One of her more daring acts was wearing full pharaonic regalia, including a false beard.
4. Hatshepsut's successor, Thutmose III, was more aggressive and set out on a harsh policy of conquest.
5. Pharaoh Amenhotep IV tried even harder than Thutmose to strengthen the powers of the throne, but Amenhotep worked hardest at changing religion.

Using The Three Degrees

■ In general, for one-syllable modifiers add *-er* to form the comparative and *-est* to form the superlative.

sweet, sweet**er,** sweet**est**

This is the **sweetest** apple I have ever tasted.

For some words, spelling changes occur when you add *-er* and *-est.*

sad, sa**dder,** sa**ddest**

blue, blu**er,** blu**est**

easy, eas**ier,** eas**iest**

Sometimes it may sound more natural to use *more* and *most* instead of *-er* and *-est* with one-syllable modifiers.

sour, **more** sour, **most** sour

That was the **most sour** lemon I have ever tasted.

■ For most two-syllable adjectives, add *-er* to form the comparative and *-est* to form the superlative.

gentle, gentl**er,** gentl**est**

The black dog is **gentler** than the brown one.

happy, happ**ier,** happ**iest**

My dog is the **happiest** one in the neighborhood.

Use *more* and *most* if *-er* and *-est* sound awkward.

helpful, **more** helpful, **most** helpful

No one was **more helpful** than Rita.

■ For adverbs ending in *-ly,* always use *more* and *most* to form the comparative and superlative degrees.

quickly, **more** quickly, **most** quickly

I am able to run **more quickly** in cold weather.

■ For modifiers of three or more syllables, always use *more* and *most* to form the comparative and superlative degrees.

delicious, **more** delicious, **most** delicious

I think pears are **more delicious** than apples.

■ *Less* and *least,* the opposite of *more* and *most,* can also be used with most modifiers to show comparison.

Rosa is **less talkative** than Daryl.

Bea is the **least talkative** person I know.

Exercise 2 Using Degrees of Comparison

Write the word or words that would complete the following sentences with the correct degree of comparison of the modifier in parentheses. (You may need to use the positive degree as well as the comparative and superlative.)

The Early Civilizations of the Middle East

1. Civilizations rose ____ in the Middle East than they did in most parts of the world. (early)
2. More than 5,000 years ago, the ____ civilizations known to historians developed in that region. (old)
3. For the approximately 2,000 years that the Sumerians ruled Mesopotamia, religion played an ____ role. (important)
4. Among the ____ Sumerian deities were Inanna, goddess of love and war, and Nanna, the moon god. (important)
5. To honor their deities, the Sumerians built ____ shrines and temples. (grand)
6. It is believed that thousands of workers labored hard for years to build the ____ temple in the empire. (grand)
7. In artists' sketches, each story was ____ in area than the one directly beneath it. (small)
8. The top story of the temple, which dominated the entire city, was the ____ of all the stories. (small)
9. The Babylonian empire, which succeeded the Sumerian, was ____ than the Sumerian empire. (strong)
10. Hammurabi, a famous leader, issued a single code of law that centralized the government ____ than it had been centralized under Sumerian rule. (tightly)
11. The code regulated trade and commerce ____ than ever before. (precisely)
12. The code also provided ____ regulations than before for marriage and divorce. (strict)
13. Punishments for violating the laws in the code were harsh, and the ____ penalty of all was death. (harsh)
14. Babylonia fell to the Assyrians, who were the ____ rulers ever to control Mesopotamia. (harsh)
15. The Assyrians were the ____ warriors on horseback. (fast)
16. Within their vast empire, the Assyrians built a ____ system of communication. (speedy)
17. Encompassing almost all of the Fertile Crescent, the Chaldean empire may have been the ____ of all the Middle Eastern empires. (large)
18. One famous leader, Nebuchadnezzer, constructed ____ fortifications and buildings. (impressive)
19. None was ____ than his own elaborate palace with its lush hanging gardens. (impressive)
20. These gardens, known as one of the seven wonders of the world, were built in Babylon, the ____ city in all of Mesopotamia. (famous)

18.2 Irregular Comparisons

A few modifiers have irregular forms.

Modifiers with Irregular Forms of Comparison		
Positive	**Comparative**	**Superlative**
good	better	(the) best
well	better	(the) best
bad	worse	(the) worst
badly	worse	(the) worst
ill	worse	(the) worst
far (distance)	farther	(the) farthest
far (degree, time)	further	(the) furthest
little (amount)	less	(the) least
many	more	(the) most
much	more	(the) most

Exercise 3 **Making Correct Comparisons**

Complete the following sentences with the correct degree of comparison of the modifier in parentheses. (The positive degree is used in four sentences.)

SAMPLE Lea's drawings are __________ than mine. (imaginative)
ANSWER more imaginative

The Art of Drawing

1. Drawing is one of the ____ art forms of all. (old)
2. Even though they drew on some of the ____ surfaces, prehistoric people created colorful images on rock or clay. (bad)
3. During the Middle Ages, parchment was one of the ____ drawing surfaces available. (good)
4. Partly because silk wore ____ than other materials, Eastern artists often used it as a drawing surface. (well)
5. Since the 1400s artists have preferred using paper, which costs ____ than parchment. (little)
6. Though they worked in ____ conditions than present-day artists, artists of centuries ago produced excellent drawings. (bad)
7. Leonardo da Vinci and Michelangelo were among the ____ artists of the High Renaissance. (good)
8. Rembrandt and Goya produced ____ drawings than many of their contemporaries. (much)
9. Many people believe that Pablo Picasso advanced the cause of art ____ than any other artists of the twentieth century. (far)
10. Today people will travel ____ than ever to see exhibits of his work. (far)

Exercise 4 Writing Correct Comparisons

Write the word or words that could complete the following sentences with the correct degree of comparison of the modifier in parentheses.

SAMPLE Belinda is the _________ cyclist in our school. (fast)
ANSWER fastest

Babe Zaharias, All-Around Athlete

1. Many people consider Mildred "Babe" Didrikson Zaharias the _________ all-around athlete of this century. (good)
2. Babe Zaharias excelled in _________ sports than any other athlete, male or female. (many)
3. Of all the sports in which she participated, she was _________ in basketball, track and field, golf, skating, and lacrosse. (outstanding)
4. Zaharias rose to national fame _________ than most other athletes of her generation. (quickly)
5. In high school, she held numerous track-and-field records and was the _________ female basketball player in the country. (fine)
6. During the 1932 summer Olympics, held in Los Angeles, Zaharias performed _________ than ever before, breaking several world records. (good)
7. From 1940 to 1950, she achieved the goal of establishing herself as the country's _________ golfer, winning every possible United States and British title (successful)
8. Zaharias, who won the U.S. Open in 1948, 1950 and 1954, could drive a golf ball _________ than most other golfers. (far)
9. Despite a major operation, Zaharias still played _________ than any other competitor in the 1953 National Women's Open. (skillfully)
10. When Babe Didrikson Zaharias died in 1956, the country lost one of the _________ of all athletes. (talented)

Exercise 5 Writing Sentences That Make Comparisons

Select five of the irregular modifiers from the list on page 666. Write a sentence for each, using the positive and comparative degrees of the modifier.

SAMPLE far
ANSWER Chen can throw the ball quite <u>far</u>, but Bernice can throw it <u>farther</u>.

18.3 Double Comparisons

■ Do not make a double comparison by using both *-er* or *-est* and *more* or *most.*

INCORRECT	Texas is ~~more~~ bigger than Oklahoma.
CORRECT	Texas is bigger than Oklahoma.
INCORRECT	That is the ~~most~~ funniest joke I have ever heard.
CORRECT	That is the funniest joke I have ever heard.

Exercise 6 Correcting Double Comparisons

Write the correct form of the comparison in each of the following sentences.

Winston Churchill, British Statesman

1. Today we recognize Sir Winston Churchill as one of the most ablest statesmen in world history.
2. Churchill's star shone most brightest when he was Great Britain's prime minister during World War II.
3. His courage, eloquence, and faith in victory inspired the British to endure more greater hardships than they had ever before known.
4. One of the most happiest sights during the war was Churchill himself, a cigar in his mouth and two fingers raised in a victory salute.
5. Although he had stuttered as a boy, Churchill gave more clearer speeches than any other leader of his time.
6. Churchill was also one of the most liveliest writers of the day.
7. As a schoolboy, however, he had been the least carefulest student in his class.
8. Physically, Churchill was one of the most fittest leaders of the war.
9. He loved the rough, active life of a soldier, but he also had a more quieter side, which he expressed in some of his excellent paintings.
10. No other British leader of the twentieth century is regarded with more higher esteem.
11. The United States was more closer to entering the war than had seemed possible a year before.
12. Churchill and President Roosevelt developed the most strongest friendship of any wartime leaders.
13. Meeting in Yalta in 1945, Churchill and Roosevelt faced one of their most toughest challenges.
14. What was the most fairest way to divide control of postwar Europe?
15. Even more better than his postwar speeches was Churchill's six-volume series, *The Second World War,* which won him a Nobel Prize.

Exercise 7 Correcting Comparisons

Rewrite the following sentences, correcting the comparisons. If a sentence needs no correction, write *correct.*

Family Dogs

1. Dad had said that bringing two puppies into the house would be the goodest move our family could make.
2. When he brought them home from the animal shelter, the collie weighed littler than the shepherd.
3. Now the collie is more heavier than the shepherd.
4. Dad chose the collie because it had the sadder eyes of all the dogs at the shelter and he felt sorry for it.
5. The shepherd caught his eye because it had the most prettiest markings.
6. Both dogs have the most sweetest dispositions imaginable.
7. They are more happiest when they are right by our sides.
8. Raising two puppies is hardest than raising just one.
9. When one acts frisky, the other seems to act even friskiest.
10. With two dogs to care for, I have most responsibilities than before.
11. To give them the better care possible, I have had to give up pleasures I once enjoyed.
12. The situation is even badder when one of the dogs is ill.
13. The iller the dog feels, the more time someone must spend with it.
14. The shepherd appears to be in best health than the collie.
15. Since I am the most oldest of three children, it is my responsibility to walk the dogs every morning.
16. Sometimes I wish that the dogs were least playful on their morning walks around our neighborhood.
17. Whenever I am feeling weary, they seem to feel especially adventurous.
18. Then they try to run faster than ever before, dragging me along with them for blocks at a time.
19. I think that each day both dogs try to run further than the day before.
20. Last week, the shepherd ran off for the gooder part of the morning.
21. No one was happiest than I when he finally returned home.
22. The shepherd, whose sense of smell is more acuter than the collie's, was attracted by picnic leftovers in the park.
23. These leftovers were tastiest treats than his regular canned dog food.
24. In recent months, the dogs have become more easiest to train than they were when we first got them.
25. Their training is going the best than before.
26. Now they respond to simple commands most readily than before.
27. Of the two, the collie is gooder behaved than the shepherd.
28. The shepherd is the most stubbornest dog that I have ever known.
29. Sometimes the shepherd is least cooperative than a mule.
30. Raising two young dogs has definitely been entertaining and has brought this family closest together than ever before.

18.4 Incomplete Comparisons

- Do not make an incomplete or unclear comparison by omitting *other* or *else* when you compare one member of a group with the group.

UNCLEAR Crayfish are more like lobsters than any animal.
CLEAR Crayfish are more like lobsters than any **other** animal.

UNCLEAR She reads more books than anyone.
CLEAR She reads more books than anyone **else.**

Make sure that you are comparing like things.

UNCLEAR The population of Texas is greater than Oklahoma. [One state's population is being compared illogically with everything about another state.]
CLEAR The population of Texas is greater than **that of Oklahoma.**
CLEAR The population of Texas is greater than **Oklahoma's.** [The word *population* is understood after *Oklahoma's.*]

UNCLEAR The duties of a traffic officer are more complex than a game warden. [The duties of a traffic officer are being compared illogically with a person, namely, a game warden.]
CLEAR The duties of a traffic officer are more complex than **those of a game warden.**
CLEAR The duties of a traffic officer are more complex than **a game warden's.**

Exercise 8 Making Complete Comparisons

Rewrite each of the following sentences to correct the incomplete comparison.

The Art of Flamenco

[1]Since discovering flamenco music, I have become more interested in the culture of Spain than in any other country. [2]Flamenco songs and dance are associated more closely with the Gypsies of southern Spain than with anyone. [3]Flamenco may have been influenced more by medieval Arabic music than by any tradition. [4]After listening to a performance of flamenco music, I am now convinced that flamenco is more dramatic than any music. [5]The rhythmic patterns of flamenco music are more complex and elaborate than American folk music. [6]The tones of a flamenco guitar's nylon strings are softer than a steel-stringed guitar. [7]In a flamenco performance, the dancer's role is just as important as the singer. [8]The gestures of a flamenco dancer are more extravagant than a ballerina. [9]As flamenco dancers whirl, strut, and strike dramatic poses, they exude more passion than any performer. [10]If I could, I would rather learn flamenco dancing than anything.

18.5 *Good or Well; Bad or Badly*

- Always use *good* as an adjective. *Well* may be used as an adverb of manner telling how ably something is done or as an adjective meaning "in good health."

Natalie is a **good** speaker. [adjective]

Anita feels **good** today. [adjective after a linking verb]

Daniel speaks **well.** [adverb of manner]

Mr. Chong is not **well** right now. [adjective meaning "in good health"]

Always use *bad* as an adjective. Therefore, *bad* is used after a linking verb. Use *badly* as an adverb. *Badly* almost always follows an action verb.

The machine made a **bad** copy. [adjective]

The air smelled **bad.** [adjective following a linking verb]

I felt **bad** about your losing the race. [adjective following a linking verb]

His cut is bleeding **badly.** [adverb following an action verb]

Exercise 9 Choosing the Correct Modifier

Write *good, well, bad,* or *badly* to complete each sentence.

Training a Dog

1. Generally it is __________ to begin training a dog when it is about eight weeks old.
2. In order to respond to training, a dog must feel __________ and be in good shape.
3. To train a dog successfully, owners need a great deal of patience and ready access to a __________ training manual.
4. For large or ill-behaved dogs, professional obedience training can result in pets whose temperaments are __________.
5. Some dog owners do not understand that if they communicate __________, their pet will not obey.
6. Communicating __________ means issuing simple, direct commands in a consistent manner.
7. Because repetition only confuses a dog, it is __________ to give a command only once.
8. It is best to speak firmly and clearly—not loudly—when reprimanding a dog that has behaved __________.
9. Both physical and verbal abuse are __________ for a dog; abuse creates fear in an animal but does not make it behave well.
10. Experts agree that nearly all dogs are eager to please their masters and feel __________ when they misbehave.

Exercise 10 Using the Correct Modifier

For each sentence, write the correct modifier in parentheses. Then write whether the modifier is used as an *adjective* or an *adverb.*

A Dog's Life

1. Elizabeth Marshall Thomas writes (good/well).
2. Her surprise best-seller, *The Hidden Life of Dogs,* speaks (good/well) of dogs.
3. The theme of her book is that dogs do many things as (good/well) as human beings.
4. There are, of course, things that dogs do (bad/badly) or cannot do at all.
5. Some critics of Thomas's book claim that she condones dogs' behavior even when it is (bad, badly).
6. Thomas believes that dogs live (good/well) if their lives are filled with love and intellectual pursuits.
7. According to Thomas, dogs have a "conscience" and feel (bad/badly) about some of the things they do.
8. Thomas's dog Koki skulked around the house for days because Koki knew that she had been (bad/badly).
9. On the other hand, if a dog feels (good, well) about its behavior, it is likely to show this by acting happy.
10. When one of her dogs acts (bad/badly), Thomas usually finds a logical explanation for its behavior.

Exercise 11 Correcting Comparisons

Rewrite each of the following sentences, correcting the incomplete or incorrect comparison. If a sentence contains no errors, write *correct.*

Dogs and Cats

1. I believe that dogs are more like human beings than any animals.
2. I'm convinced that the brain of a dog is more complex than a cat.
3. A cat's brain doesn't seem to be wired as good as a dog's brain.
4. Dogs lead lives that are fuller than cats.
5. Dogs seem to have more stronger emotions than cats do.
6. Cats seldom, if ever, feel bad about things they have done, even when someone is reprimanding them.
7. Dogs' emotional needs may be as great as human beings.
8. What dogs seem to want more than anything is the company of other dogs.
9. What cats want is good food, preferably mice.
10. If someone wrote a book about cats, the book would probably sell even more copies than dogs.

18.6 Double Negatives

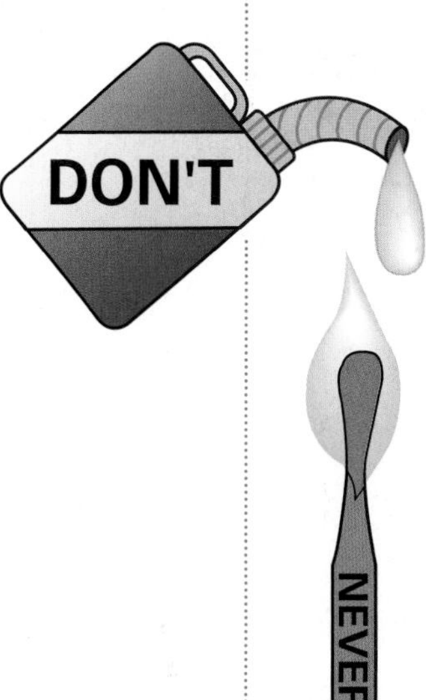

■ In general, do not use a double negative, two negative words in the same clause. Use only one negative word to express a negative idea.

INCORRECT	I didn't see ~~no~~ accident.
CORRECT	I did**n't** see **any** accident.
INCORRECT	He doesn't know nothing about my plans.
CORRECT	He does**n't** know **anything** about my plans.
CORRECT	He knows **nothing** about my plans.
INCORRECT	She ~~never~~ tells no lies.
CORRECT	She **never** tells **any** lies.
CORRECT	She tells **no** lies.
INCORRECT	We haven't hardly eaten our breakfasts.
CORRECT	We have **hardly** eaten our breakfasts.

Exercise 12 Avoiding Double Negatives

Rewrite the following sentences, eliminating the double negative in each.

Boa Constrictors

1. Boa constrictors do not inject no venom into their prey.
2. Still, I would not want no boa constrictor for a pet.
3. Boa constrictors kill birds and rodents by not allowing them no air.
4. Once captured in the boa constrictor's coils, a bird or rodent cannot do nothing.
5. The boa constrictor is big, but it cannot be compared with no anaconda, or python.
6. Boa constrictors cannot swallow no cows, horses, or people.
7. After a meal, these snakes do not eat nothing for a week or more.
8. Often they do not do nothing; they just sleep and digest their food.
9. Boa constrictors can survive for many months without no food at all.
10. Unlike many other snakes, boa constrictors never lay no eggs.
11. Though my friend Jeremy has one, I wouldn't want no boa constrictor for a pet.
12. There aren't scarcely any snakes that appeal to me.
13. Jeremy shouldn't never have brought his boa constrictor to school.
14. He thought it wouldn't never escape from its bag.
15. He didn't have no clue where the snake was after it escaped.
16. First he pretended that he didn't know nothing about all the commotion.
17. He couldn't hardly keep pretending for long, though.
18. There wasn't nobody in the class who didn't know he had the snake with him.
19. Jeremy hadn't hardly expected to become a school celebrity.
20. He won't bring no snakes to school again anytime soon.

18.7 Misplaced and Dangling Modifiers

■ Place modifiers as close as possible to the words they modify in order to make the meaning of the sentence clear.

Misplaced Modifiers

Modifiers that modify the wrong word or seem to modify more than one word in a sentence are called **misplaced modifiers.** Moving the modifier as close as possible to the word it modifies or revising the sentence will correct this problem.

MISPLACED **Proceeding with care,** we stood at the foot of the mountain and watched the determined mountain climbers. [participial phrase incorrectly modifying *we*]

CLEAR We stood at the foot of the mountain and watched the determined mountain climbers **proceeding with care.** [participial phrase correctly modifying *mountain climbers*]

MISPLACED The mountains delight many visitors **in their autumn splendor.** [prepositional phrase incorrectly modifying *visitors*]

CLEAR The mountains **in their autumn splendor** delight many visitors. [prepositional phrase correctly modifying *mountains*]

Exercise 13 Identifying Misplaced Modifiers

Write the misplaced modifier in each sentence. If a sentence is correct, write *correct.*

1. Dumping more water on an already flooded state, California is hit by still another torrential rainstorm.
2. The winter storm battering northern California for days has worked its way down the coast to the southern counties.
3. Howling through mountain passes, a highway winding through the Sierra Nevada is forced to shut down due to heavy winds.
4. Built in the 1960s, officials estimated that three months would be needed to rebuild a bridge.
5. Most meteorologists attributed the storm to a recurring Pacific weather phenomenon known as El Niño.

Dangling Modifiers

Dangling modifiers do not modify any word in the sentence. By supplying a word that the dangling phrase can sensibly modify, you can easily correct this error.

DANGLING **Digging in the field,** a Native American village was found. [participial phrase logically modifying no word in the sentence]

CLEAR **Digging in the field,** archaeologists found a Native American village. [participial phrase modifying *archaeologists*]

DANGLING **After digging for months,** the find was all the more satisfying. [prepositional phrase logically modifying no word in the sentence]

CLEAR **After digging for months,** the archaeologists deemed the find all the more satisfying. [prepositional phrase modifying *archaeologists*]

DANGLING **Feeling proud of our find,** our dinner that night was a celebration. [participial phrase logically modifying no word in sentence]

CLEAR **Feeling proud of our find,** we made our dinner a celebration. [rewrite supplies a word for phrase to modify]

Placement of *Only*

■ Place the adverb *only* immediately before the word or group of words it modifies.

The meaning of your sentence may be unclear if *only* is positioned incorrectly.

UNCLEAR Bertina **only** has breakfast on Sunday. [Does she have just one meal on Sunday? Does she skip breakfast every day but Sunday? Is Bertina the only person (in a group) who has breakfast on Sunday?]

CLEAR Bertina has **only** breakfast on Sunday. [She does not have lunch or dinner.]

CLEAR Bertina has breakfast **only** on Sunday. [She does not have breakfast on any other day.]

CLEAR **Only** Bertina has breakfast on Sunday. [No one else (in Bertina's house) has breakfast on Sunday.]

Exercise 14 Identifying Misplaced and Dangling Modifiers

Write any incorrect modifier in the following sentences. Then write *misplaced* or *dangling* to identify the kind. If a sentence contains no errors, write *correct.*

SAMPLE Renting huge rafts, rivers become accessible to city people.
ANSWER Renting huge rafts—misplaced

Outdoor Adventures

1. Looking for adventure, white-water rafting, mountain climbing, and bungee jumping have become popular vacation activities.
2. Adventure travel, now a billion-dollar industry, has grown rapidly in recent years.
3. Thousands of people sign up for rafting trips through the Grand Canyon each year.
4. Ranging in difficulty from Class I to Class IV, knowledgeable river guides lead inexperienced rafters.
5. Unlike an amusement-park ride, rafters often find their trip down the rapids unpredictable and strenuous.
6. Interested in glaciers and icebergs, the untouched wilderness of the Yukon territory can be very appealing.
7. Some tourists enjoy watching the mountain gorillas with sloping heads and dense black fur that make their home in central Africa.
8. Filled as they are with hidden dangers, some vacationers find ice climbing and rock climbing especially challenging.
9. Climbers in the best physical shape should only climb glaciers.
10. Extremely vigorous outdoor adventures push people to their physical limits.

Exercise 15 Correcting Misplaced and Dangling Modifiers

Rewrite the following sentences, correcting the misplaced or dangling modifier in each.

A Day in the Park

1. Driving carefully down the road to the park, the accident was avoided.
2. I saw two squirrels riding my bike in the park.
3. Searching for wildflowers, poison ivy was found instead.
4. We caught a butterfly using a net.
5. Making a nest for their young, Alex and Maria saw two birds in a big tree near the parking lot.
6. Carmen only dreams of being a forest ranger; she knows it is what she wants to be, and no other career interests her.
7. Because of their huge size and strength, many backpackers and campers in the park fear grizzly bears.
8. Myung only knows which trail leads to the waterfall; he won't tell anyone else where it is.
9. Stuck fast on the hook, I had trouble removing the fish that I caught in the lake.
10. After planning for months, the outing was a big success.

Exercise 16 Correcting Misplaced and Dangling Modifiers

Rewrite the following sentences, correcting the misplaced or dangling modifiers in each.

Toni Morrison, Novelist

1. During her childhood in Lorain, Ohio, Toni Morrison was surrounded by poor, hardworking people and steel mills with little opportunity to get ahead.
2. Finishing high school with honors, Howard University in Washington, D.C., accepted Morrison as an undergraduate.
3. Constantly on the road during the summer, her acting talent shone in the productions of the university's theater troupe.
4. Attending graduate school at Cornell University, William Faulkner and Virginia Woolf were the subjects of her thesis.
5. Graduating in 1955, jobs in education and publishing followed.
6. Until 1969, when her novel *The Bluest Eye* was published, Morrison had edited only books, not written them.
7. In *The Bluest Eye,* a young girl is described by Morrison wishing for blue eyes exactly like Shirley Temple's.
8. With the curious name of Milkman Dead, Morrison created a powerful character in her third novel, *Song of Solomon.*
9. Becoming increasingly aware of his family heritage, the author convincingly pictures Milkman Dead.
10. Some critics liked Morrison's novel *Tar Baby,* but others said that the characters only were stereotypes.
11. Described by some as the last classic American writer, one critic put Morrison in a category with Poe, Twain, and Faulkner.
12. Only *Beloved* was the book written by Morrison to win the Pulitzer Prize.
13. *Song of Solomon* only won the National Book Critics Circle Award.
14. Having won such prestigious literary awards, Princeton University offered Morrison a teaching position.
15. Morrison wrote *Jazz,* angry at the injustices experienced by African American women.
16. After many months of writing, it was published.
17. Heartbreaking and powerful, readers were mesmerized by the story woven by Morrison.
18. Writing with passion, the main characters in *Jazz* formed a triangle of jealousy, murder, and redemption.
19. With their daring themes and lyrical passages, readers admire Toni Morrison's novels.
20. Given for distinguished literary work of an idealistic nature, in 1993 Morrison won the Nobel Prize for Literature.

Exercise 17 Adding Modifiers to Sentences

Revise the following sentences, adding modifiers as indicated in parentheses.

Summer Programs

1. Many parents have begun their search for the right summer program for their children. (Add *planning ahead.*)
2. Parents collect as much information as possible. (Add *knowing how difficult the decision is.*)
3. Information helps narrow the choices. (Add *though sometimes overwhelming.*)
4. Children need help sorting out the possibilities. (Add *often unsure of their decision-making ability.*)
5. Various programs are available at public libraries and recreational centers throughout the county. (Add *many of them free.*)
6. Some programs have a residency requirement and a small nonresident surcharge. (Add *offered by county agencies.*)
7. College dormitories provide housing for some programs. (Add *empty during summer months.*)
8. Children can find any kind of camp. (Add *suited to their interests.*)
9. There are nature camps, history camps, and even astronomy camps. (Add *designed for aspiring astronauts.*)
10. Students with experience in digital photography can enroll in the animation program at the computer arts camp. (Add *only* to make clear that others cannot enroll.)

Exercise 18 Correcting Modifiers

The following paragraphs contain 10 errors in the use of modifiers. Rewrite the paragraphs, correcting the errors.

Apprenticeships

[1]Going to college is a good way to train for some, but not all, kinds of work. [2]Apprenticeship is probably a more better way to train to be a carpenter, for example. [3]Apprentices never gain no practical skill without on-the-job experience. [4]As their training progresses, they learn various job skills good. [5]After about four years—more longer for some trades and not so long for others—they become experts. [6]Then the wages received by these skilled workers are better than the unskilled workers.

[7]The construction industry is more crowded with registered apprentices than any field. [8]There are many different occupations that require apprenticeship. [9]Having varying interests, some fields are more attractive than others. [10]Apprenticeship programs have entrance exams and minimum age and education requirements. [11]If you want to become an apprentice, the best thing you can do is find out about your chosen field while you are still in school. [12]Sometimes you will find that the most good thing to do is to finish college first. [13]Not wanting to miss out on a college education, colleges today train a growing number of artists and craftspeople. [14]Nevertheless, many people believe that the close relationship between master and apprentice only can provide suitable training.

Exercise 19 Correcting Modifiers

Rewrite the following sentences, correcting any errors in the use of modifiers.

Arthurian Sites

1. My summer vacation was more better than any I ever took before.
2. While traveling in England, places associated with King Arthur were my primary destinations.
3. Located on the coast of Cornwall, our tour guide pointed out King Arthur's legendary birthplace at Tintagel.
4. When I learned that no one really knows where King Arthur was born—or even whether he actually lived—I felt badly.
5. I didn't let nothing keep me from seeing Cadbury Castle, which may have been the real Camelot.
6. Are the Arthurian sites in Glastonbury more numerous than any other city in England?
7. Standing at King Arthur's legendary grave site, the ruins of Glastonbury Abbey surrounded me.
8. I missed visiting the possible sites of Sir Lancelot's northern castle, because I didn't feel good.
9. Hanging in the hall at Winchester Castle, I gazed intently at what is supposed to be the table top of the Round Table.
10. My tour of Arthurian sites provided me with the most fondest memories of my vacation.

Exercise 20 Writing Correct Comparisons

Write 10 sentences, following the directions given in each of the items below.

SAMPLE Use the comparative of *happy* as an adverb.
ANSWER I worked *more happily* after I realized that I was almost finished.

1. Use the comparative form of *tiny* to compare the size of two objects.
2. Use the superlative of *little* (meaning amount) as an adjective.
3. Use the modifiers *good* and *well* following the appropriate kinds of verbs.
4. Use the comparative of *far* to compare distance.
5. Compare two games or activities of your choice, using the superlatives of *good* and *bad.*
6. Write a sentence comparing the population of New York with the population of Oregon.
7. Use the comparative form of the modifier *many.*
8. Express the same idea in two sentences. In one, use the negative *never;* in the other, use *ever.*
9. Use the modifier *only* to explain that you have art class one morning a week.
10. Use the participial phrase *reviewing all the grammar* in a sentence.

UNIT 18

Grammar Review

Using Modifiers Correctly

Alessandro Giuliani, the hero of Mark Helprin's epic novel *A Soldier of the Great War,* is a young Italian student whose life is turned upside down by World War I. In this passage, which has been annotated to show some of the kinds of modifiers covered in this unit, Alessandro is returning on foot from Germany to his family estate in Rome.

Literature Model

from A Soldier of the Great War

by Mark Helprin

Comparative form of the adjective *high*

Positive form of the adjective *far*

Superlative form of the adjective *far*

Correctly placed prepositional phrase modifying *end*

Positive form of the adverb *violently*

He crossed six ridges, each higher than the one preceding it, before he came to the point where he would not see trees until he was in Italy, and when he cleared the forest he was confronted by a world of glaciated mountains. In the dusk, they were a dusty-rose color and the distance to them appeared so vast that he thought it would take a month to reach them, but it was only a trick of light and shadow, and they were neither as far nor as high as they seemed to be.

Here and there in the snow-covered pastures were hay-filled cabins where he could find shelter from the wind. He sought the one farthest from any farmhouse or village and closest to the great glacier upon which he would soon be walking. Several hours after dusk he stopped at the end of the meadows, in a place where the glacier was so close that he could feel the rivers of cold air that flowed from it and carried its sounds—the muffled sound of a locked wheel skidding on a steel rail, thunder-like cracks, a barely perceptible rumble, as if from a giant piece of furniture being pulled slowly across a rough floor. . . .

He awoke at midnight, shivering so violently that he found it difficult to get to his feet. He buttoned his clothes tight, bloused his pants in his socks, put on every item of wool he could find, and burst out the door, almost falling

Using Modifiers Correctly

down the slope that descended to the tongue of the glacier. The moon was down, his head throbbed, and his fingers were too stiff for him to have opened his food even had he been warm enough to try to eat.

He had to use both axes. The crampons were not necessary, and he would never have been able to strap them on anyway. After struggling up a short fractured ice wall by pulling himself forward with his arms, he was on the glacier. It rose gradually toward a line of mountains that then shot straight into the sky like the spray of a wave exploding through a sinkhole. With luck he would have a moon or a sky clear enough to let the starlight through, and with more than luck he would reach the peaks by daylight.

Correctly placed phrases modifying *he*

Review: Exercise 1 **Making Correct Comparisons**

The following sentences describe World War I and Alessandro Giuliani's involvement in it. For each sentence, write the proper comparative or superlative form of the modifier in parentheses.

1. World War I was called the Great War because ________ men fought and died in it than in any other war up to that time. (many)
2. The nations that fought in World War I assembled the ________ number of soldiers and armaments ever seen. (great)
3. Before the war, Alessandro joined the navy in the belief that wars were fought ________ at sea than on land. (safely)
4. Ironically, he was then sent to fight in the naval infantry and survived some of the ________ battles of all. (dangerous)
5. Alessandro later deserted when German and Austrian forces shattered the Italian front lines; it was Italy's ________ defeat of all in the war. (bad)
6. Desertion was usually punished by the ________ penalty of all: death by firing squad. (severe)
7. The Italian army chose to punish Alessandro's desertion ________ than usual, however; he was simply sent back to fight the Austrians. (harshly)
8. After he was taken prisoner by the Austrians, Alessandro fared ________ than other prisoners did. (good)
9. After Austria's collapse, Alessandro slipped cautiously through enemy lines amid the ________ confusion imaginable. (bad)
10. Every step Alessandro took toward the glacier led him ________ from the enemy and closer to his homeland and to freedom. (far)

Review: Exercise 2 Correcting Double Comparisons

Some of the following sentences elaborate on scenes from *A Soldier of the Great War* that are not reprinted in this textbook. Other sentences describe the Alps and glaciers. For each sentence, write the correct comparison. If a sentence contains no errors, write *correct.*

1. The Alps are probably better known than any other mountains in the world.
2. On the lower slopes of the Alps, many varieties of trees flourish, but the most highest slopes are almost bare of vegetation.
3. The more taller peaks attract many competent climbers; among them were the characters Alessandro and his friend Rafi.
4. Making his escape from an Austrian prison, Alessandro chose the most straightest path to Italy and his home.
5. Alessandro climbed until he was more higher than the tree line and within sight of the glaciers.
6. A glacier is a slowly moving river of ice and snow that stays frozen even on the most hottest summer days.
7. There are more than a thousand glaciers in the Alps; the most largest is the 16-mile-long Aletsch Glacier.
8. The most riskiest part of Alessandro's escape from Austria was his crossing a vast glacier at night.
9. Sharp-spiked crampons give climbers a more firmer foothold on the ice than plain climbing boots do.
10. More skillful than most amateur climbers, Alessandro chose not to wear crampons and used only his two ice axes to climb onto the glacier.
11. The glacier on which he climbed was in a more warmer climate than many other glaciers.
12. Glaciers are found both in polar regions and also in more temperate climates.
13. Glaciers become larger when more snow falls and more smaller when snow melts.
14. A glacier moves more slowly when it reaches an area that is less steeply sloped.
15. The steeper the slope, the more faster a glacier generally moves.
16. Many glaciers in the Alps are mountain glaciers that begin on the most highest slopes.
17. When compressed into a granular mass by more snow on top, the old snow starts to slide slowly down the slope.
18. The movement causes the mass to become more further compacted into glacier ice.
19. The slowest glacier moves about an inch a day; the most rapidest one, several hundred feet.
20. Climbing on glaciers is often more dangerous than climbing on rock.

Review: Exercise 3 Correcting Incomplete and Unclear Comparisons

The following sentences describe World War I and Italy's involvement in it. Rewrite each sentence, correcting any errors of incomplete or unclear comparison. Some of the sentences can be revised in more than one way. If a sentence contains no errors, write *correct.*

SAMPLE World War I shaped Alessandro's life more than any event.
ANSWER World War I shaped Alessandro's life more than any other event.

1. The First World War, which involved all the major powers of Europe as well as the United States, produced carnage greater than any previous war.
2. The use of aircraft, tanks, and machine guns made the Great War more impersonal than any war.
3. Some observers believed that British and French soldiers fought more bravely than anyone.
4. The Central Powers—Germany, Austria-Hungary, and the Ottoman Empire—were united as much by geography as by anything.
5. When fighting began in May 1915, Italy's army was less prepared than France or Britain.
6. For months the Alps, more than any place in Europe, were the site of many battles between the Italian and the Austrian forces.
7. The Isonzo River, in northern Italy, was the site of more battles than any other location on the Italian front.
8. After a devastating battle in 1917, Italy's position was weaker than Austria.
9. The Italian offensive of 1918 forced an Austrian retreat more successfully than had any Italian attacks.
10. By the time World War I ended in 1918, Italy had sustained a million casualties, more than in any war in its history.
11. More civilians were affected by World War I than by war.
12. Technological innovations made survival on the battlefront more difficult than earlier wars.
13. Bigger and better battleships and submarines revolutionized naval warfare.
14. Chemical warfare, more devastating than any form of warfare, was introduced.
15. Was the cost of rebuilding Europe higher than the war?
16. Italy's Prime Minister Vittorio Orlando, a delegate to the Paris peace conference, opposed the peace plan more than any delegate.
17. Italy's primary goal was more nationalistic than the other Allies.
18. Italy wanted control of the former Austrian territories more than anything.
19. Orlando took a greater interest in the punishment of Germany than in any other issue discussed at the peace conference.
20. The Italian delegation only walked out of the peace negotiations.

Review: Exercise 4 Choosing the Correct Modifier

The following sentences describe a mountain-climbing expedition that Alessandro and his friend Rafi took before Alessandro enlisted in the Italian navy. For each sentence, write the correct form of the modifier in parentheses. Then write whether the modifier is used as an *adjective* or an *adverb.*

1. Leaving the train, Alessandro and Rafi felt (good/well) about the next day's climb.
2. They carried enough equipment to ensure that the expedition would go (good/well).
3. A novice climber, Rafi needed Alessandro's expertise (bad/badly) to keep him safe.
4. Soon, however, Rafi was climbing safely and (well/good).
5. The climbers deftly hammered small spikes, called pitons, into the cliff, for it was essential that the pitons hold (good/well).
6. Once the pitons seemed to have been placed in the rock (good/well), the climbers snapped clips—carabiners—to the pitons.
7. The safety line they slung through the carabiners would not snag (bad/badly) on outcroppings of rock.
8. With Alessandro in the lead, they inched up the face of the cliff, sidestepping any footholds that looked (bad/badly).
9. Their muscles were aching (bad/badly) as they hammered pitons into the cliff.
10. Since they were feeling (good/well) about the day's work, they rested and planned the next day's climb.

Review: Exercise 5 Correcting Double Negatives

Rewrite each sentence, eliminating any double negatives. If a sentence contains no errors, write *correct.*

1. Most novice climbers don't know nothing about the basics of mountaineering.
2. Hiking is the least perilous type of mountaineering; it is not no riskier than walking.
3. Rock climbing and ice climbing should not be undertaken by no beginner without expert supervision.
4. Mixed climbing, a combination of rock climbing and ice climbing, is not meant for novices neither.
5. Climbers not wearing boots with cleated rubber soles should not begin the ascent.
6. It would be unusual for beginning climbers not to feel no jitters when they start.
7. Except when climbing on ice or snow, no more than two climbers should never be tied together on a single rope.
8. Climbing instructors never waste no time before explaining the proper use of pitons and carabiners in securing the rope.
9. Nonclimbers never have any idea of the tight teamwork climbers must develop.
10. Most careful climbers do not have hardly any serious mishaps.

Review: Exercise 6 Correcting Misplaced Modifiers

The following sentences describe the scene from *A Soldier of the Great War* that follows the passage featured in this workshop. Rewrite each sentence, correcting misplaced modifiers. If a sentence has no errors, write *correct.*

SAMPLE Shining silently in the cold night air, Alessandro gazed at the stars.
ANSWER Alessandro gazed at the stars shining silently in the cold night air.

1. Alessandro was constantly on the lookout for dangerous crevasses walking across the glacier.
2. Possibly obscuring deep chasms, he avoided any thin patches of snow.
3. The bleak vista lay before this lonely man stretching into miles of darkness.
4. The danger of crevasses recently cut into the glacier haunted the soldier.
5. He ran across the icy surface burning with fierce determination.
6. Perfectly hidden from view by a snowdrift, Alessandro narrowly avoided a pair of crevasses.
7. Alessandro leaped into the air beyond the point of feeling fear.
8. Alessandro completely lost all sense of time falling into a wide canyon.
9. Miraculously, he landed on a soft bed of snow in a kneeling position.
10. When he found that he had only survived by a miracle, he began to laugh.

Review: Exercise 7 Correcting Dangling Modifiers

The following sentences are based on the passage from *A Soldier of the Great War.* Rewrite the sentences, correcting each dangling modifier. In some cases you may need to reword the entire sentence. If a sentence contains no errors, write *correct.*

SAMPLE After crossing six ridges, trees did not appear again until he was in Italy.
ANSWER After crossing six ridges, he did not see trees again until he was in Italy.

1. Leaving the forest, a world of glaciated mountains stretched toward the horizon.
2. Rising vast in the distance, Alessandro was amazed by the mountains' immensity.
3. Tricked by the play of light and shadow, the mountains seemed distant to him.
4. Surveying the snow-filled pastures, hay-filled cabins dotted the landscape.
5. Offering shelter from the wind, Alessandro chose the cabin farthest from any settlement.
6. After walking for several hours after dusk, Alessandro stopped at the edge of the meadows.
7. Feeling the rivers of cold air, the proximity of the glacier was certain.
8. Rumbling almost imperceptibly, he was awed by its tremendous power.
9. Hoisting his body upward, the ice wall was scaled only with great difficulty.
10. Given a combination of luck and skill and perseverance, the peaks would be reachable by daylight.

Review: Exercise 8 Adding Modifiers to Sentences

The following sentences describe Alessandro and his friend Rafi's mountain-climbing expedition. Rewrite the sentences, adding modifiers as indicated in parentheses. (There will be more than one way to rewrite some sentences.)

1. Alessandro and Rafi began their preparations for their mountain climbing expedition. (Add *making their plans early.*)
2. They packed lightweight, high-energy foods. (Add *wanting to be sure they had nourishment for their journey.*)
3. Rafi was an inexperienced climber, but Alessandro was ready to help him. (Add *who was not used to such heights.*)
4. Novice climbers could easily lose their footing and very possibly their lives. (Add *climbing alone.*)
5. Alessandro reviewed the use of pitons and carabiners with Rafi. (Add *not knowing how much Rafi remembered.*)
6. Alessandro was in the lead, and Rafi followed behind him. (Add *because he was more competent.*)
7. Rafi could watch Alessandro's climbing strategies and copy them. (Add *by letting him go first.*)
8. Alessandro and Rafi inched their way up the face of the first cliff. (Add *checking their footholds carefully.*)
9. The expedition was more of a physical challenge than the two men had first believed. (Add *that they had dreamed about for so long.*)
10. The two men were extremely pleased at the progress they had made in a day. (Add *filled with challenges.*)

Review: Exercise 9

Proofreading

The following passage describes the artist Albert Bierstadt, whose painting appears on the opposite page. Rewrite the passage, correcting the errors in spelling, grammar, and usage. Add any missing punctuation. There are twenty-five errors.

Albert Bierstadt

[1]Born in Germany, Albert Bierstadt (1830-1902) was brought by his parents at the age of two to New Bedford, Massachusetts. [2]When he was twenty-three. [3]He returns to Germany to study painting. [4]He often traveled to Switzerland and Italy and made countless sketches of mountain landscapes becoming intrested in landscape painting.

Albert Bierstadt, *Sunrise on the Matterhorn,* after 1875

[5]Bierstadt returned to New Bedford in 1857 and the next year he joined a surveying expedition to the Rocky Mountains. [6]Their size and beauty overwhelmed him, he made many pencil and oil sketches. [7]When he was twenty-nine, moved to New York City and set up a studio there. [8]His huge landscape paintings commanded higher prices than those of anyone.

[9]His training in Europe maked him a master at drawing and oil sketching. [10]Making preliminary sketches from nature, his works were completed in the studio.

[11]Like many of his fellow artists, the unspoiled grandeur of the West was a frequent subject of Bierstadt's paintings. [12]His romantic paintings of the West become a symbol of national pride.

[13]Famous for his unusual technique, Bierstadt's paintings combined enormous scale with the delicatest suggestions of light and shadow. [14]The painting on this page which was based on sketches made during his travels through the Alps, is typical of his' style. [15]The delicately lit peek looks least real than the trees in the foreground.

[16]The hero in Mark Helprin's story crosses the Swiss Alps wanting bad to return home. [17]Here Bierstadt portrays one of the most grand of all the Swiss mountins the Matterhorn. [18]Does the painting remind you of Helprin's description of the "trick of light and shadow" that can make the Alps appear to be more distanter and more unreachable than they really are?

Review: Exercise 10

Mixed Review

Read the following brief biography of Mark Helprin. Then rewrite the sentences that follow it, correcting any errors in the use of modifiers. If you need to obtain information to complete your sentences, consult the biography.

Mark Helprin

Born in 1947 in New York City, Mark Helprin attended Harvard University, earning a bachelor's degree in 1969 and a master's degree in Middle Eastern studies in 1972. He then joined the Israeli armed forces, where he served in the infantry and in an elite unit of the air force. After further study at Princeton and Oxford universities, he moved to Brooklyn and began to write fiction. Helprin submitted a dozen stories to the *New Yorker* magazine before two stories were finally accepted at once. In 1975 he published *A Dove of the East and Other Stories;* two years later his first novel appeared. *Ellis Island and Other Stories* won the National Jewish Book Award in 1982, and Helprin was also awarded the prestigious Prix de Rome by the Institute for Arts and Letters. Helprin published his popular novel *Winter's Tale* in 1983. *A Soldier of the Great War* was published in 1991.

1. Helprin performed good as both a scholar and a soldier before turning to a literary career.
2. After settling in Brooklyn, writing became his primary pursuit.
3. The *New Yorker* magazine did not accept none of the first twelve stories that Helprin submitted.
4. The reviews of his third book, *Ellis Island and Other Stories,* were more positive than his first book, *A Dove of the East and Other Stories.*
5. Generally speaking, to Helprin most romantic fantasies are more vivider than most realistic tales.
6. Of all of Helprin's books, *Ellis Island and Other Stories* only received the National Jewish Book Award.
7. Racing over frozen winter landscapes, Helprin's novel *Winter's Tale* describes the exploits of a flying horse.
8. The heroes of Helprin's novels are adventurers who defeat evil beings with great courage and virtue.
9. In *Winter's Tale,* the hero is pursued by creatures called Short Tails, who are eviller than anyone.
10. A skilled mountain climber, Helprin's novels often depict courageous mountaineers on treacherous slopes.

Writing Application

TIME

For more about the writing process, see TIME Facing the Blank Page, pp. 109–119

Modifiers in Writing

Good writers use modifiers correctly and position them carefully to make their meaning clear. Notice, for example, the use of the italicized modifiers in this passage from "Tuesday Siesta," a short story by Gabriel García Márquez that has been translated into English by J. S. Bernstein.

> *Keeping to the protective shade of the almond trees,* the woman and the girl entered the town without disturbing the siesta. They went directly to the parish house. The woman scratched the metal grating *on the door* with her fingernail, waited a moment, and scratched again. An electric fan was humming inside. They did not hear the steps. They *hardly* heard the slight creaking of a door, and immediately a cautious voice, right next to the metal grating. . . .

Techniques with Modifiers

Try to apply some of García Márquez's techniques when you write and revise.

❶ Place modifiers as close as possible to the words they modify.

MISPLACED MODIFIER Keeping to the protective shade of the almond trees, *the town . . .*

GARCÍA MÁRQUEZ'S VERSION Keeping to the protective shade of the almond trees, *the woman and the girl . . .*

❷ Will moving a modifier make your meaning clearer? Compare the two positions of the prepositional phrase *on the door.*

CONFUSING PLACEMENT *On the door,* the woman scratched the metal grating with her fingernail . . .

GARCÍA MÁRQUEZ'S VERSION The woman scratched the metal grating *on the door* with her fingernail . . .

❸ Try not to create double negatives, especially with *hardly* and *scarcely.*

DOUBLE NEGATIVE They *couldn't hardly* hear the slight creaking . . .

GARCÍA MÁRQUEZ'S VERSION They *hardly* heard the slight creaking . . .

Practice On your paper, practice these techniques by revising the following paragraphs.

Born in Aracataca, Colombia, many of Gabriel García Márquez's stories and novels are set in small Latin American towns. *One Hundred Years of Solitude* portrays the history of the remote town of Macondo, one of the most popular books ever published in the Spanish-speaking world. Many critics, symbolizing the turbulence of Latin American politics, think Macondo and the people living there eccentric.

Magical and at times surreal, the author has a distinct writing style. After winning the Nobel Prize in literature, many new readers from all over the world were attracted to García Márquez. The author, who, in my opinion, doesn't have no patience for human rights abuses, has also won praise worldwide for his humanitarian efforts.

UNIT 19

Usage Glossary

19 Usage Glossary

Certain usages of English are preferred by most educated speakers and writers. The glossary in this unit presents some aspects of preferred usage that are particularly troublesome. It shows you how to choose between words that are often confused, and it advises you to avoid certain words and expressions when you are speaking or writing for school or business.

a, an The article *a* is used when the word that follows begins with a consonant sound: *a ticket.* Words that begin with a sounded *h* or the "yew" sound are thus also preceded by *a: a hurricane, a eulogy, a uniform.* The article *an* is used when the word that follows begins with a vowel sound or an unsounded *h: an umbrella, an hour.*

a lot, alot This expression, which means "a great number or a large amount," should always be written as two words. Some authorities advise that you avoid it completely in formal English.

> **A lot** of television programs show too much violence.

a while, awhile An article and a noun form the expression *a while.* Often the preposition *in* or *for* precedes *a while,* forming a prepositional phrase. The single word *awhile* is an adverb.

> She'll speak in **a while.**
>
> She'll speak for **a while.**
>
> She'll speak **awhile** before showing the filmstrip.

accept, except *Accept* is a verb meaning "to receive" or "to agree to." *Except* is occasionally used as a verb or a conjunction, but much more frequently it is used as a preposition meaning "but."

> Miki will **accept** the invitation to lunch.
>
> The restaurant is open every day **except** Monday. [preposition]

affect, effect *Affect* is a verb meaning "to cause a change in" or "to influence." *Effect* as a verb means "to bring about" or "to accomplish." As a noun *effect* means "result" or "that which has been brought about."

> Daily exercise will **affect** your health. [verb meaning "cause a change in"]
>
> Daily exercise will **effect** a positive change in your health. [verb meaning "bring about"]
>
> Daily exercise will have a good **effect** on your health. [noun meaning "result"]

ain't *Ain't* is never used in formal speaking or writing unless you are quoting the exact words of a character or real person. Instead of using *ain't,* say or write, *I am not; she is not;* and so on.

all ready, already *All ready,* written as two words, is an adjective phrase that means "completely ready." *Already,* written as one word, is an adverb that means "before" or "by this time."

Lloyd was **all ready** to go at seven o'clock, but his friends had **already** left without him.

all right, alright The expression *all right* should be written as two words. Although some dictionaries acknowledge the existence of the single word *alright,* this spelling is not generally accepted as correct.

I hope the baby is **all right.**

all the farther, all the faster These are informal expressions. It is much better to use *as far as* and *as fast as* in speaking and writing.

Reno was **as far as** I wanted to go.

Is this **as fast as** you can walk?

all together, altogether *All together* means "in a group." *Altogether* is an adverb meaning "completely" or "on the whole."

The actors joined hands and took a bow **all together.**

Altogether it was a very good play.

amount, number *Amount* and *number* both refer to quantity, but *amount* refers to nouns that cannot be counted, and *number* refers to nouns that can be counted.

A huge **amount** of lava spurted from the erupting volcano.

A **number** of volcanoes are still active today.

bad, badly See Unit 18.

being as, being that Although these expressions sometimes replace *because* or *since* in informal conversation, you should always avoid them in formal speaking and writing.

Because bears are hibernators, they sleep during the winter.

Since the movie has already started, let's come back later.

beside, besides *Beside* means "located at the side of." *Besides* is ordinarily used to mean "in addition to."

The cat sat **beside** the refrigerator.

Besides losing my gloves, I lost two buttons from my coat.

between, among *Between* should generally be used when comparing one person or thing with another person or thing or with an entire group.

It was difficult to choose **between** ice cream and pudding for dessert. [Two desserts are compared.]

What is the difference **between** this opera and others by Verdi? [One opera is compared with the entire group of Verdi's operas.]

Among is generally used to show a relationship in which more than two persons or things are considered as a group.

Tim's great-grandfather had lived **among** the Iroquois.

Exercise 1 Making Usage Choices

On your paper, write the correct word or expression from each pair in parentheses.

George Washington, Our First President

1. General George Washington fought with great determination for (a/an) independent United States.
2. As leader of the Continental Army, Washington tried to make sure his troops were (alright/all right), even though a great (number/amount) of them had poor health and low spirits.
3. Washington's courage and determination to win (affected/effected) his soldiers, improving their morale.
4. After his stunning victory, Washington rested (a while/awhile) at home at Mount Vernon on the Potomac River.
5. When delegates from the states met (all together/altogether) to write the Constitution, they chose Washington from (among/between) all the delegates to be their leader.
6. Washington was asked to (accept/except) the office of president after the vote of the first Electoral College.
7. President Washington was (all ready/already) widely known and respected when he took office.
8. As the first president of the United States, Washington did (alot/a lot) to shape the duties of his office and to (affect/effect) a responsive administrative system to lead the nation forward.
9. (Beside/Besides) showing strong leadership, Washington went (all the farther/as far as) he could go to mold the young nation into a strong republic.
10. It (ain't/is not) at all surprising that the capital of the United States was named in honor of Washington.

borrow, lend, loan The verb *borrow* means "to take something with the understanding that it must be returned." The verb *lend* means "to give something with the understanding that it will be returned." *Loan* should be used as a noun. Although *loan* may be used as a verb, *lend* is the preferred usage.

Mari wants to **borrow** Victor's bicycle. [verb]

Victor will **lend** her the bicycle if she puts air in the tires. [verb]

Mari asked her aunt for a **loan** so she could buy a bicycle. [noun]

bring, take *Bring* means "to carry from a distant place to a closer one." *Take* means "to carry from a nearby place to a more distant one."

Bring the dog when you come to our house on Saturday.

Don't **take** the dog when you go to the Bradleys'.

can, may *Can* implies the ability to do something. *May* implies permission to do something or the possibility of doing it.

You **may** go skiing this weekend if you **can** find a place to rent the necessary equipment.

can't hardly, can't scarcely These expressions are considered double negatives, since *hardly* and *scarcely* by themselves have a negative meaning. Do not use *hardly* and *scarcely* with *not* or *-n't.*

Juliana **can hardly** believe that she is taller than both her mother and her brother.

I **can scarcely** hear my television program when my neighbor plays the drums.

could of, might of, must of, should of, would of The helping verb *have,* not the preposition *of,* should follow *could, might, must, should,* or *would.*

I **could have** danced all night.

I **might have** won the singing award if I had not lost my voice the day before.

different from, different than The expression *different from* is generally preferred to *different than.*

Square dancing is **different from** ballroom dancing.

doesn't, don't *Doesn't* is a contraction, or shortened form, of *does not* and is used with *she, he, it,* and singular nouns. *Don't* is a contraction of *do not* and is used with *I, you, we, they,* and plural nouns.

My mother is one commuter who **doesn't** mind long bus rides.

Most subway riders **don't** expect comfort.

emigrate, immigrate *Emigrate* means "to leave one country to settle in another." *Immigrate* means "to enter a country in order to live there permanently." With *emigrate* use *from,* and with *immigrate* use *to* or *into.*

Roberto will **emigrate** from Mexico this spring.

He will **immigrate** to the United States.

farther, further Use *farther* to refer to physical distance. Use *further* to refer to degree or time.

Compact cars can go **farther** on a gallon of gasoline than full-sized cars can.

Argue no **further**—I will do as you suggest!

Exercise 2 Making Usage Choices

On your paper, write the correct word or expression from each pair in parentheses.

Abraham Lincoln, a President of the People

1. As a young man, Abraham Lincoln had to (borrow/lend) money in order to open a store.
2. (Because/Being that) Lincoln always dealt fairly with people, he earned the nickname Honest Abe.
3. As president, Lincoln (could of/could have) isolated himself, but his style was (different from/different than) that of his predecessors.
4. If I had to choose (between/among) the Gettysburg Address and Lincoln's second inaugural address, I would choose the second inaugural address as the better speech.
5. Other issues (beside/besides) slavery divided the North and the South.
6. Toward the end of Lincoln's first term, the Civil War was going (badly/bad) for the North.
7. Many people who (emigrate/immigrate) to this country know all about Lincoln.
8. I (can't hardly/can hardly) believe that a great man like Lincoln was assassinated.
9. (Can/May) we borrow this biography of Lincoln? Ted (doesn't/don't) know where ours is.
10. Ann will (bring/take) the biography with her when she comes back on Sunday.

fewer, less *Fewer* is generally used to refer to things or qualities that can be counted. *Less* is generally used to refer to things or qualities that cannot be counted. In addition, *less* is sometimes used with figures that are regarded as single amounts or single quantities.

Why did **fewer** people come to this year's gallery opening than last year's?

There is **less** space in the new building than there was in the old one.

The rent in the new gallery is **less** than 400 dollars a month. [The money is treated as a single sum, not as individual dollars.]

good, well See Unit 18.

had of The word *of* should not be used between *had* and a past participle.

I wish I **had known** that you were ill.

hanged, hung When your meaning is "put to death by hanging," use *hanged.* In all other cases use *hung.*

Although Benedict Arnold escaped punishment for his treachery in the American Revolution, his messenger, John André, was caught and **hanged** as a spy.

Clara **hung** her oil painting in a prominent place in the school auditorium.

in, into Use *in* to indicate location "inside" or "within" a place. Use *into* to indicate movement or direction to a place, generally from the outside to a point within.

The onions were **in** the stew.

The chef put the roast **into** the oven.

irregardless, regardless Both the prefix *ir-* and the suffix *-less* have negative meanings. When they are used together, they produce a double negative, which is incorrect. Therefore, you should use *regardless* rather than *irregardless.*

Regardless of the heat, the workers at the steel mill remained on the job.

this kind, these kinds Because *kind* is singular, it is modified by the singular from *this* or *that. This* and *that* should also be used with the nouns *sort* and *type* (*this type, that type, this sort, that sort*). When the plural *kinds* is used, the plural form *these* or *those* modifies it. *These* and *those* should be used with the plural nouns *sorts* and *types.*

This kind of exercise is challenging.

These kinds of exercises are easy.

That sort of fruit is delicious.

Those sorts of fruits are delicious.

Exercise 3 **Making Usage Choices**

On your paper, write the correct word or expression from each pair in parentheses.

Theodore Roosevelt, a Man of Determination

1. Theodore Roosevelt's ancestors (emigrated/immigrated) from Holland during the 1640s, (bringing/taking) their belongings with them.
2. Roosevelt fought so (good/well) in the Spanish-American War that he gained national attention.
3. Many of President Roosevelt's policies were (different from/different than) those of his predecessor, William McKinley.
4. Roosevelt's conservation efforts went (farther/further) than those of any previous president; he (could have/could of) been an influence on nature groups.
5. An enthusiastic leader, Roosevelt put a great deal of energy (in/into) his work.
6. (These kind/These kinds) of qualities made Theodore Roosevelt a good president, (regardless/irregardless) of his faults.
7. If I (had/had of) known more about President Roosevelt, I might have seen the merit in much that he did.
8. Even those people who criticize Roosevelt (doesn't/don't) deny his great determination.
9. Theodore Roosevelt wrote no (less/fewer) than forty books.
10. Hunting trophies (hanged/hung) on the walls of his home.
11. Roosevelt was a president who had an unforgettable (effect/affect) on the people of the country.
12. They (could hardly/couldn't hardly) ignore his bravery.
13. Because he kept right on talking after he was shot while making a speech, people (accepted/excepted) him as a hero.
14. Some critics believe that Roosevelt (took/brought) many imperialistic viewpoints to the presidency.
15. Others say those viewpoints were not so (different from/different than) what many politicians of his day believed.

lay, lie *Lay* means "to place" or "to put" something down. It always takes a direct object. *Lie* means "to recline" or "to be positioned"; it does not take an object.

Lay the bar of soap on the edge of the sink.

I like to **lie** under a warm blanket in the winter.

Occasionally there is confusion in sorting out the principal parts of these verbs. Notice the similarities and differences between the two.

BASE FORM	lay	lie
PRESENT PARTICIPLE	laying	lying
PAST FORM	laid	lay
PAST PARTICIPLE	laid	lain

He **laid** the bar of soap on the edge of the sink this morning.

Last night I **lay** under my warm blanket and slept soundly.

He had **laid** his toothbrush down beside the soap.

I have **lain** under those wonderful blankets on every chilly night.

learn, teach *Learn* means "to gain knowledge." *Teach* means "to instruct" or "to give knowledge to."

I **learned** to speak Swahili.

My sister Midori **teaches** organic chemistry at Yale.

leave, let *Leave* means "to go away" or "to depart." *Let* means "to allow" or "to permit."

Lian had to **leave** the auditorium.

The usher **let** her use the house telephone.

With the word *alone,* however, you may use either *let* or *leave.*

Leave me alone. **Let** me alone.

like, as Use *like,* a preposition, to introduce a prepositional phrase. Use *as,* a subordinating conjunction, to introduce a subordinate clause. Many experts believe that *like* should not be used before a clause in formal English.

Kathleen sings **like** an angel.

Maya thinks **as** I do in this matter.

loose, lose Use the adjective *loose* when you mean "free," "not firmly attached," or "not fitting tightly." Use the verb *lose* when you mean "to have no longer," "to misplace," or "to fail to win."

That button is so **loose** I'm afraid I will **lose** it.

passed, past *Passed* is the past and the past participle form of *to pass. Past* is used as an adjective, a noun, a preposition, or an adverb.

The challenger in the race **passed** the leader. [verb]

I paid many bills this **past** month. [adjective]

San Antonio is a city with an interesting **past.** [noun]

Make a sharp right turn **past** the bank. [preposition]

When did the bus drive **past?** [adverb]

precede, proceed Use *precede* when you mean "to go or come before." Use *proceed* when you mean "to continue" or "to move along."

In a dictionary, the entry for *airplane* **precedes** that for *airship.*

An airplane can **proceed** at a faster speed than an airship.

raise, rise The verb *raise* means "to cause to move upward" or "to lift up." It always takes an object. The verb *rise* means "to get up" or "to go up." It is an intransitive verb and never takes an object.

We will **raise** the flag at six o'clock tomorrow morning.

They will **rise** at seven o'clock for exercise.

reason is, because *Because* means "for the reason that." Therefore, do not use *because* after *reason is.* Use either *reason is that* or *because* alone.

The **reason** Leroy entered the marathon **is that** he enjoys long-distance running.

Leroy entered the marathon **because** he enjoys running.

respectfully, respectively Use *respectfully* to mean "with respect." Use *respectively* to mean "in the order named."

The basketball champion shook the president's hand **respectfully.**

Ann and Arlene are my aunt and cousin, **respectively.**

says, said *Says* is the third-person singular of the verb *say. Said* is the past tense of *say.* Do not use *says* when you mean *said.*

Enrique always **says** that he is just an average pianist.

Last week my teacher **said** I was ready to perform in public.

sit, set *Sit* means "to be seated." It rarely takes an object. *Set* means "to put" or "to place," and it generally takes an object. When *set* is used to mean "the sun is going down," it does not take an object.

Before a show starts, many people find it hard to **sit** quietly.

The stage manager **set** the flowers on the mantelpiece.

The lighting designer saw to it that the sun **set** in a blaze of color.

than, then *Than* is a conjunction. Use it in comparisons and to show exception.

Winston is more athletic **than** Carl.

The winner is none other **than** last year's champion, Rashida.

Then is an adverb and is mostly used to refer to time. *Then* is also used to mean "soon afterward," "the time mentioned," "at another time," "for that reason," "in that case," and "besides."

Sam was an inexperienced cook **then.**

You bowl first, and **then** it will be my turn.

By **then** we will be experts.

If you won't try it, **then** I will.

this here, that there Do not use *here* and *there* after *this* and *that.*

I want to look at **this** newspaper.

Please hand me **that** lantern.

where at Do not use *at* after *where.*

Where is Salt Lake City?

who, whom See Unit 17.

Exercise 4 Making Usage Choices

On your paper, write the correct word or expression from each pair in parentheses.

John F. Kennedy, a Vibrant Leader

1. One reason John F. Kennedy is still admired is (because/that) he showed exceptional leadership qualities.
2. As a young man, Kennedy toured Europe, talking to heads of state to (learn/teach) their political views.
3. (These kind/These kinds) of situations helped prepare Kennedy for the presidency.
4. When Kennedy took office, he (raised/rised) the nation's morale with his inaugural address.
5. Kennedy declared that "the torch has been (passed/past) to a new generation of Americans."
6. Much of his charm (lay/laid) in his fine speaking ability.
7. (Like/As) you would expect from people interested in the arts, the Kennedys invited many performers to the White House.
8. During the missile crisis, Kennedy refused to (leave/let) the Soviet Union keep missiles on the island of Cuba.
9. Kennedy's decision to (precede/proceed) with a naval blockade of Cuba was a difficult one.
10. It was painful for Americans to (loose/lose) such a young and vibrant leader.

Exercise 5 Making Usage Choices

On your paper, write the correct word or expression from each pair in parentheses.

Franklin Roosevelt, a President During Hard Times

1. Many people (said/says) that Franklin Roosevelt was a great president.
2. After being stricken with polio in 1921, Roosevelt had to work harder (than/then) ever to maintain an active life.
3. (This/This here) paralysis struck when he was thirty-nine.
4. Warm Springs, Georgia, was (where he took treatments/where he took treatments at).
5. Roosevelt did not (set/sit) idly during the Depression.
6. People (who/whom) had lost everything looked to Roosevelt for hope.
7. The Tennessee Valley Authority and the Works Progress Administration were, (respectively/respectfully), a natural resources corporation and an employment program.
8. After Pearl Harbor was attacked, Roosevelt, (then/than) in his third term, led the country into World War II.
9. In February 1945 at Yalta, Roosevelt and Winston Churchill met with Joseph Stalin, with (who/whom) they planned Germany's defeat and its postwar occupation.
10. After Roosevelt's death on April 12, 1945, President Truman (respectively/respectfully) proclaimed a national day of mourning.

Exercise 6 Make Usage Choices

On your paper, write the correct word or expression from each pair in parentheses.

Puerto Rico, Past and Future

1. When Christopher Columbus reached Puerto Rico in 1493, the Arawak (already/all ready) inhabited the island.
2. Columbus and the Spanish explorer Ponce de León landed on the island in 1493 and 1508, (respectfully/respectively).
3. (Awhile/A while) after Ponce de León founded the island's first Spanish colony, he became its governor.
4. Spain ceded Puerto Rico to the United States in 1898, but nineteen years (passed/past) before Puerto Rico was designated a U.S. territory.
5. In 1952 (a/an) effort to establish the Commonwealth of Puerto Rico was approved by the citizens and government leaders of both Puerto Rico and the United States.
6. Since then the debate (between/among) Puerto Ricans has been about whether the island should be a commonwealth, an independent nation, or a state.
7. For decades, more Puerto Ricans have lived in the city of San Juan (then/than) in any other community on the island.
8. (Irregardless/Regardless) of the problems that occurred after World War II, Puerto Rico has one of the highest standards of living among the Caribbean islands.
9. Due to urbanization, (fewer/less) Puerto Ricans live in rural areas.
10. Perhaps (farther/further) debate about Puerto Rican statehood is inevitable.

Exercise 7 Making Usage Choices

On your paper, write the correct word or expression from each pair in parentheses.

Native American Place Names

1. I have found that (a lot/alot) of Americans don't know that many place names are derived from Native American languages.
2. If you (ain't/aren't) sure about the derivation of a place name, see if it is explained in a dictionary or an encyclopedia.
3. The (amount/number) of place names in the United States is more than 3.5 million.
4. We (can/may) make a list of Native American place names in our state.
5. Many place names aren't very (different than/different from) their source words.
6. (Beside/Besides) adopting tribal names, such as Dakota and Delaware, as place names, settlers often adopted descriptive Native American words, such as *yaphank,* which means "river bank" in Algonquian.
7. My trip to Meddybemps, Maine, (learned/taught) me two things: that the name comes from an Algonquian word meaning "plenty of alewives" and that an alewife is a type of small fish.
8. A (loose/lose) translation of the Ojibway word *kichi* is "big"; Kichi Lake, in Minnesota, received its name from the Ojibway word.
9. *Nebraska* is a Sioux word that means "a wide, flat river"; the word refers to the Platte River, which (lays/lies) in the southern part of the state.
10. Although the names of Pennawa Creek, Florida, and Penacook, New Hampshire, look similar, their meanings—"turkey" and "sloping place"—are quite (different from/different than) each other.
11. The Mississippi River is not as long as the Nile River or the Amazon River; the Gulf of Mexico is (all the farther/as far as) the Mississippi River goes.
12. (Because/Being as) so many Cherokee were forced to migrate to Oklahoma during the nineteenth century, Cherokee is a common place name in that state.
13. A town in Oklahoma is called Pawhuska; (this/this here) word means "white hair."
14. I've learned that the word *ponca* comes from *pa-bonga,* meaning "sacred leader," but I don't know how it (could have/could of) become the name of a town.
15. The Native Americans of Acoma, which is located on a mile-high mesa in New Mexico, named their pueblo (good/well); *acoma* means "sky city."
16. (These kind/These kinds) of place names appear to be among the oldest names in North America.
17. The large (amount/number) of lakes in Minnesota may be why the Dakota used the words *minne,* meaning "water," and *sota,* meaning "reflection of sky upon water," to name the region.
18. The banks (beside/besides) the Olentangy River in central Ohio are streaked in red; hence, the river has an Algonquian name meaning "place where paint is found."
19. The hills for which Massachusetts was named (lie/lay) near Massachusetts Bay.
20. May I (borrow/loan) your book so that I can research the name Nippersink?

Exercise 8 Making Usage Choices

On your paper, write the correct word or expression from each pair in parentheses.

Spirituals

1. The first time I heard a spiritual, I was surprised by the (affect/effect) the music had on me.
2. I had heard that spirituals were known as sorrow songs, yet I didn't find the music (all together/altogether) sad.
3. In fact, the inspirational lyrics and haunting melody made my spirits (raise/rise).
4. My friends agree that these songs don't make them feel (bad/badly) but, rather, inspired and hopeful.
5. When I decided to do some research on spirituals, the first thing I did was to go (in/into) the library's audio room.
6. I then (preceded/proceeded) to locate such songs as "Go Down, Moses," "Michael, Row the Boat Ashore," and "Steal Away."
7. I decided to (sit/set) all my research books on the table and concentrate on the music.
8. Even now, I (can hardly/can't hardly) believe how inspiring I found these songs of hardship and faith in religious salvation.
9. If you listen closely to a spiritual, you (can/may) hear how the verses alternate with a refrain.
10. The lyrics of some spirituals express the singers' desire to have the cruel world (leave/let) them alone.
11. I listened to a tape of the singers Dock Reed and Vera Hall, (who/whom) researchers recorded in the 1930s and 1940s.
12. The recording was made with primitive equipment, so the sound quality is (alright/all right) but not excellent.
13. Before starting my research, I (had/had of) thought that spirituals originated in America.
14. Some people (doesn't/don't) believe spirituals originated here, since there are African elements in many of them.
15. Spirituals did not achieve international popularity until the Jubilee Singers, an American group from Fisk University, (brought/took) their act to Europe in the 1870s.
16. It (must of/must have) been quite an experience to hear those powerful songs sung by such beautiful voices.
17. By the early twentieth century, the spiritual had begun to be treated (like/as) a true artistic form: songs were published and performed by choral groups and symphony orchestras.
18. African Americans such as Paul Robeson and William Grant Still were (accepted/excepted) around the world as fine performers of spirituals.
19. The reason spirituals are an important part of our musical heritage is (because/that) they have influenced many other types of music, from folk to gospel.
20. Last week my friend Jeanine (says/said) that she would be going to the library to learn more about spirituals.

UNIT 19

Grammar Review

Usage Glossary

The following quotations deal with different aspects of our relationship with nature. Conflicts with nature, the need for harmony with nature, and the wonders of nature are all discussed by poets and novelists. The quotations, some of which appear in translation, have been annotated to show usage items covered in this unit.

Literature Model

Quotations About Nature

The articles *a* used before a word beginning with a consonant and *an* used before a word beginning with an unsounded *h*

To see a World in a Grain of Sand
And a Heaven in a Wild Flower,
Hold Infinity in the palm of your hand
And Eternity in an hour.

From "Auguries of Innocence" by William Blake

May used to suggest possibility

It may be that the stars of heaven appear fair and pure simply because they are so far away from us, and we know nothing of their private life.

From *The Romantic School* by Heinerich Heine, translated from the German

The intransitive verb *lie*

The whole secret of the study of nature lies in learning how to use one's eyes.

From *Nouvelles Lettres d'un Voyageur* by George Sand, translated from French

The conjunction *than* used in a comparison

I like trees because they seem more resigned to the way they have to live than other things do.

From *O Pioneers!* by Willa Cather

Doesn't used with a singular pronoun

Something there is that doesn't love a wall,
That sends the frozen-ground-swell under it
And spills the upper boulders in the sun,
And makes gaps even two can pass abreast.

From "Mending Wall" by Robert Frost

Surrounded by the voracity of nature, Aureliano and Amaranta Ursula continued cultivating the oregano and the begonias and defended their world with demarcations of quick lime, building the last trenches in the age-old war between man and ant.

From *One Hundred Years of Solitude* by Gabriel García Márquez, translated from the Spanish by Gregory Rabassa

The preposition *between* used to show a relationship between two elements

Mankind's true moral test, its fundamental test (which lies deeply buried from view), consists of its attitude towards those who are at its mercy: animals.

From *The Unbearable Lightness of Being* by Milan Kundera, translated from the Czech by Michael Henry Heim

The relative pronoun *who* in the nominative case because it is the subject of a clause

Review: Exercise 1 Making Usage Choice

The following sentences describe the seasons of the year. On your paper, write the correct word or expression from each parentheses.

1. In many areas of this country, each season—spring, summer, autumn, or winter—is (different from/different than) every other season.
2. There is however, (less/fewer) difference in the seasons in the southern United States than in other regions.
3. In the spring, the geese fly by the thousands across the prairie sky, (emigrating/immigrating) from their southern winter habitat.
4. Thawing snow fills the streams and rivers with (a lot/alot) of water, sometimes bringing on flooding.
5. The warmth of summer (affects/effects) all plant life, bringing green lawns, buzzing insects, and brightly colored flowers.
6. By June most people have (hanged/hung) their sweaters and jackets back in the closet and are eagerly anticipating the hot summer months.
7. Warm summer weather invites youngsters everywhere to jump (in/into) swimming pools.
8. Summer (proceeds/precedes) the coming of autumn, when the weather usually turns cooler.
9. I wish you (could of/could have) seen the brilliant orange, red, and yellow colors of the autumn leaves in Vermont this year.
10. In the winter, all trees (accept/except) the evergreens are bare, brisk winds blow, winter storms leave a white carpet of snow, and streams and rivers freeze solid into thick layers of ice.

Review: Exercise 2 **Making Usage Choices**

The following sentences describe endangered and extinct animals. On your paper, write the correct word or expression from each parentheses.

1. (Because/Being as) dinosaurs are so popular, people flock to museums to see their skeletons.
2. Dinosaurs roamed the earth for 120 million years (all together/altogether).
3. I wish someone would (learn/teach) me more about dinosaurs.
4. The (number/amount) of dinosaur species that populated the earth was greater than I had imagined.
5. (Irregardless/Regardless) of how many dinosaurs there once were, they all became extinct.
6. Many animals are (affected/effected) adversely when their habitat is altered.
7. The black rhinoceros and the giant panda, which roam over sub-Saharan Africa and China, (respectively/respectfully), are both endangered.
8. (Where at/Where) do grizzly bears, lynxes, and red wolves live?
9. If people are not careful, they might (loose/lose) these animals permanently.
10. Far too many animals have (already/all ready) become extinct, thus diminishing the world's biological resources and sometimes upsetting the delicate balance of nature.

Review: Exercise 3 **Making Usage Choices**

The following sentences discuss topics related to astronomy. On your paper, write the correct word or expression from each parentheses.

1. (This here/This) machine is a telescope, which is used to view the moon, stars, comets, planets, and other celestial bodies.
2. Scientists will travel (farther/further) than most other people will to get a good view of a total eclipse of the sun.
3. Earth revolves around the sun, just (like/as) the other eight major planets of our solar system do.
4. Our solar system (lies/lays) within one swirling arm of the Milky Way galaxy.
5. The Milky Way acquired its name from our view of it as (a/an) hazy, luminous, milk-like band of stars enveloping the night sky.
6. (Farther/Further) in space, beyond the Milky Way, lie perhaps 100 billion other galaxies.
7. The Milky Way galaxy alone has no (fewer/less) than 200 billion stars.
8. The reason stars appear to twinkle is (that/because) the turbulent motion of Earth's atmosphere distorts the light that comes from them.
9. The sun and the moon appear to (rise/raise) and set in the sky.
10. Perhaps one day we will be able to travel easily (between/among) the stars.

Review: Exercise 4 Making Usage Choices

The following sentences relate to the study of ocean life. On your paper, write the correct word or expression from each parentheses.

1. Some people believe that life (don't/doesn't) exist in the icy depths of the oceans.
2. Oceanographers, however, (can't hardly/can hardly) enumerate the various kinds of life found in the oceans of the world.
3. You must (bring/take) special equipment with you when you explore the ocean depths.
4. (Beside/Besides) being the home of fish and mammals of normal size, the oceans are home for plankton, which are microscopic animals and plants.
5. On a television documentary I saw the other day, an oceanographer (says/said) that *plankton* is a Greek word meaning "wandering."
6. Plankton drifts through the upper levels of the sea rather (than/then) in the depths.
7. (These kind/These kinds) of living organisms become food for other marine life.
8. My cousin, (who/whom) I believe is an expert on ocean life, told me that many deep-sea fish have fantastic shapes.
9. I (should of/should have) joined my cousin on her last deep-sea adventure.
10. My cousin said that she always thought my idea of a deep-sea adventure was to (sit/set) my fishing line in the water and wait for a fish to bite.

Review: Exercise 5 Making Usage Choices

The following sentences describe rain forests. On your paper, write the correct word or expression from each parentheses.

1. Many people feel that it is not (alright/all right) to exploit rain forests.
2. If care is not taken to preserve these forests, they will be gone after (a while/awhile).
3. Some plants seem to thrive (irregardless/regardless) of where they grow.
4. Plants that grow (well/good) on the forest floor are the same kind as those that thrive in dimly lighted buildings.
5. Far below the forest's green canopy, the ground is interlaced with streams and rivers formed in times (passed/past).
6. No one knows the exact (number/amount) of plants and insects in the rain forest.
7. If you travel to a rain forest, you will want to (bring/take) a camera with you to record on film the beauty of the extraordinary scenery.
8. I was able to capture the exquisite detail of the plants because my friend had (loaned/lent/borrowed) me a special, high-resolution camera.
9. Only after several years of training (can/may) a nature enthusiast identify many of the different forms of wildlife in a rain forest.
10. As I (preceded/proceeded) through the forest on my last visit, I encountered a band of monkeys rapidly making their way through the treetops.

Review: Exercise 6 **Writing Sentences with Correct Word Usage**

Choose five of the pairs of words below. For each pair, write a sentence using each word.

bring/take	between/among
good/well	in/into
doesn't/don't	bad/badly
who/whom	lay/lie
fewer/less	farther/further

SAMPLE ANSWER
a. Our yard has *fewer* weeds this year than our neighbor's yard has.
b. We have had *less* rainfall this year than we've had in several years.

Review: Exercise 7

Proofreading

The following passage describes the life and work of Louis Comfort Tiffany, whose stained-glass window is reproduced on the opposite page. Rewrite the passage, correcting the errors in spelling, grammar, and usage. Add any missing punctuation. There are twenty-five errors.

Louis Comfort Tiffany

[1]Louis Comfort Tiffany (1848–1933) was the son of Charles Lewis Tiffany a gem merchant and the founder of the famed Tiffany and Company, manufacturers of fine silverware. [2]The younger Tiffany became excepted as a designer of distinctive glass. [3]Louis Tiffanys' designs reflected the Art Nouveau style of the passed, particularly the late nineteenth century. [4]The reason this here art movement came into being was because the handcrafting of objects was being revitalized as a reaction against the intense industrial activity of the late 1800s. [5]The movement toward handcrafted objects was meant to give naturel beauty and artistic impact to ordinary objects. [6]Art Nouveau was different than other art forms because it characteristically used rounded edges and iridescent colors.

[7]Louis Tiffany began his career making stained-glass windows as the one shown on the opposite page. [8]He used many kinds of colored glass, including opaque glass opalescent glass, and "satin glass," which was developed around 1880. [9]Each piece of glass generally would of contained more then a single color or kind of decoration. [10]The glass pieces were joined together with lead beading and then they were framed in a variety of ways. [11]In the work on the next page, Tiffany sat a natural outdoor scene in a stylized wooden frame.

[12]A increasing amount of artists and writers of this age struggled to "get back to nature." [13]They hoped to counteract the affects of industrialists, who were

Louis Comfort Tiffany, *Autumn Landscape,* 1923

scavenging the land for raw materials. [14]The literary quotations in this review explores our relationship to nature. [15]We seprate ourselves from nature in our homes and our buildings, and yet you long to act naturally. [16]This conflict among human ways and the ways of nature are reflected in Tiffanys stylized window which celebrates nature in an all together self-conscious, highly crafted way.

Review: Exercise 8

Mixed Review

The following sentences provide information about authors. On your paper, write the correct word or expression from each parentheses.

1. Writers often focus on nature, (like/as) many other artists do.
2. Knowing the details of an author's life can help a reader (farther/further) understand that person's writings.
3. In addition to being a poet, the English Romantic author William Blake was also (a/an) artist and illustrator of his own works.
4. The nineteenth-century German composer Robert Schumann had to choose (between/among) many of Heinrich Heine's poems when he was composing the song cycle *Poet's Love.*
5. (Being that/Because) George Sand was troubled by the poor treatment of women in her time, she often wrote about social injustice.
6. Willa Cather frequently wrote about people who had (emigrated/immigrated) to the United States to farm the prairie lands of the Midwest.
7. Robert Frost, (who/whom) many people admire, won four Pulitzer Prizes for his lyrical poetry, most of which describes the people and landscapes of New England.
8. Frost's work, (besides/beside) being highly romantic, also contains much irony.
9. The reading public probably (doesn't/don't) know that Nobel Prize-winning author Gabriel García Márquez founded an organization for human rights.
10. The poet and novelist Milan Kundera agreed to (accept/except) French citizenship in 1980, after his political writings cost him his Czechoslovakian citizenship.
11. As a young man, Blake admired Michelangelo and Dürer, artists of Italy and Germany, (respectfully, respectively).
12. In his later years, Blake created (less/fewer) poems than in his youth.
13. Earning a law degree was (as far as/all the farther) Heine went in his law career.
14. One (couldn't hardly/could hardly) call Sand a conventional woman of her time.
15. Many years (past/passed) before critics recognized Sand's literary stature.
16. The reason Cather wrote about pioneers is (because/that) she lived among them during her childhood in rural Nebraska.
17. Cather's love of the American landscape greatly (effected/affected) her writing.
18. When Robert Frost went to England in 1912, he (took/brought) with him vivid memories of his native land.
19. In *One Hundred Years of Solitude,* García Márquez (sets/sits) the family saga in the fictional town of Macondo, a place much like his own hometown in Aracataca, Colombia.
20. Strains of pessimism keep Kundera's novels from being (all together/altogether) humorous.

Writing Application

TIME

For more about the writing process, see TIME Facing the Blank Page, pp. 109–119

Word Usage in Writing

The following passage from "The Most Beautiful Place on Earth" by Edward Abbey contains words that writers sometimes use incorrectly. Read the passage, concentrating on the italicized words.

The view is open and perfect *in* all directions *except* to the west where the ground *rises* and the skyline is only a few hundred yards away. Looking toward the mountains I *can* see the dark gorge of the Colorado River five or six miles away, carved through the sandstone mesa, though nothing of the river itself down inside the gorge. Southward, on the far side of the river, lies the Moab valley *between* thousand-foot walls of rock, with the town of Moab somewhere on the valley floor, too small to be seen from here. Beyond the Moab valley is more canyon and tableland stretching away to the Blue Mountains fifty miles south.

Techniques with Word Usage

Try to use these words correctly when you write and revise your own work.

1. *Except* is most frequently used as a preposition meaning "but." It should not be confused with the verb *accept,* meaning "to receive" or "to agree to."

INCORRECT USE The view is open and perfect in all directions *accept* to the west . . .

ABBEY'S USE The view is open and perfect in all directions *except* to the west . . .

2. The verb *rise,* which means "to get up" or "to go up," never takes an object. It should not be confused with *raise,* which always takes an object.

INCORRECT USE to the west where the ground *raises* . . .

ABBEY'S USE to the west where the ground *rises* . . .

Usage Glossary

Practice Practice correct usage by rewriting the following passage, using a separate sheet of paper. Choose the correct word from each pair in parentheses.

The most beautiful place in my city is a large park where I can ride my bike on weekends. Some cities have nothing (accept/except) block after block of high-rise buildings, so I think I'm lucky to live close to a green, wooded area. Every Saturday morning, as soon as the sun (rises/raises), I'm off on my bike along the trail that winds through the park. At one point the path divides, and it's always hard to decide (among/between) the two forks. One leads (in/into) dark, secluded woods. The other goes (passed/past) an area that the city rents out to people who want to (rise/raise) their own vegetables. One of the women (who/whom) gardens there always offers me one of her luscious red tomatoes. I say politely, "No, thanks," but one of these days I just (can/may) (except/accept) her generous gift. The only thing missing on these Saturday outings is someone to talk to. I'm hoping that my classmate Justin will buy a bike. (Among/Between) all my friends, he's the one who would most enjoy Saturday mornings in the park.

UNIT 20

Capitalization

20.1 Capitalization of Sentences

■ Capitalize the first word of every sentence.

Traditionally, a comedy ends with a marriage between the principal characters.

Have you read her latest novel?

Capitalizing Quotations

■ Capitalize the first word of a direct quotation that is a complete sentence.

Robert E. Lee once wrote, "**D**uty is the sublimest word in our language."

"**H**appiness lies not in the mere possession of money," he observed. "**I**t lies in the joy of achievement."

The first word of a quotation should not be capitalized unless the entire quotation can stand as a complete sentence or begins with a capital in the original text.

The ecologist reminded the audience to save "**t**he air, the water, the animals, and the trees."

An indirect quotation should not be capitalized. An **indirect quotation,** often introduced by *that,* does not repeat a person's or a document's exact words.

Amendment VI of the U.S. Constitution states that **a**ccused persons have the right to a speedy trial.

Capitalization

Exercise 1 Capitalizing Sentences and Quotations

On your paper, rewrite the following sentences, correcting any errors in capitalization.

The Words of Thomas Paine

1. writer and political theorist Thomas Paine wrote, "it is the object only of war that makes it honorable."
2. he pointed out that those who expected to reap the blessings of freedom must "Undergo the fatigue of supporting it."
3. "every spot of the Old World is overrun with oppression," wrote Paine in *Common Sense.* "freedom hath been hunted round the globe."
4. Paine observed that In its best state, government was a necessary evil and that In its worst state, government was intolerable.
5. "Suspicion is the companion of mean souls," Paine wrote, "And the bane of all good society."

Capitalizing with Parentheses

- Capitalize the first word of a sentence in parentheses that stands by itself. Do not capitalize a sentence within parentheses that is contained within another sentence.

Webster's first dictionary encouraged a distinctive American spelling of British words. (**F**or instance, the British word *honour* was replaced by the American word *honor.*)

A major cotton-producing state in the antebellum South (***a**ntebel-lum* means "before the war") was Georgia.

Exercise 2 Capitalizing Sentences and Quotations

On your paper, rewrite any of the following sentences that have errors in capitalization, correcting the errors. Write the word *correct* if a sentence has no errors.

1. one line of Langston Hughes's poem "Dream Deferred" asks, "what happens to a dream deferred?"
2. In 1934 Chiang Kai-shek (He was the Chinese Nationalist leader) said that the Chinese people would improve the nation if they could live "Artistically."
3. Helen Keller said that One can never consent to creep when one feels an impulse to soar.
4. Emerson argued, "Nothing is at last sacred but the integrity of your own mind."
5. in his moving speech of surrender, the Nez Percé leader Chief Joseph said, "from where the sun now stands I will fight no more forever."
6. Abraham Lincoln said that Frederick Douglass was "the most meritorious man of the nineteenth century." (He must have been impressed with Douglass's strong leadership.)
7. Golda Meir (She was a prime minister of Israel) said, "to deny oneself various comforts is also easier in talk than in deed."
8. Marian Anderson once said that when there is money, there is fighting. (she meant that greed encourages conflict.)
9. The first line of Gabriela Mistral's poem "Rocking" is "The sea rocks her thousands of waves."
10. Anaïs Nin wrote, "one handles truths like dynamite."

Exercise 3 Using Capitalization in Writing

On your paper, write a short paragraph about the philosophy of Benjamin Franklin as expressed in the maxims he published in *Poor Richard's Almanack*. In your paragraph include the quotes below, either as direct or indirect quotations. Make sure that your sentences are capitalized correctly.

1. "But dost thou love life, then do not squander time, for that's the stuff life is made of."
2. "Lost time is never found again."
3. "Early to bed, and early to rise, makes a man healthy, wealthy, and wise."
4. "He that lives upon hope will die fasting."
5. "Laziness travels so slowly, that poverty soon overtakes him."

20.2 Capitalization of Proper Nouns

■ Capitalize a proper noun.

A common noun should not be capitalized unless it is the first word of a sentence. In proper nouns composed of several words, do not capitalize articles, coordinating conjunctions, and prepositions of fewer than five letters within a proper noun.

1. Names of individuals

John **F.** **K**ennedy	**G**randma **M**oses
Kareem **A**bdul-**J**abbar	**S**hirley **C**hisholm
Rita **M**oreno	**S**andra **D**ay **O'C**onnor
Uncle **S**am	**T**oshio **M**ori

2. Titles of individuals

■ Capitalize titles used before a proper name and titles used in direct address.

President Lincoln	**G**overnor Pete Wilson
Queen Elizabeth II	**C**ardinal O'Connor
Chief Tecumseh	Yes, **G**eneral. [direct address]

■ In general, do not capitalize titles that follow a proper name or are used alone.

At the White House, the **p**resident greeted Alberto Fujimori, the **p**resident of Peru.

■ In general, capitalize a title that describes a family relationship when it is used with or in place of a proper name.

Dear **C**ousin Yuki,	*but*	My **c**ousin Yuki sews.
Did you see **F**ather?		my husband's **f**ather
Won't you write, **U**ncle?		What did your **u**ncle write?
A few days later, **M**other wrote to us.		My **m**other arrived yesterday.

3. Names of ethnic groups, national groups, and languages

African **A**mericans
Apaches
Americans
Chinese
Spanish
Russian

Capitalization

4. **Names of organizations, institutions, political parties and their members, and firms**

   Environmental **P**rotection **A**gency

   Knights of **C**olumbus

   Ohio **S**tate **U**niversity

   the **C**ongress

   General **M**otors

   a **D**emocrat

   the **R**epublican party

Do not capitalize the word *party.* Common nouns such as *court* or *university* are also not capitalized unless they are part of a proper noun.

Kim has to appear in **d**istrict **c**ourt today.

Their case is now before the **C**ourt of **A**ppeals for the **F**ederal **C**ircuit.

Teresa visited the **U**niversity of **T**exas.

Teresa enjoyed her visit to the **u**niversity.

Exercise 4 Capitalizing Names and Titles

On your paper, rewrite the following names, titles, and sentences, adding capital letters as necessary. Write *correct* if the item is already capitalized correctly.

1. governor george pataki
2. senator nancy kassebaum
3. uncle paul and his father
4. the populist party
5. the community college
6. brown university
7. secretary of state thomas jefferson
8. federal trade commission
9. Sign here, admiral.
10. traffic court
11. bell Atlantic corporation
12. nelson mandela, the president of South Africa
13. georgia o'keeffe
14. pope constantine
15. chief justice william rehnquist
16. What did you say, grandma?
17. boy scouts of America
18. first city bank
19. swahili
20. japanese americans

5. **Names of monuments, bridges, buildings, and other structures**

   Tomb of the **U**nknown **S**oldier
   Delaware **M**emorial **B**ridge
   Empire **S**tate **B**uilding
   Sears **T**ower
   Grand **C**oulee **D**am
   the **T**aj **M**ahal

6. **Names of documents, awards, and laws**

   the **D**eclaration of **I**ndependence
   Treaty of **V**ersailles
   Nobel **P**rize
   the **M**agna **C**arta
   an **O**scar
   Sherman **A**ntitrust **A**ct
   Civil **R**ights **A**ct of 1968
   Fourteenth **A**mendment

   Do not capitalize short prepositions that appear as part of the name.

7. **Trade names**

   A **F**ord
   Crest toothpaste
   Kraft cheese
   Sanka

8. **Geographical terms**

■ Capitalize the names of continents, countries, states, counties, and cities, as well as the names of specific bodies of water, topographical features, regions, and streets.

   Africa
   Brazil
   Kentucky
   Essex **C**ounty
   Denver
   Pacific **O**cean
   Lake **E**rie
   Snake **R**iver
   Midwest
   Rocky **M**ountains
   Great **R**ift **V**alley
   Mojave **D**esert
   Long **I**sland
   Tropic of **C**ancer
   Southeast **A**sia
   Pennsylvania **A**venue
   Forty-second **S**treet
   Central **A**merica

9. **Names of planets and other celestial bodies**

   Jupiter
   Venus
   Polaris
   Alpha **C**entauri
   the **L**ittle **D**ipper
   the constellation **P**isces
   the **M**oon
   the **S**un

Capitalization

Capitalize *earth* only when the word refers to the planet, but in that case, do not use the definite article, *the.*

Mercury, **V**enus, and **E**arth are the planets closest to the **S**un.

There will be an eclipse of the **M**oon at midnight.

We looked from the sky above to the **e**arth below.

10. Compass points

- Capitalize the words *north, east, south,* and *west* when they refer to a specific area of the country or the world or when they are part of a proper name. Do not capitalize them when they merely indicate direction.

the **S**outh	*but*	**s**outh Florida
East **G**rand **R**apids		**e**ast of Grand Rapids
North **D**akota		**n**orth Texas

Exercise 5 Capitalizing Proper Nouns

On your paper, rewrite the following sentences, correcting capitalization errors.

Visiting Washington, D.C.

1. Washington, D.C., is located on the potomac river.
2. The capital city was built on land ceded to congress by virginia and maryland.
3. An engineer from france, Pierre Charles L'Enfant, designed and partly laid out the city with the help of Benjamin Banneker, an african american surveyor.
4. D.C. stands for the district of columbia.
5. Its avenues are named after The states; pennsylvania avenue is one of the most famous.
6. The central point of The design of The city was the Capitol.
7. Tourists come from all over the world to visit such famous attractions as the Washington monument, the Vietnam veterans memorial, and the national air and space museum.
8. The senate's working copy of the treaty of Versailles is housed in the national archives.
9. A rough draft of the declaration of independence is on display at the library of Congress.
10. Tourists stand in line for hours to tour the white house and possibly catch a glimpse of the president and his family.
11. They also take time to visit George Washington's home at Mount Vernon, which is located several miles South of the city.
12. In warm weather, many tourists spend time boating and fishing on nearby chesapeake bay.
13. Class trips from high schools in the north, south, east, and west visit Washington in the spring.
14. Many people enjoy The cherry blossom festival.
15. Still others drive to the beaches along the atlantic ocean to enjoy the Sun and sand.

11. Names of most historical events, eras, and calendar items

Boston **T**ea **P**arty	the **R**enaissance
Persian **G**ulf **W**ar	**T**hanksgiving **D**ay
Battle of **G**ettysburg	**T**ang **D**ynasty
French **R**evolution	**F**ourth of **J**uly

A historical period referring to a general span of time should not be capitalized.

the **f**ifteenth century	the **s**ixties
the **m**edieval **p**eriod	**t**urn of the **c**entury

■ Capitalize the days of the week and the months of the year, but do not capitalize the names of the seasons (*spring, summer, autumn, fall, winter*).

They will be here all **s**ummer, beginning the first **S**aturday in **J**uly.

12. Religious terms

■ Capitalize names of deities, religions and their denominations and adherents, words referring to a supreme deity, and religious books and events.

God	**S**outhern **B**aptist **C**onvention
Allah	**B**uddhists
the **L**ord	**Q**ur'an
Judaism	**B**ible
Hinduism	**E**aster
Christianity	**Y**om **K**ippur

13. Names of ships, planes, trains, and spacecraft

USS ***I**ndependence*	***S**ilver **M**eteor*
***A**ir **F**orce **O**ne*	***C**olumbia*

14. Names of school courses

■ Capitalize only those school courses that are the name of a language or the title of a specific course. Do not capitalize the name of a subject.

Japanese	*but*	a **f**oreign **l**anguage
Economics 101		**e**conomics
Advanced **C**alculus		**c**alculus

Capitalization

15. **Titles of works**

The Pearl [novel]
Washington Post [newspaper]
Grolier Encyclopedia [reference book]
"**T**he **M**onkey's **P**aw" [short story]
Song of Myself [poem]
"**A**merica the **B**eautiful" [song]
Beauty and the Beast [movie]
Calla Lily with Red Roses [work of art]
Much Ado About Nothing [play]
Out of Africa [memoir]

Always capitalize the first and last words of a title or subtitle. Capitalize all other words except articles, coordinating conjunctions, and prepositions of fewer than five letters.

- Capitalize articles (*a, an,* and *the*) at the beginning of a title only when they are part of the title itself. It is common practice not to capitalize (or italicize) articles preceding the title of a newspaper or a periodical. Do not capitalize (or italicize) the word *magazine* unless it is part of the title of a periodical.

"**T**he Open Boat" *but* **t**he *Post-Dispatch*
"**A** Christmas Carol" a *Time* **m**agazine article

Exercise 6 Capitalizing Proper Nouns and Explaining Why

Write the following items, adding capital letters where necessary. For each item, explain why you did or did not add capital letters.

SAMPLE gulf of mexico
ANSWER Gulf of Mexico—name of a specific body of water

1. university of texas
2. hillary rodham clinton
3. the golden gate bridge
4. the *new york times*
5. laotians, scots, turks
6. captain McShane
7. aunt marilyn and my uncle jack
8. a republican
9. the atlantic charter
10. the pure food and drug act
11. apple computer, inc.
12. pulitzer prize
13. the first monday in october
14. the northwestern united states
15. first district court
16. appalachian mountains
17. the reformation and renaissance
18. the big dipper
19. world history II and my history class
20. new testament
21. "the star-spangled banner"
22. wheaties cereal
23. Labor Day
24. uss *constitution*
25. Sunset Boulevard in hollywood, california

Exercise 7 Capitalizing Sentences and Proper Nouns

On your paper, rewrite the following sentences, correcting capitalization errors.

The Chippewa People

1. In my history class, I learned about the Chippewas, who were once among the most powerful culture groups of north America.
2. In canada chippewas are known as ojibways; both names are derived from a word that describes the group's traditional moccasins.
3. The chippewas, the ottawas, and the potawatomis—all members of a governing body called the Council of Three Tribes—lived peacefully near the shores of lake Superior for several hundred years.
4. During the Seventeenth Century, the chippewas fought and defeated the sioux to the West, the Kickapoos to the South, and the iroquois to the East.
5. The Chippewas fought with the french against the british in the 1760s, yet they sided with the british in the american revolution.
6. By 1871, when the United States congress stopped making treaties with native americans, the Chippewas and the government had signed forty-two Treaties.
7. In the Winter of 1973, the leaders of an organization called the american indian movement seized a piece of federal land in north dakota; it was the site on which the battle of wounded knee had been fought in 1890.
8. The language of the chippewas is related to several other languages still spoken today, including algonquian, cheyenne, arapaho, shawnee, and cree.
9. Perhaps the most famous chippewa was not a real person at all; rather, he was the hero of Henry wadsworth longfellow's poem *hiawatha.*
10. Today, tens of thousands of chippewas live in cities in the midwest and canada.
11. They also live on Reservations in the provinces of manitoba and ontario in canada.
12. The leech lake reservation is a well-known Chippewa Community in minnesota.
13. For years, a medicine man living in south Dakota has been a spiritual leader for many Chippewas.
14. One of the first questions young people ask him is "what is a native american?"
15. This respected man, whose name is leonard crow dog, says Being a native american is to be spiritual. (another well-known modern-day medicine man is Pete Catches.)
16. One of the most prolific Chippewa writers is the Poet Gerald Vizenor, author of the highly acclaimed book *white earth chippewa.*
17. Responding to Native American activism, congress passed a number of laws, including the indian education act of 1972.
18. According to president Richard Nixon, the primary objective of the legislation was "To strengthen the Indian's sense of autonomy without threatening his sense of community."
19. In a poignant poem called "indian," a student at cloquet junior high school reveals what it is like to be a Chippewa today.
20. This poem and other poems and essays written by young Native Americans have been published in a book called *rising voices.*

20.3 Capitalization of Proper Adjectives

■ Capitalize proper adjectives (adjectives formed from proper nouns).

The following are some of the kinds of proper adjectives that should be capitalized:

1. Adjectives formed from names of people

Elizabethan literature	**S**hakespearean actor
Jeffersonian principles	**N**ewtonian physics
Machiavellian character	**A**ristotelian philosophy

2. Adjectives formed from place names and names of national, ethnic, and religious groups

Roman candle	**A**frican **A**merican leaders
Chinese checkers	**P**uerto **R**ican heritage
Irish linen	**J**ewish history

Many proper nouns do not change form when used as adjectives.

Senate majority	**O**scar-winning performance
New **Y**ork debut	**R**embrandt exhibit
Vietnam veteran	**W**hite **H**ouse statement

Some proper adjectives that are in common use are no longer capitalized.

venetian blinds	**r**oman numerals

Exercise 8 Forming Proper Adjectives

Form a proper adjective from each of the proper nouns listed below. Consult a dictionary if you need help. On your paper, write the adjective plus a noun that the adjective could modify.

SAMPLE Israel
ANSWER Israeli music

1. Italy
2. Queen Victoria
3. Southwest
4. Sweden
5. Alaska
6. Saturday
7. Buddhism
8. Boston
9. Passover
10. Grammy
11. Karl Marx
12. Charles Dickens
13. Latin America
14. Taiwan
15. Chicago

Capitalization

Exercise 9 Capitalizing Proper Adjectives

On your paper, rewrite the following sentences, correcting capitalization errors. Write the word *correct* if a sentence has no errors.

Marisol Escobar, Sculptor

1. Marisol Escobar was born into a wealthy venezuelan family living in Paris.
2. The name *Marisol* is a combination of the spanish words *mar y sol,* meaning "sea and sun."
3. Even at a young age, Marisol was fascinated by central and south american art.
4. She was especially drawn to aztec and mayan art.
5. Art critics describe Marisol's work as a cross between modern art and Folk art.
6. Many of her wood and clay figurines are pre-Columbian in style.
7. Her work is displayed in several famous european museums.
8. Some of her more whimsical pieces are in the collections of various american museums.
9. A Marisol Exhibit in Washington, D.C., featured wooden caricatures of well-known public figures, including the british royal family.
10. Today Marisol is a new york city Resident who spends most of her time creating new art.

Exercise 10 Capitalizing Proper Adjectives and Proper Nouns

On your paper, rewrite the following sentences, correcting capitalization errors.

Gordon Parks

1. A kansas native, Gordon parks has become one of america's most productive and versatile artists.
2. At the age of twenty-five, Parks decided to move to the chicago area and become a Professional photographer.
3. After holding a successful one-man Photography exhibit, parks served in the military in Europe in the united states office of war information.
4. Returning to the United States after world war II, Parks worked as a filmmaker for a new jersey oil company.
5. Soon afterward, *life* magazine hired parks as a Staff Photographer.
6. In the field of photography, parks's awards include magazine photographer of the year (1961) and Syracuse university's newhouse award.
7. Parks has also published such novels as *the learning tree,* an Autobiographical work called *A Choice Of Weapons,* and a book about photography entitled *a Poet And His Camera.*
8. Parks is also a composer, and his musical work entitled *first concerto for piano and orchestra* won favorable reviews.
9. When he directed a movie version of *the Learning Tree* for Warner brothers, parks established himself as the first African american film director at a major hollywood studio.
10. At a white house ceremony in 1988, this distinguished new york resident was honored by president Reagan as one of the twelve recipients of the national medal of arts.

Summary of Capitalization Rules	
Capitalize	**Do Not Capitalize**
He told us to turn to page 506 for the rules of capitalization. (**T**here was no page 506.)	He told us to turn to page 506 (**t**here was no page 506) for the rules of capitalization.
She said, "**H**e liked it very much."	She said that **h**e liked it very much.
Attorney **G**eneral Janet Reno	My **a**ttorney advised me.
Will **G**randmother visit us?	My **g**randmother is eighty years old.
Ohio **S**tate **U**niversity	a **u**niversity in Ohio
Joslyn **A**rt **M**useum	the **a**rt **m**useum in our city
Mr. **S**oapy soap, **D**azzle toothpaste	Buy **s**oap and **t**oothpaste.
the **F**irst **A**mendment	The committee added an **a**mendment to the bill.
Atlantic **O**cean, **T**imes **S**quare, **E**ighth **S**treet	the **s**quare at the end of the **s**treet overlooking the **o**cean
Jupiter, **V**enus, **M**ars, **E**arth	the **p**lanets
the **A**merican **C**ivil **W**ar	The country was on the verge of a **c**ivil **w**ar.
Qur'an, **E**aster **S**unday	**s**acred **b**ook, **h**oliday
German, **A**rt **H**istory II	**f**oreign **l**anguage, **h**istory
Senator Barbara Mikulski	the **s**enator from Maryland
President Jimmy Carter	a former **p**resident
First **D**istrict **C**ourt	**c**riminal **c**ourt
South **P**acific	**s**outh of Honolulu
the **S**tone **A**ge	the **f**ifth **c**entury
"**T**he **B**irthmark"	a **s**hort **s**tory
Friday, **A**pril	**s**ummer, **w**inter

Exercise 11 Using Correct Capitalization in Your Writing

Imagine that you are visiting a friend in another state. On your paper, write several sentences of dialogue between you and your friend, discussing the places you would like to visit. Use a variety of proper nouns and proper adjectives. Capitalize all sentences, direct quotations, and proper nouns and adjectives correctly.

Exercise 12 Identifying Correct Capitalization

On your paper, write the letter of the one item that is correctly capitalized in each of the following pairs.

1. **a.** Countee cullen said, "good poetry is a lofty thought beautifully expressed."
   b. Countee Cullen said, "Good poetry is a lofty thought beautifully expressed."
2. **a.** the Supreme court
   b. the Supreme Court
3. **a.** the chair of the Joint Chiefs of Staff, General John Shalikashvili
   b. the chair of the joint chiefs of staff, general John Shalikashvili
4. **a.** In what year did President Lincoln sign the Emancipation Proclamation?
   b. In what year did president Lincoln sign the emancipation proclamation?
5. **a.** Gabriela Mistral was the first latin american writer to win the nobel prize for literature.
   b. Gabriela Mistral was the first Latin American writer to win the Nobel Prize for literature.
6. **a.** Diana Chang wrote the novel *The Only Game in Town.*
   b. Diana Chang wrote the novel *the Only Game in Town.*
7. **a.** I took American History II and a course in mathematics at Stanford University.
   b. I took American History II and a course in Mathematics at Stanford university.
8. **a.** Hindu shrine
   b. hindu shrine
9. **a.** Even though the calendar says otherwise, many people consider Memorial Day to be the beginning of the summer season.
   b. Even though the calendar says otherwise, many people consider memorial day to be the beginning of the Summer season.
10. **a.** Explore the southwest.
    b. Explore the Southwest.
11. **a.** I read the article in *the St. Louis Post-dispatch.*
    b. I read that article in the *St. Louis Post-Dispatch.*
12. **a.** We met Jim Thompson, the former Governor of Illinois.
    b. We met Jim Thompson, the former governor of Illinois.
13. **a.** Hello, Officer.
    b. Hello, officer.
14. **a.** He said that the concert was sold out.
    b. He said that The concert was sold out.
15. **a.** He reminded us that Earth is the planet between venus and mars.
    b. He reminded us that Earth is the planet between Venus and Mars.

UNIT 20 Grammar Review

Capitalization

The British writer Bruce Chatwin spent several months walking through southern Chile and Argentina, and *In Patagonia* resulted from that journey. In this passage, Chatwin describes one of Patagonia's more famous residents, the outlaw Butch Cassidy. The passage has been annotated to show some of the rules of capitalization covered in this unit.

Literature Model

from In Patagonia

by Bruce Chatwin

Person's name

Name of an institution

Name of an organization

Trade name

Name of a religious group

First word of a sentence

Name of an ethnic group

Butch Cassidy, in those years, was drover, horse-wrangler, mavericker, part-time bank-robber, and leader of men; the sheriffs feared him most for the last of these accomplishments. In 1894 they gave him two years in the Wyoming State Penitentiary for stealing a horse he hadn't stolen, valued at five dollars. The sentence soured him to any further dealing with the law. And, from 1896 to 1901, his Train Robbers' Syndicate, better known as The Wild Bunch, performed the string of perfect hold-ups that kept lawmen, Pinkerton detectives and the railroad in perpetual jitters. The stories of his antics are endless; breathless rides along the Outlaw Trail; shooting glass conductors from telegraph poles; or paying a poor widow's rent by robbing the rent man. The homesteaders loved him. Many were Mormons, outlawed themselves for polygamy. They gave him food, shelter, alibis. . . . Today he would be classed as a revolutionary. But he had no sense of political organization.

Butch Cassidy never killed a man. Yet his friends were seasoned killers; their murders drove him to fits of remorse. He hated having to rely on the deadly aim of Harry Longabaugh, the Pennsylvania German with evil blue eyes and a foul temper. He tried to go straight, but there was too much on his Pinkerton card and his pleas for amnesty went unheard. Each new robbery spawned another and added years to his sentence. The costs of operating became unbearable.

In the fall of 1901 Butch met the Sundance Kid and his girl, Etta Place, in New York. She was young, beautiful and intelligent, and she kept her men to heel. Her Pinkerton card says she was a school teacher in Denver; one rumor has it she was the daughter of an English remittance man called George Capel, hence Place. Under the names of James Ryan and Mr. and Mrs. Harry A. Place, the "family of 3" went to operas and theaters. (The Sundance Kid was a keen Wagnerian.) They bought Etta a gold watch at Tiffany's and sailed for Buenos Aires on S.S. *Soldier Prince.* On landing they stayed at the Hotel Europa, called on the **Director of the Land Department,** and secured 12,000 acres of rough camp in Chubut.

"Are there any bandits?" they asked. They were glad to hear there were none.

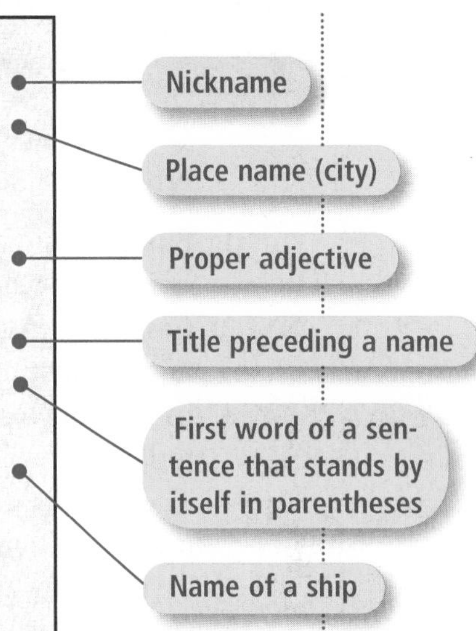

Review: Exercise 1 Capitalizing Sentences

On your paper, rewrite the following sentences about Butch Cassidy, correcting any errors in capitalization. If a sentence has no errors, write *correct.*

1. Robert Leroy Parker (Also known as Butch Cassidy) borrowed his nickname from a friend named Mike Cassidy.
2. the same friend also taught Parker many of his "outlaw" skills. (Mike Cassidy was a hired hand on the Parker ranch.)
3. By 1892 Butch Cassidy was well known throughout the West as a Horse Thief.
4. Cassidy's motto was that He would never rob a person with whom he had "Broken bread."
5. When Cassidy asked for a pardon, the Wyoming governor said, "will you give me your word that you'll go straight?"
6. "can't do that," Cassidy said. He did promise, however, that he would never again "molest the state of Wyoming."
7. Years later, a friend told the governor that. He should have made Cassidy promise to leave Utah alone as well.
8. the Sundance Kid (His real name was Harry Longabaugh) was a dead shot and had a "Foul temper."
9. When asked whether he would ever give himself up to the law, Longabaugh answered, "they'll never take me alive."
10. Interestingly, Cassidy's Pinkerton file described him in this way: "He is a gentlemanly sort of man."

Review: Exercise 2 **Capitalizing Proper Nouns and Proper Adjectives**

On your paper, rewrite the following sentences about Butch Cassidy, correcting any errors in capitalization. If a sentence has no errors, write *correct.*

1. Butch Cassidy grew up on a ranch near Bryce canyon, utah, and spent much of his spare time reading Dime Novels about Jesse James.
2. Cassidy's reputation as the Robin Hood of the West was probably exaggerated but not wholly unjustified.
3. In the Nineteenth Century, the Pinkerton Agency did work similar to that done today by the federal bureau of investigation.
4. The Cassidy Gang accidentally blew up thousands of dollars during a holdup of the union Pacific railroad.
5. Trying to escape, they mistakenly stole horses belonging to a republican senator from nevada.
6. Joe lefors, portrayed in paramount's movie *Butch Cassidy and the Sundance kid,* pursued them.
7. For three years, the north American outlaws lived quietly on a patagonian Ranch.
8. Cassidy knew that Argentina, Peru, and the Amazonian nations were not Jeffersonian republics: if caught, he would have no assurances of legal rights or due process.
9. Cassidy gave himself away in 1908 when he stole a mule during the theft of a payroll for a bolivian Mine.
10. After dozens of soldiers attacked the outlaws' hut, they found butch and sundance dead, one wearing Etta's tiffany watch.

Review: Exercise 3

Proofreading

The following passage discusses photography in general and the photograph of Butch Cassidy's Wild Bunch shown on the opposite page. On your paper rewrite the passage, correcting the errors in spelling, capitalization, grammar, and usage. Add any missing punctuation. There are twenty-five errors.

Early Photography

[1]the evolution of photography was given a boost in 1837 by Louis-Jacques-Mandé Daguerre of france. [2]Daguerres' process involved the exposure of a polished silver plate to the vapors of iodine (this process formed a sensitive layer of silver iodide). [3]After exposing the plate in the camera, daguerre developed the image with mercury vaper.

[4]The announcement of Daguerre's discovery spurred an english photographer named Henry fox Talbot to develop his own photographic process, which used a paper negative. [5]The photographic process we use today is based on Talbots

negative-to-positive principle. [6]not merely a technical expert, Talbot had an eye for beauty and composition as well. [7]According to the Art historian kenneth Clark, "fox Talbot was the first photographer who could properly be called a great artist."

[8]Indeed, the significance of the Photographic camera at first seemed more artistic than practical but it soon has far-reaching effects in many areas. [9]For the first time in history, the World was made visible and accessible. [10]Photography changed our view of ourselves and the World around us. [11]Because there was now a precise means to show what things looked like, science and teknology flourished. [12]Communication was also affected by the advent of Photography: magazine and newspaper reporting became more pictorial.

[13]The photograph shown here of butch Cassidy and his gang was taken in 1901 during the final days of Americas Wild west—a period that began after the Civil war. [14]Butch Cassidy was a charming character with an easy smile but he was an outlaw, nonetheless. [15]Cassidys gang received the name the Wild Bunch because of the uproar they caused while unwinding in town after a hard day of rustling. [16]Do you find it ironic to see the members of the Gang sitting in such a serene and genteel pose?

Photographer unknown, *Butch Cassidy and the Gang,* 1901

Review: Exercise 4

Mixed Review

On your paper, rewrite these sentences about Bruce Chatwin, correcting any errors in capitalization. If a sentence has no errors, write *correct.*

1. In the early Sixties, Bruce Chatwin walked away from a "Brilliant future" at Sotheby's, a fine-arts auction house.
2. At Sotheby's, Chatwin attributed his expertise in part to his scant knowledge of chinese porcelain.
3. In time he developed what he termed "A horror of things" and quit his job to write for the *london Sunday times.*
4. he announced his departure with a Telegram stating that he had "gone to Patagonia for six months."
5. Chatwin's strength was writing travel books. (two of the most popular are the semifictional *The songlines,* about australia, and *In Patagonia.*)
6. Chatwin's love of travel began during world war II, when his Father was a naval Officer.
7. Even harrowing experiences as being arrested (in Africa), being harassed, or catching tropical diseases did not dull Chatwin's appetite for travel.
8. Chatwin's himalayan trek convinced him that A person's true home is on the road, not in a house.
9. Chatwin's keen eye made him the pride of his publisher, Viking Press.
10. Chatwin's world was a confusing place full of Legendary tales, Myths, and strange truths.
11. Chatwin described Patagonia as "The uttermost part of the Earth."
12. He was fascinated by this southernmost place in south America, where the darwinian theory of the "survival of the fittest" had been formulated.
13. He owed his interest in Patagonia to a distant cousin, captain Charles Amherst Milward, whose ship sank at the entrance to the strait of Magellan.
14. In a cave in chilean Patagonia, Milward found the frozen remains of a Prehistoric animal, a toothless mammal.
15. The sea captain shipped the skins and bones he recovered from the ice to England, where he sold them to the British Museum.
16. Chatwin returned from Patagonia on a third-class Ship.
17. He acknowledged that he could not have written the book *in Patagonia* without the help of Milward's Daughter Monica Barnett, who lived in lima, Peru.
18. Chatwin won the 1982 whitbread award for his books *the Viceroy Of Ouidah* and *On the Black Hill.*
19. He also received the Hawthornden Prize in Great Britain.
20. "Chatwin's studied style," wrote John Updike in a *New Yorker* Magazine review, "Touches on the epic."

Writing Application

TIME

For more about the writing process, see TIME Facing the Blank Page, pp. 109–119

Capitalization in Writing

William Least Heat-Moon, a Native American of Sioux ancestry, chronicled his journey across the less-traveled roads in *Blue Highways: A Journey into America.* As you read the passage below, pay special attention to his use of capitalization.

> **W**est of the gorge lay verdant rangeland, much of it given to a buffalo herd maintained by the **A**rizona **G**ame **C**ommission; the great beasts lifted their heads to watch me pass, their dark, wet eyes catching the late sun. To the north rose the thousand-foot butt end of the **V**ermillion **C**liffs; the cliffs weren't truly vermillion, but contrasting with the green valley in the orange afternoon light, they seemed so.

Capitalization Techniques

Like William Least Heat-Moon, you should apply the rules of capitalization when you write and revise your own work.

❶ Capitalize proper nouns that name specific topographical features or monuments. Do not capitalize common nouns or adjectives unless they are part of a proper noun.

PROPER NOUN Vermillion Cliffs

COMMON NOUNS AND ADJECTIVES cliffs, vermillion

❷ Capitalize the names of organizations.

PROPER NOUN Arizona Game Commission

COMMON NOUN game commission

❸ Do not capitalize *north, south, east, west* when they indicate direction, except as the first word in a sentence.

INCORRECT VERSIONS west of the gorge lay verdant rangeland . . . To the North rose the thousand-foot butt end . . .

LEAST HEAT-MOON'S CORRECT VERSIONS West of the gorge lay verdant rangeland . . . To the north rose the thousand-foot butt end . . .

Capitalization

Practice On your paper, revise the paragraph below to make 25 changes in capitalization.

Arizona

As a result of the treaty of Guadalupe Hidalgo in 1848, mexican lands North of the gila river became part of the territory of new Mexico. A southern section of land was added by the so-called Gadsden purchase in 1853. Arizona, which became the forty-eighth state in 1912, is rich in legend and american folklore. Tombstone was the site of the west's most famous gunfight (This battle took place at the O.K. Corral), and it was in Arizona that chief Geronimo surrendered after 25 years of fighting. today, the State is home to 14 native American groups living on 20 Reservations. (the largest reservations are the navajo, hopi, Fort Apache, and Papago reservations.) Throughout the year, especially in the Spring, tourists come to experience first-hand the scenic beauty of Arizona and to visit such natural wonders as the grand canyon, the Petrified Forest, and the painted desert. The Hoover dam and the reconstructed london Bridge are also popular attractions.

UNIT 21

Punctuation, Abbreviations, and Numbers

21.1 The Period

- Use a period at the end of a declarative sentence and at the end of a polite command.

DECLARATIVE SENTENCE	My father came to America when he was not yet twenty-one. —Yoshiko Uchida
POLITE COMMAND	Look in the story for five quotations from Uchida.
	Please read them aloud.

Exercise 1 Identifying Use of the Period

Identify each of the following sentences that should end with a period by writing *declarative* or *command* on your paper. If a sentence is neither a declarative sentence nor a polite command, write *no period.*

Japan's Natural Features

1. Read the following sentences carefully
2. You will learn many fascinating facts about Japan
3. Did you know that Japan is an island country in the Pacific
4. Locate Japan on the world map
5. Japan is made up of four large islands and many smaller ones
6. Mountains and hills cover most of the country
7. These beautiful landforms have long been a source of inspiration to poets and painters throughout the world
8. Please open your books to the section about Japan's highest and most famous mountain peak, Mount Fuji, or Fujiyama
9. Mount Fuji is on Honshu, Japan's largest and most heavily populated island
10. Can you find Mount Fuji on your map
11. An inactive volcano, Mount Fuji last erupted in 1707
12. The volcano rises 12,388 feet above sea level
13. In winter, snow covers the mountain's rugged peak
14. In summer thousands of tourists climb the mountain for a view of the crater
15. Consider now how Japan's breathtaking mountains are both an asset and a problem
16. The Japanese Alps attract tourists to the country, thus aiding the economy
17. However, the mountain range covers so much land area that the coastal regions are overcrowded
18. Only one-seventh of Japan's land is suitable for farming
19. How have the Japanese compensated for this scarcity of farmland
20. They farm efficiently and cultivate high-yielding crops, such as rice

21.2 The Exclamation Point

- Use an exclamation point to show strong feeling and indicate a forceful command.

  What a colorful garden**!**

  How exciting the game is**!**

  Pay attention**!**

- Use an exclamation point after an interjection expressing a strong feeling.

  Wow**!** Ouch**!**

Exercise 2 Identifying Use of the Exclamation Point

The following items are declarative sentences, polite and forceful commands, interjections, or exclamatory phrases. Identify the correct type of punctuation for each item by writing *period* or *exclamation point* on your paper.

1. How noisy this class is
2. Please pay attention to the presentation on Japanese arts
3. Many Japanese paintings portray the beauty of life in Japan
4. What rich colors the artists used
5. Color priming from wood blocks is very popular
6. Look out
7. We'll pass around this modern wood-block print by Umetaro Azechi
8. Wow
9. What a gorgeous screen painting
10. Japanese sculpture is also outstanding
11. The sculptors worked mostly with wood
12. Please note that some sculptors also used bronze and clay
13. Such fascinating music
14. Traditional Japanese music is made with gongs, drums, flutes, and *samisens* (banjo-like instruments)
15. Oh, my goodness
16. How beautiful Japanese architecture is
17. Most of the houses are small, simple, and unpainted
18. Everyone, please listen now
19. Japanese drama is also worth mentioning
20. How very lively *kabuki* drama is
21. By comparison, the *No* drama is slow-moving
22. The actors in a *No* play often wear special masks to represent emotions
23. *Kabuki* dance-dramas are more popular than *No* because they are easier to understand
24. What a surprise
25. Japanese men have traditionally played women's roles in *kabuki* drama

21.3 The Question Mark

■ Use a question mark to indicate a direct question.

Was W. E. B. Du Bois born in 1868 or 1869**?**

Should I ask my history teacher**?**

Who knows the answer**?**

Do not place a question mark after a declarative sentence that contains an indirect question.

My friend asked whether W. E. B. Du Bois was born in 1868 or 1869.

I wondered whether I should ask my history teacher.

He asked whether anybody knew the answer.

Exercise 3 Identifying Use of the Question Mark

The following items are either direct questions or declarative sentences that contain an indirect question. Identify the correct type of punctuation for each item by writing *period* or *question mark* on your paper.

World Languages

1. How many languages are spoken in the world today
2. My friend asked our Spanish teacher whether she knew how many languages exist today
3. Señora Lopez wondered how anyone could know the answer to that question
4. Do you know that estimates have varied from 3,000 to 10,000 languages
5. How can we possibly count all the languages, plus the dialects within each language
6. More important, what actually counts as a language
7. Our teacher asked whether we realized how difficult it is to complete a linguistic survey throughout the world
8. How can linguists stay current when languages are constantly dying or being discovered
9. A linguist would want to know what factors were considered in the survey
10. The question of how many languages are spoken worldwide does not have a simple answer
11. Have you heard the theory that most of the languages spoken today are descended from one ancient language
12. Linguists hotly dispute whether the theory is valid
13. Some scholars ask how there can be so many similar words without a shared ancestral language
14. Is it ever possible to verify or disprove such a theory
15. Did you know that "baby" words such as *papa* and *mama* are common to many languages in the world

Exercise 4 Using End Punctuation (Part 1)

Rewrite the following sentences, adding periods, exclamation points, and question marks where they are needed.

Major-League Baseball

1. Major-league baseball has often been called the national game of the United States
2. What an exciting sport it is
3. I asked how many fans crowd into baseball parks each year
4. How many more Americans, do you suppose, watch the games on television
5. How did such a popular sport get its start
6. Children in colonial Boston were probably the first to use bases with bat-and-ball games
7. Note that these colonial games probably developed from the English sport of cricket, a bat-and-ball game in which each team defends its wicket
8. Should we credit Abner Doubleday for originating the game
9. In 1839 in Cooperstown, New York, Doubleday developed a diamond-shaped field with four bases and named the game *baseball*
10. Did you know that the National Baseball Hall of Fame and Museum opened in Cooperstown one hundred years later

Exercise 5 Using End Punctuation (Part 2)

Rewrite the following sentences, adding periods, exclamation points, and question marks where they are needed.

Willie Mays, a Great Baseball Player

1. Baseball fans are forever arguing about who the greatest baseball player was. Which player would you choose.
2. Many people would name Willie Mays as an all-time great player.
3. In 1951 Mays entered major-league baseball as a center fielder for the New York Giants and quickly became a hero to the fans.
4. For years there was a spirited rivalry in New York involving Mays, the Yankees' Mickey Mantle, and the Dodgers' Duke Snider
5. When the Giants moved to San Francisco, Mays electrified the fans there as well
6. He will always be remembered as a fearless base runner and an exceptionally gifted fielder. What a fantastic catch he made in the 1954 World Series
7. Many people wonder whether there will ever be another outfielder as spectacular as Mays
8. Mays's hitting statistics were also impressive. Do you know that he hit 660 home runs and had a career batting average of .302
9. How many players have hit more homers than Mays did Only a small number have.
10. In 1979 Mays was elected to the National Baseball Hall of Fame. Some still wonder why the vote was not unanimous

21.4 The Colon

Colons to Introduce

1. Lists

■ Use a colon to introduce a list, especially after a statement that uses such words as *these, the following,* or *as follows.*

My grandparents' garden contains **these** flowers**:** camellias, pansies, peonies, tulips, marigolds, and chrysanthemums.

Perform **the following** operations to start a car with a stick shift**:** (1) step on the clutch, (2) put the car into first gear, and (3) turn the ignition key.

Maria's class schedule is **as follows:** English, history, and math.

If a list immediately follows a verb or a preposition, do not use a colon to introduce it.

The author Alice Walker **writes** poetry, articles, essays, and fiction. [The list follows the verb *writes.*]

Do not leave for your trip **without** your toothbrush, toothpaste, comb, and brush. [The list follows the preposition *without.*]

2. Illustrations or restatements

■ Use a colon to introduce material that illustrates, explains, or restates the preceding material.

You can see how bitterly cold the winters are in Alaska**:** On a windy morning your breath freezes into ice crystals in front of you.

A complete sentence following a colon is capitalized.

3. Quotations

■ Use a colon to introduce a long or formal quotation. A formal quotation is often preceded by words such as *these, the following,* or *as follows.*

Lincoln began the Gettysburg Address with **these** famous words**:** "Fourscore and seven years ago our fathers brought forth on this continent a new nation . . . "

When poetry quotations take up more than one line and prose quotations take up more than several lines, they generally appear below the introductory statement and are indented.

Stephen Crane makes this admission in his poem "Truth"**:**

For truth was to me
A bread, a wind . . . .

Exercise 6 Using Colons Correctly

On your paper, rewrite each of the following sentences, adding colons where they are needed. If a sentence has no errors, write *correct.*

Famous Words

1. In our literature class, we memorized famous lines by these writers T. S. Eliot, Emily Dickinson, Edgar Allan Poe, and Federico García Lorca.
2. Noted architect Frank Lloyd Wright once made the following observation "What is needed most in architecture today is the very thing that is most needed in life—integrity."
3. Physicist Albert Einstein placed great value on imagination: He believed that imagination is more important than knowledge.
4. According to the Italian poet Petrarch, five great enemies to peace are avarice, ambition, envy, anger, and pride.
5. In "The Still Voice of Harlem," Conrad Kent Rivers writes the following "I am the hope of your unborn."
6. This famous sentence is from a book by Stephen Crane "He wishes that he, too, had a wound, a red badge of courage."
7. An old Native American saying goes something like this "When you were born, you cried and the world rejoiced. Live your life in such a manner that when you die, the world cries and you rejoice."
8. Abolitionist Theodore Parker defined the American ideal as a government of *all* the people, by *all* the people, for *all* the people.
9. Poet Walt Whitman was referring to the death of Abraham Lincoln when he wrote the following lines

    O powerful western fallen star!
    O shades of night—O moody, tearful night!
    O great star disappeared—O the black murk that hides the star!
    O cruel hands that hold me powerless—O helpless soul of me!
    O harsh surrounding cloud that will not free my soul.
10. Consider the following observation by Mother Teresa "If you judge people, you have no time to love them."
11. Robert Frost once compared poets and baseball pitchers "Both have their moments. The intervals are the tough things."
12. Addressing a Wellesley College commencement, Barbara Bush, wife of then-president George Bush, made this remark: "Somewhere out in this audience may even be someone who will one day follow in my footsteps and preside over the White House as the President's spouse. I wish him well!"
13. The Declaration of Independence lists these unalienable rights life, liberty, and the pursuit of happiness.
14. The artist Georgia O'Keeffe explained her purpose in these words "I had to create an equivalent for what I felt about what I was looking at—not copy it."
15. Emily Dickinson, one of the most quoted of all poets, was little known before her death only six poems were published in her lifetime.

Other Uses of Colons

■ Use a colon between the hour and the minute of the precise time, between the chapter and the verse in biblical references, and after the salutation of a business letter.

5:45 P.M.	1 Kings 11:1–13
8:30 A.M.	Madam:
Proverbs 8:22–31	Dear Sir:

Exercise 7 Using the Colon

Rewrite the following sentences, adding colons where they are needed. Two items will need two colons.

Quotations

1. "There are two times in a man's life when he should not speculate when he can't afford it and when he can."

   —Mark Twain
2. The Chinese philosopher Lao-Tse described his "three treasures" as follows

   The first is deep love,
   The second is frugality,
   And the third is not to dare to be ahead of the world.
3. Dear Company Officers

   Please send me the following a prospectus, a copy of your annual report, and an application form.
4. Toni Morrison says the following about her work "I always know the ending; that's where I start."
5. Dorothy Parker asked to have this epitaph engraved on her tombstone "Excuse my dust."
6. A haiku by Ezra Pound follows

   The petals fall in the fountain
   the orange-colored rose-leaves,
   their ochre clings to the stone.
7. These famous words are engraved on the Statue of Liberty "Give me your tired, your poor . . . "
8. The following quotation appeared in Eleanor Roosevelt's autobiography, *This Is My Story* "No one can make you feel inferior without your consent."
9. After he stepped onto the moon on July 20, 1969, astronaut Neil Armstrong spoke these words at 4 17 P.M. "That's one small step for a man, one giant leap for mankind."
10. In reading Genesis 21 1-21, keep in mind that *Sarah* means "princess" and *Isaac* means "laughter."

21.5 The Semicolon

Semicolons to Separate Main Clauses

- Use a semicolon to separate main clauses that are not joined by a coordinating conjunction (*and, but, or, nor, yet,* or *for*).

The acting and directing ability of Orson Welles is considered phenomenal, **and** his film *Citizen Kane* is still studied and appreciated.

The acting and directing ability of Orson Welles is considered phenomenal**;** his film *Citizen Kane* is still studied and appreciated.

- Use a semicolon to separate main clauses joined by a conjunctive adverb (such as *however, therefore, nevertheless, moreover, furthermore,* and *consequently*) or by an expression such as *for example* or *that is.*

A conjunctive adverb or an expression such as *for example* is usually followed by a comma.

In her youth Mary Cassatt was strongly discouraged from any artistic endeavors**;** nevertheless, she later became one of America's foremost painters.

Many of her associates were world-famous artists**;** for instance, she was strongly influenced by the great French painters Edgar Degas and Edouard Manet.

Exercise 8 Using Semicolons with Main Clauses

On your paper, write each of the following sentences correctly, adding semicolons where necessary.

Mary Cassatt, American Artist

1. Mary Cassatt was born in 1844 to a wealthy Pittsburgh family she later studied at the Pennsylvania Academy of Art.
2. Cassatt's father wanted her to remain in the United States nevertheless, she moved to Paris, France.
3. Edgar Degas became her close friend she relied on him for guidance and counseling.
4. Cassatt's paintings are Impressionist in color however, her delicacy of line resembles that of Japanese prints.
5. Cassatt became famous for her paintings of mothers and children in everyday situations for example, she depicted mothers holding, hugging, and bathing their children.

Semicolons and Commas

- Use a semicolon to separate the items in a series when these items contain commas.

  Notable abolitionists were Harriet Beecher Stowe, who wrote *Uncle Tom's Cabin;* Frederick Douglass, who spoke out against slavery; and Harriet Tubman, who led many slaves to freedom through the Underground Railroad.

- Use a semicolon to separate two main clauses joined by a coordinating conjunction when such clauses already contain several commas.

  Leonardo da Vinci pursued a wide range of subjects, including mathematics, music, astronomy, and engineering; but he always returned to his primary interest, which was, of course, art.

Exercise 9 Using Semicolons in Sentences with Commas

On your paper, rewrite the following sentences, adding semicolons where they are needed.

The Arts in Renaissance Italy

1. The Medici family, especially "Lorenzo the Magnificent," became the most famous patrons of the arts in Renaissance Italy, and they summoned poets, philosophers, and artists to the city of Florence.
2. Artists such as Leonardo da Vinci, Michelangelo, and Sandro Botticelli reflected the spirit of the Medici court, for they tried to portray a world of beauty, grace, and nobility.
3. Botticelli's *La Primavera* depicts Venus, who is the goddess of love, Zephyr, who portrays the warm wind of spring, Flora, who is transformed into spring, Mercury, who holds the symbol of medicine, and the three Graces, who symbolize poetry, art, and music.
4. The famous painter Leonardo da Vinci is also considered a great sculptor, architect, and scientist, yet no existing sculptures and buildings, nor any specific inventions, can be attributed to him.
5. Michelangelo's most famous achievements include *The Last Judgment,* a fresco that covers the altar wall of the Sistine Chapel, the dome for St. Peter's Church in Rome, which he designed, and his sculptures *Evening* and *Dawn* on the tomb of Lorenzo de Medici.

Exercise 10 Using the Semicolon

On your paper, rewrite the following sentences, adding semicolons where they are needed.

The Purpose of Art: To Instruct or Delight?

1. "Persons attempting to find a motive in this narrative will be prosecuted persons attempting to find a moral in it will be banished persons attempting to find a plot will be shot."
2. Mark Twain attached the preceding notice to *Huckleberry Finn* he felt that too much analysis made art less enjoyable.
3. "The trouble with music appreciation in general is that people are taught to have too much respect for music they should be taught to love it instead." —Igor Stravinsky
4. Among Stravinsky's compositions are the operas *Oedipus Rex, The Rake's Progress,* and *Mavra* the ballets *Petrouchka, The Firebird,* and *Pulcinella* and three symphonies.
5. Stravinsky lived in Saint Petersburg, Russia Paris, France and the United States.
6. Oscar Wilde agreed with Twain and Stravinsky he said that art should be pleasurable rather than instructive.
7. On the other hand, some writers and artists try to combine pleasure with instruction they seek to teach and delight simultaneously.
8. Simon Ortiz, who is of Acoma Pueblo descent, does not write simply to entertain his readers rather, he wants to impart knowledge about his heritage.
9. In his art, Diego Rivera portrays the hard life experienced by some Mexicans he also shows the arrogance of their oppressors.
10. Capturing the imagination of their public is enough for most painters, writers, and musicians other creative people, wanting to raise consciousness, use art to instruct.
11. Leo Tolstoy once observed that art was neither a pleasure nor an amusement instead, art was a great matter.
12. By contrast, Pablo Picasso was unconcerned with art's role in instruction his only concern was that his paintings evoke emotion.
13. French painter Georges Braque also placed great emphasis on art's emotional role for example, he felt that art was created to disturb.
14. Still other creative people believe art has purposes beyond instructing or delighting in fact, they regard art as revolutionary.
15. Many artistic people have agreed that art inspires revolution, including Paul Gauguin, a painter of South Seas scenes, Jean-Louis Barrault, a French actor, and Mihajlo Mihajlov, a Russian writer.
16. Gauguin said art was either a revolutionist or a plagiarist it could not be otherwise.
17. Barrault went a step further he regarded art as a permanent revolution
18. Mihajlov stated that art was a direct challenge to communist totalitarianism consequently, one true artist was more dangerous than any political adversary.
19. Walter Savage Landor agreed that art creates change he regarded every great writer as a great reformer.
20. British writer John Ruskin provided an eloquent definition of art he defined good art as that in which the hand, the head, and the heart of the artist go together.

21.6 The Comma

Commas in a Series and with Coordinate Adjectives

■ Use commas to separate three or more words, phrases, or clauses in a series.

Alaska, Texas, and California are our three largest states.

The movie was long, dull, and humorless.

They have traveled on land, by sea, and in the air.

I enjoy reading stories, writing articles, and listening to poetry.

Preheat the oven, beat the eggs, and sift the flour.

When the items are separated by conjunctions, commas are unnecessary.

The movie was long and dull and humorless.

Nouns used in pairs (*eggs and bacon, salt and pepper*) are considered single units and are not separated by commas. The paired nouns are set off from the other nouns or groups of nouns in a series.

The storm brought thunder and lightning, high winds, and heavy rain.

■ Place a comma between coordinate adjectives that precede a noun.

Adjectives that are **coordinate** modify the same noun to an equal degree. You can tell whether adjectives in a sentence are coordinate by reversing their order or putting the word *and* between them. If the sentence sounds right, then the adjectives are coordinate.

It was a warm, starry, fragrant evening.

Avoid placing a comma between adjectives that precede a noun if they sound strange with their order reversed or with *and* between them. In general, do not use a comma between adjectives that describe size, shape, age, color, and material.

The big old oak desk stood in one corner of the room.

Some, but not all, of the adjectives in a series may require commas between them.

A noisy, dusty Japanese truck roared down the street.

Commas and Compound Sentences

■ Use commas between the main clauses in a compound sentence.

A comma should be placed before a coordinating conjunction (*and, but, or, not, yet,* or *for*) that joins two main clauses.

I told Eartha what he said**,** and she advised me to forget it.

I picked up the clay jar carefully**,** yet it crashed to the floor.

When two very short, closely linked main clauses are connected by a coordinating conjunction, you may omit the comma between them unless it is needed to avoid confusion.

Alicia opened the door and Manuel came in. [clear]

Alicia opened the door for the dog and the cat ran out. [confusing]

Alicia opened the door for the dog**,** and the cat ran out. [clear]

Exercise 11 Using the Comma (Part 1)

Rewrite the following sentences, adding commas where they are needed. For the sentence that needs no comma, write *correct.*

Hispanic Culture

1. Hispanic culture is complex diverse and rich in many historical traditions.
2. It has been a vibrant vital part of American life ever since Spanish friars settled in the Southwest in the sixteenth century.
3. People may think Hispanic culture is Spanish but it has also been influenced by Latin American and Caribbean cultures.
4. The influence of Aztec culture can be seen in the popular striking paintings of Carlos Almaraz, a Mexican American.
5. Almaraz's paintings combine beauty oddness power and tranquillity—qualities found in Aztec art.
6. Music from the Spanish-speaking Caribbean islands—Cuba the Dominican Republic and Puerto Rico—sparkles with rhythms brought to the Americas by enslaved people.
7. The lively, syncopated rhythms have been borrowed by such popular American rock groups as the Talking Heads.
8. Hispanic literature is also popular and English translations of Hispanic books are eagerly sought.
9. The works of the Mexican poet and essayist Octavio Paz the Colombian novelist Gabriel García Márquez and the Argentine novelist Julie Cortázar have influenced many American writers.
10. There is no doubt that Hispanic culture will continue to influence enrich and enliven American life.

Commas and Nonessential Elements

1. Participles, infinitives, and their phrases

■ Use commas to set off participles, infinitives, and their phrases if they are not essential to the meaning of the sentence.

He read, engrossed, until the doorbell broke his concentration.

I am not very thirsty, to tell the truth.

If participles, infinitives, and their phrases are essential to the meaning of a sentence, do not set them off with commas.

The girl watching us is my sister. [The participial phrase tells which girl.]

To study my notes would not help you much. [The infinitive phrase is used as the subject of the sentence.]

2. Adjective clauses

■ Use commas to set off a nonessential adjective clause.

A nonessential (nonrestrictive) clause provides additional information about a noun. Considered an extra clause, it does not change the meaning of a sentence but adds to it. It is therefore set off with commas.

Jackson Pollock, who was an American painter, was born in 1912. [*Who was an American painter* is a nonessential clause.]

Do not use commas with an essential adjective clause. An essential (restrictive) clause gives necessary information about a noun and is thus needed to convey the exact meaning of the sentence.

One of the few American writers whom she read was Langston Hughes. [*Whom she read* is an essential clause.]

3. Appositives

■ Use commas to set off an appositive if it is not essential to the meaning of a sentence.

A nonessential (nonrestrictive) appositive provides additional information and is therefore set off with commas.

Lucha Corpi, teacher and author, has published many poems.

A historic city, New Orleans was originally settled by the French. [The appositive, *A historic city,* precedes the subject.]

An essential (restrictive) appositive is not set off with commas because it gives necessary information about a noun.

Both the *Iliad* and the *Odyssey* are traditionally attributed to the poet Homer. [The appositive, *Homer,* identifies the poet.]

Commas with Interjections, Parenthetical Expressions, and Conjunctive Adverbs

■ Use commas to set off interjections (such as *oh* and *well*), parenthetical expressions (such as *on the contrary, on the other hand, in fact, by the way, to be exact,* and *after all*), and conjunctive adverbs (such as *however, moreover,* and *consequently*).

Yes**,** I hope to build my own home one day.

The beautiful and historic city of Philadelphia**,** in fact**,** is three centuries old.

After all**,** we did the best we possibly could under extraordinarily difficult circumstances.

We drank two bottles of orange juice last night; consequently**,** we did not have enough left to make the punch today.

She intended to use the money to buy an expensive stereo**,** nonetheless.

Exercise 12 Using the Comma (Part 2)

Rewrite the following sentences, adding commas where they are needed. For the two sentences that need no commas, write *correct.*

Chinese Pioneers

[1]Thousands of pioneers from China lured by reports of riches rushed to California after gold was discovered there in 1848. [2]Gold Mountain the name these Chinese immigrants gave California tells more about their expectations than it tells about the reality they found. [3]The seven-thousand-mile journey across the Pacific Ocean which often took more than three months drained the pioneers both physically and financially. [4]Chinese men who had arranged passage on credit found themselves in debt to the steamship company for several years. [5]Chinese miners did receive wages; nevertheless the amount they received was usually less than that paid to non-Asian miners.

[6]On the bright side the Chinese miners tireless laborers often succeeded where others had failed. [7]They often worked in abandoned mines hoping to find what previous miners had overlooked. [8]There they sifted through gravel heaps to extract the last traces of gold dust that the others had failed to notice. [9]These Chinese miners determined to succeed persisted despite the severe hardships they faced. [10]To succeed in the United States was to tell the truth far more difficult than they had imagined.

Commas with Introductory and Antithetical Phrases

1. Prepositional phrases

- A comma after a short introductory prepositional phrase is not incorrect, but the only time it is necessary is if the sentence might be misread without the comma.

  Among those running**,** women were well represented. [The comma is needed to prevent misreading.]

  Before the election the candidates will participate in two debates. [A comma would not be wrong but is not needed.]

- Use a comma after a long prepositional phrase or after the final phrase in a succession of phrases.

  During the coldest part of winter**,** she caught a bad cold.

  On the first Wednesday after the first Monday of each month**,** our book group meets.

If the prepositional phrase is immediately followed by a verb, do not use a comma.

Among the candidates in the race for mayor were three women from our part of the city.

2. Participles and participial phrases

- Use commas to set off introductory participles and participial phrases.

  Gesturing forcefully**,** the speaker held her audience spellbound.

  Running after my cats**,** I sprained my ankle.

3. Antithetical Phrases

- Use commas to set off an antithetical phrase.

In an **antithetical phrase,** a word such as *not* or *unlike* qualifies what comes before it.

Alaska**,** not Texas**,** is the largest state in the United States of America.

Australia**,** unlike New Zealand**,** is an island that is considered a continent.

Commas and Adverb Clauses

- Use commas to set off all introductory adverb clauses.

  Because it was a beautiful day, we decided to have a picnic.

- Use commas to set off internal adverb clauses that interrupt the flow of a sentence.

  Our outing, although it was well planned, did not run smoothly.

In general, do not set off an adverb clause at the end of a sentence. (If the clause is parenthetical or the sentence would be misread without the comma, however, the clause should be set off.)

We went home early even though we weren't tired.

Exercise 13 Using the Comma (Part 3)

Rewrite the following sentences, adding commas where they are needed. If a sentence is correct, write *correct.*

Jasper Johns and Robert Rauschenberg

1. Throughout the long history of art only a few artists can be said to have changed the course of painting.
2. One candidate might be Jasper Johns because many critics consider him to be the most influential of modern artists.
3. Because Jasper Johns and Robert Rauschenberg have influenced each other it is interesting to compare their work.
4. Putting aside their traditional training both artists preferred to work with abstract images.
5. Their finished works although they were carefully planned and executed sometimes look haphazard.
6. In the middle of a splash of paint and beside a scrap of newspaper Rauschenberg placed a light bulb.
7. Confused by such unusual combinations art critics have held differing opinions ever since they first attempted to interpret Rauschenberg's work.
8. Although the critics were puzzled at first they eventually realized that the everyday objects Rauschenberg used took on new meanings in his work.
9. The use of everyday objects by both artists was meant to be symbolic not absurd.
10. Everyday articles such as light bulbs and brooms became mysterious and beautiful things unlike ordinary light bulbs and brooms.

Additional Uses of Commas

1. Titles of people

■ Use commas to set off titles when they follow a person's name.

Maria Lopez, Ph.D. George Allen, governor of Virginia

Alberta Jones, D.D.S., will address us.

2. Addresses, geographical terms, and dates

■ Use commas to separate the various parts of an address, a geographical term, or a date.

Lancaster County, Pennsylvania, is known for its farms.

Please forward my mail to 6390 West Nassau Circle, Englewood, CO 80110, until Thursday, June 20, 1996.

Tuesday, April 1, 1996, was the day I won the scholarship.

Use the following forms for letter writing:

6390 West Nassau Circle
Englewood, CO 80110
April 1, 1995

If only the month and the day or the month and the year are given, do not use commas.

July 4 July 1776

3. References

■ Use commas to set off the parts of a reference that direct the reader to the exact source.

Refer to John Steinbeck's *The Pearl*, pages 37–47.

We rehearsed act 2, scene 3, of Lorraine Hansberry's *A Raisin in the Sun*.

4. Direct address

■ Use commas to set off words or names used in direct address.

Carlo, are you sure that you can get tickets for the game?

Remain in your seats, students, until the lecture is over.

Please don't forget to call me tomorrow, Anna.

5. **Tag questions**

■ Use commas to set off a tag question.

A tag question—such as *shouldn't I?* or *have you?*—suggests the answer to the statement that comes before it.

You checked your baggage**,** didn't you?

You haven't read that book**,** have you?

I should return the book to the library**,** shouldn't I?

6. **Letter writing**

■ Place a comma after the salutation of an informal letter and after the closing of all letters.

Dear Juan**,**	Dear Aunt Miriam**,**
Sincerely**,**	Love**,**

Exercise 14 Using the Comma (Part 4)

Rewrite the following letter, adding commas where they are needed. (Nineteen corrections are needed altogether.)

714 Williams Road
Charlottesville VA 22901
September 12 1997

Dear Greta

How have you been? I hope that you and your family are in good health. Did I write last time that we are moving? Our new address is 62 Channing Way Cranbury NJ 08512. I hope we will be all moved in by the first of next month.

I am enclosing a copy of the famous speech you requested. You haven't already found a copy of it have you Greta? The original speech was published in the September 9 1963 edition of *Newsweek* page 21. You can use it for your English assignment can't you?

On August 23 1963 there was an important civil rights march in Washington D.C. The march was led by Dr. Martin Luther King Jr. who was a church leader and a political activist. Dr. King believed in nonviolent protest and put his beliefs into practice. He organized a boycott of the segregated bus system of Montgomery Alabama in December 1955.

I hope the speech and this information will be helpful to you Greta.

Your friend
Tamara

Misuse of Commas

Do not use a comma before a conjunction that connects a compound predicate or a compound subject.

INCORRECT	The quarterback threw the ball**,** and then slipped.
CORRECT	The quarterback threw the ball and then slipped.
INCORRECT	The quarterback**,** and the running back are good athletes.
CORRECT	The quarterback and the running back are good athletes.

If two main clauses are not part of a series, do not use a comma alone to join them. Remember to add a coordinating conjunction or use a semicolon.

INCORRECT	The North Carolina state flag is red, white, blue, and gold**,** the state flower is flowering dogwood.
CORRECT	The North Carolina state flag is red, white, blue, and gold, and the state flower is flowering dogwood.
CORRECT	The North Carolina state flag is red, white, blue, and gold; the state flower is flowering dogwood.

A comma should not be used between a subject and its verb or between a verb and its complement.

INCORRECT	What she thought fit to do**,** was beyond me.
CORRECT	What she thought fit to do was beyond me.
INCORRECT	On our vacation we will bring**,** our tent, snack food, and beach clothes.
CORRECT	On our vacation we will bring our tent, snack food, and beach clothes.

Exercise 15 **Using Commas Correctly**

Each item contains one or more examples of incorrect comma usage. On your paper, rewrite each sentence to make it correct. You may need to delete commas, use a semicolon in place of a comma, or add a coordinating conjunction with the comma.

The Fascinating World of Seashells

1. The enormous diversity among seashells, makes them one of nature's most delightful creations.
2. Seashells come in all different sizes, and have spectacular patterns.
3. Some shells are fragile and easily broken, others are solid and sturdy.
4. What some people do not know, is that a shell is the outer skeleton of a soft-bodied animal known as a mollusk.
5. The five main classes of shells are, gastropods, bivalves, tusk shells, chitons, and cephalopods.

21.7 The Dash

On a typewriter, indicate a dash with two hyphens (--). On a computer, you may be able to make an actual dash. Refer to the manual of your word processing program for instructions.

A comma, semicolon, colon, or period should not be placed either before or after a dash.

1. Dashes to signal change

- Use a dash to indicate an abrupt break or change in thought within a sentence.

What was it—I paused to think—what was it that so unnerved me in the contemplation of the House of Usher?

— Edgar Allan Poe

2. Dashes to emphasize

- Use a dash to set off and emphasize supplemental information or parenthetical comments.

The crowd marveled as fifty pounds were lifted by the circus performer—using one finger.

The circus performer—using one finger—lifted fifty pounds.

Exercise 16 Using the Dash

On your paper, rewrite the following sentences, adding dashes where needed.

Forging Steel at Valley Forge

1. On July 3, 1775, George Washington he had served as commander-in-chief of the Virginia militia assumed command of the Continental Army.
2. One winter the army camped at Valley Forge, an easily defensible site so many people thought located 15 miles from Philadelphia.
3. Few soldiers if indeed they could be called that had ever heard of Valley Forge.
4. Washington himself designed the huts simple log cabins for his troops.
5. That winter was long snow fell early and bitterly cold.
6. The soldiers already exhausted, freezing, and hungry soon found themselves barefoot.
7. Life in Valley Forge an unbearable nightmare for everyone dragged on.
8. Yet Valley Forge a place where boys became men and men became soldiers played a crucial role in the war.
9. The unwavering commitment shown by General Washington he worked alongside his men and earned their devotion also inspired the troops.
10. Washington he developed his military skill by trial and error emerged from his defeat at Valley Forge with a well-trained and loyal army.

21.8 Parentheses

■ Use parentheses to set off supplemental material.

Parentheses, like commas and dashes, are used to set off supplemental material. Commas are used to set off material that is closely related to the rest of the sentence. Dashes are used not only to set off—but also to emphasize—material that abruptly interrupts the sentence. Parentheses are used to set off material that is incidental to the main statement but is nevertheless important enough to include.

Minnesota **(**named after the Dakota Sioux word meaning "cloudy water"**)** was explored by French scouts.

1. With complete sentences

If a complete sentence within parentheses is contained within another sentence, it is not capitalized and requires no period. If a complete sentence stands by itself within parentheses, both a capital letter and a period are required.

As gold and silver mining waned **(m**ining declined in the 1870s**)**, cattle became Nevada's principal source of revenue.

Nebraska contains two of the widest and flattest rivers in the country: the Missouri River and the Platte River. **(T**he name *Nebraska* comes from the Native American word *nibrathka,* meaning "flat water."**)**

2. With a comma, semicolon, or colon

■ Always place a comma, semicolon, or colon *after* the closing parenthesis.

Although Death Valley may appear barren (it is often called a desert**),** many plants and animals flourish there.

Pioneer towns had few women (more than half the population of Seattle were bachelors**);** in 1864, however, a settler brought a group of widows and orphans to Seattle.

Washington State is the site of these fur-trapping posts (all built before 1833**):** Spokane, Walla Walla, and Nisqually.

3. **With a question mark or exclamation point**

- Place a question mark or an exclamation point *inside* the parentheses if it is part of the parenthetical expression.

  There is a city named Clinton (named after American statesman De Witt Clinton**?)** in almost every state.

  Many names have been suggested for the Black Hills of South Dakota (surprisingly, they were almost named the Purple Mountains**!).**

- Place a question mark or an exclamation point *outside* the parentheses if it is part of the entire sentence.

  Did you visit the famous cowpoke capitals of the Old West (Dodge City, Cimarron, Wichita, and Abilene**)?**

  How surprised I was to find out that the Alamo was originally a Franciscan mission (the Mission of San Antonio de Valero**)!**

Exercise 17 Using the Dash and Parentheses

Rewrite the following sentences, adding dashes and parentheses where they are needed. Use the marks of punctuation indicated in parentheses at the end of each sentence.

The Story of Anne Frank

1. Anne Frank wrote a remarkable diary about her life in Amsterdam during World War II. She and her family were born in Germany but had moved to Holland before the war. (parentheses)
2. The diary addressed to an imaginary friend named Kitty has been published in over thirty languages. (dashes)
3. Anne, her parents, an older sister, and four friends eight persons in all went into hiding during the Nazi occupation of the Netherlands. (dashes)
4. Their hiding place was an unused section of an office building. In Dutch their secret apartment was called *het achterhuis,* which means "the house in the back." (parentheses)
5. The eight persons hidden in the apartment had to avoid making any noise. How could they have remained so quiet for so long? (parentheses)
6. The diary begun in June 1942 and ended in August 1944 covers Anne's life from the age of thirteen to that of fifteen a significant period in a girl's life. (parentheses, dash)
7. One entry tells how pleased she was who wouldn't be? to find out that a boy she liked also liked her. (parentheses)
8. Another entry reveals that she felt that her hopes could not compete with "the ever approaching thunder" the misery and destruction sweeping through Europe. (dash)
9. When Anne and the others were eventually discovered and taken prisoner, the diary was left behind. The diary was later found along with some short stories and sketches and was published in 1947. (dashes)
10. Anne Frank died in the concentration camp at Bergen-Belsen, Germany, in March 1945. She was not even sixteen. (parentheses)

21.9 Quotation Marks

Quotation Marks for Direct Quotations

■ Use quotation marks to enclose a direct quotation.

Place quotation marks only around the quoted material.

Introductory or explanatory remarks may be set off from the actual quotation with a comma.

The Mexican American poet Marina de Bellagente wrote, "You cannot put a fence around the planet earth."

"I celebrate myself, and sing myself," wrote Walt Whitman.

(For the use of colons to introduce quotations, see page 737.)

■ When a quotation is interrupted by explanatory words such as *he said* or *she wrote,* use two sets of quotation marks.

Each part of the quotation should be separated from the interrupting phrase with two marks of punctuation, such as two commas or a comma and a period. The second part of the quotation should begin with a capital letter if it is a complete sentence.

"Luis Tiant," Reggie Jackson once declared, "is the Fred Astaire of baseball."

"I never think of the future," wrote Albert Einstein. "It comes soon enough."

Quotation marks should not be used in an indirect quotation.

ORIGINAL QUOTATION	"I never intended to become a run-of-the-mill person," said Barbara Jordan.
INDIRECT QUOTATION	Barbara Jordan said that she never intended to become a run-of-the-mill person.

■ Use single quotation marks around a quotation within a quotation.

My instructor replied, "Sarah Bernhardt said, 'An artiste with short arms can never, never make a fine gesture.'"

■ In writing dialogue, begin a new paragraph and use a new set of quotation marks every time the speaker changes.

"What grade you in now, Raymond?"

"You got anything to say to my brother, you say it to me, Mary Louise Williams of Raggedy Town, Baltimore."

"What are you, his mother?" sasses Rosie.

—Toni Cade Bambara

Barbara Jordan said that she never intended to become a run-of-the-mill person.

Quotation Marks with Other Marks of Punctuation

1. With a comma or a period

- Always place a comma or a period *inside* closing quotation marks.

"Everything had its wonders, even darkness and silence**,"** wrote Helen Keller, who was blind and deaf from a young age.

Gwendolyn Brooks has said, "Poetry is life distilled**."**

2. With a semicolon or a colon

- Always place a semicolon or a colon *outside* closing quotation marks.

Lorraine Hansberry wrote "On Summer**";** this essay tells how her feelings about the season changed over the course of her life.

There are two Spanish verbs that mean "to be**":** *ser* and *estar.*

3. With a question mark or an exclamation point

- Place the question mark or exclamation point *inside* the closing quotation marks when it is part of the quotation.

My friend asked, "How did you persuade your mother**?"**

My father kept saying, "That's incredible**!"**

- Place the question mark or exclamation point *outside* the closing quotation marks when it is part of the entire sentence.

Why did he say, "This is only the beginning**"?**

How wonderful that she will print your story "Winter**"!**

If both your sentence and the quotation at the end of your sentence need a question mark (or an exclamation point), use only one question mark (or exclamation point) placed *inside* the quotation marks.

When did she ask, "Will the car be fixed in time**?"**

I ran when he yelled, "Come quickly**!"**

Do not use a comma after a quotation that ends with a question mark or exclamation point.

"That's incredible**!"** my father said yet again.

Quotation Marks with Titles and Unusual Expressions

1. With titles of short works

■ Use quotation marks to enclose titles of short works, such as short stories, short poems, essays, newspaper and magazine articles, book chapters, songs, and single episodes of a television series.

"Chee's Daughter" [short story]

"The Road Not Taken" [poem]

"On Summer" [essay]

"Welfare Reform Debated" [newspaper article]

"Climates of the Earth" [chapter]

"America the Beautiful" [song]

"A Stranger Comes to Town" [episode in a television series]

2. With unusual expressions

■ Use quotation marks to enclose unfamiliar slang and other unusual or original expressions.

My roommate calls clumps of dust "dust bunnies."

Exercise 18 Using Quotation Marks

Rewrite the following sentences, adding quotation marks where they are needed. For the sentences that need no changes, write *correct.*

Albert Einstein

1. Albert Einstein's uncle taught him algebra. It is a merry science, he told the boy. When the animal that we are hunting cannot be caught, we call it *x*.
2. The young Einstein was often called oddball.
3. One of Einstein's teachers is supposed to have said to him, Your presence in this class destroys the respect of the students; and someone else apparently told him, You will never amount to anything, Einstein.
4. I am a horse for a single harness, Einstein later said, not cut out for tandem or teamwork.
5. Einstein published a paper called The Influence of Gravity on the Propagation of Light.
6. If Einstein's theory should prove correct, said physicist Max Planck, he will be considered the Copernicus of the twentieth century.
7. Was it in 1916 that Einstein published his paper General Theory of Relativity?
8. Einstein believed—amazingly so at the time—that time and space could disappear!
9. In the 1950s, Einstein said he was ready to introduce his unified field theory, in which gravitation, electromagnetism, and subatomic phenomena are explained in one set of laws.
10. The most incomprehensible thing about the world is that it is comprehensible, said Einstein.

21.10 Italics (Underlining)

Italic type slants upward and to the right. (*This is printed in italics.*) On a typewriter or in handwriting, indicate italics by underlining. (<u>This is underlined.</u>) On a computer you can actually use italic type. Refer to your software manual for help.

Italics for Titles and Foreign Words

1. With titles

- Italicize (underline) titles of books, lengthy poems, plays, films and television series, paintings, and sculptures, and long musical compositions. Also italicize the names of newspapers and magazines, ships, trains, airplanes, and spacecraft.

The Color Purple [book]	*Appalachian Spring* [ballet]
The People, Yes [long poem]	the *Baltimore Sun* [newspaper]
Macbeth [play]	*Newsweek* [magazine]
On the Waterfront [film]	U.S.S. *Constitution* [ship]*
The Civil War [television series]	*Yankee Clipper* [train]
American Gothic [painting]	*Air Force One* [airplane]
Venus de Milo [sculpture]	*Sputnik I* [spacecraft]

*Do not italicize abbreviations such as U.S.S. in the name of a ship.

- Italicize (underline) and capitalize articles (*a, an, the*) written at the beginning of a title only when they are part of the title itself. It is common practice not to italicize (underline) the article preceding the title of a newspaper or a magazine. Do not italicize the word *magazine* unless it is part of the title of a periodical.

The Red Desert	*but*	the *Boston Globe*
A Farewell to Arms		a *Reader's Digest* magazine

2. With foreign words

- Italicize (underline) foreign words and expressions that are not used frequently in English.

Because Einstein was unconventional as a child, he was considered an ***enfant terrible.***

Do not italicize such words if they are commonly used in English.

Apple pie **à la mode** is my favorite dessert.

Italics with Words and Other Items Used to Represent Themselves

- Italicize (underline) words, letters, and numerals used to represent themselves.

Why does the author of that poem use the word ***essence*** instead of ***life***?

While I was carefully proofreading my essay, I noticed that the ***i*** and the ***t*** were reversed in the title.

In order to complete the mathematical equation, I needed to find the values of ***s*** and ***y***.

Exercise 19 Using Italics

Rewrite the following sentences, underlining the parts that should be italicized.

Noteworthy Americans

1. Lorene Cary's book Black Ice is a memoir of the author's experiences as one of the first African American students at St. Paul's, a boarding school in New Hampshire.
2. When Will I See You Again, painted by Martin Wong, realistically depicts an image from the artist's neighborhood.
3. Américo Paredes, a professor who has also served as editor of the Journal of American Folklore, has written about Mexican proverbs, or dichos.
4. Paredes points out that although the formal word for proverb in Spanish is refrán, many Mexican Americans use the word dichos, meaning "sayings."
5. Mary Tyler Moore has been successful on television in her highly popular comedy series The Mary Tyler Moore Show and later in movies as the star of such films as Ordinary People.
6. A short-lived magazine of the late 1980s was Lear's, created by Frances Lear for women age forty and older.
7. Novelist N. Scott Momaday won a Pulitzer Prize for his book House Made of Dawn in 1969, but he is perhaps best known for The Way to Rainy Mountain, a collection of stories and legends of the Kiowa people.
8. The well-known American composer Aaron Copland was awarded the Pulitzer Prize for his ballet score Appalachian Spring and later received an Academy Award for his film score for The Heiress.
9. Mark Harris once wrote an entire comic novel that consisted of correspondence supposedly composed on a defective typewriter; the work lacked the letter f throughout.
10. The Puerto Rican artist Arnaldo Roche Rabell's emotional and expressionistic style is evident in such paintings as Blind Dreams and You Tell Me If This Is Not an Omen.

21.11 The Apostrophe

Apostrophes with Possessives

1. Pronouns

■ Use an apostrophe and *-s* for the possessive of a singular indefinite pronoun.

An apostrophe should not be used with any possessive pronouns.

one**'s** time	*but*	**his** duty
somebody else**'s** clothes		**its** paws

2. Singular nouns

■ Use an apostrophe and *-s* to form the possessive of a singular noun, even one that ends in *-s*.

the man**'s** collar	Mexico**'s** landscape
the dress**'s** hem	George Burns**'s** humor
The heiress**'s** instructions	Dickens**'s** novels
the fox**'s** lair	Max**'s** father

Some exceptions to this rule do exist, however. When forming the possessive of ancient proper nouns that end in *-es* or *-is*, the name *Jesus*, and expressions that contain sibilants (*s* sounds) close together, such as *appearance'* sake and *goodness'* sake, add an apostrophe only.

Aristophanes**'** plays	Jesus**'** followers
Isis**'** temple	Xerxes**'** army

3. Plural nouns ending in *-s*

■ Use an apostrophe alone to form the possessive of a plural noun that ends in *-s*.

purple mountains**'** majesty	the Hawaiian Islands**'** charm
the gloves**'** size	the *Ladies*' *Home Journal*

4. Plural nouns not ending in *-s*

■ Use an apostrophe and *-s* to form the possessive of a plural noun that does not end in *-s*.

the men**'s** department	Women**'s** Medical Center
the deer**'s** antlers	the geese**'s** eggs

Punctuation, Abbreviations, and Numbers

5. **Compound nouns**

- Put only the last word of a compound noun in the possessive form.

  my mother-in-law**'s** camera
  the district attorney**'s** victory
  the heir apparent**'s** throne
  the surgeon general**'s** warning

6. **Phrases**

- In a phrase or combination of names, add an apostrophe and *-s* to the last word only.

  the President of the United States**'s** inauguration
  the director from Hollywood**'s** last movie
  Chief Medicine Crow of Montana**'s** delegation

7. **Joint possession versus individual possession**

- If two or more persons (or partners in a company) possess something jointly, use the possessive form for the last person named.

  Shiro and Suki**'s** home
  Barnum and Bailey**'s** Circus
  Gilbert and Sullivan**'s** operettas

- If two or more persons (or companies) possess an item (or items) individually, put each one's name in the possessive form.

  Jorge Amado**'s** and Jorge Luis Borges**'s** novels
  Mozart**'s** and Beethoven**'s** music

8. **Expressions of time and money**

- Use a possessive form to express amounts of money or time that modify a noun.

It is also correct to express the modifier as a hyphenated adjective. When that is done, the possessive form is not used.

five dollar**s'** worth	*but*	a five-dollar contribution
one minute**'s** pause		a one-minute pause
a day**'s** journey		a one-day journey
six day**s'** rest		a six-day rest

Punctuation, Abbreviations, and Numbers

Apostrophes with Contractions and Special Plurals

1. With contractions

■ Use an apostrophe in place of letters omitted in contractions.

A **contraction** is a word formed from two words that have been combined by omitting one or more letters. Contractions are generally formed from a subject and a verb or a verb and an adverb.

I'm	*formed from*	I am
you're		you are
it's		it is, it has
doesn't, don't		does not, do not

■ Use an apostrophe in place of the omitted numerals of a year.

the World Series of '83   the fall television season of '97

2. With special plurals

■ Use an apostrophe and *-s* to form the plural of letters, numerals, symbols, and words used to represent themselves.

Only the letter, numeral, symbol, or word should be italicized (underlined), not the apostrophe or the *-s.*

Your *a*'s are indistinguishable from your *o*'s.

All of the *8*'s had been typed as *3*'s.

Exercise 20 Using the Apostrophe

Rewrite the following sentences, adding apostrophes where they are needed and *-s* wherever necessary.

American Performers

[1]Lets imagine that we are compiling a list of actors and actresses names for a biographical dictionary of American performers. [2]Under the *c*s wed include Kevin Costner, a popular contemporary actor, and Claudette Colbert, a brilliant actress of the thirties and forties. [3]We mustnt forget to include Bill Cosbys name, because hes essential. [4]He and Whoopi Goldberg would probably appear on everybodys list of excellent performers. [5]We would also include Graham Greene, the Native American performer who received critical acclaim for his performance in *Dances with Wolves.* [6]Under the *m*s Id expect to see a good many names. [7]My friend Maxs choice is Pat Morita, whose performance in *The Karate Kid* movies entertained audiences everywhere. [8]Then theres Rita Moreno, whose role as Anita in United Artists *West Side Story* earned her wide praise. [9]After an hours time we would have a much longer list, including Julia Roberts and Susan Sarandons names. [10]My friend James first choice is Tom and Dick Smothers, one of show business best comedy teams from the past.

21.12 The Hyphen

Hyphens with Prefixes

Hyphens are not usually used to join a prefix to a word. The following are some exceptions:

- Use a hyphen after any prefix joined to a proper noun or a proper adjective. Use a hyphen after the prefixes *all-*, *ex-* (meaning "former"), and *self-* joined to any noun or adjective.

pre-Columbian	all-encompassing
un-American	ex-governor
mid-August	self-addressed
post-World War I	self-employed

- Use a hyphen after the prefix *anti-* when it joins a word beginning with *i-*. Also use a hyphen after the prefix *vice-*, except in *vice president.*

anti-inflationary	vice-principal
anti-inflammatory	vice-chancellor

- Use a hyphen to avoid confusion between words beginning with *re-* that look alike but are different in meaning and pronunciation.

re-count the ballots	*but*	recount a story
re-lay the tiles		relay the message
re-mark the papers		remark on her condition

Exercise 21 **Using Hyphens with Prefixes**

On your paper, rewrite the following sentences, adding hyphens where they are needed.

The American Revolution

1. The desire for selfgovernment among British colonists grew steadily during the preRevolutionary War period.
2. Antimonarchy and antiimperialist forces prevailed, and the Continental Congress prepared for allout war with Britain.
3. Not only was the British army considered the best allaround fighting force, but it also had the support of the proBritish Iroquois Confederacy.
4. At first British leaders remarked disdainfully that most American soldiers were self-taught.
5. After carefully recreating their government, the exBritish colonies became the United States of America.

Hyphens with Compounds

1. Compound adjectives

■ Use a hyphen in a compound adjective that precedes a noun.

When a compound adjective follows a noun, it is usually not hyphenated.

up-to-the-minute news	*but*	The news was up to the minute.
a nine-year-old boy		The boy was nine years old.
a well-educated girl		The girl is well educated.

An expression is not hyphenated when it is made up of an adverb ending in *-ly* and an adjective.

a happily married couple	the beautifully prepared dinner
a mainly green interior	the amazingly bright child
a nicely decorated house	the perfectly grand day

2. Compound numbers

■ Hyphenate any spelled-out cardinal or ordinal compound number up to ninety-nine or ninety-ninth.

forty-five	eighty-eighth
twenty-first	sixty-seventh

3. Fractions used as adjectives

■ Hyphenate a fraction used as an adjective or as a noun.

two-thirds majority	two-thirds of the members
one-half liter	one-half of a liter
one-eighth mile	one-eighth of a mile

4. Connected numerals

■ Hyphenate two numerals to indicate a span.

pages 354-392	1884-1903
April 1-6	15th-16th centuries

Hyphens to Divide Words at the End of a Line

When a word must be divided at the end of a line, it should be divided between syllables or pronounceable parts. If you are unsure of the correct place to divide a word, check your dictionary.

- In general, if a word contains two consonants occurring between two vowels or if it contains a double consonant, divide the word between the two consonants.

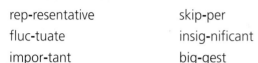

rep-resentative	skip-per
fluc-tuate	insig-nificant
impor-tant	big-gest

Exercise 22 **Using Hyphens**

Hyphens must be added to seven of the following sentences. On your paper rewrite those sentences, adding the hyphens where they are needed. If a sentence contains only words that need no hyphens, write *correct.* Then make a list of all the italicized words, showing where each would be divided if it had to be broken at the end of a line.

Looking at Statistics

1. Statistics can tell us an extraordinarily broad *spectrum* of things about Americans.
2. In 1830, for instance, nearly three-fourths of the U.S. population lived on family farms; today one in *fifty* Americans lives on a farm.
3. There is a clear cut trend toward *urban* living.
4. A look at the *almanac* reveals the wide ranging salaries of United States governors—going from just under $56,000 to well over $100,000 a year.
5. During a period of fifty years (1935 1985), the average annual income of a person *working* in the United States jumped from less than $500 to nearly $14,000.
6. American women, however, continue to earn less than men; on average, for every *dollar* that a man earns, a woman earns sixty nine cents.
7. By the year 2000, the number of Asian Americans and Native Americans in the work force is *expected* to experience a two thirds increase.
8. Whereas most Americans work for others, a significant *number* of adults are self employed.
9. The fast growing Hispanic population is having a great impact on American *culture* and society.
10. One widely known statistic is that more and more African Americans are *holding* public office.

21.13 Abbreviations

Abbreviations are shortened forms of words. They are used to save space and time and to avoid wordiness. For example, it is more concise and easier to write *800 B.C.* than to write *800 years before the birth of Christ.* Periods follow most abbreviations. For guidance on how to write a particular abbreviation, check a dictionary.

- If an abbreviation occurs at the end of a sentence that would ordinarily take a period, do not add an additional closing period

  I am going to Washington, **D.C.**

- If an abbreviation occurs at the end of a sentence that ends with a question mark or an exclamation point, use the period for the abbreviation *and* the second mark of punctuation.

  Have you been to Washington, **D.C.?**

  I can't wait to go to Washington, **D.C.!**

Capitalization of Abbreviations

- Capitalize abbreviations of proper nouns.

  Dwight **D.** Eisenhower
  135 Claremont **Ave.**
  U.S. Department of Labor

The names of many organizations and agencies, whether pronounced letter by letter or as words, are abbreviated by using the initial letters of the complete name without periods.

NAACP YMCA CIA FCC UN NATO

Capitalize these abbreviations related to historical dates:

A.D. (*anno Domini*), "in the year of the Lord" (since the birth of Christ); place before the date: **A.D.** 66

B.C. (before Christ); place after the date: 336 **B.C.**

B.C.E. (before the common era; equivalent to *B.C.*); place after the date: 1000 **B.C.E.**

C.E. (common era; equivalent to *A.D.*); place after the date: 60 **C.E.**

A.M. (*ante meridiem*), "before noon"; place after exact times: 2:45 **A.M.**

P.M. (*post meridiem*), "after noon"; place after exact times: 10:30 **P.M.**

State Abbreviations

In ordinary prose, spell out state names. When addressing mail, however, use the abbreviations of state names that appear in the list below. (*Note:* No comma appears between the state postal abbreviation and the number in a zip code.)

Alabama	**AL**	Montana	**MT**
Alaska	**AK**	Nebraska	**NE**
Arizona	**AZ**	Nevada	**NV**
Arkansas	**AR**	New Hampshire	**NH**
California	**CA**	New Jersey	**NJ**
Colorado	**CO**	New Mexico	**NM**
Connecticut	**CT**	New York	**NY**
Delaware	**DE**	North Carolina	**NC**
Florida	**FL**	North Dakota	**ND**
Georgia	**GA**	Ohio	**OH**
Hawaii	**HI**	Oklahoma	**OK**
Idaho	**ID**	Oregon	**OR**
Illinois	**IL**	Pennsylvania	**PA**
Indiana	**IN**	Rhode Island	**RI**
Iowa	**IA**	South Carolina	**SC**
Kansas	**KS**	South Dakota	**SD**
Kentucky	**KY**	Tennessee	**TN**
Louisiana	**LA**	Texas	**TX**
Maine	**ME**	Utah	**UT**
Maryland	**MD**	Vermont	**VT**
Massachusetts	**MA**	Virginia	**VA**
Michigan	**MI**	Washington	**WA**
Minnesota	**MN**	West Virginia	**WV**
Mississippi	**MS**	Wisconsin	**WI**
Missouri	**MO**	Wyoming	**WY**

The postal abbreviation for the District of Columbia, for use on envelopes only, is **DC**.

Exercise 23 Using Abbreviations

On your paper, write the abbreviations for the italicized words or phrases in the following sentences. If an abbreviation should not be used, write *correct.*

1. The *Young Men's Christian Association* has been promoting family and recreational activities since *anno Domini* 1844.
2. The *United States* Capitol is located in Washington, D.C.
3. One zip code for Fargo, *North Dakota,* is 58103.
4. The *Federal Aviation Administration* establishes regulations for airline companies.
5. Many Americans begin work at 9:00 *ante meridiem* and end at 5:00 *post meridiem.*

Abbreviations of Titles and Units of Measure

1. Personal titles

■ Use abbreviations for some personal titles.

Certain titles, including *Mrs., Mr., Ms., Sr.,* and *Jr.,* are almost always abbreviated. Professional and academic titles, such as *Dr., M.D.,* and *B.A.,* are also usually abbreviated. When they are used before a full name, the titles of government and military officials and members of the clergy are frequently abbreviated.

Mrs. Elizabeth Dole	**Gov.** Tommy Thompson
Ms. Amy Tan	**Sen.** Carol Mosely-Braun
Dr. Joseph Fernandez	**Rev.** Jesse Jackson

2. Units of measure

■ Abbreviate units of measure used with numerals in technical or scientific writing but not in ordinary prose.

In the list below, the abbreviations stand for plural as well as singular units:

ENGLISH SYSTEM		METRIC SYSTEM	
ft.	foot	**cg**	centigram
gal.	gallon	**cl**	centiliter
in.	inch	**cm**	centimeter
lb.	pound	**g**	gram
mi.	mile	**kg**	kilogram
oz.	ounce	**km**	kilometer
pt.	pint	**l**	liter
qt.	quart	**m**	meter
tbsp.	tablespoon	**mg**	milligram
tsp.	teaspoon	**ml**	milliliter
yd.	yard	**mm**	millimeter

Exercise 24 Using Abbreviations (Part 2)

Write the abbreviations for the italicized words or phrases in the following sentences. If no abbreviation should be used, write *correct.*

1. *Governor* Nellie Tayloe Ross of Wyoming, elected in 1924, was the first woman to hold that office in any state.
2. Among the guests were *Mister* Diaz and his daughters.
3. *Doctor* C. Everett Koop was the surgeon general during George Bush's administration.
4. The pitcher stood 60 *feet* 6 *inches* from the batter and glanced at first base.
5. Add 20 *milliliters* of water to the formula.

21.14 Numbers and Numerals

In ordinary prose, some numbers are written out in words, and some are expressed in figures. Numbers that are expressed in figures are known as *numerals.*

Numbers Spelled Out

- In general, spell out cardinal and ordinal numbers that can be written in one or two words.

  The Senate consists of **one hundred** members—**two** senators from each of the **fifty** states.

  The building is **sixty-eight** feet tall.

  Juanita was the **thirty-sixth** person waiting in line for concert tickets.

- Spell out any number that occurs at the beginning of a sentence.

  Two thousand twenty-eight people were at the concert.

  Twenty-nine students are in our class.

Exercise 25 Using Numbers

On your paper, rewrite the following sentences, spelling out numbers where necessary.

The Inca Empire

1. The Inca Empire dominated the Andes region of South America for more than 1/3 of a century.
2. 2,200 miles of Pacific coastline were controlled by the Incas.
3. The 8th Inca ruler was the first to be called *Sapa Inca,* meaning "emperor."
4. 150 miles a day was not an uncommon distance for a team of Inca runners carrying messages throughout the empire.
5. The mighty Inca Empire was destroyed in only 3 years by the Spanish explorer Francisco Pizarro.
6. In 1531 Pizarro made his 3rd expedition to Peru, determined to conquer the rich and powerful Inca Empire.
7. 180 men went with Pizarro when he sailed from Panama to Peru.
8. At the start of his expedition, Pizarro had only 27 horses and 2 pieces of artillery.
9. Pizarro and his men were the 1st Europeans to reach the interior of Peru and confront the Inca ruler.
10. Within 50 years of the Spanish conquest, there was little trace of the once-glorious Inca civilization.

Numerals

- In general, use numerals to express numbers that would be written in more than two words.

  The Homestead Act allowed each farmer to claim **160** acres.

  The speed of light is **186,000** miles per second.

When a large number can be written as a mixed number followed by the word *million* or *billion,* the numeral should appear in decimal form.

  The television station was purchased for **$86.5 million.**

- If some numbers of a category can be written out while other related numbers should appear as numerals, use all numerals.

  Of the **435** members of the House of Representatives, **50** were newly elected.

1. Money, decimals, and percentages

- Use numerals to express amounts of money, decimals, and percentages.

  $19.50 | **2.5** pounds
  $6.25 million | **57** percent

If an amount of money can be expressed in one or two words, however, it should be spelled out.

  seventy-six cents | **sixty thousand** dollars

2. Dates and time

- Use numerals to express the year and day in a date and to express the precise time with the abbreviations A.M. and P.M.

  The First Continental Congress met on September **5, 1774.**

  The president was to meet the ambassador at **3:15 P.M.**

Spell out expressions of time that do not use A.M. or P.M.

  The ambassador's meeting was scheduled for **three** o'clock.

- To express a century when the word *century* is used, spell out the number. Likewise, to express a decade when the century is clear from the context, spell out the number.

  The greatest decade of the **twentieth** century was the **twenties.**

- When a decade is expressed as a single unit, use numerals followed by *-s.*

  The **1920s** were known as the Jazz Age.

Punctuation, Abbreviations, and Numbers

3. Addresses

■ Use numerals for streets and avenues numbered above ten and for all house, apartment, and room numbers. Spell out numbered streets and avenues with numbers of ten or under.

526 West **111th** Street	**52** South **Ninth** Street
Apartment **6D**	Room **8**
18 East **12th** Avenue	**866 Third** Avenue

4. References

■ Use numerals to express page, line, act, and scene numbers.

Look on pages **9** and **24** for references to Arthur Ashe.

Read paragraphs **3** and **4** on page **360** of my Chinese cookbook.

We danced in scenes **1** and **2** of the community ballet.

Exercise 26 Using Numbers and Numerals

Write out the following sentences, making any necessary changes in the use of numbers and numerals.

Wilma Rudolph, Sprinter

1. One of the fastest female runners of the 20th century, Wilma Rudolph won 3 gold medals at the 1960 Olympic games.
2. Besides placing 1st in the women's one-hundred-meter and two-hundred-meter dashes, she pushed her team to victory in the women's four-hundred-meter relay.
3. Rudolph's feat is all the more astonishing because she was not able to walk until she was 8.
4. Her birth weight was low, well under 5 pounds, and she suffered from a series of illnesses that left her, at the age of 4, without the use of her left leg.
5. By the time Rudolph entered high school, she had recovered so well that she excelled in basketball; in 1 year she scored eight hundred three points in 25 games.
6. At the Millrose Games in nineteen hundred sixty-one, she ran the 60-yard dash in six and nine-tenths seconds; she broke that world record 2 weeks later.
7. 11.3 seconds was her time in the one-hundred-meter dash at the 1960 Olympics—a time she bettered by one tenth of a second on July nineteen, 1961, when she set the women's world record.
8. At 5 feet 11 inches and one hundred thirty pounds, Rudolph was tall yet extraordinarily graceful.
9. After her Olympic victory, she toured Europe, greeting 1,000s of people and traveling more than two thousand miles.
10. During the nineteen sixties Rudolph retired from running while still in her 20s; she then devoted herself to developing track-and-field teams for girls.

UNIT 21 Grammar Review

PUNCTUATION

Eudora Welty has spent most of her long and productive life in Jackson, Mississippi, where she was born in 1909. This seemingly sheltered life has not been without risk, for "all serious daring starts from within," as she says in her memoir, *One Writer's Beginnings.* In this excerpt from that book, she reminisces about her father's family and alludes to her mother's, the Andrewses. The passage has been annotated to show some of the rules of punctuation covered in this unit.

Literature Model

from One Writer's Beginnings

by Eudora Welty

The Weltys were originally German Swiss; the first ones to come to this country, back before the Revolutionary War here, were three brothers, and the whole family is descended from them, I understand—it seems to hark back to German fairy-tale tradition.

My father is not the one who told me this: he never happened to tell us a single family story; could it have been because he'd heard so many of the Andrews stories? I think it was rather because, as he said, he had no interest in ancient history—only the future, he said, should count. At the same time, he was exceedingly devoted to his father, went to see him whenever he could, and wrote to him regularly from his desk at home; I grew up familiar with seeing the long envelopes being addressed in my father's clear, careful hand: Jefferson Welty, Esquire. It was the only use my father made of the word; he saved it for his father. I took "Esquire" for a term of reverence, and I think it stood for that with him; we were always aware that Daddy loved him.

An English Welti, who spelled his name thus, with an *i*, wrote to me once from Kent, in curiosity, after an early book of mine had appeared over there; he asked me about my

Semicolon to separate main clauses

Dash to indicate a change in thought

Period at the end of a declarative sentence

Colon to introduce a restatement

Apostrophe to indicate a contraction

Question mark to indicate a question

Commas to separate elements in a series

Apostrophe and *-s* to indicate the possessive forms of *father*

Comma to separate two main clauses that are joined by a coordinating conjunction name. My father, who had never told us anything, had died, and this was before my mother set herself as she did later to looking into records. Mr. Welti knew about the whole throng of them, from medieval times on, and the three brothers who set forth to the New World from German Switzerland and settled from Virginia westward over Pennsylvania, Ohio, and Indiana before the Revolutionary War. "I expect you know," wrote the British Mr. Welti, "that one unfortunate Welty fell at Saratoga."

The only part of his letter that would have interested my father is that about the St. Gotthard Tunnel and the Welty who pushed it through. The fact that this same Welty had been President of Switzerland seven times running would have caused him to say "Pshaw!", his strongest expletive. (That my mother's strongest exclamation was "Pshaw!" too rather took away some of its force for both of them.)

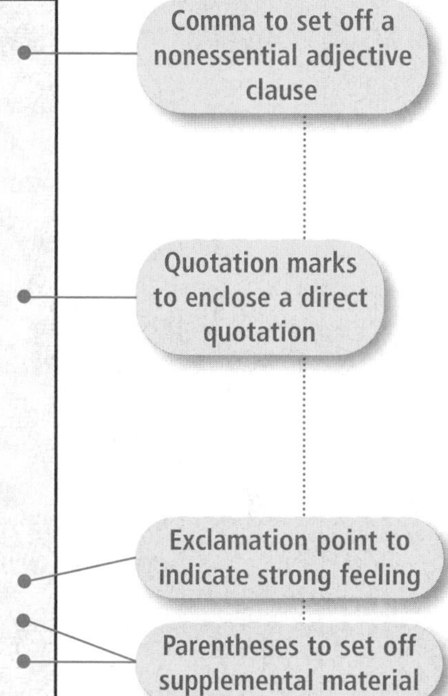

Review: Exercise 1 Using End Punctuation

The following sentences describe some of Eudora Welty's early teachers. On your paper, rewrite each item, correcting any errors in end punctuation. If an item contains no errors, write *correct.*

1. Don't most people vividly remember at least one teacher from their childhood. One of Eudora Welty's most memorable teachers was Miss Duling.
2. Can you imagine a prim woman, wearing a black-and-white checked dress, a long red sweater, black stockings, and black high-top shoes. Wow.
3. What a perfectionist Miss Duling seemed to Eudora?
4. Miss Duling was intolerant of excuses and pretensions. The governor's daughter, named Lady Rachel, was just plain Rachel to Miss Duling.
5. Miss Duling asked the Mississippi legislature to compete in a spelling match with her fourth-grade class?
6. Who won the spelling match. Welty hints that the class did.
7. Miss Eyrich, Welty's physical-education teacher, was also memorable.
8. How her booming commands terrorized reluctant runners?
9. Mrs. McWillie, a stern fourth-grade teacher, once overhead Welty and a friend using improper grammar.
10. The furious Mrs. McWillie asked which of the girls had used an incorrect verb form? Why, she even threatened to report them to the principal.

Review Exercise 2 Using Colons and Semicolons

The following sentences tell about Eudora Welty's love of reading. On your paper, rewrite each sentence, correcting any errors in the use of colons and semicolons. If a sentence contains no errors, write *correct.*

1. Eudora Welty's parents valued reading: therefore, they purchased books that would delight as well as instruct.
2. Books in the Welty library included those by the following authors; Mark Twain, Ring Lardner, and Charles Dickens.
3. Welty was exposed to books at an early age: books were a favorite gift in her household.
4. *Our Wonder World,* one of Welty's favorite sets of books, contained: legends about Robin Hood and King Arthur, fairy tales by H. C. Anderson, and fables by Aesop.
5. One critic describes Welty's *One Writer's Beginnings* as follows, "This splendid little book will itself be remembered and used and loved."

Review: Exercise 3 Using the Comma (Part 1)

The following sentences describe Southern writers. Rewrite each sentence, adding the material in parentheses in the place indicated by the caret. If the material is *not* essential to the meaning of the sentence, add commas. If it is essential, do not add commas.

SAMPLE Writers∧have contributed greatly to the body of memorable American literature. (who are from the South)

ANSWER Writers who are from the South have contributed greatly to the body of memorable American literature.

1. The Mississippi writer∧is considered to be among the greatest authors of the twentieth century. (William Faulkner)
2. Faulkner∧wrote a saga about life in Yoknapatawpha County. (who won a Nobel Prize in 1949)
3. He depicts in these books∧a changing South. (that feature the Snopes family as protagonists)
4. The Southern author∧is Alice Walker. (whom I enjoy most)
5. Alice Walker∧writes about African Americans. (whose most famous book is *The Color Purple*)
6. ∧Flannery O'Connor did grow up in Georgia. (Yes)
7. O'Connor∧depicts eccentrics and outcasts. (by the way)
8. She writes about a character∧. (who is called The Misfit)
9. Carson McCullers∧depicts an isolated café owner and a hearing-impaired person in one of her novels. (another Georgian)
10. ∧*The Member of the Wedding* focuses on a lonely Southern girl. (one of the most famous of McCullers's works)

Review: Exercise 4 Using the Comma (Part 2)

The following sentences describe the Southern settings used by some American writers. On your paper, rewrite each sentence, adding or deleting commas where necessary.

1. The South is often the setting in works written by Eudora Welty Harper Lee and Walker Percy.
2. Lee grew up in Alabama and she used a small, Southern town as the setting for her only novel *To Kill a Mockingbird.*
3. *To Kill a Mockingbird* won a Pulitzer Prize in 1961; subsequently it was made into a movie.
4. By the way the main characters in *To Kill a Mockingbird* seem much like the young Eudora Welty and her father.
5. Walker Percy grew up in Birmingham, Alabama but his novels are set in various locales throughout the South.
6. Although Percy called his view of the world "cold-eyed" and "despairing" his books are popular.
7. Percy's first novel, *The Moviegoer,* is about a young affluent New Orleans stock-broker searching for a new direction in his life.
8. His settings create a mood that is at once grotesque, and humorous, and disturbing.
9. Writers such as Zora Neale Hurston, Alice Walker and Truman Capote left the South but the region remained a presence in their writing.
10. For example Capote's "A Christmas Memory" is a story set in Monroeville Alabama

Review: Exercise 5 Using the Dash and Parentheses

The following sentences are about the Saint Gotthard Tunnel, which one of Welty's ancestors helped build. Rewrite each sentence, adding dashes or parentheses where needed. Use the marks of punctuation indicated in parentheses at the end of each sentence.

1. The masonry-lined tunnel it is more than nine miles long connects Andermatt to Airolo in the Swiss Alps. (dashes)
2. Did you know that the tunnel, at its highest point of elevation, is 3,786 feet 1,154 meters above sea level? (parentheses)
3. The project after a decade of construction was finally completed in 1882; it was part of the Saint Gotthard Railway. This line connects Lucerne, Switzerland, to Milan, Italy. (dashes, parentheses)
4. The tunnel was costly in human terms hundreds lost their lives during its construction; it was also a financial burden the company almost went bankrupt several times. (two pairs of parentheses)
5. This tunnel a massive undertaking cut the traveling time between Milan and Lucerne to ten hours. (dashes)

Review: Exercise 6 **Using Quotation Marks and Italics**

These sentences are based on other parts of Welty's memoir. On your paper, rewrite each one, adding quotation marks or italics (underlining) when necessary.

1. Welty loved listening to music: first, lullabies like Rock-a-Bye Baby and, later, selections from the opera Carmen.
2. Using today's slang, someone might call Eudora's mother's avid reading totally awesome; she read everything from novels such as Jane Eyre to scientific works.
3. Eudora is going to be a writer, we can imagine one of her teachers saying, because she loves fine literature.
4. Welty learned the meaning of words such as somnambulist by watching The Cabinet of Dr. Caligari and other films.
5. Welty relates that the first book she ever bought was In April Once, by William Alexander Percy, a Mississippi poet. The first poem in the volume was entitled Home.

Review: Exercise 7 **Using the Apostrophe**

Rewrite each of the following sentences, adding or deleting apostrophes where necessary. If a sentence has no errors, write *correct.*

1. *One Writers' Beginnings* is about Eudora Welty's early life.
2. Both parent's love for her was steady but unindulgent; its apparent in the book.
3. Their children's success in life was partially due to the Weltys high regard for education.
4. Welty also describes the trip to her Grandma Andrews's house in West Virginia.
5. Grandma Andrews (Mrs. Weltys' mother) must have been pleased with her son-in-law's adoration of her daughter.

Review: Exercise 8

Proofreading

The following passage describes the artist Winslow Homer, whose painting appears on the opposite page. Rewrite the passage, correcting the errors in spelling, usage, and grammar. Add any missing punctuation. There are twenty-five errors.

Winslow Homer

[1]American artist Winslow Homer (1836–1910) was born in Boston Massachusetts. [2]When he was 6 his family moved to the nearby town of Cambridge. [3]Where Homer first developed a love for the outdoors. [4]By the time he was 19 Homer had apprenticed himself to a Boston lithographer. [5]Uninspired by the work there he became a free-lance illustrater for *Ballou's Pictorial,*

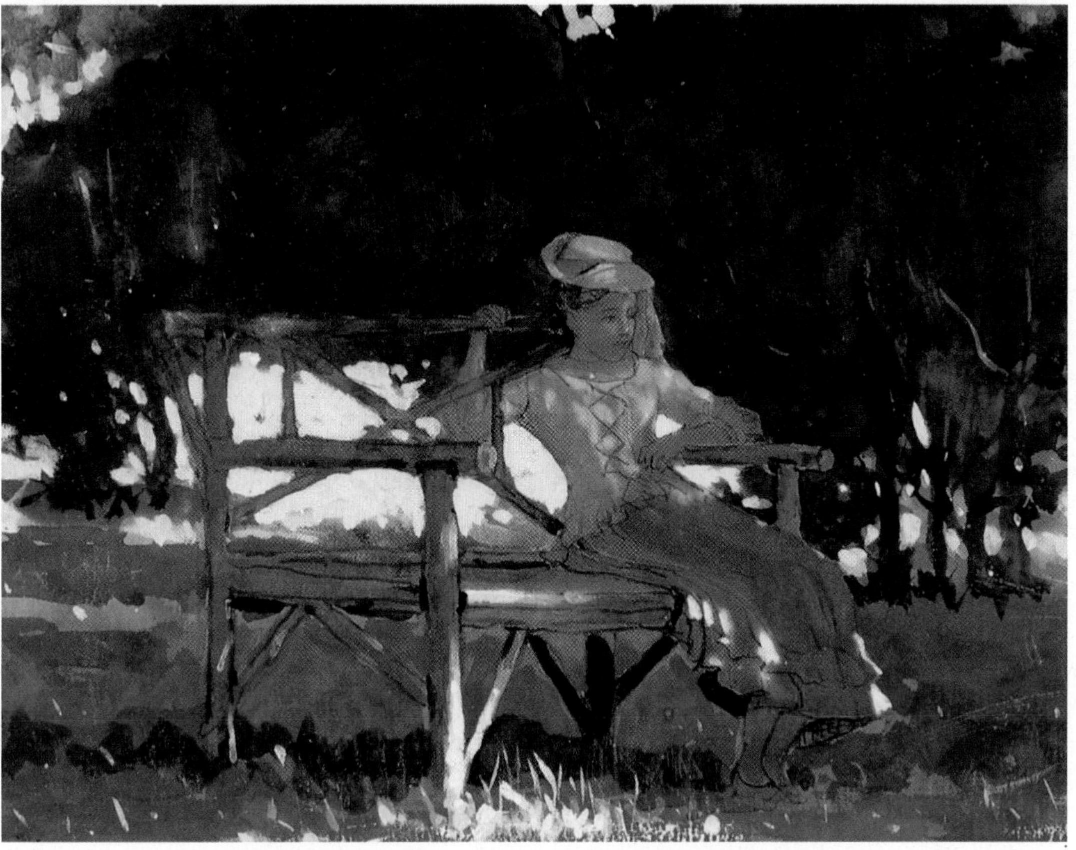

Winslow Homer, *Girl on a Garden Seat,* 1878

a Boston periodical and for *Harper's Weekly,* a New York magazine. [6]He moved to New York in 1859 and he continues to make illustrations for *Harper's Weekly.*

[7]When the Civil War began *Harper's Weekly* sent Homer to Virginia to document the fighting along the front lines. [8]His well drawn illustrations of the war were accurate and lacked heroic exageration.

[9]After the war ended Homer turned to painting scenes of contemporary country life. [10]The painting above is typical of Homers work after the war. [11]Like many of his paintings, it was executed in watercolors a medium in which he excelled. [12]Using only a few brush strokes he was able to convey an entire world of light, shadow and color. [13]Homer's paintings always reflected his love of nature recording life acurately without being sentimental. [14]His nature scenes, where the land and sea predominate are very popular. [15]Powerful examples of Homer's trust in nature.

[16]It is easy to imagine that either Eudora Welty or one of Weltys' relatives is depicted in the painting above. [17]The portrait shows a young woman who is prosperous she symbolizes all the young women of her time and class.

Review: Exercise 9

Mixed Review

The following sentences are about Eudora Welty and her family. Rewrite each sentence, correcting all errors in punctuation.

1. The author, Eudora Welty, was born in 1909 in Jackson, Mississippi (the state's capital.
2. Her parents who valued reading purchased books for their children.
3. Welty first attended a womens' college in Mississippi: but she graduated from the University of Wisconsin.
4. In 1936 Welty published her first short story "Death of a Traveling Salesman:" moreover she followed it quickly with two collections of stories.
5. "Place", Welty once said, "has the most delicate control over character; she then discussed the role of setting in the fiction of William Faulkner, Emily Brontë and Thomas Mann.
6. Welty's characters sometimes labeled with the word grotesque evoke the atmosphere of the small-town South.
7. Among the memorable characters in Welty's stories are these; Phoenix Jackson, in "A Worn Path," Leota, in "Petrified Man," and Marian, in "A Visit of Charity".
8. After reading the story *A Worn Path,* some readers have asked, "Is Phoenix' grandson really dead"?
9. Another character the narrator of "Why I Live at the P.O.", vividly describes her eccentric relatives.
10. Welty's novel "The Optimist's Daughter" won a Pulitzer Prize in 1973. (It's main characters resemble her parents)
11. Her ancestors on her fathers side who were of German Swiss background) arrived in America before the Revolutionary War.
12. Weltys' father said that "he was not interested in ancient history."
13. However her father did keep in touch with his own father, Jefferson Welty Esquire, for whom he had a deeply felt regard.
14. "It was the only use my father made of the word he saved it for his father," wrote Welty in her memoir *One Writer's Beginnings.*
15. As a result Welty always held the term Esquire in great respect.
16. After her father died an English Welti, who spelled his name with an i told Welty about her ancestors.
17. Three Welty brothers left German Switzerland for the Americas, and settled in Virginia Pennsylvania Ohio and Indiana before the Revolutionary War.
18. Welty said her father would have been interested in the following information one Welty helped push through construction of the St. Gotthard Tunnel.
19. Whenever her mother, and her father, became excited, they would exclaim "Pshaw"
20. Welty wrote of both her fathers family, and her mothers.

Writing Application

Colons and Commas in Writing

In the following passage from *Blue Highways: A Journey into America,* William Least Heat-Moon describes the fear of being stranded in a snowstorm while attempting to drive across rural America. His careful use of colons and commas enlivens the experience. Examine the passage, focusing on the punctuation in the italicized items.

> I wondered how long I might have to stay in the Breaks before I could drive down. *The cold didn't worry me much: I had insulated the rig myself* and slept in it once when the windchill was thirty-six below. I figured to survive if I didn't have to stay on top too long. Why hadn't I listened to friends who advised carrying a CB? *The headline showed darkly:* FROZEN MAN FOUND IN AVALANCHE. The whole night *I slept and woke, slept and woke, while the hail fell like iron shot, and thunder slammed around, and lightning seared the ice.*

Techniques with Colons and Commas

Try to apply some of Least Heat-Moon's techniques when you write and revise.

1 When introducing information that explains preceding material, use a colon for emphasis and economy of style.

WITHOUT COLON The cold didn't worry me much because I had insulated the rig myself . . .

LEAST HEAT-MOON'S STYLE The cold didn't worry me much: I had insulated the rig myself . . .

2 Use commas to vary sentence length and to set off ideas. Least Heat-Moon's sentence is less choppy but still emphasizes each separate occurrence.

WITHOUT COMMAS I slept and woke. I slept and woke. The hail fell like iron shot. The thunder slammed around. Lightning seared the ice.

LEAST HEAT-MOON'S STYLE I slept and woke, slept and woke, while the hail fell like iron shot, and thunder slammed around, and lightning seared the ice.

TIME

To find more suggestions about using details and emotions, see the **TIME *Facing the Blank Page***, pages 109–119.

Practice On your paper, revise the following passage, correcting all punctuation errors.

Called a pine snake east of the Mississippi the bullsnake puts on quite a show when it feels threatened. The snake swells up. It hisses loudly. It vibrates its tail. It lunges toward the enemy. Be on your guard The snake is not merely bluffing. It bites. Fortunately, it's bite is not poisonous and a person will recover from one physically, if not emotionally. Bullsnakes are sometimes referred to as a farmer's best friend. They eat large numbers of mice, rats, and gophers that consume crops. These snakes live primarily in these dry habitats open pinewoods and sandhills and brushlands and deserts. They are also found on grass covered prairies.

"Around her neck she wore strings of false pearls, on her arms bracelets of imitation gold, and combs set with glass jewels."

—Guy de Maupassant

Portrait of a Woman,
17th Century

Part 3

Resources and Skills

UNIT 22

History and Development of English

22.1 How Language Began

Walk along a busy street in any major metropolitan area—New York, London, Mexico City, Tokyo—and look at the signs in the storefronts you pass. Chances are you'll see signs in a variety of languages from many different parts of the world. Where did all these languages come from? How did language itself originate? No one knows for sure, but linguists, people who study the history and development of languages, have proposed some interesting theories.

Bow-Wows and Yo-he-hos

According to the bow-wow theory, language may have begun when people imitated the sounds they heard in the natural world. Imagine some early hunter returning to his family group after discovering a pond alive with ducks. The hunter communicates his discovery by making a quacking sound. The other hunters in the group nod excitedly and grab their weapons. Was this the first sign of the ability to form words having meanings?

Theories of Language Origin			
The Gesture Theory argues that gestures were accompanied by sounds that eventually came to mean what the gesture meant.	**The Ding-Dong Theory** states that primitive people instinctively reacted to every sensory experience with a specific vocal expression.	**The Pooh-Pooh Theory** suggests that language arose from instinctive emotional cries expressing pain, joy, disappointment, anger, and so on.	**The Musical Theory** proposes that language arose from song or that speech and music developed together.

A second attempt to account for the origin of language is referred to as the yo-he-ho theory. A fourteenth-century French scholar named Noiré observed that when people engage in hard physical labor—moving a heavy rock, for example—part of the effort involves trapping air in the lungs by closing the vocal cords. During brief moments of relaxation, the vocal cords open, and involuntary grunting and groaning noises are made. Noiré suggested that these sounds may have evolved into words that meant "heave" or "lift."

Other theories of language origin have been proposed, such as the four listed and described in the Theories of Language Origin chart. None of these theories accounts for the complexity and richness of human languages. Still, each theory suggests a possible explanation for how people learned to talk to one another.

A Mother Tongue?

Since the late 1700s, linguists have known that certain languages are closely related to other languages, indicating these differing languages developed from a common source. Did all languages originate from one common language—a "mother tongue"? Is it possible that the earliest humans in one part of the African continent created a language that, through contact with other groups of people elsewhere, slowly spread throughout the world? Or did different varieties of human speech begin in different places on the earth with different people? Again, we don't know. What we do know is that a very long time ago, human communication became human language.

Exercise 1

For some years, scientists have attempted to teach chimpanzees and gorillas to "speak" human language through typing, sign language, and other methods. Other scientists have tried to decode the "language" of dolphins, whales, and other creatures. Investigate one of these attempts at human-animal communication and write a brief report. Present your report to the class.

Wordworks

Acronyms

From *A* to *Z*

In this fast-paced society of ours, it seems everything has speeded up. We have bullet trains, supersonic airliners, 150-mph sports cars, and instant satellite and e-mail communications. We even have a speeded-up language, thanks to acronyms. Acronyms are words formed from the initial letters of other words that make up a phrase. Acronyms can make communicating quicker, easier, and more creative.

Acronyms can take two forms. One type of acronym is a word that is pronounced as a sequence of letters. Examples include *LA* (*L*os *A*ngeles), *CD* (*c*ompact *d*isc), *SUV* (*s*port-*u*tility *v*ehicle), and *DJ* (*d*isc *j*ockey).

A second type of acronym is pronounced not as a sequence of letters but as a word. These acronyms are usually formed by using the first letter of each word in a phrase: *swat* (*s*pecial *w*eapons *a*nd *t*actics). Other acronyms you're probably familiar with include *scuba* (*s*elf-*c*ontained *u*nderwater *b*reathing *a*pparatus), *radar* (*ra*dio *d*etection *a*nd *r*anging), and *laser* (*l*ight *a*mplification by *s*timulated *e*mission of *r*adiation).

The French bullet train, or *train à grande vitesse* (TGV)

Genuine acronyms develop as a natural process of abbreviation. Reverse acronyms, however, are deliberately created. For example, during World War II, the U.S. Navy created a special force of women to perform volunteer work. The navy called the women *Waves* and said the acronym stood for women accepted for volunteer emergency service. It is thought, however, that the navy first came up with the clever name and then created a phrase to support it. That's how reverse acronyms work.

ACTIVITY

Game (Great Acronym-Making Endeavor)

Try your hand at creating reverse acronyms. First choose a word; this will be your acronym. Then work out a phrase that supports the acronym. Here are two examples from *The Oxford Guide to Word Games*, by Tony Augarde: shovel (sharp hand-operated vertical earth lifter) and brain (box retaining assorted interesting notions). You might want to use the title of a film: *Jaws* (just a white shark). Share your reverse acronyms with your classmates.

22.2 From Speaking to Writing

Browse through an international bookstore and you'll see books written in many languages using different writing systems. Choose one book written in Chinese, another in Japanese, and a third in Greek, and what will you find? Each of these languages uses a different type of writing system.

Chinese is written using a logographic writing system: each character (there are about fifty thousand of them) represents an entire word. Japanese uses a writing system called a syllabary: each of the approximately fifty characters represents a syllable, or a group of sounds. Greek, like English, uses an alphabet: each of the twenty-four characters in the Greek alphabet represents a sound. All of these writing systems enable people to write what they say and read what they've written. Although these systems have vastly different numbers of characters, each system is capable of expressing a world of ideas.

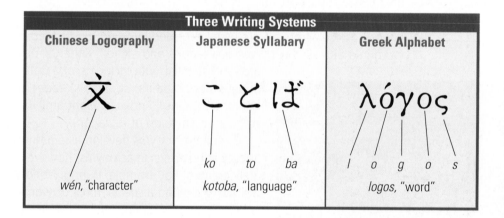

Three Writing Systems		
Chinese Logography	**Japanese Syllabary**	**Greek Alphabet**
文	こ と ば	λόγος
	ko *to* *ba*	*l* *o* *g* *o* *s*
wén, "character"	*kotoba*, "language"	*logos*, "word"

Picture Writing

Did people always have writing systems? No. In fact, although spoken language probably originated several hundred thousand years ago, language scholars think that the first fully developed writing system got its start much later—about 5,500 years ago—with hieroglyphs, or picture writing.

Hieroglyphs were pictures that represented objects or ideas rather than words or sounds. This type of writing emerged in many parts of the world at about the same time. You may have seen illustrations of the Egyptian hieroglyphs of northern Africa, in photographs of Egyptian tombs. However, the Hittites, the earliest inhabitants of what is now the country of Turkey, also used hieroglyphs. And half a world away, in Central America, the Maya used hieroglyphic writing to record important information about science, religion, and other aspects of their culture.

Sounds and Symbols

Picture writing, however, proved cumbersome and limiting. Over time, the pictures became streamlined, enabling complex information to be conveyed more efficiently. In Sumer, an ancient region in what is now southeastern Iraq, cuneiform symbols underwent this kind of streamlining.

Cuneiform consisted of about six hundred wedge-shaped symbols. At first, these symbols represented objects and ideas. At some point, however, some of the symbols came to be associated with specific sounds as well. For example, the cuneiform arrow symbol represented the object "arrow." The word for "arrow" was pronounced *te,* so the arrow symbol came to represent the syllable *te* in all the words in which that syllable occurred, regardless of their meaning. Cuneiform was changing from a logography to a syllabary.

Cuneiform, 1800 B.C.

We Get Letters

Another milestone in the development of writing systems took place along the coasts of what are now Syria, Lebanon, and Israel. By 1000 B.C. the Phoenicians, the people who inhabited the coastal region, had developed a great trading and manufacturing civilization. Their society demanded a written language that was easy to use and learn. So the Phoenicians slowly adapted their existing writing system, finally arriving at one that included just twenty-two characters. Each character in the system represented a single consonant sound. By 900 B.C., the Phoenicians had created an alphabet.

The Greeks further refined the Phoenician alphabet by adding characters that represented vowel sounds. This Greek alphabet proved so useful for expressing and communicating ideas that it has remained virtually unchanged for nearly three thousand years. All of the alphabets in use in Europe today have their origins in the Greek alphabet.

Exercise 1

Collect a variety of books, newspapers, or magazines that use different writing systems for a class display. You may find examples from reading materials in your home, or you may be able to photocopy examples at your community library. You may also be able to obtain examples from the Internet. Try to find examples of Cyrillic, Hebrew, Japanese, Latin, Chinese, Arabic, and Greek writing. Create a chart to display your findings.

Wordworks

MALAPROPISMS

Pullet Surprises

Have you ever unintentionally misused a word with humorous results, as in the following bloopers?

Rich? He's a malted [multi] millionaire!

The ancient city of Pompeii was buried in moldy [molten] lava.

Larson 2·16

©1987 Universal Press Syndicate

"So, until next week — Adios, amoebas."

These humorous mistaken uses of words are known as malapropisms, from the French expression *mal à propos*, meaning "not appropriate."

In 1775 playwright Richard Sheridan popularized the notion of malapropisms in *The Rivals* through the character of Mrs. Malaprop, who humorously bungled the English language with such utterances as "She's as headstrong as an allegory [alligator] on the banks of the Nile."

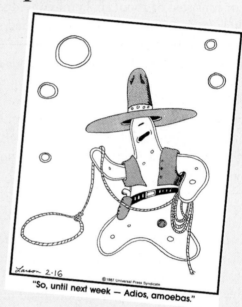

Today, malapropisms are also called Pullet Surprises, after a statement in a student essay from Miss Amsel Greene's high school writing class: "In 1957, Eugene O'Neill won a Pullet Surprise [Pulitzer Prize]." Pullet Surprises, according to Miss Greene, are "marvels of ingenuity and logic," like these:

"The doctor prescribed milk of amnesia [magnesia]."

"The flood damage was so bad they had to evaporate [evacuate] four cities."

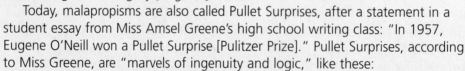

Excuse Me?

See if you can figure out and correct these malapropisms.

1. They put her in an exhilarated class.
2. We couldn't understand his Scottish derelict.
3. The cotton crop was ruined by bold weasels.
4. He plays both guitar and mandarin.
5. She gave him a diamond that sparkled at every faucet.
6. He sent the package by partial post.

22.3 Indo-European Language Family

Have you ever investigated your family tree to discover who your ancestors were? If so, what did you find? Some people have been surprised to discover a famous—perhaps infamous—relative perched on one of the tree's branches. Family trees are sometimes literally drawn as trees, with branches representing family groups and leaves representing individuals. This diagram shows relationships clearly.

It may surprise you to discover that languages have family trees too—in the sense that languages are related to one another, perhaps with a common source. English, for example, is a member of the Indo-European language family, which is shown on the next page. This vast language family includes most of the languages of Europe as well as those of Iran and India.

As the language tree shows, English belongs to a branch of Indo-European known as Germanic. English shares its linguistic history with the other Germanic tongues, including Yiddish, which derives from Middle High German and is spoken today by eastern European Jews and their descendants in many parts of the world. Another Germanic language is Afrikaans, a language spoken by some white South Africans. Afrikaans derives from Dutch, which was the language of the first white Europeans to settle in South Africa.

The Indo-European languages are believed to have a single "parent" language, although no such parent has yet been found. Language scholars think it is unlikely that direct evidence of this language will ever be found.

Selected Language Groups of Europe

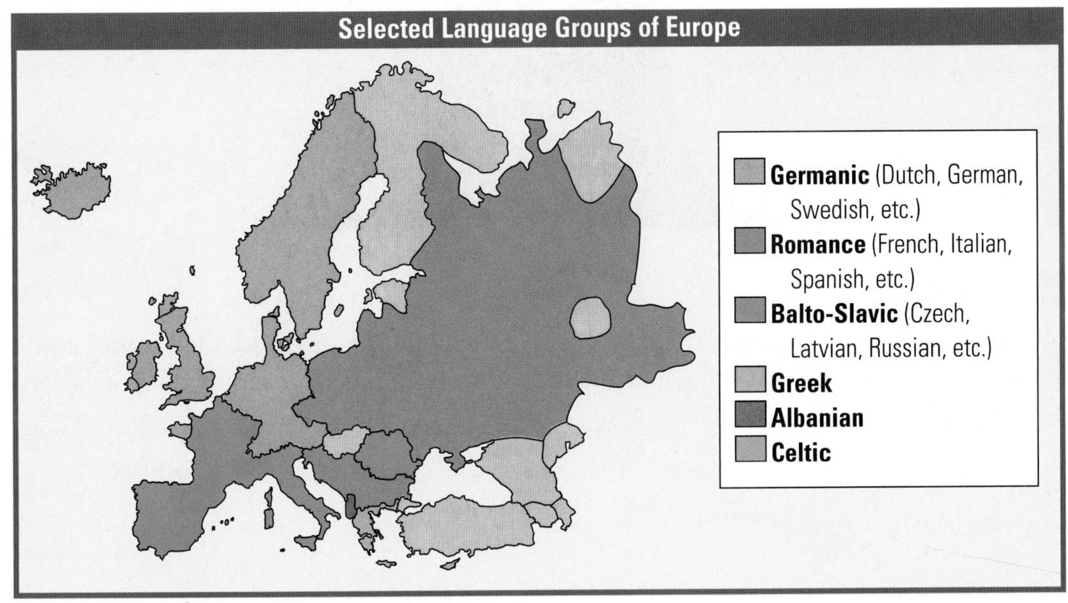

History and Development of English

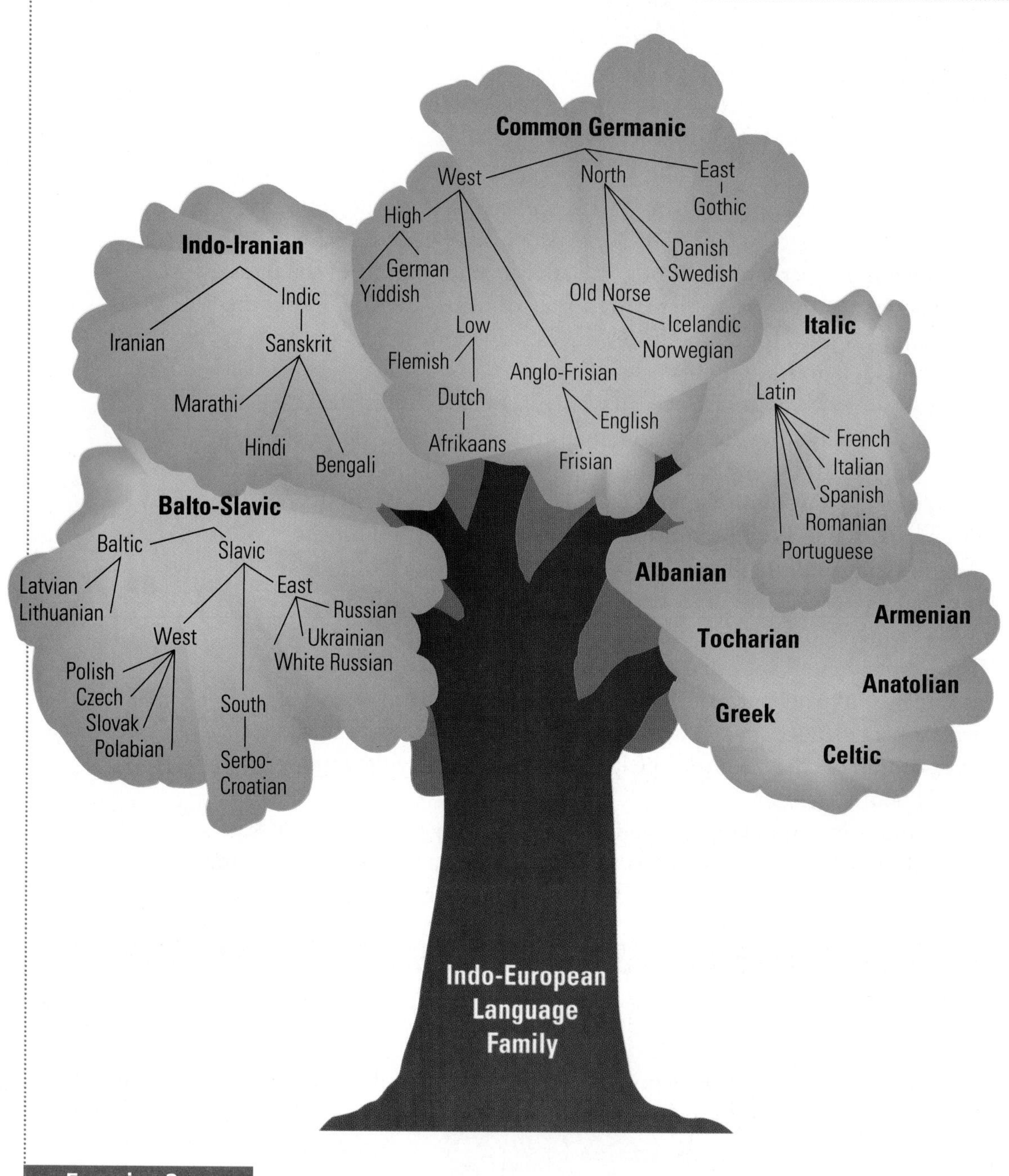

Exercise 2

Study the Indo-European language tree. Which languages are descended from Latin? Eastern Slavic? To what branch of the Indo-European language family does Sanskrit belong? Icelandic? Latvian?

History and Development of English

Wordworks

Idioms

Don't Have a Cow, Man!

You're walking to algebra class one day, and a friend introduces you to Michel, a newly arrived French foreign exchange student. He speaks some English, but he still has a lot to learn. As you're talking, you suddenly realize you're going to be late for class. "Yikes! Michel, I gotta go. If I'm late for algebra again, Mr. Kim will have a cow!" You expect a laugh from your new friend, but instead Michel gives you a puzzled look. Why?

Time flies!

Well, you used an idiom, a phrase whose real meaning cannot be understood by putting together the meanings of the individual words that make up the phrase.

Some of our most colorful idioms have fascinating histories. *Eat humble pie* means "to be forced to admit a mistake or to accept insult or shame." In medieval England, the master of the manor was the only one allowed to hunt game. When he shot a deer, he kept the meat and gave the innards, or "umbles," to his servants, who would make pies from them. *Eat humble pie* meant being forced to accept the least desirable food.

Buy a pig in a poke means "to buy something sight unseen." Centuries ago in England, a farmer would carry a piglet to market in a sack, or *poke*. Dishonest farmers might substitute a stray cat for the valuable piglet and then sell it to some trusting person who did not bother to check out what he was buying.

ACTIVITY

Test Your Idiom IQ

With a partner, see if you can match each of the idioms in the left column with its correct definition in the right column.

1. Sow wild oats
2. Put your shoulder to the wheel
3. Off-the-cuff
4. Pull up stakes
5. Throw in the towel
6. Johnny-come-lately
7. Put on the dog
8. According to Hoyle
9. Lose face
10. Raise Cain

A. To work very hard
B. To do foolish or bad things as a young person
C. To move to another city or area
D. By the rules
E. To be humiliated
F. To become angry and cause a scene
G. To give up
H. A newcomer
I. Unplanned or prepared
J. Make a flashy display

22.4 Old and Middle English

Can you read these three lines of poetry? They're from *Beowulf*, one of the most famous poems in the English language.

Hafa nu ond geheald husa selest
gemyne mærþo, mægen-ellen cyõ,
waca wiõ wraþum!

Yes, *Beowulf* is written in English—Old English, the earliest form of the English that is spoken today by people in many areas of the world.

Old English was the language of the inhabitants of Britain from about A.D. 449 to 1100. The Celts had been living in Britain under Roman rule for several centuries when Rome withdrew its legions to battle invading barbarians back home. The Celts were left defenseless against a series of invasions by the Picts and Scots from the north and west; Germanic-speaking Saxons, Angles, and Jutes from western Europe; and the Scandinavians. Britain soon became Engla Land, "land of the Angles," and the principal language was largely West Germanic with Scandinavian and Latin influences. This language was Old English.

Old English had three important characteristics. First, it was an inflected language. That means Old English nouns, pronouns, and adjectives had case endings to indicate their function in a sentence—for example, subject or object.

Second, nouns as well as pronouns had grammatical gender. A noun was masculine, feminine, or neuter. Adjectives and certain other modifiers had three sets of endings, and each was used with a noun of a specific gender.

From Old to Middle English

597 Pope Gregory I orders Christian missionaries to Britain to convert the heathens. Monks open schools and teach Latin. Latin words relating to learning and religion enter English: *master (magister), candle (candela), temple (templum).*

100 B.C. | A.D. 400 | 500 | 600 | 700

55 B.C. Julius Caesar invades Britain and claims it for the Roman Empire. Latin vocabulary is introduced into Celtic.

A.D. 449 At the Celts' request, Germanic Saxons, Angles, and Jutes arrive to defeat the Picts and Scots. The conquerors then turn on the Celts, subjugating them. Celtic is gradually replaced by the Germanic languages of the invaders.

Finally, Old English was characterized by irregular word formation. There were many ways to form the plurals of nouns and the past tense of verbs.

Middle English

By about 1100, enough cumulative changes had occurred to signal the beginning of a great transitional period for English. This period, Middle English, lasted until about 1450.

How did Middle English differ from Old English? Read these lines from Geoffrey Chaucer's "The Nun's Priest's Tale," written in Middle English.

We alle desiren, if it might bee,
To han housbondes hardy, wise, and free.

This text is much easier to understand than the Old English of *Beowulf.* The changes were more than just cosmetic, however. Compared with Old English, Middle English was grammatically simpler. Grammatical gender began to disappear, as did inflected case endings. Irregular verb forms gave way to regular forms, and the addition of *-s* to a noun became the standard for forming plurals. Unfortunately, these changes were not applied to all words. That's why we still have irregular verbs and plurals today. *Oxen,* the irregular plural for ox, dates back to Old English and is still in use today!

Exercise 3

Look up each of the following words in a dictionary. Write the word as it was formed in Old or Middle English and the language from which English borrowed the word. Look in the front of your dictionary for an explanation of abbreviations.

1. city (Middle English)
2. priest (Old English)
3. adjourn (Middle English)
4. ugly (Middle English)
5. school (Old English)
6. altar (Old English)

1066 William the Conqueror (right) defeats King Harold II at the Battle of Hastings, ushering in a period of French domination over the affairs of England. Many French words relating to government enter English: *authority (auctorité), liberty (liberté), pardon (pardoner),* and *verdict (verdit).*

800 | 900 | 1000 | 1100 | 1500

865 A large Viking army invades England. Decades of raids follow, and Vikings conquer half the country. Vikings contribute many words to English, including *law (log), skin (skinn), sky (sky),* and *die (deyja).*

1100 The Old English period ends and Middle English begins. English grammar begins to undergo simplification.

Wordworks

Weasel Words

New, Different, and Improved!

Have you ever purchased a skin cream that you thought promised a clear complexion after a few applications? Have you ever used a new toothpaste, expecting it to give you a dazzling smile? Chances are the ads for these products used phrases like "new and improved formula," "helps give you a brighter smile," or "fights oily skin." Such phrases are full of weasel words—*new, improved, helps, fights*—words that seem to say one thing but that turn out to mean something quite different.

ACTS FAST!

Cleans most surfaces!!!

Spring Fresh Scent

The term *weasel word* is derived from the habits of the weasel, which robs eggs from other species' nests. The weasel makes a small hole in the eggshell and then sucks out the yolk and the white, leaving just an empty shell. The emptied egg looks whole, but it is actually hollow. Weasel words are just like that egg—not what they appear to be.

Weasel words work because most people don't pay very close attention to the words they read and hear. Look at that toothpaste claim—"helps give you a brighter smile." What does the word *help* really mean? *Help* simply means "to give assistance or aid." *Help* is a weasel word. To get that dazzling smile you still have to brush after every meal, have your teeth professionally cleaned twice a year, and floss regularly.

Think about the claim "fights oily skin." Does this slogan say the shine will disappear from your face? Does it claim your troubled skin will magically clear up? No, of course not. The promise, like the remnants of the weasel's meal, is not what it appears to be.

Weasel Watch

While watching television or skimming magazines, list the weasel words you find in advertisements or hear in political speeches. Besides the ones mentioned above, other important weasel words to watch for are *works* (not the same as *performs*); *virtually*, as in "leaves glasses virtually spotless" (*virtually* means "almost," not "entirely"); *like*, as in "gives you skin like peaches and cream" (what qualities does skin have in common with peaches and cream?). Share your collection of weasel words with your classmates.

22.5 Modern English

By the 1590s, when William Shakespeare asked the famous question that begins his "Sonnet 18," the transition from Middle English to modern English had taken place.

SHall I compare thee to a Summers day?
Thou art more louely and more temperate:
Rough windes do ſhake the darling buds of Maie,
And Sommers leaſe hath all too ſhort a date:
Sometime too hot the eye of heauen ſhines,

With the exception of some words such as *thee, thou,* and *hath,* Shakespeare's vocabulary could easily be mistaken for contemporary English. In fact, aside from some spelling, vocabulary, and pronunciation changes that would take place over the next century or two, the language spoken in Shakespeare's time was essentially the English we speak today.

Modern English, as the English spoken after 1450 is called, continued the trends of Middle English. English was no longer an inflected language—word order, not case endings, determined the function of words in sentences. Grammatical gender was gone—modifiers no longer needed gender endings to match the gender of the nouns they modified. And thanks to a marvelous new invention, standardization was beginning to take hold of the language.

Prior to the mid-1400s, all written English was handwritten. Then around 1440, Johannes Gutenberg and some associates began using movable raised type on a printing press. In 1476 William Caxton built and began operating the first printing press in England, and English hasn't been the same since.

Printed matter was now available to a much wider audience than ever before. Because London was the center of England's printing industry, the Londoners' ways of speaking and writing soon spread throughout the country. Pronunciation and spelling became more standardized. There were still inconsistencies in written English, but printers were doing their best to bring order to the language.

Contemporary English

None of the changes that transformed Old English into modern English happened overnight. The evolution of a language is a slow process, and often changes aren't even noticed until decades or centuries later.

Even now, the English you speak continues to evolve. New words have entered the vocabulary from foreign sources: *tai chi* and *feng shui* from Chinese, *caffe latte* and *paparazzi* from Italian, and *ayatollah* from Persian.

Middle English
"Whan that Aprille with hise shoures soote
The droghte of March hath perced to the roote . . ."

Modern English
"O Gertrude, come away!
The sun no sooner shall the mountains touch
But we will ship him hence."

Contemporary English
"Roger, Houston. I copy. Over."

New technology, new ideas, and other innovations demand the creation of new words: *infomercial, euro, search engine, hyperlink, morph.* Some existing words have taken on new meanings: *mouse, rap, network.*

Grammatical shifts are also taking place. The verb *read,* for example, is sometimes used as a noun today: *Barbara Kingsolver's new book is a good read.* The noun *audible* (which originally was an adjective meaning "able to be heard" but took on a new meaning in football as "a new play called at the line of scrimmage") has now been transformed into a verb: *The quarterback audibilized his way out of a potential loss of yardage.*

One fact about the English language is certain. English is a living language, always changing, always growing. Perhaps several hundred years from now, language scholars will look back at the early decades of the twenty-first century and conclude that important changes were taking place in English during this time.

Exercise 4

You can keep track of some of the changes taking place in the English language. Create several pages called "Language Watch" in your journal or another notebook. Label individual pages "New Words," "Existing Words with New Meanings," "Current Slang," "New Acronyms," and "Grammar Shifts." Whenever you run across a word that fits one of these categories—in your reading, in talking with friends, as you listen to radio or television, and so on—add it to your "Language Watch" files, and date the entry.

Wordworks

JARGON

Clips and Red Dogs

The exasperated supervisor hands a sheaf of papers to her young assistant and says, "Try a new slug, and a new cutline, too. And see if you can come up with a new head." What is this person talking about? Fishing with a cutline and slugs? Or maybe one boxer slugging another? Or is it science fiction? "We're ready for the head transplant, doctor."

In this case, *slug* doesn't have anything to do with slimy sea creatures or with punching somebody out. *Slug, cutline,* and *head* are newspaper jargon, the specialized language used by newspaper people. A *slug* is a story name, a *cutline* is a caption, and a *head* is a headline.

Most trades and professions have their own kind of jargon, or specialized language. Doctors use jargon. Lawyers use it. Auto mechanics, educators, and engineers use it. Even football players use jargon, such as the words you may have recognized in the title above and in the cartoon.

Jargon often sounds like gibberish to people outside the profession. But jargon can enable people within a specialized group to communicate quickly and clearly. Take, for example, this exchange between two medical professionals:

"Her vitals are failing. BP is low. Start an IV and order an MRI. Call Code Blue!"

Confusing? Maybe to you. But when a patient's life is hanging in the balance, it's much quicker than saying:

"This patient is in danger. We're having trouble detecting a pulse and respiration. Her blood pressure rate is falling. Let's inject her arm with an intravenous tube and then order a magnetic resonance image. Call immediately for an emergency team and a cart with resuscitator and other equipment."

ACTIVITY

Name That Profession!

How many kinds of jargon can you recognize? For each of the following examples of jargon, name the field or profession in which it is used. Then explain what the jargon means. Use a dictionary if necessary.

1. RBI
2. differential
3. tort
4. hacker
5. cross-check
6. stet

UNIT

23 Library Resources

23.1 Arrangement of a Library

Libraries today offer numerous services. You can do research for a term paper, take out a book to read for pleasure, borrow a video or a CD, use the Internet, find out about events in your community, and much more.

Understanding Classification Systems

Libraries organize books on the shelves by *call numbers,* which can be thought of as addresses for the books on the shelves. Call numbers are based on classification systems. Most public and school libraries use the Dewey decimal system, while most university and very large libraries use the Library of Congress system.

Dewey Decimal System

In 1876 librarian Melvil Dewey divided the world of knowledge into ten broad categories, which are still in use today. Under the Dewey decimal system, books are organized according to the following numerical system:

Dewey Decimal System

Category Numbers	Major Category	Examples of Subcategories
000–099	General works	Encyclopedias, bibliographies
100–199	Philosophy	Ethics, psychology
200–299	Religion	Theology, mythology
300–399	Social sciences	Law, political science, education
400–499	Language	Dictionaries, foreign languages
500–599	Sciences	Chemistry, astronomy, mathematics
600–699	Technology	Medicine, engineering, agriculture
700–799	Arts	Painting, music, theater, sports
800–899	Literature	Poetry, plays, essays
900–999	History and geography	Ancient history, biography, travel

These general categories are subdivided further into subcategories; for example, under the broad heading, technology, which comprises all the 600s, the 620s are engineering books.

Books are shelved numerically by Dewey decimal number and then alphabetically by author. For example, books on the history of the *Titanic* will be shelved in 910.453, but the book by Steven Biel will be filed before the one by Paul Quinn.

Public libraries usually do not use call numbers for fiction. Sometimes fiction books are designated by the letter *F* or the abbreviation *Fic* or by the type of novel; for example *SciFi*, or *YA* for young adult. Fiction books are filed alphabetically by the author's last name. If a library has several books by the same author, they are shelved alphabetically by title.

Library of Congress Classification

The Library of Congress (LC) system is used mostly by larger libraries. The LC classification system divides all knowledge into twenty-one general categories. Each category is assigned a letter, as shown on the chart.

Like the Dewey decimal system, the LC has subcategories, identified by additional letters and numbers.

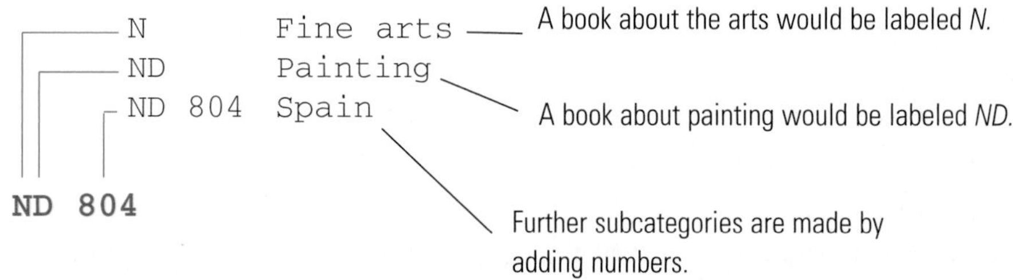

Category Letter	Major Category	Category Letter	Major Category
A	General works	N	Fine arts
B	Philosophy, psychology, religion	P	Language and literature
C–F	History	Q	Science
G	Geography, anthropology, recreation	R	Medicine
H	Social sciences	S	Agriculture
J	Political sciences	T	Technology
K	Law	U	Military science
L	Education	V	Naval science
M	Music	Z	Bibliography and library science

Table: Library of Congress Classification System

Special Sections Many libraries group special categories of books, such as reference, biographical, local history, and oversize books, in separate collections. The catalog display screen will direct you to those areas.

An *R* or *Ref* identifies a reference book. You would look for this book in the reference area.

Guinness book of world records

Ref **McWhirter, Norris,** comp.
031 Guinness book of world records [1st ed.] New York,

Library Resources

23.2 Locating Books and Other Library Materials

How do you locate a book, video, or compact disc when visiting the library? Use the online catalog to find a complete listing of the library's holdings (all the materials that the library owns). Online catalogs allow you to search by author, title, subject, or keyword, among other options. The most direct way to search is a title search. Keep in mind that some books may have the same title. To be certain the record you have found is for the book you want, make sure that it is written by the correct author. If you want to know all the works by that author in the library, enter the author's name. Always use the last name first. For example, if you want to know which books by Willa Cather the library owns, you type in *Cather, Willa.* The computer will show you a numbered list of all the books by Cather that are in the collection. The list will be alphabetical by title. Remember that the articles *the*, *a*, and *an* at the beginning of titles are skipped and not alphabetized.

When you search by subject in a library, you must use the specific word or phrase selected by the Library of Congress. For example, if you key in *Japanese Cooking* for a subject, you will find nothing because the heading actually should read "Cookery—Japan." If you find no results for your search, always use the same term in a keyword search. The keyword search will find many books on your topic; in fact too many, because it will pull up titles of songs and books and parts of books. To solve this problem, scan the titles retrieved until you find one that seems like it might be on your topic. Open that record and search for the book's Library of Congress subject headings. Then go back and do a subject search under that heading to find materials on your topic.

SEARCH TIP

1. **DOUBLE-CHECK THE SPELLING** If you type *mathmatics* for *mathematics,* you will find nothing on that subject.
2. **TRY SYNONYMS FOR YOUR WORDS**
3. **THE COMPUTER WILL ALSO ALLOW YOU TO LIMIT YOUR SEARCH BY DATE OF PUBLICATION** You can also limit by format—for example, searching only for videos or only for books.
4. **EACH TIME YOU FIND A BOOK ON YOUR TOPIC, PRINT OUT THE CALL NUMBER** That way you won't forget it by the time you reach the shelves.

Sample Search Result

Screen One If you are searching for a book on the subject of *canyons,* select *Subject* and hit the *Enter* key.

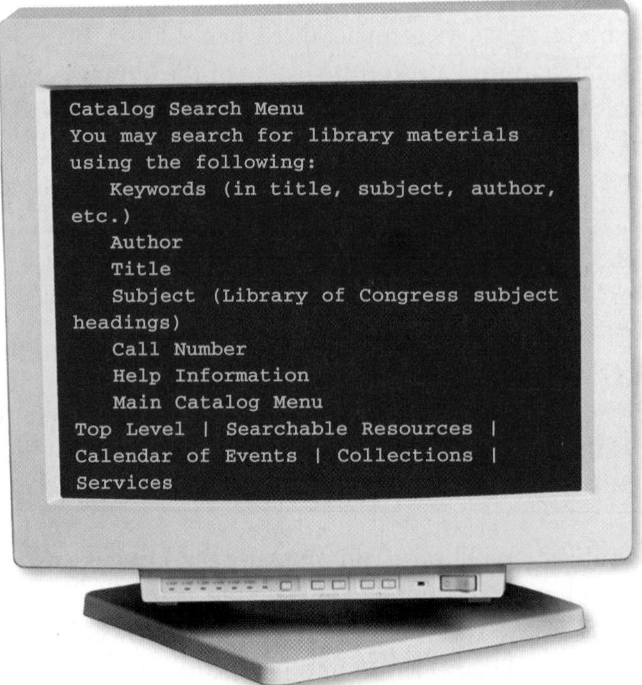

Catalog Search Menu
You may search for library materials using the following:
Keywords (in title, subject, author, etc.)
Author
Title
Subject (Library of Congress subject headings)
Call Number
Help Information
Main Catalog Menu
Top Level | Searchable Resources | Calendar of Events | Collections | Services

Screen Two The second screen provides the Library of Congress subject headings that include the word *canyons.* In this case, you might choose category 6, which includes guidebooks for canyons of the southwestern United States.

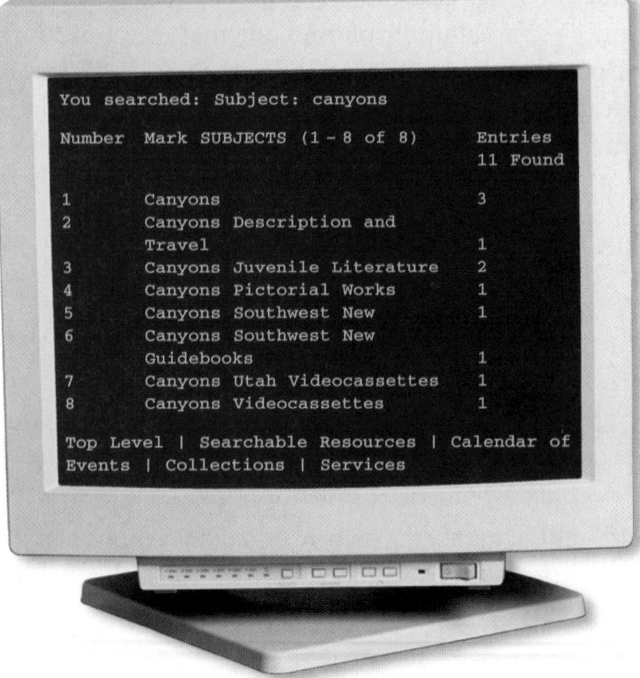

You searched: Subject: canyons
Number Mark SUBJECTS (1 - 8 of 8) Entries 11 Found
1 Canyons 3
2 Canyons Description and Travel 1
3 Canyons Juvenile Literature 2
4 Canyons Pictorial Works 1
5 Canyons Southwest New 1
6 Canyons Southwest New Guidebooks 1
7 Canyons Utah Videocassettes 1
8 Canyons Videocassettes 1
Top Level | Searchable Resources | Calendar of Events | Collections | Services

Screen Three Category 6 brings you the following reference. Note that this final display provides specific information about the book, including title, author, call number, subject headings, publisher, date, number of pages, price, and whether the book is a first edition.

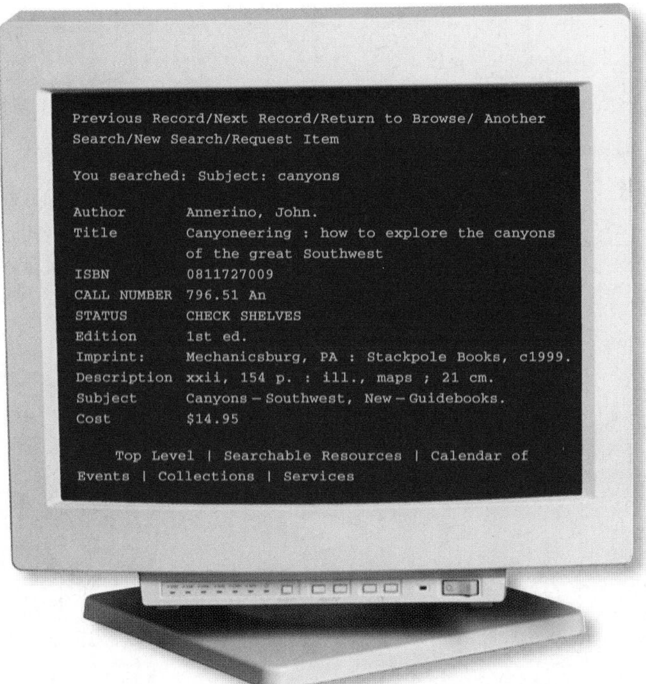

Previous Record/Next Record/Return to Browse/ Another Search/New Search/Request Item
You searched: Subject: canyons
Author Annerino, John.
Title Canyoneering : how to explore the canyons of the great Southwest
ISBN 0811727009
CALL NUMBER 796.51 An
STATUS CHECK SHELVES
Edition 1st ed.
Imprint: Mechanicsburg, PA : Stackpole Books, c1999.
Description xxii, 154 p. : ill., maps ; 21 cm.
Subject Canyons – Southwest, New – Guidebooks.
Cost $14.95
Top Level | Searchable Resources | Calendar of Events | Collections | Services

Exercise 1

Use the catalog to find one book on each of the following topics. List the author, title, call number, and publication date for each book you find.

1. Space exploration
2. Pompeii
3. Celtic mythology
4. Black holes
5. Collected works of Edgar Allan Poe
6. Triathlons
7. Biography of Nelson Mandela
8. African American poetry
9. Polar exploration
10. History of jazz

Sections of a Library

Learning about the organization of a library will help you use its many resources efficiently. Most school and public libraries are organized into the same general sections. The map below shows these sections.

Circulation Desk To apply for a library card or to check out or return materials, stop at the circulation desk. This desk is also the place where any books that you have requested will be held for you.

Young Adult and Children's Sections Books and materials that appeal to teens and to young children are kept in the young adult and children's sections.

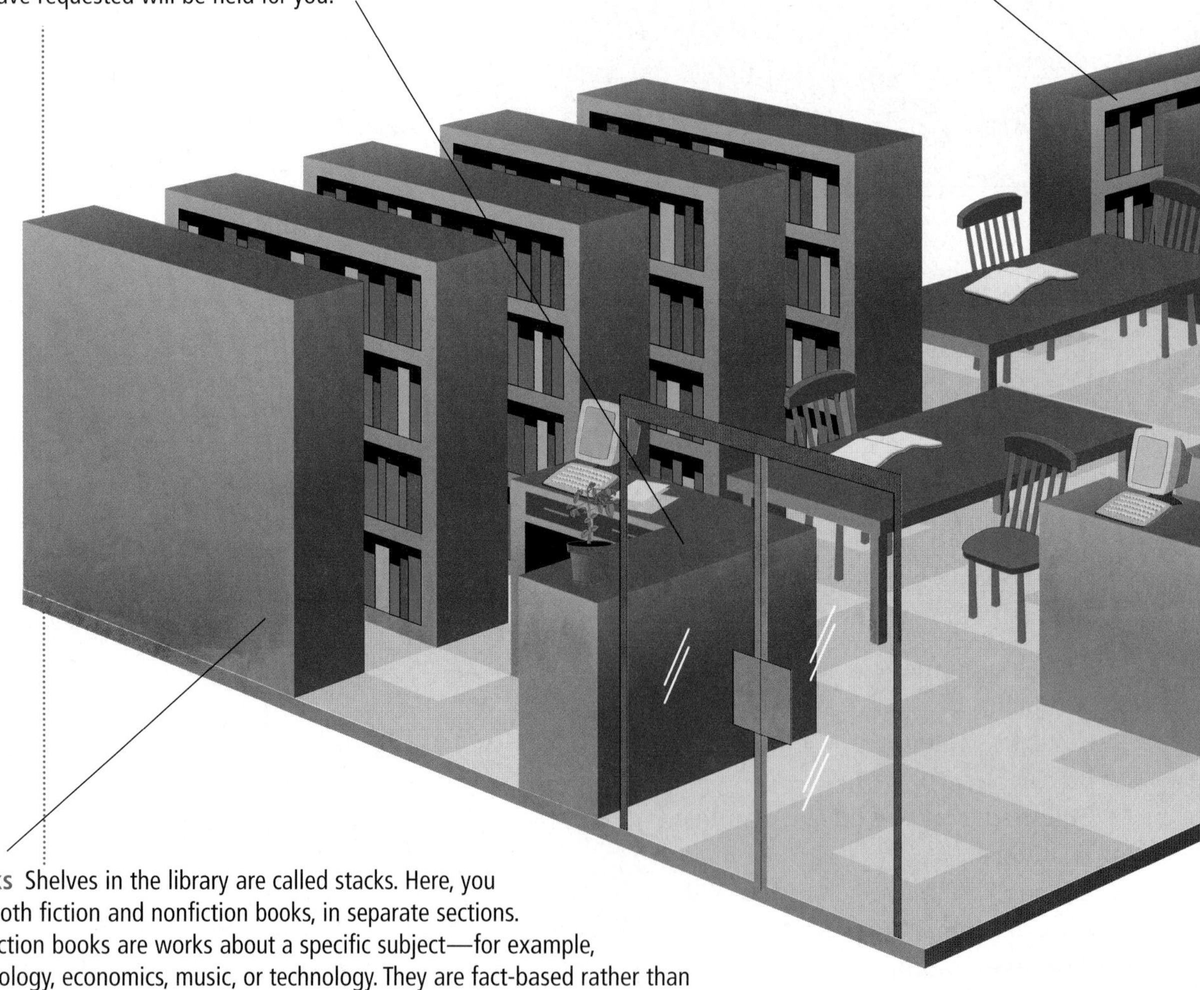

Stacks Shelves in the library are called stacks. Here, you find both fiction and nonfiction books, in separate sections. Nonfiction books are works about a specific subject—for example, psychology, economics, music, or technology. They are fact-based rather than imaginative. Fiction books, including novels and short stories, are considered works of the imagination. Although poems and plays are imaginative works also, they may be shelved under "Literature" in the nonfiction section.

Library Resources

Reference Section Available here are reference materials, which include encyclopedias, dictionaries, almanacs, and atlases. These cannot be checked out of the library. Librarians will show you how to use these resources and help you formulate an effective search strategy.

Audiovisual Materials The audiovisual (AV) department offers a wealth of multimedia sources. Included in the AV section are videos, compact discs, audiocassettes, and even circulating computer software. Many audiovisual departments have listening rooms, where library users can try out different materials.

Periodicals Section Current magazines and newspapers are stored in the periodicals section. You can also find bound and microfilm copies of older magazines and newspapers.

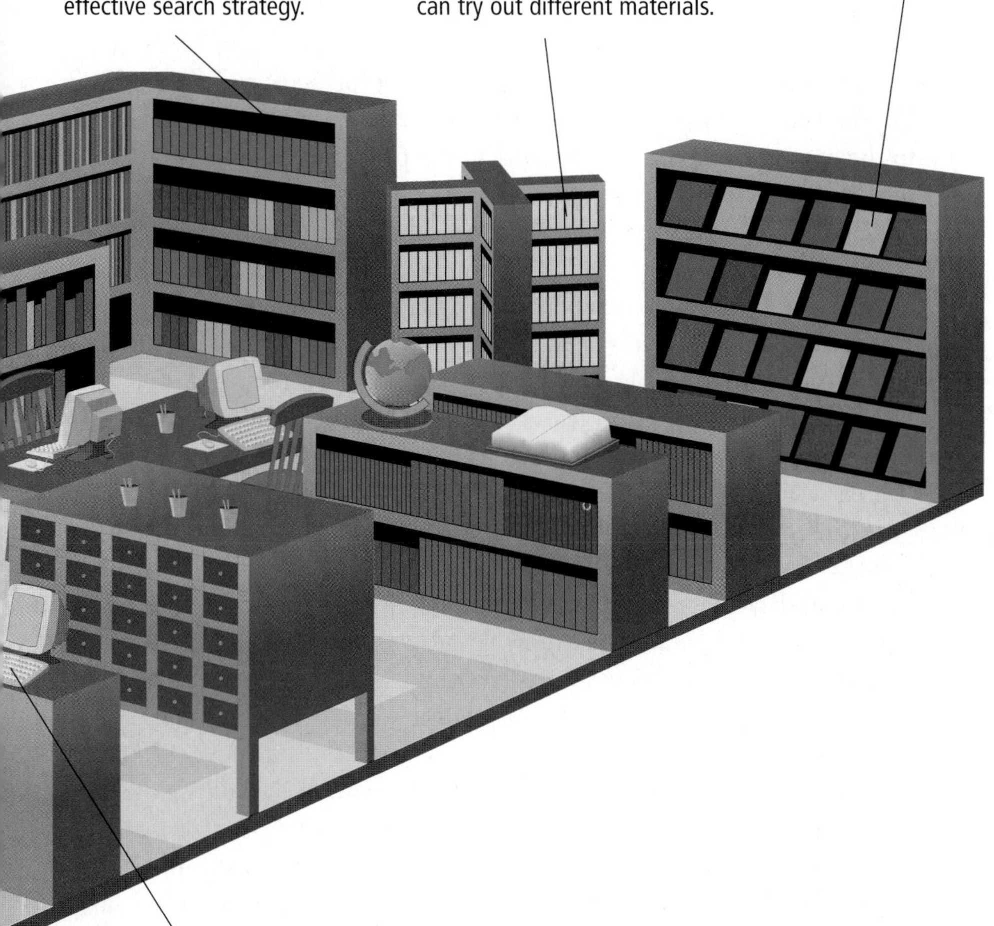

Online Resources Depending on the individual library, computer indexes and electronic databases may be found in the reference section and/or in the periodicals section. In some libraries, these electronic resources are networked throughout the library and are available on most computers. Most libraries have a special section for Internet computers.

Exercise 2

In which section of a library might you find these items?

1. *Africa: A Biography of the Continent*
2. *Premiere* magazine
3. *Mozart's Requiem* (a compact disc)
4. *Encyclopedia of Endangered Species*
5. *The Joy Luck Club* (a novel)

23.3 Searching for Periodicals

Until the early 1990s, almost all searching for magazine and newspaper articles was done by using printed indexes, and then by searching either bound periodicals or microforms (copies of magazines and newspapers stored on film). Today, magazine searches can be done electronically on the Internet and on various databases. A database is a collection of electronic files that are easily retrieved by a computer. However, if you are searching for older information, such as a magazine source from the early 1980s or before, you still need to search the older way. Scan for your topic in a bound copy of *The Readers' Guide to Periodical Literature* and then follow your citation to the correct issue of the magazine in the periodical section.

But often you will search online. Most libraries provide two different types of electronic databases: general periodical ones, and ones specific to a subject. *The Electric Library,* which searches newspapers, general magazines, maps, and TV and radio transcripts, is an example of a general periodical database. *Social Issues Resource* is an example of a database that is focused on one main subject area, sociology and current social problems.

All databases share common features. Most offer the option to do a basic search or a more advanced search. Each has a query screen. On it you key in your search term(s)—either one word, or a search phrase. Some databases allow you to search by subject, but for many databases the *default* setting (the one that appears first) is a keyword search. The *refine* option lets you limit your search by date. It also lets you do a new search with a more specific search term. Many databases allow you to use natural language—you ask the question the way you would ask a friend. Some databases will let you limit your search to full-text articles only. Some will let you limit your search to one format only, such as maps.

After your search is finished, check the display results carefully. Note if the results are displayed in chronological order or by order of *relevancy. Relevancy* means that the search results share a close logical relationship with your topic. The one with the closest relationship will be listed first, and so on.

Sample Periodical Search

This search was done using a database called *MasterFILE Premier,* which searches current magazines and newspapers. The researcher, looking for information on connections between the Internet and radio, has used the keywords "internet and radio" and has limited the search to periodicals published between January 1999 and October 1999.

Sample Screen Examine the first ten references that came up for this search. An *X* indicates *Full Text*—that is, the entire text of the article is available.

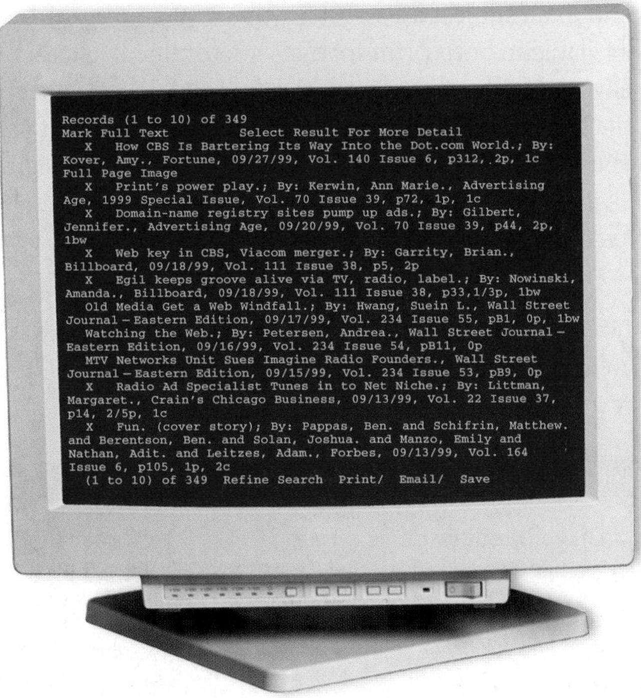

Look over your display results carefully. The display screen gives you important information about each article, including the title, author, source, date of publication, length, and availability of photographs or other graphics. The abbreviations *c* and *bw* stand for *color* or *black-and-white* images.

Exercise 3

Look at the sample screen and answer these questions.

1. Which of these periodicals did a cover story on this topic? Why might a cover story be more valuable than just any story?
2. How many of these articles have full text available?
3. You have only one hour to finish researching your report. In what ways might you refine your search?
4. You need to illustrate your report. Which of these articles has a full page image? Is the image in color or in black and white?

Library Resources

23.4 Using Reference Sources

Libraries offer many reference sources to answer all types of questions and in all subject areas. Today these reference sources are almost always available in both print formats and online. General reference works will satisfy many of your research needs. They do not take much time to survey and they provide excellent background information. If you do not locate what you need, you may have to move on to more specialized reference sources.

General Reference Works

General reference works include sources such as encyclopedias, dictionaries, atlases, and yearbooks. Online versions of these sources are available and may provide video, film, and audio clips in addition to traditional text and photos.

General Reference Sources	Examples
Encyclopedias include general information on a variety of topics.	*World Book Encyclopedia* (print), *Britannica Online, Encyclopedia Americana* (print and online), *Encarta* (online)
Almanacs provide statistics, lists, and detailed coverage of last year's events.	*Times/Information Please Almanac* (print and online), *World Almanac* (print)
Atlases are collections of maps. They often include special maps on climate, land use, history, and other topics. **Gazetteers** are geographical dictionaries.	Atlases: *Times Atlas of the World* (print), *History Atlas of North America* (print), *The World Factbook* (online) Gazetteers: *Merriam-Webster's Geographical Dictionary* (print), *Columbia Gazetteer of the World* (print), *The U.S. Gazetteer* (online)
Biographical Reference Works give life histories of noteworthy individuals.	*Current Biography* (print), *Dictionary of American Biography* (print), *Biography Index* (online), *Literature Resource Center* (online)

The Internet

Your public library will also provide access to the Internet, a valuable reference tool. The Internet provides information on any subject—text, images, sound, and video, as well as a way to contact experts. Since it provides the most current news, the Internet can be your first source for any late-breaking news. It also provides full text of speeches, laws, and excerpts of many books. On the Internet, you can search the catalogs of world-class libraries, such as the Library of Congress and the New York Public Library.

Search Engines Since there are so many Internet sites, the best way to find useful information on the Internet is by using a *search engine.* Search engines send out software agents called *spiders* that search every link they can find. If you do not find any usable sources with one search engine, try some others. They each search the Internet differently, and no single search engine will search comprehensively.

Online Libraries Online libraries on the Internet are important reference sources. They offer links to many information sources that can answer your specific reference questions. One advantage of these sites is that they are available twenty-four hours a day. You can connect from home if you have access to a computer and a modem. A disadvantage of these sites is that there are no librarians available to help you find the information you need quickly. Examples of excellent online reference sites include *The Internet Public Library,* sponsored by the School of Information at the University of Michigan, and *Thor: The Virtual Reference Desk* +, the online resource site of Purdue University Library.

Evaluating Internet Sources The Internet is not a perfect research tool, however. Much information on the Internet is unreliable. Always evaluate what you see when you scan a Web site for information. Ask yourself whether it is current, and if it was put there by a reliable source. In addition, check more than one source on the Internet to see if the information corresponds. Many libraries list recommended Web sites, which are ideal starting places for Internet research. (See Unit 7, "Research Paper Writing," page 320, for guidance on evaluating sources and detecting bias.) For any Web site you use, ask yourself the following questions.

1. Is the material authoritative? Who sponsors this site? Is it a government agency, a business promoting its own products, a nonprofit organization, or a private individual? The most reliable sites are sponsored by the government, universities, libraries, and similar reliable organizations.
2. How current is the information? A site that has not been updated for three years may be too old for your purposes.
3. Look over the screens. Are there many errors, misspellings, typos? If so, the person may also have been careless with the accuracy of the information.
4. Is the site easy to navigate? Or are you lost in a sea of words and images?
5. Are there links to other helpful sites? Although it isn't absolutely necessary, the linking feature is an important and useful addition.

Online Search Terms

Abstract A summary of an article or information source.

Database A collection of information resources which can be searched electronically. Some databases, such as Biography Index, only search a specific subject; others, such as Nexus/Lexus or the Electric Library, search all subjects.

Discussion Groups An online location where you can ask questions or discuss problems and current events. Discussion groups on the Internet exist on almost every topic, such as the environment, pets, music, and sports.

Full Text Indication that all of the article is present online. However, sometimes full-text articles do not include charts and graphics.

Hit The term for a successful result after you have searched online.

Internet A computer network is composed of many smaller computer networks. The Internet is the largest computer network in the world.

Relevancy In computer searching, how closely your search results answer your search query. Many databases and search engines display results in a hierarchy from the most relevant to the least. These relevancy relationships are usually given in percentages.

Search Engine Computer software that browses the Internet for places where your words appear. Examples are Yahoo, Goober, Lycos, and Ask Jeeves.

URL (Universal Resource Locator) An address for a Web site. It contains the computer name, directory name, and name of the Web page.

World Wide Web The part of the Internet that provides information in various formats, including print, sound, photos, graphics, and video. Links allow you to move from place to place.

Exercise 4

Use general reference works to answer the following questions. Use at least one encyclopedia, one almanac or yearbook, one atlas, and one biographical reference work. After each answer, indicate the reference source you used.

1. Where was Madeleine Albright born?
2. Who won the Nobel Peace Prize last year?
3. When did Brazil win its independence?
4. What is the average temperature in Bombay, India, in January?

Exercise 5

Ask your librarian to recommend two search engines. On both search engines, look for references for the same topic—a topic from one of your classes. Are there differences in the information you found on each search engine? Which of the two search engines would you prefer to use if you were doing research for a term paper? Why? What are some of the most promising references you found? Explain. Report on your findings to the class.

UNIT 24

Using Dictionaries

24.1 General Dictionaries

A dictionary is an alphabetical listing of words with their definitions, called entries. Most dictionaries of the English language fall into one of three categories—unabridged, college, school—based on their size and comprehensiveness. The characteristics of each type of dictionary are shown at the bottom of this page.

The Main Entries

Look at the sample dictionary page on page 813 to familiarize yourself with the organization of entries in a dictionary. Two features of the page, the guide words and the pronunciation key, help you find and understand dictionary entries.

Types of Dictionaries

Unabridged Dictionaries 250,000 or More Entries

Characteristics
- Extensive word histories
- Detailed definitions
- May be in several volumes
- Found mostly in libraries

Examples
- *Random House Dictionary of the English Language*
- *Webster's Third New International Dictionary*
- *Oxford English Dictionary*

College Dictionaries About 150,000 Entries

Characteristics
- Detailed enough to answer most questions on spelling or definitions
- Widely used in schools, homes, and businesses

Examples
- *Random House Webster's College Dictionary*
- *American Heritage Dictionary of the English Language*
- *Webster's New World Dictionary*

School Dictionaries 90,000 or Fewer Entries

Characteristics
- Definitions based on students' backgrounds
- Emphasizes common words

Examples
- *Macmillan Dictionary*
- *Webster's School Dictionary*

kaolin / keep

Guide words indicate the first and last entry on the page **kaolin/keep**.

ka·o·lin (kā′ə lin) *also,* **ka·o·line.** *n.* fine white clay used chiefly to fill and coat paper and to make pottery and other ceramics. [French *Kaolin,* from Chinese *Kao-ling* name of a mountain (literally, high hill) in China where it was first obtained.]

ka·on (kā′on) *n.* *Physics.* subatomic particle of the meson group. See **subatomic particle** for table. [*Ka* the letter *k* + (MES)ON.]

ka·pok (kā′pok) *n.* light, fluffy fiber obtained from the seedpods of the silk-cotton tree, used as a stuffing for life preservers, pillows, and mattresses, and as an insulating material. Also, **silk cotton.** [Malay *kāpoq* cotton tree.]

kap·pa (kap′ə) *n.* tenth letter of the Greek alphabet (Κ, κ), corresponding to English *K, k* and sometimes *C, c.*

kappa meson, kaon.

ka·put (kə poot′, kä-) *adj.* *Informal.* defeated, destroyed, or ruined. [German *Kaputt,* from French *capot* without tricks (in the game of piquet); literally, hoodwinked, from *capot* hooded cloak, going back to Late Latin *cappa.* See CAPE[1].]

Ka·ra·chi (kə rä′chē) *n.* largest city and former capital of Pakistan, a port in the southern part of the country, on the Arabian Sea. Pop. (1975 est.), 2,800,000.

kar·a·kul (kar′ə kəl) *n.* **1.** sheep of a breed originally native to central Asia, having a narrow body and a broad tail. The young karakul has a coat of curled, gray or glossy black fur which becomes long, coarse, and gray or brown when the lamb matures. Height: to 3 feet at the shoulder. **2.** caracul. [From *Kara Kul,* lake in Turkestan, where it was first raised.]

kar·at (kar′ət) *also,* **car·at.** *n.* unit of measure used to express the fineness of gold, 24 karats equaling pure gold. Fourteen-karat gold is 14 parts gold and 10 parts alloy.

ka·ra·te (kə rä′tē) *n.* Japanese system of unarmed self-defense in which the hands, elbows, knees, and feet are used to strike an opponent at various vulnerable points of the body. [Japanese *karate* literally, empty hand (in the sense of weaponless).]

Karl-Marx-Stadt (kärl′märks′shtät′) *n.* city in southern East Germany, formerly known as Chemnitz. Pop. (1977 est.), 310,770.

Kar·lo·vy Va·ry (kär′lô vē vär′ē) town in northwestern Czechoslovakia, a famous health resort. Pop. (1977), 61,000. Also, **Carls′bad;** *German,* **Karls′bad.**

Karls·bad (kärlz′bad′, -bät) *German.* Karlovy Vary.

Karls·ruh·e (kärlz′roo′ə) *also,* **Carls·ruh·e.** *n.* city in southwestern West Germany. Pop. (1977 est.), 275,828.

kar·ma (kär′mə) *n.* **1.** Hindu and Buddhist doctrine that the morality of a person's actions determines the status of the person's future incarnations. **2.** fate; destiny. [Sanskrit *karma* action, fate.]

Kar·nak (kär′nak) *n.* village in Egypt, on the Nile, site of a large group of ancient temples. Karnak is located on part of the site of ancient Thebes.

kar·roo (kə roo′) *pl.,* **-roos.** *also,* **ka·roo.** *n.* **1.** dry tableland of southern Africa. **2. Karroo.** vast plateau region in the southern part of the Republic of South Africa, in Cape of Good Hope province. [Afrikaans *karo,* probably from Hottentot *garo* desert.]

karyo- *combining form* nucleus of a cell: *karyokinesis.* [Greek *karyon* kernel, nut.]

kar·yo·ki·ne·sis (kar′ē ō ki nē′sis, -kī-) *n.* mitosis. [KARYO- + Greek *kinēsis* movement, motion.]

Kash·mir (kash′mēr, kash mēr′) *also,* **Cash·mere.** *n.* area in the extreme north of the Indian subcontinent, disputed by India and Pakistan, each of which occupies part of the territory. Area, 86,024 sq. mi. Pop. (1971, excluding Pakistan-occupied area), 4,617,000. Also, **Jammu and Kashmir.** —**Kash·mir·i** (kash mēr′ē), *adj., n.*

Kashmir goat, goat native to India, Tibet, and other regions of Asia, raised esp. for its fine, soft undercoat, which is used to make cashmere wool. Also, **Cashmere goat.**

Ka·tan·ga (kə täng′gə, -tang′-) *n.* former province in the southern part of Zaire, now known as **Shaba.**

Kat·man·du (kät′män doo′) *also,* **Kath·man·du.** *n.* capital of Nepal, in the central part of the country. Pop. (1971), 150,402.

Kat·te·gat (kat′ə gat′) *also,* **Cat·te·gat.** *n.* broad arm of the North Sea between Denmark and Sweden.

ka·ty·did (kā′tē did′) *n.* any of a group of large green grasshoppers, family Tettigoniidae, having long threadlike antennae. The male produces a shrill, rasping noise by rubbing its wings together. [Imitative of this sound.]

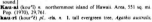

Katydid

Kau·ai (kou′ī) *n.* northernmost island of Hawaii. Area, 551 sq. mi. Pop. (1970), 29,761.

kau·ri (kour′ē) *pl.,* **-ris.** *n.* **1.** tall evergreen tree, *Agathis australis,* found in Australia, New Zealand, and California, having broad flat leaves. Also, **kauri pine.** **2.** fine, ever-grained wood of this tree, used in shipbuilding. **3.** resin obtained from this tree, used esp. in making varnish and linoleum. [Of Maori origin.]

kau·ry (kour′ē) *pl.,* **-ries.** *n.* kauri.

Kay, Sir (kā) rude and boastful knight of the Round Table who was the foster brother and steward of King Arthur.

kay·ak (kī′ak) *also,* **kai·ak.** *n.* **1.** Eskimo canoe made of animal skins stretched over a light framework of wood or whalebone, having a small opening in the center for a paddler. **2.** light, highly maneuverable canoe resembling this, used esp. in sports and usually covered with canvas. [Of Eskimo origin.]

Kayak *(def. 2)*

kay·o (kā′ō′) *pl.,* **kay·os.** *n.* knockout in boxing. —*v.t.,* **kay·oed, kay·o·ing.** to knock out in boxing.

Ka·zakh·stan (kä′zäk stän′) *n.* republic of the Soviet Union, in the Asian part of the country. Official name: **Kazakh Soviet Socialist Republic.** Area, approx. 1,048,300 sq. mi. Pop. (1965 est.), 11,853,000.

Ka·zan (kä zän′) *n.* city in the European part of the Soviet Union, near the Volga River. Pop. (1970 est.), 869,000.

ka·zoo (kə zoo′) *pl.,* **-zoos.** *n.* toy musical instrument consisting of a tube containing a strip of catgut or a piece of paper that vibrates and produces a harsh buzzing sound when the player hums into the tube. [Probably imitative.]

kc., kilocycle.

K.C., Knights of Columbus.

ke·a (kē′ə) *n.* New Zealand parrot, *Nestor notabilis,* having a sharp, hooked bill and predominantly olive-green plumage. It feeds on fruit and insects in the summer, but in the winter may feed on carrion or attack and kill sheep by tearing their backs to eat the kidney fat. [Of Maori origin.]

Keats, John (kēts) 1795–1821, English poet.

ke·bab (kə bob′) *also,* **ke·bob.** shish kebob.

kedge (kej) **kedged, kedg·ing.** *v.t.* to move (a boat or ship) by pulling on a rope attached to a small anchor that has been dropped at some distance. —*v.i.* (of a boat or ship) to move by kedging. —*n.* small anchor used esp. in kedging. Also, **kedge anchor.** [Of uncertain origin.]

keel (kēl) *n.* **1.** main timber or steel piece extending lengthwise along the center of the bottom of a ship or boat and supporting the entire frame. **2.** part in an aircraft, esp. an airship, corresponding to a ship's keel. **3.** any structure or part resembling a ship's keel. **4.** *Archaic.* ship. **5. on an even keel,** in a state of stability; steady; balanced: *His clear-headedness helped keep everyone on an even keel.* —*v.i., v.t.* **1.** to capsize or nearly capsize; turn over: *The boat keeled when the wind came up.* **2. to keel over. a.** to turn bottom up; capsize. **b.** to fall over suddenly; topple; collapse: *to keel over in a faint.* [Old Norse *kjölr* lowest timber along the bottom of a ship.]

Keel

keel·boat (kēl′bōt′) *n.* flat-bottomed river boat having a keel but no sails, propelled by being rowed, towed, or poled, formerly used to carry freight in the western United States.

keel·haul (kēl′hôl′) *v.t.* **1.** to drag (a person) under the keel of a ship from one side or end to the other as a form of punishment. **2.** to rebuke or punish severely. [Dutch *kielhalen,* from *kiel* keel + *halen* to haul.]

keel·son (kel′sən, kēl′-) *also,* **kel·son.** *n.* long beam running parallel with and fastened to the main keel of a ship in order to strengthen it. [Of Germanic origin.]

keen[1] (kēn) *adj.* **1.** having a fine cutting edge or point; able to cut or pierce easily; sharp: *a keen sword.* **2.** having or showing great mental sharpness; clever; perceptive: *a keen mind, a keen understanding of a subject.* **3.** highly sensitive or acute, as a sense or sense organ: *keen eyes, a keen sense of smell.* **4.** vividly felt or experienced; intense; strong: *a keen sense of loss. The hounds followed the keen scent.* **5.** of a piercing, penetrating, or cutting nature: *A cold, keen wind blows in from the ocean.* **6.** enthusiastic; eager: *Kate is keen about traveling.* [Old English *cēne* wise, brave.] —**keen′ly,** *adv.* —**keen′ness,** *n.* —**Syn. 6.** see **eager.**

keen[2] (kēn) *Irish. n.* wailing lament for the dead. —*v.i.* to wail loudly for the dead. [Irish *caoinim* I wail.] —**keen′er,** *n.*

keep (kēp) **kept, keep·ing.** *v.t.* **1.** to retain in one's possession, power, or control: *I told Joan she could borrow my sweater but not keep it.* **2.a.** to cause to continue in some specified place, condition, relation, or position: *to keep things in order, to keep the door open, to keep a child*

at; **ā**pe; c**ä**r; **e**nd; m**ē**; **i**t; **ī**ce; h**o**t; **ō**ld; f**ô**rk; w**oo**d; f**oo**l; **oi**l; **ou**t; **u**p; **ū**se; t**u**rn; si**ng**; **th**in; **th**is; **zh** in treasure; ə in **a**go, tak**e**n, penc**i**l, lem**o**n, circ**u**s   561

The first entry on the page is **kaolin**.

The last entry on the page is **keep**.

Pronunciation key uses well-known words to indicate how to interpret the pronunciation symbols **a**t; **ā**pe; c**ä**r; **e**nd; m**ē** . . .

Homographs Two or more words that are spelled the same but have different meanings and histories are listed as separate entries. Such words are called homographs. For example, *sole* could mean "the bottom of a foot," "acting alone," or "a type of fish." Since these three meanings are so distinct from each other, sole is listed as a main entry three times. Each is labeled with a small, raised number. Notice the different meanings and histories of *real*[1] and *real*[2] shown on the next page.

Entry Information Most often you probably look up a word to find a definition. However, entries also provide other information, such as

- correct hyphenation of words with more than one syllable
- pronunciations
- preferred spellings when alternate forms of words are acceptable
- inflected forms of the main entry word, such as plurals, adverbs, or adjectives
- part or parts of speech
- cross-references to synonyms, words with the same or similar meanings, and to antonyms, words with opposite meanings

Etymology Many entries also include an etymology, which is the history of a word. For example, the word *telephone* comes from two Greek words—*tele* ("far off, afar") and *phone* ("voice, sound"). From etymologies you can also learn when a word is derived from another, such as *atomic* from *atom.*

Look at the following dictionary entry for *real* to review the elements of an entry.

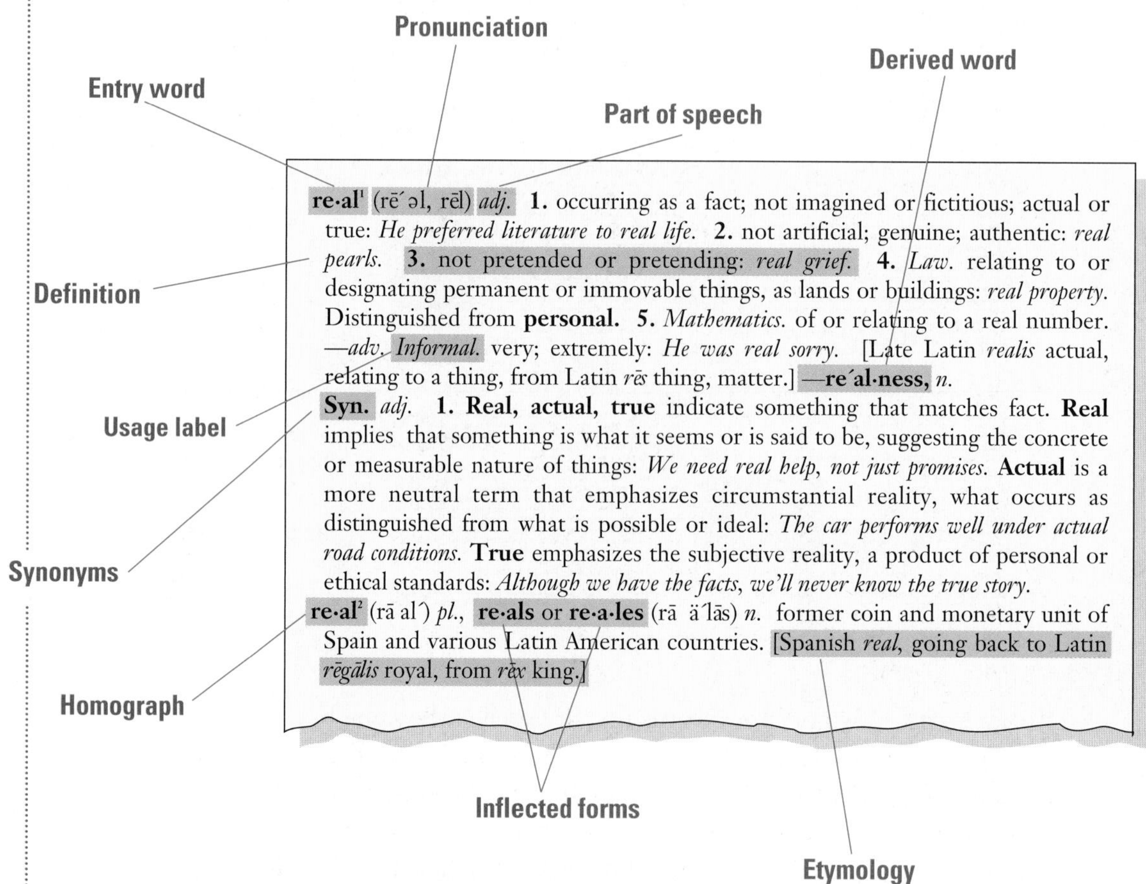

re·al[1] (rē´ əl, rēl) *adj.* **1.** occurring as a fact; not imagined or fictitious; actual or true: *He preferred literature to real life.* **2.** not artificial; genuine; authentic: *real pearls.* **3.** not pretended or pretending: *real grief.* **4.** *Law.* relating to or designating permanent or immovable things, as lands or buildings: *real property.* Distinguished from **personal. 5.** *Mathematics.* of or relating to a real number. —*adv. Informal.* very; extremely: *He was real sorry.* [Late Latin *realis* actual, relating to a thing, from Latin *rēs* thing, matter.] **—re´al·ness,** *n.*

Syn. *adj.* **1. Real, actual, true** indicate something that matches fact. **Real** implies that something is what it seems or is said to be, suggesting the concrete or measurable nature of things: *We need real help, not just promises.* **Actual** is a more neutral term that emphasizes circumstantial reality, what occurs as distinguished from what is possible or ideal: *The car performs well under actual road conditions.* **True** emphasizes the subjective reality, a product of personal or ethical standards: *Although we have the facts, we'll never know the true story.*

re·al[2] (rā al´) *pl.,* **re·als** or **re·a·les** (rā ä´lās) *n.* former coin and monetary unit of Spain and various Latin American countries. [Spanish *real,* going back to Latin *rēgālis* royal, from *rēx* king.]

Usage Guidelines A dictionary entry also provides you with guidelines on usage, meaning the way words are used in different contexts. Labels identify situations in which the word can be used appropriately. For example, the definition of the word *dig* that means "to understand" is labeled "slang." This usage label tells you that this meaning of *dig* does not belong to standard English.

Many dictionaries include a phrase or a sentence illustrating the use of a particular definition of a word. In some dictionaries these phrases and sentences are quotations from actual pieces of writing, in which case the dictionary may also identify the writer and the date of the piece.

Common usage labels are described in the table located at the top of the next page.

Usage Information in Dictionary Entries		
Type of Information	**Description**	**Example**
Capitalization	Indicates when a particular meaning of a word needs to be capitalized	**confederate . . . 2. Confederate.** citizen or supporter of the Confederate States of America.
Special field usage	Identifies a definition used only in a particular activity or area of study	**travel . . . 7.** *Basketball.* To walk or run illegally while holding the ball.
Regional usage	Indicates words with special meanings in certain geographical areas.	**submarine . . . 3.** *Chiefly Northeastern and North Midland U.S.* a hero sandwich.
Usage note	Provides guidelines for using (or not using) words in particular situations	**oyez . . .** ▲ used to announce that court is in session and to ask for silence.
Out-of-date usage	Labels words as archaic (used only in special contexts) or obsolete (no longer used)	**transport . . . 4.** *Archaic.* to kill.

Special Sections

Many dictionaries also include special sections, such as a biography section listing famous people and a geography section describing cities, countries, and other places.

Accessing Dictionaries on Computers

Today, many dictionaries are available on compact disc (CD-ROM). You can also access dictionaries on the Internet. Online dictionaries allow you to enter a search word to find the definition. For some words, you also get an illustration. Online dictionaries also offer features such as help with spelling, word games, language tips, and amusing facts about words. Some online dictionary services allow you to access many general and specialized dictionaries in one search.

Exercise 1

Use a school or college dictionary to answer the following questions.

1. Who was Haile Selassie?
2. What are the past and past participle of *tread?*
3. Is *theater* or *theatre* the preferred American spelling?
4. What are the origins of the homographs spelled *bow?*
5. What synonyms or antonyms are given for *spectator?*

24.2 Using a Thesaurus

One special type of dictionary is a book of synonyms, also known as a thesaurus. Such a book can help a writer find colorful, precise words about any given subject. The best-known thesaurus is *Roget's,* first developed by a British doctor, Peter Mark Roget, in 1852. Roget grouped together words related to the same basic concept, such as *improvement,* into categories. He then developed an index to the categories. Thesauruses exist today both in this original form and an updated, dictionary form.

You can also access thesauruses electronically—on CD-ROMs, on the Internet, and even on some word processing software.

Original Form

Using Roget's original thesaurus is a simple two-step process. First, you look up a word in the index to find the category under which it is listed. Then you look up the category to find synonyms for the word. For example, look at the following thesaurus entries for the word *change.*

The index lists many categories for change. Category 139 lists synonyms for the meaning *alteration.*

change
n. alteration 139
alternate 149.2
conversion 145.1
differentiation 16.4
petty cash 835.19
substitution 149.1

Category 139 lists synonyms for change that mean *alteration.*

Commonly used words are printed in boldface type.

139. CHANGE

.1 NOUNS **change, alteration, modification; variation,** variety, difference, diversity, diversification; **deviation,** diversion, **divergence; switch, turn,** turnabout, about-face, **reversal,** flip-flop [informal]; apostasy, defection, change of heart; **shift,** transition, **modulation,** qualification; **conver-sion, renewal,** revival, revivification; remaking, reshaping, re-creation, redesign, restructuring; realignment, **adaptation, adjustment,** accommodation, fitting.

Dictionary Form

A variation of Roget's original system is even simpler to use. A thesaurus in dictionary form presents words in alphabetical order. A regular word entry is followed by a few synonyms and cross-references to one or more related major categories, as in the entry for *grow.*

> **grow,** *v.* raise, plant, sow (FARMING); vegetate, germinate, sprout (PLANT LIFE); fill out, wax, accumulate (INCREASE).

If you can't find an appropriate synonym under the regular entry, try one of the major categories, which are in parentheses. Under a major category entry you will find nouns, verbs, adjectives, and adverbs all related to one main idea. Major categories include cross-references to antonyms. The following excerpt shows the entry for *increase.*

> INCREASE—*N.* **increase,** raise, rise, boost, step-up; addition, increment, accrual, access.
>
> **growth,** surge, swell, rise, accretion; accumulation, overgrowth, spread.
>
> [*abnormal bodily enlargement*] giantism, gigantism, elephantiasis, acromegaly.
>
> *V.* **increase,** enhance, aggrandize, augment, add to, heighten, aggravate, intensify, step up, raise, lift, boost, up; multiply, propagate, redouble, magnify, exaggerate, maximize, lengthen.
>
> **grow,** surge, swell, fill out, inflate; wax, accumulate, rise, skyrocket; overgrow, overrun, spread.
>
> **expand,** distend, dilate, inflate, swell, develop, extend, spread, stretch, widen; enlarge, pad, amplify, bulk.
>
> **enlarge on** (*a subject, etc.*), amplify, develop, dilate on, elaborate on, expand, expatiate on, extend.
>
> *Adj.* **increasing,** etc. (see *Verbs*); accretive, crescent, crescive, incremental, increscent, addititious, cumulative, accumulative.
>
> See also ADDITION, EXAGGERATION, SPREAD, SWELLING. *Antonyms*—See DECREASE, DEDUCTION.

Major category

Synonyms for increase

Subcategories

Cross-references to other major categories

Cross-references to antonyms

Exercise 2

Use a thesaurus to find two synonyms for each word below. Then write an original sentence to illustrate the meaning of each synonym. You may wish to check the exact meaning of each word in a dictionary before you use it in a sentence. Share your sentences with the class.

1. want (verb)
2. angry (adjective)
3. hold (verb)
4. like (verb)
5. near (adverb)
6. deny (verb)
7. throw (verb)
8. good (adjective)
9. condemn (verb)
10. place (noun)

UNIT 25

Vocabulary

25.1 Building Vocabulary

Most words that you know you learned through active conversation and through listening and reading. One way to learn new words is by analyzing the passage in which they appear.

Analyzing Specific Context Clues

You can often figure out the meaning of a word from its context— the words and sentences surrounding an unfamiliar word. The following chart describes five different context clues and lists the words that help you interpret those clues. In the Example column, clue words are in bold type. Unfamiliar words and the context that helps you interpret the meaning of those words are in italics.

Interpreting Clue Words

Type of Context Clue	Clue Words	Example
Definition: The meaning of the unfamiliar word is stated in the sentence.	which means also known as in other words or	The course emphasized *demography*, **which means** *the study of changes in human population.*
Example: The meaning of the unfamiliar word is explained through other illustrations.	for instance such as for example like	He was the president's *amanuensis*; **for instance**, he *took dictation and copied manuscripts.*
Comparison: The unfamiliar word is similar to a familiar word or phrase.	likewise also similarly as	Consuela had a height *phobia*; **likewise**, she *feared caves.*
Contrast: The unfamiliar word is the opposite of a familiar word or phrase.	however but on the contrary unlike	We were *pertinacious* about the topics; **however**, we were *flexible* about the time of the meeting.
Cause and Effect: The unfamiliar word describes a cause in a sentence in which the effects are understood.	therefore since because when as a result	Otis was typically *loquacious*; **therefore**, the rest of us were unusually *quiet.*

Analyzing the General Context

What if there are no specific context clues to help you figure out an unfamiliar word? Often you can deduce a meaning of a word because you know other words that appear with it, as in the following sentence: The bowl contained apples, oranges, plantains, cherries, and plums. You may not know that plantains are a fruit similar to bananas. However, because the other items in the list are fruits, you might assume that plantains are a type of fruit.

Sometimes you can begin to figure out the meaning of a word by determining its part of speech. You can use this approach even if practically no words are familiar. For instance, Lewis Carroll began his poem "Jabberwocky" with these two lines: "'Twas brillig, and the slithy toves / Did gyre and gimble in the wabe." Even though Carroll made up most of the words, you can still begin to figure out their meanings.

Start with the word *toves*. You know that *toves* is the subject of the sentence because it is performing some kind of action— "the slithy toves did gyre and gimble in the wabe." The article *the* provides another clue; *the* appears only before nouns. From these two clues, you can figure that *toves* is a noun. In fact, given the plural *-s* ending, *toves* probably means "more than one tove."

Another way to figure out an unfamiliar word's part of speech is to compare the sentence in which it appears to similar sentence constructions. Look at the sentence "'Twas brillig," which means "It was brillig." *Brillig* follows a verb of being, *was*, and could therefore be a noun or an adjective. Think of other times when you have used or read a similar sentence construction. *Brillig* might describe the weather—"It was chilly"—or indicate the time of year—"It was spring."

Remembering Words You've Learned

Increasing your vocabulary improves your reading and writing skills and your chances of scoring well on standardized tests. The following tips will help you remember new words you encounter.

Tips on Learning New Words

1. **Write** down new words in a notebook. Just writing the word will help you remember it.
2. **Check** the meaning and pronunciation of the new word in a dictionary. Looking up a word helps you learn its meaning. Include this information in your notebook.
3. **Relate** the new word to words you already know. Associating its spelling or meaning with a familiar word makes a new word easier to remember.
4. **Practice** using the word in your writing and conversation. Using the word repeatedly is the best way to remember it.

Exercise 1

Each of the following passages contains an italicized word that may be unfamiliar. Determine the meaning by examining the context. Look for the context clues described in the chart on page 819. Write the italicized word and its meaning. Then indicate the strategy used in each case by writing *definition*, *example*, *comparison*, *contrast*, or *cause and effect*.

1. Television in the 1950s portrayed a *homogeneous* national population; however, the United States actually included a number of different ethnic groups.
2. Our biology teacher told us to rely only on *empirical* evidence—that is, our careful observations and experiments.
3. The beginning of Beethoven's *Sonata Pathétique* is to be played in *grave* tempo—like a funeral march, only slower.
4. Early tribes were usually *nomadic*, but because of the development of agriculture, some tribes stayed in one place.
5. The defenders of the western bridge were undefeatable, and since the defense of the eastern bridge was also *insurmountable*, the attacking forces gave up.
6. The woman was a true *miser;* for instance, she never donated to charities and spent very little money on presents.
7. At the fall of Berlin, *anarchy*, or complete disorder, prevailed until Allied forces took control.
8. Our creative writing teacher instructed us to use a *pseudonym* to hide our real identities. I chose "Lian Chen" as my pen name.
9. Do not keep *volatile* substances in places where they will be exposed to extremely high temperatures, because they may explode.
10. The Empire State Building is among New York City's tallest *edifices*.

25.2 Word Parts

Another way to figure out the meaning of a word is by analyzing its parts. The main part of a word is its **root**. When the root is a complete word, it is sometimes called a **base word**. The root or base word is often combined with a **prefix** (a word part attached to the beginning of a word), a **suffix** (a word part attached to the end of a word), or another root to form a different word.

Consider a word you already know—*unbreakable*—and look at its parts. Added to the base word *break* are the prefix *un-* and the suffix *-able*. The prefix *un-* means "not." The suffix *-able* means "capable of." Therefore, *unbreakable* means "not capable of being broken."

Word Roots

While prefixes and suffixes can give hints about a word's meaning, the most important clue is the root. The following diagram shows several words that have been formed from the Latin root *spec*. From what you know about the words given, what do you think *spec* means?

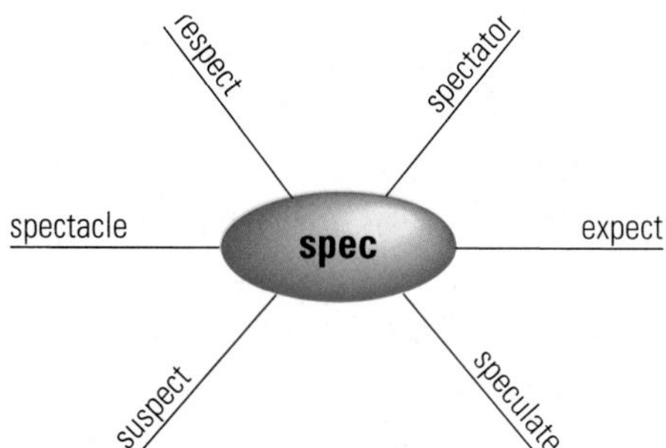

As you might have figured out, *spec* means "to look at." The next diagram shows several words. See if you can figure out which root the following words share and the meaning of the root.

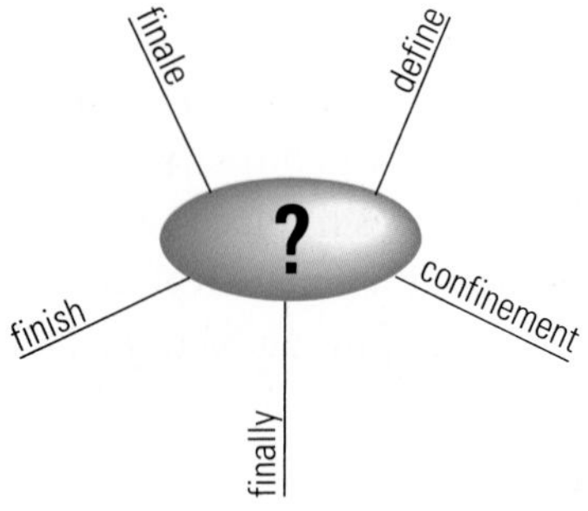

The root of each of these words is *fin*. What do you think *fin* means? All the words relate to some kind of ending, like *finish*, *finale*, and *finally*, or limitation, like *define* and *confinement*. Therefore, you can deduce that *fin*

Vocabulary

means "end" or "limit." The root *fin* comes from Latin. Nearly half of modern English general vocabulary comes from either Latin or French. Many other roots come from Greek or Anglo-Saxon words.

When you are trying to determine the meaning of a new word, think of words that might share a root with it. The meanings of these other words might give you clues to the meaning of the unfamiliar word. The following chart lists some common roots and some words that share them.

Analyzing Word Roots

Words	Meanings	Roots
aqueduct aquarium	means of moving water tank of water	*aqua* means "water"
astronaut astronomy	traveler among stars study of stars	*astro* means "stars"
biology autobiography	study of living things story of a person's life written by that person	*bio* means "life"
century centimeter	a hundred years measurement equal to one hundredth of a meter	*cent* means "hundred"
chronological synchronize	arranged in time order cause to happen at the same time	*chron* means "time"
democracy epidemic	rule by the people rapidly spreading among many people	*dem* or *demo* means "people"
geology geocentric	study of the earth measured from center of the earth	*geo* means "earth"
anonymous pseudonym	with no name known or acknowledged pen name	*nym* means "name"
agoraphobia monophobia	fear of open spaces fear of being alone	*phobia* means "fear"
portable transport	capable of being carried to carry across	*port* means "carry"
inscribe scribble	to write or mark on to write messily	*scrib* means "write"
constrict stringent	draw together; bind strict; severe	*string* or *strict* means "bind"
unique unified	one-of-a-kind joined into one	*uni* means "one"
revive vivisection	bring back to life operation on a living animal for science	*viv* means "live" or "alive"

Prefixes

Prefixes are important tools for building, and learning, new words. Prefixes change the meaning of words, sometimes drastically. Certain prefixes, such as *un-* and *in-*, can even reverse the meaning of a root.

The following chart lists other prefixes and their meanings. You will see that some prefixes can have more than one meaning. Note how some prefixes can change the meaning of a word.

Analyzing Prefixes

Words	Meanings	Prefixes
amoral atypical	without morals not typical	*a-* means "without" or "not"
coauthor colead	write together lead together	*co-* means "together"
contradict contrary	to act in opposition opposed	*contra-* means "opposed"
demote deduction	move down in rank conclusion drawn from reasoning	*de-* means "from" or "down"
dishonest distrust	not honest lack of trust	*dis-* means "lack of" or "not"
emit expel	send out drive out	*e-* and *ex-* mean "out"
illegal immoral insignificant irregular	not legal not moral not significant not regular	*il-*, *im-*, *in-*, and *ir-* mean "not"
international interject	among nations to throw between	*inter-* means "among" or "between"
microscopic microwave	invisible to the naked eye very short electromagnetic wave	*micro-* means "small"
misplace mistreat	put in wrong place treat badly	*mis-* means "wrong" or "bad"
monochromatic monogamy	of one color marriage with one mate	*mono-* means "one"
prearrange preliminary	to arrange beforehand coming before the main action	*pre-* means "before"
replay recall	to play again to call back	*re-* means "again" or "back"
submerge subzero	to place under water below zero	*sub-* means "under" or "below"

Suffixes

Suffixes are letters added to the ends of words to create new words with new meanings. Many suffixes also change the original word's part of speech. Remember the example of *unbreakable* at the beginning of this lesson? When added to the verb *break*, the suffix *-able* forms a new word with a new part of speech, the adjective *breakable*. With certain words, the spelling of the original word may change slightly when a suffix is added, as with *forgivable* (*forgive* + *-able*).

The following chart lists other suffixes, their meanings, and the parts of speech they form. See if you can figure out the meaning of the suffix by looking only at the first two columns in the table.

Analyzing Suffixes

Words	Meanings	Suffixes	Part of Speech Formed
occupant dependent commandant	one who occupies one who depends one who commands	*-ant* and *-ent* mean "one who does an action"	Concrete noun
boredom freedom	state of being bored condition of being free	*-dom* means "state" or "condition"	Abstract noun
shorten quicken enliven	to cause to be short to cause to be quick to cause to be lively	*-en* means "to cause to be"	Verb
fearful hopeful	full of fear full of hope	*-ful* means "full of"	Adjective
crystallize minimize	to become a crystal to make minimal, or smaller	*-ize* means "to become" or "to make"	Verb
hopeless treeless effortless	without hope without trees without effort	*-less* means "without"	Adjective
quickly slowly	in a quick manner in a slow manner	*-ly* means "in the manner or way mentioned"	Adverb
kindness fondness darkness	state of being kind state of being fond quality of being dark	*-ness* means "quality" or "state"	Abstract noun
furious joyous	full of fury full of joy	*-ous* means "full of"	Adjective

Exercise 2

Divide into groups of three, and have each member in a group write down the meaning of one word from each of the following groups of words. Use a dictionary if necessary. After you share your definitions, decide as a group what root the words share and what the root means.

1. philosophy, bibliophile, philanthropy
2. autocratic, technocrat, bureaucratic
3. photophobia, photography, photosynthesis
4. beneficial, benevolent, benefactor
5. mortician, immortality, mortuary

Exercise 3

Rewrite each of the following sentences, replacing the underlined words with a single word that uses a prefix. You may want to change the word order in some cases.

1. Cooperating with <u>workers with whom you are employed</u> makes work more enjoyable.
2. Many countries have experienced recessions <u>after a war.</u>
3. The journalist <u>spelled incorrectly</u> the senator's name.
4. Students can improve their grades by changing study habits that are <u>not efficient.</u>
5. When a doctor recommends surgery, many patients decide to be <u>examined again</u> by another doctor.

Exercise 4

Rewrite each of the following sentences, replacing the underlined words with a word that uses a suffix. You may want to change the word order in some cases.

1. Jon noticed that when he runs, his heartbeat <u>is made quick.</u>
2. The hero of the tale, Beowulf, is <u>without fear.</u>
3. Mel Allen and Red Barber both helped <u>to make popular</u> radio broadcasting of baseball.
4. As she left the garage, Joan gave her car keys to the <u>one who attended to</u> parking.
5. The eyewitness showed <u>a state of being willing</u> to cooperate with the police investigators.

UNIT 26

Spelling

26.1 Improving Your Spelling

As a writer, you want readers to understand your ideas. Using correct spelling in your writing will enable your readers to focus on what you have to say. One of the best ways to become a good speller is to be an avid reader; the more you see a word, the better you will remember it.

You can improve your spelling in other ways too. First, you can learn some basic rules that will help you spell correctly. Second, you can pay attention to spelling patterns in order to take better guesses as you try to spell new words. Third, you can check your spelling with an authoritative source.

Basic Spelling Rules

The following rules, examples, and exceptions will help you master the spellings of many words.

Spelling *ie* and *ei* Many writers find the rules for certain combinations of letters, like *ie* and *ei,* difficult to remember. One helpful learning strategy is to develop a rhyme to remember a rule. Look at the following rhyme for the *ie* and *ei* rule.

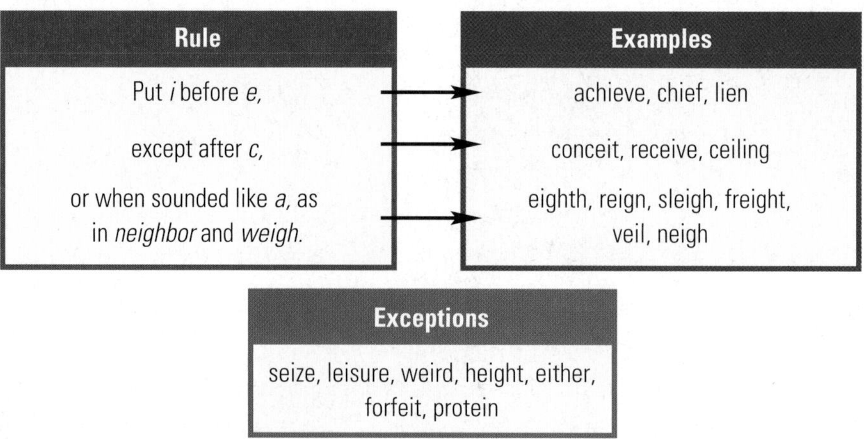

Rule
Put *i* before *e,*
except after *c,*
or when sounded like *a,* as in *neighbor* and *weigh.*
Examples
achieve, chief, lien
conceit, receive, ceiling
eighth, reign, sleigh, freight, veil, neigh
Exceptions
seize, leisure, weird, height, either, forfeit, protein

Spelling *-cede, -ceed,* and *-sede* Because various letters in the English spelling system are sometimes pronounced the same way, it is often easy to make slight spelling errors between two different letters. The similarity of pronunciation between *c* and *s* accounts for the confusion in spelling words ending in *-cede, -ceed,* and *-sede.* Because there are only four exceptions, however, you should be able to memorize them.

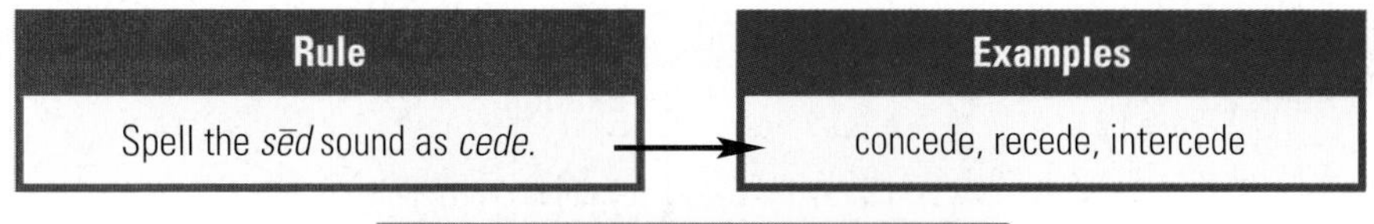

Exceptions

One word uses *-sede* to spell the *sēd* sound: *supersede.*

Three words use *-ceed* to spell the *sēd* sound: *proceed, exceed, succeed.*

Spelling Unstressed Vowels Notice the vowel sound in the second syllable of the word *or-i-gin.* This is the unstressed vowel sound, and it can be spelled several ways. Dictionary respellings use the schwa symbol (ə) to indicate it. To help spell words with unstressed vowels correctly, try thinking of a related word in which the syllable containing the vowel sound is stressed. The chart below shows examples of this process.

Spelling Unstressed Vowels

Unknown Spelling	Related Word	Word Spelled Correctly
leg_l	le**gal**ity	legal
fant_sy	fan**tas**tic	fantasy
host_le	hos**til**ity	hostile
opp_site	op**pose**	opposite

Adding Prefixes When adding a prefix to a word, keep the original spelling of the word. If the prefix forms a double letter, keep both letters.

dis + appear = disappear   ir + regular = irregular
mis + direct = misdirect   co + operate = cooperate

Suffixes and the Silent e Many English words end in a silent letter *e.* Sometimes the *e* is dropped when a suffix is added. The following chart shows when to keep and when to drop the *e.*

Adding Suffixes to Words with Silent *e*

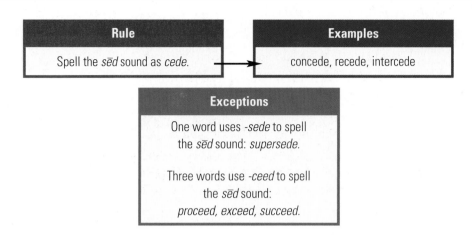

Rule	Examples
When adding a suffix that begins with a consonant to a word that ends in silent *e,* keep the *e.*	place + -ment = placement rare + -ly = rarely
Common exceptions	*awe + -ful = awful* *judge + -ment = judgment*

(*continued*)

Adding Suffixes to Words with Silent *e*	
Rule	**Examples**
When adding a suffix that begins with a vowel or *y* to a word that ends in silent *e*, usually drop the *e*.	excite + -able = excitable shine + -y = shiny
Common exceptions	*mile + -age = mileage*
When adding a suffix that begins with *a* or *o* to a word that ends in *ce* or *ge*, keep the *e* so the word will retain the soft *c* or *g* sound.	change + -able = changeable trace + -able = traceable
When adding a suffix that begins with a vowel to a word that ends in *ee* or *oe*, keep the *e*.	agree + -able = agreeable canoe + -ing = canoeing

Suffixes and the Final *y* When adding a suffix to a word that ends in a consonant + *y*, change the *y* to *i*. Do not change the *y* to *i* when the suffix begins with *i*.

try + ed = tried copy + ing = copying

When adding a suffix to a word that ends in a vowel + *y*, keep the *y*.

joy + ous = joyous convey + ed = conveyed

Doubling the Final Consonant When adding a suffix to a word, you sometimes need to double the final consonant before adding the suffix. Double the consonant when adding a suffix that begins with a vowel to a word that ends in a single consonant preceded by a single vowel, if the original word

- is a one-syllable word: dip + ing = dipping; stop + age = stoppage
- has an accent on the last syllable, and the accent remains there after the suffix is added: occur + ence = occurrence
- is a prefixed word based on a one-syllable word: reset + ing = resetting

Based on the preceding rule, you would not double the final consonant when

- the accent is not on the last syllable: develop + ing = developing
- the accent shifts when the suffix is added: refer + ence = reference
- the final consonant is preceded by two vowels: train + ing = training
- the final consonant is preceded by another consonant: remind + er = reminder
- the word ends in a consonant and the suffix begins with a consonant: reck + less = reckless

Adding *-ly* When adding *-ly* to a word that ends in a single *l*, keep the *l*. When the word ends in a double *l*, drop one *l*. When the word ends in a consonant + *le*, drop the *le*.

real + ly = really dull + ly = dully terrible + ly = terribly

Adding *-ness* When adding *-ness* to a word that ends in *n*, keep the *n*.

sullen + ness = sullenness keen + ness = keenness

Forming Compound Words When joining a word that ends in a consonant to a word that begins with a consonant, keep both consonants.

after + noon = afternoon key + board = keyboard

Forming Plurals English nouns form plurals in many ways. Most nouns simply add *s*. The following chart shows other ways of forming plural nouns and some common exceptions to the patterns.

General Rules for Plurals

If the Noun Ends In	Then Generally	Examples
ch, s, sh, x, or *z*	add *-es*	wish ➛ wishes crutch ➛ crutches
a consonant + *y*	change *y* to *i* and add *-es*	cannery ➛ canneries baby ➛ babies
a vowel + *y*	add *-s*	day ➛ days key ➛ keys
a vowel + *o*	add *-s*	studio ➛ studios stereo ➛ stereos
a consonant + *o*	generally add *-es*	potato ➛ potatoes cargo ➛ cargoes
Common exceptions	but sometimes add *-s*	*silo* ➛ *silos* *halo* ➛ *halos*
f or *ff*	add *-s*	reef ➛ reefs
Common exceptions	change *f* to *v* and add *-es*	*leaf* ➛ *leaves*
lf	change *f* to *v* and add *-es*	half ➛ halves wolf ➛ wolves
fe	change *f* to v and add *-s*	life ➛ lives knife ➛ knives

A few plurals are exceptions to the rules listed on the previous page or present some other special problem, but they are easy to remember. The following chart lists these plurals and some examples.

Special Rules for Plurals	
Special Case	**Examples**
To form the plural of proper names, add either *-s* or *-es.*	D'Amico ➛ D'Amicos Sanchez ➛ Sanchezes
To form the plural of one-word compound nouns, follow the general rules for plurals.	penknife ➛ penknives blackberry ➛ blackberries
To form the plural of hyphenated compound nouns or compound nouns of more than one word, generally make the most important word plural.	father-in-law ➛ fathers-in-law attorney general ➛ attorneys general
Some nouns have irregular forms. These nouns do not follow any rules.	man ➛ men ox ➛ oxen
Some nouns have the same singular and plural form.	series ➛ series deer ➛ deer

Learning to Spell New Words

As you read, note unfamiliar words and words that you recognize but that look hard to spell. As you write, pay attention to any words that you have difficulty spelling. Then try the process shown below.

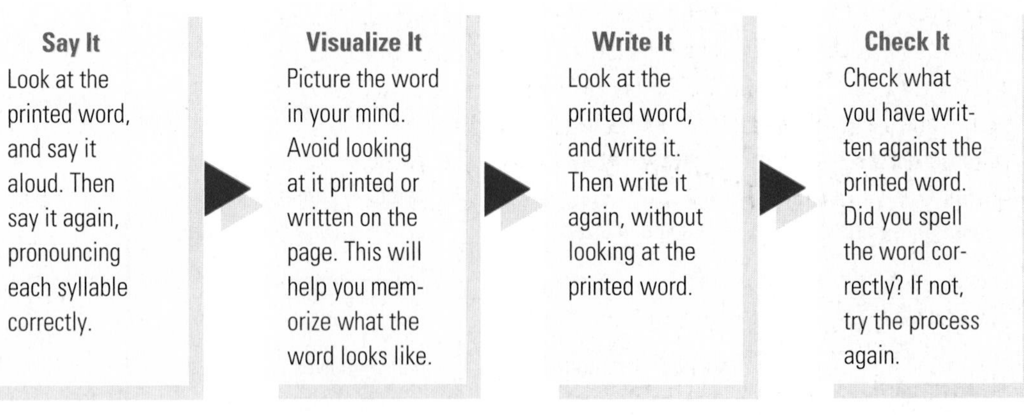

Remember that the dictionary is a source for finding the correct spelling of words. You might ask, How can I look up a word if I don't know how to spell it? Frequently you will be able to spell enough of the beginning of a word to find it in the dictionary. If you don't find a word in the first place you look, think of other probable spellings. Once you have located the correct spelling of a word, use the process described above to learn the word.

Exercise 1

In each group of words, find the one word that is misspelled. Write the word correctly. Cite the rule that applies to the spelling of the word. If the word is an exception to a rule, note that as well.

1. yield, freight, concieve
2. exceed, supercede, accede
3. sincerely, responsiveness, engagment
4. sheriffes, scarves, thieves
5. headdresses, stone crabs, commander in chiefs

26.2 Spelling Difficult Words

One very useful strategy for learning difficult words is to develop a personal word list. What words do you frequently misspell? Include those words in your personal word list. Study the words, using the four-step process you learned in Lesson 26.1, page 832.

Developing memory devices is another helpful strategy for learning to spell difficult words. Imagine, for example, that you have trouble remembering if the word *tomorrow* has one *m* or two. You might think of the sentence "Tom will arrive tomorrow" to help you remember that *tomorrow* begins with the letters *t-o-m.*

Frequently Misspelled Words

Following is a list of words that many people often misspell. Which words on the list do you have difficulty spelling?

Words Often Misspelled			
accidentally	conscientious	immediate	precede
accommodate	conscious	incidentally	prevalent
advertisement	definite	jewelry	proceed
allot	descent	laboratory	receipt
all right	discipline	library	recommend
arctic	elementary	maintenance	rhythm
attendant	eligible	mischievous	schedule
ballet	embarrass	misspell	separate
business	fascinating	niece	technique
cafeteria	February	occasion	technology
canceled	foreign	original	theory
canoe	forty	pageant	traffic
changeable	government	pastime	usually
colonel	height	pharmacy	variety
commercial	hippopotamus	physical	villain

Easily Confused Words

Some words are easily confused because they contain similar sounds. Other confusing words are homophones, words that have the same pronunciation but different meanings and spellings. Study the following list of easily confused words. Are there any words on the list that you confuse?

Words Often Confused	
accept **except**	to agree to take; to assume; to approve: We accept your plan. but; to omit: I remembered everything except my ticket!
affect **effect**	to influence; to act upon: I'm sure the book will affect her. a result: What effect did the movie have on him?
formally **formerly**	politely; officially; according to custom: We addressed him formally. previously: The principal was formerly a teacher.
lose **loose**	to misplace; to drop: Did you lose your assignment? free; not confined; not tight: My clothes are loose since I lost 10 pounds.
passed **past**	moved through or by; completed satisfactorily: I passed you in the hall. the time before the present; ended; over: You can't change the past.
principal **principle**	the head of a school; first; main: My principal concern is for the victims. a basic truth; a rule of conduct: The principle of fair play is important.
stationary **stationery**	fixed; unmoving: The plane appeared stationary in the sky. writing paper and envelopes: Rhonda preferred simple stationery.
than **then**	in comparison with: You studied harder today than yesterday. at that time; next: He did his chores, and then he played soccer.

Exercise 2

For each sentence below, determine which word in parentheses correctly completes the sentence.

1. Is Mexico City or Acapulco the (capital/capitol) of Mexico?
2. That store sells (stationery/stationary) of every color.
3. What were the (affects/effects) of the tornado?
4. Put your money away, or you may (loose/lose) it.
5. Will you (accept/except) this gift?

UNIT 27

Study Skills

27.1 Studying Effectively

Some students seem able to study and remember large amounts of material in short periods of time. Why? Part of the answer lies in how effectively students use appropriate study strategies.

Taking Notes in Class

Taking notes during class discussions and lectures can help you remember what you hear. While taking notes, you think about and rephrase the information.

Outlining Your Notes One common and very useful way of organizing notes is the modified outline form. Like the outline you might write for a research paper (see Lesson 7.2 in Composition, pages 328–331), notes in outline form summarize the main ideas and supporting details of a lecture. However, unlike formal outlines that you write, your notes need not follow precise guidelines about parallel structure or number of entries. By highlighting the main ideas and the relationships among them, an outline makes reviewing the material easy.

Recognizing Signals Signal words, such as *first*, *most importantly*, *on the other hand*, and *finally*, indicate important information or point out relationships among ideas. Such words help you know what to write down.

The speaker's voice and gestures also provide clues. By suddenly speaking more loudly or quickly, or by punctuating a point with an emphatic sweep of the hand, the speaker may be signaling an important point.

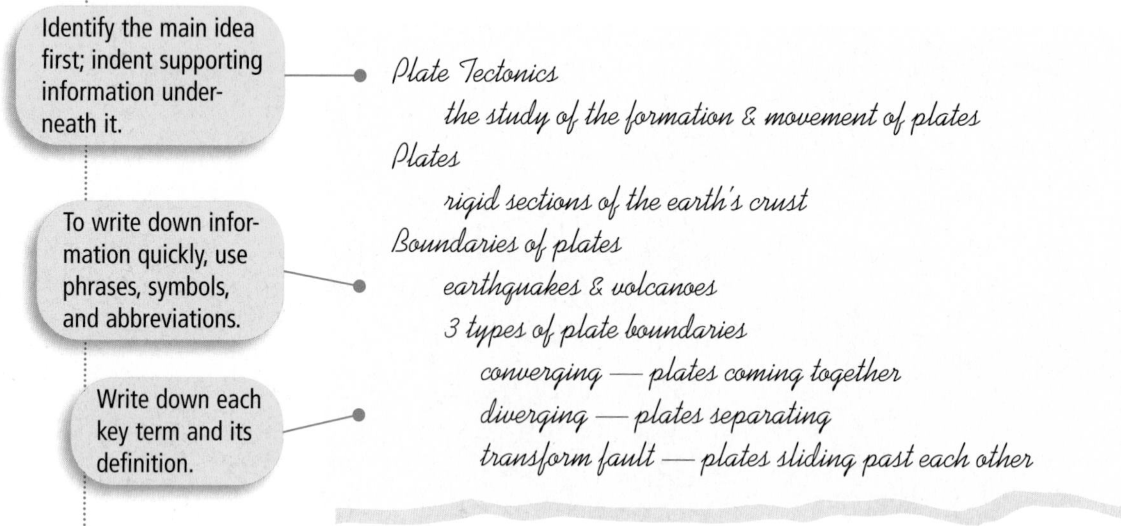

Identify the main idea first; indent supporting information underneath it.
To write down information quickly, use phrases, symbols, and abbreviations.
Write down each key term and its definition.
Plate Tectonics
the study of the formation & movement of plates
Plates
rigid sections of the earth's crust
Boundaries of plates
earthquakes & volcanoes
3 types of plate boundaries
converging — plates coming together
diverging — plates separating
transform fault — plates sliding past each other

Study Skills

Using Study Time Wisely

Most studying occurs outside of class. Whether in study hall, in a library, or at home, you want to make the most of your study time.

Recognizing Your Learning Style You can improve your studying by identifying how you learn best. People learn in a variety of ways—by reading, discussing, writing, drawing diagrams, and so on. If you learn best by discussion, meet with a friend to talk about your schoolwork. If you learn best by writing, try rewriting the lesson you are studying.

Preparing to Study Planning your study time wisely lets you make the most effective use of each minute. Here are some tips to help.

Tips on Planning Your Study Time

1. Study at the same time and place each day. Doing so makes studying a habit; your mind will be prepared when the time comes.
2. Update your list of assignments and due dates weekly. This will help you stay aware of what you need to accomplish.
3. Break down long assignments into stages. Many assignments include researching, reading, and writing stages.
4. Estimate the amount of time each stage of each assignment will require.
5. Don't plan to study one subject for too long. Many students find that changing subjects every thirty to forty-five minutes keeps their minds fresh.

Studying Effectively When you actually sit down to study, you can increase your efficiency by following the guidelines listed below.

Tips on Studying

1. Set objectives for each study session. Identifying what you want to read, write, or learn helps you focus your efforts.
2. Take notes while reading. The act of writing down information helps you remember it.
3. Create tables, charts, or diagrams. Seeing information in a different form can help you understand and remember it better.
4. Begin your study session with the hardest assignment. This way you can tackle the toughest work while you are freshest.
5. Summarize what you've learned at the end of each study session. (See Lesson 1.2 in Composition, pages 12–15, for information on keeping a learning log.)

Reading and Remembering

Knowing what your purposes are when you read and keeping track of how well you've understood what you've read are two critical study skills. Match your strategies to your purposes and use whatever methods you need to be sure that understanding does not break down. As with most skills, there are a variety of strategies to help you accomplish your purposes.

Three Ways to Read Before you begin to read, think about what information you want to learn from the material. Do you want a general idea of the topics covered? Are you looking for a specific fact or definition? Or do you want to learn everything in the passage? The highlighted text that follows shows the information you would learn from reading a passage in three different ways: skimming, scanning, and in-depth reading.

Skimming is glancing over the text to identify main ideas by reading chapter and lesson titles, words in bold or italic type, and topic sentences.

Scanning is glancing over the text in search of specific information by looking for key words.

In-depth reading is reading over the text carefully to absorb new ideas and facts.

Family and Government Promoting order was Confucius's principal concern. He believed that everyone had a proper role in society. If each person would accept that role and perform the related duties, social and political disorder would end.

Individuals, Confucius taught, should live according to principles of **ethics** — good conduct and moral judgment. Ethics began with respect for family, especially elders, and reverence for the past and its traditions. Ethics should govern each person's behavior in these five primary relationships: ruler and subject, parent and child, husband and wife, old and young, friend and friend.

Each reading style is useful for certain times. Here are a few suggestions for when each style might be appropriate:

- **Skimming** is useful when you're previewing material for a general overview, determining main ideas or an author's purpose, or deciding whether a book covers a subject you're interested in.
- **Scanning** is useful when you're reviewing key terms, looking for a detail to support an opinion, or searching for specific information.
- **In-depth reading** is useful when you're reading for the first time and learning new concepts, or when you're evaluating the information presented or preparing to explain the information to someone else.

The SQ3R Method An effective method for learning and remembering written information is known as SQ3R. The name comes from the steps in the process: survey, question, read, record, and review. Applying this method can help you remember what you read. Look at the chart below to find out how to use this method in your studying.

Survey		Question		Read		Record		Review
Preview the material by skimming. Read heads, highlighted terms, and the first sentence of each paragraph. Look at all pictures and graphs.	▶	Ask questions about the material. Your questions might begin with *who, what, when, where, why,* and *how.*	▶	Read the selection carefully. Identify the main idea of each section. Take notes and add questions to your list.	▶	Write answers to your questions without looking at the text. Make brief notes about additional main ideas or facts.	▶	Check your answers in the text. Continue to study the text until you can answer all questions

Mnemonic Devices Rhymes, sayings, or words, called mnemonic devices, help you recall basic information and can also help you remember what you study. The list below gives some examples. By looking for patterns in what you study, you can develop your own mnemonic devices.

Common Mnemonic Devices

Purpose	Word or Phrase
To remember that the order of scientific classification of living things is *k*ingdom, *p*hylum, *c*lass, *o*rder, *f*amily, *g*enus, and *s*pecies	*K*ing *P*hilip *c*ame *o*ver *f*rom *G*ermany *S*aturday.
To remember that the person who runs a school is a principal, not a principle	A principal is a pal.
To remember that the lines of the treble clef are the notes *E, G, B, D,* and *F*	*E*very *g*ood *b*oy *d*eserves *f*udge.
To help you interpret centigrade temperatures	30° is hot, 20° is nice; 10° is cool, 0° is ice.
To remember that the order of the planets from the sun is *M*ercury, *V*enus, *E*arth, *M*ars, *J*upiter, *S*aturn, *U*ranus, *N*eptune, and *P*luto	*M*y *v*ery *e*xcellent *m*other *j*ust *s*erved *u*s *n*ine *p*ickles.
To remember that the order of colors in the spectrum is *r*ed, *o*range, *y*ellow, *g*reen, *b*lue, *i*ndigo, and *v*iolet	Roy G. Biv
To remember that the five Great Lakes are *H*uron, *O*ntario, *M*ichigan, *E*rie, and *S*uperior	homes

Evaluating What You Read

Another study tool is critical reading. In critical reading, you might ask yourself questions such as the following: Is this statement true? Are these connections logical? Do I agree with the values underlying this writer's viewpoint? Remember that even well-researched and carefully considered writing can contain mistakes or reflect an author's bias.

Identifying Facts and Opinions One step in evaluating writing is recognizing the difference between fact and opinion. A fact is a statement that can be verified or proved true. The proof of a statement might come from direct experience—something you saw or experienced yourself—or from an authoritative source, such as a reference book or a quotation from an expert on the subject.

An opinion is a personal judgment. Since opinions are expressions of someone's beliefs or feelings, they cannot be proved either true or false. Opinions can provide useful information, but to be valid they should be supported by evidence.

The following chart shows examples of facts and opinions and how to separate them from each other.

Distinguishing Facts from Opinions

Statement	Fact or Opinion
1. Sammy Sosa was the first baseball player to hit sixty homeruns in two consecutive years.	**1.** Fact: It is easy to confirm through newspapers and reference books that Sammy Sosa was the first baseball player to hit the sixty homerun mark in two consecutive years—1998 and 1999.
2. Sammy Sosa is the best baseball player of the twentieth century.	**2.** Opinion: While facts might be used to support or oppose this idea, it is a matter of one's personal view. It cannot be proved true.
3. The Hubble Space Telescope was launched on April 24,1990, aboard the space shuttle *Discovery*.	**3.** Fact: Reference books, newspapers, and newsmagazines can provide evidence to support this statement.
4. Manufacturers' carelessness caused severe flaws in the Hubble Telescope mirror.	**4.** Opinion: Although some experts have presented evidence to support this idea, other experts remain unconvinced of the connection.

Interpreting and Evaluating Figurative Language Writers sometimes express ideas using figurative language, a word or phrase used in an imaginative, rather than literal, sense. Similes, metaphors, and idioms are

Study Skills

examples of figurative language. For example, in a U.S. history textbook, you might read Theodore Roosevelt's advice on United States foreign policy: "Walk softly and carry a big stick." He meant that the United States should be cautious in foreign affairs but willing and able to use a powerful military. Be attuned to figurative language so that you can pick up on the subtleties of the materials you read. You will be better able to evaluate an author's message.

Exercise 1

Reorganize the following notes into a modified outline. Use abbreviations and symbols when possible.

Types of reptiles: between six and seven thousand species of reptiles are alive today; most of these are classified into one of four orders

Squamata includes lizards, such as iguanas and Gila monsters, and snakes, including pythons, rattlesnakes, and garter snakes

Chelonia includes reptiles with shells, such as turtles and tortoises; some live on land, others in fresh water, others in salt water; all members of this order lay their eggs on land

Crocodylia includes reptiles such as crocodiles and alligators, also caimans and gavials; crocodiles have longer, thinner snouts than alligators; unlike alligators, the fourth tooth on their lower jaw is visible when their mouths are closed

Rhynchocephalia includes tuatara; these reptiles look like lizards, but are more closely related to dinosaurs; they live off the coast of New Zealand

Exercise 2

Use the SQ3R method to study a lesson that your teacher assigns. Then write a paragraph analyzing whether or not the SQ3R method helped you.

Exercise 3

Identify at least two facts and two opinions in the following paragraph.

The slider is a major-league baseball pitcher's best friend. To the batter, the pitch looks like a fast ball. Even the pitcher's motion is the same as the motion for throwing the fast ball, so there's no hint about what's coming up. The ball will start out in a straight, easy-to-hit line toward the center of the plate. Then, suddenly and unexpectedly, the ball changes direction. It doesn't change much, mind you, just enough to turn solid hits into foul balls, pop-ups, and easy grounders. It's not surprising that every hitter hates the slider and every pitcher can't wait to serve one up.

27.2 Reading Graphs and Diagrams

Writers often use charts, diagrams, tables, and other graphics to present information. By using a graphic, writers can also make relationships between ideas easy to see. A clear graphic usually has the following components:

- title—a phrase that summarizes the main topic of the graphic
- labels—words or phrases that show the organization of the information in the graphic
- data—words or numbers that provide the actual information in the graphic

Tables

Tables present large amounts of information. They are often used to compare one or more characteristics of a list of similar items. For example, a box score for a baseball game lists each player's name and the number of hits, at bats, and runs batted in for each. At a glance, you can see who had the most hits, who had none, and so forth.

The table below shows the population of four major cities in the United States between 1850 and 1996. Notice how easily you can compare the changes in these cities.

Populations of Four Major Cities in the United States, 1850–1996

City	1850	1900	1950	1990	1996
New York	696,115	3,437,202	7,891,957	7,322,564	7,380,906
Los Angeles	1,610	102,479	1,970,358	3,485,557	3,553,638
Chicago	29,963	1,698,575	3,620,962	2,783,726	2,721,547
Houston	2,396	44,633	596,163	1,637,859	1,744,058

You can read most tables horizontally (across) or vertically (down). By looking across the row labeled "New York," you can see how the population of that one city changed over time. By looking down the column labeled "1950," you can compare the population of all four cities in one year.

Pie Charts

Tables can show characteristics of several items, but pie charts, sometimes called circle graphs, focus on the parts that make up one whole item. In a pie chart, each slice of the pie represents one part of the whole. A pie chart easily and quickly shows you how big the slices are in relation to each other.

Because they are mathematical parts of a whole, percentages are often shown in pie charts. In the pie chart shown here, the circle represents the entire world population in 1988. Each slice shows a specific region's population as a percentage of the world's total population.

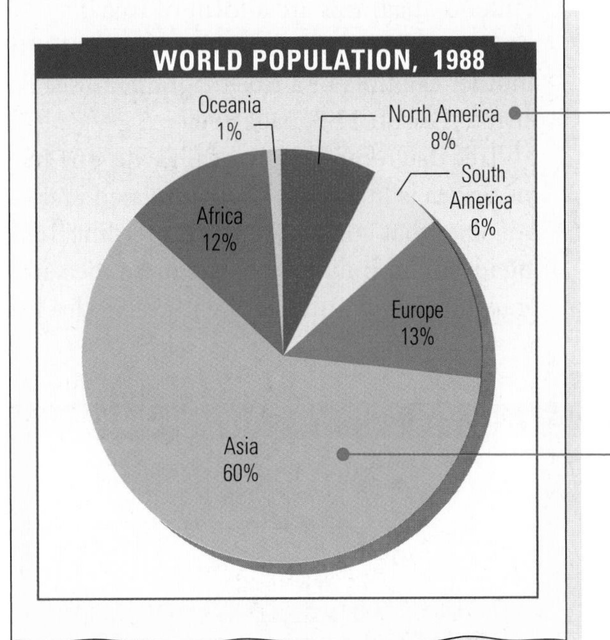

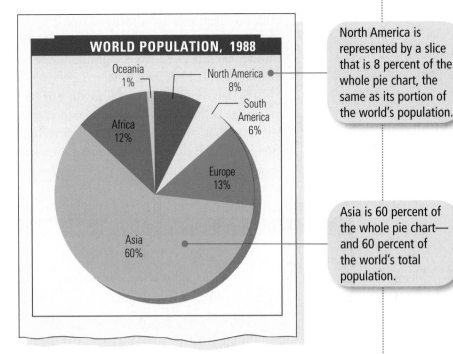

North America is represented by a slice that is 8 percent of the whole pie chart, the same as its portion of the world's population.

Asia is 60 percent of the whole pie chart—and 60 percent of the world's total population.

Line Graphs

Line graphs can show changes over a period of time. You will often see them in books, magazines, or other news media to show trends or variations in statistics.

To read a line graph, first look at the labels on the axes. The axes are the main vertical line and main horizontal line that make up the graph. The labels tell you what is being compared and the time interval over which the data is being reported.

On the following graph, the vertical axis shows the number of immigrants entering the United States. The horizontal axis shows the year.

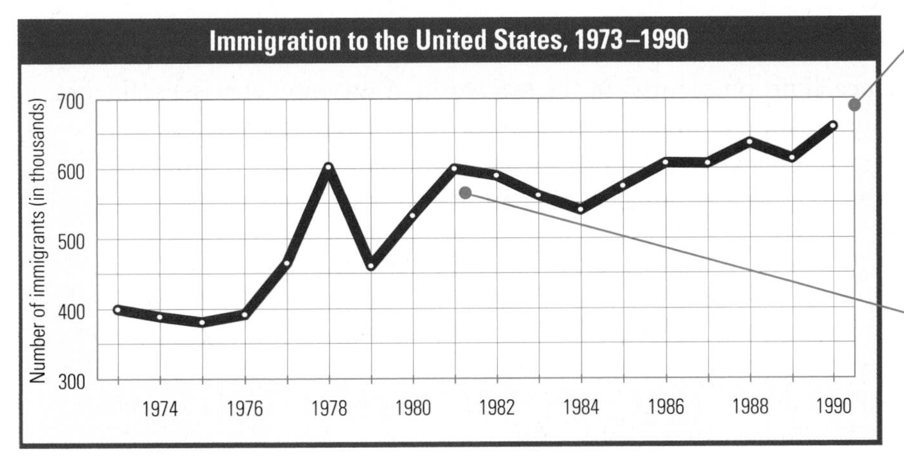

The line's highest point indicates that immigration was highest in 1990.

In 1981 the line intersects at 597. Because the data is given in thousands, this means that about five hundred ninety-seven thousand immigrants arrived in 1981.

Tree Diagrams

Unlike the previously discussed graphics, tree diagrams rarely show numerical data. Instead, they show relationships between things or ideas.

Sentence diagrams are a form of tree diagram. They show how words in a sentence relate to one another. An organizational chart for a company is another example of a tree diagram. To see an example of a tree diagram, turn to Lesson 22.3, page 790.

Tree diagrams usually begin with one main idea. In this example, the main idea is literature. Closely related ideas are linked to the main idea by branches that connect to the center line. Ideas related directly to the branching ideas and indirectly to the main idea are connected to the branches. The branches can continue on, with each idea leading to others.

Nonfiction is a type of literature, so it branches off the main idea.

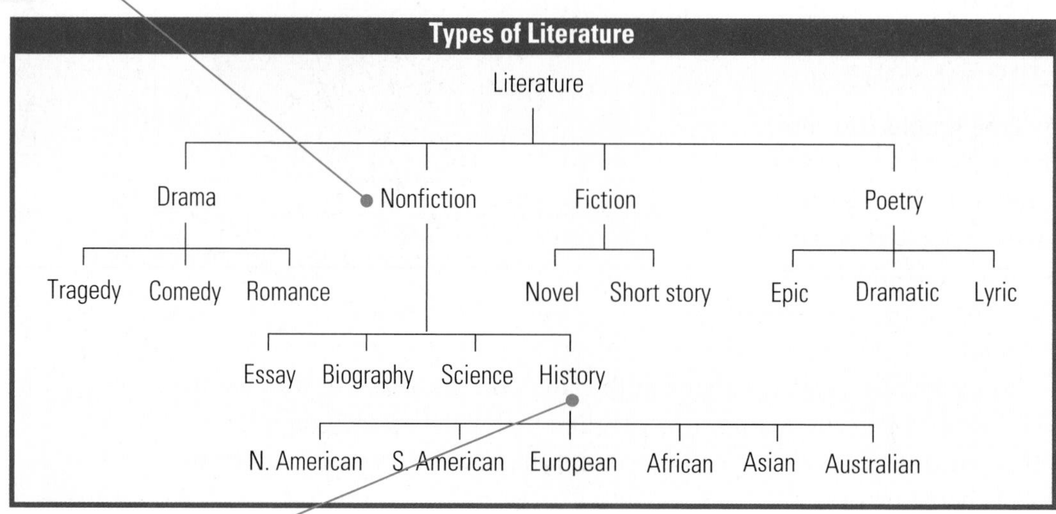

History is a type of nonfiction literature. You can divide it further into smaller categories.

Scales

A scale is a line segment divided into categories that represents a specific distance, time, or quantity in the real world. A thermometer is a scale that measures temperature. In mathematics, scales demonstrate relationships among numbers. For example, a scale might show the relationship between positive and negative integers on a number line.

Map Scales Scales are commonly used on maps. A map scale tells you that a certain number of inches or centimeters on the map represents a specific number of miles or kilometers. By finding the number of inches between Boston and Denver on a map of the United States, for example, you can determine the number of miles or kilometers between the two cities.

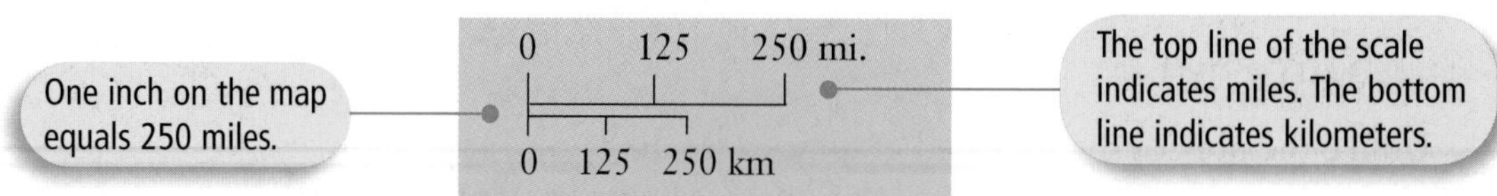

One inch on the map equals 250 miles.
0 125 250 mi.
0 125 250 km
The top line of the scale indicates miles. The bottom line indicates kilometers.

Study Skills

Time Line A time line shows events during a given period of time by representing time as a line. The space between the events on the time line is proportional to the amount of time that passed between the events. For example, a line segment three inches long could represent a period of three hundred years, with one inch equaling one hundred years.

Time lines are often used to show key events leading up to a major event. The time line below shows developments in space exploration.

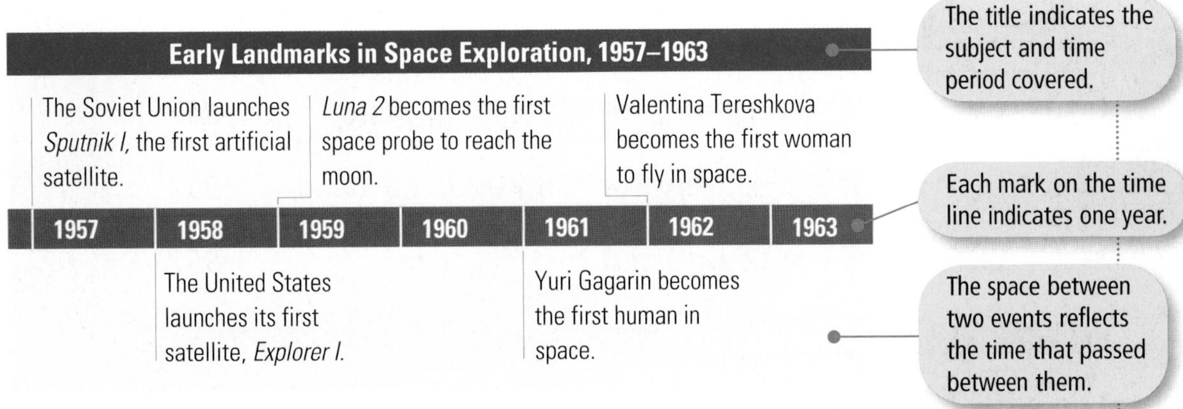

Exercise 4

Answer each of the following questions about graphs and diagrams studied in this lesson.

1. Which type of graph or diagram would best show changes in the cost of a college education over the last thirty years? Why?
2. Which type of graph or diagram would best show what portion of a twenty-four hour day you spend sleeping, going to school, eating meals, and doing other daily activities? Why?
3. Which type of graph or diagram would best compare the average high temperature, average low temperature, and average precipitation in ten U.S. cities? Why?
4. Which type of graph or diagram would you use to show the relationships among different types of foods? Why?
5. Which type of graph or diagram would you use to show the order in which various forms of music, such as classical, jazz, blues, and rock-and-roll, developed? Why?

Exercise 5

Find and copy two different graphics from books, newspapers or newsmagazines, or create a graphic of your own, using information from a current news source. Write a short statement identifying and explaining the information in the graphics you found or in the one you created. Share your visual representations with the class and explain the illustrated information.

UNIT 28

Taking Tests

28.1 Preparing for Classroom Tests

On exam day, you walk into class at the appointed hour. How do you feel? Overwhelmed and panicky? Or confident and relaxed? How you feel and how you perform have a lot to do with how well prepared you are for the test. The following time line suggests steps you can take in preparing for a test.

How to Prepare for a Test

10 9 8 7 6 5 4 3 2 1 TEST

Ten days or more before the test
Find out about the test. By writing down any information your teacher provides about the test—when it will be given, what it will cover, and so on—you can plan your study time effectively.

Eight days before the test
Gather your information. Review your textbook, quizzes, homework assignments, class notes, and handouts. By keeping all of your papers in one folder, you'll save time gathering study materials.

Six days before the test
Test yourself. Develop your own study questions about main ideas and important details, and practice answering them. Writing down your answers allows you to check what you have learned.

Four days before the test
Form study groups. Meet with members of your class to review material. Try to answer one another's study questions. Explaining information to a peer is one of the best ways to learn the material.

Day before the test
Sleep well the night before a test. Spreading your study time over several days will give you enough confidence to go to bed at your regular time the night before a test.

Day of the test
Eat a good breakfast. Students who eat a full meal the morning of a test usually score higher than those who don't. Eating well helps you remain alert during the test.

Taking Objective Tests

Many of the tests you take during high school will be objective tests. These tests ask for very specific information about material you've studied.

The most common type of objective test item is multiple choice. Each item includes a specific question or an incomplete sentence, and four or five responses. You are to pick the response that best answers the question or that best completes the sentence. When selecting the best response, consider the following tips.

Tips for Answering Multiple-Choice Items

1. Read the item carefully. You need to know what information you are looking for.
2. Read all the responses provided. Even if the first response seems almost correct, a later response may be better.
3. Eliminate any responses that are clearly incorrect. This helps you focus your attention on the responses that might be correct.
4. Be cautious about choosing responses that contain absolute words—*always, never, all,* or *none.* Since most statements have exceptions, absolute statements are often incorrect.

The following item might appear on an earth science test. As you read it, focus on what information is being asked for and how you would select the correct answer.

Note that the item calls for "first clues." Choice *a* is accurate, but since it does not list "first clues" it is incorrect.

Since this statement includes the words *all* and *perfectly,* you should select it only if you are sure it is correct.

This statement is incorrect because it is factually wrong. The answer is *c.*

```
What were the first clues that led scientists
to believe that the continents of the earth
were once connected as a single landmass?
a. Alfred Wegener, a German meteorologist,
   proposed the theory of continental drift.
b. Scientists found that all continents could
   be fitted together perfectly like a puzzle.
c. Similarities in ancient climates, fossils,
   and rock structures seemed to link separate
   landmasses.
d. Scientists discovered ancient historical
   records describing a giant landmass called
   Pangaea.
e. all of the above
```

Taking Tests

The chart below describes other types of objective test items and provides some suggestions for answering them.

Tips for Answering Objective Test Items		
Type of Item	**Example**	**Tips**
True-False	_____ Soil erosion on the earth's surface is a natural process unaffected by human activities.	If any part of the item is false, the correct answer is "false." Since the last phrase of this item is wrong, the answer is "false."
Short Answer	Why is the planet Venus known as Earth's twin?_______________	Use complete sentences to help you write a clear response. "Venus is almost exactly the same size as Earth."
Fill-in	The most important prophet of the _____ faith was Muhammad.	After completing the sentence, read it again to check that your answer is grammatically correct. In the example, "Islamic," not "Islam," would be the correct answer.
Matching	_____ an Indian leader who emphasized nonviolence _____ a German leader who led the Nazi party _____ a Chinese leader who led a communist revolution _____ an American leader who started the New Deal a. Mao Zedong b. Mohandas Gandhi c. Franklin Roosevelt d. Adolf Hitler	Note in the directions whether some responses can be used more than once or are not used at all. Quickly read each list to become familiar with the choices. Do easy items first to limit the number of choices for the difficult ones.

Using Time Wisely

Because test time is usually limited, you will need to use your time efficiently. First, read the directions carefully. If any are unclear, ask questions. Respond to each item on the test, answering the easier ones first. Skip difficult items rather than dwelling on them. When you have answered the easier items, go back and answer hard items that you skipped earlier. Save some time to review your test before handing it in.

Exercise 1

Read the paragraph below, and use your test-taking strategies to help you answer the questions that follow.

The Arabian Peninsula is a wedge of land of about one million square miles between the Red Sea and the Persian Gulf. The peninsula is made up of two distinct geological regions. In the west is the Arabian Shield, made up of a huge mass of igneous and metamorphic rock. To the north, east, and south lies the sedimentary region, once submerged in seas in geologic times, subsequent to the formation of the shield. As part of the sedimentary region, the southern coasts and the coasts of the Red Sea and the Persian Gulf experience extreme humidity, particularly in summer. Much of the interior of the peninsula, however, is hot and dry. Drifting sand dunes cover most of the southeastern part of the peninsula. This area, about the size of Texas, is so barren that it is called the Empty Quarter.

1. Why is part of the Arabian Peninsula called the Empty Quarter?
   a. It is completely uninhabited.
   b. The landscape is barren.
   c. Drifting sand dunes make travel dangerous.
   d. none of the above
2. The sedimentary region of the Arabian Peninsula
   a. includes the Arabian Shield.
   b. is always hot and dry.
   c. is made of a huge mass of igneous and metamorphic rock.
   d. experiences extreme humidity in the summer.
3. True or false: The Arabian Peninsula is about the size of Texas.
4. Contrast the two regions that make up the Arabian Peninsula.

   ____

   ____
5. The Arabian Peninsula is located between the ______ ______ and the ______ ______.

Taking Tests

28.2 Preparing for Standardized Tests

Along with the exams that you take in each class, you will often take standardized tests—tests designed to measure your general knowledge, abilities, and interests. They are called standardized because the results are compared with those of other students around the country who have taken the test. The performance of a large group of students provides a standard by which to measure individuals who take the test.

The Purpose of Standardized Tests

You might take a standardized test for one of several reasons. The chart below lists and describes the basic types of standardized tests.

Three Types of Standardized Tests

Type	Purpose	Examples
Ability	Ability tests use questions about different subject areas to evaluate your general learning skills and to predict how well you will do in college.	Stanford-Binet tests Preliminary Scholastic Aptitude Test (PSAT)
Achievement	Achievement tests measure your knowledge in specific content areas, such as American history or algebra.	Tests of Achievement and Proficiency
Aptitude	Aptitude tests discover your individual talents and interests. They can help you choose an educational program and a career suited to your needs.	Differential Aptitude Test

Types of Items

You can prepare for standardized tests by reviewing general areas of knowledge, such as English usage and grammar, math, science, and social studies—areas that the tests usually cover. In addition, you can prepare for tests by learning about the types of questions presented. The following pages show examples of commonly used formats for test items and hints for answering each kind.

Reading Comprehension The objective of reading comprehension items is to measure your ability to understand what you read. You will be presented with a passage and asked a series of questions—usually multiple-choice—about it. All of the information you need to respond will be in the passage. Skimming the questions before you read the passage will help you know what to look for. However, you should read the passage completely before answering any questions. Read the passage below, and answer the questions that follow.

According to Muslim tradition, the ʿAbbasid caliph al-Ma'-mun (mah MOON) founded the House of Wisdom at Baghdad in A.D. 830. This research center specialized in the translation into Arabic of Greek, Persian, and Indian scientific texts. It was believed that al-Ma'-mun staffed the center with salaried Christian, Jewish, and Muslim scholars who used Arabic to share ideas from different intellectual traditions. These scholars were thought to have performed scientific experiments and mathematical calculations, carefully studying and building upon the ideas of the ancients. The House of Wisdom, therefore, served as a catalyst for many mathematical and scientific achievements in the Islamic world.

To answer this question, you need to pick out the main idea of the passage. Since *d* summarizes the entire passage, it is the correct answer.

1. Which of the following would be the best title for this passage?
   a. Islamic Translation
   b. Islamic Scholars
   c. Abbasid caliph Ma'mun
   d. The House of Wisdom
   e. none of the above

Answer *a* seems correct, but never answer a question until you have read all the choices. Since *b, c,* and *d* seem correct also, the correct answer is *e*.

2. The House of Wisdom scholars
   a. were paid for their efforts
   b. translated scientific texts into Arabic
   c. had different backgrounds
   d. based their work on the ideas of previous scholars
   e. all of the above

```
3. The point of view shows that the author
   a. doubts the existence of the House of
      Wisdom
   b. is objective about the subject
   c. has contempt for the ancient sciences
   d. is biased in favor of Islamic
      achievements
   e. believes that science is the most
      important area of study
```

Since the author avoids praising or condemning the information, *b* is the correct answer.

Synonyms Tests that ask you to identify synonyms require you to select from a list of words one that is closest in meaning to another given word. Look for the best choice; no two words have exactly the same meanings. Study the example below.

```
_____ perimeter
a. circle
b. middle
c. direction
d. circumference
```

All of the choices describe space in some way. Only *d* describes the distance around, so it is the correct response.

Sentence Completion This type of test item is designed to assess your ability to complete sentences with logical and grammatically correct words. You generally need to choose one or more missing words from a list to complete a sentence. Consider the following example.

```
The paralysis of his leg, rather than _____ his
expectations, actually _____ his drive to
succeed.
a. lowering/heightened
b. redefining/acknowledging
c. limiting/lessened
d. clouding/confused
```

Identify the relationship between the first and the last parts of the sentence.

The words "rather than" and "actually" suggest that the two parts express opposite ideas. The words in *a* are the only pair that are opposites.

Items Testing English Skills

Standardized tests often include sections that evaluate your knowledge of written English. Items might ask you to identify usage problems, grammatical errors, and incorrect sentence constructions.

English Usage Tests of English usage often ask you to identify a variety of mistakes in the following areas:

- grammar
- spelling
- capitalization
- subject-verb agreement
- pronoun references
- improper word choice

Often English usage items include a sentence in which several words or phrases are underlined. Each underlined part is lettered. You are to identify the part of the sentence that includes an error and mark the corresponding letter on your answer sheet. Many items include a choice *e*, which states that the sentence contains no error. Following is a typical example.

The word "affect" is incorrect; the correct word would be "effect."

```
The fall of the Berlin Wall has had a positive
    a                         b
affect on the human struggles around the world
  c                                  d
for freedom and peace. no error
                          e
```

Sentence Correction In these items, you will be given a sentence with one section underlined and choices for replacing the section. Choice *a* usually is identical to the section in the sentence; choose it if the sentence is without error. The other choices suggest other ways to word the section. Tests often include common errors such as wordiness, lack of parallel construction, and awkward wording. Try the following example.

Identify the problem in the underlined section. In this example the two parts in the section are not parallel.

Find the choice that corrects the problem you identified. Choice *d* is correct because its structure is parallel.

```
Ms. Sanchez's plan for redesigning the city's
public transportation system is finan-
cially feasible and has a sound structure.
a. is financially feasible and has a sound
   structure
b. has good financial feasibility and has a
   good structure
c. is financially feasible and sound in
   structure
d. is financially feasible and structurally
   sound
```

Taking Tests

Analogies While vocabulary items test your knowledge of word meanings, analogies test your ability to see the relationships between word meanings. An analogy item may contain a pair of words separated by a colon, and four or five other pairs of words. You are to choose the pair with the same relationship as the first pair. Here is an example.

```
praise : insult ::
a. admire : like
b. waste : devour
c. chide : encourage
d. provide: redistribute
e. entertain: study
```

Identify the relationship: *praise* is the opposite of *insult.*

Identify the pair showing the same relationship: *chide* is the opposite of *encourage.* Therefore, c is the correct answer.

To improve your scores on analogies tests, develop your vocabulary. See Unit 25, pages 818–826, for tips on building your vocabulary. In addition, practice identifying the relationship between two items. Following are some of the common relationships used on analogies tests.

Analogy Relationships

Type	Examples
Cause and effect—one word causes or is the result of the other word	tornadoes : damage boredom : yawn
Opposites—one word is the opposite of the other word	happy : sad poor : rich
Users—one word uses or is used by the other word	doctor : stethoscope mechanic : wrench
Synonyms—the two words share a general meaning	elated : happy ready : prepared
Time sequence—one word comes before or after the other word	lunch : dinner sunset : sunrise
Characteristic—one word is a characteristic of the other word	leopard : carnivorous steel : hard
Category—one word is a specific item in the general category of the other word	broccoli : vegetable jazz : music

Standardized tests are sometimes given outside of regular class time. You may need to register to take some tests, such as college entrance exams. If so, register early to ensure that you can take the test on the day you need. In addition, follow the tips in the chart below.

Tips for Taking Standardized Tests
1. Show up ready for the test. Try to arrive early so you can relax before beginning.
2. Sleep and eat well before the test. Get enough sleep the night before the test so that you are well rested. Eat a good breakfast so you don't get hungry during the test.
3. Pace yourself during the test. You usually have a limited amount of time to take the test, so don't get stalled on hard items. Skip them and move on.
4. Repeatedly compare the item numbers in your test booklet and answer sheet. Be careful to put your answers on the proper lines.
5. If time permits, check your answers. If you are not penalized for guessing, fill in answers for any items you might have skipped.

Exercise 2

Use the test-taking strategies described in this lesson to help you complete the following items. Write your answers on a separate piece of paper.

1. Which of the following is the best synonym for *analogous*?
   a. different **b.** representative **c.** incongruous **d.** alike **e.** agreeable
2. Choose the word that best completes the sentence below.
   _______ his many hours of hard work at the computer, he realized that his progress was insignificant.
   a. Despite **b.** Because of **c.** Through **d.** Besides **e.** By
3. Examine the sentence below and decide if it contains an error in standard English usage. Mark the correct letter.

   All the students <u>who attended</u> (a) the assembly <u>were instructed</u> (b) to leave <u>his or her</u> (c) books <u>in the cafeteria.</u> (d) <u>no error</u> (e)
4. Decide whether the underlined portion of the sentence below needs correcting. Pick the best correction from the choices that follow.

   As public outrage over contaminated foods becomes stronger, <u>people who will demand</u> more organically grown vegetables and fruits.

   a. people who will demand **b.** people that will demand **c.** people will demand **d.** people demanding **e.** people who have demanded
5. Choose the pair of words whose relationship is most similar to the following pair.

   paintings : frame ::

   a. photographs : margin **b.** brooms : handle **c.** spectacles : rim **d.** faces : hair **e.** globe : universe

Taking Tests

28.3 Standardized Test Practice

INTRODUCTION

The following pages of exercises have been designed to familiarize you with the standardized writing tests that you will take during the school year. These exercises are very similar to the actual tests in how they look and what they ask you to do. Completing these exercises will not only provide you with practice, but also will make you aware of the areas you might need to work on.

These writing exercises—just like the actual standardized writing tests—are divided into three sections.

Sentence Structure In this section, pages 858 to 865, you will be given short passages in which some of the sentences are underlined. Each underlined sentence is numbered. After you finish reading each passage, you will be asked questions about the underlined sections. The underlined sections will be either incomplete sentences, run-on sentences, correctly written sentences that should be combined, or correctly written sentences that do not need to be rewritten. You will need to select, from the four choices that you are given, which best rewrites the sentences if they contain mistakes.

Usage In this section, pages 866 to 873, you will also be asked to read short passages. However, in these exercises, a word or words in each passage will be omitted and a numbered blank space will be in their place. After reading the passage, you will need to determine which of the four provided words or groups of words best fits in each numbered space.

Mechanics Finally, in the third section, pages 874 to 881, you will be asked to read short passages that have parts that are underlined. You will need to determine if, in the underlined sections, there is a spelling error, capitalization error, punctuation error, or no error at all.

Writing well is a skill that you will use for the rest of your life. You will be able to write more accurate letters to your friends and family, better papers in school, and more interesting stories. You will be able to express yourself and your ideas more clearly and in a way that is interesting and engaging. These exercises should help to improve your writing and to make you comfortable with the format and types of questions you will see on standardized writing tests.

Standardized Test Practice

Read each passage. Some sections are underlined. The underlined sections may be one of the following:

- Incomplete sentences
- Run-on sentences
- Correctly written sentences that should be combined
- Correctly written sentences that do not need to be rewritten

Choose the best way to write each underlined section and mark the letter on your paper. If the underlined section needs no change, mark the choice "Correct as is."

Bears are known as animals that hibernate. Ironically, though. Bears do not actually hibernate. (1) In fact, they fall into a deep sleep during the winter. There are several factors that make a bear's sleep different from true hibernation. Most important may be the bear's body temperature, it remains relatively constant compared to that of true hibernators. (2) A bear's body temperature will drop from 100 degrees to 93 degrees during its "hibernation." A true hibernator will have a body temperature that is the same temperature as the surrounding environment. Small animals can hibernate because their bodies warm and cool quickly. (3) Bears are large animals, so it requires a lot of energy for them to change body temperature.

1 A It is ironic, though, bears do not actually hibernate.
B Ironically, though that bears do not actually hibernate.
C Ironically, though, bears do not actually hibernate.
D Correct as is

2 F Most important may be the bear's body temperature, which remains relatively constant compared to that of true hibernators.
G Most important may be the bear's body temperature. Remaining relatively constant compared to that of true hibernators.
H Most important, the bear's body temperature, which remains relatively constant compared to that of true hibernators.
J Correct as is

3 A Small animals doing this hibernation because their bodies warm and cool quickly.
B Small animals can hibernate. Because their bodies warm and cool quickly.
C Small animals can hibernate because their bodies warm. And cool quickly.
D Correct as is

<u>Tucson's Six-Finger Fred was such a good thief that many said he could never be caught.</u> (1) In 1896, he robbed sixteen banks and seven jewelry stores. <u>However, an anonymous letter put the police on his trail. In February 1897, he was almost caught in his hideout.</u> (2) But, Fred escaped the police yet again. <u>In the fall of 1897, the great Brazil Topaz came through Tucson, authorities were sure Six-Finger Fred would try to steal it.</u> (3) They put the jewel under close guard. The jewel was safe all night.

They put the Topaz in a black felt bag and loaded it onto a wagon bound for California. However, when they opened the bag in San Francisco, the Topaz was gone! In its place was a lump of coal and a note that read, "Better luck next time, S-F F."

1 **A** Tucson's Six-Finger Fred being such a good thief. Many said he could never be caught.
B Tucson's Six-Finger Fred was such a good thief, many said he could never be caught.
C Tucson's Six-Finger Fred being such a good thief, that many said he could never be caught.
D Correct as is

2 **F** However, an anonymous letter put the police on his trail to catch him in February 1897, when he was in his hideout.
G However, an anonymous letter put the police on his trail, and in February 1897, he was almost caught in his hideout.
H An anonymous letter put the police on his trail. In February 1897, he was almost caught in his hideout however.
J By February 1897, police almost caught him in his hideout, and they also had an anonymous letter.

3 **A** In the fall of 1897, the great Brazil Topaz came through Tucson, and authorities being sure Six-Finger Fred would try to steal it.
B In the fall of 1897, the great Brazil Topaz coming through Tucson. And authorities were sure Six-Finger Fred would try to steal it.
C In the fall of 1897, the great Brazil Topaz came through Tucson, and authorities were sure Six-Finger Fred would try to steal it.
D Correct as is

Standardized Test Practice

Read each passage. Some sections are underlined. The underlined sections may be one of the following:

- Incomplete sentences
- Run-on sentences
- Correctly written sentences that should be combined
- Correctly written sentences that do not need to be rewritten

Choose the best way to write each underlined section and mark the letter for your answer. If the underlined section needs no change, mark the choice "Correct as is."

Nathan stood with his family, watching the plane taxi to the gate. His brother Daniel was finally coming home. Daniel had been studying in Italy for the last eight months, Nathan couldn't wait to hear all about it. (1) No one in Nathan's family had ever been to Europe. Just last year, while a freshman at college, Daniel had accepted a scholarship to study abroad. (2) Daniel, an art major, would study with the masters. Architecture was his main interest. He had written a paper on the Sistine Chapel and received admission to the special program. (3)

1 A Daniel had been studying in Italy for the last eight months. Nathan waiting to hear all about it.
B Daniel studying in Italy for the past eight months. And Nathan couldn't wait to hear all about it.
C Daniel had been studying in Italy for the past eight months, and Nathan couldn't wait to hear all about it.
D Correct as is

2 F Just last year, while a freshman at college, Daniel had accepted something, it was a scholarship to study abroad.
G Just last year, while a freshman at college. Daniel had accepted a scholarship to study abroad.
H Just last year, while a freshman at college, Daniel had accepted. A scholarship to study abroad.
J Correct as is

3 A Architecture was his main interest, and he had written a paper on the Sistine Chapel, and he had received admission to the special program.
B Architecture was his main interest, and after writing a paper on the Sistine Chapel, he received admission to the special program.
C Architecture, which was his main interest, had written a paper on the Sistine Chapel and received admission to the special program.
D Architecture was his main interest while he had written a paper on the Sistine Chapel and received admission to the special program.

Opening night had finally arrived. Joseph had an important job. Joseph operated the spotlight. <u>Standing above the theater in a booth, Joseph watched the audience file into its seats. He watched the musicians enter the orchestra pit.</u> (1) It was going to be a great show. <u>Joseph could hear the crowd murmuring with excitement, he could sense that it was almost time to begin.</u> (2) The house lights were turned off. That was Joseph's cue. <u>When the applause died down. He flipped the switch on the spotlight.</u> (3) A woman stepped onto the stage and into the light. <u>Joseph knew the performance would be perfect even before the actress spoke her first line.</u> (4)

1 **A** Standing above the theater in a booth, Joseph watched the audience file into its seats while he watched the musicians enter the orchestra pit.
B Joseph watched the audience file into its seats and the musicians enter the orchestra pit standing above the theater in a booth.
C Standing above the theater in a booth, Joseph watched the audience file into its seats and the musicians enter the orchestra pit.
D Standing above the theater in a booth, Joseph watched the audience file into its seats because the musicians enter the orchestra pit.

2 **F** Joseph could hear the crowd murmuring with excitement, and he could sense. That it was almost time to begin.
G Joseph could hear the crowd murmuring with excitement, and he could sense that it was almost time to begin.
H Joseph could hear the crowd murmuring with excitement. And he could sense that it was almost time to begin.
J Correct as is

3 **A** When the applause died down, he flipped the switch on the spotlight.
B The applause died down since he flipped the switch on the spotlight.
C The applause. It died down when he flipped the switch on the spotlight.
D Correct as is

4 **F** Joseph knowing the performance would be perfect even before the actress spoke her first line.
G A perfect performance. Joseph knew it even before the actress spoke her first line.
H Joseph knew the performance would be perfect. Even before the actress spoke her first line.
J Correct as is

Standardized Test Practice

Read each passage. Some sections are underlined. The underlined sections may be one of the following:

- Incomplete sentences
- Run-on sentences
- Correctly written sentences that should be combined
- Correctly written sentences that do not need to be rewritten

Choose the best way to write each underlined section and mark the letter for your answer. If the underlined section needs no change, mark the choice "Correct as is."

Adaptive radiation is a term that many scientists use to describe one way in which species arise. (1) Adaptive radiation can occur when the members of a species in one area adapt to local surroundings and become different from those in other areas. The result is that one species. Becomes two or more. (2) For example, at least thirteen different species of finch have developed on Ecuador's Galapagos Islands, each with a beak adapted to local foods. The ground finch has a strong beak, while the cactus finch has a long, thin beak. Each bird adapted to the food nearby. They eventually developed into distinct species. (3)

1 A Adaptive radiation is a term that many scientists use. To describe one way in which species arise.
B Adaptive radiation is a term that many scientists use it describes one way in which species arise.
C Adaptive radiation is a term that many scientists use. Describing one way in which species arise.
D Correct as is

2 F The result is that one species becomes two or more.
G The result is that one species, becoming two or more.
H The result that is one species, it becomes two or more.
J Correct as is

3 A Each bird adapted to the food nearby distinct species eventually developing into.
B Each bird adapted eventually developing into, because of the food nearby.
C Each bird adapted to the food nearby, eventually distinct species being developed.
D Correct as is

Wilbur and Orville Wright built one of the first airports. They did this in 1900. (1) The Wright Brothers have been credited with inventing the airplane. This first "airport" was actually just a shelter at Kitty Hawk, North Carolina, where the Wright Brothers conducted their flying experiments. Kitty Hawk was the perfect place for these experiments, it was a barren stretch of sand. (2)

Later, the Wright Brothers moved their "airport" to Kill Devil Hills near a high dune that proved a good launching place. On December 17, 1903, Wilbur Wright succeeded in making the first manned, sustained, powered flight. (3)

1 **A** Wilbur and Orville Wright built one of the first airports because it was 1900.
B In 1900, Wilbur and Orville Wright built one of the first airports, and that's when they first built it.
C Wilbur and Orville Wright built in 1900 one of the first airports.
D In 1900, Wilbur and Orville Wright built one of the first airports.

2 **F** Kitty Hawk was the perfect place for these experiments because it was a barren stretch of sand.
G Kitty Hawk was the perfect place for these experiments, it being a barren stretch of sand.
H Kitty Hawk was the perfect place for these experiments. It was a barren stretch of sand.
J Correct as is

3 **A** On December 17, 1903, Wilbur Wright in making the first manned, sustained, powered flight.
B On December 17, 1903, Wilbur Wright succeeded in making the first manned, sustained flight, and he also succeeded in making the first powered flight.
C On December 17, 1903, Wilbur Wright succeeded in making the first. He made manned, sustained, powered flight.
D Correct as is

STOP

Standardized Test Practice

Read each passage. Some sections are underlined. The underlined sections may be one of the following:

- Incomplete sentences
- Run-on sentences
- Correctly written sentences that should be combined
- Correctly written sentences that do not need to be rewritten

Choose the best way to write each underlined section and mark the letter for your answer. If the underlined section needs no change, mark the choice "Correct as is."

Radio sportscasters make listeners at home feel that they are actually at the event. This job was much more difficult years ago. Radio announcers were often not even at the game. (1) In the early days of radio, live broadcast signals could not travel as far as they do today. Some games were played in remote parts of the country. Announcers had to recreate the game for listeners who could not receive the signal. (2) They did this in an interesting way. Sportscasters received updates by telegraph. They used these updates to fuel their broadcasts. (3)

1 **A** This job was much more difficult when radio announcers were often not even at the game years ago.
B Radio announcers were often not even at the game years ago since this job was much more difficult.
C Years ago, this job was much more difficult because radio announcers were often not even at the game.
D Years ago, radio announcers were often not even at the game because this job was much more difficult.

2 **F** Some games were played in remote parts of the country, so announcers had to recreate the game for listeners. Who could not receive the signal.
G Some games were played in remote parts of the country, then announcers had to recreate the game for listeners who could not receive the signal.
H Because some games were played in remote parts of the country, announcers had to recreate the game for listeners who could not receive the signal.
J Correct as is

3 **A** Sportscasters received updates by telegraph, and they used these updates to fuel their broadcasts.
B Sportscasters received updates by telegraph when they used these updates to fuel their broadcast.
C Fueling their broadcasts were the updates that the sportscasters received by telegraphs.
D Sportscasters received updates by telegraph and these updates were used to fuel broadcasts.

<u>Cathy sells antique glassware, she keeps it in her basement.</u> (1) During a hurricane last year, many towns in Cathy's area were flooded. Some even declared a state of emergency. <u>People were advised to stay inside their houses. Roads were blocked off.</u> (2) Cathy kept many boxes of antique vases and glasses in her basement.

<u>It was after the hurricane passed. Cathy had to wash the glass, which had gotten dirty in the flooded basement.</u> (3) Cathy set up several barrels of water in her yard, some with soapy water and some with clean rinsing water. She must have washed several thousand glasses!

1 **A** Cathy sells antique glassware that she keeps in her basement.
B Cathy selling antique glassware. She keeps it in her basement.
C Cathy sells antique glassware. that she keeps in her basement.
D Correct as is

2 **F** People were advised to stay inside their houses, because roads were blocked off.
G People were advised to stay inside their houses that the roads were blocked off.
H People were advised to stay inside their houses, and roads were blocked off.
J Roads being blocked off and people being advised to stay inside their houses.

3 **A** It was after the hurricane passed, and Cathy had to wash the glass, and they had gotten dirty in the flooded basement.
B After the hurricane passed, Cathy had to wash the glasses, which had gotten dirty in the flooded basement.
C It was after the hurricane passed because Cathy had to wash the glass, which had gotten dirty in the flooded basement.
D After the hurricane passed, Cathy had gotten dirty in the flooded basement washing the glass.

STOP

Standardized Test Practice

Read each passage and choose the word or group of words that belongs in each space. Mark the letter for your answer.

If you have ever played with two bar magnets, you probably discovered that the ends with opposite charges attract one another. A compass __(1)__ under this basic scientific principle. The needle of a compass is actually a tiny, lightweight magnet. This magnet __(2)__ to the Earth's magnetic field. Like a bar magnet, the Earth has two oppositely charged poles. The south end of the compass needle is therefore attracted to the Earth's North Pole. This is why a compass needle always points due north. A compass is a very useful device, often providing lost travelers with the __(3)__ route home. You may find that you can read a map __(4)__ with a compass in hand.

1 **A** operate
B operates
C will operate
D has operated

2 **F** will be attracted
G was attracted
H is attracted
J had been attracted

3 **A** quicker
B quickest
C most quick
D most quickest

4 **F** clear
G most clear
H more clearly
J clearliest

Louis Pasteur developed the process now known as pasteurization in the mid-1800s. __(1)__ discovered that many diseases and infections are caused by microorganisms. Some of these microorganisms __(2)__ in fluids, including the milk we drink. When milk is pasteurized, it is heated for a specific period of time. This process __(3)__ most bacteria and other harmful microorganisms. Pasteurization also __(4)__ to keep food fresh and prevent spoilage. Before Louis Pasteur introduced pasteurization to the world, many people contracted diseases from milk and other food products.

1 **A** You
B We
C They
D He

2 **F** are found
G found
H had been found
J will be found

3 **A** killed
B is killing
C kills
D has killed

4 **F** help
G helps
H helped
J had helped

STOP

Standardized Test Practice

Read each passage and choose the word or group of words that belongs in each space. Mark the letter for your answer.

Have you ever stood out in a field on a summer evening and watched the fireflies twinkle in the moonlight? Fireflies do not perform this spectacle for the benefit of human __(1)__. The fireflies' glow is actually part of a complex mating ritual. With over fifty species of fireflies, it is difficult for fireflies to find the appropriate mate. Male fireflies __(2)__ through the air, flashing specific patterns. On the ground, female fireflies of the same species respond with __(3)__ own corresponding pattern. This is how the male firefly knows it is safe to land. Depending on how many species are in the air, you may see a multitude of different patterns. Some are __(4)__ than others.

1 **A** viewer
B views
C viewers
D viewed

2 **F** float
G floated
H had floated
J will float

3 **A** our
B their
C your
D its

4 **F** complex
G more complex
H most complex
J complexer

Throughout history, ___(1)___ farmers have had to find ways to protect their crops from birds and other pests. The American farmers of the eighteenth century used scarecrows. These straw men looked realistic enough to frighten animals away. The ancient Egyptians also devised a clever way to defend ___(2)___ fields. Using four poles, they suspended large nets over nearby trees. When a flock came to roost, the net ___(3)___, capturing the birds.

Early Japanese farmers ___(4)___ on a different trick. They would hang dirty rags and fish skeletons from sticks and would place these sticks out in the field and set them on fire. The smell was enough to drive the birds and animals away.

1 **A** imagine
B imaginative
C imagined
D imagination

2 **F** your
G its
H their
J our

3 **A** has been dropped
B is dropped
C was dropped
D have been dropped

4 **F** relied
G will rely
H are relying
J rely

STOP

Standardized Test Practice

Read each passage and choose the word or group of words that belongs in each space. Mark the letter for your answer.

While perusing an old family scrapbook, Hector noticed several handwritten letters. He wondered how people __(1)__ without computers. He could not imagine life without __(2)__. Fascinated, Hector read all of the letters, paying attention to the penmanship. Everybody in his family seemed to have beautiful handwriting.

Hector asked his grandfather about it. "Why is your handwriting __(3)__ than my scribbles?"

Hector's grandfather explained that he __(4)__ penmanship at school. "You don't need to write as much as I did," said Grandfather, "because you do your homework on the computer and you only send e-mail."

1 **A** will manage
B managed
C managing
D had been managed

2 **F** it
G us
H them
J you

3 **A** beautifulest
B most beautiful
C more beautiful
D beauty

4 **F** has been taught
G is taught
H was taught
J were taught

Have you ever admired the stamp on a letter you received? You might consider becoming a philatelist. A philatelist is someone who collects and ___(1)___ postage stamps. Each country issues ___(2)___ own stamps. The United States releases over a hundred different stamps a year.

Of the thousands of images, some of the ___(3)___ are of historical figures, animals, sports stars, or popular cultural heroes. A stamp collection can be organized according to country, theme, or type. Some people ___(4)___ to the beauty of stamps, while others are interested in their history and monetary value. The next time that you see a stamp on a letter, consider cutting it out and starting your own collection.

1 **A** will study
B is studying
C studies
D has studied

2 **F** his
G our
H your
J its

3 **A** most popular
B more popularly
C popularly
D popular

4 **F** will be attracted
G was attracted
H has been attracted
J are attracted

STOP

Standardized Test Practice

Read each passage and choose the word or group of words that belongs in each space. Mark the letter for your answer.

Since humanity's __(1)__ days, bridges have been built to make getting from one place to another possible. The world's longest bridge over ice-covered water, called the Confederation Bridge, __(2)__ from Prince Edward Island to New Brunswick in the Canadian northeast. The 12.9 kilometer bridge __(3)__ in May of 1997 and is open 24 hours a day, seven days a week.

Safety considerations played a major role in the design of the bridge. The owners of the bridge made sure that it was curved in order to keep drivers alert. __(4)__ also included 7,300 road drains to keep precipitation from collecting on the bridge.

1 **A** most earliest
B more earliest
C earliest
D earlier

2 **F** stretched
G had stretched
H stretches
J will stretch

3 **A** completes
B completed
C had completed
D was completed

4 **F** They
G Them
H Us
J She

One of the biggest problems facing cartographers, or people who make maps, is the fact that the Earth is round. Since a flat map, called a projection, can't __(1)__ show the curved surface of the Earth, it will always distort the way the Earth looks to some extent. Some projections, including the very __(2)__ Mercator projection, show things in more or less their real shape, but distort their relative sizes. Others, such as the Lambert projection, show the continents in more or less __(3)__ relative sizes, but are forced to distort their shapes.

You can tell how much distortion a map has by looking at its lines of latitude and longitude. The latitude lines should be parallel and equal distances apart. Longitude lines should be farther apart at the equator, and should __(4)__ at the poles.

1. **A** more accurate
   B accurate
   C accurately
   D most accurater

2. **F** commonly
   G common
   H more commoner
   J most commonly

3. **A** their
   B your
   C its
   D our

4. **F** converge
   G had converged
   H was converging
   J converged

Standardized Test Practice

Read each passage and decide which type of error, if any, appears in each underlined section. Mark the letter for your answer.

Every summer, <u>kids attend Edward's Summer camp to learn</u> (1) how to use the Internet. Many of them have never used the computer for more than playing video games. At the camp they <u>learn to use the many infomative sites on the Internet.</u> (2) They also learn about the origins of the Internet.

<u>The Internet was originally created in 1983 by the United States defense department</u> (3) and was further developed by the National Science Foundation. At first, only researchers and scientists used this network. Now the Internet connects millions of computers. It is used <u>for banking, publishing, business, and even shoping.</u> (4) Students use it to research papers, and many people write to each other <u>through e-mail because it is faster than regular mail.</u> (5)

By the end of the summer, many of the kids will have built their own web sites by using a programming code called HTML. <u>Some will even deside that the Internet can be more fun than video games!</u> (6)

1 **A** Spelling error
B Capitalization error
C Punctuation error
D No error

2 **F** Spelling error
G Capitalization error
H Punctuation error
J No error

3 **A** Spelling error
B Capitalization error
C Punctuation error
D No error

4 **F** Spelling error
G Capitalization error
H Punctuation error
J No error

5 **A** Spelling error
B Capitalization error
C Punctuation error
D No error

6 **F** Spelling error
G Capitalization error
H Punctuation error
J No error

Bicycles are a great means of transportation and also a source of pleasure for many people. Actually, (1) it was not always so easy to ride a bicycle. The first two-wheeled rider-propelled machine appeared in 1818. (2) It was made of wood and the seated rider moved simply by pushing his feet along the ground.

The most practical early version of the bicycle was invented by the michaux family of Paris in the 1860s. (3) Its iron and wood construction and lack of springs earned it the nickname "boneshaker." It was driven by pedaling cranks on the axle of the front wheel. To increase the distance it covered for each turn of the cranks, the front wheel was enlarged. In england, this bicycle was popularly referred to as a "penny-farthing." (4) The nickname came from the smallest and largest british coins of the time (5) and referred to the small and large wheels of the bicycle.

In fact the bicycle would be reinvented several times more (6) before becoming the quick and sturdy two-wheeler we know today.

1 **A** Spelling error
B Capitalization error
C Punctuation error
D No error

2 **F** Spelling error
G Capitalization error
H Punctuation error
J No error

3 **A** Spelling error
B Capitalization error
C Punctuation error
D No error

4 **F** Spelling error
G Capitalization error
H Punctuation error
J No error

5 **A** Spelling error
B Capitalization error
C Punctuation error
D No error

6 **F** Spelling error
G Capitalization error
H Punctuation error
J No error

Standardized Test Practice

Read each passage and decide which type of error, if any, appears in each underlined section. Mark the letter for your answer.

Mr. Louis Alvarez
First Class Publishing
301 Rio Grande
Austin, TX 78701

Dear Mr. Alvarez:

It was a pleasure meeting you yesterday. The tour of your office was very informative; I really enjoyed learning about the publishing Industry. (1) As I mentioned to you, I am interested in many aspects of the publishing business, including editing marketing, and sales. (2)

I hope you will continue to consider me as a strong candadate for the position at your company. (3) A summer internship with a professional publishing house is a wonderful opportunity. It is a chance for me to gain firsthand knowledge as well as valuable life experience. (4)

Thank you for your consideration.

Sincerely,

Marcia Dooley

1 **A** Spelling error
B Capitalization error
C Punctuation error
D No error

2 **F** Spelling error
G Capitalization error
H Punctuation error
J No error

3 **A** Spelling error
B Capitalization error
C Punctuation error
D No error

4 **F** Spelling error
G Capitalization error
H Punctuation error
J No error

The ancient greeks held the first Olympic Games centuries ago. Their Olympics (1) were much different from the Games of today. For example, the ancient Olympics had fewer events. Some of these events included the following, boxing, running, chariot racing, and wrestling. (2) The Pentathlon, one of its most famous contests, actually combined five different events. Of all the compatitions, perhaps the most difficult was the armored race. In this event, Olympic (3) athletes ran the length of the stadium while wearing a full suit of armor. This armor could weigh as much as sixty pounds. There are images of the ancient Olympic Games on the pottery and other artwork of the period. (4)

1 **A** Spelling error
B Capitalization error
C Punctuation error
D No error

2 **F** Spelling error
G Capitalization error
H Punctuation error
J No error

3 **A** Spelling error
B Capitalization error
C Punctuation error
D No error

4 **F** Spelling error
G Capitalization error
H Punctuation error
J No error

STOP

Standardized Test Practice

Read each passage and decide which type of error, if any, appears in each underlined section. Mark the letter for your answer.

Cryptography, or code breaking is a highly important aspect of wartime strategy. (1) Although they work far from the battle, code breakers are central players in any army.

One of the most brilliant code breakers in the Second World war was Commander (2) Joseph J. Rochefort. He worked in Pear Harbor, Hawaii. He was obsesive about his work, and went (3) for long periods without eating or sleeping in order to break the Japanese codes.

In 1942, Rochefort realized that the piece of Japanese code "AF" really meant Midway Island. However, (4) his superiors were not sure he was right, so Rochefort designed an experiment to test his hypathesis. He told the people on Midway to send (5) a message out about water trouble on the island. He knew the Japanese would intercept the message and decode it easily. The next day he picked up a japanese transmission about (6) water trouble on AF. He knew he was right.

1 **A** Spelling error
B Capitalization error
C Punctuation error
D No error

2 **F** Spelling error
G Capitalization error
H Punctuation error
J No error

3 **A** Spelling error
B Capitalization error
C Punctuation error
D No error

4 **F** Spelling error
G Capitalization error
H Punctuation error
J No error

5 **A** Spelling error
B Capitalization error
C Punctuation error
D No error

6 **F** Spelling error
G Capitalization error
H Punctuation error
J No error

Native to Tasmania and southern and eastern australia, the platypus (1) is a strange animal indeed. It is a mammal, but it lays eggs. It has dense fur, like a beaver's, and has a bill that resembles a duck's. The platypus (2) is a semi-aquatic animal. The platypus lives in a long burrow, which it digs by the banks of rivers. With its flat tail and webbed feet, the platypus is very agile in the water. Useing its elongated snout, the (3) platypus can stir up the mud at the rivers bottom where it finds food. (4) The platypus subsists on a diet of worms shellfish, and insects. A shy animal (5) by nature, the platypus is rarely observed in the wild.

1 **A** Spelling error
B Capitalization error
C Punctuation error
D No error

2 **F** Spelling error
G Capitalization error
H Punctuation error
J No error

3 **A** Spelling error
B Capitalization error
C Punctuation error
D No error

4 **F** Spelling error
G Capitalization error
H Punctuation error
J No error

5 **A** Spelling
B Capitalization
C Punctuation
D No error

STOP

Standardized Test Practice

Read each passage and decide which type of error, if any, appears in each underlined section. Mark the letter for your answer choice on your paper.

"Look out below!" George bellowd loudly (1) as he tossed the rope down into the hole. Once his end of the rope was tight he leaned toward the opening (2) of the mine and listened carefully.

"All is well down here, called the foreman from (3) deep inside the mine. He had climbed the fourty feet to the bottom of the well (4) earlier in the day and had been working ever since. However, when he had tried to climb back up the Iron ladder that was fixed to the wall of the mine, (5) one of the supports had broken. He had been waiting for George to arrive with a rope that was sturdy (6) enough to get him out of the Bullhorn Gold company's mine. (7)

Slowly the foreman reached the mouth of the mine, struggling, with George's help, to hoist himself out onto the ground.

1 **A** Spelling error
B Capitalization error
C Punctuation error
D No error

2 **F** Spelling error
G Capitalization error
H Punctuation error
J No error

3 **A** Spelling error
B Capitalization error
C Punctuation error
D No error

4 **F** Spelling error
G Capitalization error
H Punctuation error
J No error

5 **A** Spelling error
B Capitalization error
C Punctuation error
D No error

6 **F** Spelling error
G Capitalization error
H Punctuation error
J No error

7 **A** Spelling error
B Capitalization error
C Punctuation error
D No error

Lila slowly opened her jewelry box and peeked inside cautiosly (1) at the contents. Since she had been a child growing up in the mountains of colombia, she had dreamt of having (2) her very own emeralds. For generations her family had worked as gem stone cutters', (3) but had been too poor to afford any of the prescious stones for themselves. (4)

"I almost can't believe that you are real," she whispered to the stones. You are too lovely (5) and too perfect to belong in my jewelry box." Lila paused as she thought about how the stones had come to be in her possession. Her Father had saved every spare penny for many years to buy these stones (6) for Lila as a gift. Yesterday, the day before Lila was to be married, her father had given her two emerald earrings. (7) Now, as she prepared to leave for the church, she took the gems out and put them on.

1 **A** Spelling error
B Capitalization error
C Punctuation error
D No error

2 **F** Spelling error
G Capitalization error
H Punctuation error
J No error

3 **A** Spelling error
B Capitalization error
C Punctuation error
D No error

4 **F** Spelling error
G Capitalization error
H Punctuation error
J No error

5 **A** Spelling error
B Capitalization error
C Punctuation error
D No error

6 **F** Spelling error
G Capitalization error
H Punctuation error
J No error

7 **A** Spelling error
B Capitalization error
C Punctuation error
D No error

STOP

UNIT 29

Listening and Speaking

29.1 Listening Effectively

Your ability to listen effectively can help you be more successful in school, sports, jobs, and personal relationships. Studies show that the average person comprehends only about half of what he or she hears and remembers only about half of that. In this lesson, you'll learn how to improve your listening comprehension.

Listening Actively

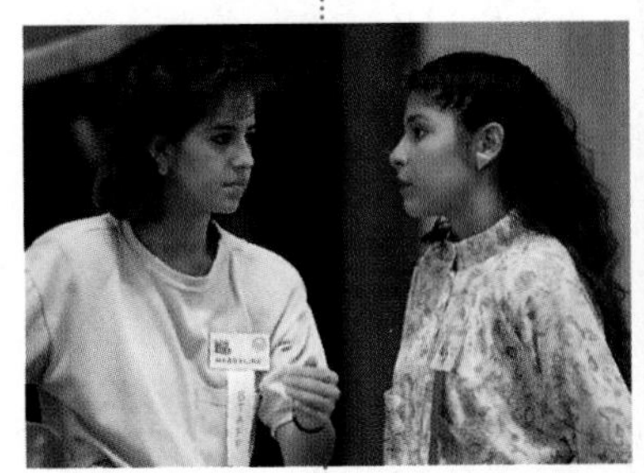

Whether you're listening to a friend, a coach, or a teacher, you need to do more than just hear what the person says. Only by listening actively will you be able to understand, interpret, and respond to what you hear. The chart below shows some important types of active listening. Keep in mind, however, that these types of listening cannot really be neatly separated. For any particular situation, you will probably need to use a combination of these types of listening.

Types of Listening

Type	Example
Empathic listening: understanding and responding to another's feelings	Participating in an informal conversation with a friend who needs advice
Critical listening: separating facts from opinions and evaluating the speaker's message	Listening to a persuasive message such as a political speech or a commercial
Reflective listening: identifying main ideas and thinking about their implications	Listening to an informational message, such as a history lecture
Appreciative listening: enjoying and interpreting a performance	Listening to a spoken performance of a short story

Even though particular listening situations differ greatly, you can still benefit from understanding general strategies for active listening. The following chart presents such strategies.

Active Listening Strategies

Prepare to Listen

- **Eliminate physical distractions.** Make yourself comfortable and put away whatever you're working on.
- **Clear your mind of other thoughts.** Don't think about your schedule for the day or what you're going to do over the weekend.
- **Adopt a positive attitude and an open mind about what you are going to hear.** Don't prejudge the speaker or jump to conclusions about the message before you have listened to everything the speaker has to say.

(continued)

Listening and Speaking

Active Listening Strategies

- **Identify the situation and the types of listening called for.** Does the situation call mainly for empathic, critical, reflective, or appreciative listening?

Listen to the Message

- **Focus your attention on what the speaker is saying.** Don't jump ahead and think about what you want to say next.
- **Maintain your concentration by finding something of interest in the message.** Don't doodle, daydream, constantly look around, or become impatient for the speaker to finish.
- **Take notes if the situation calls for it.** Note taking is often useful for classroom presentations, speeches, and interviews.

Interpret the Message

- **Summarize the message.** Identify the purpose of the message and the main ideas or themes.
- **Reflect on what you hear.** Ask yourself: Does this information sound reasonable? Does it conflict with anything else I know?

Respond to the Message

- **Ask questions.** Clarify ideas and terms you don't understand and ask questions that relate to the topic.
- **Discuss the message.** Compare your interpretation with the interpretations of others.
- **Assess the message.** What significance or consequences does the message have for you or for others?

Analyzing and Evaluating What You Hear

The Active Listening Strategies on pages 883–884 can help you understand and interpret the messages you hear. But in certain situations, you'll want to do even more. Some situations—such as persuasive messages and performances of poems, short stories, plays, and other literary works—require you to critically analyze and evaluate what you hear.

How to Evaluate Persuasive Messages You hear many persuasive messages—from friends, teachers, and parents; on the radio or television; and from a variety of other sources. Some of these messages are reasonable and worth acting on; others are not. How do you decide? Review Unit 6 Persuasive Writing on page 276. You can also use the following questions to analyze and evaluate persuasive messages.

Evaluating Persuasive Messages

- **Purpose.** What is the purpose of the message? In other words, what is the speaker trying to get people to do?
- **Audience.** To what audience is the message targeted?
- **Facts/opinions.** What are the facts and what are the opinions in the message? Do the facts support the opinions or claims? What necessary facts or opinions are missing?
- **Errors in reasoning.** Does the message contain errors in reasoning, such as overgeneralization?
- **Persuasive techniques.** What kinds of persuasive techniques—such as loaded language, celebrity testimonial, and exaggeration—are used in the message? How does the message appeal to people's emotions?
- **Values and biases.** What values or biases does the message reflect? How do these values compare to yours?
- **Your opinion.** After analyzing the message, form your opinion. Do you agree, disagree, or need more information?

How to Evaluate Literary Performances Some literary works, such as poems and plays, are intended to be read aloud or performed. But even short stories and essays sometimes come alive more fully in a performance than in a silent reading. You can use the following questions both to assess literary performances and to improve your own performance of literary works.

Evaluating Literary Performances

- **Voice qualities.** Does the performer effectively use such voice qualities as volume, stress, tone, and pronunciation to present the work?
- **Body language.** Does the performer use body language—including posture, eye contact, facial expressions, gestures, and movements—to engage the audience and bring the work to life?
- **Literary elements.** What element of the literary work—such as character development, plot, imagery, rhyme, or figurative language—does the performance emphasize? What is the effect of this element?
- **Your rating.** How would you rate the performer's interpretation of the literary work? Why?

Exercise 1

Practice the Active Listening Strategies as you listen to an in-depth news program, a panel discussion, or an interview of a public figure on radio or television. Prepare and present an oral report on what you heard. Your report should include the following:

- a summary of the purpose of the message and the main ideas
- your reflections on the message
- a description of the significance or consequences of the message

Exercise 2

Listen to a television commercial that you like and use the questions in the Evaluating Persuasive Messages chart to write an analysis and evaluation of the commercial. Present your report orally to the class.

Exercise 3

Use the Evaluating Literary Performances chart to create a critique form. Then work with a partner to videotape each other performing a poetry reading. Watch the videotape and complete a critique form for both your performance and your partner's. Compare your evaluations with those of your partner. Make a list of goals for yourself for future presentations.

Exercise 4

Obtain an audiotape or videotape that contains a poetry or short story reading. Listen actively to the presentation and then fill out a critique form evaluating the performance.

29.2 Speaking Effectively

Think of some recent situations when you had to use your speaking skills. Have you spoken to a friend on the phone recently? Have you presented a report for one of your classes? Have you given anyone directions? Have you made a speech? Different types of speaking require different skills. In this lesson, you'll learn how to speak effectively when talking informally and when making formal speeches.

Speaking Informally

You speak informally all the time. Whether telling your friends about a television show you saw, explaining the causes of World War I when called on in class, or giving directions to the supermarket, you are speaking informally. In informal speaking, you do not usually plan what you will say, and often others do as much talking as you. The chart describes some typical informal speech situations.

Tips for Informal Speaking

Type	Description	Hint
In-person and phone conversations	Conversations are the most common and least formal speaking situations. Subjects are usually spontaneous and varied, and each party both listens and speaks. A phone conversation, however, usually has a more defined purpose.	Letting others speak without interruption helps encourage participation of all those engaged in the conversation. A phone conversation will be more effective if you explain your reason for calling. Be sure to call at a time that is convenient for the person you are phoning and keep the call to a reasonable length.
Announcements	Announcements provide brief, important information about events, meetings, projects, and other such occurrences. Announcements should be clear and give all necessary details.	Encouraging questions after the announcement helps to ensure that you have clearly communicated the necessary information.
Giving directions or instructions	Providing directions or instructions usually involves an explanation of a procedure or process.	Present your points as a series of logical steps. Speak slowly and be sure the listener understands. Encourage the listener to ask questions. You might even ask questions yourself to help your listener understand.

Preparing and Delivering Formal Speeches

Formal speeches are prepared, rehearsed, and then delivered at a prearranged place and time. Preparing a formal speech involves many of the same steps as writing a research paper or a persuasive essay. However, a speech actually involves more steps, as outlined here.

Think About Purpose and Audience Once you have a topic, decide on your purpose for making the speech. Do you want to persuade your audience, inform them, or entertain them? You may end up doing all three—an audience that is entertained is more likely to listen attentively, and an audience that hears solid evidence is more likely to be persuaded. Write a clear statement of your purpose, such as "I want to persuade my audience to participate in our community's recycling program."

After clearly defining your purpose, identify your audience. What age group and economic class do they belong to? Do they live in a large city, a suburb, or a small town? Determine what your audience knows about the topic, even interviewing some of them if possible. What concerns or preconceived ideas do they have? What misinformation might you need to correct? Then think about the kind of language that fits your audience. You may need to tailor your vocabulary to your audience and explain any technical terms.

Research the Topic Do library and Internet research to gather facts, examples, and experts' opinions on your topic. Conduct polls and interviews when appropriate. Study the information you gather and write a clear statement of your thesis. Then select accurate, relevant evidence and examples from reliable sources to support your thesis.

Organize an Outline Choose a pattern of organization that fits your information and your purpose. Outline your information using your thesis as the controlling idea. At this point, consider whether visual aids might be useful.

Draft and Revise Use your outline as a guide to draft your speech, following the standard structure of an introduction, a body, and a conclusion. If you are preparing a persuasive speech, review the appropriate appeals and rhetorical strategies for persuasive writing on pages 310–313.

In your introduction, think of a way to grab your audience's attention. You might consider one of the methods listed in the following chart.

Methods for Introductions	
Tell a compelling story	Two years ago, my older brother was riding in a car that was hit by a drunk driver.
Ask an intriguing question	If you could change one thing about yourself, what would it be?
Use an interesting quote	There is a saying by the Chinese philosopher Confucius that applies to learning: "I hear and I forget. I see and I remember. I do and I understand."
State an amazing fact or statistic	Americans are using up a disproportionate amount of the world's resources. The United States alone consumes 25 percent of the world's energy.

In your conclusion, you might provide an interesting twist that sums up your speech. For example, if you began with a question, you might state it again and give the answer. Whatever method you use, always strive for a strong finish that drives home your message.

Revise your speech, just as you would any other work of informative or persuasive writing. Read your speech out loud and make further changes so that it flows smoothly. You have to be able to say what you write. If your sentences are too long, shorten them. If you stumble over a group of words, change them.

Prepare Materials Some speakers read from manuscript pages; others speak from an outline or note cards. Some even memorize their speeches. If you are not required to use a particular method, choose the method that works best for you and your situation. If you read your speech, prepare a double- or triple-spaced manuscript with wide margins. If you choose to speak from an outline or note cards, use your written speech to prepare these materials. Underline topic sentences, number supporting points, and transfer the ideas to an outline or note cards. Number manuscript pages, outline pages, or note cards at the top.

Practice and Deliver Your Speech Practice your speech in front of a mirror. Ask a friend or relative to listen to your speech or to videotape it. As you rehearse, pay attention to the points listed in the following chart. Even if you read your speech, be sure to make frequent eye contact with your audience, especially at the beginning and end of sentences.

Guidelines for Delivering a Speech

Verbal Techniques

- **Volume.** Speak loudly enough so that everyone in the audience can hear you.
- **Pronunciation.** Speak clearly, pronouncing all the words.
- **Pace.** Speak at a moderate speed, but vary the rate and use pauses to convey your meaning.
- **Tone.** Speak in a lively tone.
- **Emphasis.** Stress important words and ideas.

Nonverbal Techniques

- **Posture.** Stand up tall with your head straight.
- **Eye contact.** Make eye contact with people throughout your audience.
- **Facial expressions and gestures.** Vary your facial expressions to reflect what you are saying and use natural gestures to reinforce your ideas.
- **Visual aids.** If appropriate for your topic, use charts, diagrams, graphs, or video clips to enhance your speech and convey important information.

Invite questions and comments When you complete your speech, ask if there are any questions or comments. Answer questions honestly and respectfully. Use this question-and-answer period to correct misunderstandings, to repeat points that your listeners may have missed, and to learn what you could have made clearer in your speech.

Exercise 5

Following the guidelines provided in this lesson, prepare, practice, and deliver a brief persuasive speech in which you propose a solution to a problem in your school or community. Apply the Active Listening Strategies presented on pages 883–884 as you listen to the speeches of your classmates and use the questions in Evaluating Persuasive Messages on page 885 to provide feedback for each speaker.

29.3 Working in Groups

You participate in many groups—families, classes, study groups, teams, clubs or organizations, and work groups. To contribute in positive ways to any of these groups, you need good listening and speaking skills as well as an understanding of how to function in a group.

In a study group or discussion group, members typically have definite roles, such as group leader, recorder, and participants. The group leader guides the discussion and keeps the group focused on the topic or task. The recorder takes notes and records decisions. The participants contribute ideas, respond to the ideas of others, and vote on decisions. A group operates most effectively if members follow guidelines like those listed in the chart below.

Guidelines for Working in a Group

- **Be prepared.** Complete any assigned reading or research before the group meets.
- **Focus on the issue.** Don't bring up unrelated topics.
- **Listen actively.** Make an effort to understand each person's viewpoint and don't interrupt when someone is speaking.
- **Show respect**. Recognize that each person has something worthwhile to contribute. An effective group draws upon the different strengths of its members.
- **State your ideas clearly and concisely.** Don't talk on and on so that others have little chance to speak.
- **Respond constructively to the ideas of others.** Explain why you agree or disagree with someone's idea, providing reasons or evidence.
- **Encourage everyone to participate.** If someone has not spoken, ask for his or her opinion.

Exercise 6

Form a small group and choose a group leader and a recorder. Hold an informal, twenty-minute discussion on the following questions: What are high schools doing to deal with the rise in teenage violence? What *should* they be doing? After the discussion, evaluate how well your group functioned, based on the Guidelines for Working in a Group. Then give a brief summary of your discussion to the rest of the class.

29.4 Conducting an Interview

Listening and speaking skills are also crucial in conducting interviews, which is a valuable way of gathering information. The following guidelines will help you conduct an effective interview.

Guidelines for Interviewing

Prepare for the Interview

- Research the subject and learn about the person you will interview.
- Prepare a list of five or more *who, what, where, when, why,* and *how* questions. Avoid questions that require just a yes or no answer. For example, instead of *Do you agree with this idea?* ask *What do you think of this idea?*
- If you plan to tape the interview, make sure your tape recorder works. If you plan to take notes, make sure you bring along two pens that work and a pad of paper as well as your list of interview questions.

Listen Actively During the Interview

- Take notes or tape-record the interview. Ask for the correct spelling of the person's name and of any unfamiliar places or terms the person uses.
- If necessary, ask the person to explain or repeat statements you do not understand.
- Ask intelligent follow-up questions.
- At the end of the interview, thank the person.

Follow Up after the Interview

- As soon as possible after the interview, write a full account of everything you remember, referring to your notes or your tape.
- If necessary, contact the person to clear up any points of confusion.
- Write the person a thank-you letter.

Sample interview notes

Note the date of the interview.

Nov. 16, 2000

Interview with Elena Paz, Owner of Paz Landscape Architects

- college major — sociology
- couldn't get job that she enjoyed in that field
- took an interest in landscape architecture
- got entry-level job in landscape architecture business
- went back to school to study landscape architecture
- graduated and started own business
- after much hard work, business became extremely successful
- has just created a Web page for her business

Verify the spelling of the person's name and the company name.

Jot down just a few words to capture questions and answers. These words will jog your memory when you write up a full account of the interview later.

Exercise 7

Interview a parent or another adult about his or her occupation, following the guidelines given in this lesson. Write a full account of your interview and ask the person to check the account for accuracy. Also ask the person to give you feedback on how you conducted the interview. Share highlights of your interview in a brief oral report to the class.

UNIT 30

Viewing and Representing

30.1 Understanding Visual Messages

Think of the last time you watched television, listened to a radio broadcast, saw a feature film at a theater, or visited a Web site as part of your research for a school project. In each case, you were turning to mass media for entertainment or information. In many cases, what you see and hear in mass media presentations will not only entertain and inform you, but will also persuade you in one way or another. Whether you realize it or not, media presentations help shape your attitudes, values, and behavior. They not only reflect your culture, but they also help create it.

Developing *media literacy*—the ability to understand, interpret, analyze, and critique media messages as well as create your own—will help you recognize the ways media messages might influence your thinking and your life. The goal of this unit is to help you gain such media literacy.

Interpreting Visual Design

With the exception of radio, all the mass media send visual messages. Being aware of the techniques used in developing visual messages will help you to interpret the messages you see and to understand and analyze the ideas that are presented. To understand the design of a visual image such as a photograph or illustration, you examine its *composition,* or arrangement of elements. The following chart lists some basic elements in the composition of a photograph or illustration. Although the actual effect of an element depends on the overall context of the picture, as you will see in the chart, various effects can be achieved by manipulating each element.

Elements of Visual Design		
Element	**Example**	**Some Possible Effects**
Shape	Circle	Suggests wholeness, lovableness, softness
	Square	Suggests firmness, stability
	Triangle	Suggests unity, balance, or tension
Line Lines can be real (the edge of a building) or implied (a person's gaze). Lines can be used to direct a viewer's attention or to suggest a mood or theme.	Straight lines	Point or lead to something
	Curved lines	Suggest motion, warmth
	Vertical lines	Suggest dignity, status, power
	Horizontal lines	Suggest peace, stillness
	Diagonal lines	Suggest tension, energy

Viewing and Representing

Elements of Visual Design (cont.)		
Element	**Example**	**Some Possible Effects**
Color or Tone	Cool colors (blue, green, gray)	Convey calm, emotional distance
	Warm colors (red, yellow, orange)	Convey energy, vibrancy, warmth
	Bright colors	Convey joy, action, excitement
	Subdued or pastel colors	Suggest innocence, softness, serenity
	Light tones	Create happy, playful mood
	Dark tones	Convey sadness, mystery, dullness
Texture	Smooth, flat	Might suggest emptiness or something modern and streamlined
	Rough, woven	Might convey wholesomeness, naturalness, a feeling of home
	Silky, shiny	Creates sense of luxury
Positioning of subjects The positions of figures grouped together can show how the artist views their relationships to one another.	Center of frame	Conveys stability
	Top of frame	Conveys importance, power
	Bottom of frame	Conveys inferiority, weakness
Light A viewer's eye naturally travels to the most lighted area.	Bright light	Draws the eye to a specific area; creates a cheerful mood
	Dim light or shadows	Creates a sense of mystery or doom
Space	Large space around subject	Draws attention to subject; isolates details; can create a sense of openness, vastness, emptiness, loneliness
	Little space around subject	Makes subject seem dominating, overwhelming

To understand how elements of visual design work together in a photograph, study this picture of two high school students, which appeared in a magazine feature story about the lives of teenagers. Several items in the picture show aspects of teen culture—school books, a decorated school locker, and popular styles of the time, including athletic shoes and flared jeans. Those items alone inform viewers about teen life. However, the photographer has used certain techniques to send a stronger message. Note how the diagonal lines created by the students' legs draw the viewer into the picture. The subdued lighting and predominance of muted tans and browns add a feeling of warmth and softness to the picture. And the students' position in the center of the frame with lots of space around them, together with the students' relaxed poses and smiling faces, combine to create a positive portrait of friendly, happy teenagers who have an equal, easy-going relationship.

A viewer might look at this photograph and think that the photographer simply shot a realistic portrait of these two teenagers. But the photographer made a conscious decision about where to shoot the picture, what elements to include and exclude, how to position the students, and what facial expressions to try to capture. If the photographer had chosen instead to use very dim light and capture the students scowling instead of smiling, the resulting photograph would have conveyed a completely different impression. Every photograph presents one view of a subject from a particular perspective.

Exercise 1

Use the Elements of Visual Design chart to describe the effects of lines, shapes, positioning of subjects, color, light, and space in this 1998 photograph of John Glenn's return into space at the age of seventy-seven. Summarize the ideas that the photograph conveys about the relationships among people, their heroes, and technology in U.S. culture.

Film Techniques

The basic elements of visual design apply to the media of motion pictures and videos as well as to photographs and illustrations. In addition, motion picture and television directors—even the creators of video games—use a wide variety of film techniques to tell stories and to convey messages. The following chart describes some of these techniques and the effects they can have.

Basic Film Techniques		
Technique	**Example**	**Possible Effects**
Camera angle	High (looking down)	Minimizes status of subject
	Low (looking up)	Emphasizes status of subject
	Straight-on (eye level)	Puts viewer on equal level with subject; promotes identification with subject
Camera shots	Close-up (magnified view)	Promotes identification with subject
	Long shot (wide view)	Establishes relationship between characters and a setting
	Reaction shot	Shows effect of one character on another or of an event on a character
Lighting	High-key (bright, even)	Creates cheerful, optimistic mood
	Low-key (producing shadows)	Creates gloomy, eerie mood
	Lit from above	Subject seems to glow with significance
	Lit from below	May raise audience apprehension
Movement	Slow motion	Emphasizes movement and heightens drama
	Blurred motion	Suggests speed, confusion, or dreamlike state
Editing (selection and arrangement of scenes)	Sequence of short shots	Builds tension, creates a rushed mood
	Sequence of long shots	May convey a feeling of stability
Special effects	Artwork and miniature models	Can be filmed to appear real
	Computer enhancement	Can create composite images or distort qualities of a character or scene
Background music		Evokes audience's emotional response, sets mood, reinforces theme

Examine the elements of visual design and the film techniques used in this still from the movie *Jurassic Park* (1993). This reaction shot shows the characters' amazement as they wake up to see a brachiosaur grazing on the leaves of a tree in which they had slept. Sunlight streams onto the characters from above and behind, lighting up their faces and casting shadows on the tree. The shadows and the blue and green colors of the tree dominate the picture, creating a slightly eerie though calm mood. The characters' bodies form a circle within the radiating branches of the tree, emphasizing the close relationship that has developed between them after their escape from a *Tyrannosaurus rex.* Because of the straight-on camera angle and the long shot, the viewer identifies with the characters' situation. These design elements and film techniques combine to help engage the audience with the characters, who have bonded through a harrowing experience and have kept their ability to be awed by a wonder of nature. Like many scenes in the movie, this one was created using special effects, including a fifty-foot model tree.

Exercise 2

Study the still below from the movie *Jurassic Park.* Use the Elements of Visual Design and Basic Film Techniques charts to help you identify at least three elements or techniques used in the scene and to analyze their effects. Share your analysis in a brief oral report to the class.

30.2 Examining Media Messages

Photographs, movies, and television programs typically seem to capture scenes from life just as they are. For example, although the photograph on page 897 seems realistic, it represents only a portion of the high school student population in the country. Not all students wear athletic shoes and flared jeans. Keep in mind that all media messages are constructed for a purpose and show only a particular view of life from one perspective. Even in a documentary that you might consider strictly factual, a director has made many decisions about how to shoot scenes, what information to include and exclude, and what effects to strive for. To fully understand what you see and how it can influence you, you need to be able to analyze, or **deconstruct,** media messages. This lesson will help you develop that skill.

Identifying Media Genres

Every day you are exposed to a variety of forms of media. These forms, or genres, can be grouped into four main types: print, broadcast, film, and Internet. *Print media* include newspapers, magazines, fliers, books, product packaging, and other materials that convey messages through printed words and images. *Broadcast media* consist of radio and television, in which sounds alone or both sounds and moving images are transmitted to a wide public audience. *Film media* include movies and videotapes, which also consist of sounds and moving images. The *Internet* contains a wide variety of Web sites that consist of some combination of printed words, still and moving images, and sounds.

The form of a media message can affect its meaning and how you interpret or respond to it. For information on a specific topic, you might choose between several types of presentation depending on the kind and amount of information you need. For example, for a quick look at the main news events of the day, you might turn to a newspaper. Another quick source could be a news service on the Internet, which would have links to other articles related to the news items that catch your attention. However, you might gain a fuller appreciation of the impact of a news event—for example, of civil unrest somewhere else in the world—from watching a TV newscast than you would from reading about it in a newspaper article. The moving images on TV have a strong impact and often arouse a stronger emotional response than print does. To learn more in depth about the causes of the problem, you could refer to a book or view a film documentary. Imagine that the United States was involved in a war and you gained all your information about events from the newspaper. How might your view of events and reactions be different than if you watched the live TV news coverage? Which source might give you more comprehensive information? Which might make you feel more personally involved?

Exercise 3

Watch a TV newscast for coverage of a foreign war or conflict and take notes on what you learn. Then check the Internet and read a newspaper to find coverage of the same event. Create a chart comparing and contrasting the coverage in the different media, the impressions you gain from each, and the impact that each has on you.

Analyzing Media Messages

As you look critically at a media message—whether it's a print advertisement, an online research resource, or a popular movie—you need to analyze how and why it was created. The following chart describes how to deconstruct a media message.

How to Analyze a Media Message		
Identify	**By Asking Yourself**	**Example**
source	Who made this? How does the source affect the message?	A dairy industry organization sponsors an ad in a national newsmagazine promoting the nutritional value of milk.
purpose	Why was the message made? Is it meant to inform, entertain, or persuade?	The purpose of the ad is to persuade people to buy milk. Another purpose seems to be to inform people about nutritional benefits of milk.
target audience	Who is the message intended for? How has the content been shaped to appeal to the intended audience?	The ad is targeted to middle-aged adults. It shows the middle-aged cast of a popular TV sitcom drinking milk. The middle-aged audience should relate well to the show's cast.
main idea or theme	What is the intended message?	Men and women should drink three glasses of milk each day to get enough calcium in their diet.
design elements and/or film techniques	How are design elements or film techniques used to communicate a message or manipulate a viewer's response?	The actors in the photo are bathed in a golden light that makes them appear healthy, warm, and lovable.

How to Analyze a Media Message (cont.)		
Identify	**By Asking Yourself**	**Example**
elements that reflect a specific culture	What cultural values and assumptions are reflected in this presentation?	Good health and youthful looks are important. People would like to look and act like attractive actors.
persuasive techniques glittering generalities	Does the message make sweeping claims that are impossible to support?	The ad implies that everyone who drinks milk will be as glamorous and look as young and healthy as the actors do.
logical fallacies	Are the statements in the message logical, or are there errors in logic?	The argument that people need calcium in their diet is based on fact, but drinking milk is not the only way to get this nutrient.
symbols	Does the message use symbols that stand for popular ideas or values?	Milk itself is a symbol of health and youth.
celebrity testimonial	Do admired celebrities add to the message or endorse the product?	The ad uses celebrities to endorse a product.

Exercise 4

Use the questions in the How to Analyze a Media Message chart to write an analysis of a print ad targeted to teenagers. Then create a print ad of your own promoting the same product or service and write an explanation of the techniques you use in your ad.

Exercise 5

In a small group, discuss the influence that such media as TV shows and commercials, movies, magazines, and radio programs have had on your ideas about the following topics:

- romantic love
- the importance of physical beauty and standards of beauty
- the importance of material success to a person's happiness
- the kinds of things you want to own and buy

After your discussion, choose one of these topics and write an editorial in which you give your opinion on the media's effects on your perceptions and those of your classmates.

30.3 Making Your Own Media Messages

A good way to understand media messages and the decisions behind them is to produce your own media presentation. This lesson provides guidelines for producing two forms of media messages: videos and Web pages.

Making a Video

The creation of a video requires the skills and cooperation of several people. Depending on the topic of your video and the way you choose to present it, you might need people to fill any or all of these roles:

- **Director:** coordinates the activities of the group members and supervises the filming of the video
- **Researcher:** finds background information on the topic and the interviewees
- **Scriptwriter:** writes and revises the script
- **Storyboard designer:** prepares a series of simple sketches of each video scene to go along with the dialogue or narration
- **Interviewer:** prepares questions to ask the interviewees and conducts the interviews
- **Narrator:** reads the script during the filming
- **Camera operator:** films the interviews and other shots

Some members of your production team may take on two or more roles. For example, the scriptwriter might also function as the researcher and narrator. Making a video provides an opportunity to try out different roles and learn new skills.

Consider the elements of visual design and the film techniques described in the first section of this unit as you plan and produce your video. Make sure that you have a clear focus for your video and that you can summarize that focus in a paragraph. The following chart provides additional guidelines for carrying out a video project.

TIPS ON PRODUCING A VIDEO
1. **Begin by brainstorming.** In your group, discuss these questions: What is the purpose and focus of the video? Who are the intended viewers? What do they already know or think about the subject? What information do we need to find out? What scenes will we shoot? You may want to have a group member write down these questions and the answers as they arise in the discussion. *(continued)*

TIPS ON PRODUCING A VIDEO

2. **Use a storyboard to help in planning.** A storyboard provides a blueprint for shooting your video. It consists of simple sketches of the sequence of scenes you will shoot, with the dialogue or narration for each scene. You want your video to tell a story—so create a beginning, middle, and end. Include scenes that set the stage, show the location, or provide details that enrich the story.
3. **Vary your scenes.** Mix long camera shots that show a location with closer shots that focus on a single subject. Shoot from different angles and heights to achieve different effects. Vary the length of the shots you take as well.
4. **Work with good lighting.** Shoot in strong light—outside during daylight or inside near windows and with all the lights on. Set up your own lights if necessary.
5. **Shoot with editing in mind.** To make it easier to edit scenes later, leave a little room before and after each scene by letting the camera run. Reshoot scenes that don't turn out well.
6. **Create a polished final product with careful editing.** At the editing stage, you can eliminate bad footage, add music and sound effects, and insert titles. You also can mix short cuts and long cuts to achieve the pacing you want.
7. **Ask for viewer feedback.** After you present your video, ask the audience to fill out a questionnaire or participate in a discussion to give you feedback. Ask viewers to state the main idea of your video and to comment on how effectively it was conveyed. In addition, elicit their comments on the pacing, the camera techniques, and the audio and visual quality.

Exercise 6

Working in a small group, choose one of the following video projects to undertake:

- a six-minute documentary designed for adults, describing a contemporary fad
- a movie review show for teenagers
- an instructional program for people who do not use computers on how to produce fliers or books on a computer

Decide on a topic and agree on roles for each group member. Then work together to plan, write, shoot, and edit your video. After presenting the video to the class, hold a discussion to gather feedback from your audience.

Creating a Web Site

You can create a Web page that incorporates photographs, graphics, text, and even sound using a software program or hypertext mark-up language (HTML). A good Web site is attractive, informative, and easy to follow. The following guidelines will help you design a Web site that meets those standards.

Guidelines for Developing a Web Site

1. **Begin with a clear purpose.** Identify your intended audience and make sure you have something useful to share. Your home page, or main page, should convey what the site is about in a way that gets viewers' attention.
2. **Plan your site.** View other sites on your topic or similar topics and brainstorm ideas about what to include. Design a layout for each page that is logical and easy to follow. Create a flowchart showing how the pages of your site will be connected.
3. **Keep the design simple and consistent.** Use only a few colors and fonts for your site. Unify the pages by using the same background color and by repeating a logo or icon that identifies your site. Avoid a busy background that detracts attention from your message. Keep key design features consistent on all the pages.
4. **Be sure the site is quick to download.** Viewers will give up if your home page takes too long to download. Keep the images small enough and few enough so that the page downloads quickly. For the same reason, don't embed music on the home page. Instead, put the music on a linked page.
5. **Make the site easy to navigate**. Use a clear, simple navigation scheme on all your pages. Make all your pages accessible from your home page within four or fewer clicks.
6. **Keep the text short and easy to read.** Break up information into short and medium-length sections and put the sections on linked pages. Use a font that is easy to read and a background color that provides enough contrast for reading ease. Carefully proofread and correct all text.
7. **Test your site and revise it.** Ask your friends or classmates to visit your site and test how well it works. Make a form similar to the one below and ask them to complete it.

Evaluating a Web Site

Characteristic	Comments
Location: Do search engines find it using logical searches?	
Ease of Use: Does the site download quickly? Can you navigate the site easily? Do all the images download?	
Design: Is the site visually appealing? Are colors, fonts, photos, and other graphic elements used effectively?	
Content: Is the information easy to understand and useful?	

Exercise 7

Working again in a small group, rethink your video project and turn it into a Web site. Ask classmates to visit your site and complete an evaluation form similar to the one above. Use the responses you receive to revise and improve your site.

UNIT 31

Electronic Resources

31.1 Electronic Resources and the Writing Process

Writing well is a process that requires much editing and revision. A computer with word processing software has many advantages over writing on paper with pencil or pen. A computer allows you to write and revise without time-consuming recopying. You can move words, sentences, or paragraphs from one place to another with a few mouse movements. You can store copies of many versions of your work or, if you prefer, you can keep your work on the same file—adding, deleting, correcting, and revising until you're satisfied with what you've written.

Generating Ideas

Often the hardest part of writing is thinking of a good idea. The choices are endless, and a blank computer screen can be intimidating. Are there topics that you have enjoyed writing about previously? Use one of these topics as a starting point. Or think about something on your mind that you might want to explore through writing. If you are completely out of ideas, the following list of writing formats might spark some creative thoughts.

- Song
- Questions
- Description
- Explanation
- Letter
- Critique or review
- Proposal
- Endorsement
- Newspaper article
- Opinion column
- Script or play
- Poem
- Character sketch
- Short story
- Essay

Collaborating with one or more other students is also a great way to jump-start your creative juices. You might even collaborate with a pen pal via e-mail over the Internet. You and a collaborator could decide to write a two-person play, with each of you writing his or her own part. Or you might want to write a piece debating an issue, each of you taking one side of the issue.

Begin by brainstorming. On an electronic file, compile a list of random thoughts or questions that you can revise as your plans take shape. In fact, you might find it useful to start a special electronic file for your writing ideas. Call the document "Writing Ideas" and add to it whenever you get a new idea. Look through the file when you're in search of something to write about.

At the prewriting stage, you should also consider your purpose and your audience. What do you hope to accomplish? For example, will you write an essay that will appeal to your fellow students or are you trying to impress your teacher? Do you want to provide a comprehensive guide to the restaurants in town or write a review of one specific restaurant? Do you wish to enlighten your readers, persuade them, entertain them, or do you have some combination of purposes? With your audience and purpose in mind, you will be better able to define your project.

Finding Information

If you are really stuck for ideas, the Internet may be a source of inspiration. Surf the Net and see what Web sites appeal to you. Is there something you would like to share with other students? There are sites that publish student writing. Perhaps they are looking for a certain type of submission that you can try your hand at. With a little luck, you can be an Internet author.

Once you have a topic, you can use the Internet as an informational resource. Information from the Internet can be downloaded to your hard drive or printed out directly to your printer and saved as reference material. Information can even be cut and pasted directly into your project document. Don't forget to include the source of each item you download. You may need to credit that source in your paper, especially if you rely on it extensively or quote from it. You can learn more about citing Internet resources on pages 336–341.

You'll also want to evaluate the information you find on the Internet. Anyone can start a Web site and claim to be an expert on some topic. You must decide whether the information you find can be trusted and is worth using. Don't be misled by a flashy, elaborate Web site. Think about what's on it. Is the information useful to you? Does it appear to be accurate? Can you confirm it from a second source? Is the writer a recognized authority on the topic?

Planning and Organizing

As you begin planning and organizing a piece of writing, word processing is a great asset. Most programs allow users to work with more than one document open at a time. Thus, if you have a separate document for your prewriting notes, you can keep it open while you are writing your first draft. Then you will be able to drag and drop material from the notes into your draft. You can also easily copy the thoughts you have into a new file and expand them into an outline. Make each main idea a heading and then drop and drag the details under the main ideas they relate to. As you work, you may think of other details you can add.

Also think about your introduction and conclusion. The introduction can state the thesis that the paper supports, with the conclusion summarizing your arguments. Or the introduction can be a quotation or story that sets the mood. As a result of the ease of editing, word processing encourages you to experiment with different ideas. If you write something terrific that does not fit your current piece of writing, save the work in a separate file for use at another time.

Writing the Paper

Once you have created your outline, with main ideas and the details that support the main ideas, you can begin drafting the body of the paper.

Drafting You might want to begin drafting your piece by simply expanding your outline. Try turning your main ideas and supporting details into sentences. Then keep expanding as needed. Don't worry about including too much. You can cut out what isn't necessary during the revising stage. Anything that doesn't work can be easily dropped, replaced, or revised.

Among the advantages of using a computer for writing is a word processor's ability to produce macros. A **macro** is a single instruction that stands for a sequence of operations. For example, suppose you were writing a report in which you knew you would have to repeatedly type "Perry's Victory and International Peace Memorial National Monument." You could create a time-saving macro in which one keystroke would produce all eight words, properly spelled and capitalized. Check out your word processor's ability to create macros. It could save your fingers a bit of work.

Revising and Editing Read your work over carefully. Have you gotten all your ideas across? Do your arguments make sense? Then use your word processing software to help fine tune the writing. Most word processing programs have a spelling checker. In a few seconds, this tool will check the spelling of every word in a document. However, remember that a spelling checker can only identify words that are in the computer's memory as correctly spelled words. If you use a wrong word but the word is correctly spelled, the spelling checker will not know the word is wrong. The program may also question proper names and foreign words even when they're correctly spelled. There's no substitute for a careful personal proofreading.

The ability to include headers and footers is available as part of many programs. With these tools, you can include the title of the piece, your name, the date, and the page number either at the top of every page (header) or at the bottom of the page (footer). Don't confuse a footer with a footnote, which provides your reader with a reference for the resources you use to write the paper. Many word processing programs also provide you with the ability to insert automatic footnotes and endnotes, a very handy tool when you need to write a research report.

Publishing Word processing programs offer you many options for dressing up your work. You can experiment with different fonts, make words **bold** or *italic* or ***bold and italic,*** change the size of the type, add bulleted items, and put lists into columns. Most programs also allow you to add illustrations and graphic elements—photos, artwork, graphs, and maps—to your work.

Many word processing programs also include some of the features of more-complex desktop publishing programs. These features will allow you to design professional-looking reports, newsletters, and brochures. They may include predesigned templates with attractive layouts you can use or adapt to meet your personal needs and tastes. Working with classmates, you can collaborate to produce an attractive collection of class writings or to start a school literary magazine.

Exercise 1

Working with a few classmates, write an article about using word processing for school work. Base the article on the software you currently use. Your audience is fifth-or sixth-grade students who are familiar with computers but have not yet used such software.

31.2 Research and Resources

Research is an important part of all writing—from history reports to novels about rabbits. Research is the tool that helps you provide the most accurate information possible and furnishes information to help you make your stories believable and your essays authoritative. Your school or local library is a terrific place to start looking for information. Online resources are accessible through the click of a mouse button. For many topics, Internet resources rival—and may even exceed in importance—such traditional resources as books, magazines, and newspapers. If you want to learn about an upgrade for a particular piece of computer software, for example, the Internet is your best bet for the most up-to-date information.

The Internet

Think of the Internet as an enormous web that stretches around the world and has no center—hence the term *World Wide Web*. There are distinct components: business, education, and government, for example. A site's URL (uniform resource locator, or Net address) will tell you the type of organization that created a particular Web site. (See the Technology Tip on this page.) Sites offer information and resources, and specific software programs help you navigate through hundreds of millions of Web pages to find what you need.

You also have the ability to communicate within the Web through e-mail, chat rooms, and newsgroups. Thus, there is a world of information available to those who are willing to search.

E-mail Electronic mail, or e-mail, is one of the most-used features of the Internet. E-mail allows you to exchange messages with anyone else in the world who has an e-mail account. You can even send the same e-mail to many different people at the same time. E-mail is available twenty-four hours a day, seven days a week, and can be sent and received almost instantaneously. You can correspond with an expert on a topic you hope to write about and include the expert's answers to your questions in your paper. Remember, however, that not everyone is available instantly. Thoughtful responses take time, so you will need to allow a few days for people to respond to your requests. Following is list of a few sites where you can find answers to your questions or information about where you can find answers. Note that none of these sources will do your homework for you, but they can give you valuable advice to help you do it.

Technology Tip

You've no doubt heard radio or television ads giving Internet addresses ending in "dot-com.") The *.com* ending indicates a commercial (for-profit) business. Here are a few more common endings:

.edu (educational organization)
.org (nonprofit organization)
.gov (government)
.mil (military)

Sites outside the United States use a two-letter ending that indicates the country of origin. For example,

.br (Brazil) *.ng* (Nigeria)
.ca (Canada) *.sy* (Syria)
.fr (France) *.vn* (Vietnam).

Site	Web Address (URL)
Homework Planet	http://www.homeworkplanet.com
Infoplease	http://www.infoplease.com/homework/
Kids Search Tools	http://www.rcls.org/ksearch.htm
Awesome Library	http://www.awesomelibrary.org/student5.htm

Chat Rooms Imagine a clubhouse where a different discussion is occurring in each room. You can come and go as you please. Chat rooms are like clubhouses, except in chat rooms people communicate via written computer communication rather than by voice. Chat rooms are areas of the Internet where people who have similar interests gather.

There are thousands of chat rooms, hundreds just for teens alone. Some of these teen chat rooms are devoted to general teen discussions, others to specific topics like dating or school work. Since chat rooms are on the World Wide Web, you can often find interesting discussions among young people from many different countries. A Web search will lead you to chat rooms on almost any topic you can think of. Once in a chat room, you can participate in the discussion or just observe. To take part, you simply type a statement or question into your computer. Others in the chat room can respond to you from their computers.

Before you become active in a chat room, you should always look for and read carefully the chat room's membership requirements, rules and regulations, and list of FAQ's (frequently asked questions). Doing so will keep you from asking questions that have been asked and answered previously.

Newsgroups There are newsgroups devoted to discussions of thousands of topics—for example, the uses of particular software programs or computer games, teen concerns, discussions about popular recording artists or movie or TV stars. Like a chat room, newsgroups bring together people with a similar interest. Newsgroups, however, do so via e-mail rather than in real-time discussions. You can send an e-mail with a comment or a question to the group. Your message goes out to all group members, which may be hundreds of people. Any member can respond to you. Newsgroups provide a great way of learning from people who know more about a topic than you do.

Exercise 2

1. Compose an e-mail message and send it to five people you know. Ask each one to provide you with the URL, or Internet address, of one or more favorite Web sites. Investigate each site and start a list of sites that you think are worth visiting often.
2. Use a search engine to find a chat room that interests you. Visit it and report to the class on what you find.

CD-ROMs and DVDs

While the Internet has loads of information, you often have to sift through a multitude of data to find what you want. Software packages or CD-ROMs (compact disc read-only memory) have been created that contain comprehensive information on specific topics. These CD-ROMs include encyclopedias, dictionaries, atlases, and a variety of other helpful references, many of which contain video clips, animation, and sound as well as text. Check with your school or local library, which may have a collection of such disks that you can consult for your research projects.

DVDs (digital video discs) are a more recent technology. It would take about eight CDs to hold as much information as a single side of a DVD. The storage capacity of a DVD is so great that an entire full-length motion picture can be stored on a single disc. In addition, the video and audio qualities are superior to those of other data storage software. DVDs with feature films are already widely accepted. Because of their huge capacity, they are likely to eventually replace CD-ROMs for computer data storage, software programs, and games.

Finding and Tracking Sites

The best way to find the specific information you want on the Internet is through a search engine. Type one or more keywords into a search engine and within seconds you'll get a list of dozens (or even thousands) of sites that may contain the information you need. On most search engines, brief descriptors will help you sift through the hits for those most likely to help you. The use of well-chosen keywords will keep you from getting too many irrelevant sites.

Your browser will let you keep track of the sites you have visited and would like to return to. (These sites are called Bookmarks or Favorites, depending on which browser you use.) Think of them as an address book for online content. If you think you may want to return to a site, all you need do is pull down the Bookmarks (or Favorites) menu and select the command that will save the site's URL for you. To return to the site, you pull down the menu again and select its name.

Exercise 3

Choose a favorite author and use a search engine to find one or more Internet sites devoted to that author and his or her works. Use the sites to answer the following questions about the author you chose.

- When was his/her first book published?
- How many books did he/she publish?
- What was the longest time span between published books?
- What other writers were writing at the same period of time?

31.3 Communicating Visually

Have you ever noticed that some documents are so dense and wordy that you have a headache when you look at them? Such documents are packed with words. There are no headings and no breaks between paragraphs; it is hard to distinguish among the different ideas that are presented. In fact, you can barely read such documents. They are poorly designed because the publisher did not take readability into account.

Everything from the style and size of the font, or letters, to the size of the margins and the length of the page contribute to the appeal of a document. As a writer you should try to make your writing easy to read as well as interesting.

Different Forms, Different Styles

The many different forms of writing have different styles. The form of haiku is very specific—three lines of verse containing five, seven, and five syllables respectively. Newspaper pieces usually have multiple narrow columns with a headline followed by a byline. The headline is bold and centered; it jumps out from the page. The stories usually have very short paragraphs, sometimes as short as a single sentence. Newspaper articles may also contain photographs with a caption and charts, graphs, or maps.

In The News

MSU, UM fall
Spartans lose to Arizona; Duke defeats Michigan
Sports, 1C

Lions ready
Detroit victory against Tampa means first place
Sports, 5C

Mostly cloudy
High 42; Low 36

In the Free Press

Top 100
Michigan's best artists, entertainers of century
Entertainment, 1K

Death on 401
Couple's dreams dashed on Canadian highway
The Way We Live, 1J

The Detroit News AND Free Press

Metro

Sunday, December 12, 1999

"There are probably six centers in the world that can do what we're doing here, and half of them are here in southeast Michigan."

Doctors implant tiny gold markers like this in prostate tumors to help locate cancer.

New cancer treatment cuts pain, aids recovery

Radiation therapy improves

Advances begun in state may affect millions

By Sarah A. Webster

GOP agenda puts squeeze on Detroit

Some call legislation racist. Lawmakers say they're helping city.

Analysis

Modern safeguard

Behind tensions

With a word processing program, design elements such as headers, font style, and alignment can be accessed from the tool bars at the top of the window. These elements make your writing readable. However, too many different styles can make your writing as difficult to get through as a piece that has no distinguishing characteristics.

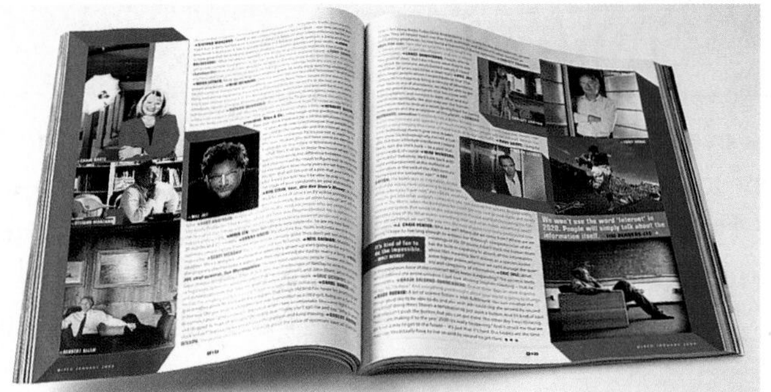

Does this page look like it would be easy to read?

There are specific style guides that provide rules of usage and instructions on how to write well. Many of these guides are also available on the Internet. Following are several simple rules to get you started.

- Keep the style simple.
- Do not use too many fonts. For most of your writing, one font for your main text and one font for headings is enough. If you are producing something more elaborate, such as a brochure or a Web page, you might consider using more.
- Use generous margins. Margins of one to one-and-a-half inches left, right, top, and bottom will frame your text nicely.
- **Bold**, <u>underlining,</u> and *italics* indicate extra importance, but don't overdo these elements. If you try to make everything look important, nothing will be emphasized.
- Bulleted lists (like this one) or numbered lists can help make your ideas stand out.

Exercise 4

Look through your portfolio for a piece of your writing you particularly like. Use word processing software to redesign the presentation for a particular audience. Suit the design to your intended audience. Share your design and your thoughts about it with your classmates.

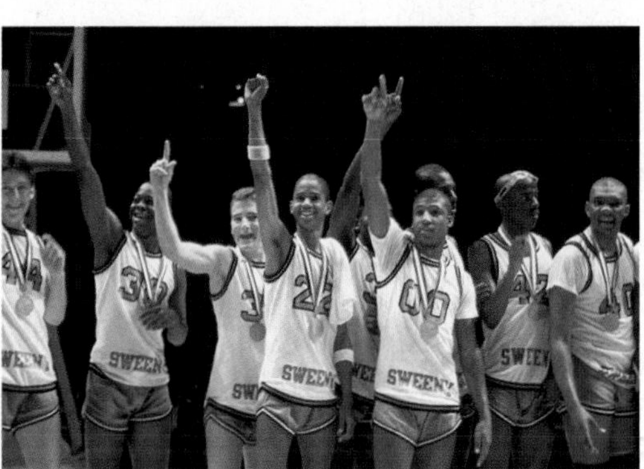

Graphics and Writing

Visual images—photographs, artwork, graphs, charts, and tables—enhance your writing. It is easy to imagine the joy of winning a sports championship, but a photo of the enthusiastic faces of the team shows how they cherish their triumph. Images also help with difficult explanations. You could write that ice cream consumption varies considerably from season to season. You could then state the percentages for each season. However, a graph like the one on this page provides all that information much more vividly.

Color-coding parts of a graph makes the parts stand out more clearly. In the ice cream pie chart, it is easy to identify the different seasons since each is a distinct color. On a computer with graphing software, or with your word processing program if the program includes a graphing function, you can enter data into a table and convert the data into several types of graphs.

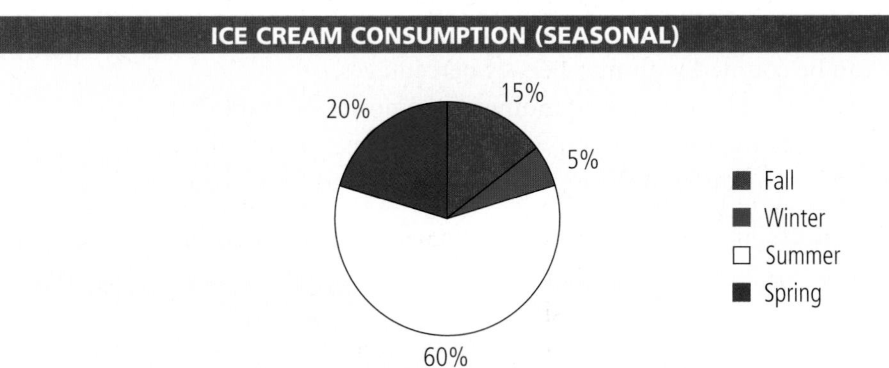

Word processing software allows you to include all kinds of graphic elements within your written text. Check your software to see what options you have for the creation of tables, graphs, and other artwork. The Help function of the program will help you learn to use these tools. Simply create a graphic image and then copy and paste your image into your written text in the same way that you copy and paste text.

Graphic Explanations

Graphics can help you make clear some concepts and processes that are difficult to explain in words. Notice how clearly the family tree on page 920 shows that children with four different last names are all cousins descended from great grandparents Mary and Paul Smith. (The letter *m* in the diagram stands for "married." Each generation of children is shown below the parents.)

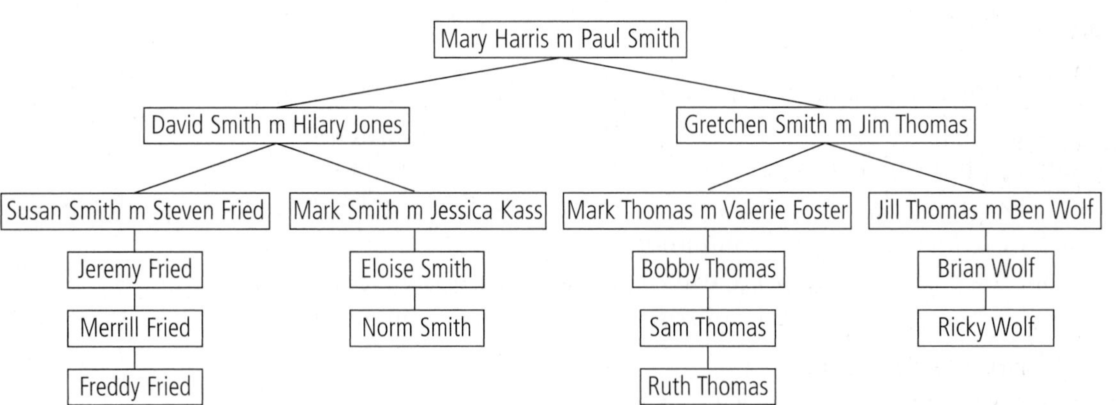

Choosing the right kind of graphic is important. Charts and tables can help you sort and organize information in various ways. Your class schedule at school is a chart. It is divided into days and times; your classes are written into the slots. However, your class schedule would be extremely confusing if you tried to graph it as a pie chart. Graphs are excellent choices for comparing items that can be counted with numbers or percentages.

The best way to gain a better understanding of the power of graphics is to experiment. Try creating different graphics with the same information. This will help you see the difference and to better understand how various concepts can be best illustrated.

Exercise 5

1. Gather some data about your school, your class, or a group within your class. Use computer software to convert your data into a graph.
2. Create a table in your word processing program and use it to organize information about ten of your favorite movies. Include at least four categories of information, such as title, year of release, featured stars, and director. You might also want to rate each film. Name the categories in headings at the top of your table.

31.4 Visual Analysis

Have you ever thought about how you get your information? Do you read a newspaper or magazines? Do you watch the news on television? Do you listen to something other than music on the radio? Do you look for news and other information on the Internet?

Have you ever tried to **deconstruct** the media? *Deconstruct* means "take apart." For example, have you tried to take apart the content of a news story or a television comedy so that you could look at how each part works and how the parts work together to transmit messages to you?

Technology and the Visual Media

Movies, television, and television commercials have several important similarities. They all hope to capture and hold your attention. Some even want you to suspend your belief in reality and enter the visual world they have created. These visual productions contain many of the same elements as a story. They are set in a particular time and place. They (even most commercials) have a plot and characters. Like books and other writings, they cover everything from reality-based news reports and documentaries to science fiction.

Movies and television also provide viewers with experiences they might not otherwise have. Technology has made these experiences all the more realistic. Wearing special 3-D glasses in an enormous theatre, you can watch swimmers scuba dive off the Great Barrier Reef and feel like you are there. With advanced stereo sound projection, you can almost feel the reverberation as bombs drop during a World War II movie. With a superior script, you can feel and share the stirring emotions of a great drama.

Technology has caused a revolution in television and movie production. Satellites allow pictures to be broadcast from halfway around the world. Computers blur the lines between fantasy and reality. You watch on television car chases between the police and fugitives as they actually happen. Animals seem to talk, and animated characters share the screen with real actors.

As computers and software become more sophisticated, what they create becomes more believable. Watch an old science fiction movie and you can almost see that the space ships were plastic models shot at close range. Yet, when you watch more-recent movies, the computer-generated aliens look as real as the actors.

Since many people tend to believe what they see, visual productions have a relatively easy time capturing the audience's imagination.

The Medium and the Message

Different forms of writing have different lengths in which they can tell their story. A poem may only be several lines, while a novel can go on for hundreds of pages. Likewise television ads tend to last between fifteen and sixty seconds, while most television shows are thirty to sixty minutes in length. A feature film has the luxury of telling its story in two hours or more. The amount of time available has an impact on the plot and character development in a story and on the depth of detail in a documentary. The longer you have, the more in-depth you can go. As with poetry, however, the requirements of a shorter form mean that you must be more exacting in what you produce.

Sights and Sounds

Next time you watch a movie or a television program, pay attention to the set. Notice the amount of detail the set designer has included in order to make that set as believable as possible. In a kitchen set, not only is there food in the refrigerator, but there may be crumbs on the counter, silverware in the dish drain, and a credit card bill on the counter. It looks like a kitchen in anyone's home.

Once you are aware of the surroundings, listen carefully to the soundtrack. Notice how the music varies depending on the emotions the scene tries to evoke. Notice also the sounds added to the scene, other than the actors' voices. Sounds and music are a tremendous tool for setting the mood and manipulating the emotions of the audience.

Lastly, the angle of the camera and the choice of shots affect the storytelling process. The longer the camera dwells on a character's face, the more emotion an actor can show. If the cinematographer zooms in on a subject, that subject takes on greater significance. The camera is the mechanism advancing the story. Are the individual shots long or short? Rapid cutting of a series of short shots can add to the excitement of the scene.

Critical Viewing

Many of the skills you learned for critiquing other people's writing can be applied to the visual realm. Compare the plots of a sixty-second television commercial, a thirty-minute television show, and a movie. Were the characters or actors believable? Did the story capture your attention? How many characters were in each? How many different scenes were there? How many different cuts of the camera? What was the critical turning point of the plot? How did the musical score accentuate this action? Were all the plot twists resolved?

Not many of us evaluate the visual stories in movies, television, and commercials. We tend to watch placidly, without noticing how the filmmaker is manipulating the story. In addition, uninvolved participants and channel surfers seldom realize that even slapstick comedy may have a message.

Learn to watch television and movies with a more critical eye. What is the producer trying to sell you? What message is the program conveying? What effects made a movie especially entertaining? If a news story is particularly compelling, ask yourself whether the most important element was the interviewer's technique, the subject matter, or the visuals. Find ways to use similar techniques in your own work.

Exercise 6

Compare a thirty-second television commercial, a thirty-minute television show, and a movie. Ask yourself such questions as:

- Who made each of them and for what purpose?
- How many characters were in each?
- How many different scenes were there?
- About how many shots did each have in a half-minute period?
- How was the camera used in each?
- How were music and sound effects used?
- What rhythms did the editing create?
- How did all these elements combine to produce one or more messages?
- What messages did you detect?

Working in a small group, discuss and compare your findings and conclusions.

31.5 Producing in Multimedia

Multimedia is the merging of written text (the written word), sound (speech, music, sound effects), and images (photos, graphics, video clips) into a single presentation. Productions can be as relatively low-tech as a slide show with a tape recorder or as high-tech as your own Web page with video and audio clips. Some multimedia productions are created to be viewed in a linear fashion, as the author assembled it. Other productions include hyperlinks that allow the user to choose the paths they want to take. Presentation and hypertext software packages can help you create a multimedia production, and you can begin with just a little help from the program itself.

Following are three relatively easy ways to create a multimedia production.

Camera, slide or overhead projector, screen, and tape recorder.	Use 35-mm slides or overhead transparencies for the visuals (text and images). Use a tape recorder for narration, music, or other sounds.
Computer with speakers, monitor, and a microphone	Use presentation software to create a computer-based slide show combining text, graphics, images, and sound.
Computer with speakers, monitor, and a microphone Also useful: digital camera, video camera, scanner (to scan and digitize images)	Use a hypertext program to combine text, graphics, images, and sound to create a series of "cards" that can be viewed in a sequence.

Multimedia Techniques

If multimedia is the merging of text, sound, and images, the possibilities of what you can create and how you create it are almost endless. You could create an animated flipbook with text captions and an accompanying soundtrack that is played on a tape recorder. Or you could create a DVD that details the history of moviemaking.

In multimedia, as in writing, different subjects lend themselves to different forms. A multimedia production about the history of your hometown might start with several old photos, perhaps accompanied by an interview with a historian or one of the town's founders. More pictures showing the town's gradual development could be followed by video footage of the town as it currently looks and your own reflections presented in text and words.

If you have a great deal of historical information, you might provide links to sidebar stories that users can explore as they wish. You would probably want to use presentation software to create this production and allow users some freedom in following paths of their choice.

By comparison, if you are doing a biography of one of the town's founders, you could choose to create a more linear story, beginning with the founder's birth and moving chronologically into the present. You could also use presentation software for this production so that you could incorporate digitized still photos, slides, home movies, and sound. However, you might require that the user go through the production sequentially, in the order you created it.

Creating a Project

Presentation software provides you many tools with which to create a multimedia production. Start by thinking about the look and feel of your project. Is your goal to entertain, to inform, or to persuade? Who is your audience—people around your age, older people, young children? Or will the audience be a mixed audience? Once you've determined your purpose and audience, choose an appropriate background for your slide template. (Multimedia software programs generally call each different screen a *slide* or a *card.* We'll refer to the different screens as slides.) If each slide is presented on the same background, there will be consistency throughout the presentation. On the other hand, if your topic calls for variety or distinct segments, you can vary the backgrounds and the templates.

Next you can add a few simple hyperlinks to your template. Arrows can be inserted that the user can click on to move from slide to slide. Another hyperlink might take your user back to the first slide—the title slide, or "home." The presentation software makes adding these features fairly simple. The software program's Help function helps you put your presentation together and does the programming for you.

After completing the background, you'll need to set up fields for your text and graphics. A field is an area you define into which you can add either text or images.

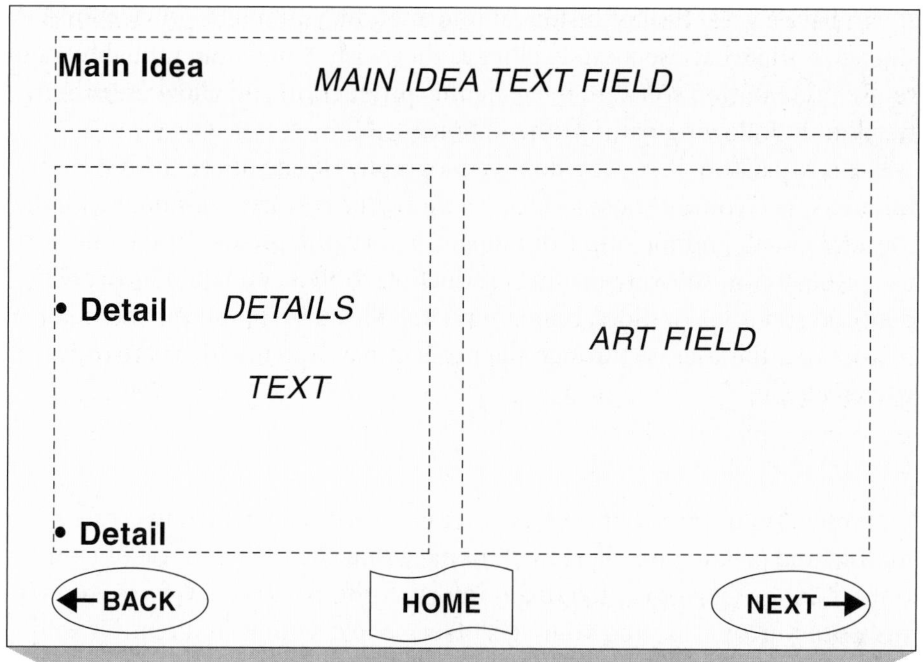

This sample slide background is one possible design. The number of ways you can use the space on a slide is limited only by your imagination.

Next, script what you want to say. You might want to start drafting your script with word processing software. After you've completed and revised the script, you can cut and paste the text into the appropriate slides. Another alternative is to storyboard your multimedia presentation. Create a table with separate columns for slide number, text, sounds, and images. Each row of your table will describe one slide in your presentation.

Storyboard: Making a Multimedia Presentation			
Segment	**Text**	**Sounds**	**Images**
1	Title: Making a Multimedia Presentation by Jesse Sanchez	Music: to come (something lively)	Opener artwork: sample slide
2	None	Narration: Anyone can make a multimedia presentation.	Photo of me at the computer
3	None	All you need is a computer, presentation software, and an idea.	Photo of presentation software box

Electronic Resources

Think of each slide as a separate part of an outline, with no more than one main idea per slide. Remember not to overload the production with extras (too much information, too many colors, too many different things happening in each segment). If the images are particularly powerful, you may not need any text. Likewise, you may use a narrator and not need any written text. Start with a title slide. At the end of the presentation, include a slide (or more if needed) to credit your sources.

Presentation software usually has word processing and slide show tools. The word processing tools—such as the variety of fonts and the spelling checker—are similar to what you are familiar with. You will also have the choice of how you want the show to progress, for example, by adding fades or dissolves between slides.

Evaluating a Project

You have spent countless hours creating a multimedia project that you think is great. How can you be sure? Use the following checklist for evaluating your project.

- ✔ Does the project flow?
- ✔ Are the ideas easy to understand?
- ✔ Will users be able to navigate through all the links?
- ✔ Are there too many fancy cuts and fades that could distract the user?
- ✔ Have I achieved my purpose and addressed my audience?

Once you have gone through your presentation yourself, set up a dress rehearsal with a friend. First create an evaluation sheet. Then have your friend go through the production. Since multimedia is ultimately viewed by an audience, collaborating with a friend is probably the best way to make sure you have accomplished your goal. Often what an author thinks is obvious is not obvious to the viewer. You may have left out information or provided too much information. Listen to your reviewer's comments and try not to take criticism personally. Remember your friend is helping you. You might also want to view other people's work and note what you like or dislike. Adapt ideas you like to your own project. Like everything, being a good multimedia producer takes practice.

Exercise 7

Working with a group, create an ad campaign for a favorite movie. Plan presentations for a variety of media: print, radio, television, and billboards. Prepare for personal appearances on talk shows with group members playing the host and the star guests.

Writing and Language Glossary

This glossary will help you quickly locate grammatical and other terms useful for writers.

A

Abstract noun. *See* Noun.

Active voice. A verb is in the **active voice** if the subject of the sentence performs the action.

Adjective. A word that modifies a noun or pronoun by limiting its meaning. An adjective may tell *what kind, which one, how many,* or *how much.*

The **positive degree** is the simple form of the adjective.

The **comparative degree** compares two persons, places, things, or ideas.

The **superlative degree** compares more than two persons, places, things, or ideas.

Adjective clause. A dependent clause that modifies a noun or pronoun. *See also* Clause.

Adverb. A word that modifies a verb, an adjective, or another adverb by making its meaning more specific. Adverbs tell *how, when, where,* and *to what degree.*

The **comparative** form of an adverb compares two actions. (*more quickly, better*) The **superlative** form compares three or more actions. (*most quickly, best*)

Adverb clause. A dependent clause that modifies a verb, an adjective, or an adverb. *See also* Clause.

Allusion. A reference in a composition to a well-known character, place, or situation from a work of literature, music, or art or from history.

Analysis. The act of breaking down a subject into its separate parts to determine its meaning.

Anecdote. A short story or incident, usually presented as part of a longer narrative.

Antecedent. *See* Pronoun.

Appositive. A noun or a pronoun placed next to another noun or pronoun to identify or give additional information about it. (My cousin *Lonnie* is going to Guatemala this summer.)

Argument. A statement, reason, or fact for or against a point; a composition intended to persuade.

Article. The adjectives *a, an,* and *the.* **Indefinite articles** (*a* and *an*) refer to one of a general group of persons, places, or things. The **definite article** (*the*) indicates that the noun is a specific person, place, or thing.

Audience. The person(s) who reads or listens to what the writer or speaker says.

Auxiliary verb. *See* Verb.

B

Bias. A tendency or inclination that prevents impartial consideration of an idea; a quality to consider when producing or evaluating persuasive writing.

Bibliography. A list of the books, articles, and other sources used as reference sources in a research paper.

Body. The central part of a composition that communicates the main idea identified in the introduction.

Bookmarks/Favorites. The feature on many Web browsers that allows the user to save addresses of Internet sites so that the sites can be accessed quickly.

Brainstorming. A group activity in which people generate as many ideas as possible without stopping to judge them.

C

Case. The form of a noun or pronoun that is determined by its use in a sentence. A noun or pronoun is in the **nominative case** when it is used as a subject or after a linking verb, in the **objective case** when it is used as an object, and in the **possessive case** when it is used to show possession.

Cause-and-effect development. A kind of organization that involves examining the reasons for actions or events and the results of those actions.

Character. An individual involved in the plot of a work of fiction. **Round characters** have different traits, some of which may be contradictory. **Flat characters** are those which display one dominant trait. **Static characters** do not change. **Dynamic characters** show development in the course of a story.

Characterization. The techniques a writer uses to reveal character. Characterization may be **direct,** revealed through the description of the character and the character's own words and actions, or **indirect,** revealed through what other characters think and say about the character.

Chronological order. The arrangement of events in order of time.

Clarity. The quality of a piece of writing that makes it easy to understand.

Clause. A group of words that has a subject and a predicate and is used as part of a sentence. Clauses fall into two categories: **independent clauses,** which are also called **main clauses,** and **dependent clauses,** which are also called **subordinate clauses.**

An **independent clause** has a subject and a predicate and can stand alone as a sentence.

A **dependent clause** is one that cannot stand alone as a sentence. It may be restrictive or nonrestrictive.

A **nonrestrictive clause,** also called a **nonessential clause,** is one that is not needed to make the meaning of a sentence clear. (Mae Jemison, *who comes from Chicago,* gained fame as an astronaut.)

A **restrictive clause,** also called an **essential clause,** is essential to the meaning of a sentence. (A free doughnut will be given to everyone *who arrives before 9 A.M.*)

Cliché. An overused expression. (*quiet as a mouse*)

Climax. The point of greatest emotional intensity, interest, or suspense in the plot of a narrative.

Clustering. A technique for generating writing ideas, which involves writing a word, circling it, and surrounding it with other words and phrases.

Coherence. The quality of a paragraph or composition in which sentences are clearly and logically connected; also called cohesiveness.

Cohesive writing. A type of writing in which sentences and paragraphs are logically connected to one another.

Collaboration. The process of working with others on writing or other projects.

Collective noun. *See* Noun.

Colloquialism. A casual, colorful expression used in everyday conversation.

Common noun. *See* Noun.

Comparative degree. *See* Adjective; Adverb.

Compare-and-contrast development. A type of organization used in expository writing that examines similarities and differences in order to find relationships and draw conclusions.

Complement. A word or phrase that completes the meaning of a verb. The four basic kinds of complements are **direct objects, indirect objects, object complements,** and **subject complements.**

Conceptual map. A graphic device that develops a central concept by surrounding it with examples or related ideas in a weblike arrangement.

Conclusion. A restatement or summing up of the ideas in a composition that brings it to a definite close.

Conflict. The struggle between opposing forces that lies at the center of the plot in a story or drama.

Conjunction. A word that joins single words or groups of words.

Coordinating conjunctions (*and, but, or, nor, for, yet*) join words or groups of words that are equal in grammatical importance.

Correlative conjunctions work in pairs to join words and groups of words of equal importance.

Subordinating conjunctions join a dependent idea or clause to a main clause.

Conjunctive adverb. An adverb used to clarify the relationship between clauses of a compound sentence. (The team lost the game last night; *consequently,* they will not play in the tournament.)

Connotation. The thoughts and feelings associated with a word, rather than its dictionary definition.

Constructive criticism. Comments on another person's writing made with the intention of helping the writer improve a particular draft.

Context. The words and sentences that come before and after a specific word and help to explain its meaning.

Conventions. Correct spelling, grammar, usage, and mechanics.

Coordinating conjunction. *See* Conjunction.

Correlative conjunction. *See* Conjunction.

Credibility. The quality of a speaker or writer that makes that person's words believable.

Critical analysis. The consideration of the elements of a literary work to examine, organize, evaluate, or draw conclusions about them.

D

Declarative sentence. A sentence that makes a statement.

Deconstructing. Breaking down into component parts, or analyzing.

Deductive reasoning. A way of thinking or explaining that begins with a general statement or principle and applies that principle to specific instances.

Definite article. *See* Article.

Denotation. The dictionary definition of a word.

Dependent clause. *See* Clause.

Descriptive writing. Writing that uses sensory details to convey a dominant impression of, for example, a setting, a person, an animal, and so on.

Desktop publishing. The use of computer programs to format and produce a document that may include written text, graphics, and/or images.

Dialect. A variation of a language spoken by a particular group of people. A dialect may be regional (based on location) or ethnic (based on cultural heritage).

Dialogue. The conversation between characters in a story, play, or novel.

Diction. A writer's choice of words and the arrangement of those words in phrases, sentences, or lines of a poem.

Documentation. Identification of the sources used in writing research or other informative papers, usually in the form of endnotes or footnotes, or using parenthetical documentation.

Drafting. One of the steps in the writing process; the transforming of thoughts, words, and phrases into sentences and paragraphs.

E

Editing. One of the steps in the writing process in which a revised draft is checked for standard usage, varied sentence structure, and appropriate word choice.

Editorial. An article in a newspaper or other form of media that expresses a personal opinion about a subject of current or general interest.

Either-or reasoning. A logical fallacy that limits possibilities to two opposite choices, ignoring other valid possibilities.

Elaboration. The support or development of a main idea with facts, statistics, sensory details, incidents, examples, or quotations.

Ellipsis. A mark of punctuation, consisting of three spaced periods, that indicates the omission of one or more words.

E-mail. Short for electronic mail; messages, usually text, sent from one person to another by way of computer.

Emphatic form. *See* Verb tense.

Essential clause. A subordinate clause that cannot be omitted without changing the intended meaning of a sentence.

Evaluation. Making a judgment about the strengths and weaknesses of a draft in content, organization, and style.

Evidence. Facts or examples from reliable sources that can be used to support statements made in speaking or writing.

Exclamatory sentence. A sentence that expresses strong or intense emotion.

Explanatory writing. *See* Expository writing.

Expository writing. A kind of writing that aims at explaining an idea or presenting a process; also called informative or explanatory writing.

Expressive writing. Writing that emphasizes and conveys the writer's feelings.

F

Fact. A piece of information that can be verified from direct experience or from an authoritative source.

Feedback. The response a listener or reader gives a speaker or writer about his or her work.

Fiction. Literature in which situations and characters are invented by the writer.

Figurative language. Words used for descriptive effect that express some truth beyond the literal level. Figures of speech such as similes, metaphors, or personification are examples of figurative language.

Foreshadowing. Clues that hint at events that will occur later in the plot.

Formal language. Language that uses correct grammar and omits slang expressions and contractions. It is especially common in nonfiction writing that is not personal.

Freewriting. Writing for a specific length of time without stopping or limiting the flow of ideas.

Future perfect tense. *See* Verb tense.

Future tense. *See* Verb tense.

G

Generalization. A statement that presents a conclusion about a subject without going into details or specifics.

Genre. A division of literature. The main literary genres are prose, poetry, and drama. Each of these is further divided into subgenres.

Gerund. A verb form that ends in *-ing* and is used as a noun.

Glittering generality. An attractive claim based on insufficient evidence.

Graphic organizer. A visual way of organizing information; types of graphic organizers include clustering, graphs, tables, time lines, and tree diagrams.

H

Home page. The location on a Web site by which a user normally enters the site. A typical home page may explain the site, summarize the content, and provide links to other sites.

Hyperlink. A highlighted or underlined phrase or word on a Web page that, when clicked, moves the user to another part of the page or to another Web page.

Hypertext. Links in some text that can be clicked with a mouse to take the user to another document or to a different section in the same document.

I

Idea map. *See* Cluster.

Ideas. In writing, the message or theme and the details that elaborate upon that message or theme.

Idiom. A word or phrase that has a special meaning different from its standard or dictionary meaning. (*In the same boat* is an idiom that means "having the same problem.")

Imagery. Language that emphasizes sensory impressions that can help the reader of a literary work to see, hear, feel, smell, and taste the scenes described in the work.

Imperative sentence. A sentence that makes a request or gives a command.

Independent clause. *See* Clause.

Inductive reasoning. A way of thinking or explaining that arrives at a conclusion by examining a series of examples.

Infinitive. A verb form that usually begins with the word *to* and functions as a noun, adjective, or adverb in a sentence.

Informative writing. *See* Expository writing.

Intensifier. An adverb that emphasizes an adjective or another adverb. (*very* important, *quite* easily)

Interjection. A word or phrase that expresses emotion or exclamation. An interjection has no grammatical connection to other words.

Internet. A worldwide computer network that allows users to link to any computer on the network electronically for social, commercial, research, and other uses.

Interpretation. An explanation of the meaning of a piece of writing, a visual representation, or any other type of communication.

Interrogative sentence. A sentence that asks a question.

Interview. A question-and-answer dialogue that has the specific purpose of gathering up-to-date or expert information.

Intransitive verb. *See* Verb.

Introduction. The beginning part of a composition, in which a writer identifies the subject and gives a general idea of what the body of the composition will contain.

Inverted order. The placement of a predicate before the subject in a sentence. In most sentences in English, the subject comes before the predicate.

Irregular verb. *See* Verb tense.

Jargon. Special words and phrases used by a particular trade, profession, or other group of people.

Journal. A personal notebook for freewriting, collecting ideas, and recording thoughts and experiences.

Learning log. A journal for clarifying ideas about concepts covered in various classes.

Lexicon. A wordbook or dictionary.

Listing. A technique used in generating ideas for writing.

Literary analysis. The act of examining the different elements of a piece of literature in order to evaluate it.

Logical fallacy. An error in reasoning often found in advertising or other persuasive writing. *See* Glittering generalities; Either-or reasoning.

Main clause. *See* Clause.

Main idea. *See* Thesis statement.

Media. The forms of communication used to reach an audience; newspapers, radio, TV, and the Internet reach large audiences and so are known as mass media.

Memoir. A type of narrative nonfiction that presents an account of an event or period in history, emphasizing the narrator's personal experience.

Metaphor. A figure of speech that compares seemingly unlike things without using the word *like* or *as.* (The girl's aloof *manner* was her *armor* against snubs.)

Mood. The feeling or atmosphere that a writer creates.

Multimedia presentation. The presentation of a piece of writing accompanied by other media, such as music, video, and visual art.

Narrative writing. A type of writing that tells about events or actions as they change over a period of time and often includes story elements such as character, setting, and plot.

Nominative pronoun. *See* Pronoun case.

Nonessential clause. A clause that adds information but is not absolutely needed to express the meaning of the sentence.

Nonfiction. Prose writing about real people, places, and events.

Nonrestrictive clause. *See* Nonessential clause.

Noun. A word that names a person, a place, a thing, an idea, a quality, or a characteristic.

An **abstract noun** names an idea, a quality, or a characteristic.

A **collective noun** names a group of people or things.

A **common noun** names a general type of person, place, thing, or idea, characteristic, or quality.

A **proper noun** names a particular person, place, thing, or idea.

Noun clause. A dependent clause that functions as a noun.

Number. The form of a noun, pronoun, or verb that indicates whether it refers to one (**singular**) or to more than one (**plural**).

O

Objective pronoun. *See* Pronoun case.

Onomatopoeia. A word with a sound that suggests its meaning. (*buzz, clink, pop*)

Opinion. A belief or attitude that cannot be proven true or false. Readers and writers should clearly distinguish opinion from fact.

Oral tradition. Literature that passes by word of mouth from one generation to the next. Oral tradition often reflects the cultural values of a people.

Order of importance. A way of organizing details in a paragraph or composition from least to most or most to least important.

Organization. The arrangement of main points and supporting details in a piece of writing; the internal structure of a piece of writing.

Outline. A systematic arrangement of main and supporting ideas, using Roman numerals, letters, and numbers for a written or an oral presentation.

P

Paragraph. A unit of writing that consists of related sentences.

Parallelism. The use of a series of words, phrases, or sentences that have similar grammatical form.

Paraphrase. A restatement of an idea in different words that retains the meaning, tone, and general length of the original.

Parenthetical documentation. A specific reference to the source of a piece of information; it is placed in parenthesis directly after the information appears in a piece of writing.

Participle. A verb form that can function as an adjective. Present participles always end in *-ing*. Although past participles often end in *-ed*, they can take other forms as well.

Passive voice. The form of a verb used when the subject of the sentence receives the action of the verb.

Peer response. The suggestions and comments provided by peers, or classmates, about a piece of writing or another type of presentation.

Personal writing. Writing that expresses the writer's own thoughts and feelings.

Personification. A figure of speech that gives human qualities to an animal, object, or idea.

Perspective. *See* Point of view.

Persuasive writing. Writing that aims at influencing a reader's opinion and actions.

Phrase. A group of words that acts as a single part of speech in a sentence.

A **prepositional phrase** consists of a preposition, its object, and any modifiers of the object. A **verb phrase** consists of one or more auxiliary verbs followed by a main verb.

Plagiarism. The dishonest presentation of another's words or ideas as one's own.

Plot. The series of events that follow one another in a story, novel, or play.

Poetry. A form of literary expression that emphasizes the line as the unit of composition. Traditional poetry contains emotional, imaginative language and a regular rhythm.

Point of view. The perspective, or angle, from which a story is told. Most writing is done from a first-person, third-person limited, or third-person omniscient point of view.

Portfolio. A collection of various pieces of writing, which may include finished pieces and works in progress.

Positive degree. *See* Adjective.

Possessive pronoun. *See* Pronoun case.

Predicate. The verb or verb phrase and any of its modifiers that make an essential statement about the subject of a sentence.

Preposition. A word that shows the relationship of a noun or pronoun to some other word in the sentence.

Presentation. The way words and design elements look on the page.

Presenting/Publishing. The last step in the writing process, which involves sharing the final writing product with others.

Prewriting. The first step in the writing process, which includes deciding what to write about, collecting ideas and details, and making an outline or a plan. Prewriting strategies include brainstorming, clustering, word webs, and freewriting.

Prior knowledge. The facts, ideas, and experiences that a writer, reader, or viewer brings to a new activity.

Progressive form. *See* Verb tense.

Pronoun. A word that takes the place of a noun, a group of words acting as a noun, or another pronoun. The word or group of words that a pronoun refers to is called its **antecedent.**

Pronoun case. A personal pronoun refers to a specific person or thing. Personal pronouns have three **cases**—nominative, objective, and possessive. *See also* Case.

Proofreading. The last part of the editing process that involves checking work to discover typographical and spelling errors.

Propaganda. Information aimed at influencing thoughts and actions; it is usually of a political nature and may contain distortions of truth.

Prose. Writing that is similar to everyday speech and written language, as opposed to poetry and drama.

Publishing. The preparation of a finished piece of writing, often using available technology, so that it can be presented to a larger audience.

Purpose. The aim of writing, which may be to express, discover, record, develop, reflect on ideas, problem solve, entertain, influence, inform, or describe.

Regular verb. *See* Verb tense.

Representation. A way in which information or ideas are presented to an audience.

Research. Locating information on a topic from a variety of sources.

Restrictive clause. *See* Essential clause.

Review. An analysis and interpretation of a subject presented through the mass media.

Revising. The stage of the writing process in which a writer goes over a draft, making changes in content, organization, and style in order to improve it. Revision techniques include adding, elaborating, deleting, combining, and rearranging text.

Root. The part of a word that carries the main meaning.

Run-on sentence. Two or more sentences or clauses run together without appropriate punctuation.

S

Sensory details. Words that appeal to the senses—sight, hearing, taste, smell, and touch.

Sentence. A group of words expressing a complete thought. Every sentence has a **subject** and a **predicate.** Sentences can be classified by function or by structure.

A **simple sentence** has only one main clause and no subordinate clauses.

A **compound sentence** has two or more main clauses.

A **complex sentence** has one main clause and one or more subordinate clauses.

A **compound-complex sentence** has two or more main clauses and at least one subordinate clause. *See also* Declarative sentence; Exclamatory sentence; Imperative sentence; Interrogative sentence.

Sentence fluency. The smooth rhythm and flow of sentences that vary in length and style.

Sentence variety. The use of different types of sentences to add interest to writing.

Setting. The time and place in which the events of a story happen.

Simile. A figure of speech that compares two unlike things, using the word *like* or *as.*

Spatial order. The arrangement of the details of a setting according to their location—for example, from left to right or from top to bottom.

Standard English. The most widely used and accepted form of the English language.

Style. The writer's choice and arrangement of words and sentences.

Subordinate clause. *See* Clause.

Subordinating conjunction. *See* Conjunction.

Summary. A brief statement of the main idea of a composition.

Superlative degree. *See* Adjective, Adverb.

Supporting evidence. *See* Evidence.

Suspense. A literary device that creates growing interest and excitement leading up to the climax or resolution of a story. A writer creates suspense by providing clues to the resolution without revealing too much information.

Symbol. An object, a person, a place, or an experience that represents something else, usually something abstract.

Tense. *See* Verb tense.

Theme. The main idea or message of a piece of writing.

Thesis statement. A one- or two-sentence statement of the main idea or purpose of a piece of writing.

Time line. A line, usually horizontal, divided into equal segments, each of which represents a specific interval of time; a helpful device for organizing events in chronological order.

Time order. The arrangement of details based on when they occurred.

Tone. A reflection of a writer's or speaker's attitude toward a subject.

Topic sentence. A sentence that expresses the main idea of a paragraph.

Transition. A connecting word or phrase that clarifies relationships between details, sentences, or paragraphs.

Unity. The quality of a composition in which all the sentences and paragraphs support one main idea.

URL. The standard form of an Internet address; stands for Uniform Resource Locator.

Venn diagram. A graphic organizer consisting of two or more overlapping circles; used to compare items that have both similar and different traits.

Verb. A word that expresses action or a state of being and is necessary to make a statement.

Verbal. A verb form that functions in a sentence as a noun, an adjective, or an adverb. The three kinds of verbals are gerunds, infinitives, and participles. *See* Gerund; Infinitive; Participle.

Verb phrase. *See* Phrase.

Verb tense. The tense of a verb indicates when the action or state of being occurs. The **present tense** names an action that happens regularly. The **past tense** names an action that has happened, and the **future tense** names an action that will take place in the future.

All verb tenses are formed from the four principal parts of a verb: a base form *(swim)*, a present participle *(swimming)* a simple past form *(swam)* and a past participle *(swum)*. A **regular verb** forms its simple past and past participle by adding *-ed* to the base form. *(jump, jumped, jumped)* An **irregular verb** forms its past and past participle in some other way. *(drive, drove, driven; begin, began, begun)*

In addition to present, past, and future tense, there are three perfect tenses: present perfect, past perfect, and future perfect.

The **progressive form** of a verb expresses a continuing action with any of the six tenses. To make the progressive forms, use the appropriate tense of the verb *be* with the present participle of the main verb.

The **emphatic form** adds special force, or emphasis, to the present or past tense of a verb. For the emphatic form, use *do, does,* or *did* with the base form.

Voice. A writer's unique way of using tone and style to communicate with the audience.

Web site. A location on the World Wide Web that can be reached through links or by accessing a Web address, or URL. *See* URL.

Word choice. The vocabulary a writer chooses to convey meaning.

Word processing. The use of a computer for the writing and editing of written text.

World Wide Web. A global system that uses the Internet and allows users to create, link, and access fields of information. *See* Internet.

Writing process. The series of stages or steps that a writer goes through to develop ideas and to communicate them.

GLOSARIO
DE ESCRITURA Y LENGUAJE

Este glosario permite encontrar fácilmente definiciones de gramática inglesa y términos que usan los escritores.

A

Abstract noun/Nombre abstracto. *Ver Noun.*

Active voice/Voz activa. Forma verbal usada cuando el sujeto de la oración realiza la acción.

Adjective/Adjetivo. Palabra que modifica, o describe, un nombre (*noun*) o pronombre (*pronoun*), limitando su significado. Un adjetivo indica *qué tipo, cuál, cuántos* o *cuánto.* Los adjetivos aparecen en varias posiciones en la oración.

Positive degree/Grado positivo. Forma simple del adjetivo.

Comparative degree/Grado comparativo. Adjetivo que compara a dos personas, lugares, cosas o ideas.

Superlative degree/Grado superlativo. Adjetivo que compara más de dos personas, lugares, cosas o ideas.

Adjective clause/Proposición adjetiva. Proposición dependiente que modifica un nombre o pronombre. *Ver también Clause.*

Adverb/Adverbio. Palabra que modifica a un verbo, adjetivo u otro adverbio, haciendo que su significado sea más específico. Los adverbios responden a las preguntas *cómo, cuándo, dónde, de qué manera* y *qué tan seguido* sucede algo.

Comparative/Comparativo. Compara dos acciones (*more quickly, better*; en español: *más rápido, mejor).*

Superlative/Superlativo. Compara tres o más acciones (*most quickly, best;* en español: *el más rápido, lo mejor).*

Adverb clause/Proposición adverbial. Proposición dependiente que modifica un verbo, un adjetivo o un adverbio. *Ver Clause.*

Allusion/Alusión. Referencia en un texto escrito a un personaje, lugar o situación muy conocidos de una obra literaria, musical, artística o histórica.

Analysis/Análisis. Acción de descomponer un tema o escrito en distintas partes para encontrar su significado.

Anecdote/Anécdota. Narración breve o incidente que se presenta como parte de una narrativa más larga.

Antecedent/Antecedente. *Ver Pronoun.*

Appositive/Apositivo. Nombre colocado junto a otro para identificarlo o agregar información sobre él. (Mi prima *Lupe* va a ir a Guatemala este verano.)

Argument/Argumento. Afirmación, razón o hecho en favor o en contra de algún comentario; texto escrito que trata de persuadir.

Article/Artículo. Nombre dado a las palabras *a, an* y *the* (en español: *un, uno/a, el, la*). *A* y *an* son artículos **indefinidos** (*indefinite articles*), que se refieren a cualquier cosa de un grupo. *The* es un artículo **definido** (*definite article*); indica que el nombre al que precede es una persona, lugar o cosa específicos.

Audience/Público. Persona (o personas) que lee o escucha lo que dicen un escritor o un hablante.

Auxiliary verb/Verbo auxiliar. *Ver Verb.*

B

Bias/Tendencia. Inclinación a pensar de cierta manera que impide la consideración imparcial de una idea; importante de considerar al producir o evaluar un texto persuasivo.

Bibliography/Bibliografía. Lista de los libros, artículos y otras fuentes que se utilizan como referencia en una investigación.

Body/Cuerpo. Parte central de una composición que comunica la idea principal identificada en la introducción.

Bookmarks/favorites/Marcadores/favoritos. Característica de muchos buscadores de red que permiten guardar direcciones de Internet para entrar a ellas rápidamente.

Brainstorming/Lluvia de ideas. Actividad de grupo por medio de la cual se generan ideas al hacer una lista de todo lo que se nos ocurre sin evaluarlo.

C

Case/Caso. Forma de un nombre o pronombre que se determina por su uso en la oración. El nombre o pronombre está en caso **nominativo** (*nominative case*) cuando se utiliza como sujeto o después de un verbo copulativo; en caso **acusativo** y **dativo** (*objective case*) cuando recibe la acción del verbo; y en caso **posesivo*** (*possessive case*) cuando se utiliza para indicar posesión o propiedad.

Cause and effect development/Desarrollo de causa y efecto. Técnica de organización que examina las razones y los resultados de las acciones.

Character/Personaje. Individuo presentado en la trama de una obra de ficción.

Round character/Personaje redondeado. El que tiene una variedad de características, algunas de las cuales pueden ser contradictorias.

Flat character/Personaje plano. El que tiene una característica dominante.

Static character/Personaje estático. El que no cambia.

Dynamic character/Personaje dinámico. El que se desarrolla a lo largo de la narración.

Characterization/Caracterización. Técnicas que utiliza un escritor para crear sus personajes. Puede ser **directa,** por medio de descripción y de las palabras del personaje, o **indirecta,** por medio de lo que dicen de él otros personajes.

Chronological order/Orden cronológico. Organización de detalles de acuerdo con el tiempo en que sucedieron los acontecimientos o acciones.

Clarity/Claridad. Cualidad de un escrito que lo hace fácil de entender.

Clause/Proposición. Grupo de palabras que consta de sujeto y predicado y que se usa como parte de una oración.

Independent clause/Proposición independiente. También llamada **proposición principal** (*main clause*); tiene sujeto y predicado y hace sentido por sí misma.

Dependent clause/Proposición dependiente. También llamada **proposición subordinada** (*subordinate clause*); tiene sujeto y predicado pero depende de la proposición principal. La proposición dependiente puede ser:

Restrictive o **essential clause/ Proposición restrictiva** o **esencial,** que es necesaria para el significado de la oración. **Nonessential** o **nonrestrictive clause/Proposición** o **esencial o no restrictiva,** que no es necesaria para entender el significado de la oración.

Cliché/Cliché. Expresión usada con demasiada frecuencia *(blanco como la nieve).*

Climax/Clímax. Momento donde ocurre la mayor intensidad emocional, interés o suspenso en la trama de una narración.

Clustering/Agrupamiento. Técnica para generar ideas que consiste en escribir una palabra, ponerla dentro de un círculo y rodearla con otras palabras y frases.

Coherence/Coherencia. Cualidad de un párrafo o composición en que las oraciones tienen una relación clara y lógica; también se llama cohesión.

Cohesive writing/Escritura coherente. Tipo de escritura en que las oraciones y párrafos están lógicamente relacionados entre sí.

Collaboration/Colaboración. Proceso de trabajar en equipo para escribir un texto o realizar un proyecto.

Collective noun/Nombre colectivo. *Ver Noun.*

Colloquialism/Expresión coloquial. Expresión informal y pintoresca que se utiliza en la conversación diaria.

Common noun/Nombre común. *Ver Noun.*

Comparative degree/Grado comparativo. *Ver Adjective; Adverb.*

Comparison-and-contrast development/ Desarrollo por comparación y contraste. Técnica de organizar ideas, señalando sus similitudes y diferencias a fin de ver relaciones y sacar conclusiones.

Complement/Complemento. Palabra o frase que completa el significado de un verbo en una oración. En inglés hay cuatro clases básicas de complementos: **directo** (*direct object*), **indirecto** (*indirect object*), **de objeto** *(object complement)* y **predicativo (atributo)** (*subject complement*).

Conceptual map/Mapa conceptual. Recurso gráfico que desarrolla un concepto central rodeándolo con ejemplos o ideas relacionadas a manera de red.

Conclusion/Conclusión. Afirmación que resume las ideas de una composición, antes de ponerle punto final.

Conflict/Conflicto. Lucha entre dos fuerzas opuestas que constituye el elemento central de la trama en un cuento u obra de teatro.

Conjunction/Conjunción. Palabra que une dos palabras o grupos de palabras.

Coordinating conjunction/Conjunción coordinante. Las palabras *and, but, or, nor, for, yet* (*y, pero, o, no, para, aun*) unen palabras o grupos de palabras que tienen igual importancia gramatical.

Correlative conjunction/Conjunción correlativa*. Las palabras *both . . . and, just as . . . so, not only . . . but also, either . . . or, neither . . . nor* (*tanto . . . como, así como, no sólo . . . sino, o . . . o*) son palabras en pares que vinculan palabras o frases de igual importancia.

Subordinate conjunction/Conjunción subordinante. Une una idea u proposición subordinada con la proposición principal.

Conjunctive adverb/Adverbio de coordinación. Adverbio para aclarar la relación entre las proposiciones de una oración compuesta. (El equipo perdió anoche; *por lo tanto,* no jugará en las finales.)

Connotation/Connotación. Pensamientos y sentimientos relacionados con una palabra, más que con su definición de diccionario.

Constructive criticism/Crítica constructiva. Comentario sobre lo que escribe otra persona, con la intención de ayudar a que mejore el borrador.

Context/Contexto. Palabras y oraciones que vienen antes y después de una palabra y ayudan a explicar su significado.

Conventions/Reglas de escritura. Normas que regulan la ortografía, la gramática, el uso y la puntuación de un escrito.

Coordinating conjunction/Conjunción coordinante. *Ver Conjunction.*

Correlative conjunction/Conjunción correlativa*. *Ver Conjunction.*

Credibility/Credibilidad. Cualidad de un hablante o escritor que hace creer sus palabras.

Critical analysis/Análisis crítico. Consideración de los elementos de una obra literaria para examinarlos, organizarlos, evaluarlos o sacar conclusiones sobre ellos.

D

Declarative sentence/Oración afirmativa. Oración que declara algo.

Deconstructing/Desensamblar. Separar en componentes o analizar.

Deductive reasoning/Razonamiento deductivo. Pensamiento o explicación que parte de una afirmación o principio generales y los aplica a casos específicos.

Definite article/Artículo definido. *Ver Article.*

Denotation/Denotación. Definición de una palabra que da el diccionario.

Dependent clause/Proposición dependiente. *Ver Clause.*

Descriptive writing/Escritura descriptiva. Tipo de escritura que da detalles sensoriales para comunicar una impresión predominante de un escenario, persona, animal, etcétera.

Desktop publishing/Edición por computadora. Uso de programas de computadora para formar un documento con texto escrito, gráficas y/o imágenes.

Dialect/Dialecto. Variedad de lenguaje hablado que usa un grupo particular. Un dialecto puede ser regional (de un lugar) o étnico (de un grupo cultural).

Dialogue/Diálogo. Conversación entre personajes en un cuento, obra o novela.

Diction/Dicción. Palabras que escoge un escritor y cómo las utiliza en frases, oraciones o versos.

Documentation/Documentación. Identificación de las fuentes que se emplean para escribir un documento u otros textos informativos; generalmente se ponen como notas al pie, al final del texto o entre paréntesis.

Drafting/Borrador. Paso del proceso de escritura; transformación de ideas, palabras y frases a oraciones y párrafos.

Editing/Edición. Paso del proceso de escritura en que se revisa que el borrador corregido tenga un lenguaje estándar, una estructura sintáctica variada y la elección adecuada de palabras.

Editorial/Editorial. Artículo en un periódico u otro medio que expresa las ideas personales y la opinión del escritor.

Either-or reasoning/Razonamiento excluyente. Falacia lógica que limita las posibilidades a dos alternativas opuestas sin tomar en cuenta otras posibilidades válidas.

Elaboration/Elaboración. Sustento o desarrollo de una idea principal con hechos, estadísticas, detalles sensoriales, incidentes, anécdotas, ejemplos o citas.

Ellipsis/Puntos suspensivos. Signo de puntuación que consiste en dejar tres puntos con espacios iguales para indicar que se están suprimiendo una o varias palabras.

E-mail/Correo electrónico. Abreviatura de correo electrónico; mensajes, generalmente textos, que se envían por computadora.

Emphatic form/Forma enfática. *Ver Verb tense.*

Essential clause/Proposición esencial. Proposición subordinada que no puede omitirse sin cambiar el significado de una oración.

Evaluation/Evaluación. Juicio sobre las fallas y los aciertos de un texto en borrador en cuanto a contenido, organización y estilo.

Evidence/Evidencia. Datos o ejemplos de fuentes confiables que sirven para sustentar afirmaciones escritas o habladas.

Exclamatory sentence/Oración exclamativa. Oración que expresa una emoción fuerte o repentina.

Explanatory writing/Texto explicativo. *Ver Descriptive text.*

Expository writing/Texto descriptivo. Tipo de escritura que informa al público presentando información y explicando conceptos e ideas; también llamada escritura informativa o explicativa.

Expressive writing/Texto expresivo. Texto que realza y transmite los sentimientos del escritor.

F

Fact/Hecho. Información que puede comprobarse a partir de la experiencia directa o de una fuente reconocida.

Feedback/Retroalimentación. Respuesta del escucha o lector al mensaje de un hablante o escritor.

Fiction/Ficción. Literatura donde las situaciones y los personajes son inventados por el escritor.

Figurative language/Lenguaje figurado. Palabras usadas con un efecto descriptivo que expresa una verdad más allá del nivel literal. Los tropos, como el símil, la metáfora y la personificación, son ejemplos de lenguaje figurado.

Foreshadowing/Presagio. Pistas o claves que utiliza un autor para advertir a los lectores de los acontecimientos que ocurrirán más adelante en la narración.

Formal language/Lenguaje formal. Lenguaje que utiliza una gramática correcta y omite contracciones y expresiones coloquiales. Es adecuado para textos de no ficción, que no son de carácter personal.

Freewriting/Escritura libre. Búsqueda de ideas escribiendo durante un tiempo determinado, sin detenerse ni limitar el flujo de ideas.

Future tense/Tiempo futuro. *Ver Verb tense.*

Generalization/Generalización. Afirmación que presenta una conclusión acerca de un tema sin entrar en detalles específicos.

Genre/Género. Clasificación literaria o de otro medio. Los principales géneros literarios son la prosa, la poesía y el drama. Cada uno se divide en subgéneros.

Gerund/Gerundio. Verboide que termina en *-ing* y se usa como nombre (en inglés).

Glittering generality/Generalización deslumbrante. Afirmación atractiva sin pruebas suficientes.

Graphic organizer/Organizador gráfico. Manera visual de organizar la información, como el agrupamiento, las tablas, las gráficas, las redes y los árboles de ideas.

H

Home page/Página principal. Página por medio de la cual un usuario entra normalmente a un sitio de Web. Por lo general, explica el sitio, resume el contenido y proporciona vínculos con otros sitios.

Hyperlink/Hipervínculo. Oraciones o palabras sombreadas o subrayadas en una página en red que al activarse con un clic conectan al usuario con otra parte de la página o con otra página de la red.

Hypertext/Hipertexto. Vínculos en algunos textos que con el clic del ratón el usuario llega a otro documento o a una sección distinta del mismo documento.

I

Idea map/Mapa de ideas. *Ver Cluster.*

Ideas/Ideas. En composición, el mensaje o tema y los detalles que lo elaboran.

Idiom/Modismo. Palabra o frase cuyo significado es diferente del significado estándar o de diccionario. (*Hacer la vista gorda* es un modismo que significa "pasar por alto".)

Imagery/Imaginería. Lenguaje que describe impresiones sensoriales para que el lector de un texto literario pueda ver, oír, sentir, oler y gustar las escenas descritas.

Imperative sentence/Oración imperativa. Oración que exige u ordena algo.

Independent clause/Proposición independiente. *Ver Clause.*

Inductive reasoning/Razonamiento inductivo. Pensamiento o explicación que parte de varios ejemplos para llegar a una afirmación general.

Infinitive/Infinitivo. Verboide que comienza con la palabra *to* (en español termina en *-ar*, *-er* o *-ir*). En inglés se usa como sustantivo, adjetivo o adverbio en la oración.

Informative writing/Texto informativo. *Ver Descriptive text.*

Intensifier/Intensificador. Adverbio que refuerza un adjetivo u otro adverbio (*very* important, *quite* easily; *muy* importante, *bastante* fácil).

Interjection/Interjección. Palabra o frase que expresa emoción o exclamación. No tiene relación gramatical con las demás palabras.

Internet/Internet. Red mundial computarizada que permite comunicarse electrónicamente con cualquier computadora de la red para buscar información social, comercial, de investigación y de otro tipo.

Interpretation/Interpretación. Explicación del significado de un texto, de una representación visual o de cualquier otro tipo de comunicación.

Interrogative sentence/Oración interrogativa. Oración que hace una pregunta.

Interview/Entrevista. Diálogo a base de preguntas y respuestas cuyo propósito es obtener información actualizada o de expertos.

Intransitive verb/Verbo intransitivo. *Ver Verb.*

Introduction/Introducción. Sección inicial de un texto en la que el escritor identifica el tema y da la idea general de lo que contendrá el cuerpo del mismo.

Inverted order/Orden invertido. Colocación del predicado antes del sujeto. En la mayoría de las oraciones en inglés, el sujeto va antes del predicado.

Irregular verb/Verbo irregular. *Ver Verb tense.*

J-L

Jargon/Jerga. Terminología peculiar de una profesión, comercio u otro grupo de personas.

Journal/Diario. Libreta personal en la que con toda libertad se anotan ideas, pensamientos y experiencias.

Learning log/Registro de aprendizaje. Diario para aclarar ideas sobre conceptos tratados en varias clases.

Lexicon/Léxico. Diccionario.

Listing/Lista. Técnica para generar ideas a partir de las cuales se escribe un texto.

Literary analysis/Análisis literario. Examen de las diferentes partes de una obra literaria a fin de evaluarla.

Logical fallacy/Falacia lógica. Error de razonamiento que se encuentra con frecuencia en publicidad o en escritos persuasivos. *Ver Glittering generality; Either or reasoning.*

M

Main clause/Proposición principal. *Ver Clause.*

Main idea/Idea principal. *Ver Thesis statement.*

Media/Medios. Formas de comunicación usadas para llegar a un público. Los periódicos, la radio, la televisión y la Internet llegan a públicos muy grandes, por lo que se conocen como medios de comunicación masiva.

Memoir/Memoria. Tipo de narrativa de no ficción que presenta el relato de un hecho o período de la historia, resaltando la experiencia personal del narrador.

Metaphor/Metáfora. Tropo que compara dos cosas aparentemente distintas sin usar las palabras *like* o *as* (*como*). (*Él es una roca.*)

Mood/Atmósfera. Sentimiento o ambiente de un texto escrito.

Multimedia presentation/Presentación multimedia. Uso de una variedad de medios como video, sonido, texto escrito y artes visuales para presentar ideas e información.

N

Narrative writing/Narrativa. Tipo de escritura que narra sucesos o acciones que cambian con el paso del tiempo; por lo general tiene personajes, escenario y trama.

Nominative pronoun/Pronombre nominativo. *Ver Pronoun case.*

Nonessential clause/Proposición no esencial. Proposición que agrega información pero que no es absolutamente necesaria para expresar el significado de la oración.

Nonfiction/No ficción. Literatura que trata sobre personas, sucesos y experiencias reales.

Nonrestrictive clause/Proposición no restrictiva. *Ver Nonessential clause.*

Noun/Nombre (o sustantivo). Palabra que nombra a una persona, lugar, cosa, o a una idea, cualidad o característica.

- **Abstract noun/Nombre abstracto.** Nombra una idea, una cualidad o una característica.
- **Collective noun/Nombre colectivo.** Nombra un grupo de personas o cosas.
- **Common noun/Nombre común.** Nombra a cualquier persona, lugar, cosa o idea.
- **Proper noun/Nombre propio.** Nombra a una persona, lugar, cosa o idea específica.

Noun clause/Proposición nominal Proposición dependiente que se usa como nombre.

Number/Número. Forma del nombre, pronombre o verbo que indica si se refiere a uno (**singular**) o a más de uno (**plural**).

O

Objective pronoun/Pronombre personal de complemento directo o indirecto. *Ver Pronoun case.*

Onomatopoeia/Onomatopeya. Palabra o frase que imita o sugiere el sonido que describe (*rattle, boom;* en español: *pum, zas*).

Opinion/Opinión. Creencia o actitud; no puede comprobarse si es falsa o verdadera.

Oral tradition/Tradición oral. Literatura que se transmite de boca en boca de una generación a otra. Puede representar los valores culturales de un pueblo.

Order of importance/Orden de importancia. Forma de acomodar los detalles en un párrafo o en otro texto escrito según su importancia.

Organization/Organización. La disposición y el orden de los puntos principales y los detalles de apoyo en un escrito; estructura interna de un escrito.

Outline/Esquema. Organización sistemática de ideas principales y secundarias con números romanos, letras y números arábigos para una presentación oral o escrita.

P

Paragraph/Párrafo. Una unidad de texto que consta de oraciones relacionadas.

Parallelism/Paralelismo. Uso de una serie de palabras, frases y oraciones que tienen una forma gramatical similar.

Paraphrase/Parafrasear. Reformulación de un pasaje en palabras diferentes que conservan el significado, el tono y la longitud general del original.

Parenthetical documentation/Documentación parentética. Referencia específica a la fuente de la información que se pone entre paréntesis directamente después de ésta.

Participle/Participio. Verboide que se usa como adjetivo. El participio presente siempre termina en *-ing* y el participio pasado por lo general termina en *-ed.*

Passive voice/Voz pasiva. Forma verbal usada cuando el sujeto de una oración recibe la acción del verbo.

Peer response/Respuesta de compañeros. Sugerencias y comentarios que dan los compañeros de clase sobre un texto escrito u otro tipo de presentación.

Personal writing/Escritura personal. Texto que expresa los pensamientos y sentimientos del autor.

Personification/Personificación. Tropo que da cualidades humanas a un animal, objeto o idea.

Perspective/Perspectiva. *Ver Point of view.*

Persuasive writing/Texto persuasivo. Tipo de escritura, generalmente de no ficción, encaminado a llevar al lector a aceptar el punto de vista del escritor mediante la lógica, la emoción, la súplica o la sugestión.

Phrase/Frase. Grupo de palabras que funcionan como unidad en una oración.

Prepositional phrase/ Frase preposicional. Consta de una preposición, su objeto y cualquier modificador del objeto; puede funcionar como adjetivo o adverbio.

Verb phrase/ Frase verbal. Consta de uno o más **verbos auxiliares** (*auxiliary verbs*) seguidos del verbo principal (*main verb*).

Plagiarism/Plagio. Presentación deshonesta de palabras o ideas ajenas como si fueran propias.

Plot/Trama. Serie de sucesos en secuencia en un cuento, novela u obra de teatro.

Poetry/Poesía. Forma de expresión literaria compuesta por versos. La poesía tradicional contiene un lenguaje emotivo e imaginativo y un ritmo regular.

Point of view/Punto de vista. Relación del narrador con la historia. La mayoría de las obras están escritas en primera persona, tercera persona, o tercera persona omnisciente.

Portfolio/Portafolio. Colección de obras creativas que representan el logro de un artista o escritor.

Positive degree/Grado positivo. *Ver Adjective.*

Possessive pronoun/Pronombre posesivo. *Ver Pronoun case.*

Predicate/Predicado. Verbo o frase verbal y sus modificadores que hacen una afirmación esencial sobre el sujeto de la oración.

Preposition/Preposición. Palabra que muestra la relación de un nombre o pronombre con otra palabra en la oración.

Presentation/Presentación. La forma en que se ven en una página las palabras y los elementos de diseño.

Presenting/Presentación. Último paso del proceso de escritura que implica compartir con otros lo que se ha escrito.

Prewriting/Preescritura. Primer paso del proceso de escritura: decidir sobre qué se va a escribir, reunir ideas y detalles, y elaborar un plan para presentar las ideas; usa estrategias como lluvia de ideas, organizadores gráficos, notas y registros.

Prior knowledge/Conocimiento previo. Hechos, ideas y experiencias que un escritor, lector u observador lleva a una nueva actividad.

Progressive form/Durativo. *Ver Verb tense.*

Pronoun/Pronombre. Palabra que va en lugar del nombre; grupo de palabras que funcionan como un nombre u otro pronombre. La palabra o grupo de palabras a que se refiere un pronombre se llama **antecedente** (*antecedent*).

Pronoun case/Caso del pronombre. Forma del pronombre que se determina por su uso en la oración. El pronombre está en caso **nominativo** (*nominative case*), en caso **acusativo** y **dativo** (*objective case*) y en caso **posesivo*** (*possessive case*), dependiendo de su función en la oración. *Ver también Case.*

Proofreading/Corrección de pruebas. Último paso del proceso editorial en que se revisa el texto en busca de errores tipográficos y de otra naturaleza.

Propaganda/Propaganda. Información encaminada a influir en los pensamientos o acciones; en general es de naturaleza política y puede distorsionar la verdad.

Prose/Prosa. Escritura que se diferencia de la poesía por su similitud con la dicción y los ritmos del lenguaje común.

Publishing/Publicación. Presentación de una obra escrita terminada mediante el uso de la tecnología, para darla a conocer a un público amplio.

Purpose/Finalidad. Objetivo de la escritura: expresar, descubrir, registrar, desarrollar o reflexionar sobre ideas, resolver problemas, entretener, influir, informar o describir.

R

Regular verb/Verbo regular. *Ver Verb tense.*

Representation/Representación. Forma en que se presenta información o ideas al público.

Research/Investigación. Proceso de localizar información sobre un tema.

Restrictive clause/Proposición restrictiva. *Ver Essential clause.*

Review/Reseña. Análisis e interpretación de un tema presentado por lo general a través de los medios de comunicación masiva.

Revising/Revisión. Paso del proceso de escritura en que el autor repasa el borrador, cambia el contenido, la organización y el estilo para mejorar el texto. Las técnicas de revisión son agregar, elaborar, eliminar, combinar y reacomodar el texto.

Root/Raíz. Parte de una palabra que contiene el significado principal.

Run-on sentence/Oración mal puntuada. Dos o más oraciones o proposiciones seguidas, cuyo significado es confuso debido a su inadecuada puntuación.

S

Sensory details/Detalles sensoriales. Lenguaje que apela a los sentidos; los detalles sensoriales son elementos importantes de la escritura descriptiva, sobre todo en la poesía.

Sentence/Oración. Grupo de palabras que expresa un pensamiento completo. Cada oración tiene **sujeto** (*subject*) y **predicado** (*predicate*). Las oraciones se clasifican según su función o según su estructura:

Simple sentence/Oración simple. Consta de una sola proposición principal y no tiene proposiciones subordinadas.

Compound sentence/Oración compuesta. Tiene dos o más proposiciones principales.

Complex sentence/Oración compleja. Formada por una proposición principal y una o más proposiciones subordinadas.

Compound-complex sentence/Oración compuesta-compleja. Consta de dos o más proposiciones principales y por lo menos una proposición subordinada. *Ver también Declarative sentence; Exclamatory sentence; Imperative sentence; Interrogative sentence.*

Sentence fluency/Fluidez oracional. El ritmo suave y suelto de las oraciones que varían en longitud y estilo.

Sentence variety/Variedad de oraciones. Uso de diferentes tipos de oraciones para agregar interés al texto.

Setting/Escenario. Tiempo y lugar en que ocurren los sucesos de un cuento, novela u obra de teatro.

Simile/Símil. Tropo que compara dos cosas esencialmente distintas, usando las palabras *like* o *as* (*como*).

Spatial order/Orden espacial. Forma de presentar los detalles de un escenario según su ubicación: de izquierda a derecha o de arriba hacia abajo.

Standard English/Inglés estándar. La forma más ampliamente usada y aceptada del idioma inglés.

Style/Estilo. Forma en que un escritor elige y organiza las palabras y oraciones.

Subordinate clause/Proposición subordinada. *Ver Clause.*

Subordinating conjunction/Conjunción subordinante. *Ver Conjunction.*

Summary/Resumen. Breve explicación de la idea principal de una composición.

Superlative degree/Grado superlativo. *Ver Adjective; Adverb.*

Supporting evidence/Sustento. *Ver Evidence.*

Suspense/Suspenso. Recurso literario que genera interés y emoción para llegar al clímax o desenlace de una historia. Un escritor crea suspenso al proporcionar pistas sobre el desenlace pero sin revelar demasiada información.

Symbol/Símbolo. Objeto, persona, lugar o experiencia que representa algo más, por lo general, abstracto.

T

Tense/Tiempo. *Ver Verb tense.*

Theme/Tema. Idea o mensaje principal de una obra escrita.

Thesis statement/Exposición de tesis. Exposición de la idea principal o finalidad de una obra en una o dos oraciones.

Time order/Orden temporal. Organización de detalles en un texto escrito según el momento en que ocurrieron.

Tone/Tono. Reflejo de la actitud del escritor o hablante hacia un sujeto.

Topic sentence/Oración temática. Oración que expresa la idea principal de un párrafo.

Transition/Transición. Palabra o frase de enlace que aclara las relaciones entre los detalles, oraciones o párrafos.

U-V

Unity/Unidad. Integridad de un párrafo o composición; coherencia entre todas las oraciones o párrafos para expresar o sustentar una idea principal.

URL/URL. Forma estándar de una dirección de Internet. (Son iniciales de *Uniform Resource Locator.*)

Venn diagram/Diagrama de Venn. Representación visual que consta de dos círculos que se traslapan, usado para comparar dos cosas con características comunes y diferentes.

Verb/Verbo. Palabra que expresa acción o estado y que es necesaria para hacer una afirmación.

Verbal/Verboide. Forma del verbo que funciona como nombre, adjetivo o adverbio en la oración. Los verboides son: participio *(participles)*, gerundio *(gerunds)* e infinitivo *(infinitives). Ver Gerund; Infinitive; Participle.*

Verb phrase/Frase verbal. *Ver Phrase.*

Verb tense/Tiempo verbal. El tiempo de un verbo indica cuándo ocurre la acción.

Present tense/Presente. Indica una acción que sucede regularmente.

Past tense/Pasado. Indica una acción que ya sucedió.

Future tense/Futuro. Indica una acción que va a suceder.

En inglés todos los tiempos verbales están formados por las cuatro partes principales del verbo: base derivativa (*base form*) *(swim, nadar)*, participio presente (*present participle*) *(swimming, nadando)*, pretérito simple (*simple past form*) *(swam, nadó)* y participio pasado (*past participle*) *(swum, nadado)*.

Un **verbo regular** (*regular verb*) forma su pretérito simple y su participio pasado agregando la terminación *-ed* al infinitivo. Los verbos que forman su pretérito y participio pasado de otra forma se llaman **verbos irregulares** (*irregular verbs*).

Además de los tiempos presente, pasado y futuro hay tres tiempos perfectos: presente perfecto (*present perfect*), pretérito perfecto (*past perfect*) y futuro perfecto (*future perfect*).

Cada uno de los seis tiempos tiene una forma **durativa** (*progressive form*) que expresa acción continua.

Emphatic form/Forma enfática. Agrega fuerza especial, o énfasis, al tiempo presente o pasado de un verbo. Para la forma enfática se usa *do, does*, o *did* con el infinitivo.

Voice/Voz. La forma única que tiene un escritor o escritora de usar el tono y el estilo para comunicarse con los lectores.

Web site/Sitio Web. Sitio de World Wide Web que puede ser alcanzado mediante vínculos o una dirección Web o URL. *Ver también* URL; *World Wide Web.*

Word choice/Léxico. El vocabulario que selecciona una escritora o escritor para presentar un significado.

Word processing/Procesador de palabras. Programa de computadora para escribir y editar un texto.

World Wide Web/World Wide Web. Sistema global que usa Internet y permite a los usuarios crear, vincularse y entrar a campos de información. *Ver también Internet.*

Writing process/Proceso de escritura. Serie de pasos o etapas por los que atraviesa un escritor para desarrollar sus ideas y comunicarlas.

*Este término o explicación solamente se aplica a la gramática inglesa.

Writing and Research Handbook

What are some basic tools for building strong sentences, paragraphs, compositions, and research papers? You'll find them in this handbook—an easy-to-use "tool kit" for writers like you. Check out the helpful explanations, examples, and tips as you complete your writing assignments.

Writing Effective Sentences

A sentence is a group of words that expresses a complete thought. Every sentence has a subject and a predicate. An effective sentence communicates an idea clearly and reads smoothly. Try these strategies as you write and revise your sentences.

Varying Sentence Structure and Length

Even when the subject matter is interesting, many sentences in a row that sound alike or that have the same grammatical structure can be dull. You can make your writing lively and interesting by varying the structure, or pattern, of your sentences. You can give your writing impact by varying the length of your sentences.

Varying Sentence Openers A sentence doesn't always need to begin with the subject. Vary your sentence openers with these techniques.

- **Start a sentence with a descriptive word.**

  Outside, the line to enter the theater stretched around the block.

  Eager and expectant, the crowd waited for the concert to start.

  Nervous, the sound crew rechecked the microphones.

  Suddenly the lights in the auditorium dimmed.

- **Start a sentence with a phrase.**

  Behind the curtain, the performer waited for his cue.

  Looking into the crowd, the entertainer spotted his brother and smiled.

  Dressed in a shiny suit, the rock star strutted onstage.

- **Start a sentence with a clause.**

  While the crowd cheered, the band began to play.

  As the lead vocalist sang his greatest hits, backup singers provided perfect harmony.

  After the concert came to an end, the band filed offstage.

Varying Sentence Structure Use a variety of sentence patterns to make your writing more effective and more interesting to read.

- **Use a simple sentence to state an idea directly. A simple sentence has only one main clause.**

  Marian Anderson was an African American opera singer.
  She sang for a huge crowd at the Lincoln Memorial in 1939.

- **Use a compound sentence to show two or more ideas of equal importance. A compound sentence has at least two main clauses.**

  Marian Anderson worked hard to develop her voice, but she was refused admission to a music school.
  She was a pioneer in the performing arts, and she never let prejudice stand in her way.

- **Use a complex sentence to show the relationship between two ideas. A complex sentence has at least one main clause and one subordinate clause.**

  Because Europeans would accept an African American opera singer, Marian Anderson performed in Europe for ten years.
  In 1955 she became the first African American singer to perform at New York's Metropolitan Opera House, where she received a standing ovation.

Check It Out

To learn more about clauses and sentence structure, see Unit 13, pages 542–573.

Varying Sentence Length Many short sentences in a row make writing sound choppy. Add style, rhythm, and emphasis by varying the length of your sentences.

- **Combine short sentences into longer ones.**

  Short The country-and-western song was sad. It told the story of a lonely man. The man missed his family.
  Combined The sad country-and-western song told the story of a lonely man who missed his family.

- **Alternate shorter sentences with longer ones.**

  The singer strummed his guitar. He sang about the troubles of a poor farmer, the power of a kind woman, and the pride of a patriotic soldier.

Check It Out

For more on how to improve your style by varying sentence length and structure, review Unit 8, Sentence Combining, pages 358–385.

Using Parallelism

Parallelism is the use of a pair or a series of words, phrases, or sentences that have the same grammatical structure. Use parallelism to call attention to the items in the series and to create unity in writing.

Not Parallel A pulled muscle can feel stiff, sore, and cause pain.
Parallel A pulled muscle can feel stiff, sore, and painful.
Parallel A pulled muscle can cause stiffness, soreness, and pain.

Not Parallel The average person uses fourteen muscles to smile and forty-three muscles for frowning.
Parallel The average person uses fourteen muscles to smile and forty-three muscles to frown.
Parallel The average person uses fourteen muscles for smiling and forty-three muscles for frowning.

Not Parallel Lifting weights builds strong muscles; do stretches to develop flexible muscles.

Parallel Lifting weights builds strong muscles; doing stretches develops flexible muscles.

Parallel Lift weights to build strong muscles; do stretches to develop flexible muscles.

Not Parallel Riding leisurely on a bike burns about three hundred calories per hour, but seven hundred calories are burned when you race on a bike for an hour.

Parallel Riding leisurely on a bike burns about three hundred calories per hour, but racing on a bike burns about seven hundred calories per hour.

Parallel Three hundred calories are burned when you leisurely ride a bike for an hour, but seven hundred calories are burned when you race on a bike for an hour.

Remember to use parallel structure in charts, graphic organizers, or visual aids you include in a composition. Also use parallelism in the formal outline you create when writing a research report. Study this portion of an outline for a report on the Olympic Games.

Not Parallel

A. History of Olympic Games
   1. In 776 B.C. first Olympic Games in Ancient Greece
   2. Greece—site of first modern Olympic Games in 1896
   3. 1900 was the first year women athletes competed in the Olympic Games

Parallel

A. History of Olympic Games
   1. First Olympic Games held in Ancient Greece in 776 B.C.
   2. First modern Olympic Games held in Greece in 1896
   3. First Olympic Games opened to women athletes in 1900

Drafting Tip

You can expand the power of parallelism beyond the reach of a single sentence or pair of sentences. Try using parallel structure throughout a paragraph or an entire composition by repeating similar words, phrases, or clauses for emphasis and rhythm.

Revising Wordy Sentences

Have you ever listened to a friend tell a two-minute story in ten minutes? You probably wanted to interrupt to say, "Get to the point!" The same is true with writing. You don't want to wade through extra words to find the writer's point. Be sure to show your readers the same consideration by getting to the point and making every word count. Here are some tips for revising wordy sentences.

- **Cut needless words.**

  Wordy I believe that all the high school students who go to Willow High School should really make every effort to volunteer in community service programs.

  Concise Students at Willow High School should volunteer in community service programs.

- **Rewrite sentences beginning with empty phrases such as *there are* and *it is important to note that*.**

  Wordy There are some students already working on a homework help line for younger kids.

  Concise Some students already work on a homework help line for younger kids.

- **Change verbs in passive voice to active voice.**

  Wordy Plays at nursing homes are being performed by drama club members.

  Concise Drama club members perform plays at nursing homes.

- **Reduce clauses to phrases and phrases to words.**

  Wordy Students who act as volunteers make a choice to help improve the community.

  Concise Student volunteers choose to help improve the community.

- **Reduce the number of prepositional phrases.**

  Wordy Four of the students in my class are teaching senior citizens who are unable to leave their homes how to use a computer.

  Concise Four classmates are teaching computer skills to homebound senior citizens.

TRY IT OUT

Write five sentences about music, sports, or another topic that interests you. Use what you've learned about writing effective sentences.

- Use a variety of sentence types, lengths, and structures.
- Use parallelism.
- Be concise.

Writing Effective Paragraphs

A paragraph is a group of sentences that relate to one main idea. An effective paragraph develops a single idea and brings that idea into sharp focus. All the sentences flow smoothly from the beginning to the end of the paragraph.

Writing Unified Paragraphs

A paragraph has **unity** when the sentences belong together and center on a single main idea. Here is a helpful strategy for building a unified paragraph: State the main idea in a topic sentence and then add related details.

Writing Topic Sentences A **topic sentence** is a concise expression of your most important idea. It gives your readers the "big picture"—a general view of what you want them to know. A topic sentence can appear anywhere in the paragraph—at the beginning, middle, or end. A topic sentence at the beginning of an expository paragraph (a paragraph that conveys information) can communicate the key point right away. A topic sentence in the middle can unify the sentences that come before and after it. A topic sentence at the end can summarize the essential details of a paragraph, leaving your readers with a strong statement of your main idea.

Revising Tip

To unify a paragraph, omit details that do not relate to the topic sentence.

Elaborating Topic Sentences Elaboration gives your readers a more detailed picture of the main idea stated in your topic sentence. Elaboration is a technique you can use to include details that develop, support, or explain the main idea. The following chart shows various kinds of elaboration you might try.

Topic sentence: Zoo animals need protection during hurricanes.	
Facts and statistics	In 1992 a devastating hurricane killed more than fifty birds at the Miami Metrozoo.
Anecdotes	One animal panicked during the storm; it ran around in circles and yelped.
Reasons	During a hurricane, an open-air habitat is a dangerous place for a zoo animal, so plans are now in place to move animals to safer enclosures in case of emergency.
Descriptions	Zookeepers herd the long-legged pink flamingos into the rest room, where they safely stand, quietly waiting for the storm to pass.
Examples	Mammals such as lions, tigers, bears, and monkeys are kept safe in concrete pens.
Quotations	One zoo director said, "The animals just have to ride out the storm like everyone else."

Writing Coherent Paragraphs

A paragraph has **coherence** when all the sentences flow smoothly and logically from one to the next. All the sentences *cohere,* or "stick together," sensibly. To make your writing coherent, choose a pattern of organization that is appropriate for your topic and use transitions to link ideas.

Check It Out

For more about organizing your writing, see pages 72–74.

Organizing Paragraphs A few basic patterns of organization you can use to arrange the sentences of a paragraph are listed below. Choose the pattern that helps you meet your writing goal.

- Use **chronological order,** or time order, to tell a story or to explain a process.
- Use **spatial order** to order your description of places, people, and things. You might describe the details in the order you see them—for example, from top to bottom or from near to far.
- Use **order of importance** to show how you rank opinions, facts, or details—for example, from most to least important or the reverse.

Using Transitions Linking words and phrases, called **transitions,** act like bridges between sentences or between paragraphs. Transitions, such as the ones shown below, can make the organization of your paragraphs stronger by showing how ideas are logically related.

To show time order or sequence

after, before, finally, first, last year, later, meanwhile, next, now, second, sometimes, soon, yesterday

To show spatial relationships

above, ahead, around, beyond, down, here, inside, near, on top of, opposite, under, within

To show importance or degree

above all, first, furthermore, in addition, least important, mainly, moreover, most important, second

Using Repetition Another transitional device is the repetition of key words or phrases. To make connections between sentences stronger, you can repeat identical or similar words. Note the repeated key words in these two closely linked sentences.

Rosa Parks's *political actions* strongly *influenced* the Civil Rights movement of the 1950s and 1960s. What is the legacy of her *political influence* today?

Check It Out

For more about transitions, see pages 74 and 130.

Paragraph Unity and Coherence Checklist

- ✔ Is the main idea stated clearly in a topic sentence?
- ✔ Do all the sentences relate to the main idea?
- ✔ Are all the sentences arranged in an order that makes sense?
- ✔ Do transitions link the sentences together and help show the order of your thoughts?

TRY IT OUT

Copy the following paragraph on your paper. Underline the topic sentence. Cross out the sentence that interrupts the unity and is unrelated to the topic sentence. Add a transition to make a clear connection between two of the sentences.

Here is how to use an incredible Japanese invention that supposedly translates the sounds your dog makes into words. First fasten this tiny gadget to your dog's collar. Encourage your dog to woof, bark, snarl, or howl. Finally press a button that interprets the dog sounds and plays them back as phrases or sentences. Dogs also use body language to communicate their feelings.

Writing Effective Compositions

A composition is a short paper made up of several paragraphs, with a clear introduction, body, and conclusion. An effective composition presents a clear, complete message about a specific topic. Ideas flow logically from one sentence to the next and from one paragraph to the next.

Making a Plan

The suggestions in the chart below can help you shape the information in each part of your composition to suit your writing purpose.

Drafting Tip

You may need two paragraphs to introduce your topic. For example, the first can tell an anecdote; the second can include a thesis statement that expands the point of the anecdote.

Introductory Paragraph

Your introduction should interest readers in your topic and capture their attention. You may

- give background
- use a quotation
- ask a question
- tell an anecdote, or brief story

Include a **thesis statement,** a sentence or two stating the main point or central idea you will develop in the composition.

Body Paragraphs

Elaborate on your thesis statement in the body paragraphs. You may

- offer proof
- give examples
- explain ideas

Stay focused and keep your body paragraphs on track. Remember to

- develop a single idea in each body paragraph
- arrange the paragraphs in a logical order
- use transitions to link one paragraph to the next

Drafting Tip

Be sure that you do not introduce new or unrelated material in the conclusion.

Concluding Paragraph

Your conclusion should bring your composition to a satisfying close. You may

- sum up main points
- tie the ending to the beginning by restating your main point or thesis in different words
- make a call to action if your goal is to persuade readers

Using the 6+1 Trait® Model

What are some basic terms you can use to discuss your writing with your teacher or classmates? What should you focus on as you revise and edit your compositions? Check out the following seven terms, or traits, that describe the qualities of strong writing. Learn the meaning of each trait and find out how using the traits can improve your writing.

Ideas The message or the theme and the details that develop it

Writing is clear when readers can grasp the meaning of your ideas right away. Check to see whether you're getting your message across.

- ✔ Does the title suggest the theme of the composition?
- ✔ Does the composition focus on a single narrow topic?
- ✔ Is the thesis—the main point or central idea—clearly stated?
- ✔ Do well-chosen details elaborate your main point?

Organization The arrangement of main ideas and supporting details

An effective plan of organization points your readers in the right direction and guides them easily through your composition from start to finish. Find a structure, or order, that best suits your topic and writing purpose. Check to see whether you've ordered your key ideas and details in a way that keeps your readers on track.

- ✔ Are the beginning, middle, and end clearly linked?
- ✔ Is the order of ideas easy to follow?
- ✔ Does the introduction capture your readers' attention?
- ✔ Do sentences and paragraphs flow from one to the next in a way that makes sense?
- ✔ Does the conclusion wrap up the composition?

Revising Tip

Use the cut-and-paste features of your word processing program to experiment with the structure—the arrangement of sentences or paragraphs. Choose the clearest, most logical order for your final draft.

Voice A writer's unique way of using tone and style

Your writing voice comes through when your readers sense that a real person is communicating with them. Readers will respond to the **tone** (or attitude) that you express toward a topic and to the **style** (the way that you use language and shape your sentences). Read your work aloud to see whether your writing voice comes through.

- ✔ Does your writing sound interesting?
- ✔ Does your writing reveal your attitude toward your topic?
- ✔ Does your writing sound like you—or does it sound like you're imitating someone else?

6+1 Trait® is a registered trademark of Northwest Regional Educational Laboratory, which does not endorse this product.

Word Choice The vocabulary a writer uses to convey meaning

Words work hard. They carry the weight of your meaning, so make sure you choose them carefully. Check to see whether the words you choose are doing their jobs well.

- ✔ Do you use lively verbs to show action?
- ✔ Do you use vivid words to create word pictures in your readers' minds?
- ✔ Do you use precise words to explain your ideas simply and clearly?

Revising Tip

Listen carefully to the way your sentences sound when someone else reads them aloud. If you don't like what you hear, revise for sentence fluency. You might try adding variety to your sentence openers or combining sentences to make them less choppy.

Sentence Fluency The smooth rhythm and flow of sentences that vary in length and style

The best writing is made up of sentences that flow smoothly from one sentence to the next. Writing that is graceful also sounds musical—rhythmical rather than choppy. Check for sentence fluency by reading your writing aloud.

- ✔ Do your sentences vary in length and structure?
- ✔ Do transition words and phrases show connections between ideas and sentences?
- ✔ Does parallelism help balance and unify related ideas?

Conventions Correct spelling, grammar, usage, and mechanics

A composition free of errors makes a good impression on your readers. Mistakes can be distracting, and they can blur your message. Try working with a partner to spot errors and correct them. Use this checklist to help you.

Check It Out

See the Troubleshooter, pages 386–411, for help in correcting common errors in your writing.

- ✔ Are all words spelled correctly?
- ✔ Are all proper nouns—as well as the first word of every sentence—capitalized?
- ✔ Is your composition free of sentence fragments?
- ✔ Is your composition free of run-on sentences?
- ✔ Are punctuation marks—such as apostrophes, commas, and end marks—inserted in the right places?

Presentation The way words and design elements look on a page

Appearance matters, so make your compositions inviting to read. Handwritten papers should be neat and legible. If you're using a word processor, double-space the lines of text and choose a readable font. Other design elements—such as boldfaced headings, bulleted lists, pictures, and charts—can help you present information effectively as well as make your papers look good.

Evaluating a Composition Read this sample composition, which has been evaluated using the 6+1 Trait® model.

Beyond Sisyphus: The Power of Positive Thinking

In the essay "The Myth of Sisyphus," Albert Camus explores how a person should respond to a cruel fate. In Greek mythology, Sisyphus must roll a rock to the top of a hill, only to have the rock roll back down to the bottom. Sisyphus begins again, and the process continues through eternity. According to Camus, Sisyphus rises above his fate by scorning it: "There is no fate that cannot be surmounted by scorn." I disagree with this statement. Instead, I would say, "There is no fate that cannot be surmounted by trying."

Two real-life examples support my position. Both Christopher Reeve and Florence Griffith Joyner have shown that "trying" to overcome misfortune can bring personal success and fulfillment.

A 1995 horse-jumping accident left actor Christopher Reeve paralyzed from the neck down. But Reeve, a real-life "superman," holds fast to his dream that someday he will walk again. Despite his physical disabilities—or because of them—he established the Christopher Reeve Paralysis Foundation, which annually raises millions of dollars for spinal cord research and assists people with such injuries. Unlike Camus's version of Sisyphus, Reeve faces his challenges with hope and courage rather than scorn. He sums up his winning attitude: "I think a hero is an ordinary individual who finds strength to persevere and endure in spite of overwhelming obstacles."

Florence Griffith Joyner, the Olympic track superstar who died of a heart attack in 1998 at the age of 38, surmounted overwhelming obstacles herself. "FloJo," as she was nicknamed, grew up in a large family living in a poverty-stricken neighborhood of Los Angeles. The conditions of her childhood didn't favor her dream of "making something of herself," but she beat the odds with her winning attitude. After her death, President Clinton remembered her outstanding achievements—both on and off the track: "Though she rose to the pinnacle of the world of sports, she never forgot where she came from, devoting time and resources to helping children—especially those growing up in our most devastated neighborhoods—make the most of their own talents."

Viewing unfortunate circumstances with "scorn" is not the best attitude to hold. We must not allow ourselves to think we are like Sisyphus, prisoners of our fate. Like Christopher Reeve and Florence Griffith Joyner, we can find creative and courageous ways of coping with difficult situations instead of feeling like victims. We can succeed in turning a seemingly hopeless situation into a personal victory.

Organization The opening captures readers' attention with key background information and a thought-provoking quotation.

Ideas The thesis statement states the central idea. The writer presents a logical plan for supporting the thesis in the body paragraphs.

Word Choice Precise words emphasize the contrast between the writer's view and Camus's.

Sentence Fluency Sentences of varying length and structure help the writing flow smoothly.

Conventions The composition is free of errors in grammar, spelling, usage, and mechanics.

Voice The writer's voice sincerely communicates a personal message to readers.

Writing Effective Research Papers

A research paper reports facts and ideas gathered from various sources about a specific topic. An effective research paper blends information from reliable sources with the writer's original thoughts and ideas. The final draft follows a standard format for presenting information and citing sources.

Exploring a Variety of Sources

Once you've narrowed the topic of your research paper, you'll need to hunt for the best information. You might start by reading an encyclopedia article on your topic to learn some basic information. Then widen your search to include both primary and secondary sources.

- **Primary sources** are records of events by the people who witnessed them. Examples include diaries, letters, speeches, and historical documents (such as the Declaration of Independence). Primary sources also include photographs, posters, interviews, and radio and TV news broadcasts that include eyewitness interviews.
- **Secondary sources** contain information that is often based on primary sources. The creators of secondary sources often conduct original research and then report their findings, shaping the information they've gathered in their own way. Examples include encyclopedias, textbooks, biographies, magazine articles, Web site articles, and educational films.

Research Tip

Look for footnotes at the bottom of a page. Look for endnotes at the end of a chapter or a book. Look for a bibliography at the end of a book.

When you find a secondary source that you can use for your report, check to see whether the author has given credit to his or her sources of information in **footnotes, endnotes,** or a **bibliography.** Tracking down such sources may lead you to more information you can use for your report.

If you're exploring your topic on the Internet, look for Web sites that are sponsored by government institutions, famous museums, and reliable organizations. If you find a helpful site, check to see whether it contains links to other Web sites you can use.

Evaluating Sources

As you conduct your research, do a little detective work and investigate the sources you find. Begin by asking some key questions to help you decide whether you've tracked down reliable resources that are suitable for your purpose. Some important questions to ask about your sources are listed in the box on the next page.

Ask Questions About Your Sources

✔ **Is the information useful?**
Look for sources that are closely related to your research topic. Dig deep; you may find a single chapter that pertains to your topic within a longer work.

✔ **Is the information easy to understand?**
Look for sources that are written at a reading level that's right for you.

✔ **Is the information up to date?**
Look for sources that were recently published if you need the most-current facts and figures.

✔ **Is the information trustworthy and accurate?**
Check to see whether the authors document their sources of facts and support their opinions with reasons and evidence. Also check out the background of the authors. They should be qualified experts on the topic that you're researching.

✔ **Is the information balanced and fair?**
Read with a critical eye. Does the source try to persuade readers with a one-sided presentation of information? Or is the source balanced, approaching a topic from various perspectives? Be on the lookout for **propaganda** and for sources that reflect an author's **bias,** or prejudice. Make sure that you learn about a topic from more than one angle by reviewing several sources of information.

Giving Credit Where Credit Is Due

When you write a research paper, you support your own ideas with information that you've gleaned from your primary and secondary sources. But presenting someone else's ideas as if they were your own is **plagiarism,** a form of cheating. You can avoid plagiarism by citing, or identifying, the sources of your information within the text of your paper. The following chart tells what kinds of information you do and don't need to cite in the body of your paper.

DO credit the source of . . .	DON'T credit the source of . . .
• direct quotations • summaries and paraphrases, or restatements, of someone else's view-points, original ideas, or conclusions • photos, art, charts, and other visuals • little-known facts or statistics	• information found in many sources—dates, facts, and ideas considered common knowledge • your own unique ideas

Citing Sources Within Your Paper The most common method of crediting sources is with parenthetical documentation within the text. Generally a reference to the source and page number is included in parentheses at the end of each quotation, paraphrase, or summary of information borrowed from a source. An in-text citation points readers to a corresponding entry in your **works-cited list**—a list of all your sources, complete with publication information, that will appear as the final page of your paper. The Modern Language Association (MLA) recommends the following guidelines for crediting sources in text. You may wish to refer to the *MLA Handbook for Writers of Research Papers* by Joseph Gibaldi for more information and examples.

- **Put in parentheses the author's last name and the page number where you found the information.**

  As *Time* magazine once noted, "Gorbachev seemed eager to stop talking about change and to begin making it happen" (Moody 41).

- **If the author's name is mentioned in the sentence, put only the page number in parentheses.**

  Time magazine journalist John Moody once noted, "Gorbachev seemed eager to stop talking about change and to begin making it happen" (41).

- **If no author is listed, put the title or a shortened version of the title in parentheses. Include a page number if you have one.**

  Mikhail Gorbachev won the Nobel Peace Prize in 1990 "for his leading role in the peace process which characterizes important parts of the international community" *(Nobel).*

Check It Out

Read a model of a research paper on pages 349–356.

Preparing the Final Draft

Ask your teacher how he or she wants you to format the final draft of your paper. Most English teachers will ask you to follow the MLA guidelines listed below.

- Create a heading in the upper left-hand corner of the first page with your name, your teacher's name, and the date on separate lines.
- Center the title on the line below the heading.
- Number the pages one-half inch from the top in the right-hand corner. After page one, put your last name before the page number.
- Set one-inch margins on all sides of every page; double-space the lines of text.
- Include an alphabetized, double-spaced works-cited list as the last page of your final draft. All sources noted in parenthetical citations in the paper must be listed.

On the next three pages, you'll find sample style sheets that can help you prepare your list of sources—the final page of the research paper. Use the one your teacher prefers.

MLA Style

MLA style is most often used in English and social studies classes. Center the title *Works Cited* at the top of your list.

Source	Style
Book with one author	Witham, Barry B. *The Federal Theatre Project: A Case Study.* New York: Cambridge UP, 2003. ["UP" is an abbreviation for "University Press."]
Book with two or three authors	Hoy, Pat C., II, Esther H. Schor, and Robert DiYanni. *Women's Voices: Visions and Perspectives.* New York: McGraw-Hill, 1990. [If a book has more than three authors, name only the first author and then write "et al." (Latin abbreviation for "and others").]
Book with editor(s)	Komunyakaa, Yusef, and David Lehman, eds. *The Best American Poetry 2003.* New York: Scribners, 2003.
Book with an organization or a group as author or editor	Smithsonian Institution. *Aircraft of the National Air and Space Museum.* Washington: Smithsonian Institution Press, 1998.
Work from an anthology	Cofer, Judith Ortiz. "Tales Told Under the Mango Tree." *Hispanic American Literature.* Ed. Nicolas Kanellos. New York: HarperCollins, 1995. 34–44.
Introduction in a published book	Weintraub, Stanley. Introduction. *Great Expectations.* By Charles Dickens. New York: Signet, 1998. v–xii.
Encyclopedia article	"Jazz." *Encyclopaedia Britannica.* 15th ed. 1998.
Weekly magazine article	Franzen, Jonathan. "The Listener." *New Yorker* 6 Oct. 2003: 85–99.
Monthly magazine article	Quammen, David. "Saving Africa's Eden." *National Geographic* Sept. 2003: 50–77.
Newspaper article	Dionne, E. J., Jr. "California's Great Debate." *Washington Post* 26 Sept. 2003: A27. [If no author is named, begin the entry with the title of the article.]
Internet	"Visit Your Parks." *National Park Service.* 1 Oct. 2003. National Park Service, U.S. Dept. of the Interior. 3 Nov. 2003 <http://www.nps.gov/parks.html>.
Online magazine article	Martin, Richard. "How Ravenous Soviet Viruses Will Save the World." *Wired Magazine* 11.10 (Oct. 2003). 17 Oct. 2003 <http://www.wired.com/wired/archive/11.10/phages.html>.
Radio or TV program	"Orcas." *Champions of the Wild.* Animal Planet. Discovery Channel. 21 Oct. 2003.
Videotape or DVD	Hafner, Craig, dir. *The True Story of Seabiscuit.* DVD. A & E Home Video, 2003. [For a videotape (VHS) version, replace "DVD" with "Videocassette."]
Interview	Campeche, Tanya. E-mail interview. 25 Feb. 2004. [If an interview takes place in person, replace "E-mail" with "Personal"; if it takes place on the telephone, use "Telephone."]

CMS Style

CMS style was created by the University of Chicago Press to meet its publishing needs. This style, which is detailed in *The Chicago Manual of Style* (CMS), is used in a number of subject areas. Center the title *Bibliography* at the top of your list.

Source	Style
Book with one author	Witham, Barry B. *The Federal Theatre Project: A Case Study.* New York: Cambridge University Press, 2003.
Book with multiple authors	Hoy, Pat C., II, Esther H. Schor, and Robert DiYanni. *Women's Voices: Visions and Perspectives.* New York: McGraw-Hill, 1990. [If a book has more than ten authors, name only the first seven and then write "et al." (Latin abbreviation for "and others").]
Book with editor(s)	Komunyakaa, Yusef, and David Lehman, eds. *The Best American Poetry 2003.* New York: Scribners, 2003.
Book with an organization or a group as author or editor	Smithsonian Institution. *Aircraft of the National Air and Space Museum.* Washington, DC: Smithsonian Institution Press, 1998.
Work from an anthology	Cofer, Judith Ortiz. "Tales Told Under the Mango Tree." *Hispanic American Literature*, edited by Nicolas Kanellos, 34–44. New York: HarperCollins, 1995.
Introduction in a published book	Dickens, Charles. *Great Expectations.* New introduction by Stanley Weintraub. New York: Signet, 1998.
Encyclopedia article	[Credit for encyclopedia articles goes in your text, not in your bibliography.]
Weekly magazine article	Franzen, Jonathan. "The Listener." *New Yorker,* October 6, 2003, 85–99.
Monthly magazine article	Quammen, David. "Saving Africa's Eden." *National Geographic,* September 2003, 50–77.
Newspaper article	Dionne, E. J., Jr. "California's Great Debate." *Washington Post,* September 26, 2003, A27. [Credit for unsigned newspaper articles goes in your text, not in your bibliography.]
Internet	U.S. Dept. of the Interior. "Visit Your Parks." *National Park Service.* http://www.nps.gov/parks.html.
Online magazine article	Martin, Richard. "How Ravenous Soviet Viruses Will Save the World." *Wired Magazine* 11.10 (October 2003). http://www.wired.com/wired/archive/11.10/phages.html.
Radio or TV program	[Credit for radio and TV programs goes in your text, not in your bibliography.]
Videotape or DVD	Hafner, Craig, dir. *The True Story of Seabiscuit.* A & E Home Video, 2003. DVD. [For a videotape (VHS) version, replace "DVD" with "Videocassette."]
Interview	[Credit for interviews goes in your text, not in your bibliography.]

APA Style

The American Psychological Association (APA) style is commonly used in the sciences. Center the title *References* at the top of your list.

Source	Style
Book with one author	Witham, B. B. (2003). *The federal theatre project: A case study.* New York: Cambridge University Press.
Book with multiple authors	Hoy, P. C., II, Schor, E. H., & DiYanni, R. (1990). *Women's voices: Visions and perspectives*. New York: McGraw-Hill. [If a book has more than six authors, list the six authors and then write "et al." (Latin abbreviation for "and others").]
Book with editor(s)	Komunyakaa, Y., & Lehman, D. (Eds.). (2003). *The best American poetry 2003.* New York: Scribners.
Book with an organization or a group as author or editor	Smithsonian Institution. (1998). *Aircraft of the National Air and Space Museum.* Washington, DC: Smithsonian Institution Press.
Work from an anthology	Cofer, J. O. (1995). Tales told under the mango tree. In N. Kanellos (Ed.), *Hispanic American literature* (pp. 34–44). New York: HarperCollins.
Introduction in a published book	[Credit for introductions goes in your text, not in your references.]
Encyclopedia article	Jazz. (1998). In *Encyclopaedia Britannica.* (Vol. 6, pp. 519–520). Chicago: Encyclopaedia Britannica.
Weekly magazine article	Franzen, J. (2003, October 6). The listener. *The New Yorker,* 85–99.
Monthly magazine article	Quammen, D. (2003, September). Saving Africa's Eden. *National Geographic, 204,* 50–77.
Newspaper article	Dionne, E. J., Jr. (2003, September 26). California's great debate. *The Washington Post,* p. A27. [If no author is named, begin the entry with the title of the article.]
Internet	U.S. Dept. of Interior, National Park Service. (2003, October 1). *National Park Service.* Visit your parks. Retrieved October 17, 2003, from http://www.nps.gov/parks.html
Online magazine article	Martin, R. (2003, October). How ravenous Soviet viruses will save the world. *Wired Magazine, 11.10.* Retrieved October 17, 2003, from http://www.wired.com/wired/archive/11.10/phages.html
Radio or TV program	Orcas. (2003, October 21). *Champions of the wild* [Television series episode]. Animal Planet. Silver Spring, MD: Discovery Channel.
Videotape or DVD	Hafner, C. (Director). (2003). *The true story of Seabiscuit* [DVD]. A & E Home Video. [For a videotape (VHS) version, replace "DVD" with "Videocassette."]
Interview	[Credit for interviews goes in your text, not in your references.]

INDEX

A

D

E

F

G

H

I

J

K

L

M

N

O

Q

R

T

U

Y

Acknowledgments

Text

Unit One From *Blue Highways: A Journey Into America* by William Least Heat-Moon. Copyright 1982 by William Least Heat-Moon. By permission of Little, Brown and Company.

Unit Two From "Bombing Down the Interstates Nuclear Loads Carry Safety Questions" by Mark Trahant. *Arizona Republic*, January 21, 1990. Reprinted by permission of Pheonix Newspapers, Inc.

"My Furthest-Back Person-The African" by Alex Haley. Copyright 1972 by Alex Haley. Reprinted by permission of John Hawkins & Associates, Inc.

Unit Three From *Equator* by Thurston Clarke. Copyright © 1988 by Thurston Clarke. Reprinted by permission HarperCollins Publishers, Inc.

The lines from "Corsons Inlet" are reprinted from *Collected Poems, 1951-1971*, by A. R. Ammons, by permission of W. W. Norton & Company, Inc. Copyright 1972 by A. R. Ammons.

"The Solace of Open Spaces," from *The Solace of Open Spaces* by Gretel Ehrlich. Copyright 1985 by Gretel Ehrlich. Used by permission of Viking Penguin, a division of Penguin Putnam Inc.

Unit Four From "Perseus and the Gorgon" by Bobby Norfolk. Reprinted by permission of Bobby Norfolk and Folktale Productions.

"User Friendly" by T. Ernesto Bethancourt, copyright 1989 by T. Ernesto Bethancourt. From *Connections: Short Stories by Outstanding Writers for Young Adults* by Donald R. Gallo, Editor. Used by permission of Dell Publishing, a division of Random House, Inc.

From *Tortuga* by Rudolfo A. Anaya. Published by University of New Mexico Press, 1720 Lomas Blvd. NE, Albuquerque, New Mexico 87131. Copyright 1979 by Rudolfo A. Anaya.

Unit Five From "Drowsy America" by Anastasia Toufexis. Copyright © 1990 Time Inc. Reprinted by permission.

From *A Book of Bees . . . and How to Keep Them* by Sue Hubbell. Copyright 1988 by Sue Hubbell. Reprinted by permission of Darhansoff & Verrill Agency.

Unit Six "A Plague on Tennis" by Mark Mathabane. Reprinted by permission of the author.

Unit Seven From *The Concord Review*, Fall 1990, Volume Three, Number One. Copyright 1991 by The Concord Review, P.O. Box 661, Concord, Massachusetts 01742. Reprinted by permission.

Photo

Cover KS Studios; **vi** Ralph J. Brunke; **vii** (t)Eric Futran, (b)Wadsworth Atheneum, Hartford/ Ella Gallup Sumner and Mary Catlin Sumner Collection; **ix** (t)Giraudon/Art Resource, NY, (b)*THE CIVIL WAR: Confederate Ordeal*, photograph by Larry Sherer © Time-Life Books, Inc; **x** (t)Stephen Kennedy, (c)Michael Holford, (b)Art Resource, NY; **xi** (t)The Howard University Gallery of Art, Washington, DC. Permanent Collection, (c)Billy E. Barnes/Tony Stone Images, (b)Ralph J. Brunke; **xii** James Porto; **xiii** Eric Futran; **xiv** (t, c) Stephen Kennedy, (b)SCALA/Art Resource, NY; **xv** PhotoDisc, Inc; **xvi** (t)Andy Keech/Photo Trends, (bl)Zao-Grimberg/The Image Bank, (br)courtesy The Collection of Mildred Hart Bailey; **xvii** Roger Tully/Tony Stone Images; **xviii** (t)HMS Images 1990, (b)P. Markow/FPG International; **xix** Milwaukee Art Museum, Gift of Mrs. Edward R. Wehr; **xx** The Metropolitan Museum of Art, Gift of Robert W. de Forest, 1925; **xxi** PhotoDisc, Inc; **xxii** (l)Artville, (r)PhotoDisc, Inc; **xxiii** Artville; **xxvi** PhotoDisc, Inc; **xxv** Carmen Lomas Garza; **xxxii-1** The Corcoran Gallery of Art/CORBIS; **2-3** Michael Boys/CORBIS; **4 5** Chel Beeson; **6** (t, bl)Chel Beeson, (br)Ralph J. Brunke; **7** Ralph J. Brunke; **8** SCALA/Art Resource, NY; **11** Carmen Lomas Garza; **12 16** Stephen Kennedy; **17** Ralph J. Brunke; **20** John G. Herron/Stock Boston; **21** Eric Futran; **24** Courtesy Mrs. Mary Weatherall; **27** Henri Rousseau, *The Sleeping Gypsy,* 1897. Oil on canvas, 51"x 6'7" Collection, Museum of Modern Art, NY. Gift of Mrs. Simon Guggenheim; **32** file photo; **33** The Oakland Museum, Bequest of Abilio Reis; **35** Courtesy Bernice Steinbaum Gallery, NY; **37** Field Museum of Natural History, Chicago; **39** Michael Boys/CORBIS; **40-41** Nathan Benn/CORBIS; **42** Monty Roessel; **43** Eric Futran; **44 45** Ralph J. Brunke; **55** Edna Davis Jackson; **56** Eric Futran; **60** Greg Mancuso/Stock Boston; **63** Art Resource, NY; **64** Reprinted by permission: Tribune Media Services; **68** Sisse Brimberg; **72** Paul Explaining Pictures to Mie Kakigahara, Tokyo, February 1983. Photographic Collage 30 3/4 x 42 1/2". © David Hockney; **76** ©The Estate of E.B. White. Courtesy Olin Library Department of Rare Books at Cornell University; **77** Eric Futran; **82** The Far Side cartoon by Gary Larson is reprinted by permission of Chronicle Features; **86** Eric Futran; **87** Stephen Kennedy; **90** The Far Side cartoon by Gary Larson is reprinted by permission of Chronicle Features; **93** Courtesy Muzeum Narodwe w Poznaniu, Poznan, Poland; **101** Wadsworth Atheneum, Hartford, Ella Gallup Sumner and Mary Catlin Sumner Collection; **108** Nathan Benn/CORBIS; **120-121** Douglas Peebles/CORBIS; **122** Jerry Bauer, Courtesy Julian Bach Agency; **124** Eric Futran; **125** Graphic House/FPG; **126** J. W. Meyers/Stock Boston; **128** Courtesy Bernice Steinbaum Gallery, New York; **131** Blackbear Bosin, Courtesy The Philbrook Museum of Art, Tulsa, Oklahoma; **134** Stephen Kennedy; **135** The Cleveland Museum of Art, Anonymous Gift; **136** Reprinted from Green Lantern #15 Copyright 1991 DC Comics, Inc. All rights reserved. Reprinted by permission. Art by M.D. Bright, Romeo Tanghal, Anthony Tollin; **140** Robert Bishop; **145** Milwaukee Art Museum, Gift of Mrs. Edward R. Wehr; **146** Giraudon/Art Resource, NY; **157** Frederic Remington, *The Fall of the Cowboy,* 1895. Oil on canvas (1961.230) Amon Carter Museum, Fort Worth, Texas; **159** Ann Taylor; **163** Douglas Peebles/CORBIS; **164-165** Richard Reynolds/TxDOT; **166** Stephen Kennedy; **167** (t)Michael Holford (b)Eric Futran; **168** (t, c) Stephen Kennedy, (b) Chattanooga Free Press. Photo by Laura Walker; **169** Stephen Kennedy; **170** Ralph J. Brunke; **174** from *THE CIVIL WAR: Confederate Ordeal.* Photograph by Larry Sherer © Time-Life Books, Inc; **176** (t) Robert Tringali Jr./Sportschrome, Inc., (b) Sportschrome; **179** Courtesy Donald Morris Gallery, Inc; **180** File Photo; **183** Des Moines Art Center, Purchased with funds provided by the AVA Program, 1982.7; **187** Gilberto Ruiz/Courtesy of the Barbara Gillman Gallery; **188 192** File Photo; **196** Nasjoonalgalleriet, Oslo, Norway; **199** Private Collection, Courtesy of the Texas Gallery, Houston. Photo by Bill Kennedy; **204** file photo; **209** Fundación Rufino Tamayo/ Art Resource, NY; **213** Richard Reynolds/TxDOT; **214-215** Simon Fraser/SPL/Photo Researchers; **216** Ellen Denuto; **217** Eric Futran; **218** (l) Billy E. Barnes/Stock Boston, (r) Ralph J. Brunke; **219** Peter

Southwick/Stock Boston; **220** Eric Haase; **223** Russian Museum, St. Petersburg, Russia; **224** Wyoming Division of Tourism; **227** The Howard University Gallery of Art, Washington, DC. Permanent Collection; **228** Ralph J. Brunke; **231** M.C. Escher/Cordon Art-Baarn-Holland/Art Resource, NY; **232** Bettman/CORBIS; **239** Alma Thomas (American, 1891-1978). *Iris, Tulips, Jonquils and Crocuses,* 1969. Acrylic on canvas, 60 x 50 in. The National Museum of Women in the Arts. Gift of Wallace and Wilhelmina Holladay; **240** Billy E. Barnes/Tony Stone Images; **243** Collection of the Chase Manhattan Bank, N.A; **244** Kent Knudsen/Stock Boston; **248** Dave Clendenen; **252** Reprinted by permission: Tribune Media Services; **258** Erich Hartmann; **266** file photo; **268** Scala/Art Resource, NY; **271** Art Resource, NY; **272** Ernest Lawson 1873-1939, *Garden Landscape,* 50.8 x 61.0. The Brooklyn Museum. Bequest of Laura L. Barnes; **275** Simon Fraser/SPL/Photo Researchers; **276-277** Joseph Sohm/ChromoSohm/CORBIS; **278** Ralph J. Brunke; **279** (l)Eric Futran, (r)Steven Wohlwender; **280** Eric Futran; **282** James Porto; **284** Rainforest Action Network; **285** Jonathan Franklin/Courtesy of the Collection of Wendy Spatz; **286** Ralph J. Brunke; **289** Courtesy of Roslyn Oxley Gallery, Paddington, Australia; **292** Courtesy of the National Wildlife Federation, photo by Ralph J. Brunke; **294** Larry Pierce/The Image Bank; **296** Consumers Union of United States, Inc., Yonkers, NY 10703; **300** Courtesy of Elgin Syferd/Drake and the Idaho Travel Council; **301** SCALA/Art Resource, NY; **302** Herman © 1976 Jim Unger. Reprinted with permission of Universal Press Syndicate; **306** Ralph J. Brunke; **314–315** The Bridgeman Art Library Ltd; **319** Joseph Sohm/ ChromoSohm/CORBIS; **320-321** John McAnulty/CORBIS; **328** Eric Futran; **336** The Granger Collection; **342** Courtesy HIstorical Pictures Services, Inc.; **346** Courtesy of Historical Pictures Service; **358-359** CORBIS; **386-387** Al Young/CORBIS; **436** SuperStock; **493** Ando Hiroshige, Japanese, 1797-1858, Imagiri Promentory for Maizaka from the Hocido Tokaido, 1833 color wood-block print 266 x 351 mm Elvehjem Museum of Art, Univeristy of Wisconsin-Madison; **503** Andy Keech/Photo Trends; **519** SCALA/Art Resource, NY; **529** Zao-Grimberg/The Image Bank; **539** Magnum Photos; **545** Roger Tully/Tony Stone Images; **571** The Carnegie Museum of Art, Pittsburgh, Museum Purchase; gift in memory of Elizabeth Mellon Sellers from her friends. 74.17; **609** Courtesy Ashmolean Museum, Oxford; **621** P. Markow/FPG International; **633** Stanley I. Batkin; **642** HMS Images; **659** Courtesy of the Collection of Mildred Hart Bailey; **687** The Metropolitan Museum of Art, Gift of Mrs. Earl W. Koeniger, 1966 (66.114); **709** The Metropolitan Museum of Art, Gift of Robert W. de Forest, 1925 (25.173); **729** Bettman/CORBIS; **755** AP/Wide World; **777** The Mary and Sylvan Lang Collection, Marion Koogler McNay Art Museum, San Antonio, Texas; **780–781** Archivo Iconografico, S.A./CORBIS; **783** Susan Anderson; **785** John Elk III/Stock Boston; **785-797** (gears)VCG/FPG International; **787** SCALA/Art Resource, NY; **788** The Far Side © 1987 Universal Press Syndicate. Reprinted with permission; **792** (l)SCALA/Art Resource, NY, (r)Courtesy Ashmolean Museum, Oxford; **793** Bettman/ CORBIS; **796** (l)The Bridgeman Art Library Ltd./Art Resource, NY, ©Martha Swope, (r)NASA; **797** By permission of Johnny Hart and Creators Syndicate, Inc; **813** File Photo; **898** Reuters/Gregg Newton/Archive Photos; **900 901** The Kobal Collection; **918** (t)Aaron Haupt, (b)Bob Daemmrich/Stock Boston.